Letters of
TED HUGHES

Selected and edited by

CHRISTOPHER REID

faber and faber

First published in 2007
by Faber and Faber Limited
Bloomsbury House,
74–77 Great Russell Street,
London WC1B 3DA
This paperback edition first published in 2009

Typeset by RefineCatch Limited, Bungay, Suffolk
Printed in England by CPI Mackays, Chatham ME5 8TD

A CIP record for this book
is available from the British Library

ISBN 978-0-571-22139-4

2 4 6 8 10 9 7 5 3

Contents

Illustrations

Editor's Introduction

This is not the first book of writings by Ted Hughes to appear after his death. It follows Paul Keegan's edition of the *Collected Poems* (2003) and Daniel Weissbort's *Ted Hughes: Selected Translations* (2006). Both of these are products of editorial intervention and interpretation, since the author himself, obviously, was unable to watch over them as they were shaped from the available material and offered to the world. *Letters of Ted Hughes*, however, goes a step beyond them, in being the first book to exhibit publicly words that he wrote, sometimes confidentially and unguardedly, for purely private consumption. So the editor's job has involved certain liberties and risks.

Big as it is, *Letters of Ted Hughes* represents only a small fraction of Hughes's epistolary output. An edition in three or four volumes, each just as big, could have been assembled, with the guarantee that no page would have been without its literary or documentary value. Many precious things – penetrating illuminations, facts not widely known, paragraphs of ingenious and cogent reasoning, and flights of sheer verbal exuberance – have had to be sacrificed to produce a book of manageable size that would nonetheless serve as companion to one of the greatest and largest poetic oeuvres of the twentieth century. (I say 'poetic', but Hughes was also a supremely original writer of imaginative and critical prose.)

Something must be said, therefore, about how the letters here came to be chosen. A personal note may help.

The first letters of Ted Hughes that I read were, naturally enough, those he wrote to me when I was his editor at Faber and Faber, during the last eight years of his life. They were like none I had ever received before. Dealing with publishing affairs, they were invariably direct and businesslike, with an extra ingredient of confidentiality and candour that at first surprised me. In addition, though – the extra extra – they were written with so much more concentration, force, choiceness of expression, vocal immediacy, grace and wit than the occasion usually, if ever, demanded. The word that perhaps best suited them was *generous*. It soon became clear that here was a writer who, even on the most ordinary occasions, could not write at less than his full stretch, or give his reader – not a readership, but a single pair of eyes – anything short of his best performance.

I was not surprised, as I read the letters that individuals and institutions have made available to me, to find that Hughes dealt with almost all his correspondents in this open-handed fashion. What I had not expected was that the habit should have been established so early. The letters that have survived from his childhood and the years of his National Service and studies at Cambridge are, inevitably, fewer than those of later times, but they are enough to show that he had already worked out what the formal and expressive possibilities of a letter were, and how he could make the most of them.

News of recent happenings and comments on them were, of course, the main point, but, at least from Cambridge onwards, the minor incidents of everyday life, as reported by him, seem to amount to more than that. An undercurrent of priorities has begun to assert itself. With a precocious maturity that must have been fostered by his unusual teenage reading, in which Shakespeare, Yeats, Jung, folklore and Robert Graves's *The White Goddess* dominated, Hughes appears already set on a deliberate journey. These are letters of learning and looking forward. Written to family members – his brother Gerald and sister Olwyn, in particular – they recount frankly and pronounce emphatically, and their language has an optimistic flourish and forthrightness to it. When judgements are uttered, they more often than not turn out to be lifelong. What is unmistakable is the writer's will to find his own way, in his own way.

This early discovered style of spontaneity, exercised in family communiqués, proved as fit for the task as Hughes's correspondence grew. Cambridge friends – again lifelong – and literary associates were treated in the same spirit. In the case of Sylvia Plath, to whom he wrote a remarkable series of letters in October 1956, when they lived apart briefly for reasons that are given on page 33, the language was not radically modified to achieve the note of loving care and encouragement that may surprise believers in a certain die-hard literary myth – or 'Fantasia', as Hughes himself tended to call it in later letters to friends. And in the last two decades of his life, when scholars and students sent questions and he replied, sometimes at lavish length, a similar, trusting note is heard.

Both in letters of the last kind, when specifically biographical information has been sought, and in less formal reports to family and close friends, Hughes tells his correspondents a great deal about his life. This book is not, however, a biography in disguise. I hope that from the chronological arrangement of my selection, and the notes that accompany it, a compelling and satisfying narrative will emerge, so that to read it from start to finish would indeed be the best way of addressing it; but the story is above all that of Hughes the writer, from the literary predilections that are first voiced in letters from Cambridge, and subsequent remarks about early work in progress, to the painstaking clarifications of textual points that he gave to enquirers in his last years, when he was able to survey, without evident vainglory, a body of work that none of his contemporaries could match. Much biographical material is caught up in this, of course, and the episodes involving the suicides of Sylvia Plath and Assia Wevill, and the death of Wevill's daughter Shura, are retailed as fully as the partial – in a double sense – nature of the telling will allow. The main thrust, however, is from project to project, from book to book.

Subplots and digressions tend to have a bearing on this central narrative, and the letters that concern such matters as fishing, wildlife, the damaged environment, the state of the nation, class, education, religion, astrology, shamanism, or the non-literary arts spring unmistakably from the same sensibility that produced such volumes as *River*, *Moortown*, *Remains of Elmet*, *Wolfwatching*, *Cave Birds* and *Gaudete*. The letters about fishing, for instance, are here largely for the verve of the descriptive writing, but I also had in mind the famous analogy, in *Poetry in the Making*, between the creation of a poem and the capture of an animal. If I could not find at least a twofold reason for including a letter not on some overtly literary topic, then I would generally decide to drop it.

The reader will find a number of letters in which Hughes ventures to comment on public or political matters. I should have liked to represent more of this side of his interests. In the early and middle eighties, he devoted a large part of his time to campaigns to clean up the polluted, exploited and neglected rivers of Devon. This demanded a lot of letter-writing and the letters that came out of it show how fully he was committed to the research and lobbying that were necessary. As he amassed evidence and read the scientific papers, he became a true expert, well able, for instance, to face interrogation at public inquiries. I wish I could have included at least one such letter here – if only to throw light on the disciplined intellect behind such a mighty structure of exposition and argument as *Shakespeare and the Goddess of Complete Being* – but their technical complexity and immersion in the unresolved political moment would have made them impossible to annotate except at inordinate length, and I have decided, with regrets, to leave them out.

Another regret has been that I could not include more letters in their entirety. The single paragraphs or passages that I have taken from larger contexts will, I trust, have earned their place here, and without too jarring an effect of dislocation; but much of the pleasure of receiving these letters must have been in the appreciation of their shapeliness, and I am conscious that that has sometimes had to be forfeited. It would require a separate study to show how that sense of design, that intuition of the right note for the occasion and the right length to sustain or vary it, was achieved. One curious fact, which will have been observed by anyone who has handled either the originals or their photocopies, is how often letters end exactly at the bottom of a page, and yet appear to say as much as, and no more than, the occasion warranted. This happens more often than not. It is as if the size of whatever page Hughes had to hand was like the template a baroque composer would have heeded when writing an allemande or a minuet, or the limited number of bars a New Orleans clarinettist would have had available for improvisation. But my comments have already wandered into speculation, when all I meant to convey was my feeling that a considerable factor in the delight these letters afford is Hughes's treatment of them, if not as an art form, then as a pretext for the exercise of his artistic instincts. In other words, the poet in him, the maker of cadenced sentences and rhetorical patterns, seldom rested.

Readers of these transcripts will miss other pleasures, too. Not the least is Hughes's handwriting, which changed greatly in some aspects at different periods of his life and under pressure of different moods, but, even when hastily flung down, or hindered by some uncooperative writing implement, is always a sure vehicle of the writer's character. The momentum of those cursives, when his hand is galloping, in combination with slashed t-crossings and emphatic down-strokes, catches the eye before anything else and makes an unmistakable impression of total engagement with immediate business. An example of this can be seen opposite and in plate 6.

Legibility may sometimes have suffered in consequence and, while I have become a fairly adept disentangler of knotted letters, there are a few cases where I have had to admit defeat. These are marked in the printed text. A more pervasive problem has been what to do with Hughes's spelling mistakes, which occur liberally in both manuscripts

the Greek Helios. (as 'god's linen' – i ariel – is not greek)
Phaeton was a type of ritual royal victim –
Hippolytus etc. – identified with the god-king fast to
duration of his fatal chariot ride or royal institute.
though as you say – the main point in Ariel is
the divine paternity – the divine urge to make the
attempt the knowledge of the divine fate.
Apollo as sun-god of poetry & learning has a link
with the Celtic god Lugh who has a link with his
two daughters love the same man. Complications. The
father promises his blessing if both will give the man
up. When one refuses, he banishes her to a crane
& out into the Atlantic, hundreds of years. Many
variants of this – to one end: the sea-god Mannanan
makes a bag of her skin. This is the crane bag &
(which the god his (dead etc) carries the alphabet
In the Welsh version of the myth – more intact –
daughter is Creiddylad (Welsh: crey = heron)
this So Cordelia is direct line of descent from the
cranes that formed the Greek alphabet via the crane-skin
bagful of letters the treasures of learning. Ariel is
a 'code' – of a kind – for Cordelia.
? Lear + Edmund as Shakespeare's way of restoring
Geoffrey Monmouth's anecdote to the original myth –
behind the version of the Mabinogion fitting Gwion
+ Taliesin back into their cyclic battle for Creiddylad
behind which is the Egyptian Horus + Set cyclic
battle for the Eye which is – want for it –
the Daughter (and wisdom) of the Sun god. When she is
separated from her father (torment by Set) she becomes a
raging lioness – the kingdom falls into confusion. The
original 'god's linen' (Israelites stole it in Egypt).
So Ariel = Phaeta = Cordelia = raging lioness =
Eye of divine wisdom = the crane-skin bagful of the alphabet
etc etc Give or take a few negative capability factors.
Medusa was the night mask that covered the day of
the alphabet when it was Greek – the Gorgon to scare off
the uninitiated. I should mention the whole will
– in which case, a note, you should have some blame.
Love to all Ted

(left margin) She has something of this – the non-god threads into a bagful of letters.

(left margin) She has something of this – what she didn't know I did.

Second and final page of TH's letter to Charles Tomlinson, 15 August 1989 (reduced from original A4).
(Source: The Harry Ransom Humanities Research Centre, The Univeristy of Texas at Austin).

and typescripts, and with his idiosyncratic punctuation and sometimes wayward grammar and syntax. I have wanted to do as little correcting as possible, and yet a text constantly interrupted by scholarly '[*sic*]'s and other uses of square brackets would have been intolerable for most readers. With the purpose of keeping square brackets to a minimum, I have arbitrarily divided spelling mistakes into two classes: the first, those I judge to have been the result of haste or inadvertency, which I have silently corrected; the second, those that turn up so reliably that they look like studied and stubborn eccentricities. Such pet errors include 'develope', 'mentionned', 'attatch', 'checque', 'daffodill', 'discoursive', 'alltogether' – and the reader will come to recognise others. (As a peculiar refinement of this editorial problem, there is the odd instance where I have been persuaded to 'correct incorrectly': e.g. the 'cacaphonous' that appears in Hughes's letter to Keith Sagar of 19 January 1986 was actually typed 'acacphonous', which I might have printed as 'cacophonous' had he not obviously intended his own favoured version of the word.) Certain names, too, sometimes those of good friends, are spelt with mixed accuracy. I have let such solecisms stand, because, even if Hughes would have preferred them to have been put right in the publication of a literary text, here they serve a special function, signalling an attitude of mind, a streak of untamed nonconformity or disobedience to school rules, that I believe to be eloquent of his character.

Oddities of punctuation are even more abundant, and most of these I have preserved as well. Hughes's use of the dash to open a parenthesis that is not then closed with one is a frequent habit, and, although it can be confusing when first encountered, the reader, in my experience, not only soon gets used to it, but learns to appreciate it as part of his characteristic sentence music. Missing commas and full stops, the pairing of single with double inverted commas, lists lacking their expected commas, and such like, I have tended to keep as Hughes wrote or typed them. What I have interpreted as accidents of no expressive value are a different matter, as when simple hurry seems to be to blame, or a comma may have dropped down and be lying concealed in the pen-strokes of the line below, or a full stop has presumably jumped off the edge of a page of typescript. In such cases, I have corrected silently. Errors in grammar, of which a singular verb following a plural subject would be a common example, I have generally left uncorrected, on the grounds that they are the sort of mistake that might be made in private conversation and so enhance the flavour of intimate speech.

The last book of poems Hughes published before he died was *Birth-day Letters* – intimate speech raised to the level of art. One assumes from the title that, although they lack salutations and signings-off, these poems, addressed to his first wife Sylvia Plath, were conceived as letters because Hughes had learnt, through many years of steady practice, that communications of a nominally occasional nature might still be capable of bearing great weight. An actual, postal correspondence stands behind another late work, *Shakespeare and the Goddess of Complete Being*, which grew from the series of letters about Shakespeare that Hughes sent to the Swedish theatre director Donya Feuer in 1990. The letters that follow this introduction encompass the emotional truthfulness of the first book and the intellectual rigour of the second, as well as the full range of attitudes, moods and manners in between.

A note on dates

The editorial dating of some of these letters has been a tricky matter. Before the early 1970s, Ted Hughes rarely put a date at the head of any but his most official items of correspondence. When he did so, that is the date the reader will find here. In a fair number of cases, when either the recipient kept the envelope, or the letter was written on an airmail form, a postmark has supplied the date – a reliable enough guide to its place in the chronology of a selection like this, even though it is evident that some letters were written in bursts, over a number of days, or held back before being taken out and posted. Postmarks, however, come in degrees of legibility, and I have spent a lot of time peering through magnifying glasses at some of the more faint and fuzzy marks applied by provincial and urban post offices without getting a clear answer. In such cases, the reader will find a date proposed in square brackets.

Square brackets, in general, signify my own uncertainty about the dating of an item. A few undated and unpostmarked letters offer suf-ficient internal and circumstantial clues to allow me to give a firm date, free of brackets, but more often I have let the reader see that the date given is conjectural. In the most elusive instances, the brackets simply hold the word 'Undated', but there are many shades of uncertainty, and some full dates that appear in brackets are quite likely to be correct – only the clinching evidence is lacking.

In a book of a different kind, with room to include full scholarly apparatus, the means of arriving at all such dates would be spelt out; but the economy of this book is different. So I must ask the reader to indulge the imprecisions he or she will meet here. When, as will no doubt happen, it is shown that some of the dates I have suggested are wrong, I shall be apologetic, but not surprised. Hughes scholarship is in its early days, and the subdivision dedicated to tracing the poet's every step through a study of his letters and miscellaneous documentary ephemera is not going to be short of work.

Christopher Reid
2007

Acknowledgements

My biggest debt of gratitude is to Carol Hughes, who asked me to edit this book. She has watched benignly and patiently over the entire operation, giving advice and encouragement, answering my innumerable questions and offering judgements, while leaving me unimpaired editorial freedom. The opinions that are expressed in my footnotes and that may be inferred from my choice of letters – that is, all sins of commission and omission – are entirely mine. So let me thank her warmly now for what has been an act of the greatest trust. I hope it has been justified.

According to custom, I ought now to distribute my thanks to helpful individuals in descending order of my indebtedness; but in this case, even if it were possible to make such discriminations, it would be invidious and give an utterly misleading impression. What struck me at once when I started to look for letters three or four years ago was the evident collective recognition that a book of this kind was urgently needed. The goodwill that has come from almost all directions has been wonderfully sustaining. I believe it has arisen from a belief, shared not just by Ted Hughes's nearest and dearest, his family and close friends, but by the widest spread of readers and admirers as well, that, despite his undoubted literary eminence, his true stature has not yet been recognised. There is also, of course, the dismaying fact that, for a large part of his life, he was the most crudely vilified of writers, and those who knew him personally, or have understood him at all well through his writings, have long wanted this injustice to be put right. The acclaim that greeted *Birthday Letters*, published in the last year of his life, was a clear sign that things were about to change, but the process of restitution needed to go further, and I have felt the demand for it as a powerful surge, propelling this book in the direction it has taken. I have come to regard all those who have lent help, not as soloists, each with his or her earned place in the billing, but as a chorus. Alphabetical order, therefore, seems the appropriate way to thank everybody. The list below includes both members of Ted Hughes's immediate family and people who never met him; those who have supplied their private correspondence and given me generously detailed information about it, as well as others whose only contribution was a courteous expression of regret that they could not help, or a passing word of encouragement.

So, for sundry acts of assistance and kindness, my thanks go to Dannie Abse, Graham Ackroyd, Jayne Albaya, A. Alvarez, Hana Amichai, Siv Arb, Simon Armitage, Neil Astley, Deepika Bahri, Lord Baker of Dorking, L. W. Baker, Jill Balcon, Michael Baldwin, Stephen Barber, Anne Voss Bark, Robin Barlow, Lisa Baskin, Gillian Bate, Kenneth Bernard, Howard Blake, The Rt Hon David Blunkett, MP, the late John Bodley, Pat Borthwick, Jack Brown, Professor Jerome Bruner, Anne-Lorraine Bujon, Robert Butler-Sloss, Tony Buzan, Richard Carrington, Anne Carson, Judy Carver, Judith Chernaik, Sir Robin and Lady Chichester-Clark, Edna Chilton, Desmond Clarke, Renata Clarke, Olivia Cole, Barrie Cooke, Ian Cooke, Wendy Cope, William Corbett, Professor Neil Corcoran, Ron Costley, Dr Coline Covington, the late Professor C. B. Cox, Hilary and Donald Crossley, János Csokits, Lady Cummins, Neil Curry, Andrew Davidson, Milan Djordjević, Gavin Drummond, the Very Reverend John Drury, Susanna Duncan, Professor Philip Edwards, Marianne Egeland, Lord Evans of Temple Guiting, Ruth Fainlight, the late John Fairfax, Jane Feaver, Paul Felver, Maggie Fergusson, Donya Feuer, Dr Ian Firla, Angela Fisher, Aisling Foster, Professor Roy Foster, Nick Gammage, Dr Nicola Gardini, Anthony Garnett, Dr Alison George, David Gerard, Terry Gifford, Dr Iris Gillespie, Rosemary Goad, Esther Godfrey, the late Fay Godwin, Edward Goldsmith, George Gömöri, Lord and Lady Gowrie, William Graves, Martin Green, John Greening, Geordie Greig, Trevor Grove, Frederick Grubb, the late Thom Gunn, the late Shusha Guppy, Professor John Haffenden, Nicholas Hagger, Donald Hall, the late Michael Hamburger, Saskia Hamilton, Shelagh Hancox, Terry Hands, Josephine Hart, Professor Hugh Haughton, Mark Haworth-Booth, M. Hunter Hayes, Marie and Seamus Heaney, Drue Heinz, DBE, Katarzyna Herbert, Lady Heseltine, Dr Franklin J. Hildy, Selima Hill, Shaun Hill, Mark Hinchliffe, Richard Hollis, Anna Hopewell, Matt Howard, Sandra Howard, Frieda Hughes, Glyn Hughes, the late Nicholas Hughes, Olwyn Hughes, Dr John Hurst, Daniel Huws, Sir Bernard Ingham, Nicki Jackowska, Peter Jay, Nicola Joss, Jutta and Wolfgang Kaussen, Peter Keen, Gene Kemp, John-Paul Kernot, Satoshi Kitamura, Mike Kitay, August Kleinzahler, Victor Kovner, Simon B. Kress, László Kúnos, Sheila Lawes, Andrew Lawson, Gregory Leadbetter, R. J. Lloyd, Christopher Logue, Herbert Lomas, Tom Lowenstein, Joanna Lumley,

Joanna Mackle, Gordon MacLellan, Janet Malcolm, Ian Marriott, Harold Massingham, Derwent May, Patricia McCarthy, Roger McGough, Gary McKeone, Paul Merchant, W. S. Merwin, Jon Michaud, the late James Michie, Professor Karl Miller, the late Adrian Mitchell, John Moat, John Montague, Pete Morgan, Blake Morrison, Andrew Motion, Paul Muldoon, Richard Murphy, Les Murray, Lucas Myers, Stephanie Nettell, Dr Sophie Nicholls, Christopher North, Edna O'Brien, Dennis O'Driscoll, James Olney, Charles Osborne, Michael O'Sullivan, Sir John Parsons, the Reverend Howard Pask, Lindsay Paterson, Anthony Paul, Lissa Paul, Tom Paulin, David Pease, Sir Michael Peat, Camillo Pennati, Monica Pennington, Joseph Petraglia, Katherine Pierpoint, Frank Pike, Christopher Pilling, Jill Pirrie, Piers Plowright, Christine Prosser, the late Mark Purdey, Rodney Pybus, Craig Raine, Jay Ramsay, David Rankin, Jeremy Reed, Clare Reihill, Adrienne Rich, Dame Diana Rigg, Paul Roazen, Neil Roberts, Annie Robinson, the late Paul Roche, Judith Rodriguez, Professor Jacqueline Rose, Anthony Rudolf, Barrie Rutter, Keith Sagar, Lawrence Sail, Andrew Sant, Frances Stonor Saunders, Jan Scammell, Michael Schmidt, Doreen Schofield, Keith Schuchard, Professor Ronald Schuchard, Gaia Servadio, Miranda Seymour, Sonu Shamdasani, Penelope Shuttle, Dan Sicoli, Dennis Silk, Alan Sillitoe, Charles Simic, Posy Simmonds, Dave Sissons, Dr Ann Pasternak Slater, Margaret and Michael Snow, Ben Sonnenberg, Lady Natasha Spender, Professor Jon Stallworthy, Anne Stevenson, Stephen Stuart-Smith, Tim Supple, Graham Swift, George Szirtes, Stephen R. Tabor, Ronald Tamplin, Emma Tennant, Janice Thomson, Ann Thwaite, Anthony Thwaite, Robert Tilling, Professor Caroline Tisdall, Brenda and Charles Tomlinson, Patricia Tormey, Deborah Treisman, William Tucker, Ann Vaughan-Williams, Paul Warwick, Vicky Watling, Daniel Weissbort, Teresa Wells, Tom West, Francis Wheen, Jane Whitbread, David Whiting, Clive Wilmer, Renée Wilson, Ashe Windham, Anna Woodford, Gillian Woolven, Carolyne Wright and Kevin Young.

Individuals, too, at the libraries and archives where I have sought material and information, have shown efficiency and courtesy sometimes far beyond what was due. Let me, therefore, now thank Erin O'Neill at the BBC Written Archives Centre, Caversham Park, Reading; Jonathan Barker at the British Council, London; Jamie Andrews, Christopher Fletcher, Sally Brown and Michelle Paull at the British Library; John Wells at the Department of Manuscripts and University Archives,

Cambridge University Library; Sir Michael Peat, Private Secretary to HRH The Prince of Wales and The Duchess of Cornwall, Clarence House, London; Sheila Noble at Special Collections, Edinburgh University Library; Charlotte Berry, Archivist at the Old Library, University of Exeter; Paul Keegan, Matthew Hollis, Katherine Armstrong, Vic Gray, Erica Somers, Rachel Alexander, Kate Burton, Anne Owen and Ron Costley at Faber and Faber; Robert MacLean at the Department of Special Collections, Glasgow University Library; Helen Roberts, Senior Archivist at the Brynmor Jones Library, University of Hull; Rachel Cosgrave at Lambeth Palace Library; C. D. W. Sheppard and Clare Everett-Allen at Special Collections, the Brotherton Library, Leeds University; Patricia Methven, Director of Archives at King's College, London; Sally Halkyard, Modern Literary Archivist at the John Rylands University Library, Manchester; Chris Hollifield of the Poetry Book Society; Chris McCabe at the Poetry Library, Royal Festival Hall, London; Jacky Hodgson, Head of Special Collections at the University Library, Sheffield; Tony Brown at the R. S. Thomas Study Centre, University of Wales, Bangor; Dr Tony Trowles, Librarian, Westminster Abbey; Pamela Clark at the Royal Archives, and the Hon. Lady Roberts, Librarian and Curator of the Print Room, Windsor Castle; Seamus Helferty, Principal Archivist, Archives Department, and Michelle Agar, University College, Dublin; Dr Heidy Zimmermann at the Paul Sacher Foundation, Basel; Prof. Dr Vasilije Krestić, Director of the Archive of the Serbian Academy of Sciences and Arts, Belgrade; Bronwyn Lea at the School of English, Media Studies and Art History, University of Queensland; Wilgha Edwards, Special Collections Co-ordinator at the Australian Defence Force Academy, Canberra; Elizabeth Grady at the Department of Immigration and Multicultural Affairs, Australian High Commission, London; Apollonia Lang Steele, Special Collections Librarian at the University of Calgary; Christopher G. Petter, Special Collections Librarian, and Danielle Russell, Rare Books Librarian, at the University of Victoria; Cecilia F. Roberts at Boston University Libraries; Stephen E. MacLeod at Special Collections and Archives, University of California, Irvine; Stephen Enniss, E. Kathleen Shoemaker, Naomi Nelson, Teresa M. Burk, Keith Nash, David M. Faulds, Kathleen Carroll, Elizabeth Chase and Jenny Heil at MARBL, Robert W. Woodruff Library, Emory University; Jenny Rathbun at the Houghton Library, Harvard University; Madeline J. Gibson at the Rare Book and Special Collections Library,

University of Illinois; Anthony Tedeschi, Michael L. Taylor and Saundra B. Taylor at the Lilly Library, Indiana University; Roland Goodbody and Nancy Mason at the Milne Library Special Collections and Archives, University of New Hampshire; John D. Stinson at the Manuscripts and Archives Division, New York Public Library; Ann Butler at the Elmer Holmes Bobst Library, New York University; Ellen M. Shea at the Schlesinger Library, Radcliffe Institute; Wm. Kevin Cawley at the Archives of Notre Dame University; Polly Armstrong at Special Collections, Stanford University; Lisa Richter and Rachel Hertz at the Harry Ransom Humanities Research Center, University of Texas at Austin; Katie Lee at the McFarlin Library, University of Tulsa; Lesley Leduc at Yaddo; and June Hadassah Can at the Beinecke Rare Book and Manuscript Library, Yale University.

I am especially grateful to Emory University for the award of a Woodruff Library Research Fellowship.

Christopher Reid
2007 (revised 2009)

A note on the paperback edition

I am grateful to readers and reviewers of the first edition of this book who brought to my attention the mistakes and deficiencies that they found there. Let me now warmly thank Elizabeth Barrett, Neil Corcoran, Clive Fairweather, Nicola Gardini, Frieda Hughes, Olwyn Hughes, Daniel Huws, Christopher Levenson, Lucas Myers, Tom Paulin, Colin Raw, Anna Ravano, Caroline Remington, Keith Sagar and Anthony Thwaite for helping me to correct and improve the text for this paperback.

C. R.
2009

Ownership Abbreviations

Ownership of each original letter is noted in the text. Where letters are owned by individuals or their estates, whether or not names are given in full, identification will be straightforward; where they belong to library or university collections, an abbreviated form is often used. The key to the abbreviations is as follows:

BBC: BBC Written Archives Centre, Caversham Park, Reading.

Beinecke Library: The Beinecke Rare Book and Manuscript Library, Yale University.

Cambridge: Cambridge University Library, in MS Add. 9451 – courtesy of the Syndics of Cambridge University Library.

Dublin: UCD Archives at the James Joyce Library, University College Dublin.

Emory: Manuscripts and Rare Books Library, Robert W. Woodruff Library, Emory University.

Faber: The Faber Archive – courtesy of Faber and Faber Ltd.

Houghton Library: by permission of the Houghton Library, Harvard University, where the call numbers for the two items are, in chronological order, MS Am 1905 (622) and MS Am 1905 (623).

Hull: Brynmor Jones Library, University of Hull, as part of the Philip Larkin Estate Archive, reference codes for these letters being, in chronological order, DPL2/3/8/9, DPL2/3/8/12, DPL2/3/105/8 and DPL2/3/75/28.

Leeds: Brotherton Collection, Leeds University Library.

Lilly Library: courtesy of the Lilly Library, Indiana University, Bloomington, IN.

New Hampshire: Milne Special Collection, University of New Hampshire Library.

Paul Sacher Foundation: The Chou Wen-chung Collection at the Paul Sacher Foundation, Basel.

Sheffield: Main Library, University of Sheffield.

Texas: The Harry Ransom Humanities Research Center, University of Texas at Austin.

Tulsa: Department of Special Collections, McFarlin Library, University of Tulsa.

Victoria: University of Victoria Special Collections, reference for the letter to Graham Ackroyd of 20 May 1960 being the Ted Hughes and Sylvia Plath Collection, 1997-174, file 6.1, and for the letter to Robin Skelton of 15 October 1975, the Robin Skelton Fonds 1981-026, box 4, file 20.

Windsor: The Royal Archives, Windsor. The letter of 24 March 1989 to Her Majesty Queen Elizabeth, The Queen Mother appears by permission of Her Majesty Queen Elizabeth II.

LETTERS OF TED HUGHES

1947/8

Ted Hughes was born on 17 August 1930 in Mytholmroyd, West Yorkshire. He was the third and youngest child of Edith (née Farrar) and William Hughes, a carpenter. In 1938, the family moved to Mexborough, a mining town in South Yorkshire, where William opened a newsagent's and tobacconist's shop.

Following his sister Olwyn, who was two years older than he, TH received his secondary education at Mexborough Grammar School. His brother Gerald, older by ten years, had been his guide and companion in exploring the countryside around Mytholmroyd, but he had left school before the move to Mexborough, working at a variety of jobs that included a spell as a gamekeeper in Devon, then serving in the Royal Air Force during the Second World War and emigrating to Australia in 1948. In Gerald's absence, TH shared outdoor adventures and an enthusiasm for the local wildlife with a school friend, John Wholey, whose father was head gardener and gamekeeper of the Crookhill estate, outside the town. Edna Wholey was John's older sister.

To Edna Wholey

[Undated 1947/8]   Ms Emory

Cherie Edna,

I have seen many strange things in my 17 years; things which, if allowed to roam at will through Whipsnade, would undoubtedly frighten to death the half of the animals which didn't bolt on sight. I have seen things which, when placed before a camera that posterity may wonder at their form, invariably shattered the lens, burnt the film and slew the photographer. I have seen things which, when taken within the city limits (To the extreme personal peril of the man responsible) stopped all traffic in the streets, paralysed the policemen and covered with green mould the money in the tills inside the shops. I have seen things which, when put on public view, slew the onlooking population by the thousand, melted the iron bars which encased it and leaping for freedom, reduced the room which contained it to general matchwood and lumber. All these things, which once held places of high wonder in my imagination, are now reduced and are dim and forgotten in the dust of eternity, for they are eclipsed; their day is ended; their brief light is extinguished in the aura of this modern wonder which is come upon me; and on the pedestal which once held aloft these wonders is placed a new phenomena. This will indeed startle the dust rimed skeletons of the dead, and bring them staring from their tombs, gazing in awe and wonderment on this iniquity of all time. It will fill the empty sockets of their skulls with a fearful fire and send them trembling in terror back to the cold clay and the darkness of the dead. For they will have gazed on the fault of God, the mistake of the Almighty they will have gazed on Edna, and will depart, terrified [. . .]

A single sheet, covered on both sides, is all that remains of this undated letter.

1949

On leaving Mexborough Grammar School, and having gained a Scholarship to
Pembroke College, Cambridge – partly through the intervention of his English
teacher, John Fisher (see footnote to TH's letter to Fisher and his family of 31 July
1960) – TH chose to serve his two years' compulsory National Service in the Royal
Air Force, before continuing his education. His first posting in uniform was to RAF
West Kirby, in the Wirral.

To Edna Wholey

[Undated 1949]   Ms   Emory

My dear Edna,

Your letter was among the best surprises I've had this side of my
civvies. I asked for your address from Johnnie, so I suppose he's gone one
better and given you mine. This life is all right in a way, but its next
thing to life in prison, and I'm writing this in my first loose time tonight,
and yet it's ten Oclock. I'm pretty lucky with my room-companions, but
fell badly in the years cruel end. Edna, I've seen rain and I tell you this
isn't rain, – a steady river, well laced with ice, tempest and thunder,
covers all this land, and what isn't concrete has reverted to original chaos
of mud water fire and air. Morning and evening its one soak and the
sun's more and less a sponge, and lately comes up frozen quite stiff. At
first the discipline was savage, and one youth broke down, but it relaxes
daily as we grow neater. At present there's a bed-tipping fight over half
the room. We have a new N.C.O. who comes in by night and talks, and
refueses to be savage. The food is scraped from I don't know where, but
parcels from home eke out my straining appetites longing. Nights are a
great comfort, for my bed's warm. The first fortnight, nay 3 weeks, has
flown by, and in 2 more weeks I have a 48, then at Xmas 5 days, and a
week after, after my training, 7 days, so I might see you, and shall if you
are home 10 minutes while I'm home. But bashfully. I am e'en shorn
and shining atop. I resemble a post that has been beaten till the tops turn
over so you won't love me any more for the spectacle of horror I am.

Gerald seems well, and writes home good merry letters. He paints a lot, and earns a lot, fishes lots, swims lots, shoots lots, and lacks nothing but home, and that will bring him in another year. Naturally I haven't heard from him yet here. It's a horrifying thought to think me 20–21 when I emerge from this morass, but then it's Cambridge so it's balanced.

I'll write more tomorrow, as its after lights out. Its tonight, which was, in the line above, tomorrow. Another day slipped under my boots, just out of my hands, behind the walls from my eyes, in no time at all. I've read a little, and now I write a little. I haven't seen the horizon today for fog, and tonight its cold. I have been eating most of the night hog from home. I shall be 19½ when I see you, and as you say it's a marvel that youre only 3 or 4 years topside of me. When I'm 20 I'll regard you as more or less my age, whereas before I've always been acutely conscious of your seniority. Now I'll tickle you familiarly like Mars, and not a boy in short pants. Tee hee. I look forward to seeing Crookhill, though in Winter. Proud to see you remember mi verses, ill as they are, but its your poem, and when I'm inurned in a temple over trafalgar square, you'll be able to point it out to grandchildren etc. Tonight for some reason I'm rather dull, Edna, to forgive mi tedious eloquence. How's Peter. I demand he combs, polishes, trims, aligns hair by hair, and warms his beard daily, curling the extreme tips, and blanco-ing any sidewhiskers, and carries his dragon-killing sword whenever he moves with you abroad, for your guardian must fain be glorious to the eye, and dreadful to the discourteous, so keeping up my standard. Noone must speak to you who has not a line of crowned ancestry that goes 7 times round his waist, otherwise he must speak through Peter or me, that you be not polluted by contact with base minds. I bow and sweep off my beret whenever I think of you, and if it is raining, I doff my great-coat and spread it in the mire, that the thought, so gloriously adorned as with yourself, may go undefiled. At Xmas shall I kiss your fingers at all partings and on each occasion have a gorgeous golden rose embroidered on the sleeves of my tunic. I shall also take you forth and carve our names together in a yew tree, haloed with stars, moons, leap-ards, and all symbols of moons of Diana. We now possess a grama-phone which you must hear at work, and I must have your opinion on the wreck of my hair. But goodnight Edna, write back, and something may happen to me to tell you. A friend of mine, also in these blue corporal be-ridden toils, took pneumonia on a drenched route march, and has bedded in hospital for 3 months as a T.B. suspect. That's a sober note to end my letter on a worldly plane, though Lord knows it's little enough inspired, but a better time will send you a better letter.

Lots of love, your fond Ted.

A simple but expressive drawing of a hammered post, in the margin, illustrates TH's new hair-cut.

A '48' was a forty-eight-hour leave.

By 'mi verses', TH almost certainly means the poem 'Song' ('O lady, when the tipped cup of the moon blessed you'), the earliest to be included in his first collection *The Hawk in the Rain* (1957). TH explains the special value he placed on this poem in his letter to Nick Gammage of 15 December 1992.

Peter was a bearded acquaintance of Edna Wholey's, at teacher training college.

1950

After a transfer to RAF Patrington, in the East Riding of Yorkshire, TH was to spend the remainder of his National Service there, plotting flights on map tables and screens, and using the relative isolation of his new posting to do a lot of reading.

To Edna Wholey

[Spring 1950]   Ms   Emory

My very dear Edna, my address is now
    2449573 A.C.2. HUGHES E J
      OPS. SECTION
        ROYAL AIR FORCE
        PATRINGTON
        NR HULL
          Yorks.

I'm waiting to begin a course for Fighter Plotting. The camp is only ¾ the size of the garden, with the Radar gear sitting all round in the wilderness. Every morning we travel from Sutton (20 mins from Hull) which we share with a fire-fighting training section, out 18 to Pat, and return at 5 at night. There are so many people they have nothing to do, and the atmosphere of the place is generally inert. Today I foiled them. I calculated cunningly which would be the last to go onto the transports, as we're all drawn up on parade waiting, and thereby escaped the journey, as there weren't enough transport wagons, as often happens. I was making off with a gay song to some secret sequestration, when a W.O. charged up, roaring like the North Wind, and harnassed me to a truck and a shovel, and indicating a small Vesuvius of coke, cried, "Shovel it in." I admit, Edna, I resorted to unfair, supernatural means. With sundry charms, I took on an appearence of enormous labour, and bewitched my 5 comrades in disaster into following my example, but they weren't so clever at only appearing to work, so they filled the truck in no time, and I retired to my idleness with a roused vigour, while they dragged outworn shells of bodies to whatever the NAAFI thought cruel enough to minister. I have read all day. Last week I brushed the guard-room aside and had a 36 at home, as I can run it in a hour when the train's going the right way. This weekend I'll be off again for a 48, if the gods think fit to relieve me from my divine duties of watching my 19th Spring burn in a dirty, wheezy, rickety rusty-limbed old R.A.F. stove, one of Ceasar's cast-outs, for thats the summit, the Olympus, of my R.A.F. endeavour. No, I lie! my 20th Spring.

It's a good thing they're going to throw me out soon enough to think over all the things I might have done, and not stop me thinking till gravestones and things take the job over for them, likely employees. I'll write again when things shall stir. Till then I'll be content that yourself's looking at the same sun as myself. I do more reading than I've done for many a month. Everything good to you and, – seperate note, – a kiss. Ted.

The dating of this is based on TH's (revised) calculation that it is his '20th Spring'.

Some RAF locutions: 'out 18 to Pat' = 'out at 6 p.m. to Patrington'; a 'W.O.' is a Warrant Officer; and the 'NAAFI' – Navy, Army and Air Force Institutes – ran service canteens. By '5 at night', TH means 5 a.m.

To Edna Wholey

[Undated 1950]   Ms   Emory

My most dear Edna,

This letter will probably be reaching you in 1952 or 3, as I'll have to float it in a bottle through this sad weather. I have been on an excellent new job for a week or two, which may or may not continue. There is little work, no officers, an excellent little sleeping hut, way away among fields by the sea. The immediate precincts are 3 or 4 inches under sea level, and full of hollows, where the rains of this season are becoming tidal, and full of strange beasts. Whenever any transports approach us to bring drinking water or coke or such, they bog like tanks in Burmese war-films, and we are invited to bring forth our pulleys, grappling irons, iron nets, strong arms etc to haul the bemired truck to dry land. Cruising upon these seas that fill our garden and fields is a small herd of wicked bulls. They look in at the doors the windows, lick the chymney, try to ride our bykes and bully everything and everyone without respect, so that, in the occasional low tides, we rush out with catapults and drive them roaring off. And amid all these distractions, – truck extractions, bull destructions, and impending death by water, – I have to call up my strongest demons to rally an imaginative peace, wherein I may fancy forth a letter. I saw such a miserably short presence of you, and that obscured by sundry bulky bodies, last time you were home, that I've been wondering when you'd next be home. I spent the week after, – no the Monday rather, – collecting flowers in a hailstorm, and found a bagfull, although I was alone. I hope you won well on my legacy in that prematurely decimated monopoly bout. I think 2 people are the outside limit to be playing any one game. I spend much of my time imagining sundry games for two, that I have plotted forth, and shall try out when I get a suitably enthusiastic partner. Live exultantly and well with all my wishes –

Seas of Love, Ted.

To Edna Wholey

[Undated 1950]   Ms   Emory

Last night as I was coming down the field I heard a commotion in the hedge, and after a while, out trundled a hedgehog, merry as you like, and obviously out for a good time. I thought he might make a jolly companion for an evening so I brought him in. After a while I noticed he had disappeared and later heard a noise just like the sobbing of a little child, but very faint, and it continued for long enough. I traced it to a pile of boxes, and there was my comrade, with his nose pressed in a corner in a pool of tears, and his face all wet, and snivelling and snuffling his heart out. I could have kissed him for compassion. I don't know why I'm so sympathetic towards hedgehogs. Once when John & I threw one in the pond, it nearly broke my heart to see it swimming to the shore. It must be that they're something my affection can't touch, and as through all my life the things I've loved best have been prickles towards that love, hedgehogs have become a symbol of such unrequiteable desire, and move me so nostalgically. I carried sad Harry outside and let him go – he wouldn't even roll up he was so sad.
[. . .]
   Those young bulls have grown too big to ride our bykes, so last week they turned to the car of a Warrant Officer who lives in a caravan at the field top, but this car was electrified against thieves, – more for pure fun

than thieves really – and when the eldest bullock, with a merry oath, sprang to the steering wheel to drive it into the sea, he was kicked nearly over the hedge by some 230 volts and spent the rest of the night cursing outside our window as if we were responsible. There really was a din for a time. We're hoping they won't come back to our bykes. When I came home from 48 last week, at 11.30 Sunday Night, I had to cross over 200 yards of field to this place. As I came out of the village I could hear these 4 bullocks conspiring just inside their gate. All the way over that field, in pitch darkness, they followed me 5 yards behind, and occasionally one would romp off into darkness, and come charging back, utterly invisible, only their hooves heard. When I got in, I had three hairs that looked as if they had nearly begun to turn grey. Had it been day I could have thrown them down; as it was I have sneered at them ever since.

About the Mexborough hedgehog incident, Edna Wholey writes, in the notes kept with her letters at Emory University: 'Here I think they were ashamed for they fished it out. Ted wrapped it in his jumper and they took it home. When Mum and Dad came down the drive there was the hedgehog rolled up in the kitchen towel in front of the range steaming away.'

1952

TH had taken up his place at Cambridge in the Michaelmas term of 1951, initially as a student of English Literature. The earliest extant letter from Cambridge to Olwyn Hughes (below) – dated by reference to the death of King George VI, on 6 February 1952 – is from his second term there.

To Olwyn Hughes

[February 1952]   Ms   Emory

Sometimes I think Cambridge wonderful, at others a ditch full of clear cold water where all the frogs have died. It is a bird without feathers; a purse without money; an old dry apple, or the gutters run pure claret. There is something in the air I think which makes people very awake. I have joined the Archery club and am very keen. This weekend I am into London to see Joan & Gerald in their natural habitat; the weekend after into Bedford, staying at Edna's. I grudge these weekends because we dedicate our weekends to the most magnificent eating – Chinese food & Indian.

Most of today I wrote my essay on the ballads, but do you know what I normally do? I get up at 6, and read a Shakespeare play before 9, and sometimes half an hour's Chaucer as well. Then I range all day among readings & writings. That early bout puts me ahead all day. My two friends, an Irishman and a Cornishman, the first two I made, are the wildest things in Cambridge. Intellectual talk is very rare because people have no beliefs. Now the King is dead. This term we have very few lectures, but what we have are really superb. One Mr Rylands, who was last year a slow motion dissecting xperiment on Pope, is talking of – speech & action in Shakes' Plays. He has produced Gielgud from time to time – his lectures are big acts but funny, and lively – full of anecdotes and interesting little ideas and today he xelled himself. Lots of things that I have known for a long time but never really caught, – up he brings them with a lovely story. Do you know that we are the first Elizabethans since Shakespeare wrote Hamlet? Sixty glorious years!

I have been poring upon prophetic writings, which predict England struggling until 1960, and from then on, because of her dominions, becoming more powerful than ever it's been. Now these lunatics have come raging up, and are in ecstasies over the publishing possibilities of my "Journal to Olwyn". I shant get peace for an hour, so I'll write more anononanonanonanonaonanonanon.

TH's brother and his Australian wife Joan were on a rare visit to England.

The 'Irishman' referred to was Terence McCaughey, a fellow-student of English at Pembroke; the 'Cornishman', David Morton, whose nickname, Cass, is given in the next letter to Olwyn Hughes.

'One Mr Rylands': George ('Dadie') Rylands (1902–99), Fellow of King's College, who cultivated connections with the wider literary world, particularly with the Bloomsbury Group, and with the London theatre.

To Olwyn Hughes

[Spring 1952]   Ms   Emory

Dear Olwyn –

This is Monday, about the 18th. Last night I came back from a week-end with Edna & her husband Stanley. [. . .] On Saturday they took me to Woburn Park – that's near Bedford – where I saw squirrels, and hares quite tame and thousands of deer and rare antelope, deer as far as you could see over a great park, and all colours from white through every brown to black, and curious pheasants with tails like rockets, and white emus, and somewhere was a herd of bison which we didn't see. At night we went to their local rep. which was quite fun – and a guest actor – Ralph Lynn – old 60 odd drawing room comedy Noel Coward vintage, all very dated – reminded me of Hilda somehow – but quite amusing. The play was rookery nook, whatever that is. A trifle, without licqueur, spirit etc.

Then on Sunday it rained as it will, and we sat and I read Thurber who isn't nearly so funny as he used to seem, though the collection was a late one, and not out of his prime. Then I played records to Edna & her spouse while they did odd jobs. And at evening I came home. A very pleasant break I conclude, and it cost me only a bottle of sherry, though it was good sherry.

Last week we had really the maddest merry party that we've had. We had dinner in Cass's room, he's the Cornishman who's like a blonde thinner Aubrey Beardsley, delicately on the recovered verge of the same sickness but with more life than a wood-full of cats. We must have drunk a lot of wine and the food was delectable for by 8 oclock we were really inspired – we didn't sing catches – we made music – à la Orchestra, and some of it, especially the end of one movement, was really astonishing. When we tried to repeat it we couldn't bring it to a close and it went on and on. Then it developped into the kind where somebody says not much, and everybody lies and laughs like an alarm clock. The next one is on Thursday, but will be broken up by 8-30, and Terence and I shall go to the theatre to A Midsummer Night's dream.

Last week we went to see "La vie Commence demain", and really aren't the French naïve – enthusiastically naïve – I mean about ideas and such. It was of a Frenchman who came to Paris for holiday to see all the historic curiosities, but met a high journalist who introd. him to Sartre, Picasso, Gide etc, to learn about tomorrow. Much of it was of atom-bombs and obsolete aircraft, and the attitude of resolution over fear which followed the atom-bomb, – all very outmoded it seemed. One fascinating biological part, which didn't really need a main feature film. Picasso wisely said nothing, and I think he looks very fine. Corbusier the architect wanted to give man the natural environment of his natural life, because only so can he function happily and more fully – which is one of my own pets. Sartre, of course, said nothing. Gide wittered like a plucked bird. When the French are homing an idea, they seem to be acting a part, don't you feel, as if they don't really understand, unless of course, its about art, and then they're the only people who seem to be able to do it at all. I can't carry on just now, but I'll fill out later. While I think – all the superficial people think the Beethoven is grotesque – all the real ones rave after a while. I have it stuck in the frame of Gerald's picture along with Napoleon, Keats, and the astrological maps for August & February. – To one side I have a little vol. of Botticelli open at Simone Vespucci. Elsewhere are books, books, books, words, words, words, and as yet I haven't progressed with my murals, though not cooled at all.

This is Thursday, and in a little while I must go to supervision, and I am sitting out my bedmaker, who is making purposeful noises in the next room. I had a little letter from you the other day. This afternoon it is archery and tonight it is dinner out and a play. Last night Terence and I went to a small concert in St Catharine's, which was very pleasant, and the orchestra passably good. Now I look back nothing seems to have happened. Last night I had tea with Mr Camps, and he too thinks the syllabus is too superficially wide, and so much more a knowledge of opinions about literature, than a real knowledge. I aired my belief – the old bards used to have to learn huge set tomes and become so intimate with them, that they became part of their mind. And just as one thinks with adopted ideas, so, if one studied say, just Shakespeare for 3 years intensely, it would be thereafter your mind, and an anchor for all other reading or art. This seems to be one of his pet ideas too. But of course nothing will ever be done, because it is a life long term policy, and nobody's prepared to forgo immediate advantages. I must be away again.

This is Sunday Night. This afternoon I went to a Beethoven Concert, by Adrian Boult and his Boys. Played Leonora I, and 8th, and Eroica. Leonora I and 8th were fine, but suffered wherever grip and momentum and furor were required, – they got through because of their music, but the Eroica, which is a Creative act to hear, was just bled white, – all the fiddlers ticking like a field of mere grasshoppers, or conjurers' assistants, while Boult's hands fluttered in the void like Shelley's for effect. On Thursday I think, I went to see the old Vic do a Midsummer Night's dream, and I never saw anything so pleasant. The tangle of loves in the wood was burlesqued but certainly not to death. Helena was the sort who was uproarous to hear every time she spoke. Even her serious speech – about her schoolday friendship with the other one, brought the house down, although she tried to do it quite straight. It was all production, but none the worse for any of it I thought – Day Lewis' wife played Oberon, or is it Titania. And now Auden has produced another Vol. of Poems called "Nones". I went into a bookshop the other day and began to look for Dylan Thomas' new book of poems before I realised he hadn't produced any, or one, rather.

I had a letter from Gerald and Joan the other day, Joan very xcited about the King's Funeral etc, – Gerald very sardonically witty. He says he's painted three magnificent pictures, and will lend them to my room, until he exhibits them in Aussie. Today I started a Mural, a huge Adam and Eve, terribly falling, which surprised me for success, and I sketched a simply fearsome Satan wheeling over them. I've just heard a programme on Henry Moore – the Irish Novelist – because Terence is having a Moore period to Counter my Yeats, but as Yeats always topped Moore in their endless inter-spite, I have it. I am reading Moore's

Biographies which are full of lovely anecdotes – one – Synge had produced some play – and after a reading Yeats leaned forward and said "Euripides", and then, after a pause, afraid he hadn't been striking enough, said "No – Aeschylus." Also a secretary, giving an account of Moore, said he had absolutely no conversation, but often said "Always eat good food", which would be mixed occasionally with "Read Pater for a style."

We had our first Spring day Yesterday, and so many people were feeding the ducks that I think several died. I'll send you a Dylan Thomas too.

Look after yourself
and write
Love
Ted.

The actor Ralph Lynn was then in his seventieth year, and *Rookery Nook* was a farce by the not much younger Ben Travers.

The humorous writings of *The New Yorker* contributor James Thurber (1894–1961) had been favourite reading for TH in his teens.

La Vie commence demain (1949) was a documentary film by Nicole Védrès.

The Beethoven thought to be grotesque by 'all the superficial people' was a prized death-mask. Where TH mentions 'Simone Vespucci', he presumably means Simonetta, of whom Botticelli made a number of portraits in profile.

A 'bedmaker' is a Cambridge college servant. Antony Camps was TH's moral tutor at Pembroke, and TH would have had to appeal to him when seeking to change from English to Archaeology and Anthropology, as he eventually did in his third year.

Sir Adrian Boult's 'Boys' were the London Philharmonic Orchestra. Helena was played by Irene Worth in the touring production of *A Midsummer Night's Dream*, in which Jill Balcon ('Day Lewis' wife'), who recalled the fact, played Titania.

For 'Henry Moore', read George Moore, Irish novelist and memoirist (1852–1933).

To Gerald and Joan Hughes

27 August 1952   Ms   Emory

Dear Pumpkin & Croft,

if this doesn't reach you at Colombo, then Ceylon has shifted since I addressed it. I have no great news which is new news; only everything is in the same denuded expression as you left to it. The brass on the cat's face is considerably thinner, and it is worn out from trying not to look like an ornament during your last looting days. What cat? did I hear you say, or was it the cracking of a locust in Palestine as he ranged into our dynamic wavelength. Well Pa brought in another Grilpe, not so carefully coloured as Grilpe I, and not as old and with a long spike on the end of its tail. At first it did nothing but howl about the house like a sheep-shearing. I suspect you have taken Grilpe I's mouse in the lightness of your fingers, but I made an ordinary paper mouse. And now it is my delight to enrage Grilpe II. So far it hasn't got Grilpe I's indolence, it goes frighteningly berserk instead, – plays conventionally enough but suddenly snarls and spits like a whip cracking and growls like a big dog. It is also a mountaineer, and climbs up your trousers as you stand. When it gets bigger I think it will eat men. It washes itself until its wrists look to be sore.

We had a letter from Olwyn who is delighted with her new work. I prophesy a time when I shall be living on her income, – I shall call it "the interest of her debts". Pa is up at Court on Thursday, to pronounce evidence and damnation on the Dobroyd boys. Yesterday I had a clash with the owner of the moor, though I was luckily unarmed. It is the best grouse season for years they say. So we could have been quicker than we were and noone need have known. Tomorrow I shall visit a barber's – I've been letting them get their strength up. The records that I ordered came, but so far not yours.

[. . .]

I trust you, Gerald, are painting, as your religion demands [. . .]

Love, Ted

This letter is addressed to the Orient Line shipping agent in Colombo, where it was to catch RMS *Orion* as it passed through, taking Gerald and Joan Hughes home from their holiday visit to Britain. 'Pumpkin & Croft' are typical of the joke names with which TH would often start letters to his brother and sister-in-law in these years.

To Gerald and Joan Hughes

[Late 1952]   Ms   Emory

Dear Gerald & Joan, –

Now if you're not painting, brother Gerald, you should be. This black certainly has a talent for handling watercolours, but I envy it no more than I envy a mirror its ability to reproduce every detail that it looks into. It's just not art, water-colour paint technique it certainly is, but there's no more art in it than in a photograph. These mirror-people are popular while they're producing, they always were, because it's remarkable to see such a labour of detail and exactness, but the pictures contain nothing xept paint. Why do you suppose those huge photographic landscapes and scenes out of the Romantic revival are ignored now, far greater things in their way than your Black's. And why do you suppose people sell their roofs and daughters to buy the little scribbles on bits of Greek pottery. When a man becomes a mirror he just ceases to be interesting to men. But when a man produces just a little scribble with real life and joy in it out of himself it lives forever because it actually is a bit of life and exuberance which people like in their company. You should read more Blake and his opinions on art, because he reacted in anticipation of the huge mirror movement which is still on, xept for the Picasso styles, and most of those are scenery under a state of sensation, not images re-imagined, as Picasso's own are. To paint a likeness is to short-circuit your artistic invention and vivacity. Blow your nose on Rembrandt and Constable and the dutch school and the later Italians. Study El Greco, and Michaelangelo who re-imagined everything. Whenever an artist is transferring to paper he is wasting paint and fooling himself. If you're painting straight out of yourself, painting trees and rocks as they please you to imagine them, you could be a good painter. But when you're measuring out scenery and bushes you've joined all the other extraverted failures. The Black's pictures just disgust me as being the very extreme of this dehumanised worthless material tendency. But nowadays people only live as they reflect their environments, so they best appreciate all the barren extraverted symptoms, but in the great ages people lived in their minds, and their environment became transfigured with human life, which is still valuable. No person is interested in a dull reproduction of appearences in the end. Everyone is interested solely in human life and the evidences of its most powerful interior episodes. Anyway it means that if you try to paint more like the black you will destroy what is really valuable in your own style, which is interior and very personal. My friend has a medium-sized picture of a moon setting over a sea-shore. I have studied and studied that and at last swore it was a coloured photograph. But it's not, it's a painting and not worth 5/- on any stall. Any fool can become a mirror if he practise hard, but only half a dozen in an age can be artists.

This is an antidote against the Black, however much the Australian's like him. You must remember that any permanent art produced in Australia would have a very limited appeal, because it's too material and outward-looking as it has to be as a nation. It's an impossible civilisation for art xept of the futile feeble mirror kind.

Looking at the Black's you don't get the impression of a tremendous or even an ordinary spirit, only of tremendous labour of reproduction and all his genius gone into mere technical skill.

You should look over a few books on Chinese and Japanese prints, and Cave art, and the early Cretan & Greek. That delicate, distinct symbolic quality is what you have, and what all good artists have until they get into bad habits. Then of course you should paint more, other-wise when the spirit comes along for a good thing, you're out of practice.

I've been down Mytholmroyd today to be measured up for a pair of flannels, precarously enough. Walt isn't so well. He could pop any day. Vic is in great form, and will go to an art-school. I drew what I thought was a very good lion leaping, but she copied it and improved on it. This astonished me, because drawing from objects or photographs where she has to discover her own line, she's not as good as that. It really was good. I shall buy her a few books of drawings for her to copy and practise. I've worked it all out by parental temperaments, zodiacs, and such, and decide that she will probably be very good one day, because she's more than Hilda can stifle. I go back to College on Thursday. Today I saw Johnny off to Nigeria, and tomorrow I shall shoot off all the ·22 ammo that I possess, before it gets too old to shoot off at all.

I haven't received those pictures yet. Happy new year
Ted.

Pa is looking very well & so is Ma. On Sunday we walked back over the moors from Haworth.

The 'black' artist disparaged here was Albert Namatjira (1902–59), Australian watercolourist of the Western Aranda tribe.

Walt, who 'could pop any day', was TH's maternal uncle, Walter Farrar, prosperous Mytholmroyd mill-owner. He died in 1976, in his eighties. Walter's sister Hilda had an only daughter, Vicky, who attended Huddersfield College of Art.

To Olwyn Hughes

[Undated 1952]   Ms   Emory

Swift is the only stylist. The excellence of any other writer is in some peculiar charm or some private strength of which the wielding is enviable but secret by nature of its being so private, original or unusual. Swift's excellence is a talent for clarity simplicity and power. His inimitable peculiarities are in choice of subject, or tone, but his writing is the bed-rock from which every writer must start. It is the norm of the language, and you can't go wrong to imitate it: it is the restrained side of every private peculiarity. Copying other writers leads people into all manner of blunders in taste, because they mimic those mannerisms for which they have no innate propensity themselves. Copying Swift's peculiarities can only refine the fundamental qualities of literature, clarity, precision, conciseness and power, of which everyone contains the original capacity.

[. . .]

Most important is to be able to enter a word like a continent. Meditate on the individual words, then you'll use them by an act of imagination, and with effective power, not merely flip them out of a jargon memory in a conventionalised encompassing of a flavoured thought. Then as often as you can, just write. Swift's one of those writers I wish I had by heart – Next to Shakespeare and Chaucer and before all others. Get a paragraph you like, learn it and often repeat it, and you'd be amazed how you can energise whatever you write just by conscious reference of tone or use to that one charge. Forget subtlety, and the ephemeral fringe of sensation, or organised thought and co-ordinated important use of words will forget you.

To my sister on her beginning her literary career.

These two excerpts are from a letter, or note, of which only half a sheet, covered on both sides, remains. Olwyn Hughes herself cannot recall the occasion, but it may be the moment in late 1952 when she moved to Paris, to take a secretarial job with the British Embassy. After working for various international organisations, she eventually joined the theatre and film agency Martonplay.

During her brother's teens, Olwyn had shared a number of her literary enthusiasms with him, persuading him, in particular, to take Shakespeare seriously.

1953

Before the end of his second year as an undergraduate, TH had undergone the crisis that led to his abandoning English Literature as an academic study. The dream that emboldened him is told in 'The Burnt Fox', the second piece in TH's prose collection *Winter Pollen*, as well as in his letter of 16 July 1979 to Keith Sagar. For his final year, beginning in the autumn of 1953, he was a student of Archaeology and Anthropology.

At some point, between the letter printed below and a previous one to Gerald and Joan Hughes, dated 10 August 1953, in which the subject is not raised, he seems to have turned his thoughts towards emigrating to Australia, to join his brother. Precisely when he took the formal step announced in the letter to his parents that I have provisionally placed some months later has not been ascertained.

To Gerald and Joan Hughes

25 November 1953   Ms   Emory

Dear Gerald & Joan,

Thanks for these marvellous vicarious holidays you're supplying me with. My new prayer is that everyone doesn't realise what a paradise Australia is, and fill it as if it were their normal Hell. I'm trying to get an extra year here, and I shall then have a teaching diploma, with which I shall not starve in Australia, nor live on the edges of your plates. Teaching is really a kind of compromise with the demands of real life, but I wouldn't mind it for a year or two. I should never stick down in a school in the bottom of a rut the shape of an industrial town's back street. It has lots of free time too. It will do until I free my hands. Olwyn writes leasurely from Paris where she leads a happy indolent existence, with every promise of enormous fortunes I'm sure. Sooner or later one of the three of us will pull out a real gold-laying goose, and then the other two can enjoy their life's ambition, to lean back and parasite in luxury. I asked Ma to make me some curtains for my differently sized windows, and asked for them to be green. She made them and had them dyed. I received the wrong number of curtains, monstrously wrong sizes, and almost jet black all of them, absolutely useless – Lord knows what we can do with them, – blindfold elephants. I have a new power-scheme. My daily charge now always contains six eggs whipped in a pint of hot milk, with a great handful of brown sugar – a delicious soup. This is besides meals. I buy meat and roast it in front of my fire, which brings people slavering from the other side of college to cram their nose in my keyhole. I do this in the middle of the night. I go to bed about 11, and get up at 2-30 in the morning. Then I work, and sing, and spring about amusing myself and draw grotesque figures on my walls until about 7, then I go to bed until 9-30. By this means I get two first sleeps, and feel fresh as a flower. The second (7–9-30) sleep is always full of the most marvellous dreams, and this is the best part of my day. This is like leading two lives. The night is so still and empty, and I'm alone in it so completely, that it's like the great pursuits, shooting and fishing and smirking at the distance. Piano playing comes on very slowly, but I have less will power than a gorged louse, and tend to neglect it. I wish you could see my room – it's the very epitome of an artist's studio without any nonsense. I never hear from Johnny, so maybe the nigs have got him in a pot, and Alice in with him for seasoning. My new study is Archaeology – I learn all about the beginning of life and everything since, which I shall delight to expound to you. So far Croft has kept silence. Even about our mutual profit, I mean the scheme whereby I invent plots, and you, Croft, elaborate them with passions and apt exclamations. You could become internationally famous – you're Gemini, and according to antique authority have a literary talent, which of course you're letters prove. So look to it. Say "Send me fifty plots to warm the pen-nib," and delight my hopes. So you can work your fingers to little grooved bones, and I can count the revenue, which is the height of my miserable ambition, to be such an accountant. How's painting?

Love, Ted.

1954

At the end of his third Cambridge year, TH completed his undergraduate studies and gained a 2nd-class BA degree. Although there was talk of his studying for a Diploma of Education, he is not known to have enrolled for any such course. Instead, he spent the next year and a half in miscellaneous employment that included – in something like this order – jobs at London Zoo, in a rose nursery, as a security guard and in the script department of J. Arthur Rank, for which he read books that were being considered for cinematic treatment. He seems, too, to have gone back to Cambridge often. TH's letters yield only the scrappiest information about this period and few can be dated with certainty.

To Gerald and Joan Hughes

23 February 1954   Ms Emory

Dear Gerald and Joan,

I really think I've made a record silence this time. Where did I stop? Have I written to you since Xmas? Well it is now almost very soulful Spring, xept in that new things are chary of display, because when they came out admiring each other in the December deceitful weather, they were most brutally and directly hit in the eye by the December honest weather, whereupon we froze up. There I suppose I stopped. There was such a freeze here that the Cam had four inches of ice, – the swans had to hop to let the ice get under, and then they dropped back onto it and walked. Everyone had to wear skates. But no snow. Only in Wales where ponies and birds froze solid. And when that passed, here it is very unremarkable climate, neither hot nor cold, weather with its coat over its arm and damp umbrella rolled so to say, glancing up occasionally at its skyline, or deducing from the flight of birds. I am teaching myself perfect freedom. I do what I want just xactly when I want in such matters as sleep, food, acquaintance etc. I suppose most people do really – but no, they do not. When I feel hungry I eat, when sleepy I sleep – anywhere – just stretch out and sleep. And this is a great reservoir of recuperative effects. Also the nagging harnass of conforming exhausts me I discover. I am built for a very quiet life, or else this sort where I do just as I like. When I work at some work eventually it will have to fit my scheme, because I could never suffer to be slowly killed by conforming to the absurd hysterical impersonal clock-kingdom legislation, or daily commercial round. However these metaphysical matters have rude heads, and should never have appeared on this page. Imagine my exquisite possessions: here I sit, having had the will-power to arise at 8 and wash my nylon shirt, now waiting, composing letters in a profound and intricate geometry of lights and shades, according to the modest emerging my room makes of a morning, merely waiting until it is time to buy herring roes, and these I shall deliciously fry, and devour, and so on into my entered day. This is discovering the great secret of possessing my soul in patience, not to be perfected in a hurry. The great first principle is that the clamour of the world is just wrong, and on a mistaken tack. That frees you from following its every stir as though it were a thing preparing to leap at you, you just let it go, confident that what you are missing would be extravagant squandering of spirit and no good, and from it select just such opportunities as are best suited to your inclinations, because when you are free from servile obedience to the noise, your inclinations are your needs. All this very slowly, – not more than one venture of virtuousity in a day, – there's no reason why you shouldn't live only one life, why try to live another nineteen, and succeed only in living one twentieth, because life is never measured in xtent. When I rock my desk and watch my ink wobble I am as delighted and sufficed as I can be. Isn't this a very philosophical religious letter? All this is straight out of the Bible. How is Dostoevksy? Balzac? When I come out there, I shall expect two learned characters. Write and tell me secrets.

Love   Ted.

Not in the habit of disclosing either his name or his address in the space provided on airmail letter forms, TH in this instance has put: 'Jack Happygraft / Houses of Peerlymount / Calcutta'.

To Edith and William Hughes

[May 1954]   Ms   Emory

Dear Mom & Dad,

   I am going to surprise you with this letter. I have filled in emigration papers for Australia. When I shall get a boat I don't know – may be months or a year. There is a girl here that I shall take with me if I still feel like it, and probably marry her before I go. She is willing to do anything as you see from the fact that she is willing to do this, which is the extreme any of things. She is a nurse and from some angles looks very like me, everyone says. Don't immediately imagine that I am being gulled. I kick her around and everything goes as I please. Unless I make this very decisive step I shall float and float remaining in England. I dread anything but going to Australia as quickly as possible. This loitering at University in a pretence of education is rapidly becoming nothing but self-deception, and I shall be no better for another day of it, now that I am sick of it. I don't imagine that Australia is a simpleton's paradise, but the psychological impetus I shall get by being a newcomer and a beginner together will carry me much farther than struggling up one more weary rung here on the old ladder in England, almost all rungs of which I have learned to despise. In Australia the bottom rung is endurable because all the rungs are possible. However this letter is merely to get you used to what have been vague ideas having become facts and actual circumstances.

If my boat sails before the Dip. Ed. course, I shall sail on it. If it sails during the course I shall sail on it. I shall do as much of the course as I have time for, but sail when my boat sails. If I had enough money I would sail as quickly as I could get a berth, but this cheap (£10) emigration scheme takes its time and ours. I wonder if Walt would like to come along. If he would pay our fares I would set about getting tickets tomorrow, and might get them on the next boat or this summer. Otherwise I shall have to go on the emigration boat.

This ridiculous xam begins next week. I despise myself for having allowed myself into such a position that such an exam is the concern of my time and attention. This is really fiddling while Rome burns. The men that walk out of University are invariably the strongest minded most intelligent ones. The fools cannot see it as unimportant, and if they carelessly neglect it because they are fools, they get frightened and are recognisable on all sides, some commit suicide, one last week. The weak-minded ones procrastinate and at the expense of all their time retreat to the lowest corner of the lowest tripos. The conventional ones, and the ones secure in predetermined destinies and professions, go quietly through with what they began. The individual ones protest and mock but do it, unless they are so determined or intelligent they find it as easy to walk out.

Love,   Ted.

The Australian government had offered assisted fares to young British people wishing to emigrate there – an offer with a strict time limit. Whenever it was that TH applied, he kept the option alive until the last moment, when the matter was in effect decided by his marriage to Sylvia Plath in 1956.

The 'ridiculous xam' is presumably the first, or one, of the papers TH was about to sit for his finals.

To Gerald, Joan and Ashley Hughes

16 October 1954   Ms   Emory

Dear Gerald, Joan & Snatchgrubbington –

Wave this before Ashley's eyes, crying – look at our millionaire relation, Ashley, future security etc. I wrote to you imparting the circumstances and promises of my latest scheme, – mink-farming. I have written to Australia House, and they tell me mink are definitely "out". Canada house tells me it is cheaper and easier to breed mink in the British Isles, and that the climate is better even than Canada, – various details. Now. I am going to do this – whatever. It would mean that within eight years we could be secure for the rest of our lives – and by then I shall be writing very saleable sentences, as is already appearing. There's nothing I want to do so much as come to Australia, and especially now, to get in at Ashley's education, but I would be without any but the most struggling of professions, and I should be a responsibility to whoever touched me. I am going next week onto a mink farm – a big one – with a very experienced man who has promised to show me everything – the one a mile from the new house. I can live cheaply at home, write morning and night, poach deer, – there are deer now up Hardcastles, – and generally prepare myself to start. Here's an American, wealthy and full of energy, an Irishman, – full of benevolence, who promise to provide everything in the way of contacts for food, capital, – so long as I get the skill. I see it as an extension of my trapping over Old Denaby – it's not as if I'd been brought up as a commercial traveller anyway. I am amassing lots of information on it, and I'm sure I can be making £12000 in four years – without tax & cost – if I have a one man help at that time. Now this seems to me a far better bet than coming to Australia immediately, & scraping round. In this way both you and me & Olwyn too – if she will support me for the first two years as she promises – can be independent within three years. Now here is a suggestion I hope you will not treat with horror – Up to three years I can do all the work myself – or up to two at the least – Olwyn will work to keep me, and I shall of course write. Not even feeding will be much expense until the fourth year. Once I have started – with land, cages, feeding supplies, 15 mink, – I am all set for a fortune. There is only one snag – I shall need more than my own labours to breed enough mink to make the money possible. Now if you come over, say, in the second year, or even earlier, you & Joan could work to keep us and the mink alive, and Olwyn too would be working, and I would be writing, and I would be tending the mink, and you would collect the food in a little van or something from the feeders every morning before you go to work – from the butchers, or whatever – the farm will be near a food supply – until – so on until – wham, in the fourth Spring there is work for all of us, also about £2,000 from the 3rd year sell off of surplus males, then in the fifth Spring £12000, and, if we like, double the breeding stock again, – there would be enough of us to do it – most of the work's just carrying food round – and that would mean in the 6th Spring £24000, or we could keep it steady at a lesser figure. This isn't a dream – there is only one condition – that you keep mink of only the finest quality, which, of course, we shall take good care to do. There aren't very many of the very best mink, and yet they're cheap enough. After 8 months on a mink farm – covering all the important stages – I shall know enough to select a good stock – I already wouldn't be fooled on several points. After ten years – or we could cut it down to lazy proportions – you could slope off to Australia again to buy hotels, Walt would have died of envy – write quick, quick. Ted.

Ashley Morris was Gerald and Joan Hughes's first son, born 11 August 1954.

The mink farm was one of a number of money-making schemes, enthusiastically researched by TH and proposed to his brother, in the hope of coaxing him back to Britain.

Old Denaby lies south-east of Mexborough.

1955

Olwyn Hughes returned from her job in Paris to stay with her parents in the summer of 1955, making rough dates possible for the first few of these letters. TH's exact location at any particular time may be hard to fix, but it is clear that Cambridge continued to attract return visits.

To Olwyn Hughes

[May/June 1955]   Ms   Emory

Dear Olwyn,

I wonder how you're surviving. You should be doing something besides, – writing those articles, – to make your stay worth-while perhaps. I'm glad you liked the poems. They're nothing that I can bear to read now. The first one has the best and the worst points. The second has three good verses to begin with, but flat, like a picture, and static, and the end is ridiculous. The third is at least a complete style, but in that particular instance too much on one note I think. But it is speech – the whole mind moving together – not a particular lyrical strain defined – death of language that. I would like my metaphors as in proverbs, not as in metaphysics. And the sound of a single voice argueing – not the atonal voicelessness of most verse now.

Everybody down here is doing exams at present, so it's very quiet. During the mornings I go to work. I'd do something else, I think, but ever since I came down here I've had athlete's foot, which at times has made it uncomfortable to get about. It's clearing up now, in fact it's cured – but my feet and hands are covered with little rags of dead skin and unsightly blotches of new.

I seem to have spent most of the week dishing up information on this author and that for the desperates, and everyone I know seems to be a desperate. The argument of Shelley's defence of Poetry I remembered from Mex. Gram. My host – a monstrously built Pisces – 24 stone – has so far done the whole exam on quotes I selected. He has a gift for flannel and a journalistic approach which is perfectly suited to the few bare

28

crumbs of knowledge I've pointed out for him – rather like Roger Owen only knows less – can reel off a Daily Mirror leader article on any incident before the incident is over, everything in neat order.

Written on the back of a letter to TH's parents, accompanying a package of laundry, this is either incomplete or unsigned. The poems TH had shown his sister cannot be identified, but they may have included items that were first printed either in the Cambridge magazines *Delta* and *Chequer*, which were now taking his work, or in *Saint Botolph's Review*, which was to be launched by his own circle of friends in February 1956.

TH's 'host' was Michael Boddy, a student at Queens' College.

To Edith, William and Olwyn Hughes

[Summer 1955]   Ms Emory

Here I am in Baldock, in a labour camp, ready to break from my bed at 6 in the morning to fiddle with roses. If I can get my tent pitched out there near the job I shall save almost everything, and shall then have enough money to live well till either my next job, or this B.B.C., which is slowly under way. The people in the B.B.C. are more nauseous than any other external objects I ever encountered. I don't think I'd like to work with them much.

I worked in London for two days at Regent's Park Zoo. It was good food and everything else bad.

[...]

I shall know today whether I can pitch my tent at this rose job, – and then my address will be, I think, Hitchin Post Office, but as the Rose gardens are quite a way from Hitchin there may be some nearer place.

The job is following round the expert as he grafts expensive rose-buds onto common bushes, and doing all the trimming-and-tying up-with-raffia – a back-breaking job apparently, but outside, and with roses, and with good employers.

The small, lined sheet on which this is written is torn at the bottom, so only excerpts are possible. TH was never an employee of the British Broadcasting Company, although he later came to write and present radio programmes for it. His job at the time was with the Hertfordshire firm of Ena Harkness & Co.

To Edith, William and Olwyn Hughes

[Summer 1955]   Ms Emory

I am out of Baldock Hotel at last, after four nights in there, which came to 32/- – the most expensive item of this episode I hope. The fellow I work with in the rose garden is the leading man in local rep., a very nice fellow, who is all day long asking me such questions as

'Ted, as stones grow older do they grow larger or do they grow less?" or

'Ted, where did all the water in the sea come from, surely it didn't all just rain?" – and "Why doesn't water wear away?" – he made one or two enquiries of a more practical bent and got me a little camping site in an orchard behind a pub, 500 yards from work – so now I can save all my money, and it should be full rate next week.

[. . .]

Everything is perfect. This is perfect country, perfect weather, perfect money. The people are appalling – horrible unhappy snoots & crumbs – this is the fringe of suburbia, where the very wealthy and the very emulous live – the sides of the roads are lawns, the towns are garden cities, with "People's Halls", and notices outside large buildings "Ladies' pleasant evening" – every lane is a drive to a huge house or a field of priceless cattle, or seedling rare flowers or a golf course, cricket ground, bathing pool. Very strange! But the open country is lovely.

To Lucas Myers

[Autumn 1955]   Ms Emory

Dear Luke,

I have come for two days. If I cannot sleep on your floor – not without Mrs Hitchcock's blessings this time – I shall move on.

                                             Ted

I have gone to eat.

Lucas Myers (b.1930), an American student at Cambridge, was living in the dining-room of St Botolph's Rectory, Cambridge, when TH left this note there. Earlier in the year, Myers had occupied a chicken coop in the garden, with TH occasionally sleeping under his bed or pitching his tent outside. All this, however, ceased when Myers's moral tutor insisted he make more orthodox living arrangements and Helen Hitchcock, his indulgent landlady, invited him to move indoors.

To Gerald and Joan Hughes

10 October 1955   Ms   Emory

My life lately has been such a turmoil I haven't felt like writing to anyone, though I'm sure I don't have to wait till I have special news. At present I'm living in London again. I shall have to get a proper respectable job because if I don't Ma will just worry herself away. So I'm trying to get onto Television, or the B.B.C., or into films. Once I've got some experience I could come to Australia and work much more profitably. I have a friend who's an agent for American T.V. and I gave him a bunch of plots for T.V. plays the other day – (they have teams of apes to write them up as T.V. plays) – and he accepted two. If he's accepted them it's likely his boss will accept them too – and they pay anything up to 1000 dollars. I had an interview for Ealing Studios – the film co – to start as a supervisors assistant or something – miserably paid – but I could force in film scenarios, and once I got skillfull at that we'd all be rich. The other day I won £25 on a newspaper competition. At present I work as a security guard – sitting in a little office at a girder-factory all night – I spend the whole time writing and I draw £8 a week, so it's O.K. till I get something better. I feel very angry at the bottom though. If I were to do what I really wanted and went on a trawler in the North Sea for the Winter, my Ma would take to her bed. I shall have to become respectable – but I shan't stay in London longer than to get qualifications to move profitably elsewhere. My idea is to save everything for about five years, then buy a house in Oxford or Cambridge & farm it out to students & nurses at £3 a room – offer a landlady free living in the basement. One of my acquaintances does this, and spends his time pottering about the world on the income. Then two and three houses. What different lives we would lead if we had a bit of money.

If we could get a line of houses running, there'd be no need to buy aircraft parts. Another branch would be garages – half a dozen brick garages here and there in small towns – 10/- a week. If I could paint as you can Gerald I would long to buy not a house for yourselves, but a house in Melbourne that you could fill with lodgers – one per room – get so much security, – then paint. If you send me a dozen of the best sort of your paintings, I can guarantee £15 to £20 each here in London. Everybody who sees your pictures says the same. It's not as though you toiled over them either. I'm sure you could average one per week and more likely two, – and after the first thirty it would be £30 each, then £40. Good God, you're mad not to exploit that vein. You could earn more on it anyway than you do at work – not £6 each but £15.

1956

Saint Botolph's Review, edited by David Ross, appeared on 25 February 1956. TH and Lucas Myers were among its contributors; others destined to be TH's lifelong friends were Daniel Huws and Daniel Weissbort. The magazine was launched with a spirited party, at which TH and Sylvia Plath met. An American graduate student, on a Fulbright Scholarship, studying for an MA in English at Newnham College, Plath was sufficiently striking in her looks and behaviour, and had published enough poems in student magazines, to have caught the attention of the *Saint Botolph's* group, who had quickly decided that she stood for the kind of poetry to which they were opposed. Her own account of the meeting with TH, and their immediate mutual attraction, is given in *The Journals of Sylvia Plath 1950–1962*.

What followed – rapid romance, marriage, honeymoon in Spain, return to England and Cambridge – can be traced through the letters below. The period of separation, while Plath was back in Cambridge negotiating her position as a secretly married student, and TH was either in Yorkshire, at his parents', or in London, yielded a unique exchange of letters. Eventually, TH would join his wife, they would find a flat in Cambridge, and he would take a teaching job while she continued her studies.

To Olwyn Hughes

[Early 1956]   Ts   Emory

I discovered the other day that one can live in Hungary even more cheaply than in Spain. Is that so? It would be a better place to live than Spain – Spain being the oven-top that it is. I have considered applying through the appointments board for a lecturing job in Madrid, which is apparently possible. A scheme that calls itself the Mango, and which is fairly well paid. Meanwhile I heard the other day that Jo Lyde has been offered a lectureship – in English Literature – at Toulaine Univ., in New Orleans. What is life like in Hungary? Not so many tourists as Italy etc I imagine.

I live on at this, but not with much zest. We are still trying to finish our comedy script, which is really beginning to look quite promising. I get no time for writing.

They are running a season of Japanese films at the Everyman

Hampstead. I saw 7 Samurai the other night. Very impressive. Extraordinarily sentimental in a way that isn't at all offensive. The only passion possible on the English screen at present is anger, or indignation. Nothing like Kikuchiyo's – the clown – when he held the little baby outside the burning mill.

As for the Attila translations I thought that was fixed. I'm waiting for literal translations in three versions. Even a selection of thirty would be enough. There would be no hope of earning money by it, of course, but it would be worth doing.

I reviewed a novel the other day written by the ex-Cambridge youth who lives in one of the cottages down in the bottom of Hardcastles. It was exceptionally dull. [. . .] The best thing I have read for a while is "I am 15 and I do not want to die" which you will have heard of.

This is two days later. I had a letter from Gerald and Joan. When I arranged to emigrate on the previous occasion – in 1954 – I asked the Auss. to defer my passage for a year. That was up last summer. Now they are enquiring from Gerald whether I want to take it up now, and if I do not then I have had a cheap passage for good because they don't like being monkeyed about when so many people are dying to be there on the next boat. I feel this is forcing my hand rather, but as I do intend to go within the year – after a stay abroad as I've mentionned up above – I suppose I should not lose the chance of a cheap passage just for the sake of 5 or 6 months in Europe this side of my 27th year. In fact, out of that very confused last paragraph you may pick my intention – which is to go to Australia just as soon as the Auss. enquire at this end whether I still want to go. I shall stay two years at least then go through America. This does not mean that I shall not have free months this summer to come to Europe.

I have discovered my secret. I only write poems when I am busy writing prose at the same time, and also when I am taking regular exercise. I published one or two poems in a magazine which were not very satisfactory, but they drew some very gratifying criticisms from the right kind of people. If I could write whole poems as good as odd little bits I'm sure I really would have something, and something quite different from the meanness and deadness of almost all modern English verse – with which I feel not the slightest affinity. And writing these poems is only a case of giving myself the leasure and the stimulation. I am as interested in the Attila enterprise as you are.

TH's interest in Hungary – thinking of moving there; enquiring about the poems of the Hungarian Attila József (1905–37) (whom he habitually refers to as 'Attila'); giving praise to the newly published *I Am Fifteen – and I Don't Want to Die*, by Christine Arnothy, Hungarian-born French author, whose first-person narrative is set in war-torn Budapest – closely predates the country's disastrous confrontation with the USSR. Olwyn Hughes, living and working in Paris, had made friends there with a circle of Hungarian émigrés that included the poet János Csokits (b.1928), who was later to become a friend and collaborator of TH's, and the violinist Ágnes Vadas, who married Lucas Myers. This group had passed on their passion for József's poetry to Olwyn.

'Toulaine' should be 'Tulane'.

'7 Samurai': Akira Kurosawa's 1954 film, in which Toshiro Mifune played Kikuchiyo.

To Terence McCaughey

[Early 1956]   Ts   British Library

Dear Terence,

You're a creepget, without qualifications, keeping so quiet for so long, hiding your address.

I suppose Mac has told you most things. I have occasionally met him in London, where we come together like two drowners in mid-Atlantic, – Homer's metaphor. I have occasionally interrupted his duties in Cambridge where, each Saturday, he supervises the erks that Hodgart can no longer bear to look at. They are an unrelievedly dull pack. Hodgart speaks nostalgically of the English Faculty as it was three years ago, and he might well. We slumped, and draped, and exhaled crass vapours when it came to supervision, but these – they have invented a new thing, a posture from beyond the black bog. Nevertheless, I have not failed to find Mac issueing poop at every orifice, and very glad to be doing it.

Do you know that I work with J. Arthur Rank? I am a shit-shoveller. Literally. I read everything that is written, and that an author's vanity can think will make a film. I make a synopsis of each piece, and say how suitable for a film I think it is. I intend to do it for another fortnight, and then I shall leave. Everybody there is – in Bradley's phrase – as far up everybody else's arse as they can get.

I'm not very well equipped really to live outside a college, that's the truth, however badly equipped I am to live inside.

Danny Huws and Luke Myers and I produced a magazine. We called it St Botolph's Review – not a very good choice of title, everyone took it for a Parish magazine. Except for the few that bought it. They complained that it was obscene. The best thing about it was the party we had on the night of its first day out. We held it in a large fine room which belongs to the Women's Union – a room with large stained glass churchish windows. Mac played, all drank, more women than men, we left the place smashed, windows out, polished floor like a dirt-track. The bill will come one day. Pity you were not there.

[. . .]

   This is not a very graceful letter, Terence, but correct its faults with an answer. Tell me how cheaply one can live in Dublin. I wish to write and publish a certain thing but I get no leasure in London. My life in London in fact is no life. Automatism in a stunned half-wake. I had the honour of considering just how suitable for a film Ulysses would be. I spoke my mind. But the Americans are going to film it? How? Some of the scenes, lots of the dialogue. But. I read a biography of Joyce – the one with surrealistic representations – jigsawed photographs – of certain periods of his life. I never read a more stupid book. "He returned to Dublin the following year and found it unchanged (it could hardly have changed in a year) . . ." and that sort of thing. Write. This is the first letter I have written for a month.

Ted

Written from 18 Rugby Street, a house in a run-down Bloomsbury terrace, where TH lodged when needing to stay in London. It was owned by the father of Daniel Huws, fellow-contributor to *Saint Botolph's Review*.
   MacDonald ('Mac') Emslie, a Pembroke graduate writing a thesis on words and music in the seventeenth century, played piano at the *Saint Botolph's* party.
   Matthew Hodgart had been TH's and McCaughey's director of studies at Pembroke in their first year.

To Edith and William Hughes

[March 1956]   Ms   Emory

It's beautiful Spring down here around Pinewood, but in London it's not nearly so noticeable. My eyes have been aching a bit lately and going wonky for spells, but it's only reading all this stuff – I shall do this job for about another month, not longer, then do as I told you.
   I went to a Party in Cambridge the other weekend, which was very

bright, and everything got smashed up. This weekend Luke was staying in London with me – but nothing really happens – all the life here is outside you – there's never time for anything else. In fact, it's a complete waste of time, its earning a little money, but losing absolutely everything else. And I should be sorry to think that the people at Pinewood were to be my company. I've discovered one thing – and that is that the only sort of life I can lead is to do exactly what I want, which means to write. This job makes me feel guilty. I shall have about 160 or 70 pounds when I leave. Forty of this I shall take with me to Italy – live there till I'm spent up or fed up – writing, then come back and go to Australia for two years.

To Lucas Myers

18 March 1956   Ts   Emory

Dear Luke,

I shall expect you any day.

If you have time, drop me a note and tell me when you are coming. If you see Sylvia Plath, ask her if she's coming up to London, give her my address. Get her somehow, free lodgings for her as for you.

I have been given an ultimatum by the Australian immigration authorities. Two years ago I deferred my application for a free passage, and my time is now up. If I do not take it now, I cannot have another chance, and whenever I go will have to pay full fare. As I intend to go within a year anyway, I think I shall agree to go as soon as possible. My sentences aren't making sense are they. Anyway, it means that I shall definitely be going within nine months, but as their are long waiting lists for passages, it may well be the full nine months before my turn comes.

See you this week sometime.

Don't forget Sylvia, and discretion.

                                                  Ted

To Sylvia Plath

[March 1956]   Ms   Lilly Library

Sylvia,

That night was nothing but getting to know how smooth your body is. The memory of it goes through me like brandy.

If you do not come to London to me, I shall come to Cambridge to you. I shall be in London, here, until the 14th.

Enjoy Paris

Ted.

And bring back <u>Brandy</u>. Two bottles – broach one to please the customs.

Sylvia Plath visited TH at 18 Rugby Street on 23 March, the evening before her departure for Paris and a tour of Europe. In the poem '18 Rugby Street', in *Birthday Letters*, TH remembers the date as 'April 13th, your father's birthday', but he seems to be muddling two separate visits: the first on the eve of Plath's journey out, the second following her early return. The note above must have been written after the first.

To Sylvia Plath

9 April 1956   Ts and ms   Lilly Library

Sylvia,

On Friday I shall be home about 8 – expect you then.

On the principle that to every sentence of prose there should be six of verse –

Ridiculous to call it love.
Even so, fearfully I did sound
Your absence, as one shot down feels to the wound,
Knowing himself alive

Only by what most frightens, the suddenly
Anxious and kneeling sky, clouds, trees,
The headlong instant that halts, stares, comes close
With an incredulous ghastly eye.

That man struck looks up:
A bird, gathering the world in its throat – one note
About to be heard –, stands, beak agape:
What ghostly hands his hearing strains to it!

One cry – then death, all into darkness.
Hands here were as inadequate, –
Wherever you haunt earth, you are shaped and bright
As the true ghost of my loss.

38

Boddy was my guest here until the other day – finally pawned his tape-recorder to me – for ten pounds – and left. Can you smuggle brandy?

Ted

Sent to Plath in Paris.

To Olwyn Hughes

22 May 1956   Ts and ms   Emory

Cher Olwyn,

On the 22nd of June I shall come to Paris. The present date is 22nd of May. Between those two dates sits one fat month. Now.

I have airily irresponsibly vacillatingly conceded to my affections and decided that I shall spend the next year teaching English in Madrid. Or at least, at first teaching English, later perhaps whatever else is most convenient and possible for one who intends to use all his spare time on himself.

[. . .]

I have met a first-rate American poetess. She really is good. Certainly one of the best female poets I ever read, and a damned sight better than the run of good male. Her main enthusiasm at present is me, and she thinks my verses are as good as I think they are and has accordingly and efficiently dispatched about twenty five to various immensely paying American Mags. So. She has published stories and poems in some of the top American journals. If you're in Paris on the 22nd I'll introduce you. She is Scorpio Oct 27th, moon in Libra, last degrees of Aries rising and has her Mars smack on my sun, which is all very appropriate.

I hope for no good of this letter because today the sun opposes a conjunction of Saturn and the moon, and Mars opposes Jupiter which is back on my sun. Defy these stars.

My life is peaking, and my writing at last going with me method. I shall write to you more fully later tonight. I have decided that correspondence with certain people is a necessity.

I shall send you what poems I write from now, because now I'm writing steadily well – and not well in a fashionable or trite way either.

Love,

Ted.

Enjoy Cannes.

Later tonight. For the last month I've lived about the strangest life I ever did live. The main thing about it – and the thing that has saved it from being just absurd – is that I've written quite a bit. As I'm miserable and fit for nothing if I don't write continuously, I shall from now on shape my life round writing instead of squeezing writing into my life where I can.

Written from 12 Tenison Avenue, Cambridge, where Lucas Myers was living. Between this letter and the next, on 16 June 1956, TH and Sylvia Plath were married at the church of St George the Martyr in Bloomsbury. The only relative in attendance was Plath's mother, Aurelia. TH did not admit the marriage to his own family until he and Plath had returned from their Spanish honeymoon, although he declares that he *will* marry her in the next letter, to his parents, from Spain, where she is plainly with him, and in the one after, to his sister.

To Edith and William Hughes

[Summer 1956]   Ts   Emory

Dear Mom and Dad,

After all our comings and goings we have arrived here where we shall stay until September. We have been here three days, and I have already written eight or nine animal fables which I am going to bring out as a childrens book for grownups also. I shall make a few drawings too. They are far more what I wanted them to be than I ever thought I could make them. With luck, I may make some money on them. I have about five other projects, too. One of them is to finish my long fairy story, which went very staggeringly in England. But I am sure there is nothing quite like these fables. Also the other day I heard that I had sold another poem in America. This time to the Nation, which is an international monthly full of articles by all kinds of bright people, and usually with about five poems. No, a weekly I think. It publishes the best American poets, and will be very good for my reputation and succeeding sales. As it is only a short poem, and as I'm not known, I shall only get about $12 for it.

We stayed in Paris about a fortnight, but had to book our train to Madrid as France was getting too expensive. So I just missed seeing Olwyn when she suddenly said she was coming back to Paris earlier than she had intended. We stayed in Madrid about five days – again it was expensive. Luckily Sylvia has about 270 dollars which she earned on stories. My last 50 pounds is with Olwyn. We saw a bullfight. We had a fine ringside seat, just above the place where all the back-ring buisiness went on, and the place too where most of the fighting took place.

It was very disappointing. The bull isn't a savage raging murderous thing at all. It's angry, naturally, and towards the end very angry, but throughout it only chases the cloaks, never the men. The moment a man stops waving his cloak, even if he is only two or three paces away, the bull stops. Most of the time it just stands, looking bewildered, while the men with cloaks try to get it to charge. At first there are several men with cloaks – muletas they are called – and these take it in turn to put the bull through its paces, so far as they can and dare. The good ones have it charging through the cloak under their held out arm, the bad ones go headlong for the safe slits in the fence of the ring with the bull goring at their trailing cloak. Even the good ones are running headlong after standing and dodging two or three charges. The bull at this point is very lively. Not quite fierce yet, but quick to join the game. This goes on for about ten minutes, and the bull begins to pant.

Then in comes a man on the horse. Two men on horses actually but one is a standbye. The horse is blindfolded, and padded on the right side with a mattress thing that hangs down to its ankles, so that it can do no more than creep. The man is in armour up to the waist, and carries a long spear. There is a washer about four inches from the point to prevent it going too far in. He parks himself on the edge of the ring, with the padded side of the horse – which is his spear side – facing outwards and towards the bull. Meanwhile the muletas are trying to lure the bull in short rushes, up close under the horse. The horseman levels his spear. The idea is to bring the bull so near the horse, that it charges that, and the horseman meets it in the shoulders with his spear. This happens inevitably. The muletas bring the bull, tossing and snorting, within about ten paces of the horse, then they all fold up their cloaks and efface themselves. The bull looks round, sees no cloaks, so charges the biggest thing in sight, which is the horse. The horseman receives the bull's shoulders – the very top of its neck – on the end of his spear. This doesn't stop the bull, not anything near it. The bull now begins to lift the horse about like a doll. The mattress pads the horse, otherwise it would be dead in seconds. The bull's horns are about 18 inches long, and the bull is furious with the pain in its shoulders, where the spearman is working and twisting his spear. The idea of wounding the bull here, is to weaken the tossing muscles, and start the blood flowing to weaken the whole bull.

The bull works on the horse for two or three minutes, often lifting it – horseman and all – clear of the ground, and all the time little boys are beating the blindfold horse from the other side, to keep it up against the bull where the spear can work, and to keep it square to the bull. Once a bull catches a horse end on, horse and man are done for. That actually happened in one, as I shall tell you.

The horses are pathetic. They behave throughout like ninth hand furniture in an old attic.

In the end the muletas decide the bull has had enough, whip out their cloaks wide under its nose, and draw it away to the middle of the ring. One of these muletas is the matador – the man who eventually is to kill the bull – but at present he is playing with the rest, using an ordinary orange cloak.

By now there are great waves of blood welling out of the hole in the top of the bull's shoulders, pouring down its sides, running down its forelegs. It is panting more desperately and hanging its head much lower than when it first came jaunting into the ring.

Now the horseman moves to another part of the ring, to give another part of the crowd their moneysworth. The buisiness with the spear comes again. This is the most exciting and disgusting part. To see a bull heaving a horse and rider into the air, the man only keeping astride by leaning on the spear he has in the bull, is unusual enough. And all this about ten paces from you.

After this second time, the horsemen are over. They leave the ring, and leave the bull to the muletas. The bull is now a very changed animal. With two great holes in the top of its shoulders, it looks to have a kind of cape of blood. The muletas are keeping it going, not letting it rest.

Then one of them runs out with two arrow things – bound with ribbon and tipped with barbed points, – called bandilleros. He stands in the middle of the ring, very pretty in his colours, high on tiptoe, holding the arrows above his head, their points downward and together, one in each hand. He dances up and down to attract the bull. At last it charges him, and he runs towards it. As they meet, he drives the two arrows down into the top of the bulls neck, where the two holes are already, and as the bull tosses its head upwards and backwards at the pain, he slips past on one side. This looks very dangerous. They do this twice too. So the bull is now standing in the middle of the ring, panting like a little mouse, still losing blood at about a pint a minute, a sag in its back and its head hanging, and the four arrows standing up foolishly on its shoulders. These arrows sway and tear in the neck muscles during what follows.

Now the matador proper comes out. He has a crimson cloak and a dummy sword. He begins to draw the bull backward and forward in short charges under his cloak. This is where all the famous skillfull bullfighting comes in. He stands, within two paces of the bull, holding the cloak out to one side as you know, and giving it provocative little trembles. At last the bull charges – at the cloak. The near horn shaves him, sometimes takes the lace off his tights, but he never moves. Or shouldn't. The bull comes out under the cloak, turns, baffled, and charges again. The matador too has turned and receives the bull as before. He tries to get a close series of turns like this non stop. Then he folds the cloak, turns his back on the bull, and walks toward the crowd holding up a hand for applause. If he is a good dramatist, he often has the crowd wild by this moment, and the effect is striking.

Sometimes, if the bull is reluctant to charge, he will kneel to receive it, so that the near horn shaves his chest, and his chin is bloodied by the bull's side. It's lucky they don't get their eyes poked out by the waving arrows.

After enough theatre, the matador changes his dummy sword for a real one. They were sharpening it just down in front of us. Now after a few more turns, the matador chooses the right moment and drops his cloak down in a fold, in front of him. The bull, looking at the cloak, is looking at him. If it charges the cloak, the matador goes up in the air or stays on the horns. But the matador keeps the bull still, by being still, by some sort of suggestion conveyed to the bull somehow that it must not move. And he sights along his sword, holding the handle at his chin. Then he dashes forward, very quick, and runs past the bull on its right side, leaving the handle of the sword showing between the bull's shoulders among the arrows, with its point presumably in the bull's heart. The bull tosses its head and begins to move around very uncomfortably, shaking itself and sometimes bellowing. All the muletas dash in and begin to work the bull with their cloaks, surrounding it closely and making it swing this way and that. Usually the sword misses the heart, and the bull is up and about for long enough. But after the muletas have worked it for a while, it begins to stagger, the long sword is still straight through it. The matador stands by, watching. The bull backs to the fence. I saw six bulls killed and only one was killed by the first sword. Usually a little man nips in with a dagger, and gives it two or three quick jabs behind the ear, or else the matador does it with a special sword. Then it lies down like an ordinary bull in a field. One or two more little stabs, and it is dead. The crowd cheers or boos, accordingly as the matador has performed. If he has performed very well, he is given the bull's ears, and runs round the ring, holding them up to show the crowd, while the women throw handbags at him and the men throw wine-bottles.

One of the bulls was more intelligent than the others. It didn't just charge blindly at the cloak, and then stare round astonished when it came out on the other side. It ran in on its toes, shaking its horns from side to side. It was also twice as fierce and quick as any of the other bulls. Nobody dared go near it. The muletas waved their cloaks once and then ran. Finally they got it under the horse, and it was speared once. That was enough. They couldn't get it near the horse again. Whenever it saw the horse ahead, it shied off and chased after a man. So the horseman tried to manoevre his horse to get near the bull, as the horse wouldn't come near him. He was just turning his creeping horse, when the bull spotted his chance from the other side of the ring. He came across like a shot, and met the horse head on. The horse folded on the bull's horns, and the spearman, who had been at the wrong angle to bring his spear to meet the charge, came over the top. As the horse toppled off sideways, the spearman came square onto the horns, face down. The bull went on heaving, thinking it was still tossing the horse. The muletas dashed in, and tried to draw the bull away from the horse, while others tried to lift the man off the horns. He was finally flung off, and staggered to the edge of the ring, where he fell. When they picked him up you could see the great holes in him. Whether he died later or not I don't know.

The matador had a hard time with that bull. There was no fancy bullfighting with it. At one time it chased him flat out, and tore the seat of his tights with one horn. But at last it was killed, and the crowd booed as its body was dragged out.

Its surprising how much a bull learns during a fight, but by the time it's learned it, it's too late. It is full of holes and has no blood left.

After Madrid we came to Alicante, which is a kind of seaside resort with a long beach. From there we came up the coast and are now renting a little flat in a fishing village, where we spend all our time writing and swimming in the sea. It is very pleasant. We buy a pound of fresh sardines for 4d.

I am certainly going to marry Sylvia. By the time I come home in the end of September I shall be married. I'll bring her home for a week before her term starts. Don't tell anyone because it mustn't get back to

Cambridge. Married women aren't allowed at Newnham and she is on a grant there for another year which is worth several hundred pounds.

When I come home, I shall stay for a couple of weeks, then come back here with Walt if he is still keen to come. There is marvellous leasurely lying in the sun. Wine and brandy are still cheap. I shall teach here. My Spanish is coming on steadily. Next summer I shall go to America and lecture for a year in some American college. Then come back, and probably teach for a year in Italy.

Don't be frightened of Sylvia being a drag. It's obvious from what's happened since I met her that she is anything but. She is a very fine cook, and a much more certain money-earner than myself. Her parents were German. She has no father, and her mother is very nice, extremely kind etc. I met her for a few days in Paris. German Americans that is. She is very very bright, and has an offer to lecture at Smith College next year, which is the top American woman's college, and in which she was aforetime the top star, mentally. That job alone should be over two thousand a year. Her American academic qualifications are all the very top [*page torn at this point, with only a few words from remaining sentences legible*]

TH and Plath reached Spain in July, having passed through Paris on the way, but, unluckily, just when Olwyn Hughes was attending a conference in the south of France. After Madrid – where it was 'vilely hot', as TH tells Olwyn in a letter of 20 July, and where he and Plath saw the disillusioning bullfight – they found their way to Benidorm, not then a town crowded with holiday-makers. They established their lodgings at 59 Tomas Ortunio, from where this letter was sent.

To Olwyn Hughes

[August 1956]   Ts   Emory

Since I came here I've written nine animal fables. They are original and I think they are very good. I have written them absolutely simply. I shall do a few drawings to each, and publish them as a book this next winter. I'll show them to you when I come to Paris. Also I wrote one or two poems. Which you could trade to that Botteghe man if you still know him. I have another project which I may be able to write up as a long short story – again in a kind of fable style. It's about a man who captures an angel, and begins to show it in a cage, for a fee. And the consequences. It's a full scale subject, but I shall do it through his eyes, and so not get tangled in theology or anything.

45

[. . .]
My fables are really very good. It's true that I am incapable of writing a story in ordinary familiar prose style. I think the reason is that I look at things in a completely moralising and stylised way. You'll see what I mean when you read my fables. It's nearest model is Swift, I'm sure. But much simpler. Sylvia is as fine a literary critic as I have met, and she thinks about my ordinary prose narrative style just as you do. But my fables she cries over and laughs all together and they are obviously very successfull with her. Now if these would sell.

The animal fables on which TH was working in Spain were eventually published as *How the Whale Became* (1963). The 'Botteghe man' may be Eugene Walter (1921–98), who was for many years assistant to Marguerite Caetani (1880–1963), editor of the literary magazine *Botteghe Oscure*. 'O'Kelly's Angel', which fits the description TH gives here, being about a man who cages an angel, was eventually published in the story collection *Difficulties of a Bridegroom* (1995), where TH says he wrote it in 1954.

To Gerald and Joan Hughes

7 September 1956   Ms Emory

Dear Gerald & Joan,
    Many happy returns. And these are the most precise greetings that you will receive. Reason: it is 5 past nine by the Hebden Bridge clocks. 36 years exactly since you were born. Did you know that they thought you were born dead? And you were dead, too, till Ma said, 'Slap him, he'll wake up," and so they did and you did. A sobering thought for a drunken birthday. You notice that I am making no excuses for my having not written. Alas, what a life I lead. But suddenly it – my life – has grown the most promising prize-winning ears, (you are to imagine that it – my life – is a rabbit.)
    I was all set to come to Australia, and very pleased at the thought of meeting you. But I was melancholy at the thought of spending important growing up years in Australia, which, so far as writing goes, is a dead letter. However I had nothing better to do. I very much wanted to come fishing & shooting with you, but I didn't want to write in Australia. I didn't want to write in England either, which is still quite a bit worse than I ever said it was. So I went to Spain with an American poetess. As a result of her influence I have written continually and every day better

since I met her. She is a very fine critic of my work, and abuses just those parts of it that I daren't confess to myself are unworthy. I have sold two poems to two leading American Magazines with very interested letters from the editors. And I have written a book of childrens & grown-ups animal fables which surprised even me. I am writing other things, and for the first time am satisfied with my progress. After she's finished this next year in Cambridge I shall go to America with her, marry her, and stay there a year teaching. Then return to Italy, then Germany, then Russia, a year in each, learning the languages and teaching English. This will go on. At present, this is a hypothetical plan for the next years. If I grow wealthy, as is possible, this will be changed. My plan is to earn enough money to buy you a dairy farm in perhaps Wales. Would you take it? This winter a Bill comes through Parliament which will permit the taking of bets in premises not used exclusively for that. In other words Pa can be a bookie, and he is quite decided. He is already a bookie in a small way – which is dangerous – and yet he makes enough to pay all the rates and to pay for their holidays. So with his, and with mine, which, I hope, will soon be prodigious, there will be every possibility of launching some venture such as a dairy farm. Once you had a dairy farm you could fly to and fro at your pleasure. Between Australia and England. And most of all, your children will grow up on a farm, without which kind of childhood a person is not worth anything. However, if you swear, angrily and righteously, that you will never betray your beloved overseer so far as to neglect him for the sake of a lot of cows, you may well argue me into thinking of something else. With two Leos you will have to look out. Your new one is certain to be pretty artistic. It will be very moody, over impressionable, over-excitable, over-voluble, all good vices out of which, if you will feed it young enough with enough weird, terrifying, strange, bizarre experiences, may well make it smarter than the normal cut of Australian. If you don't tell them three stories a day, the most fantastic you can invent, you are helping to fill up the world's dullness with two more sleeping heads. Love to all

Ted.

'I shall . . . marry her': TH and Plath had planned a second wedding ceremony, a fully public celebration, to take place in the USA when they moved there in 1957, so what TH tells his brother is not strictly untrue. But he has still not revealed his marital status.

To Donald Carne-Ross

15 September 1956   Ts   BBC

Dear Mr. Carne-Ross:

I heard from Mr. Peter Redgrove that you showed some interest in a tape recording of a part of <u>Gawain and the Green Knight</u> that I made at his place. If you are still interested in taking fuller recording of this, and perhaps making a program of it, I shall be glad to do the reading.

I intend to come to London sometime during the week beginning the 24ᵗʰ of September. If you could write and let me know when it would be convenient for you to make a recording I could easily make my visit then.

Shall I work it up into a program? It would be a series of programs actually: an initial program giving the very little bit that is known about Gawain—history, origins, authorship, etcetera—followed by a brief outline of the first part, followed by a reading of the first part. Then three more programs giving outlines and readings of the other three parts. In reading time, each part takes about thirty minutes—the third perhaps a little more.

Thanking you for your time and consideration, and hoping to hear from you soon, I am

Yours sincerely,

Ted Hughes

Donald Carne-Ross, a producer in the Talks Department at the British Broadcasting Corporation, was influential as a spotter and employer of poetic talent. The poet Peter Redgrove (1932–2003) had been a near contemporary of TH's at Cambridge, where he edited the magazine *Delta*.

The neat layout, style of paragraphing (not followed above) and spelling of 'program' all suggest that this letter, written from the Yorkshire home of TH's parents, was typed by Sylvia Plath. Dashes in the original are formed by three hyphens that join words and leave no gap – a style that TH would adopt, when typing, after his move to the USA.

To Donald Carne-Ross

21 September 1956   Ts   BBC

Dear Mr. Carne-Ross,

Thank you for your letter. I should certainly like to record some modern verse, in lieu of Gawain.

I suggest the "Wreck of the Deutschland", "Tom's Garland', several sonnets, by Hopkins. Also one or two late Yeats – "The Second Coming", "Phantoms of Hatred". A very fine thing is "The Tunning of Elinour Rumming" by John Skelton, also "Speke Parrot", but these are rather long.

I shall come to the B.B.C. by 10.30 on Thursday. Looking forward to meeting you then, I am

Yours sincerely,
Ted Hughes

To Sylvia Plath

[1 (and 2) October 1956]   Ts   Lilly Library

Darling Sylvia Puss-Kish Ponky,

it is ten oclock at night and after writing this I shall go to bed which is still just as we left it this morning in our hurry. How were the porters? And when you got back to Whitstead was it piles of mail at the door or just Janine. I had to stay at Leeds for an hour, so I bought a glass of milk and a HOROSCOPE and read our indifferent fortunes for the month – all very non-committal and unconvincing as usual. Sums of money, heavy expenditure, outbursts of passion all likely it says as always. I shall buy no more but go now on my own predictions. One excellent thing I predict about you is that you will be famous and another is that you come into vast fortunes and happiness by marriage to an amazing strange provider of these. You will see all this for yourself when you learn to prognostic. I came back to Hebden Bridge sitting opposit to a woman who had the first finger missing off her right hand, and whose horrible daughter carried a woven carrier like ours that dripped and trickled from under a load of celery. What it dripped and trickled I don't know – the situation never developed. When I arrived home I felt unsettled – I couldn't read I couldn't write, I couldn't eat, and least of all could I sit in this place, so I went a walk. I intended to go just a little way down Hardcastle wood and there sit and watch until I felt like reading. I was so unsettled, though, that I finished up at the far end of the valley in about twenty minutes, wet through with sweat and gasping. I eventually went up into that little side valley where the rhodedendron thickets are and there I sat. I began to read and I read about an hour. Twice rabbits came to within ten feet of me – quivering with nerves – almost ready to drop in

49

nerveous breakdown they look when they know something's wrong but not what. I read on 100 pages then was interrupted by a cat. A black and white cat. It sat within fifteen feet of me, on a rock, and began to stare me out – very offensive. When I threw a sod at it, it just flattened and went on staring. I couldn't go on reading – the cat completely disturbing the landscape. It wasn't an interesting wildcat, and while it was there no interesting wild thing would come near, so I moved off and came home, ousted by a cat. I have read most of Count Bel, today – I have been able to do nothing else. It's a fantastic account of futile wars fought not between two armies but regiments forced into service, picked from the mass of Goths, Bulgars, Huns, Franks, Persians etc at odd battles, against the rest that hadn't been picked. A conquered army was immediately enlisted as a new division of the conqueror's army. Under the slightest adversity the whole lot either deserted to the enemy or dispersed at night. It would make wearisome reading except for all the titbits of intriguing detail that Graves puts in. That among the Goths and Huns – the larger part of the world's population at that time – homos were castrated. And such like.

Nothing else at all. Tonight I read Yeats for about an hour, and I shall do this. An hour in the morning and again at night. Up to the inventing of Caxton's press, and for most people long after all reading was done aloud. Most people were incapable of reading silently. And Eliot says that the best thing a poet can do is read aloud poetry as much as he can. This should be sound. Silent reading only employs the parts of the brain that are used in vision. Not all the brain. This means that a silent readers literary sense becomes detatched from the motor parts and the audio parts of the brain which are used in reading aloud – tongue and ear. This means that only one third of the mental components are present in their writing or in their understanding of reading – one third emotional charge. This explains Amis and Wain and the rest, –. Painting is successful within its limits using only this part of the brain because it uses exclusively visual symbols. But only a fraction of a verbal idea is visual. And these people, besides naturally lacking the other essential components of ear touch muscle etc are frightened of a visual effect for theoretical reasons. The only thing they can do then, is to cultivate arch attitudes, or a hocus of mathematical dexterity, which deceive only their own inferior breed which in an age of silent cram-readers are crowded over every page they care to write. The wind will get rid of those people, and there's no need to argue them away. This is quite true though –

Beethoven composed singing and roaring and walking very fast and so did Dostoevsky – not singing but vociferating. So read aloud a lot, and read aloud poetry as you walk to and fro in your room timing the metre to your steps. This would be ideal, but you'll think it too ridiculous.

[. . .] I am now going to make a cup of Chocolate a la Tomas Ortunio and retire. Lonely bed. The way I miss you is stupid. I have wandered about today like somebody with a half-completed brain-operation. But the life we have decided is the best. I must go to Spain. Then we shall have all our lives. You keep watch on our marriage Sylvia as well as I shall and there is no reason we shouldn't be as happy as we have said we shall be. Don't let any stupid thing interfere. Goodnight darling darling darling darling

This is from the first of a series of letters written after Plath had returned to Cambridge, to re-enter student life as a (still secretly) married woman, while TH remained with his parents in Yorkshire. An appendix in the form of an essay on Cambridge eccentrics, written to help Plath with a novel she was planning – presumably the never-completed *Falcon Yard* – has been omitted. Whitstead was Plath's hall of residence at Newnham College, and Janine, possibly, her close American friend there, Jane Baltzell.

TH was a proficient reader of horoscopes and was later, briefly, to think of earning his living by that means (see the early-1957 letter to Olwyn Hughes).

Robert Graves (1895–1985), on whose novel *Count Belisarius* (1938) TH reports, was already revered by him as the author of the anthropological treatise *The White Goddess* (1948) – less so as poet or novelist.

By 'Amis and Wain and the rest', TH means the group of poets ranked under the banner of 'The Movement', including Kingsley Amis (1922–95) and John Wain (1925–94).

To Sylvia Plath

[3 October 1956]   Ts   Lilly Library

Dearest darling Sylvia,

What have I done today? A mouse could not find it if a second of honest labour were a pound of toasted cheese. The impression is that I have come down an everest of indolence on my yes my bum. I was roused by the nearest thing to your own ponky warmth, which was the wonderful letter. A relic for our fifteenth child's fifteenth child. Then I dozed up. dozed downstairs, and as I recollect pieced together a melancholy missive or mooning of verbs. Forgive me that. Then I posted off your parcels and came back to think about my T.V. play. I thought about it for about half an hour, got a clear look at all my characters, and began to write it. I realise that if I had thought about it for much longer, I could not have written it. The plot is ridiculous, I dare not tell you what it is. But I shall write it out, and so might get back the fluency with which I wrote the Hag and Law in the Country of the Cats. The thing to do in thinking about anything is not to try and get a clear mental picture of it, or a distinct mental concept, with all its details there, vivid in your brain, but to try to look at the actual thing happening in front of you. I find a clear distinction between these two types of thinking about a thing. As soon as I begin imagining the thing happening in my world, everything comes right. That's not quite it. It's as though in the first way of thinking I thought about the thought, taking the thought and forcing it into shape or realness. In the second way it's more like the process of memory, I think straight to the thing and am not conscious of any mental intervention. That latter way I'm sure is the best way. Does the same thing happen with you. The second way I get the feel, weight, sound, every nuance of atmosphere about a concrete thing. The first I get a barren feeling abstraction, though the picture may be of a concrete thing. I am trying to get three hours of thinking in a day. Not thinking perhaps, but one hour of remembering, one hour of discovering plots and themes, and one hour of definite and applied consideration of something that interests, some part of a theme. This is apart from any thinking or imagining that goes on ordinarily. If I can keep this up I'm sure I can change myself, and I wish I could make you do it.

Last night I began to read Wallace Stevens aloud, starting from the back because I've recently read all the poems in the beginning. I like Stevens continually, but every poem lets you down. You don't have a Stevens do you? If you have, sell it. Don't forget to send me that book with the Dylan Thomas letters in it. I would like to read what else is in it too.

It's been a miraculous day. I suppose English People talk about the weather because it really is a spectacle. Its been raining and blowing and sunning all at once, all day, with the most incredible huge crowded brilliant skies. As I sat at my window, about two, I was looking at a little dark mark in the grass about three fields away, when suddenly it began to move. It ran up and ran down then ran into the wall. One dark mark among millions of others, I think it was a weasel or a stoat. But that's not the curious thing. As I was staring, waiting for it to run out again and show its credentials a little more clearly, I saw a big red thing running down the middle of the field just above it. A flock of geese in the middle of the field separated and stood politely to let the red thing pass which was no other than Jack fox his merry self, in no great hurry, going down towards the wood.

Has Janine turned up? When she does, turn her out after five minutes. The gel will want a guide and who better than my ponk. Well my ponk don't. The book and the letter and the navel, read write reflect. The coy poem about Rose-gardeners of Graves that you read I heard too tonight. There was a programme of his reading about a dozen new poems, that one of them. Very dry. In some article Hodgart said "Miss so and so speaks of Graves as lacking real poetic imagination, and I can see what she means." Well, so can I. But he's good I think within very narrow limits, with a very barren bit of ground. One poem was a song called "A beach in Spain" and was about young married couples, honeymooning in Spain, flirting with the wrong ones, and had a little refrain 'Oh how can you regain / Love lost on honeymoon / In Sunny Spain.' Maybe youve come across it in your New Yorker safari. None of them impressed me, but Graves has a kind of disinfected enunciation, a crumb accent no less, states everything so far under that nothing at all is heard. There was one interesting one called "Gratitude for a Night-mare". The nightmare of course means the presence of unresolved highly charged states of mind, and the presence of the demon, the poem dictator. In other words peaceful sleeps go with minds shut to the visit-ation. Graves apparently, for a long time, went unvisited by nightmare, and began to fear, says his poem, that playing the celebrity in Majorca and finding life easy, had disqualified him, and scared the demon off. At last, one night, he jerked awake, moaning and trembling and in a sweat, and groaned "All's well" as he reached for a cigarette with trembling fingers.

Here is my second plot by duty. Can you remember the one I gave you over Tomato mess in Tomas Ortunio? If not I'll write it out. Meanwhile here's number two. Don't expect too much, but if I send one every day, by the end of the year we may have plots to last you for a while, five at least good. Here is this. A young newly married couple decide they will live an idyllic life, they will buy a little cottage far in the country, keep goats and a few chickens and live carefree. What attracts them to this is shortage of cash, need for solitude for a period for some reason, general disillusionment with the city – all these are disguises for the real motives, which are – each is jealous of the other, being very possessive of the other, and in their city social life great strain and provocation, each secretly fears, will be put on this passion. So, first, they want to keep each other for themselves alone and away from temptation. Secondly, being newly married they honestly think that each other's company is all they will ever need. Thirdly, they genuinely like the country. As many reasons as you like. But the only place they can buy, and they get it cheap enough, is a large farmhouse. This is of course even better than a cottage. They live awhile, very happy awhile. They begin to hanker after a little social life. They invite a couple of friends out. The friends are amazed – they are city friends – why don't the young marrieds, they ask, turn the place into a wonderfull inn. The two think about this. They are bit by bit attracted by the idea. They have no money so there is no chance of their making the change, and so they dare think about it as rapturously as they like. It becomes a thing with them. They invite other friends out to their 'Inn' as they already call it, who encourage them in the idea. Suddenly they are left so much money they can make the alterations and do. Success. For a while. They have now brought the city into the country. Their friends are staying with them continually, and, because they are their guests, albeit paying, they are in closer, and more exclusive, and lonelier contact with them than before, more concentrated contact than before – what vile phrases are coming up – anyway the upshot is that the young wife begins to worry about the husband with his old girl-friend or even a new, who visits, and so does he about her and her beaus. Result, they find they have turned their country dream into a vicious city hot-spot or the equivalent as far as they are concerned. They sell the hotel, and buy another cottage, not so far in the country this time. They will now on not entirely ignore the city, and during those last decisive weeks at the inn their marriage was tried hard and proved good. What a rotten plot. Can you pick any sense out of that? I should think you can copy it out in about one third the words.

When I have written out what follows I shall go down and fill in one line of the pools for you and one for me. No there isn't room to copy it out. I'll wait till the next sheet, and for the time being go down and kick a hole in Littlewoods the size of our fortune. These terrific astral blessings should come to even more than they are doing, according to the book. There, I have pricked you out eight most likely teams. Now I shall turn in. I wonder if you are turned in yet, or are you mooning out

54

over Whitstead lawn and Barton Backs. The poem which I have spent most of the day writing is The Horses of the Sun, or the Mark of a Modern Apollo. Is Thurber clearing the Fable market. I don't know whether my sense of humour has changed, but those recent fables in N.Y. didn't strike me as anything like as funny as the old Thurber stories and Fables, or even, for the most part, as funny at all. Do you think? Goodnight puss, goodnight little puss, little soft places little puss, I wish you were still here or rather I wish I was still there I would kiss you slowly from toe up. I neglected you. That's one of my most tormenting thoughts that I didn't suck and lick and nibble you all night long and its a thought I shall never let myself in for again once I've had chance to mend it. More tomorrow. Kiss you for me, Sylvia, and again and again and fall asleep kissing your arm.

It's true how you feel amputated in some way – like your octopus. Its now like a man who's just lost a leg or some vital interior organ that I feel – I sit around in a daze of shock, I feel there are some things I can no longer do, or only half do, or do awkwardly and without pleasure – this feeling is vivid & constant. I love you everything and you write terrific letters –

Love love love love
Ted.

Wallace Stevens, whose *Collected Poems* had been published in 1954, had died in 1955. Plath admired his work.

'A Bouquet from a Fellow Roseman' must be the first poem by Graves that TH refers to; it and 'Gratitude for a Nightmare' were included in his 1958 collection *5 Pens in Hand*. TH makes three lines of the two he quotes correctly – bar orthographical differences – from the uncollected 'Song: A Beach in Spain'.

Neither the story plot here, nor any of those offered in subsequent letters to Plath, seems to have been used by her.

Littlewoods, the gambling firm, had set up in business with their 'football pools', a system of betting on the results of a certain number of matches.

'The Horses of the Sun, or the Mark of a Modern Apollo' sounds like 'The Horses' (*The Hawk in the Rain*).

To Sylvia Plath

[4 October 1956]   Ts   Lilly Library

Dearest Sylvia kish and puss and ponk,

I was lousing in bed this morning at the one eighth emerged stage, when ma came in with your letter. I wish you had been in bed with me there to open it. Joy, Joy as the hyena cried. Now you are set. I never read six poems of anyone all together in Poetry. It means the wonderful thing. It will spellbind every Editor in America. It will also be a standing bottomless battery to charge what you write from now on, because you are almost certain to sell nearly everything you write now. Besides any other qualities they may have, your poems are eminently saleable. Joy Joy. It must be very near, when Editors will be requesting a poem. Joy Joy. Two a week, from this on, or you're betraying your luck. And think what poems you have in reserve. I wonder why they didn't accept The Shrike, which is one of your best I think, but perhaps it is a little ghoulishly melodramatic for them. Still it is a certain good one, and a certain seller. And the Glutton. This is the best thing yet, and according to the planets is exact right, and according to the planets should continue for on over a year with a particularly dense patch over this christmas. So pour them out. Right in Cravenson's eye, and his keeper, Spender's.

Since you went I have done nothing. Almost nothing. I composed a rather silly plot for a T.V. play, which I shall write out however. Yesterday I read and wandered about. I went down into the wood after dark and sat for a long time. I came back and wasted what was left in trying to write a poem, very bad, in fact, now destroyed. I suppose I shall have to get used to this new condition. I'm relieved to hear about the coat. My providential distrusting self! I had the very vague wonder if it was there, but I have such a clear memory of leaving it at Rugby St. And the Camp-bed. The next step is to sell that camp-bed, which is just a burden, though a brand new one. How to get it up here is the problem, unless when I go to London for the B.B.C. I call for a few hours at Cambridge.

I should think, when we have come this far in three months, and with all the best prognostics yet to come into effect, that we should be well away by the time we reach America. You will just about certainly get the Borestone now, this year and next O Joy.

I want to get your books off before twelve, so this note which is coming with them cannot be much longer. Write to Botteghe Oscure. And remember all the day that I love you all the day and every minute inside and outside, and think about you every minute's end and am very cold at night and sleep badly. Last night I couldn't get to sleep at all. There has just been a fall of soot down the chymney and now I am sneezing in the smell of it. Keep writing and turn all your lacks to good poems and I'll try and do the same. It is strange here just now – bright sunlight on all the fields and yet heavy hail hammering the windows.

56

Ma is very pleased at the news but I think a little bit jealous. All my love for you Sylvia

This is not my today letter but a note.

[*No signature*]

On 2 October (see *Letters Home*), Plath had heard that *Poetry (Chicago)* had accepted six of her poems. 'Cravenson' looks like TH's contemptuous name for Christopher Levenson (b.1934), poet and editor of the Cambridge magazine *Delta*, whom Plath had dated the previous year and who had angered F. R. Leavis and his followers when he innocently invited the poet Stephen Spender (1909–95), a hate-figure in the Leavis camp but not in any sense Levenson's 'keeper', to read at Downing College.

Plath submitted work for, but never won, a Borestone Mountain Award for Poetry.

To Sylvia Plath

[5 October 1956]   Ts   Lilly Library

Dear Sylvia

Your letter came alone alas with no Carne-Ross and nothing else but no worse for that. Well, at your end a great deal of preparation most boldly broached. Don't feel too guilty at speeding through those Chaucer books – there isn't room for six different books on Chaucer – ergo, all must be the same or at least a variation of at the most two. But note each chapter, have a few sheets of notes from each book, then, even though under torture you could not inform of them anything but arrant lies and nonsense, your conscience will be fortified. By knocking down these Goliaths early, the necessary tomes on every wretched letter-back scribbling rhymer, you will develope a conscience before which every fresh obstacle will surrender. Plough through them and call it penance, or at least so that you can henceforth dogmatise on the inanity of all such and show your scars. Today has been a continuation of yesterday so far as the sky showings are concerned. Prodigal genius. At dusk the sky was pure washed stretched green, still wet and runny, with brilliant illumination on the landscape. Then from the north, covering the whole breadth of the sky, came a lid of black cloud, and under it the land black. It drew slowly over the whole sky. At one stage a great advance of it overhung the green west sky, and hanging from it, black against the green were great trailing swaths of falling rain, like a long black fine mane. Or like many manes hanging down between the side by side pressed bellies of cloud. I never saw anything like it. Earlier, at three in the afternoon, I went a little walk because all I've done all day is get up again and walk around. Anyway I'd just got fairly down into the wood when it began to hail. I stood under a leaning tree and watched the hail, for an hour, filling the valley up. Leaves were coming off, the wood was sodden and seeping. Poor creatures to make house in that. Later, tonight at nine, I walked down toward Hebden and was stopped by a Police car. They checked me over as if I were some wild man, and seemed very keen. I kept asking them in a very superior tone whether they were looking for anyone in especial, and they eyed me for a time from behind their torch glares. Then one muttered, for my benefit and obviously very much against the secretive other pseudo-subtly, that "The description is very similar." I convinced them I was a local peasant, and they drove off. The fact is, I'm unrecognisable and look like a strange beast unless you're with me. I came round the bottom of the wood and up through Heptonstall, intending to buy some fish and chips. I was just stepping up into the fish and chip shop – where we never went – when two little girls ran out with their arms full of wrapped fish and chips, when they saw me one let out a scream. They recovered and went off. But that's the sort of thing which will soon dement me.

What have I done today. A great deal of nothing. I wrote a bit at my silly play. I shall tear through it now and get it away and burned, but I must go through to the end and the last word. I finished Graves Belisarius. His excuse for writing this kind of book is that he wants to write history and he wants to make it interesting and he wants to make a living. Doubtless he does the last. But when a situation that was presumably actual fact, is given a fictional cause, when the veritable mummy of Belisarius is given Graves' anaemic voice, the contrast is intolerable and both parts are discredited. It gives me that perpetual twist in the stomach that an apparent fake does, things are just not falling true, and yet the fact that the external situation of these characters is true and historically vouched forces you to think the whole is true. The result is something vicious I am sure. A great deal of History does come over, but the relationships between the main people, which is one of the most interesting things in history especially when as is usually the case you are given only external events to judge them by, are in Graves books determined for you and not at all convincingly. He has the prissiest sense of the grand, or the terrible, or of rage or energy of any sort. And when he tries to be witty, as he does interminably, the results are a fantastic heaving to and saluting of remote historical allusions that leave the whole page with a kind of blank look. Here is verses I dug up and altered, two or three lines I changed –

Old wives in their day
Had sure cures for this
Changeling, this Vanity
That has corrupted the eye
Even of the faithfull lookingglass.

Vanity, Vanity
I read in a book
How you with your wizened ears
And your snake's twisted eye
Once I could, with the hearth-muck
Have swept out of doors,
Or flung on the fire back,
Or else flogged, until
Your yell brought with one stride
Your mother through the house-wall
Out of the black wood.

Or I could have brewed beer
In a half egg-shell;
Or made black pudding of a whole
Hog, eyes, hooves, hair;
Or ploughed with a cockerel
Harnassed back to front;
Or hung our cat on a nail
And as it screeched to and fro
Fiddled in counterpoint,
Till you should confess,
With one bloody shriek
At so much newfangleness
Your fifty centuries thunderstruck
And wailed into the hill.

But I do not do so:
The times are so vile
I rock your cradle and as I croon
Fondly I smile
Into your hideous eyes

Because it is a hundred to one
At the baby show
You would win first prize.

There were new developments across the field today. When I walked out in the morning to post your letter I saw a beautiful cow in the road side, different from any cow I ever saw, a different shape, and a rich wild chocolate brown with wild wiry swirly hair. It was grazing at the road side.

Later, back in my room, I looked across the field, and saw this same cow in the lower field with the little calf walking obediently behind it. To and fro it was wandering, very restlessly, and the calf going pace for pace with it, bumping its nose on her buttock. The horse was grazing in the top field. Suddenly it looked up, and stared in obvious amazement and fury at what was going on in the lower field with its little calf, its little friend, its own dove. Away goes the horse to the rescue of its own rights, and then, very intelligently proceeds to separate the cow from the calf and drive the cow into the upper field. The little calf tried to run after the cow, whom it seemed to prefer, but the horse headed it off as neatly as if it had a rider, and headed it off repeatedly, but the little calf, full of a new love finally broke through into the top field and chased after the cow. The horse now began to drive the cow into corners. It dodged out of one and another but in the third, the near corner, when the horse came charging straight at it, it jumped the fence and ran away up the road. The calf stood with its head over the fence, mooing. The horse ran round for joy. About an hour later I looked up and there was the cow again back in the upper field with the calf, and the horse grazing in the lower. As I watched, again – recognition, rage, to the rescue by horse, and desperation by calf, and headlong flight a la Ventas by cow, to corner, to corner, to the far corner, which is a wall, but no matter, over went cow, and horse watched it warningfully walk away up the field to join Wilf's herd. The little calf stuck its head over that corner now, and mooed. Now I am turning in. I read John Skelton aloud for about an hour tonight. I love the cartoons. The unicorns one is wonderfull. I wish Carne-Ross would hurry. As soon as he speaks, we meet. I love you I love you, I love you I love you your

Ted.

The poem 'Old wives in their day', with its discernible trace of Robert Graves, was never published.

A plot outline on a third sheet of typescript, about a weak wife murdering her bullying husband – 'Too melodramatic and obvious?' TH himself asks – has been omitted.

To Sylvia Plath

[6 and 8 October 1956]   Ts   Lilly Library

Dearest Sylvia,

Saturday night, and no letter from my ponk. Is she dead? Has half the world dropped off?

This morning I could work up absolutely no interest in my stupid play, nor had I spirit for anything else. Yesterday I felt like writing but today – blank. I have read somewhere in Freud that when a person is suddenly deprived of someone he loves and has built into his life, his working powers often fail temporarily, though I should have thought they would be stimulated. I read a bit, dawdled a bit, and finally went out with my Yeats intending to read on the moors. I went up where it was luminous that evening, and there I sat reading Yeats aloud until I was frozen and my fingers were numb. Then I set off walking in the opposite direction to back home, and followed the skyline all the way around, on the moor, not feeling a bit tired, though I walked from three until 7-30. No luck on the Pools. It's amazing how far you can be out. Tonight again I just cronked, that's the perfect word for it. I slumped in a heap. Wasn't even interested in books. And now I'm going to bed early and perhaps I'll feel more like writing tomorrow.

I dreamed fiendishly and unrememberably all last night and woke twice without bedclothes. This morning I got up at six and went out to shoot a rabbit because we have no meat for Sunday. It was a lovely morning, with the sun's rays broadening up into the sky at a steep angle and all the bellies of the clouds red. I couldn't see the rabbits for some reason. I kept walking absent-mindedly straight into them, and away they would be. At last I managed to get one. I came back. It was still useless to try to write, so I read the introduction to the legende of goode women in a whisper, and ruminated, until eleven. Then out of sheer tedium – tedium isn't when there's nothing to do but when for some reason you're too distracted to do anything, too vaguely disquieted, Spleen I suppose, but I miss you very much. Anyway I went down and I did the rabbit as you would have done – only I put all the spare packets of soup in and piles of Bisto and those things. The result was good. But I'd made it too stiff. The rabbit was cooked and good, but it hadn't boiled as it would have done in a thinner mixture, with the result that it was tough, it didn't fall off the bones as yours did, you couldn't suck the bones. However, it served. I heard you once say to your mother I think that you suspected a man who was quick about the kitchen. I think the two extreme types like the kitchen – but with a difference. The hardened bachelor raids it, and the utter domestic woos it. The dangerous one – and I think this is the one you must have meant – is the hardened bachelor who woos it, or even the still soft-green bachelor who woos it, because that means he has made himself his own wife, and if in this way then probably in many other ways. I think queers must be courters of kitchens.

This afternoon, stupefied, I lay on my bed in a half dream from three until seven – you see how my days pass. I can put it down to the conjunction of the moon and saturn, but I wish you were here. Tonight, on the subject of the above I made a near nursery rhyme, very weak and not to be considered any further by you:

Very pleased with himself was little Willie Crib
When he found the little elf-girl under his bib.
He took her to his bedroom, he put her in a box,
He could hardly get to sleep for taking little looks.

She had his mother's voice, she had his mother's face
But she loved him most when he was in disgrace.
She accompanied him everywhere and noone could see her
nor hear her soft endless kisses at his ear.

He grew to be a gay young man, up and down town,
Every girl's secret was to get him for her own,
But his elf she would grow angry, she would hurry him away
"None love you as I do for all that they say."

Little Willie Crib he gadded up and down,
He swigged his fiery gaiety with a little frown,
With this girl, with that girl, then with a bitter laugh –
After two looks at any one his elf would drag him off.

"I see" said his elf at last "You are not to be trusted"
And round about his neck her two arms she twisted –

"Whoever you take in your arms" she said "Now,
You shall be but pressing me the closer to you."

And however Willie vowed to the girls in his arms
They could never get closer than the touch of his palms
And all his fierce kisses fell upon his elf,
Which left the girls imagining he had kissed himself.

There, You will think I am in my dotage. But what set me off on this
weak spiritless canter was reading this Blake:

Little Mary Bell had a fairy in a nut,
Long John Brown had a devil in his gut;
Long John Brown loved little Mary Bell
And the fairy drew the devil in the nut-shell.

Her fairy skipped out and her fairy Skip'd in;
He laugh'd at the Devil saying 'Love is a Sin.'
The Devil he raged and the Devil he was wroth,
And the Devil entered into the Young Man's broth.

He was soon in the Gut of the loving Young Swain,
For John ate and drank to drive away Love's pain;
But all he could do he grew thinner and thinner,
Though he ate and drank as much as ten men for his dinner.

Some said he had a Wolf in his stomach day and night,
Some said he had the Devil and they guessed right,
The Fairy skip'd about in his Glory, Joy and Pride,
And he laughed at the Devil till poor John Brown died.

Then the Fairy skip'd out of the old nut shell,
And Woe & Alack for Pretty Mary Bell!
For the Devil crept in when the Fairy skip'd out,
And there goes Miss Bell with her fusty old Nut.

Splendid. To say it's carelessly worked out is to show just how it
surmounts all that.
Have you read the Everlasting Gospel – Blake? Read it as antidote to
your Augustine. Now I shall take a bath, and after this go to bed early. I
wish this fit would pass but all I can do makes no difference. If I were in
some other place. If I were in some other place.
Monday morning and much better. First of all your two letters clear

the weekend with one swipe. But your two letters came alone. No B.B.C. but I have a feeling it will be sometime this week.

I hope you didn't drop any clues for Miss Abbott's ferret nose. Probably between them, Miss Abbott and Mrs Milne, and with the aid of all their innocent applied agents – South Africans, Malays, Pygmies, third-apes etc – you are being sounded and unpicked, and charted and reduced to your parts. However your new veiled Southpaw approach I should think is a match for their craft. Read Blake, as I diviningly said last night, as antidote for all your christian philosopher trash, and it is trash, all completely crooked, and shouldn't be given the name thought at all. Schopenhauer somewhere talks about the English Philosophers and laments the way they all have Religion, and a stupid allegiance to some dogmatic egotist of the post-Christ school, that stands in the midst of their thought like a great rock, and fouls all the free flowing currents. They make me foolishly angry, so righteous and vicious and at bottom selfish, at bottom stupid and timid. The whole pack are contemptible. And when you realise that there has not been a monastery, nor a church foundation of any sort, not a single post of any ecclesiastical dignity, that has not from the start been the perch of avarice, greed, cruelty, and tyranny, you marvel why they are still given so much attention.

I'm glad you like the inn-plot. It is better than the other, which was rather silly. Moreover it has a strong practical matrix, a really interesting concern with how to reconcile the city which nobody likes but which fascinates everybody, and the country which everybody loves but nobody wants to live with. In fact, I can take my choice. Either I brutally murdered a girl in Glasgow and have been seen – at various stages – making my way down into East Lancs where I am thought to be hiding up; or late last Wednesday night, when two sisters were walking home up Old Town, across the valley from here, I jumped down out of the wood into the middle of the road in front of them, stark naked. If I did, I left my shorts in the wood where the police found them. Here it is again. –

> On his side, embrangled in adult passion, he had
> Scarcely uttered his first cry under her
> Raven-winged fall of hair, her nightfall of hair,
> Her blood-drop lips, a skin whose snows were over his head
> When they both dropped through to nurseryland, and she saw

The wolf, the wolf, had her by the hand, his mad
Grin dividing her body as he licked blood
Of her own dear mother off his black ugly jaw –

Whereon, gathering her petticoats, she ran, ran
Following her shriek through the glowering wood where the red
Robins and the wrens cried "Wolf" – a sob ahead
She got to the cottage and staggered in

Shrieking "Mother". When that youth tiptoed
To the lattice, whispering her name, he met
Pressed against the glass the long black fresh-bloodied
Muzzle of her mother grinning out.

I think that gets the grisly end as well as any I've tried yet, and makes the setting definitely fairytale. For the first time since you left I'm beginning to feel like writing again. [. . .] Love to you my kish and my puss and my dearest Sylvia my wife love & love your Ted

Like the notebook poem about Mary Bell and John Brown, Blake's *The Everlasting Gospel*, begun *c.*1818 and never finished, remained unpublished for more than a century. It starts: 'The Vision of Christ that thou dost see / Is my Vision's Greatest Enemy' – and keeps up this pugnacious tone as far as it goes. TH never published either his own 'near nursery rhyme' or 'On his side, embrangled in adult passion'.

Another of TH's story plots, what he himself calls 'a sentimental one', about a woman's reunion with a lost lover, has been omitted.

To Sylvia Plath

[9 or 10 October 1956]   Ts   Lilly Library

My dearest Sylvia,
    my wakings at least are pleasant and go a long way to make up for the bad sleeping. Last night I was frozen in bed. First of all I like the poem. No lack of sophistication either. The movement is very good – firm, discreet, passionate. And the statement open, not tortoised in imagery. I can't find anything in it to criticise, except perhaps – what does an almanac do? An almanac is a calendar. How does a calendar vouch for a fact that is geographical. The implication is that your removing from one place to another, from your kingdom to a million counties away, was fastened to a certain date, and the pastness of

that date on the calendar is a too blunt reminder of that removing. Its complicated to get over in so little, but I think it works. I think it's good, and not to be slighted by any up-nosed disowning modesty. It's smoother than the glutton – the movement is more inevitable, and the words all of a family. I like it.

You are right about the New Yorker. I think Luke's poems might get in, particularly the ballade, which has just the kind of gaucherie they seem to countenance, and Fools Encountered which is as good as anything I've read in there. His kind of 'poeticalness' would catch the New Yorker I think. I know what you mean when you describe your reactions to the New Yorker. But the thing to remember is that all these people are publishing not according to some abstract New Yorker standard – they're all writing what they find they can write and writing it as well as they can. Who does Salinger copy? or Eudora Welty? All the good ones have invented their own manner in their own private rooms. If you write whatever attracts you, and you write it as hard as you can, and as rich, then you can't miss, and a pox on your imitators who will be the new breed of outnumbering gnats. Just write it off, in your own way, and make it stand up off the page and jump about the room – then even if you're writing about your Aunt Aegrotat's animated carrots it will sell. I wonder why Thurber's declined?

I had a letter from Peter Redgrove, who has finally fought through to contact with Carne-Ross, and who writes to inform me that the committee of the B.B.C. have accepted my Yeats Programme and that I shall be hearing from Carne-Ross in a day or two. Good. Joy in fact. With one programme I may well have a more lucrative qualification than a whole aeon of enunciating to Andalusian Hotel Keeper's imbecile sons. When I go there I shall take Hopkins and Skelton and try to arrange for a reading of the Wreck and maybe the Tunning of El. Rumming, which would both be long good hauls. I will tell you the day as soon as I hear then you can prepair a decamping. We'll stay the night in a hotel. And I shall kiss you into blisters.

The suit O Sylvia and the Jacket. Wonderful. They're my favourites ever. The first clothes I've ever had that I didn't put on for lack of better. Pa marvelled and amazed and I believe Ma will now sleep better. I shall come down to London in the Jacket and my dark pants. Sleek sleek sleek. If only something would sell out on the stalls we are now set to begin misering and amassing bullion. The thought of your Poetry acceptances is like a little you. You must be swaggering. But don't crack. I suppose the horde is descending about now and you're dizzy with invitations and so unsettled by the storming of feet into the city that you're accepting them out of sheer distraction. I shall be glad to be out of England and away from the thought of you down there sixteen shillings away, open to every knave's nice manners and charming conversation while I sit here and stare at the skyline like an old stone.

I heard a kind of morality play by George Barker the other night, or part of it. I suppose nobody in the history of the tongue has raved more than he about the history of the heart. His whole career has been ruined by an ambition to be mantic and oracular as Dylan Thomas, when he might have been a good sort of minor byron. I now know why the police stopped me.

Plot: SHE is a kind of recluse. Leaves the city, is wealthy enough to buy a cottage in the hills, in a beautiful lonely place. She has a car and runs to the nearest township for supplies. She has something to do. Maybe she writes, maybe she does something else. Anyway her house is the picture of what a lone and lonely woman would make of it. She manages. She becomes strange, and the townspeople say she is mad. You are never quite sure whether she is mad or not. She leads a very lonely time, and the birds come to her door etc. One day she gets back from town to find a man in her house. A young man, good-enough-looking, strong looking, but exhausted. He is fast asleep on her bed, and she cannot wake him. He is dreaming wildly. She is frightened. She wonders [*next line-and-a-half x-ed over*] she sits and watches. It never occurs to her to go for help. He wakes, and she is reassured. She makes him a meal. Almost nothing is said. He does certain things about the house. He leaves at dusk. Next morning he appears again – obviously he has slept in the woods. He goes on doing things about the house. She is alarmed at the way he takes over. He begins making gadgets to make life in that spot easier. He digs a garden. He plants it with every presumption of hoping to see good plants there. What is she feeling all this time. They hardly ever speak, but there is a union. She misses him when he goes out. Still he is sleeping in the woods. He never looks at her directly, yet his presence is open and easy. All kinds of wifely longings begin to stir in her. He always brushes off her monosyllabic enquiries monosyllabically. They grow closer. Some thing happens and they come together – they lie together. Some drastic crisis brings this about. That next day the police arrive with dogs. Now all the time he has shown an uneasiness at the mention or possibility of visitors. A figure on the land-scape has more than once sent him to the woods. Now the police take him. She is desolate. Her recluse instincts have been utterly ousted by her wifely ones. After a fearful day or two she goes to town, thence to the city to see what has become of him. There she learns that he is wanted for murder. Murder of his wife. What does she do?

This is a situation at least. LOVELOVELOVELOVEMYPONKMY-KISHPUSS.

As for the New Yorker, I don't know. Perhaps one ought to be able to strip off these little poems as a kind of exercise, but I fancy it would be death. Obviously the snail man has got the method, and writes those things as hacks turn out comic strips. There's no question of serious writing, or imaginative flight, or serious or meaningful sequence of rhythms or imagery, or really grasped detail. They are just plain bad. They don't even have charm. The snail one doesn't anyway. And to let themselves be taken by such a catch-dollar method of dividing the line makes the whole joke too obvious and entirely at the expense of the New Yorker. They ought to have printed it as prose and paid him a cent a line at that. But it is eminently a magazine of parlour pieces, and not of serious writing, not the peoms. Teaparty pieces. Birthday card rhymes. The kind of ornament on the page that the designs of advertisements also provide. A place for the eye. But nothing. And yet I should think that something good and very smooth-mannered would get in. I think that is the key – smooth-manners.

I like the poem about statuary very much, the first verse without exception, and the second. In the third "Let break an elegiac tear" reminds me of "Now break a giant tear for the little known fall" and somewhere else he "Put a tear for joy in the unearthly flood." Also there is a traffic confusion I think in "Fierce flaring game of Quick child" – do you think "Quick flaring game Of child, leaf or cloud" because the "Fierce flaring" are two consecutive likenesses, and have been too often the double tap of the hammer. Let me explain that. When a blacksmith hits the hot iron, he hits the iron, where he wants, with one hard effect-ive blow, and lets then the hammer bounce off to the side once a light tap on the anvil – this makes the whole swing easier, and by the time he lifts his hammer again he has thought, and can do the work more rhythmically this way. Well in verse the tendency is to follow an adjec-tive that's working with an idle timing one, so that adjectives tend to go in pairs. Well in 'fierce flaring' an old couple has come up, and the one to go I think should be the fierce for the same reasons that you would give me if I had written "Fierce flaring." And "Quick flaring" animates both quick and flaring. Also don't you think you should bring a stronger relationship between the elegiac tear that you break and the safe-socketedness of the statues eyes? I think you should. This isn't fully clear and vivid. Keep the idea of their stony lasting stare, but change your Dylan tear to some other contrast. Also, in the second verse, your final 'It' comes well after 'Tip', but in the last verse your 'Rock' comes as a surprise unprepared for. But I like the poem. It's worth working over. The first two verses are your apocolyptic "Black and white" but fixed in the children and the park, which is something you have hardly done before.

Now I'm looking at your second letter which has the news. Well let him give Monsier Weeks a great kick, and apply leverage, bribes, force and blackmail in every department. Still, if they look at them hard enough, long enough, even though they send them back, they may remember my name. Also I hope they give them chance to grow on them. That is good news about the fables. Do as you say, but get them off before the end of the month. I think you are right about the others. A book of mixed stories is a much less daunting prospect than two books of nine of each type. I will set about that in Spain, and try and have them shaped out to begin writing then. Are you keeping up with your novel notes? Do, because these seasons won't come again, and Autumn is Cambridge's private display. We mustn't let slip that man's goodwill and readiness.

I had begun to dislike "Circus in three rings" but I am certain "Firesong" has already titled some already book of poems. There must be ways of discovering whose and when and where.

As for the changeling, that was 'Light Verse'. The ending is a bit fortuitous, but to stop at eyes leaves you recovering your balance uncomfortably. Also there is then no explanation no consequence of the 'So vile times'. I will try to devise a close. It isn't worth sending out.

And as for the Horses of the Sun, I look at it now with horror. The prospect of doing to it all that needs doing. It certainly was rough, and strained. I will not attempt to explain or defend any of it, until I've thoroughly revised it.

I like this second poem too. You are beginning to knit your poems together unchallengeably. Everything goes perfectly here until "Pierced side". You have been giving to think of a side gaping and mangled and bloody, but 'Pierced' – in the context of literal and violent detail, means merely stabbed, with a blade, leaving a thin slash, or cut, or small hole. Something like 'Open' would give a much rawer more vulnerable terrible sense.

I'm not sure about 'cursed' to hear. In that context a comparatively mild word would do more. 'Cursed' is straining to keep up with the rest, and is a worn word anyway. The next line I don't like. Phoenix's are theatre props. The next two lines are two of the best. The next line is not so felicitous. I think there's better than hiss or is it – I've only just seen this – that the world is the daft goose? If so I think you should switch the penultimate line. Change it somehow – it doesn't present the subject, it isn't vivid and the rest is so much. I love you, Sylvia, all day, all night when I can't sleep. Thinking about you and just blankly missing you has brought me to a standstill. I love you I love you I love you. I shall come to London on Friday, so get an exeat for that night. If Carne-Ross invites me down before then, I shall stay on. If not, I shall tell him I shall be in London. Love love to my wife

Ted.

This letter seems to have been written in two parts, in response to separate letters of Plath's, the second possibly arriving before TH's reply to the first had been sent.

'Monologue at 3 a.m.', with its 'snake-figured almanac / vouching you are / a million green counties from here', is the first poem TH discusses. 'Touch-and-Go' is the second – and it is interesting to note that, when TH came to edit Plath's *Collected Poems*, he placed it, not close to either 'The Glutton' or 'Monologue at 3 a.m.', which share a page in the main body of the book, but under 'Juvenilia'. There, the lines on which he comments are rewritten as 'Let my transient eye break a tear / For each quick, flaring game / Of child, leaf and cloud'. The third poem, 'Crystal Gazer', was also revised before eventually appearing in *Collected Poems*.

Of the poems that TH discusses in the second part of this letter, 'Circus in Three Rings' is among the 'Juvenilia' of Plath's *Collected*, while 'Street Song', with its last line 'This cracked world's incessant gabble and hiss', is in the main body.

The radio play by the poet George Barker (1913–91) was *The Seraphina*.

The 'snail man': 'The Garden Snail', an eye-catching poem with prosodically questionable line breaks, by Robert A. Wallace, had appeared in the 8 September 1956 issue of *The New Yorker*.

Edward Weeks was Editor of the *Atlantic Monthly* from 1938 to 1966.

The remarks about 'novel notes' and 'Cambridge's private display' relate to Plath's projected novel *Falcon Yard* (see note on letter to Plath of 1 (and 2) October).

To Sylvia Plath

[11 October 1956]   Ts and ms   Lilly Library

Dearest Sylvia,

I got your letter this morning of the train time. I shall pick you up either off the train, or, if my bus is a bit late, in the waiting room at King's Cross. Don't get so upset. If there is such a thing, this next year will be a real character expander for you, dealing with all those people when you know them through and through.

I see you're having Holloway – Queen's golden boy. What for?

As for Mrs Milne – there ought to be some way of finally settling her. . . .

A funny thing. I don't think I told you this. Last September about this time our ginger cat, which was just about half grown, followed Pa down to the bus-stop and was never seen again. Never until the day we got the kitten, that is. The morning we got little smoggleshonks here – who's going mew mew and coming up my chair arm – our ginger cat, now just about fully grown and a beauty, came running up to Pa at the bus stop. For three mornings it came up to him. This morning when I went out for some bread it came running across to me. Everyone says it's a stray, and seems to live off charity. So I brought it back. It doesn't seem to recognise the place particularly, or maybe it's that it recognises it utterly, without question, and has already forgotten its year absence. Anyway it looks around mildly, laps milk, goes to sleep – until it sees little Nymcrimping, then it growls and backs and hisses. So I don't know what we shall do. I wish they'd make friends. I suppose they will in time, but meanwhile little Nymcrimping will have a time.

Last night a hedgehog came into the garden and we all went out to have a look at its face. Long and pointed with black eyes deep in brown bristly hair, and a wet wet snuffly nose.

While we're on noses – Holding the ladder has got me a cold in the head which is a fine thing to have contracted at this time. However, it's only a slight one, and only in my head – not in my stomach where it would have stuck. The worst of it is a slight headache. I'm dosing myself with hot milk and treacle and brandy and aspirins so if this letter is a little dopey blame aspirin.

I think that's an idea about the little poems. Why don't you try it. Single it down to your humour and vividness in lines of two or three words, and a slight difference in verse form from that Wallace or whatever his name was. I think a poem must be a great responsibility for a life and soul of the party such as NY is, whereas with a tiny trickle of song-strain nobody can take exception, and far more people can take notice. Unless they were solid stuff I wouldn't put your name to them. Call it washing doorsteps for bread. I will try a few. I suppose they're not easy to write but they're ridiculously easy compared to a poem.

Plot: Man and a woman have been married ten years, trying to have a baby for the last eight. They are both immensely wealthy. For the first two years of their marriage, they said "Let's enjoy ourselves before settling down with a family" and so they did in their way, but pretty soon the keen domestic family spirit in both of them cut their rather barren pleasure stretch short. They returned to America, settled in a suburb, he with some position in his father's company, and set to, to get offspring. Nothing happens. None come. For eight years they try, maybe for fourteen, but it's no good. The doctor's answer is 'no reason why not', and so they go on trying, but with less and less zest. Meanwhile the magnificently equipped home is waiting, the wife walking about imagining her happy shouting brats swarming. There is a paradise garden, equipped as a children's playground – one of the main reasons for their buying this house. There is a nursery runs all along the top story with wide windows, and odd wheels of toys from the big family that had it previously. Still no children come. They despair.

Then, one day, as she stares bored out at the garden, the wife sees a little child, a little girl, a scruffy slobbery ill-kept but pretty girl. She hardly dares but she does – call the girl in. She gives her cakes, cleans her, asks her where she lives, but the little girl only gobbles and looks delighted, says something – 'grockles' and laughs or so. The wife dare hardly think. She steals into next rooms, and surprises herself walking in on the child, she watches it, she stands in further rooms and listens to it playing with the toys she has set it among. Who does the child belong to? She is certain that it has been abandoned – some slut not wanting the bother of it has set it down in a rich person's garden. This is more than she dare hope.

When husband comes home she shows him her new acquisition as delightedly as if it had actually been her own. He of course immediately ponders the legal questions, the justice of the thing, the necessity of taking trouble to find out where the child belongs – if in fact it has been abandonned, then, perhaps, they may be aloud to bring it up. The wife is angry – give it back to the neglectful slut who must own it? And she shows him in high indignation the rags it was dressed in. He too wants this child – it takes to him straightaway. His wife brings up every unreasonable reason for keeping the child and saying nothing, while the husband considers what shall be done formally to assure that this heaven-sent gift really can be theirs. The woman in fact is not sure whether this isn't a gift straight from God. She is quite light-headed with delight and apprehension and hope.

There are no slums in the whole town where such a child could have come from. It certainly seems to have dropped out of nowhere. He rings up the police and enquires if a child has been lost. None reported.

They keep the child a whole week, perhaps not so much, but enough to make them confident that it is theirs and to give them a real taste for this child. The wife begins to treat it confidently like a mother. It shows extraordinary cleverness in some way – perhaps it can make things. Anyway it is enough to set her dreams soaring of what an education they will give to it . . . in the midst – at the very peak of this dream, there comes a knock on the door.

She goes, opens it, and her heart crashes. Standing at the door is a filthy beribbonned benecklaced bebraceletted swart greasy gypsy woman, with a child on her shoulder, another trailing from her hand, and another standing behind and peering round. Without preliminaries she asks, matter-of-factly, for her girl. The wife doesn't know what to do. Give her darling back to this? Back to living rough and pro-spectless as gypsies do? Back to the very opposite of everything the wife thinks the child should have. She almost refuses, almost defies the gypsy woman, but before she can speak, with a cry, the little girl rushes past her to the gypsy. Without a word the gypsy turns and walks away down the long beautifully kempt drive, trailing all her children. Perhaps the woman calls desperately to the little girl by the name she has given her, but the little girl ignores her. The wife is left standing over her hole in the earth. She turns back into the house. Everything is as the little girl left it. She sits stunned. Suddenly there is a little knock on the door – a child's knock. She runs to the door – refusing the hope. At the door stands the little scruffy gypsy boy. "Can I have her clothes. My mum's sent me back for her clothes." He hands her the beautiful expensive things in which she had dressed the girl, and waits expectantly.

Very sentimental. There are gypsies in America, though I'm not sure of their status. All over Europe they are as they would need to be for this story. This is a reversion of the old tale popular with english children's writers of the gypsies stealing a child. I'm sure it could be done. I'm rather proud of this one.

It is a heavy thing, but can you bring the camp-bed to London. Or the coat. Take your choice. No. Bring the coat. Yes, the coat.

DONT FORGET THE D. THOMAS LETTERS.

All my love to Sylvia my wife my ponk my kish my puss. Tomorrow is very near and when you read this it will be today. I shall write a letter to your mother, thanking her for the map, but I will bring it to London as I don't know her address. I suppose we can consider Carne-Ross's apparent interest to have me read my poems – I hope he means record this time, but only if he does mean me to record them, to buy the reading, as an acceptance. I wrote to him yesterday and told him that it is true I am intending to leave for Spain towards the end of this month, but that the date is still uncertain. I wondered, in my letter, if he could fix a reading of the Wreck of the Deutschland or of Skelton's Tunning of El. Rum. before I go. I thought I would give him time to operate the committee buisiness if he is interested in such readings, then perhaps I could make them next Friday which in his letter he called a free day. I also meant to offer my services, while I am in London, for any odd bits of reading in other programmes – usually in poetry readings they have several readers – but I didn't want to send a begging letter. I'll ask him that when we see him. All all all all all, all my love. Bring to London what you have written. We will see the Tate this time. Your Ted

'Fate Playing', in *Birthday Letters*, may be an account of what happened to TH and Plath's plan to meet in London, although it is in the wrong place chronologically.

John Holloway (1920–99) had recently been appointed Fellow of Queens' College. As one of the poets associated with The Movement, whose programme was regarded by its detractors as aridly rational and small-scale, he occupied a position far from that of either TH or Plath.

To Sylvia Plath

[15 October 1956]   Ms   Lilly Library

My dearest Sylvia, –

This is Monday morning about 11. When I came to Rugby St Dan was here, and I spent the rest of Sunday moping and reading.

I got up this morning feeling like writing, and with a clear idea how to begin Snatchcraftington, so this afternoon I shall write some of that. Just now I've been out trying to get Carne-Ross, but, says the operator, his office is empty, not even a secretary, so I shall try again a bit later. [. . .]

That was a well-used weekend, and we did well not to go wandering over London. I feel much better that we just stayed.

[. . .]

Dan has some good books here. In one – that I've been reading – is a collection of the curious myths – divining rods, the seven sleepers of Ephesus, mermaids etc –. The chapter about mermaids is terrific. He translates accounts by priests etc, who seem to be hurried in numbers to every mermaid catching, – close descriptions of mermaids, with small monkey heads, coarse wiry black hair, short necks, sharp teeth, cod-eyes, cartilaginous ribs, and a whimpering kitten mew – length in centimetres, four-jointed fingers, etc.

Do you remember the shop – near the Y.W.C.A., opp the British Museum – where Theosophical Books were advertised – where we stopped after coming from the ghoul's shop, and pointed, and I said that looks like the shop to have books on the tarot. Well, today I called. There is a whole shelf-full of books on Astrology, and one or two only on the tarot – there may well be more than I saw. They had the one we bought – at 21/- – and another – at 5/- – which told more or less the same elementary facts. I shall go again, and look more closely. I shall see Peter Redgrove tomorrow and ask him where he got his Tarot.

This is just a short note with no plot. Tomorrow I shall give two. For my darling wife, for my Sylvia, for my ponk, my kish, my puss, and from her big toe up by quarter inches to the tip of her longest hair, kisses, and lickings and love.

> Love love love love love love from
> your Ted.

'Dan' is Daniel Huws, with whom TH was staying at 18 Rugby Street, while in London for his negotiations with the BBC. (Most of the omitted sections of this letter concern TH's attempts to pin down Donald Carne-Ross, largely from a public phone box.)

'Snatchcraftington' was a fantastical story for children, on which TH worked for some time, inconclusively.

The book about myths and wonders was *Curious Myths of the Middle Ages* by S. Baring-Gould (1877).

To Sylvia Plath

[18 October 1956]   Ms   Lilly Library

My dearest Sylvia –

No news yet. Another delicious letter from my kiss puss. What's happened to your dreams? Probably now you've started writing all that out, you have – as you say – exorcised it, or at least got it under control. Perhaps it's been pushing and glooming and corrupting your imagination for long enough. But if you keep up a detailed vivid looking at things, and not at all things, your dreams will go on improving, till you're the angel of your own paradise. Try writing them out each morning.

Don't be taken back by those rejections, but don't send them straight out. Do as you are doing, sending out your latest. If you keep up your writing you will see, after a few weeks, where you can improve the rejected ones, or whether they are better let lie. Keep writing your Cambridge notebook, remembering incidents from last year and writing them up. The Cravenson episode would be a perfect chapter. The American letter-writer another. Each one will grow slowly. Write the definite ones first.

How much reading do you do a day? Do you get through the books? Are you browsing with appalled boredom through the English book of verse – Oxford of English I mean? Do, however. Bill with these antiquities, and coo over them, if only to deceive a degree, – keep at them. The minor Elizabethans are interesting and all alike. Try and see what their favourite gimmicks are, how they use metaphors, their rhythms, – the personal dramatic and yet colloquial tone of voice, as different from the late 17th & 18th whose tone of voice is personal and dramatic but flat literary. Note the artificial complexity of Donne's followers. A difficult period is mid-18th century onwards, when glorification of gardens turns to glorification of wild Nature as seen from over a silken cravatte. But with a little reading, and a little reading into the background – their lives in S. Johnson's lives of the poets etc – you will see this more easily and instinctively than me. You never will understand a poet of the past unless you know thoroughly and can imagine the exact cast of popular temperament. And you only pick this up by nibbling in all kinds of seemingly useless places, – but mainly too by imagining vehemently all that you read.

Books like Defoe's "Journal of the Plague Year", and bits of diaries. This is one of the first novels and one of the most terrifying books I ever read. Get it. You'd read it quickly. Browse a lot, but don't let browsing obscure and dissipate your main line of singleminded reading.

There. That's a page of dogma.

I'm spending my time here copying out, in all necessary detail, curious stories and tales out of all these hystory books and mythology books. Mostly Welsh & Irish, but some plain general mediaeval. None of the books are much but some of the stories are. I may find a use for them. Many pretend to be history, and are just the sort of thing that several English journals buy – "Everybody's" for instance. But they may do one day for romantic pot-boiling T.V. play plots.

The North American Indians thought: in the beginning there were just men. These men were peaceful, happy, glorified their maker. But they had tails. Long sleek lithe silky tails, that they adorned with knick-knacks, trinkets, paint, perfumes, and indulged as their one vanity. Gradually they forgot their God. They became arrogant & quarrelsome. Then God sent down a scourge, something to make them remember they had a maker, – He cut off their tails. Then, out of their tails, he made women. These women still show all their old characteristics – trailing around after men, dangling themselves with ornaments, painting, perfumeing, and trying every trick to get back where they came from.

I had a vast piece of steak today.

How are all the sitters, and scowlers, and yitterers, and oglers? Do you make proper coffee all day? Do they come in and sit? And be sly?

I dreamed about you continually last night, in all kinds of places and confusions. We shall meet next week. A week since we met! I wish this was that or was next week, Sylvia. I wish this year were over and our wedding in America were over and I were just laying you down on the bed. All all all all all love Your

Ted.

Everybody's, a weekly magazine that included a story in each issue, ran until 1959.

To Olwyn Hughes

[October 1956]   Ms   Emory

Dear Olwyn,

A great many things have happened since I last saw you. When are we going to meet? I hope to be setting sail next week, with Walt, for Southern Spain, and I intend to take life up in Granada. I shall expect to see you there, – but don't go by train. Train in Spain, unless its first class, is cattle-travel.

Do you still know that poetry Editor of Botteghe Oscure? I sent some poems to them – the dregs they were, but two of them were rather better. I received all back, the other day, except those two. There was a scruffily typed rejection, but no explanation for the missing two poems. And they were in some old envelope – not the neat stamped addressed that I sent. I take it they separated the two for further perusal, and sent the rest back when they saw them lying around. I shall write, if my secretary in chief has not already written. She's had some good fortune lately. She sold a long rather bad poem to The Atlantic Monthly, which is one of <u>the</u> Mags in America, for $50. Then, last week, Poetry Chicago accepted six of her poems – one or two of them her best, and her best is good – and is making an official debut. Perhaps you'll meet her in Spain, where she'll come for her vacs. She's not bla American at all, but very enthusiastic. Very unpretentious, very German in some ways – works herself till she drops. And she certainly has a startling poetic gift. I have nothing of hers at hand or I'd send you some. I'll tell her to send you some, and some of my latest too which are now coming on.

[. . .]

Sylvia is born the 27th October, has Mars in 24 of Leo, and the last degree of Aquarius rising, with Saturn in 29 of ♑, on the cusp of the twelfth, which is suicidal, – especially opposite Mars in the 6th. All correct. She has the moon in Libra, & ♃, ♀ & ♆ in the 7th house. Here is the horoscope of your conception which is 9 moons to the minute pre to birth, according to gynae-cologists.

Great pity you weren't at home to read my fables. You'll have to read them in the book now. As you haven't written for so long I've no idea what you're doing. That was a good photograph of you that Vicky brought. Write & tell what you're doing.

Love,

Ted.

Plath reports the *Atlantic Monthly*'s acceptance of 'Pursuit', which TH here calls a 'long rather bad poem', to her mother on 2 September, and *Poetry (Chicago)*'s of six poems on 2 October (see *Letters Home*).

To Sylvia Plath

[20–22 October 1956]   Ms   Lilly Library

My dearest Sylvia –

two letters from you today. The first melancholy sad, the second its antithesis. I suppose you got my letter today, on the rejection of the fables. I wonder if they read them. Anyway, – as I told you – I shall try with the detatchable four in Manchester.

I have started writing Snatchcraftington, and shall do a bit each day. It is clear now. Snatchcraftington appears, attracts all the children as he somersaults through the streets, stops in the market-place, turns into a 3 masted ship, comes out on the bridge and calls the children aboard for a free trip to Africa. The children hang back, and before he can bring persuasion to bear, a policeman comes forward and tells him to be off. The P. clears off the children, and turns back to get particulars off Snatch, finds him turned to a crow and flying away over the roofs. Next Snatch appears to a few boys, & turns into a space-ship, offering a free-trip to Mars, back by dark. Before the boys can get in, they are again interrupted – so on. You see it is definite, and I can see as far as the first main episode – the kingdom of the bright particles, – clearly. I want to introduce my character, my little boy, as quick as I can. It is very simpleminded, but not moreso than Keats Cap & Bells.

Peter Redgrove told me the other night about this Poetry competition. He obviously hoped I wasn't entering. As his first question was "When do you think of bringing out a poetry book" and as my answer was, implying all delay and tardiness "Oh next spring maybe" he told me of the competition. I wasn't greatly interested, because I have got used to thinking of my book as minus most of the poems I have, i.e. supplemented with what is yet to be written. But I now see that coming out under these people – though they are an opposition, rather than a means – it would plant my merit firmly in every editor's confidence. So. I will. And I wish I could get back into a writing spell, to add at least five, before they go in. I will try that too.

Today I went with Danny to the National Portrait Gallery. Have you never been there? Beautiful cast of Keats, of Blake. Pictures of Donne, and the rest. A superb cast head of Yeats. I came away utterly exhausted. It was a very strange thought – out of the English civilisation there are the selected works, the civilisation over. So few good ones. So many half-good, careless, ill-defined works, like Dryden, Southey, Swinburne etc. There are none very modern. Yeats is one of the latest.

I don't know what you're doing tonight – Saturday at eight to make me suddenly nightmarishly depressed. I kept trying to think of reasons why I should feel so miserable. Then a dog started howling of all things.

I shall find out on Monday just what the Education department of the American Forces is, and what it desires. £15 for 2 nights is –. I am almost ready to do horoscopes for money. I shall try, too, to sell the Calum-makers on Monday.

I shall write no more now, but more tomorrow. I think of you more and more Sylvia, though not distractedly now. If I could get quiet somewhere I could use this time. Though this is quiet enough. The only sound I hear all day is the street, but I do hear that all day, every minute of the day. I love you from your toes to your ankles to your knees to your thighs to your hips to your navel to your nipples to your shoulders to your throat to your mouth to your nose to your eyes and then in to the end of you. All my love every minute.

Do you see that Merwin has collected his sloppings over into a book, called 'Green with beasts', which just about sums up a swamped foundering arkfull of sick apes.

This is Sunday. Or rather Monday morning at one. Oh Sylvia. Where are you? I could crush you into my pores. I've never passed such days. A soulless existence, in that I live purely the presence of this shape and weight, – all my sense is utterly with you.

This afternoon Dan & I walked over to Than's. And there I've been until just a minute ago. So today I've done no writing. We've been trying to convey thoughts – Than was the only good receiver. When we thought of branding-iron, he said electric-welding Rod, which is nearly exact, and spit, and ski-man with those spiked pole things – very good. He picks casual thoughts up much better than the main image. When I looked at the picture of a man smoking a pipe – he was trying to pick up 'fireworks' – he said 'man holding a pipe'. When I quite casually thought of hand in glove – he was trying to pick up 'freeze' – he said 'foot in a sock'. And so on.

I'm behind with plots aren't I? Only I thought of one today which I shall try and make seriously into a T.V. play. The general theme is that a young man doesn't get rich until it's too horribly late.

> The day after he left he was not
> Recognisable on any calendar:
> His heart went on so wretched a foot
> Every instant cut it, crying 'her'.
> Each beat's pang dragged her absence to it.

Oh I am ill at these numbers. [*Illegible word*] quote. I think of your mouth and your brown eyes. You have drawn on the back of this book a face just like you. I have no picture of you punk except what I think of endlessly.

I want you to receive this tomorrow so I'll write no more. All my love to you Sylvia,

your Ted.

'I suppose you got my letter': TH had written on 19 October reporting that his animal fables had been turned down by the BBC Children's Department, on the grounds that they were 'too abstract and nebulous in conception and execution'. The four he was proposing to send to the BBC at Manchester were the tales of the Owl, the Whale, the Tortoise and the Polar Bear, all eventually included in *How the Whale Became*.

The competition mentioned by Peter Redgrove was for the New York Poetry Center's First Publication Prize, which TH did enter. The judges were Marianne Moore (1887–1972), W. H. Auden (1907–73) and Stephen Spender (1909–95).

TH's prose fable 'The Callum-Makers' – the invented and unexplained word 'callum' is spelt in various ways, and one notebook version has the title 'Stories about you bastard English' – remains unpublished.

W. S. Merwin (b.1927), US poet living in London, whose work TH came to admire, was not yet an acquaintance.

'Than' was Nathaniel Minton, a Cambridge friend and contributor to *Saint Botolph's Review*.

The quotation with which TH challenges Plath is from *Hamlet*.

To Sylvia Plath

[22 October 1956]   Ms   Lilly Library

First of all I think your poem's good. I'm not sure about "green wilderness" [*inserted above*: this green is the wrong one I think, not – *with arrows to show 'green', and not 'wilderness', was the doubted word*] The shift of tone in it is masterly. I think it's about the most accomplished poem you've ever written. The most well-mannered, or graceful. I'm not sure either about 'clear-cut' – 'snowflake' perfect but not 'clear-cut'. That doesn't irk me so much as the other, – but the distinctness gets away in these last two lines of this verse – just slightly – and I think its in 'clear-cut', though it may be in 'glittering'. There's a terrific interplay of images and movement, – it 'comes off' – vile phrase – perfectly. The subject – being short-story matter and descriptive – may seem to you slight, but I don't think that's in question. It's just a good poem, and I bet you get it published first try. Your verse never goes 'soft' like other women's.

By the same post as your letter this morning came one from Olwyn, suggesting that I enter for the Observer Play Competition. I shall try and write a play. I have a very romantic idea for a play, which I will describe to you when I've got it clearer. I shall write it in verse, because that cuts out most competitors. Even the worst dramatic critics have a reverence for verse-plays for some reason. And I think I can write dramatic verse. Though whether I can sustain a play to the end without exaggeration or melodrama, I'm not at all sure. The subject will give verse scope. It's generally the delinquent idealism of a youth, opposed by the saturnine respectable propriety and conformity of his parents, relations, and the law. He's a youth who refuses the world, and will be high pressure. He wants to make his own separate corner, a civilisation of his own, on his own terms – but needs a wee bit capital. And anyway his parents and relations are relying on him taking up the family buisiness. He will break himself, and break them in the conflict, but in the end he will not be broken. He will get up again, though they will not.

82

I shall need to regulate my thoughts a good deal before I can carry this out.

I think the main thing is to make it simple. I don't want any static mangling maundering Tchekovian half-hour interludes. The main effects, at ideal, would be ritualistic. I saw – on Than's T.V. yesterday – an excerpt from the Russian ballet doing Romeo & Juliet. I never saw anything like it. Effects – of pathos and beauty and sorrow – that make modern stage look mean and paltry. Problems, and haggling are nothing, unless they're lifted out, and made more. Like Family Reunion.

It will be something to write a play seriously and to the end. I would like it clean of arbitrary stage tricks – tea-pourings, cup-droppings, telephone-ringings, street effects off, – I shall imagine the whole thing to terrific music.

Plath had sent a draft of 'Spinster', which in her *Collected Poems* suppresses 'green wilderness' in favour of a 'rank wilderness of fern and flower' – though 'an intricate wilderness of green' was allowed into her 1958 poem 'Yadwigha, on a Red Couch, among Lilies'. In 'Spinster', the second criticised phrase becomes 'Exact as a snowflake'.

There is no record that TH ever began a play of the 'romantic' kind he describes here.

To Sylvia Plath

23 October 1956   Ms   Lilly Library

My dearest Sylvia,
  I've just sent off the telegram. I didn't ring, because the lodge would infallibly have eavesdropped – merely by holding their receiver to their ear. And what they would have heard – anyway, let any startling news be delivered to the authorities by you, deliberately, and according to your strategy, if any are to be delivered at all. Not picked out of our whisperings by their long calliper ears.
  I've been thinking about this too Sylvia. I think we shouldn't confuse it in letters. We can say nothing to the purpose in one way letters. I've already written two sides, and it was all just argueing one way then the other. By Saturday we shall both have clearer minds about it. One thing: to spend our first year – which is longer than most marriages last anyway – apart, seems mad. But do nothing. Don't ask Dr Krook anything yet. Let's talk about it on Saturday, which is only three more days.

I received an envelope from Carne-Ross this morning, returning to me Bishop Farrar, Six Young Men, Egg-head, September, Two wise generals, The Hag, Roarers in a ring, Bawdry embraced, the drop of water. He suggests I do 'Bishop Farrar" – "It seems to me" he says "that this one comes off more completely than any of the others." These are not all I gave him. I must have a great bout of revision. I am sure it would be best to pick out about 25 poems, and publish those. Here are two or three changes I see I want to make in the water-drop.

I will show Carne-Ross your poems, and recite to him your list of achievements – hair-raising. I'm sure he'll do you at least as much honour as he's done me, and publish one.

London is murderous. I tried to write a poem yesterday, and the result was ghastly. Drab stodgy exhausting filth and exhausted faces and exhausted streets. The trouble with London – all its ghosts have gone. The richness of a place, is the richness of the ghost impressions that it retains. It's an old fable and a convincing explanation, that neither ghost nor fairy will remain where there has been mechanism, petrol and oil. There's no aura left here. Its dead in exactly the same way as a corpse is dead – its soul has been ground out of it. Imagination, sensation, can find nothing in it. And the air's exhausted, full of fumes and stale petrol and stale oil and exhaust. And dreary hordes of people moving in complete helplessness.

If I were to stay in England, £50 a week would not keep me in London. This has been an awful fortnight, and I can't see that I've done anything in it.

[. . .]

Hold on, darling Sylv., till Saturday. I dreamed last night that I, a little boy, was fishing and hooked an enormous fish, then I, grown, came up and landed it for the little boy. I said 'Take a good look at it, because you'll probably never see a bigger one.' Then, a hundred yards away up the bank, I saw a lithe animal – like a fox only more of a ferret, – yellow red and very shark-faced. I whistled on my finger and it came rushing down, straight up to me, and began licking my face. I wish all this would mean something. Probably the fish is just the B.B.C.

I think it definitely better to make a formidable body of about 25 poems.

The last thing I did last night was write to you, and the first thing I'm doing this morning is write to you. So I'll cut it short. I meant to try & write a poem this morning. Keep things controlled darling puss, darling kish and ponk and we'll work it all out best. I'll get a hotel for Saturday night – a better one if I can. Maybe now, while we're needing money, we ought, I ought to make the effort to earn, which is only in England.

One thing. If the Fulbright were to hear you are married, your money would almost surely stop, or be halved. Find out that.

Above all, save every whisper until Saturday, save every little bit of you. I can hardly remember you without feeling almost sick and getting aching erections. I shall pour all this into you on Saturday and fill you and fill myself with you and kill myself on you.

It seems crazy of me not to earn.

I will come back with you on Sunday. If I were to stay in England and earn wouldn't all our problems be solved? It will be time to go to Spain etc when we both go together, and are not faced with a financial steeplechase, but just with jigging on.

I love you

Your husband, Ted.

After weeks of havering, during which Plath's main worry had been that the Fulbright Commission would deprive her of her scholarship on hearing of her marriage, she and TH were moving towards a resolution: she would confess her status to both the Commission and the Newnham authorities, while TH would shelve his plans to move to Spain for a year. As it turned out, there was no objection to the marriage from either official quarter.

The omitted passage concerns detailed corrections to poems of his own that TH wanted typed, followed by comments on poems of Plath's which elude identification.

To Lucas Myers

16 November 1956   Ms   Emory

Dear Luke,

To explain this address, and rumours you have probably been receiving, let me tell you that Sylvia & I were married on June 16th – same day as I got the acceptance for Bawdry Embraced. Under the impression that Newnham allowed no married students, we were going to keep this secret until next June. But she began to receive letters – from the Passport Office & such – addressed to Mrs S. Hughes, so she took the initiative – wept here, raved there, while I, in the background, got a flat here in Cambridge – inspired move as it turned out – and in conclusion here we are: Sylvia the first married undergraduate, and myself looking for a job. One of the conditions of her being allowed to continue her studies was that her husband must live in Cambridge.

The flat is good – a downstairs floor – extremely cheap. Upstairs lives a South African scientist – chemist really – who hates the English because they will have nothing to do with his discoveries – he has over-turned the whole chemic premise of modern chemistry of a certain sort and is hailed as this and that wonder in Canada, Australia & South America so he says, but in England – "Idle bastards to the least." He takes it out of his wife between three and four in the morning.

We sent your poems to New Yorker. The New Yorker is a closed ring to all but poems. I was sure they'd buy Fools Encountered or the bal-lade. 'They' sent them back, and now they are at Poetry Chicago and have been for some time. I'd give all you have to Tate, and let him publish them if he will. Tell him which ones are at Poetry – it shouldn't make any difference – most magazines don't mind where it's been printed before (though some do) and I'll let you know just which ones are accepted – which news you relay to Tate, all very rapidly. The main thing is to get all your poems into his hands.

Why don't you send something to 'Nimbus' – Wright liked your poems, and Nimbus is the only respectable English Magazine. Soon enough, by force of natural necessity, there will evolve an enormous dog with a bum-gut like a cement-mixer to crap directly and continuously over the offices and personnel of Encounter & London Mag.

What are you doing? Your letters were many and full when they were, but now they are old.

There are rumours in the likeness of sweeping plagues, and in the likeness of the racing seizing bed-fever. Of your tearing the tops off the seven hills on a 360 cc twin cylindered Grapalotti motorcycle. Also of your living in a five storied palazzio – à la byron (to see whom at his windows crowds waited all day in the streets below) – the ground floor full of spare beds for acquaintances, the first floor the kitchen of the next door restaurant, the next floor a menagerie of 39 subtly var-ied bawdristes, the next floor a single padded dark cell with a circular bed in the centre, and the top floor a bare room – one-spidered – with a bare chair at a bare table, on the bare table a dried-up ink bottle, beside the dried-out ink bottle a pile of foolscap, on the top sheet of the pile, at the top of the top sheet, these words written "Write for three hours at least each day at this table," and three months dust thick on them. A dead sparrow a husk on the floor. These rumours, I might add, can be caught out of the air, even at this distance, with a meat-hook.

I am curious to know more. Enumerate folly, appraise bawdry, give calendar dates, Rome time, and sketches wherever possible.

Did you ever begin your long poem? I would like to hear about it. Is David around?

I've now sold six poems. I got some reading on the B.B.C. Their payments amount up according to some inscrutable ratio, very profound mathematics it seems to me, whereby, for once in the world, they pay about 5 times as much in the end as they offered in the beginning.

Harpers, did you know, are holding a poetry contest. The entry has to be sixty pages (poems) by someone who has published no book (of poems). The judges are Spender, Auden, Marianne Moore. The prize is publication in America & England. Under these conditions, I should think that book will be about the only first book of poems ever to make any money. I have written a great deal since I saw you, some of it, I think, better than I have ever written. I can manage about 50 odd pages – 30 or so poems, only a few that you've seen. Considering the enemy – that Trinity – I have small hopes. But all kinds of people are beginning to show an interest in a few poems I gave to Redgrove. He is very generous – he reads them everywhere, all his various poetry societies. And I've no doubt that mainly through him I shall soon be able to sell something in England. I wish I could get a proper theme for a long poem.

Did Dan tell you of how we worked the ouija board – the glass turned upside down on a smooth table in a ring of the letters of the Alphabet. We were at Jim's. Jim, his girl friend, Dan & I each put a finger on it – on the glass. We then asked it questions. We got someone who called himself Pan. He told Jim 'Love fallen on rich soil." He told Dan to "Cut out drudgery. Go to Ireland and pray." It told me "In England do you never starve" – which is vague enough. We asked it if it knew Shakespeare. It said Yes, but not personally. We asked it to recite its favourite line and it spelled 'Never, never, never, never, never' – out of Lear. We then asked it to go on, but it refused. It said 'I forget.' We forced it a little and it wrote

"Why shall I ever be perplexed so.
I'd hack my arm off like a rotten branch
Had it betrayed me as my memory."

It didn't know where this came from. Nor do I. I've a vague memory of the last two lines. It said all manner of strange things – spelling them out, letter by letter, and quite irresistibly. We asked it to recite some of its own poetry and it recited

"Nameless he shall be
The myriad of daughters
Tending his image
Washing the mountainslopes with tears
To slake the parched plains."

It said it lived in Tibet. When we asked whether it's poetry was good or not it spelled out "Qui scit."

Another time I did it with Sylvia. We got one who swore, gave out the most incredible obscenities, and kept refusing, saying "I'm tired." Later we got another called Jumbo, who said she was a vixen and when we asked her where she lived she said "In core of nerve" – we pressed, asking what it was like there, whether it had mountains etc, whether it was happy, and it said "I've world enough." Then we asked it to predict whether certain magazines would accept poems – and it got these right. This week we've had it give us the result of the football Pools.

The Atlantic Monthly chose the very worst of a batch I sent them, and Poetry Chicago chose the weakest again of theirs. To the Nation I sold what is just about my best I think.

If you are thinking of leaving Italy next summer – having earned a year's keep – I know of a farmhouse which you may get for a mere retaining fee. It belongs to a cousin of my mother's and is in good shape. They won't have ordinary lodgers, because such make demands – repair this, supply that. Yet they don't want the place to drop apart from neglect. Tell me if you're interested.

I'll write no more, the fire's fumes are poisoning this room.

Ted

'To explain this address': TH and Plath had moved into a flat at 55 Eltisley Avenue, Cambridge. Myers was now in Rome. While he was abroad, Plath had offered to type his poems and send them to magazines. TH and Myers were in the habit of setting each other poetic assignments, and Myers's 'Fools Encountered', which had appeared in *Saint Botolph's Review*, was the stanzaic and metrical model for TH's own 'Bawdry Embraced'. 'David' was David Ross, editor of that magazine.

Daniel Huws records that the ouija session took place at the flat of his erstwhile Rugby Street lodger, Jim Downer, in Great Portland Street, London W1 (see footnote of letter to Daniel Huws, 15 May 1959). The three lines of 'quotation' offered by Pan after cajoling seem to have been original to him, as indeed was the sample of his 'own poetry'. Jumbo's enigmatic answer, 'in core of nerve', is hard to read in TH's hand, but is confirmed by his account of the same incident in a letter to his parents, where 'Core of Nerve' is given capital letters. The phrase occurs, too, in Plath's 'Dialogue over a Ouija Board'.

Of the poems offered to US magazines, 'Bawdry Embraced' had been taken by *Poetry (Chicago)*; 'The Hawk in the Storm' (which would later be revised as 'The Hawk in the Rain'), by *Atlantic Monthly*; and 'Wind', by the *Nation*.

To Aurelia and Warren Plath

[December 1956]   Ms   Lilly Library

Dear Sylvia's Mother & Warren,

I don't think it's possible to add any news to any letter by Sylvia, but I do add my best wishes for a Good Xmas and a happy New Year. Our few seconds over the phone was too tantalising – but its not what news is exchanged that makes such a phone-call important or worth-while. It had a wonderful effect on Sylvia, and it's certainly the best present the Aldrichs could have thought of.

After my first three weeks at school I hardly know what to do with all this free holiday time. I tell myself I'm just resting. I never thought teaching could be so hard – you were right when you said it's often not much more than playing the warder to a gaol-full. But sometimes, I think, I succeed in getting through to them, then they sit up.

They're working-class children, which means that as they grow up they take over mental habits, – the mental habits of the working class, – which are in fact a stupidity. At eleven years they are quick, bright, interested, full of possibilities and promise: at fourteen they are copying their elders – their brightness has disappeared – they are dull, cloddish, stupid as brutes. Literally. 'Who was Hitler?" I ask. "A leader of the French Resistance in the Boer War" they say, – after my forcing their memories –

Or "Three threes, quick?" I ask.

"Nine, sir."

"Are they nine? Are you sure they're nine?" I ask.

"er – eight, sir. No, sir, five, sir."

Then from all over the class – 'Twelve, sir', 'Sir, sir' 'Fifteen sir' – hands fly up to correct the poor idiot who thought 3 × 3 were nine. This illustrates the complete distrust they have of their own mental

89

processes. They all know it's nine, but none of them will believe it. When I ask the very young ones – 3 × 3? they say "Nine, sir" – and nothing I say can make them think it might be otherwise. It's disheartening to realise that the difficulty of teaching them something comes of not innate stupidity on their part, but a stupidity gradually adopted from the general outlook of the class to which they belong. But what an experience! Life purely as a writer would be suicidally narrow – purely as a musician, or as a painter, perhaps not – but a writer lives on relationships to people, & observation, as no other kind of artist does. Even so, his life as an observer and as a person involved in relationships will crush him as a writer unless he keeps up a full-time writing life as well – two lifes at once in fact. Difficult.

I am applying pressure to get Sylvia started on her novel. She is reading a novel about Cambridge which is having very fair success in sales & reviews – and that will set her off. There's not the slightest question – hers would be infinitely better. If only she'd get into it.

Our home is fine. And each day, when I get home, Sylvia has a speciality ready out of her cook-book.

We keep receiving little items from you – two steak-knives arrived just after the butcher had delivered a massy piece of steak. Then some delicious cookies. The only negative in the general sum of our good fortune at present is the Cambridge-winter – it's like living at the bottom of a stagnant swamp. We stoke our fire and put our feet up.

Have a good Xmas, & pass our Best Wishes onto Betty and Dwayne.

With love
Ted.

Don't believe those crook's gallery photographs.

'Arrived Dec 24, 1956' is in Aurelia Plath's hand at the head of the first sheet.

TH had begun teaching at the Coleridge Secondary Modern School in Cambridge in November.

1957

This is the year in which, after marrying his American wife, TH found the USA exerting its strongest influence on the course of his life. The collection of poems that, with Sylvia Plath's help, he had submitted for the Poetry Center's First Publication Prize, won it, and Harper & Row became his first publisher – although Faber and Faber, in London, which subsequently took the book, issued it earlier so that it would be eligible as a Poetry Book Society Choice. Harper's edition of *The Hawk in the Rain* came out in September. In June, TH and Plath sailed across the Atlantic, so that she could take up a teaching job at her alma mater, Smith College, in Northampton, Massachusetts. Far from home, TH consolidated the habit of keeping in touch with old Cambridge friends, adding Daniel Huws and Daniel Weissbort to Lucas Myers and members of his own family as his most regular correspondents.

Where his own work was concerned, it seems that the writing of plays became more of a preoccupation at this time, to the extent that, in his letters, they sometimes overshadow the poems for which he is now better known.

To Aurelia and Warren Plath

21 January 1957   Ts   Lilly Library

Dear Sylvia's mother and Warren,

This is a long guilty lag since I received your load of splendid presents. Our kitchen was transformed in a few minutes from a kind of Nomad scratching to a gleaming American annex. As for the shaving set, and the wallet, and the tie, and the pen, well – they make thanks look just silly. As we were going up to Yorkshire Sylvia asked me what I would really like for Xmas, and after thinking ineffectually for an hour I finally decided that about the only thing I needed was a shaving set. Through several years mine has grown to look like something the dog plays with, a rusty old razor and a bedraggled begnawn brush, enough to confirm the bearded lady to eternal beardry. As for a wallet, I had an old ill-stitched fold of leather that clung on to notes by magnetism or else just did not cling on to them at all. In fact, you divined my needs with something like clairvoyance.

The book of paintings we sent you really stood out in the shop, and there were many others, – but not one of them near it in quality of reproductions or in the actual selections.

Sylvia and I write pretty constantly. I suppose she's told you how we get up at six. I hope to make that even a little earlier, it's easy enough if we go to bed early, and the moral boost it gives outweighs an hour's sleep. She has written one or two very good poems lately, – it rather looks as if she's beginning another spate like the one that produced those this month in Poetry Chicago, though she's come some distance beyond those. Her book is startling. The individual poems are dazzling and disturbing enough, but more than that, they add up to each other – most books of poems stale their effect because the poems somehow break each other down, betray each other, outyell each other – Sylvia's are cumulative. This is especially surprising because her individual poems have such a brilliant and emphatic finish.

We're just breaking open one or two possible new markets here. A chance with the B.B.C. which is quite a strong one I think, and strong too in profits and reputation. Today Sylvia has written a sonnet on the subject "Mayflower" – set by one of the Oxford Colleges, for a 15£ prize. Her sonnet is strong and good, but excellence is hardly in question in these contests. The dons' dreams are still with Rupert Brooks and Rudyard Kipling.

Today a little young woman with a voice like a precocious double bass boy came to look at the flat upstairs and it looks as though she's our future neighbour. She seemed quite nice, and her husband's an American airman. She mentionned that she rarely goes out and that she has a big radiogram. If that means that we're in for a permanent high power jazz background, we have our own weapons and shall not hesitate to attack. Our weapon is the Grosse Fuge – [*inserted above*: By Beethoven], which, I know from experience, to someone who hasn't got to know it for the greatest work of art in existence sounds like an ear-trumpet into the ninth circle of the cats' hell. Our gramaphone also steps up a terrifying volume – the floor shakes, flakes of plaster fall from the ceiling, and after ten minutes at top pressure every nasty neighbour within a hundred yards is on their knees at the door and knocking timidly and pleading ... We'll be glad to get someone in up there though. I suppose you know better than us just how eerie a half empty house can be.

My schoolboys are pretty much as I thought them at first. First impressions have been pathetically confirmed. But they have good hearts, even the little crooked ones who steal money out of my desk have good hearts. I have met one or two of the very oldest boys – most of which left at Xmas – who were utterly corrupt. Boyish good nature had gone as an unsuitable qualification for their slouching gum-chewing shirking race for notoriety as a local tough-egg. I beat their heads for their insolence in a last stand for authority but I don't suppose I redeemed any. My work is almost entirely that of a policeman, and I'm only just learning how actual teaching can be squeezed in. The one answer is – give them work and more work, and when they've done bad work frighten them by a display of apparently serious temper – rip up the paper etc – and when they've done good work praise them in front of the class and sit down beside them and kindly show them how they could have improved it. The desperate attempt to get back into my favour when I've just been angry with one is a real guarantee of the success of this method. Perhaps I'm not old and set enough, not enough of an unapproachable father-figure, to be really successful with this type of boy. I'm still very much a younger brother, the one who finds it a battle to get out of the youngest generation even to his death, while an elder brother grew out naturally when his younger brother was born. It's certainly one of the sobering experiences in my life.

Sylvia reads out your long fascinating letters. I'm getting a very definite idea of America – of your America from them. One thing that interests us: Sylvia has been told that prices are jumping there – could you give us the prices of the common things, whatever thing comes into your head as you write out the list. Sylvia by the way is becoming the most superlative cook I ever encountered. She adds one Ace dish each week.

Love to you both
Ted

From 55 Eltisley Avenue.

To Olwyn Hughes

[23 February 1957]   Ts   Emory

Dear Olwyn
    This morning I had news and a half. You remember the contest for

which I was getting those poems into a book, and that Auden, Spender and Marianne Moore were going to judge? I have won it. This means that the book will be published in America and England, with the considerable publicity of having such selectors, and probably a forword to establish me officially as someone who at least someone has declared worthwhile in print, and I draw royalties from the first volume and on. I must be the first poet to draw royalties from a first book, with a few exceptions.

You must celebrate it mildly and at not too great expense. I had a telegram this morning from New York and Sylvia has not stopped dancing since – it is music for a month.

My first reaction was a horrible feeling of guilt at what I had committed, and I went to read the poems over to see if they were really as dull as I dreded they were. I immediately saw fifty things I wanted to change and I'm appalled that I let most of the poems out in such an unfinished state.

Have you got a job yet? or decided what to do? Keep me well posted until you are settled again. I had a setback about my astrology. I tried to put the advert in, but they wouldn't take it. "We small papers daren't risk it" was what they said. There are all kinds of laws about witchcraft and fortune-tellers, and maybe the wording of my advert infringed them. Perhaps if I try on a larger paper with just – "Send £1 for horoscope in full" I could do it. This is the 23rd, so just see what my horoscope is, because its the best personal stroke of good fortune that I suppose I've had ever. Jupiter on the cusp of the fifth if I was born at one exact. Mars near my moon. Moon opposite my ascendant. It's much better for Sylvia – the sun on her ascendant degree – Jupiter near her moon – perhaps not.

Anyway celebrate it. I hope my fables have a success. I'm full of ideas for books and for a certain style of fantastic super-realistic type of play. I saw Eliot's Sweeney Agonistes done on the stage the other night along with a translation of Euripides Hippolytus – the style occurred to me and I immediately thought of several subjects. I'm trying to write a more straightforward play at present – the theme is the conflict between the conservative traditional principles that make character strong, (but which in this case can mean only death of the hero and his wife and unborn child,) and the sheer expediency and opportunism of keeping yourself safe and your skin whole no matter what (Which in this case means leaving the ancestrally held farm and a sick mother and an aged furiously heroic old father to certain death again.) The hero chooses the former and dies consequently.

It is melodramatic because it is slightly unreal because whatever I write is slightly fable and larger than life no matter how I try to make it ordinary or natural. Still, this quality needn't disqualify it, if I can cut out the melodrama, or so stylise the melodrama that it becomes a symbol. The melodrama in this case is the very sudden violent death of three men on the stage – I excuse it saying that they are not really my characters, not characters of the main play, they are three who appear to establish the threat in the first place under pressure of which the subsequent action unfolds. All this is shockingly vague and fuzzy but the plot is a bit much to tell you here.

Please make a decision quickly and establish yourself again. Get clear of unfortunate people, as they certainly infect your fate. Make a big step. Paris is stale. Get a hypnotist to stop you smoking.

Ma is now so much better that she can walk down Hardcastle's.

> Love, look after yourself. Eat well
> and speculate hopefully.
> Ted.

In a letter to her mother dated 24 February, Sylvia Plath tells her that the telegram announcing the award of the Poetry Center's First Publication Prize 'came at about 10:30 yesterday morning'.

'Jupiter on the cusp of the fifth' indicates good fortune in respect of creativity and romance.

To Gerald and Joan Hughes and family

24 February 1957   Ms   Emory

Dear Gerald & Joan etcetera –
this is the 2nd of two letters. Thank you Joan for your letter and thank you Gerald for yours. Sylvia was very pleased with them because she's the most superstitious fanciful apprehensive diffident creature in the world, and what she's met so far of this family has bewildered her a bit. She adores Walt – and she's rather like him in a curious way – they bring each other out extraordinarily. After a year in America we shall go to Italy and invite Walt to live with us – from there we'll try & get to Australia for a year or so. Two years won't be long – look how the last 6 have flown since you were here – and I shall get Walt to Australia yet.

That will settle your problems, I hope. If not then I have the potential to earn five times Walt's fortune and not be too long about it either, and Sylvia will probably earn more than me, – and that too will solve your problems, if you will permit me to consider your security – i.e. a dairy farm or such – as my bank, or rather – your property as my, our, security. So don't let any stupid Englander annoy you.
[. . .]

Though I haven't been fishing for 7 years I dream every single night that I am fishing. Often it is the canal at home – vastly altered, sometimes flowing swift & very deep, with sharks, – mostly it is Crookhill. I have every kind of fishing adventure. There's always a big fish – and whenever I dream I catch that, the day after I sell a poem. One night I dreamed I caught the grandfather pike at Crookhill – at the corner near the out-flow. You and Johnny were pulling at its fins, and I was heaving down the slope – we had twenty feet of it out – and still most of it was in the pond. The next day I sold my first poem and got married. Sylvia is my luck completely. In these fishing dreams my great enemies are eels. Joan, I cannot tell you your horoscope till I know the year. Was it /29? Brendon will definitely be artistic – too emotional – extremely fortunate – mentally overactive – develope him now. Show him every dawn & read to him endlessly.

Love Ted.

In Plath's story 'The Wishing Box', in *Johnny Panic and the Bible of Dreams* (1977), a dream of a mighty fish, similar to the one recounted here, is attributed to the character Harold, whose inexhaustibly fertile inner life is the envy of his wife Agnes.

To Daniel Huws

[April 1957]   Ms   Daniel Huws

The nerve from the ear, which was originally exclusively – as it still is partly – to do with the sense of balance & movement, is connected directly to the Medulla – the oldest part of the brain, which controls & receives sensations from all the muscles & organs of the body. Now the nerve from the eye is connected to quite a recent part of the brain, and is associated with the areas that seem to have nothing to do but are apparently responsible for abstract & constructive thought, & speculative. This is interesting. Obviously, I think, people like Wallace Stevens house their demon where the eye-nerve enters – so that everything is arbitrary & colourful & partial & questionable. Whereas Wyatt & Crowe-Ransome house theirs where the ear enters – so that in them everything is inevitable & final & bottomless & unquestionnable as the response of glands or the harmony of moving muscles. And in Hopkins I think its possible to see the uncomfortable & incomplete concert of the two. The former – the eye – only interprets things from outside, in a domineering speculative way – the latter, the ear, expresses movements from inside, in a servantish & obedient way, that have already quite definitely & completely occurred. This is the argument for the superiority of the latter kind of poetry, from Chapter XVII subdiv 7C/964, Para 98c, note 8, Vol 127 "Hot air on the unutterables in aesthetics" by Martin B. Plunger Umpledefunct.

TH had got to know Daniel Huws during his third year at Cambridge. Huws was at Peterhouse, over the road from Pembroke College, and they met at The Anchor, a pub that TH, Terence McCaughey and others from Pembroke frequented.

This is a small part of a letter that includes the birth charts, drawn by TH, of Sigmund Freud, James Joyce, Robert Graves and the American poet John Crowe Ransom (1888–1974), Freud and Joyce being culturally dominant figures of the time, while Graves and Ransom were poets for whom TH and Huws shared admiration.

The heading gives TH's parents' address, where TH and Sylvia Plath stayed between her exams and their departure for the USA.

To Gerald, Joan, Ashley and Brendon Hughes

[May 1957]   Ts   Lilly Library

Well, my life lately is splendid, wonderfully repaired from what it was. Marriage is my medium. Also my luck thrives on it, and my productions. You have no idea what a happy life Sylvia and I lead or perhaps you have. We work and walk about, and repair each other's writings. She is one of the best critics I ever met and understands my imagination perfectly, and I think I understand hers. It's amazing how we strike sparks. And when we're fed up of that we walk out into the country and sit for hours watching things. We sit by the river and watch water-voles and when they come near Sylvia goes almost unconscious with delight. She's the most responsive alert creature in the world, about everything. I squeal and rabbits come out. The other night outside a wood I squealed to no effect for about quarter of an hour and was just thinking there was nothing left alive when an owl that must have flown up at ground level suddenly rose in my face and tried to land on my head. Very good. It's the first time I've ever got one so near.

America is waiting with arms open. I've got my visa after blood tests etcetera, and we sail on the 20th of June. My book comes out in mid-August, my birthday I suppose. The New York Poetry Center have offered to give a party for me, which would mean that I would meet several poets and make useful contacts. Over here one or two literary nabobs are saying very flattering extravagant things about me, seeing that America has as it were snatched me from under their nose. This is very different from the life I led a year or more ago.

Ma is a great deal better. I think my recent good fortune has rejuvenated her about fifteen years. The most pleasing sensation I get from my prize-winning and acclamation is when I consider how this in a way realises some of Ma's fairy-tale dreams. However, it has not yet started, and the real thing will begin in about three years.

Paul Brendon, Gerald and Joan Hughes's second son, was born on 22 August 1956.
 'The Owl', in *Birthday Letters*, gives a version of the encounter described here, while Sylvia Plath's poem 'Faun' gives another.

To Edith and William Hughes

[10 May 1957]   Ms   Emory

This morning we got specially good news. Faber & Faber wrote to me & told me that Mr T.S. Eliot likes my poems very much indeed, congratulates me on them, and they will publish the book. (Eliot is chief oracle at Fabers)
[. . .]
I shall be the first poet ever to publish his first book in both countries, and only about the 3rd to publish any book of poetry simultaneously in both countries. Dylan Thomas & Auden have beaten me to that I think. However, it's not a patch on what my third book will be, in another year or two. The poems I'm writing now, – the one or two, – show a change. This first book is really very immature. I'm very slow.

TH fails to give the date, but the letter home in which Sylvia Plath conveys the same news supplies it.
 T. S. Eliot (1888–1965) was a director of the publishing firm Faber and Faber.

To Olwyn Hughes

20–23 June 1957   Ms Emory

Thank you for the letter. Also the 1000. I don't think we shall be able to use it. We don't get into Cherbourg until 10, and then, I hear, noone is allowed ashore. So I'll send the note back, and you can buy a steak tartare.

The days at home were ill-starred. Don't criticise Sylvia too badly about the way she got up and came after me. After her exams etc I suppose she felt nervy – she did, that was obvious. But the Beacon is too small for five or six people – especially if one of them has an obsession about resting. And everyone was walking in and out & up and down continually. She admires you more than any englishwoman she's ever met. Her immediate 'face' when she meets someone is too open & too nice – 'smarmy' as you said – but that's the American stereotype she clutches at when she is in fact panic-stricken. Or perhaps – and I think this is more like it – her poise & brain just vanish in a kind of vacuous receptivity – only this american stereotype manner then keeps her going at all. She says stupid things then that mortify her afterwards. Her second thought – her retrospect, is penetrating, sceptical, and subtle. But she can never bring that second-thinking mind to the surface with a person until she's known them some time. She's hard to bring out, in fact. You saw how much better she was the last day. Don't judge her on her awkward behaviour. I'm sure you see what she's really like. She's no angel, but there's a balance to her worst side. She has a miserable past, which I'll tell you about gradually. She's had enough experience to respect your life & your experience, and she judges harshly enough, ruthlessly enough, of people, to see that you're extraordinary, and prize you. [. . .]

We had a very pleasant last evening at home. Hilda & Walter came up, and we drove across to the New Delight, where everything was very convivial for a couple of hours, in spite of the Wigan sandwich-bar decor. Harry Ogden came up, at Hilda's instigation, to take photographs. He saw that his stories of the Manchester blitz had an effect on Sylvia, so for over an hour we got all the goriest episodes – that Harry's wife, veteran nurse – had experienced. Walter all but fell asleep.

We got on board the Queen E. at 1 oclock. We're down nine or ten seperate flights of stairs, eighty yards along a corridor, fifteen yards to the right, and here in a room 10 ft by 10 by 10. The finest thing is the food – all included in the fare. It is steak, steak, steak – if you wish. And excellent big thick tender steak. Five courses to each meal, & many choices of dish. So it is easy to run a perfect diet of meat, greens & fresh fruit. [. . .]

Thanks for the clipping from the Observer. I suppose it's fair. I think Wilbur is all that's there said of him, but more too. Apart from the virtuoso whimsical descriptive writing, which they admire for its +7 and deplore for its –77, he has written three or four original beautiful finished poems, [*inserted at end of paragraph and connected by an arrow*: Such as "Beasts", "Piazza Piece", "Toad", the one about eating on a mountain, potato, several. Durable.] which they do not acknowledge at all. It's time these Oxford Cambridge hole-in-the-wall literary hedge-priests stopped throwing everybody into the fire because they're not the Shakespeare-cum-Donne that dogma demands. But they won't stop. I haven't read Thom Gunn's book. I agree with you about Logue. I will add bits & bottoms to this, till I can post it within sight of the Statue of Lib.

June 21ˢᵗ Evening Midsummer night or is it tomorrow. No. I've just looked it up and it's not till 23ʳᵈ. We have been going & going, the sea flying past, and yet we're only just off the West Southernmost bit of Ireland – not off the continental shelf yet. Last night I had the most unusual dreams – the main theme was a murderer, who took his victims to an old empty house, summoned the spirit of the house – in darkness – and accused his victim-to-be before the spirit of the house – or asked what the sentence was. Then the victim was given chance to defend himself or herself – but they were each time cut short by this voice from the dark empty house, sentencing them. The murderer then attacked them. He buried the bodies anywhere – under pavements, in gardens. I was both detective and observer. Although it was so morbid it was a pleasure to dream at all – spontaneous mental life seemed to have died out. Today however I was in good form, and I got ideas for about twenty fable style stories, one or two might make poetic plays, one or two are realistic. I haven't been so awake for years. I've been trying to think of even one, for weeks.

The food came at us again today, head high. Fish, griddle cakes, eggs, steak, curry, the Lord knows what. But the air is such that we are hungry at bed-time. I am reading the Bible. I think it is my favourite book. I read the spirit of the Lord as the King of the ouija-board Pans, i.e. the one who does not come until you have walked through the fire. The whole makes now bottomless sense. All the obscure sentences now make sense. 'The foolishness of God is greater than the wisdom of the wise" etc. Paul was someone who spoke direct from Tibet or wherever it is that Pans live, so that when he says that drunkards, thieves, the covetous shall not see the Kingdom he meant that the psychological & physiological consequences of these pursuits – drink, thieving, hoarding etc – dissipate or worse the spiritual clarity & concentration & inwardness that's necessary before you hear the pans & the Pan speak at hallucinatory voltage & appear. In the mystery religions – of which Christianity was originally one – Christ & Pan were interchangeable, the prototype figure was.

The Atlantic is uninteresting. Ships pass occasionally. The sea is dazzling & quite calm. The wind off it scorches your face. Even the sunset was bald & headachy, though everybody crowded to the rails to watch it. There is a slow slight roll to the ship, which you never notice until you're on the stairs – then you think a storm must be springing up. You feel slightly drunk continually – and I suppose that's your usual sense of the roll. The horizon moves between the line of the edge of the deck & the line of the rail – up ten or so seconds, down ten. The smoke blows over the decks, & you're continually creepy with a sense of the hot sootiness of the air. Between readings at the Bible I'm reading Henry James short stories

[. . .]

23rd. Yesterday was really accursed. I don't know whether it was the catastrophe of novelty, and the overshadowing of the next long three days on a desert island with a thousand howler monkeys, or just the freezing cloud that settled over the ship at about 11 a.m. Or just the fact of still enduring after 2 days of three five course meals a day. But the depression was black and absolute. It was difficult even to speak. The only thing salvaged was a film we saw, with Errol Flynn, the sandbag head in person. Fists and fires, amnesias and anathemas, Istanbul, diamonds, and a persistence to the far end of the second hour. That, in its turn, was redeemed by the film we saw today – 'The Great Man', with José Ferrer. One of the best films I've seen for a long time. Have you seen it? All close, & T.V., and character and real dramatic development. And Rank made it!

Today has been much better. After about an hour in the sun – during which a whale passed, about 200 yards from the ship, going along just under the surface & heaving clear of the swell every few seconds, – we had lunch – I now eat nothing but the brains, the hearts, and the essences. Meals, in fact, have become the main enemy. There's a kind of sly malice in the way every time you look up its time for another meal, and though you sit down only intending to drink fruit juice & eat fruit, somehow these are hidden inside sides of salmon and bombs of Turkey.

The sea was generally about as calm as Windermere. I thought it would be flowing hills. After 'The Great Man' we found our way out onto the bows. We had thought this was reserved for the 1st Class, but it's exclusively for the Tourists. For the first time I got the sensation of crossing the Atlantic – the heroic bid. You lean over the rail, and the bows hollow in under you so that you're standing in fact on a shelf about 30ft – not more – above the bow wave. The bow-wave is the speciality. The sea was at that time rougher than I've seen it – that is, it was choppy, with white horses, but brilliant Prussian blue under a clear sky. Just a kind of vertebrae of little clouds along the horizon, pink popcorn clouds. The bow-wave was blinding-white, with a great clear rainbow in the spray all along the breaking edge of it. We are about two miles above the sea-bed – maybe a bit more. The sight of the bows towering up into the sky and towards the empty horizon was fine.

Dated the day of embarkation and with his mother-in-law's address at the head of the first page, most of this letter was written at intervals during TH's and Sylvia Plath's crossing of the Atlantic on board the liner *Queen Elizabeth*. Between her exams and their leaving for the USA, they had stayed at his parents' home, The Beacon, in Heptonstall Slack, West Yorkshire. During a visit of John Fisher, TH's old English teacher, and his wife Nancy, Plath had upped and left the house, mid-conversation, in a silent rage.

The correct titles of the poems by Richard Wilbur (b.1921) that TH refers to are 'Beasts', 'Piazza di Spagna, Early Morning', 'The Death of a Toad', 'The Terrace' and 'Potato'. Thom Gunn's second book of poems, *The Sense of Movement*, had recently appeared. The critic and poet A. Alvarez (b.1929) had reviewed it and Wilbur's *Things of this World* together in the *Observer* on 16 June, dismissing Wilbur's work as 'so determinedly accomplished' that it would never amount to more than that.

Earlier in the year, the poet Christopher Logue (b.1926), after joining Tristram Hull as co-editor of *Nimbus*, had rejected a submission by TH.

'The foolishness of God . . .': TH misquotes 1 Corinthians 1:25, 'Because the foolishness of God is wiser than men'.

The Errol Flynn vehicle must be *Istanbul* (1956). José Ferrer both directed and starred in *The Great Man* (1956); J. Arthur Rank, whose association with the film seems to have amazed TH, had been his employers briefly.

To Gerald and Joan Hughes

[Late June 1957]   Ms   Emory

Next day we came up to Sylvia's home, which is in Wellesley, Mass. as you know of course. The country we passed through was all wide low estuaries and rocky woods. The kind of scene that makes you think continually of Red Indians & smoking encampments. I never saw so many blackbirds – all with vivid red flashes on their shoulders. We got here, rested, then opened our wedding presents. Luckily so far we've got only superb stainless steel cutlery, magnificent pans etc – the sort of thing that will make a nomad life easier rather than harder. The thought of settling to a comfortably housed life gives Sylvia the jimjams almost as badly as it does me. The truth is, too, of course, that a comfortably housed life in America is an officially entered numbered trap in the rat-race. The great sin in America is 'not-to-be-able-to-mix', & the greatest cause of people being sacked from jobs is that they don't mix, they're a bit too unusual. So everybody's in everybody else's arms, and all burstingly happy & well-adjusted so far as their facial expressions go.

[. . .]

At present I'm still meeting all the friends & relations, which is interesting but a bit wearing. The houses are splendid here – each in its little grounds. The food, the general opulence, is frightening. My natural instinct is to practise little private filthinesses – I spit, pea on shrubbery, etc, and have a strong desire to sleep on the floor – just to keep in contact with a world that isn't quite so glazed as this one. But I'll learn my position. It's good too for me to be surrounded by a world from which I instinctively recoil. I mightn't waste quite so much energy here. For all this though there's something – a great deal – about what tiny bit I've seen, that I like. The birds are interesting – the robins are big as thrushes & shaped like them. The jays – which are everywhere, – are smaller than ours, and give the impression of being bright blue all over. They make a smacking rawk like ours. There are lots of others. Last night I saw fireflies – twinkling in and out like little aircraft on fire.

There are skunks – though I haven't seen them. I'm going to get some fishing tackle and keep myself buried as deep in what these 85ft long Cadillacs cannot touch, as I can. I never saw so many cars & so huge. Those illustrations of the highways of the future – vast butterfly crossings with hundreds of cars like wingless airliners streaming in every direction through wooded countryside – that's what its like just round here. But the real American phenomena is the kindness of these folk. Even in the literary reviews – which in England are just cauldrons where everyone donates his most-literary, therefore most-vain, therefore bittermost gall to boil the heads & hearts of everyone they (Everyone) can get hold of – here the reviews are surprisingly honest, outspoken, but not venomous. They attack each other mercilessly – but openly. I will pick out the most interesting sentences in the reviews of my book and send them on. Did I tell you that it comes out over here on Ma's birthday?

[. . .]

Sylvia has just come out with a glass of beer, a chicken sandwich and a lobster sandwich. There is a tiny yellow wrenlike bird called a chicka-dee sitting just above me. When I inspect my past life I have made a spectacular climb by steps of pure luck. A facility in falling not on my feet, so much as into a full-length reclining posture onto a fifteen foot depth of down-cushions, the ducks of which down are entering by the main door roasted, bespiced, dispensing odours & appetite in all directions equally – Etc. There is no explanation for it, though astrology, of course, explains it all.

To Lucas Myers

22 July 1957   Ms Emory

Dear Lucas,

Your letter was the first here. 'Here', is a little wooden house in a Christmas Tree forest, with all fittings, squirrels on the roof, chipmunks under the floor. There is a screened verandah where from 7 a.m. to 2 p.m. I write, or rather, I sit over a page – my thoughts at present are stones in a wall. I'm gratified to hear that you are publishing poems. How many have you altogether now? Robert Frost published his first collection 15 years after he had completed it, and after he had completed several others – so all his life he's had five or six books on hand. When he was young he put a number of poems aside – now he's bringing them out one by one – 'something new'. This is hearsay. Your letter was full of news. Are your parents in England now? Or are they going on to Italy? 'The palm-wine-drinkard' came out about 4 years ago and Dylan Thomas reviewed it in the Observer. If I see it I will buy it, though I fancy to you it might have unique importance as being your spiritual autobiography, ghost-written & foisted on some innocent, – the unique charm, that is, of another man hanging for your crime.

I was interested to hear about Berlin. Perhaps you could tutor privately. Did you know Anthony Hecht? He's at Smith, apparently. If America is good for nothing else, it is good for my composing strophes & antistrophes to the real world. The real world retreats a bit here. Sterilised under cellophane. I am attempting to rebegin my education, in that I am reading all the main authors, in chronological order, and reading each author through, and each work at a sitting. To keep this resolution in good conscience there is in Northampton one of the best libraries in America. So it is called.

[. . .]

Also I am reading all Shakespeare in what I consider the order of their being written, approximately. This is a deliberate project. Of Henry VIII only <u>Act I</u> Sc I, & II, <u>Act II</u>, Sc III & IV, Act III [Sc I *inked out*] & first half of Sc II – up to 'And then to breakfast with what appetite you have.", and finally Sc I of Act V are Shakespeare, the rest is Fletcher. These are distinct as black & white. When you bear this in mind it makes the play easier to read, because you're not saying 'How dull & senile" all the time, you just say "Fletcher." Have you read 2 Noble Kinsmen? It is of about the same date composition. The Shakespeare in it is incredible in that it seems at first better than Shakespeare – but the rest, a great deal – is Fletcher. "Late Shakespeare" gets the blame for a lot of Fletcher.

How Scholarly & bald my wit grows!

I think this next year I shall try private tutoring – priming for literary exams. When I consider how my affable familiar has sabotaged my every attempt at a normal profession, and sabotaged my whole life while I constrain it so, and how very affable & very magically helpful & luck-bringing it is when I entertain it & its inventions, its fantasticalia, its pretticisms and its infinite verballifications – then I think it would be the best & most sensible course to make a career of humouring it. If you humiliate your devils, they avenge themselves, by paralysing your outer efforts. They operate like minor Furies. Forgive me this blither. I read the first four pages of William James on 'Pragmatism' and that, and the quiet here, have filled me with theories like an intellectual. No. The main evidence in favour of a life doing nothing but write & nose into other folk's affairs only in so far as you need exercise, is that your dreams become long & coherent & beautiful. Give my greetings to Than, Dan, Danny, David & Helga, as you see them. The Sewanee Review bought two poems that are in my book. Spender took one that is new. I will write in an envelope & send you one or two. Do not think that your buying fifty copies of my book will save you from the copy yours by right.

Ted.

Writing from Eastham, Massachusetts, TH addresses this to 'E. LUCAS MYERS, COCK OF BULLS', care of an address in England.

As a wedding present to TH and Sylvia, Aurelia Plath had paid for the summer rent on the cottage described here.

The Palm-Wine Drinkard, magical-picaresque first novel by the Nigerian Amos Tutuola (1920–97), came out in 1952.

Anthony Hecht (1923–2004) had published his first collection, *A Summoning of Stones*, in 1954.

In omitted paragraphs, TH asks after mutual friends or passes on family news. In the final one, 'Helga' is Helga Kobuszewski, who, as Helen Hitchcock's German au pair, moved into the chicken coop at St Botolph's Rectory when Myers vacated it. She married Daniel Huws later in 1957.

Stephen Spender, co-editor of the magazine *Encounter*, had accepted TH's 'Thrushes'.

To Olwyn Hughes

22 August 1957   Ms   Emory

What a place America is. Everything is in cellophane. Everything is 10,000 miles from where it was plucked or made. The bread is in cellophane that is covered with such slogans as de-crapularised, re-energised, multi-cramulated, bleached, double-bleached, rebrowned, unsanforised, guaranteed no blasphemin. There is no such thing as bread. You cannot buy bread. And fifty processes that side of the wrapping these loaves saw the last molecule of their original wheat. Garlic comes in little boxes – 2 garlics to a box – covered with manager's and directors' names & the multiple vitamins injected to keep the flavour even though the garlic in appearance is black-rotten. Everything is a bit the same. It is to be survived by dint of killing & eating raw – flies, spiders, mice, by eating grass & pine-needles, and by drinking under horse-troughs. This is my main impression of America – it is a temporary expedition, in which we're living on food we brought to last the expedition out. And we mustn't put up houses to last more than a year because we shall soon be going. And everything is a temporary fixture and we've so much to get done before we leave that there's no time to do more than sleep & hurry. There's something like a temporary mountain-top expedition, too, in the way everybody's so friendly, and nobody knows anybody else's family history, and nobody ever bothers to get to know anybody except on purely temporary and facetious terms. Little I know about it. Maybe it's different when you live & work in a place. Northampton was fairly English – all the shops & streets huddled together – so maybe that will be more congenial. But most of America is a boundless suburbia. Most of New England that is. Wellesley in particular, that is.

To Gerald, Joan, Ashley and Brendon Hughes

27 August 1957   Ms   Emory

Dear Gerald & Joan, and Ashley & Brendon,

Let me try & bring you up to date. We are now on Cape Cod. This is a long arm of low land hooking into the Atlantic. All down the outer side of it is marshes and great beaches. Woods cover most of the arm. It is just turning from a desolate sandy outpost, where people survived out of the habit of the species rather than by help from their environment, into the hot secret summer resort of the New York & Boston rich. The woods are full of little wooden cabins, for which the landlords charge up to £25 a week. The folks bring their families, or business men bring other men's wives or so on, & they relax up and down the main arterial road in immense cars travelling at 83 m.p.h., or on the beaches. At any time you may count 10 to 15 wealthy pink-paunched overgrown porky Nettletons struggling to disentangle their reels, along the beach. However, Sylvia & me are hidden away. Her mother bought us this cottage – Dowry almost – for the summer. Hoping that we would relax & write. At first the cost of the place $70 a week so got on my nerves that I couldn't do anything. A too-costly article paralyses my appreciations. It paralysed Sylvia too. We sat, we got brown on the beaches, we idled, for 3 weeks. Then we had a black week, in which Sylvia lay helpless with sheer depression, and I went about with a melon grafted onto the side of my head – a corpulent drumming devil in the likeness of an abscess & swelling – the abscess right in my ear. This black week broke last Sunday the 3rd or 4th when we rode five miles to the nearest Doctor. It was strange because a long tedious spell of 98° per day broke with it. The rain fell as I have never seen it. Thunder was continuous. I saw 3 trees that lightning had just struck within 20 yards of the road. Anyway the Doctor's magic was good. The ear had cleared up by Tuesday, Sylvia cleared up, and suddenly we have begun to write like angels and apply our brains like the bits of electric drills. I am writing one children's story per day before 9 a.m. These are a sort that really should sell. The publishers showed such interest in my last year's attempt – which I wrote without having a notion of what children read at what age, and which were hopelessly abstract. Now I am doing better. I am writing for about age six. A paragraph of simple story to each full page picture. Maybe if I practised a bit each day I could do the drawings too within a year or two. Now if I can keep this up – one a day – and I can, and if I can sell them, – as I shall soon, either because they are good, or become good through practice, or both & my shortly-to-be-bandied name as a poet, – then that will be quite a wage, and leave my whole day after 8-30 or so for more strenuous lofty attempts. These stories come to me absolutely naturally so I'm not prostituting my imagination. I would like to produce a classic volume – about 5,000 – children's stories. I shall bring in all the situations & characters etc out of all the fairy tales, animal tales etc that I have read & I have read millions in the last six years. Now if I could do that it would be a classic because there would be so much in it for desperate parents. At present there are countless children's books, mostly bad, all different, very few that you want to read 2x – so parents don't know what to buy – they just buy one here & one there. I hope I have these stories coming out by the time Hengist & Horsa are of an age to open their ears & eyes.

You would love it here Joan. We are surrounded by pine trees. We have a verandah on which we eat. Every single necessary tool is in the kitchen, & big refrigerator, & hot water. Sylvia is princess of cooks. American food is overpowering. Your letter Gerald coincided with our emerging from dumpdom and greatly helped. Your statements concerning the slavery of the mind to the tyranny of the spare tyre is absolutely sound philosophy & psychology. I have made a pact with Sylvia that when I don't want cream-chiffon pies, & all the other fairy palace dishes it's not because she isn't an exquisite cook but because she cooks for relaxation while I eat only by necessity, so that there must come occasions when the most Himalayan heaps of pork & sour cream cannot so much as brighten my eye. Her fault is – and it is a fault that she acknowledges – is that when she's faced by some tedious or unpleasant piece of work she escapes into cooking. During her exams my weight rose from 195 to 205 lbs. Every time I looked up there was a dish that called straight to my lean years in London and hypnotised a stomach made simple-minded by ma's random recipes. However when she's working & enjoying it we live on meat & fruit and that's how I prefer it. Every now & again – after about 10 days West Yorkshire belly-parsimony – I plunge headfirst into this world made of meringue, lobster newburg, 112 flavoured pre-fruited ice-cream and so on, and let my heels disappear. Where we are living all next year – Northampton, Mass. – is right in the woods. Deer, rivers full of big trout. I'm buying tackle for my birthday. One poem sold can fit me out, and I'm at the stage now where I sell pretty well everything I write, though poems don't grow on trees. Or if they do, they grow only one on every millionth tree. Everybody here hunts & fishes. But they're mostly a bit like the Chicago washing-machine-makers – you remember. They drive about loaded with armour, they buy shooting permits, & in the end maybe they shoot the foot off a local farmer. On Cape Cod the deer season lasts for one week. During that week the cape crawls with boozing parties having a remote resemblance to 90 gun cruisers. Last year 7 deer were shot and 7 deer-shooters. True fact. We're looking forward to the pictures because we have none. Happy birthdays to the two Kings. Tell lots of details about their doings in your next letter.

Love, Ted.

'Porky' Nettleton was the young son of a Mexborough butcher.

To Lucas Myers

[October 1957]   Ms   Emory

My not writing to you has been little sister to my not writing at all, anything, since July, as if my head & hands were off. So I keep my hands in my pockets except for the five seconds during which I blow my nose, (assuring myself both head & hands are still extant), and in my thought I invoke water. Floods. Black rivers. By these means, within five years, I shall compose a line. Perhaps.

[. . .]

Sylvia is teaching. At present I am doing nothing – I sit for hours like the statue of a man writing, no different, except that during the 3rd or 4th hour a bead of sweat moves on my temple. I have never known it so hard to write. I have never, of course, tried to write before. Since I came I've got about 4 poems which seem to me an improvement. Publishing all the poems I had has done one thing – made it impossible to go on writing in that fashion. I shall get a part-time job I think.

[. . .]

We have a very pleasant flat here – we look into tree-tops out of every window, and next door is a park of 5 or 6 acres, more perhaps, full of trees & squirrels. Two years will be our stretch in America. I haven't seen much of Smith yet, but what sniffs I have had were old mushroom in my left nostril, indeterminate in my right. I will give you details as I observe them. The girls – their numbers & their surpassing likeness one to another & their machined glaze of hyper-health – are almost unnerving. Chromium dianas.

My book over here has not been reviewed yet, except once in some publisher's magazine of which I heard by hearsay. That was 'laudatory'. Edwin Muir made some kind remarks in the New Statesman this week. He says my poem The Jaguar is better than Rilke's panther – the kind of remark that provokes more derision than curiosity perhaps. I have often noticed when I have been fishing that a good start means a bad day & vice versa, so I look eagerly for direct frontal attacks.

You must write & give details of your days. You cannot be too detailed. Until I can fasten some associations into this place my days are dull as an empty house.

TH and Plath were now settled at 337 Elm Street, Northampton.

The passage about the invocation of water alludes to a technique for summoning his poetic resources that TH practised, and with which Myers was familiar.

The poet and translator Edwin Muir (1887–1959) had reviewed *The Hawk in the Rain* in the 28 September issue of the *New Statesman*, saluting the newcomer as 'a remarkable poet . . . outside the currents of his time'.

To Daniel Huws

[Late October 1957]   Ms   Daniel Huws

Dear Dan,

Thank you for your letter & for the poems. I like them all. 'The Survivors' is terrific, and I admire the way you recount the episode without letting – to coin a monster – the solution of your meanings precipitate into mere narrative. In that poem of mine called Two Wise Generals, the phrase 'you & I' at the end of the fourth line was origin-ally 'you, love, & I" – so the whole poem enacted an allegory. But when I took out the 'love', the poem slipped into cold & cornered narrative. Your 'love-in-idleness' is perfect, without anyone having to go round pulling it up in bunches.

I have brought out your Dante translation, The Dragon & the other Botolph poems. Have no hopes, but you may be surprised. Most American editors can recognise nothing but the American mir-ror glaze in poetry – hence Poetry Chicago. Your poems – to their great advantage – have none of this, but as a result will crawl with difficulty where the democracy dances as of right. (They have a way of treating milk over here – they 'homogenise' it – this means that no matter how long the milk stands the cream can never rise to collect at the top.) (They don't mind going without cream so long as they get no blue milk.) But I have high hopes. I saw a translation of that same Dante some time ago in a Kenyon or a Hudson & it was just so much more democracy. Your translation must be one of the most extraordinary in English. I take my whole idea of Dante from it. Translating poetry – Welsh & Italian (& German) will probably earn you as much as translating prose. For one thing the Quarterlies over here take it readily – it has such an air of "serious creative scholarship & high culture". If you can translate other Dante as beautifully as that sestina, then there is a chance that the better paying Magazines would take it.

[. . .]

Nothing much happens here. On Sunday we went into New York. The Poetry Centre and Harpers had fixed up a reading & reception to boost my book & honour me. The place was packed. Russ was there. Afterwards I was swamped by dowagers who wanted to know why 'Bawdry Embraced' wasn't in the book & maidenly creatures wanting my signature in the book. One took the book back, after I'd signed it, & said "And what I want to say is "Hurrah for you"," goggling her eyes. Nobody of any note was there, though one or two sent their apologies. I had hoped to see at least Merwin. It was very much a poetry-fancier's event. I met the woman who pirated Ulysses – very fine.

I saw a review of my book in the Observer by Alvarez. Have you seen Alvarez's poems? Very crabby little apples. He scattered a great many names, Lawrence, Thom Gunn, Lowell, Coriolanus. He accused me of stealing twice from Shakespeare. One was that I used the word 'dispropertied' – & so did Shakespeare, (The Oxford Dic. cites Coriolanus as precedent) I don't know what the other theft is. In the end he deigned to be 'impressed' and conceded me fair words. It was a very undergraduatish review.

This year I shall do nothing. I sit down at 8-30 to 9 every morning & write prose until 12-30. I am already getting the habit & a feeling, occasionally, of skill.

Huws's 'The Survivors' was included in his first book, Noth (1972), but left out of the later selection of his poems, The Quarry (1999). His Dante translation, 'Al Poco Giorno', concludes the latter.

The reading and reception to announce the US edition of The Hawk in the Rain were given on Sunday 20 October, at the Poetry Center of the Young Men's and Young Women's Hebrew Association (now the 92nd Street Y) in New York. Russ Moro, who attended, had been an American student at Cambridge. The US poet W. S. Merwin, who was absent, did not – according to his wife Dido's 'Vessel of Wrath: A Memoir of Sylvia Plath' – meet TH and Plath until 'the end of '57 or the start of '58 at the apartment of Jack and Maire Sweeney'. By 'the woman who pirated Ulysses', TH may have meant either Margaret Anderson (1886–1973), founder and editor of The Little Review, who serialised Joyce's book in her magazine, or her co-editor Jane Heap (1883–1964).

A. Alvarez was the Observer's poetry reviewer and already known as a maker of reputations. His review appeared in the paper on 6 October. In it, he commented on TH's 'rather set, heroical, misanthropic swagger', opined that he was 'often "literary", in the debilitating sense', but concluded that there were 'half a dozen pieces here which only a real poet could have done'.

To Olwyn Hughes

[Autumn 1957]   Ms Emory

Have you read anything about or by Goethe? I have just read the 'conversations with Eckermann'. He is extraordinarily sane & his intelligence is so completely & at every point also <u>common sense</u>. Along with this, I have been reading Nietsche. Nietsche appears strained, overemphasised, headachy and a fool in his ravings against the barbarity of Germany (which is at the bottom of everything he says) whereas Goethe says "I can never hope that my works can become popular. The best I can hope for is that wherever a man emerges from the mass to the height of understanding something of what I have written, then what I have written will help raise him a little further." He dismisses the barbarity of Germany as an unfortunate but unalterable actuality. His presence is so vivid in these conversations. He says "When the barometer is high I find I work easily, but when it is low I become sluggish. So whenever the barometer is low I deliberately make a greater effort – and so get things done." There is this practicalness in everything he says. He has the same horoscope as you almost. First degrees of Scorpio rising, born 28th August. Same type of face too, don't you think?

[. . .]

Life here is fairly pleasant. I am in very good humour, so I get lots done, though no more poems. Since the Sewanee asked for more poems I've had the jinx. Sylvia is creaking under her burdens. This, for her, except insofar as it is a trial of character by ordeal, is a year lost. She works every hour she wakes almost. She certainly won't have to teach again.

Did you get the Yeats & the Auden? I would be grateful if you were to send an Elouard. Is there anything else you would like? The more I study my aspects, the more I am convinced that ♄ is my lucky planet. Everytime it is strongly aspected, things are good. I sent my book off at the beginning on ☉ ♂ ♄.

TH went on to produce as many as forty translations of poems by the French poet Paul Eluard (1895–1952) (see Daniel Weissbort's *Selected Translations of Ted Hughes*).

The symbols that end this extract mean 'Sun conjunct Saturn'; it is unusual to regard Saturn, which astrologers associate with the rigours of experience, as a 'lucky planet'.

To Gerald and Joan Hughes

[December 1957]   Ms   Lilly

I think I have just written you a long letter. White Xmasses are the rule in this part of America and a most slovenly snowfall has duly fallen, & still lies in spite of 3 or 4 days quite hot sun. How is your nursery for books? Let the two amuse themselves – don't kill them with T.V. It's terrifying to see this American race turning into gaping automata – audiences, consumers, – "Show me, amuse me, feed me." Do you all go fishing together yet? If Brendon is kindhearted then you should recite & recite to him. Then when he grows up he'll have the means to express himself in his head, & won't have to start learning 10 years too late. What are his tastes. Does he draw? Write a few pages autobiography – hour to hour over three days.

Unsigned note filling the back of a Christmas card, inside which Sylvia Plath has penned her own, more newsy, note.

1958

At the end of January, TH started teaching at the University of Massachusetts, Amherst, as an instructor in English Literature and Creative Writing.

In his few typed letters of 1958, TH now habitually employs the three-hyphen, unspaced dash that Sylvia Plath may have introduced him to. At the same time, his handwritten dashes had already been growing longer and more emphatic. So it seems appropriate, at this point in the present text, to switch from short to long dashes for both ts and ms letters.

To Daniel Weissbort

[Early 1958]   Ms   Emory

This is a letter straight back, while the replies are still itching on their cues. I was pleased to hear from you needless to say—your fate has been one of my favourite mysteries.

You give a terrible picture of the factory. Maybe you didn't intend to, but one mention of Music-while-you-work conveys Hell complete to me. Music-while-you-work, the daily mirror, these are the exhalations of the cancer in the English spine. During my 2 years in the R.A.F. most of my energy went in resisting the light programme. I used to wake up in the middle of the night and hear it going on in my head—in possession as it were, which was much like if not so bad as, quite, waking up & coughing blood. The thought is the same in both cases: "It's got me: it's got a hold: I shall never be the same."

Still, there must be immense compensations. Getting control of some practical relationship with the world objectifies a lot of emotion that otherwise remains subjective, unfocussed, & eventually distorts more & more. This is the great growing up act, I suppose. Your feelings towards other people as competitors in existence, & towards yourself as a man who has got to be at least as efficient as the average in getting money enough to live, are made firm & confident—so that you are liberated from them.

You are right about England. It is a vicious doghole for the most part. One half has a bellyful of acid and old iron, that's the articulate part, and the mass, the proletariat, is a great senile toothless hairless white ape, blind, tied etcetera.

[. . .]

America is about as insufferable as England, but there are possibly more compensations. Neither country is fit to live in. Yet who wants to be an exile. The only thing is to become autonomous, and for that you need several people dedicated to rejecting the balderdash of every-thing contemporary, and living according to the best of the past, and as if there were no future. Impossible as all other Utopia's. Survival, as in Dan's poem, is essentially a mangled creature—a horror to itself. There is no more beauty or nobility to be expected from our societies. Here in America it is all "Grab what you can boys, this land belongs to everybody, the land of plenty"—follows greed, vulgarity, & the horrible superficiality of a race without any principles left either to impose on itself or defend. In England it is "This is my garden: you shall be summoned for this trespass"—follows envy, spite, mealy-mouths, prissy complacency & the horrible stuck-in-the-solid-concreteness of having only one principle to defend & defend & defend—that nothing more can be given or taken in this land so Nobody Must Make A Move or else—"you shall be summoned for this."

Daniel Weissbort (b.1935) had been an habitué of the Cambridge pub, The Anchor, opposite his College, Queens', and contributed to *Saint Botolph's Review*. From 1957 to 1961, he worked for his father at Albion Knitwear Ltd. *Music while You Work* was the name of a daily radio show, put out by the BBC's Light Programme as anodyne accompaniment to manual labour.

The poem by Daniel Huws is 'The Survivors' (see letter to Huws of late October 1957).

To Lucas Myers

[Early 1958]   Ms   Emory

Dear Lucas,

This letter is drooping at the mouth, trailing at the coat, & standing speechless, but has no excuses for its extreme & bemonthed laggard-ness. In fact, now that it is actually getting written is the first weekend in 2 months that I have had not time to fill the pen preparatory, spread the paper invitativo, reverse the hearse of actuals into a howling arriving cradle of promising would-bes, debouche this brain's botchings onto the apparent excellence of breath, kill the sick pig and cry 'pheasant', as it were.

The truth is, that I have taken a job. As a teacher. As no more dignified labour was possible, (there is a slump, & many people out of work in this town) and as our life here consumes a few dollars each month more than Sylvia earns, I was put to this. I shall teach 14 weeks—which is ½ an academic year—at the University of Massachusetts. I take two classes three times a week on a "Great book" course—Milton's shorter poems & Samson Agonistes, Goethe's Faust Pt I, Crime & Punishment, Keats, Wordsworth, Yeats, Thoreau's Walden, 5 plays by Moliere. Then I take a class of Freshmen 2 × a week—their's is composition, grammar etc. Then a class of "Creative Writers".—I will tell you in my next letter (my first class is in 4 days time) what this chimera is as to heads, wings, diet, droppings etc. The money will get us back to Europe nicely next summer.

So I am in the thick of Samson Agonistes.

I am looking forward—we are looking forward—to seeing your novel. It is certain to be excellent, and I hope you can hit a market too. Put me in there the rumour of a woman being delivered of a Gorilla & when the Newspapers & Birth Report Research Statisticians get round there damn me if they didn't find the mother a gorilla too, a splendid 957 lb specimen, & she married happily these seven years to the Mayor of Harrogate. Do you have "the tearing of the cat"? A symbolic episode to be included henceforth in all great works. Do you know the Bacchae? That includes a fine "tearing of the cat" episode— "Enter Agave with her son's head . . ." thoroughly worthy the great name of Greece. Only in my next work—in progress—the son enters with the head of his father (thinking it the head of a lion, as Agave does hers). You see, I have read Hamlet, as Euripides had not. As the Holy Father claims his son, the father in the flesh is killed. Only more complicated. No promise at all of a market for this. Yet you see how profound the episode is. The cat in all cases is the elemental spirit that has housed in or fallen in love with some material object; and as a race the cats are distinguished from the Godhead—Holy Father & Holy Mother—King & Queen of the elementals, housed in the man himself, & in love with him.

You will now conjure this last paragraph into the mental image of a cat, mentally tear that cat,—relieve yourself of it, now that I have been so discourteous as to burden you with it.

To tell you the truth, Lucas, I am a little weary of this place—New England—and work at my life here as one takes satisfaction in walking with a lame leg. "This takes skill." I have written a little, particularly just lately—I sold a children's story to Jack & Jill—which is the children's magazine put out by the same people as put out the 'Slicks'. That is encouraging—a success in an extremely competitive professional market, & entirely on my own terms. Sewanee eventually accepted 4 poems—they accepted 2, then asked for more, & I sent them a rather obscure bunch—of which they chose the two simplest & slightest. I have 23 poems now. But I think that is finished until June. Teaching does not stop you writing, but it stops—dowses the illumination at the source. Don't you find that? You do, I know.

One reconciling circumstance—I did not seek this job, it sought me, and so came with as much likeness to a gift from God as to a temptation of the devil. Teaching in these Universities is the death of the artist in whatever person tries it, but for 14 weeks I hope to get some experience in collecting my wits in front of an adult audience, and improvising nonsense to look like excellent workaday sense. Also it will be to the mortification of idleness. Still, it would have been better if I could have existed without it. I shall not quickly be caught in a small American town again.

The most useful thing about this last year so far is that it has forced Sylvia out of several of her easy delusions. Younger brothers can never really grow up with the completeness of elder brothers—that's why they compensate with overgrowth in their subconscious minds—but teaching for a short period—until you have control of that situation—is like having suddenly a lot of younger brothers & sisters, so that a great deal in one grows up that never otherwise would. Sylvia would have been an adoring Smith Sophomore all her life but for this job—which has very brutally disenchanted her. Now she sees what an utter kindergarten the whole place is, and she is really a different person.

Write about your life in Paris. I haven't heard from Olwyn for a while, though I haven't written to her either. Describe who comes & goes, and how, and with what refinements.

Huws junior is to be born this month I believe. Do you know what date? Than wrote, & said Helga looked as though it might be twins. He also said that Danny W. was enjoying business. That David Ross led an obscure job-hunting life.

Did you see the "New Poets of England & America." The editor was

John Hall, and the whole is 343 pages of verse that might have been written by any one person, but most probably by John Hall.

Now you have started, don't you think that rather than escape into a job for a year you ought to keep writing? You are at the age now as I am where jobs are no longer 'experience'—only delay & obstruction, and your best experience—& the only absolutely necessary experience—is now that of your own thinking & writing. If you write nothing but bad nonsense for 3 years you will have done more & be nearer what you want to be than if you had ascended to 2nd mate on the Queen Mary in that time, or travelled along every line of lat° and every line of long° as marked on Mercators. Good advice from a grandfather.

Ted.

[*Two marginal insertions, the second with arrow pointing to final paragraph*]

Have you read Conrad's "The Secret Sharer"? It's about the best short story I've ever read.

"Words of wisdom are more intolerable than blows with a club" Chiai-F'ang—by which he means they do not enlighten, but stun, as here exemplified.

The phrase 'Creative Writers' appears in magnified letters and flaunts conspicuous inverted commas.

The play in which 'the son enters with the head of his father', could be *The House of Taurus*, on which TH worked while at Yaddo in the autumn of 1959 and which we know, from Plath's report to her mother, was based on *The Bacchae* by Euripides. It has not survived.

By the time TH's 'Billy Hook and the Three Souvenirs', which bears a narrative resemblance to the ballad of 'Thomas the Rymer', appeared in the July edition of *Jack and Jill*, it had been 'castrated' – as he put it in a letter to his brother. The 'Slicks' were popular magazines printed on coated paper.

The editor of *New Poets of England and America* was Donald (not John) Hall (b.1928). TH may have confused him with either John Hall Wheelock, editor at Scribners, who had invited Sylvia Plath to submit work for a three-poet volume in a series introducing young American poets, or J. C. Hall, the British poet. Poems by TH were included in the 1962 revised edition of Donald Hall's anthology.

To Lucas Myers

[Early 1958]   Ms   Emory

I think work is probably an escape from the responsibility of writing—once you've contracted the responsibility. The way to really develope as a writer is to make yourself a political outcast, so that you have to live in secret. This is how Marlowe developed into Shakespeare. Think what a precise detatchment this would give to all your observations—at the same time making all your life, and the only possible life, inward. This is how Dante developed into Dante, & Joyce into Joyce. The other way is to go deaf. Also, the instinctive effort to communicate through this separation goes into your works. Deaf is not so good. Another way is to be in a state of continual infatuation, without any possibility of requital. Another way is to have a Dionisius of assertion buried under an absolute paralysis of shyness and a nature confused by emotional impressions. Another way is to fall in love with your 'affable familiar', or contrive that she fall in love with you, or both.

Don't let teaching depress you. It is a valuable study in characters—of your students. And if you are teaching something you didn't know before it is a good way of making that knowledge your own. Also it is a great means of coming at a type of maturity, if you can adapt to it—especially if you're a younger brother. The way I taught grammar was to write a fairly simple but not too simple sentence from Swift on the board, and had them write five sentences copying the structure etc exactly, but with different subject & words. Quite dumb people do this very easily, and the example goes like magic through all their writing—if you do it regularly. This is the only successful method of teaching grammar I've used.

Myers, too, had recently taken up teaching, at the University of Maryland's extension in France and at language schools in Paris.

To Daniel Huws

[End of February 1958]   Ms   Huws

At present I am teaching. I teach three days a week, eleven hours in all. It is no good for anything except money unfortunately. It is amusing. I take of all things (among others) a creative writing class 8 students, 3 beautiful, one brilliant & a very good person. I know almost nothing about writing generally—I just have theories about a few ultraspecial refinements which authorise me to dismiss the works of all but about 6 writers who ever lived without another thought. Now I am being forced to have these other thoughts, and elaborate on the skillful effects of tedious short-story writers. There are a thousand million masterpieces of the short-story in America, and more living masters than you could recite in a day. Some day the fashion will pass maybe, like the 3 volume novel.

To Lucas Myers

[March 1958]   Ms   Emory

What are you writing now your novel is finished? Poems? I got started on a broad theme—and I had several poems mapped out which would be variations or rather distinct & separate assaults on this main theme from one angle or another. This kept a drift of thought & imagery, and was successful, in that the poems were well-prepared in my mind when I came to them, and in none of the poems did I feel the burden of having to get everything into this one poem. I speak as if there were 60 poems— I only wrote the first 5. One useless. The Acrobats which Olwyn has, was the last I wrote. By that time I had momentum, & the poems got the feeling that I didn't care whether they came out or not because if they didn't I could scrap them & try another and so they were coming out at just about the speed I could copy them out. Maybe they're no better for this—they're a certain type of poem I suppose. I feel to have no connection with them at all, which isn't the feeling where I have taken trouble & found the writing hard.

This must be the advantage of writing a long work though,—the next stretch is always preparing in your mind, and the organisation of the poetry must be so much deeper & smoother for having been developed with fair definition for a good time in your unconscious mind. The disadvantage of writing a poem here & a poem there, on this & on that, is that not until you begin writing does your deeper mind begin working on this particular poem, & you have written nonsense & confused yourself before the real poetry begins coming up through the cracks of what you have stiffly & coldly written. All the mass of miscellaneous poetry in your mind has to realign itself to the sudden demand. If you plan the poem ahead, & work towards it to give it the feeling of responsibility & urgency, as you work towards a part of a long work, then by the time you get to it it is ready assembled & comes up whole. Maybe. This is apart from the poems that come of their own accord—and which ought to come more promptly if you could train them, make—nonsense. One page of nonsense.

With the exception of 'Acrobats', specifically named here, the poems resulting from TH's 'assaults' on a 'main theme' cannot be identified, but they presumably included some that would also go into his next book, *Lupercal* (1960).

To Olwyn Hughes

[Late March 1958]   Ms   Emory

On the anniversary of my meeting Sylvia (the 2nd) and the anniversary (1st) of receiving the telegram that my book had won its prize, we both sold a poem to Mademoiselle—a high-heeled chrome-glaze woman's monthly—for 60 dollars. A nice sentimental touch. Also Harper's bought 2 poems—'Relic' (did I send you that?) and an early version of 'Of cats' which I sent, I believe, to Luke. Also the New Statesman bought 'Crow Hill'. All the poems for my second book are a little out of favour. They are hard-headed. I have tried so hard to take nothing for granted in matters of cadence & rhythm, that sentiment & warmth has seemed like a proscribed outlaw. In an effort to express myself trenchantly & controlledly, I have kept out softness. I think depth & wholeness of sentiment is the only important matter in any art,—the only permanent thing: technique, atmosphere, fantasies etc will become old-fashioned no matter how far-ahead they seem when they first appear. Only the sentiment, affection, lasts. Hence Chaucer etc. I have passed through a necessary stage maybe, towards making my writing my own and developeing the wholeness & solidness of my thoughts & the verbal expression of them, but I now have the longing, very strong, to bring in all that I have troubled to keep out, and to scapegoat my ice-age I have written the most impersonal i.e. the deadest, poem yet, which I will send along. 'The Creation of Adam.'

Sylvia is having her holidays, and in 5 days has written more than for the previous 14 months, and better, I think, than ever. An art Magazine 'Art News' asked her to write some poems on certain paintings which, they said, they could illustrate with reproductions of the paintings. This is easy for her. Paintings inspire her. Quite seriously. She had in mind certain Rousseau, certain Klee early drawings, one or two others. She took the copies from the art library—splendid one—here at Smith, and has lived in a state of ecstasy for five days, writing in all 6 quite long poems. The one she wrote today is about her best ever. She sits & writes for about 12 hours at a stretch, and gets too excited to sleep. What she'll do when she's doing nothing but writing for month after month I don't know. I've been reading a great book—a biography of Klee with hundreds of his sketches & paintings. Very interesting. He painted continually, and produced several hundred works a year—paintings & etchings. Rousseau's development is interesting. Nothing is known of his from before his 36th year, and he didn't get to his jungle pictures until his old age.

Another thing I've been going through lately—the Journals of the Psychical Research Society—1880 onwards. The most wonderful accounts of hypnoses, automatic writings, ghosts, double personalities etc—much superior (the hypnoses & double-personalities) to what you find in psychology, because in these accounts the whole thing was new, much more of a mystery, & set down more interestingly—not explained away. I was surprised to find one theory stated & famously supported which I thought was my own— this was that in right handed persons the left side of the brain has charge of all consciously-practised skills, capacities etc, but in the right lobe is the subconscious, or something deeper, a world of spirits. This is a half-baked sort of idea, but I had thought of it because I've noticed that many people's right eye has an utterly different expression than their left, a different brilliance etc. One of Dostoevsky's pupils was so completely expanded that no iris showed. The whole side of the face is different, but the effect is most noticeable in the eye. This made me think that the side of the brain corresponding to the funny eye must be in a different state of excitement than the other, and have different concerns.

Alone of the poems by TH that he names above, 'The Creation of Adam' was not included in *Lupercal* and its identity is uncertain; but the catalogue at Emory has two entries that may be germane: one for 'Triptych: The Creation of Adam', the other for 'Running to Paradise', of which 'The Creation of Adam' is a variant title.

The poems Plath wrote as the result of a commission from *Art News* are identified in TH's notes to her *Collected Poems*, where he explains: 'Throughout this time [1958] SP found writing difficult. She resorted to set themes, and deliberate exercises in style, in her efforts to find release.' She herself reports this long-delayed burst of creativity in a letter to her mother dated 22 March 1958.

To Olwyn Hughes

[June 1958]   Ms   Emory

Yesterday we went into Boston to find an apartment for next year, as we're determined to live on our savings for a year. Last year (writing nothing & working most of the time) we earned about $1400 on writing alone, so if we write continually we ought to earn something. And even if we don't, I don't care. I'm going to waste no more time on employers.

About a month ago I opened a magazine in the Barber's shop and saw a photograph of a street on Beacon Hill in Boston called Acorn Street. (Beacon Hill is the stronghold of ancient Boston—hasn't changed since early Henry James, is like York or Chester—Cathedral city charm, the only in America) This street was almost too narrow for cars, & had grass growing between the cobbles. The very place to be quiet & in pleasant surroundings, and yet in the middle of Boston. This became my ideal, in thinking of what sort of district we would like to get into in Boston. Anyway, the renting agent wasn't optimistic, & it was going to be even more difficult to find a place now, since we don't want to move into it until Sept 1st. But he dug up a place, and took us to see it. Very small. Each main room (of the two) had a little bay window —5th floor—looking out over the rooftops, (very jumbled & ancient & interesting) onto the Charles River one way, the park the other way, Louisberg Square, where all the characters in Henry James live, the other way, and directly below, opposite our front door, the very view down Acorn Street that I had seen in the Magazine. Isn't that strange? It's a good address too—9, Willow St. Next September we move in. I like Boston as much as any city I've been in.

Last week we were in New York. I don't like that. It's like living in an underground terminal. Soot, noise, weariness, cheapjacks, and the most pathetic Bohemian district, called The Village, that is on earth. If Chelsea is 5 removes from the Left Bank, this is 50 from Chelsea. The Bowery is very interesting—purple drunks asleep across the pavement.

124

Also South Ferry, the very tip of the island, is like Holborn. We went to see Oscar Williams, who proliferates the anthologies. He is using Bishop Farrar, The Hag, and Thought-fox, to end his new 'Pocket book of Modern Verse." A little bright nice huckster, ¼ Welshman ¾ jew. Dylan T's bosom crony. (Haven't I told you all this)

Sylvia recorded some poems for the Poetry Library at Harvard. Each one she writes is an advance on the last. Sweeney, who is in charge of the poetry library, ran an amusing course with his students there. First, all year, they read Yeats, Eliot, Pound, Auden etc, & certain critical essays (by poets only), and finally he gives them about 30 books of verse—recent, English & American, that they're not likely to know (they're graduate students from other faculties), and from these they're to make an anthology of 30 poems—using which poets they like & not more than 3 poems by any one—and write a long introduction. Phillip Larkin's & mine were the favourites. Phillip Larkin you'll have heard of. He's a librarian in Hull—about 36—very good gentle poet. But this was gratifying. Perhaps it shouldn't be.

[. . .]

The poem about the bull has taken a great deal of writing and is as bare as it is (i.e. unmetaphored & without fanciful flights) because it has steadily insisted that I redo it to what in bad translation would look like prose, I suppose. But the effect is powerful, I think. It is the bull on Oats' farm over old Denaby, but also of course a creature within the head—. I got the idea from the Taurus of those astrology books. Grackles are a bird here. Rather like jackdaws, but not much bigger than blackbirds. Their cry is exactly that "Grackle". They are ridiculous, somehow.

There was a review of my book in Antioch Review. Reviewing 8 poets, he gave me 4 pages. He criticised the blood & thunder acutely (it is miserably splashed all over, now I see it more clearly) misunderstood the conclusion of Jaguar, but then selected what he liked, very shrewdly, and called me an "occasionally great poet" and so on, and compared other poets in his review with me, disastrously to them. He had the hitherto non-existent virtue of seeing what is good and is bad in the very bad bits. I'm surprised. Pleasantly. I'm sure I shall be attacked soon. Fulsome praise of one reviewer provokes 3 others to malice. In the later reviews of most books the battle is with earlier reviewers. This should begin on mine. And the book is full of ineptitude, too—over half the poems were a fierce attempt to get writing after weeks of idleness, or months. Their violence is mostly impatience, perhaps. I'm amazed now I look back on the reviews its got.

You should write and give an account of what is going on in Paris.

There was an art festival in Boston this last weekend which we visited when we were down there. The park—in the middle of Boston—is full of marquees, & the marquees are lined with paintings, sculpture etc. Also they have concerts, folk-dancers, and some poet or other to receive an award & give a reading—this time it was Marianne Moore.
[. . .]

Marianne Moore was delightful. The audience sat in the open, under trees. She's the worst reader alive—mixes up remarks with the poem so you can't tell one from the other, and reads with a kind of plum in her mouth. But she's engaging. Do you know her poems? Tell me what writers you're interested in reading, and I'll get you the books.

Remember Corbière.

We went to a restaurant in Boston, full of Italians celebrating—or filled up with—a birthday, and a sailing for Europe. Shouting, dancing, singing, orchestra two-piece (the boy played a clarinet) playing very ancient shepherd-like songs, cake for everybody. This kind of unself-consciousness makes it easier to live—to have it around, I mean. I ordered Calamara because that means Octopus—I got one little octopus about as big as a mouse, the rest shrimps & fanciness. They have a magnificent fish market in Boston, and fresh fish—marvel of marvels!

TH and Sylvia Plath paid a visit to New York soon after her last day of teaching at Smith, 22 May 1958.

Plath made her Harvard recording on 13 June, at the invitation of John L. Sweeney (1906–85), Professor of English and curator of the Woodberry Poetry Room at Harvard.

A big tear puts the central, omitted paragraph beyond retrieval, and creates difficulties of interpretation in the paragraphs on either side.

The poem about the bull was 'The Bull Moses' (*Lupercal*). The explanation of grackles must have some separate context.

Marianne Moore is less affectionately treated in TH's 'The Literary Life' (*Birthday Letters*).

'Remember Corbière': because Olwyn Hughes was at this time supplying TH with French poetry.

To Aurelia Plath

[Early July 1958]   Ts   Lilly Library

Dear Sylvia's mother,

today is the second of a wonderful spell of relief. The sudden heat came too quickly and too strongly for us to adjust to, so we were a bit demoralised and I lost two night's sleep. The change has restored us miraculously to industry and mood. Sylvia has a new interest which I suppose she's told you about. We found a little bird at the foot of a very high tree. It looked to be dead, but when we payed attention to it it showed itself quite interested. We brought it back, and now Sylvia feeds it chopped steak every couple of hours or so. No bird in Massachusetts gets fed so well, or looked after so carefully. It ought to have an unusual personality. It's amazing how quickly it seems to have acquired a little character and identity, quite important, and not at all to be neglected.

On Monday we went up the mountain again, this time walking from the very bottom and in terrific heat. Probably that was the deciding blow in our three day knockout. We all but caught a ground-hog, a little fat brown furry rat-bear of a creature. It couldn't run very fast, so backed up under a bank and chattered its teeth at us very gallantly. We watched it for quite a long time, but it wouldn't move from its position till we had gone. All kinds of birds, insects, flowers, none of which we seem to know the name of, to our grief. How ignorant we are. Because these are the things we really should know, much more than who is the villain in the Bostonians.

Attempting to keep just a little fit in the paralysing heat I put my neck out. I'm writing a story in which one of my main characters slips a disk, or says she slips a disk. This isn't the first time I've noticed how often something I'm writing about tends to materialise in real life in some way. Sometimes frighteningly. This is a mild case, fortunately. But uncomfortable. Another of the characters in the same story wins 75000 pounds on the football pools so we're waiting confidently.

I brought a load of books out of the library. Two of them by Rachel Carson, books about life in the sea which are wonderful. Sylvia is in raptures. I started one yesterday and couldn't put it down till I had finished it completely.

Writing is going steadily. Sylvia has written two or three first class poems, as strong as anything she has done, and I think the unbroken practise is necessary—her style and self are changing so rapidly that it is a continuous labour to bring the two together. This is one of the main problems in poetry writing I think, bringing your style to unity with your experience. It would be easy if your experience weren't continually outgrowing itself. As it is one's style is always just a bit out of date.

I thought we would naturally go down and pick up Warren, but I was imagining the distance to be about the same as between here and Wellesley, which I would have seen for nonsense if I had bothered to think for a second. As it is, probably you're right. It would be very nice, though, for him to be just picked up and be in a way home immediately.

This letter, I see, wouldn't get very full marks in a typing class, or even in an English class. One has to be very strict to check all the mind's little punning and inverting games, which don't matter and are all part of the essentially dreamy operation of composition for oneself. However, just mentally reprimand them.

I have recently written one very good poem, I think very good and so does Sylvia, and am writing other things. We are both about twice as industrious at this as we were at teaching, the way it should be. Look after yourself. Best to Grampy.   Love,   Ted.

Sylvia Plath tells the story of the maimed bird in a letter to her brother dated 9 July 1958, so a July date looks acceptable here.

The two books by Rachel Carson were *The Sea around Us* (1951) and *Under the Sea Wind* (1955).

To Olwyn Hughes

[Summer 1958]   Ms   Emory

Your long letter came today, full of news. I'm glad to hear you're so pleasantly settled. And that Luke is too. I shall write to him today. Where did you get the idea that we were living in New York? We shall be here at No. 337 until Sept 1st. Then at 9, Willow St, Boston.

Your remarks about the poems are always important to me & good. Sylvia has cut the verse out of her ghost poem which gives the rhetorical catalogue of common ghosts, beginning "Into sanity". And finished the previous line with a stop, & worked the first phrase of the following verse into the following sentence. Much better. She wrote a beauty about Fiddler crabs—very direct & lucid, not so elaborate. 91 lines. The

New Yorker bought it and the Nocturne one that you have for about £1 a line. $350 altogether.

The Pig, you say, is literary. I hoped it wasn't. The 3rd verse I thought was particularly me. Relic is rather grey, but it's texture struck me as being the same as Thrushes. Cat & Mouse you are quite right about. First I cut out that 4th verse completely, & changed the beginning of the last, but in the end the style is too coldly elaborate for its situation & the situation too pat. I like the end. So I've cancelled it from the canon. I'm sending you another in similar style—an anecdote—"Wilfred Owen's Photographs". "Lines in mid-air" is stylised & has a tone, or is nothing. I was very moved by it when I wrote it, but that doesn't mean anything. Tell me how you think Water-lily compares with October dawn in my book. I'm trying to make my style more closely woven & subtler in pitch—the poems in my book seem crude in pitch for the most part, & the tone too single-voiced. So these poems lately have been more quietly written, & are smaller subjects for the most part. But I find them more satisfying. Tell me how you like Bull. I wrote it out in some confused shape two or three months ago, then didn't want to touch it because it seemed too good a subject to spoil with tinkerings. But then I dreamed the bull came to me—just wandered up. So I finished the poem next day. It's about my favourite.

A reviewer in Poetry Chicago picks out my most obvious faux pas, in my book, & dismisses the whole book. He is quite young, and writes very brash cocky verse, so he is probably a defeated contestant. His review was stupid throughout, so it didn't trouble me. The Sewanee Review was quite intelligent, though he likes people like William Jay Smith, who is about the corniest poet alive. His own verse—Luke will know it. Your idea of a reviewer's verse very much modifies your idea of the authority of his opinions on verse.

We are sending Luke a little book.

Luke can stay with us as long as he likes, either here or in Boston, and I certainly hope he comes for some time, a week at least. Boston I hope. I would like him to meet Robert Lowell, who is incredibly like him in some ways.

Love

Ted

Plath's 'ghost poem' was 'The Ghost's Leavetaking', based on a painting by Paul Klee and one of the six that had been commissioned by *Art News* (see letter to

Olwyn Hughes of late March). 'Mussel Hunter at Rock Harbor' is the 'beauty about Fiddler crabs', and 'Hardcastle Crags' (titled 'Night Walk' in *The New Yorker*), the 'Nocturne'.

Of his own poems mentioned here, TH was to keep five – including 'Cat and Mouse' – in *Lupercal*, while 'Lines in mid-air' is not easily identified. The third verse in 'View of a Pig' is the one about thumping the carcase 'without feeling remorse'.

The *Poetry (Chicago)* reviewer was the poet Galway Kinnell (b.1927). In his review (Vol. 92), he complained that 'the reader is kept at several removes from reality by layers of turbid metaphor', and concluded that the volume contained no 'important' or 'finished' poem.

To Gerald and Joan Hughes and family

[Late August, with additions dated 7 and 8 September, 1958]   Ts and ms   Emory

Our year in Northampton is almost over, thank God. Of all plastic cellophane wrapped places on earth, this is the prototype. [. . .] I have led an utterly unreal life for a year, because there is no friendship with these people, only acquaintance. All churning over the same mechanical trash, which passes for modern criticism etc (naturally our contact has been mainly with the English Literature faculty). My spell of teaching at the State University near here was amusing, a sort of Marx brothers episode, and a great relief. Luckily Sylvia is unique to live with, and we have largely amused ourselves. Since June when school finished, we have written, or pretended to write, or got ready to write, and at last, this last couple of weeks, have actually got writing. I hope we keep this momentum up all through this next year. We have acquired a marvellous room in Boston next year. Boston is an old city, and the "hill", which is the old centre of it, is rather like the old english cathedral towns, stone, alleys, queer old families, and all life there seems unself-conscious and more European than in these frightful inland executive suburbs. There are European restaurants, a dense foreign population, and above all endless fresh fish. I shall cheer when I see my first dead herring.

I meant to get some fishing over here, but I was a bit deflected by the fact that there is an air over all American sports, I don't know how to define it. As if all those duck-shooters who were going out daily to make washing machines, you remember, were actually driving past the factory for a few hours and going fishing because fishing was a sport for the man of the house, and only tough woodsy guys got round to it and so on. In

130

America a calendar picture, say, of a fishing episode, is of some bronzed pipe-smoking lawyer-cum-doctor-cum-truck-driver-cum-your-honest-neighbour plated and belted and buckled from head to foot in all those frontierish looking accessories, gaffs, nets, bowie-knives and the rest, healing over in a tarzan-tearing-the-arms-off-the-ape-stance as he surfaces some proud king of the deeps, and in the background, just on land will be shown the family beach-wagon in three colours drawn up with the back open showing the hams, steaks, squashes, and so on or perhaps they will all be actually laid out on a cloth on the pine-needles, while the R.K.O. wife smiles at the five bouncing boys in their woodsy outfits. No I'm spoiling it. But that is the tendency. That is the image of the fisherman in the American mind. Now the same image in the English mind is of some clown sitting in pouring rain fishing in a pool that has a great notice "Petrol Dump". Something of that sort. But there's a difference. One can go fishing in England without feeling that you're taking part in some national Let's All Be Good Americans campaign, and be sure that any fish you catch won't have tattooed on its underside "I'm an American too so treat me well and cook me with FRENCH'S HOTCHA SAUCE." Something like that. So I haven't gone fishing. But when we get near the sea I shall go. In fact we shall go when we go to visit Sylvia's mother next week down Cape Cod. Sylvia loves fishing, and has luck.

[. . .]

I have been reconsidering your paintings, Gerald, and I think their secret is they are visions. That is, you don't paint what you see in front of your eyes, but what you see in front of your eyes summons a similar scene out of the other side of your imagination and that is the one you paint. If this is true, your paintings should be permanent, no matter how easily you do them. At the other side of the imagination is a brilliant world which has no part in our lives. This is a psychological fact. You get glimpses of it in certain dreams, under drugs sometimes, and very rarely in art. This is the world that the saints are trying to get at, with all their fastings and prayers;—in spite of the blasphemy of that interpretation, it is true. The reason we are all trying to get at it, is because for some reason or other, it is a world of untouchable beauty, freshness, and satisfaction. This gets into the work of certain painters. Have you seen the early countryside paintings of William Palmer? They are generally an evening scene, with a new moon. Also Turner. Also Blake. These people have it. Also those chinese paintings have it characteristically. It is very rare. I think you have it, in your watercolours. That's why you should go on painting those barren landscapes etc. It is the final quality that Namatjira lacks. I look for this in all arts, and I'm sure this is the one criterion I have always unconsciously used in selecting what I like. That must be why I like so very little, though I admire a great deal that I do not like.

With any single artist, it is generally a certain type of subject that brings the visionary touch out in him. With Turner it was sunsets over parkland. With Palmer it was new moons. With you it is The Waste Land. Or seems to be. Maybe you can do it with other things too. You did it with these pheasants blowing up over the brown trees that we have on our mirror. Also, how are you progressing with your children's story books?

'R.K.O. wife': i.e., as in a film made by the US production company Radio Keith Orpheum Pictures.

By 'William Palmer', TH must mean the visionary British landscape painter Samuel Palmer (1805–81).

To John L. and Máire Sweeney

[November 1958]   Ts   Dublin

Dear Jack and Maire,

This is a shamefully late date to be thanking you for your several notes, the 'Listener' cutting, and the enquiry about the recording. We are settled very pleasantly in two small rooms with a charming view over rooftops to the Charles to Cambridge—in the tall thin building that you must have been able to see from your back windows. Sylvia's working part-time at the Mass. General Hospital, to get back in touch, but I think she'll be finishing there next week. I read, and occasionally write. I have a draft of a monstrous play—monstrous in nature and features, not so much in size—and I work at that now and again. Also we have a few more poems.

Life is very calm—a country sort of life. We've had pleasant evenings with the Fassetts, and have seen Lowell once or twice, and Frost once or twice—Frost monologueing and running his horn into everything. I suppose you knew William Alfred. We went to see his Hogan's Goat in the Sanders Theatre. It was quite well performed in most of the parts. I'm not sure what I thought of the play—we were on the balcony for the first half and what bits drifted up were too barbarously Irished to decipher. We went downstairs for the second half and that was much better, and interesting, some parts a bit harshly melodramatic but quite large lumps had been cut out, so they were probably to blame. The staging wasn't too effective. They tried to make it simple and Elizabethan but only made it ragged.

I saw Merwin's 'Drunk in the furnace' in the Partisan and thought it really excellent. His verse as you say Jack is getting much solider—mainly by his cutting out the arbitrary rhetorical and fantastical development of his ideas and purging the metaphysics, and by strengthening the consonant beat. This is what's obvious, anyway.

Do you know

The great bull of Bendylaw
Has broken his band and run awa
The King and a' the king's court
Cannot bring that bull about.

That's inevitability for you.

Boston is a great refreshment after the closets of Northampton. If we get cash enough, but not enough to go to Europe, we might well stay here another year.

Here is a poem 'Pike'—celebration of a totem, straightforward, romantic.

Sylvia sends her love. She's at work at present.

Ted

Plath had recorded poems for Stephen Fassett, a recording engineer with a studio on Beacon Hill, late in 1957.

Hogan's Goat, many times rewritten by William Alfred (1922–99), is a verse play set in the Irish community of Brooklyn, where the author grew up. The Sweeneys were its dedicatees.

Merwin's poem 'The Drunk in the Furnace' was to lend its title to the collection he brought out in 1960.

Plath's 1959 poem 'The Bull of Bendylaw' was a response to the fragment TH quotes from Child's *English and Scottish Popular Ballads* (1883).

To Daniel Huws

25 November 1958   Ms   Huws

Dear Dan,

Many happy returns to Helga & many happy returns to Mary's Ascendant, and a Merry Christmas to all three of you.

How did the British Museum turn out? That would be about as congenial a job for you as exists in London, wouldn't it?—not nervously exhausting, with learned Colleagues. And generally to belong to the place must be very fine.

Nothing much happens over here. I read & amuse myself. Boston is a really excellent city—Liverpool, Mile-End, Manchester, parts of Manchester, a bit of York all crushed onto a peninsula about a mile across and a mile & a half long. There seems to be a great deal of loose living here, and I never saw so many hip-flask size whisky & brandy bottles lying on the pavements & in doorways. Sylvia has been working part-time at the psychiatric clinic & brings wonderful stories of family rape, diabolic possession, people who can't see their feet and so on. Imagine what would happen to Liverpool if all the factories were to stop & the docks were to close—it approaches that here. Wrinkled bristly sodden Irish faces everywhere. There are seven tattooists & 3 gypsy fortune tellers in view from one place—a main Charing cross sort of junction of streets. Tattooing is an extremely bloody job—have you watched them?

I suppose you heard about the £300 Guiness prize. What a pity that didn't happen where I could have celebrated in kind and at large. Luke was here when we got the letter, and we went out to celebrate a little (celebrating is inhibited here). There was a letter along with it asking if I would accept & enclosing a copy of the rules. After a while we re-read these rules & decided the poem was not eligible. So we spent a depressed afternoon. However, it seems we misinterpreted a slightly ambiguous sentence. The judges were McNeice, Laurie Lee and some Irishman who died soon after making the decision.

That was interesting about Danny's story. The possible comfort to be derived from it, is that he must have a deeper artistic conscience than he knows, and that it is active. The discomfort—that his filial sense of duty is a militant devil.

We've met Robert Frost once or twice recently. He's very old now, & a bit deaf. But talks continually, & very amusingly. He has very good stories about Edward Thomas who was a great friend of his, apparently. Also about Pound—they are all very funny about Pound & completely to Pound's discredit. I met Pound's son too—Omar, who teaches 'Chinese History' at a private school here. His mother, Pound's wife, is Yeats' daughter by Mrs Shakespeare, & this Omar has a really recognisable look of Yeats. He's not Ezra's son, however, in fact. An interpolation, by an unknown hand. He's rather a mousy creature.

We met the monster Brinnin—monster is not exaggeration either. The glassiest slimiest creature I ever met, just about. Done a rich sun-ray lamp tan, with pale blue eyes, wears an English style blazer & cricket sort of shirt & smiles & smiles. Also, we met Richard Eberhart, who is a sort of bounding rubber ball of a man, very genial, a bit mechanical.

I was sorry to hear about Danny's father. What is he going to do with the factory? How is Than? That's to say, I hope he's well, since you told me very precisely how he is. Do you ever see Mac now? I occasionally get one of his letters. He seems to be happier in Cambridge. He once had the cheek to tell me I couldn't get away from Cambridge, & what a baby I was for my Alma Mater. I'm saving that for him.

You say Edward Thomas has no 'lines'. What about

"That most ancient Briton of English beasts,"

—meaning a poet with a welsh name, of course.

I have just discovered Hardy. Preposterous & very novelettish, but completely genuine, & unconscious of literary 'mode'. One of the two sources of Crowe Ransome. The other source, the main one, is a poem by Campion called 'Love's Pilgrims'—first line "What fair pomp have I spied of glittering ladies." I like the songs very much. I haven't heard the tunes yet. Are they your tunes? Greetings to Helga, & to Mary.

Ted

TH had received First Prize in the 1958 Guinness Poetry Awards. Judges were Louis MacNeice (1907–63), Laurie Lee (1914–97) and Seamus O'Sullivan (1879–1958).

John Malcolm Brinnin (1916–98) was the author of *Dylan Thomas: An Intimate Journal*. Published in 1955, two years after Thomas's death, it made public the extent of the poet's drinking and womanising. Richard Eberhart (1904–2005) was a poet and writer of verse plays.

The line by Edward Thomas (1878–1917) is from his poem 'The Combe' and describes the persecuted badger.

It may have been 'Vision by Sweetwater', in which John Crowe Ransom invokes 'a dream of ladies sweeping by', and of 'bright virgins . . . Flowing with music of their strange quick tongue', that connected Ransom with Thomas Campion (1567–1620) in TH's mind. TH also speaks of Ransom's music in his second interview with Ekbert Faas (Appendix II of *Ted Hughes: The Unaccommodated Universe*), citing 'moments in [his] work which have a Shakespearean density'.

1959

To Leonard and Esther Baskin

[January 1959]   Ms   British Library

Dear Leonard & Esther,

We hope you are enjoying the first of an excellent year, and wish you plenty of luck and inspirations. I don't know what date we shall be coming up there, but before then—and within a fortnight—we ought to produce a Pike and a Bullfrog, I've at last found quite a good picture of a pike. The skull of a pike would have been best, since the pike in the poem are not really the living, but I shall have to be literal and make it a pike in flesh. I found this the other day, so I shall do the drawing today or tomorrow, and send it to you. This library is terrible on Bull-frogs. The Dickerson book isn't there, and what frog-books there are are all surgical. There is one work, supposedly on all American frogs: it has a few handsome plates, but the accounts of the specific frogs are 1st grade nature studies. The best fact in the bullfrog piece was evidence that they eat ducklings, which surprised me.

The exhibition was magnificent. My favourites: the big Marat facing the entrance, Death among the thistles—the engraving, the Angel, the crows—especially the etching of the dead one—, and Love me love my dog. This last is tremendously dense and deep.

We're delighted to hear the book is so near completed. Are the drawings ready? Mrs Mcleod seemed quite excited about it. This is a pleasant tumbledown city. It has plenty of fresh fish—a great change after the Northampton preservatories. It has Atlantic weather too, but the pigeons have started wobbling round & ruffling in circles encourageingly.

Our best wishes for a good year—with Tobias to help you.

Ted.

The checque is for a copy of the 7 deadly Sins.

TH and Sylvia Plath had met the artist, sculptor and printer Leonard Baskin (1922–2000), who was teaching in the art department at Smith, and his wife Esther, through an English-faculty colleague of Plath's. 'Pike: A Poem' was the first of many collaborations between TH and Baskin, whose Gehenna Press produced it as a broadside, with a woodcut by Robert Birmelin (b.1933). According to Baskin's widow, Lisa, although he had not set up Gehenna as a vehicle for his own work, he regretted never having illustrated 'Pike' himself. It is not clear from the correspondence why TH needed to provide his own drawing – perhaps for anatomical or stylistic guidance?

The item that the library lacked was Mary Dickerson's *The Frog Book* (1906).

Emilie Warren McLeod edited children's books at Harper & Row and wrote books for children.

To Leonard Baskin

[January 1959]   Ms   British Library

Dear Leonard,

Relieved to get your letter. The pike's head is exactly like a pike's head—but a pike's head under a fishmonger's slab among cod's heads and herring heads, abstracted of all but a sheepish surface. My other efforts were over-sensationally vicious—I've seen too many fantastic-ally gaping pike on fishing-tackle advertisements. I thought the danger ought to be underplayed—but I'm afraid the result was as you so exactly describe.

Maybe something like a skull, or even just a jawbone, would be most subtly explosive—illumine the undermeaning of the poem a bit and not over define the real pike in it. But I'm sure that whatever you do with it will be the perfect thing. The poem looks more & more like my best piece, just about.

How is the night-creature book coming? And what's the new idea?

I hope you're doing well and pleasantly, with Toby enlarging visibly. Boston is fine, flourishes on its muck—what Northampton lacks is muck.

Don't wait to discuss the pike business with me—our coming up there is vague even as a possibility.

Here's my latest work—

Oyez, Oyez,
    I let ye to wut
That our cat Gilbert's
    Dead o' the gut.

—traditional style.

    Love from us both to you all three,

Ted.

TH had sent his own drawing of a pike with a previous letter.

    The 'night-creature book', *Creatures of Darkness*, in which Baskin illustrated a text by his wife, would eventually appear in 1962. Sylvia Plath's poem 'Goatsucker' was written for it, but not in the event included.

To Edith and William Hughes

[Early 1959]   Ms   Emory

Dear Mom & Dad,

    I've just written to Hilda & Vic, after receiving your letter with the account of Vicky's cropping. What is Vicky doing exactly—what about these possible Art Colleges etc? The tablets I enclose are miracle-workers. I believe they are mainly Vit C, which is what citrus fruits contain. Anyway, they are cold-proof. Take one a day, two if you have a chill. Neither Sylvia nor I have had so much as a sneeze all winter—taking these daily. I will try & get more. Strong Orange-lemonade would be nearly as good, but you would have to take it daily, in big doses. This is the only thing to keep out colds. Do you have goloshes, Dad? You mustn't have kept up your breathing, because that's a great protection against colds, for some reason or other.

    I think I've finally got my day into shape. Simplemindedly, it all depends on my going to bed early. After an early night—10-30 ish—the whole quality of my energy seems higher, I get more done, & much better, and am generally happier. I don't know why it should be any different to go to bed at 10-30 & get up at 6-30 than to go at 12-30 & get up at 9, but in fact there's no comparison between the respective days that follow these. Probably it's a moral effect,—after being told almost nightly all my life to go to bed early, I have a clear conscience & good spirits when I obey. I've often noticed how important are little things like that.

    Dad, if you want an inexhaustible supply of really good really exciting detective novels ask for the novels of <u>Georges Simenon</u>. He was French, is American, but his books are published in England. He is the greatest detective writer alive, & finishes a book in eleven days—the psychology perfect, the technical details exact.

The Pennines in April poem came out in the Spectator of Dec 26th. Another came in the Spectator Jan 2nd. The London Mag bought 3 of my poems, but I'll tell you when they're due. "The month of the drowned dog," is because November reminds me of a drowned dog, and is a general impression of the sodden lifeless appearence of the land, & the fate of the life on the land which I talk about in the rest of the poem. Olwyn was wrong about the gang of cats, but I misled her. These are ordinary cats. All keepers shoot cats. I need about 5 more poems, longish ones, for a book. I'll have these in no time.

The other night we went with Robert Lowell to a reading by Allen Tate. Their photographs are on the back of that 'Modern Verse', & their poems in it. Lowell only has one poem in there, but he's easily the best of all the Americans under fifty—easily & far away. He goes into the mental hospital now & again and occasionally gets dangerous, as you'll be able to believe when you see his photo. However, he's about the most charming & likable American I've ever met, very like Luke in some ways. Allen Tate is about 60—he is Luke's cousin. He is an excellent poet too, though his obscurities are wilful. He's almost an alcoholic & has wasted his gifts more or less on whisky & criticism—though his criticism is quite interesting. He has a splendid poem in that Anthology called "Ode on the Confederate dead"—that's on the Southerners killed in the Civil war. He's a Southerner, of course. That's one of my favourite American poems. He's a brisk charming little man, chipper is the word for him. We went to Lowell's after, & Tate got drunker & drunker.

Lowell is a fisherman, quite keen. He calls the poem of mine "Pike" a masterpiece.

Did you read that Edwin Muir died? He's been sick a long time. But he was still writing excellently. I wrote to him towards the end of last year, just a note. It's the Cambridge climate got him—that really is a drowned dog county.

Mrs Prouty, Sylvia's fairy godmother, sent us tickets for a play the other night, & we sat on the third row among the minks. Then we went into the dentists. My teeth are keeping well, but here they scour & pick at them as no English dentist would dream of doing, just as a matter of course, & polish them. The New York party was amusing, half amusing. Nothing else has happened. We're in a quiet spell. Yes, one thing has happened. We decided quite definitely to make our base in England. I'm not quite sure where, and I'm not quite sure what I shall do, but no doubt the right job will invent itself, income until we free ourselves. That's a lovely photo of Olwyn. I wrote her the other day. Now I'll write Gerald. Sylvia's going to add a sheet.

[*No signature*]

The poet Allen Tate (1899–1979) had been selected by Robert Lowell as something of a father figure when, in his early twenties, Lowell arrived uninvited at the Tate family home and, finding no room for him, pitched a tent on the lawn. The poem of Tate's that TH praises is actually 'Ode to the Confederate Dead'.

   Olive Higgins Prouty (1882–1974), author of *Stella Dallas* and *Now, Voyager*, among other novels, had taken an interest in Sylvia Plath as a student at Smith, when Plath won a writing scholarship endowed by Prouty. She had paid for Plath's medical care after her attempted suicide in 1953 and would continue her interest in her protégée until Plath's death in 1963.

To Daniel Weissbort

21 March 1959   Ms   Emory

I would like a letter full of gossip,—which I can't really pay for. My gossip is of a sort of public kind. Do you know Robert Lowell's poems? He has a new book coming out in April, from Fabers. I'll be interested to hear your response. It's quite new I think, though for a fairly rarified taste. He's an excellent man, and about my only gossip is that I see him occasionally. He goes mad occasionally, & the poems in his book, the main body of them, are written round a bout of madness, before & after. They are mainly Autobiographical. AutoBiography is the only subject matter really left to Americans. The only thing an American <u>really</u> has to himself, & <u>really</u> belongs to, is his family. Never a locality, or a community, or an organisation of ideas, or a private imagination. Also, while being completely open to the guidance of what is expected of them—as in 'the Lonely Crowd'—they are swamped by the reviews, magazines, etc, from all individuality. As soon as I begin to write to England I begin to get critical of this place. Ordinarily, I hardly react to it.

   Are you writing much? Is Dan? I sent some of his poems to the Nation, I don't know whether they'll take anything. American taste in poetry is basically, aside from sophistications & hep, like their taste in cars. The indigenous literary form, gradually becoming predominant as indigenous forms do after invasions, is the advertisement. Ponder that. I mean it seriously. American & English poetry are already as far apart as

French & English. I think poetry is either cultivated or perverted or extinguished by national character, & in countries of the wrong character the hugest & most excitable geniuses come to nothing. Its my belief that American character is now entering a phase about as favourable to poets as, say, Norway's is. I think England is in such a phase too, but the small artists there are pretty individual. In America, they're all the same. Tumbleweed country.

Lowell's imminent book of poems was *Life Studies*. In 'Autobiographical' and 'AutoBiography', TH appears to have added the prefix as an afterthought.

David Riesman's *The Lonely Crowd* (1950) is subtitled *A Study of the Changing American Character*.

To Olwyn Hughes

[April 1959]   Ms   Emory

Robert Lowell's new book came out the other day. I asked Faber to send me one of their edition, which hasn't arrived yet. He's been building up to another manic climax over these last weeks—he was on milk only, about a month ago. It's extraordinary how his tension seems to centre about his book. He published his main book in 1945 or so, which is fantastically good. He got the Pulitzer prize for it & was acclaimed great poet etc. 3 or so years later, his next book was an absolute dud—unreadable, feeble etc. Since then he's written almost no new poems & gone in & out of hospital regularly (mental hosp.) This last year he wrote these new poems in an utterly new style, all about his relatives (the Lowells who speak only to God). He's very apprehensive as to how it will be received, and talks continually—or too often— about how it won't be liked, how it oughtn't to get any prizes since he has lots of money and is already established, and so on. Sylvia goes to a class he gives at Boston University once a week, about Poetry. Usually he is very quiet, shy, whispers (a real mad whisper) but this time he burst in, flung the tables into a new order, insulted everybody, talked incessantly. And if anyone made a remark (such as—they had mentionned Dr Zhivago—one youth's that Dr Zhivago seems too full of coincidence) he held his head saying "Yes, yes, that's enough, this is intense enough as it is." Then he went on to promise the boy an A for the course if he wrote that up and got it published in a review—all flung out. He told them, elegiacally, that he hadn't been able to see any of them much outside class because he had to see his psychiatrist so often, as he had only just come out of McLean's (the mental hospital he came out of over a year ago). Then he recommended McLean's to them as a really fine place, only what a pity it was so expensive,—too expensive for them, he supposed. Then he went on, like a deathbed speech, how he had loved teaching them, that he never wanted any of them to publish a ragged line that he wouldn't be proud of, because he didn't want any one to say that he was an incompetent teacher—etc. He drove straight from the class, we heard afterwards, to McLean's—where he now is, under supervision. This was the day before his book came out. He gets quite homicidal.

Lord Weary's Castle (1946) was the volume that had won Lowell his first Pulitzer Prize; it was followed by *The Mills of the Kavanaughs* (1951). In the quatrain about Boston ('home of the bean and the cod') that TH misquotes, the Lowells 'talk only to Cabots', while it is the Cabots who 'talk only to God'.

To T. S. Eliot

15 April 1959   Ts   Faber

Dear Mr Eliot,
    I would like to thank you for your kind support of my application for a Guggenheim Memorial Fellowship, which was successful. I think I shall use the Grant in Rome.
    My play is not really to be imagined from the meagre hints I gave in the Project. I first conceived it as a sort of opera. Sundry modifications have imposed themselves since then, however. Now I couldn't say what it resembles, but it does begin to have its own colour and verse and impetus.
    I hope you are well, and enjoying April.
                                        Yours sincerely
                                        Ted Hughes

TH did not use his Guggenheim award to visit Rome, but the play outlined in his application may have been *The House of Taurus*, on which he worked while at Yaddo, the writers' and artists' colony in Saratoga Springs, NY, where he and Sylvia Plath would stay in the autumn.
    Whether the author of *The Waste Land* was enjoying April is not recorded.

To Daniel Huws

15 May 1959   Ms   Huws

Dear Dan,

Since we shall be moving out of this place at the end of June, I'm giving you Sylvia's mother's address, which is permanent. Your letter came yesterday, naturally, since I wrote to you the day before. Yet I didn't write out of simple telepathic impulse,—my definite impulse was as you will see when you receive that letter (which I sent ordinary mail.) You must have written with a sort of prescience.

As I tell you in that letter, we are coming to Europe in November. I got a Grant, nominally to be taken in Rome, but we shall call at England, deposit our belongings & cat, see a few people, then go onto Italy & if nothing supervenes spend the first months of 1960 wandering around Italy & Greece & thereabouts. Then we shall come back to England. It's going to be a puzzle deciding where to live.

I like the ap G. very much—it's about the most moving of them. This sort of thing is all but meaningless to Americans—for which you have to take into account the way their whole life is condensed on the superficies of the moment. Relation to a changing past, & to all the various pleasant enviable periods of it, they are without, and get no pleasure from contemplating it. These translations to them are simply strange speeches suspended in vacuum. Also, poetic language is getting to be more or less consonant with I IEP talk over here. I can't describe the terrifying lack of inwardness about America. I think periods of poetry pass because the national character becomes anti-poetic—beauty, & form & metrical laws become meaningless, & that's happened over here. As in England. But it's too obvious & wretched & complicated to bother with. Behind all these million poems weekly there is nothing individual or human—no brain, just a slightly circumscribed spy-hole into the deathly sargasso of paper-back popularised philosophico-sociologico-aesthetic-critick-tock mechanism that passes for modern intellectual life. They feel that somehow their numbers must prove they're right, but you've only to think of glancing through a foot-high pile of Quarterlies & weeklies to realise they aren't even plunderable as scrap. A living defunction.

Your letter was really very inspiriting. The Boddy passage was amusing—especially the Daniel event. I haven't had Luke's address for months, or my sister's to get to him through her. Who goes to the Lamb now? We will have a Guiness [*word, possibly 'party', obscured by blot*] when I get back, to celebrate my winning. What a superior alternative if they had given me the freedom of Guiness products, for, say, ten years. I'd have thought twice before not taking it. I thought about living near Cambridge, but I'm susceptible to all catarrhs etc. Then I thought about living on the downs somewhere. Somewhere very countrified, but not completely buried. If I could manage a windfall, I still think Landlording in Oxford or Cambridge would be my ideal, for all its troubles. Joe Lyde writes that he's been left a house in Wales where he's going to retire for two years & write his novel. His experiences over here have been the characteristic burlesque sort, being beaten up by his father-in-law etc. I'm pleased to hear about Jim. What did he do with his girl friend?

My main bit of news in my other letter, was that a magazine over here bought The Fox, translation of ap G. It should keep your thirst for a week or two.

I met Crowe Ransome the other week, little whimsical gentle man. He read his poems as you can't imagine. 'Wind' was "Wined" and "wounds" were "wownds"—and such a strange grandmotherish story-telling way of speaking them, very good. He's making the most terrible changes in the poems. The one called "What Ducks Require" which is one of my favourites, he's completely ruined. I meant not to tell you about The Fox, since I wanted it to be a pleasant surprise in my other letter. It should be about $12. Write soon.

Ted

Huws had sent TH some of his own translations of the Welsh poet Dafydd ap Gwilym (*fl.*1340–60). He had planned a volume of them, but abandoned the idea after the appearance of Joseph P. Clancy's *Medieval Welsh Lyrics* in 1965 (see letter to Daniel and Helga Huws of September 1965).

'Jim' was Jim Downer, a commercial artist who for some years lived in the top flat of 18 Rugby Street. Another flat of Downer's, in Great Portland Street, was the setting for the events related in 'Ouija', in *Birthday Letters* (see letter to Lucas Myers of 16 November 1956). TH wrote a children's book, which Downer illustrated, but which has never been published.

John Crowe Ransom was at this time editor of the *Kenyon Review*.

To Lucas Myers

19 May 1959   Ms   Emory

I was reading Carlos Williams recently. I admire some of his short poems very much—one in particular about a sea & some flowers. When he is at his best, I find him infinitely more satisfying than, say, Stevens. Patterson repels me—the pretension of 'great mission' about its banalities. His preoccupations—sexy girls, noble whores, the flower of poverty, tough straight talk—are the soft-centred usuals of that most brainless American romanticism—E.E. Cummings chief Christ. In a way he's a genius, but prevailingly a fool, and essentially a huckster—only selling what he swears & believes is genuine. His tedious iterations of the factness of the fact, as if all life had condensed on the superficies of our momentary surroundings. Also, his attitude to words seems to me very naïve, if not brainless. He says somewhere that he takes the words as he finds them,—as objects, in fact, with perfectly honest faces—and uses them like that. So that where he is not being purely descriptive, where he tries to make a more general statement, he is straightforward garbage-can paper-back synthetics—such as "girls whose imaginations have no peasant traditions to give them character"—I forget how he typographs that. But he's an intense unique flavour when he's good, and there's something bracing & tonic about him generally. His irreverence for poetic tradition is a bit like the pig in the palace, though. He's one of the first symptoms & general encouragements of the modern literary syphilis—verseless, styleless, characterless all-inclusive undifferentiated yelling assertion of the Great simplifying burden-lifting God orgasm—whether by drug, negro, masked nympho, or strange woman in the dark. And the obverse of this—damning of all constructed civilisation, including all poetry that has not been gasped out with vomit or orgasm. [. . .]

Don't you really like the Yeats before Byzantium? There's something spoiling my taste for Yeats. Maybe I knew him too well. Something inflexible about him that disagrees with me at present.

TH is misquoting William Carlos Williams's poem 'To Elsie', where Williams depicts 'young slatterns' who are 'tricked out . . . with gauds / from imaginations which have no // peasant traditions to give them / character'. The other Williams poem could be 'Flowers by the Sea', from *An Early Martyr* (1935).

To Lucas Myers

19 June 1959   Ms   Emory

Now behind every word of Hart Crane is no human being at all—just an electronic noise. Hart Crane himself, I always feel, is a frayed over-strained single string no longer able to give out a sound. The quality is unhuman, unreal. There is no face, no eyes, no blood heat—just, as I say, an electronic note. Now behind each word in Crowe Ransome's poems is a whole human being, alert, sensitive, reacting precisely & finely to his observations. In this respect he resembles Shakespeare. Most poetry, particularly modern poetry, is quite without this whole-ness—men make their whole style out of one filament of the thick rope of human nature. You get the rope solid in Proverbs, ballads, songs, Shakespeare, Chaucer, Skelton, Webster—but never after 1688 (the Restoration) except maybe in Burn's dialect poems. This lack is what Eliot calls 'dissociation of sensibility", but being American he didn't perceive that the causes for this apparent dissociation of sensibility are in the inter-conflict of upper & lower classes in England, the develop-ment of the English gentleman with the stereotype English voice (and the mind, set of manners etc that goes with the voice) & the tabu on dialect as a language proper for literate men. The only poets speaking dialect since 1688 up to this century were Wordsworth, Keats & Blake. However, I'll write out my thoughts on this at greater length. It's a weighty stylish subject, since the fortunes of English poetry are bound up in it.
[. . .]
Your remarks about 'gesture' interested me very much. Both of us run to "gestures" I think. Still, the best moments of Shakes, Donne, Yeats, even Eliot, are "gestures" in your sense. But in all that I've written since my book this "gesture" is just what I've been trying to avoid. There's a natural war between inspiration & the fixed system of the ego—this latter can only be bypassed by personae, provisional egos ('gestures'), or by being melted down. This last seems to me a very precious & enviable experience at present. I have one or two minisculae, just lately, that are "gestures" all right, and unlike anything I've written. The aston-ishing thing about Shakes' sonnets is that without mythologising, or dramatising, or using any but merely decorative metaphors, he can raise such things as a direct & fairly matter-of-fact reproach to his ami for

snubbing him, to first-class intensity, perfectly objective art, in a dense atmosphere of imagination.

Hart Crane: US poet (1899–1932) and a powerful influence on some US poets of the 1950s.

To Esther and Leonard Baskin

[Early July 1959]   Ms   British Library

Dear Esther & Leonard,

The day after tomorrow we go off on a trip around the States—Mexico via California & Canada—with a car & a tent.

Thank you Leonard for your willingness to consider doing a design for my book. I'll tell you how it goes. The general drift of the poems is—"Man as an elaborately perfected intestine, or upright weasel."

How are you enjoying this weather? Toby must be like a blackberry.

I was walking across the park in Boston the other day, hot afternoon, middle of the festival, plenty of people about, when I saw a bat on the path. I thought it was a black slug pushing at a brown leaf at first. It was directly under a big tree, so I suppose it fell in its sleep. It didn't want to be picked up—snarled at me, little furry pig face, and tried to crutch itself along on its wing joints. I put it back on the tree trunk & it went scrambling away upwards, upside down, snarling downwards and shrieking. Its teeth just pricked my finger in one place, so now I'm waiting for rabies.

How is the night-creatures? Have you got a contract yet? I have a book of 8 poems for children—each poem is about a relative: a sister who is really a crow, an Aunt who is devoured by a thistle, so on. American publishers are shy of it—all the characters being metamorphotic or psychotic or otherwise too natural for the "How to relate to your child" public on which the bald heads in publishing depend. Fabers are going to publish it in England.

Between our trip & going to Yaddo I doubt if we shall manage to visit Northampton, but before we sail we certainly shall.

Sylvia joins with her love, & to Tobias,

Ted.

Here are the poems we read that time at Smith.

In this instance, Faber and Faber had made the initial offer to publish *Lupercal*.

The '8 poems for children' were to be published as *Meet My Folks!* – which, in a letter of 14 May to Charles Monteith, his editor at Faber, TH teasingly calls a 'sort of "Life Studies" '. The poems enclosed with the present letter were 'Pike', 'To Paint a Water-Lily', 'Of Cats', 'Thrushes', 'Relic', 'Shells' and 'Bull-Frog'.

TH and Plath's summer tour of the USA was to be followed by a two-month residence at Yaddo. After spending Thanksgiving with Aurelia Plath, they returned to Britain on the SS *United States*.

To Olwyn Hughes

[Summer 1959]   Ms   Emory

The Feast of Lupercal was a Roman festival held on 15th of February, in honour of Zeus as a Wolf. Nobody knows how it originated, but it came from Mt Lycaon in Greece, & combined sacrifices of goats & of a dog (—originally of a wolf, I suppose) It was mainly a fertility rite. Various bachelors stripped naked & ran a certain course through Rome (Mark Anthony ran, & at the end of the race offered Caesar the crown 3 times). They were splashed with the blood of the dog & the goats, & carried thongs cut from the skins of the goats. Women who wanted a child stood in the way of the runners & held out their arms which the runners lashed with the thongs as they went past—this was supposed to make the women fertile. It's strange how since the title occurred to me an entire vision of life seems to have grown up for me around the notion of God as the devourer—as the mouth & gut, which is brainless & the whole of evil, & from which we can only get certain concessions. But no sermons. The whole idea makes a metaphor of the Holy Family, and logically poses love—all derivatives of mother-love (of Mary, you see)— as the only protection against evil (—the natural appetite of everything living to devour everything else). (The lower orders of life do not have any love—no mother-love: the adults devour their own offspring as they find them—their world is entirely evil.) When I look through them, almost all the poems I have in this batch are about nothing else but this. God, the Creator, isn't protective love, but simply absolute power—the irrefutable authority of the need to devour to live: so God in the individual is his own power & assertion, but as He appears in every other living thing is evil—for this individual. This evil in other beings is unalloyed, save by some derivative of protective mother-love. I am not describing it clearly, because I am not really wanting to talk about it all.

148

But it seems to me the essential meaning behind everyone's obsession with crucified Christ, with the Virgin Mary, with the questionable character but supernatural force of God (and with the reducing God to simple creative or electrical (unhuman, amoral—devouring, evil) energy,) & most of all with some vague redemptive heal-all—Love (capital L). It is basically a simple family situation.

To Charles Monteith

8 August 1959   Ts   Faber

Being aware how much the character and dignity of Faber book production are valued, I make this following query very tentatively. By separate post I am sending you the proof of an engraving—actually a representation of the deadly sin Avarice—by Leonard Baskin, the American sculptor and engraver. I'm not sure that he's known at all in England, but over here he's generally considered about the finest engraver alive: you will see from the proof how beautiful and intense and delicate his work is. (He also has a printing press—The Gehenna Press. His books are collector's items.) He is interested in my poems, particularly this last lot, and suggested that he might do a sort of emblem for the book. He is thinking of a wolf's head, within a circle— quite small, perhaps an inch in diameter. I realise that to include such a design—either on the jacket and the title page or just on the title page— would be less a modification of your style than a clear departure from it. But Baskin is an extraordinary artist, and as he is so perfectly tasteful and experienced in these matters, and as I feel something in the inner nature of his work is so kin to the inner nature of my own (quality apart), I would like to know what the Faber council thinks of my enquiry.

Charles Monteith (1921–95) was TH's editor at Faber and Faber, and his main contact with the firm until Monteith's retirement in 1981. The letter from which this paragraph is taken deals primarily with Faber's acceptance of TH's new collection of poems. Although the Feast of Lupercal was connected symbolically and etymologically with the she-wolf that fostered Rome's founders, Romulus and Remus, no wolf-design of Baskin's was incorporated in the Faber edition.

To Edith and William Hughes

[Summer 1959]   Ms   Emory

As we entered the park we were given a leaflet informing us the bears were not to be fed, were to be avoided etc, but within ¼ of a mile of the entrance we saw a bear's backside filling a turned over trash-can, while a whole party of folk were sitting eating their lunch at picnic tables nearbye. We saw 19 bears in the 30 or so miles between the Park entrance & the place we camped. They lay on the roadside or even in the driving lane. One or two had little cubs. Cars stopped at every one, & people took pictures & threw sandwiches. Our first night I was wakened by the clatter of the trash-can lids as the bears did their rounds. The trash-cans within the camps are buried, with lids like man-holes, but the bears open them up, scoop everything out & sort through it carefully. There was a trash-can 10 ft from our tent, another two across the way, another one a little further up. I heard them "sniff, sniff, sniff" around the tent. The first day—the one on which I began this letter—we went fishing on the lake, caught 6 trout fairly easily. We cooked them all, make it easier to keep what we couldn't eat immedi-ately. Tuesday we went round the park looking at the geysers, whole valleys are full of these things—most are just holes in the caked white ground—steaming, & bubbling water, a really hellish landscape, sul-phur smell. Now & again one will begin to froth & jet, then burst up in a tower of water—boiling. Some go off in steady jets, others in succes-sive explosions, some are regular & play every hour or 5 hours or once a day, others are irregular & play any time. Some haven't played for 50 years, others began only last year. Some of them, when they're not playing, are caverns of blue steaming slightly boiling water, others are white empty bottomless caves. One or two boil coloured mud, one is just a crevice of erupting black mud. We got back very late from that trip, & drove the last twenty miles with the petrol tank registering empty. But we did get back, & there was a big black bear upended in our trash can. He ran off among the tents as we pulled up. All night the bears were sniffing round. About 3 a.m. I awoke to a sudden crash. We leave most of our stuff out on the table, & I imagined a bear had knocked our pans off. Other bumps & thumps followed—from the direction of the car, then the sound of a tin being rolled. Sylvia could see the bear eating at something. I was sure it had opened the boot & got at our food supply—it sounded to be dragging out such heavy things. It went back to the car "sniff, sniff"—more bumps followed. I looked out & saw it looking through the far rear window. As I watched it got down & wandered away up the camp—a huge brown bear. We thought better of going out to see what it had done. We could hear the bears working the camp over, clattering pans off tables & opening trash cans. An hour later the bear came back to our car. It was clear that it had got into the back window now. We heard it sucking at our oranges. Once a car went past & the bear ran to hide behind our tent—hitting a guy rope & shaking the whole place. As it got lighter the bear finally wandered off. I went out & found that it had torn out the rear side window: we must have left it a fraction of an inch open. It had lifted out Sylvia's red bag, opened a tin of biscuits in there & eaten them all. Then it had pulled out a bag of oranges & crunched & sucked each one. That was all. I don't know what most of the knockings & tearings were—it sounded to be tearing the whole car apart. Next morning Sylvia was talking to a woman in the wash-room who had come over from one of the other camps because of the bears there. She & her husband had meant to sleep in the open, just in sleeping bags. On their first night a woman from a tent about 50 yards away went out in the dark to scare a bear from her pans. (People get very familiar with them, usually they will run off if you shout & clatter a pan, & most of the time they behave like great tame dogs). This bear she shone her flashlamp at (a foolish enough thing but people do it often enough) whereupon it came straight at her & killed her on the spot. That was the Sunday night we came into the park. The woman who told Sylvia this had spent the following nights curled up in her car. The following nights we smeared kerosene round the windows, & draped a kerosene rag over the broken window—a tip we learned too late—and were troubled by no more bears. We saw 67 in all, while we were in the park. The following day we moved to a place further from trash cans. The bears came that night before dark, & people were chasing them through the camp, clattering pans. They'd all heard of our window, you see, & were nervous. But the next night they'd forgotten. The brown bear arrived about 7-30. Some child shouted "Here he is." People stood round in a group watching him methodically emptying trash cans, then, as it got a bit darker, they began shining their lights on him & taking flash photographs. So somebody else will get killed up there soon I suppose.

From Yellowstone National Park, Wyoming. Sylvia Plath used some of the details of these events in her story 'The Fifty-Ninth Bear' (1959), in which a wife and husband engage in the competitive counting of bears, until number fifty-nine kills the husband. TH's poem 'The 59th Bear', in *Birthday Letters*, reflects on the 'need' in Plath that 'Transformed our dud scenario into a fiction'.

To Aurelia and Warren Plath

14 August 1959   Ms   Lilly Library

> As we crawled over Nevada's oven top
> Honky tonks & mirages drank our drop;
> God knows California was one itch
> Of sunburn lotion, bugs, and the lousily rich;
> Burned black, bled white, we fled fast into Texas,
> There dust & dulness came near to annex us;
> Next, in Louisiana's leafy slum
> We stewed our bones, being to great poverty come;
> Setting our noses North for Tennessee
> We proceed, on irreducible hand & knee.

Lines on the back of a postcard mailed in Sewanee, Tennessee.

To Daniel Huws

3 December 1959   Ms   Huws

Dear Dan,

Thankyou for the letter, and for the invitation—which I would like to accept. I'll ring you up as soon as we get in London. If you don't have a phone, we'll just come—don't be bothered about missing us, I still have a key and we could sit on the stair. The boat gets in on the 14th of December, and it should be in the afternoon. We should get to London about 6.

This trip is nicely in time. Another year in America would have worked a permanent petrifaction on my glands. As it is I'm recovering already—more vitality & zest than I've had since I left England.

I have a book of short poems coming out in April or thereabouts—much better than my earlier ones, but all gravely crippled by the awful emotional dryness I've felt over here. Also, this type of exile has driven me to nostalgic themes, and altogether I feel as if my brain had been bound up in sewn leather. Most of the poems are metaphors for this state of psychic hibernation. I was noting the other day which ones had reference to Graves' White Goddess, and out of 41 pieces there are only about 6 that are not direct representation of her or her victims.

Sylvia is pregnant & should be delivering some time in March. It's wonderful how the prospect of such responsibilities concentrates one's mind. After a trip to see Luke I think we shall live in London. See what can be done again with life there.

I was interested to read your remark about Mac. Is he living in Cambridge? And Lyde? Sylvia detests Lyde.

Is your study of other languages than Ancient Welsh & Irish? Are you still hopeful of doing something in the museum. If you were I imagine this year will be a useful qualification. With your Saturn opposition I imagine you're having to force your way.

I met one of these new English novelists the other day—Andrew Sinclair, who was the editor of Granta in 1955. He's about 24 & has written 3 novels. There's a whole literary generation spluttered into presence since Colin Wilson, apparently, all taken very seriously & all committed to combining Christ Kierkergaard & the daily mirror in their own persons. This Sinclair was quite nice. He spoke of the others with despair.

I look forward to a glass of beer—the beer over here is unspeakable & unspewable,—like the sucking of pennies. I got a letter from Dan Weissbort, who seems to have been going through a trying time, but haven't heard from Than.—to whom I owe perhaps 3 letters.

I hope Mary & Helga are thriving. Which part of Rugby St do you live in? Up or down. However, it's nice to hear you're extending properties. I hope I can manage the same, in time. Greetings to Helga & Mary till we see you

Ted

TH and Plath had been invited to stay with the Huwses at 18 Rugby Street on their return from the USA, and they did so while they looked for their own place to live.

Andrew Sinclair (b.1935) and Colin Wilson (b.1931) had both enjoyed precocious successes: the first with his novels *The Breaking of Bumbo* and *My Friend Judas,* and the second with the best-selling socio-philosophical tract *The Outsider.*

1960

On their return to Britain, TH and Sylvia Plath set about the exhausting and dispiriting task of looking for a London home, somewhere they could afford to live and work. In the end – with the help of W. S. Merwin and his English wife Dido, whom they had met in Boston, through the Sweeneys, and who were to become close friends during their time in London – they found a small flat at 3 Chalcot Square, NW1, close to Primrose Hill. Immediate prospects were the birth of their first child, expected at the end of March, and the publication of *Lupercal* in April. Completed in the last months of 1959, Plath's first collection, *The Colossus*, did not yet have a publisher, but it would be out, with Heinemann, in October.

To Chou Wen-chung

1 January 1960   Ts   Paul Sacher Foundation

Dear Wen-chung,

Thank you for the long letter. I will say immediately that I regard your suggestion of the two themes as a gift from the Powers. Both my dramatic and poetic interests direct me straight toward such work.

I am acquainted with both books. I once made a small selection from the Jatarka stories.

If you could sketch out your own rough ideas about the form, sequence of parts, and length of these two pieces, I could begin to work up my own ideas accordingly. Then we could correspond regularly as the text grows in more detail. Even if you eventually decide you cannot use what I produce, I shall not regret the time and concentration spent on such work. You can be sure I shall not offer you anything that disappoints me. By May or June it should be clear whether my text is going to interest you, and whether we can work together.

You will see that I am already in Europe. After you left Yaddo the weather turned to more or less steady downpour and our numbers washed away to a bare six. Still, I got a great deal done—my play, among other things. The play is, I believe, unperformable save as a curiosity, but among its extravagances I did achieve here and there what I set out to do. I will send you some of the pages. After a year or two at other things I shall rewrite it, and pull it into a shape which will, I think, be much more interesting to you than the one it's in at present.

I was pleased to see your work so well received in San Francisco. I have plenty of respect for certain modern composers, but it is very rare that any of their music strikes my imagination directly and makes me wish to have it as part of my life. Your own music did strike me in this way. Nothing could please me more than that we should combine successfully in these two proposed works. The astrological aspects for initiating this are pretty good, whatever else. Let's hope they have some significance.

Meanwhile, I wish you a very happy and productive New Year,

Ted

The Chinese-born composer Chou Wen-chung (b.1923) had lived and worked in the USA since 1946. TH and Plath had met him at Yaddo. He had proposed to TH that they work together on musical settings of two texts, the Jataka stories – Sanskrit tales illustrating precepts of Mahayana Buddhism – and the *Bardo Thödol* (or *Tibetan Book of the Dead*), of which the latter was his own more urgent priority. TH produced an ambitiously conceived libretto later in 1960 (see Daniel Weissbort's *Ted Hughes: Selected Translations*), but for practical reasons the score was never written.

To Aurelia and Warren Plath

11 January 1960   Ms   Lilly Library

One of our worries, over the past two weeks, has been how you must be worrying about our not writing. However, you would excuse us if you could have seen our tribulations. I don't think there's been any period in my life when I felt luck to be so against me. The series of strokes of sheer ill-luck began to look like some deliberate superhuman conspiracy against us. We searched London from top to bottom—flats opened & closed, always just behind us or just in front of us. This would have been bad enough if we had been sitting in an office watching them flicker on and off as small lights on a large mural map of London. But we were running the enormous distances between chance & chance—often on foot, which was exhausting, sometimes by taxi, which took all our money. Added to that was a cold spell equal to anything I felt in America. However, we finally ran something to earth, or I hope we did. I put my signature to the lease, though considering the frightful competition for flats in London, and the general trend of our luck, I wouldn't be a bit surprised to find that some desperate ruthless customer had bribed us out of place. It's a pleasant very light flat with one bedroom, one living room, one kitchen, and a bathroom. We would have preferred one more room, but flats are not to be had for the wishing, and several circumstances convinced me that it would be foolish to prolong our search. The main one being, of course, March 27ᵗʰ.

TH and Plath were expecting their first child to be born on 27 March, but Frieda Rebecca arrived on 1 April. Her birth is described in TH's letter to Lucas Myers of 22 April.

To David Gerard

2 February 1960   Ts   David Gerard

Dear Mr. Gerard,
   It is very gratifying to reach such a reader as yourself, who are aware enough of my 'bangs' and my various literary debts (to Hopkins among the rest) without resenting my book for them.
   Since publishing that book I have been able to make an interesting observation. The reviews it received—even the very good ones—did not help at all. When I think of them I feel chilled with the whole writing business: something to do with the 'official' air they have, the exposed public tribunal atmosphere. But when I think of the various letters I have had from readers I have never met I feel a distinct urge to begin writing more, at once. This relationship with unknown readers, being secret and conspiratorial, is apparently a very natural part of the underground operations that poetry seems to demand.
   Yes, the Hughes strain is partly Welsh.
   Thank you again for your letter,
                                    Sincerely,
                                    Ted Hughes

To Lucas Myers

[Early 1960]   Ms   Emory

I was in the Lamb one night with Dan and we met David Wright. He had read my book—Lupercal—in proof, because he was one of the

156

judges for the Poetry Book Society choice, (which was given to Peter Levi.) He said he didn't like my book—"too American"—and so downed it, he "thought it oughtn't to be encouraged." This to my face—enough of a draught of that sad circle for me. The other judge was J.C. Hall, who had attacked the Hawk in the R. What a dim muddy glow there is lighting this goldfish bowl of the English intelligentsia. Nothing exists for them later than 1948, or outside the Charing Cross noise perimeter. America—the word itself, pronounced, acts on them like an obscene private joke. Europe is a "hard cutaneous" area over the two frontal lobes. They are damply steaming compost of bile, saliva, & disinte-grated copies of Penguin New Writing,—the pustulence of their own canker, the fungi that sits & swells & sweats & stinks wherever English literature is gathered together.

David Wright (1920–94), South African-born poet, had moved to Britain before the Second World War. His 'sad circle' included such poets as George Barker and John Heath-Stubbs.

To John Lehmann

9 April 1960   Ts   Texas

Dear Mr Lehmann,

   I am very conscious of the honour you do me, inviting me to review for The London Magazine. I would have answered earlier, but we received a baby daughter on April Fool's morning and that seems to have kept things busy.

   Of the Critical Literature produced over the last six or eight years I am almost completely ignorant and feel it would be an injustice to the authors of such works if I were to begin reviewing their books now. If, however, you should occasionally receive Folk-Lore studies or collections, song or ballad collections, or books on Pre-Christian, Eastern or Primitive Religion to review, I would be thankful for the chance to try my hand at them. I imagine you don't often get that sort of thing, though, which is a pity: one of the most interesting literary events, for me, of the fifties—Paul Radin's "Trickster Cycle of the Winnebago Indians"—crept out into a few libraries as if it were a work only for the most curious kind of scholar.

Thank you again, for the invitation.

Sincerely

Ted Hughes

John Lehmann (1907–87) was a dominant literary figure of the time. Associated with the Bloomsbury Group in his youth, he founded the magazine *New Writing* in 1936 – it became *Penguin New Writing* in the war years – and was later editor of the *London Magazine*. TH went on to place poems and stories with the *London Magazine*, but wrote no reviews for it.

To Lucas Myers

22 April 1960   Ms   Emory

Dear Luke,

On the 31st of March the weather, which had been draughty, sleety, & treacherous, turned very mild—and there was a delicate spring evening of the most delicious sort. So we walked out & across Regent's Park. Sylvia felt very well,—impatient. At 1-45 in the morning she awoke, & said she thought it had begun—everything was wet. So she padded around, grumbling. She had just recovered from 2 weeks flu, and after several nights of no sleep had taken two sleeping pills. She was so determined not to have the infant on April Fool's day that she felt sure she wouldn't and, so, that she could safely take these pills. The contractions began almost at once, 15 minutes apart. I rang up the midwife who rode leisurely across London on her bicycle—just to make sure that "things got going nicely" and intending to go back, finish her sleep, have her breakfast & return about 9 with anaesthetics & so on. The contractions were soon coming every 5 or 10 minutes, stronger & stronger & more & more painful, apparently. Sylvia was quite depressed—she thought this was just the first stages of something that was going to go on for 20 hours or so. The midwife was a little Indian woman, very good & sensible, but adamant, obviously, for natural drugless childbirth. She was thinking of going off again at about 4 when Sylvia said she wanted to push—this desire comes as the beginning of the next stage. The midwife examined her inside & out & said O.K. she could push. The next minute she showed me the black hairs on top of the baby's head—& showed it to Sylvia in a mirror, very merrily. Apparently the main pain stage is over when they begin to push & the pushing itself seems to be a relief. She rang up the doctor, who had no anaesthetics—being at home—either. However, he came along. The effect of the sleeping pills seemed to be wearing off, so Sylvia could cooperate—the business is like backing a lorry round a tight bend in a narrow alley full of parked cars. When the mother is stupified with drugs—the usual condition, especially en Amerique—she can do nothing, perhaps not even push, and everything has to be done in a numb fumbling half-lit way. But they seemed to know just when to tell her to stop, to start, to lean over a little. The baby's head appeared like a mushroom & the midwife guided it every second. Then all at once it slid clean out—looking exactly like a pink translucent balloon, baby-shape, smeared all over with a whitish cream like wet flour. The cord was round its neck, but not tightly. A little girl. In the same second that it came clear it gave a little sneeze, and muttered to itself & began to move its fingers. The afterbirth came five minutes later. The whole business took 4½ hours—which is almost record time. The baby opened its eyes a few minutes after that. Sylvia was amazed. So was I. There is something intensely surprising about seeing it appear. Also something infinitely disastrous & shocking about it—even about this very unmessy one. What worked on her, I hope, were my hypnotisings. For the past month I've been putting her to sleep at nights—telling her to lose her toes, release her feet, so on, up her body, telling her she's getting sleepy, can't open her eyes etc, to relax & relax & relax, & that she's going to have an easy short delivery, that she can leave it all to the spirit who has it in hand etc. You might try it with Cynthia, if she's suggestible. What makes me think it partly worked is that I've been able to have her do other things, have her period start at a certain time & be over in two days, so on. Our Frieda Rebecca is beautiful of course [. . .]

As ever   Ted

To Olwyn Hughes

[May 1960]   Ms   Emory

We had dinner with Eliot & Spender & their wives—very pleasant. Eliot is whimsical & pleasant—at the same time very remote. He talks staring at the floor between his feet—when he's sitting—& looks up only to smile at his wife. His smile is like that of a person recovering from some serious operation. Spender chattered so much that he wrote us a letter afterwards apologising—but he was charming, I didn't expect to like him at all & found him almost congenial. They talked—exclusively—of the Bloomsbury group & its satellites, literary gossip. Eliot isn't at all unguarded in his remarks. He has huge thick hands—unexpected.

The dinner party, at the home of T. S. Eliot and his wife Valerie, was on 4 May.

To Esther and Leonard Baskin

14 May 1960   Ts   British Library

Dear Esther & Leonard,

We're finally established here, in a small flat in one of the most interesting corners of London—Victorian genteel houses overtaken by an Irish, Greek, Cypriot & Italian creeping damp. We have 5 square miles of lush grass, containing flowery trees, bird sanctuary, hill overlooking all London, excellent zoo, starting within 100 yards. We hear the seals regularly & occasionally the lions & wolves. All this within about 10 minutes of the centre.

On April 1st, at 5:45, Sylvia produced a little girl. She's pleased with herself since she had it at home, without anaesthetic, in 4½ hours, and one hour later got up and phoned her mother in America, & has been in pristine form ever since. We call the girl Frieda Rebecca—using Rebecca. Visitors comment on her mouth—very delicately & voluptuously formed at this stage—and her eyes which are enormous & stare intently like a bird's. She's just begun to smile—she's generally very good.

Up to the birth of Rebecca our life was a scramble—to find a place to live, to furnish it—after a fashion—to decorate it & so on. Inner life decamped. Now I'm trying to get one or two things going again & was thinking the other day about the Metamorphoses. My book came out a couple of weeks ago—with a very simple inoffensive cover. I sent a copy off which you should be getting any day. One or two people have criticised the cover for lack of imagination. Some of the printing—see the third poem—is lousy.

We got a handsome picture of Seated Man With Owl, from <u>Time</u>, I think. How would you go about getting your things shown over here?

160

We would like a catalogue of your works, if there is one, the catalogue of the ones you've priced.

I suppose Tobias is now a boy—as distinct from a baby, I mean. It's surprising how they change every single day: you feel you could really educate them now if only you knew the right symbols. Probably if you let them watch sunrise every morning, flew them over the city in a balloon, kept them in a purple room, let them sleep among cattle & so on—these memories as they got buried would become nuclei for unique regions of mind & spiritual gifts. But instead you just let them go on squalling. Though Rebecca is very attentive to singing.

We were wondering how the night-creature book got on. Did I tell you how Emilie McLeod coached my children's book up to the last stage, then decided that she wanted the whole thing different—frightened of the big words. She seems more interested in yours though, & we want to know how it goes on.

You must be enjoying your trees & garden again now. One of these days—now that I'm organised—I intend to look up all the back numbers of the appropriate magazines & find photographs of vermin-poles in the hopes of starting you off on something.

Love to you both, & Tobias
from the three of us,
Ted

To Graham Ackroyd

20 May 1960   Ts   Victoria

Dear Mr. Ackroyd,

Your letter gave me a great deal of pleasure & I liked your paintings—particularly the Death of Bird on Country Lane. I don't know why death should interest us so much. Perhaps, with the collapse of every belief & the nuclear disenchantment of every hope, death remains as the one invariable, the one indestructible thing in Creation. The one image of the truth.

I would be honoured to hang one of your paintings on my wall. The only decorations I have are a wood-engraving of Tobias and the Angel—who looks more like the Angel of Death—and a woodcut of a dead boar—both by Leonard Baskin, the American artist, whose theme is exclusively death.

You must live in a pleasant place, if pheasants walk on your lawn.
Sincerely,
Ted Hughes

Graham Ackroyd (b.1920) is both a poet and a painter. In a later letter, not included here, TH gave him advice about finding a gallery in London to show his work.

To W. S. and Dido Merwin

[June 1960]   Ts   Emory

Except for three days during the moon's negotiations with Saturn which were properly cold and wet we have had a beautiful May—the one month I would not happily spend outside England. Blossoms, gardens, perfumes, loaded trees, deep grass, people lying about half naked. I spent the first two weeks in the study immunising myself from the books. Since then things have gone smoothly and I think I may have finished my tragifarcical melodrama in very rough slovenly verse. It materialises uncertainly somewhere between a mime of supernatural essences and a Peter Ustinov fantasy—the Ustinov type being a genre I detest. This piece has a sort of extravagance of language and emotion which gives it some life. Also, not until I was casting about for the right way to end it did it begin to dawn on me what the whole thing was really about: it had seemed to fall into two very separate halves, but in fact at the mid point it simply turns over, and the person who dominates the first half in one form is the same as the one who dominates the second half in another: his relationship throughout is with one woman. This is very vague. If Sasha Moorsom thinks it recoverable and a possible programme I will try and get a copy to send you.

We went the other night to see the Pinter play, The Caretaker, which has been so much praised. It was entertaining in a light way but then from the half way mark boring. The theme is his usual one: the id emerging in some decrepit disgusting vindictive form and threatening the isolated dried-up ego. This is really the English subject at present, the national malady being the awful inadequacy of the public school ego-kit, the do-it-yourself perfect gentleman kit, its point-of-death isolation, and the corresponding shrinkage and forlorn rottenness of the national id so that the whole outfit resembles the stuffed head of a white walrus mounted on the tail of a bad herring. The failure of

Pinter's plays, as far as I'm concerned, lies in his utter lack of any imaginative dimension, the obviousness of the Jungian ego-id formula, and the triteness of his language, or rather the triteness of the experience of his characters. The wit is very sharp in a drawing room comedy way and you laugh at it readily—flattered to know that something very ominous is intended also. Afterwards, you go off with an impression of the lightest entertainment.

Written when the Merwins were in France. During their absence from London, TH had been encouraged to use W. S. Merwin's study in St George's Terrace, near Chalcot Square, and Sylvia Plath had begun to write her novel *The Bell Jar* there.

Sasha Moorsom (1931–93) was a BBC radio producer.

The Caretaker, by Harold Pinter (b.1930), had opened at the Duchess Theatre, London, on 30 May. Combined with the report that 'we have had a beautiful May', this suggests a date in early June.

To Olive Higgins Prouty

21 June 1960   Ts   Lilly Library

Dear Mrs Prouty,

By now you will have the notes for LUPERCAL. Your long letter came this morning and made me realise that in those notes I haven't answered most of the things you will be curious about. You really are a gratifyingly intensive reader. Your remark about the tramps surprised me, but it's quite true. The notes should give a sort of broad background for each poem, somewhere to start from. The other little knots I'll have to unravel as you point them out. For instance, the last four lines in the book mean

"Maker of the world
(who conduct the living spark of man's spirit
from generation to generation, throughout the ages,
as long as man goes on being born into a body)

Touch this woman, whose spirit seems dead, and kindle
her with the living spark.

The book is being well-received here and I believe they're reprinting it, which means it's had an unusual sale for poetry (though not many compared with other sorts of books, perhaps 1500)

Our flat is at its best, with a view onto thick leaves at front and back. The park nearbye is blooming, we're in the middle of a heat wave, American temperatures, and little Frieda Rebecca has discovered that she needn't squawl at the top of her voice to make her sounds—she's found her talking voice and is inventing curious new noises every day, quite like a language at times. Sylvia is sitting here feeding her and she looks all round wildly with her great popping blue eyes. She smiles now whenever you smile at her, and sometimes even when you speak her name. Sylvia is marvellous with her,—no fuss, very efficient and endlessly patient. We've been taking photographs and if any come out we'll send you one.

The park here is much larger than Boston common—it must be several square miles and has wide beds of roses that are now full out. We go out there and sit and read and sometimes picnic. The other day we gave ourselves a party with a bottle of champagne my sister sent us. From our hill—Primrose Hill—you can see the whole of London lying like a small-scale map, St Paul's seems to be just below us, though in fact it's half an hour away by tube.

Sylvia is at last getting back to writing two or three hours a day. W.S. Merwin—an american poet who married a sort of English Society woman a good deal older than himself—has lent us his study. His wife owns a large house about three hundred yards away and theyve both gone off to France for the summer. They have a farm in the country there (they don't farm it, just live and laze there, and let the local peasants farm it.) They will be away until September. So now Sylvia goes to the study in the morning and I go in the afternoon. I've written a verse-play which may be good for something, and now I'm going to try and get another going. This is what I would really like to do and it's a matter of time. Verse plays are a puzzle because nobody has written one that has established a method and form. So you have to invent right from the start, picking a hint up here and another there.

On Thursday we're going to meet the poet W.H. Auden—the same firm publishes his books and mine, and we're invited to a cocktail party given in his honour. We've been to one of these parties before. There is unlimited champagne, the main attraction.

Did Sylvia tell you about the Somerset Maugham Award? It's a sum of money which I <u>must</u> use abroad, for not less than three consecutive months, sometime in the next three years. I wrote and thanked him and received a pleasant note back. He says he will be coming to England the end of the summer and hopes we can meet. So we'll give you a detailed account of that.

Are you going away for the summer? I think we shall sit tight for another eighteen months at least, and think over the removals, tours, visits, spectacles, departures and arrivals of the last nine months, which have been crammed as never before. I hope we shall write something: we'll keep you supplied with copies of whatever appears.

Sylvia joins in sending love,

Ted

Olive Higgins Prouty's 'remark about the tramps' probably relates to TH's poem 'November', in *Lupercal*. The last three-and-a-half lines in the book go: 'Maker of the world, / Hurrying the lit ghost of man / Age to age while the body hold, / Touch this frozen one.'

The park is Regent's Park, the far side of Primrose Hill from Chalcot Square.

TH had heard about the Somerset Maugham Award, given for *The Hawk in the Rain*, in March.

To Olwyn Hughes

[Summer 1960]   Ms   Emory

Our objection to Auden wasn't to his sloppy slippers—it was the inner circle at Smith sacked him because of those. My objection to Auden, & Sylvia's I think too, is to so much of his poetry, as you say yours is. As a person he seems to be very engaging—I say this after reading an essay by him in Encounter, on Falstaff. At the Faber party I scarcely spoke to him, since he was overpowered by the Blue-haired hostesses that seem to run those meetings. Sylvia talked quite a lot to McNeice & Spender, and I talked to Eliot. Auden has a strangely wrinkled face, like a Viking seaman—that sort of tan & wrinkles. Like a reptile—though not squamous, not unpleasant. Lively brown eyes. The impression was pleasant. Spender was drunk—silly-giddy like Mabel Brown at her 9 year old birthday party. McNeice was drunk & talked like a quick-fire car salesman. Hedli Anderson, the singer, was there—trophy from the Spanish Civil War—drunk, her green eyelids coming up seconds too slow & not quite far enough. Eliot has been ill. His wife was supporting him. She is so Yorkshire you would smile. [. . .] He holds her hand or stands with his arm around her. We talked about the need to have a job in country's not your own if you are to see it other than as a tourist; of Coleridge's grave—which was in the playground of a school where he taught, though he didn't know it at the time; of Criterion—for which, he said, he did most of his reading, & for which he wrote many of his essays; of his smaller poems—like the 'landscapes'—I asked him if these were a picking of a great number of such short poems, but he said no, they are the lot; & of verse-plays—he said he was writing another or thinking about it, and I promised to let him see my piece. I felt to get on so well with him—though he's charitable & tactful & no doubt gives most people the feeling—that I must send him my play then go talk to him about it, as he invited me to.

[. . .]

Have you ever read Emily Dickinson's poetry? I've just rediscovered her. She wrote hundreds & hundreds of these small incredible poems— lived a more or less isolated spinsterish life in the small churchy town of Amherst, in Mass.—contemp of the Brontes, save that she lived to 56. I've just known small selections of her poems before—but now I've got hold of a volume. The most unself-conscious poetry ever, the most intensely occupied with her thought,—Shakespearean language & genuine. Makes Crowe Ransome etc seem like Museum pieces. I will send you some.

The Faber reception at which W. H. Auden, Louis MacNeice and Stephen Spender were guests was held on 23 June. Auden had spent two months in 1953 as a visiting lecturer at Smith College, on one occasion reading his poems to an audience that included Sylvia Plath, but there is no record of his exclusion by the 'inner circle' there. Both TH and Olwyn Hughes in fact admired many aspects of Auden's poetry.

To John, Nancy, Angela and Francis Fisher

31 July 1960   Ms   Angela Fisher

Dear John, & Nancy & Angela & Francis,

In your present after-term invalid state I imagine you'll feel more like receiving a letter than writing one. Suspended now till the results I suppose—that sudden revelation of traitors & secret sympathisers.

I don't know whether we shall be able to manage it, with our new daughter, but I would like to come up through Mexborough this August. Are you going on holiday? If you could let me know what dates you'll not be at home I could arrange our visit to avoid those. Our time, at present, is free. I don't know when employment's going to force our defences, but certainly not before October.

This Spring I've been trying to write a few things, but as usual most of the time seems to have frittered itself away. I wrote a tragi-farcical melodrama in verse, fairly fantastic, which the B.B.C. will put on in Autumn. I wrote it at great heat, but now I'm not so sure. Because it moves in a super-real dimension, a sort of dream dimension, it seems over emotional & over-eloquent, but there's no poetic drama in any other dimension, as far as I can see. Normal people don't speak like that, but the stresses that break them down from within are trying to get things expressed in even more violent & complete language. Realistic drama seems to me to leave the reality unexpressed & I mean also unsuggested. But that is no competitor to poetic drama, any more than Mrs Dale's diary is—though that fascinates people too. People are fascinated picking their fingers.

We live very quietly here. After a great effort, I excluded myself from the literary world. Now we see just our friends. Once you've written a book, the possibilities of dissipation are terrifying. There are cocktail parties at Faber & Faber now & again & we go there because the champagne is plentiful. We met Auden there at the last one, though I hardly spoke to him, and McNeice to whom I didn't speak either though Sylvia talked to him about half an hour. Spender was there, like a silly giggly girl. And Eliot was there with his wife, so I mainly spoke to Eliot. I've met him three times now—the first time we scarcely spoke, the second time was at his home, for dinner, with Spender, and the whole evening went under a torrent of Bloomsbury chat from Spender, but this third time I was able to communicate and he seemed to be getting used to me. He speaks just as he reads his poems, funereal & measured. He seems very old, & is supposed to be quite ill, though I believe he's always been supposed to be quite ill.

I occasionally see poems by Massingham in magazines & so on. What is he doing now? Do you have any new bright sparks?

If I were rich enough I would send the school a copy of Emily Dickinson's collected works—burial of the axe. I feel there is an axe to be buried—indeed, I feel part of it in my head. However, as I'm not so rich I'm sending a volume under my own pseudonym. My relationship with that Grammar School has been thrust back at me again & again since I saw you at Xmas, till it's grown almost to a problem.

Are you all well? I don't suppose I shall recognise Angela & Francis, though I'm sure Mexborough & its approaches haven't changed much.

We call our daughter Frieda—after an Aunt of Sylvia's, sole survivor of her father's family. And curiously enough the only person our Frieda shows any resemblance to at all is her namesake. She's very lively & very merry & a great blessing, in the real sense.

I'm enclosing a bagatelle—the first part & the last part I wrote when she was new. The middle part when she was a bit more humanised. I don't know what you make of my more recent poems, I suspect you'll like them less and less—some of them seem very odd to me.

Well, we look forward to seeing you

Edward

At Mexborough Grammar School, John Fisher (1914–80) had been TH's English teacher from the 5th form onwards, and it was he who effectively – to use TH's word, reported to the editor by Fisher's daughter Angela – 'shoe-horned' him into Cambridge, sending a selection of his pupil's poems to back up his application to Pembroke. Another of Fisher's gifted pupils had been the poet Harold Massingham (b.1932).

TH's 'tragi-farcical melodrama' was *The House of Aries*, which Sasha Moorsom was to produce for the BBC. *Mrs Dale's Diary* was a genteel radio soap opera.

To Aurelia and Warren Plath

22 August 1960   Ms   Lilly Library

Dear Sylvia's Mother & Warren,

Well, here we are at The Beacon. A necessary holiday, I think. London seems to be a load on the nerves, even when you live as quietly as we do. On my birthday we went up to Hampstead Heath—a stretch of country 2 tube-train stops North of us—with a bottle of wine, a bowlful of salad, and a chicken & ham pie from the food-shop in Piccadilly, Fortnum & Masons, which caters I've no doubt specifically for the royal family & the American Ambassador—deep carpets, sturgeon's tongues, bowing uniformed attendants, cassowary brains in melon syrup. Our chicken pie is one of my three favourite foods—the other 2 vary according to what Sylvia is cooking next, but the Fortnum & Mason pie stands firm. On Hampstead Heath, after regaling ourselves & reciting our triumphs of the year, we fell into a drowse so deep & pervading that I was made curious—I never relax like that even in bed.

Then it occurred to me that we were, for the first time in 6 months, out of the constant half-audible rumble of the huge wheel of London, and were under trees. That decided me that we need a holiday. So here we are at the Beacon. We've spent this first 24 hours in bottomless torpor, sucking in this enormous blissful silence.

I think this must be the most beautiful spot in England—how you'll love it next summer! You must come up here, instead of challenging the map of Europe, and stay for a week or two. Ma & Pa are looking better than they have for years. Correspondingly, the garden here is just one blaze. My mother is a random gardener, but persistent, and the house is surrounded by flowers—roses at the window, honeysuckle on the walls. To celebrate our arrival, a mole threw up two hillocks on the lawn this morning—the first mole this year, and a snipe—a very shy & quite uncommon moorbird—landed in front of the house. The silence here is overpowering—because the hills seem to embody it—you can see it—everything is spellbound by it. The nearest approach to it is in the far West, where the prairies had the same feeling. When you leave the door open here it seems to come right into the house. Sylvia is in raptures, she hasn't been so exalted since we came to England. And little Frieda's response is to sleep & sleep & be no trouble at all. We have some very true-to-life photos of her now, which will make you proud. In one of them she looks extremely like Aunt Frieda.

Sylvia had a letter the other day from Harper's asking if she was thinking of making a book of stories or a novel—they had seen her story in the London Magazine. And she sold two poems—just exercises—to the New Yorker. I wish we had a place up here to spend the odd summer months in—the inspirations would flow.

Tonight Sylvia got my Dad talking about his experiences in the 1st War—that always starts a great entertainment. It's quite amazing how whole evenings pass away in this kind of reminiscence—all the past is raked up as something intensely interesting & highly amusing. It isn't that they live in the past at all, but the whole past is kept alive & very present. It's the sort of thing I miss very much when we're in London, and now Sylvia's getting addicted to it.

We have both, with a great shock, discovered Emily Dickinson. There is a 3 volume edition of her poems & I would like to get it for Sylvia's birthday, so if you could casually mention the price of it I will order & have it sent from a New York bookshop. She's America's greatest poet, without a doubt. Now this is all about <u>us</u>. How is the summer? Keep in the sun. Love from us all,

Ted.

To Olwyn Hughes

[Undated 1960]   Ms   Emory

Thistles was a sort of Picasso thistles—the plant, you see, from an academic point of view, being the nucleus of associations on the whole more important in the piece than the plant. Also a sort of Walt Disney thistles, and Klee thistles. Not really thistles. Their plume isn't red, each has several plumes, etc. It's a scherzo, not very serious. The idea of the decayed Viking was really the main one—the one I'd had before & been amused by.

'Thistles' appeared in the *Times Literary Supplement* on 9 September.

To Aurelia and Warren Plath

[About 17 December 1960]   Ts   Lilly Library

Dear Aurelia and Warren,

Well, if I were to go through this year in anything approaching detail, it would make a ten volume opus. So much has happened, odd in every way, and life has assumed such imposing forms. It must be the busiest most preoccupied year I've ever spent—bad for some things, rich to look back on.

It's not true that only women have children, for instance. I think the general psychological upheaval is quite as severe for the father. This was complicated, as an illness might be, by the fact that when I got back here (having left in 1957 as a complete unknown) I found myself really quite famous and was deluged by invitations to do this, give readings, do that, meet so-and-so, etc, and many doors were comfortably wide open that I had never dreamed of being able to enter and places such as the B.B.C., which I had been trying to penetrate for years, suddenly received me as guest of honour. Naturally I wanted to take advantage of some of this, telling myself that there was a real advantage there to be taken, and so, besides the profound inner revolution caused by Frieda's arrival, I had to manage also the profound inner revolution of becoming something of a public figure. The first of these revolutions was natural and welcome and good in every way; the second was unnatural, cruelly against myself, and I think cost me a great deal more in the way of energy. So, on the whole, when I look back at this year, I see struggle. However, out of it have come many improvements. I've won both revolutions: the paternal forces are in power, a sort of golden age, and the forces of publicity, exposure to the curious public, acceptance into the circle of complacently pronouncing literary busts, have been routed and crushed. The interference of 'literary life' had begun almost to drain our home. And 'literary life', closely examined, turns out to be a chance juxtaposition of individuals who wish to be known as "writers" held in a semblance of community by the watchfulness of their mutual envy and malice. To enter 'literary life' is in fact to enter a small windowless cell, empty, under a stunning spotlight, and left to your own devices in the knowledge that millions of invisible eyes are watching through the walls. It's not 'life' at all, you see. And it cuts you off from life. However, it had to be tasted at first hand. And I remain with the few possibly real advantages, such as very good contacts with the B.B.C., good terms with certain editors and one or two figures in the infinitesimal London grant-giving circle. Though I might have had these anyway.

I mention all that first because it really lies over the whole year like a battlesmoke through which everything else has to be recognised if possible.

Our writing has been bad-good. Bad in this way: Tending Frieda and recovering from having her (and coming to London, scrambling for a flat, decorating it, striking roots through the stonework) really absorbed Sylvia utterly until a month ago. You can imagine she was worried about what might have happened to her writing, fearing that it might have depended on an inner plan which had now been entirely reorganised. However, since then she has written five poems better than anything in her book, and so much larger, with her humour and oddness in them, and completely alive. Also, she has begun to write stories for the Women's Magazines. This is an episode to itself. Sylvia was confused and her writing ambitions to a certain extent corrupted by the Academic taste for the so-called 'art-story'—stories that concentrate on the 'poetical' nuance of a situation or some fashionably frivolous style of treatment. This kind of story had its prestige boom just over the years that Sylvia went to college. Her teachers, misguidedly in my opinion, required this sort of thing of her in classes, and such episodes as Mademoiselle also tended to persuade her that rare and tremendous prestige was waiting for the successful writer of just such pieces. As a result of that 'boom' the literary and arty periodicals of those years are jammed with bits and pieces that now seem absurd, pretentious, artificial, and finally unreadable. This is the kind of story that Sylvia has been telling herself is her kind. The truth is, that her demons are such as can find no place in such stories—she needs stories in which people get killed, get born, get married etc. And I think Women's Magazine stories may well be the means of her learning how to write about life directly and boldly and full-scale. She's going into it with tremendous energy and determination, and this is a definite 'form' of writing, it has a definite audience. Art stories have really no form and nobody really knows what their audience is. This is the first time she's decided to write these. Before, she's always thought that she might write an art story that would somehow also be a Woman's Magazine story and so on. The thing that has really deterred her from writing these stories before is that she had no plots. However, when she says "I want a story about such and such"—indicating some subject very vaguely, then we sit down and within half an hour we have a wonderful vigorous real plot, it just jumps into life between us. So far we've composed four, each one better than the last: neither of us lets the other get away with any absurdity or fogging over of an improbable detail. We work out the characters in detail, the motivation, the setting: we make a clear chart of the moment to moment suspense, the devices for titillating a reader, the concealments and promises and omens that make a reader's imagination supply everything the writing doesn't. And we make sure it has a more or less essential shape, cutting out every piece that doesn't by it's very situation have willy nilly some suspenseful interest. Sylvia has written two of these: the first one she's very pleased with, the second even more. The agreement is that she doesn't show them to me till she gets one published. She has had to change our plots slightly as she wrote—which means that the story took on life and from what she has told me of the changes they are all improvements. This having a plot mapped out in front of her gives her freedom to spread herself and concentrate on the characters and their doings without always worrying about the "effect". Even if these first stories don't sell in their present version, they are all plots which when she's had some experience she will be able to rewrite and sell—they are real plots. So much for Sylvia's writing.

Mine has been somewhat devastated by "literary life" or rather by the inordinate disturbances that such a life sets up in me, so I feel to have done nothing. The little verse-piece for voices which you so generously went to see and make notes on, I wrote in a few days last April. Since then I've written a story called The Harvesting, which is easily my best, I think: it's about a man out shooting a hare who finally seems to turn into the hare—only seems to, I don't make it definite. It's a moral fable, you see: when you hurt something or somebody else, there is also a spirit in you which receives the hurt. (This was really one of the two main ideas at the bottom of The House Of Aries, and if those taking part in the discussion had reread the lines about

"When you shut the door against the face,
Rejecting the beggar's face,
What shape, in your heart's darkness,
Turns away forever."

they would have caught it, but I'll come back to that.)

Besides The Harvesting I wrote a story which should really have been a tour de force, but distractions caused me to betray it. It's about a youth who comes to London and begins to bump into a girl, a particular girl, again and again; everywhere he goes, he sees her, and this particularly upsets and intrigues him because in London one of the terrifying circumstances is that each time you go out you see thousands of faces you have never seen before and will never see again—there is not one of them you will see again or have ever seen before. He begins to think some strange fate is in operation—he begins to think he glimpses the laws behind coincidence etc.. The main character in the story was to be London, just evocations of various parts of London at various times. But I misfired with it. It makes a sort of story, but nothing like it should have been. So, when time comes, I shall rewrite it as it deserves. Besides these two stories (I have ideas for about fifteen) I wrote this oratorio for the Bardo Thodol, The Tibetan Book Of The Dead. I've just sent off a final version. That will be something for you to hear: it's quite awesome. It's the progress of the soul during the 49 days between death and rebirth, a sort of Buddhist Mass. I really enjoyed doing it, though I spent all the summer months just getting the material into shape and telling myself I ought to be working harder at it. However, if the musician, Chou Wen-chung is ready for it, in himself, it could easily be a terrific musical work as it provides wonderful opportunities. He wants to do it

173

with an illuminated backcloth, showing the various deities as they rise before the soul, and the various lighting effects of the different regions through which the soul is driven by his furies, and with a dancer—to mime the events of which the chorus and solo sing. So, when this work is completed you shall both have tickets.

Besides that I've written seven or eight small poems: on the whole a step or two beyond those in my book, but nothing like what I feel like doing.

The House Of Aries ought not to have been acted because (a) there was no action (b) there was no 'character', except perhaps, a little bit, in the Captain (c) the 'argument' was utterly obscure and not to be seen through a stage representation. Finally (d) the thing simply didn't do what it set out to do: I wrote it hastily, even casually, without thinking out its implications, without taking trouble to give it any of the additional interests—such as theatrical ones, for instance—that might have redeemed it. Altogether, I was a bit horrified when I saw what I had let out into the public.

However, for what it was, it amounted to this: the whole second part is, in a very definite sense, Morgan's dream. Now you must excuse me if for a minute I speak a bit pretentiously and give the play an explanation which could not possibly be read into it unless I said that was actually what I was trying to write about: essentially, Morgan I intended to represent, roughly, the discursive sort of intelligence which is separated from the sympathetic emotional life WITHIN THE INDIVIDUAL. Elaine represents that sympathetic emotional life, within the same individual. The other characters represent other 'psychic entities'—the wife is the digestive tract, the mayor the circulatory system and so on. Now, all these characters are created out of a whole—the Self. The great desire of the Self is to act as one, as an undivided being, with all its faculties and processes present and working together. But . . . a big BUT . . . . discursive intelligence has become what it is, helped by the labours of the various thinkers and taught so to each succeeding generation, only by ridding itself of everything unpredictable, obscure, mysterious, ambiguous and emotional. In other words, a division has been created in the Self, between a briskly busy discursive thought-process, logical, with an air of infallibility and precision, arrogant because it thinks it works according to eternal rational laws, and the whole emotional animal life of consciousness which is on the whole impressionable, passive, and only positive in its intuitions—which cannot support

174

themselves with argument—and when its emotions become positive, at which time they are of course anything but reasonable and predictable. So now, the discoursive intelligence is characterised by restless, almost impatient, sometimes even feverish point to point to point activity: it is characterised, in fact, by a curiosity which searches everything that comes before it. What is it looking for and why is it in such a hurry?

This restless 'discoursive rational abstract' mind is supposed to be characteristic of our Western civilisation, and when it's mentioned in that capacity it is also usually described as a symptom of some sort of malaise. Primitive peoples don't possess it, and the great efforts of Eastern philosophers has been spent devising means of getting rid of it. The point is, that this "Morgan" is searching for the SELF, it is searching for reunion with the whole being from which it has become, by its character, cut off. Its activity is desperation, a terrific longing which is always frustrated—always frustrated because as soon as it does approach reunion it becomes frightened: reunion into the Self can only mean the death of its own separate individuality.

So now you have the motivation of Morgan's facetious cruelty toward Elaine. Elaine is not the whole remainder of the Self, of course, but she is the emotional representative of it, and Morgan's spite is turned equally on the wife and the Mayor and the bog. His frustration of course, plus the fear of the reunion that he feels would be his salvation, are the roots of his twisted spite—always directed against the thing he desires and fears.

Now, this is the interior or domestic situation. And this is what the first part is about.

Morgan's frustration builds for itself a dream-figure: an ideal accomplisher of his own desires, a conqueror, smashing down all opposition, taking what he wants with impunity just wherever he wants it, and with the seemingly divine sanction of political law and logical right behind him. This is the Captain. I infer, you see, that militarism is just the public manifestation of the qualities innate in "discoursive intelligence". This ties up with what I was saying earlier: cruelty—wherever it is the cold deliberate 'logical' kind—is an outer manifestation of what is primarily an act of the Morgan against the Elaine, or of the Captain against the Elaine, within the individual. And any person whose intelligence is in fact severely separated from his emotional life is willy nilly a public menace: he automatically projects his inner situation. This is the kind of mind behind the Atomic Bomb, Germ Warfare etc, and behind Science in general, in my opinion. In Jung's opinion too, I believe: no doubt that's where I got the idea. It's the cause of the huge human suspicion of "science"—because the scientific mind must operate, if it is to operate accurately, without the emotional human thing.

Anyway, so much for the House Of Aries. I'm afraid I've been very obscure. And tedious.

You were dear to make notes, Aurelia, and I was really interested to know what they did with it. You were right, you see, about the second part being Morgan's dream. However, I now feel I must instantly redeem myself with a really dramatic play, which is on its way, and perhaps—in the planning of it and writing of the first act—the best thing I have produced this year.

So much for my writing.

I meant to break this letter up into paragraphs, because I know long paragraphs are hard on the attention, single space.

Sylvia has just come back from the B.B.C. where she has been recording her poem A Winter Ship which is to be part of a review broadcast, in which her book is called "the best first volume of poems since, say . . ." then they mention a book published eighteen months ago. Another review I am going out now to try and procure, so that you may have it in this letter.

Dreary dull sky. Black scratchy trees. Smoky housetops. Damp street and square. Nobody about.

Little Frieda is wrestling in her pen. We took her out to tea the other night and she sat on Sylvia's lap, gnawing a rusk, smiling round, humming to herself now and then, watching, <u>for three hours</u>. That's how happy and good she is. She is very self-sufficient in entertaining herself. The other day I looked into the bedroom, hearing her croon, and there she was leaning over the top bar of her crib, chin on her folded arms—standing. Ever since then she's been pulling herself upright. She's showed no inclination to sit, though she kneels.

First thing in the morning, when I pick her out of her crib and take her into the bedroom, she bursts into laughter at the sight of Sylvia. She has a real gurgling laugh. About one third of her repertoire of sounds are made on the <u>in</u> breath not the out.

Well, we're taking our Tarocq up to Yorkshire tomorrow. We've spent this last week looking forward to the change, it's quite stopped us doing anything else.

176

Have a merry Xmas, a merry merry xmas. We shall have some festive photographs to send you.   Love

Ted

In a letter to her mother and brother, written 'about 17 December' (see *Letters Home*), Plath advises them against taking TH's 'elaborate metaphysical explanations' of his play 'too seriously'. The 'really dramatic play' with which TH followed *The House of Aries* was *The Calm*.

1961

The dissatisfaction with London that TH had already recorded was growing. Sylvia Plath's health was suffering, too, with a bad cold in January, then a miscarriage at the beginning of February. At the end of February, she was in hospital to have her appendix removed. In spite of successes, acceptance of work by magazines, commissions, and TH's accumulation of laurels – the Somerset Maugham Award for *The Hawk in the Rain* in 1960, the Hawthornden Prize for *Lupercal* on 24 March 1961 – the pleasures of the 'literary world' were showing threadbare. The purchase of Court Green, the house in Devon that became theirs at the end of August, was intended to provide an escape.

To Lucas Myers

[Early 1961]   Ms   Emory

I'm sending you all the poems I've written since I came back here—most of them in the last month. [*Arrow to marginal addition:* in another envelope.] Most of last year I wrote nothing, or complete confusion. I had continual dreams of being in falling houses, & now I read that this is the classical dream of the breakdown & reformation of your personality. I can believe that. Last year was a sort of death-march, except for Frieda, and I'm sure most of my exhaustions, nervous tics of all the kinds I had always thought impossible for me, came from my turning from a youngest son into a father of sorts. Did you go through any of that?

Your Rosamond is about parallel to Frieda, who has the effect of some highly effective religious ritual in the way of bringing life. My American years in retrospect from this look like a barrenly spiritless time, & Lupercal seems to me to suffer from the lack of the natural flow of spirit & feeling [*addition in left-hand margin:* just as you criticised it] which it takes as its subject [*addition in right-hand margin:* (it takes the lack as subject, I mean)]. The feelings in it are fished up out of experiences which still held some light even in those otherwise dark three years. I would prefer to write more freely & widely for a bit, maybe more superficially. It seems more possible now anyway, since Xmas.

178

These poems are very different from the earlier ones, don't you think? I think of 'Pibroch' and 'Eucharist' as main-line ones, and the others as marginal—about equal to Pennines in April in Lupercal, though more interesting I hope.

The play was so awful I can't bear to send it you. I've got a draft of another full-length one which is much better, & written in a real way—I feel the characters are speaking in it, & what they say is strange to me. In the other one it was my voice tediously all the time & very general & vague & cliché.

I wish you lived here. I started a regular invocation of power which worked so well I did nothing but write pretty well all day for a month, & found it very difficult to stop. The outlines of about 150 poems came to me at odd moments—whenever I looked for them they came up. The 'Theology' in Dully Gumption was one of the notes & so was Poltergeist [*marginal addition:* Poltergeist isn't much]—I found I couldn't change them to anything better, & 'Theology' is the sort of thing I could never have written normally. Anyway, if you were here we could have these invocations & mesmerise each other into states of high productive power. 'Wino' was another note. [. . .]

While I've been enjoying all this thaw of my three year freeze, Sylvia's been going through a poor time, with bouts of flu, a grumbling appendix which she's to have out, & sundry malicious planetary foistings. Perhaps she'll pick up when she's had the thing extracted—I believe they poison & filter toxins into your blood slightly but effectively the whole period of their disaffection.

[. . .]

I'm having a pleasant time at the Zoo—I have a season ticket & go nearly every day & draw the animals & look at them a bit more closely than I have done heretofore. Also, I've started inspecting London as if I were a tourist—going to the law-courts, the galleries, the museums, all the things I would regret neglecting if I were to leave London tomorrow. At the old Bailey last week I saw a youth aged 21 that very day, accused of raping a 14 year old girl. The charge of rape was dismissed—the girl had had an abortion at eleven, and several other youths were suspects as fathers of this child for which, finding her belly irrepressible & calling brazenly to the neighbours, she now selected him. But the judge fined the boy £25, with £35 towards costs, and 6 months in prison, for committing sexual intercourse with the girl's consent. Would you raise a son in this country? That's not just the natural war of the generations. On my statistics, 950,000 15 year old, & under, girls are out after males of any condition nightly, with small red lamps on the clitoris & hooks in their hands to get a good purchase on the shoulder-blades, & an average 8,000,000 inches of penis are trapped nightly by these sophisticated means—that's by girls of 15 and under. Yet the judge can sit in Court No 1, at the Old Bailey, & treat one of the victims, a mere item of prey, as if he had come swimming up the Thames with seventeen heads, and his shark-form phallus directed at Buckingham Palace, the one such prodigy in the history of Europe.

Sylvia's book is being extremely well-received. There is a slight reaction noticeable in the manners of these reviewers—reaction from the 'spot the influence' coon-hounding. Now they say 'Obviously so-and-so has read so-and-so, Swattworp, Tripletit, & Gutterdunce, but these influences are wholly subdued to the unique original note etc.' This isn't a bad thing either. Poetry is a good deal harder to detect, for these people, than smiles from familiar faces, & it's a virtue in them to recognise that it might be a more valuable thing to find. Among small U.S. reviewers this reaction hasn't taken place—the rhinoceros there is 'a pretentious tapir-sort of beast, heavily dosed with dear old elephant. The tail is a lift straight out of pig. The feet, for all their technique, are simply stork, inverted. And the horn, which he brandishes tediously, is the old over-flogged Unicorn, with a slightly modernising twist," and so on. I'm sending one or two of her more recent poems which I hope you'll agree, are better than anything in the book.

Rosamond, Myers's eldest daughter, had been born on 1 May 1960 – a month after Frieda Hughes.
   'Pibroch', 'Theology', 'Wino' and 'Gog', of which 'The Eucharist' is a variant title, were all to be included in Wodwo, and 'Poltergeist' in Recklings. 'Dully Gumption's College Courses' was a set of poems in a tone somewhat liberated from TH's usual.

To W. S. Merwin

[26 February 1961]   Ms   Emory

We had a pleasant evening with Dido last night at Whiting's play "The devils". It's a play would interest you a great deal—I haven't read Huxley's book by some fluke, but I can see I must. As a play, it suffers a little bit from the same ailment as Saint's Day—a slight, but sometimes fatal incoherence of the intellectual pretensions. He has wonderful dramatic ideas, but doesn't have the drive or grasp to make a team of them. His plays seem to me to be founded in a real imagination, sinister & very odd, but actually constructed & written by a sometimes rather precious actor—the actor exploits the ideas for his momentary eyebrow lifts or smiling insinuations—too much smiling insinuation—& doesn't quite know what to do with the idea rolling about in full view like an actor who's fallen downstairs offstage somewhere & staggered onstage rubbing his head, staring at the audience, trying to remember, & stark naked. Also, inevitably when you consider the subject, there was a great deal of ceremonial robe trailing, effulgent processionary entrances of bishops & kings. But the really wonderful things in the play seemed to me to be Whiting's rather than the subject's. A perfect genius for bringing one scene on on top of the previous at such a moment that the new scene seemed to be evolving out of the minds of the characters in the present scene. Not very clearly put. Some fear, under-running a scene, would grow, to a climax—then enter the new scene, as the fear being irresistibly realised, the fearing characters of the previous scene being still on stage, thrust into the dark corners. Or the working of two scenes on the stage at once so that each seems to be a projection of the mind of the other—Grandier lying in his cell, while the abess (is she an abess?) grieves for him on the forestage. Or the Abess shrieking with mental & you suppose spiritual agony on the forestage, while Grandier is being physically tortured at the back of the stage.

The Devils by John Whiting (1917–63), who also wrote Saint's Day, was a dramatic treatment of Aldous Huxley's The Devils of Loudun.

To Olwyn Hughes

[Early 1961]   Ms Emory

I'm enclosing a few poems—the Observer's printing them. Except for Gog they're all odd-thought poems—poems I could never write before because I didn't know how to, and now I get them very rapidly & slyly—and perhaps too easily. Still, I don't think these could have been much more than they are. I'm tired of the kind of poem that gets one little grain of a notion & erects a great architecture of verse about it. These spring directly out of themselves & stop when the impulse stops

& its their own fault if there isn't more to them. I don't feel to have my shoulder behind any of them, except one or two of the lines in Gog. When I write the next central pieces they'll be like nothing else. "Wodwo" came as a complete little lizardy voice. I tried afterward to put punctuation in, but that seemed to ruin it, so I left it as I wrote it. I think if ever I publish these in a book, I'll lump them & others like them all together & call them "Dully Gumption's table-talk."

Dated by reference, in an omitted passage, to Whiting's *The Devils*. Neither 'Gog' nor 'Wodwo' seems to have been taken by the *Observer*, but both were published, in different magazines, in the course of 1961.

To Aurelia and Warren Plath

22 April 1961   Ms   Lilly Library

Dear Aurelia & Warren,

   This should get to you at least as soon as the birthday cards, so let me wish you again happy birthdays, and many happy returns.

   Since I last wrote a great deal has happened in one way or another—I said that without thinking & when I look more closely I see that really very little has happened. The impression of great happenings stems mainly out of Frieda's staggering developments. You will just sit & watch her all day long, Aurelia. At this minute Sylvia is sitting at the window reading the mail—several checques—& Frieda is standing up in her pen laughing at everybody. No, now she's thrown her ball out & she's bawling at everybody. Sylvia's been writing at a great pace ever since she's been out of hospital & has really broken through into something wonderful—one poem about 'Tulips' which she's going to send to this Poetry Festival—they commissioned her—is a tremendous piece. Her poems are in demand more & more. The Poetry Center in New York wrote asking her if she'd be over there to give a reading. That appendix must really have been plaguing her for years—a steady drain of toxins into her system possibly for the last five years. Anyway now she's renewed. I think the ten days in hospital were a good rest from Frieda too.

   By the time you get here Aurelia I hope we'll have a car. Poetry prizes of the last two years will just about buy it. We haven't got one before because I refuse to buy a second-hand car here—knowing as little as I do about them—unless it's an old insect for £10 or so, and Sylvia refuses to buy that sort. So we're getting a new one. A sort of small station wagon—possibly you've seen them, Morris 1000. They're extremely popular over here, & are the nearest thing to what we want among the various models available. Now we'll be able to see something of England—train-fare, trouble of luggage plus Frieda, has kept us imprisoned this last year & it's worth some outlay of cash to be freed & able to go where we like—since we are free & not rooted in jobs. I hope we shall be able to take you to Cornwall, Devon etc, & feed you on strawberries & clotted cream, & lie in the sun a bit.

I went on T.V. the other day, talking for 5 minutes about my children's book. There was a huge 6 ft blow-up of the grandfather picture. Sylvia watched—a huge studio, with many different sets, odd characters sidling about in costume,—other parts of the programme, which was a sort of bundle of interviews with 'People in the News'. I've been in the news a bit too much lately, I'm beginning to feel news-burned.

I'm just finishing a play—a real play. No resemblance to that other at all. 8 people wake up on a desert island without memory—or with only floating fragments of memory. I'll send it to the poets' theatre so you'll be able to see it. Though it may be good enough to go further—& it may not. There's a good chance of a good performance over here—the best director in England is interested in it (he hasn't seen it yet). All the posts of power—or the main ones—in the literary world over here are now filled by people who were my contemporaries at Oxford or Cambridge & many of them vague acquaintances. It's the first time, I imagine, the very youngest generation has ever had such complete control. They're all eager to promote their own 'age-group', luckily for us. We look forward very much to receiving you here, keep well meanwhile.

Love, Ted.

Plath had offered 'Tulips' – described by TH, in a letter to Olwyn Hughes, as 'an absolutely inspired poem . . . a real torrent' – in response to a commission from the 'Poetry at the Mermaid' Festival (see the following letter to Daniel and Helga Huws). TH's own contribution, which he told Olwyn he had 'mewled & pewled together . . . in a husk of my styles', was 'My Uncle's Wound', which he never collected.

The 'real play' he had just finished was *The Calm*, of which there are some pages at the British Library, and some, the backs of which Plath used for drafts of poems, at Smith College.

To Daniel and Helga Huws

[July 1961]   Ms   Huws

Dear Dan & Helga,

As is the rule, your letter interrupted one of mine in preparation.

Since you left, our life has been a bit of an upheaval, & there are no prospects of it settling before Xmas, since we have to go off on the Maugham travel money in September. We shall sit down somewhere in Italy, & ruminate. We procured a car, thanks to one of Sylvia's fairy godmother's, & that's lessened the opression of London a bit, & enabled us to go seek a house somewhere pleasant—several possibilities at present, one of which we shall have to secure some time this month.

Frieda has just started running about—opening drawers & doors & issueing a stream of Japanese, with the beginnings of translation—app-uh, for apple, ooo-en, for open, daddy for all men—no mama yet. Her grandmother's over at present, taking the strain in one sense. Sylvia is four months gone with an inevitable irony—a Capricorn. It may sneak into Aquarius.

We spent two weeks in France, leaving Frieda with Sylvia's mother, but I wish we had gone almost anywhere else. I'm sure now that I detest the French, France & everything touched by them. When we go abroad this September, we'll cross to the Hague, & go down through Germany, rather than be robbed in France again.

I've no gossip, except of the most public kind, since the only people I've seen since you left have been such public blasted statues as played in the Mermaid Festival of poetry—we saw one day of it. John Wain is very odd—very friendly, & quite nice, but gashed & scarred in the literary battledore, much of his personality seems determined by his expectation of being attacked in a review—he's full of ready bile to reply with. I met Richard Murphy there, who owns a 30ft hooker & spends 6 months taking tourists out fishing off the coast of Galway, & 6 months writing poetry. He's unexpected—English Public School finish, manners & appearence of a fastidious cleric, but very fresh, & very nice.

I don't know when we shall be able to get up there & see you. Most likely not before spring, and it depends how our househunting goes. I'd like to find a place in Devon—we have one or two lined up. But all that's in the air. We'd be quite near you if we could get there. This Maugham travel money is proving a bit of a plague,—just as we are being forced to move to a new house, it's forcing us to go abroad: the alternative is turning down the cash—out of which we hope to save some.

Is Madelin speaking Welsh exclusively now? And how is life in general?

I'm including some dry goat-droppings—sole remains of life on this last somewhat stony year & a half. It must be pleasant, in one way, to have place & time, private & regular, & know that you can blame nothing & nobody but yourself for what your pen releases. I look forward to that time, anyway.

How is life among the Welsh, I Ielga? How are the shops? How is the place to live in? Do you go picnics? And how is Lucy? We bought 3 quite handsome chairs, finally, one a rocker, & ousted some of the Merwin's stuff. Do you go to sales & so on? We found an inexhaustible (apparently) supplier of Windsor chairs at Haworth, near where my parents live—quite cheap, though not dirt-cheap. We spent a week up there, introducing Frieda to 500 or so baby pigs. She's a great one for animal noises—she barks at dogs, moos at cows. Her latest game is running round with a ball of fluff that looks nothing like a chicken, though it is actually intended to be a chicken, & going 'tweet tweet tweet' in a high unnatural voice.

I'm seeing David on Saturday—I think he's still living on his own.

Sylvia sends her affectionate greetings to you all four

Ted.

This appears to have been written some time between the unhappy holiday at the Merwins' place in the Dordogne – described by Dido Merwin in her appendix contribution to Anne Stevenson's Plath biography *Bitter Fame* – from which TH and Plath returned in mid-July, and the end of the same month, when, in a letter to her son (included in *Letters Home*), Aurelia Plath reports on their discovery of Court Green, the house in Devon which was soon to become their home. Commitment to Court Green meant that TH was never able to use his Somerset Maugham Award for the purpose for which it was intended, namely, to spend some time abroad, but he was given the money anyway.

Nicholas Hughes turned out a Capricorn, of which the governing planet is the sombre Saturn.

John Wain had directed the 'Poetry at the Mermaid' Festival, at the Mermaid Theatre in London. The Irish poet Richard Murphy (b.1927) was at this time living on the Connemara coast, where he earned his living as skipper of a boat plying between Cleggan and Inishbofin and taking tourists on fishing expeditions.

To Leonard Baskin

[August 1961]   Ms   British Library

Dear Leonard,

Ever since you went I've been wondering if you'd write, since that last day was unpleasant for us too. If you're still curious to know the cause—or what was probably the main cause—it was that Sylvia hadn't been able to do any work all week in the middle of her first longish work which had been going like gunpowder up to that point, and she was upset at the same time at taking no part in your visit except to cook and so on. So your sharp remarks to her on that Friday hit her with a special irony.

We've now rectified one of the basic circumstances of that trouble. We've sublet 3 Chalcot square, for good, and bought a house in Devon—a house with 6 bedrooms, a stable with 3 stalls, a spare 2 room cottage, a big vegetable garden, an extensive orchard and 2½ acres of land. Also a thatched roof. It's an old farm—part of it 11th Century. There's a prehistoric tumulus or fort-mound in the orchard. It's a knock-out. We're having the owner clear out the population of wood-worm and death-watch beetles before we move in, this weekend.

So now maybe I'll be able to write something without the hourly intervention of the domestic order. We're only just in time (a year late more exactly) since we're expecting a sister for Frieda in January.

Are you back at work? How is your exhibition doing? And what's the hope for a show of your drawings, via the dishonourable?

Your visit was such a great thing in so many ways—regret that the last day went wrong has been a constant thought with me. I wondered if you were as taken by surprise with it as I was, and as helpless to correct it.

Anyway, to hell with it, where it belongs.

I'll write you in greater detail of our apple harvest, the superb Palmer country etc, when I'm among it.

Did Esther rejoice in your loot? You got a haul. Does Toby want to come on a holiday? In a few years you'll be able to send him and he can live in our cottage, tutor Frieda & the other, for a while.

Sylvia sends her love to you all, & I do too
                                        Ted

In his most recent letter to TH, dated 28 June 1961 – and headed with a large ink drawing of the naked Agamemnon – Baskin had expressed his bewilderment over an 'awful' visit to Cambridge with TH and Plath, and wondered if he had been 'somehow responsible' for the 'cold un-generosity of that day'.

To Daniel Weissbort

[Autumn 1961]   Ms   Emory

Dear Danny,

The invitation to your wedding came in the middle of our removal from London, & by the time I looked round it was long past & you in bliss—at least I trust you're in bliss, & if you're not quite I hope short time will bring you there, & long time keep you there, Jill & yourself.

I had been reckoning on coming all year—but then I had <u>not</u> been reckoning on leaving London.

As you see, we're in Devon—peace, space, London departed like a headache. So from now on I hope my life will be privacy, my own thoughts, my own amusements, my own time, with occasional raids on the world. London was beginning to build (had built!) an ants' nest between my ears that never gave me peace. But as I say, the 200 miles have exterminated that miraculously. We have a sort of farmhouse in a rather grim little village—but are quite private in our two acres, with apple trees, fancy trees, garden, outhouses etc. Some day, we hope, it will be ours   at last a place to dump things.

And where are you? In one of your houses? Or still honeymooning or what? Marriage is a nest of small scorpions, but it kills the big dragons. I'm an advocate, so have nothing but congratulations & good wishes, my very best wishes, for both of you. Meanwhile, drop a line, Danny, now & again,

Ted

Weissbort married Jill Anderson on 17 September 1961. He owned, not 'houses', but a house, which he let.

To Olwyn Hughes

[Autumn 1961]   Ms   Emory

I agree with you about Thom Gunn's book & so does Sylvia. Much better than his last, & in a narrow & rather sterile way, very good indeed. Nobody can praise it full-heartedly, because in a way it's an exercise in style. At the same time, it's a completely skillfull exercise, & in it he does things that were out of his range before, & the language is his own. Before, his language was general, & common to a number of writers, all fairly bad. His main subject in this book is the clean delimi-tation of a thing, without illusory marginal suggestions, without sec-ondary meaning, & this is a natural image of his desire to reduce his language to what is controllable, known fully to him, & his own, which results in emptying it of associations & secondary richness,—all natural developments of his concern with deliberate will, reason & wit. The worst thing about it, is that as he refines these predilections, the poems become less & less human—less profound psychologically, & so they begin to lose weight. They become less like statements & more like witticisms. I'm ordering Faber to send you a copy.

This is the place to be allright. I planted about fifty strawberry bushes a while ago, & they seem to have taken. In addition to my 71 apple trees, 3 cooking pear trees, 4 plum trees (two in very bad shape), 3 wall pear trees, I have ordered four peach trees, two greengage trees, two nut trees, four eating pear trees, a grapevine (we have a small greenhouse) & a dozen black-currant bushes. In a good year we should make quite a little income off fruit alone, not to mention the incredible pleasure of wandering among your own fruit trees eating one apple here & one plum there, or retiring to the top of your prehistoric mound with a small pile of selected fruits, & surveying your domains.

Thom Gunn's new book was *My Sad Captains*.

To John Montague

[Autumn 1961]   Ms   Montague

Dear John Montague,
    I've been meaning to write to you ever since I saw that "review" of your book in the New Statesman. I trust it didn't affect you. Davie is a kind of parasite in the crutch & armpits of poetry very common in the States—a strident proclaimer of the latest O.K. notions all sure to be found in a pitiful form in his own latest verse. He's a grotesquely shrunken silly imitator of Pound, forty years after the phenomenon. He's the old receptacle of every other critic's—particularly the American

battalion—dud cartridges & empty cases & he's trying to fit them all together, not dropping one, into a semblance of armament, but of course there's a new lot every quarter (with the quarterlies), so poor old Davie's kept busy. He's the mincy mean know-all kind of little office snot—a standard English type—gone into Literature, & in the branch of poetry his own practice is about the measure of his understanding—all creak & no cart. So up & down with him.

What are you doing now? We've just moved to the country to gather breath—London was a bit wearying. I hope to get into something here or at least amuse myself more efficiently than I was doing in London. Let me know how the Magazine goes—I will send something when I have it, for when you can use it.

Do you know Patric Creagh? I've just seen a proof of his book—the second two sections very good.

I liked the Eluard very much, though I'm too late now to do anything with it. I had intended to send it to Silkin at Stand, with some other things. I'd love to see Eloges.

I only stayed at the Mermaid the one day, then cleared out of London, and again we'd moved down here when you had the reception at the Embassy. If you're ever down this way—unlikely event—call on us, please.

I'd like to see your long poem. Have you published your stories anywhere? Stories are something to keep going at. I have about four, & I'd like to get about 6 more like them. They seem to help me write verse—get the machine going unself-consciously, very necessary in my case.

Send some poems to John R. Stevens, HUTCHINSON EDUCATIONAL LTD, 178–202 Gt Portland St, London W.1., he's the editor of a Gramaphone record Anthology who asked me to ask whoever I thought might want to, to send 6 or so poems for him to choose from, published or not. Keep well.

Meanwhile, all the best

Ted H.

'Davie' was Donald Davie (1922–95), poet, academic, and associate of 'The Movement', who had written what John Montague (b.1929) has described to the editor as a 'very condescending' review (*New Statesman*, 29 September 1961) of his first British publication, *The Poisoned Lands*.

TH had seen Patrick Creagh's *A Row of Pharaohs*, as a recently appointed selector for the Poetry Book Society – which had made *The Hawk in the Rain* its Summer Choice in 1957. The job involved comparing and selecting the best from all volumes published for a number of consecutive seasons. In this instance, TH was looking at books by George Barker, John Holloway and Derek Walcott, among others.

At about this time, too, he was translating the poems of Paul Eluard (1895–1952), possibly with an edition by Penguin in mind. Reporting to Olwyn Hughes, who had supplied texts, he wrote: 'In a way, Elouard is just what I need. I'm much too objective & matter of fact to be melted down by him, but he does encourage my own fluencies. His absolutely musical way of building a poem up is something the stupid good manners & scissor-fencing of english modern poetry doesn't permit among its précieuses.'

Jon Silkin (1930–97) was a poet and editor of the magazine *Stand*.

Eloges was the first collection by the French, Guadaloupe-born poet Saint-John Perse (1887–1975).

To A. Alvarez

[Late 1961]   Ms   British Library

Dear Al,

I'm sending you this piece—which I described to you or mentionned earlier in the year but didn't show you—because Sylvia is insisting now on trying to sell it & though I've no fear that you'll want to publish it in the Observer, you'd better see it, according to contract. I didn't send it out before, not because I dislike its rhetoric, I don't, but because if it's published too publicly it becomes a bit of a testament.

I'll be sending you some proper pieces soon—there's opportunity here. The days are about 55 hours long, so Devon must get all London's, plus Chalk Farm's—7.

David Wevill & wife took over our flat—quite by chance, I'd never met him though I'd met her glancingly. Some of his poems are good in an unusual way, don't you think? He showed me about 60, and I'm sending you 3 which I don't imagine you'll have seen but which seem to me first rate.

When you next come climbing King Arthur's cliff's you must apply your brakes at about Taunton, which should slow you down sufficiently to turn in at our gate & come in & stand on our bare cheerless floors for a while, & maybe eat an apple. We'd be very glad to see you.

My duties as Poetry Book Society Choice judge have begun—with Holloway's 'The Landfaller's', indescribable, & George Barker's 'View from a blind I'. The first is unrelieved, the 2nd lightly relieved—full of an odd odour of the most ordinary Auden, oddly.

Did I tell you, or did Thom Gunn tell you, that we're editing an Anthology of Young-American-Poets-not-yet-published-over-here. We were asked for about 6, but we seem to be stuck at 4. Nemerov (whom I like less & less) Bowers (whom I like resistingly), William Stafford (very good on his ·5 degrees of the compass, otherwise the worst of the Creative Writers) & Simpson, who has one or two new poems which are knock out. But in the whole four we've still only got a sort of Piltdown man. Have you any suggestions. There are piles of writers who write more brilliantly & excitingly, in their moments, than any of these four, but they have only moments, so far as I'm aware & most of them are sports of the Carlos Williams Rexroth cross, a doomed & detestable breed on the whole, & congenital lightweights.

Are you keeping all right?

The only kiln-building plans I've found are too complicated, or <u>were</u> too complicated,—I'll consider them now I have time & space maybe. But there's a very simple biscuit kiln which I shall sooner or later find out how to build then I'll send you the directions—if you haven't already bought an electric one, which is probably the smartest answer.

Are you writing anything? If you get bored, persuade Faber to do a 600 poem edition of Emily Dickinson, & edit & introduce it—they ought to, Eliot's violated her & ought to go far now to make an honest woman of her. And send it me to review.

When are you going to write some more poetry reviews?—you've no idea how attentive we provincials are. Review the new edition of David Jones In Parenthesis, perhaps.

I have your copy of 'Imitations'—I've been secreting it rather than keeping it because my daughter tore off the cover—the front cover at least, & I've been nonplussed about sending it back as it is. But I will send it now, & put on a fresh cover—for which this is the explanation.

All the best
Ted

TH and A. Alvarez had met in 1960, when Alvarez, after writing an unreservedly enthusiastic review of *Lupercal* for the *Observer*, had been asked by the paper to interview the author. As well as being the *Observer*'s main poetry reviewer, Alvarez chose poems to be printed there, but he does not recall the terms of the contract according to which TH had felt obliged to offer 'Dully Gumption's Addendum'. The poem, in any case, was to have its first airing in *Poetry (Chicago)* in May 1962.

David Wevill (b.1935) was a Canadian poet and the third husband of Assia Wevill (née Gutmann).

TH mentions four of the poets whose work would eventually be included in *Five American Poets*. The fifth was Hyam Plutzik (1911–62). William Carlos Williams (1883–1963) and Kenneth Rexroth (1905–82) were not admired by Alvarez, either.

Imitations, Robert Lowell's book of translations, some very free, from a wide variety of languages, was published in 1961.

1962

The birth of TH and Sylvia Plath's son Nicholas was the event that dominated the beginning of the year. TH, however, was increasingly busy beyond Court Green, making trips to London, for instance, to record radio programmes, which included a talk about the then little-regarded British poet Keith Douglas (1920–44), who had died of shrapnel wounds in Normandy. In his letters, TH continues to present life in Devon as a paradise of tranquillity and abundance, but there were strains in the marriage that went unreported, and they were ultimately tested by the visit of David and Assia Wevill over the weekend of 18 to 20 May. It appears that TH and Assia, who had met before without consequence, fell in love with each other then; and, sensing something of the kind, Plath saw her visitors off in a mood of tension and unvoiced rage. Thereafter, although he and Assia would meet clandestinely in London, TH remained based at Court Green, until a flare-up during a visit by Aurelia Plath drove him away.

To Charles Tomlinson

[Early 1962]   Ms   Texas

Dear Charles Tomlinson,

Thanks for the nice long letter & the invitation to trout. I hope to be driving up North in Spring & that should bring us through your country—we'll call on you. I don't imagine you've much need to come to Devon from where you are, but when you do you must certainly call here. We've a sort of rectorish farm-house in a village, lots of room thank God, outhouses, a bit of land & orchard—just what I like. We're on the Taw—a great trout river, which I hope to inspect next season. It's a change to have a base, where one can dump everything—without already calculating the removal.

I'm glad to hear you got some things you liked for the Anthology. I wonder what writers you chose. When I was helping to edit that P.E.N. book last year, two facts struck me—the proud & English sent nothing, while a swarm of excellent little pieces turned up from people I'd never heard of. One inspired poem called "Potato-pickers" I thought must have been written by a 13 year old turned out to be written by somebody in an asylum near Oxford. There's obviously tons of talent in this country, but it can't somehow grow up.

Your place sounds idyllic. You should hang the traps over the fire-place to keep out witches in the shapes of hares, weasels and single wandering hands.

Both my wife & I look forward to seeing your new book. Fifty poems! They must be great leaves up that way, or is it the oracular trout.

Yours

Ted Hughes

The poet Charles Tomlinson (b.1927) was in the process of editing a British edition of *Poetry (Chicago)*, which would appear in May. His 'country' was Gloucestershire. With Patricia Beer and Vernon Scannell, TH had edited *New Poems 1962: A P.E.N. Anthology of Contemporary Poetry*, which included B. A. Hill's 'The Potato Field'.

To Esther and Leonard Baskin

[Late January 1962]   Ms   British Library

Happy New Year. That heading has been lying around for a fortnight— my procedures having been disrupted by the arrival of a <u>son</u>. 17th January, at 6 minutes to midnight. Sylvia handled it very well, though he was a bit big—9 pounds eleven ounces. At one stage he seemed to get stuck, but finally he came out with a pop, very near. I never saw anything quite as ugly as he in his first few minutes—the skull plates had closed as far as they could, so that he looked brow-less, with a terrifying expression of ferocity, swarthy, eyes going in every direction, a blue weal like a circlet over his brow—where he got stuck inside and took the strain, evidently. But by morning he'd recovered his humanity, & even took on a family likeness to Frieda. Now he's thriving—a very calm steady child, unlike Frieda, who was wilful from her very first day. So that's our main recent event. Husbands go through just as much as wives on these occasions. I wasn't aware of being troubled or excited or even very involved, but the next day—! I was flat.

[. . .]

My own affable familiar ghost has been absent for some time—driven off by the trivial outer adjustments of my life very likely. I hope it will

194

come back with something a bit different from what's gone before—
which is O.K., but not more than a start, not more than hawking &
spitting. I'll be sending you a script of the radio-play I wrote—very
gruesome in a sketchy way. It's on the air this next week—Feb 1ˢᵗ, the
eve of the day which the Indian astrologers have chosen for the end of
the world.

Nicholas Farrar Hughes was born on 17 January 1962.
   Douglas Cleverdon's production of TH's play *The Wound* was broadcast by the
BBC Third Programme on 1 February.

To John L. and Máire Sweeney

29 January 1962   Ms   Dublin

Dear Jack & Moira,
   We finally gave Creagh the prize—not with furious enthusiasm, but
confidently.
[. . .]
   The recommendation was George Barker's book 'View from a blind
I." "The ballad of Yucca flats" is very good, but the rest————. He used
to have a wild flair for verbal detail which was good in an atrocious
way that's gone. He now resembles, as a rule, Auden at his bland
dullest, as you'll be surprised to see. It wasn't a very bright crop.
Walcott, the West Indian, has a sort of dash & fluency, but he's a medley
of the Treece, Gascoyne, Tiller styles, the apocolyptic Xmas decoration
style, which I've swallowed long enough.
   I've been nursing for several weeks—nay, months—<u>thanks</u>. For
'The Cattle-Raid of Cualnge". It's the prize item of my small library of
essential literature—mainly mythology, or folk-tales of a particular
sort (like the Ananzi stories, many African stories, the Ainu stories,
the Trickster cycles etc), which I hope I shall now be able to expand.
Thanks, Jack, very much.
   This last year hasn't been very good for poetry, or much else either.
We made a desperate bid to escape the prime folly—London—& even-
tually settled in here, a nice old house, biggish, bit of land, orchard etc,
quiet. So far adjustments, tittivating, & the arrival of a son this last
week—Nicholas—have troubled the centre of gravity, but I thrive now
as I always thrived best—in a half-vegetable existence. And Sylvia loves

it. And Frieda blossoms on it. So there are nothing but relieved sighs on this score, & something may come of it this spring. Sylvia's not written much this year but what she's written is her best.

Bill's gone to the U.S. I see—for good, I dare say. He belongs there now, & I daresay, he'll find a literary circle there that didn't exist for him before. He's a part of the appetite for the "New Poetry" [*arrow to marginal addition:* translations of Neruda etc.]—as his recent verse shows. It's an interesting movement, but so far it's all second-hand. He's easily the most distinctively himself of the whole bunch. But his most recent pieces (the one about a child born blind in a recent Nation) seem to me to be becoming more evasive than suggestive, & exploiting his genius for metaphor, in which he always tended to be a bit facile. But with him, I'm sure this is a phase. He's becoming the most accomplished poet of his generation, very obviously.

Well, Sylvia sends her love, & please pass our greetings to Agatha & Steve,

as ever
Ted

In a Green Night was Derek Walcott's entry for the Poetry Book Society Choice. Henry Treece (1911–66), David Gascoyne (1916–2001) and Terence Tiller (1916–87) were the poets whom TH identifies as unassimilated influences on Walcott.

Joseph Dunn's translation of the Irish epic *The Cattle-Raid of Cualnge* had been available since 1914.

W. S. Merwin ('Bill') had indeed left London to settle back in the USA.

To Aurelia and Warren Plath

1 May 1962   Ms   Lilly Library

Dear Aurelia and Warren,

Since I read Sylvia's letters to you, as often as I can get hold of them before she dashes off out with them, it seems that we're communicating regularly—this is my first letter since we last saw you. The first heave of the struggle with this place is over, and for a week we've had Cape Cod weather—Cape Cod August weather I mean. Sylvia's actually brown. The daffodills are a perpetual court-ball—every day some stunning new variety bursts out in a drift. Today it was a tall slender white narcissi with a big golden eye. Twenty or thirty times a day Sylvia staggers &

exclaims—hit by a fresh wave of the wonders of this place. The cherry trees are loaded with purple blossom just on the point of exploding. A little peach tree I planted beneath Sylvia's study window has five blossoms. All the apple trees are getting ready. You would hardly recognise it now, Warren. Internally, it's transformed—very comfortable. Externally, it is soaked with hot sun from morning to night, & like a great aviary. Sylvia's been loading her flower beds with seeds, & I've been sowing the vegetable garden—martial rows of beans & peas appearing almost immediately. This year, I'm going to burden Sylvia with preserving jars—we mustn't let the harvest get past us again. Already the rhubarb is threatening the house. Frieda, of course, is the great blossom. It's amusing to see the way she's beginning to own "Baby Nick" as she calls him. Very concerned when he cries, & if he's out in his pram at the time she runs & rocks him, which stops him successfully. Baby Nick is completely different from her—though they're alike in some features, shape of their eyes & eyelids. He has a most complicated smile—Frieda's is just a 1,000 kilowatt radiance. He gives the impression of being sage. Whereas Frieda's a bit of a tempest. However, when you get here, Aurelia, Nicholas will be smiling all round, & you'll not be able to leave Frieda. I think Sylvia's happier here, now the good weather's come, than she's been since I've known her. Also, she's writing very well, which seems to be the main thing. Since she left America, she's lost the terrible panic pressure of the American poetry world—which keeps them all keeping up on each other. As a result, she's developing her own way & will soon be a considerable genius. Her poem "Tulips" made something of a stir—she had a letter from Howard Moss about the reactions. This is a very satisfying life—producing steadily, in these surroundings, and with all this to work at. And we both needed it, since we'd both got to be such outstandingly fleet rats in such a hectic race. Literary life is more exhausting, nervously, than most, because it works with nothing definite or regular, it is a continuous improvisation of reality out of illusions & fantasy, without set limits or hours. One needs to provide substance & duties to the life—as we've done by coming here. Looking forward to seeing you. Another Letter following.   Love   Ted.

To Gerald, Joan, Ashley and Brendon Hughes

[Early May 1962]   Ms   Lilly Library

Your latest letter was waiting for me when I got back from fishing this morning. I go about twice a week onto the Taw, just below the village, where the river is about as big as the Hardcastle river, but more winding, sunk 10 feet beneath its banks that are thick with trees & bushes, going among round hills covered with sheep. I get up at 5, just first grey light, & am at the river in about ten minutes. I fish with a worm, wading slowly up the river & casting upstream into the likely runs. This morning I got four fish, 2 of them ½ lb & very strong, another just a bit lighter—it had been mauled at some time by an otter or a big cannibal trout—and one only 9 inches long. I put back one about the same size, & lost one about the same size. I pricked & lost several others,—just a tug & a thump or two. There are much bigger trout in the quiet pools & deep places, but I haven't yet connected with any or devised tactics to. It's a very swift river, so spinning is a bit of a problem though I suppose it would be possible. They're wonderful mornings, though, the birds coming to inspect me, pheasants crowing & drumming their wings, kingfishers bolting up & down, the banks full of primrose clumps & daffodills & aconites. I occasionally go to the sea, but all my trips so far have been little more than reconnaissance, & I don't have proper tackle for casting out far enough—though I'll alter that this year. The lowest 5 or 6 miles of the Taw, the tidal reach, is free fishing—for sea-trout etc, & I shall be going down there this next month.

In the letter she tags on to this one, Sylvia Plath mentions her delight in the cherry blossom – suggesting a rough date.

To W. S. and Dido Merwin

24 May 1962   Ms   Emory

Dear Bill & Dido,
    We're sorry to hear about your ailments. The gall-bladder complications sound grisly. I think of the gall-bladder as one of the vital centres, along with the prostate gland & the cerebellum—inside all Defences. To

have the scalpels in there—the thought is painful. I hope you're both now out of your several agonies. Over here, the Spring has arrived, five weeks late, but a tide of weeds that I hope will stop soon. And the rhubarb growing 2 inches a day, threatening the house. The house & environs are possessed by about 15 swifts—a bird I have neglected, I see. Their shits come like sling-shots, & lime white. You step outside, & they're coming up the house-side like a gang of hoods, & zip past all round your head. They go up into their nest-holes like bullets into earth. One fell in the yard the other day, by some freak, & flopped about for quite a while before it got off again—rising vertically from the ground for about a yard, its wings going like a humming bird's, then off forward like a shot. We're all absorbed in country pleasures. I introduced Frieda to a baby crow the other day & it nipped her—so she now recognises crows as far as she can see them.

Thank you Bill for the Neruda. I heard the programme—you read them wonderfully well, with authority, & the poems were exciting to hear. The unfortunately named Critical Quarterly will publish probably all together—you should be hearing from them. Are they pretty literal, the translations? I imagine they're completely literal. Also, thanks for the odd pieces. I particularly liked the Roumanian Otter & Wolf song, the Pampas Indian songs, & the Arab recollection. I'll send back what the C.Q. won't use. How about your own stuff, are you knocking that out? Of what I've seen, I've liked the one in the Nation about the singer, & the bowsprit poem in the N.Y. The longish one in the Nation, relevant to the child born blind, was effective with the commentary. It arrived, of course, the morning of the day on which Sylvia was to produce Nicholas. As for my own stuff, I've written nothing. I'd got to the point of writing purely out of nerves—so now I'm quite content to let that tension relax & smooth itself out. Then maybe I'll be able to hear myself speak. I've written up that dream I told you about—of course you heard it, Dido. And I'm writing a morality play "Difficulties of a Bridegroom"—moral: "What you are afraid of overtakes you", something of a joke. What's happening about the London House? I haven't been up into that quarter for months. I imagine the super-flats will be up there. London seems further & further away, thank God.

Are you in the thick of the American new wave? Don't listen to them too closely—the Carlose Williams cult. You're already so far beyond them. Is there anything very new, any new body very real? I haven't read anybody born after 1932 that's interested me in the slightest—it can't be my senility yet, & there must be some geniusses around. 1942 should have been a vintage year. I've just read Voss, by Patrick White—the most staggering book I've read for a year or two. I thought novels couldn't touch me. Sylvia sends love. Send news,   Ted.

W. S. Merwin has been one of the USA's most versatile and prolific translators. An early advocate of Pablo Neruda (1904–73), he was to publish a version of the Chilean poet's *Twenty Love Poems and a Song of Despair* in 1969.

To Olwyn Hughes

[June 1962]   Ms   Emory

Do you want a copy of the Gunn/Hughes selected poems—nothing in it you haven't got. I originally made a larger selection, with some of my prize pieces at the end. Then when the proofs came, I saw I had about twice as much as Thom Gunn. Also, it struck me that I had thoroughly gutted both books, & my selection would supply all anybody would ever want. So I cut off the last section, & now I'm not very satisfied with what remains, though it's all right. I'm sending you the Alvarez Penguin. His judgement is a bit shaky, I think—witness the Boyars, the Aymis, the Fuller. He's sold 10,000 copies of it in its first month. There must be a poetry boom.

I wish you'd send me the volumes of Montale & Ungaretti. Something to counter the influence of the Observer & new Statesman. Any magazines. I feel a bit cut off—sick of English magazines, & not seeing many American.

[. . .]

I'm writing another radio piece, a complete dream this time, but more imaginatively constructed than the last in that the background to the whole thing is—coming & going at the necessary moments—a sort of drumbeat to a song with a certain refrain. Very short scenes, or conversations, weigh in on this. Sometimes the drumbeat becomes church bells, sometimes jazz, sometimes just a beat, but always reverting to its little refrain sung in African style by female voices. I got it from an African song. It's the hero's wedding day. He has answered an advert for a husband, & is going through the interviews etc with the bride's family, expostulations with his friends & associates. Then it becomes probable that he is being had by a society of ritual murderers,

& isn't going to get a bride at all but a man-eating tiger. It ends with "here comes the bride", & just as it's become certain that he's to be fed to this tiger, it's not a tiger after all, but a genuine bride. The implication is that by his resolution in following the whole thing through, he has forcibly converted the tiger to a beauty—all inwardly, of course. It depends on an atmosphere surpercharged with metamorphoses, an utter confusion of narrative expectations—a generally bewildering effect. It's an extravaganza, a scherzo, & perhaps indulgent—but if I can get it excessive enough, it will do. I want it to be an insult to decently Puritan artistic means. It's fault is unreality, of course, but if the conversations have character, & if the hero keeps sane, it might become real in some way. It's not just fantasy. I haven't got to the last scenes yet, which will be the trickiest.

[. . .]

I think the kind of writing—the only kind—to go perfectly with writing poetry, is writing films—which is simply an exercise in realistic & infinitely detailed imagination & life-size situations, not another bungling affectation of language—as novels & stories & plays are. If I could do as I've planned, with 9 months free to write verse, I'd spend an hour a day just imagining films. I've got one very good idea, a bit plotted, but I'll write it out & send it.

The Faber volume of *Selected Poems* by Thom Gunn and Ted Hughes, published in May, linked two poets who were in no sense allies, although they later grew friendly. Alvarez had just brought out his Penguin anthology, *The New Poetry*. Its introduction proposed a renunciation of the 'gentility principle' that had, the editor asserted, dominated British poetry for too long.

The new radio play was *Difficulties of a Bridegroom* – not to be confused with the story collection with the same title that TH published in 1995.

To Charles Tomlinson

[June 1962]   Ms Texas

I've been studying 'Poetry Chicago' carefully, ruefully & gravely. It makes an interesting issue, in an odd way. The Donald Davie poems are odd—like the stubborn practising of a theory of poetry. Very interesting, but perhaps only to one's taste for theories, & I don't think he does anything that Lowell in his poems since Life Studies doesn't do genuinely. I like 'Sculptures in Hungary' best of these. This making a sort of mobile of related images to turn & twinkle at each other is a pleasing sort of poetry—particularly when it happens naturally, as in your own recent stuff. With you it's a means of saying other things, but I think Davie's just making Mobiles.

[. . .]

Are you producing flowingly & meltingly & abundantly? I have a few things—dwarfs & cannibals mainly, but the general prognosis seems better than for two or three years i.e. I'm not bothered about trying to write anything other, since my potatoes are rumbling in the earth like contented elephant herds, my beans full of bear's nests & cottages, my peas wandering the neighbourhood & assaulting the local beauties, my turnips groaning, my radishes booming like bitterns in the dew, my onions threatening the house, my spinach singing quietly. And now somebody's given us a beehive or housefull of muses, all rhyming & labouring—so that by the laws of compensation I am forced to relax, as I trust you are too, or are you in the thick of papers?

Letter undated, but placeable roughly by the May date of Tomlinson's British issue of *Poetry (Chicago)* and by the delivery of the beehive, reported in Sylvia Plath's letter to her mother of 15 June 1962.

The other poets included by Tomlinson were Donald Davie, R. S. Thomas (1913–2000), Norman MacCaig (1910–96), F. T. Prince (1912–2003), Peter Redgrove and Thomas Kinsella (b.1928); and there were prose 'Statements and Perspectives' by various writers.

To Ben Sonnenberg

2 July 1962   Ts   Emory

Glad you think the Magazine of translations might be a good idea. I wouldn't have dreamed of it either if some of those American translations, particularly one or two pieces from the very youngest generation of German poets, had not given me more than any English or American originals for some years. To be influenced is perhaps evil, or rather the weakness in us that permits any influence but for our further true development, is evil, but it's better to be destroyed quickly, if we are weak, than go on protecting our inanity with deliberate cautious ignorance. And if we're not weak, then it's as well to know everything, and interesting too.

If you could keep your perceptions open for rumour of any benevolent foundation likely to back such a Magazine, I'd be grateful. Naturally, I thought you'd be more enlightened about the fish at that fathom than I am—

[. . .]

I've been open to stunnings just lately, it seems. The other day we saw Francis Bacon's Exhibition at the Tate. I saw a small exhibit of his in 1960, and couldn't specify my sensations, beyond a general revulsion. But seeing such a range of his work, and the businessmen, and particularly the latest three studies for a crucifixion, I was bowled over. It's a shock, not entirely disappointing, to find your deepest inspirations set out with such final power. The weight and colouring of his latest things put me in mind of the things Picasso was doing in the late thirties and forties, but then by comparison Picasso seems decor and even a little evasive. I had begun to think I was simply insensitive to contemporary painting, but now I can resume something of my self-respect and assure myself that I'm simply fanatically selective.

As a wealthy American with literary aspirations, Ben Sonnenberg (b.1936) had been living in various parts of Europe, including London, where he and TH had met. TH first put his idea for a magazine of translations to Sonnenberg in a letter of 22 June, and later Sonnenberg gave money to help *Modern Poetry in Translation* get started.

The Tate Gallery in London had mounted a retrospective exhibition of the paintings of Francis Bacon (1909–92).

To Olwyn Hughes

[Late summer 1962]   Ms   Emory

Dear Olwyn,

Thanks for the offer of help etc. The only help I need is cash—in an account of my own—to free my operations, since the prolonged distractions of the last 9 months have cut down our output & so our funds, & now all I can earn, or much of it, is needed to keep the three heads fed & happy. However, the need isn't so desperate—so far, the money-spirit has proved a friend indeed, & earned quite a bit lately. My only concern is to swell a private account.

Things are quite irrevocable. My idleness & deference to other people's wishes is superficial compensation for a completely inhuman will. About 2 months ago, just as the climax was arriving, I dreamed

Hitler came to me, furious, demanding that I carry out the commands instantly. The most extraordinary set of dreams alltogether has been going along with this. And quite a burst of writing.

I have another radio thing, only 30 minutes but in some ways better than the Wound & quite as deeply involved in my life—the realistic frame in which this dream-flight on a drum is set is fairly detailed & odd—but as soon as the B.B.C. had agreed to it, everything happened to me exactly as I'd written. Even to running over a hare (I've never run over anything before) selling it for a certain price at a certain shop in London, what I did with the cash, & the dialogue—to the phrase, & with the exact person involved. All one morning it occurred—the most extraordinary queer thing in my life. Keep it to yourself. I'll send you the play as soon as I get copies from the B.B.C.

I'm cheered about 'The Wound'. I could write these things very rapidly & become more skilled, & shall, as soon as I get some solitude to work in, & prolonged stretches without the awful intimate interference that marriage is. I'd heard they pay up to £500. I have some film scenarios outlined, which I'll send. Ma says you're coming to London, to work? I'm just thinking of leaving England. I'd like to connect with some journal, then go slowly round the world for 3 or 4 years, & learn the main languages, & write travel things to finance it.

I'm rapidly becoming editor of a Magazine of translation, backed by Gulbenkien. I want it about the size of Encounter, 2 × a year, publishing modern poetry only, from other languages—destroy Larkin's affable familiar. I have enough for a first issue.

Faber's commissioned me to edit a selection of Keith Douglas' poems, of which I'm very fond. With an introduction. I'll gradually become the guiding taste at Faber's, when Eliot retires—it would be an amusing coup. I suggested they do Douglas.

I'm aghast when I see how incredibly I've confined & stunted my existence, when I compare my feeling of what I could be with what I am. What I am, is completely a consequence of certain ideas which I arrived at quite rationally & imposed like laws. Such as my decision, when I read Jung when I was 18, to inhibit all conscious thought & fantasy, so that my unconscious would compensate with an increased activity— maybe it worked, but it rendered me so incapable of mental control & deliberate mental play that my whole life has been shut up in a self-imposed curfew. I've had the most terrific labours to get back the flow of mind & memory that used to be quite spontaneous, & should be, if one's not to become an infantile sort of gloom-cloud of repressed utterance, occasionally producing fantasies. There's a list of about 7 such curious deliberate laws which just about account for my condition & the bottom of it all is the fear of becoming different from what I am—which is infantile enough. However, by progression I now have Leo in the Ascendant instead of Cancer, which just about expresses the change I feel.

My earnings are gradually becoming steady. My books earn about £7 a week, which is amazing. Most of it is reprints in Anthologies, & such things. If I've done nothing else, I've written more perfect Anthology pieces than anybody alive—something for all tastes. Also, since poetry creates its own audience, the longer my stuff lies around the more necessary to people it becomes or seems to. I've got to the stage now where they rediscover poems in Hawk in the Rain. For instance, '6 young men' was more or less ignored as just another piece about a photograph, in Movement form—it's now become the example of what that whole Movement genre, with inspiration, could be capable of, it's beginning to justify all those people & their rhymes.

I'm now creating two other poets. One, experimental & lyrical, one very rigid formalist, descriptive detailed reportage, no liberties taken. These are the two extremes I feel I need to keep going—the first frees me & prevents me taking the puritanical virtues of 'good verse' too seriously, the other frustrates me but exercises my attentiveness to objective detail & full development of ideas. My own poems barge midway, exploiting the qualities of the extremes without reducing myself to or losing myself in either. The products of both these poets are very easy to write—since I've no self-consciousness about them, they are real play. And they're very saleable. You keep this to yourself of course. This is one of the lyrical ones—not very extreme, about Heptonstall of course

Black village of gravestones
Head of an idiot
Whose dreams die back
Where they were born

Skull of a sheep
Whose meat melts
Beneath its own rafters
Only flies leave it

Skull of a bird
the great geographies
Drained to sutures
Of cracked windowsills

Life tries
Death tries
The stone tries

Only the rain never tires

I'll have them publish books.

I'm trying to fix Sylvia up in Spain for the winter. Then, by next Spring, have this spare cottage renovated & a Nanny living in, let her write & be company for her. Besides, as soon as I clear out, she'll start making a life of her own, friends of her own, interests of her own. If she wants to buy her half of the house gradually, fair enough. Write to me at the Beacon. I shan't be there, but they'll forward it.

Love   Ted

Written between TH's flight from Court Green in July and the trip to Ireland that he and Plath made in September, hoping to find a house for her to spend the winter in, the Spanish plan – mentioned in the final paragraph – having been dropped. For the time being, TH was staying in Dido Merwin's mother's flat in Montagu Square, London w1.

The 'radio thing' was *Difficulties of a Bridegroom*, of which TH says more in the letter to Olwyn of 10[?] February 1963. The Faber commission had come about after TH's broadcast talk on Douglas.

The Gulbenkian Foundation did not concern itself with the magazine *Modern Poetry in Translation*, which TH and Daniel Weissbort eventually got off the ground in 1965, until 1972, when it provided funds for issue no. 13/14, devoted to Portuguese poetry and edited by Helder Macedo.

There is no record of TH having sent poems out under any alias, at this time or later. The poem here, 'Heptonstall', appeared frankly with his name when *The New Yorker* printed it on 27 February 1965. The text in *Wodwo* has differences of wording, punctuation and layout.

To Vicky Watling

[Late summer 1962]   Ms   Watling

Dear Vicky,

I laughed out loud when I heard the splendid news. Congratulations.

And best wishes. Marriage, of course, is a bloody monster, but it eats up many little snakes.

These secret marriages must run in the blood—you are now in the Farrar Underhand Society of Elopers, of which Ma is honorary chairwoman (don't mention this) Albert the patron saint, Hilda the secretary, myself the white elephant, yourself the dark horse.

Where are you going to live? I want to know because of a secret life I am trying to get going. I want an address in Yorkshire from which I can pretend to send poems under one or two names other than my own. I'm going to invent a rival poet, or perhaps two, who will gradually become much better than me—then the people who resent me for one reason or another, will line up to support one of my rivals (i.e. me). Also, I shall feel freer to write all kinds of stuff without endangering my reputation—since it's on reputation alone that I make my living, or on what my reputation attracts in the way of lucrative commissions.

All you will have to do—if you're willing at all—is, when the poems are returned to your address from the Magazines, stuff them into other envelopes addressed to other Magazines, & repost them. I'll supply you with all the addressed envelopes. You send the checques to me. Would you do it?

The first name will be <u>John Major</u>—ancestor of Pa's.

Don't on your life tell anybody about this. Nobody but yourself & Sylvia will know. Make this your first secret from your spouse too, if you can. Since you're probably the best secret-keeper in existence, I don't hesitate to let you in on it.

What's your new name?

Bring him down as soon as you can. We've a great apple crop this year, so if you can come in 3rd week September, or 2nd, you can fill up the back of the car.

Love to you Vic, & much happiness

Ted

Written in response to the news that his cousin Vicky (née Farrar) had married in secret.

To Olwyn Hughes

[September 1962]   Ms   Emory

Dear Olwyn,

The two letters were very good to find here. I've just been 7 days in the West of Ireland, with Sylvia—the holiday she's been struggling towards for the last weeks, and which has given her great ideas about living on the coast of Connemara till next March or so, instead of in Spain. She even found the house. A friend of ours, Richard Murphy, an Irish poet whose first good but somewhat staid first book has just been accepted by Fabers, lives out there—he runs two fishing boats for tourists all summer, & writes all winter. They seem to get on, & he'd be company for her—decayed aristocracy. He gets on my nerves rather. Though I quite enjoyed the place. In fact that coastline must be one of the most beautiful & unspoiled in the world.

The news of the snoop was interesting. But she knew more or less where I was. She couldn't possibly have thought I was in Yorkshire. She got to know all sorts of curious details, though—I put it down to clairvoyance, which works at full power where other women are concerned. Yes, it's just like her, to employ a snoop.

There's no problem, though, so long as I can keep up the cash. Sometimes she wants a legal separation, sometimes a divorce at once. I've left her in Ireland, while I attend to one or two small things, & I shan't be back at Court Green until Oct. 1ˢᵗ—by then she'll probably be wanting a divorce, & have started it up.

In her manner with other people she's changed extraordinarily—become much more as she was when I first knew her, & much more like her mother, whom I detest. You're right, she'll have to grow up—it won't do her any harm.

I hear you met Dido. They've just given me open house to their place in France—whether they're there or not. Sylvia had estranged them drastically—even from me. You ought to apply for a job at Fabers.

Love

Ted

I suggested Faber publish Keith Douglas' poems—they've commissioned me to edit it, with introduction.

TH and Plath had joined Richard Murphy in Cleggan, Connemara, on 13 September. An account of the visit, which was fraught with unhappiness and cut short, on TH's part, when he left abruptly to go fishing with the painter Barrie Cooke, is given in Richard Murphy's memoir, *The Kick* (2002). Plath's visit terminated in unwarranted ill feeling towards her host.

To Gerald Hughes

[December 1962]   Ms Emory

Dear Gerald,

Olwyn's sent me a letter you sent her, and you're quite right. All this business has been terrible—especially for Sylvia, but it was inevitable, and now the storm-centre of it recedes into the distance, I can only be relieved that I've done it. The one factor that nobody but quite close friends can comprehend, is Sylvia's particular death-ray quality. In many of the most important ways, she's the most gifted and capable & admirable woman I've ever met—but, finally, impossible for me to live married to. Now we're separated, we're better friends than we've been since we first met. Mainly because we see each other only about once a month, if that. The main grief for me is that a life that had all the circumstances for perfection, should have been so intolerable, and that little Frieda loses a father & I lose little Frieda. She's been my playmate for 2 years & become absolutely a necessary piece of my life. Now we're trying to get a biggish flat in London where Sylvia can live with the two children— only in London can she get a girl to live in & look after the kids, & she needs that if she's to write & work. When they're in London I can visit them regularly. They'll spend their summers in Devon. That's the plan. Meanwhile, I'm feeling a lot better except for dreaming about Frieda about every night.

Any chance of you coming to England? If I can amass the cash, I shall have some time in South America this next year—I'm thinking of it.

I left the car with Sylvia so now I'm driving around in a 1950 Ford van a friend's loaned me. Very inadequate, but O.K. I suppose I ought to buy another of my own.

I'm writing this at the Beacon. Ma & Pa seem very well, though Ma is troubled with rheumatism in her knee which slows her up & must be painful. Everything very still, misty, silent.

I'm off today to read poems to the assembled heads of Hull

University—a doubtful exercise, this poetry-reading. I keep thinking I'll stop it.

Sylvia's stories of all the women in London are exaggeration, of course, though it was cruelly unfortunate that the one woman Sylvia envied for her appearence should happen to get tangled up in my departure. That hurt her more than any other thing. But it's done.

Are you allright?

Love

Ted

To Olwyn Hughes

[December 1962]   Ms   Emory

I've got a little flat in Soho—just North of Charlotte St, exactly where I wanted it. A bit like a hotel room, but nice, & a very pleasant district—3 licensed betting offices within shouting distance.

Sylvia has finally, by a series of extraordinary flukes—which she calls her witchcraft—acquired the top two floors of the house in which Yeats lived as a child—Fitzroy Road, which leads onto Primrose Hill, 200 yards from the Chalcot Square flat. Very nice. £10 a week, which is extremely low, & a lease which allows her to sublet it for her own price at any time. So she'll advertise in the U.S. & let it for 5 summer months at £25 to £30 a week—should be easy, 80 dollars is doss-house rent in the states—and so she'll make the whole year's rent while she lives at North Tawton. A great relief to me.

[. . .]

Sylvia & I are great friends—though it's better I keep clear of her. I shall see Frieda. Apparently she talks about me all the time. She brought a dead shrew into the house the other day, holding it by the tail, & said "Look. Shrew fed up."

The 'Soho' flat was at 110 Cleveland Street, in the part of London w1 more commonly known as Fitzrovia. Plath's flat was at 23 Fitzroy Road, nw1.

To Donald Hall

[Undated 1962]   Ts   New Hampshire

Dear Don,

Here's a manuscript I would like you to read and pass on, if you will, to the powers at Wesleyan with a strong recommendation that it be published.

David Wevill's 27, lived outside Canada for the last 8 or so years (he's Canadian.) As you'll see, he's by quite a bit already the most interesting poet and probably the first real poet that Canada's produced. When he's good, it seems to me he's very good indeed, and not in any predictable or merely skillfull way. Alvarez agrees with me. I would like to recommend it in measured superlatives, but I don't want to put you on the defensive before you start to read it. You'll see the unusual combination of elements, the flexibility of language, and the genuine intuition with words, the original procedure of the whole works, as well as I do. Write back to me anyway, as soon as you can, with your reaction.

If you write to David Wevill, or meet him, ever, my name must not be mentionned—not on any condition. This isn't just modesty. And please don't carelessly mention that I sent you this manuscript, as that may get back to him.

How is the Douglas business proceeding? I would be glad to give some blurb, and so would Charles Tomlinson—he'd be strong support over there.

                              Yours
                              Ted

In the event, David Wevill was not taken up by Wesleyan University Press, for which Donald Hall sat on a selection committee.

Hall, who had in effect introduced Keith Douglas to TH through his anthology *New Poets of England and America*, was trying to find a US publisher for him.

1963

In the early hours of 11 February 1963, Sylvia Plath used the gas oven in her Fitzroy Road flat to kill herself. Her children, asleep in another room, were unharmed. The reasons for her suicide have been the subject of endless speculation, and readers of this book will find TH's own hypotheses in letters that follow. The effects of her tragic action on the direction his private life and writing were to take can also be traced there.

To Olwyn Hughes

[10 February 1963]   Ms   Emory

Dear Olwyn,

Here's the 'Difficulties'. The production was not too good, I thought, but it's effect was infinitely superior to "The Wound"—much richer than I expected. The most original passage, & what I thought would be the most impossible to do—the part where he's converted into numbers, with the tiger roaring—was hair-raising, really exciting. If you want some production notes I'll send them.

The women sing like African tribeswomen—flat, derisive etc.

The conversation between Sullivan & the first woman goes at great speed.

The chorus where his mutilated soul is brought back to the world 'bring his body" etc, should go with heavy driving momentum, not slow.

As a thing in itself, I think it's much more a work of art than the Wound. The day after I posted it, I drove up to London, ran over a hare (by pure chance—it's impossible to do it deliberately) sold it to a butcher's in Holborn & he gave me 5 bob. I spent it on roses—4 I got for 5/-, smashed two, & gave 2 to Assia.

I'm doing another now called The Dogs, about a man & a woman—infinitely richer & more artful than either of those. Also, I've borrowed a tape-recorder, so now I know what it sounds like—very delicate business, detecting the phrase or passage which is interesting to read but boring to hear.

[. . .]

The idea in the Bridegroom, is that running over the hare triggers off the drama inside Sullivan's head—the situation prepared there in consequence to his going to meet this girl. Essentially, the idea is that Sullivan must first of all recognise & dismiss—by some ordeal or other—the supernatural women which project themselves onto the real woman, & prevent him seeing her as real—as herself. Once he's dealt with his instinct to do this, he can meet that real one. The hare is the tiger is the women is his blood is all kinds of things, I'm not quite sure. But he has, so to speak, to kill it, master it, or at least meet it & recognise it, before he can get on with real outside life with a real woman. The thing he gets control of in this way, i.e., the instincts he gets under control, he can then offer to her in acceptable form—the roses. There are two roses, because one is for that other dual-tiger-hare-woman, not present but sacrificed.

Tell me what you think. The poachers are the first phase of the inner story, the rest of it the second.

Love   Ted

Written from 110 Cleveland Street, and accompanying the script of *Difficulties of a Bridegroom*. Douglas Cleverdon's production of the play was broadcast by the BBC Third Programme on 21 January 1963, close to a year after *The Wound*, and a year before *Dogs: A Scherzo*, both by the same service and with the same producer.

The date is a guess, based on the assumption that the letter was written between TH's hearing the broadcast and his learning of Sylvia Plath's death two days later.

To Olwyn Hughes

[February 1963]   Ms   Emory

Dear Olwyn,

On Monday morning, at about 6 a.m. Sylvia gassed herself. The funeral's in Heptonstall next Monday.

She asked me for help, as she so often has. I was the only person who could have helped her, and the only person so jaded by her states & demands that I could not recognise when she really needed it.

I'll write more later,

Love
Ted

TH now gives 23 Fitzroy Road as his own address.

To Daniel and Helga Huws

[February 1963]   Ms   Huws

Dear Dan & Helga,
   Sylvia killed herself on Monday morning.
   She seemed to be getting in good shape, she was writing again, she
was making enough money, getting all sorts of commissions, good
reviews for her novel—then a series of things, solicitor's letters, etc,
piled up, she flared up, the doctor put her on very heavy sedatives—and
in the gap between one pill & the next she turned on the oven, and
gassed herself. A Nurse was to arrive at 9 a.m.—couldn't get in, & it
was 11 a.m. before they finally got to Sylvia. She was still warm.
   The Funeral's in Yorkshire on Monday.
   I was the one could have helped her, and the only one that couldn't
see that she really needed it this time. No doubt where the blame lies.
   I shall look after Frieda & Nick here, & get a Nanny of some sort.
                                                    Ted

The postmark gives the date as 18 February, a Monday and, therefore, the day
of Plath's funeral. Probably this was written earlier, then posted locally, after a
delay.

To Aurelia Plath

15 March 1963   Ts   Lilly Library

Dear Aurelia,
   It has not been possible for me to write this letter before now. Jean,
the Nanny, is wonderful with Frieda and Nick, and already very
attached to them, especially to Nick. She is even better than I thought
she would be. Now that she's used to us she's not so shy. She comes
from a small village on the coast of Dorset, and there's a true country
peace and sureness about her. Nick is his old self, and both walks odd
steps and speaks odd words. Frieda has started talking in quite long
sentences and talks constantly. She's also much less selfish now she's
calming down, and when we have guests she plunders them and takes
everything to Nick. It is not a bad thing for her to have somebody as
calm as Jean. It would be disastrous for her to lose me now.

214

I shall never get over the shock and I don't particularly want to. I've seen the letters Sylvia wrote to my parents, and I imagine she wrote similar ones to you, or worse. The particular conditions of our marriage, the marriage of two people so openly under the control of deep psychic abnormalities as both of us were, meant that we finally reduced each other to a state where our actions and normal states of mind were like madness. My attempt to correct that marriage is madness from start to finish. The way she reacted to my actions also has all the appearence of a kind of madness—her insistence on a divorce, the one thing in this world she did not want, the proud hostility and hatred, the malevolent acts, that she showed to me, when all she wanted to say simply was that if I didn't go back to her she could not live. Only in the last month suddenly we became friends, closer than we've been for two years or so. Everything seemed to be prospering for her, and we began to have happy times together. Then suddenly her book about her first breakdown comes out, fifty other hellish details go against her, she became over-agitated, begged me to leave the country because she couldn't bear to live in the same city, my presence was weakening her independence, and so on, then very heavy sedatives, then this. If I hadn't been so blindly involved in the struggle with her, how easily I could have seen through all this! And I had come to the point where I'd decided we could repair our marriage now. She had agreed to stop the divorce. I had that weekend cancelled all my appointments for the next fortnight. I was going to ask her to come away on the Monday, on holiday, to the coast, some place we had not been. Think of how it must be for me too.

We were utterly blind, we were both desperate, stupid, and proud— and the pride made us oblique, she especially so. I know Sylvia was so made that she had to mete out terrible punishment to the people she most loved, but everybody is a little bit like that, and it needed only intelligence on my part to deal with it. But the difficulties caused by that, the fact that on the surface the situation was no more difficult than the normal one for separated couples—it was better than most in that she had money, fame, prospering plans and many friends—all these things delayed the workings of our reconciliation.

I don't want ever to be forgiven. I don't mean that I shall become a public shrine of mourning and remorse, I would sooner become the opposite. But if there is an eternity, I am damned in it. Sylvia was one of the greatest truest spirits alive, and in her last months she became a great poet, and no other woman poet except Emily Dickinson can begin to be compared with her, and certainly no living American.

So now I shall look after Frieda and Nick and you are not to worry about them. I will write as often as I can about them. Frieda has just gone to School—she wakes up shouting to be taken to school, and she's very good there, mixes well and has two special friends. Jean is putting Nick down. This Nanny costs only £6 a week and does absolutely everything. She has a day and a half off each week.

I didn't know how to start this letter and now I don't know how I can end it. I'll write again, and tell you my plans.

Love
Ted

To Assia Wevill

[27 March 1963]   Ms   Emory

Assia,

I tried to ring you this morning. I wanted to see you. Nothing we said the other day was right.

If you & David are going to part, it must be easier for both of you now, than after a month more of general misery.

As things are, it is bad for all of us. If you come to me, David suffers. If you go to him, you suffer, and does he stop suffering? I don't see how it can make him happy again, just to hand yourself over to him as a prisoner or a body, unless he's not at all concerned how you are feeling, and quite happy to have you even against your will.

I haven't been able to do anything since yesterday but think how we can do this. But the only alternatives are that David accepts the way you feel, or he refuses to accept it. If he accepts it, there's some hope for all of us—though a painful one for him. If he refuses to accept it, what hope is there for you, or for him, or for me. If what you've said really happens, then you'll go to pieces. He'll go to pieces in the mess. And I add one mistake to my other one. I've concentrated all my life now on these two children & on what you and I might do, & you say you want nothing but that, and I've believed you so far that if now you stay with David I don't know what I shall do.

I feel tied up in everything I say about this by David's claim on you.

He hopes & believes what you feel is temporary & will change,

216

whereas I believe it's permanent. So it's up to you to act as you do feel, & demonstrate which of us is wrong. There's no other way of solving this.

You know what I feel. If my feelings about you had been moveable at all, this last 6 weeks would have moved them, but it hasn't, it's just shown me how final they are, and particularly this last weekend. This isn't to say that my feeling for you is stronger than anybody else's, such as David's, ever could be, but that it's complete, and you can rely on it completely, if you choose to. But it's up to you now to choose.

Will David let you live away from him, and with me, for six months? Anything shorter is silly. You say you want to leave him now. If you still want to live away from him then after 6 months, how can he claim you, except by law, which he must feel is as meaningless as you do.

I'll ring you this morning   Ted

To Aurelia Plath

13 May 1963   Ts   Lilly Library

Dear Aurelia,

I have delayed writing to you for several reasons, circumstances which have confused my original attitude to you and made it difficult to know what to say, without being simply incredulous. But let me explain my thoughts to you.

As you understand, your coming over this June presents me with a manifold problem. Naturally, you want to visit the children, but while our memories are still so very raw, this is going to need thoughtful handling. For one thing, what is your state of mind going to be while you are with them? There is a danger, I fear, that you may slip into simply mourning over them, almost as if they were Sylvia, as indeed they are—Frieda especially. Or, if you avoid the oppression of that, will you be tempted to something much worse, I mean to force-feed them love—to satisfy your feelings for Sylvia, and to make up for Sylvia's love for them which they no longer have. This could be terrible. Your feelings for Sylvia, like mine, no longer have any worldly object, so they are free to develope an unearthly and perhaps even religious intensity—and if these feelings are turned onto a substitute, such as Nick and Frieda, then their consciousness is forced into a world of unreal abstraction, feelings they cannot understand, which cripple their sense of reality and falsify their nature. This is not theory, in that I have been the victim of just such feelings when I was far more capable of fighting them than these children are, and the effect on me was to make me to all practical purposes mad, to alienate me from the world and from myself. And with such a person as yourself, Aurelia, so eager not to reserve any feeling you feel may be good, the impulse to envelope them with this kind of love may be an irresistible and quite unconscious impulse. If you could be sure of treating them naturally, that is to say in an easy and relaxed way, it would be good for you to see them, but I dread the effects of that tense, watchful anxiety for them and everything about them which, I think, helped to make Sylvia's life so much more difficult than it need have been, difficult as it was at times—I mean a more or less constant state of terror that something might go wrong, then panic when it does, even if it's only missing a train. What makes me fear that such feelings of not-alltogether realistic anxiety may be your guiding motives at present, are the rumours of things you have said which I hear inevitably from the U.S., together with certain questions which Warren put to me when he was over—questions which could only have been framed in a mind very ill-informed and perhaps misinformed about the state of affairs—and your own desire to hear from my acquaintances over here details about our life which you fear I might not think necessary to supply, and which—in all justice—it should not be your concern to know. This naturally makes me feel the subject of investigation—not a state to be suffered complacently. It also sharpens my perhaps mistaken sense of your antagonism to any course of life I may now choose which is not American, or which is not a public and resigned posture of remorse and self-immolation over Sylvia's name. Please, Aurelia, do not make the mistake of thinking that the way I caused Sylvia to suffer was any indication of my real feelings for her, which are simply unaltered. Because of what I describe above, my love for her simply underwent temporary imprisonment by something which can only be described as madness, as much an attempt to free myself from the strangling quality of our closeness as by any outer cause. My love for her simply continues, I look on her as my wife and the only one I shall ever marry, and these two children are ours. Understand this, and please be watchful for any tendencies in yourself to make a battleground of Nick and Frieda, either now or in the future. My life will no doubt go through several strange interludes, but who is to say that these may not be the best luck they could have? We cannot protect their lives too much from life, otherwise when it does arrive it may be more than they can take, or something they feel not quite their element. I am sure you will endorse all this, and it may be the legion of talebearers have dramatised things somewhat, as they have done all along. But you see how things stand. And in the light of this, you will see how easy it is for me to conceive of your visit over here simply or largely as investigation into circumstances, a checking-up, and the rest of it, and you know how natural it is to resent that. I had hoped it would be possible to avoid moving into opposition, no matter how concealed, but unless you can leave my life and the lives of the children to me, then it is inevitable. Then, as I say, you will have no alternative but to forego a close relationship to the children, or make a battlefield of their loyalties.

Your remarks about Court Green illustrate, I think, the slight unreality of your thinkings about this business. Can you imagine me living, with the children, in the rooms and corners of Sylvia's greatest happiness and worst grief, the site, in fact, of my crime against her, against myself, and against every human thing. It is impossible to consider 'historical interest' in such a place. I wish to feel my share of the guilt to the full, but I also want to live and see these children live not crippled by it. And can you imagine Frieda and Nick growing up with the memories of those villagers? You could not wish to seal us off where your memories are sealed off. We have to create a life which will not succumb backwards into Sylvia's Magnetism, so perhaps we shall have to make unusually vigourous leaps. Surely you understand this, and realise that we must be allowed to live without supervision from curators of the past, no matter how well-intentionned they may be.

I intend to purchase a place in Yorkshire, perhaps in the dales, where the children will have all the advantages of a semi-country life, a rooted home among rooted people, and belonging to my family. It may be that Hilda will retire and live with us, as she wishes to retire and is particularly fond of the children, especially Nicholas whom she loves, she says, more than she ever did her own daughter. She tells me you have invited her to live with the children, with you, in the U.S. I think you must be thinking fantastic thoughts to come to such an idea—and such thoughts, I fear, you will be bringing with you.

Nick and Frieda are thriving. Nicholas runs about and Frieda is very proud of his advances. He feeds himself, chatters weird language, and eats enormously. Sylvia's upset about his eye was apparently unfounded. The slight cross was an optical illusion caused by the unusually deep fold of skin over the inner eye-corner, which made the pupil in that eye look nearer to the nose, and seem almost to disappear when he looked to the right. But the eye is quite straight, and as he grows, the fold is disappearing. I will send you snaps of them.

My writing, which has now reached a fairly steady level of proficiency is going quite well, provided I avoid interruptions, and our income is in order. I am steadily getting Sylvia's poems published in Magazines, then I shall have them all published in one volume, and perhaps the poems of the Colossus reprinted with them, so everything will be together.

Meanwhile, please consider all that I have written here as my attempt to forestall too impulsive actions on your part, concerning the children, and to show you quite openly what I have been forced to think. It may be that all I have said has grown from a delusion and is unnecessary, and I trust that it is so.

As ever
Ted.

Hilda Farrar, TH's maternal aunt, had been helping him to look after the children.

To Gerald and Joan Hughes

19 June 1963   Ms   Emory

Dear Gerald & Joan,

I've been thinking that I'll hang on to Court Green. I'm likely to sell it for much less than it will be worth in future as a country resort for Frieda & Nick etc. Meanwhile, if you're feeling like a change, and would like to review the farm-market without breaking yourselves on rent, etc, why not come over & live in it—for as long as you like. Plenty of room for all of us.

Farms in Devon tend to be very expensive—since retiring to a farm in Devon is every Colonial Governor's, Prizefight promoter's & Advertising Agency Director's dream—the countryside is creeping with medals, titles & Jaguars. If they're not expensive, they're tiny & obviously a struggle—$^1/_3$ the farms in Devon change hands every 5 years. Though I'm sure it's with small farmers as in all other occupations—most of them don't use much sense.

Farms in the North are much cheaper. I gave a lift just last week to a youth who had been to 3 farm sales—all over 30 acres, none went for over £3,000. One, good grazing, good buildings, 75 acres brought

£2,900. That was in the Lakes—in Cumberland, rather. Life up there is not quite so pinned by suburbs & the mentality of the South either—

I hope to have quite a bit of cash within the next 2 years. I don't know if I'm being sanguine. But I'd like to be turning enough over to make whatever farm we do take—if we take one—a healthy hope. I mean, we shan't be relying on just milk, in case of a disaster.

Tell me what you think of coming over to live in Court Green for a while—even just as a holiday.

Frieda & Nick are with Hilda—both much happier than they were, since they've now got playmates. I'm trying to sublet—for a slight profit,—this place in London.

Sylvia's mother is in England for a month—which means another four weeks of nerves, just in case I thought things might be settling down. Olwyn's here, on her way back to Paris. We've just been for a huge Chinese meal at a place down in the East End—supposedly the best in Europe, & not at all expensive. Unbelievably delicious food.

Ma is fine—much better for her rest. We're trying to persuade them to put central heating in the Beacon, where the air is so damp the pliers, & saws & nails in the drawers rust in a week, the window-fittings rust away, the sheets feel damp if nobody's slept there for a week. All that must have some effect, if you tend to suffer rheumatism at all.

I keep writing odd things, but this confusion is not good for regular application which is very necessary for me. It makes life seem a bit of a battle on seven fronts. All I've ever been interested in is simplifying my existence so I could write, & all I've ever done is so involve myself with other people that now I can't move without horrible consequences of all kinds, on all sides. So I'm having to learn to let a few things take care of themselves.

Olwyn sends her love   Ted

To Michael Baldwin

[Autumn 1963]   Ms   Baldwin

Dear Michael Baldwin,

Thank you for the 2 books. I haven't read either of them yet, but I'll drop you a note when I do.

It struck me after writing the review of "A World of Men" that my interpretation might be completely wrong—I was only reassured by the book's title.

D.A.N. Jones' retort to your letter in the N.S. is a real example of our particularly English brand of stupidity. What he's saying is "Don't be emotional." He is incapable of drawing a moral distinction between fighting with weapons that kill only the people who are trying to kill you, and fighting with weapons that kill everybody. His letter seems to me a criminal offence of sorts. I can imagine what a jolly good no-nonsense sort of chap he is. You were answered, of course, by your "superior officer", so what did you expect. Christ knows why he's allowed to review anything.

Yours

Ted Hughes

TH's review of two books by Michael Baldwin (b.1930), including the novel *A World of Men*, had appeared in the *Listener* (21 February 1963), where he had called the writing 'radiant and unalterable . . . clean and alive at every point.' Baldwin, whom he had not yet met, then sent him two earlier books, one of which, *In Step with a Goat*, an account of soldiering, had been the subject of a disparaging review by D. A. N. Jones in the *New Statesman* (6 September 1963). When Baldwin had written to complain of misrepresentation, Jones had used the opportunity to add 'superior officer' remarks.

To Assia Wevill

[3 October 1963]   Ms   Emory

Asseenke—

I got down here screwed up like a guitar string & spent the rest of the day trying to ease up, sitting around drinking coffee & eating apples & starting one book after another.

Our evening on Primrose Hill should have been our norm—not a freak occasion. Does it still work on you? Let it. Because if you don't, there's no future but stupid finaglings. I'm so sick of them I can't go on with one more, they're too debasing & ruinous.

It's completely different down here—so strange to be here without the electrical cloud. The peace is bewildering—I spend a lot of time just standing about. I saw a door in the yard, on one of the outbuildings, that I'd never seen before. I opened it—a big shed, as big as the kitchen at Fitzroy Rd. All the time we were here I never even noticed it. It's full of interesting barrels and stone jars. How weird to think that Sylvia never knew about it, never looked in there.

I've just been on to phone you and the fault that cut us off was as usual on the Primrose Line—they couldn't reconnect me. O Assia—I could hear you saying Hello Hello Hello, & rattling the phone, and I was saying Assia! Assia! and you just went on saying, Hello Hello. Then you got very faint, then there were buzzings & voices.
[. . .]
I'm just settling into a stew of scribbling and meandering. I shall do more in the next month than I've done in the last year, as you'll see. I'll bring up the play next week, and be on to another. I'm going to see if it's possible to write myself out—just for an experiment.
[. . .]
Are you exhausting your appetite for Seafood? How is it that I can never get you to eat anything, but with Ducker you eat 9 oysters—all in high spirits and laughing your head off & being overwhelming I expect.

It's up to you.

Everybody down here listened to Sylvia's broadcast. They're all painfully friendly.

What are you doing? Keep a journal and send it. I might come through this weekend as I go to collect the kids—it's almost as quick.

Everything with me is as it was, Assia.

Ted

TH was now back at Court Green. Assia Wevill was at 23 Fitzroy Road.
'Sylvia's broadcast' was a memorial radio programme by A. Alvarez.
Passages omitted from this letter contain insignificant literary news.

To Aurelia and Warren Plath

[October 1963]   Ts and ms   Lilly Library

Dear Aurelia and Warren,

It's been rather a long time since I wrote. I was negotiating to buy a large and very beautiful house/farm in yorkshire, in its own valley. I felt that if I could not easily live in Court Green again, I must find a place at least as good for Frieda and Nick. But the prospective purchaser of Court Green delayed and delayed, until it began to seem possible that I might live here and not throw away all the work and love that was put into it. So I just cancelled the sale—the buyer's very ambiguous ditherings made that simple. Anyway, I'm back here now, with Frieda and Nick in the small room, and Olwyn and Hilda temporarily helping. Certain things about living here are difficult, but not to have come back would have been worse eventually.

It took us about twelve hours to get down here, driving very slowly and with frequent stops. Frieda had been terribly excited about it for several days, packing everything she could move, all the ornaments and pictures she could find. So she was car-sick the first hour of the trip. Then she recovered, and as usual blamed Nicky for being sick (he wasn't) and was no trouble at all the rest of the way, sang and conversed. She holds long conversations now. When there are no other children near, she becomes like an adult: it is completely like being with an adult—the sense she gives you of being completely tuned in to all your feelings and unspoken thoughts, and quite understanding them. Obviously what she has gone through has developed her in an unusual way. Nick slept and sang and ate, and never once cried the whole way. Frieda became quite anxious about finding the place. I suppose she thought we were taking a terribly long time. When she got out of the car in the dark she looked all round, asking if this was Court Green, then went into the house, looking around. I was apprehensive about her reactions. But I haven't been able to tell whether it's all new, or whether she remembers it completely and just takes it all for granted. She knows her way around, and knows everybody we meet, but she never reminisces—perhaps it's an unnatural thing for a child of her age to do. We met Elsie, the little hunchback, the other day and she and Frieda greeted each other. She's only about a foot taller than Frieda. "My, how you've grown," says Elsie. "Yes I have," says Frieda. Then, after a pause: "You haven't, have you." People in the village are being incredibly kind and pleasant, and Elizabeth and David have been a great help. We went up on Dartmoor the other day to fly a kite David had bought at a jumble sale. It was the third day—the day the reactions to everything hit both Nick and Frieda, but the kite was a great cure. Then we took her to Bideford and she became quite wild about the sea. We waded, and chased gulls, and found little crabs and caught shrimps in the pools. She was all for refusing absolutely to come away, and we only got her away by saying we were now going to the swings. There are some swings nearbye, luckily. That was the day we bought a lovely little bed for her for 25 shillings—after Winnifred had rather caught me into buying one off her, neither so pretty nor in such good shape, for ten pounds. Elizabeth talked to her, fortunately, so now we're only borrowing Winnifred's bed. They are only 13 pounds brand new. Now both Frieda and Nick are thoroughly at home, absorbed all day with the million interesting things there are to do down here. Olwyn is making jam and bottling fruit—it's not a good year for apples, but a surprisingly good one for plums. For the first time the plum tree in the yard corner has fruit—and it's loaded. Both Hilda and Olwyn are relaxing too to the tempo of life down here. Frieda's cat Skunk has returned so now she has him and two ginger kittens. We kept the kittens—½ grown cats actually, in the barn till they get used to their new home. Yesterday Skunk, who is very rough, swatted at Frieda with his claws, so she told him very strictly that he was a naughty pussy, and if he didn't mend his ways he'd have to live in the barn with the other cats. I hope you are keeping well. Faber & Faber have asked if they may publish Sylvia's poems and I think they will give better advertisement, & better distribution than Heinemanns. The Colossus was never in the shops. Also, they have offered a special royalty, which would go into an account for Frieda & Nick—so I shall send the M.S. to Fabers.

[*No signature*]

A note in Aurelia Plath's hand says the letter was received on 18 October.
  Elizabeth and David Compton were Devon neighbours who had looked after Court Green in TH's absence.

To Donald Hall

[Late 1963]   Ms   New Hampshire

I hope you got a few more poems of Sylvia's, before the proofs went too far. Her MS is still here with me. I'm negotiating with publishers.

  I'm glad you like the poems. I don't agree with your remarks about them in the review. It's a pity remarks in print look so absolute.

  Other people's weaker poems look like anybody's, or somebody else's, but her least successful efforts were unique—like a completely original substance, even the very artificial ones.

  When you criticise her for using the impact of her sufferings in place of the impact of art, it seems to me you misread them. What you're saying really, is that at last she managed to get through—she managed actually to say something of her own, in verse. What a feat! For a change, and at last, somebody's written in blood.

Whatever you say about them, you know they're what every poet wishes he or she could do.

At the same time, I imagine you know as well as I do, she was incapable of writing without a dozen or so purely formal devices going along with her, in the way of design, & music, recurrence & development—and these are there in the poems you mention, plus. When poems hit so hard, surely you ought to find reasons for their impact, not argue yourself out of your bruises. If I cavil a bit, it's because I hate to see cavilling, when something like those poems has occurred. And you seemed to cavil a bit, in that review.

Did you see any English reviews of the 5 American Poets? I was genuinely surprised. They read like 1948. I can understand it though. Their apparent contempt for, say, Bowers (dull as he is, on the whole) is really a sort of self-contempt. Their underestimation of Simpson is an extension of the prevailing English repressive outlook, our military army-of-occupation heritage.

Nobody liked Plutzik, who seems to me quite inspired at times, & speaks like a man, where the others speak like birdwatchers.

I'd have liked to include other people—maybe, if this one pays, they'll do a second, as I believe you suggested. But quite a few Americans are already published over here, in one form or another.

I've just sent back the Douglas proofs—ratty, ant-bitten print they've used, I'm afraid, like "Imitations." I told them about your efforts in the States, so I doubt if they're thinking of doing anything in that direction.

In a friendly review of *Five American Poets*, in the October 1963 number of the magazine *The Review*, Hall, who was an admirer of Plath's work, had voiced reservations about it, in an attempt to counterbalance the more exaggerated and sensationalising claims that had been made for it since her death. He wrote: 'Some of the most powerful of Plath's late poems – like "Lady Lazarus" and "Daddy" in *Encounter* – are not really the best ones. They have power over us by shocking us with content, and the poem has remained largely unwritten.'

Faber's *Selected Poems of Keith Douglas* was published in February 1964, suggesting, albeit vaguely, a date for this letter.

To Aurelia and Warren Plath

16 December 1963   Ts   Lilly Library

Frieda and Nick are now getting very excited about Xmas. Some time ago I bought them three coloured mice, and had ordered a new cage for them, since the cats were always interfering with the old one. This morning the cage came and Frieda thought it must be Christmas if presents for the mice have come. "We'd better open all those other parcels" she said. I explained that Father Christmas was just visiting last night, to find out what was wanted at this house, and sure enough a few minutes later Frieda heard him going over in his aeroplane. The mice are quite important at present. She took them all out a few days ago, and spread a blanket over them, 'because they ought to get plenty of sleep'. But of course they all ran away. We recaptured two. Then there are two goldfish and a catfish. Daddy fish, Frieda fish, and the catfish is Nicky fish. Everything goes into families.

[. . .]

At present, everything is stories. Each night I have to tell her two or three, and again first thing in the morning. There is a character called Frooda who goes all over the place and does all kinds of things. I've discovered that whatever Frooda learns, Frieda knows next day, and this has all kinds of possibilities. Frieda is very keen that Frooda shouldn't get ahead. She's invented a beast called the Lagerlock—I think it's a cross between dragon and weathercock, but it's very terrible and there are vast numbers of them. Sometimes she gets the upper hand, and gobbles them all up. Nicky is sometimes a Lagerlock, and it's ten to one that every car you pass on the road is full of Lagerlocks going to a party.

1964

To Aurelia and Warren Plath

5 January 1964   Ts   Lilly Library

DEC. 20th: Last night I bought some plastic model animals, and gave her the giraffe. The bedtime story was all about this giraffe, and at last it began to call to all the animals in the world to come and live with Frieda and Nick, because they were such happy children and treat their toys so nicely, and all night long they would be walking towards Court Green and maybe by morning one or two would have arrived. Then early this morning I put a penguin beside her bed, but as it's so tiny she never noticed it. She got dressed in her red pants, Nicky in his new green marvellous suit. Frieda looks like a baby Father Xmas of a sort of Toyland, and Nick looks like a holly tree with berries. She told me no animals had arrived, so we went back to look, and when we found the penguin she could hardly believe her eyes. She's talked about it ever since. [. . .] DEC 23rd: They've both been angelic all day. Yesterday while I was chopping wood in the orchard, Frieda came out, all wrapped up, to watch. We're now on the last of the poplar logs—not very good wood for burning until it's been thoroughly dried out. As I chopped, a great strip of old bark fell away, and exposed a colony of woodlice, centipedes and a few worms. Frieda was in raptures. "Stop, stop", she cried. And we had to carry them all to safety, especially the worms who are her particular friends. The other morning when Frieda woke she found a "Crockledile" on her heater, come in the night all the way from Egypt. Next morning she found nothing, so I supposed it was because she'd been naughty with Nick the evening before and made him cry. So all that day she was angelic—even though they're so excited about Xmas, or rather Frieda is and Nick picks it up. This morning she found no animals and was very upset, because as she said she'd been so good so they'd all come, so I asked her if she'd looked on the stair. Sure enough on the stair were a polar bear and a kangaroo. [. . .] Our old friend Lucas was here all last week and will be staying with us again after Xmas. He has a little daughter in America just as old as Frieda, so she gets all his attention and is becoming very attached. He tells her stories all day. Her appetite for stories is absolutely insatiable. Nicky stands listening like a statue.

The letter from which the excerpt above is taken, although written and posted separately from that of 16 December 1963, continues the reassuring Christmas narrative.

To Assia Wevill

[9 February 1964]   Ms   Emory

Sweetness—

that last day was the first of a relapse into some grisly kind of flu for me. The train back was tropical forest inside, Arctic outside—so yesterday dragged by half-conscious,—today's a sore throat, & Monday will be a cough with pains, & Tuesday tubercolosis—Anyway, it's good for letters. My life has gone over completely to the production of letters.

Tell me a few things.

What if I'd just put the phone down on Thursday, when you said you were so busy & in a bad temper?

When you'd spent Wednesday describing to me how & just how completely you'd planned me out of your future moves, why did you pretend to be angry on Thursday morning at what you interpret as my lack of confidence in you? Something else must have made you angry.

In fact, the more I think about it, the more strange it seems, that on Thursday morning you were ready to tell me to disappear, & on Thursday afternoon & Friday were so affectionate. Maybe those two days were just an illusion.

I wish it didn't all seem so fishy, in retrospect.

There's one explanation for that, and other things, which is that to get your revenge & for self-respect & compensation-just-in-case, you took Liliana's gossip as fact, added it to your general humiliations from last year, & have been investing your Insurance in somebody else. If that's so, it's O.K., but don't go on nursing the dream of our living together—because that dream feeds exclusively on trust, & nothing else will turn it to reality.

If it were to live on your letters, it would prosper—they ring sincere, or I'm a fool. And if it were to live on me, it would prosper—but on your moods, your oblique plans, your mistaking of my name, nothing prospers but my wondering what's really going on.

You know what I feel, my sweet Assia, about what might be, & will be—if you're a good enough tightrope-walker for a few months, & if I can go on producing as I have done this last month—. If you can't fasten your feelings in that, there's no hope. If you can't live under the surface, but need to be playing some game all the time & winning obvious sums, there's no hope.

You say you want me to repeat it all now & again, as if it were from me that the single-mindedness had to be dragged—but you know I'm single-minded in all my long-term desires.

So tell me a few things.

Maybe all this comes out of your sickness.

If you distrust Thursday afternoon & Friday, you must be nutty.

I got a lot of checques in the mail—improvement.

The letter ends abruptly, unsigned. In the months following the last letter to Wevill printed here (3 October 1963), TH, when not in London, wrote frequently to keep her up to date with a heavy programme of work that included the early film-script version of *Gaudete* – to which she seems to have contributed ideas – as well as other projects designed to make money.

To Siv Arb

10 February 1964   Ms   Arb

Dear Siv.,

This is partly in reply to a letter you wrote 5.12.63. Of course I remember your visit, and I remember most of what we said.

Here is 'the Earth-Owl', and I am getting you a copy of Sylvia's novel. Also, I'm enclosing one or two of Sylvia's poems—for your magazine if you like, or to pass on to Lars Backstrom, to whom I'll be writing soon.

I've written a film scenario, in detail, which I think is outside the scope of any English director, and so I thought first of all of trying to have Ingmar Bergmann read it, or some similar Swedish director. In theme, it's somewhat in line with his sympathies, I think. Could you get him to read it—do you know anyone who knows him & could ask him to read it? I imagine he's pretty hard to get at. But if you can, I'll send you the script.

I hope you're doing well.

Yours

Ted

Having introduced TH's poetry to Sweden in 1961, in the magazine *Rondo*, Siv Arb had visited TH and Sylvia Plath in Devon on 25 April 1962. Later, she translated a number of Plath's poems, again in *Rondo*, and put together a collection of them, *Dikter*, in 1975. Lars Backstrom: Swedish poet, critic and translator.

The film scenario was an early stab at the themes of *Gaudete*. In a subsequent, undated letter, TH writes to Arb: 'I sent that script to Vilgot Sjoman, but he returned it—not suitable for him. I think I'll re-write it as a novel—then see if anybody'll pick it up. In its present form it's a bit melodramatic—a real idea, though, I think.' Vilgot Sjöman (1924–2006) was most famous for his taboo-breaking film of 1967, *I Am Curious (Yellow)*.

To Daniel Weissbort

12 February 1964   Ms   King's College, London

Dear Danny,

It is great news that you are stirring up so much electricity about the Magazine. I <u>was</u> up last week, but a locally-confined cataclysm more or less put me out of action, & I found your long letter when I got back.

The costs sound terribly steep. I've been thinking all along of a fairly scrappy looking thing—just to keep the spirits thinking it needs their help, they desert something that gets too efficient, they like to feel needed, I'm sure.

I haven't heard from Hull, but I've written again. I've asked for a detailed description of the procedures of their distribution & how they could help us.

Since you're assembling a front of interested helpers, we might well appeal directly to Gulbenkian.

I'm enclosing a letter—self-explanatory—with addresses of Americans, but I'd like to keep it English, wouldn't you? There's something in that American translaterese that's too glib in their way, better to use the English brand. The menace with English translators is lack of momentum & flair—they're all stilted & minced up, Senior Parlour consciences. But there are good ones.

I think it's important not to go off at half-cock. Let's make the first issue good—now those American translations would do later on, but they have been published in the States—twice & thrice. If we're going to use them at all, that is.

I'd like to make one of the early issues on Ferenc Juhasz—the Hungarian. That would be striking, wide appeal, & not done in America. [. . .]

I'm coming up Friday—I'll give you a ring. I shall be in the red Lion, which is in that street between St James' Square & that street parallell to & South of Piccadilly, from 1 oclock on. See if you can see her before then. Greetings to Jill & Hercules   Ted

Alan Sillitoe is an excellent translator & very keen on this mag—he has some translations of Vallejo much better than the American, & he's learning Russian, could get the books, has met the poets—he's a Communist of course. But would you like to ring him? BAY 5572. Say I gave you his number, & this is the magazine moving into its possibly practical phase. He knows a pile of people too.

By now, TH and Weissbort were on course to bring out the magazine that in 1965 would appear, initially in the form of a broadsheet on Bible paper, as *Modern Poetry in Translation*. Ferenc Juhász (b.1928), author of 'The Boy Turned into a Stag Cries Out at the Gate of Secrets', was not in fact to be included in the first issue, although at about this time TH made his own version of Kenneth McRobbie's translation of the poem (see *Ted Hughes: Selected Translations*, edited by Weissbort). Alan Sillitoe (b.1928), novelist and poet, was on the masthead among the magazine's 'advisory editors', and the featured poets, most of whom were given generous spreads, were Yehuda Amichai (1924–2000), Zbigniew Herbert (1924–98), Miroslav Holub (1923–98), Ivan Lalić (1931–96), Czesław Miłosz (1911–2004), Vasko Popa (1922–91) and Andrei Voznesensky (b.1933) – the last translated by Weissbort.

'See if you can see her': i.e. a Hungarian contact mentioned in the omitted passage.

To Charles Monteith

7 April 1964   Ms   Faber

Dear Charles,

We were hoping to be able to come to the party on Thursday, but of all things I've been conscripted as a juror, at the Exeter assizes, for that very day. It happened before, then they cancelled me at the last minute—which I expected to happen again this time.

I'm just arranging Sylvia's poems. There were two things I ought to have mentionned before—could I have a say in the design of the jacket, & in the print used? For instance, I'd like the cover to be red, the print either black or yellow, preferably black. That was what she imagined. Very simple, just the colour—the print. Another detail: she prided herself on having a remote Mongolian Ancestor. The national emblem of Mongolia is a horseman riding into the sunrise. Her title poem "Ariel" is about riding on horseback into the sunrise, and she played with the idea of having that emblem, small, on the cover, though she couldn't decide whether she preferred a rose.

For the print, she wanted it large—she was pained by the small print of the Heinemann "Colossus". She liked the print of "The Hawk in the Rain"—big and black.

I hope the designer will be willing to do something with this.

All the best,

sincerely
Ted

TH's suggestion for the cover design of Sylvia Plath's first posthumous collection, *Ariel*, was not followed. On 13 January 1965, he wrote to Monteith: 'I've just received a copy of the dust-jacket of Ariel from Mr Volpe. It was a bit of a shock: they always are. I'm writing him a little note about it.' Berthold Wolpe (1905–89) was the German-born designer whose highly personal use of type and hand-drawn lettering made the covers of Faber books unmistakable during the years of his association with the firm.

To Gerald and Joan Hughes

14 July 1964   Ms   Emory

Dear Gerald & Joan,

Things here are going on fairly normal. It's been one of the most overpowering Springs I remember—everything seemed to come together. It's looking a bit more burned out now, & the land here has just vanished under weeds. I scythe for an hour a day, but don't really make much headway. The soil is so incredibly rich. There are foxgloves in the front garden a foot taller than I am. Hilda came the other day, for two weeks. She's looking very well—younger than ever. Also, Ma is much better—looking really well, & years younger, and walking again. Olwyn is a bit ill—but she's just doped with cigarettes. I've bet her £50 she can't stop, so she pretends to have stopped. The reason her life has been such a drifting fog for 15 years, is that she's been smoking 50 a day for just that period of time.

The kids are doing well. Nick is a very tough-minded little bloke—alltogether a very strange & violent little kid, a little Napoleon. Frieda goes to school & is just a delight. Joan, you seem to have made an impression on them—that room is Auntie Joan's room, whoever stays in it. And we still occasionally hear what Auntie Joan did.

We met Henry Williamson the other day—he wrote Tarka the Otter (If you haven't read it, read it—about a Devonshire Otter). He was a great Fascist, dreamed he had been called to do for England what Hitler did for Germany, etc, and made a great mess of his life with Hitlerism. But he's full of the most amazing anecdotes about birds & animals—you'd love him, Gerald, though he's a bit of an old sod. We've several extremely interesting friends down here.

Why don't you come over for a bit longer, and make a provisional dabble in the antique & 2nd hand trade—there's quite a good living in it, & a very interesting one. You could fix to supply some stuff to Australia. I read of an American Antique scout who was over here. He commissioned a junk dealer in Brighton to collect chamber pots—victorian & floral as possible, which he thought of selling in the States for punch-bowls. So this junk dealer collected over 2,000 chamber-pots, ready for the American to collect in the spring. He was going to get a very high price for them, so he'd collected diligently. Then that winter the American died & this man in Brighton is stuck with 2000 chamber pots.

The boar's tusk arrived, very fine, but Frieda immediately carried it off to her treasure box, her precious box, she calls it. It must have been quite a big boar.

I've stopped griping myself about the crowds & the rubbish—it would kill you, if you set yourself against it. The millions are pouring down here into the coastal resorts but I see nothing of them.

Did you get the Keith Douglas poems, Gerald? Answer this.

Are the boys all right? Keep thinking about coming over here for good—house in Ireland, or something, or as a junk dealer scouring the sales all over the country, while you keep a shop—or just a Head-quarters. It can be a good thing. Love from all,   Ted

The Court Green ménage at this time included TH's sister, who in November 1963 had given up her professional career to look after his children. Edith Hughes was often in poor health.

Henry Williamson (1895–1977) published his most celebrated work, *Tarka the Otter*, in 1927. TH read it again and again as a child. Williamson also wrote a number of books on his experiences in the First World War, and his infatuation with Hitler may have sprung from, or been reinforced by, his belief that Britain and Germany should never fight again.

To Lucas Myers

28 August 1964   Ms Emory

I got a magnificent book to review—"Shamanism"—it's a classic scholarly review of the whole field. Voodoo is just one small section, an aberrant development. Your eyes will pop. You'll be glad to know that your (& my) obsession with physical disintegration, being torn into fragments & fitted together again, is the great Shaman initiation dream, & that after such a dream, an Asiatic knows that if he does not take up serious shamanising he will die. He then spends some years learning the myths, & the details—makes his drum, his dress etc, & sets out to collect familiar spirits. You'll be able to fit your last two years into the general introduction to the style of life that has obviously claimed you. But it's interesting to hear that it's the beginning of something new, rather than irreperable damage to whatever was there before—the beginning of the real thing. Shamans say if they don't shamanise pretty often, they get sick, 'in the head'. Anyway, the powers be with you meanwhile [. . .]

TH's review of Mircea Eliade's *Shamanism* and Idries Shah's *The Sufis* appeared in the *Listener* on 29 October 1964. Myers's marriage had broken down.

To Peter Redgrove

[Undated 1964]   Ms Emory

I see Graves' Hebrew Mythology is out—that's one of the richest deposits of all, much more imaginative than the Greek, & much more apposite. I find the world behind Job etc more interesting than the world behind the Bacchae. It has the great grace too of not having been fingered over by schools & Universities & the educators of Gentlemen for the last 600 years.

Hebrew Myths: The Book of Genesis by Robert Graves and Raphael Patai appeared in 1964.

1965

Assia Wevill would give birth to her only child, Shura – full name, Alexandra Tatiana Elise Wevill – on 3 March 1965. TH continued to work, in Devon, on different projects, one of them a suite of poems based on the zodiacal symbolism he had discerned in playing-cards. Wevill had agreed to illustrate them.

   The other main collaborative venture, this one with his old Cambridge friend Daniel Weissbort, was the pioneering magazine *Modern Poetry in Translation*, which would appear in the autumn.

To Assia Wevill

[7 February 1965]   Ms   Emory

Sweetmouth, all our difficulties blow up out of these long absences. And out of your occasionally tactless doings—you'll have to admit that. And out of mine sometimes. But you mustn't get depressed about it—you're all chemical & fagged & warped around that infant at present, so don't trust your reactions. Just put them out of gear, disconnect.

   Do you know what oppresses me? the thought that you save my letters. You said recently—I forget what, but enough to make me think some day somebody might get hold of those letters & make hay. Assia, I'm foolishly oppressed enough as it is with bloody eavesdroppers & filchers & greedy curiosity, & if you're going to be sitting on all that for some Suzette suddenly to lay her hands on, then I can't write freely. As it is I'm always expecting my notes to get intercepted so I don't write a fraction of what I would.

   Past experience is bad enough to cope with, but it clears itself—it doesn't really oppose our present lives, whereas those letters & that diary of yours do. They're in our way. They've already caused enough trouble. So please burn all my letters.

   If it ever strikes you that my letters are cool or cramped, now you know why.

   In fact, in my letters I sometimes get perverse about that reader over your shoulder.

Which is all wrong & swinish. Sweet Assia, I'll see you next week &
tell you why.

As with almost all the surviving letters from TH to Wevill, this one is unsigned.

To Assia Wevill

[14 February 1965]   Ms   Emory

Sweetness, are you feeling better. Be well & weller. I feel I hardly saw
you this last week—I was just getting to see you when it was Waterloo
Station. I'll see you for longer & longer stretches. I'm arranging things
much better, bit by bit.

I see in my notes for the scene of the stair & the visions, that the first
vision is a green hill, the tree, & a moon—nothing else. So the moon is
OK, & belongs.

The lines for the plum-blossom are:

The plum-tree has battled the whole way
Up the hard road of the roots, its mouth full of stones.
The buds of the plum-tree are scarred veterans
Full of last words, the old saws of zero.

But the plum-blossoms open
Volcanoes of frailty,
Mouths without hunger but to utter
Love, love, to each other.

It's winter again today here—very many snowdrops & more coming.

Keep the paintings going, & write to me. I'm cleaning my story up—
I'll send you a copy if I type it before I come. I should finish it today &
tomorrow.

Take it easy, & don't get gloomy, & don't get chemicalised, & don't
get too depressed with the Pushkin. I'm sitting here, surrounded by my
rubbish.

Babel, the tower, was 7 stairs—each one a different colour, according
to one of the planets.

Sweet little Asseek, sweet love.

The lines about the plum-tree were to become part of the poem 'Plum-Blossom', in
TH's *Recklings*, published as a limited edition by Turret Books in 1966.

During the last weeks of her pregnancy, Wevill read Pushkin's *Eugene Onegin*, in which the character of Tatiana, while loving the hero of the poem, marries another man instead.

The letter was the first of a series addressed to 'F. Wall Esq', at 25 Belsize Park Gardens, London NW3, where Wevill now had a flat.

To Assia Wevill

[February 1965]   Ms   Emory

Sweetling, now are you truly & wholly & entirely & winningly better? And drawing? Your note about Miss N. arrived. Interesting. She gazed around, & annotated, I take it. Your remarks were interesting. Interesting.

Nothing happens here. Henry Williamson came last night. He's a sweet old boy, but I'd just got going. He stayed so late he stayed all night. He's still in bed. "I looked in & saw lumps of him" said Nicky, this morning. He's full of anecdotes of about the twenties—Churchill, Aldington, T E Lawrence, Ezra Pound etc. And about his farm. He got quite tight, we went to a pub near. He began to orate about Christ & Hitler, leap about, put horns on his head.

The stuff about the monkeys is good.

I rewrote my story again yesterday. Here I am, 34½, utterly unprepared, unequipped, like the naivest beginner, full of the trash I've let myself be absorbed into, that I have to shovel out, day after day. God knows if there's still anything genuine at the bottom. Also, writing plays & preferring plays, has destroyed my conviction about stories—about ordinary, linear stories.

Freezing here today—cast iron.

My tiger claw is from the right forefoot of a tiger shot in Bengal in November, last year.

What are you up to? Who was your 'elderly' admirer with the mimosa.

Keep very carefully going around but don't treat yourself too preciously, otherwise you'll get alarmed. What a relief when you have a bawling substitute for all this!

There are no new flowers, only old snowdrops, so here is a special issue

TH's pen drawing of a desert flower, with various creatures on it or climbing it, and a snake half-concealed beneath its leaves, ends the letter. Similar drawings, of solitary flowerings in desert landscapes, adorn other letters of TH to Wevill of this period.

The tiger's claw was a gift from Gerald Hughes, who had visited India.

To John and Nancy Fisher

[Early 1965]   Ms   Angela Fisher

I live down here with Frieda & Nicholas—for the last year & a half Olwyn's been looking after them extremely well. Here is one of Nicholas' stories

"There was a huge, huge great, great mouse and a wolf lived inside it and drank all the mouse's blood and made a hole and came out and then he went to a big hole a great river came out of it and the wolf drowned to the bottom and a big ship split straight in two and the ship was split when it was filled with people and they were all split in two at the sides and a big hunter came walking and he shot the wolf and the wolf sank to the bottom of the river and turned to ice and made the river higher. And the hunter mended all the people and they all went home. And another wolf came and a soldier shot it & it turned to ice & the ice turned to snow and the soldier walked on the snow. And a shark came with a gun between its teeth & shot another wolf and this wolf turned to ice & then to snow and the shark swallowed the man and the blood turned to ice. And then all the wolves turned to wild ones and jumped out of the river and ran to a window where a lot of men with big big swords and guns killed them & chopped them up & put them in a pan with a lid & cooked them. And the mouse turned into a big stone with legs and a big fierce shark's teeth like a shark and a man came with a great sword & chopped its head off & then it changed again and was a wild whale walking & it gobbled the man & the man turned to ice. No the man didn't turn to ice he turned into big horrors, big stones, and he broke in half."

Isn't that magnificent? He was 3 in January. It's a bit bloody-minded but then he has Frieda to contend with. He recites it with great force & earnestness.

To Richard Murphy

9 March 1965   Ms   Tulsa

Dear Richard,

It was a nice surprise hearing from you. The sweaters are beautiful—
that wild heath-grass green! Even though they flew down out of the
prevailing wind you must let me send Mrs Coyne a little present—I'll
think of something she'll like. Frieda & Nick wear them all the time, &
they came just in time for this last freeze-up.

I like the poem—I can see your difficulties needless to say. I was
going to ask you to delete the mention of the way she died—though it's
common enough knowledge, it's not actually publicised. The main dif-
ficulty is going to be with Frieda & Nick. If Sylvia were not such a
spectacular public figure, it would be well enough to tell them when
they're grown up. But as it is, some schoolkid is likely to tell them
before I do, if it's made all that public. Sylvia's poems figure largely in
school curricula.

What an insane chance, to have private family struggles turned into
best-selling literature of despair & martyrdom, probably a permanent
cultural treasure.

There are about 15 more poems of that order, and about 30 of the
sort she rejected but which simply show that she was incapable of writ-
ing a line that wasn't unique & inspired in some way or other. In about
4 years Faber will do the whole lot.

I like the last version of the poem best, except I'm sorry to lose 'Gone,
you write from a graveyard'—that verse. It's beautifully solidly modelled
& strong, the whole piece.

I've done not much for 2 years. Most of it's gone on Journalism—
none that I'm ashamed of, but all of it a waste of application, finally.
And on writing radio plays. I've brought one long work out of it—a
drama in about 7 scenes, highly poetical & theatrical, which has been
amusing to compose & which may have hidden virtues. Most of its
visible qualities are vices. It's a sort of Alchemical Marriage, I now
realise, though it began as a grand demolishing of in-laws.

An amusing phase has arrived in the Gallipoli project. I occasionally
see Teddy Lucie-Smith—he asked how I was getting on with Gallipoli,
& I said 'So far I've done nothing'. I haven't felt the touch yet to open
it up—I don't want just to plough into it coldly. Anyway, he says

he's assembled vast piles of notes on Gallipoli & is all set for a grand work—in time for next March I suppose. I don't know whether to feel challenged or hilarious. He's forced my hand, I feel. I think he intends to do long narrative stretches—general survey pieces like football commentary—interspersed with shorter illuminations & historical diagnostics. It might be quite interesting—it will be interesting to see what he manages, at any rate.

I think I'll do a collection of lunatic ballads. Or a collection of about 7,000 short biographies: as—

"Gerald Greenwood, 6 ft 1 ins, 18 years 3 months, a Todmorden weaver, played left wing for Rochdale, wrote every other day to Muriel Sharpe (later Mrs Westlake), son of Arthur Greenwood, pig farmer, descended of a lineage unbroke for 160 million years, now without issue, somewhat depressed, though having just won 4/3 & a packet of woodbines at Housey-housey, missing the rain, nagging at his ulcer caused by the strange foreignly Southern braying of the officers, walks behind a pile of oilcans to pea and unfortunately encounters a piece of shrapnel the size of a horse's head coming at invisible velocity in the other direction. Feeling nothing, he sees the landscape collapse like a jigsaw, & without regret, remembrance, understanding, resentment, or any mental flourish whatsoever, ceases to be."

No, no good. It wouldn't do. A series of derisive ballads would be one way of getting a grip on it. To approach the whole thing in derision would give the pathetic heroisms their correct setting and perspective too.

I know Henry Williamson very well here—have you read anything of his? He wrote Tarka the Otter etc long ago, & many semi-autobiographical fictions since. He's a wonderful old boy.

Last night I heard Thom Gunn's long poem 'Misanthropos'. Its about the last man—after a war. A quite simple schema: he first of all wants to destroy his consciousness, the vile human machine of sophistical errors, he honours the minimal virtues—to keep control, to guide one's actions with a modest balance, surrendering to no mystery or ideology etc. He becomes an animal. He finally meets other men—& by a spontaneous act of sympathy for one of them (who is slightly hurt) recognises his own instinct for community with them. It ends with his total committment to mankind, in a spirit of friendship—a solidarity against the nothingness & the merely bestial & the irrational etc. Roughly that.

It's faults, I think, come from its sticking so close to a generalising theoretical form: man is horrible—he has all but destroyed his species in a war; but the nothingness of insensate matter is worse; there is a possible sanity, even in the worst circumstances; cosmic law is one thing, the moral law, by which we must live if at all, is another. I'm doing him an injustice: but he starts from such ideas, rather than from recreation of the circumstances that might have given them life. The poem is a bit thin & mental. It's strength and virtue though is that it's theoretical procedure goes on in very pure language, interesting verse, & certain pure, clear, lovely pattern, sane poise, & some sort of personal authenticity in the ideas put forward. The verse is the mode of the sanity he advocates: with nothingness on one side, & bestial destructiveness on the other, it's possible to live balanced & alert—is what he's saying, & the verse & language has something of the virtues he proposes, balanced, alert, & strong.

What a long letter.

Well, write again. Are you coming to England. I'm sometimes in London—if I knew when you'd be there, we could meet.

Pass my good wishes to Mrs Coyne & thank you again.

Yours
Ted

Mary Coyne, Richard Murphy's nearest neighbour in Cleggan, on the Connemara coast, knitted Aran sweaters as gifts for friends. Murphy's poem 'For Sylvia Plath' was never included by him in any collection.

The play that was 'a sort of Alchemical Marriage' sounds like *Difficulties of a Bridegroom*, which appears to have undergone many changes between its broadcast as a radio play and its reconfiguration for the stage. TH's allusion is to the Rosicrucian document, John Valentin Andreae's *The Chymical Marriage of Christian Rosenkreutz* (1605).

Edward Lucie-Smith (b.1933) was to publish a limited edition of his poem *Gallipoli Fifty Years After* in 1966.

Thom Gunn's 'Misanthropos', in seventeen sections, is the centrepiece of his 1967 collection, *Touch*.

To Daniel and Helga Huws

[March 1965]   Ms   Huws

How are you both. I've been intending to write to you and send you a copy of Sylvia's book—I will. But at present I'm in London, and shall be until the 15th, so I wondered if you felt like a Holy Sequestration from affairs of the world, imbibing the waters & the effulgences of the Holy City, this weekend.

Here is the book by the best of the youngish German poets, which seemed to me perhaps in your vein, Dan. Look at 'verteidigung der wölfe gegen die lämmer' on page 29, to begin with. Some of the others are a bit journalistic, perhaps. The idea would be to translate the whole lot, as roughly as you please, if you like them. When money arrives (if ever) we'll divide it with a spade, and also pay twice. You'll be interested to see the things we've got for the first issue—Slavic etc.

How is the new member? Stop at nine, or the tenth will be Pan, with hooves.

Ariel, 'Sylvia's book', came out in March 1965.

The quoted German poet is Hans Magnus Enzensberger (b.1929), a few of whose poems Huws did subsequently translate. The 'new member' was a daughter, Louisa.

To Harold Massingham

[Spring 1965]   Ms   Massingham

Dear Harold Massingham,

Thanks for the proof—very exciting stuff. There's twice as much cash this year: two bursaries of £750 each. Don't raise your hopes—everybody's entering their favourite. Jack Clemo nearly got it last year—not only on the strength of his poetry, but also because he lives & has always lived in poverty, is blind, a severe case of bare survival, & so on. I imagine he'll come up again.

The bursary shouldn't go just to impoverished writers, but if a good poet's poor in cash, sympathy sways every judgement that doesn't unbalance itself going deliberately against such a possibility.

Martin Bell, who got it last year, has a reasonably paid job.

The way they're going to do it this year is: the sponsor writes a short critique & introduction, & submits a sample of the work. This is read, fingered, thumbed, kneaded, chewed over, digested etc—by each of a committee of, I think, 8. There will be a short list of maybe 6 manuscripts. So your manuscript will be looked after, never out of the Arts Council, but it will be out of my hands. The only question is, do you mind submitting your proof? I'll clip it with a strong spring clip. I only ask this, because places like Texas buy proofs—eventually.

This proof would have a greater effect on the judges than a typescript. They all secretly worship the master & main font on the public page.

I'll write to you again about the translation business—I'm glad you're interested.

Yours

Ted Hughes

TH had agreed to sponsor the poet Harold Massingham, who was from a younger generation at Mexborough Grammar School, for an Arts Council bursary. The proof was of Massingham's first book, *Black Bull Guarding Apples* (1965). The application was unsuccessful. Jack Clemo (1916–94), the Cornish poet, was both deaf and blind. Martin Bell (1918–78) earned his living as a teacher.

To George MacBeth

[Undated 1965]   Ts   BBC

Dear George,

I intended to ring you today—I'll write now in case I get displaced from ringing you tomorrow. I'd like to read the poem, Hawk Roosting, but I'd prefer not to take part in the discussion—the poem's my contribution, after all. If it is about violence. I wrote it to a text: "The truth kills everybody," and if the truth is, ultimately, a totalitarian system, then my poem is also topical. I don't see it as having anything to do with random, or civil or even elemental violence. If you could get all those people going at heat, it should be great entertainment—a very good idea. But I think my poem is about Peace. I'm eager to hear what else can be made of it.

I'm enclosing a poem for your programme—two poems in fact, both of them written nearly two years ago. The short one, Heptonstall, the New Yorker took but I've no idea whether they published it. The other one the Observer took, 18 months ago, paid me for it, then lost it and don't seem to want another copy. I'll let you see a bunch of other things in a month or two, but I hope you'll want to use these. The wolf one started off as a tribute to Johann S. Bach—wolves howl in concert, in harmony, and for pleasure.

I hope to be in London the week after next—I'll give you a ring.

Yours

Ted

The poet George MacBeth (1932–92) worked at the BBC and produced many of TH's broadcasts, including his 1963 talk on Keith Douglas. TH's reading of 'Hawk Roosting' was to form part of the edition of *Poetry Now* recorded at the Edinburgh Festival and transmitted on 3 September 1965. 'Heptonstall' was published in *The New Yorker* on 27 February 1965, but, like 'The Howling of Wolves', which the *Observer* printed on 10 January – possibly without TH's noticing – seems not to have been taken up by MacBeth.

To Ben Sonnenberg

[Summer 1965]   Ms   Emory

Dear Ben,

How are you. Each time I come up there I ring GRO 4521 & get no answer. The other day I even called.

Olwyn's been reading your plays & was properly impressed—no doubt she'll be writing to you.

Just after your last letter I went to Italy to this Festival at Spoleto. Good entertainment. Neruda read very memorably. Ingeborg Bachmann, the Austrian, was memorably present. Evtushenko appeared for 1 hour, & performed, which I did not like. Not nearly so impressive as Voznesensky, that boy. Miroslav Holub, the Czech, was there—truly marvellous poet. We've got about 15 of his pieces in the Magazine.

Pound appeared—under a vow of silence, evidently. He listened to questions, but said nothing. He read—but I missed that.

The first issue of the Magazine is primed—except for a small detail or two. It will be good. All the poetry is good—one of the best collections you will have opened for some months.

35 or so poems by Poppa, the Jugoslav. 15 by Holub. A play—with about 10 poems in it—by Zbigniew Herbert, the Pole, plus 2 or 3 poems. A couple of pieces by Juhasz the Hungarian—plus fill-ups by other Poles, other Jugoslavs, perhaps other Hungarians. Plus, perhaps, some pieces by Mihail—an excellent Israeli poet. He doesn't fit politically—but which issue would he fit? Poetically, he does fit. Plus, also, perhaps, some pieces by Voznesensky—if we don't put them in this issue it will maybe be too late, since all kinds of people are translating his poems en masse—Lowell, Auden etc, and he's a bit of a band-wagon. Ideally, the next issue ought to be a Russian issue.

I'm typing up my Alchemical Marriage—disappointing experience, though I'm sure it's got something, & it's suggested many things. I'll let you see it & you give me your comments. Supposing you had actors who all spoke verse as well as it's imaginable, instead of worse than believable, it would be a theatrical 1½ hours.

Have you any more plays I might read?

Greetings to your wife

As ever

Ted

The Spoleto *Festival dei Due Mondi* was one of the first such international literary gatherings. TH had been invited at the suggestion of Stephen Spender. The other guests named here were Pablo Neruda, from Chile; Ingeborg Bachmann (1926–73); Yevgeny Yevtushenko (b.1933), who is adversely compared to his fellow-Russian Andrei Voznesensky; Miroslav Holub, from Czechoslovakia; and the exiled American, living in Italy, Ezra Pound (1885–1972).

'Mihail' seems to be TH's mishearing of the name of the Israeli poet Yehuda Amichai (1924–2000), who was later emphatically confirmed in TH's admiration and became a close friend.

To Assia Wevill

18 August 1965   Ms   Emory

Dear sweet little love sweet Asseeke sweet love sweetness & sweetest

My birthday passed in average confusion & melancholy, screamings & dullness. Vicky cooked a colossal curry, that knocked me out. The heat attended faithfully from dawn to dusk. But it was all a bit by the way.

The only wrong circumstance about children is their noise—their squabbling. Otherwise, they'd be O.K., really & thoroughly to be desired, if also they could fly & go for a week without food.

Thank you for the Ad. dimensions. Could you get the other?

Danny is storming me with letters, as the magazine creaks into life. But we're getting lots of customers.

Days down here are a desperate series of last-stands against the domestic demons. Mail has decided to investigate me again, too. It's all slowly turning me into a monster of self-defence. As it should have done 10 years ago.

The dream has one very bad interpretation that I don't want to make. It has others.

If I post this now, you'll get it tomorrow morning. I'll make some Jacks & Kings & Aces today.

Sweetness lovely sweetness

TH's birthday was 17 August.

The 'Jacks & Kings & Aces' were the poems on which TH and Wevill were working together. He would include samples in his letters to various correspondents, Richard Murphy and A. Alvarez among them, at this time.

To Charles Tomlinson

[Summer/Autumn 1965]   Ms   Texas

Dear Charles,

How goes it?

I suppose you're up to the hilt in the Amazon, or touring the Encantadas, or translating Profkiewitzeritzoskowoskowoskinsko, into dragon-flies, Aztec scarabs, Minoan dance-amulets, & brass monkeys.

Life here proceeds in average dullness & confusion.

Thank you for the list of translators. The first issue is already excellent—I think.

Keep an eye open for us, will you, for eager students who will distribute copies, sell them at readings, at dramatic performances, or pick them up off your desk, leaving the 2/6. Comes out, October.

If we can sell 1,000 copies, we can proceed to the next.

Would you like to be an advisory editor? Wish you would. To dignify our part, & to generate parental concern within your own proper bowels for our productions, & to advise.

I saw Pound the other month—like a resurrected Lazarus: dead button eyes, beautiful old man though. Spoke to noone, listened patiently. Also saw Neruda—he read torrentially for about 25 minutes off a piece of paper about 3″ by 4″. Then he turned it over, & read on.

We have some very interesting stuff coming up in the next issues.

The magazine's about the size of the Daily Mirror—12 pages, solid verse. 2/6. Surely Bristol could absorb a hundred or two?

I've just written a monstrous drama—a cave-drama. I'll send you a copy when I get it reproduced.

All the best to you all

Ted

Riddle 712/K¾

I am fons et origo.
Astonishment and disbelief attend me.

247

I am seven colours.
I have turned my face away from man.
What am I?

Answer: A baboon's arse.

Now that *Modern Poetry in Translation* was almost ready, the question of how to distribute it had to be tackled.

Tomlinson was himself an admired translator and taught at Bristol University.

The 'cave-drama' must be *Difficulties of a Bridegroom*, the cave in question being Plato's, and the alchemical practices of the Neoplatonists lending their structure to the work, as they do in TH's 1978 *Cave Birds* – subtitled 'An Alchemical Cave Drama'.

To Daniel and Helga Huws

26 September 1965   Ms   Huws

Dear Dan & Helga,

Thank you for the lovely book. What a mass of stuff! But what a funny coincidence, too, especially that he should use the seven syllable lines. Though I don't think he gets the effect of art & poise with them that you do—anywhere near. I'm reading them a few a night.

Your poems are in fact at Hutchinson's. I didn't do anything with them for a long time after Faber sent them back, and after James Michie, who liked them very much, said that his firm was keeping off poetry. I wanted to send them to where James Reeves is editor & finally did send them to Hutchinsons—though I have a feeling he may be at Longman's.

Before I do any more with the Children's Book, do you want to reshape it, & concentrate just on the game. The editors complain about the irrelevant business at the beginning—red herrings under the Aunts' skirts etc.

I've just finished my 13 scene cave-drama, which is infinitely the best of my efforts in that line. I'll send you a copy when I get one. I quite like it.

Are you returned from Greece, reading this, or not gone. My Aunt has just been in Greece, & got involved in an incident. She & 3 or 4 other Yorkshire worthies were admiring the Athenian crowd when it parted and a jeep shot through, full of soldiers, one of whom hurled a tear-gas bomb, at my Aunt, more or less. They ran off up an arcade. She was delighted.

Our translation magazine is suddenly emerging to show us its real dimensions—an absolute horror of business, correspondence, sub-officials, agents, & hurry. Danny's fled to Ostend, wisely.
[. . .]

Love to Helga and the four Queens

Ted

P.S. This letter has been lying here for about 2 weeks.

URGENT: Could you send that copy you have of 1001 Nativities? (I'll send it back in a few days) We'd be very grateful—Olwyn's translating & slightly Anglo-Americanising those French Astrology books, & she wants a few famous birthdays.

The 'lovely book' was Joseph P. Clancy's *Medieval Welsh Lyrics* (1965), which included a poem from which the title of *The Rattle Bag* (1982) was to be taken.

The collection of Huws's own poems that TH was showing to publishers was eventually accepted by Secker & Warburg, and appeared as *Noth* in 1972, with a jacket blurb by TH. Huws's children's book was never published. The poet James Michie (1927–2007) was an editor at Heinemann.

The phrase 'Four Queens' – i.e. the Huwses' four daughters – refers back to the court-card poems which TH had added to his letter, but which are omitted here.

Leo's *1,001 Notable Nativities* (1917) was an astrological 'Who's Who'.

To Gerald and Joan Hughes

15 November 1965   Ms Emory

Dear Gerald & Joan,

By the time you read this I shall probably be residing in Ireland. I got key in hand, correct side of door, after something of an earthquake, but greatly helped finally by Olwyn's suddenly earning about £400. So now I'm alone, long blissfull days of absolute peace, the kids in wonderful form—very easy suddenly. Anyway, along with this arrived a terrific conviction that I need to get away from Court Green for some months, & perhaps settle my centre of gravity somewhere outside England, and Ireland arrived as the first place to try, & along came a chance to rent a big well-set up House on the Galway coast for £2 a week till March 31st.

So I'm off, with the kids, in a fortnight, while Ma & Hilda plus—later—pa, come down to Winter at Court Green.

I shall try to locate a permanent place. You can get big beauties still, here & there, for £3000, and in Ireland (next to no tax) I shall flex my dorsals and reap that in no time. Here, I've simply lost interest in earning cash—I already pay 8/9 in the pound tax, and that's after knocking off £1200 expenses. When I earn more—the tax seems to be scraping my barrel before the year's out. Also, I've decided I don't want Frieda & Nick to grow up in this rotten English civilisation—Frieda is already getting tainted, yet I want them to speak English. Also, I want to live where the life flows unselfconsciously in people & with lots of freedom. Also, fishing & shooting is in dead centre of the visual field. And as an omen, this knocker friend of mine (who would break your heart, every week he gets a small fortune in lovely objects, & sells them off to dealers for a pittance) gave me a beautiful double-barrelled twelve bore, right barrel slightly knocked at the muzzle edge, but otherwise good—left barrel just like glass, beautifully chased, lovely hammers, light walnut stock—a real gent's gun, probably worth 40 or 50 quid. He got it for 10/-. Last week he got what he thinks is an El Greco (multi-thousands) but which the National Gallery, & Christies & Sotheby's, the big art auctioneers think is a Magnasco, worth probably £500. He got it for £10 off a couple of old rich farmers. When he'd got it into his car, he was sick in the hedge with excitement. He's a marvellous little bloke—just needs a manager or a hard-headed partner. But the stuff he finds! He wants to come to Ireland, where the junk supply is still pretty untapped. He's a great merrymaker (devout Catholic, half-Irish half-Italian, little fat bloke) and he's constantly ringing up "Hey, I've got two ducks"—then we have a feast. Next week it's going to be a swan—he's found a farmer with a lakefull of swans. Well, think about coming to view the prospects.   Love to all,   Ted

P.S. Christmas books on the way.

The need to get the 'key in [his] hand' is a recurring theme of TH's correspondence with his brother. The Irish house he had found, with the help of Richard Murphy, was Doonreaghan House, in Cashel, Galway.

TH's friend, the 'knocker' – i.e. dealer in antiques and bric-à-brac – was Michael Dyton, with whom Assia Wevill would later become a business partner. Alessandro Magnasco (1667–1749) was an Italian Rococo painter.

To Lucas Myers

10 December 1965   Ms   Emory

My great drama collapsed disappointingly. My mistake. Too literary. But its a wonderful schema for a long series of pieces of verse, and I shall keep bits of the dialogue plus three whole scenes—the most spectacular, which are also quite interesting as verse.

My fault was to attend to the content etc of the verse, rather than simply listen to characters whom I imagined real. That's the dilemma. The moment I begin to ripen up the writing, I lose sight & sound of an actual character speaking. When I simply listen to imagined characters, of course they speak quite natural prose. But whereas the final effect of the former is artificial & literary, the final effect of the latter is real. The charm is to see & hear characters who seem real, yet who surprisingly speak in verse, or in something more stylised than prose. I think its probably better to put all the complications into the situation, & let the speech be what you hear. Late in life, when the brains shrinkage has shrivelled everything into a mustard-seed, it will all happen together naturally.

The play that had 'collapsed' was *Difficulties of a Bridegroom*, which TH had offered to the Arts Theatre, London. Turning it down on 27 September 1965, the director Peter Hall (b.1930) wrote that he couldn't 'accept it as a valid piece of theatre', finding it characterised by 'over-blown metaphors' that made everything 'seem rhetorical and empty'.

1966

In February, TH, Frieda and Nicholas Hughes, and Assia and Shura Wevill moved to Doonreaghan House, with the idea – not to be fulfilled – of eventually settling in Ireland. In the letter immediately below, TH still gives Court Green as his address. At the end of March, the tribe would transfer to Cleggan Farm, becoming neighbours of Richard Murphy.

To Aurelia and Warren Plath

[March 1966]   Ts   Lilly Library

Dear Aurelia and Warren,

Olwyn sent your letter on to me, about the Lois Ames business. She first wrote to me six months ago. I don't have her letter here, but as I remember she didn't ask for permission directly, she phrased it more vaguely, so I understood her to be inviting me to participate in a volume of reminiscences rather than asking for permission to do so definitive a work as the one she seems to have described to you. My first reaction was anger, since I assumed she was some journalistic publicist who wanted to make a quick book, a flash sort of close up, taking advantage of the great stir which Sylvia's poetry is already beginning to make over there, as I hear. My second reaction was more divided, since if the book was to be only reminiscences, a superficial introduction to Sylvia as a person, then even if Miss Ames did make something out of it, it would help to spread Sylvia's fame—though I doubt if that will need any help after May, when her book of poems appears. A biography of the modern, popular sort about some exciting creative figure, a fuller description and interpretation than the sort of thing I understood Miss Ames to be planning, is just the sort of thing I shall resist. The secret motive, usually of such books, is simply to cut the subject down to size, show how like the rest of us they really are. They are destructive in every way, and compromise the public life of the poetry. But a small account, reminiscences from acquaintances, I thought, might not be a bad thing. A full biography could not be attempted without your full cooperation and mine, and I refused mine. I should have written to you, telling you that she would most likely be approaching you, but my usual dilatory busyness deferred that. I was wondering if you would in fact also refuse—I very much hoped (and assumed) that you would. Miss Ames wanted to come over to England and ask me questions etc over a period of time and it was this sign of her insensitivity that decided me to have no part of it, beyond perhaps, confirming facts such as dates. Because I realise, too, that if Miss Ames is in fact a determined journalist we could not stop her publishing some sort of book—though we could make it difficult. To guide her at least a little way, I gave her one or two names of people who held Sylvia in high regard—Dorothea Krook of Jerusalem University was one, perhaps the only one I gave.

However, perhaps the better solution is, now you've met Miss Ames, to defer the whole thing as far into the future as possible. You must have sized her up, and will know whether she's amenable to a request.

The TRI-QUARTERLY REVIEW is doing a number largely devoted to Sylvia's work, and apparently Lois Ames is contributing something to that. The Editor Charles Newman, University Hall 101, Northwestern Univ., Evanston, Ill., mentioned that she is quite well qualified—I'm not quite sure what that means.

I got everything arranged with Harpers completely to my satisfaction, you'll be glad to hear, and the book should be coming out in May. I hear from friends of mine at various Universities in the States that Sylvia's poems are already a holy text among the students, and that in large groups she is the sole admired influence. I predict a future for ARIEL somewhat like the Catcher in the Rye, but broader and of course permanent.

I should long since have written thanking you for the beautiful things that came at Christmas. Everything since then has been a bit of a turmoil. However we're finally here, in a really lovely spot. I left some beautiful snaps at Court Green, but I've taken some others here and I'll be sending you copies. It's a very large house—Frieda has a bathroom to herself—beautifully light and well-fitted, about a hundred yards above the sea, or rather the beach of a calm rocky bay. We have almost as many daffodills as at Court Green. The weather is the surprise. It is about like an average English May—bright warm days, occasional wind and sea-squalls. The house is well-heated, but often enough the air coming in at the front door—straight off the Atlantic—is warmer than the house. The children are in Paradise. Nicky is now a boy. He is extremely intelligent. The other day he said to me: "What is very warm, and yellow, but doesn't burn its paint off, and it's in this room?" The answer, believe it or not, was the sun's light. I wish I could have recorded his guiding hints and red-herrings while I was trying to guess (I couldn't guess, though it is as you can see a legitimate riddle). Frieda is the best companion in the world. I suppose you heard about her sudden blossoming as a dancer—that was astounding. At present she's making a whole world for her Percy Panda. One good effect of coming here was that we escaped the bewildering variety of toys. Frieda brought just one—a puppet Panda. She's made a house, built the furniture from little assembly kits, made the beds the carpet etc. At this minute she's making the wall-paper—very beautiful it is too. She makes the rooms out of the cartons the groceries come in. Her painting and drawing grow like magic. She has filled an exercise book with pictures and I'm thinking of entering one or two for the National Children's Art competition we have—I've never seen an entry under seven. She has great supplies of colouring things. But she likes to use exactly the proper type of paint or crayon for the job she has in mind. Her general ability surprises every-body. They have made several friends among the locals and they disap-pear among the cottages. At the end of this month, we're moving to another place which will most likely be the one we'll come back to in Autumn. It's large, Victorian, and part of a prosperous farm. Herons roost and nest in the grounds. A lovely sand bay about 100 yards away. The local school is, I'm told, the best in Galway—the children get the top county scholarships. The children around here are a fine lot— bursting with life, with the most charming manners I've ever seen any-where. Frieda isn't going to school here (in this present place)—I thought just an odd month at a school she wouldn't be returning to would have more bad effects than good. I have found a very good Irish help, a girl who's used to the work, and has taken greatly to the chil-dren, as they to her. As for me, I'm able to work all day long and at last I am getting something done.

I'm sure you'll be pleased to hear that for the next five years I shall be an honorary member of the Philosophischen Fakultät at the University of Vienna, on a salary of two thirds a working professor's salary, which works out at $4800 a year about, and the contract is that I simply exercise my poetic talent. I am not allowed to earn more than an equiva-lent amount besides—or rather I have to report the fact if I happen to. (Please keep this to yourselves) [*This last sentence added by hand.*]

254

My mother and Father will be moving to Court Green soon, for a few months, as my father has sold his little shop, and dreads being inactive, and I have plans for Court Green which he can help to fulfillment. I'll have the whole place repainted inside and outside, re-roofed, and an extension of the house built into the barn. Also, if someone is living there I can employ a gardener for two or three days a week to recover the grounds. Then when you come over next year you can take your choice of living there, or coming here. If you came here, you could possibly live in the house where we are now living. It's rented in the summer for what are—for England or Ireland—rather high fees, but perhaps I could help a little with those. Also, next time you come, we must arrange that you have a car.

How is little Jennifer keeping? Frieda and Nicholas send her their love and greetings.

Otherwise, is everything going well?

So: my commitment's to Miss Ames' projects are nil—beyond the wish to make sure that if she collects reminiscences from anybody, she collects them from the right people. The idea of a biography is an awful constant turmoil to me, and I'm sure it must be worse to you. If you would like to ask her to defer her enquiries till further notice, I think it would be a good idea. She would obviously collect material wherever she could, but at least there wouldn't be the painful presence among our acquaintances of an authorised heady-eyed questioner and note-taker. I feel I failed to do the proper and sensible thing in not simply referring her straight to you, since the permission surely rests mainly with you.

How is Mrs Prouty—I think about her very often, and Dot and Joe. I hope they are all well.

I'm planning to leave for Germany towards the end of May. We shall stay somewhere in the South—I'm leaving it to the German Embassy in London to actually find me a place in one of the old towns I have listed.

Meanwhile, Aurelia, keep well. And remember that in anything to do with publications about Sylvia, my wishes are entirely subservient to yours.

After the end of this month, our address will be Cleggan Farm, Cleggan, Galway. But perhaps it would be best if you continued to write to Court green if you write after the middle of May.

Frieda and Nicholas send love and kisses

Ted

I suppose you heard that 'Life' is doing an article about Sylvia, to appear about the time of her book. I've only heard about it indirectly.

I've just discovered the note about Lois Ames. Charles Newman says "She is quite a remarkable woman—I came across her by accident—through Anne Sexton—she is utterly free of academic pretensions and the sort of gossipy agressiveness which characterises so many of our graduate students, her analysis is as compassionate as it is thorough—like every good biographer she subjects her research to constant revaluation. . . . . I think you will be pleased by the depth of her concern with Sylvia's work, as well as her caution."

Lois Ames never published a book of the kind TH seems to have feared here. Dorothea Krook (1920–89) had been a research fellow at Newnham College and Sylvia Plath's admired supervisor. The Fall issue of the *TriQuarterly Review* would include articles by A. Alvarez, Lois Ames and Anne Sexton ('The Barfly Ought to Sing'), as well as TH's 'The Chronological Order of Sylvia Plath's Poems' and a selection of poems by Plath.

'Little Jennifer' was Warren Plath's daughter.

The visit to Germany was put off, when TH was persuaded that he should stay in Court Green and look after his parents.

Not *Life* magazine, but *Time*, was to include an article on the background to *Ariel* in its issue of 10 June 1966.

To Gerald Hughes

[April 1966]   Ms   Emory

This place is a mild paradise for me at present. We moved yesterday, from our sumptuous home, to a much older, wilder place—£2 a week, a house annexed to a big farm (big for this region) at the top of Cleggan Bay—right on the West Coast. I have a great ramshackle roomfull of silence to work in. I look out at a heathery hillside, & if I stand I see the Open Atlantic. The village is about 1 mile away. Its a blue, still day. I've worked fairly steadily for 6 weeks & now I'm going quite smoothly, & plenty of improvement still in hand. The kids are brimming over. Assia is here with me and a complete success. We have a good local girl, Teresa, helping us. (Their local average wage, hotel job, is £3 a week. Average man's wage—£7-10-0. Tin of sardines: 2/-. Honey 4/- a ¾ lb jar. Everything 10% to 30% more expensive than England. So I just don't see how people live—evidently it's mainly on checques from children abroad.)

This morning I went fishing to a lake about 2 miles away—I took Frieda & Nick. Blue, dead still morning. The lake was like glass. Within an hour I had 3 fish—lovely trout. The first about 1½ lb, the second—3½, the 3rd, again about 1½ lb. The second is the biggest trout I've ever seen alive. I've let the children hold the rod awhile each time, to arouse any dormant passion for the art they may have. Frieda thinks it's cruel—[*marginal insertion:* (but she's quite keen)] Nicky is very keen. Connemara is all like the moorland going over from the top of Hardcastles towards Colne—but with twelve high granite peaks sitting in the middle of it. And lakes everywhere—terribly lonely & eerie lakes. I went fishing to a big remote one last week—took F & N—and it hailed, it blew, there were three concentric rainbows, the mountains rose up & sank down, & finally I caught a sea trout about ½ lb. But later I heard they've been trying to rouse a monster in that lake—one of the Plesiosaur type that are in Loch Ness & others. Several locals have seen it evidently.

Written from Cleggan Farm.

To Aurelia Plath

19 May 1966   Ts   Lilly Library

Dear Aurelia,

This is just a note in great haste. First of all, thank you for the lovely dress of Frieda's. She will be writing to you. And the little bag goes with her every day to school. Where she is, by the way, a great success. She can't wait to be off in the mornings.

I wanted you to see the draft of the enclosed notes, which I've written for the symposium on ARIEL, which is to appear in the next issue of the TRI-QUARTERLY MAGAZINE. It was extremely difficult to make it even as objective as it is. I have a fear that I may have said one or two things which, if I could see it from a greater distance, I would not approve. At the same time, I do not wish to set afloat the impression that she was just another ordinary person and the poems were some sort of fluke which in time we shall see through. I wanted to give a suggestion of the extreme temperatures of her genius. I don't think there's any avoiding the fact that she will become a literary legend—already is.

I wanted the notes to set an order to the poems—it's an important clue to their unity. And I wanted to set just enough factual notes to the more obscure pieces to make the strong close link evident between her poems and her real world. At the same time, I wanted to set in the forefront, at as early a stage in the great inevitable exegesis as possible, the claim that Sylvia was not a poet of the Lowell/Sexton self-therapy, or even national therapy, school, but a mystical poet of an alltogether higher—in fact of the very highest—tradition. I didn't want to press this claim too hard, though I think I have a right to say what I think about it, and I think my claim, even if it raises some temporary would be debunkers, will eventually stand. There is simply nobody like her. I've just finished re-reading all Emily Dickinson for a small selection, and my final feeling is that she comes quite a way behind Sylvia. As for Lowell etc, if he is a fine doctor, she is a miracle healer. There is no comparison. But I want to avoid seeming to set myself up as the high priest of her mysteries—and so I've limited myself in these notes to the lowest order of editor's facts.

I hope you will not allow yourself to get too overwrought when ARIEL appears, and that you will hold the public stare at a distance.

We're leaving here this weekend, shall be at Court Green for a while, a week or two, then Germany—address there still not definite. The German Embassy in London is fixing me a place in the Black Forest. My mother and Father at Court Green are seeing to my renovation schemes, which seem to be going O.K. Finally, as I've realised, the only way to deal with a place of that kind is by application of cash.

Frieda and Nick shout happy birthday. Keep well. And please pass my regards to all.

as ever
Ted

P.S. Could you just point out whatever in my notes gives you the slightest qualm, and I'll change it. If you could let me have the copy back, with the parts marked.

To Richard Murphy

21 June 1966   Ms   Tulsa

I've been meaning to write to you every blessed day, but I've returned to a round of interruptions that reminds me of yours. I'm trying not to lose the habits of work I managed to develope in Cleggan.

Germany's off—can't afford to take the tribe, and can't leave them: too fissile, friable etc. Besides, I can't easily contemplate going deeper into 'arrangements' etc. Things are fine here—beautiful in fact—if I can keep working.

Assia has gone into business with this antique-collecting friend of mine, and they're turning stuff over that would make your eyes pop.

TH, Assia Wevill and their assorted offspring had by now returned from Ireland to Court Green, where TH's parents were in residence.

To Aurelia Plath

13 July 1966   Ms   Lilly Library

Dear Aurelia,

Your letter only confirmed what I have been feeling more and more strongly—that "Ariel" should never have been published in the U.S. Though I never expected it to become such a big-scale sensation. The malice of the 'Time' article was simply 'Time's' usual style—nobody, caught there, escapes. It was much less vicious than I expected. They are simply disgusting. So high-minded about the 'plain realistic facts' that they get them all wrong. All they are after really is a sensational article—to keep their name in the Time office etc. I refused to speak to any of them, & so did several others of Sylvia's friends here and in the States. But some of the gossip legends are as wild as they are widespread. I trust you'll pay no more respects to the publicity machine. The 'Time' article was made up from several reports, I think. It surprised me, having heard of their disciplines & tough-mindedness, how shallowly they followed the story up.

But all that will pass. What will not pass, I'm afraid, is the effect the book will have on teenagers at college who set her course up as a holy example. This is already happening, I hear. And all the insane rubbish talked about the 'fatal' nature of her gift, that she could not come back from these poems, etc, only makes their worst effect much worse.

The truth is, I'm convinced, that the poems, which were nearly all completed by the end of November 62 (ending with the bee-poems, that was to be "Ariel"—the last word was to be "Spring.") had cured her. What really set things going, on top of everything else, and in spite of the fact that we were beginning to get on again and bought a bottle of champagne to celebrate it, was her novel being published on Jan 19th—then the reviews. That novel was the accursed book, that required the tranquillizers.

So please don't get fouled in reacting to the generalised malice & pseudo-psychologising of those reviewers. With a story like Sylvia's, everyone treats it as a mysterious dream—a sort of free space for them to air their own nightmares & self-suspicions. I now treat all reviews as pseudo-poems on a certain subject: I do not look for any evaluation of the subject, since it's used simply as a theme, a pretext, for the reviewer's self-expression. $9/_{10}$ of the time, I'm justified. The reaction to the book in England was so sane, by comparison, & so humane. The best plan, is to read nothing of those reviews. I'll be writing again.

Love
Ted

To Robert Lowell

14 September 1966   Ts   Houghton Library

I've been meaning to write, to thank you for the introduction to Ariel: it was very good of you and an exciting piece in itself. I've wondered since if it was a sane thing to publish the book over there—no doubt as holy text it will push several girls over the brink. And the backlash onto her family has been considerable.

I hope you're keeping well and productive. I've been absorbing your last book. LIFE STUDIES seemed to take itself to the limit in that direction, but this book seems to be full of new openings in all directions. ALFRED CORNING CLARKE shows that Life Studies wasn't the end of that road, and also looks like a wholly fresh start. I put a book of pieces together with about five stories and a radio play—coming out next Spring. It brings the other two books to a close. What I've been getting since is a bit more to my taste. I'll send a copy.

Robert Lowell had written a foreword exclusively for the US edition of *Ariel* (1965). His own collection, *For the Union Dead*, published the same year, included the poem 'Alfred Corning Clark', a wry elegy.

260

To Daniel Huws

27 October 1966   Ms   Huws

Things are smoothing out here. Assia is a very keen gardener & has made everything very nice. My mother has been ill quite seriously all summer—partly precipitated by the Irish girl who made more trouble than I thought we had potential for. My parents are still here—mother too ill to move. She's had pneumonia 3 times in 18 months, which never retreats beyond asthma/bronchitis. Some osteopath has just this last week or two almost cured her with a diet of orange juice & boiled onions—a meal of one, then of the other. But she's still too weak to move much.

But Nick & Frieda are prospering greatly, satisfactorily. And I've been writing lots in the history, songs, discourses, bedtime stories & general doggerel of one, Crow. Crow is very crude, nearly illiterate, very rough, & has not heard of most things, but he's a relief, after the poems I put all together & sent off a couple of months ago. I'll send you some of his primitive attempts when I get the courage to see them in type.

The poems 'sent off a couple of months ago' would be published in 1967 as *Wodwo*, which, as TH had told Robert Lowell in his preceding letter, also contains prose stories and a play.

To Richard Murphy

9 November 1966   Ms   Tulsa

Dear Richard,
    Your hospitality was a feat, considering the odds against you. It was an extremely pleasant visit for us. Thanks again.
    We got back without too much adventure. I obeyed a sudden little red light on my dashboard & pulled in at a big piratical repair garage in Ballinasloe, where my dynamo was removed & a £7-15-0 reconstituted model put back in—three hours. I didn't suspect too much, since my old dynamo's done 62,000 & they're only supposed to do about 30,000. But a historical Irish character, a real horse-thief, entertained me throughout with accounts of his coups—on cars not horses—selling for £500 a van he got in exchange for a lame dog, selling for £350 a Morris (like mine) that he bought for £15 & so on. With all the devices for

rejuvenating his engines & bodywork. I'd never heard real bragging before, I realise.

I overshot Dublin—very exhausted & finding no parking—but I managed to stop in Bray.

Everything back here is more or less in one piece—usual corruptions, usual family coup d'états, usual shatterings of fragile sentimental treasures, usual heaps of loathly ashes in the flower-beds, place nearly burned down with the bonfire, children regressed to unrecognisable savages, usual wild tales—not the entertaining sort that travellers bring back but the consequential sort they return to. However, the proverb now in power is "Retire from trouble & sing to it."

Alberti's coming to the Festival. He's an Alpha performer—I saw him in Spoleto. I now have 6 Alphas—it's already a crashing list. If everybody accepts, I shall have to flee—fate will have taken me too literally.

Assia's struggling with her kingdom—somewhat fractured in her absence, but it's repairing.

Here's a copy of the Magazine, issue 2—dismiss your djinns for an hour, & peruse it. The first things are my favourites.

When the power of the dog begins to work, Mrs C will be struck silent from the toes up, all labour in Connemara will be taken over by the Sidhe, & finalised in one night. An immense bejewelled Albatross, banking over the house, will crap the entire cargo of a Spanish treasure galleon into the garden, Clifden will become a volcano, supplying fire heat to the whole of Connacht. An ancient school of ollaves, unhoused by your septic tank, will take up new positions of eternal rest on your lawn, invisible but audible, reciting their repertoires ad infin in funereal distinct tones, well satisfied to stay there.

I'll send you some pieces of mine, when I type them. Meanwhile, may the dog guard the battle, & thanks again.

Yours

Ted

TH omits the date, but a note added by Assia Wevill gives it. They had just paid a brief return visit to Ireland.

Rafael Alberti (1902–99), Spanish poet of the generation of Lorca, had been one of the readers at Spoleto the previous year. TH had invited him to read at Poetry International – the London festival of which he was a founder and (for a while) director – in 1967.

The second issue of *Modern Poetry in Translation*, edited by Edward Lucie-Smith and devoted to French poets, had been published in the summer.

To Daniel Weissbort

[December 1966]   Ts   King's College, London

Dear Danny,

Glad to hear you got out there finally. I've been wondering just where you'd be in order to land the Greek things accurately on you, so you can expect them by separate post. The whole lot reads quite impressively—though it isn't a full coverage. He wasn't interested in the more surrealist younger ones—his tastes being to translate Sophocles, which he does. Tell me what you think of it all.

The great thing about living in peaceful country for a short spell is the way it combs all the distraction out of you. Then there's a brief moment of equilibrium before you begin to topple the other way into the domestic nest till you have to flee back to the city to get the family lice combed out of you. I'm beginning to think the only arrangement is to live in a small park, and your room is in the top of a tree about 500 yards from the family creche. I'm seriously thinking of taking a room and leaving every morning at 8-30 to go and sit in it—not just to escape, but to relieve everybody of my idle presence. Also to try and recover that blissful evening feeling of having come home from work. As it is, I neither work nor play, I'm never busy for long enough to feel I can enjoy the distractions. All day long as you know it's this petty struggle between the two. The impression of enormous energy having been exerted is really the battle you've had against yourself.

The kids are on holiday at present and I've managed to make some Station Routine Orders—26 rules, which they stick to infinitely better than they ever did to mere instructions. It's made quite a change.

I've been writing a foolish children's play about nebuchadnezzar and the fiery furnace. I'm committed to writing another two—one about going out to grass for seven years, and one about Daniel in the lion's den. I make them ryme very rigidly with octosyllabics and the effect is very odd, like puppets. My saga about the Crow is therefore at a standstill though it was going very well.

> Greetings to Jill. Keep well.
> Ted

The 'Greek things' were translations of contemporary Greek poets by Paul

Merchant, son of TH's Devon friends Moelwyn and Lynne Merchant.
  The children's play is *The Head of Gold*.

To Robert Lowell

29 December 1966   Ts   Houghton Library

Dear Cal,

I was stunned to get your note this morning. It's a shock to find that what I said in that article can be taken in that way.

I wrote the article in a struggle against a million cross-qualifications and undercurrents. I had resolved to write nothing about Sylvia's poetry because I knew from one or two brief attempts I made earlier that it dragged me into a morass of feelings I simply could not deal with in words that would sound like reasonable discourse. Yet I wanted to say something unqualified about what seems to me best in her poetry. I realised well enough that whatever I said in praise would sound, as you say, like uxorial fatuity, and that anything I might say in detraction would be something much worse. But her poems are public property as well as my private life, and I felt I must say one or two things.

I dragged you and Anne Sexton in because the linking of your three names in every blessed review has become an automatic reflex that seems to me to obscure differences that are much more important than the links, and a main obstacle to anybody approaching her poems—as the latest comer to the group. And I tried in a clumsy, battering upwind way to indicate at least one essential difference that it obscures. Then everything got twisted up in those images about the torture cell and the masks laid out. I was trying to discriminate in kinds. I was trying to define Sylvia's poetry as something that moves in spirit or in the dimension of spirit rather, and to distinguish it in this way from yours and Anne Sexton's which seem to me to share at least this, that they move in the dimension of nature and society. I can only blame the tastelessness of the images I used to express this on the nightmare three weeks slogging struggle the article descended into as I wrote at it, the blind capsized battle I had to say anything at all, where everything seemed to be overstatement or false statement and where I had no longer any real bearing on my readers. And if my method seems to imply a disparagement of your poetry and Anne Sexton's I can only say that emphatically wasn't my meaning and that my own preferences lie with poetry that moves—like Shakespeare and Tolstoy after all—in the dimension of nature and society. And it is the other kind of poetry which I feel needs the defence, and it was to forestall the charges of those who looked in her poetry for certain essential elements that they find in yours that I wrote the article at all. But I now realise that in the general blindness and deafness and struggle against myself to grind out my promise to the Tri-Quarterly I committed something ghastly, as I had feared I must, and had been once more dragged down into a struggle where my judgement vanished.

I've described all this to you because I can't leave you not understanding the crosswinds and headwinds and near-darkness in which I arranged those sentences and how I buried my head in those accursed images and how far I was from intending any belittling of you or Anne Sexton or any overcasual lumping of your poetry together. If it had lain in my argument I would have said something about the vast difference between your poetry and Anne Sexton's as it appears to me all right, but I was concerned to modify the cliché only so far as Sylvia's poetry is concerned. In the early drafts I brought you both in because without the combined operation of you and Anne Sexton Sylvia would never have written what she finally did, and it seemed wrong not to mention you. But that was before I got dragged into the struggle. Please understand how this happened with me.

To lay out the good qualities of one sort of poetry, even in a rhapsodic way, doesn't to my mind imply any discrediting of other sorts of poetry from which it is first distinguished, though I know that's the common strategy—so much so that pure habitual reflex might easily misunderstand my sentences. To take a sideswipe at anybody in a pseudo display of critical integrity is dead against everything in me. And that in all my writing the first person I have given pain of this sort to is you, of all people, has sickened me. To say I apologise just seems inadequate. Please write to me soon.

Yours
Ted

For background to TH's *TriQuarterly* article, see his letter to Aurelia Plath of 19 May. On the same date as writing to Lowell, TH sent a similarly placatory letter to Anne Sexton.

'Cal', an abbreviation of Caligula, was Lowell's nickname.

1967

The publication of his third collection, *Wodwo*, and his continuing, if diminished, involvement with London's first Poetry International Festival (see letter to Richard Murphy of 20 January) were TH's principal public activities of the year. At Court Green, Assia and Shura Wevill remained part of the household until unresolved frictions between Wevill and TH's parents forced her to return to London in the autumn.

Aside from these public duties and private upheavals, TH's main preoccupation was now the developing story of *Crow*.

To Charles Monteith

17 January 1967   Ms   Faber

Is it possible for you to fix the publication date?—for May 9th. I'll tell you why I ask. I've spent thousands of hours studying Astrology, and I would like some recompense in being able to choose the birthdates of my books. I've sent off all three to the chosen hour—so far with goodish results. The first two came out well-timed. This year, May 9th is the day of days. I'd be interested, actually, to see if it would prosper as well as that day says its progeny should. Before or after is not much good for that kind of help. Please try and fix it. May 9th is a Tuesday.

Wodwo was in fact published on 18 May 1967.

To Richard Murphy

20 January 1967   Ms   Tulsa

The Poetry Festival lost a lot of feathers. I was all set to cram London with geniusses, when John Lehmann etc decided I ought to be restrained— evidently. So the Festival could only be 5 foreigners, 5 Americans, and 5 English. It was those 5 English I was trying to avoid. So I withdrew from main directorship—which I had somehow stumbled into, & Patrick Garland is now in control, while I 'advise' or something of that sort. I'm advising that the 5 English be as old as possible—Graves, Macdiarmid, Basil Bunting and—I thought—Austin Clarke. David Jones was the 5ᵗʰ, but evidently he's not likely to agree—or, if he agrees, likely to get a word out.

[. . .]

I got writing some new things—very plain ballad fables which will be O.K., I think, if I don't write more than about 40. They are the various Songs, bed-time stories, parables & visions of The Crow—who sings on one base, brutish note. I'll send you some when I get them typed.

[. . .]

I'm editing a Faber paperback of Emily Dickinson—very hard to cut her down to the shortness they want. I wrote a children's book—an Iron Man who defeats a Space-Bat-Angel-Dragon (who comes out of a wandering star) by the ordeal of fire. The Iron Man gets white hot—on an oil-fired grid—3 times. The Dragon gets white hot—on the sun—only twice, & then surrenders, & becomes a slave of the earth, flying round & singing the music of the spheres which brings peace to the whole earth. I'll send you a copy, when it comes out.

Have you ever read A Patriot's Progress, by Henry Williamson—excellent. Very concentrated account of trench fighting—which he's since disowned. He's disowned it because it was only his notes—nearly raw, which is just what's good about it.

With its inclusion of a Scot, Hugh MacDiarmid (1892–1978), an Irishman, Austin Clarke (1896–1974), and a Londoner who, in his writing, made much of his Welsh heritage, David Jones (1895–1974), TH's proposed 'English' contingent looks like an attempt to outmanoeuvre those wishing to constrain him. Robert Graves, only half-Irish, did appear.

Both *A Choice of Emily Dickinson's Verse* and *The Iron Man* were published in 1968.

To Daniel Huws

[March 1967]   Ts   Huws

Dear Dan,

How are you keeping? It seems a long time since I wrote. Here is RECKLINGS, pig's litter, and a preposterous pretentiorisation of better days. RECKLINGS is what I threw out of the nest the better to fatten my great cuckoo, WODWO, which will take wing in May, Wodwo being a false singular for Wodwos, which is an apocopated plural for Wodwoses, which is middle English for Orang Outan.

Otherwise—a busy year. Nonsense upon nonsense, each multiplying all the others, with all its brothers and none without triplets or grandmothers. A first labour of Endymion, completed in supine triumph.

Here live Assia and Shura who is a very beautiful little charmer now aged two, Frieda and Nick, who thrive, my father, who thrives, and my mother, who came on holiday a year ago and has ever since been too ill to move. So I got a hut up in the top of my orchard and there I fall back when I'm routed. But most things are about balanced now.

The translation people never applied to me. My non-support doesn't seem to have had any effect. How are the translations going?

A friend of mine is doing an Anthology for Penguin of Irish Poetry, beginning to present, so I wondered why not do a Welsh. If you are interested, write to Olwyn and she will apply a bone-crushing grip to Penguin. You could mullingly idle it all together on those interminable summer afternoons in the Library when all the rest of the staff are chasing in desperation the head librarian all round and about the streets of Aberystwyth he laughing maniacally stark naked shaming you all.

I've just been in London one night, first time for quite a while. I read verses to the students of the Central School of Speech and Drama where Joe works. Harry Fainlight was there. He's suddenly become a mysterious element in my life. For instance one day last week I got a letter from him in the morning post. Five minutes later, 9 a.m., he appeared on the doorstep. 9 p.m. that night I put him on a Paddington train in heavy snow. A day and a night passed. Next morning, a letter from Harry postmarked Nottingham. Five minutes later, when I come in from pissing against an apple tree, he is sitting in the kitchen. At eleven a.m. I put him on a train for Paddington. That night, 11 p.m. I'm sitting having a drink and in comes Harry. Next day at 2 p.m. I try to get him on a train for Paddington but he resists and insists on disappearing onto Dartmoor. Faber are reading his book of poems and he must be thinking I'll turn red or blue at the moment they decide yes or no and so completely sleepless (he never slept all those days of his visits) he's keeping me under observation.

We were sitting drinking after this reading the other night, since he'd appeared on the back row, when in came our old friend Thom Gunn, with red Indian bead necklace dangling to his navel, Tony Tanner in his right holster, Tony White in his left, seven-day-out-beyond-the-frontier beard, having within the three hours landed hot from New York which had been no more than his skip in a hop skip jump from San Francisco. Joe had singled out Harry F. to sit on. So while I was worrying about Harry, who admits to morbid paranoia, in came Danny. There was nowhere for him to sit at all, so after about five misheard words he went off back to Jill and his castle, so then I worried about him. Then Harry got up and left. Then I was worrying about both Danny and Harry. And so my evening was ground into the dirt.

Do you have Luke's address. I only have a doubtful one. It's about a year since I wrote to him.

Are you and all your little muses well? Are you contemplating the infernal marsh of your garden?

Love to Helga

Ted

Recklings was published in January 1967, in a numbered and signed edition of 150 copies, by Edward Lucie-Smith's Turret Books. In referring to 'pig's litter', TH simply gives the dictionary definition of the title.

Brendan Kennelly's *Penguin Book of Irish Verse* appeared in 1970.

Harry Fainlight (1935–82) was the brother of Ruth Fainlight, whom TH and Sylvia Plath had got to know, with her husband Alan Sillitoe, on their return to London in 1960. Fainlight was, like his sister, a poet. He published just one small book, *Sussicran* (1965), and is the subject of TH's elegy 'To Be Harry' (1982). TH's Cambridge friend Joe Lyde taught at the Central School. Thom Gunn was living in San Francisco. Tony Tanner was a don at King's College, Cambridge, and wrote on US literature. Tony White (1930–76) had been an actor of outstanding talent and promise, but left the profession suddenly to support himself by manual labour.

To John and Nancy Fisher

11 March 1967   Ts   Angela Fisher

My writing got moving again this last year. I proved again the Universal law that the more you concentrate on anything inside the head, obstacles, devils and the general worldly barrage seize the opportunity to attack full strength. So my year has been a succession of beautiful take offs that crashed beyond the end of the runway. However, you'd be amazed how persistent I've become so I make a kind of staggering headway. Just lately I've got on to something quite new, from my point of view—so much so that I feel disinclined to publish it till I've emptied the vein for fear it gets pirated. It may be my dotage, too, there's that possibility.

I collected the salvageable parts from what I'd produced between 1960 and 1966 and it will come out in May. About fifty poems and five stories and a radio play arranged in a sort of narrative. The pieces on their own are O.K., several of my better things, but read as a connected work and interpreted properly it's a rather sickly book. But it's the end of a phase, not the phase I trust. The stories cover all three books— they're very close to the poems and show how things connect up. I quite like the book, but it's dismaying to think what I didn't write. And I'm sure the chance doesn't return, everything changes all the time, and there are only the new arrangements in I hope the new ways, i.e. closer and closer. But the field is always wider and wider, and the habits stronger and stronger. So after writing naturally on a simple scale to begin with it's become a napoleonic campaign, unless I desert.

Perhaps you heard about my Schools programmes. They will come out in one book, with an anthology of about thirty poems added to the poems already quoted in the programmes. It will be a sort of primer plus Anthology. It's hard to think who might be able to use it. It falls between all stools. Nevertheless, I think it's worth publishing and I'd like to dedicate it to you, John, and to Pauline. I hope you won't object to being made Ancient Mariner to that particular bird (as far as the getting it round your neck goes. You needn't breathe a word about it.)

The book of 'salvageable parts' was *Wodwo*.
The collection of 'Schools programmes', *Poetry in the Making*, also appeared in 1967, with a joint dedication to Pauline Mayne, TH's other English teacher, and 'John Edward Fisher'.

To Vicky Watling

11 March 1967   Ts   Watling

Dear Vic

You let us know the exact dates of your descent into this ninth circle and there will be some preparations. The domestic factory/sweatshop/ foundry which I own and which is now running reasonably smoothly with not more than eight screams a day seven pints of blood lost 15 guineasworth of equipments cups plates etc three inches of floor worn off corners ground smooth twelve tons of food fed into the seven ovens with a net product of one dirty nappy, one inch of baldness, two wrinkles (permanent) and one desperate howling laugh into the darkness and silence which comes down at about 1 a.m., all this cannot take one new adjustment without a complete overhaul and three or four days propaganda to all personel. In other words, if you take us by surprise, the house will fall on us all and you will be over.

Otherwise, we'd be delighted for you to drop in any time. As it is, we'll be delighted for you to come when you say—Ma is already getting into position, smile aimed at the door edge. As you know, she gets out of bed for about five minutes per day. She's really pretty ill. Health goes through the elephant's mouth and it returns through the ant's anus. Dad is fine. Wherever I could get one nail, he has driven two. Anything that looks as if strength could rip it loose, he has ripped loose and screwed back into place with eight inch screws. He's built a greenhouse nearly from scratch, a big shed. He's allright, though I think they both get a bit homesick now and again.

Are you both teaching your heads off and on again twice a day? What you need is a cafe down here where we can come and gorge free. In return for a few wormy apples every October.

So we look forward to seeing you

love
Ted

William Hughes had sold his shop at 17 Crown Street, Mytholmroyd, in February 1966, and he and Edith Hughes were now staying at Court Green. They had intended to return to their home in Heptonstall, but Edith's increasing ill-health made her virtually a permanent resident in Devon.

János Csokits

21 April 1967   Ms   Emory

Dear Janos,

At last my lame hand gets to the paper. Thank you for the snaps. The cold winter sunlight—lovely. Very good souvenir of your visit, which we both enjoyed very much. There are times, with this factory of domestic machinery (children, ailing mother, bored father, the million articles each to be patted & stroked regularly) that it seems impossible to spare one minute to turn & look at the world & other people. Your visit was a great relief, really.

Here are three books. 'Ariel' by Sylvia, is in a class apart. She truly became the most phenomenal genius just before she died. In English, there is nothing quite so direct & naked & radiant—yet complicated & mysterious at the same time. As you will see.

My own earthen labours must be looked at on a different day. "Recklings", the thin grey book, is a collection of bits & pieces which didn't seem to me to fit into WODWO—not good enough or simply irrelevant. WODWO is one long story—the key piece is "The Wound" which is a close literal transcript of a dream repeated to me in full detail, as a film, twice on the same night. I'm sure you'll fit everything together.

I'm gradually getting things moving. Are the translations stirring? An American sent me some fine pieces by Miklós Radnoti—really good English poems they turned out to be.

I'll be sending you our next issue soon. Danny W., co-editor of the Magazine, is, as you guessed, more riddled with fatal complexes than any creature still on its feet. He's quite a good poet.

Give me a brief critique of WODWO. What you said about 'closed' and 'open' Universe was as shrewd & penetrating a remark as I shall hear about the change in my verse from Lupercal to Wodwo.

I haven't got down to touching those versions of your pieces yet—I want to be in concentrated & fluent fettle before I do, which as yet I am not.

There seems a likely chance that we shall be in Germany for one month this summer—not quite sure when. I'll keep you informed.

Is the new poem going to your satisfaction? I will send you some new pieces of my own, some songs of the Crow, when I've got them into focus. Dreary obligations have used me up lately—activities that were neither life nor a substitute for life. Just limbo.

Thank you for the invitation to Spain. Nowhere I would more like to come—but Germany, heavily financed, is all I shall be able to manage.

Meanwhile, Assia sends her greetings, & hopes the jaundice is now in the last stages of a flying retreat. So do I. And all the best things taking its place   Yours

Ted

When Olwyn Hughes brought him and János Csokits together in the early 1960s, TH had offered to help the exiled Hungarian poet translate his work and the two began a correspondence. During one of Csokits's visits, in the course of which TH asked him to edit a Hungarian *Modern Poets in Translation*, Csokits had looked at TH's most recent poems, destined to appear either in *Wodwo* or in *Crow*, and had contrasted their 'open universe' with the 'closed' one of *The Hawk in the Rain* and *Lupercal*.

Miklós Radnóti (1909–44), Hungarian poet of Jewish ancestry, was shot dead after the evacuation of the labour camp in which he had been interned. The language of his poems is noted for its unwavering objectivity and precision.

TH eventually visited Germany, with Assia Wevill, in 1968.

To Robert Graves

20 July 1967   Ms   Graves Trust

Dear Robert Graves,

Thank you for coming to the Festival. I hope you think it was worth it. Some of the other evenings were more grotesque but none had quite that variety.

I've been intending to write to you for years, to thank you for your poems and for The White Goddess—which I regard as the chief holy book of my poetic conscience (confirmed again, after the Festival). Somebody gave me a copy when I was 17.

Some day I hope we'll meet for a longer time.

                              Yours sincerely
                              Ted Hughes

The White Goddess had been a school-leaving gift from TH's English teacher, John Fisher.

To János Csokits

6 August 1967   Ms   Emory

Dear Janos,

Thank you for the long painstaking letter. It is really about the best total judgement the book has had. Quite right, it's a transit camp. It's a clearing house, so I can feel more clearly about what comes next. Also, it's a record—for me—of a rather baffled time. The order of the poems is not chronological, but arranged around the following theme: after an undisturbed relationship with the outside natural world, I receive a demand from behind—from a subjective world. The main event of the

273

book—and of my life from 1961–2 onwards—is this invitation or importuning of a subjective world, which I refuse. I think I did refuse—or rather, I deferred. And I paid for it quite heavily. The Rain-Horse is the record of the importuning, & the refusal. The consequence of the refusal was a mental collapse into the condition of an animal. 'The Harvesting' is a story on the theme: the man turns into the hare at the moment he shoots it. The Wound—which was a dream I dreamed twice on one night—is a parallel fable. I refused the invitation, & so I was forcibly abducted. (All this is interpretation afterwards.) The Suitor is a story of death & the maiden & is a prophecy—I wrote it in 1962, January, almost under dictation. The Suitor is me, the man in the car is me, the girl is Sylvia, the Stranger is death, & the situation turns me into an animal—as Gog. Also, the girl is my spirit of light, my Ophelia.

All the poems in the first part are what I wanted to save, that were before the event, & yet seemed related to it. The stories are episodes of the event—as you'll see. 'The Wound' is a traditional journey to the land of the dead. As I understood the dream at the time, it all takes place in a few seconds when the protagonist's heart stops. Throughout the action, the dreamer is lying prone.

The poems in the second part are poems after the event (though some were written quite a while before it. But prophetic poems don't come in order, in my experience.). My own criticism of the whole book is that it's too subjective—too dominated by a long nightmare in which I was for the most part incapable of projecting my notions into a world of real action, incapable of real detachment.

Also, in no single poem do I feel to have created something that really surprised me. At the same time, there's an awful lot of me in it.

I'm taking the second 2 parts of Gog, and 'Karma' out of the American edition—it's amazing how you hit my own feelings in your criticisms of the individual poems. (Also, I had already decided to take out the titles in 'Wings')

Anyway, now you know why I put the poems in that order. It was just a way of putting the book together, really, since I didn't write a single one of them with this construction in mind. Also, I thought if I arranged them in this way, they would work powerfully to bring me back to the objective world where my talent really belongs, and where I begin to have some control of my life again. The 7 years are over—and I think the book has had a great good effect on me. I hope you'll think so, when you see what I've been doing.

So much for all that.

Pilinzky is in London—Olwyn met him & liked him extremely. The local Hungarians are apparently putting pressure on Danny Weissbort, for the Hungarian issue—but as far as I'm concerned, you are editing that, and I don't want to compromise you.

There's no hurry.

I'm keeping far out of the Magazine now. It has involved me in such irrelevant struggles. I don't want to be a poetry telephone exchange operator. But the Magazine is growing at a ferocious rate—covering America like a space-weed.

Was Spain a relief? And how is the liver? And the writing?

My mother's very ill—in hospital, hardly able to move now, & in pain. But the children are flourishing.

Olwyn is also flourishing. She signed up Pilinszky & all his works (as his agent). How about yourself & Bikitch? Are you likely to disgorge a novel?

Keep well, and let us hear from you soon. Assia sends her greetings.

Yours

Ted

Although János Pilinszky, whom TH was later to serve as translator, had visited London as reported here, it seems that he and TH were yet to meet.

Gábor Bikich (1923–2002) was a Hungarian poet, friend of Csokits and, like him, an exile.

To Anne Sexton

9 August 1967   Ts   Texas

Dear Anne,

I hope you're back and enjoying peace. It was so nice having you come down here—it completely redeemed the general unease I felt about Mrs Ames. After all, I liked her and was quite convinced that there's nothing suspect about her motives for writing the book about Sylvia—though I did suspect that when she started.

Aurelia is here at present, with the children at a seaside resort. She really is an extraordinary woman. Every time I meet her I'm more impressed.

[. . .]

Don't you worry about reviews. I've just been getting a load of them too. Both kinds are bad, but the favourable are worst I think. They tend to confirm one in one's own conceit—unless they praise what you yourself don't like. Also, they make you self-conscious about your virtues—just as when you praise a child for some natural charm. Also, they create an underground opposition: applause is the beginning of abuse. Also, they deprive you of your own anarchic liberties—by electing you into the government. Also, they separate you from your devil, which hates being observed, and only works happily incognito. Also, they deprive you of your detachment from the scene into which you are injecting your work, by making you a visible part of the scene. Also, they satisfy ambition, which only works from a radical discontent and public neglect. Also, they banish your spirit helpers, as when the eskimo hunter enters opens a gift shop and buys a car. Also, they falsify your life, by forcing an identification of you and your poems: your poems earn the praise but you read it and accept it. Etc Etc. Whereas bad reviews are like a humiliation: you feel you must conscript every reserve including God and the Devil, and produce the absolute reality that will withstand everything. They send you into the wilderness.

Anyway, you've no need to worry. When you've got it you've got it—you don't have to bother about poetry, you just have to be truthful (which is where the brain and all its hideous lies leap in, I know).

That bone meal has to be taken regularly, but if you take too much you'll grow bone all over like a crab, so take it easy. My book is coming out in the States in November—I've taken a few dud pieces out, and put one or two in for interest's sake. I'll see you get an American copy.

Keep well. Let me hear from you now and again.

Yours

Ted

Anne Sexton (1928–74) was among the US poets who had appeared at Poetry International. After Sexton's death, Lois Ames, about whose plans to write a biography of Sylvia Plath TH had been wary (see letter to Aurelia and Warren Plath of March 1966), was to edit with Linda Gray Sexton a volume under the title *Anne Sexton: A Self-Portrait in Letters*. The UK edition of Sexton's *Live or Die* had just appeared.

To Hana and Yehuda Amichai

[Late 1967]   Ms   Beinecke Library

Dear Hannah & Yehuda,

I suppose you've given up hope of ever hearing from me again. After the Festival, I lapsed into complete, inert non-communication—this is the first letter for weeks, I haven't even been paying bills.

The Old City sounds wonderful. You must have caught it in its best moments—before it fills up with a permanent population of sightseers, all hoping to be taken for or to become items in the museum. It will probably become a Sargasso sea of the world's loosely drifting poets, then it will breed monsters.

We've been having upheavals. As a first step to us leaving Court Green & Devon, Assia has gone to London. Situation here too intolerable. She'll work there—get a well paid job—till I can pull out of here with the kids etc. A straggling act of migration.

She finished the small edition of translations and they really are good, all of them. As soon as she'd gone over them for the last time, I felt I must write to you straight off to tell you how good they were—they're excellent, in fact. I think they are the best of all I've seen, of translations of your poems, Yehuda. Also, finances have been fixed for the best of all possible worlds—limited edition with Cape, full edition with Penguin. Have you heard yet from my sister?

The rain's pouring down, it's now dark, at seven oclock, the leaves are blowing about, our big elm tree is roaring exactly like a sea. This is a Devonshire you didn't see—it will continue, more or less, till March.

I've been writing a bit—I'll send you copies.

How are you both? Keep in touch. At present, the translation magazine is trying to muster an issue of Hungarian poetry, but the Hungarians are still tribal—Goths, huns, Ostrogoths, one against the other in a totally murderous state of mind. So my co-editor & I will probably get bumped off in a literary quarrel. The Hungarians in London have refined & intensified their qualities, they are the worst. I'll be writing. Love to you both. Ted

Yehuda Amichai had been a guest of Poetry International, and his poems presented there in translations by Assia Wevill, under her maiden name of Gutmann. Wevill, who had had a successful career in advertising before moving in with TH, was planning to re-enter the profession.

1968

While his work on *Crow* continued, TH had also accepted a commission from the National Theatre and the director Peter Brook (b.1925) to contribute to a production of Seneca's play *Oedipus*, adapting a translation that had already been provided by David Anthony Turner. In the event, TH came up with a completely new script.

At the beginning of the year, Assia Wevill was living in St John's Wood, London NW8, and supporting herself and Shura by a job in advertising. In spite of TH's visits, it is clear that she was feeling ever more isolated. In mid-February she was in hospital, being treated for cystitis.

To Assia Wevill

[17 February 1968]   Ms   Emory

Sweet Asseenke—what's happening? Whoever the 2 envelopes went to they didn't come here—neither of them.

I rang you up last night but you must have had a visitor. Maybe you'll ring me & talk to me.

I'm redoing the Oedipus bits. Quite good progress. I've got back to the right point. It was real rubbish I'd done last week.

Luke is here sitting studying & writing all day. Those plays have pulled him together. He's in very good form, very easy guest.

The kids are or were completely out of hand—it's been a battle to get them back, Nicky getting the worst of it because he goes off furthest. Very exhausting & depressing. Things are better now.

Have they located your ailment precisely yet? What are they doing about it? How many bottles of champagne now?

Sorry to be so miserable a visitor last week. I felt terribly apprehensive about what I'd done for the Oedipus—whereas when it's O.K. I feel quite without qualms. Just see how Frieda's picking up my thoughts. Here is her latest

My Secret Garden

As I run through the thicket

As I run to the ivy to the wall
As I run down the garden path
I find a door under the ivy
I go in the door I run around
   the secret garden twice.
I see a pond with a crocodile in it.
I see an angel.
I see elves and fairies.
I see apple trees and tulips.
I see ghosts and primroses.
In a den in a corner of the secret garden is a bear.
There is a crow dancing on top of the den.
Butterflies are flying about.

This was her essay. She wrote it out like this, then joined it all up to look like prose in her schoolbook.

Luke got me a beautiful life mask & death mask of B.

Everybody has terrible colds—this morning I had a sore throat.

Be home by Wednesday, & be better. This Oedipus seems to be rocking the atmosphere for me—horrible little dreams, perpetual horrible feeling. But you brighten me up with a letter very soon. Love love

Addressed to Wevill at the Middlesex Hospital, London w1. The item that Lucas Myers had given TH was a replica of Beethoven's death mask.

To Leonard Baskin

2 March 1968   Ts   British Library

Dear Leonard,

How are you after these two years or so of silence. Please send me a few sentences of news.

The CROW project did not fade, it's grown into a folk epic which will be the length of a novel—Bushman prose but more poems than prose. God has a nightmare—a Voice attacks him. He cannot understand what is wrong. Man comes to heaven and asks to be permitted to cease to exist since life is too awful. God is flabberghasted hearing these words from his prime creation. The Voice scorns man and God his creator. God finally challenges the Voice to do better. The voice creates Crow. Crow goes into the world and God tries everything to destroy him, pervert him, educate him out of himself etc—an epic of ordeals. This style of prolonged forging gradually transforms indestructible Crow into a superbeing who gets sacrificed.

All through, are a great many apocryphal legends about Crow—some of which I enclose. Mainly Crow sings songs (God also sings songs and many of the objects and beings which Crow meets sing songs). I enclose one or two of Crow's songs. No songs are typical because Crow himself gets transformed at every stage. But his songs are all in crowtalk—which is as base and crude and plain and ugly a talk as I can devise though I haven't yet quite hit what I shall get. I enclose one or two of his songs.

What if we do a short book now of some of these pieces, then perhaps another book and another. Then finally when the whole epic is complete your drawings would be a tremendous series, and if I can go on and finish as I've started my part will also be OK.

I've just finished translating Seneca's Oedipus for The National Theatre—I'll be getting typescripts this week and I'll send you one. If it appeals to you, maybe you could help make that a saleable book. It's come off better than I expected—I hope you'll like it.

I inscribed the enclosed copy of WODWO long ago—last May. That's the end of my first period—as I remember you saying with a difference.

I hope you're well, prospering, progressing. You've been constantly in my mind all this last year and it's an immense relief to have finally written you this letter. Hope I'll hear from you soon, some news.

as ever
Ted

The volume that was to be published in 1970 as *Crow: From the Life and Songs of the Crow* had its genesis in an exchange of ideas between TH and Baskin early in their friendship. Baskin's images of birds with anthropoid features fascinated TH, but his proposal of a series of short books on the theme was never followed through. By 'Bushman prose', TH is alluding to *Specimens of Bushman Folklore* (1911) by the German philologist Wilhelm Bleek (1827–75), a work he greatly admired.

To Peter Redgrove

[Undated 1968]   Ms   Emory

Until I got this much more taxing invitation to write a translation of Seneca's Oedipus for the National Theatre. They had a translation by a

Scotsman—a chatty but quite lively version that had been on N. Irish B.B.C., and they wanted me to 'go over' it. They'd contracted him—paid him etc. So I thought they wanted something slight. Peter Brook producer. Gielgud Oedipus. Irene Worth. However, it's turned into a complete soul-searching type of rewrite. The first translation has vanished. Peter Brook's directing is more like prolonged group-analysis of everybody concerned—so I've got extremely involved. But I'm fairly pleased with my text,—I've hit an abbreviated sort of style. But the whole thing is a battery of these long narrative speeches—it's really a piece of epic, broken between 3 or 4 voices, with short passages of very formal dialogue. The characters are going to stand motionless beginning to end, the chorus is going to be a 'mob' stationed all round the audience on those pillars at the Old Vic. It will depend on terrific momentum. Lasts about 1¼ hours. You must come up and hear one of the rehearsals when they get going. Meanwhile, I'll try and visit you and show you the text. I've written in one quite long speech for Jocasta, several shorter ones—and it needs another long one. I've got over the eyes in Sphynx/womb/hell/body/forbidden/questionmark/mother/darkness/death etc—a very absorbing Proteus. At the end, he's going to have an obscene satyr 'happening' & I've devised one maybe too obscene, but too appropriate not to try and use—serpent, cunt, totemic penis, drums, a gigantic ritual fuck on stage—a serpent penis 30 feet long & full of people.

Seneca's Oedipus opened at the Old Vic on 19 March. Sir John Gielgud (1904–2000) played Oedipus, Irene Worth (1916–2002), Jocasta. A less ambitious 'happening' than the one TH sketches here was staged.

To Gerald Hughes

15 March 1968   Ms   Emory

I've a feeling I'm on the brink of making a lot of cash, & various circumstances point that way. The bloke directing this play 'Oedipus'—which opens next Tuesday—is one of the best most imaginative directors in the world, and we get on very well together. He's invited me to do a cycle of short plays—absolutely on my own terms as far as style etc goes—which he's going to set up in a great hall he's been loaned in Paris. It's more or less an invitation to create my own theatre, my own kind of play, whatever actors I want—since any actor falls over to be directed by this Peter Brook. Anyway, alltogether the opportunities are such as no writer was ever offered before so suddenly & so out of the blue. Since I've never had any play produced etc by even the worst director, until this Oedipus. This Oedipus is terribly crude, bad in many senses, but in the main one it is good—in that the further I've dragged it into my own territory (out of all conventional modern theatre even away from the avant garde) the more uniquely effective it is. It's bad insofar as the original Roman play is fearfully melodramatic, & the main actor, Sir John Gielgud, wonderful man though he is, is incapable of acting like a demon or speaking like a Stone-age witchdoctor—which is necessary, & which the younger actors can manage. He speaks in the usual high tragedy English convention. I'll describe it all in another letter. The terrible thing is—how my time-wasting, my non-working, has caught up with me. I ought to be so much better prepared than I am. In fact, I'm not prepared at all. I have my poetical scrap iron, but this business needs bronze. So I have to melt down my iron, & recast it to do the work of bronze. But it will never be bronze. So I shall have to set the fashion for iron—which may be a failure, a mistake, a waste etc. The whole thing may come up against the fact that my will to write poems is stronger than my will to write plays.

To Aurelia Plath

1 July 1968   Ts   Lilly Library

Dear Aurelia,

If all goes as it should the children should be flying on the 6th August, and they will be with you for three weeks. They are getting very excited about it. Frieda studying the world map at four in the morning.

I'm sorry I sent you that disappointing letter earlier. You better than anybody will understand how many fronts I feel to be operating on—several of them that I'm by nature very unfitted for. I keep trying to find the key that will solve them all, but I have a growing feeling that before I find it I shall have to lift myself and the children completely out of the situation we are in, and try and start absolutely afresh. I daresay that's what I would have done but for this freakish business of my parents. My mother has heard today that her knee—and she seems pretty well except for one point on her knee that will not heal, where she had the metal hinge put in—is not in the opinion of the specialist responding to treatment and will therefore have to be stiffened—i.e, the hinge taken out and the joint locked. So she will then be on two stilts. So she is very depressed, my father very depressed. And myself somewhat baffled. I was banking on them moving back to Yorkshire this next week. I get on with them quite well, they are endlessly good with the children, but there's no doubt that their presence is simply suspending my life. And the only solution, it seems, is for me to leave them here and move myself. If I find them a cottage here, they will be here for good and I shall be in a way more responsible for them than ever. It wouldn't be so bad if they didn't interfere in a million ways, and absolutely instinctively, calamitously, with my life. I'm in the foolish position of trying to seal them off from me, for the time being, at the same time as they live in my house. The only solution, apart from removing myself and the children, is to forcibly send them back to Yorkshire and let the hospitals up there do what they can to replace the hospitals down here.

Anyway, I'm sure you've a good idea of what it is like, and the effect this sort of thing has on everything else.

Added to that, I'm in the middle of things I should have done years ago, which is enough in itself to absorb all my attention at every minute.

Did Olwyn write to you about THE BELL JAR being made into a film etc? Please don't feel any pressure from that. Please tell me if you have the slightest qualms—I certainly have. I would prefer it not to be done—since whatever cuts are made etc, the film makers will inevitably take every sensational and sentimental advantage. As for publishing it over there simply as a book—again, I think not. I imagine you seeing it on the bookshelf of everybody you know, as it would be, and it seems to me I should ask you not to think about whatever the book might earn for the children—the money is as likely to do them harm as to do them good. It's true that copies of the English Edition are sold over there, but they're not easy to get—it's not really on the market, and nobody you know is likely to see a copy. You aren't going to see it displayed in bookshops, with foolish advertising phrases.

Anyway, keep well. The children are getting old enough now to appreciate the difference of places, and one reason I desperately want to get my life watertight again is so that I can take them around to a few of these invitations I get to go all over the world—I have standing invitations to Czechoslovakia, Russia, India, Israel, Jugoslavia and of course the U.S. a hundred times over.   Yours   Ted

The 'disappointing letter' for which TH apologises was written to dissuade Aurelia Plath from paying a visit to Britain.
   Larry Peerce's film *The Bell Jar*, based on Sylvia Plath's novel, was released in 1979.

To Sheila Roberts

[Autumn 1968]   Ms   Sheila Lawes

Dear Miss Roberts,
   I'm afraid I can't tell you much about my work. There's a book "Poetry In The Making", by me, published by Faber & Faber, which gives something of my general ideas about poetry. It's a school book.
   My work for children, particularly in the little plays you mention, is not quite what I wanted. Two or three of the plays came off quite well on Radio. But they are not really worth bothering about. I wrote them because I was asked to, and I needed the cash at the time. They were very well received, I believe.
   I wrote a children's book titled The Iron Man—published by Faber & Faber. Apart from being a story I told to my own children, I intended it as a blueprint imaginative strategy for dealing with a neurosis. That is, ideally anybody familiar with that story will have a plan of action for dealing with neurosis in themselves. It is a story intended to cure the mentally sick, & to put people in contact with their real nature. To some extent, I think it is successful. Though it is difficult to measure things like that, of course. I'm afraid it's not easy to explain either.
   I hope you like Silkin's poems—he seems to me extremely gifted, much moreso than he gets credit for.
                                        Yours sincerely
                                        Ted Hughes

Sheila Roberts was a student at Lancaster University, planning a dissertation on TH's children's books and the work of Jon Silkin. She had written asking for advice.

284

To John and Nancy Fisher

[22 October 1968]   Ms   Angela Fisher

Dear John & Nancy,

Thank you for the magazine. I like especially 'Suffrage or Suffering' and 'Ad Infinitum'. Also 'Violence'. Also, very much, the two designs on page 12, especially the fish.

I've got myself involved in a major piece of sacriledge. Peter Brook evidently did a production of King Lear some time ago—perhaps you saw it. Paul Schofield as Lear. Now he wants to make a film of it. Not a film of the play—like Richard III or Olivier's Hamlet, but a film of the story, using whatever in the text doesn't sound unreal in a film. (like the Japanese Macbeth "Throne Of Blood", & like the Russian "Hamlet"). So he wants me to rewrite the text !! !! !! So the opening speech becomes something plain, simple—not measured & musical. He's quite right, I think. The whole world of Lear is in the verse, but when you're manifestly supplying that world in something else i.e. in the visible (over-visible) film, the world visible in the film, and the world audible in the verse, are two different worlds, different orders of symbolism, that just destroy each other. We can't manage both simultaneously. I agreed to do it mainly to prevent anybody else doing it, but in fact I'm quite enjoying it. It makes me appreciate what an over-focussed & over-simplified thing cinema is—compared to verse anyway. I think I'm trying to do an impossible thing, actually. What happens is—most things go. The present state of the 1st speech is

> Lear: Give me the map there.
>   We are growing old
>   it is time we unburdened ourselves
>   of all these cares of government
>   and prepared ourselves for death.
>   Cornwall
>   and you our no less loving son of Albany,
>   we intend to bestow their inheritance
>   on our daughters
>   now
>   to prevent strife after our death

The Princes France & Burgundy—suitors to our young-
est, Cordelia—you too shall be answered here.

This is our decision. We have split our kingdom into
3 parts. Now my daughters—which of you shall we say—loves us
most.

etc.

What goes (apart from most things) is the carrier wave, the larger
than lifeness, the slight hypnosis. A lot might have to come back. Love
to all   Ted

In a letter to John and Nancy Fisher of around Christmas the same year, TH reports:
'You'll be glad to know the King Lear project has fizzled out as far as I'm concerned.
I got completely sick of it, had bad dreams about it etc, & finally I've pulled out. It
was a mistake to get involved.'
   In Peter Brook's 1971 film of *King Lear*, with Paul Scofield in the title role,
and Irene Worth as Goneril, the screenplay is credited to Shakespeare and Brook
alone.

To Assia Wevill

[Late December 1968]   Ms   Emory

When I got back here Gerald & Joan had just arrived from Australia—
they brought their holiday forward. Otherwise by now I would be
with you. They leave this weekend. Your misunderstanding of me
that last evening was as terrible as ever. But I felt I could not go
on promising until I had actually cleared myself with some action.
I saw that what I had done was probably what had been making you
ill too.

I have not put the children to school because I want them to start
there. I am coming down to find a school and some temporary lodging
for us, until we can find a place big enough for all of us.

I know quite clearly what has been making me so ill. I want to start
afresh with nothing whatsoever from earlier times—no furniture, place,
mementoes etc. I intend to get free of it and cut everybody but you
out of my life completely. You'll see that I'll fulfill all my promises
eventually.

Yesterday Gerald & I drove to Mexborough & to the pond where
I used to catch all the pike. The lodge, where my friend had lived, was

a ruin. The garden was a forest. We went down to the pond, and it had shrunk to an oily puddle about twenty feet across in a black basin of mud, with oil cans & rubbish. Nicky had brought the fishing rod and he made a few casts into the poisoned looking water among the rubbish. It was horribly depressing. My name carved on the trees. It began to pour with rain. Then I made one token cast—a ceremonial farewell— and there among the rubbish I hooked a huge perch. The biggest I ever caught. It was very weird, a complete dream.

1969

Assia Wevill was granted a decree nisi in October 1968 and her divorce from David Wevill became final in February 1969, by which time she had already moved to a flat by Clapham Common, London sw4. Edith Hughes died on 13 May.

To Charles Monteith

19 February 1969   Ts   Faber

Dear Charles,

   Sorry for the delay, but may I have another week to decide about the Emily Bronte selection?

   Is there any possibility of your doing in the same series a selection of Shakespeare's shorter pieces. I'm always amazed that there is no single portable book where I can read all my favourite passages from the plays etc. One result of the reverence that leaves the big speeches buried in the plays is that only scholars and actors doing that play ever read them. I don't think extracting 'beauties from the plays' is so reprehensible, except to the fanatics who read their complete Shakespeare steadily and constantly. The big passages aren't so dependant on their context that they become small and empty when they're read separate. Along with the passages from the plays (no passages at all from some plays, one or two only from others) there would be a selection of the sonnets and the short poems. If you think this would be possible, I would love to do it. After all, it would be the best book of poetry in English (after the complete works.)

   I suppose the Penguin selection has taken care of Blake.

                              Yours
                              Ted

TH was never to edit *A Choice of Emily Brontë's Verse*, in the Faber series that had included his 1968 Dickinson selection, but his idea for a similar treatment of Shakespeare was taken up at once, and the text delivered a few months later (see letter to Monteith of 23 June). *A Choice of Shakespeare's Verse* – US title: *With Fairest Flowers while Summer Lasts* – appeared in 1971. Jacob Bronowski's

Penguin edition of William Blake's *Poems and Letters* (1958) had been a popular success.

To Richard Murphy

8 March 1969   Ms   Tulsa

Dear Richard,

How are things at Hull? Very busy, very preoccupation, very involvement, very cacaphony, I imagine. Are they a rebellious lot? I read an account in the T.L.S. of some Arts Festival at Essex and I thought "If North means worse what does that make Hull?"

It will be interesting to hear your account of it all. I'm on the point of nearly deciding poetry should be made as inaccessible as possible, never taught in schools, forbidden in Universities, 5 times as difficult to get printed. The students I meet now are not at all interested in poetry, but in the style of life certain poetry has got attached to. They're interested in one of the modern Bohemias or other. This is the mob that fills the spectacular readings, & its the mob that buys the Penguins etc.

I got going on my Crow thing very busily. Slowly turning into something mostly unpublishable I think—too something or other. I've got a lot of short pieces but they make more sense with the prose story which is what's not too elevated. A super-crude prose which will probably leave me psychically deformed.

Will you still be there around March 19th? I'm coming up to Yorks then—& shall stay up a day or two, and I'd drive over to Hull if you'd be there—say on the 21st.

I was going to be in Leeds in Feb—but the snow nipped that.

Enclosed one review you've probably seen.

I've had flu on & off for about a fortnight—then it laid me right out. Now up & nearly active once again.

Have you been out to Withernsea etc where I spent the flower of my youth. It would be interesting to stroll around and see how much time has passed on certain faces—shockingly much or surprisingly little. It's just beginning to be shockingly much, everywhere else.

It will be nice to hear from you—what it's been like.

Are you managing to write anything?

Yours

Ted

Murphy had taken up the Compton Lectureship in Poetry at Hull University, at a time when political discontent among university students was at its most vocal and active.

Withernsea, near Hull, was close to Patrington, where TH had spent the 'flower of his youth' in National Service (see letters to Edna Wholey of 1950).

To Celia Chaikin

14 April 1969   Ms   Emory

Dear Celia,

I should have written to you long ago but I've felt so absolutely smashed and not capable of talking to anyone about what happened. Your letter was a lot of support to me. I always liked you in your letters, and in what Assia told me about you, and you said just what was needed. I've gone through these last weeks in a daze. Everything has become horrible to me, I cannot believe how I never knew what was really happening to her. Our life together was so complicated with old ghosts, and dozens of near-separations over the years, but we belonged together so completely and so deeply, that her repeatedly testing me, saying that we'd better separate for good, were just like a bad habit, part of our old difficulties, and so when she repeated it on that last day over the phone, it was nothing new, nothing we hadn't got over dozens of times before.

I feel now my life has gone completely empty. I know if I had only moved—if I had only given her hope in slightly more emphatic words in that last phone conversation, she would have been O.K. But I was totally exhausted, and nearly off my head with other distractions. Usually, one of us could pull the other out of it, but on that day we were both exhausted—and then she acted so quickly. If only she'd gone away for a week, anywhere, she'd have jerked me out of my apathy & confusion. Little Shura was the most wonderful little girl, full of fire. And really beautiful. I'm certain she finally did it in one of those crazy devilish moods. She didn't even ring any of her friends.

I've no idea what I'll do now. Leave this unlucky house, maybe go back to live in Ireland.

The various things have gone off to you. They'll be there in about 3 weeks, I imagine. Assia was my true wife and the best friend I ever had, it's with me every minute of the day and night. Please write occasionally

love   Ted

290

Celia Chaikin, Assia Wevill's younger sister, had settled in Canada, as their parents had done.

After a house-hunting expedition to Tyneside, where TH and Wevill appear to have found a house that suited them both, he had returned – via Manchester, where he gave a poetry reading – to Court Green, and she to her flat in Clapham. On 25 March they spoke again, by phone, their conversation ending in argument, as it had done many times before. Shortly after that, Assia killed herself and her daughter.

To Aurelia Plath

14 April 1969   Ts   Lilly Library

Dear Aurelia,

I'm sorry I haven't been communicative through this last ghastly year. It has been a struggle to do anything at all, I have lost every single battle. Fortunately, Frieda and Nick are in very good shape, doing well at school, healthy and all that I could wish.

I shall make another attempt now to get away from this house which has gradually become a hell for me—of paralysis and apathy as well as of other things. Assia and I thought some atonement could be made for Sylvia, but this house made sure we were dragged into the utmost nightmare.

This last horror has maybe taught me one thing. Sylvia's death threw my whole nature negative. I now see the senseless cost of that, for others as well as myself and I must in some way set everything behind me if I'm to carry on at all. I see very well how I must live and maybe I shall manage it if I can find the right help.

There is a famous Quaker school in the south of Ireland, recommended to me by friends of mine who are professors at Trinity College, Dublin. I am going over there next week to investigate that.

The children talk incessantly about coming to the States this year. Would you like them? For how long? Nicky is growing very tall. He'll get more out of it this year, returning there to something familiar.

Please don't let Winifred know about Assia and Shura. The gossip will go straight to the children and I do not want them to know until we are established somewhere else. And Winifred tells all.

The dress arrived just in time for Frieda's birthday. Thank you for that and for everything else.

love

Ted

To Patricia Tormey

[April 1969]   Ms Emory

Dear Pat,

I feel terrible having got that ring off you at that moment but when I saw it I saw I would have got it for Assia because it is more like her than anything I ever bought her. It seemed so uncanny you should have made it just now and with me watching it arrive. I don't know what I shall do with it. When I saw it I thought I must bury it with her ashes and I think I shall.

I will try and give you something in return, not payment, but something I value. I think it's the most beautiful ring. I never wanted to get hold of any other like this one.

love

Ted

The funeral of Assia and Shura Wevill was on 31 March. After it, Edward Lucie-Smith took TH, Olwyn Hughes and the Irish-born jeweller Patricia Tormey (b.1941) to lunch. The gold ring that TH speaks of is one that Tormey had recently made. He had noticed it on her finger as the three of them were returning to Olwyn's Hampstead flat. She gave it to him and, in return, TH gave Tormey a netsuke that he prized.

To Charles Monteith

23 June 1969   Ts Faber

Dear Charles,

Here is the Shakespeare Selection. It is rather long, but I think the real point of it is to be long, and so include both the well-known good and the not so well-known good. It would not be longer than some of your paperbacks. And being long, it will be big enough for readers to be constantly finding something new in it. A short selection would be little more than a pedestal for the greatest most famous. You couldn't make a selection of the less well-known passages and leave the well-known assumed well-known. Perhaps you could. Anyway, I hope you'll agree that the point of this one is to be pretty long, pretty big.

Perhaps another selection of the other dramatists could follow it. Webster, Marlowe etc—again a big one.

I've spent a long time writing a long introduction to this selection, but finally I think this brief piece is best. My ignorance of Shakespeare scholarship wouldn't recommend me, and it is no place to brandish opinions and interpretations, I think.

Thank you very much for sending the note to my Insurance Company.

Yes, I was pleased about the prize—very surprised.

Yours
Ted

A few days later, having despatched the scissored-and-pasted text of *A Choice of Shakespeare's Verse*, TH writes: 'I should have mounted the cuttings on stiffer paper—the glue wouldn't have made such a mess, and my daughter was a bit enthusiastic with it on the last stages.'

The prize TH mentions was the Premio Città di Firenze.

To Leonard Baskin

16 July 1969   Ts   British Library

After all this time, greetings again. How is life going?

Mine has been going up and down lately, mainly down, though I'm well enough and now and again productive in a fashion. Crow has dragged my life into its vortex and the quicker I get it finished the better —but everything tries to frustrate it. How do you feel about it still?

There are quite a number of short poems, plus a longish seven chapter adventure in a sort of verse—a bit horrible, so much so that at one point I stopped, it was affecting my mind and everybody round me. But too late to stop. So now I'm pushing on. If I can get to the end I hope the end will redeem the rest somehow.

[. . .]

I have two nice children who make life a great pleasure. They come to the States every summer. I had a third, a little marvel, but she died with her mother.

I'm just moving to Yorks—bought a nice big house up there, lots of room for you to come and stay. Devon is dissolving me in its lush, superheated leaf-sleep. Everybody falls asleep down here. And it hasn't been lucky for me.

The 'big house' in Yorkshire was Lumb Bank, spectacularly situated on the edge of Heptonstall and not far from where Edith and William Hughes had lived. TH, who had contemplated buying it in the months following Sylvia Plath's death, this time made an offer on the day of his mother's funeral. It was accepted immediately.

To Gerald, Joan, Ashley and Brendon Hughes

19 August 1969   Ms   Emory

Dear Gerald and Joan, and Ashley and Brendan—

I've just written you one letter, but these little stamp-backs are just enough to get the froth off, the scum, and the floating dead flies, all of which you must spit out.

The Kangaroo skins adorn my chairs envied by everybody.

The leopard skin hat, Joan, was not stared at in stupefied incomprehension, but was stared at in some disbelief that anybody could let such an object go. Joan, it will be the collar of my eventual fur coat of Jacob. I now have ermine, mole, jaguarandi (a little S. American leopard) otter, kangaroo. I want a couple of foxes and maybe a mink or two. Plenty of mink down on the river.

I found another dead badger the other day—skin no good, but I'm getting its teeth for my rosary. Also, other bones for sundry operations, anklets, drumsticks etc. If I get to be eighty, I want to resemble a red Indian shaman.

So eagle-claws, fox-skulls & teeth, fox-skins—all desirable. God's first-hand artefacts are going to be so scarce, I want a few nearbye. Or rather, I don't like to think of them just being rubbished into the useless and already hugely superfluous dust.

How is the guitar? I expect you over here, Ashley, in a year or two, coming across country, painted in 7 colours, capering & strumming, with hordes of demented girls trampling the neighbourhood. Remember Uncle Ted's First Law of Music: if it isn't the devil, it isn't music. None of that wet marshmallow crooning. Also, Uncle Ted's Second Law of the Musical Phrase: Lay hold of it, as a tiger lays hold of a pig.

Are you in his group, Brendan? I've discovered a great instrument for you—the Bodhran, pronounced Bowran. It's an open goatskin drum, native to Kerry, Southern Ireland, the ancient wardrum of the Celtic tribes, and before that, a witch doctor's ghost drum. It is the most hair-raising sound on earth. An Irish friend of mine

294

who plays 12 instruments, writes songs, makes records etc, is making me one. Quite simple: stretch a goatskin over the frame of a gardener's riddle.

Going to bed now. Dad's just brought in a glass of brandy in hot water with sugar, very good.

Walter is looking after Barbara—doesn't bear imagining, though there are worse things. Hilda is stewing in contented retirement. Olwyn is flourishing. Etc.

I bought a new car—exactly like the old one, but maroon, and new. Very pleased with it.

Nick & Frieda are in the States. By degrees, the mind's elastic ceases to resemble old rope. I shall be getting back into twang just ready to greet their invasion.   Love

Ted

To Richard Murphy

10 October 1969   Ms   Tulsa

Dear Richard,

Here I am ensconced. It is very beautiful—marvellous house etc. I'm pleased with all of it.

My only reservations are psychological/metaphysical interpretations of the move in general and its consequences on the vital spark. If I relax & sink in, I'm finished. But if I can make great extensive forays from here, it will turn to profit. As it is, for the first time in my life since that brief spell in Galway I can work for 12 hours a day. So now I'll groom & curry Crow.

I like the new pieces immensely. 'The Battle' was clearly a great thing to have done, for your relationship with modern Ireland. I'm sending you a book which I think you'll like. This is just a note in a hurry. If you're over—call. Is there any more of Hull? I'm hoping so.

I'm still thinking of a place in Ireland. I need another pole—not Devon or London, out of England.

Frieda, naturally, bagged the room you bagged. However, all the rooms are pretty good.

Charles showed me photographs of the consecration. I'm still studying what to donate. How about a pair of foxes?

Some St Kilda mice. Foxes might be very good. They wouldn't be able to damage the birds too much. They would level off the rabbits.

Keep well. Write a note.

Yours

Ted

This move has been a great thing for Frieda & Nick—and that was the main motive.

I'm enclosing a letter to Claddagh, accepting £5 fee, just in case they had outlined to you anything different for contributors/participants. If it's O.K., perhaps you could just post it off. £5 is fine for me.

Written from Lumb Bank, where TH had moved with his children, and with Brenda Hedden, with whom he had been conducting an affair, and her children. He had taken part in a performance of Murphy's *The Battle of Aughrim*, for Claddagh Records in Dublin. Murphy tells the story of how he himself bought barely accessible High Island, with its derelict hermitage, off the Connemara coast, in *The Kick*.

To Gerald Hughes and family

27 October 1969   Ms   Emory

My production line is going O.K. Either I've done something unusual and got beyond everybody (in England & the U.S. at any rate, where most good writers are a bit deadlocked at the moment) or I've followed a personal peculiarity and merely produced a Heath-Robinson monstrosity. Only time will tell. But since my tradition—what I set my writing against—is the primitive literatures, the absolute bedrock productions of nature, which I find most congenial anyway, and which seem to me the vital and unchangeable tradition, then I think what I'm doing will always be there. It will be invisible to all those who hardly know that tradition exists (almost all literateurs) and whose brains have been constructed by the aberrations of recent civilisation. But since I've seen my other books gradually create an audience out of people who to begin with were full of superior opinions I guess this will do the same, though it might take longer. The whole collection is called 'The Life and Songs Of The Crow.' My Crow has been created by God's nightmare (actually the voice of God's mother whom God has buried alive and forgotten). God's whole effort is to discourage Crow to the

a Gerald, Olwyn and Ted Hughes, late 1940s
b Sylvia Plath, TH, and William and Edith Hughes, outside The Beacon, the Hughes'
ome in West Yorkshire, possibly September 1956
c TH and his uncle, Walter Farrar, mid-1970s

2a TH and Sylvia Plath in Boston, Massachusetts, 1958/9
2b Sylvia Plath and TH returning to Britain on the SS *United States*, December 1959

a TH with Nancy and John Fisher, 1974
b Daniel and Helga Huws with TH, late 1970s
c Lucas Myers, David Ross and Daniel Weissbort, April 1995
d Terence McCaughey

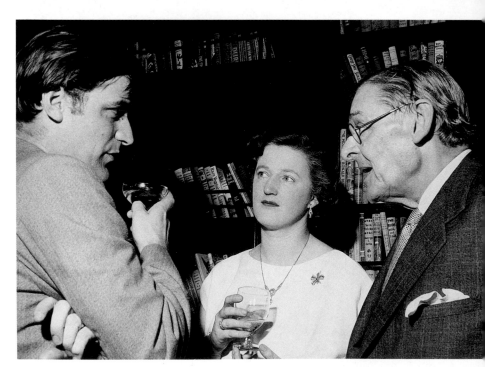

4a TH, T. S. Eliot, W. H. Auden and Stephen Spender at a party at Faber and Faber,
23 June, 1960
4b TH with Valerie and T. S. Eliot at the same party

a TH with Frieda and Nicholas Hughes, April 1962

b Warren and Aurelia Plath, December 1955

5c Richard Murphy,
early 1960s
5d Ben Sonnenberg

Dear Gerald,

CLEGGAN FARM
CLEGGAN,
Co. GALWAY, IRELAND   Ap 66

Well, your note of poorish news has just come. However, so long as we shall at least see you. And this time we must try and scan some new possible line of action — so you can break that locking nut system. Try and think of some research I can be doing that might be of use — for instance I can tell you here in the whole of Connemara there is not one good garage. Every single one is a scratch job. Just as Paul & Alice told you about Willcan.

This place is a mild paradise for me at present. We moved yesterday, from our sumptuous house, to a much older wilder place — £2 a week a house annexed to a 'big farm (big for this region) at' the top of Cleggan Bay — right on the west coast. I have a great vanshackle room full of silence to work in. I look out at a heathery hillside, + if I stand I see the open atlantic. The village is about 1 mile away. It's a blue, still day. I've worked fairly steadily for 6 weeks + now I'm going quite smoothly, + plenty of improvement still in hand. The kids are brimming over. Olwyn is here with me and a complete success. We have a good local girl, Teresa, helping us. (Their local average wage, hotel job, is £3 a week. Average man's wage —£7-10-0. Tin of sardines: 2/-. Honey 4/- a 3/4 lb jar. Everything 10% to 30% more expensive than England. So I just don't see how people live — Evidently it's mainly on cheques from children abroad.)

This morning I went fishing to a lake about 2 miles away. — I took Frieda + Nick. Blue, dead still morning. The lake was like glass. Within an hour I had 3 fish — lovely trout. The first about 1½ lb, the second — 3½, the 3rd again about 1½ lb. The second is the biggest trout I've ever seen alive. I let them children hold the rod awhile each time, to arouse any dormant passion for the art they may have. Frieda thinks it's cruel — (but she quite keen). Nicky is very keen. Connemara is all like the moorland going over from the top of Hardcastles towards Colne — but with twelve high granite peaks sitting in the middle of it.

6 First page of TH's letter to Gerald Hughes of April 1966

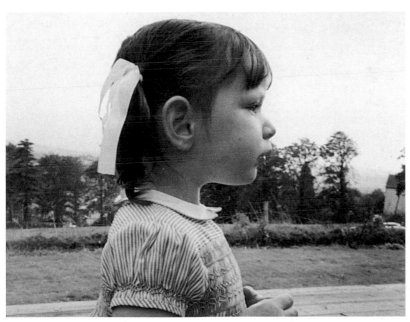

7a Assia Wevill, mid-1960s
7b Shura Wevill, 1968

8a Nicholas and Frieda Hughes with TH, on holiday in Scotland, early 1971
8b Peter Brook and TH in Teheran, summer 1971
8c TH, Frieda, Nicholas and Carol Hughes at Persepolis, summer 1971

point of making him no longer want to live—but Crow is indestructible, and in an imbecile sort of way un-outwittable, and eventually he <u>eats</u> God (he is forced to eat him) and liberates God's mother in the form of God's mother's daughter i.e. the daughter not of God but of the Creation, the mother of all the gods, and her he marries. After his terrific experiences he is a half-man (no longer a Crow made of solid black.) Though of course he is always a man as well.

From the second of three airmail letters sent to his brother on the same day.

To Daniel Weissbort

[Autumn 1969]   Ts and ms   Emory

Dear Danny,

Thanks for the letter. You sound about as confused as I am. Yes, I think the answer is flight. I thought I was fleeing from Devon. I've ended up with twice as much as I had, and all the things I want to keep lost. Nevertheless, real flight would have managed it. Real flight has not been tried. I was reluctant to move, thinking it would prevent me finishing my Crows. I was right. The whole Heath-Robinson but happily working factory that was producing them has fallen to bits, so I'm now assembling what I've got, which will be quite a lot. But not the most important part. In my saga Crow descends to Hell then climbs out to Paradise or a sort of quasi Crow Paradise. Unfortunately, when I got him right at the bottom of hell and being forced to eat his doppelganger and finding his bride in fragments and before he could get her together again (in process of which he was to become a skeleton scattered over the earth) at that happy moment everything went to hell and my sporadic efforts to get him out of it in convincing shape have been hopeless. My trouble is, I need two weeks now before I get to the point where I begin to get what I want. And each time I've got there—about three times—something's happened to break it up after one or two pages. Mostly I just haven't got there. End of lament over Die Fragmente.

It is galling, though, to have had a really good and fruitful idea like that one, and then bungled it so horribly. I think I've past it now. I need a new hero. Perhaps Crow reconstituted in Hell is no longer Crow. Maybe I'm plugging the wrong hero.

I would like to explore the little editions possibilities among our-selves. The trouble is, when you publish them yourself, you're honour bound to sell them at their price. Whereas if you're first buyer, you can then charge what you like. Not much of a point there.

Mostly, I would like to publish yours, Dan's, odd things of mine, and perhaps wherever we find something else that seems to us worthy of the series, and do them really beautifully—maybe very small, yes with woodcuts etc, in a small edition, and a slightly larger edition, dirt cheap, in bound-proof form. Even if we did not run for long, it would step both you and Dan into the benighted keyhole visual field of ordinary publishers.

At present, there are so many collectors of my pieces that one issue, signed, and sold about five guineas, would float the first three securely. Then the other two would catch up. If we made it a series, and didn't include duds, and made them handsome, we could hook collectors on the series. Since publishers etc are among the collectors the books don't just disappear—don't seem to, and we could sell the proof-bound copies around also. We would undersell Penguin. We could sell them as MPT publications, and gather all the kudos under one emblem.

So, let's think further on it. If we could start quick, I could assemble some of my unpublished Crows. I've let Merchant have about nine—though all published, for a limited edition he's producing on a handset press. Another fellow, Alan Tarling, I've promised some to. He produces lovely little books. But I'd like to publish the main lot of them soon. Perhaps we could make a book of the ones I don't put in the main lot. Anyway, we should start.

Hope you're all well
Ted

I'll not invite you up just at the moment—things are in turmoil. But soon Court Green will be empty—and you could go there any time. Or come here—here will be peace I hope by then.

I've decided I've been trying to write verse in completely the wrong way for some years. I've been excluding the real thing. I institutionalised the mode of one or two successes in 1962—and got myself stuck on the board of management. So my best 7 years have passed in error and futile strife. Are they the best 7 years? Everybody's life, between 30 & 40, seems to be special chaos—when you reap what the innocent eagerness of your twenties sowed, and before you can wise up. We are now wising up.

The fine printing of limited editions enjoyed something of a boom in the late 1960s. Talk about a collective venture of the kind TH toys with here, and in other letters of the time, did not lead to action, although Olwyn Hughes's Rainbow Press was started in 1971 in much the same spirit.

To Thom Gunn

1 December 1969   Ms   Estate of Thom Gunn

Dear Thom,

Here is my Yorkshire address. I'm not quite sure why I moved—one reason was, Devon was sending me to sleep. It has that effect on people—notorious for it. Decomposition of the will. All the electrical points rust up. Moss grows in under the toenails.

I am <u>nowhere</u> with the Anthology. My life this past 2 years has been so demoralised & chaotic, any kind of study has been impossible— beyond me. But I agree—I think we should go through everything. I started on Dryden—whom I've never read—and got far enough to real- ise that this was a job for anchorites or life. You can't just skim Dryden and remain very definite about what's outstanding.

Here is a copy of Oedipus. It was really fascinating to do. I worked with the company all along—started in November, and didn't produce my final text till February. Performance in March. First thing I realised— verse was too static, metaphor too literary. Or verse conducted me to a literary speech. Next thing: any word outside a tiny vocabulary seemed too civilised. Also, any complexity of sentence. I gradually got down to a hammering ugly plainness and finally hit the right note, where every- thing went like an express from start to finish. Much of it seems very crude—even in its own style—but all my efforts to correct it produced something too fine, or turned, and I was stuck with plumber's lead.

The performance was elaborate. A revolving golden box—sides down, a crossroads; sides up—a mystery package, Oed. & Joc. enclosed etc. Chorus drummed, hissed, wailed etc. A chorus member tied to every pillar of the old Vic—each shouted a different phrase. Finale, Jocasta impaled herself on a spike set up on the stage—sat astride it, held it, then drove herself as if down on it, most spectacular death, people fainting left & right. Finally, a 9 foot high golden phallus unveiled & left for the audience to stare at.

But the best performance was two nights before opening. Brook set all actors on stage, like a football team photograph, then they went through it at double speed, and without any inflexion of voice—just flat. No movement. The idea was to break them from verbal habits acquired up to that point. But the result was truly shattering. Two of the cast fainted. I suggested to Brook he stage the whole thing just like that, and I daresay he would have liked to.

Anyway, the way to read it is in one go, and as if the whole thing were set in a stone desert, in ruins, terrific sun, little fat mulatto characters, complete aboriginal barbarians.

I hope you're keeping well, and productive. I've greatly liked what I've seen recently—the ones about England. Keep well   Ted

TH and Thom Gunn had been commissioned by Faber to edit an anthology of English poetry. It never materialised.

To Leonard Baskin

15 December 1969   Ms   British Library

Dear old Leonard,

I hope you haven't had a year of such poor luck as I've had.

I'm half-inclined to suspect CROW.

There are now about 45 poems concerning Crow—so I'm calling it a day, and publishing them.

Whether people like them or not, they are my masterpiece. Insofar as I can manage the likeness of a masterpiece.

I'm sending you a copy of the typescript.

Are you still interested in supporting the text with some visible Crows? I'm considering changing my U.S. publisher—so nothing's fixed over there yet. Faber will do them over here.

Crow was your suggestion remember.

I'm also sending you a copy of my Oedipus—which made me think often of you.

Are you well? I really hope so. And productive. I think of you very often. Is the Gehenna press still going. If it is, is there any possibility of a limited edition?

I hope you like my Crows.

Let me hear from you very soon. I've got a spare house now over here if you want to come & live in a Samuel Palmer for a few months. Love as ever Ted

The 'spare house' was Court Green.

1970

In the last months of 1969 and the early part of 1970, TH showed versions of *Crow* to friends and professional associates, receiving their comments and tinkering with the text. Even after he had handed it to Charles Monteith, at Faber and Faber, it went through changes in both size and internal arrangement, before taking shape as the book that was to be published in October 1970. An augmented edition would appear two years later.

To Moelwyn Merchant

30 January 1970   Ts   Paul Merchant

Dear Moelwyn,

Sorry to be so delayed writing. I've been in Ireland. Here is the complete text of what I shall publish. Could you let me have it back very soon—within a day or two, because it is my only copy of many of the poems and I have some readings coming up, from 5th Feb onwards. If you like, you could maybe get it photostated then look at it at leisure.

The trouble with the series is that the last third is missing—the whole section where Crow, having touched the bottom, climbs to the top. Maybe that will be another book.

The line you query about. Speaking Crow, God speaks simply Crow in his actuality, Crow is the word made flesh, without any further need to make his being articulate. What disturbs Crow is that the stones etc are also the word made flesh, or at least made material, just as real in this sense as he is. And he understands too that the Logos is unconcerned about the consequences of its multiple creative act—that it loves and speaks Crow and lead which do not love each other. So Crow realises there is a big god who creates many sons, each one a god and indivisible within itself from its father, but all antagonistic to each other. So Crow realises this god is two faced. Within himself the god is smiling. But out of every other created object it is frowning. So this poses alternative lives: to live outside the practical struggle, outside the oppositions, and in a sense a little outside created objects, where the God is still one and all smiles, or to live in the struggle, and in the world of created objects, where the fiat of God has been delegated to egos each in opposition to every other, as if God had created as many replicas of himself as he creates objects and beings, and so filled the Universe with Gods each one thinking it is Himself, and each one representing His will. So in this poem Crow is seeing both alternatives at once. That is nowhere near as clear as the poem.

Keep well both of you—
Ted

Moelwyn Merchant (1913–97) had taken holy orders in 1940 and served as a curate during his time as lecturer at Cardiff University. TH had got to know Merchant and his wife Lynne in the 1960s, when Merchant was Professor of English at Exeter University. Their shared interests in both Shakespeare and spiritual matters were aired in numerous letters.

To Yehuda and Hana Amichai

11 March 1970   Ts   Beinecke Library

Dear Yehuda and Hana,

You must have thought long ago that I must have had a brain operation to remove all traces of former life. If you knew how much and how continually I've thought of you and the more time passed the less and less able I was to write and the more and more I wanted to. After Assia and Shura died I did not know how to write to anybody. I carried your letter around unopened. I carried her sister's and her father's letters around unopened. I was just paralysed, and I'm still not much improved. I've been swallowed up this last year. I made a move to get away and of all places I moved to a house that she and I once tried to buy.

I haven't written anything for a year. I was writing a long series of poems about a Crow being, a sort of saga that puts this Crow through all sorts of extremes. At the absolute nadir it dragged me into a great depression, and Assia with me, and then the thing happened. So I have this depressing collection of poems about a Crow.

It is great news that you're visiting England. Let me know what week exactly and I'll be there. Would you like a free place to stay? I could arrange for one very easily.

If only Assia and me had come to Israel!

I would like to come now. I'm trying to make a move this year, give myself a shake, see if I settle back in a different pattern.

I'm sorry you are not coming Hana. I think of you both as one unit so much that Yehuda alone will seem like a draught. A little bit like one.

So much has happened to you this last year you must have almost forgotten this glass case, where nothing alters—three years ago just like yesterday.

My sister's phone, in case you've lost it, is SWISS COTTAGE 5108.

Don't get too tangled in that war.

love

Ted

'If only Assia and me . . .': Assia Wevill had grown up in Israel.

To Ben Sonnenberg

23 March 1970   Ms   Emory

Dear Ben,

Very sad to hear your news. What was it about this last year? It's left nobody whole—certainly no couples.

I also am endeavouring to piece together my much-fractured vessel of peace—not a lot of success, but the promise is good. I got a new house—lovely spot, handsome building—disaster. Relatives (too neighbouring) and my own folly soon exploded it. So here I am where I was, with kids that much older, & still none of their problems solved.

I finished my CROWS—or rather, I stopped writing at them. I got him right to the bottom of the inferno where in piecing together the fragments of the beloved he himself is reduced to a scattered skeleton—and at that point the world intervened. So there his bones still are. I haven't written a word since—for a year to the day. A lot of what I wrote is very much my best, and here and there, and in one piece in particular, I touched something. If only I can get back to that point. I'm publishing about 60 of the poems in the Autumn. Baskin is doing an edition de luxe with engravings on the Gehenna press—he suggested writing about the Crow in the first place.

Somebody has offered £20,000 (not dollars) for Sylvia's M.S.—of all the worksheets of Ariel, that is, (most of the poems, with 5 or 6 sheets per poem), some odd notes, a couple of diaries etc. I fancy they may be worth quite a bit more in time, and I'm in no hurry to sell them. I might sell them for half as much again. But how could I raise money on them without selling them? How could I pawn them to somebody for, say, 5 years, for a fair sum? Is there any possibility you could suggest? If there is, could you drop me a line soon?

How is the theatre world in N.Y.? Have you any projects? I've been thinking I would like to try plays—very short, & in verse. Single episodes. Recitations. Gods, demons, etc. Infinite scope for productions over here—acting companies everywhere, all starved for material, all ready for anything.

I hope you're keeping up, getting into production,—it's the only way short of masks, dances, and blood sacrifice.

Any thoughts of coming over here?

affectionately
Ted

As TH's letter to John and Nancy Fisher of September 1970 makes clear, the last *Crow* poem he had written – 'a year to the day' – was 'A Horrible Religious Error'.

To Frank Pike

[Undated 1970]   Ms   Faber

What I meant to ask—can CROW be brought out on October 1st? It's a Thursday. Would you ask Charles? Newton and Kepler are in agreement, that is a great day in heaven. Why not exploit it.

From a letter otherwise concerned with *A Choice of Shakespeare's Verse*, then in preparation. *Crow*'s eventual publication date was 12 October.

To Peter Redgrove

[March/April 1970]   Ms   Sheffield

Penelope Shuttle was one of the two people I ever sent a fan letter to. A story of hers in one of those Calder triptychs—written when she was 17. I haven't seen her novel. I'd never seen such sensitive, clairvoyant writing—it was so sensitive I couldn't see how it could survive. Is it surviving? I was afraid she might go avante gardish—intellectual renovations in the French style. I suspect novels which are long poems—you get neither novel nor poetry. It seems to be alltogether too easy. An intellectual production unit sets up & the stuff pours out on one glassy electronic note. But in that story the whole nervous system was feeling its way through every word.

I stopped writing just over a year ago and have entered a state since that I thought I was too robust and sane to succumb to. I'm having to believe that my guardian angels who I always thought were on my side are now having a game with me—I act on my initiative & they stop me in the most paralysing way. I follow what seems to be their will—and they reverse it, then reverse it again. I do everything except write. But this folly has so disrupted my domestic kingdom that I cannot get an hour's peace for arranging & re-arranging that, or worrying about it. I seem to have been populated by the deceased who go on requiring God knows what of me & permit me very little. The one advantage in all this is the scope it gives for a really effective campaign of self-discipline & self-examination, but—. The whole mess stems from self-indulgence & self-absorption & the general inferno invoked by poetry. And general indolence. And general evasiveness. A higher command of attributes that couldn't see through the digging of a ditch.

I'm glad you're productive. It's helpful to live with somebody self-disciplined & concentrated. And I'm sure Miss Shuttle is an aerial of unique properties. I hope the other things are not too distressing.

My Crow book comes out in October. 59 poems—out of about 90. The long beautiful saga has not come to anything—I simply could not hammer out the style I wanted. Maybe I will. It keeps on hanging around. It's a permanent dismay that I didn't press straight on when I got to the point—I'm not sure I shall be able to get back there again. There were moments when I really felt my bones open.

Peter Redgrove and Penelope Shuttle (b.1947) had met in July 1969, in Zennor, Cornwall. In February 1970, after the break-up of his marriage, she moved to Falmouth to live with him. In 1967, her novella, *An Excusable Vengeance*, had shared, with prose pieces by Carol Burns and J. A. Dooley, volume 6 in the Calder & Boyars 'New Writers' series.

To John and Nancy Fisher

[September 1970]   Ms   Angela Fisher

I hope you like my Crows. There are about 50 more—some of which I should have put in. It will be interesting to see the reactions. It will be invisible to all those guardians of 'concrete specificity' and 'pragmatic scrutiny of the everyday actual' etc—but their world has well enough proved itself a prison, I think, for me. I'm sure the book's got something special. But I've lost all sense of how it will strike somebody who hasn't been staring at it for 2–3 years. What it's got may not be very pleasant.

The last one written was page 37—one day before the event that closed down the works. When I wrote the last line—all very rapidly, on a train—I received a terrific blow on the head, from nowhere. Nobody near me.

I'm glad I'm clear of it—even though I wish I had more like page 74 and 79. That's where I'll go on from, when I get airborne again.

What I wanted was more positive ones—where the last line would give me a kiss, possibly.

The 'event that closed down the works' was the deaths of Assia and Shura Wevill. The poem on page 37 was 'A Horrible Religious Error'; on page 74, 'Lovesong'; and on page 79, the second of the 'Two Eskimo Songs', 'How Water Began to Play'.

To Richard Murphy

[October 1970]   Ms   Tulsa

Sorry for the long silence. Herewith CROW. I'm very glad to be rid of it—I hope it means I now come from under the shadow of his horrible little wing. I wish I'd got more of it. When I remember how I flapped around, wasting time, running around Festivals, writing Opera librettos, reviews etc, and in general herding my goosish follies from one confusion to another, just when I was in the thick of Crow, I could skin myself. This last year has seen the culmination of my idiocies and the near-complete disintegration of any writing talent I had. The bits of prose I've tried to write have been ludicrous. Verse, I haven't even tried. So I feel in a bit of a baffled position. I either succumb—or do something which might well outstrip all possible follies. I can't quite muster the nerve for that—since all my wild leaps inevitably land on the kids. Just as they land on me whenever I try to sit still. Boarding school is looming as the answer. So much for my silence.

[. . .]

It will be interesting to see the reaction to my Crows. So much is taken for granted—i.e. all obvious, pragmatic scrutiny of the everyday actual—that it can't fail to be missed by many beady eyes. Alas, God, heaven, hell, Serpent etc will get slotted into drear old slots. Yet it seems O.K., whenever I open it & look at it, & some of it still alarms me. But I've lost all sense of how it will strike someone unfamiliar with it—how it looks alongside everything else.

1971

In August 1970, TH had married Carol, the daughter of a Devonian farmer, Jack Orchard. In February 1971, they travelled to Israel, TH to participate in a reading tour organised by the British Council. In March, TH and Richard Murphy set off on another reading tour, this one of the USA, for which Murphy's friend Tony White accompanied them as agent and road manager. Then, in April, the Hugheses were in Paris, at the Hôtel l'Aiglon, so that TH could work on the spot with Peter Brook and his company, the International Centre for Theatre Research, creating a drama they would take to the Shiraz-Persepolis Festival in Iran in the summer.

To Gerald and Joan Hughes

[February/March 1971]   Ms   Emory

You'll have been thinking my long silence has some special signifi-cance—quite right. This last six months has been the bitter end of this last two years. From the age of about 16–17 my life has been quite false, and since Ma's death & Assia's this false arrangement has been falling to pieces with great drama. Finally, I think I've reached the end of it—where I can begin again. Not easy to describe & probably not interesting. It's left me in a strange state, feeling I now have to begin again from scratch, in myself. I imagine I've reached the end of it, in that everything appears to me in quite different terms—the hellish feel-ing has lifted off somewhat, and I'm getting active again. It has meant the end of all sorts of dreams—temporarily, I hope. But the situation was desperate, and such things as putting F & N into boarding school instead of us all living happily together in some blissful country place seem to have been quite small sacrifices, considering the alternatives that kept rearing their nasty heads.

Anyway, I'm now getting going and my aim is to build myself up to the point where I can once again live in a house in a decent spot & live the enviable life. As it is, all I can manage is a very confined arrangement of things where working comes first—putting everything before my writing is just what caused all my disasters. It's not that the writing needs to be good or anything in particular,—it only needs me to work at it a few hours a day. Otherwise, as I've proved for about seven years, I go crackers and live in a most horrible atmosphere. Also, as I say, everything in me now seems to be on a completely different basis—as if my real life had been suspended since age of 16 or 17. Perhaps it really has. Anyway, suddenly everything & my attitude to myself seem so utterly different, it will be interesting to see what comes of it—if anything. The key was—[*short phrase obliterated*]. That removed something absolute—though it took me a while to realise it.

Lumb Bank seems so horrible, I think I shall have to get rid of it. Court Green not so much—though I couldn't possibly live there for quite a while. Somehow or other, Carol has hung on, and I mustn't inflict all that past on her any more than is inevitable. She's very sensitive to it—in fact I don't know how she stands it. The best thing will be to start somewhere afresh—some quite new place, which will be absolutely hers. We're tentatively looking around here & there.

To Nicholas Hughes

[March 1971]   Ms Emory

Dear Nick—
    The stag is jumping over a tired hyena. The rabbit is listening for its bomb to explode. The leaves are hiding a man playing a piano.
    But Nicholas is fishing in the lake on the other side of the hill.
                                        Love Daddy

On the back of a postcard showing a detail from the tapestry 'The Unicorn at the Fountain', in the Cloisters Collection at the Metropolitan Museum, New York. Both Nicholas and Frieda Hughes were by this time boarders at Ibstock Place, a school in Roehampton, London sw15.

To Peter Redgrove

[Spring 1971]   Ms Emory

It seems a long time since I wrote to you. When life has swallowed you, after chewing, there is still the being digested to go through and the osmosis into all active parts & organs, until what gets shat out in the clear air & sunlight & universal peace is no longer qualified to speak of what has passed.

So silence, like a behemoth gone off, speaketh, inadequately, reasons for my hitherto silence.

However, some condition of self-determination having now arrived, I think about writing to you and asking how goes it all. I imagine you've been going through the stomach of the crocodile. I trust by now you have been shat out to some advantage. I look forward to hearing a bulletin, however symbolically couched.

[. . .]

These things are beginning to have a hilarious side but only after destroying a whole year in very strange darknesses. I imagine the whole situation got tangled with something much deeper, since A's death & my mother's. I could spend the rest of my life trying to understand it. The one benefit of it all is that everything—the whole of my life so far, the world, all the great works, have undergone a simultaneous re-interpretation on an infinitely bigger scale than before. My main anxiety is that I might never have the time etc to catch up with it all, that I might turn too little of it to account. It requires a complete change in my life, to get into gear with what's happening.

I'd like you to meet my wife. She's from Devon, daughter of a farmer, half Welsh, very young, not very interested in literature but with perfect taste & judgement for what really counts in what she does read. Part gypsy—family name was Orchard, which is a West Country gypsy name. Exceedingly good for me.

It would be nice if we could meet & have two or three days, & talk.

I visited Israel—never believed I could be so moved & impressed by the place. The rock—where Abraham was to sacrifice Isaac—inside the Mosque, on the old foundations of the temple, must be the most electrical place on earth. But Jerusalem is alltogether overwhelming. So is Bethlehem, which I didn't expect, & so is Mosada. Then I went to the States for 2 weeks & had a pleasant scramble around the colleges with Richard Murphy and Tony White—who used to be an actor at Cambridge. Maybe you remember him. Then Carol & I took the children to Scotland, where we toured around & camped by the Lochs. After my ten years or so in the underworld everywhere I go astonishes me—I feel quite naive, the way I react to these places.

I don't know whether it really is astrological, but nearly every-
body I know seems to have been going through some first-intensity
transforming drama this last couple of years.

Redgrove would have been 'going through the stomach of the crocodile' because of
the emotional and financial fall-out from the break-up of his first marriage.
    'Mosada' is usually spelt 'Masada'.

To Frieda and Nicholas Hughes

26 April 1971   Ms   Emory

Dear Frieda and Nick,

We are staying in a room on the 5th floor of this hotel, right on a
corner. The hotel narrows to a point like a slice of cake, and we are
at the point. So our rooms are a peculiar jigsaw of shapes—triangles,
parallelograms and shapes like squashed matchboxes. We have a tiny
kitchen shaped like a tent on end and just about as convenient to cook
in.

Yesterday I found a fishing tackle shop which sells weird things. For
instance, meat tablets—which you put inside a small plastic cannister
(supplied) and fasten just above your bait. The tablet dissolves, as water
enters the perforations inside the cannister, and the meat smell flows
out, attracting fish towards your bait. That's the idea. Also, they have
special ointments for annointing your bait, to attract fish. Also, they
have spectacles with special lenses, so you can look through the shine on
water and see fish—quite expensive.

I haven't yet received your letter, Nick, telling about the rods. When
you have the cash, we'll go to a big tackle shop and you will see that
there are many many different makes of rod—all good, and plenty of
them O.K. for you. 8 or 9 ft would be O.K., same as for you, Frieda.
Now this is how to earn some cash. <u>Method</u> (1) For every story you
write me, you get 1/- (one shilling) if it's good, 6^{d} (sixpence) if it's quite
good, 1^{d} (one penny) if it is not good.

<u>Method</u> (2) Good painting or drawing—one shilling each. (Nothing if
they are careless)

<u>Method</u> (3) Practise making memory lists, so when we meet at the

weekend you can earn 1/- (one shilling) for each list you do both forward and backward without mistake.

Method (4) Similes—that is, when you say so-and-so is like a so-and-so. For every good simile—threepence. Make lists. We look forward to the weekend. love Dad

To Hana and Yehuda Amichai

[Late spring 1971]   Ms   Beinecke Library

Here we are, living in luxury in L'Aiglon—on the Bvd Raspail. I'm having a wonderful time inventing completely crazy scenes for a great goulash mix-up of Prometheus, Calderon's "Life is a dream", and Hercules Furens. I connect them all together, then develope the episodes where they criss-cross each other—anything can happen. Absolute liberty, so long as I stick to my mythology—which has become a continuation of Crow (my Prometheus has a black brother). For parts of it, I've invented a language called Orghast—('Orghast' means 'sun'—so 'Orga' means 'Being'—'Urgith' means Death—'ghast' means spirit or life—etc.) it is fascinating inventing a language.

The whole thing, or what we eventually make of it, is going to be performed at Persepolice—on the ruined Palace of the Gods   so probably the Iranian Ancestral spirits will descend, & add a scene or two impromptu.

This is just the thing for the moment—just right. Here in Paris I'm absolutely cut off from the English flock of harpies & the rest—a great relief.

Life is a Dream, by the Spanish playwright Pedro Calderón de la Barca (1600–81), is about the moral conversion of a tyrannical king. TH seems to have called on his knowledge of Seneca's *Hercules Furens* when greatly expanding the role of Hercules in his treatment of Euripides' *Alcestis*, near the end of his life.

To Richard Murphy

[June 1971]   Ms   Tulsa

Dear Richard—
    Many thanks again for the hospitality those few days. It was a much

too brief visit, but very worth while. What did Kieran make of his fish? I found the fish-hook we extracted from his dog's lip—a treble with one bend pulled right out of line—and Frieda made a relic of it. She cried most of the way to Letterfrack for her lost dog. It had one or two big ticks, and we'd been warning Frieda—as you know. On the boat she got wildly excited—she'd found a tick on her leg—a darling tick from her darling dog. So she made a relic of that too.

We came back down the East side of Lough Corrib. I would absolutely like to live somewhere near the top—somewhere near Maam maybe. So we'll concentrate on that area—and Northward by Lough Mask. So anything you chance to hear of—or any way we can get to know about small (or biggish) properties going there—either to sell or rent—we'd love to hear about.

Here's a list.

(1) In mid air—over mid-Atlantic.
(2) A congregation of gulls, storm petrels, seals—the text, the service.
(3) The voice in the well
(4) 7 Apocryphal legends about High Island
(5) The Saint's curse on desecrators.
(6) High Island as a radio receiver of cosmic or historic signals—variously tuned by the weather.
(7) <u>Fifty</u> metaphors of High Island
(8) High Island considered as a woman
(9) High Island considered as a man
(10) Ireland as a graveyard of bachelors, a nursery of little girls (there seem to be hordes of little girls—I noticed it in 1954. Carol noticed it this time)
(11) High Island as an orchestra and a choir
(12) Seven kinds of sea—emissaries to High Island
(13) An audit of duties, non-duties masquerading as duties, duties masquerading as non-duties
(14) Stations in the decline and fall of Inishboffin.
(15) A rogues gallery

All considered only as starting points—Also, each exercise to cover 3 pages in order to make a habit of flow & release. Also, under Beethoven's dictum to pupils: "Never mind the wrong notes—go through to the end." Very good dictum as dicta go. I have accepted your

314

offer—from January this year, your address was my official base for tax operations. Keep well—

Ted.

P.S. Persia is an exhilarating place—so far.

TH and the family had taken a fishing holiday in Ireland, before the working visit to what was then still called Persia.

'Here's a list': in his memoir, *The Kick*, Murphy recounts how, as a stimulus to his writing, TH and Tony White set him a number of literary exercises, with penalties and rewards to be exacted and paid in champagne. This came to be referred to as the 'Champagne Method'.

To Frieda and Nicholas Hughes

[June 1971]   Ms   Emory

Dear Frieda and Nick—

how are my two lovelies. Here I am, flying about 5,000 ft (nearly a mile) above the Persian desert. Sandy rose, with blue shadows, like a beach when the waves have left it rippled. Little green shadings of oases here and there. Yesterday we visited the ruins of Persepolis—which Alexander burned—where we are going to give the play. On the way out we passed several caravans of camels. In one place, two huge eagles. We were choosing the actual site of the play, and it looks as though we shall be doing it at some tombs cut into enormous red cliffs. As we looked at the place, and tried out all its echoes, an eagle came to watch—circling overhead for about 10 minutes. (I can see a little scatter of black tribesmen's tents (the tents black, not the tribesmen) on the desert below.) It is very hot and will get hotter—but the ice cream and melons are delicious. I didn't see any scorpions, but there are plenty. And snakes too.

I've been thinking that we should have fished that lake differently. We should have let ourselves drift across it on the rubber boat, and sunk our lines quite deep, with worms, and simply let them trail quite deep and slow right across the lake. However, next time, it will be loch Corrib, where there are pike of 40 pounds, and trout of 15. And salmon of 50. And lots of rivers.

Now we are crossing strange crumpled mountains, like collapsing piles of builder's sand. Now it's a desert of perfect sand, just like a beach. Now theres a spiked mountain like a Witch's hat.

Keep working hard. Keep practicing your memory trick, but don't tell the others how you do it. Write me a letter. I miss us all being together, but we soon shall be. Love to both of you & hugs & kisses

Daddy

P.S. One thing there are millions of here is toads. Also, quite a few lizards. Now we are coming down into Ispahan airport. Suddenly it is all green, I see gardens, orchards, a green river, herds of goats and bump—we're down.

An old fort out there—four towers and brown walls. More black goats. The heat is 72°F—not too bad. Now 15 helicopters standing like shrimps. Everything is done by helicopter in these deserts. love again. Daddy

To Lucas Myers

[September 1971]   Ms   Emory

Dear Luke,

We've just got back from Persia—fantastic 3 months. I wish I'd kept a journal. But I was either too busy or too exhausted. We started off all living in a Palatial corrupt new hotel, run by gangsters. 35 actors— French, English, American, a Japanese Noh actor, 2 Africans, Brook & his wife & me & one or two miscellaneous. During the day I wrote in my room, while the actors exercised & so on at an old tumbledown beautiful palace in the middle of Teheran. Now and again I had a day at the palace. Very slowly and laboriously I made a play out of (a) story of Prometheus, (b) Calderon's Life is a dream (c) Mannichean cosmology (d) Persian Creation mythology (e) sundry folk-lore & mythology. My idea was to make many scenes all inwardly related but without any particular narrative sequence. Very early I invented a language for it. After a while, I moulded it all into one mythology so complicated and multi-dimensional that I've already completely lost my way in it—but it helped me produce the scenes. Deep discussions with Brook at every stage. Finally, I had a play about 1½ hours, with odd passages of Greek (from Prometheus Bound) a passage of Latin (from Seneca's Hercules

Furens) & much Avesta (sacred texts of the Zoroastrians, as pronounced by a dotty inspired Kurdish woman. She's unearthed the original pronunciation—by inspiration—& teaches it. Her own readings of it are some of the most amazing beautiful sound I ever heard—she's something very original. So she taught our actors.) The rest of the play was in my invented language—more or less a method of frustrating the actor's inclination to speak merely verbal rattle of seeming meaning and forcing him to dig up something authentic from his midriff. It was a sort of musical notation really. Very successful. Much drumming, & the whole range of cries.

Then we went off to Shiraz and lived in a filthy hotel during the very hot days and worked at night 50 miles out in the desert at the tomb of Artaxerxes III—above the ruins of Persepolis (which Alexander burned at the request of his concubine). The tomb was a small natural Theatre cut in the side of the mountain (the mountain onto which fire first descended from heaven, according to the Zoroastrians). Marvellous acoustics, a low door leading into the vault. The play was a series of episodes—not easy to describe. A series of musical moments, with plenty of murder & extreme demonstrations—but the whole thing totally mysterious, very exciting. The star turn was the African (from Mali)—a real demon. The sort of cave-drama I would never have thought possible. Absolute dream come true. We performed it, eventually, at night, during the Shiraz Festival. One of the performances was so completely stupefying the audience sat afterwards for 15 minutes in dead silence. There were piles of critics there who all responded with gratifyingly befuddled astonishment. The whole thing was almost hilarious. An American lady, Margaret Croydon, New York Times, was there—quite a lady. So she'll probably be writing something. I wish you could have seen it.

Also, parallel to that, we did an improvised play. I reshaped the story of Difficulties of a Bridegroom, & the actors developed it, with improvisation—and we performed that in a mud village, very primitive place. Great success. We performed the serious play in another village & that was a bit of a fiasco—they couldn't follow it after 20 minutes. You realised a million things that a play needs. What we're going to try to do, is make a repertoire of plays combining both extremes, & take them all over the place. Brook wants to go to Africa next year, performing in the villages. I seemed to learn a lot.

My feeling is that if you were living in Paris again you could somehow be in on all this. What I'm doing now—in a vague way—is devising situations which we can work up into the sort of play that will go on equally well in Jur-al-duluj, population 43 & 12 goats, and in Peking.

The Persian venture was one series of weird episodes. We rehearsed inside a ring of bayonets. If you went to pee, you risked getting shot. The caviare was first-rate. The half-dysentery was universal—even the Persians got it. The mountains were unearthly, with beautiful lizards. Condors. It was something to stand in front of the tomb of Darius—which is cut into a beautiful rosy cliff, 50 ft up—and see a negro standing in the tomb-door reciting the speech of Darius' ghost from Aeschylus' PERSIANS (written to glorify the memory of Salamis for the Greeks) to the Persian Queen (the real, living, present one).

Frieda & Nick came out, too. They didn't have much of a time—all you can do by day is swim, so they swam. We caught a scorpion or two, and the whole campaign was dominated by the effort to catch a lizard, one of the big, handsome dragonish ones, with ruffs. In vain.

Carol also came. So far, marriage has more than redeemed itself. At last, I've made a wise move.

I'm trying to get back to writing some verse. Crow is O.K., but it's no more than knocking on the door really. Now that Carol has everything so watertight, I'm going to try doing what I should have done 10 years. Just drop everything, & see how far I can get by working at nothing but verse for 6 months. If there's anything there, I'd better be getting it now. That's my feeling, late in the day.

[. . .]

Are you hearing much about the Sylvia mania over there? Her book has been in the best seller list since April. If you can get me Al Alvarez' article in the New American Review, I'd like to read it. For some reason he's very cagey about showing it to me. I've missed Elizabeth Hardwick's article too. One or two New Yorkers I've met tell me she's the sole topic of literary conversation this last 3 months. Two new books of her poems I'm sending you.

Well, why not come & live in Europe & enjoy the rest of life? You can always live free in one of my places, between your more active sallies. Xeroxing is absolutely tied up here. But how about publishing?

> Keep well. Carol sends her greetings. My greetings
> to Erica (& Martha if you ever see her.)
> Ted.

Margaret Croyden is the author of *Conversations with Peter Brook 1970–2000*.

The first US edition of Sylvia Plath's novel *The Bell Jar* had come out earlier in the year, while *Crossing the Water* and *Winter Trees* had been published in Britain.

'Erica' was the novelist and poet Erica Jong (b.1942), a New York friend of Myers.

To Gerald and Joan Hughes

26 September 1971   Ms   Emory

Strange coincidence the other day. We were driving down from London, and on a long lovely stretch a mile East of Mere, in Wiltshire, when Carol saw a dead badger at the side of the road. It was hot weather, & already a bit high, but not too bad, and the biggest badger I've ever seen, with a beautiful coat, so I stowed him in the back of the car, intending to get his teeth & bones if not his skin. For one stupid reason and another I left him a day, & was too late to skin him. Two days later, we were going back up to London to collect the kids and take them up to Yorks for the weekend—we wanted to collect some books etc. So on the road, one mile West of Mere, there was a beautiful fox just killed—too badly smashed to skin, but head perfect—so I hid him in the hedge. We were marvelling at this—to see a badger & a fox on two consecutive runs, and I was measuring the distance from the fox to Mere, & from Mere to where we'd found the badger, to see if it was exactly the same distance between each of them & the town, and when the exact distance came up on the milometer, we were going exactly over the spot where we'd found the badger, and so I said "It was exactly here", & pointed at the side of the road, and there about three yards off my finger end was <u>another</u> dead badger. This time smaller, & skin not as special. But I hid him in the hedge. Then as we came back down after the weekend I stowed the head of the fox and this other second badger in polythene bags & brought them back.

I imagine the second was mate to the first—probably smelt his death on the road & sat there mourning for two or three nights till a lorry came along & killed her on the same spot. So now they lie together in my ossuary, attended by the head of a fox.

To Frieda Hughes

26 October 1971   Ms   Emory

Dear Frieda,

Today I was sitting in my hut, eating an apple, and reading, (and in fact I was eating apple after apple, because if we don't all eat as many as possible (and if possible as many as is impossible) then we shall never eat all our apples). So there I was. Then first, a jenny wren flew on top of my door—which stood open. We looked at each other and he decided I was not a Daddy longlegs or a spider, but something quite uneatable. He flew off. Then I heard a rustling in the brambles and I thought "A weasel is coming to investigate me", so I waited. The rustling stopped. Then it started again. Then it stopped. I went to the door, very quietly. I squeaked, like a mouse. Then like a rabbit. The rustle did not rustle. So I waited. Then, suddenly, a rustle. I went towards it. It stopped. Now I was under the thick foliage of the hollies of the hedge. I looked everywhere. I rustled, I kicked the dead leaves, I separated the brambles. Then, out of my eye-corner, I saw an eye watching me. Up on the hedgebank, at the mouth of a hole, watching me, was a [*new page* . . .]

HEDGEHOG.

Now he's asleep in a tin inside my hut.

love
Daddy

To Peter Redgrove

27 October 1971   Ms   Sheffield

Enclosed—a bagatelle. The introduction is really notes for what ought to be a book. But I leave that sort of book to that sort of writer. Not one scholar in a hundred knows Shakespeare well enough to guess whether I have something or haven't. Not one in a hundred of those hundreds has the nose for the poetry to know what I'm distinguishing in the total Himalayas of Shakespearean ore. You'll see what I mean.

I would like to go into the plays King Lear & later in more detail—because there the thing gets complicated, but proceeds absolutely according to the way I indicate. Noone ever went to more trouble to write an apologia for a selection of verse. I sweated musk, ambergris, and skunk-fat.

The enclosed item was *A Choice of Shakespeare's Verse*, recently published.

To A. Alvarez

[November 1971]   Ms   British Library

Dear Al,

As a friend, please reconsider your writings, talks etc about Sylvia's suicide. It was enough before, without the details. Obviously you can't unwrite them, but I do ask you to set a quick limit on how far you popularise them—among mechanical parrot-teachers etc.

It is humiliating to me, & to her mother & brother, to have her last days exhumed in this way, as you do in your memoir, for classroom discussion. Whatever motive or intention you put upon your writing of that piece, what you have done is supplied it to classroom discussion, you know there is no other real audience for it. It is interesting purely & simply as further notes to the poetry. You would be the first to point out—if the context were different—that such notes are superfluous to any appreciation of the poems. In fact, they are guaranteed to corrupt a real appreciation of the poetry with a sensational involvement of another sort. Those close-up shots of her last days, your theories & interpretations derived from what you saw or what I told you (and I didn't tell you half) are not only superfluous to the poetry, they are an intrusion on the present and future of her family—there are only three of us can tell you whether they are or not, on concrete evidence, and now I am telling you for all three of us that they are. The mechanical so-called objectivity of higher Lit. Crit. is unscrupulous enough in the cynically low opinion it has of the real power of words & in the way it cannot be bothered to distinguish between remarks made on paper and their consequences in real life—and most of that one can't do anything about, it is all part of the brutalised righteousness of journalism, but your view is wider and I'm expecting you to be open to some appeal.

Whatever Sylvia may be for your readers & for you, for her mother & me & her children she is something different, she is an atmosphere we breath. This is something apart from remembrance, it is a world imposed on us by the public consciousness of her and of our inevitable relationship to her. Your memoir has simply increased that atmospheric pressure intolerably—you have supplied details & interpretations in a form that is now being taken as the official text. I thought you were sensitive to this sort of atmospheric persecution, because it is a sort of persecution. It was enough & too much before. Nobody could have written that scenario of her suicide but you (or me) and I cannot see how you persuaded yourself it was necessary. I would like to know what purpose you think it's going to serve. You kept saying you would show me what you were writing about her—why didn't you? For you it was something you wrote, no doubt against great inner resistance, for your readers it's five interesting minutes, but for us it is permanent dynamite.

You tell yourself maybe it is all literary history, she belongs to the public, she gave herself to the public etc. You know that is rubbish. She didn't give her family, & she didn't hand over the inner life of her children to the officiation of critics. A heart-attack laid her mother out two months ago, but I'm even more concerned what role your article is going to play in the lives of Frieda & Nicholas. What do you think its effect will be? Either when they come to read it (nobody but a lunatic would give it to them) or when some precocious schoolfriend gives them the savoury details as you recount them? The first shock will be one thing—(a shock they might have been spared if you'd put your article in a bank-vault). The long-term effect of that slow motion close-up movie will be another. I would have credited you with more imagination. Can't you see that they won't be able to get it out of their minds? They won't be able to escape it—because you've programmed their acquaintances, the general public vividness and popularity of the story is not going to let them forget it. The poems, & the novel, & the bald fact of suicide, left things general, crossroads of many interpretations, open in all directions, ordinary amnesia could have dealt with that, just the natural anaesthetic of being allowed to forget or shape it into acceptable form. But this detailed, exclusively painful artistically vitalised record of yours is going to break down that sort of defence. Surely you can see all this. The whole subject you deal with is what Sylvia made of her father's death—yet you somehow didn't remember how history tries to repeat itself even without human help, it didn't occur to you that her children are left with an even more dangerous situation than hers & with all her vulnerabilities.

For you she is a topic for intellectual discussion, a poetic/existential phenomenon—basically it doesn't matter a damn to you what she did & you'd find any new details fascinating. But for F. & N. she is the absolute centrepin—they have made her very important, the moreso because of her obvious absence throughout the mess I've been making of replacing her these last years. Their image of her—of what she did & was—is going to decide their lives. You know these things work out seriously. Yet you've defined their mother's pose—and set it up as the official final public version (the schools will make sure of that)—in an absolutely disastrous way.

As I say, in spite of everything, before your details it was vague, it was a mystery. But now you have defined the whole thing, and handed it to the public. In a real way, you have robbed them of her death, of any natural way of dealing with her death. This will add up through every year they live. For you & everybody else it is fading fast—you've solved the mystery of <u>exactly what happened & how</u>. (You've given a version anyway). But for F. & N. it has not yet properly begun, the presiding fact of their future will only really dawn on them when somehow they meet your memoir. Then what sort of dramas will your details start up in their inner life? You've defined their guardian angel for them in a pose that is going to make things as explosive as possible for them—as if their lives weren't already going to be enough of a minefield.

She isn't their guardian angel any more—you've made a public statue of it, a school & University cultural monument. In a real sense, you've given their inner life away for them. Whatever audience you imagined & wrote so painstakingly for—all that business about the existential work-out of mental events—you completely forgot your only real audience, the audience whose lives your words really are going to change. You were searching out details to enthral your academic audience & didn't realise you were sticking electrodes in her children's brains. How can you ever say anything about pain?

They had enough of the facts & the truths, living in the mausoleum Sylvia left for them. What your memoir supplies is not just facts (so few of the facts—so many fictions & mere speculations trying to be facts) but poison. Poison is no less poison for being a fact. There are some poisons they oughtn't to be made to eat. And these are poisons that you alone have brought into existence, in this memoir.

You know all this I'm sure, yet somehow you've rationalised it all away. I can only think Sylvia's death has become a theme for some involvement of your own—some private tie-up that's fouled your judgement. If so, for Christ's sake step back & see what you're doing. Sylvia is still very much alive in these two children—you can't reinvent her according to your theories just for the curiosity of the mob, nor for your own private satisfaction either. Not if you're setting up any standards of sense.

However you regard it, Sylvia's writings were considerable treachery against her mother, and together with her suicide they were maybe something worse against her children—but critics use the incidental poetry to convert all this into a general licence for ransacking the lives of her family—and for no purpose whatsoever, it enlightens nobody, it does nothing finally but entertain in a sophisticated fashion, it is higher entertainment, or it is matter for students to stuff into answers & theses—again for no purpose whatsoever except to get the grades & the jobs. It doesn't even have the justification of an artistic compulsion. The whole occupation is completely frivolous. There was a place here for some sane critic to point out the rights & the wrongs in the humanity of it, and lay open some of the violations going on under the guise of fashionable commentary. I'm absolutely amazed to see you joining that mob. Imagine what Lawrence would have said about it.

What makes it so much worse is that it was so totally unnecessary. And that it was written by you—the very person most likely to know that there are quite a few things more important than literature—more important even than great poetry, let alone memoirs.

Anyway, I'm relying on you now to push those details & snapshots & the rest no further.

Yours
Ted

Another thing. Not even temporary insanity would explain your completely false remarks implying that there was some sort of artistic jealousy between Sylvia and me. All that banal theorising about the muses etc—that is simply the crudest light-minded speculation, as you should know. If you do know, what made you print it in that ex-cathedra fashion, as facts about our life, which you, as an intimate confidential uniquely-in-on-the-scene friend can be relied on to get right? Is your audience that much in need of theories?

You must have alternative theories that would do us more justice and perhaps even be closer the truth & would maybe even reflect better on you.

What makes you think you can use our lives like the text of a novel—something on the syllabus—for facile interpretations to keep your audience of schoolteachers up on the latest culture?

You saw little enough of us. Both of us regarded you as a friend, not a Daily Mirror T.V. key-hole rat-hole journalist snoop guaranteed to distort every observation and plaster us with his know-all pseudo-psychological theories, as if we were relics dug up from 10,000 BC. Of our marriage you know nothing—but you can't even give us the benefit of your ignorance. You have to rack us with your mechanical blasé theories.

It is infuriating for me to see my private experience & feelings re-invented for me, in that crude, bland unanswerable way, and interpreted & published as official history—as if I were a picture on a wall, or some prisoner in Siberia. And to see her used in the same way.

You are false to the facts and you shame yourself in the way you insult the privacy & confidences of two people who regarded you as a friend.

Please stop toting us around like a flea circus, and do what you can to change what you have written.

And just in case you aren't sure, none of this letter is to be journalised in any form.

I was going to send you this letter yesterday. Today Sunday I see you haven't resisted the cheapest stage of all.

Nothing can excuse the swinish mindlessness with which you are exploiting this. You seem determined to push our misfortune in this business to the limit.

If you cannot stop your next installment I shall do everything to stop it. I am first of all asking you yourself to withdraw it.

Ahead of the publication of A. Alvarez's book *The Savage God*, his study of suicide, which included an intimate account of Sylvia Plath's story, extracts were serialised in the *Observer*. Replying on 15 November to TH's protest, Alvarez wrote that his account had been 'written with great care and as a tribute to Sylvia'; that he believed it better for the children 'to see this, which is at least written with some kind of consideration and feeling for their mother, than a cloud of vague and malicious rumours'; and that he was powerless to prevent serialisation in the *Observer*, as his publishers held the serial rights. Finally, he reminded TH that he had always judged him and Plath to be 'the most gifted poets of this generation'.

1972

After the theatrical experiments that had come to fruition at Persepolis, and that had excited curiosity far beyond, TH's creative association with Peter Brook continued into 1972 with a dramatisation of the twelfth-century Persian classic, *The Conference of the Birds* by Farid ud-Din Attar. A first-hand account of how Brook's multinational troupe toured this show through the villages of Nigeria is given in John Heilpern's *Conference of the Birds* (1977). TH chose not to accompany them.

To the Editor of the *Observer*

17 January 1972   Ts   Emory

Dear Sir,

I thank Mr Ricks for his two columns of lyrico-critical prose, and I understand his ill-will and indignation. I hadn't forgotten, in making my selection of the verse, that Shakespeare is jealously guarded museum property, with a great many curators.

There would be no sense in replying to his review, even to point out that perfect example of reviewer's reflex in his mechanical attribution to two essays by Lawrence (which I happen never to have read) ideas which I got from quite different places, if he hadn't invented something which really ought to be corrected.

He shows unprofessional disregard, it seems to me, for the precision of argument he elsewhere affects to require of others, in attributing to me the opinion that Eliot was in some way 'prissy'. This is not my opinion at all. The word 'prissy' is Mr Ricks' contribution—what he would probably call 'irresponsible interpolation'. He jumps to his conclusion from my remark about 'the dissociation of sensibility'—said to have occurred in Eng. Lit. in the 17th century—being an understatement. If I had quoted every source for my remarks in that essay there would be more scholarly sweepings than text. On one of the few occasions that I met T.S. Eliot, in 1960 and 61, I happened to say I wish I understood better what he had implied by that phrase 'dissociation of sensibility' in the context of the 17th century, and his reply was 'I'm afraid it was something of an understatement.' I cannot imagine how anyone who ever met Eliot could describe him as 'prissy'. The main impression he left with me was of something moving with indeflectible force and weight—moreso than in anyone I ever met.

Yours sincerely
Ted Hughes

Christopher Ricks (b.1933) was at this time Professor of English at the University of Bristol. His review of *A Choice of Shakespeare's Verse* had appeared in the *Observer* on 16 January.

To Peter Brook

[Undated 1972]   Ts (photocopy)   Emory

Dear Peter,

I'm sending a copy of the U.S. version of the Shakespeare passages because it is more interesting. Also I'm enclosing the lineage of trans-formations of VENUS—as she appears in the long poem Venus and Adonis—throughout the plays, so he will get a clearer idea of what I mean—I hope. Considering the basic story to be a combination of the two long poems, Venus and Adonis and Rape Of Lucrece, as I've out-lined in the introduction, then pretty well every play—or at least the big poetic moments of every play—can be fitted to it, as it reappears in some form or other in each one. From the Lineage I'm enclosing, he'll be able to see what I mean, and so he'll be able to put any Venusian passage in its place and proper relation to other parts. So in CORIOLANUS—where there are no whores, no sexual ravings—the VENUS role is taken by the city of Rome itself, with his wife and mother in the middle of it. Close Parallel in TIMON the Venus role goes to Athens—which is abused like Babylon itself, the Great Whore itself. The point is, each play carries on the debate about VENUS—or whatever it was she was, is.

If the idea is feasible, of making a performance out of a grand syn-thesis of this sort, then I could let him have the lineages for the other three main characters—Tarquin, Adonis and Lucrece. Also a tree of the Metamorphoses, splittings, interchangeable correspondences and so on. The Flower moments, Music, Tempests etc all fall regularly in place.

All that could be very entertaining to a Shakespeare addict, if it didn't revolt him completely, but it would be even more interesting to take the lineages backward—into the Reformation conflict events, and earlier religion and mythology, using texts from Egypt, Israel, Mesopotamia etc, of which there's a mass as you know, and which are full of songs, hymns, charms, curses, prayers etc or just straight narrative which fits Shakespeare's fable perfectly.

Also, it could be opened out to include Shakespeare's contemporary history in brief glimpses—Elizabeth and Mary Tudor go straight into the Venus lineage.

Then it could be brought forward, using Milton's Paradise Lost and Samson Agonistes as a continuation of Shakespeare's series (Webster too). The Venus lineage would then come on into Delilah, Guilty Eve, the Serpent, and Hell, and the Tarquin sequence into Satan, and the Adonis sequence into Samson and Christ). Then it would spread out and include Cromwell and the Civil War and the witch persecutions as a natural culmination.

The Natural culmination would be a satyr play epilogue. Plot—something like this. Heath is a monkey in a very tatty, overpainted Adonis mask. Wislon is an identical monkey in a saggy Tarquin mask. Lucrece would be Princess Anne, and Venus would be a schizophrenic female gorilla in Regent's park.

Sc I: Earthquake. The escaped gorilla pursues Heath, under a sky-full of blazing prodigies, into the Reptile House. He turns as he runs, emptying his derringer into her, mortally wounding her, but still fleeing, until in the gloom of the Reptile House he mysteriously vanishes.

Sc 2: Wislon emerges like a crocodile from the Thames at Westminster, purges the Tories, throws away his Tarquin mask, dons an Adonis mask and forcibly marries Princess Anne while a Loch Ness Monster bellowing in death-agonies churns up the Serpentine.

Sc III: Heath emerges glistening from high tide at the Isle of Dogs, dons a Tarquin mask, and leads the dockers against Westminster, promising the new age, and every man to be a King.

Sc IV: Civil War, London the Battlefield, coinciding with a National Flower Festival and freak cloudbursts. Heath crushes Wislon to death under a piano, and Princess Anne is carried in raped to death by dockers. Heath tears the Adonis mask off Wislon, and dons it over the top of his Tarquin mask. Wislon's monkey body is stuffed and given to the L.S.E. Heath pardons the dockers, dedicates all his prize money to the extermination of gorillas, closes all theatres and zoos, puts a colossal tax on vaginas, and marries the organ in Westminster Abbey. England plunges into another three hundred years of catatonic stupor.

[. . .]

Anyway, if Andre would like to do something using the Shakespeare passages, please tell him I'd be delighted to make what I meant a little bit clearer, if I can. Or perhaps he'd prefer to use them in some much simpler way. Could you get this copy sent on to him?

What I'm feeling the Birds needs at the moment is some quite different contrasting type of material. Perhaps that will be easier to locate when the basic sequence is more developed.

I hope Natasha is well.

[*No signature on this copy*]

The 'U.S. version of the Shakespeare passages', *With Fairest Flowers while Summer Lasts*, was published in May 1971, six months before *A Choice of Shakespeare's Verse* in Britain.

In the sketched 'satyr play', 'Heath' is Edward Heath (1916–2005), then Britain's Conservative Prime Minister, and 'Wislon' (TH uses the nickname bestowed by the satirical magazine *Private Eye*), Harold Wilson (1916–95), Leader of the Labour Opposition.

Peter Brook is married to the actress Natasha Parry.

To Peter Redgrove

[Undated 1972]   Ms   Sheffield

The other day we acquired a badger—saved it from execution, more or less. From a condemned pet-shop where the animals were all being destroyed—(bears, kangaroos etc—all diseased, lousy etc). We can't liberate it—it was caught as a cub. So we feed it—her, & talk to her, & try to befriend her. So far, she responds only up to a point. But badgers are something special—you see how they got their rôle in Japan. They have a goblin gleeful intensity about them—and stronger than you'd believe possible.

330

The Tanuki badger (*Nyctereutes procyonoides*), which is a different beast from the British badger, but equally shy, figures commonly in Japanese folk stories as a trickster, shape-shifter and merry fellow. Porcelain models of Tanukis are placed in or outside pubs throughout Japan.

To Aurelia Plath

7 July 1972   Ms   Lilly Library

This latest project is—for me—more complicated. It is based on a great Persian Sufi classic poem, called The Conference of the Birds. All the birds are gathered by the hoopoe—and they undertake a journey to enlightenment. It is a remote original of Dante's Divine Comedy & many other Western works. Our actors are the birds, and I invent (a) all the incidents of their journey (b) the stages of their journey (c) their language. The actors explore the limits of everything I give them—and these are actors (3 American, 3 English, 2 French, 1 German Jewish/ Negress, 1 African from Mali, 1 Japanese,) who have now been together 2½ years, & whom I know better than my closest friends. Peter welds it all together into a performance. Whatever any of his critics say, he is an extraordinary man—very gentle but very strong, & so much more knowledgeable & wise than his detractors. Just lately, I've discovered the ideal way to write this work, & it has become very exciting for all of us. The Company goes to Africa in November, tours through Nigeria, playing to the villages, & of course we're all invited—in fact, I shall more or less <u>have</u> to be there. But I'm being wary, because Nigeria "The white man's grave"—is even less of a joke now than it used to be. Yet the adventure seems such an opportunity. I think we might go for 2 or 3 weeks.

To Lucas Myers

[July 1972]   Ms   Emory

Dear Luke,

   Good to hear things are going well. Also, here, quite well. I alternate between deep rural torpor and Paris with the actors. The great new thing at present is the way I've shaken off literary life etc. I get no mail, & the last trampling footprints of London are fading on the margins.

I'm really getting back that feeling of privacy & seclusion which I haven't felt since 1962. The other day was my first visit to the flat since you left—so that sausage was my London representative, completely mouldy.

My last two visits to Paris were breakthroughs—I discovered a way of writing those scenes which made everything previous obsolete. I enclose 2—give you some idea. We have several characters now—a Fool, a drunkard, a soldier, an ogre/hag, a sort of maniac/saint/coward/ rebel/tyrant, a slave, a lover, a charlatan, a trickster Caspar Hausar, & 3 women—will be four. All the men also double up as women with black, blonde & red wigs. Each of the actors can theoretically play any part— and each character is a sliding scale, so Fool is at one end imbecile and at the other end Holy man. To make it more coherent (it is getting phenomenally incoherent) I try to give each actor a 'line'—a sort of story. The idea then is to weave all the stories together, so the whole sequence will be like a maze of mirrors & echoes. They are all also birds on a journey. I'm trying to make 6 or 7 main sections—first one is the love gone wrong section, as the birds are called to their journey, then an ogre/hag section, then a section where all are lost & searching through the deserts of space, then a soldier/tyrant section & so on. Each of the scenes is basically an exercise for the actors—rather than a scene, though now they are becoming scenes. It's got very interesting, & all the actors are excited. The last 2 weeks (they've now gone off—2 months holiday) they developed beyond any expectation. They became concentrated & quite inspired. I've written 60 of these scenes, & there will be maybe another 40 or 50.

However, it effectively prevents me writing anything else. And I would really prefer to be writing something else.

We're still looking for bits of land, or something to invest the Kids' money in. The trouble is, from the moment the money materialised, the pound has gone crazy, land prices have doubled, house prices quadrupled or more—absolutely unbelievable. A year ago, we could have bought quite a big farm—now we could hardly buy a small-holding.

It's a good idea to get some land. Get it near water if you can. Olwyn's latest excitement is—she's handling the manuscripts of the 2 IRA leaders. She's sold it in the States, but no English publisher dare take it on.

Keep well—Carol sends her love

Ted

By 'the Kids' money', TH means what had been earned from the unexpected, runaway success of *The Bell Jar* in the USA.

To Daniel Huws

24 September 1972   Ms Huws

I had qualms about writing that paragraph about your book—and I regretted the 2 or 3 other paragraphs I'd written for other people's books, which were really no more than interesting, because I wanted what I said about yours to look like something more than a hired opinion. Also I wanted to say the important thing without making the sort of judgement which would merely provoke perverse reviewers—they're all perverse for the time they're reviewing—into merely countering my move & showing how much smarter than me they were, showing how wrong I was etc. After the first review, all subsequent reviewers write against that review, or correcting it to their own visible advantage—they don't write about the book.

I felt the whole book was very fine, and indestructible. True & unforgettable, and not like anybody else. It can't fail to be recognised. It's a touchstone—it comes as a reproach to most poetry.

Daniel Huws's first book of poems, *Noth*, had been published by Secker & Warburg. TH's jacket blurb commended Huws's 'natural style of excellence, invisible to fashion and for so long to publishers too, which is the real, rare, durable thing'.

To Leonard and Lisa Baskin

[November 1972]   Ms British Library

A few things have changed. Persia ushered 1971 past in fairly acceptable numbness—that year was my nadir. Big chunks of my U.S. trip have followed the earlier parts of my life into amnesia. Superflux of deaths & exits, maybe. The Peter Brook involvement trailed on—pretending to be little but in fact devastating great tracts of time. He went off to West Africa with his actors—to perform for 3 months among the tribes & villages—and thinking of all the loot I might pick up I was tempted to go. But it has become seriously clear to me that unless I collect my wits and step through the door that Crow opened & get to

333

what there is beyond all that—beyond all those brief sketches & notes & blueprints & crude charts of the territory—then I shall go on sitting in stupor whether the seat is in North Tawton or Caffa—(where the Black Death came flying over the walls as infected corpses). Anyway, I've been getting my machinery going. If I can get what I've been sitting on all these years, I'll be somewhere.

Biological warfare of the kind described by TH, first recorded at the Siege of Caffa, in 1346, is supposed to have been the means by which the Black Death entered Europe from the Crimea.

1973

Having bought various pieces of property and farmland in the course of 1972 and early 1973, TH and Carol Hughes set about acquiring livestock. By this time TH had involved Carol's father, Jack Orchard, an experienced farmer, in the enterprise.

To Peter Redgrove

[March 1973]   Ts   Emory

Dear Peter,

Thanks for the letter. Full of fascinating things. Not only As above so below, but As inside so outside.

I'm enclosing a piece I did for the Shakespeare Birthday Celebration at the Globe Theatre—which I see you took part in last year. It reflects—remotely—some of the things in your letter, as you'll see. It derives from the note to my selection of Shakespeare's verse—about the unity of the poetic theme. That was maybe over-brief and too reduced, for the sixth form or lay reader I imagined buying such a selection. But I didn't want to burden myself with a book. The theme in the verses is—metamorphoses of whatever it was that appeared as Venus in Shakes Venus And Adonis, throughout the plays (and throughout England at the same time). And the Metamorphoses of what appeared in that poem as Adonis, and of the relationship between the two. There are actually three characters in that poem—the other vital one is the Boar. So these explosive substances are closed in the pot together at the start, and the plays are interim records of what working follows. There are two ways of looking at the whole thing: As Shakespeare's natural attempt to save his sanity—in a final transcendence, the marriage of Miranda and Ferdinand, and so as a successful feat of survival, a successful salvaging of the Puritan ideals of the time from the natural matrix which opposed and denied them, and so as a successful assertion of civil reasonableness and rationalist objectivity such as went on into the 17th Century and on and on right up to the 'intelligence' of now, a progressively emptier

335

and more mechanical twitter of those same puritan ideals. From that point of view, The Tempest is adored by modern english readers who are tuned to that waveband, and regarded as a glorious spiritual triumph. They disregard the family of Sycorax, her real nature and meaning, that she is all that Shakespeare has left of his original Venus, and that Dan Cupid of those earliest plays and poems has degenerated to Caliban. So from the second point of view Shakespeare recorded, somewhat helplessly, what was actually going on in the English spirit, which was the defamation, subjection and eventual murder of what he first encountered as Venus—the Mary Goddess of the Middle Ages and earlier. In other words he recorded the most horrible of all disasters—the declaration of war against the natural (real) world and natural fellowship with it and in it, by a pseudo intelligence which is now on the point of culminating its logics and natural bent in destruction of the world and all life. In my verses I bring in some of the antecedents, the latencies of the situation in archaic Palestine, Babylon and Egypt. So the poem sets up Shakespeare as the crucial record of the real inner story of the whole of Western History. But very abbreviated and in bagatelle style.

Milton took the theme up (Sycorax/Caliban have become Satan, Ferdinand and Miranda those two wretches Adam and Eve) Venus has become Delilah, Adonis Samson) but also helped promote the conflict to a showdown—the Civil War. With notorious repercussions in his own life. Since then I see Blake, Wordsworth, Keats, Hardy, (Hopkins), Yeats and Eliot, to name the most obvious, as records—made at upheaval intervals—of Nature's attempt to correct the error, supply the natural body of things and heal the torment. The whole psychoanalytical movement becomes the activist wing, poetry becomes nature healing or nothing—using all the natural techniques ever evolved, the conservation movement—a new thing of the last ten years after all—is the popular form of the first dawning awareness that we have inherited a disaster that blights every detail of life. None of this is in the poem, but it shows you how I regard the ideas—which have grown like feathers the dead end of things. And it's a literary historical comment rather than a poem.

The Cottage is a definite offer. Two bedrooms, one room downstairs plus a small kitchen. Outside toilet. (Bath in the empty flat in the main house—sixty yards away.) It's in that valley below my parent's house—halfway down the hill. Rent would be just to cover rates (nearly nothing). Could keep a cow etc. No hurry to decide. It adjoins another cottage like it, which I let to some student for ten shillings a week—he goes there in his holidays I believe. It was lived in regularly until last summer. The flat in the main house needs quite a bit doing to it, but meanwhile it would be an excellent place for one of you to work away from the other.

Think seriously about it. It would be a good place to save money until you absolutely do have to work again. Meanwhile, whatever strings I can find to pull I'll pull.

Best to Penelope

Ted

Peter Redgrove's own note at the head of the letter records that it was received on 6 March.

The piece for Shakespeare's birthday was 'An Alchemy', which appeared in Graham Fawcett's anthology, *Poems for Shakespeare* (1973), then in Keith Sagar's critical anthology, *The Achievement of Ted Hughes* (1983), but never in any of the collections TH himself presented to the world.

The cottage was in the grounds of Lumb Bank. TH's offer came as Shuttle and Redgrove were contemplating leaving Falmouth, but they stayed and it was never taken up.

To Keith Sagar

[September/October 1973]   Ms   British Library

Dear Keith Sagar,

Sorry to be so long answering your letter with the M.S. of your book. I find it very difficult to clear up my reactions to its contents.

Whatever person I've projected, in the body of my poems, will have to bear whatever ideas people have about him. I've freed myself fairly successfully from too great a concern about his fate. What does disturb me, I'm afraid, is to see him identified with me—in the details of my life. It is ridiculous, of course, but the sense of constriction and over-exposure I feel, reading the biographical parts of your book, is something I would rather be spared. I would be extremely grateful if you could delete anything of that sort.

A great concern of mine, over the past few years, has been to disperse in myself that sense of <u>the wrong audience</u>—which is so inhibiting, & falsifying, & wearisome. The more concentration one achieves, the more one is aware of its real enemies. By wrong audience I mean all those who, without being the people for whom you write, yet

337

have a strong idea about you and enough scraps of your hair & nails. I'm trusting you'll understand. I'm always telling people about myself, then always regretting it when I see myself outlined in the 3rd person.

Your book made me regret the months & even years I've yielded to the serpent Ophiuchon—who always appeared, to the day, when I had at last managed to take a real step. But he wasn't always ugly.

Best wishes

sincerely
Ted Hughes

Keith Sagar (b.1934) had sent TH a draft of the introduction and first four chapters of *The Art of Ted Hughes* (1975; revised edition 1978), partly to give him the opportunity to comment on the biographical material that had been included. After his initial, wary reaction, TH suggested very few changes – some of which involved providing additional biographical information.

'Ophiuchon' seems to be TH's own name for the serpent grasped by Ophiuchus, serpent-bearer associated with the healer Asclepius.

To Keith Sagar

[November 1973]   Ms   British Library

Dear Keith Sagar,

Thankyou for the letter & the Crow chapter. This chapter seems somehow the best. You certainly get my drift better than anybody else I've read. The book (Crow) is mostly blueprints, route-maps, reconnaissances, etc—so it needs creative as well as sympathetic imagination, not just critical attention.

I'd forgotten Marvell's lines. I was paraphrasing—as he was—"the Gnostic commonplace". I came to it as an apocryphal explanation for Crow's colour—a sort of joke.

2 statements in your interpretations contradict what I intended—

In 'A horrible Religious Error' the serpent is—in a way—a form of Crow's own creator. He/she is a consistent figure throughout the overall story.

In 'Crow's last stand', Crow's reactions, through the 3 first stanzas, correspond to separate phases of intensifying psychological pain— where the forms of hilarity & anguish are indistinguishable.

338

The lines 'From one of his eyes . . . " to ". . . in a column", are transcript from the Tain—description of Cuchullin's battle-fury.

If a poem doesn't work as an event in itself, no armorial embellishments from its distinguished lineage can help it—they rather embarrass it, I think. But if it works, then they help—they enrich it. To him who has etc. I wonder now if I wouldn't have defended my bird from the common reaction—that he's a disgusting creature, evil omen etc—if I'd been a little more forward with his lineage.

Crow as the totem of England (history of Bran—his ravens—the tower of London)

Crow in early Celtic literature—the Morrigu, the death-Goddess, a Crow, & the underground form of the original life-goddess—as Hecate was of Aphrodite etc.

Apollo the Crow god. Crow in China. Crow among the Siberian peoples & the North American Indians. Crow in Alchemy.

Crow is a modern evil omen bird only insofar as he is a fallen god—he is Anathema because he was originally Anath.

Except that my main concern was to produce something with the minimum cultural accretions of the museum sort—something autochthonous & complete in itself, as it might be invented after the holocaust & demolition of all libraries, where essential things spring again—if at all—only from their seeds in nature—and are not lugged around or hoarded as preserved harvests from the past. So the comparative religion/mythology background was irrelevant to me, except as I could forget it. If I couldn't find it again original in Crow, I wasn't interested to make a trophy of it.

The poetic works that summarise cultures—as in Eliot, Joyce, David Jones—and those whose gyroscope is the vision of a new culture (vain as that dream must be)—as in Lawrence—are very distinct kinds, I think—both doomed to different kinds of failure. Doomed, probably, because both imply the two extremes of a culture at the point of collapse—so the one is loaded with obsolescent material, & the other is too naive—implies an exclusive attitude, in opposition to too much, and a visionary projection which reality will always find wanting.

In the small scope of my operations I tried to get the best of both worlds. Crow's account of St George is the classic nightmare of modern English intelligence in particular—as Hercules Furens was of the Roman. I tried to dissolve in a raw psychic event, a history of religion & ideology rooted in early Babylonian Creation myth, descending through Middle Eastern religions, collision of Judaism & its neigh-bours, the mannichees & the early Christians & the Roman Empire, the reformation & its peculiar development & ramifications in Englishness, down to linguistic philosophy & the failure of English intelligence in the modern world—failure in comprehensiveness, depth, flexibility, & emotional charge. Which seems to me true & true again. The immediate source of the fable is a Japanese folk tale—where the exclusive, hubristic, ossified professionalism of a Samurai, & the madness behind it—unacknowledged because it contains everything rejected & ignored—is analogous to the sort of 'intelligence' my protagonist relies on. That's not a very good poem—but it's a real part of my story. But it's only part of my story because I could exclude from it the Japanese tale—Hercules Furens—the whole repetitive history of the militant ethos.

As for the style—I simply tried to shed everything. It was quite an effort to get there—as much of an effort to stay there—every day I had to find it again. It was like hanging on to the 9.5 second 100 yards. I tried to shed everything that the average Pavlovan critic knows how to respond to. It was a wonderful sensation when I finally got there. My idea was to reduce my style to the simplest clear cell—then regrow a wholeness & richness organically from that point. I didn't get that far. 'Horrible Religious Error" is a sort of fable of the idea of the confronta-tion in the style, I suppose, (mainly it's Crow mis-recognising the object of his quest)—but that was the last poem, March 20th 69, on the train leaving Manchester.

Since then I've written virtually nothing. The Prometheus sequence is an expression of limbo—limbo in Persia, but limbo. A numb poem about numbness.

But things have looked up a bit lately.

I'd be grateful if you could let me see your final draft. I'll assume this copy is only interim, until I hear from you.

Yours

Ted Hughes

On 9 October, Sagar had sent TH the chapter on *Crow* from *The Art of Ted Hughes*. In it, Sagar had suggested that, because of their obscurity, the opening lines of the poem 'A Kill' might appear merely 'a lame attempt to revamp' certain of the paradoxes in Marvell's poem 'A Dialogue between the Soul and the Body'.

In 'Crow's Account of St George', England's patron saint uses numbers as his weapons in an orgy of slaughter that climaxes in his running 'dumb-faced from the house / Where his wife and their children lie in their blood'.

To Hana and Yehuda Amichai

12 November 1973   Ms   Beinecke Library

Dear Hannah & Yehuda

We have been thinking of you constantly lately. The first days of the war I worried all the time. I'm disgusted with our Government—really sickening lot they are, but typical. I'm a bit surprised that Israel ever depended on them—they should have stockpiled spares long ago. What are you all feeling about it now? Is it still touchy, do you think? Maybe the one good chance is that the Arabs have had a big whiff of Russian takeover and are too smart to want any more. They don't need to read Aesop's fables.

What a horrible war, though.

I trust you're all back together in Jerusalem.

Everything here goes O.K. After my two invalid years with Peter Brook I extricated myself at last—and we bought a farm. Now we breed beef cows & sheep. Carol's father looks after everything—we're his reserve manpower for critical moments. I'm getting quite a hand at overpowering a lamb. Writing & farming mix like motor engines & gelignite. So I try to keep out of it—but it's difficult, farming's fascinating. I got going writing a bit lately, I'm gently easing myself back into literacy.

Started learning Hebrew, tentatively.

I released the badger—caught her, took her five miles away, & let her go. About a week later I was coming across the fields at night & I met this badger, which followed me & wouldn't be scared away. The only badger I ever met. So I suppose that was Bess.

Frances is sending me your book, Yehuda—I'm looking forward to it. Is there an English publisher?

Olwyn is trying to buy a house in London—nearly too late. House prices in England have multiplied in the last year. Write & tell us everything is O.K. Carol sends her love & so do I

Ted

Yehuda Amichai, who had served as a soldier in some of his country's earlier conflicts, enlisted again as an Army Reservist in the October 1973 war between Israel and its invaders, Egypt and Syria. His *Songs of Jerusalem and Myself* had just been published in New York.

A fuller account of TH's dealings with his pet badger is given in 'Bess My Badger', in *What Is the Truth?* (1984).

To Frieda Hughes

[20 November 1973]   Ms   Emory

Dear Frieda,

Here is some stuff about Julius Caesar and Cleopatra. In your library there must be quite a few books that will give you lots more details.

The history of Rome etc, about that time, is immensely complicated, naturally, and it is not always easy to pick out just what you need, in the books. But you will need more than I tell you. And since <u>the whole point</u> of projects is to teach you something—or to get you familiar with something—you must read something on your own.

The best place to find out about Cleopatra is in a book, which every library possesses, called <u>PLUTARCH'S LIVES</u>. That contains the biographies of many famous Greeks & Romans. The one you must read is the <u>last half</u> of the life of <u>ANTONY</u>. Antony was a friend of Julius Caesar's—he recited the funeral oration over Caesar's dead body—who later shared the rule of the Roman Empire with Caesar's adopted son—Caesar Augustus, (Caesar Augustus was first called Octavius Caesar—then Augustus when he became Emperor.) Antony & Cleopatra had a long disastrous life together—as you will read. While telling about Antony, Plutarch tells all about Cleopatra. You <u>must</u> read that. It's quite short.

In the same book, there is also a life of Julius Caesar, but in that life Plutarch gives only a couple of paragraphs to Cleopatra. But you must read those 2 paragraphs.

However, there is a very good play to be made out of the story of Julius Caesar & Cleopatra. Or a very good film. If you wrote it as a film script, you could not only write the dialogue, you could describe the scenes. You could even describe camera scenes where there would be no dialogue, and you could flit to & fro across the Roman world as you never could in a play. You could show gladiatorial combats, terrible battles, the blazing library etc. As well as all the close-ups & whisperings.

As you read, make a note of <u>everything</u> that would make a good camera shot, or a bit of a scene.

When you're writing a play or a film, you can alter things—can press 3 events into one, shift characters round etc. Invent scenes. Bring in strange things.

I'm sending you a book called Pharsalia. The last Chapter (Chapter X) gives <u>one version</u> of Caesar's visit to Egypt—written by a man who hated Caesar (and whom Nero had executed). (Chapter 8 describes Pompey's murder)

For Julius Caesar, read the Life of Julius Caesar in that book by SUETONIUS—which had the life of Nero in it, also. It should be in your school library, in the Classics section.

Also, in the biography section, you must have lives of Caesar, and Cleopatra, or both.

Also, in Encyclopedias.

Also, in Histories of Rome, Histories of Egypt.

(Also, read the bit about Caesar & Cleopatra in that book PLUTARCHS LIVES.)

To begin with, find a map of the Roman Empire, in a history book of Rome, & trace it out. Get some idea of it.

Before you write your play, write out—in notes—everything you can find, relating to Julius Caesar or Cleopatra or ancient Egypt, which <u>you think</u> you might somehow be able to drag in to your play. Or Film. Just jot a note. Even a couple of words, such as "Cleopatra's long nose". (She did have a long nose)

These notes are all part of your project—you will present them <u>as well</u>. You may not be able to include more than a tiny bit of them in your play, but they will all be part of your understanding—the hidden $^7/_8$ of the $^1/_8$ visible tip of your iceberg.

Then break up the story into <u>scenes</u>. As many as you like. (In Shakespeare's "Antony & Cleopatra" there must be 50 scenes. All he read was Plutarch's Lives.)

You can write the scenes as you like—as you go along—in any order—then fit them together at the end. If you write it as a film, you can add bits all over the place. Describe lilies on the Nile. Caesar shooting a hippopotamus etc.

You can bring in whatever you like—a party of Sudanese negroes bringing a white elephant for Ptolemy—and the elephant runs amok in the great fire. Ghosts of Cleopatra's ancestors. Anything.

Anything, so long as it uses the peoples & things of those days, & so long as your <u>main story</u> goes forward pretty clearly.

A good idea is to try and write it all out as a cartoon—like Asterix. That helps you get familiar with all the ins & outs—and get control over it.

It would be a good idea, I think, (if you write it as a play,) to write it in rhymed verse—or the sort of verse you wrote the witch story in. That would make really interesting drama. You might well do something unusual. That verse was very <u>dramatic</u>.

Also, if you write about Caesar or Cleopatra saying ordinary things in an ordinary way, you might as well be writing about anybody. Whereas ordinary people don't talk in verse—and you want your characters to sound extra-ordinary, or rather out of the ordinary.

Anyway, just you plough into it & mainly try to <u>make it interesting to yourself</u>—then it will be good.

We'll be seeing you this Sunday.

Love

Daddy

P.S. What's the name of your English teacher? I want to thank him for sending those poems.

Frieda Hughes had just begun her first school term at Bedales, in Hampshire.

1974

To Ruth Fainlight and Alan Sillitoe

[January 1974]   Ms   Lilly Library

I'm doing up the house in Yorkshire. I'm going to lease it to the Arvon Foundation. Have I told you about them? Friends of ours down here (John Moat—very strange novelist & poet) bought a big farmhouse, & he invented this organisation which employs, for a few days at a time, 2 poets (mainly poets), to live in this farmhouse with about 14 students, & the idea is that everybody will write poetry. If you get an invitation to take one of these courses, you should take it—because it works on the poets very much as it works on the students. It is completely successful. People who've never written a line begin to flow with poetry. A very intense erotic ecstatic atmosphere developes. (It's quite isolated.) Maybe you should come separately. Would you come? I'm asking now if you'd come to this one in Devon, but the new branch in Yorks, in this house of ours, might be more to your tastes. If I tell John Moat you would come, he would ask you like a shot. He's quite an unusual fellow—very original & genuine. The thing is highly organised.

[. . .]

We have some beautiful beasts. I'm getting quite involved in them. Impossible not to. They're giving me more than I give them. I was quite intensely enmeshed in their world when I was an infant—but I felt I was losing it. Fishing isn't enough. But now this working on this land & these animals has given it all back double. I feel to be waking up for the first time in my life.

Also, it's a revelation to watch at close quarters somebody like Carol's father (he does all the real work)—from farmers in unbroken line as far back as they can trace. He's a mobile archive of know-how & understanding—and the perfect attunement.

TH had been associated with the Arvon Foundation, which continues to organise writing courses, almost from its start. The writers John Moat (b.1936) and John Fairfax (1930–2009) had got it going in 1968 with a course at Beaford Arts Centre, in

Devon, at which TH had been the guest reader. Sceptical at first, he became a total convert and served on various committees in the years that followed. Lumb Bank, the refurbishment of which took up much of 1974 and proved expensive, was leased to the Arvon Foundation as its second centre in 1975. Moat's own account of TH's involvement is given in *The Founding of Arvon* (2006).

To János Csokits

25 February 1974   Ms   Emory

Dear Janos,

After 2 years or so in one limbo or another, I'm getting back to a few things. First job, is to finish these translations of Pilinsky.

You'll recognise yours—they are not much changed. The others came from Pilinsky himself or Gomori (I think, but I'm not sure). Obviously it would be best if they came from you. Could you look over these and note any far-out errors? I started marking the points I'm doubtful about on the poem called NOON—but I stopped—because I'm not really sure about <u>any</u> of it. [*Addition in left-hand margin:* Or any of many of the others. Until I get your word.] I hope it isn't an awful labour. If you could mark in the correct literal meaning wherever I seem to have got lost.

I'd like them to be as literal as possible. Some of those we did long ago seem to me very fine English poems—and they are almost entirely your words.

The book is all set up to be printed as soon as these are finished.

Are there any others you think would go well?

I omitted 'Apocrypha'—it's simply too difficult. Though I imagine it's one of the best in the original.

I feel I've somehow made 'Frankfurt 1945' too smooth. The type that come over best are the bleak simple ones—like "Under the Winter Sky." What is the middle verse of 'Cold World'. I can't make sense of it, in the version that came to me. (Could you also check the rest of that poem. It's nearly one of the really effective ones.)

How are you, Janos? Olwyn mentionned you had new daydreams of living here. If only you could, somehow.

We now have a farm. You haven't met my Aries wife yet, have you? Her father looks after it—for me, it's just exercise & concern. When the dark age arrives, I'll set myself up as a primitive herdsman,—eat my own animals. We still live here—at Court Green—the farm is a few miles away.

The Drama experiment in Persia was amusing—& I suppose it did something for me, but it dragged on through the next year. I foolishly allowed it to drag on.

Write & tell me how you are, & what is happening.   As ever
Ted

TH had been working on literal translations from the work of the Hungarian poet János Pilinszky (1921–81) that Csokits had supplied. Pilinszky's *Selected Poems*, translations attributed jointly to TH and Csokits, was published by Carcanet in 1976. TH's introduction to the volume, reprinted in *Winter Pollen* (1994), elaborates on Pilinszky's appeal to him.

George Gömöri (b.1934): Hungarian poet and translator.

To Frieda Hughes

13 March 1974   Ms   Emory

Dear Frieda,

We went into Exeter yesterday, and I bought Carol a Cammelia—just a young sapling, with one bud. They grow into big bushes. Also, I got some more lilies—problem is, where to plant them.

Proverb: Heat a stone for a thousand years, it will cool in an hour.

We enjoyed our visit. The service in the church was beautiful. And the church was beautiful too.

Proverb: For the rose, the thorn is watered.

Today's been sunny & quite warm—though it began sleety cold. Daffodils are coming in tufts. Odd celandines. Primroses here & there. Snowdrops looking tatty.

Proverb: Slowness comes from God, quickness from the devil.

If it's fine again tomorrow, I shall start the foundations of the greenhouse. It's time we started getting our seeds into frames.

Proverb: He who breaks faith, will be broken by distrust.

Proverb: The sweet is in the bitter.

Proverb: The hammer suffers as much as the nail.

The poem was in parts one of your best. It really begins "Day creeps over the horizon." The spider & the web of light are vivid. I see you got your worms in. What about real worms? The flames devouring paper is good.

Proverb: The ground is always frozen for lazy pigs.
Proverb: The used key is bright.
Carol is saying: Leave some space.   Love
                               Daddy

To Keith Sagar

23 May 1974   Ms   British Library

Dear Keith Sagar,

I came through Clitheroe the other day—but you weren't at home.

I wanted to leave the typed M.S. with you, & ask you one or two things.

Olwyn will be sending you a number of comments I made about various points—mainly factual adjustments.

Two things I would like to ask. First is—could you reduce the number of photographs to not more than one.

This concerns me directly. This mass exposure intensifies my sense of being 'watched'—(which maims all well-known writers, & destroys many). It sharpens, in any readers, the visual image of me, making their telepathic interference correspondingly more difficult to counter. (This might be laughed at, but not for much longer).

Your book, in general, of course, is going to increase both these types of harrassment immeasurably, in my awareness. Which is why I asked you to cut the biographical element to the minimum. If I were the sort who could migrate from country to country, finding a succession of acquaintances who knew nothing about me, with whom I could have ordinary relationships, I would be happier. As it is, everything written or said about me goes into the heads of the people among whom I live— so with everyone I have to allow for this unreal element. After trying to ignore it for some years, as part of the danger of the trade, I am finally having to reckon the cost. The photographs I've allowed to be published, the remarks I've made in persona, the degree to which I've let it be known that the writing's under my name belong to this particular person living this particular life, & then what others have said about me—all this seems to have an awful effect on the people round me. Now my children are becoming aware of it at school. They are beginning to realise that to some degree they are creatures in a peculiar museum— which my anonymity could have saved them from. They are having

348

to adjust their directions against the crosswinds from their mother & from me. My daughter has a quite unusual natural poetic gift—quite some stages beyond what her mother or I were capable of at that age—but she is beginning to detest the word 'poetry'. Which will be too bad if—as seems quite likely—it is going to be her only real way out.

It would be ideal if your book concerned the verse alone as if nothing at all were known about me personally—as if my name were a pseudonym.

Another favour I would like to ask, is that you make no mention of any comments I might have made. Do not thank me in the preface. Because at present, the preface gives the impression that I have approved all you say in the book—almost as if you had ghost-written it for me. No matter how you qualify & limit what details I have given you, the response to your book will be confused by these other suspicions. I've tried to give your text factual support, & to suggest my debts to certain sources & sites in the way of subject matter, but everything speculative or to do with interpretation & evaluation are anybody's own business, yours as much as mine, finally. I know how absolutely meaningless it would be to try to impose mine, or attach it somehow to the poems as if it were part of them. Finally, poems belong to readers—just as houses belong to those who live in them & not to the builders.

I'll post off the M.S. I hope you're well.

Yours
Ted Hughes

The 'typed M.S.' was the penultimate version of *The Art of Ted Hughes*. Sagar had suggested using a photograph of his subject at the head of each chapter, as he had done with a previous book, *The Art of D. H. Lawrence*.

To János Csokits

28 May 1974   Ms   Emory

Dear Janos

It was lovely to see you again—looking so internationally bronzed. I'm very much hoping you will get that job.

Obviously in the circumstances it will be good to get a good Introduction to the Pilinsky by some English or American. What I suggest is that

349

I do one—a few pages. And if possible we get somebody else—some American, perhaps, to do another. Do you know of any U.S. experts on modern Hungarian literature? There are certain to be some. I will try & find out, but you try too.

What I need for my introduction is more knowledge—even if I don't use it—of Pilinsky & his originals. The best way for me to get this, it seems to me, is for you to simply jot down notes—numbering them 1, 2, 3. Not in any order, not developed, not even sentences necessarily. Just go on until you've exhausted your responses and your knowledge.

The things I'd like a scatter of hints about are

(1) The atmosphere & temper, the texture, of his Hungarian. What's distinctive about its physical qualities.

(2) Oddities or special bias of his vocabulary, his grammatical usage, his inventions—if any.

(3) Any traceable antecedents in Hungarian literature—in style, in subject matter.

(4) His Catholicism.

(5) His biography—how much would he permit us to use. He told an extraordinary story of his upbringing in a convent—a nunnery for redeemed prostitutes. Things of that sort add great weight to his poems, I think. But are they proper to mention— what does he think?

(6) His relationship to other Hungarian writers of his generation— & slightly before & after.

(7) Account of any other writings.

(8) What is said about him in Hungary. Any quotations from articles about him that shows how Hungarians regard him.

(9) A general description of each of his books (plus their titles & dates)—of their contents, & how they were received.

(10) How he first became known.

(11) What other languages has he been translated into.

(12) Anything else connected with him no matter how remotely.

This is a big order, but I don't want you to regard it as anything more than what you might jot down on a train—just random free-association comments. Pro & con.

Maybe you could get him to supply much of it.

I shall be able to speak sincerely about him. I've lived with some of his

350

poems now for 7 or 8 years & they are still as interesting & still seem as good as ever.

This is just a note, Janos. Everything seems to be doing fine down here in the bosom of the green earth.

What we must next do is some translation of Visit to a Celestial Body. The Armageddon pieces were very bleak & final, keen & memorable. I would very much like to try.

I hope to see you again soon anyway

love

Ted

In the event, Csokits felt unable to supply answers to TH's questions, being reluctant to approach Pilinszky himself, who was under the constant watch of censors and informers at home in Hungary.

To Aurelia Plath

16 July 1974   Ts   Lilly Library

Dear Aurelia,

Fran has been here all week going over the letters finally, and I've gone through them too. I've cut out a few things—remarks about other people which might cause trouble and a few places where her remarks about me are nobody's business but mine.

It seems to me a marvellous book—or it has the makings of a marvellous book. At present it has one great fault. It is much too long. I'll try to explain this, because it is very important, for several reasons, that it should be drastically cut.

If you want that length because you want it to be a biography of her last years, I think you're making a mistake. It can't do the job. A collection of her letters to everybody, with all the varied aspects that different correspondents drew out of her filling the picture, might come nearer to it, especially if it contained extracts from her private journals.

But though she wrote to you amazingly frankly and freely, especially in the first half, there imposes itself finally one overall very limiting factor: all these letters exist within a single relationship, and this entails, eventually, beyond a certain critical mass of text, a feeling of monotony and narrowness. There are quite pronounced factors which work strongly towards this. For instance, her constant and growing and very understandable need to reassure you that the life she had chosen was not a mistake, that writing was succeeding financially etc. This hardly appears at all in her letters to other people. But in these letters it is one of the main themes. Much of this needs to be cut down.

In the early letters, which give such a dazzling picture of Smith College life in the early fifties, there is a good deal of repetitiousness of mood and response. This needs to be cleverly cut, too.

These things will have to be watched carefully, because such a terrific pressure of curiosity is going to be focussed on this book, and the response will be in any direction violent. It needs tact. I'm speaking to you frankly, because I fear you may have set your heart on a long book.

I know you want to show the full strength and consistency of her enthusiasm. But this can easily be overexposed, in this narrow context. Towards the last half, a reader begins to suspect that the emphasis on her joyful excitements is maybe part of what I spoke about—her need to reassure you. This may not have been so, you and I know that those moods were absolutely characteristic of her, but a reader can't help feeling it was so, because there is <u>so much</u> of it in comparison to other things. So then the book begins to produce the opposite effect to what I'm sure you must have hoped. So even much of this evidence of her good spirits must be cut.

These are simple matters of literary tact. Or rather not so simple. A book of this sort really has to be as judiciously fashioned as any novel. Otherwise, the good things won't work—readers will be confused in their response, and many of them—we know—will take the opportunity of thinking and saying the worst.

In my opinion, the book could easily be a best seller—not only that, it could silence forever the most vicious and stupid of her interpreters. But only if it is a fairly short book. Ideally it should leave the feeling that this is one facet, one concentrated glimpse of Sylvia's best side. All other questions should be no more than hinted at. But if the book is too long, if it makes even a gesture towards any sort of completeness, it will leave the reader with the feeling that that's all there is to it—and it will be attacked. I don't say this to justify any cutting of my doubtful role in the last part of the book. Those are some of the best letters and will cut short many far worse speculations about me going the rounds at present. But there is a chance here to present the Sylvia that most of her readers simply can't imagine because they have been so brainwashed by stupid literary commentators.

Properly edited, the book will do that and will find an immense reader-ship, I'm certain.

I've given Fran a note in the form of a letter to you, saying that I've read through the text, cut some and encouraged Francis in her instinct to cut more. She is a good and experienced editor, and sees it far more objectively—i.e. far more as the ordinary reader will see it—than either you or I. And—which is just as valuable in this case—she has it at heart to protect you and to protect Sylvia's reputation.

But it could be a good and precious book. And I'm sure it will be. [. . .]

I hope you're relaxing after your heroic labours typing that mountain of stuff. It must have been hard. Love

Ted & Carol

Aurelia Plath's edition of her daughter's *Letters Home* was in preparation. 'Fran' was Frances McCullough, editor at Harper & Row, who was later to bring out under her own name the first (exclusively US) edition of *The Journals of Sylvia Plath 1950–1962* (1982).

To Frieda Hughes

23 November 1974   Ms   Emory

Dear Frieda,

To see the Queen I had to wear morning dress. Since I've never worn it before, and I shall probably never wear it again, I don't have a suit of this sort, so I had to hire one, which means I had to make sure I got a good fit, which means I had to get to the shop that hires them in good time on Thursday morning, which means we had to go up to London Wednesday night.

Thursday morning it was pouring down. We wanted to get to the hiring shop—Moss Bros—by 10-30. But at 10-30 we were still trying to get a taxi at Olwyn's. There were simply no taxis to be had. Every taxi in London was jammed with people keeping out of the rain. So Carol & I set off to walk to the tube station. No hats. Carol borrowed a Persian scarf of Olwyn's, but it wasn't really any good. Rain poured down, grates gurgled, gutters clattered, traffic sizzled, & we sloshed. Then behold a taxi—guided by a tiny orange angel in the likeness of four letters. So we thought 'Good omen' as we sat damply & tried to dry our hair.

Moss Bros is a big clothing shop—men's clothing, & their hiring department is away at the back. An Irishman brought me a suit we thought ought to fit, and left me in the cubicle to change. First you put on the pants, pin-striped grey & black. They were a bit short. Then you put on the waistcoat—this is a weird object made of two grey wings, decorated with buttons, & fastened together with two strips of grey elastic. The idea is to get the bands of elastic somehow behind you, across your back and behind your neck, then button the two wings together over your chest, so that it seems—when you eventually get your jacket on—that you're wearing a grey waistcoat. Mine was short. Between the bottom of the waistcoat & the top of the pants, I had three inches of white shirt puffing out. I could see I was going to spend my time in front of the Queen, surrounded as I imagined by lords & ladies, pulling my pants down to cover my socks, then pulling them up to cover that waist gap from below, & pulling my waistcoat down to hide it from above, and I thought I'll look like a right hick. But then I put on the black jacket, which had long tails behind—to my knees—and only one tiny button in front, and I could see straight-off that I looked totally ridiculous. So there I stood tugging, & twisting,—shrinking my legs & shortening my shoulders, when the Irishman came back. He began to fuss, he lengthened one of the elastics, to let the waistcoat down, he whipped the pants away & brought me another pair, (too tight) whipped them away & brought me another pair—about right but very thin unpleasant material. "What's this for?" he asked, as he pulled & hitched & patted at me "Is it a wedding or something of the sort?" So I said "Well as a matter of fact I'm meeting the Queen, in about an hour." He stared at me, he shrank about six inches, his hands began to tremble, his feet got tangled in the odd pairs of pants lying about the floor. Then he tore off my jacket, "Take off those pants" he cried "All this stuff's rubbish. Let me get you the real thing." So he reappeared with a fresh armful, & fitted me up, & stroked me, & gazed at me, & picked off invisible grains of moth-dust, then he produced a silver tie, & there I was. I really looked quite presentable.

We got another taxi to the Grosvenor hotel and sat in a great gloomy room & had a drink until John Betjemann the Poet Laureate appeared. You've probably seen him on T.V. He's a very sweet man and we all liked each other straight off, so we sat there drinking our drinks, getting "slightly tight" as he put it, and working up to our dash to the Palace.

He was very nervous. "It's so immense!" he kept muttering "Such a vast place! Terrifying!"

Finally, it was time, and we went out to get a taxi in the pouring rain. Carol got one of course, & we called "Buckingham Palace, please, main entrance!"

As we drove in through the gates, where people stand with their cameras, the police recognised John Betjeman & waved us in. We drove right through that main first building & stopped somewhere—I was so busy seeing the end of the red carpet that covered the steps getting soaked in the rain that I didn't notice. There was the deputy Keeper of the Privy Purse welcoming us in through this great door. We climbed a few red-carpeted steps, and came into a huge red-carpeted hall that went away into the distance to left & right, then away up staircases again at far left & far right. We were overwhelmed by chandeliers, golden panels, giant paintings, lofty ceilings, & led into a small room— where the Queen makes her Xmas speech every Xmas day. Walls covered with paintings of ships & sea-fights. We sat down, & the Keeper of the Privy Purse appeared, jovial fellow, who poured out glasses of sherry. He said the Queen had been reading my books and had discovered words that she didn't know were in the English language, & she wanted to ask me about them. "Very good" said I. We talked about farming. He wished he'd known we were farmers, he'd have told the Queen, since she's a great breeder of cattle & horses. "I'll tell her", said John Betjeman.

Suddenly a very tall thin young man, with a beaky face, in dark blue uniform, came in. He was covered with gold braid & gold ropes & gold tassels, as if a great bundle of it had simply been draped over him. He had golden spurs. And he announced that it was really time for us to be moving, & he would show us up.

So Sir John & I followed him out & left Carol being entertained by the Keeper of the Privy Purse and his deputy.

We went into a corridor more palatial than anything I had imagined possible. All the way, the ceiling was gold-ribbed cupolas. The carpet was gold-bordered red. The walls were thickly-crusted with paintings— every square foot had a painting—portraits & scenes, gigantic & small. All the way along either side, spaced maybe four feet apart, were display cabinets—chockfull of jewel boxes, long boxes, short boxes, fat, thin, round, heart-shaped, oval—gold, silver, ivory, studded, agate, jade— anything you can think of. Every two strides, another cabinet full on

355

your left, another on your right, then two strides more & another pair. Everything gleaming & glittering under the chandeliers.

We went up a lift that was like a miniature palace. We came into a high-ceilinged elegant room, with a high wide window opening out over the back-gardens of the Palace. Full of gorgeous furniture, more pictures again, ornaments, every cranny crammed with richness. A sad, tired little lady received us—the Queen's secretary, Countess of something or other. We were to wait with her until the Queen had finished with the Ambassador to Yemen—Yemen is a tiny country near Israel. So there we sat, chatting about all sorts of things, including the Hilton Hotel which was staring at us over the trees from half way up the sky.

After a while, the door opened and a face whispered "The Ambassador is now leaving," and beyond in the corridor I got a glimpse of a wild face gazing in at us as curiously as we were gazing at him. So now it was our turn. Sir John & I got up, and the equerry—the tall young man—told me what to do. "Er, I think if you go in side by side, er, and, er, pause at the door and bow, just a small bow"—he demonstrated. "A neck bow," said Sir John, & he demonstrated too, tucking his chin in & staring down at his silver tie. "Then you go forward & the Queen will shake your hand" went on the equerry "Then you'll sit & when the conversation's over, she will ring a tiny bell—don't be alarmed. It simply means, it's over. I'm listening out here, & when I hear that bell, I open the door. The Queen will then say goodbye, may or may not shake your hand, & you will bow, & then turn to the door, & at the door face her again and bow once more."

"A neck bow again" said Sir John, practising.

"You address her as "Your majesty" the first time, & after that as "ma'am". So, we're ready."

We huddled out into the corridor, where there suddenly seemed to be about twenty people, though I think in fact there were only 2—besides us & the equerry. Sir John & I got abreast, & we stepped into this wide open doorway.

We were looking into a large room, about as big as the barn and about as high, but very light, with the same high wide windows as the other room. Quite a lot of furniture. What seemed to be a grand piano over to the right was completely covered with propped up photographs of the royal family. And there, far away across this great room, was a tiny person whom of course I recognised. Nobody else in the room at all. Just her. Then I saw Sir John seemed to have fallen asleep, with his chin sunk on his chest, so hastily I sank my chin too, & we presented the Queen with the tops of our heads. Then we stepped in, & she came beaming towards us, & the door closed behind us, and we were alone with the Queen.

Well, it was one of the most entertaining quarters of an hour. First of all, she was a complete surprise. I'd imagined her rather tall, rather solemn, rather slow, rather aloof. Not at all. She was tiny. About Nicky's size. She had a very lively expression, & spoke so openly & friendly, that I immediately got the idea she liked me as much as I liked her. "Here is the medal," & she handed it over, & we gasped & exclaimed. Actually, the medal is twice as big as I expected, & very much more beautiful. Inset in a satin bed, inside a red leather box. After we had cried & marvelled enough, she invited us to sit down, & made for a chair. She offered a chair beside her, or a couch opposite. We bumped into each other, Sir John & I, going to the chair beside her, so we recoiled together & sat on the couch, side by side, and we started to talk. Really we talked about all sorts of things. I was so delighted with her & with us, I simply can't remember what we said until she said she liked my poem about the otter. There are all sorts of strange anecdotes about that poem, so I started to tell her. She seemed so interested, I told her them all. We quite forgot about Sir John. But she finally brought him back into the conversation somehow, & we talked about the architecture of the Palace, and about the Hilton Hotel, which she dislikes very much. "I wish they'd spend as much pulling it down as they spent putting it up" she said. She was so lively and likeable, I was very disappointed when our talk paused, and she reached for her tiny bell. Ting a ling, & the door at the far end of the room opened. We got up. We bowed, we said goodbye, we began to sidle away—since it's a tradition that you never turn your back on Royalty—when she said "You're forgetting your medal"—I'd left it on the couch. She gave it to me again, & I admired it again. "I do hope it's real gold," she said. So smiling & smiling we got to the door, & bowed, & smiled again & alas it was over. The door was closed. We were led off down a corridor about 100 yards long—display cabinets on either side, crammed with treasures, walls covered with pictures. "Don't you ever stop to look at any of this," I said to the man leading us. "This is only one corridor," he said "You'd never see a quarter of it."

Carol was still being entertained. Or rather, she was entertaining. She took a snap of Sir John & I at the Palace door—in the pouring rain—and we were off. We went to drink a bottle of champagne with Sir John.

And that was it. You really would have loved it.

lots of love
Daddy

The Queen's Medal for Poetry was presented to TH on 21 November. As Poet Laureate, Sir John Betjeman (1906–84) chaired the committee that proposed recipients to the Queen.

For 'strange anecdotes' about 'An Otter' in *Lupercal*, see TH's letter to Keith Sagar of 18 July 1998.

To Gerald and Joan Hughes and family

25 November 1974   Ms   Emory

Dear Gerald & Joan & all—

How are you all after these many months? Mysterious silences will insist on descending. The final realisation that you never would come & live over here was probably what knocked me out—it was a big station in my life's journey to realise the emptiness of that dream. Part of the general stripping away of everything, lately drastic.

However, as a soft-brained astrologer, I guess you've been having a very bad time in the way of illusions. I suppose my silence has been part of a bigger design.

The farm, you'll be amused to hear, is still afloat—which is a miracle, considering the numbers of farmers going bankrupt, selling up, blowing their brains out. We're overloaded with beasts—there hasn't been a moment this last year when they were worth selling. So my hope of unloading most of our commonplace stuff, and getting a few classy cows to match the phenomenal bull we chanced to get hold of, has to be deferred. This bull is my best purchase ever—I've never enjoyed owning anything $^1/_{10}$ as much. I really love him. Carol carries photographs of him, which we display at every opportunity. It isn't just his incredible size & beauty—he has a strange, sweet nature, in every respect like an unusual person. He makes our cows seem like a pile of real rubbish.

Visited the Queen on Thursday. Had a nice talk. She surprised me—very lively & nimble, small, immediately likeable. She gave me a 3 oz gold medal for writing poetry. John Betjeman (poet laureate) led me in. Carol meanwhile entertained the Keeper of the Privy Purse.

Well, it's been the wettest year in centuries. Hay is £80 a ton—but unobtainable (last year £30). Animals starving all over the place—everybody slaughtering everything. And now this winter is already wetter than last.

The great technological folly is having its bluff well & truly called. Every day it's clearer—the Red Indians were the last sane human beings. I'm coming to Australia in March 76 with Carol.   love
                                Ted

[*Marginal addition*: I'm sending off the knives at last—blame them.]

The 'phenomenal bull' was Sexton Hyades XXXIII.

1975

To János Csokits

15 January 1975   Ms   Emory

Dear Janos,

Thank you for the letter & the poem—a beautiful poem. How is it that the poetically fruitful phases, in the adoration of the female, are the phases of difficulty—just before you are accepted fully, and after the bitterness has entered.

As a Cancer, astrologically you are now in a difficult low time, on all fronts—but it is temporary. At the moment it is actively blacker than for a long time (culminated this last weekend)—from now on it is moving toward clear light. Something to be said for astrology—even if it were utterly false. It's main instruction is, when things are good: "This is temporary—so act accordingly." And when things are bad: "This is temporary—so act accordingly." I hope to send you some of my verses soon.

Love   Ted

The 'beautiful poem' was one of Csokits's own, 'In the Dust of Eden', sent for TH to improve the translation, which he did, returning his version on 4 February.

To Daniel Weissbort

28 January 1975   Ms   Emory

How is Iowa? Your letter gave me a vivid impression. It sounds as though you have those ideal circumstances, finally—prolonged solitary confinement. I know what you mean, about the horrors of it—that's why it's so difficult to get—we avoid it with all our strength. Even when we know its absolutely necessary. We're well past the age now when the Indian Princes handed over their affairs and disappeared into the forest. I try to get it every day, but I know that's really no good—the isolation needs to extend for many days and preferably for weeks, if it's really going to work. Then one thing that happens is, our ordinary habits, all the mesh of associations & reflexes that keep us rooted so fixedly into the trivialities of the most trivial common denominator—they dissolve, we forget them. And we begin to reshape according to inner require- ment & inner events. By the age of 40, I'm sure, our outer mind & personality is hopelessly out of phase with our inner one. Unless we can make the change, I think there's nothing ahead but self-imitation & sterility & less & less life. In fact I think that out-of-phase phase starts around 30.

Those lamented imprisonments of Dostoevsky, Solzenitsyn, & the rest, weren't all wasted. When Goethe was writing a piece, he locked himself away absolutely solitary, for weeks. 6 weeks for Werther. If there was one other person even in the same house, he couldn't write a thing. So one faithful or jealous companion would have cancelled all those forceful volumes, evidently. Surely not.

The year before, Weissbort had moved to the University of Iowa as director of its Translation Program.

To Gerald and Joan Hughes and family

15 February 1975   Ms Emory

Dear Gerald & Joan & all,

The python skin came today—a beauty. Thanks very much. They're quite valuable, you know. Not that I'm concerned about their value.

The way to test a tiger skin, is to approach it surreptitiously, & give it a little rip at the edge. If it tears like cardboard—no good. If it hurts your fingers, it's O.K., even if it looks ratty. Also, remember that the skull of a tiger costs about £35. That's with teeth, of course. Even without teeth, they are desirable objects, in my tribe.

Eagles' feet still wanted.

Our new building has made farming really easy. Also, it's a great satisfaction to go & play with all the cattle. Unfortunately, having gone through an incredible number of thousands of pounds this year (20 on Lumb Bank alone, 9 on tax, etc) (God knows where it's come from), I'm now absolutely penniless, in fact considerably in debt, right at the moment when I've decided finally exactly what pedigree cattle I want— and right at the moment, too, when they're cheaper than they ever will

361

be again. Still, no matter. Some cash is due, later on. It will be too late, of course.

Main thing is, I got working again, so I'm quite happy. Playing around in Persia knocked 2 years out of my production line. Probably be worth it, later.

The brilliant probably disastrous idea dawned lately, that Dad must sell the Beacon, & get a place in North Tawton. He just doesn't want to go back up there. He's quite excited. He's even getting up before 2 p.m.

A perfect place, down at the bottom of the town, has come on the market. Small, one sitting room, a kitchen, a bathroom, and 2 bedrooms, newly renovated throughout, it's price is grotesque—£7000. But it's on the flat by the river, in a row, with easy walks in all directions, within 100 yards of the Copper Key (his pub) and 105 yards of his girl friend. It's as like King Street as still exists. It was even built, as one of a row of mill cottages, by a wool-factory that came from Mytholmroyd— that big old place down at the bottom. Anyway, if he can get a good price for the Beacon, this place will be cheap at any price he can afford, because he likes it, & it will solve really all Willy problems. We're putting the Beacon for sale at £16,500. He has £4,800 in the bank. So he'll need a bank loan for a month or two.

We're well.   love   Ted

Written on William Hughes's birthday.

To Charles Monteith

24 February 1975   Ts   Faber

Dear Charles,

Thank you very much for your letter with the comments about GAUDETE. That was exactly the kind of response I'd hoped to get. Coming back to it now, after some time, I see how I can use your suggestions. The Ancient Mariner idea had actually occurred to me. What I'd stuck on was the opposition between the general tendency of the whole thing to concentrate itself, and the need to keep open sufficient ordinary background. Also, the stiffnesses and lumpish ugliness, which was the abortive form of the sort of ugliness I was after—I'd hoped for an irreducible beautiful ugliness, like a Caesarian operation.

However, your remarks gave me just the beckoning jolt I needed, and I think it's now going better.

Also, you've assured me it wasn't completely unpublishable—isn't.

I'm glad Viking are having a rethink about the Season Songs book. I hope Faber can sort something out with them.

Do you know Michael Baldwin's writing? He writes novels, film-scripts, has written some short plays, but mainly he's a poet. I got to know him through reviewing his first novel—A WORLD OF MEN, which Peter Brook was wanting to make a film of. He seems to write everything after eleven at night—he teaches all day in a training college. He's supporting two domestic enterprises, both quite expensive, so he's under pressure. But he seems to like that, though maybe it has driven him to write things he otherwise wouldn't have done. He just tries everything.

I think he's a very powerful writer, he has a marvellous abundant natural wealth of things and energy. On a long car journey he once improvised a children's story for about an hour and a half that turned into a full scale adult child's novel—started with a pet winkle and ended up with a major situation among all the characters of a region. Absolutely brilliant and rivetting. When I asked him to write it out he complained he never has the time for that sort of thing, he's always toiling with some ambitious novel. What he needs is to give up teaching.

His poetry means a lot to me. It is completely creative and free. There seem to be several different poets in him, various pretty distinct styles, but when two or three of them combine the result is marvellous, and unique. And it's always interesting, even when they're writing on their own. He's unfashionable up to a point—because the police state in literature at the moment here is rather tight on permissions and licences, as you know. But his own attitude to his writing is completely generous and open—anything could happen in it. I think he's a remarkable writer—and still only casting about among his possibilities.

I'm going on at length because he's looking for a new publisher—he's accumulated about five. He was wondering if you would be interested and I urged him to write to you.

He's done a lot of collections for children—his own and anthologies of others. He sits with me on the Daily Mirror Children's Lit panel. He really knows that world of Educational publishing.

I hope everything is going OK with you.

Yours

Ted

TH had first mentioned *Gaudete* to Monteith at the end of 1974, writing in a letter of 6 December: 'What I would dearly like are your reactions against—those mightn't make me alter, but they would give me a test for my own feelings pro. Critics would slaughter it—it is completely vulnerable, awkward as a newborn babe, ugly, excessive etc—but after a few years it would have found a den to stay alive in I think.'

TH and Michael Baldwin were now friends, having met in the mid-1960s, when they both served as judges of the *Daily Mirror*'s Children's Literary Competition. By the time of this letter, they were in the habit of showing each other their work in typescript. Baldwin's novel *The Gamecock* was published by Faber in 1980.

To Aurelia Plath

3 April 1975   Ms   Lilly Library

Dear Aurelia,

What a pity we've got into such a misunderstanding.

I wondered why Francis had fallen so silent since she returned. She was shocked, I think, by all that I wanted deleted, and she did say that Harpers wouldn't like it.

Your letter doesn't say exactly what you want to keep—at the cost of a lawyer (probably Harper will pay for your side of the debate, but I don't suppose they'll pay for mine). I look forward to seeing their letter.

Frieda & Nick are already living in a mausoleum—I just want to cut down the furnishings & the tourist visitors & the general mess of publicity. I certainly don't want my private life with Sylvia exposed. Carol feels enough like an also-ran, & I feel quite enough of a second-hand relic husband, as it is.

Yes, I agree it's a pity I didn't wake up sooner to exactly what all that exposure would amount to. But when I did waken up, there it was. What did help to waken me up, I admit, were the letters of absolute horror from friends of mine in the States who had seen copies of the M.S.

It seemed to me, after I'd cut the letters, that though the book now lacks the sensational interest of all the inside dope on me, & though it lacks those early love-letters which Sylvia somehow sent to you rather than to me—I mean those early letters about me—nevertheless it does still give, very brilliantly & fully, her relationship with you. And I know that was what you wanted.

All I've done, really, Aurelia, is extract my private life, in an attempt to keep it private. I know that sort of thing isn't much respected in the States, especially by publishers & the mob which you know. But I thought you would respect it. I hope you're not letting them think for you. The book is fine as it is now—you shouldn't worry about it.

love   Ted

This letter picks up the argument for cutting material from Sylvia Plath's *Letters Home*, put forward in TH's letter to Aurelia of 16 July the previous year.

To Michael Hamburger

3 April 1975 Ts Leeds

Since we last met, I got the opportunity and decided to go the whole hog. I bought a farm. So far, it's proved to be the best decision I've so far managed, just about, though incredibly expensive. Also, I entered it just when the whole thing went crash. So I've farmed through the most disastrous year in the history of British farming—so I'm told. We have about 28 cows, some more beautiful than others, and a bull. From last year we have about 24 calves, and we're right now in the middle of this year's crop. One yesterday, two the day before. Also we run between fifty and two hundred sheep—a rather improvised system of buying young ewes, lambing some, selling some as breeding ewes. Carol's father, who was a farmer, manages the whole thing actually—all I do is struggle to stay uninvolved though inevitably I spend a great deal of time on it. The whole thing is too interesting to resist. It's reconnected me to the only world I belong to in any way—which I felt I was beginning to lose. And so far as I can judge it has helped my writing—mainly by making it impossible for me to gad about and showing me the real precious value of each hour, which I did not learn twenty years ago as I should have done.

On this farm there is a small farmhouse—pretty isolated, at the moment pretty ugly too, but we're doing it up bit by bit and by summer it should be very inhabitable. It would please me greatly if you would come and stay there some time. [. . .]

The real relief of this farm is that even though it makes no money it has somehow freed me from all feeling of dependance on the literary world. That is certainly something to secure. I've paid for it, of course, with a real loss of liberty—though I haven't begun to resent that yet.

TH and the poet, translator and teacher Michael Hamburger (1924–2007) had met and begun corresponding in the 1960s.

To Aurelia Plath

23 April 1975   Ts   Lilly Library

Dear Aurelia,

Harper got in touch with your solicitors asking them to draw up an agreement according to your promise in your letter to me, that the book of letters will not be published in England, except in a form and at a time that I approve. Since then I've heard nothing. Could you please get onto them and ask them to move. It is obviously in their interest to draw the whole thing out as long and tortuously as possible—the lawyer's motivation is to earn fees not solve problems—and meanwhile I'm sure Harper's will take every excuse to rush the letters out perhaps even without deleting the few letters which at minimum I would like to be removed and which I'm sure Fran has told you about. They are the letters describing Sylvia's first days with me which are of course very private to me.

I'm sorry you felt it necessary to hand this negotiation over to lawyers, and that you feel it so vitally necessary to your peace of mind to cut short our amiable discussion of the book's final form at this stage. A contract is a contract, I agree, but that sort of document is meant as a safeguard against hostilities, not as an enforced policing of reasonable agreement between friends. However, it's still in your power to do as you please in the way of concessions to me, and I'd be very grateful Aurelia if you could ask your lawyers to make the necessary moves on the two points I've mentionned. First of all, the agreement about not publishing in England except in a form I've approved (that would be called an abbreviated version of your book for English readers and the friends of Sylvia's children). Second, that you allow me to settle with Frances exactly which and which parts of the letters describing Sylvia's first meeting with me we cut out. I'm sure you like those letters, but you will see they are for me somewhat sacred documents which I would prefer not to have every college kid and viperous reviewer and thesis writer pawing over.

366

Please drop me a note letting me know this is being done, Aurelia.
I hope you are keeping well,

Ted

It took me quite a while, given my resistance to all that business, to wake up to the fact that in suggesting you use all those letters, and complying to a great extent with your first choice, I had made a mistake. What I'm now asking is that you do not allow your lawyers to persuade you to take advantage of my mistake. It isn't as though it would be of any measurable advantage to you, but they think in legal terms and to them a point conceded is a point lost.

To Frieda Hughes

[Late June 1975]   Ms   Emory

Dear Frieda,

How did the exams go? Did you manage to get into a nice fluent gallop with your answers?

The rain came just as we were finishing loading the bales—we had a wild rush to get them in, bales into the landrover, bales into Jean & Ian's van, bales into the horse-box, bales into our ears, bales into the backs of our necks, bales in our boots, bales down our shirts. So we tottered home towering & trembling & tilting & toppling & teetering. And there in front of us was some other tractor creeping along with a trailer loaded twice as high as ours, like a skyscraper. All over the countryside there were desperate tractors crawling home under impossible last loads in the very green rain.

The rain is making everything grow again. Including your alpine strawberries, which are luscious—the ones the birds don't get. Since we mowed that jungle of weed over the tennis court and the upper part of the orchard, there seem to be whole flocks of blackbirds and thrushes hunting there. And the doves. And Ginger-dandelion. He's discovered a great metropolis of mice up there, that were beyond him before. He's a fine mobile ginger flower.

It's still raining, Thursday evening.

[. . .]

Well, here we are, all aches & stretched joints, like broken down five bar gates, after our baling.

367

And here are all the holidaymakers, sitting in their sauna-bath cars under the downpour, staring at the sea, with their transistors turned up, & their ice-cream running down to their elbows, like cars stuck in a car-washer. See you very soon.

love, Daddy

For a poetic treatment of the farming activity described here, see 'Last Load' in *Moortown*.

To Robin Skelton

[15 October 1975]   Ms   Victoria

Dear Robin,

Thank you for the copy of The Poet's Calling—naturally I went through it at once, since it's a fascinating collection of remarks and quotes. At one time I thought of assembling all the tricks & devices that artists have used to help them work, to start them working, & all the disciplines etc they have invented to keep & sharpen their faculties. You have done quite a large part of that.

Naturally too I homed in on my name page 133 & noted your comment: "connection between cause & effect. . . . arbitrary."

Well, every man skin his own skunk, as the redman used to say, though mine is more like a white rabbit:

(1)——————— When God hammered Crow
                     He made Gold
Note: Re. proverb: "Beat a woman with a hammer & you make gold." Re. the technology of improving all metals by hammering them. Re Chinese Proverb: "Persistent knocking brings forth at last the golden colt."
(2)——————— When God etc . . . he made Diamond"
Note: Re: alchemical etc production of diamond in nuclear processes, as in cooling fragments of cosmic explosions etc, as ultimate form of carbon, basis of all organisms.
(3)——————— "When God crushed etc . . . . alcohol"
Note: Re: making of cider. With some reference to Eden Creation background of anecdote—i.e. heady consequences of apple. Also making of saints, crushed.

(4)——————— "When God tore Crow . . . . money"

Note   i.e. What becomes symbolic object of value & barter—pieces of gold, lumps of iron etc—the valuable thing divided small, with a bit for everybody. Also, creating abstract wealth, you create what God wants to tear up. Tearing up the valuable thing, you create abstract wealth etc.

(5)——————— When God blew Crow up . . . . day.

Note   i.e. Conflagration of basic elements makes light—the sun is an explosion.

(6)——————— When God hung Crow . . . . Fruit.

Note   i.e. Ballad about 'strange fruit'. Also, the love-daimon as fruit (apple, grape, figs etc—Dionysus & Adonis etc, Christ etc—all fruits of the tree, all tree-born.) Fruit as the sexual organs etc, basis of idea of fruit as the initiator of the generations etc, plus consequences.

(7)——————— When God buried Crow . . . . man.

Note   Re: Creation of man—difficulty of getting spirit to take on the body of earth, the coffin of flesh. God had to do it forcibly, as a rule—from spirit's point of view, this was a death (c.f. other poems in Crow & elsewhere). Also, man was created 'earth-rooted', fixed in earth, womb, grave of earth etc.

(8)——————— When God tried to chop Crow in two . . . . woman

Re: Creation of Eve—by dividing Adam, (Many other origin stories similar.) by externalising & separating female in man. But also, re-phrases "split-arsed mechanic" (woman) etc. Vagina as axe-cleft—various stories of God, trying to demolish the female with an axe, merely giving her the means to copulate & reproduce. Re: idea that death has forced organisms to invent reproduction.

(9)——————— When God said . . . . Redeemer.

Note   Re: notion that the Redeemer is what overcomes everything, the final positive victor over all temporal defeats. i.e. Spirit, in general, as redemptive energy.

(10)——————When God went off in despair etc

Note   i.e. After Christ's shout "Why hast thou forsaken me"—death commences in earnest for the mortal part of the fruit on the tree. Re also: in absence of God, in absence of Spirit value, Spirit reduces itself to mere life, surviving at all costs—i.e. what was Christ, son of God, becomes a demon devouring his fellow-sufferers.

The whole poem is a definition of Crow—(1) as the ultimate elemental value, & as the femaleness of things, & as the salvation of things. (2) as the most precious thing arrived at only through the most extreme punishment (3) as the intoxication deriving from suffering & encounter with reality (4) as what is destroyed by abstraction & exploitation (5) as the energy of the sun (6) as eros (7) as the pre-adamite spirit (8) as the inventive & creative spirit, which thrives on the pressure of death (9) as the unconquerable thing (10) as the inextinguishable tenacity of the unconquerable thing.

Keep well—Ted

Robin Skelton's *The Poet's Calling* (1975) included the remarks that, in 'Crow's Song of Himself', it was 'difficult to see the connection between cause and effect as being anything but arbitrary', that the poem was no more than 'a draft to work on', that it lacked 'punch' and was 'self-indulgently sentimental, even narcissistic'. Skelton (1926–97), poet, critic, anthologist and magazine editor, was born in Britain but had moved to Canada in 1963.

To the Editor of *The Times*

3 December 1975   Ts (Photocopy) Emory

Dear Sir,

The use of the Royal Navy to oppose the Icelanders' defence of their own waters from short-sighted exploitation by foreign fishing fleets is perhaps based on an official English policy of free-for-all, or whatever policy it is that has allowed the Russian fishing fleet, for instance, to cruise around the coasts of this Western Peninsula all summer, 'hoovering up' the sea-bed and every living thing on it.

The Icelanders know, as everybody else knows or very soon learns, that the instinct for 'havoc', the lust to kill and carry away as much as possible, comes freely into play when the hunter is off his own grounds and on somebody else's. The thrilling satisfaction of 'making a killing' in a swift raid is as deep as human nature, and legislation against it only makes it more exciting. There are countless proofs of this in the history of edible and profitable species. In fact, the logical conclusion is, that any such species has only one hope, which is to become somebody's private property and be bred for profit in a controlled way. The Iceland-ers are quite right in believing that foreign fishermen will take all they can while they can, and the greater the fear that the stocks will soon be gone, the more ruthless the final plunder. Commercial fishing has proved itself throughout history to be an exercise of just this raid and plunder. It is only when a species dwindles to the point of becoming just about unprofitable to go after, that sudden close seasons and restraints are agreed on, while the fishermen go after something else. As in the pre-sent case of the North Sea herring. But before that point is reached, who-ever applies any self-restraint in commercial fishing is simply leaving his share to others.

We don't need to go to Iceland to see this plundering instinct taking effect, or even to the massive overkill wildcat drift-netting off the Norwegian coast this last year. We don't even have to go to the Russian and French fleets that can be watched often enough from our own shores. In many places, our own fishermen plunder their own waters just as senselessly. They always have tried to catch all they could, of course, but now they have the equipment to make a difference, and many powerful rivals.

Surely there would be some point in acclaiming and doing all we can to uphold Iceland's attempt to make some intelligent defence of the fish life in her seas. We ought to recognise her action as a big step forward in controlled sea-farming, and follow it ourselves: push the limits of our fishery as far out to sea as possible, and employ the Royal Navy to some purpose policing that.

Yours faithfully
E.J. Hughes
~~M.L. Weston~~

In the third of the so-called 'Cod Wars' between Britain and Iceland, a dispute over Iceland's move to extend its fishing rights led to diplomatic rumblings and minor skirmishes at sea. NATO intervened and the following year Britain's right to fish the disputed waters was restricted.

From the crossed-out and replaced pseudonym it appears that this is a photocopy of a draft not actually sent. No letter from TH on this subject was printed in *The Times*.

1976

In February of this year, Jack Orchard died from cancer, making the running of Moortown as a commercial proposition impossible.

To Daniel Weissbort

[Undated 1976]   Ms   Emory

I've read the poems twice, quite carefully. They seemed just as good and interesting the second time. They are much fuller than those you showed me a few years ago—and their works seem much more intricate. But they have the same quality of being totally absorbed in their subject—their private train of thought. And their thoughts have the same quality of being very true searchings out of genuine painful things, with no eye to anything but the truth & justness of their words. That makes something unique.

Nobody else writes their private diary without any stage make-up or mannerism whatsoever, no matter how bold an attempt they make. Lowell is trying to do what you are doing—using all the flexibility & experimental provisional possibilities of verse to find out exactly what he does feel, or to get as near it as he can, and to set it down without any concessions whatsoever to his audience, his reputation, his ideas about poetry, or the other people in his story—but the result seems to me totally ersatz, it is all stage performance, even the careless, slovenly, loose shuffling off of imperfect approximations, on his way to closer sincerities, is all part of the act. Or it seems so. The only interesting moments are when he forgets the effort to be nakedly true with himself, & writes a formal impersonal poem about something else alltogether.

Peter Brook was experienced & enlightening about actors—even the most sensitive & gifted—in their attempts to find their true response to a situation. No matter how absolute their self-abasement, & their rendings of themselves, & their plunges into darkness—all that ever comes out is 'actorishness'. It is so rare that anything really true emerges, that to all purposes one can say it is impossible. I think it's the same with writing.

But somehow you manage to escape any sense of writing in the eye of an audience or for an audience. You manage to keep the whole thing intact, & true to yourself. That sort of thing is quite different from 'original talent' or 'unique poetic note' or 'brilliant gift' or any of those things which attract attention to writing. It's an alltogether different order of expression. It is invisible to most people, who only see impurities, which reflect the light. It is usually only visible after a long time—because it does not date. It is immensely strong, though, with a sort of passive strength—like an element of nature.

So in your poems I think you are doing something very special and, to me, infinitely valuable. I really do.

[. . .]

Most poems seem to have been composed onto paper like a drawing—that is their place & existence, they need the coherence of the paper to hold them in shape, and only an accidentally permanent surface, like paper, can give the needed support to the phrases, since they have no support of human presence. Insofar as poetry is convincingly the real speech of a real person, it seems to happen "off" the page. I think that's fairly true. And it seems unusual because the main body of all modern poetic traditions is 'objective' in the sense that it approaches a poem as an 'artefact'—like a bridge, or a car, or a modern sculpture, or a film, or a biological study, or a collage index of related information, or even a fantastic mathematics. A great mass of modern quasi-surrealist poetry seems to me fantastic mathematics—where images have become algebraic values, & flights can be taken in any direction, with a show of intricate relatedness of image to image. All that is a flow or an ebb dead opposite to the idea that the real subject of poetry might be what we really feel about what really happens to us, and the real language might be a very plain & direct business. Maybe the reason we're so affected by this last sort of poetry, when it's genuine, is that we're starved of it, & now we really need it.

There's a close inner relationship, I think, between the whole modern movement in poetry & the attitudes of technologists & scientists. Even surrealism—which is presumably its relationship to Freud—is basically analytical. The human tone of it is rigid, narrow, impersonal, 'absent'. It is incapable of making a statement which doesn't seem, in a real human situation, supercilious, bookish, inadequate, frivolous, irrelevant, etc. It's 'wildness' is all stage props, & its 'beauty' stage deportment.

All the real poetry has been the other thing, after all. The problem is that we now have highly analytical brains, & simple whole speech is something we can only sustain with great effort, like walking along the ridge of a house, or with the same clumsy effort as 17th Century alchemists trying to be analytical.

Weissbort does not recall which of his poems he had shown TH, but his style then, as now, was marked by exceptional spareness of language and an unguardedly confiding tone.

To Charles Monteith

5 February 1976   Ms   Faber

Dear Charles,

Olwyn tells me Season Songs is due to be published in May. I'm sorry it can't be earlier. If it can't, I'd like to ask how much of a favour you can do me in the matter of a date in May.

Because of the carefully selected day on which I gave you the manuscript, & because of the occurrence of certain special conditions of the earth's electrical field in May, there is a chance that Season Songs could become a text-book example for the modern Czech & French research which has now established the predictable occurrence of moments of high positive opportunity.

The day is Thursday the 13th.

If you have any other likely books lying around—that's the day. Whatever else, I would like you to apply pressure, bend rules if necessary, and help my experiment to its conclusion. If we miss the 13th May, then the first part of my plan, when I sent you the manuscript, is wasted.

"Do good, and throw it on the road," is a fine proverb, but a better one is "God is a great worker, but he likes help."

Well, like roulette, its interesting to play, even if you go on losing.

I hope everything is well. Here, it's so so—pipes burst, taps exploded etc.

I'd be grateful if you'd humour my superstition in this case, Charles.

If the 13th is impossible, the 14th at 9 oclock is still in the light. That's the moment to back your horse.

I also meant to ask you—are those manuscripts I sent, for the exhibition, still under control?

As ever

Ted

Season Songs, which had been published in the USA the year before, with illustrations by Leonard Baskin, came out from Faber, unadorned, on 13 May 1976.

To Richard Murphy

31 March 1976 Ms Tulsa

Dear Richard,

Since we spoke last, Carol's father died. Cancer got the upper hand, and he died very suddenly, early February. Big shock to me, since I'd involved my life so closely with him. Everything alters now. The farm is too much for Carol—through the winter—and now we're both doing it, much of the day, it has stopped my writing etc absolutely. No point in getting some stranger to manage it—since we're hardly farming for profit. Probably sell all the beasts this summer. Which will be a sad business. Try to keep the land, sell the grass. End of a beautiful dream. A bit too beautiful, maybe.

[. . .]

I went to Australia for a week. Took my father, to stay with my brother. Had six beautiful days at the Adelaide Festival—what a lovely lot they were. A gang of young Australian poets half-adopted me. The wine was startling—not exported. I found 3 or 4 really good young writers.

[. . .]

But what a weird ghostly glare they live in—like a primitive painting. Eerie, sinister, desolate, incredibly vivid—everything sits in this ancient sinister air, like a dream of some sort, full of hidden significance & strangeness. The birds are utterly peculiar, prehistoric antics, prehistoric cries, more like flying lizards. I just couldn't get over a constant sense of amazement. It was all just what I'd imagined, but infinitely moreso, & so beautiful. But I felt everybody was completely out of place there. I didn't see much outside Adelaide & Melbourne & Perth. Six days isn't much.

Write & send something you're writing.

As ever

Ted

TH was a guest of the Adelaide Festival Writers' Week in early March.

To János Csokits

[May 1976]   Ms   Emory

Carol's father died in early February, after a horrible drama of cancer and its treatment, its hopes & its hopelessness, & its transfigurations. A very great shock to me, since my farming was so intimately tied up with his unique archaic personality.

Since the farm cannot afford a man, we are now selling the animals. I'm not sure yet whether we shall sell the land. A beautiful dream finished.

My Uncle—the patriarch of my family and one of my dearest friends—also died, in March.

My psychological state, a close mesh of uncontrollable peculiarities & psychosomatic upsets, culminated about then. Finally, I decided the only thing was to drop everything and start writing my verse again. So now things show some signs of coming back under control.

I corrected our Pilinszky proofs—they are handsome. It seems to me a good book, a real book. Now we've started the machinations to get Pilinsky over here for the publication on August 25th. The Arts Council, Manchester University, The Critical Quarterly, and the publisher are joining forces, to apply what pressure they can to the Iron Mountain. Naturally, you will be an important part of what happens, so reserve yourself.

The uncle who had died was Walter Farrar.

To Charles Monteith

21 May 1976   Ms   Faber

Dear Charles,

Your note about a Yorkshire book came the day after I returned from up there thinking that I would now do what I thought of doing 5 years ago—a book of Yorkshire pieces, with photographs by Fay Godwin. After I'd vaguely suggested it to her, she went up there, became infatuated with the region—the S.W. corner—the old kingdom of Elmet—and is now the photographer of that whole area. (Our book never materialised.)

Just lately, I started composing odd Yorkshire pieces & the idea revived.

This isn't quite what you have in mind, I know. I just mention the coincidence.

Anyway, I'll work at these pieces & see what happens. If I can keep it to poems, it might be O.K. Once it moves onto autobiography and history I meet resistance—against giving away capital & the medicine bundle. Though no doubt there are ways of doing it.

'Gaudete' is ready now, pretty well, as far as it will ever be.

Yes, the title has exercised me, from the point of view of the customer in the shop who doesn't want to feel even very slightly a fool. Even when you have a pronunciation, there's still something odd about it. But it's stuck, as far as I'm concerned. The subtitle has always been 'An English Idyll'—but the irony of that seemed a bit precious.

The thing about incomprehensible words, of course, especially those which noone is quite certain how to pronounce (forgive me that line), is that once they've got through, and stuck, they're impossible to dislodge or dissolve. Don't you think so?

I'm inclined to stick with Gaudete. Until I hit on something which connects with the main image as properly.

According to these planets that I keep pestering you with, Season Songs is going to sell an unusually large number of copies. Is Faber prepared?

I'll let you know how things go. All the best meanwhile.

Yours

Ted

A rendering of some early church chant "Gaudete etc"—which they titled Gaudete—by the Steeleye Span group of musicians & singers— was top of the pops last year for a while. It is on a record of theirs called "Below the salt." It is worth buying. It has 2 or 3 of the most extraordinary old songs I ever heard. And Maddy Prior, their female voice, is absolutely the most thrilling singer I ever heard. Though I suppose you probably know her voice better than I do.

P.S. Somehow or other, I can't think how, I missed a verse out of the poem called "Hay", in Season Songs. If it can be inserted without too much fuss, I'll send it—for the time when it's possible. But it would mean going onto the next page. If it's very difficult, we'll leave it.

The photographer Fay Godwin (1931–2005) had only recently seen her first book published, but *The Oldest Road* (1975), a study of the Ridgeway in Berkshire, on which she worked with the writer J. R. L. Anderson, was an instant commercial success.

Steeleye Span's 'Gaudete', with its Latin lyrics, had been a surprise Christmas hit in 1973 and the band had performed it on the television programme *Top of the Pops*.

To Fay Godwin

4 July 1976   Ts   Estate of Fay Godwin

Dear Fay,

Your news shattered me. There is simply nothing to say or do but concentrate everything, and try to turn the current positive. It so happens, I've been close to two or three recoveries from that illness this year. It's one of the departments of fate where even the worst can suddenly reverse itself. If long term plans and activity can be part of that, then maybe there was something mysterious in the way our book suddenly resurrected and proposed itself. I'll outline how I think of it.

There are a few old pieces I've written from time to time, about that region, and my first idea was to collect those and add more. It all came up when my old Uncle came to stay with me—last of my mother's family except for a much younger Aunt, and a living archive of the Calder Valley, a really remarkable and eloquent fellow, mill-owner and the lot, and very close to me. His whole life at the end—in his eighties—was recounting the life of the whole region. And I thought I really must get what I can of what I grew up in there—because it is over now, with that generation. What is taking its place is utterly different, and a very strange world to me. But it is fascinating too.

So my first idea became an episodic autobiography—nothing connected. Just poems anchored in particular events and things. I don't know how much there might be, or what it will be like. But I know I do have an immense amount locked up in all that. At times it is overwhelming, when I try to release it. But I shall have to do something with it. The odd pieces I'm beginning to get look quite rich.

378

What grips me about the place, I think, is the weird collision of that terrible life of slavery—to work, cash, Methodism—which was an heroic life really, and developed heroic virtues—inside those black buildings, with that wilderness, which is really a desert, more or less uninhabitable. The collision of the pathos of the early industrial revolution—that valley was the cradle of it—with the wildness of the place. The terribleness of it was sealed by the First World War—when the whole lot were carted off and slaughtered, as a sort of ultimate humiliation and helplessness. So I grew up with the feeling that all those buildings were monuments to a great age and a great generation which was somehow in the past, and the people round me, my parents etc, were just survivors, toiling on and being religious and the rest of it, but really just hanging around, stupefied by what had happened. And as that generation finally died off—(my Uncle was the last surviving member of the King's Royal Rifles. My father is one of the last four Lancashire Fusiliers on the Yorks side of the border. So they say,) the whole region just fell to bits, the buildings collapsed, the walls collapsed, the chapels were sold for scrap and demolished, likewise the mills. A fellow called John Greenbank, was a farm-hand behind Heptonstall, became a demolisher and is now single-handed erasing the last 150 years. But that only makes what there still remains even more poignant for me. If only some of that could be caught in photographs—the way the primaeval reality of the region is taking over again from the mills, chapels, farms, pubs, bowling greens and cricket pavilions, pompous houses and rhodedendrons, walls and reservoirs, stonework of nineteenth century giants, and the black peculiarities of the three points of the triangle—Colne, Todmorden and Halifax. I realise now I was living in the last days of a Pompei.

But it was curious. When my brother walked over those hillsides with a gun he was the first person anybody had ever seen just wandering about free up there. He was regarded as an eccentric. Everybody else was clamped to his farm or to the valley bottom and convulsed with the ideals of toil. The great feeling there was that you were utterly free and alone—everybody else was at work and out of the way. It was as if I had the whole place to myself. I'd like to get something of that.

Now of course you can't walk five yards without meeting some idler, and you never see anybody working. So that great feeling of freedom is no longer there. It's a giant public park now, a sad and terrible museum.

I'm telling you all this to give you some idea of my feeling about the place. But as soon as you know when you can get up there, we'll try and arrange it to be up there together. If David Pease and his wife are away (they're just going to Spain) you could very likely stay with my Aunt—sweet lady, interesting.

I've been trying to find my copy of a book published last year called Millstone Grit, by Glyn Hughes. Did you see it. He came over from Lancashire and got interested in the Calder Valley, and now has a house there. Just his book about the region's history and his own sensations.

I'll send you some pieces as I get them together and typed. Though it will be just as fruitful for me to work the other way round too, work from your pictures—that is always a surprising stimulant.

Meanwhile, Fay, my warmest support,

yours
Ted

Fay Godwin's news was that she had been diagnosed with cancer. It was successfully treated.

To Daniel Huws

22 December 1976   Ms   Huws

Dear Dan,

I hope everything's going well. This has been a peculiar year for us. In February, Carol's father died—cancer—which left us farming full time. So I had the alternatives of hiring a man, or selling the cattle. The place earned just about enough to pay a man—but not enough to pay for his problems & the hassle. So all year we've been selling our cows & calves. [. . .]

So now we have the bare land, which at present we're renting out to neighbours. It seems quite likely I shall have to sell it to pay the Tax on Sylvia's earnings over the last 5 years.

Otherwise, everything goes on. Unloading the farm has left a great gap, much of which I filled with one folly or another, so I've written very little. I had a strong feeling of having come to the end of something, and not quite knowing how to get through to the next phase, assuming there is a next phase. But I wrote a fair amount over the last 2 or 3 years. One book coming out next year—a narrative in a kind of verse, about a changeling priest.

Much of the atmosphere of this last year has been decided by the latest wave of publications about Sylvia. I'm not at all sure how much that is affecting me, but it's affecting Carol quite a bit.

Sometimes I think I ought really to try and write it all out, as I've occasionally started doing, and then other times I ought to forget it, vanish, and start again somehow. I met a healer/spiritualist last week who told me to lie flat on the earth, splay out my arms and legs, and let it all go—release it into the astral. I feel she might be right. But then I feel you have to deal with it, too—if only to put an end to 'evasion'. What's certainly wrong is staggering along year after year, neither dealing with it nor letting it go, just getting older.

[. . .]

Frieda is 16, nearly offensively precocious, physically, and boy-mad. She is infatuated with a local motor-byke gang—mainly farm-hands and N.A.B. slobs. One of them bought her a crash-helmet—£42. Every time she goes out, she comes back with somebody else's leather-jacket crusted with badges—that's the way these youths bestow a favour, lend the girl their jacket. At school she's bored to death. Still writes unusual poetry—in fact that's developed a lot. Comes from the other personality—so I'm hoping this daft obvious one is only a phase. Lives in a fog of pop.

Nicholas is very tall, good scholar, still keeps his bees going, & spends all his time fishing & cycling. He's assembled a racing bike which cost alltogether £143. He sold nearly everything he possessed to get it. Now he's decided it's not good enough.

Met Danny the other day. It's quite wonderful how M.P.T. has put its roots down. He's in pretty good shape. Trying to get going as a publisher. M.P.T. to publish collections—big complete ones—of Popa, Herbert, & Holub. Meanwhile, he seems to be becoming a permanent U.S. fixture, in spite of his efforts to find a job over here. But he's all of a piece, & looks well.

I hear very occasionally from Luke—more often than he hears from me. He's writing plays. Danny says he's working quite concentratedly—had a conventional sort of comedy put on. Evidently he's aiming to write some popular success. I think he'd do better going his own way, but maybe he's trying to do both. Did you see his translations of Attila?

381

Xmas this year feels like redoubled imprisonment, for some reason. I feel like a complete change of circumstances, but there's less & less illusion that any change will change anything.

Enclosed is our Pilinszky translations—which I'm quite pleased with—except for the long rough ones.

I'm forgetting the biggest thing. I went to Joe's funeral. His liver collapsed. He'd a very bad last year, with repeated haemorraging & hospital. He took it all very bravely—very cheerful & plain. [. . .]

So that crams all the misfortunes into 1976, where they can be all sunk together on the 31st.

Love to Helga & all your family & to yourself

from Ted & Carol

The funeral was Joe Lyde's.

1977

Gaudete was published on 18 May.

To Keith Sagar

30 May 1977   Ts   British Library

Gaudete seems to me the best—both the narrative and the poems at the end. The narrative sketches a style of writing and a style of composition I would dearly like to be able to take further and make complete. At present Gaudete is a prototype—but not to be altered. The poems at the end seem to me about my furthest point so far, some of them. Even so, they leave me very unsatisfied.

So this whole batch of writing has an odd character for me—it looks provisional and interim. Probably because I did it when I was pre-occupied with farming and crises, that disrupted every line of thought or work.

The original film scenario of Gaudete—1964—is still extant. I haven't read it since. The subject was novel in 1964—charismatic priests, harem congregations, black magic or at least Old Religion magic in church precincts. But then of course it all became commonplace. I wish I'd kept cuttings of the priests who here or there came near to living out Lumb's situation. By 1972 I began to see what looked to me very like reminiscences of my story in other people's books—Fowles, Redgrove etc. I decided to write down the outline in simple summary form, just to stake my claim. I'd hit on that rough narrative verse—each line, ideally, a compressed paragraph—while I was writing a scenario of Burke and Wills. Once I started writing, I started to redream it, in various forms—in that way I got the whole notion of the two men, the real and the changeling, which I now see is full of potential. Also various small episodes, the bull-killing consecration of the non-man etc. I've probably told you all this.

Why an Anglican priest? How could that adventure happen to a Catholic?

The 'healing' refers to the task for which living men were carried away by spirits in various scots and Irish tales: sometimes to cure a sick person, usually to work some recovery on a woman, or deliver a child. What he actually did there is a whole separate possibility. Difficulty—if it is one—is to keep that distinct from continued Crow.

The consciousness of the original real Lumb and that of the changeling leak into each other, at times change places—a little of that in the Gaudete narrative. I didn't push it or develope it for its own sake because I wanted a story that (a) could somehow happen like that if the priest was eccentric enough (b) would rush from beginning to end with natural acceleration, like a runaway truck downhill—a small compact sequence, really a short story. Obviously, it could also have been a big sprawling fantasy of two worlds but I didn't want that.

Idea in the style was to crush an elemental dimension into the dead end of tea-cups, spectacles, bits of stone etc. I wanted the feeling of a collision—a disastrous one—between something unlimited and insatiable and something trapped and itself a trap, between a keen sense of something supernatural or at least unnatural going on while the actual world yields nothing but the commonplace visible surface of inert objects and the skins of people's faces. I don't confuse this at any point with dialogue—nobody says anything. If they do, it's indicated at a remove, as if it were the track of a fly on a window. That helped determine the style. Also part of it, a collision between a debased demonish spirit-power, in wood-goblinish form, and the sterile gentility of a Southern English village.

I wanted to suggest all that, and say nothing about it. No detail but what radiated the right feeling I've described. No explanation of cause and effect—just juxtapositions or symmetrical relationships.

Various bits and pieces that might seem 'difficult' seem to me right in the overall pattern. The goblin figure that gets into bed with Betty, for instance is a truant demon imitating Lumb and emanating from the tom-cat—he copulates with Betty's astral body, as it were. The changeling Lumb, plus his magical operations, is a doorway for the general influx of a debased demonish spirit-life—this is partly what has got control of the women. I don't say anything about this because that would be ridiculous and mechanical—and anyway it is only a way of speaking, a metaphor for feelings and energies that Lumb somehow evokes. The wolf-dream is part of what would have been a larger half of the scheme if the book had been leisurely and ample. That touches the circumstance that the consciousness of the women in this world—affected by Lumb—and that of the ailing one in the other world, the elemental one, also leak into each other. Usually it's just a whiff of the elemental one in this world, but in this case a reinterpreting dream image. But as I say, I didn't want anything of that that wouldn't work naturally into a 'realistic' sort of story—so I deliberately ignored the developments that kept trying to turn the main idea into a cosmology. I wanted to keep it to the dimension of the spirit-life of stones, rivers, starlings, rising and falling like little flames in a wet reluctant fire—sometimes there, sometimes just damp sticks. The way I think it really is.

The shift from Anglican to something like a tenth century anchorite in the West of Ireland surely has its meaning.

The fact that this—mistaken—summoning of spirit through sexual life of women is shot through the head also has a meaning I intended.

What interested me was to see if I could get all this into terms of cosy English village life, and the sort of people who live it.

It's also a story about English Maytime, about the doom and horror and otherworldliness of sexual life, a little bit.

Probably I abbreviated everything too much. But maybe not. It will take more than a few reviewers to unpick the codes. The main thing is, for it to stay alive and interesting.

Sagar's *The Art of Ted Hughes* had been out since August 1975, but TH's high rate of production meant that it was now out of date, and so Sagar had begun work on a second edition that would take into account *Season Songs*, *Gaudete* and *Cave Birds* – the context in which Hughes writes of *Gaudete* that it 'seems to me the best'. Sagar received a copy of this work in the spring of 1977 and over the summer studied it with friends and students.

The 'Burke and Wills scenario', which engaged TH for much of 1970, was never made into a film. The story of Robert Burke and William Wills's ill-fated attempt to journey across Australia and back has a kinship to that of *Voss,* the novel by Patrick White that TH admired exceptionally.

To John Greening

16 November 1977   Ms   Greening

Dear John Greening,

Sorry to have kept your 3 plays so long. I was interested to see them, and found much intrigueing stuff in them. I know what a near-impossible thing it is—to write a satisfactory drama in verse, to write satisfactory verse in a drama.

I hesitate to say anything about the plays as <u>plays</u>—because I know it needs a much more experienced eye than mine to judge the stage-effect of any piece of writing.

Within my experience, I discovered that written scenes were always too long, speeches were nearly always too long, and scenes which seemed to read naturally as dialogue became—on stage—interminable journeys on narrow rails. In other words, I learned that every half page had to contain the equivalent of a new dramatic surprise, a lump of action or its equivalent, and that in the marriage of words & action words had to be a Japanese wife, of sorts, to a frightening Samurai, an irrepressible hot-head.

But verse is a Greek or Italian wife—as a rule—to a demoralised defeated spouse. She can't stop. It's a tendency.

I don't know what the balance would be in your plays.

But the verse itself is interesting—the rough hold-all flexible quality of it is attractive. It seems to me ideal for the job.

Do you work with a group of actors? I'm sure it is the only way to learn. Nothing will educate one's natural wilfulness, in the business of writing dramatic scenes, except the mortification of seeing just how & why they fail to work, in front of an audience.

But the real power of a play is never in the language—though the language might make it a powerful poem. The dramatic power, it seems to me, is always in the action—generated by collisions, irreconcilable energies, thunderbolts from the malicious god of circumstance & fact, & the inability of events to foresee or avert their outcome. It is interesting, for instance, to analyse the first act of Othello, & add up the new themes, the new expectations, that are piled on top of each other—to create that colossal dramatic momentum.

The whole job is to make those energies real, to see through to the actuality behind forces that are merely imagined. Once you touch that actuality, I don't think it matters much how long the speeches are—that's where you feel the verse really has to be able to rise to the occasion.

I liked the Grey Wethers best—a very strong atmosphere & interesting blend of flavours.

I wish you the best of luck with your writing.

Yours
Ted Hughes

386

John Greening (b.1954) was then living in Devon and writing an MA thesis on verse drama. He had sent three of his own plays, one of them drawing on Dartmoor mythology and titled *Grey Wethers*, to TH for comment and advice. While none of the three has been performed, subsequent verse plays by Greening have.

To Gerald and Joan Hughes

28 November 1977   Ms   Emory

Dear Gerald & Joan,

Sorry to delay so long writing to you. Life has been very odd and confused lately. I'm going through a phase of feeling suffocated by the thousand daily demands—not an hour without a phone call, every morning three or four letters from people all wanting something. All wanting a day or three days of my time. Just declining somehow nevertheless entangles you. I feel like the bird that is perfectly free except for the tiny thread of nylon tying its leg to the post. But that's after a year of doing a great many readings—too many.

Henry Williamson died, & its his Memorial Service next week. I once read a sort of tribute to him, at a little celebration he had, & his daughters have asked if I'll read it again at the service. Which will mean rewriting it. They were making a film of his book Tarka the Otter while he was in hospital, and on the morning they filmed the death of Tarka Henry died.

Dad's O.K.—but the time is rapidly approaching when he'll no longer be able to live alone. He's in good form, on the whole. Just more & more vague. Gets up at 7 in the evening, sometimes.

Poked his electric fire (I suspect) and sent it up in flames last week.

It's very cold here—2″ of ice—white fields & hedges with frost. Big flocks of snipe & redwings already. So I must take him in to get a thicker suit.

Frieda's applying for Art School—she has some talent, enough to get in, real talent for design, unpredictable talent for a primitive style of painting—immune to education in art as in every other subject—which might turn out to her advantage. Her writing—of poems—seems to me phenomenal—I keep quiet about it even to myself—I can't quite believe it. Otherwise, she's a rather gorgeous dead-end kid. I go easy on her. She's very canny, at bottom, and very good—just tempestuous-wilful. Her mother plus Olwyn. 18 next April.

Nick is becoming a pretty good scholar—took his O level maths a year early and got an A. Very high marks in everything. He's still a fanatic cyclist—moreso than ever. And his mania for pike-fishing had its reward. We went to Ireland, & this pal of mine over there—angling fanatic—went with us onto some beautiful lakes in Clare. This is 3 weeks ago. Nick had talked everybody sick about the 25 pounder he was going to catch. Going over, he couldn't sleep for excitement, but dozed just enough to dream of catching mighty pike. First day, we caught a few smallish ones. So that night, he re-prepared & replanned his tactics & dreamed again about mighty pike. Next day, we caught a few more small to medium. So that night, he regrouped, & planned a fresh approach, then dreamed about mighty pike. Next day—beautiful day on a spectacular lake—he fished with the old green-heart rod you bought me long ago, and a 19th Century reel (a classic, I picked it up in a heap of junk) and hooked a huge fish. It took him 15 minutes to get it to the surface. The handles bent on his reel. He burst all the blisters on his hands (from 2 days rowing). Finally we got it out. Exactly 25 lbs. Biggest pike alive I've ever seen. Our Irish pal had only ever seen one bigger, & he'd caught thousands. We put it back, after war-dances & celebrations on a lovely green island in the middle of the lake. Nick is now hooked on Ireland. We had a marvellous time.

Otherwise, everything goes on. We're thinking of getting a few sheep to take the winter grass down, on the farm. If we let it, the hedges get trampled flat, the grounds overstocked etc.

The latest boom in antiques has been stripping the old pine furniture. Common or garden old kitchen table with a drawer now—stripped—brings £100 or more. Our ex-bobby friend has two giant cattle buildings crammed with stuff—multi-millionaire in 6 years. Desperate incessant holidays in Tennerife & the Bahamas, trying to get rid of his cash. Ships containers full to the U.S.—mostly Victorian rubbish. But handles so much—and in among it so much expensive stuff too—that he's going mad with money, almost.

Don't see much in the way of weapons. Quite a while since we bought anything. There's something in owning the minimum. Pity we can't buy time.

You should have come over & played at farming. Interesting life. I hate the feeling that certain dreams are fizzling out—in exchange for what.

Nicky keeps me up to the mark. He's wanting a boat now for our fishing trips—so no doubt we'll be getting a boat. He's an unusual talent for forcing his dreams to materialise. He just goes straight ahead—very concentrated & dogged, with no doubts about the outcome.

He's become a physical culturist. I bought him a bullworker & now he tells me his strength has increased 50% in seven weeks.

Carol is in goodish form—still missing the farm. She's ordered Sexton (our bull) back—when the farmer who's got him has finished with him (3 years up this next year.) She's transforming the grounds at present, & planning to convert the barn to one great room.

I ignore the political/economic mess. I found no problems in Ireland. (2 of my best friends over there are as entangled politically in the trouble as can be). I concentrate on making the most of what I can plunder, & salvage, & produce.

How are the happy newlyweds? Love to everybody from us

Ted

Henry Williamson had died on 13 August.

To Frieda Hughes

[Undated 1977]   Ms   Emory

Dear Frieda,

I didn't post your story today. I thought it would be better if I went through a few pages of it in detail—so you would really get a feeling of what I meant on the phone.

When you get going—and especially when there's lots of collision between the characters,—you manage it often very well indeed. The surprising oddity of the reactions & remarks is very good. And the natural flow.

But between times, where there's some slightly complicated bit of business, which isn't dramatic, & yet has to be got through, you lose interest, & your sentences tend to become careless.

(1) Remember: when you get to one of those sticky patches—for instance, bottom paragraph on page 1—the best thing, always, is to break it up into small units. Make each small unit interesting & vital in itself. Not necessarily by descriptive detail—maybe by dramatic juxtaposition. And make it brief.

That's a thing to practise: <u>dramatic juxtaposition</u>.

(2) When you get to a sticky passage it may be sticky because <u>it doesn't really belong</u>. That whole first page, for instance, doesn't really belong. It bores you.

Sometimes, in your writing, you get too closely interested, and involved, with something that's not really necessary to the story. Watch that. It always produces a tangled bit of careless writing.

(3) Imagine reading the story to a listener. Always imagine your listener. Then you'll feel instantly where something is too much, & doesn't fit.

You'd also realise, very often, how <u>little</u> it needs to convey quite a big piece of the narrative.

(4) <u>Most important</u> (1) Practise—just a paragraph at a time—copying writing, as I showed you that evening. Raymond Carver is good— because he's simple, clear, & very dramatic. And probably right for you. And you like him. (2) <u>Practise</u> reading aloud. Take a Carver story and read it—quietly to yourself, but aloud—as if to a listener. <u>Read every sentence as a separate musical speech unit</u>. Nothing will teach you more thoroughly to recognise sharp writing. Clean effective sentences.

Don't be too dismayed by all my corrections. Once you've grasped the dramatic shape of your sentences (<u>by reading aloud</u>) and recognised the difference between sharp and dull in language, you'll be very far on.

Love, Daddy (I have spent thousands of hours reading aloud)

P.S. I'm enclosing a book: read the 1st chapter & the Writing a Novel chapter—Writing about people.

The story in question has not been identified.

1978

To Peter Redgrove

[Undated 1978]   Ms   Sheffield

Dear Peter—
   Just a note.
   I read The Wise Wound in one sitting. <u>First impressions</u> are—it is the most important book about The Goddess since Graves' White Goddess, & <u>more</u> important in that it roots the whole story in physiology, & lifts it from status of vestigial remains of lost, archaic, external things (where he tends to leave it, after all) & sets it in the closest present & the inevitable future—and does so with truly convincing power & sweep. Really does make it the one & only story.
   Also, it provides a convincing physiological basis—a living, creative basis—for much of the mythologizing of Jungians, who have defined & recorded the doings of their archetypes, without seeming to feel the need to locate them properly in essential physiology. In crucial physiology.
   Also, it is far & away the most convincing & persuasive re-establishment of the real dignity & sacredness of woman, therefore of all processes belonging to her & related to her, therefore of real spirit & real nature, that I've read—in the general accumulating case against St Paul's madhouse State.
   It's a more startling, more powerful, eloquent book than I expected. Then again, I don't know what I expected.
   The first chapter is the hardest—not quite easy to read, impression of much rewriting & reshaping. But the rest of the book goes with a bang—each chapter seems whole & smooth and—to me—totally convincing. My only doubt—that small last chapter.
   I think I see which are your parts, which are Penelope's—both are equally rivetting. Between you, you do what no other book on these topics can ever begin to do—you speak 'from the inside', as if from a 'lived' knowledge, rather than an 'academic' knowledge—very important in the effect the book has on a reader's imagination. In other

words—you make big imaginative impact, in imaginative terms, without ever seeming amateurish or negligent in your concern for the scientific evidence—& a proper scepticism.

Your tact, in your attitude to the practitioners & specialists, with whom you argue, seems perfect.

What it opens to women (libbers or not) is a vista of the kingdom where they rule by right of their sex, which is the very thing they have been persuaded to relinquish, the very thing they most intimately know & are most intimately burdened with—what a shock for them, to realise, as they read, that the dreadful leaden burden is after all pure gold—with historical, physiological proof.

With luck, I think it might take off as a <u>real</u> cult book, a genuine revelation book. And that will be good for everybody, as well as incidentally yourselves. Anyway, it's long-term effect will be tremendous.

Also, it provides real system for your poetry—which will all read quite differently now.

Love to you both
& to Zoe
Ted

I've lent it to a friend—very fierce U.S. Women's Libber. I'll read it again when I get it back, & let you know my second reactions. But no matter how well you've done the job, it will take <u>time</u> to work on the established system of attitudes & assumptions—probably several years. Probably only a new generation—young girls—etc—will be able to grow up into it. That's usual after all. You aren't going to overthrow such a mightily successful taboo in one bout. So look out for dismissive reactions. But what a pity you didn't use this book to get your poetry taken on by some big U.S. house. However, I'm sure you'll produce a follow-up. I find it an exciting book. And your own excitement in the ideas is not a little of its effect & power.

In either late 1977 or early 1978, Redgrove and Shuttle sent TH a page proof of *The Wise Wound* (1978), their pioneering study of menstruation in anthropological, psychological and poetic terms. TH also saw and approved a final chapter, 'The Menstrous Traveller', which looks at Sylvia Plath's menstrual imagery, but it was never included in the book.

Zoe is Redgrove and Shuttle's daughter.

To Frieda Hughes

17 May 1978   Ms   Emory

T.S. Eliot said to me "There's only one way a poet can develope his actual writing—apart from self-criticism & continual practice. And that is by reading other poetry aloud—and it doesn't matter whether he understands it or not (i.e. even if its in another language.) What matters above all, is educating the ear."

What matters, is to connect <u>your own voice</u> with an infinite range of verbal cadences & sequences—and only endless actual experience of your ear can store all that in your nervous system. The rest can be left to your life & your character.

To Keith Sagar

7 August 1978   Ms   British Library

Dear Keith,

Sorry I couldn't get over to you. I was in a more than usual dash— my brother's here from Australia, which has foreshortened the day somewhat.

I meant to tell you in my last note. I thought your dream-story was very <u>impressive</u>. Quite convincing, interestingly & well written, and <u>unforgettable</u>.

How do you interpret it?

The beast is, I imagine, among other things, your original being in all its undeveloped aspects—primitive & still out of this world aspects. The great stakes in its head were probably—among other things—all the theories & ideas, derived from your reading etc, about this original self, which are not natural to it—i.e. have not developed naturally out of it, but have been imposed on it by you, in your thinking about yourself. These were a torture to it, a false head-load, a false crown.

The fact that you took these out—that you were able to find the beast & take those terrible stakes out, means—among the other things— that you have inwardly come to an understanding of the artificiality & wrongness of those notions, & have inwardly—by some inward change—removed them. Rejected & rubbished them. The beast weeps, because you have released him from these misunderstandings, which

393

were like monstrous electrodes of imposed signals, having nothing to do with his real truth, & because you have, by implication, recognised his real nature, & are concerned for it.

The next dream in the series he will not be blind, & probably won't even be a beast.

Interpreted like this, it records a big change in your life—the transition from an intellectualised steerage (and mismanagement) of your real power [*marginal insertion:* which actually immobilised it—'froze up' your life in some way.], to a phase in which, we hope, it will reveal its true direction & possibilities, under your understanding respect. Propitious dream. Though it depends how you follow it up in your behaviour.

No doubt there are other interpretations. But I think it's important to interpret dreams—if at all possible—positively. And this dream is so general, it seems quite clearly good.

All the best

Ted

Sagar tells the story of his dream, in which he encounters a 'great Elk-like beast', eyeless, seemingly dead and yet not, in 'A Poet and a Critic', his contribution to *The Epic Poise: A Celebration of Ted Hughes* (1999). He speaks there of the dream's resemblance to TH's story 'The Head', which the magazine *Bananas* included in its Summer 1978 issue.

To Terence McCaughey

[Summer 1978]   Ms   British Library

I'm looking for a copy of Carmina Gadelica—is there one in the University Library there? It seems to be very rare. I just can't find it.

I'm doing an Anthology of poetry for children—with Seamus Heaney—and I remember there were wonderful charms, prayers, spells etc in that book—I'm sure it was that book. Just the sort of thing we want. If you have a copy there, he could come in & go through it.

Also, what is "The Sorrows of the Deer"?

Also, is there any supply of poems etc anything resembling the piece Yeats & Lady Gregory did together: "It is late last night the dog was speaking of you" etc—ending "you have taken the moon, you have taken the sun from me, and my fear is great you have taken God from me." He (Yeats) calls it an Aran song.

TH and Seamus Heaney were gathering poems for the Faber anthology that was to be published in 1982 as *The Rattle Bag*, with a number of poems from the Gaelic included in it. 'The Deer's Cry', St Patrick's hymn, which the Celtic scholar Kuno Meyer translated and to which TH seems to be referring, was not included. The translation of 'Donal Og', the 'Aran song', is attributed in *The Rattle Bag* to Lady Augusta Gregory alone.

To Neil Roberts and Terry Gifford

29 October 1978   Ts   Roberts and Gifford

Dear Neil Roberts and Terry Gifford,

Thank you for the copy of your chapter on Cave Birds. You are indeed on the right lines and I'm very grateful for your quick appreciation of the nicer points, and of the particular blend of styles in which the thing is cast.

At one point (I don't know whether I mentionned this in my letter) I subtitled it The Death Of Socrates and his Resurrection in Egypt—with some idea of suggesting that aspect of it which is a critique of sorts of the Socratic abstraction and its consequences through Christianity to us. His resurrection in Egypt, in that case, would imply his correction, his re-absorption into the magical-religious archaic source of intellectual life in the East Mediterranean, and his re-emergence as a Horus—beloved child and spouse of the Goddess.

I cancelled that subtitle because I thought it was simply too 'curious-good'. Better if the poem operates without historical confinements or scholarly-pedantic baggage. I left in Alchemical because I did feel it needed some clue—knowing how nine readers out of every learned or poetic-professional ten will read it just as a string of arbitrary images, when in fact I put it together as deliberately as a clock.

Composing it had an extraordinary effect on me, mentally and physically—I wish I could guarantee the same effect for understanding readers.

Just one or two comments: After The First Fright is crude—at one point I replaced it—but I put it back. It has a kind of intactness, and it serves a purpose in the whole pattern. The crudity and deliberate numbness of the language is a metaphor of the real subject (I think style in verse usually is—or becomes in writing—a metaphor for the prevailing idea-mood, and it's impossible to feel the poem has reached a final

form until that has happened. It's a natural sort of mimicry, I suppose.).
The real subject here is the crude and degenerated state of the mutual
understandings between what is desirable and required, and what is
inescapably and blindly undergone. 'Civilisation' and 'Sanity' are vari-
able terms, according to what is desirable and required. What is 'desir-
able' and 'required' to what is truly suffered? In Cave paintings, there
exist many stencil outlines of hands lacking fingers, one two or more.
These are widespread. And in various surviving primitive societies, one
of the 'requirements' of mourning, is that the mourner loses a finger.
It is evidently a spontaneous instinctive 'requirement'—at a time of
bereavement. One would hesitate to call it 'civilised' or 'sane', but
where it exists, as a custom, it is a required and (by everybody else in the
society) desirable thing to do. It is part of the coherent, balanced, suc-
cessfully adapted system by which those societies manage life and their
world.

In the same way, the 'cross-shaped cut' is, or was, required and desir-
able in Japanese society in certain circumstances. Part of the fascination
of Hara-kiri is our recognition of what it implies—an ultimate confron-
tation of the real pain of pain, a deliberate, controlled translation of
psychological pain into physical pain, the absolute acceptance of pain
on its own terms. In that sense, it is an act not only of absolute courage,
but of absolute honesty. It is the symbolic act of the acceptance of the
reality of what hurts. It is part of the reverence—in that case not short of
worship—for the reality of inner experience.

The basic situation in this poem, as you'll have seen, is one of
those mediaeval disputations—but as in Rabelais and in some folk-tales
one side is a pedagoguic (that can't be spelt right) fool and the other
is a wise clown. One comes out with theological riddles, in crushing
scholastic terms, and the other replies with obscene caperings, ludicrous
non-sequiturs, profane body-talk, which turn out to be superior sense.

Next point concerns THE ACCUSED, and the term 'blood-
aberration'. There is a sense in which the 'guilt' which is here—
throughout—being judged is the guilt innate and incorporated in physi-
cal life—it is the guilt of the extraverted, beady-eyed, predatory career
of the organism making its way, clearing its space and setting up its fort
and satisfying its needs. It is the guilt of the ordinary life of the human
being up to thirty. Up to that age the organism is focussed for survival,
and the biological reinforcements are at the full. After thirty, the bio-
logical requirements have been met, the species has reproduced, and I

expect for millions of years that was the optimum age of survival. After that, decay starts and we are living a posthumous life: psychological and spiritual complexity sets in and suddenly we have to meet the bill for the actions and experiences of our first thirty years. At that point, so to speak, my drama starts. In this sense, The Summoner is our own body—our guardian companion up to the point where he becomes, gradually or suddenly, the one who arrests and brings to judgement.

Next point, in Walking Bare, concerns 'corolla'. The Corolla is the ring of flames round the sun. These are flames actually falling into the sun—the space-gas is being sucked into the sun from all sides, and as it approaches the surface it becomes incandescent. The idea is that my protagonist, on his journey, is finally approaching the crucible of the source, and now comes under its pull and begins to brighten with its power, into which he is about to fall and be dissolved. This union of questing soul and re-creative source corresponds to the union of the male and female in the poem following.

The Owl Flower, then, is also the crucible itself, the sun, the bird of flames, into which the dead Osiris sails in his coffin, the dry seed, and from which he is reborn as Horus the Falcon, or into which the questant sinks deadlocked still in his insoluble problem and from which he emerges in a form that surmounts it.

Behind this poem, I should say, is a memory of The Conference Of The Birds—twelfth Century Persian Poem by Fariq Ud-din Attar (Routledge publish it—a really beautiful book) which I worked on for a year with Peter Brook and his actors. The poem tells the story of the birds who set out to find the Simurgh—God. They are led by a Hoopoe. After adventuring through seven valleys of trial, their numbers are reduced to thirty. These thirty birds meet the Simurgh—but Simurgh means 'thirty birds'. In other words, after the inner transformations, induced by their ordeals, the questing birds meet their real selves, their sacred selves, their spiritual selves who are one with their creator.

I hope all this hasn't confused the issue. But I wanted to add a note or two to those points.

Adam And The Sacred Nine also has some memory of The Conference of the Birds, I dare say, but only hints. I don't know that any supporting story exists for that sequence.

All the best
yours
Ted Hughes

Neil Roberts and Terry Gifford were working on *Ted Hughes: A Critical Study*, to be published in 1981. *Cave Birds*, which is subtitled 'An Alchemical Cave Drama' and which had first appeared in 1975, in a Scolar Press edition of 125 copies, was now available in a trade edition.

The phrase 'too curious good' is from Shakespeare's *The Rape of Lucrece*.

'Civilisation', 'Sanity' and 'cross-shaped cut' are all terms in the book's third poem, 'After the First Fright'. 'The Summoner' is the second poem in the book.

By 'Fariq Ud-din Attar' TH means Farid ud-Din Attar. The Routledge translation of *The Conference of the Birds* is by A. J. Arberry (1966).

To Mark Hinchliffe

[November 1978]   Ms   Hinchliffe

Dear Mark,

Thanks for your letter. I'm sending this picture of your grandfather back—I'm sure you value it, & I'm afraid I shall lose it in the mass of loose papers that follows me around. Thanks for letting me see it.

Did you see the T.V. film about the Somme the other night? The writer Henry Williamson, who died recently, (you should read his war-books) knew about the incredible depth of the German Trenches <u>before the battle</u>, and nobody would believe it mattered. After the initial bombardment, of course, the Germans all bobbed up unharmed. It mattered then.

Interesting—what you say about 'Shamanism'. Odd that you say it's obsolete—or anachronistic. The body produces secretions, of various sorts, to counter physical crises. The mind & nervous system produce certain openings of psychic energy, which have standard features. Such things are not built into any century—they are built into the genes.

A very powerful healer near here—80% success even with such things as Leukaemia—went through the whole shamanic process in great detail. He's a simple man, in that he's read very little—or had read very little when it happened. Very interesting life, & loves talking about it. His 'Shamanism' is just 5 centuries ahead of 20th Century medecine, not 5 centuries behind.

I wanted to write straight off to get this photo back to you.

Yours
Ted H.

As a schoolboy in Huddersfield, West Yorkshire, Mark Hinchliffe heard TH reading and immediately began collecting all the books by him that he could get hold of. His first letter to TH was written while he was still at school. Partly with TH's poem 'Six Young Men' in mind, he had sent a First World War photograph of his grandfather, sitting on a horse, in the uniform of a gunner in the West Yorkshire Regiment.

Hinchliffe had grown interested in shamanism through TH's work, and that of Carlos Castaneda, but had assumed that the practice was a thing of the past. The local healer was Ted Cornish, whose powers impressed TH so much that he recommended him to sick friends (see letters to Daniel Weissbort of 23 October 1983 and to Philip Larkin of 21 November 1985, among others), energetically promoted his reputation and later tried, without success, to get a book about him published.

To Richard Murphy

[November 1978]   Ms   Tulsa

Dear Richard,

Nice to see you after all this time. Here is Cave Birds—more for some tastes than others. It had a strange penetrating effect on me, writing it—even though it was a commissioned task.

Our Anthology is knocking along—I'm proposing several things from the Murphy canon. Reading through it all again, closely, within 8 or 9 days of reading through & glancing into all the books of poetry published from 1920 onward, from Z backward through the Alphabet to L, at that dauntingly crammed mausoleum the Poetry Society or Arts Council Poetry Library, I was struck how your things stand up, stay fresh, grow stronger—and in general stand apart. I was also struck how so much that's been published seems so temporary & corruptible—so locked into some cliquish silly mannerism, so diffuse & temporary, already so dated & empty. Even some books published within the year—you see how they draw all their life from their immediate cultural medium, almost their newspaper accompaniment. There's really very little that's finally any good. Even some authors I quite liked faded a bit during my mass exposure—Mackay Brown I liked very much, but somehow suddenly it seems mannered & blurred.

I suppose you concede far more to a book alone in your hands after a week of no reading than you do to the same extricated with great muscular effort from jammed shelves of competitors, then read in haste among a hurry of others.

I'm trying to get going, as ever, on various half-started things—but for some astrological reason we've been swamped by visitors, and even now more are stacking themselves in the offing—long lost friends from far off places, who have nowhere to go, & who I want to see.

Your idea of the tinker story has haunted me. You've the unique chance there to make something unique.

The little book Moon-Bells was just a gathering of odd bits & pieces. The passages about the fox-hunt, the birth of the calf Rainbow, & the dead badger, are from the farm diary I told you about. Chatto asked me to do a children's book for their series—and with great reluctance Charles permitted it.

Keep well

as ever
Ted

In the event, *The Rattle Bag* included a single poem by Murphy, 'Pat Cloherty's Version of *The Maisie*' – which in a letter to Murphy of 6 December 1974 TH had called 'an unalterably final piece of writing . . . among my few favourite contemporary poems' – and two by George Mackay Brown (1921–96).

Moon-Bells (1978) was a book of poems for children, published by Chatto & Windus.

To Adrian Mitchell

[November/December 1978]   Ts   Mitchell

Dear Adrian,

This last week I was sitting every day in the poetry Library at the Arts Council going through every book that showed any likelihood of producing a poem for the Anthology For Younger Readers that somehow I've got myself into compiling along with Seamus Heaney. I started at Z (do you know Zabolotsky—Cape Editions? If you don't, you've a great beautiful surprise coming. My favourite Russian poet.) So I was trekking for days up through the densely impacted Ys and the insuperably ranked Ws—going very swiftly birdlike over the tops of their heads for the most part, and on and on, through stupefying deserts of petrified hyena turds, occasional palm, occasional blessed oasis, but in the very slow dawning light of how incredibly alike it all is somehow. In Japan they are Japanese, and among the Alacaluf there was not one lifting of the finger that was not supersaturated Alacaluf. That's how modern poetry is modern poetry. I got to glancing out into those vast regions across those mighty forests of inhabitable planets

400

where modern poetry does not at all happen, never lifts its whisper, never ventures even in capsule, and after all those are the very regions where everybody breathes and lives. Very strange experience, squeezing every morning into modern poetry, and sitting in there all day all curled up with book clamped over mouth inhaling deeply, then coming out in the five or six oclock dark onto Piccadilly again.

Anyway, that went on until I came to The Apeman Cometh, which for some evil reason I have completely missed up to now. I was so overjoyed by that book I swore I would write you a fan letter before the impulse cooled. It was such a relief, such a liberation, and it is so good.

So I came home and here is your letter waiting for me.

I must say, though, I still want to write my fan letter. I liked a lot in your earlier books, they freed me in all sorts of ways. But this book seems a whole new phase, a whole new bigger overdrive control of all your spirits—and all of a piece, intact and solid, no fumbling and no tinkering fiddle, solid and round like indestructible folk-rhyme. Anyway, it's the first book for a long time that's made me wish it was four times as long.

If May 11th is not something I've already promised, or within school holidays, yes I'd like to take part.

If you hire a hall, and invite many schools to send their O and A level enthusiasts, 25£ per school, the gate might add up. Maybe my things aren't on the East Anglia O and A. But you could try it. I raised a lot of money for Arvon doing that.

I mentionned this Festival to John Fairfax who I met at a meeting of the Arts Council Meeting the other day, and who is George Barker's nephew. I think. And a close friend of his. He thought there might be a danger of Barker reacting to the charity tone of this enterprise, no matter how much he agrees with it at the start. As if he might in the end find himself humiliated. That might be bullshit.

It struck me, though, that this would have been an occasion to start an annual Eistedfodian style Festival to raise cash for some general Fund for poets over sixty. The cash could then be given <u>as a grant</u>—a mini Nobel. I imagine few poets would challenge the Fates by refusing to take part. It might become a joyful airborne jamboree like that first International Festival in 67. Once it got established, a charity, I fancy it would be a magnet for all kinds of donations. An Annual event. This first year could have given everything to Barker.

There'd have to be a committee of wise young men to be sure it didn't go to Civil Servants retired at forty five who take up the pen at fifty nine.

Do you think there's anything in the idea—not so much for this Festival, which you've probably already got moving, but for some future launching?

I think a regular Festival of that sort could tap both the Arts Council and those loaded branches of Government that drop their reluctant usually by that time withered Civil List Pensions.

This is a slight modification of your £5,000 a year idea.

It's marvellous to hear you're so productive and in spate—that's the rewards for striking oil, which you have done.

love

Ted

TH gives no date, but this must have been written between two letters from the poet Adrian Mitchell (1932–2008), dated 26 November 1978 and 7 December respectively. The first had invited TH to read at a festival, an incidentally mooted purpose of which was to raise funds for George Barker, whose indigence was widely known.

Three poems by Mitchell were to be included in *The Rattle Bag*, and three by N. A. Zabolotsky (1903–58), the latter in translations by Daniel Weissbort. Mitchell's *The Apeman Cometh* was from 1975.

1979

By the beginning of the year, *Remains of Elmet* was with Faber and Faber and on its way to publication in May, while *Moortown* would appear on 1 October. TH was now busy with a number of highly diverse projects that included the poems for *Under the North Star*, which had been prompted by a visit to Leonard and Lisa Baskin's place in Maine, in the autumn of 1978, and the libretto for Richard Blackford's opera *The Pig Organ*, required for a production at the Roundhouse in Camden Town, London NW1, in 1980. Less publicly, he was also, as he notes in a journal, 'writing daily one passage of memories of S' – presumably Sylvia Plath.

Lake fishing had become an increasing obsession, and in July he took his son Nicholas on a unique holiday to Iceland.

To Terry Gifford and Neil Roberts

26 February 1979   Ms   Gifford and Roberts

Dear Terry Gifford & Neil Roberts,

Thank you for the typescript. I don't know whether I ought to read it—anyway, I shan't be able to for a week or two.

The point you made about 'corolla' in the poem in Cave-Birds is quite right. Technically, it should be corona. I expect I was seduced into 'corolla' by the underlying image of 'flower', and was effectively repelled from 'corona' by that word's more immediate associations—which are more than discordant—and by the element of hardness in it. So even now, fully awakened to what I've done there, I prefer to leave it as it is. Corolla in fact is just what I want there. If it were absolutely wrong technically, I still wouldn't use 'corona'—I'd have to do something else. Many thanks though for drawing my attention to it.

There is a latent conflation of corolla & corona, anyway, in the courtship of 'l' & 'n', as in the image of sun's flame-ring & flower's petals.

Yours

Ted Hughes

Between TH's letter to them of 29 October 1978 and this one, Gifford and Roberts had written to say that they were 'still confused' by TH's use of 'corolla' in the poem 'Walking Bare'.

To Philip Larkin

20 March 1979   Ms Hull

Dear Philip,

We're trying to raise money for the Arvon Foundation, which has a big indigestible debt. Just in case you haven't heard of Arvon, I'm enclosing the brochures—(maybe you could display them somewhere in the library.)

It's belatedly dawned on us that a good way to cancel some of our debt is by holding one of these Poetry Competitions for a big prize.

We quieten our sentimental conscience—with reference to the Athenian Prizes for Tragedy, the huge prizes at Celtic poetry contests in the good old days, Shakespeare's £1,000 for Venus & Adonis, etc. Fairly easily done.

Will you be a judge—along with Seamus Heaney & Charles Causley? Fee £350.

I know you don't do this sort of thing much—but I wanted to ask you before trying elsewhere.

The work is not all that much—the real rubbish would be sorted out first, before you start. And even for the rest, as you know, a glance is enough for 99·9 percent.

Look forward to hearing from you.

All the best meanwhile,

yours
Ted

I wrote you a fan letter recently—after seeing 'Aubade' in that U.S. poetry review. Then I thought you must be sick of fan letters. But I still think that's a really great poem—an event. I can't get it out of my mind.

For TH's association with the Arvon Foundation, see his letter to Ruth Fainlight and Alan Sillitoe of January 1974. Appeals to Athenian and Celtic precedents did not put off Philip Larkin, who joined the team of judges. If TH first saw Larkin's poem 'Aubade' in a 'U.S. poetry review', he must have missed it when the *Times Literary Supplement* scooped it in 1977.

To Donya Feuer

[Undated 1979]   Ts (Photocopy)   Emory

Dear Donya,

Sorry for the long delay, after my promise. The truth is, I've been at a loss just how to write. After saying I'd give you my ideas about Measure For Measure, I wasn't at all sure that my ideas were really worth communicating.

As a Director, you have to treat the play as—in a sense—a sacred text, in that you have that and only that to work on, and somehow or other you have to turn the whole thing to account, you have to treat even the apparent shortcomings of the thing as enigmas from which theatrical treasure can be extracted. Your attitude to every part of it has to be positive and creative.

Once actors, in particular, lose faith in the text—feeling that it has built in weakness or inadequacy—it is very difficult for them, in my experience, to bring real creative confidence to it. Therefore I was hesitant, in writing back to you, because I am full of doubts about the 'theatrical' adequacy of this particular play. I imagine that one of the reasons it is called a 'problem play', is that it is nearly impossible to stage in a way that will move and satisfy an audience—though it is in itself, in other ways, a manifestly fascinating work.

However, I imagine you are now so far on with the production, that any negative criticism of mine, about the play, will be harmless, with no chance of confusing you on the tightrope of your interpretation.

Negative first.

I feel the 'failure' of the play, as a work of art, derives from one main source, which is this. While Shakespeare set out to write one kind of play, selecting the plot and imagining the characters accordingly, he was surprised by the emergence, from his own mind, of a whole new body of emotional/imaginative matter which that type of plot and that mould of character was unfitted to deal with. And that happened here, because this play comes, in the series, between the two main phases of Shakespeare's work—between the early period of histories and comedies, and the middle period of mature tragedies. The transition was sudden, and the technical apparatus of the former, with the emotional/imaginative content of the latter, collide in Measure for Measure.

Up to this point, Shakespeare had mastered two main forms—the

405

history style of play and his particular brand of comedy. He pushed the history form as far as it would go, in Troilus & Cressida, and the comedy form as far as it would go, in All's Well. Whatever problems these plays pose a producer, they are satisfying works of art in that the actual matter and the expressive form are all one, and work together.

The form of the comedies, right up to All's Well, is roughly the same: courtly aristocrats permutate ingenious operatic relationships, with much switching of sexes and mistaking of identities and criss-crossed love-mismatches. Genial low life comic characters, often with comic Dickensian names (Belch, Aguecheek etc) are interwoven.

This line showed more scope for development than the histories. In Romeo and Juliet it managed tragedy, and in All's Well it controlled a new metaphysical complexity and inwardness, without losing its essential form. In All's Well the intricate plot is of the same kind, essentially, as the earlier comedies: operatic ingenious artificiality, with the same elements, and the same mannered courtiers whose pretensions are judged finally, and unmasked, by true love.

Measure for Measure is usually put after Hamlet—1604 to Hamlet's 1602, and certain passages of verse (But man, proud man, and Be absolute for death) seem to me post-Hamlet. But actual order of writing does not always correspond with actual place in inward development. The emergence of works of art way out of sequence in the progress of a developing artist's work is one of the mysteries. Usually, the anomaly is a work far in advance of what the artist is currently producing, a work that anticipates a much later stage of development. But sometimes artists regress to earlier phases—especially after a long absence from work, as a kind of recapitulation. Whether Hamlet is an example of an out of phase precursor of later things, or Measure For M. is a recapitulation of earlier things, does not really matter. The fact is that in true artistic succession, M for M follows All's Well. The affinities are very close, in plot details, and in mould of character. And there are certain things in All's Well that look like the larval form of certain things in M for M. The King's fistula, in All's Well, is the first sign of the corruption that, in M for M, has mined through the whole society. In M for M the Duke blames his own laxity for this general malady, and the plot hinges on his attempt to find a desperate cure. The obscene sinister Parolles seems to me very akin to the more openly depraved Lucio. And it is this character, in both plays, who in an odd way carries most life. It is the one character who belongs equally to both high and low life. Anyway, all that is academic. The affinities between the two plays are endless. All's Well is the honest, likeable albeit ailing elder brother of the darker, introverted, crippled and psychotic M for M.

And the point of all this is to establish that M for M is, in plan, a comedy of the first phase. That is, the plot is an artificial 'operatic' geometry of interchanging places, a clockwork symmetry of logic that suggests the formality of a court dance. That was worked out before he set pen to paper, as is quite clear. And the characters were cast in a corresponding mould—clearly imagined, again, before he set pen to paper. So, before he began to write, the mistakes were made.

Once a dramatist has made his decision to use a certain plot, he is stuck with its limitations whether he likes it or not. And once he has imagined certain characters, he has to go through with them. If it begins to dawn on him that something else is emerging from the depths of the plot, for which his characters are inadequate, then it needs a whole new start, a re-casting of the whole imaginative structure, a re-feeling and re-inventing, before he can re-imagine the characters differently, re-aligned by the new material. Novelists and playwrights who take a year to write the work can do this, but in those days things were different. Ben Jonson was a laughingstock because he took three months over a play. One anecdote mentions a playwright—unnamed—who wrote his plays straight off in three days. And plays in those days did not have to meet the massive judgement of history, as they do nowadays. They were performed a couple of times and lost. And it's clear too that Shakespeare didn't invest a tremendous amount of ego in his works. He evidently did not regard them as life-statements—as Bacon might have regarded his Advancement of Learning, or Hobbes his Leviathan, or, a little later, as Milton regarded Paradise Lost. Each of his plays was an experiment: he sets up the apparatus, introduces the ingredients and procedure, and sees how far they will take him. If it fails, he's not too concerned. He doesn't care much, if it's a play of some sort—good at least for a performance or two. He goes on to make another play. His way of correcting the experiment wasn't to rewrite the play, but to write another. He was making plays for immediate rough and ready use, like making plant-pots.

So when—if—it dawned on him, in the process of writing M for M, that his plot and his characters were inadequate controls for the explosive energies that were emerging, he simply wrote straight on, soldiered through to the last twists of his tale, and left it at that, with all its imperfections on its head. One of the great absolutely essential components of Shakespeare's generosity of production, is his carelessness, his magnanimity towards just those inadequacies of plot and in a way, too, towards his own inadequacies, his own incomprehension and human limitation. This is part of an ultimate vision of the absurdity of human actions and pretensions, which includes the arbitrary claims of human truth and the provisional vanities of art. He had no interest in perfectionism, because he regarded all psychic exploration as 'experimental'. As 'play'.

I'm afraid all that is only a tortuous way of saying that we can't rightly blame him for leaving an imperfect play, and that we ought really to take the imperfections as imperfections, and accept the fact that if we choose to deal with M for M then we are going to be dealing with a deeply flawed work. In other words, I don't believe that the inadequacies of M for M are, as I called them at the beginning, enigmas full of concealed treasures. I do believe that in a production of the play we have to treat them as such—reserving to ourselves the understanding that they are, simply, inadequacies. We have to treat them as 'given' elements, and somehow or other turn them to theatrical account. As if we were given a handful of unrelated, meaningless objects and asked to construct a meaningful drama round them. Sometimes we do better with a 'meaningless' object of that sort than with an object which is presented already organically part of a fable.

The inadequacies, then, of this sort, are scattered throughout the play in quite a fatal fashion. I expect by now you are far more familiar with them than I am.

The inadequacies of the plot are profound. The Duke's decision to relinquish the state, temporarily, to a deputy, who will be able to make the unpopular reforms that he dare not make, is credible enough, and interesting. But after that, almost everything is hard to take. The suddenness and intensity of Angelo's desire is too schematically opposite to his proclaimed character, and his surrender to it is psychologically too abrupt and simple. It is not dramatically interesting for this reason. Angelo's soliloquies, which make a show of his conscience and inward struggle, are inadequate. His character is conceived in too simple a mould, to be interesting in this situation. To turn the possibilities of this extreme situation to dramatic account, it would need a character as fully conceived as Macbeth. It is very easy to imagine Macbeth in that situation—and how interesting it becomes at once.

In the same way, Angelo's reversion to his original character, suppressing all thought or mention of his satisfied desire, is again too schematically complete and external to be interesting. Yet this action—Angelo's temptation, fall and recovery—is all the play has in the way of dramatic engine-power.

Compare it to Bertram's (very similar in some respects) temptation and fall and recovery. In All's Well, Bertram's deed is only a small part of the play's dramatic dynamo, but how much more complex and interesting it is than Angelo's. And Bertram is simple enough.

The Duke's retirement, as I say, has a certain dramatic potential—but given the plot and the characters he has stuck himself with, Shakespeare has great trouble in making the Duke subsequently interesting, theatrically. The danger is, in fact, that he becomes so boring we fairly dread his reappearance.

The minor twists and turns of the plot are all similarly short of dramatic voltage—or project a situation which is, theatrically, counterproductive. For instance, Angelo's forced marriage to Mariana is intellectually logical, but remains a cruel violation of human justice—especially against Mariana. Angelo is punished, but Mariana is compelled to live with a man who will from now on hate her even worse, and be close enough to make it felt, a man who, as we already know, is capable of any manipulative cruelty towards women. That can only have its justification in Elizabethan mores of marriage.

The tedious business of on and off executions is also theatrically null, it seems to me, and the entire last act, which essentially depends on the series of unveilings and unmaskings, must be a great problem to stage effectively, because the dramatic charge—insofar as they had any—of those veiled characters has already been exhausted.

As a working plot, then, as a mechanism of suspense and tension, the play seems to me a failure—partly because of its own perverse intricate busyness, but mainly because the characters involved are simply not interesting enough, they do not experience their situation interestingly enough. On this level, it seems to me the play is best avoided.

However, the fact remains that it is a fascinating work. We are drawn back to it, and perhaps drawn to attempt to stage it, by the imaginative intensity of its atmosphere, the strange flavour and power of its musical accompaniment, the poetic undertow of the play, and by the symbolic force of its moral scheme, the raw shocking vision of evil which it somehow opens up.

These are its positive qualities, and there is nothing quite like this particular blend and emphasis in any of the other plays. It is as if we were aware of two plays being performed simultaneously. One is an inadequately conceived over-intricate and artificial courtly comedy, theatrically not very effective, while the other is an enormously powerful poetic presentation of human corruption, folly and wickedness. We are aware of both, in reading the play. In fact, in reading the play, we are rather more aware of the second. But in a performance, we are made aware that the latter play, the great poetic play, is totally dependant on the former somewhat trivial old-fashioned failure.

So the whole problem, in producing the play, as far as I can see, is in somehow recreating the plot and characters in the light of the real matter of the poetic vision. And to this end, I think any liberties, that work, are justified.

The way to go about it, for me, would be to sink the characters a little more deeply into the poetic lava, dissolve them a little in the molten stuff that is pressing towards expression through them, suffuse them with its heat and glow, try to let them be transformed by it, and to become more open to it at every point even though this would mean disconnecting them, in some ways, from the brisk rigours of the plot.

I imagine you have done this, as any producer must—if that poetic dark fire of the centre is to be liberated in any effective form. From what you said on the phone, this has obviously been your whole effort—using each character as a lens to enlarge the vision of what is behind them in the poetry and the symbol of the situation. What I can't know, of course, is exactly what you have found.

I haven't read any criticism or commentary on Measure for Measure, but I imagine the main interpretations of the fable are pretty standard. At one extreme it can be called a play about God and the human spirit's free will—a doctrinal sort of analysis of some of the consequences. At the other extreme, it can be read as an analysis of the deep psychological terror of venereal disease—as the culmination of the deep psychological/religious fear of sex in general, and its specific effect on religious feeling in Europe at the turn of the 16/17 centuries. These things are no doubt there, but I'm not sure they are of any help in an attempt to make the play work.

What encourages speculations of this kind is precisely that famous 'coldness' of the play—as if what we had here were a deliberate intellectual analysis of some kind, where actual 'theatrical' effectiveness was of only secondary importance. And there may be something in this. Apart from the fact that he was making plays, as I said, like plant-pots, for immediate use, there seems to me plenty of evidence that Shakespeare was involved with some group of Rosicrucian or other society whose main concerns were Hermetic magic (as in Giordano Bruno) and an esoteric resolution of the religious conflicts of the day—pursuing those interests quite deliberately and methodically. Frances Yates books certainly suggest this. If Shakespeare were involved with a group of that sort (as Bacon, for instance, quite definitely was) then even if he were personally more interested in the Hermetic magic and kindred operations (which the plays suggest), he can't have been indifferent to the concerns with the problems of orthodox religion. It was feared, in those highminded secret societies, that the religious conflicts were going to destroy Europe's established order—as in England they very soon after did.

In this light, Measure For Measure can be read as a deliberate imaginative analysis—exploiting the possibilities, at the same time, for dramatic effect. It's even conceivable that in this play a deliberate demonstration was intended—a didactic demonstration of consequences etc. Because, among other things, the play is a savage analysis of the text-book puritan's moral nature. Combined with a reconciliation of the State authority (the Duke, after the correction of his excessively puritan Angelo) with the spirit of Catholicism (Isabella, who descends from her marriage with God—the nunnery—to plead for those who sin according to nature.)

In fact, if this was Shakespeare's leading concern, it is easy to see why his characters are exactly as they are—why the Duke is passive and invisible, why Angelo is so schematically simply drawn and unsympathetic, why Isabella has, in fact, the most interesting and varied part in the play, and why it is necessary for the plot to go through all those otherwise tedious drawn out intricacies of denouement. It gives meaning—of an intellectual sort—to the sacred family of innocent sinners at the core of the play, Juliet, her unborn child, and Claudio. If you imagine the play performed, as plays were performed, at a meeting of Rosicrucian practitioners of Hermetic magic and religious philosophy, you can see why it was written as it was. In that setting, it is a rather fascinating mystery play. The humanity of the characters is not so important—would even be intrusive. As in a mystery play, the characters are semi-religious symbols. That particular audience would not be watching a play about human depravity and the human attempt to be saintly, and would not be waiting to be entertained. They would be following a myth of their familiar spiritual concerns. Plays of that sort (there's a description of one in the famous Rosicrucian text, The Chymical Wedding of Christian Rosenkreutz, by Andreae, 1459) were more like mysterious pageants than public stage dramas.

However, interesting as all that is, I don't think it helps the play work, as a stage drama. If the play was written in that analytical way, for that purpose, and if it has fallen to us, as it were, by accident, then it has to be remade, not as a sacred drama, but as a dramatic exploration of immediate human life.

I have never produced the play, and I have seen it performed only once, very badly. I certainly haven't given the play's potential for dramatic performance one fraction of the thought that you have. And I'm very aware how much depends, in a case of this sort, where the play is a mystery full of unknown potential, rather than a work of disciplined intention, on exploration and experiment with actors during rehearsals.

I have always read it rather as a dramatic poem, and I think I can only speak about it as such. I don't think I have any practical suggestions whatsoever as to how it might be staged, except the one I have given— the initial act of sinking the characters back into the poetic matrix of the fable.

I relate it firstly to its place in Shakespeare's own inner development, secondly to what is condensed in it from the general atmosphere of the time's conflicts—chiefly religious conflicts and the political conflicts that swayed and were swayed by them.

In his own inner development, as I've said it comes at a moment of sudden change, or rather transformation, in Shakespeare's psychic make-up. It records a revolution, where an old worn-out style of being (of thinking and feeling, of self-image) is replaced by a new one. So it seems to me. The sudden change—from the imaginative works of the early phase, to the imaginative works of the mature middle phase which followed immediately after Measure For Measure, from Hamlet onwards—is easy to see.

I say the old ego is replaced, but in fact he is not quite replaced. He is weak and ailing (in All's Well he was already fatally ill), he can no longer control or tolerate the chaotic underworld of his nature, and so, experimentally, he abdicates. He hands over to a new ruthlessness of intellectual will, a spirit full of new untried energies, a moralist of scientific detatchment and purity. He realises his old-fashioned mediaeval laissez faire will no longer do.

What happens to him now is interesting. He has a new sympathy (why has he never tried reform before) with the new moral spirit, and adopts it, somewhat, himself, in retiring to a Friar's habit, taking religious instruction—even if only provisionally—and in attempting to rebuke the irrepressible sexuality of Lucio. But this new role is unconvincing, he is only borrowing the religion as a cover for spying, and he is ineffective against Lucio. His real nature, in other words, is the seething sexual underworld from which Lucio emerges. Lucio is like a mocking spirit from one of his own dark corners. He truly is the Duke of dark corners. Everything that Lucio says about him has an essential truth, even if not a factual one. Lucio is his own creation, just as is the whole corruption of Vienna. Part of the dramatic indefiniteness of the Duke springs from the fact that he is everywhere, and party to everything that happens. He is everywhere passive and everywhere manipulating. He is, in fact, the person to whom it is all happening, the crucible inside which all the workings are going on. He is ubiquitous but curiously null—rather like Horatio in Hamlet who also has that air of the one inside whom everything else is going on, as if the ego were visiting the soul. The Duke is rather like the representative of Shakespeare himself, attending and guiding this experiment inside his own imagination. So he does have the air, too, of a manipulating rather detatched God, and an all-powerful all-knowing Fate.

This would explain why in the play he somehow has no real identity, no real objective existence, as all the others have, in spite of their shortcomings. He is all shifts and deviousness, spyings and disguises, and unexplained instructions. As if he had abdicated responsibility of every kind, causing all kinds of suffering—because he is not himself actually involved with anybody. As if all these people were his fantasies. In the end, after Angelo has proved himself the most morally depraved sexualist and the least human righteous moralist in the kingdom, he re-instates himself, and takes for himself, without the slightest evidence of love, the woman for whom Angelo risked and lost everything. In a sense he is like a cloaked but very visible manipulator of puppets who takes his favourite and most beautiful puppet to bed with him, without her ceasing to be a puppet. He has no identity because he is, in truth, each of his puppets in turn, and all together. They are his real identity. In that way, the play is a fable of Shakespeare's relationship to his own creative

413

imagination. And I always imagine him rather like the Duke, very selfless but mercurially manipulative, a non-participant controlling everything indirectly.

By comparison Angelo is an innocent. Angelo emerges as if he had come new out of a box, or out of the Duke's hat. He has the naivety of an idealist intellectual, the undeveloped emotional nature of an abstract idea, and the human thinness of somebody committed to a moral line of action so fiercely and adamantly only because it is, in fact, in dead opposition to their real inclinations—with which they have lost touch. Familiar type of revolutionary intellectual. It is the very intensity of his extreme claims for his own righteousness, the brittle dehumanised fixity of it, the extraverted self-confidence of it, that gives such inner freedom to the underworld in him, and which makes sure he is totally unfamiliar with it, and therefore totally at its mercy, when the moment comes for it to rise. A man of more flexible and honest self-knowledge, of subtler and warmer human judgement, might have succumbed easily enough to Isabella, but not so instantaneously, and not so helplessly. So far, this is just an illustration of the psychology of love at first sight. It occurs—say in a man, when the woman appeals direct to a part of his nature with which he is totally unfamiliar, which he has never used or let into life. The more thoroughly we know ourselves, through experience, the less easily we fall in love.

What makes the distinction in Angelo's case is that his extreme idealism is fortified, most of all, directly against sexuality, any sexuality, even the slightest rumour (in Mariana's case) of indulgence. So what he is ignorant of, innocent of, and has no control over, is the whole of his sexual nature. And in accordance with the psychic law, what we disapprove of in ourselves degenerates until it becomes identical with the hated examples of the hated thing in the outer world. So the puritan extremist becomes sexually as depraved and evil as he considers sexual activity to be. He is then a walking bomb of sexual psychosis. And the more he senses the danger and depravity intensifying within himself, the more vigilant and militant he becomes against sexuality in others, helped by the natural mechanism of projection. And this, Shakespeare is saying, is the true condition of the puritan.

And now, he says, see what happens to him when he meets a beautiful woman, with a touch of the supernatural about her, a reputation of holy purity and abstinence, who tries to persuade him, with tears, that copulation is natural.

The demon that hears and steps forward, within Angelo, though it contains all Angelo's natural energy, is ignorant of any human finesse, because it has spent its life being tortured in a prison. Angelo falls instantly in love with Isabella, but his love is a completely depraved, dehumanised body of energy, denied any of the civilisation that a free negotiation with his moral intellect and with experience might have given it. It is as if somebody whom Angelo had never met suddenly shoved him out of the way, took his mask, and continued the conversation with Isabella. This is clear and simple. But the point is, that this is the only way Angelo can fall in love. The love he has to give is exclusively of this sort. His moral sense, so overdeveloped as a mechanical system, is erotically destitute. And his erotic nature is destitute morally. What is lacking from both is the human warmth and sensitivity that a natural blending of both would give. This is part of what Shakespeare is saying very clearly. That the puritan extremism not only divides the soul, and makes one part a cold machine, and the other part a sub-human animal, it destroys the most precious extra thing: sensitive loving understanding between individuals. Such as, for instance, Escalus displays in deliberately posed contrast to Angelo.

Nevertheless, Angelo's helplessness, in his love, is genuine. Depraved as it is, it still has the potential for human development. It's first thought is to release Claudio—even though it uses this merciful thought to attain its desired ends. If this ugly passion can only hold the stage, then Angelo has a future as a human being, because that passion holds the seed of his humanity.

This is also part of what Shakespeare is saying clearly. The corruption of Vienna, though it is corrupt, nevertheless contains the city's humanity. Though it throws up the whores and bawds, and though the spirit of it, in its ugliest form, takes possession of Angelo, who has come to control it, nevertheless it also throws up Juliet's pregnancy and Claudio's devotion to her. It turns out that Angelo cannot crush the whores and bawds, without sentencing Claudio to death, and throwing Juliet into prison to have her child behind bars. The corruption of Vienna, in other words, is only evil through Angelo's eyes, and in the form it takes in Angelo's own soul. In the eyes of Escalus, it is comic, fallible, helplessly natural humanity, deserving only mercy and forgiveness.

This is a very detailed excruciating portrait of the Puritan psyche, which is repulsive top to bottom, and which makes the world repulsive. It is full of a hell, a dehumanised demon living in a hell, and it makes its world full of dehumanised demons living in a hell. Only insofar as those demons manage to express their sexuality, in any form, do they hang on to the seeds of their humanity. And this is what is repulsive about Angelo.

And what is paralysed and absent about the Duke, is that he is undergoing an attack of the Angelo: he is self absorbed, preoccupied by the conflict between this new self, this Angelo, and his old self, the old reigning Duke of dark corners. Insofar as he inclines towards Angelo, he sees Lucio as a kind of Satan from the infernal depths of sexual depravity and disease, this is what he hears Lucio whispering mockingly to him. But when he recovers, and regains control of himself (of Vienna) he sees Lucio as an impudent bold wag, whose proper fate is to marry the whore he got with child. In other words, he is a man in turmoil, vacillating between puritan disgust with its clinging smell of sexual disease and an uneasy hopeful trust in marriage in a world that is all too fallibly human. He is man removed from himself, a man in transition, a man in a state of chaos, his ego in fragments, clinging to bits of vanity and shreds of authority. He is a man, finally, in conflict.

And that is what has arrived, that is the change in Shakespeare. Angelo has arrived. And from now on, Shakespeare's imagination is a field of conflict, where the spirit of Angelo, with his lofty classical ideals of purity, and his vision of sexual love as a cosmic hell of corruption, tries to stay in command.

The really active element in the play, poetically, is Lucio. He has several satanic attributes, especially if Satan is considered a demon of sexuality. He is totally unconcerned with conventional moral law, yet he is loyal to the lovers and to the cause of love. His dealings with Isabella are all in the cause of Claudio and Juliet, and in the scene where Isabella first attempts to persuade Angelo that fornication is no sin, Lucio's whispering encouragement—as if he were totally invisible to Angelo— recalls the serpent's words to Eve in the garden of Eden. He has complete social freedom from highest to lowest. He is a merry swaggering devil of sexual innuendo, a lord of punks, on all occasions, in every company. A Priapus. He identifies sexual licence with a person's humanity—this is how he redeems the loftiness of the Duke, and at the same time he makes it a mocking rebuke of the Duke's hypocrisy. He is insuppressibly self-assertive, full of high-spirited lies and improvisations.

At the same time, he is the essential Mercury in the plot, bringing the vital news to Isabella that sets everything in action.

He pops up, reeking of the stews, then plunges back in like an infernal frog.

He is the carrier of the ineradicably sexual nature of society, and whoever tries to escape from it—as Isabella and Angelo and the Duke do—he catches and re-infects. Justice, religious seclusion, cannot escape him. He brings them down with his fever, and mixes them back into humanity. Separated lovers are brought back together in the general hospital of love-malady and complications that he creates. And his natural wife is a whore. He's very consistent.

The Play was written at a critical moment in English History. First known performance was 1604, the year after Elizabeth's death and James' accession. The religious question, basically Puritan versus Anglo-Catholic, which Elizabeth had suspended rather skillfully and luckily, flared up, and it was exactly now that the Puritan pressure—which was just under the ascendant and still had forty odd years to go before it took over the country openly—suddenly rose with a real hope and new confidence, a new inevitability. In other words, the conflict between that newly confident and militant spirit and all that it opposed, and all that partly sympathised with it and would have to accomodate it, somehow, became acute and critical. In its way, Measure for Measure is Shakespeare's portrait of this moment—and it records, I think, his horrified understanding of a spirit with which he himself was all too strongly infected, the Angelo spirit. But at this point, says the play, he felt it could be controlled and humanised: in spite of it, the established order is secure, and indeed has much to learn and gain from it. The Duke, living out his experience and correction of Angelo, marries Isabel who, like Angelo, is a moral puritan, but one fully acquainted with the sexual reality of nature and society. One who partakes equally of refined spirituality and natural sexuality and merciful human understanding of human frailty.

If the play wasn't written partly with a special society of Hermetic philosophers as the intended first audience, it was certainly written for the audience at Court. Shakespeare's company had just become the King's players—under James' patronage. The topicality of the play, then, lies in its treatment of the evermore familiar and intrusive Puritan type, and the world he creates about him; and in its analysis and judgement of those things.

It was never again possible for Shakespeare to introduce the Angelo figure without destruction of the status quo, chaos, and a new order somewhat hastily patched up, until the last phase, the romantic plays where the tragic consequences are evaded by a dream sleight.

Just off the top of my head, I would try, if I were setting out to stage the play, to find ways of suggesting, as powerfully as possible, the doubleness of Angelo's nature—of suggesting, from the first moment, the imminent presence of his hidden opposite self, which is actually the real self. I would try to suggest the panic tension of the puritan personality which he asserts, the dreadful human vacuity in which it operates. Unless this apprehension is established at the start, this complex of suffering—unconscious suffering—then he is going to remain uninteresting, I think. Somehow, we have to feel—rather than openly understand—that his secret self is identical with the sexual corruption he is supposed to purge and bring under control, and that he is, somehow, himself the satan of this particular hell.

I would also look for ways of projecting the duality of the Viennese corrupt society—that it is simultaneously evil and merely joyfully licentious, that it oscillates somehow between the two according to who confronts it. Because this is part of the mysterious power and horror of the play—that the bawdy phallic abandon of the low characters has an aura, a glamour, of unspeakable evil, and almost occult depravity. That definitely is there, and there is something horribly real about it, as if we were in fact watching damned souls. The innocence of Juliet and even Isabella, and Mariana, in that setting, has a weird pathos, as if they were the Mona Lisa mystery flowers of an occult morass. As if Escalus, after his warm, merciful handling of the malefactors, were to release some horrible goblin amusement out of the corner of his eye.

That is the real poetic mystery of the play—that uncertainty about the repulsive ectoplasm of evil that repeatedly oozes from every hint of sexuality. It is hard to pin down, but all-pervasive. And the innocent lovers, Claudio and Juliet, aren't free of it—they simply gaze innocently through it. It's very strange. But a production that misses that, misses the essential thing, I think. The Puritan sees only the evil, the Lucio sees that whatever the evil may be (it may be just the horror of existence itself), only sexuality carries the seeds of humanity and joy.

The whole vision, of course, of a Universe of fundamental evil, within which love and joy and understanding make provisional little relationships, would be impossible in the framework of some religions. The play is deeply Christian, in this sense, deeply Mannichean. But that was Shakespeare. We try to be human, say the plays, but in fact we are being

418

lived by supernatural creatures, goblins from every region of space. In this setting, the clockwork of the last act has a certain pathos and dignity. If that effect could be captured on stage, much of the real gist of the poetry would be transmitted.

I imagine if intellectual lizards found the text, and performed it according to a laboriously detailed description of a conventional performance, one might get the poetic truth, something like it.

Donya, I have sat here all day and typed without moving, and I'm not sure I've set down anything that will be of the slightest interest to you. Most of what I say, I imagine, you've thought over and rejected long ago. I come from reading the play (though perhaps for the hundredth time) but you come from wrestling, on stage and in the mouths of real actors, with every phrase, twisting it for its secrets. So I can't help feeling I'm speaking from a much more superficial acquaintance with the play than you are enjoying at present.

However, at least it's chat about Measure for Measure—though not that much more rewarding thing, two-way conversation. And it's a contact.

I hope all goes well. I received an invitation to come to the first night. I'll reply, but I'm afraid it is absolutely impossible. I'm up to my neck in deferred things and pressing things, and always the real thing gets shelved.

Please don't publish any of this letter—it's been so hastily concocted, it's so long and repetitive. But I didn't want to get into a detailed, measured exploration of the text—I just know how long that would take me, once I started. So what I've given are my general feelings, general impressions, and I've given them with a strong feeling that a little practical attempt to set the play up on stage would change all my ideas completely.

All the best, then. Let me know how it goes, sometime.

[*No valediction or signature on photocopy*]

Donya Feuer, a director at the Royal Dramatic Theatre in Stockholm, who had been inspired by *A Choice of Shakespeare's Verse* to make a one-woman show, *Soundings*, from Shakespearean soliloquies, was mounting a production of *Measure for Measure* and had asked TH for his view of the work. Although they met only once and briefly, TH and Feuer remained in touch, mainly by telephone, and it was the series of letters that he sent to her in 1990 – the first dated 23 April, Shakespeare's birthday – that, after reworking, were published as *Shakespeare and the Goddess of Complete Being*.

To Fay Godwin

31 May 1979   Ms   Estate of Fay Godwin

Dear Fay,

Just got what must be your 2nd letter—haven't yet seen the one you refer to as yesterday's.

Don't let any remarks disturb you. Everybody wants to remake things their own way—everybody wants to be editor. A success upsets 99%.

Without your pictures there would have been no poems at all. Without your pictures most readers of the poems would be completely lost for a concrete setting. The poems relate to your pictures as commentaries to an original, great difficult text, and there is no question of them having any existence apart. [*Arrow to marginal addition:* See how much less impact & power Olwyn's edition has—with the lack of pictures.] My attitude to the book is mainly simple delight, that we managed to make such a rich & real world of our subject. And insofar as I'm pleased with the poems—and I am pleased—I'm grateful to your pictures for making them possible. The few poems—½ dozen or so—I wrote <u>before</u> your pictures seem to me the least interesting—more or less a continuation of my other writing—but what I did from the pictures seems to me new, and there's no other way I could have got them. And, without my first poems, no doubt you wouldn't have gone on to take the superb pictures from which I wrote the later ones, so the whole thing is one circulation, one organism, and people will eventually feel that, whatever they feel to begin with. Everybody I've spoken to has been gratifyingly bowled over, & I've noticed that most people stare mainly at the pictures. And I'm sure, in a system like the one we've constructed there, they can only read the poems to find their way deeper into the pictures. Several of my friends call it my best book—which makes me jealous for the others (but I know what they mean, they mean that mutual interdependence of poems & pictures puts my poems in quite a new category, for me, on quite a new level.) So I hope you have some friends that call it your best book too.

I don't care how it sells, for myself, because I think we've really done what we set out to do, we've really pulled it off, we've made a book that's unique, beautiful right through, & supported at every point by real things—so opinion can't alter it. I'm just sorry we're not halfway through something else, as well.

Lots of love

Ted

The Rainbow Press limited edition of *Remains of Elmet* was published in April; Faber's trade edition, in May.

To Moelwyn Merchant

1 July 1979   Ms   Paul Merchant

Dear Moelwyn,

   This is just a note to keep contact in what has for me been a rather beleaguered time—now coming to clearer views I hope.

   I've been wanting to answer at length and thoughtfully your letter about the novel. I shan't broach it now, because I don't want to do it hurriedly—and this is hurried. I should only say, that you must go ahead with it. Apart from its use to you—as a summary of a lifetime of feeling & thinking about those images & experiences—it would draw many things towards you, many helpful strengthening things. I think whatever we work at, in the way of imaginative creation, operates as a conjuration, a ritual summoning of all energies associated with the subject matter—from levels that our normal activities can rarely tap. And those energies are good or bad for us—helpful or destructive—almost in the style of demonic entities—according to our subject matter, & the moral-imaginative interpretation we make of it. It is extremely import-ant, it seems to me, that we choose our subject matter—the last point, almost, at which our choice can still operate—with consideration of those inevitable results in mind.

   And what you are contemplating is really a chance to give definition to your highest self—and summon afresh its resources—with the artistic drum. For you, too, it will gather together many vital strands in your life.

   That's how it seems, superficially & theoretically, to me, an outsider to your self-doubts & self-knowledge, writing hurriedly.

   Please give my love to the family. I'll write again, to all, at more length & leisure.

as ever

Ted

After leaving his post at Exeter University, Merchant had moved to be vicar of the parish of Llanddewi Brefi in west Wales. He seems to have sought TH's encouragement before starting on his novel, *Jeshua, Nazareth to Jerusalem* – about the boyhood and young manhood of Jesus – which was eventually published in 1987.

To Keith Sagar

16 July 1979   Ms   British Library

The fox-dream story really goes as follows: in 1953, my second year at University, I was going through some kind of crise. The problems attached themselves to the writing of the weekly essay. It became impossible for me to write a sentence, except in lucky moments. (It varied with the author in question—I remember writing fluently about Blake). The difficulties became chronic towards the end of my second year. One night I sat up late writing & rewriting 3 or 4 lines I had managed to compose—the opening of an essay about Samuel Johnson (a personality I greatly liked). I left the page on my table & went to bed. Then I dreamed I was still sitting at my essay, in my usual agonising frame of mind, trying to get one word to follow another. The door opened & a creature came in, with a fox's head, & a long skinny fox's body—but erect, & with human hands. He had escaped from a fire—the smell of burning hair was strong, & his skin was charred & in places cracking, bleeding freshly through the splits. He came across, & set his hand on the page & said "Stop this. You are destroying us." He lifted his hand away, & the blood-print stayed on the page. The hands in particular were terribly burned.

The dream had total reality. I woke soon after, & went to look at the page.

The following night, I dreamed that I woke, with the knowledge that somebody had come through my door. 2 or 3 steps led down from the door, into my room,—I could make out a tall figure standing on these steps. I got out of bed (in my dream) & went across to see who it might be. As I crossed the room, the creature opened two eyes & I saw that it was a leopard—but standing erect. My exclamation "It's a leopard" is the most vivid thing about the dream. As I spoke, it stepped towards me & began to push me back,—I resisted & wrestled for a moment, before it pushed me backwards over my armchair.

This was a less striking dream than the fox dream, but the very peculiar thing was I woke soon after lying over the chair—as if I had sat into it, over one arm, in backing from the door. I woke up because I was so uncomfortable. The leopard said nothing I remembered.

So that's the account as I remember it. I made a note of it at the time. The room was on K staircase, 1st floor, & looks out over the small courtyard halfway up Pembroke St.

These are dreams I should never have told, I expect.

I connected the fox's command to my own ideas about Eng. Lit., & the effect of the Cambridge blend of pseudo-critical terminology & social rancour on creative spirit, & from that moment abandoned my efforts to adapt myself.

I might say, that I had as much talent for Leavis-style dismantling of texts as anybody else, I even had a special bent for it—nearly a sadistic streak there,—but it seemed to me not only a foolish game, but deeply destructive of myself. I think it was something peculiar to Cambridge at that time, that nurtured it, & in particular separated the spirit of surgery & objective analysis from the spirit of husbandry & sympathetic coaching. I don't think it happened at Oxford, for instance.

'The Burnt Fox', dated 1993 and placed prominently early in TH's prose collection *Winter Pollen* (1994), recounts the first of these dreams, but not the second.

To Eric Walter White

[August 1979]   Ms (photocopy)   Faber

Dear Eric,

We just got back from Iceland. The most exhausting holiday I've ever had—thanks to the Icelandic roads, which are rarely any wider than the giant buses which come hurtling along them now & again, & which have as a rule sheer drops to right & left, sometimes an 8 ft toppling incline, sometimes 1200 ft sheer fall into <u>cloud</u>, & which are made exclusively out of lava lumps, lava gravel, & lava dust with 2500 breakback pot-holes to the kilometre, & over which I drove nearly 2000 miles. It was like driving along the top of Hadrian's wall—much more ruinous. In an unsprung landrover.

But the scenery is extremely novel, alarming & exhilarating. The people are like the dourest Scots, but more paranoic. The food is what you'd get in a small store in Galway. The weather was pretty good. Brilliant sun, icy wind, extraordinary light.

The fishing lay at 2 extremes—one, first class, probably best in the world, in the hands of 2 agencies, monopolists who stock the rivers with salmon & sell the fishing to expense account gangs of big businessmen & the international dolce vita sporting rich—£100 a day upwards (we met one group who'd paid £350 a day). Other extreme was what still belonged to the farmers, who netted it empty, as part of their crop. Met plenty of them. Camped.

Between these two, by pure chance, we hit on about 6 days of phenomenal fishing—the sort we were looking for. Dream fishing.

And I rediscovered an old friend from International Poetry Festival days—Thor Willjamson—who fulfilled every article of the heroic code —infinite cheer, infinite hospitality, infinite laborious help. Novelist, & I think pretty good.

So I've come back a bit battered—I feel I've swallowed quite a lump of Iceland & it's only gradually dissolving into particles of experience & revelation. Its a beautiful, terrible place.

Love from us, Eric. Hope to see you soon.

Ted

Eric Walter White (1905–85), arts administrator with a wide variety of interests, at this time ran the Poetry Book Society. He sent a copy of the original letter, which has not been traced, to Charles Monteith at Faber and Faber.

Thor Vilhjálmsson (b.1925), Icelandic novelist, was active in numerous writers' and artists' organisations.

To Daniel Weissbort

[August 1979]   Ts   King's College, London

Iceland was very exhausting. We hired a landrover and I drove right round it—2000 miles or so on a cinder pot-holed narrow track like the top of Hadrian's wall. Archaic out-of-this-world feeling—no wild animals (only escaped mink and foxes, and imported reindeer, none of which are ever seen), no insects except midges and about one tiny moth, and a red sea-rock tiny mite. Only five species of fish. No sparrows, starling, general small twitterers and babblers. Only terns (visitors from the Antarctic) puffins, gulls (not many) and skuas. And curlews and plovers. Many hundred kinds of duck, but confined to a few spots. So the effect is not just desolate, so much as vacant—deserted, blasted and cursed. The folk are odd—unsmiling, funless, somewhat hostile. My friend Thor is an anomaly—a real jovial Viking. The rest seem to be a cross between the most downtrodden Irish and the meanest Scots. In fact by blood they are evidently closer to the British Isles than to Scandinavia, and they look it. But we caught plenty of gigantic fish in spectacular places.

To Gerald and Joan Hughes

30 August 1979   Ms   Emory

This life in Devon would be perfect, if only I could break all the tugging little threads—most of them of my own tying. I've now got to that bad last stage, of resenting every phone call, detesting every visitor, hating every letter-writer. Very little fills the whole 24 hours.

Dad is O.K.—a bit frailler perhaps, sometimes off his food. The one male in that zoo with him died a couple of weeks ago, and that's thrown him—plus, perhaps, Olwyn forcing him with unthinking vividness to realise that he was in an Old Folk's Home—and not just staying with friends—the comfortable illusion he'd hung on to. Can't tell. When I visit him, he'll suddenly say "How long have you lived here?" I took him for a drink, the other night, and after sundry comments he suddenly said "Do you ever see Ted these days?" Took me quite a negotiation to ease him out of that one. He had a bad spate of heavy nose-bleeds recently.

How's the Australian Spring? How are the marriages? Frieda had her wedding reception here on the lawn—lovely day, average 1.5 bottles of champagne per head. She seems very happy & busy. Nicky's gone in for weight-training. He's taller than me.

Frieda Hughes married Desmond Dawe on 11 August.

To Keith Sagar

30 August 1979   Ts   British Library

Do you remember that article about Yeats in the Kenyon Review, where

Auden dismissed the whole of Eastern mystical and religious phil-
osophy, the whole tradition of Hermetic Magic (which is a good part of
Jewish Mystical philosophy, not to speak of the mystical philosophy of
the Rennaissance), the whole historical exploration into spirit life at
every level of consciousness, the whole deposit of earlier and other
religion, myth, vision, traditional wisdom and story in folk belief, on
which Yeats based all his work, everything he did or attempted to bring
about, as "embarassing nonsense". The article concerned Yeats as an
Example. Auden's example, following the example of most cultured
English sensibilities that awaken to the morally responsible life, was the
solemnly-intoned, shuffling, high-minded, pedantic, frivolous, tea-and-
biscuits Oxford High Anglicanism, dignified with whiffs of the old
incense and murmurous latin—which seems to me closer to the pride,
pomp and circumstance of the High Table than to any altar of uncut
stones.

Well, we mustn't be thrown I suppose by the sharp reaction to the
follies of the Sixties. The Sixties also produced that mass of newly
published or republished texts of the essential literatures, which were
swallowed whole by a generation that is still only in its thirties.
And it produced the whole idea of our ecological responsibility, fully
developed—maybe the crucial awakening. And the idea of ecological
interconnectedness, which is the fundamental assumption now of child-
ren under 18, is only the material aspect of the interconnectedness of
everything in spirit. But traditions—like Auden's—aren't changed by
argument, only by death of skulls and brains. Argument changes the
children, I suppose, who eavesdrop.

I'm beginning to babble, I think.

The Auden piece, published in 1948, is titled 'Yeats as an Example'.

To Stephen Spender

9 September 1979   Ms   Estate of Stephen Spender

Dear Stephen,

Thank you for the lovely little book memoir of Cyril Connolly.

I only met him once, very briefly, but I got a glimpse of his richness.

I was once in the pen-shop, top of Regent St, with Alvarez, and I
exclaimed about an extraordinary portly magnificent pen in the display

case. Alvarez also exclaimed & laughed—"It looks like Cyril Connolly." I don't know how the remark was intended—no idea what Alvarez felt about C.C.—but the comic idea seemed just right—it endeared both Cyril Connolly & pen to me. So I later got the pen, & I still use it. It was my first meeting with a Mont Blanc.

Thank you for the kind remarks about Elmet. The style was an adjustment to photographs—you know how photographs & verse normally clash. I tried to hit a dimension outside the visual finality of the picture—with minimum contradiction. Usually failed. Mainly, it's childhood impressions filtered through my mother's feelings for that landscape. She used to sit & cry, thinking about it.

My own feelings about it are slightly different—I must try to locate them. Are you still writing those verse passages of autobiography—I love those. Keep well, affectionately

Ted

Stephen Spender's *Cyril Connolly: A Memoir* was published in a limited edition in 1978. Cyril Connolly (1903–74) had presided over the London literary world as magazine editor and book reviewer.

To Terry Gifford and Neil Roberts

[September/October 1979]   Ts   Gifford and Roberts

Your remark that the narrative of Gaudete does not convey meaning gives me pause, as you can imagine.

However, I look it at like yourselves, as a commentator from the outside, and make my interpretations. Is it really about what I thought it was about? Is it about the collision of healing and creative energy with a fixed, decayed rural community that has lost all sense of spirit? Is it about the debasement of that spirit energy—brought about by the material stupor that it ought to enlighten and transform and supply? Because what I held in focus as I wrote was a sense of the spirit energy staggering through the crassness of the living cells, in this group, and emerging in its way as stupefied and benighted, and going about its mission almost somnambulist, almost unconscious, tinkering with Heath-Robinson paper-back magical operations as an instinctive but muddied attempt to re-establish contact with the real origins and the real calling. The battery image of the poem was of transcendental energy jammed—unconscious and deformed in the collision—into dead-end objects, dead-end claustrophobic egos, dilettante museum egos, second-hand bailer-twine-repaired mechanical egos, and galvanising them in perfunctory fashion, blowing their inadequate circuits. Is any of that there? As if the brilliant real thing were happening to creatures of light in another world—but these are the shadows of it, confusedly glimpsing and remembering, translating it all into puppet and monkey and routine reflex, and helpless to manage even that, broken or demonised by the flashes of it, enmired in bodily thickness and ego inertia, and overwhelmed anyway by the vegetable weight and confusion and dumb beauty of late May? Is that relevant to anything we have to live in, and is it a meaning, does it open onto any meanings?

My main problem technically was to make the implications of my theme clear, and yet at the same time make no authorial comment, no exposition, permit no discussion between characters and permit them no individual speculation that was not an immediate part of enactment. I wanted nothing that was not organically part of enactment, and that didn't contribute to a sense of claustrophobic involvement. Ideally I would free my image from the entanglement of my reader's immediate intellectual response to explicit meanings—by having no very explicit meanings, or rather no meanings enlarged on in explicit terms. I would like to liberate it into imaginative freedom behind my reader's rationale of defences, his ego's natural rejection of whatever does not belong to it, by excluding any language that directly engages that part of the mind. That's an impossible ideal, I know, but that's the aesthetic motive behind much of what is in the writing, and it explains why I excluded what I did. I don't know whether I've succeeded, except with temperaments near enough kin to my own. I know temperamental differences can be bigger gulfs than national differences.

The pattern I tried for was a centripetal maze of nuclear scenes like strobe flashes, tightening and accelerating towards a dead end centre.

I had found a language of enactment, nowhere fine or studied, nowhere remarkable in detail—tolerant of a good deal of vernacular commonplace, which nevertheless was an intense pleasure to create. My feeling for it, very hard to convey, but nevertheless a clear sensation, was a cutting into a stiff headwind at an angle sensation of harshness, a heightening that I felt mainly as a slight ugliness, a feeling of abbreviation and foreshortening, ugly as I broke through to it, but beautiful to me when I'd found it, and ideally each line a single lumped summary rather than an unfolding paragraph. What has been pointed out to me as 'grotesque', seemed to me exhilarating and beautiful and a way of combining what I felt to be truths, and still does—so it's a difference of taste, with the critic calling my taste in this instance corrupt, meaning he doesn't agree with me. The style was indispensable to the theme, nothing else released the particular thing I had located.

At the same time I wanted the language open and clear—conductive of narrative current—above everything I wanted a flowing and accelerating current of narrative momentum—not a narrated story so much as an acted-out story. This is how it comes about that at every point the intonation of the language becomes infected by the tempo and style of whatever character it's dealing with at the time—that's an inevitable part of any 'acting-out' style of telling a tale, it happens involuntarily, and it explains the variations in the tuning of the language within the overall style, and it explains too I think the misreadings of some of the book's reviewers.

I wanted something between a primitive painting, a mosaic, and a slightly speeded up early silent film—a sense of that—where things are simultaneously comic, horrible and beautiful. My feeling for the life of my characters drew on this combination in them and their moments. I wanted a sense of things happening faster than anybody wants them to happen, and in a more final way, and yet being fixed, static, like that dreadful sort of leisure in mid-accident. Hence the epic style similes etc, which became part of the natural means.

Are these meanings?

I know of course that if a poem can't win its case with its reader, then for that reader there's no case for the poem. There's very little credit, in verse: what the poem can't pay for isn't handed over. But I argue my poem's case a little, because what you say in your book will argue your opposition and in absence of any supporting voice for the meanings of the poem will sway the jury—i.e. eleven out of every twelve of your readers. So if I can qualify a little your understanding of Gaudete, I shall maybe have made it that bit more possible for your readers to read it creatively. Example, after all, is a great thing.

Gifford and Roberts had sent TH the typescript of *Ted Hughes: A Critical Study*. Chapter 6, which concerns *Gaudete*, was amended in the light of his comments. Roberts, who has come to admire the book more, seeing the function of Lumb's epilogue songs as an answer to the preceding narrative, writes about this and about the correspondence with TH in *Ted Hughes: A Literary Life* (2006).

To Glyn Hughes

[November 1979]   Ms   British Library

Dear Glyn,

Your publishers sent me a copy of Best of Neighbours. Reading it's made me realise again how much I left out of my Calder Valley book. Your book says much more about what I feel about it than mine does—mine says what my mother felt about it when I was about 5.

I've been thinking I ought to write something supplementary to mine—set down some of my—not quite hatred but something pretty sour—that is most of <u>my own</u> feeling about it. Maybe I'd have to live there again for a while.

But your book does it really—gets the place as it is. Very satisfying.

Here's a collection of my bits & pieces from this other Eden.

Keep well. Love to Roya

Ted

TH and Glyn Hughes (b.1935) were unrelated. They had met in the early 1970s and TH had paid occasional visits to the house in the Calder valley where Glyn Hughes, a Cheshire man by birth, now lived. *Best of Neighbours*, a collection of Hughes's 'New and Selected' poems, appeared in 1979. Thanking him for the gift of a copy, TH had presented him in return with *Moortown* – 'bits & pieces from this other Eden'.

Roya, Hughes's then wife, had for a while in the 1970s worked as personal assistant to Michael Henshaw, TH's accountant.

1980

To Keith Sagar

23 April 1980   Ms   British Library

Curious what you say about the Prometheus poems. Are you sure you're not being influenced by what people say about them? It's true for me too, the printing counts for a lot—the distinctness of the visual impact is inseperable from my sense of the actuality and organic fullness of the poem. The same part of the brain enjoys both. Still, I'm not absolutely self-indulgent. Those pieces are O.K., within their terms, & they serve their purpose. The other poems aren't unrelated. Earth-numb pieces all relate to events along that fringe where vivid & awakened sensation, sensitive alertness & sympathy, finds its limits—confronts what it cannot feel or share or for some reason openly contemplate— because of sheer physical limitations. It's where spirit awareness is humbled to physical body-cell confinement—and the prevailing sensation is like that in the dream where you try to see through blindfolded-ness or nearly sealed eyes something very brilliant or strange which you know is in front of you, it's a sense too of mutilation, & related to the amputated feeling after somebody's death. That's the magnet bundle of feelings holding that section in its pattern. The God, last piece, is the child in the womb, as you'll have divined.

So the first part is a life embedded in mud, body of death etc, & seeds. Prometheus is what tries to waken up inside this. Earth-numb is his failing effort to come to terms with it. Adam is his succeeding means of coming to terms with it. That's the general plan. The whole drift is an alchemising of a phoenix out of a serpent. An awakened life out of an unawakened.

Anything that was not satisfyingly inter-related, I kept out, or rather, it kept out.

Prometheus is related to the main protagonist of Earth Numb—in his various phases. The Vulture not unrelated to the 9 birds.

The death in the natural labouring external world of Moortown, which is mainly dung & death acting as a crucible for repeated efforts at

431

birth, is a counterpoint to the 'birth', in a supernatural, spirit, inner world, of Prometheus. That's it's symbolic rôle.

etc etc.

It was a case of me finding the dominant or a dominant pattern in all the stuff I had from 3 or 4 years, & making positive sense out of it, rather than negative. And as it turned out, I didn't have to wrench & remake anything, it was all there simply.

What it lacks, as a single pattern, is a sense of purposive or dramatic motive. Maybe it's better that way. But it means its growing into other people will be a slow business—as it was with Wodwo. Assuming that it isn't encapsulated by white corpuscles & rejected, like a transplanted organ.

Still, it's time to do something different.

To Doreen Schofield

1 May 1980   Ms   Schofield

Dear Doreen Schofield,

I am interested to hear that you have chosen my poem The Horses, for your specimen verse, in your Exam.

It is a poem I have rarely read out to any audience. An audience is rarely aware of the reader's (or reciter's) problems, but I cut down my own problems, in recitals, by choosing to read only those poems which, for me, recite themselves. These are the poems where the internal concentration is intact, & remains so in any circumstances. And where the musical structure—the assembly of inflections—needs no help from the performer. These poems are quite few.

But if one can stay within the poem, concentrating only on the meaning, everything else takes care of itself, I find. What the audience does not know is how—unless one is in an extremely concentrated state of mind—one's attention goes all over the place. That is when you need 'technique'—which serves, as far as the audience is concerned, just as well as the most achieved communion with the spirit of the poem, & what lies behind it. Though it leaves the 'reader' unsatisfied.

In 'The Horses' there are problems, I can see. When I first published it, I was rebuked, by Roy Fuller, for the last line—I forget what he said, but he implied that I had wooden ears, & had somehow mishandled our English verse Tradition. I hope you do not find the same difficulty.

432

Best wishes for your Exam

yours

Ted Hughes

Doreen Schofield had chosen to read 'The Horses', from *The Hawk in the Rain*, as part of a verse and prose examination at the London Academy of Music and Dramatic Art, and had asked TH for advice. Reviewing TH's first book in the *London Magazine*, January 1958, poet and lawyer Roy Fuller (1912–91) had included the last line of the poem, 'Hearing the horizons endure', in a list of the book's 'very bad patches', but without specifying his objections to it.

To Karl Miller

11 June 1980   Ts   Miller

What I'd like to do in Alaska is record every moment and detail just as it occurs. I tried something of that in Iceland last year and got a glimpse of an interesting kind of record. Trouble is, angling, (like farming) is absolutely non-verbal—it all goes on in the right side of the brain or in the sympathetic nervous system or thereabouts—it becomes physically difficult to recover any freedom of language for quite a while. I've never read anything about that odd fact. I suppose what it is, angling and farming are pretty unconscious. But in Alaska I shall try to alternate. I'll give you a ring when I get back.

Karl Miller (b.1931) had known TH since they were both at Cambridge, had published poems of his in the student magazine *Granta* and in the anthology *Poetry from Cambridge 1952–4*, and had continued to publish them while working successively for the *Spectator* and the *New Statesman*, and then editing the *Listener*. He had agreed to collect the Royal Society of Literature Award, which had been given for *Moortown*, on behalf of TH, who was about to take a fishing holiday in Alaska.

To Keith Sagar

16 July 1980   Ms   British Library

They're having a Billy Holt Exhibition, opening August 2nd, in Tod. That should be interesting. He painted giant holy canvasses—spiritual revelations of the Mills, the dark Satanic Mills as a Jerusalem—very grand & bad.

His horse, Trigger, died the other day. The vet estimated its age at 35 (human equivalent about 120) Billy rode it to Rome & back when it was 15 or 20. A white Arab—he bought it from between the shafts of a coalman's cart. I've just been rereading his autobiographies "I haven't unpacked" etc. I'd forgotten what a marvellous record they are of that world of my parents, full of the real details. He joined up same time as my father—they were 3 apart in the queue—but was so clever they gave him a more or less special Army career to himself. He invented a shuttle & lost the patent somehow—it became the standard shuttle. Fascinating chap. Glyn Hughes is writing his biography.

William (Billy) Holt (1897–1977), self-educated, peripatetic Todmorden author and artist – to whose spirit TH offers the poem 'For Billy Holt', in *Remains of Elmet* – bought his grey horse, Trigger, from a rag-and-bone man and rode him around Europe. Glyn Hughes dropped the biography.

To Karl Miller

19 July 1980   Ms   Miller

Dear Karl,

I just got back from Alaska. It was as I imagined, only many times more intensely so. Just the most fantastic land I've ever been in. Something quite different from America. And what few Americans there are there (about the same number as in Devon, 300 thousand) are mainly a selected lot—in flight from the lower States, living the free wild life & the Alaska dream. Most of them living the dream—rather beautiful dream. Extraordinary free place—everybody doing just as they please, apparently, with that vast untouched country to play in. The only restraints seem to come from the Fish & Game Wardens, the army— who've shut off great areas—and the natives, who now have so much cash—compensation & conscience money from the Alaskans—that they're employing wizard lawyers and gradually getting their territories back—and closing them to whites, pretty well.

The Americans just seem to be holidaying there—shallow scratchy hold on the surface. Average residence is about 3 years—then marriage dissolves & one or both collapse back South to the States. Can't stand the winters, the loneliness, the small variety of the society etc. Very odd temporary feel to their lives. Average age 23. So the land stays very separate, vast & archaic—with the natives as part of the natural flora & fauna. I saw quite a lot, paddled over quite a distance, caught salmon till I was actually sick of catching them (up to 50 lbs), fished alongside bears, woke up among howling wolves—the place put on its full show, completely satisfactory. Immense high wide valleys just floored with flowers—all in a brilliant preserving odd light, so the clouds looked like cut lead & everything had an extra dimension of depth & singularity. I just couldn't believe it.

The Americans there are a doubly hospitable & generous lot—all a bit lonely, & feeling isolated (from the U.S. & the world), but pleased about it, resent their connection to the U.S., & so a visitor—like me—gets a whole landslide of unexpended friendship, & everybody there seems ready to do anything to convince you what a marvellous land it is, they're so pleased with it & with themselves living in it. So I had a good time. But even so hardly uncovered a corner.

When I come up I'll give you a ring—maybe we can have lunch. Maybe I can take you to lunch. I hope the event wasn't too bald. Thank you again, Karl, for doing it. I have something for you, but it needs delivering by hand. Keep well.

Ted

To Harold Massingham

1 September 1980   Ms   Massingham

Dear Harold,

Thank you for the note.

John's death—like all those cancer deaths—was difficult & terrible. I called in on him—in hospital—just half an hour after he'd learned that it was indeed cancer. Nancy had feared all along—from the summer before, his first awareness of pains etc, that it was, and she said she'd known he was going to die. But at that meeting he was very lively & himself—just thin. Very emotional, very frightened—so aware.

Angela & I tried a few desperate measures—I brought up a healer (he's brought cancer patients back from very near death—abandoned by doctors etc), but no good. Angela hunted up all the details about the Vitamin C treatment (lengthens the life)—but John would only obey his doctors, and his doctors (who'd thought it was pleurisy till it was nearly over) dismissed the Vitamin C business as foolish.

I saw him just before he died, a skeleton, barely conscious.

The funeral was about as decent as such things can be. Big crowd. I gave a rather hastily composed address—nearly a funeral oration, which I'm reshaping as best I can. We were all very stirred up, you can imagine.

The service at the crematorium was the only one I've ever been to which had dignity. Several of my closest friends have gone through those curtains—always with the most shaming idiocies being mouthed over them by some dog-collared hack, & hideous muzak. So we asked the Minister to say nothing, except the formal funerary texts, and we played the slow movement from Opus 132. Only about ten of us there. The effect was strange. At least, we were drawn into a concentrated depth & a long intense stillness—very long & very intense. The music & the coffin there, together.

If he had been going into the ground instead of those horrible flames it would have been perfect.

Many causes of cancer—but I felt these last years, since he retired, John was trapped, in that house, that sulphurous street, that Sunday round of the same sameness, the whole vital clock forcibly stopped. A dream of starting something afresh just flapped past him, for a while, 2 or 3 swoops—then he sank back. I suppose teaching had been everything—too exclusively, too dutifully, too religiously.

How is the writing Harold? I hope you're keeping it moving.

All the best

Ted

John Fisher, who had taught both TH and Massingham at Mexborough Grammar School, died on 1 April.

To Barrie Cooke

15 September 1980   Ms   Cooke

Naturally I've been intending to write to you ever since we got back from Alaska but the problem has been—the real stopper—that there is too much, too fantastic, to tell.

However, I'll give you a very brief outline, and then we'll fill in all the details when we see you.

During my week in Fairbanks, at the 'Festival Of The Midnight Sun"—(actually a week of writers talking to & holding seminars with

436

people who wanted to write)—I made my contacts. Alaska has so few people (quarter of a million—in $^1/_6$ the U.S. area) that everybody you meet knows quite a proportion of the rest.

I made several really good contacts I could never follow up—the place is so vast, & the regions so varied. One or two who could open up the Eskimo N. & N.W.

However, most of our action came through one couple—a doctor & his wife, who knew bush pilots, fishing camp guides etc. We met them. Everybody took endless trouble. And we concentrated on the South.

In the end, we were only able to use a fraction of the openings. But we reconnoitred pretty well. We made 2 main trips.

Our couple lived in Anchorage. He was being stand-in locum for a doctor at Seward—down on the coast—so they lent us their house as a base.

First, we borrowed a canoe—aluminium—and portaged through lakes & down the Moose River to the Kenai. That was pretty surprising. Wolves howling round at night. We bumped into Moose—nearly literally. We shot past lakes where 3 lb rainbows seemed fairly common. Went too fast.

We had quite an educational time.

Ended up on the Kenai River, a mighty river, running very high. We were just in time for the run of the red salmon and the Kings.

Last year was the record run of salmon—ever—in Alaskan rivers. This year, it was reckoned just <u>twice</u> as big.

Also the fishing fleets were on strike (the Japs seem to have got control of the market & were dropping the prices) so the rivers were so full of salmon even the Alaskans were astounded.

We caught red salmon—on weighted big flies—till we thought they were very small fry. Average about 8 lbs. Tremendous fighters, in the heavy river. And delicious.

Then by a fluke we got in with a little group of King Salmon regulars. King salmon are not easy to get at. Usually it's guide business—quite expensive—boat onto river to special holes etc.

But there is just one point, where the Moose—a broad quiet river—meets the colossal glacier-green torrent of the Kenai—where you can get at them, on the Kenai, from the bank.

We'll describe that fishing to you. You should have been there. Nicky kept saying "If only Barrie were here!"

It was strange fishing. Heavy rods (our Mark IV carp rods) 30 lb line, a legered fly—with red salmon-egg red round float just by the fly, so it floated clear of the bottom. The bites were as light as tench bites. And at 30–40 yards, very difficult to hit.

In 3 days, we saw maybe 5 landed—all over 40 lbs.

Then we refined the (very crude) U.S. technique, & got three. Ours were the smallest fish we saw. Nick got one 19 lb. I got one 24 lbs, 29 lbs (& foul-hooked & landed one about 45 lbs.)

We missed about 500 bites. We saw maybe 20 hooked & lost. (The gang was about 5 strong) (We got the highest proportion of fish finally).

One of the gang, a Frenchman, a hunter's guide in winter, an angler all summer, became quite a pal. When we asked for his address, he said "You'll find me here every year all June & July."

You're allowed 5 King Salmon a year, but no matter how many he catches he never declares a score above 4.

Fish & Game wardens are everywhere. The fishing is very tightly policed.

Then we flew out to the Katmai—a very wild volcanic region. Friend lent us a 30'06 Remington—wouldn't let us go without it. Bear accidents very common.

There we hired a canoe at a small fishing camp, & set out to cross a system of lakes & rivers. As it turned out, the canoe was too small & we were lucky to get out of it alive. The lakes are so cold, you're reckoned to have—at most—5 minutes of life, once you're in.

We went about 15–20 miles, & camped. Bears everywhere. On that lake—23 miles long, 4–6 miles across—a high road of travelling red salmon ran right round it. At every point we caught red salmon. Nick got a 8½ lb lake trout. We had a great time.

But we couldn't get to the place we wanted—a great region of islands—where rainbows averaged 8 lbs & pike were plentiful. We didn't dare venture out onto the lake in our canoe—the lakes become rough as open sea in about 15 seconds—from flat calm.

We should have had a klepper—a covered in kayake—they go anywhere.

Back at the fishing camp (an incredible spot, in itself) we met the Bear Bros—who hire kleppers etc throughout that region. I put their card in my diary and out fell—out of my diary, that is—a Bear Bros card. Somebody in Fairbanks had given it to me & I'd forgotten all about it.

If I'd remembered, & we'd had a klepper, we could have done our complete voyage. As it was, we just fished ourselves stupid.

Then we came back, & had a day out at sea after Halibut. I got one 29 lbs. Masses of other strange red snappers & bass, up to 8 or 9 lbs.

Then we had a final day at the Kings (which was when Nicky got his 19 lbs & I got the 45 lb).

We had other trips lined up—but no more time.

Next time, we shall know exactly where to go, how to get there, & how to fish it.

It's just the most beautiful place I've ever been. Nicky was smitten, too. Extraordinary light & atmosphere.

Hilarious & strange event, from beginning to end.

Everything very rough. No roads—all done by little aeroplane, or canoes. And a great lot of people. All Alaska-mad. All call America "the outside".

Since we got back, the usual rubbish-wagon of trivia has buried me.

The painter and fisherman Barrie Cooke (b.1931) had met TH in the USA in 1959, since when they had shared many fishing expeditions, mostly in Ireland, where Cooke lives.

Portaging involves taking a canoe overland from lake to lake. A 'legered fly' is one weighted to counteract buoyancy.

To Lisa and Leonard Baskin and family

[September 1980]   Ms   British Library

Dear Lisa & Leonard, & all, i.e. Tobias too if he's there

Here we are on a beautiful still yellow September morning, apples wet, weed-mass all sparkling & wet, Crows talking in the elm above me, a blue-tit levering life out of some cranny in my shed wall, sky blue, clouds high.

The river is perfect, just clearing after a glut of brown yeasty flood, which will have brought up the fish. Three days ago, just before the flood, I had a 10 lb salmon—special dramatic circumstances—which I'll have smoked, so we can share it.

Cormorants come up with the sea-trout. I surprised one in a deep hole in the river—as I came to the brink, ten feet above the water, he came up from the depths, just below me. My dazed brains just couldn't make sense of it—for a wonderful three or four seconds I saw it as a small plesiosaur surfacing. It saw me before it properly surfaced & knotted itself into a simultaneously-all-directions escape scramble through the surface—it didn't dare come up into air, and it wanted to get away faster than swimming underwater. A lovely mutual scare. Spoiled the river for me. See overleaf.

[. . .]

Carol sends her much love, & so do I.

Ted

Letter headed 'The Crow's Nest'. A single paragraph and a version of the poem 'A Rival', here titled 'Verses about the Rival', have been omitted. 'A Rival' was included in *A Primer of Birds*, TH and Baskin's 1981 collection of poems and woodcuts, before finding its place in *River* (1983).

To Philip Larkin

23 December 1980   Ts   Hull

Dear Philip,

This is the list we propose, after agonising the rest of Sunday and all Monday. Like yours our list is 'tentative'.

We finally persuaded ourselves that in spite of its jabber the mass of Irish sonnets was the most considerable piece of our elected triumvirate – after reading at it a good deal.

A Walk In The Country gradually asserted itself with us as the most interesting and substantial of the rest.

Rising Damp began to crumble a bit. Letters Home I turned against quite hard and Seamus never did like it. And Charles liked it less and less.

Father Makes A Speech kept a hold – though we began to feel that the lines slipped over things and went through the motions a bit too lightly for the occasion. We all found ourselves increasingly impressed by that notorious poem about the letter and the pilot. But this third place stayed even more dubious than the other two.

You'll see that The Baboon in the Nightclub is there in the pack of followers – Seamus feels much as I do that it's a real and very remarkable poem. But we acknowledge Charles' and your opposite opinion. Though I wish I could persuade you to read it right through – as

440

a lament of some sort to Priapus, an ultimate fantasy of sexual nostalgia and the comical – gruesome – pangs of erotic jealousy – "howling unlaughed laughter". It's finally a moving poem, I think, and not unreal at all. And that style of slightly 'gay' near-cliche trying to pour its heart out seems to me skillfully manipulated for the job and perfect for the character confessing the fantasy. The casual – subtle – structure of the piece seems to me quite inspired. Your 'political' argument against it appearing too visibly in the prize list, though, is ours too.

Please let us know what adjustments you feel like making to the tentative list here. After overwhelming you with all this, we feel guilty that the three you picked out got a bit battered in our final (nightmarish) struggle to become four bodies with but a single head – or at least a single mouth-piece, and I feel we have perhaps too readily imposed freakish tastes alien to your own. I've rung all round (after six days) to see what after-thoughts Seamus and Charles had and they feel as I do that we've got it about as right as we three – (mis)using your suggestions in your absence – are likely to get it. What we need now is for you to return with your final suggestions.

Merry Christmas and Happy New Year.

The judges for the first of what would be a continuing series of Arvon Poetry Competitions – TH, Larkin, Charles Causley and Seamus Heaney – were required to do a vast amount of reading, and their final deliberations were protracted well beyond the stage reported here. Of the poems still in the running, TH's favourite remained Kenneth Bernard's anarchically ribald 'The Baboon in the Nightclub' (published in extended form in 1994), but Larkin fiercely opposed it. Andrew Motion's 'The Letter' was the finally agreed winner.

TH's letter is unsigned, having been dictated over the phone to David Pease, director of the Arvon Foundation.

1981

Once disagreements over the outcome of the Arvon Poetry Competition had been resolved, much of TH's attention went on setting the Sylvia Plath archives in order. William Hughes's health gave increasing cause for concern, and he died on 8 February.

To Gerald and Joan Hughes

[Early February 1981]   Ms   Emory

Dad is now very low. My impression is he could die any minute, & no doubt suddenly will. I go every other day now, and each time his face seems even more changed—just a tiny ancient bird now, & obviously not happy. The worst thing is the expression of misery on his face—a struggle to keep going in that awful half-pyjamas, half-blanket perpetual dripping & leaking. No longer speaks—just the odd exclamation. Has to be fed, but most times refuses food—like a little sick animal. If you decide to come, don't expect to be recognised, beyond the odd flash. Expect to be shocked.

Since he fell & broke his hip, he's declined fast. Presumably he had some sort of stroke under the anaesthetic. It's a terrible business, living on as he is now. What a rotten life he's had since Ma died—$^{1}/_{8}$ of his life.

Otherwise, we all carry on.

To Leonard and Lisa Baskin

17 February 1981   Ms   British Library

Forgive us for being absent from this launching of the work into England. You know I very much wanted to be there, and so did Carol, to honour the event as much as we could. However, I have locked my doors and am lying down.

Just to drive the point home, the devil of anniversaries made sure

I saw Dad's dead body 18 years to the day on which I saw Sylvia's. I expect they were buried on the same day too.

Since my usual technique of pressing on regardless was really no good, this time I'm going to do nothing at all for awhile.

Buried him the day after his 86th Birthday.

I thought I was quite prepared, having watched him decline for so long, & being quite sure he'd die the weekend he did die, but in fact it gave me the shock of my life. Just that sight of him.

The exhibition *Leonard Baskin: Graphics, Drawings, Sculptures* was at the Cottage Gallery, London, in February and March.

To Keith Sagar

[11 April 1981]   Ms   British Library

Odd feeling re-reading such things as Brother's Dream etc—I see what it is about much of my writing that repels people—again & again I seem to be starting some sort of fight for life that admits only rough & ready counters of language—a sort of makeshift language, as if I might have time later to verbalise the thing more adequately, which of course turns out to be quite impossible, because—evidently—the important thing is the fight. And as soon as I come to the second wind and fresh shirt of revision, I'm drawn back into the fight, & I'm soon gasping for air again. Brother's Dream has that—and Quest, I suppose. Both of which I seem to have rewritten—in other poems—several times over.

The ugliness in all that, for me & I suppose for others, is that it is a fight—and not a talk, or a marriage, or an agape, or a sweet friendship, or a debate.

Reading my prose—or rather the odd bits of self-defence (just looking at Roberts & Giffords book) I've set down here & there—I feel the fight coming on. That prose somehow expresses very little of what I want to say, as though it were said only in the tension of a fight.

Strangest of all, I've realised, it is the same feeling I used to get reading my father's letters—there was something about them so vehement, so much in over-drive, that I often couldn't read them. (He was mostly a very silent man.) Is it possible to inherit a brain-rhythm? Very curious—in a biological way, to see it in myself so clearly, really as plain as a colour in a calf. The rest of me observes it with some dismay.

When I see it in such things as my exegesis of Orghast—in Anthony Smith's book—I feel slightly horrified—I see what barren wastes of intellectualism—in the worst sense—lie in wait if I let that monster fly off with me. What a fury of ingenuities! The real relieving thing comes from elsewhere if it comes at all.

Apologies for this self-centred digression—I must feel you're interested, but this business of my father's temperament & my mother's lying side by side in me in some antagonistic arrangement has only occurred to me lately, as a way of explaining things. And as a novelty.

'The Brother's Dream', written at the time of the *Wodwo* poems but left out of that volume, then broadcast on the Third Programme and collected by TH's BBC producer, George MacBeth, in his anthology *Poems 1900–1965*, was one of the items included by Sagar under 'Uncollected and Unpublished Poems', as Part 3 of his *The Achievement of Ted Hughes* (1983). A. C. H. Smith is the author of *Orghast at Persepolis* (1972).

To Keith Sagar

23 May 1981   Ms   British Library

Dear Keith,

I think I dated all the poems I could.

Kenner is consistent—higher-minded than any of us—loyal to a poetics that would bring about an Ice-age if he were Lord of the Universe—which his tone sometimes suggests he might be. His principles set in the fifties, O.K. for some.

He's probably perceptive about some writers who suit his temperament.

But don't follow him too closely on the 'frigidity of S.P.' trail. After all, what if he's wrong? (Maybe that never occurs to him—many silent classes have polished his confidence) Lots of people didn't like her—for no reason at all. I never knew anybody else who got poison pen letters from complete strangers. And it seems to go on after her death.

Where does the 'lack of sexual imagery' trail lead?

If only I can get her notebooks etc published, you'd probably get a better idea of her. The letters merely mislead. And the poems have been overlaid with other people's fantasy visions of her.

Kenner seems to me simply wrong about The Colossus. The metrics of those poems expresses limbo—immobility of fear—inability to come to grips with the real self. If a stasis of that sort, which she experienced as psychic paralysis, is a control of 'dangerous forces'—well, he can be said to be right. But he doesn't mean that.

Ariel—March–Nov. 62—is the diary of her coming to grips with & inheriting this 'real self'. It isn't the record of a 'breakdown'. Growing up brought her to it—having children etc, & confronting the events of 1962 (and mastering them completely). (After all, in 1960, she was only 18 months out of College—nearly all the Colossus poems were written while she was still a student or teacher & the rest within the first year after.)

You know Goethe's remark about the labour & difficulty of actually laying claim to what we have inherited—and you know how few people attempt it, how few even know they need to make the effort, how some go through Primal Screams to find it etc. Well, Ariel is her record of her experience of it—of coming into possession of the self she'd been afraid of (for good reasons).

The developed strategies of the verse were invented at need, to deal with the unique self-revelations—revelations of herself to herself (only incidentally to us). You suggest you find much of it a language of dis-integration. I see it as footwork & dexterity—the honesty (nakedness) to meet the matter on its own terms, & the brave will to master it—which she did. Those poems enact a weird fusion & identity with the material & simultaneously take control of it, & possession of it.

It's a process of 'integration', start to finish. By Dec. 62 she was quite a changed person—greatly matured, and a 'big' personality. In Dec/Jan she stopped writing (no poems really from early December to late January) & set up a new home, a new circle of friends, & a new life—and had almost completely repaired her relationship to me. She had set the Ariel poems behind her as 'a-Hell-of-a-necessary phase'.

[*Arrow connects previous paragraph but one to the next*]

That's a hypnotic technique (which Crowley used to like to demon-strate)—imitating somebody, exactly, until, at some imperceptible point, the initiative passes to you, & they begin to imitate you, & can then be controlled—its the fundamental dynamics of the artistic process, but in literature nowhere so naked as in those Ariel poems, which are all little dramas. More like some painting, or music, than any other poetry.

So you see I read those Ariel poems as a climb—not a fall. A climb to a precarious foothold, as it turned out.

But she was knocked off again by pure unlucky combination of accidents. No doubt that year exhausted her emotionally. The house-making etc, the 62/63 snow & cold, the 2 kids, exhausted her physic-ally. Flu knocked her lower. Stirrers & troublemakers complicated our getting together again, in no small way. Then on Jan 23rd—I think—The Bell Jar came out—which you can guess was traumatic for her—to have all that suddenly at large. But the key factor, maybe, was that her doctor prescribed, for pep up, a drug that her U.S. doctors knew—but her English doctor didn't—induced cyclic suicidal depression in her. She was allergic to it. Probably she didn't recognise the trade name. She was aware of its effects, which lasted about 3 hours between the old pill wearing off, & the new one taking effect. Just time enough.

The group of poems she wrote in those last days record the exhaustion & resignation—and the precariously-held-off solution—always very close when she touched bottom physically.

I've been trying to find the quote in Jung where he describes the most dangerous moment of all, in any episode of psychic disturbance—it is the moment of emerging from it, after having conquered it, when the sufferer has turned her back on it—steps out of it & away—at that moment it gathers all its energy and makes a last all-out attack (which, as he says, very often proves to be fatal, because the victim has lowered her defences). If that can be weathered, he says, the episode is usually over. Relevant.

I tell you all this to qualify your attitude to the notion of her as a young woman hurtling to disintegration shedding rags of poetry—leaping into Aetna & bursting into flames as she fell.

Ariel poems are about successful 'integration'—violent inheriting of a violent temperament.

The first sign of disintegration—in a writer—is that the writing loses the unique stamp of his/her character, & loses its inner light.

Mustn't underestimate her humour either.

The real question is—what would be the interpretation of those poems if she hadn't died, if she'd gone on to write something marvellous in a different way. [*Inserted from above:* As those very last poems suggest she was about to do.] They could only have been read as the scenes of a victorious battle for so-called 'self-integration'. The whole accent of subsequent commentary would have been different. The interpretation generally given is a pure fantasy—induced by her death, which was an accident (it could have happened at any moment between 51 & 63, if she'd got physically low enough—just as it could happen to thousands who never show a symptom,) and not at all essential to the poems—except as one latent factor in her mythology.

There were other factors, just as dominant in their phase. The suicide factor, however, only needed a phase of 3 hours to remove all other factors from the succession, & seize the crown for itself.

It is more interesting to read Ariel as a series of dramas of integration—though sometimes of diabolical material—but no more diabolical than most women would become aware of in her situation.

Nobody seems to have tried this approach, that I know of. Perhaps it's less interesting.

[. . .]

Keep well
Ted

TH had tried to date the fugitive poems that Sagar was rounding up in Part 3 of *The Achievement of Ted Hughes*. When the book came out, he told Sagar: 'The collection of poems seems strange to me—strange, I suppose, in that I would never have put together just these. In fact, they make a definite, consistent effect—a real book in their own little way' (letter of 25 March 1983, not included here).

'Sincerity Kills', an essay by Hugh Kenner (1923–2003), appeared in *Sylvia Plath: New Views on the Poetry* edited by Gary Lane (1979).

Aleister Crowley (1875–1947) wrote on many aspects of the occult, while energetically cultivating a reputation for scandalous behaviour.

To Ben Sonnenberg

30 May 1981   Ts   Emory

Thank you for the invitation to write about my life. I have tried it, a little, in verse. A friend took photographs of the valley where I spent my early days—a moorland valley in West Yorks ("Cradle Of The Industrial Revolution")—and I wrote some text. It was a curious experience. I had always regarded my early life as a Paradise, from which I was wrenched at age eight. But digging down through the strata with verse—following the goblin—I found dislike, dread, even hatred. What a surprise that was. And difficult to handle. And not at all what I wanted for the book of atmospheric photographs—National Heritage photographs (the place is about 5 miles south of Haworth and Wuthering Heights).

So I skidded off, after one or two encounters, and borrowed my mother's feelings (which I keep intact, in the appropriate shrine)—more suitable. She had the right tribal allegiance to the Holy Ground and the magical dead (the last-ditch farms, the slave mills, the massacres of the first world war, and the glamour of the genetic peculiarities of the valley as a badlands (Defoe hid there).

But my own life there, I saw, resisted surgery. I would like to try seriously, before time overtakes, but I shan't promise any results.

I enclose some pages. Two about rivers (from a book about rivers) and one about a bird from a book of birds. The SALMON EGGS poem was originally a poem about Sheila-na-gig. An Irish painter, friend of mine, is making a catalogue for an exhibition of Sheila-na-gigs. Do you know these creatures? Literally, 'Woman Of The Tits'. They're the most primitive figurative sculptures in these islands—always the same: high relief frontal of a woman with her knees splayed, and her orangoutang fingers hauling wide her giantess cunt—her face peering over it. Mostly in Ireland—two or three in England and Wales, built into churches— into the walls, often on the outside, just among the rough stonework— but always much older than the church, and always very crudely cut. In my poem, I suppose that this woman is our oldest goddess (a death/ battle/love goddess) who copulated with her consort standing astride rivers (I suppose, where she also gave birth). (A suggested scholarly correction makes her Sheila-na-gog—woman of God, God's Wife. Gog in old Irish means God!)

So my verses conflate the sculpture, the goddess, the red fish eggs and the swollen wintry river. Mainly, though, as you will see, it is about salmon spawning in the River Torridge—beside which I spent too much of my time.

Sonnenberg was at this time editor of the New York literary magazine *Grand Street*. He included three of TH's poems, 'An Icon' (a version of 'Portraits', in *Birthday Letters*), 'In the Dark Violin of the Valley' and 'Salmon Eggs', in his Autumn 1981 issue.

'Shelagh-na-gig' is the conventional spelling for the relief carvings described here.

To Leonard and Lisa Baskin

2 August 1981   Ms   British Library

Sunday morning, eleven a.m. It started clear and blue, in obedience to the weather-prophets, but has now succumbed a little to clouds—of a vague and well-meaning sort. All my ash-trees & oak trees & apple trees are breathing happily—so I look out into a depth of quivering light and shadow, and my crow's nest is surrounded by woodpigeons, a large but scattered pack, who are trying to get a full choral howl going, but can't synchronise, & stumble along with swallowed hoots & aborted gobbles, & keep stopping to check on each other. Now & again they all fall silent, discouraged, till some bold bird in the distance suggests a quiet note or two, & they all start up again. I've always noticed how they practice like this on Sunday mornings.

Yesterday I got through to the last page, of the first full draft, of my grotesque & ridiculous story, which I know you will never manage to read. It's as long as a short novel. It's composed of the sort of stuff nobody can take for more than about seven pages. Not that it's so crammed with vitamin essence—but that it's so grotesque & ridiculous. Once I got to grips with it, naturally there was no way I could break off & escape, without damage to my morale. So in the end I was pushing on simply to prove to myself that even idiocy could be made to work, in an idiotic way, to its own idiotic laws. And in the end I felt I was getting somewhere, breaking down some stale old yellow fat, if nothing else. So I've regarded it as a gruesome gymnasium—not a summit conquered.

It's full of good themes—real truths of the everymanskinhisownskunk sort. But all boiled together in a crude stew. As I say, I'm telling you all this because I know you'll never read it—even when I've streamlined it, & installed new engines (considering it as an aircraft rather than a goulashe).

My notion (vain) was—if I could give it that compulsive dynamics of a Kleist story, I could make it as grotesque and ridiculous as I liked. (The only avant-gardisme left for narrative is—to make it irresistibly readable.) But since those dynamics are to be found only in Kleist (and Singer), I'm left with a debris of grotesque & ridiculous scrap—like Scott's haulage tractors at the South Pole.

Otherwise, I've been fiddling (while the brain-cells burn) at a book I started by accident.

The 'grotesque & ridiculous story' has not been identified. TH was fond of quoting the proverb, 'Every man [must] skin his own skunk' – commonly attributed to Abraham Lincoln, but regarded by TH as Sioux in origin (see letter to William Cookson of 5 November 1989). TH greatly admired the stories of both Heinrich von Kleist (1777–1811) and Isaac Bashevis Singer (1904–91).

The book he had 'started by accident' was *What Is the Truth?*, which, as he goes on to tell Baskin, had been suggested to him by his Devon neighbour and friend Michael Morpurgo (b.1943), children's writer, co-founder of the charity Farms for City Children, and the book's dedicatee-to-be.

To Lucas Myers

28 December 1981   Ms Emory

My doings touched a low low this last year, many things coming to an end, many mistakes coming to an end too I hope. One of those periods of audit. I made a new selected poems, and realise that for the last ten years I've just piddled about—everything except make a stand and confront the real thing in a concentrated way. Everything except concentrate and confront. What I've written in these years is all doodle somehow—I just never put myself behind it. I was always occupied mainly with something else. Or writing pieces for a book with somebody else. What a folly. Since 1970 I've written nothing of what I feel I should have and could have. I'd have given more time and thought to painting somebody else's house. Maybe life and folly became too interesting—unproductive folly that is. There are productive follies after all.

Depression and debt too. Our horrendous tax debt got itself solved this summer—I sold Sylvia's manuscripts to Smith. It's like coming out of a prolonged delirious illness.

Anyway, my new resolution is to write only what I want to write and get back my old conscience about the business, no matter what the results might be. It's been a ten years of odd estrangement from myself.

TH's tax problems had arisen from the unexpectedly large sums earned by sales of *The Bell Jar* in the USA.

1982

To Ben Sonnenberg

29 January 1982   Ts Emory

I've spent a month trying to write a new and somewhat more true intro-
duction for the English Edition of Sylvia's notebooks book. Arduous,
because I'm unmanageably too involved. My main drift is that she was a
particular kind of poet—her poetry recorded a very particular process,
which isn't the case with any other poet of reasonable competence. Her
whole opus is a record of the process that most poets (the ones that
count) have gone through secretly (and unconsciously) before they can
really begin. Which means, more or less, that when she died she was
almost ready to begin. But it's too elaborate or analytical a thesis to
present—nobody is that interested in the psychic economics of writing.
But that is why her writing is so odd. The closest thing to it in art are
those paintings produced by Jung's patients—you don't have to be a
Jungian to see what the analogy implies. But as I say it's no good—I've
simply mired myself in it. I mean those patients of Jung's which accord-
ing to him were going through the equivalent of the alchemical process.
Maybe she's the only spontaneous and literal case. All other poets have
a subject—or rather, an arrangement of objects. She only had the sub-
ject. (As Edgar Cayce's Voices said, at the beginning of his healing
trance "We have the body"—before they proceeded to anatomise the
ailments and prescribe. Her muse says: "We have the—whatever it
was—psychic entrails"). Then the whole thing happened in camera.
Very odd. Reports from the crucible window. Up to the end of Colossus.
[. . .]

The point about my notion of Sylvia's poetry as the X-ray record of
the history of a purely internal process is—without understanding this I
don't see how the mood, obsession, frustration etc of her journals is to
be understood.

Volume 9 of C. G. Jung's *Collected Works*, which includes *A Study of the Process
of Individuation* and *Concerning Mandala Symbolism*, has passages relating

paintings by his patients to alchemy. Edgar Cayce (1877–1945) was a US psychic and healer.

The Spring 1982 issue of Sonnenberg's magazine *Grand Street* was to include TH's essay 'Sylvia Plath and Her Journals'.

To Glyn Hughes

[Early 1982]   Ms   British Library

Dear Glyn,

Knowing well what it feels like to have no response from somebody you've showed some writing to, I feel I owe you an apology. My excuse is, after I came back from Ireland early December I'd lost your book—I'd also lost Peter Redgrove's latest, which I received about the same time.

However I've rediscovered them both.

I've tried to dissociate my natural fascination with anything written about that region from what you've actually written. I say that but I expect it's impossible.

My final impression—after reading each page with fascination unabated—is that you've done something pretty impressive. The way you've written it, the way you've made a big powerful living image of the horrible truth of that business, could only have been done by somebody who knows the place inside out. Also, it seems to me you've avoided the pitfalls—the opportunity for 'fine' writing, for getting bogged down in incidental history, for making a 'modern' comment. You've somehow solved the historical dialogue problem (you make every bit of speech sound as if it was taken down at the time—that abbreviated formality is just right), and the problem of keeping religious mania from being boring. By sticking to the inner spirit of the thing, you've made the whole thing fly along. It could have been so heavy & depressing. Most of all you've captured that nightmare—of what went into those mills & chapels & pompous houses & worn-out ginnels—it made my stomach contract—horrible recognition. That compacted, swift, point-blank way you've done it is so good.

I've refused so many people who've asked about a quote for publicity—I hate seeing my name & opinion rear their heads, & I really think it draws fire (it did for Redgrove's Menstruation books, where I last appeared in that judgement wig). But what I will do, if you like, is

452

write a short review for some local (Yorkshire) publication, send you the text, & then they can use some of that—making sure to add the name of the paper, so it's clearly from a review. I really would like to say something about it.

Love to Roya—Keep warm
Ted

TH wrote a review of Glyn Hughes's *Where I Used to Play on the Green* for *Arts Yorkshire* (March 1982).

To Daniel Weissbort

7 April 1982   Ts   King's College, London

What an odd thing to think of 'modern' English literature. I can see why Americans aren't very interested. It's a collection of eccentrics—English Parson style, like Larkin, and ever shallower whiz kids.

The real poverty of 20th century English writing has been masked by presence of Eliot, Joyce and Yeats. Lawrence is really the only representative, and what an oddball he is. But at least he has psychological depth on a major scale. Graves, Auden, Thomas etc whatever they have, seem to me small beer in comparison—and I suppose it's because they're not psychologically self-explored in a serious way, they seem internally rudimentary, by comparison. Don't you think so? The whole thing is depressing. It's some sort of poison gas pouring out of all English Institutions—numbing, smartening, trivialising, finally paralysing. One used to think it was a historical phase, but it begins to reveal itself as a self-perpetuating thing. Now that the 1948 Education Act debouchement of the masses has subsided to Pop, that smart manner is reasserting itself, I think, with a vengeance. Everything new seems to get brighter and brighter and tinier and tinier. Or is it just stupor of the fifth decade beginning to close the slits of the old visor?

Did you see the Rozewicz, and the Celan? Both lovely books. I thought the Celan was a remarkable piece of translation by Michael H. Taps something in him that no other originals have. He's doing a mountain of Goethe now. I visited him (with Leonard B. who wants to use Michael's translation of Goethe's unfinished—and never before translated—Pandora, in a Gehena Press Limited Edition) and he was working all waking hours—in a very strange state. High on work.

Adam Czerniawski's translations of Tadeusz Różewicz (b.1921), *Conversations with the Prince*, and Michael Hamburger's of Paul Celan (1920–70), *Poems of Paul Celan*, were both newly out from Anvil Press.

To Craig Raine

16 May 1982   Ts   Raine

Dear Craig,

Thank you for the long painstaking letter. [. . .]

All your points gave me pause. You're quite right about several things. That Swallow poem out—for instance. Knock the last verse off the mouse—I quite like it, but the fox came first and the detail there is necessary, as things go.

I'll look at all the metrical pieces over the next couple of weeks. I want to replace the goat piece—'each rose fails'—alltogether, and one or two of the others. Also, I really ought to have a bee. My difficulty with the lollopy rhythmical lines is that for my first writing years I wrote nothing else (Kipling), and so soon got to the point where my main pleasure in those metres is in giving them a twist—and setting some other metre, inside them, against them. So you have the two oscillating along together. The problem is—others hear them differently.

Roy Fuller quoted my romantic line 'Hearing the horizons endure' as an example of my metrical imbecility, and called it (I think) 'unsayable'. On the other hand, I was specially proud of it. In fact, it still seems to me that if you're going to say it at all, you can only say it as I want it said. It's just that Roy Fuller refuses to surrender his officer's moustache, even provisionally.

I take your doubts more seriously I might say. Where you've jibbed, there are words with something like neutral value—so if I haven't imposed something definite, it's a thick ear. In 'necks up out' (in that partridge piece), you're quite right: it's 'up' is the trip. I try to get it both ways —and presumably fail. I try to get it with a pause after 'up', as if there were a comma there, (though it's still a glottal hitch), but I try harder to get it expressivo demonstrativo 'upout'—so there's a sense of a pause after 'necks' before you hit it 'UPOUT!!!'—which makes no doubts about the spondee on 'green corn'—in fact three long stresses together 'young green corn'. Imagine it spoken in a sort of Devon-cum-Yorks rural style.

'Bedding cattle' is the straw that breaks camel's backs on those who are foolish enough to winter cattle inside.

But I'll look at all these points. I'll argue my line about 'partridges lay clutches . . . and some he lets hatch. He's'

I'm going to Ireland for ten days, so I'll finish all this off while I'm there, I hope.

Meanwhile: Eng. Lit. paper 108.

> Question 1: 'Even the loose stones that cover the highway'
>   (a) Identify author and context.
>   (b) Scan.
> Question 2: 'Young couples nimbly began dancing'
>   (a) Identify author and context.
>   (b) Scan.
> Question 3: 'Evening and morning, the steep street of Urbino'
>   (a) scan 'the steep street'.
> Question 4: Are the above quotations forgettable? If not, give reasons.

> Keep well, love to Li
> Ted

TH is replying to notes on the poems in *What Is the Truth?*, on which the poet Craig Raine (b.1944), now working at Faber, though not the book's editor, had been asked by TH to comment. Phyllis Hunt, the firm's editor of children's books, had been baffled by some of the versification and Raine took up the matter. In the published text of the poem beginning 'A grand bird is the Partridge', the bird is singular and a comma appears between 'up' and 'out'. A poem about bees – 'At a big wedding' – was added to the book, which also eventually offered a variety of goat poems, including one, about the goat as a garden pest, with the phrase 'and every rose fails'.

The first of the exam quotations is from Wordsworth's *The Prelude*; the second, from Keats's *Endymion*; and the third, from Yeats's 'The People'.

'Li' is Ann Pasternak Slater, Raine's wife.

To Philip Larkin

21 October 1982   Ms   Hull

Dear Philip,

The enclosed isn't only a memento mori. Leonard Baskin wants to make a small book of poems [*marginal addition:* (poems about

Death—main point)] on his Gehenna Press, and with each poem he'll make a drawing. Do you know any Gehenna books? The Italian who is considered by all the relevant fanatics to be the best printer & book-designer in the world, considers Leonard to be the second best. He very much hopes you'll contribute a poem. Your payment would be some copies, I expect. So the enclosed is by way of a flyer.

To encourage you, I've drawn out your horoscope overleaf. If you now take up Astrology (consult Gauquelin for the computerised evidence pro) you'll see what a remarkable map of the heavens you've been carrying around all this time, in spite of the weight.

All the best
Ted

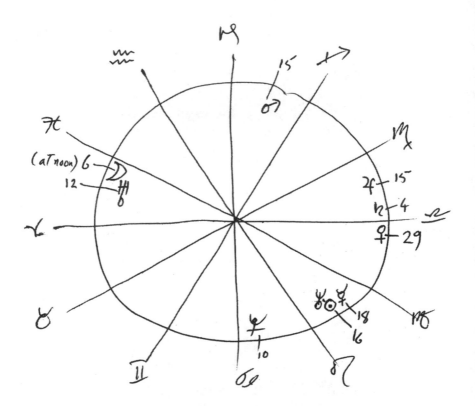

That's the map for 12 noon, 9th Aug. 22. The moon would still look full, and if you were born at about eight in the evening, which seems likely (says the ghost of Kepler), it would have moved to 10 of ♓ and would be just above the Eastern horizon.

456

If you were born about 1 or 2 a.m. (the other possibility, says this affable familiar), it would be directly overhead, & just moving from ♒ to ♓.

If neither, it would still be doing quite well.

TH encloses a pamphlet, produced by Leonard Baskin's Gehenna Press, with the title announcing 'JOHN SKELTON / UPON A DEEDMAN'S HEAD', and Baskin's etching of a jovial death's head under the title.

Michel Gauquelin (1928–91), French statistician, wrote *The Scientific Basis for Astrology*.

To Bishop Ross Hook

10 November 1982   Ts (Photocopy)   Emory

Dear Bishop Hook,

Your invitation, to take part in a discussion of ways in which representatives of the Church and of poetry might explore together ground of mutual benefit, came as a great honour. That will be a most interesting occasion, and an opportunity for acquaintance that attracts me greatly. But whether it would be appropriate for me to attend has given me some thought.

I cannot speak for other writers, but for myself I have to say that I don't know what purpose poetry serves, or what needs it supplies that people—a small number of them—should appreciate it as they do. I am not at all sure what purpose it serves for myself, when I try to produce it.

But I am very keenly aware—and the history of literature seems to me to support my observation—that poetic talent is a very unbiddable quotient in any work of verbal composition. It has only allowed itself to be directed here or there, by the writer's deliberate will, on very few occasions. History is full of examples, indeed, of poets who, on conscripting their talent for some worthy purpose, are promptly deserted by it. This independance of the authentic poetic spirit is certainly an inexhaustible subject for speculation—but I cannot see how any discussion about it can go much further than that.

At least, so it appears to me. It's true, I suppose, that for most readers of poetry, poetry seems to point, on one bearing or another, towards a spiritual life of sorts, or perhaps towards something that is a substitute for the spiritual life as it is understood by the Church. And I suppose there have been many occasions where poetry, in this way, has awakened

457

readers towards the spiritual life—readers who have gone on to a more whole-hearted self-involvement with the Church. I don't know whether poetry can be thanked for this. It may be that the superficially mystical aspect of much poetry is the first thing noticed by people who are willy-nilly starting on an inner psychological change, whose goal is, poetry or no poetry, eventually a full religious life. I think that is most likely.

At any rate, it seems to me that this incidental use of poetry as a sort of vestibule or pronaos to orthodox communal worship is one that cannot be exploited in any way.

The popular attitude to poetry—one encouraged and often enough quite strongly held by poets themselves—is that the poetic gift is a sort of biological aptitude that can be put to different uses. Every poet likes to think he would write richer and deeper plays, for instance, if he happened to write plays, by somehow 'illuminating' his drama with his poetic gift. In the same way, not a few poets have toyed with the conviction that if they were given the chance, they could create a superior sort of liturgy—more incantatory, more verbally evocative. Quite a few, after all, have produced what amount to liturgies—for their own private religion. And others—not poets, but perhaps the admirers of certain poetry—have thought poets could do the same. Most poets over thirty have been begged, at some time or other, to write a poetic drama—or have been commissioned to 'poeticise' a dramatic text. And there is a notion in the air—I have seen it expressed directly here and there—that poets might be induced to contribute to the verbal parts of orthodox Church texts.

But this attitude ignores that chief characteristic of poetry—that the spirit of it refuses to be directed. Poets would like to feel their talent is some sort of bonus—like physical strength, or swiftness, or even an aptitude for mathematics. I submit that it is very likely something quite different. I think we get a closer description of the way it has always operated if we regard it as nothing more than a facility for expressing that complicated process in which we locate, and attempt to heal, affliction—whether our own or that of others whose feeling we can share. The inmost spirit of poetry, in other words, is at bottom, in every recorded case, the voice of pain—and the physical body, so to speak, of poetry, is the treatment by which the poet tries to reconcile that pain with the world.

If this is true, then the only occasions on which the voice of poetry can operate within the body of a religion is where the pain is a religious pain—in other words, when the pain springs unambiguously from the relationship between the poet and his experience of God. In this sense, the poetry of Job and Isaiah and Revelations is the real thing: those men were the agonised nerves between God and the world, and their language sprang only from that pain. In this Century I think Eliot's Ash Wednesday is a similarly authentic religious poetic text. Though in this last case the pain is that of a man who has not yet found the God without Whom he feels he cannot live.

According to my argument, you will understand, I hope, why I think the writer who occasionally produces poetry is the very last person to venture with his specialised compass needle into the overwhelming magnetic field of the Church. This has nothing to do with his own religious beliefs. It has to do solely with the purity of his response to the source of his poetry—and that source is simply something that exists. Pain cannot be adapted—it can only be experienced.

It may be—one supposes that it unquestionably is so—that a full religious life, and particularly the Christian life, locates and embraces and redeems pain, and expresses the redemption, more fully and all-comprehendingly than any system human beings have yet devised. And it has been the case with many poets who have been drawn into the religious life, that they have attempted—sometimes successfully like Eliot, to take their poetry with them, widening the source of it from something that had been personal and particular to something communal and spiritual.

But whether they take their poetry with them, or find in their religion the real consolation for which their poetry had been only a temporary substitute, and in which their poetic talent evaporates as something no longer necessary, in both cases the same thing has happened: their former readers have lost them. The only exception to this rule that I can think of among contemporary writers is R.S. Thomas—who is also the only practising Minister among the really outstanding talents.

These considerations really have no end. But I bring them to an end in telling myself that even among the temptations and persuasions of everyday secular life, it is extraordinary difficult to do one's own job. If secular poetry is of any value, and I'm persuaded it is, to others and to myself, then I have to listen to its needs with great care, and divine its requirements in quietness and solitude, and work only according to those, and follow where they lead me. I regard poets such as myself as a sort of country healer, where the Church is Orthodox Medicine and the

National Health Service. It's a bad analogy, on many counts. But it illustrates what I think is one of the poet's duties (insofar as he has any outside his duty to himself)—it lies in the service he performs for people like himself who live round him. He may well pass on patients to orthodox medicine. But if he himself took up an orthodox training, though he might not lose his gift (it is of course the superstition that he would), he would no longer be accessible to those archaic citizens who prefer a healer to a doctor. Well, as I said, it's a bad analogy.

I have gone on far too long. I merely wanted to make my reasons as clear as I could, in saying that I feel I must decline your very kind invitation.

Yours respectfully
Ted Hughes

Bishop Ross Hook was Chief of Staff at Lambeth Palace. TH wrote at least half a dozen tellingly different drafts of his letter replying to the Bishop's invitation to join a lunch party and discussion with the Archbishop of Canterbury on 20 January 1983. Records at Lambeth Palace being subject to a thirty-year embargo, it cannot be known for sure, but TH's own photocopies suggest that the letter above, which he signed, was the one Bishop Hook received. The following letter was among the unsigned drafts.

To Bishop Ross Hook

10 November 1982   Ts (Photocopy)   Emory

Dear Bishop Hook,
Your invitation, to take part in a discussion of ways in which representatives of the Church and of Poetry might explore together ground of mutual benefit, came as a great honour. That will be a valuable event, without fail. But whether it would be appropriate for me to attend has given me some thought.

The relationship of poetry to the Church is intimate and profound, I'm convinced. But what the mood of it is I am not so sure. In face of the permanent truths of the established Church, it seems to me (I may be wrong) that poetry has a bad conscience. There is a very real sense, I fear, in which poetry can be said to live on the decay of formal religion. Poetry is forever trying to do the work of religion—as local 'healers' are perpetually setting up as an alternative to orthodox Medecine. Some very great poets have come near formulating what was, pretty well, an alternative religion—a new religion. It's the shaman streak in the poetic temperament. Sometimes this is concealed and disguised as a godlessness, a humanist materialism. This questionable relationship, between poetry and established religion, seems to be the rule.

The poets who have managed to work freely within formal religion seem to be scarce. The temperament which can manage that, or do it naturally, seems to be an exceedingly rare one. I wonder why that is.

One thing, I suppose, is sure. Real poetry, whatever it's compass bearing on the true North of the perfect spiritual life, offers to the reader a spiritual life of sorts, even if, as I say, it is only a temporal substitute for the spiritual life—a bearing, as it were, due South. I imagine this is how poets have often served as a sort of awakener to the spiritual dimension of things, for people who go on to find their real needs met by religion, by common worship, a traditional and ancient liturgy etc.

But for most readers of poetry, I fancy, that spiritual life of sorts, that substitute, it may be, is quite enough. So what most poets offer—an eccentric, home-made, semi-mystical system of images, cadences and luminous experiences, leads, in a spiritual sense, nowhere, but does serve a need. It serves those readers who would prefer not to launch out onto the real depth of spirit, but like to visit the edge of the sea, occupy their conscious minds with pretty objects washed up, and give their subconscious minds a douche of the old thrill—just a reminder that there is more to the world than the street, the office and the garden. People who regard formal and real religion as something for other peoples, and other times. In fact, they have such definite ideas about their scepticism of the full spiritual life, that any too open show of it in the poetry they might otherwise appreciate will turn them against that poet as if with a kind of logic, as if by that he lost all credibility.

This huge population—lost to the fullness of spiritual life that a Church offers—still have these needs as I've described them. At least I think so. And as a writer who finds himself accepted by them as 'a poet', I wonder if my only chance of being any service to them is in remaining as I am—writing out of my home-made system of things, in every way one of them, and being careful to make no move that will separate me from them.

My fear is, that if my compositions were to become in any way more openly engaged with formal religion (and like all other 'poets' of my acquaintance I have robbed many churches), they would lose whatever power they might at present have in turning a readers eyes, even if only

461

temporarily, towards a deeper (I hesitate to say more spiritual) view of certain aspects of life. That is a precarious sentence for a precarious apprehension.

If, by internal compulsion, I were to move toward a direct self-involvement with the Church, that would be a different matter.

I hope you will understand, therefore, when I say that I feel I must decline your kind invitation. I trust you will find a freer response from the excellent poets who have a more appropriate temperament.

To Jack Brown

10 November 1982   Ts   British Library

Dear Jack,

I apologise for this year-long silence, after you sending me Egocentricities and the letter. You know I'm a fan of yours. I find myself reading your poems with the sort of alerted interest that very little new verse raises in me these days. They're very fresh, and seem to me very real at the core, and you have your own musical secrets of progression from one point to another—a kind of original inner freedom that leaves me quite exhilarated. End of comment.

If it occurs to you, as you say, to resurrect Crow or Gaudete in any form at all, please feel absolutely free to go ahead.

I felt disappointed for you in your political impasse up there. Never mind. One thing that doesn't cease to be fertile with reversals and surprises is the womb of time.

It occurs to me more and more often that the prolonged Tory dominance—the gradual consolidation of the Eton/Oxford/Tory axis in all positions of social influence—is beginning to have a narrowing and shallowing effect on the cultural atmosphere. Many symptoms. As if the Education Act had been a sort of vaccination—and the late fifties and Sixties the immediate post-jab malaise—and now the abounding immunity.

Probably zoological. Swing of the evolutionary pendulum, among the weeds in a small garden plot. This year its all foxgloves, next year Willow-herb, next year thistles etc. Though I fancy it's a bit more sinister, in its effects—on acceptable, socially acceptable, poetry for instance. Perhaps it makes it easier to write the real thing—socially unacceptable poetry.

Whichever it is, keep at your own brand. And drop a line now and again.

Keep well
Ted

Egocentricities was a typescript of poems by Jack Brown, at that time a Labour county councillor, who had met TH at a public function in Barnsley, South Yorkshire, establishing a rapport that soon led to an exchange of letters. In his most recent letter to TH, Brown had volunteered to adapt *Crow* and *Gaudete* for stage performance.

1983

To Yehuda and Hana Amichai

14 May 1983   Ms   Hana Amichai

Yehuda, I think you are my favourite poet—on one side there are all modern poets, writing the great intercontinental express of modern poetry, coaches crammed indiscriminately with great men, brilliant women, comedians, charlatans, ninnies, etc, but all racing along the flashing rails, a resounding 150 m.p.h. concatenation of modern poetry hurtling through the century, and on the other side is you—absolutely alone and apart from them—standing I imagine on a dusty hill over Jerusalem—the sole shepherd of the voices of human beings. You've discovered a subject that seems absolutely new to poetry, and it turns out to be the human being speaking like a human being about being a human being, or rather singing like one. The undiscovered animal!

I'm trying to persuade Faber to publish it, and using every possible means, but that doesn't guarantee anything.

From the beginning of his friendship with Yehuda Amichai, when Assia Wevill had been among his translators, TH had urged British publishers to take his work on, but seldom successfully (see letter to Daniel Weissbort of 21 November 1983). Faber and Faber did not publish a volume of Amichai's until the *Selected Poems* of 1999.

To Barrie Cooke

23 October 1983   Ms   Cooke

Dear Barrie,

I've delayed sending you this, because I wanted to give you some account of Africa, maybe photographs. But Nicholas is being dilatory, getting the snaps developed.

He was on an island in Lake Victoria. He chose it, for his Nile Perch study, because last year, when he was roaming about it & went to investigate what looked like a good spot on the map, he found that

464

strong wind-currents ran between mainland & island, at one point through a 100 yards narrows—and there a German (who'd gone out to advise the Africans on fishing methods, & who after 2 years of having all his advice ignored, was reduced to amusing himself by catching Nile Perch on lures) was casting big weighted bunches of chicken feathers into the narrows. He jigged them in, & caught fish up to 60 & 70 lbs—though he said most of the big ones just ran off all his line & broke him. But he usually had 4 or 5 fish a session between 20 & 40 lbs.

When Nicky got to the same place this year, a causeway had been built—a ridge of huge rocks, carrying a road 20 yards wide—right across the narrows from mainland to island, so the long 6 or 7 mile strait, with its strong currents, had become two stagnant bays. A disaster for the fishery of the town at the causeway. The Nile Perch no longer ran through, & the stagnant water just thickened up on Bilharzia, Malaria, & the thousand fatal diseases.

Nicholas made useful friends. The local fishery inspector (the control organisation, of all the native fishing, is very active—but fairly loose) took to him, and introduced him to the chief of a fishing village right out on the North point of the Island, where one fishing station—a beach where they hauled one beach seine at a time—(though they brought one in behind the other), caught more Nile Perch than anywhere on the Kenya shore of the Lake. So he was pretty lucky. In fact, considering the other fishing beaches, some of which were quite poor (only 20 or 30 fish a day) he was incredibly lucky, since his aim was to examine & measure as many fish as possible. He lived there in the chief's hut (9 mud huts in the whole village) for 10 weeks, & gutted about 1500 fish—inspected their diets etc—and measured about 3 to 4,000. A far bigger & fuller sampling (all-sizes) than in any earlier Nile Perch research published. By the time I got there, he'd just about finished what he wanted to do, so he was free to fish with me.

It took me about 24 hours travelling to get to him from Nairobi—the last 80 miles very rough in one of those jeeps that sprout heads & arms like a crate crammed with chickens—and the last lap by canoe.

The village is called Ulugi Beach. Its the Northern tip of Rusinga Island. On the map, it's the South headland of the neck of the Kavirondo Gulf, & a perfect spot for all traffic of fish in & out of the Gulf, which is shallow & very rich water, as well as being quite enormous itself, a big arm of the Lake.

I imagine the wind currents help, at Ulugi. The wind blows NE to S.W. all morning, sometimes quite strong, & bends the current round the tip of the island, creating a near rip tide only about 200 yards out— not a rip tide, but a perfect drift. At noon, the wind drops (under the vertical overhead sun) & the lake becomes a mirror for about an hour— like a pan of molten lead, fairly fries your balls. Then after about 1 dreadful hour—(when a strange exciting thing happens, as I'll tell you later)—the wind gets up exactly opposite—S.W. to N.E.— & blows till just after dark, whereupon it changes again, back to where it started.

The village was 9 or 10 mud huts, on the slope (quite steep) over the N. facing beach. The chief's huts (3 huts—3 wives—3,000 children) were up on the neck of the ridge between that beach & another small beach 100 yards down to the west. Between the 2 beaches, the ridge ran up onto a rocky headland, covered with scrubby jungle and thorns, 2 big fish eagles (and their chick just beginning to fly) & infested with lizards about 4 feet long. There was another pair of fish eagles, on the other point of the N. beach. (In fact, canoeing down the side of the island, we saw fish eagle couples about every five hundred yards. Wherever you looked in the sky you saw an eagle.)

The chief's hut, where we slept & kept our gear, was the most marvellous location. To the West, hilly jungle-covered islands blocked most of the view of the open lake (bigger than Ireland), & to the North, 7 or 8 miles across the neck of the Gulf, mountains beyond mountains.

The chief—(a young bloke, 28 or so, who had become very attached to Nicky & tried to get him to stay, offered him a patch of land & all the materials for a hut) owned 4 beach seines—inherited from his father, who lived back somewhere among the thorns (& owned all that North end of the island.)

He (the young chief) owned the fishing rights on the two beaches. The ownership & fishing rights are complicated—archaic and modern mix of family territory & Govt. licences. Net mesh size is controlled—but everybody tends to violate it. Net length etc likewise. The fishing is done from small beaches here & there among the rocks, & from boats—with drift nets & long lines. Fishing pressure, evidently, is going up all the time. (Kenya's population has doubled in ten years, quadrupled in 30).

He has the four nets on the North beach. (The West Beach is too rocky off-shore, & nothing like as good) About a dozen canoes— strange craft, very gaudily painted, 15 or 20 feet long, a yard beam, with

3 or 4 very stout narrow seats, & they all take a mast & sail—Dhow style. He employs about 15–20 blacks to pull the nets etc—mostly his brothers. (He has 20 odd brothers, & eighteen sisters). Pays them 20 shillings a day (same cash as ours, about)

The drill is: they load the net into a canoe, take it straight out from the right hand side of the beach, to the end of its 500 yard pulling rope, then drop it across the bay, parallel to the beach, & bring the other rope in to the other end of the beach. The net is maybe 100 yards long, with a big pod, & weighted to drag bottom. Behind the beach, there's a great cairn of rocks brought up from the lake, where they've cleared the path of the net. They always drop the net in exactly the same place, & bring it back over the same ground. At that five hundred yard limit, the net goes down maybe 100 yards beyond the East headland or rather NE headland, but it's main pull is well within the bay. The fish must swing into the bay.

3 or 4 or 8 or 9 (sometimes) pullers on each rope start the pulling—a very slow job. As they bring the net in, they narrow the angle of pull, closing from the left hand side of the beach to the right, so the final pod comes ashore always on the same five yards of sand.

It takes about ¾ of an hour to get the net in, but when it's half way in they take another one out beyond & behind it, so there are always—pretty well—two nets coming in.

When the net comes to within 30 yards of the beach, the lake just erupts. The pod is <u>always</u> packed with fish. Average number is 30–40 fish. Average weights 20 to 40 lbs. And they pull an average 9–10 nets a day.

So at the end of the day, they have between a ton and a ton & a half of fish. A colossal heap of colossal fish. All Nile Perch.

Women come down towards evening, & buy fish.

Each puller can take a small fish or two from each pull (5–10 lbs)—and trade these to the women, who butcher them there & then, sling the offal into the lake, & go off up the hill with great pans, piled with fish, on their heads. What eats the offal?—a story.

The fish are loaded into a couple of the canoes—which go down to 8 or 9 inches of freeboard, & they set off under sail to a town on the Northern mainland shore. It takes about 3 quarters of an hour, & they arrive at dark, with all the canoes from other beaches, & there's a wild hurricane-lamp market. The whole lot are sold at just over a shilling a kilo. That little town is all fires for frying the fish, & smokehouses, an infernal scene of hacking and stirring.

Every night the same—any weather. One night, in a terrific storm, the wind changed too early, & caught them only 200 yards from the far shore, & blew them right back across the lake to Ulugi. How that loaded boat kept up in that storm I can't imagine. The fish are heaped above the gunwales, except for a baling space in the middle, & the men sit on top of the fish. The rudder is a big paddle braced against a foot.

Nick & I went across one night—a biggish sea, a very big load of fish, sailing into the most incredible display of lightning I ever saw. Truly like a thunderstorm on an electrified planet in a space fiction film. We got into a race with another canoe. I expect that was about the most exciting half hour of my life, under those great vertical 15 second rivers of orange or blue or green lightning, & great skyfulls of blazing thorns, & continuous overhead thunder, with great long swells coming along the gunwales, pouring in on both sides, one man bailing like mad, the rest paddling & yelling, & our sail like a map of the world in giant rips & holes, and those fish, unbelievable, their eyes glaring like orange torches—colour of the orange on traffic lights & just as bright, actually lit from the inside, very eerie & mysterious, hours after they were dead—well, I'll tell you, it was like the greatest impossible dream. And two of those fish were Nicholas'—one weighed 68 lbs, the other 82. We won the race.

After we landed, we spent the rest of the evening taking the head off the biggest Nile Perch either of us saw—it weighed 81 kilos. We tried to dry it—to bring back—but not even the Afric equatorial sun was up to it, so we left it hanging from a euphorbia tree at Ulugi, still in a cloud of flies. "Dogge-duong" it was named—Big-Mouth. It achieved some local fame.

At night, a different fishing population took over. The whole lake is covered with a tiny fish called Omena—exactly like a whitebait, brilliantly silver, size of minnow, live in the surface layer. The omena fishermen operate from the beach. They put out a hurricane lamp, suspended in a braced arch of wood, on a square raft a yard or so across, very stable—float it 50 or a 100 yards off shore. Each group has seven or eight. So at night, the lake is fringed with these bright little villages of omena lamps. Some fish them from boats, same style, on calm nights.

After about an hour, they start to pull one of the lamps in very slowly on a long line. As it comes close to the shore, they take a floating seine of very fine mesh round the back of it, then bring the two in together, very slowly, & so right up on to the sand—and the net is seething &

skipping with omenas. Next day they dry them in the sun. They're quite valuable—500 shillings a sackfull.

Along with the omenas they catch baby Nile Perch—3″ to 8″ or 9″. So we got our bait there.

Nick had his own canoe, so we set off each morning, about 9—usually had a lad to manage the boat, but we did better without. Fished till about 2.

Nick's experience had been: he went out once, with very small baits—3 or 4″—a single treble in the lip, & caught 3 in about 1 hour, up to about 25 lb. Then he went out with the chief, lowered a bait, & got a fish straight off—64 lbs. The water was too rough, so they came straight in.

So we expected good action. In fact, we never got more than 6 fish a morning—but we tended to get big ones. I jigged spoons—leaded to hit bottom (about 60 feet down in the middle of the bay) and got fish, but gradually lost all the spoons, on the very rocky bottom (only the seine's path had been cleared).

Live baits seemed best. We moved to one big treble in the lip, & another dangling free—Cooke style—and hooked more biters. Then we realised dead baits were pretty good, fished à la Lough Allen, dragged and jigged a bit nearly beneath the boat. Big leads in the strong current.

We located the hot spot—along beside the reef that ran out in shallow water from the point of eagles & lizards. It dawned on us that baits over 5″ long caught nothing under 30 lb. So we went a bit bigger, & caught bigger fish.

They took with a bang—then just anchored. In shallow water, evidently, they run for hundreds of yards. But in the depth we fished, they simply hugged the bottom, circling slowly. The fight was getting them up—& them getting back down. We began to straighten big treble on very big fish—so we took bigger trebles off some giant Rapalas. On average, we caught fish in the biggest range of the sizes that appeared in the nets. By my last morning (and Nick's) he had the top weight of 82 lb. That morning we hadn't a single bait. There had simply been none in the omena nets. Nicky went to another tiny beach, where a few omena lamps were sometimes put out, & he found one little Nile Perch—about 8″ long. So we went out with just one bait. He paddled & I fished. Since we planned to catch a monster, he persuaded me to use that Loch Lomond pike rod—which he'd been using, with 30 lb line. But on the first rock I snagged I realised the rod had been smashed

& crushed—just above the butt. I'd laid it on that cairn on the beach, & a rock—dragged up in the net—had been tossed, out of ancestral habit, onto the cairn, and of course smack & bang onto the rod. We'd thought it had missed.

So I went back to my Ugly Stik (10 ft, marvellous rod) which has much more action & life. After a while, I got a fish about 30 lb. And—it never happened before—the bait was still on the hook. We fished on & I got another—very big fish, that pulled us around for a minute, then evaporated. And the bait was still on. I trimmed it back to fish-shape with my scissors. Then I got another—and lost that. And the bait was still on—looking very ragged. More trimming, & we fished on. It was about 12-30, & we had to go in by 1-30, if we were to get back to the mainland before dark. Then a great bang, & I had another—that I couldn't move at all for a while. It moved off very slowly, pulled us round in a big circle, then to & fro across the bay. I kept the rod full arc, tip down near the water (Ugly Stiks are unbreakable). After about 30 minutes, I was more or less total cramp, but I began to get line. Then up a bit, & back down, for a while. Then up a bit more, & up. The peculiar thing about this fishing, in that depth, was that once you got the fish to within about ten feet of the surface, suddenly its weight ceased—and it simply floated up, like a balloon, completely helpless. So this huge thing bobbed up. It took us five minutes to get it over the side of the boat.

104 lbs!

Then we paddled in, packed up, & left the island—end of trip.

After that, the Spey seemed civilised enough. 4 of us got 59 fish in 5 days. Biggest, 20½ lb. My biggest—2 of 19½ lb. Average weight, about 14lb. So there were quite a lot round 15–16. I had 16 fish. All on little flies—Monroe Killers, Stoats Tails, & Yellow-haired black-bodied tubes, except for a few on a Kynoch killer harled from a boat. Exciting stuff. If the weather hadn't failed, & river started rising, on the 3rd day, I think we'd have had a lot more. Periods of 2 or 3 hours at a time with a fish in the air every moment, sometimes 2 or 3, in a ½ mile view of river.

Did you get any pike fishing?

love

Ted

[*Postscript at head of first page*]

Second thoughts: I've sent my book "River" to Sonia—where you can pick it up.

Some angling terms: 'single treble in the lip' refers to a three-pronged hook; 'Ugly Stik' is the registered trade name of a particular rod; to keep a rod 'full arc' is to apply maximum pressure; 'harling' is a method of fishing from a boat where you move from side to side trailing a fly or a spoon.

To Daniel Weissbort

23 October 1983 Ms Emory

Dear Danny,

Just got back from Canada to find your letter. By the time you get this, you'll have had the operation. I've been trying to think how you can get yourself into a position—or the best position—for fighting back, & bringing yourself out of it. My one or two fleeting glimpses of what it's like, to know you've somehow got yourself so ill, gave me a good idea of the rage against yourself, & the fright. Ted Cornish always says—the worst (he thinks, the most dangerous) thing about such illnesses is the fear. He thinks, if you can control the fright—the imagining of the worst, & the resignation, you can get the upper hand, & come out of it. He thinks a lot of his success is because he hypnotises his patient to overcome the fear—to fix their imagination on hope & miracles. On confidence in miracles. He thinks that up-beat hypnosis is crucial. Is it possible, to get yourself under a powerful hypnotist?

He also thinks, you have to escape the conditions associated with the illness, as if you were making a clean break, & a fresh start. Impossible usually, I imagine. But the illness itself often forces a clean break, doesn't it?

What would happen if you simply dropped everything, came back here, & lived on the State? Why not? Just bugger the whole set-up, live on the State, & write. Is it desirable? Lots of other people do it. Just tell everybody to fuck off.

I expect this sounds pretty irrelevant. I know even when you've told everybody to fuck off, & you've drawn your first National Assistance packet, & settled down to your Vitamin C overdoses, & your hypnosis, & your general five-year campaign-plan to put Number One back on the throne, as sole reigning monarch,—your problems have only just started. Still, they're your own problems, at least. Not the department's. And they amount to a complete fresh start, on the only things that matter—to you. Is this hot air?

I was in Africa, with Nicholas. He was on Lake Victoria, an island, with a gang of black fishermen—9 mud huts, a little beach, a seine net, a few canoes. They caught 1½ tons of fish a day. He was there 3 months, cutting the fish open, measuring their diet etc. Those fishermen had absolutely nothing—lived in the dirt, ate maize meal, sweet tea, & chapatis, & nothing else. (Sold the fish—took it 9 miles across the Lake every night). After two weeks with them, I entered a peculiar euphoria of feeling free of every anxiety—no care about chairs, beds, time of day, dirtying the carpet, who'll arrive next, whether I've done what I promised. It dawned on me—with a great unforgettable dawning—that knives & forks, locks & keys, clean shoes & appointments, concern for tomorrow, are each a huge separate world of apprehension, complicated meaningless fiddle, and nightmare unnatural dread. It was a revelation I still haven't lost the feeling of. The infinite happy security of living in the dirt like a baboon! Like a baby, I suppose, really. Still, those blacks were so full of merriment & life. And they had no anxieties because they <u>didn't want anything</u>. We offered them superior hooks—which they'd admired—but they didn't want them. They wouldn't accept them! Love from us, Danny. I'll write some more,   Ted

While teaching at Iowa, Weissbort had discovered that he had cancer of the jaw. He did not act on TH's recommendation to leave his job, but the tumour was successfully removed. Later, when it seemed that the cancer might return, Weissbort consulted Ted Cornish.
   TH did 'write some more': another letter of the same length, on the same day.

To Lisa and Leonard Baskin

9 November 1983   Ms   British Library

Since I'm bumbling happily along towards the end of Canto I Complete Lives and Songs of The Crow—pulling everything together in what seems like a satisfactory fashion—and since I know that you will never mention the fact to anybody & so it is as if I hadn't breathed it aloud (which would certainly be instant strike & close-down of the entire productive industrial complex) & so as I say I can tell you that this is what I'm doing happily and so as it seems you will have to work your own way out of the maze of syntax herein circumbombulated—

Anyway, I'm knocking off for ~~ten minutes~~ two hours to write a line. Enclosed: the ultimate text of my Notes for a Panegyric Ode. My plaque of embossed prose, in iron & copper extracted from blood.

I expect all the assumptions out of which I draw my reflections, in the Hanged Man & the Dragonfly, are so alien, you probably do have difficulty in taking it seriously. Especially as I seem to be telling you, Leonard, what in spite of what you think you are you in fact in terms unacceptable to all sane men unacceptably are. Especially to yourself unacceptably. Well, there it is. But after all, beating my head against it for ten months, a 55th of my life, I haven't finally come up with something that isn't what I do feel. It seems to me I've come up with something that I actually know.

The tone might be a bit hard to swallow for stomachs dieted on art-prose—but then "The sybil, with raving mouth etc." Objections will be lodged—against the presumption of such frail insects as yourself & myself attaching ourselves to such mighty angelic concepts. But when we've withered away, or been frazzled off, the mighty angelic concepts will remain embedded in your figures, & the personal affront will wear off—along with our fingerprints, let's hope.

[. . .]

Please summon a deep breath & read it again in this final form. If I haven't finally got my notions into clear, expressive, fully-communicating sentences—then it's beyond me. In the earlier versions, nothing was clear. Now, to my perverse ear, it all rings like a bell. (Dumb bell)

Mention of the 'Complete Lives and Songs of The Crow' – who has a single 'Life' in the 1970 published edition – is tantalising, as no such complete text is known to exist. 'The Hanged Man and the Dragonfly', which TH wrote as introduction to *The Complete Prints of Leonard Baskin* (1984), is also included in *Winter Pollen* (1994).

To Daniel Weissbort

21 November 1983   Ms   Emory

Dear Danny,

I expect my two excessive letters rang every possible wrong note for you. As soon as you feel like writing, let me hear something.

I shifted all my books into a different room the other day, & sorted them in some order—for the first time. Half a ton of modern poetry, there must be. Very strange, digging back into it—Tarn on Neruda, Bly in the Sixties, those endlessly marching Penguins. It's particularly odd at the moment—poetical climate here being what it is. I would have said the reigning Court—all around 40—are as utterly closed to it as their fathers were (Kingsley Aymis, Roy Fuller). But a student the other day sent me a College Mag more or less devoted to Holub & Herbert and to <u>imitations</u> of them. The 40 year olds in fact (Penguin Modern Poetry Motion Morrison) have already gagged—nauseated their juniors, who are casting around for alternatives, & finding what M.P.T. found. But can their curiosity survive?

You must do that Anthology of the Gang.

Nothing much doing here. Larkin's just published his Collected Prose bits & pieces, & Observer & Sunday Times & Sunday Telegraph have prostrated themselves and finally deified him. Not a murmur of suspicion. If they give the Laureateship to Spender (I imagine that's why he was Knighted, to marinade him for the Court Banquet) there'll be a revolution of English Profs & Civil Servants & probably every literate loyalist-to-his-upbringing between 56 and 65, & a 9 mile column of Don's wives will carry P.L. (born Poet Laureate almost) from Leicester to Charing Cross on the frame of a Penny farthing.

It's a brilliant, very frosty day here—thrushes, blackbirds, & redwings flocking onto the last squishy rinds of our fallen apples.

I finally more or less finished my Introduction to a book of Leonard Baskin's prints (Collected—830 odd pieces). I started it last December, I've written nothing else, & its 15 pages long. It reads like the rosary of a Notre Dame gargoyle, made of petrified hyena turds (technically known as coprolites)

It's the last prose I'll write. I don't know who it is writes that stuff, but it surely to God isn't me.

Write a word or two. Are you coming back here? Remember the Xess Vit C.

Love from us   Ted

Faber rejected Yehuda's latest book—after Oxford, calling it back after a previous editor had rejected it, had rejected it.

Sir John Betjeman had died in May, prompting a carnival of public speculation as to his likely successor.

To John Moat

22 November 1983   Ms   Moat

Dear John,

I've been thinking about our talk the other day, and the idea of asking Peter to devise a sub-Arvon Institute of Creative Research—as it might be called in the U.S.

Mainly, I've been thinking how to deal with the objections (coming from the Arvon Committee) and the reflex disapproval (from Arts Council etc), to anything that sounds like an innovation. It has to sound like growth.

It all depends, I imagine (supposing that Peter is at all interested), on the way his operation would be camouflaged.

The whole point, at bottom, is to give him a free hand, and see what happens. But that inner licence will have to be concealed behind some outer conformity—since Arvon is under such scrutiny from establishment benefactors. The outer conformity will have to show structure, and real activity—will have to be enough, in itself, to justify Peter's management, & salary.

There'll have to be an esoteric inner circle, kept secret, until it begins to produce results—and perhaps kept secret even then, & in some way kept separate from direct Arvon involvement. I'm only supposing that the slightest rumour of bizarre goings on would provide a feast for critics of the Arts Council.

So I imagine something in the shape of a Society with grades of initiation would be the model. The lowest grades would be open, under Arvon, and would simply take the ordinary Arvon type course—with picked students, presumably—to more intense stages of activity, without going beyond what might be thought of as specialised exercises for writers, which Peter could supervise, as a specialist.

To begin with, this would be the whole thing anyway. The exercises etc could be formulated, & the whole programme shown to the Arts Council, if they were curious, & would logically be the next step from Arvon courses for young writers,—a crash course in psychic disciplines of the most practical kind (such as most writers totally lack).

475

This would be more than enough to justify, to the world, Peter's Arvon College. It might be enough to attract extra support—even from the Arts Council.

If this could be got going, the inner secret esoteric grades would invent themselves, I imagine, in time, naturally, for those who could enter them. Those loftier operations could be separated from Arvon—while Arvon continues to nurture their eggs and their caterpillars.

This is vague—but that notion of a first stage of practical disciplines (for real writers, beyond the usual student stage) seems to me workable—potentially attractive to both Arts Council & Arvon.

love   Ted

P.S. I left my boots in your car. No hurry—I have others.

John Moat, co-founder of the Arvon Foundation, and TH had talked privately about this idea before it was aired at a committee meeting, where the practical difficulties of implementing it stopped it dead. When it was put to Peter Redgrove himself, who had been a frequent and successful tutor on Arvon courses, he expressed only the most cautious interest. Arvon received, then as now, funding from the Arts Council.

To Daniel Weissbort

25 November 1983　　　　　　　　　　　　　　　Ms　Emory

I'm sending the Annual to Faber, with whatever persuasion I can summon. They are flush, at the moment, their Scrooge & down-market opportunism is paying off. But one can't tell how they'll react—the staff is so peppered with fresh whizz kids, all having novel right-ish notions about what tendencies ought to be discouraged at all costs. Also, they've just published Larkin's collected reviews, & they're heavily infected, for the moment, with Larkiniosis, and as you know he's established the fatuity & silliness of all translation of modern poetry, (and, indeed, of all poetry of any kind, except his own, Gavin Ewart's, & Betjemann's—nothing else survives his spermicide). Some of the pieces are awfully good & persuasive—and he has a sort of social one-upmanship raised to such a subtle efficiency that finally you begin to feel that what doesn't meet his approval is somehow a genetic mistake, unfit for the decent society, of which Kingsley Aymis is the apotheosis. Jazz & Kingsley Aymis' sensibility & clowning are judged in exactly the same terms by which he dismisses everybody else except Barbara Pym, Thomas Hardy, Wilfred Owen. He's a sour old cuss & the whole book's outrageous propaganda for his own tastes & limitations & prejudices, but perfectly timed—philistinism has been browbeaten too long!

Modern Poetry in Translation: 1983 – in new, bigger format and with an introduction by TH – was intended as the first of an annual series. Faber had just brought out *Required Writing*, a miscellany of Philip Larkin's prose, including reviews. Gavin Ewart (1916–95) was one of the few contemporary poets deemed worthy of praise by Larkin.

To Keith Sagar

14 December 1983   Ms   British Library

The 'Milesian'—in 'Milesian encounter' refers not Greekwards but West—Irishwards. 'Greek on the Irish Sea' maybe. But more specifically as follows: 'Milesian' is the name given, in the legendary account of the Invasions of Ireland, to the Goidels—who came evidently from Spain around the 2nd Century BC, and were the last big invasion to impose a language & distinctive culture over most of the country. They set up Tara.

During I suppose the 18th Century, the remains of Irish Tales—Ossian etc—as English style culture became aware of them—were at some point called 'Milesian'. Meaning, I suppose, pre-Christian, monstrously exaggerated, incredible, Irish-fantastic, Celtic-inordinate ridiculously barbaric. The Milesians, presumably, gave the final stamp to most of the early Irish stories that survived—and even the more serious pieces from earlier, the Tain etc, must have been bundled under the one disparaging epithet. 'Milesian' came to mean, as I've said, 'ridiculously exaggerated barbaric Irish tale, perfectly incredible, typical of the idiotic hyperbolical Irish," etc.

So I used it because Skye is part of that old Irish kingdom, because the Salmon came from the Irish Sea, because the Salmon considered as a primitive Irish daughter of the nobility—of the archaic nobility—is an Irish enough idea, because all fishing tales are 'Milesian', because the kernel of fact in Milesian tales can only be disappointingly small, and anyway lost beyond investigation, as my salmon, after all my effort and excitement, was only about 4 lbs, and also I lost it, & because the setting of my encounter, which should have been consummated in the legendary conquest & ingestion of a great Irish queen in the form of a hiding salmon, was the actual setting of the real Milesian stories—the bogs, mountains etc of that sea-fringe. Because in Milesian tale style I worked up the losing of a small fish into an encounter on the frontiers of this that & the other. Because I wanted to set my poem—which I'm fond of—in the court of sympathetic indulgence and understanding, as a mini mock-Saga episode. And so on.

[. . .]

Nicholas has written up his thesis, or rather his project. He's wondering what to do next year (finishes at Oxford this next summer). Half thinks of Alaska, but seems to be veering back to Africa. Strangely enough, or not so strangely, he was talking the other day of "the very moment" that his English teacher stopped him writing poetry. He'd written a (I thought) marvellous poem about a dead salmon he found under the river bridge. He pulled it out, and noticed, as he waded there, salmon eggs coming up out of the gravel. He scooped up the gravel, & salmon eggs poured out & downstream. The fish was lying actually on top of a redd—right under the town bridge. He was about thirteen. His English teacher said, evidently "Don't try to write about things outside your experience". Nicholas said it was just like a guillotine—he cut off, from that second, from any interest in English lessons. No doubt he needed another way forward. But now he's evidently regretting it. He says he has a constant craving to be doing his potting—he makes very good primaeval animals & fish (didn't I show them to you?)—and his printing. He's an interesting mix. Some sort of artist.

'Milesian Encounter on the Sligachan' is a poem in *River*. The Sligachan is a river on Skye.

1984

To Craig Raine

23 February 1984   Ms   Faber

Dear Craig,

Suddenly recalled why the scarred, bald skull of Peter Hillmore in your dream seemed so familiar to me. Close to home.

I couldn't at the moment locate it as my own dream—which it felt like—or somebody else's, which I'd read, or what.

End of a book of mine (Gaudete), after the changeling substitute has been cancelled by a ·318 bullet through his bald skull, the real & original fellow re-appears on earth (from his absence in the other world), West of Ireland, identical in all visible features, but with his skull scarred—i.e. result of the operation that removed the other self, result of the damages incurred by the life led by that other self, the mistakes made.

Collective Unconscious strikes again.

Reg Lloyd has done some new Bookmark samples, very nice, but if he doesn't get them to you soon it will be too late. "After all, maybe Faber will think I'm doing it for love"?

I hope Li & the family are well

love

Ted   (P.T.O)

In Gaudete the cancellation of the changeling is managed by a 'gang'—semi-supernatural gang—representatives of the woman in the other world.

My idea was to have a parallel tale of the real man's experience in the other world, that would counterpoint the changeling's experiences in this one. At certain points they become aware of each other. The real man's tale did not get written—I was so concerned to abbreviate & foreshorten the changelings.

I have a scarred skull in Cave Birds too, where the 'Judgement' becomes an operation on the hero's brain 'to take something out'—i.e.

the 'growth' that corresponds to his 'crime' against a female. My playful scheme was to make it the judgement, by the underworld, on Socrates—and his resurrection, in archaic Egypt, as a Horus. The execution of the anti-feminist ironist, & his restitution as a child of Isis, living in the sun. What it actually was—3 years early—was a dim prefiguring of Leonard B's operation (which I must have connected with his first marriage) & his recuperation into his second. Leonard's skull is now a crumpled globe of scars. Using his birds—trying to find a story for his birds—I must have drawn out his story. I ought to re-write all that, & give it more context.

I'm looking forward to your book.

Peter Hillmore, the *Observer*'s gossip columnist, had appeared to Raine in a dream, with a scarred skull. The dreamer did not then know that some years earlier Hillmore had undergone a successful operation for a brain tumour, which had left him without visible scarring. TH was fascinated by the clairvoyant aspect of the dream.

TH had suggested to Matthew Evans, Faber's Chairman, that, as a publicity exercise, poems should be printed on bookmarks for insertion into all Faber books. The Devon painter R. J. Lloyd was to design the bookmarks.

Leonard Baskin had had surgery on his pituitary gland in April 1979.

Raine's *Rich* was soon to be published.

To Karl Miller

17 March 1984   Ms   Miller

Dear Karl,

I must write back straight off and say—your remarks really were exactly what I was needing. You put your finger very gently on the ailments of the Baskin piece—that I've been trying to give the bill of health, knowing too well what they are.

The trouble is, I detest it—the Baskin Introd.—and yet put so much of my real belief (in various things) into it that I can't rubbish it. Also, since it's now being printed in the book I have to acknowledge it.

It's Baskin's 1st Act Lear versus my Cordelia—only my Cordelia has said "O.K., I'll say what I feel but but but—nobody else has to hear me making my declaration because nobody would make allowance for etc etc, and while you force me to reveal the positive you being so naked

480

vulnerable etc. force me to suppress the negative"—well. There it is. He compelled me to make public declaration of my loyalty etc—in Pindaric style. But to a public that feels no loyalty to him whatsoever—in fact are inclined to be unconvinced.

Hence the terrible strain of the piece. It's genre is eulogy—Panegyric Ode, as I say. But there is no public for such things. And no convention. So I'm just afraid it will be counterproductive.

But I just needed the shock of seeing it through somebody else's eyes—to give me a sense of the audience. The solipsistical electromagnetic field of the thing became so strong I couldn't be sure that I've escaped—it warps my judgement again whenever I look at it, sucks me back in.

I can't get away from it even here as you see—going on & on.

~~Don't bother to send it back.~~ Sorry, I see you have done.

If ever you come this way, call & have a meal with us.

Ted

TH had asked for Miller's opinion of 'The Hanged Man and the Dragonfly'.

To Lissa Paul

[April 1984]   Ms Paul

(1) It's part of a continuum. Writing for children, one has a very definite context of communication. Moreover, it's one where the audience is still open. For the most part, a child knows what it feels—and what it likes, and looks at things with a comparatively unconditionned eye. Underline comparatively.

The first & last problem, writing for adults, is establishing the context of communication. Very slight differences in culture can make this quite difficult. And the defences—against what we feel & against everything that alerts us to the excommunicated feeling—are well developed by mid-teens. After that, readers are looking for support for their defences—on the whole. So, as a writer trying to pierce the defences, you're involved in a game with the defences—the defences being constructed from the minutiae of culture, of a narrow & particular culture, [*marginal addition against these lines:* All this assumes you have dealt—as the writer—with those same defences in yourself.] (in England, for instance, the culture of a class, or of a political affiliation), which is also, inevitably, a mass of fashionable & fairly temporary items, emphases, attitudes, since these cultures move only in waves of fashion.

These cultures of defence are by definition superficial—since they exist mainly to conceal/deny the real thing, & to defer the confrontation with it. Since they have no roots in that real thing (which is largely made up of things we do not want to face) they only work so long as they are novel enough to excite attention, & that is the fashionable phase. Novelty (who's the stranger coming up the road?) is an anaesthetic, in this sense. The pricking of the ears & the craning of the neck, & the adrenalin of running with a crowd towards something. The adrenalin of novelty is—so far as the real painful thing is concerned—anaesthetic.

So the writer has to communicate his reminder of the common red-hot centre through—a language of anaesthetics.

That's what it boils down to, for 99.9999% of writing.

So gifted & visionary writers are absorbed into the nothingness by the refusal of their fellow citizens to {respond to / understand} anything but anaesthetics.

Now it seems to me, children don't demand anaesthetics. One can communicate with children in a simple & whole way—not because they're innocent, but because they're not yet defensive. Providing one moves affectionately.

So, in writing for children, it seems to me there's an attractive possibility—of finding, in some way, on some wavelength of imagery & feeling, a lingua franca—a style of communication for which children are the specific audience, but which adults can overhear. In other words, it reaches adults—maybe—because assuming this is not for them, they suspend their defences and listen—in a way secretly—as children. So long as the affection is there.

This might even be logical. I'm sure one thing the defence system does is keep the child in its original state—internally excommunicated and a prisoner, but fairly intact & eager to hear, inside the concrete-faced adult. (In misery)

Well, who knows. But something of that is what draws me to write for children. Not as I've written, particularly, but as I'd like to write. [. . .]

(3) What do I like to read? I don't know why it should be, but my taste for folklore is as strong now—(but much more discriminating)—as it was when I first discovered it. In some ways, much stronger. I recently

moved my whole library. It was quite a revelation. I did it in intervals of writing something I was impatient to get on with. As I lifted each book (the whole lot got into a mess, a mountain) I had a clear absolutely sure sense of its value to me—as if its worth were being rung up on a psychic till. Lot of surprises. But the really precious books—apart from the very few sacred items—were the folklore, the mythology & works related to them. I was surprised how much I hated some books.

[. . .]

(5) No, I don't think my ideas have changed—beyond spreading a few branches.

I think(?!) my basic notion, the root of the roots, in Poetry In The Making, was—that—poetry is simply the name we give to a certain kind of writing. The closer that kind of writing gets to a total (instantaneous) release—something that satisfies & rejoices & appeases the whole organism—the more intense, as poetry, it seems to be. Verbal competence has to be taken for granted, I suppose, but my aim was to direct readers (listeners) towards certain faculties—inner concentration, inner listening, dependance on the spontaneous mind rather than on the calculating & remembering mind etc. A deliberate sort of self-exposure to an event—an inner event, where the part normally active (our manipulation of the world) becomes passive, and the part normally passive (whatever it is that registers the consequences of our manipulations—or failures of manipulation) becomes active, i.e. speaks, & renders the account.

So rather than saying 'study writing', I was saying 'practice writing', as diving to depths has to be practised.

The whole business closer to athletics than to aesthetics, perhaps. Hence my no words about 'technique'.

I don't know how adults should talk with children about poetry. As a child I never experienced written poetry as anything but tedious school food. I'm sending you a book by a friend of mine who teaches it to 11 year olds with interesting results—but it all depends on her, I think, rather than the games she uses.

[. . .]

My instinct is—in a narrative (or whatever) for children, the protagonist <u>has to win</u>. And the undesirables have to be, somehow, turned to gold, of some kind.

The basic pattern, I mean, has to fortify the digestion & general confidence of the cell. The healer's magnetism does that (according to the research, of the Healer's influence on damaged cell-cultures). And if writing weren't that, in its way, I would stop now.

But I'm sure it is that. If it's cultivated at the right depth in the writer. So that's how I see it. Its material is the unacceptable thing, & its purpose is to turn that stuff to increase & a new sort of health. So you are permitted to kill your protagonist, only if you make him, in some more important way, win.

Undated, received on 1 May 1984, this letter had its origin in conversations between TH and Lissa Paul in Toronto, at the International Festival of Authors, and in Oxford the previous year – conversations that, at TH's suggestion, modulated into a form of interview. Paul no longer has the questions with which she presented TH in Oxford, but something of their nature may be inferred from the answers he gives.

To Lisa and Leonard Baskin

6 May 1984   Ms   British Library

It was a strange experience moving my books. It made me realise how much I detest most of them. My real library—the one I'd save from the fire—is quite small. I'd save the folklore, Mythology etc. A few odd things such as Kleist, Montaigne etc. About 10 books of poetry. I discovered, for instance, that I have a deep hatred of all novels except Singer, Tolstoy, Dostoevsky, a few odd other volumes.

It isn't that I'd burn the books. But at a certain point I would happily cease to go back into the flames.

[. . .]

Do you know much about the research into the body's physical response to stress—emotional etc stress? It's extremely interesting. It involves, very heavily, the pituitary. The general drift of the mobilisations are towards defence. This appears in the psychological conscious wavebands as strategies for not feeling the real pain. Intellectually, it appears as self-consistent systems—space-capsules with all mod-cons & conveniences, circling the stricken earth. Artistically, it appears as—well, we know what. Almost all art is an attempt by somebody unusually badly hit (but almost everybody is badly hit), who is also unusually ill-equipped to defend themselves internally against the wound, to improvise some sort of modus vivendi with their internal haemophilia etc. In other words, all art is trying to become an anaesthetic and at the same time a healing session drawing up the magical healing electrics. What happens usually is—the anaesthetic rôle gradually gets stronger, as the successful (pain-distancing) methods are evolved. So the artist gradually bricks his revelatory suffering into the wall, without healing it, & without, any longer, really feeling it. So he quickly grows out of his 'inspiration'.

The source of the biologic defence & anaesthesia system is the pituitary. Or it's heavily involved.

It is interesting to see—I can see very clearly it seems to me in what I do—the anaesthetic tendencies, which displace the real confrontation that can only be solved by a real healing.

It's all very curious. It's something one always knew—but it's the first time I've seen it clearly in these terms of pain & anaesthesia. I suppose it's a codicil to my piece about the book of Prints. That fixed stare at Pain/Healing, took no account of the fact that there's another option—Pain/Anaesthesia. And that 99.999% of all art demonstrates the Anaesthetic option, because under the artist's beady eye, the old reptilian body insists on <u>suffering less</u>.

And so it encysts the wound, which thereafter petrefies & kills. Q.E.D.

I've been thinking about this in particular, because it struck me lately, with a certain waking surprise, that I've lived quite a lot of my last ten years (at least) somehow unconscious.

To Leonard Baskin

15 August 1984   Ms   British Library

I let myself be tempted by an invitation to write a programme note for Bergmann's staging of King Lear in Sweden. Several curious things struck me (all very irrelevant to a programme note.) Basically they are: in 1605, when Shakes wrote King Lear, if he was seriously ill (text suggests he was), and contemplating his will, he had to divide it among 3 women: his wife & his two daughters. His wife, it's assumed, he did not greatly care for (he lived 20 years apart from her); his second daughter, as the survivor of her twin brother (and Shakespeare's only male heir, Hamnet), I assume Shakes. could not bear to look at, after his son died in 1596, (and she could not read or write); his third daughter was said to be as clever as he was. She was his favourite, to whom, directly & indirectly he eventually left everything, and who, that year, 1605, was being courted by a (quite famous) doctor—(married the following year). Apart from this Lear-like positionning of the family entities, within Shakes' home, he also had a brother, young enough to be his son (only 2 years older than his own dead son), who was also an actor in London (at a company other than his own), and who was called of all names Edmund. Now this Edmund, of all Shakes' brothers, was the only one with a son living in 1605—in other words, was the true bearer of the Shakespeare lineage, and Heraldic priviledge, the true heir of the Shakes' dynasty. And this youngest inheritor was also called—like his father—Edmund. Moreover, he was known to be a bastard. (When he died, a year later, his death was registered as Edmund the bastard son). Now isn't that suggestive? More peculiar yet, a notorious court case, a year or two before, had concerned an old wealthy gent who was certified mad by his 3 daughters—and the youngest was called Cordelia. More peculiar yet, in the historic tale, from which Shakes took the story of King Lear dividing his kingdom between two daughters and banishing the 3rd, the youngest was called as he calls her Cordelia. More peculiar yet—and now I could a tale unfold which would bring your eyes out on long thistle-like stems of bristling & writhing nerve-rope.

But I'll stop there, though the rest is quite stupefyingly strange. The incidental conclusion—seriously—is that King Lear is also Crow—in that he is descended by plain cultural stages from the first god of all England—who was also the Crow, and by archaeological & mytho-logical/religious evidence, from Apollo (who was also a Crow god). Now, the details of all that read like a ten page paper in NATURE on the analysis of the enzymes in a rat's testicles. You know these islands got their metaphysical ballast by boat from the Eastern Mediterranean. None of it concerns King Lear, or Crow. It's just curious.

In Ingmar Bergman's 1984 production of *King Lear* at the Royal Dramatic Theatre in Stockholm, the choreography was by Donya Feuer, recipient of the letters from TH that became *Shakespeare and the Goddess of Complete Being*.

To Keith Sagar

28 August 1984 Ms British Library

I've just been reading the big Phoenix Collection of Lawrence's pieces—

straight oxygen. What is the great plastic megaphone mask of English, that gets jammed over the head of all English writers, & that he avoided? He is the only one quite free of it. Maybe what helped him— apart from the talent, the nerve etc—was marrying a German, & staying out of England.

But all (modern) English writers disappear into the Gallery Tussaud's of a non-language—which acts automatically as censor & suppressant of any real material, as if it manipulated the brain-rhythms, which I suppose it does. I opened John Fowles Mantissa the other day—a chronic extreme case, I'd say. It's very strange. It introduces into all writing a sort of struggle—Alan Sillitoe's is a full battlefield display of it. Most writers simply capitulate, & join its Civil Service, & proclaim its regulations. Others just get worn out. It's a study.

Sagar's books include a number of studies of D. H. Lawrence. John Fowles's novel *Mantissa* had appeared in 1982.

To Craig Raine

12 September 1984   Ms   Raine

Thank you for "Rich". Your strongest collection so far, I think. I like everything in it. [. . .]

The prose is enviable. Was that very difficult to get into focus? You've done it brilliantly. It's in its rightful place, too, among the poems—a map of your discoveries, your Eldorado exactly located. i.e. your father's skull, your alchemist's crucible.

You didn't mention that actual wounding of his skull when you told me that dream of Peter Hillmore's skull. It makes your dream fit my interpretation better than ever—even more deeply & inevitably than I'd supposed. Your father's inner life—especially his pain and his possession—seem to illumine the poems. You probably inherited Massa (I'd put 'invented'—but I was thinking maybe Massa helped to invent you.)

In 'A Silver Plate', the autobiographical prose piece which forms the central section of *Rich* (1984), Raine tells of his spiritualist father's spirit guide, Massa.

To Seamus Heaney

[Autumn 1984]   Ms   Emory

We've had our usual summer. Ireland in May, cracking my whip over those obstinate Loughs, seems to exhaust it. The rest just crawls along under the stampede of summer visitors—not so much visitors as holidaymakers who call. Very much as you know—but in Dublin you're kept in condition, you can manage the tumble of it. Problem of living as we do like owls in a forest, every crack of a twig prostrates us. Carol's worse than I am, so she acts as amplifier, but I'm bad. Actually, I'm beginning to realise angling is a worse goblin. It's the symbolic, elastic hold-all for all obsessions & compulsions, & it feeds on their fanatic jumpiness. So the rest of your life is emptied, while this huge polyp fills up, & begins to drag you around. It's also produced a large crop of specialist acquaintances, each with the same haggard besotted lust for another encounter. All bursting with urgent phone calls & breathless opportunities—all like Barrie. The neurosis always brings on the same symptoms. So what used to be an infantile tic has become a 24 hour convulsion of the central nervous system. When the season ended yesterday I felt huge spacious release. But straightaway a friend rings me up—a never-to-be-repeated chance to fish the bottom beats of the River Test for two nights, this next weekend, the pools jammed with fish coming in, sea-trout up to 12 lbs, he's fixed it all up, the sleeping lodge and the lot, £10 only a day, can I go, his voice trembling with fever.

Desmond Clarke (I met him briefly) sent me a copy of Station Island. Well, what a book! Station Island itself must be what you've been pushing yourself towards. It obviously took some confronting. The passages where you tackle the greatest fright seem to me the most masterful successes. And I get the feeling your real kingdom is in there—that's your way in & forward. That clear, life-size, full-frontal, direct statement is quite a triumph. To cope with 7, 8 & 9, and not be found wanting, and not in any way to demean them, confronting them so point-blank, is something exemplary. It also suggests to me what you might make of an Antigone—an indirect method might give you an even bigger release, now you've got such a grip on the nerve of it.

TH and Seamus Heaney (b.1939) had been in correspondence since the

TH and Carol Hughes outside Lurley Manor, Leonard and Lisa Baskin's Devon home, d-1970s
Carol Hughes and TH with calf, Devon, possibly 1975

10a TH with Leonard
Baskin, Cumbria, 1970s
10b Yehuda and Hana
Amichai with TH, Mexico,
August 1982

10c TH with János Csokits and János Pilinszky,
West Yorkshire, 1977/8

11a Penelope Shuttle and Peter Redgrove, 1978

11b TH and Charles Tomlinson in North Devon, 1980s

11c Philip Larkin and TH at the University of Hull, May 1975

11d TH and Seamus Heaney at Court Green, early 1980s

12a Frieda Hughes, 1980s
12b Nicholas Hughes with 24½lb pike, Castle Lough, Ireland, October 1976

a TH and Barrie Cooke on the River
rt, South Devon
b Dermot Wilson fishing for trout on
e of the southern English chalk-streams,
8os

c TH with steelhead, on the River Dean, Canada, 1987

14a TH and Charle
Monteith at Faber
and Faber, 1977

14b Jack Brown,
1980s

14c Craig Raine and TH, 1982

5a Moelwyn Merchant supervising the casting of a piece of sculpture, about 1983
5b William Scammell, 1990s
5c Nick Gammage, 2007
5d Keith and Melissa Sagar with TH, on their wedding day, 1981

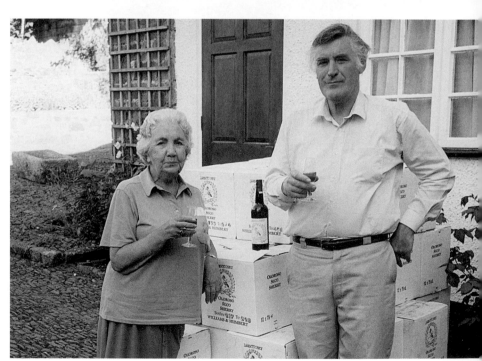

16a Her Majesty Queen Elizabeth, The Queen Mother and TH, Balmoral Forest,
May 1998
16b Hilda Farrar and TH, with newly delivered 'Laureate' sherry, at Court Green,
Devon, 1991

mid-seventies, TH appraising and encouraging the younger poet's progress from the volume *Wintering Out* (1975) onwards.

Desmond Clarke was for a few years the unusually enterprising Sales and Marketing Director at Faber and Faber.

Heaney did go on to translate Sophocles' *Antigone*, as *The Burial at Thebes* (2004).

To Lucas Myers

29 September 1984   Ms   Emory

Life is quiet. Main adrenalin at the moment provided by the exertions of escaping from disruption. Disruption of what, you might well ask. I keep writing this and that, but it seems pitifully little for the time I spend pursuing it. I wonder sometimes if things might have gone differently without the events of 63 & 69. I have an idea of those two episodes as giant steel doors shutting down over great parts of myself, leaving me that much less, just what was left, to live on. No doubt a more resolute artist would have penetrated the steel doors—but I believe big physical changes happen at those times, big self-anaesthesias. Maybe life isn't long enough to wake up from them.

To Craig Raine

3 November 1984   Ts   Faber

Thanks for the note about the selection.

One of my concerns—which you might feel is unjustified—was to keep the actual number of poems low enough, or at least to that critically low number at which the reader feels it is being given only a taste of the real feast, well below the number that seems enough of a meal. Obviously we don't want a book that though it omits a good deal of ARIEL nevertheless manages to displace it as a necessary purchase. The first list I sent has I think 21 from Ariel's 40.

After your letter and extra titles—which coincide very much with mine (and with Olwyn's)—I must say I'm inclined to take in a few more. In the early poems I relaxed to 'Hardcastle Craggs' because it's a compendium of one whole category of her early mannerisms—though I never thought it more than an exercise. I included 'Disquieting Muses' because it's such a direct description of her malevolent familiars—but even so (maybe for that reason) I always found that tone in her early work repellant. I'd gladly see those two pieces dropped from this selection. Also, though I like Winter Ship, the sharpness in it reappears to much greater effect in Suicide Off Egg Rock, a poem I like much more, but I skirted it because another overall concern that steered me a bit touched me to one side here—I mean I was concerned to keep down the death theme, or at least to restrain it from swamping the book. For the same reason I didn't include 'Two Views Of A Cadaver Room'—though that seems to me one of the successes in that same sharp manner. Your suggestions 'Night Shift' and 'Manor Garden' are two of my favourites from The Colossus, and I only kept them out on the principle of the squeeze. Of the titles from the mature phase, that you suggest, I greatly like them all, though 'Whitsun' seems to me a bit of a display counter of her souvenirs. 'Not a book poem' was her phrase for those. Of the others (among your suggestions), I ducked Face-lift because it opened hostilities between Sylvia and a friend that I haven't managed to close. I evaded Widow because I've evolved a dumb non-response to anything that might remotely touch her mother. I skipped By Candlelight—one of the very strong ones—because the image of the brass Candlestick is so elaborately private. 'Surgeon at 2 a.m.' is a poem I've never much liked—I associate it with Face-lift which seems to me much more genuinely motivated, and manages to crack the Bell Jar. Your remark about The Rabbit Catcher encourages me to drop it—and to drop Pheasant for something better. Lesbos is long—but so unlike anything else, it suggests to me a whole range of things she might have gone on to, I find it one of the most interesting.

Resolve—one of my sister's favourites—was an odd by-blow. She knew it had clues (it reminds me of the one called Bitter Strawberries—first in that selection of her 'juvenilia') but it wasn't her priority to exploit them. Her priority, I suppose, at that time, was still dictated by the metrical, kinaesthetic, tensile pattern of momentum that could take the full weight of undifferentiated undischargeable howl.

Tell me how you think the list looks if I delete

Epitaph for Fire and Flower
Hardcastle Craggs
Disquieting Muses
Winter Ship
Pheasant

Rabbit Catcher
A Secret
Medusa

And put in

Resolve
Night shift
Manor Garden
Suicide Off Egg-Rock
Wuthering Heights
Face Lift
The Babysitters
By Candlelight
Winter Trees
Letter in November
Munich Mannequins

Part of a discussion about the contents of Sylvia Plath's *Selected Poems*, which TH
was editing and which would appear in 1985.

To Ann Skea

3 November 1984   Ts   British Library

Dear Ann Skea,

Thank you for the long letter. I don't know that I can answer your que-
ries, beyond the simplest—and that not very definitively. The quotation
at the opening of the poem titled Hardcastle Crags is Chinese, Taoist—
but of the precise source I'm ignorant. I found it long ago in a giant
Encyclopedia of Proverbs from all languages—a U.S. book I think, and
quite old. I imagine it comes from some Taoist text—not from the
common stock of proverbs.

And yes the satin was as you suggest.

No, my heart doesn't sink at your description of the method you've
hit on, to deal with Cave Birds. I haven't read any commentary about
that book (though I know there have been one or two). So if I just
outline my notion of the framework I may be repeating what you
already know. The plot consists of two parallel 'stories'. In the one, the
dramatis personae are birds. In the other, a man and a woman. My

491

starting point was the death of Socrates. The crime for which he is judged, and which he expiates, in the sequence, is not the crime of which the Athenians accused him—rather the one for which (from one point of view) history holds him responsible, namely, the murder of the Mediterranean Goddess (as Mother and Bride).

His soul becomes a bird and is judged by birds. Throughout the stages of this judgement, projections are made, into a 'human world', where the man and woman enact (in static tableaux sure enough) the phase of the relationship, between male and female, which is being dealt with, at that point, in the judgement of the birds.

This judgement follows a simple course: accusation, defense, conviction for the murder, execution after an expiatory sacrifice (the cockerel), passage to the underworld. In the underworld, a different order of judgement takes place—as in the Bardo Thodol (Tibetan Book Of The Dead), the soul is confronted by everything which, in the upper world, he had rejected. He is confronted, that is, by the Goddess in various forms: if he rejects again, he would be annihilated. If he accepts, he will be resurrected. So through this phase he does accept, with difficulty. Going through the ordeals of acceptance, he is transformed. When he achieves total acceptance he is resurrected. He was accused, and executed as one of the corvidae. He is judged in the underworld by the raptores, and becoming one of them is resurrected as a Falcon. Dying in Athens as a sceptical philosopher, the patron saint of irony and dialectical reason, he is resurrected in Egypt as Horus, child and spouse of the Goddess. The human scenario of the first half presents the disintegration of the female and the anaesthetised alienation of the male, and the second half the reconstitution of the female and the reunion of the female and male. So that is my view of it. The 'alchemy' of the process operates in bringing the most debased raw materials of de-spiritualised entropy, in the matter of human relationship, to a perfect spiritualised wholeness.

That was my intent, at least, my guiding image.

Thank you for the kind words about WHAT IS THE TRUTH? It's a book I have a soft spot for. In Australia, it must read rather like a fairytale.

All the best
Ted Hughes

Ann Skea would eventually publish the results of her investigation into the mythic background of *Cave Birds, Remains of Elmet* and *River* in *Ted Hughes: The Poetic Quest* (1994).

To Peter Redgrove and Penelope Shuttle

17 November 1984   Ms   Emory

Thank you for the article & water. The article seems to me the best inclusive outline account of Yeats' 'occultism" and the only place I've ever seen his whole poetic-magic system identified as a sort of spiritual anatomising of the body of the Goddess, using Cabala as a gymnasium, preparing himself & fitting himself for the greater work. I'm quite sure you're absolutely right, & it explains how what seemed to Auden to be a giant ramshackle pseudo-metaphysical toy for a soft-headed self-delusionist, nevertheless supplied Yeats with that superior sense of reality, the sense of an all-embracing vision, the golden radiance of an unfathomable poetic source, a poetic substance that seems irreducible & universal & infinitely energised, like the source-flow of the first particles.

Curious how it's the culmination of his first vision—the Wanderings of Oisin the embrace of the moon's three aspects in conventional guise—in final terms a contemplation & dramatisation of life within the (timeless) matriarchate of the egg-maker.

Redgrove's review of Graham Hough's *The Mystery Religion of W. B. Yeats* was to be printed in the *Times Literary Supplement* of 30 November 1984.

1985

TH, Carol Hughes and their friends Clare and Michael Morpurgo had visited Egypt between 21 November and 7 December 1984. The letter below, to Leonard and Lisa Baskin, describes both the trip and the surprise that awaited TH on his return: a letter from 10 Downing Street asking if he would agree to his name being put forward for the post of Poet Laureate.

To Leonard and Lisa Baskin

[Early 1985]   Ms   British Library

Our Nile cruise came just right. After 2 weeks of readings—20 readings, 6,000 students processed in all, a peculiar progress through the hotels & beds of Birmingham, nether Manchester, & assorted other limbos. We kept clear of hospitality, got to our hotel early, and began to shape the day round a stiffish Vodka at 6-15, became experts in local television etc. I only had one bad reading—a huge school hall, about 400 kids, and a group of girls giggling & whispering in a far corner just out of reach of control. So after my hour, I was ready to commit a male-chauvinist massacre. There's nothing so exhausting & enraging as a persistent interference. And so I was escaping in evil humour when a gloomy bat-faced teacher stopped me and accused me of reading horrible sadistic ugly poems to the children. I just stared at her and thought how sick she looked—that was as far as I got in self defence. But I've made a note of the school and I'll never go near it again. After that, the Nile was a beautiful shock.
[. . .]
   We had little adventures. We went out into a town called Assint, one evening—guarded by sailors from the boat. Mediaeval city. Colossal turbulent, aimless, incessant, seething uproar of people. Afterwards, we learned it's the centre of the Moslem Brotherhood, & Europeans are warned to keep out. I fished off the back-end of the boat, at night, with the crew when we were moored, and I learned that the banks of the river, in the towns, are composted corpses of donkeys, dogs etc, and in

494

general are compacted refuse spilling from the town. We didn't catch anything, but had plenty of exciting bites, in the miasma.

I expected to see far more bird life on the river. We saw no vultures, & no peculiar creatures except a Warrener—which looked exactly like & crawled into the reeds exactly like a 6 ft crocodile—and two small lizards. Where are Egypt's lizards? I greatly liked the archaic river-side villages.

We got to almost every site early morning, and were first there— very worth doing. El-Amarus—Akhnatan's site—impressed me most, for some reason. Mainly a bare stretch of desert, & a cliff—though the tomb-carvings (in the cliff) seemed to me special there. We kept thinking—there—how Leonard must have appreciated those reliefs.
[. . .]

This Laureateship has been very peculiar. When we got back from Egypt I sat in that exhausted after-journey stupor opening the giant pile of mail, and came across a letter from 10 Downing St asking me if I'd received Maggie Thatcher's letter, and if so could I please reply one way or the other. I was too tired to react. I guessed what it meant of course, and my first pure thought was 'Here we go—how horrible.' Just dismay. Then I came to her letter, asking if I objected to my name being proposed to the Queen etc as P.L. 'in ordinary' (in ordinary?). I really felt I'd walked into a pit trap. I saw at once that refusing invoked as many demons as accepting. I'd grown very happily accustomed to the total confidence of the press (many articles openly describing him as 'Poet-Laureate-to-be') and Ladbroke's (who stopped taking bets three months ago, they regarded him as such a certain choice) and Fabers (they'd reprinted huge numbers of his books), and himself (in an interview he settled all doubts—once assumed he'd been asked and had accepted), that I couldn't imagine it not being Larkin.

Thatcher's letter to me was posted the day we left for Egypt, but as we got back on a Friday I had the weekend to think about it. Once it dawned on me that yes I had actually been asked, I supposed that Larkin must have been asked and had refused. That complicated my position. I felt disinclined to take on infinite little silly problems that he'd had the level-headedness to refuse. On the other hand, his general all-purpose No seems to me not so admirable, & there were attractions in turning mightily to my advantage what he'd shied from. So I see-sawed. For about a day I seemed quite capable of saying No. It was my old life defending its status quo. Carol didn't press. I could see she was almost gagging with trepidation. Now and again she'd say "How are the feelings—positive?" Olwyn refrained from any leverage beyond "It would be awfully good for you in America"—which seemed a long way round. Still thinking that Larkin had been asked and had refused, I kept remembering the line in King Lear, where the French King changes his mind about Cordelia—"Be't lawful I take up what's cast away." And so by Sunday nobody could have argued me out of it. So monday morning I rang them up and said Yea. Since then I've been in a strange daze—a somnambulist sort of slow flight. Something to do, maybe, with realising that I'm performing one of my mother's wildest dreams.

Evidently Larkin hadn't been asked. After the high pressure & evidently highly organised lobby that's been growing more vocal over this last year, he must feel quite odd about it. Since then—nearly two months—I've done little except write letters, mostly saying No in some variant of the 700 diplomatic & courteous kicks up the arse. Some need more thought. Lots of old friends out of remote pasts. Patron-ships, Vice-Presidencies, Guests of Honourships are falling literally like snow. I wade through letters and envelopes. I once wrote a story of a man who came to in a world of snow—simply carrying his chair in a level world of endlessly blowing snow, dreaming, when he snatched a few minutes sleep on his chair, of a real life, somewhere, elsewhere—past? future? etc. It's coming back to me as a simple prophecy. I'm beginning to delegate note-writing—but it has to be organised. The deluge or blizzard is thinning a bit. Today only seven. (And somebody even sending me 4 beautiful salmon flies—but then asked if I'd write a poem for the Anniversary of the escape from Colditz!!) Every third letter there's a request. Problem is, most people think of the Poet Laureate's rôle as a public convenience (it's the job's one inconvenience). They don't know yet that things have changed.

To Hilda Farrar

2 February 1985   Ms   Vicky Watling

Dear Hilda,

That was a lovely evening. We did truly enjoy it. I was quite amazed to find that sort of place in Todmorden—though why shouldn't they be as hungry in Tod as anywhere else.

496

I didn't get to the factory. We only just got down to Lumb Bank, the following day, and then only just managed to claw our way out. On Friday morning we decided to flee back to Devon before the freeze-up came back.

Otherwise, I had all kinds of orders for David—everybody wanting pants.

I've spent most of this week simply answering letters. Even writing very briefly, they take ages. I'm about $^1/_3$ through. All sorts of people popped up—from school etc. College. Even the rose-farm I once worked on in Hertfordshire wrote asking if I was the one who'd worked there in 1955. So Carol is expecting them to name a rose after me.

I was asked if I'd send a copy—presumably hand-written—of my christening poem to Prince Harry, to be "the first item in his collection". Did I tell you that? I have another one I wrote for Prince William (the Sunday Times asked me, at the time, so I wrote it, then desisted from printing it because Sir John was still alive), so I shall write that out too—it's his horoscope in verse. Prince William has a very strange horoscope—it has the same main features as Elizabeth I's, Victoria's, King George VI, Elizabeth II—very odd! What's odd, is that they, too, all share the same main features. Almost as if there were something in Astrology.

It was very good to see Vicky looking so bright & obviously so pleased with life.

Love from both of us

Ted

Hilda Farrar was TH's maternal aunt, and the 'lovely evening', a family celebration of TH's appointment as Poet Laureate, at a restaurant in Todmorden, near Mytholmroyd. His cousin David Farrar ran the family firm, Farrar Sutcliffe, which manufactured clothing.

The horoscope poem for Prince William, 'The Zodiac in the Shape of a Crown', was published in a fund-raising limited edition, *Four Poets for St Magnus* (1987), but not in TH's collection of Laureate poems, *Rain-Charm for the Duchy* (1992); nor is it included in *Collected Poems*.

To Terence McCaughey

7 March 1985   Ms   British Library

This new life as Laureate has its strangeness. What is most strange of all is the rôle I now play in the rusty locked-up heart of the Anglo-Saxon common man woman and child. Very peculiar. Odd effects of resonance & echo too. Everything I come out with is either (a) a megaphone blast from the peak of a mountain of soap-boxes (b) possibly the solution to the whole problem (c) an infinite sum drawn on infinite credit. So I have to be careful what inanities I come out with. Obviously it's best if I now become a silent recluse (occasional loud laugh) and never write another word. So my capital will remain unsquandered & my interest will accrue.

[. . .]

I love Sorley Maclean's poetry, & your essay has borrowed some qualities from it—there's some sort of affinity between the temper of the one & of the other. Not simply shared intimacy with Calvinist conscience. You should publish it in an English journal (maybe you have)—I mean something like Critical Quarterly, which is very open to real commentary on the real things in verse (as distinct from orthodox Lit. Crit.)

Sorley MacLean – or Somhairle MacGill-Eain – (1911–96) wrote primarily in Gaelic. McCaughey's essay, 'Sorley MacLean: Continuity and Transformation of Symbols', appeared in *Sorley MacLean: Critical Essays* (1986).

To Ohna and Terence McCaughey

14 April 1985   Ms   British Library

We sold our grass on Friday. This is Carol's day. She does all the work—result is, it's the best-kept farm in Devon. The fences are so good they're a problem. A farmer renting some grass last year scared a fox out of the middle of a big field—it ran to the fence <u>and couldn't get through.</u> ! ! It ran all along the fence, trying every likely looking place. Finally, it went through a gate at the end.

On Friday, it rained almost horizontal, icy, N.E. rain, very heavy. So there was Carol & the Auctioneer, their backs to the rain—addressing the crowd of farmers who'd come to bid, & who had to make their bids into the rain. Very odd sight. Field after field. Carol & the Auctioneer, hoods over their heads, leaning back into the rain, and twenty yards away, a row of streaming, sodden farmers, with their backs turned, also leaning back into the rain. Farmers on principle never wear hoods, so there they all were, trying to shrink under their collars, & rain pouring off every jutty, frieze, eyebrow, nose end, projecting upper lip, ear-lobes, elbows, coat-fringe—like gargoyles under a fountain. And squinting round to make nods or flick up a finger, as the bidding went. As it was, on some fields she made the highest price ever given for grass in Devon.

To Renée and Dermot Wilson

6 June 1985   Ms   Renée Wilson

What a jewel of a three days it was, for me. With that kind of weather, my Irish fishing companions would have despaired—they need a cloud, before they'll tie on a fly. I've always suspected they make too much of it! But there wasn't a moment, with you Dermot, when it didn't seem like exactly the right moment.

I've been trying to work out whether you 'structured' the fishing, or whether it just fell out that way. That first day on the Itchen was "difficult", in the way I'd been led to expect. My Beacon Beige felt like a W.D. helicopter, my casting like a lion-tamer breaking in a new whip, and me like a water-buffalo dragging a rice-plough. (I expect that's what it looks like on the photographs.) Then on the Avon, I only gradually got the hang of it. But the number of walloping rises there, at least, gave me a vivid sense of the possibilities. And on the second day, as I got the wavelength, & began to focus, and it began to dawn on me that I was, after all, in Hampshire/Wilts, the real delight of it began to settle on my head. The notion of performing in an old English Mystery Play—as performed historically in the Houghton Club & the Piscatorial Society— began to make me realise how ill-dressed I was for the part. A lot of the pleasure after all is in taking on the traditional robes etc. I didn't even have a fishing rod! Or maybe I can say I had a wand—something not unlike a composite angle-rod, part hickory, part willow, part whalebone—and was more authentically equipped, in that detail, than most. But my Gye net! I feel it wasn't far off a bound pack of dynamite.

The 3rd day, I felt, came just as I was ready for it. If that had come first, I wouldn't have been able to slip into it so intensely—I would still have been crusted with Salmonising monotonous deep-wader's trance & waiting for a pull, in a waste of fishlessness, Spey-style.

As it is, I remember every second of that magic day as if it were happening right now. It was one of the most delightful days of fishing I've ever had—and for me everything about it was unique. I shan't ever forget the siege of that fish under the reeds on the far side, that would neither take nor stop rising—with its aides fore & aft to draw the fire.

The whole visit was a rich pattern of surprises,—our evening meals, the Museum, the fishing hut, the monster in the pool. And the novelty of the places, & the landscape. I enjoyed every word, and every minute.

As guest of the Wilsons, TH had spent three days fishing on the rivers Itchen, Test and Avon. He had never before fished the Hampshire and Wiltshire chalk-streams, where the dry-fly technique, on which Dermot Wilson had written a classic manual, is the same as on other rivers, but the fish are livelier and tastier. A Beacon Beige is a kind of fly; a Gye net is used to land salmon, not trout. The Houghton Club is an exclusive fishing club on the Test.

To Lydia Clement and Alison George

29 July 1985   Ts   Clement and George

Dear Miss Clement and Miss George,
    Thank you for your letter. If I answered your question it might stop you worrying, but it would not help you. You know that when you answer a problem, you kill it. And it might be a fruitful problem.
                                Best wishes,
                                Ted Hughes

As 13-year-old schoolgirls, Lydia Clement and Alison George had been reading TH's story 'The Rain Horse', and had written to ask what the horse symbolised.

To Nicholas Hughes

10 August 1985   Ts (carbon copy)   Hughes

Since I got back naturally I entered the turmoil. Surprising rains—rivers almost constantly up and brown. There hasn't been more than one day that we could sit out in the garden. The roses went over before we could really relish them. Main event was the appearance of two peacocks, on the lawn. At first Carol shooed them off—they flew. Then one came back and we seem to have adopted it. When she calls, it comes lumbering across at a heavy Dinosaur sort of lope, and picks up the bits of bread etc she scatters. Yesterday it appeared in the yard. It's moulting all its tail feathers. At the moment it has about three left. The doves keep their noses at the evolutionary grindstone. New little pairs keep creeping out of the dovecote, and the cats or a hawk keeps trimming the flock. At the moment we have one slate-coloured (survivor of two that attatched themselves) and one with a slate fringe on its tail—another incomer. Plus the whites. I'm not sure how many—they never seem to get above about eight.

TH and Nicholas Hughes had shared a fishing holiday in Alaska from 13 June to 3 July.

To Stephen Spender

16 November 1985   Ms   Estate of Stephen Spender

I've always thought your early work was the most alive poetry of that time, and still think it's probably true. One of their problems (the poems) was that they became <u>too well</u> known at the time. But they became so, I'm sure, for a very good reason, and now the generation of your enviers and your resentful sons is either dying off or ageing into sense, it's becoming clear. So I think. By 'alive', I suppose I mean—your nakedness to yourself, the way the most primitive & immediate levels of your feeling can easily show right at the surface of your writing. It never happens in Louis McN., and in W.H.A. only in those early half-somnambulist poems—This lunar beauty—that voice.

But the same thing (to my mind, at least) appears throughout your writing, and is very strong again in these more recent diary-like pieces. These are some of my favourites. I wish you'd done a bit of that all your life. Not so much a matter of images as tone—atmosphere, a presence.

I expect you know that besides being yoked all your days with Auden in public, you're yoked with him in heaven too—not just both Pisces, but your moons linked in Gemini—considerable odds against it.

Spender had sent TH his *Collected Poems 1928–1985*.

To Philip Larkin

21 November 1985   Ts   Hull

Dear Philip,

I sent the enclosed pieces to the other members of the Queens Gold Medal Committee a couple of days ago. I delayed sending yours because I wanted to write a longer note, and delayed writing the note because until now I've been unsure whether I should write it at all.

I hope you're holding ill-health at a distance. Ever since I heard you'd been into hospital I've been wanting to communicate something which for some reason I've assumed you'd reject outright. Enough of an assumption to keep putting my letter off. But the impulse to write keeps intruding. It is an intrusion, to give it this form now—I don't like it either but I like the alternative less.

I simply wanted to let you know somehow of the existence of a very strange and remarkable fellow down here, quite widely known for what seem to be miraculous healing powers. I've known him quite well for about eight years, watched many of his 'cures' very closely. His own history is odd enough—after forty years as an increasingly helpless invalid, with ankylosing spondilitis, forty years spent largely in the hands of doctors, and eventually in the hands of healers, he was told by a healer (in a trance!) that he could be healed only if he himself began to heal others. So he started, had phenomenal results, and now after about ten years you wouldn't say he'd ever had a day's illness, and certainly not that his spine on X-ray is just a dissolved blur (I've seen the X-ray). He heals three days a week, and says he gets through about 70% of the people who come to him—those 70% are mainly complete cures. He's called Cornish.

He heals every kind of illness. Recently he held a party with twelve guests—all ex-patients of his: six of them had been terminal cancer, six with cancer in some earlier phase—all now quite clear. A man came to him who had only ever had one functioning kydney—the other had stayed rudimentary from birth, size of a hazel nut, and had never worked. Now his good kydney had collapsed, and he was living on the machine. After about five sessions with Cornish the one kydney had repaired itself and was working perfectly, while the other had started to grow and function as a healthy kidney. The case was written up in Lancet as a mystery. A Truro doctor came to Cornish with a disabled shoulder—the bone much eaten away with arthritis. During the next year as he felt the shoulder improving the doctor had X-rays of it taken at intervals. Cornish gave him treatment about once a month. At the end of a year the shoulder was back to normal—painless and the bone actually regenerated, as the last X-ray shows. X-rays are in Truro museum. The Okehampton ex-Postmaster came to Cornish with such acute angina that he couldn't keep his hands raised for long enough to shave, and couldn't walk more than fifteen paces without the pains bringing him to a stop. After about five minutes of treatment, this man had some sort of heart-crisis—Cornish thought he'd killed him—recovered, went on with the treatment, walked out, and was never again able to bring on the angina pains no matter how he exerted himself. You'll know the calcified condition of the heart's blood vessels in angina. Many other 'miraculous' healings of this sort—literally many hundreds.

As I say, I've watched many of these cures, I've sent many people to him, I've been his patient myself. He explains his 'power' as some sort of energy that flows from him and galvanises the patient's own auto-immune system. I've read U.S. research into what goes on under a healer's hands, where cell-cultures—in a laboratory—were deliberately injured, first, then given a few seconds of the healer's attention. The experiment was repeated many times, with different gifted healers, and the conclusions were that whatever was happening, the effect on the injured cells was to heal them in—on average—one tenth of the time it would normally take them to heal themselves.

It isn't absolutely necessary to meet him. All he seems to need is name, details of place—but best of all contact over the phone.

You see why I hesitated to write. Doctors dismiss this sort of treatment as coincidence, credulity, or they put it down to the hypnotic effects of a magician's suggestion. On the other hand many doctors come to Cornish and are healed.

His phone number is Okehampton (Devon) 3193. I shall tell him about you, and that there's a remote chance you might ring. I shan't mention this to anyone else.

He's pretty well known. He was invited to Germany recently to treat an entire hospital. I asked him why there isn't a mile long queue to his door and his reply was: People are afraid of it. (This kind of healing).

Please don't write back or mention this again—no point. But the impulse to tell you all this has been recurring more and more strongly. I just wanted you to become aware somehow or other that this fellow exists.

Meanwhile I very much hope you're getting well.

Ted

These poems are probably reaching you too late to be of any use. If they do make any difference, and there were any way for you to indicate thumbs up, down, or whatever intermediate angle, maybe you could ask someone to ring the palace Monday. But I shan't expect to hear from you. There are still some of the books I haven't seen.

Larkin was a member of the committee that, under the Poet Laureate's chairmanship, recommended poets for the Queen's Medal for Poetry. He was in hospital, being treated for the cancer of the oesophagus that would kill him a month later, and never consulted the healer, Ted Cornish.

1986

To Dermot Wilson

5 January 1986   Ms   Renée Wilson

I should have written back to you pronto, because my 'yes' was instant-aneous. It's an opportunity for me to do some small pleasing thing for yourself and Renee. Also,—the heady achievement of sharing a platform with Sir Michael! I shall try to get him to deliver some speeches from Troilus & Cressida. He's the best speaker of Shakespeare—the very best—I've ever heard. Makes it sound like his own natural speech—but full of everything, with power, & a whole world behind it. I get chills remembering it.
[. . .]
   Thank you for the irresistible invitation to cast a fly, over those bewitched waters, with a real rod. This time, I'll bring some of my Irish Friend's Copydex spents—really phenomenal tying, and very pretty. By phenomenal tying, I don't mean artistically superb—though his are nice—so much as deadly-looking, & in effect deadly, & curious.
[. . .]
   Ed Zern is marvellous. Some of the things in those books (which I've now belatedly released—into Conrad's clutching hands) make me laugh even remembering them. Very fine writer. Well, wonderful America! They have a wonderful way of enjoying those wonderful places.

In answer to the Wilsons' request that TH read with the actor Sir Michael Hordern at a fund-raising event for the Salisbury Arts Centre, which took place on 5 December 1986. The invitation was to return and fish the waters TH had visited earlier in 1985 (see letter to Renée and Dermot Wilson of 6 June 1985). A 'spent' fly is the female who is dead, or dying, on the surface of the water after laying eggs.
   Ed Zern (1910–94) was a humorous US writer on hunting and fishing; Conrad Voss Bark (1913–2000), journalist and broadcaster, was a mutual fishing friend.

To Craig Raine

11 January 1986   Ms   Raine

I'd just about yielded to Peachy's solicitations (partly out of curiosity to
see what comes with the name), I'd even decided to read Aubade, which
seems to me quite a poem—summary of all Philip's negatives—when I
slipped on an icy wall top. Flat top of a low wall that looked simply like
wetness in the rain. My left foot skidded away right—I cart wheeled,
propellor-fashion—caught the edge of the wall-top with my left eye-
brow (skull came through the mask round the edge of the socket) hard
enough to set me spinning on the axis of my spine, so I landed rolling.
Very finally judged connection. A friend followed me over—slipped the
same, but only cut his leg.

TH had intended to read 'Aubade', the poem he had praised in his letter to Philip
Larkin of 20 March 1979, and one that resoundingly forswears the consolations of
religion, at the Memorial Service for Larkin in Westminster Abbey on 14 February
1986, but instead he read a passage from *Ecclesiasticus*.
    The friend who had 'only cut his leg' was Daniel Weissbort.

To Keith Sagar

19 January 1986   Ts   British Library

Your comment about the Lions interested me. Here's how it came about.
Just before the Queen Mother's birthday The Daily Express asked if I had
any tribute ready for her—presumably they would have liked to print it. I
didn't answer, but then about five days before the day I read that one of
her more celebrated ancestors was a scots Lord known as The White
Lion. It occurred to me that she's the focal point of odd coincidences: her
maiden name Lion, her birth-sign Lion and the fact that she's astrologic-
ally very typical, a text book case, in that facially she somehow resembles
a Lion (especially the eyes—even moreso when she was younger—and
the profile), and her role as bearer of the mythic crown in a collective
psychic unity where the totemic symbol of union was the Lion. I thought
something might be made of this that would amuse her to read.
    This starting point went into complications, once I began to reflect
that the Lion is the only totem under which the British Isles have ever
approached a state of unity, as one Federation with a reasonably shared

506

family feeling, and that their history as a united people of the lion culminated—and collapsed—in her reign, in the 2nd World War, which she seemed to survive as the sole sacred representative of the idea of unity under the Lion (which she upheld apparently quite alone and in her own person after she had absorbed all the Royal qualities of her reign, on the death of King George. In the poem I keep the Queen out of it, on the understanding that she represents something different and new, and not relevant here.)

As I say, my idea was to write something she herself might get some pleasure from. The thing had already become rather arcane. Casting it into the form of a fable gave some hope of a simplification, and of bringing narrative leverage to bear. But it introduced a whole set of new problems that I hadn't clearly foreseen, in that it shifted everything back into my own super-totemised childhood. This was partly deliberate, since my own real feelings about this Lion totem are there (as I imagine everybody else's are, if they have any), and I thought I might be able to tap them. But those feelings are too obscure I suppose for a poem that has to be simple. My early days are tangled in lion ideas. The idea of Being English, of my father having won the war (when I was about four) etc was all tied up with lion. I was disappointed (I remember where I sat thinking about it) that my name didn't begin with L. When the war came and we were painting posters endlessly all mine were simple scenes of the giant lion in action. But that was simple enough (and common property I expect) compared to the purely accidental fact that it always seemed to me my mother looked a bit like a lion, compounded by the maybe quite odd circumstance that I identified her, from when I was quite young, with the Queen Mother. The actual resemblance is probably fairly slight, but it was enough to do the trick at the occult level where those tricks are done. Maybe this is a common English delusion (Marrying one of the Royal Family is one of the common English dreams).

Anyway, these incidental dramatic twists meant that I found myself involved with that whole business of mother as representative of the Queen as representative of the Crown centre of psychic wholeness and unity and harmony—in an immediate but quite unmanageable and also irrelevant way. My footsteps through that sucking ooze are visible from verse to verse.

The most I could do with it was to project an Eden—not just a childhood land of the animals, but a land of communal protective care, where all natural internecine impulses are suspended, before the fall into division, difference and conflict. In this land every creature, of whatever kind, is also, psychically, a lion—as in a totem group. Enjoying the spiritualising harmony of a benign symbol—which is also the life-giver and the sun.

The Wolf and the Hyena are simply two predatory types of the residential fauna of this land (island), which are all types of dog. I don't actually say that because I didn't want to raise the complications it would entail. I didn't want any allegorising to hog the scene. But I take it the natural British totem is Dog. If you take away the lion you have cacaphonous Dog show. Before Lion appeared, this was a Dog-show, dog-fight, dog-hole etc. Hengest and Horsa commented on the fact, and what a pity it was to leave such a fine land to such creatures. This nation of domesticated cannine curiosities I take to be what the Romans left behind—having bred them for amusement and servile use (400 years—12 generations—a long time among dog-breeders). The Anglo Saxons and the Vikings found them simple prey and they brought in the Wolvish. So in the national mix I take the Wolvish to be the purer strain of Norse and Anglo Saxon, and the hyena to be the native british strain of opportunistic collaborator, joining forces in the common business of preying on the dog-show.

Now the lion, in this English mystery, came into being as a unifying self-mastery, the emanation of the whole genetic blend, when it attained self-control, self-restraint, and a common purpose. Then all the separate varieties (as in Macbeth) sunk their differences in the general species, and even the wolf and the hyena suspended their inclinations, and all let themselves be raised into the single-mindedness of another order of animal, all became subordinate faculties of the body politic and leonine, all imbued with the general self-respect of Lion, a common Lion self-confidence. So the cannines had real existence, but they united in the shared fantasy of a lion existence, and over them all presided a visionary lion, which incarnated itself, as collective visions do, in a single real representative, in this case, I suggest, the Queen Mother. The Wolf and the Hyena, as the armed and violent and enterprising, concealing for awhile or transforming or sublimating their natural inclination to plunder and devour, become the 'guardians'. In other words, in this unified and harmonised system of potential havoc, the predators are the very ones who become the protectors.

And this Lion-likeness, being such a powerful form of self-esteem and self-confidence, which all share in the collective psychic unity, is regarded as 'sacred'—there's a religious attitude towards it. (Was!)

This is what I understand to be the real meaning of Monarchy, of which the Monarch is the actual and visible guarantee and assurance. Monarchs aren't created by the individuals of a group. They can only reign if they are created by the unity of a group, and all their trapping are investiture projected from that dream-level of unity.

[*Last two paragraphs bracketed and linked to the following, in ms:* You're saying this isn't desirable—but I'm saying rather that it's simply a fact. And loss of the sense of the sacred axis is loss of depth & coherence. And where do most people get that sense from?]

Now these Roman dog-varieties, the native islanders, i.e. the medley in possession post 450 AD, were formerly something else. The Mare is (for the poem's purpose) the Totem of those Celts that came in from the East or rather the South East corner, and the Raven is the Totem of those Celts who came in from the West—from Ireland and the Mediterranean.

The First—later in time—left their Totem cut into the chalk. The second left their Totem in the Tower—Bran's Raven, guardian of his buried head, surviving earliest god, etc.

These are the widest possible shorthand generalities obviously.

The peoples of these two Totems had been genetically transformed in the Roman Hypocaust, from which they trickled out as a lot of dogs.

What I further had to keep out of the piece was the general sense that the Lion passes away with the Queen Mother. What's left after her is the breakdown of the Federation, the tribes seceding into their old local allegiances. Resurgence of the alignments of the Civil War which was itself a resurgence of the oppositions of Norse and Anglo-Saxon, Anglo-Saxon and Celt, Celt and Roman, Celt and Celt. The Pull for home rule in Scotland Wales and Northern Ireland are signs of it. That's why the Lion for me can be nostalgic pageantry but the Crow quite real, in its way. Incomprehension of the Lion in that piece is also a sign. The country's falling to bits.

I saw that the Lion piece was, in spite of all my efforts to make it quite simple, too complicated. So the second piece was intended to be again simple—but without any internal complications. Even so, maybe the notion of 'a people's dream' is no longer part of common understanding.

From the start I'd wanted to bring in salmon. The Queen Mother is President of the Salmon And Trout Association, and it's known that salmon fishing has always been her sport. But I didn't want to drop the last chance of a unifying totem. The ultimate Totem is a fish as you know. And the ultimate totemic fish because of its peculiar life is salmon. So my idea was that, since political unity at the level of the Lion has gone, and since all the fragments are now recoiling into their differences, the totem of the only unity to which one can appeal is not Christ as a fish, because even that is not general enough, but the fish as the totem of the sexual creation, the weaver at the source. And that's how I tried to combine mentionning salmon as the nucleus of an obsession, and projecting an image of a universal totem, a global unity.

It may sound overelaborate but that's the general idea from which I tried to make something as simple and clear as a hymn—since I was still trying to write something she herself might quite like.

Anyway, there it is. I understand the dislike. Verse written semi-privately or as if semi-privately to someone else and yet published openly is always somehow offensive. False interpretations are like the air—always there at 15 lbs per square inch. Worse things too.

You don't have to defend it, Keith. You only have to say you don't like that kind of verse. And who can write in an amiable way to any member of the royal family without it looking like flattery? Can't be done.

'The Dream of the Lion' is the first of 'Two Poems for Her Majesty Queen Elizabeth The Queen Mother on her Eighty-fifth Birthday', included in *Rain-Charm for the Duchy*. The Queen Mother's maiden name was Bowes-Lyon. Sagar, who had defended TH's acceptance of the post of Poet Laureate and given a lecture with the title 'Ted Hughes: The Laureate as Shaman', had expressed his misgivings about what he saw as the imperialist tendency of the poem and its air of flattery.

To Nicholas Hughes

20 February 1986   Ts (carbon copy)   Hughes

I caught the peacock yesterday. He's stripped the buds from all Carol's spring flowers in the yard, and round the front. Clare and Mike said they'd take him at Nethercott, as a curiosity for the Schoolkids. So I rigged up the Ambassadeur and the green carp rod, and laid out a long line with a big noose around a patch of monkey nuts in the yard. He walked straight into it. In fact, he saw the noose, and stepped into it with special care. First strike, I had him. Up he went. A peacock is a startling sight in the air, the underside is all flaring smoky black, so it was like playing a big black rocket for a minute or two, till he landed and stood moping. I tightened up towards him, and caught him under a blanket. He fought actually for only about ten seconds.

Clare and Michael Morpurgo are the friends mentioned. They did indeed take the peacock, which was soon eaten by a fox.

To Barrie Cooke

7 March 1986   Ms   Cooke

We had a grand opening day on the deadly Torridge. The Salmon & Trout Association had their annual dinner, near here.

A friend of mine, who has a beautiful 2 miles of the Torridge (not the Nethercott stretch) is the Chairman, and Michael Hordern, the actor, was guest speaker. Nick Grant was also down. And the S. & T. Association National Director—fellow I like.

The day after the dinner was 1st day of the season, so we fished on the Chairman's stretch. The river was frozen, in places, right across, and in most places there was 2 or 3 yards of thick ice fringing it—thick enough to stand on. So very few places to fish. I got a frozen salmon out of our freezer—about a 7 lb fresh fish from last year, and while Sir Michael was fishing down a long fast run I fished behind him. Everybody was primed. I hooked the frozen salmon front of the dorsal fin & tied the cast round him to get a side pull, then lobbed it out into the run. It landed with a great crash. "Fish!" I yelled. It played rather well. I'd wanted to get a stone into it to take it down, but it was frozen too solid. Still, it churned about, and occasionally flailed its tail fin at the surface, & flashed. "Come & land it"—I yelled to Sir Michael "Let's have a picture of you". The cameras were ready (but hidden). But Sir Michael, as an experienced fisher, refused to take another man's rod. Still, he came clattering & hobbling up the bank "Is it fresh? Yes," he cried "It's fresh. It looks fresh." Then somebody had a brainwave, & gave him a net. He crashed out through the ice with the net. "It's foul-hooked, I think," I shouted. "Yes, it is, it's foul-hooked" he assured us, & then with a gallant plunge, he netted it out of the frozen river, about 20 yards below me. He staggered up the shingle with my fish—which still had a sort of Z crook in its tail, from the freezer—and dumped the net. Then bent down to unhook the fish and "Good God" he cried "It's actually frozen solid! It's frozen absolutely solid!"

Nick Grant: then chairman of Duncan Lawrie Ltd, the private London bank.

To Nicholas Hughes

[Undated 1986]   Ts (carbon copy)   Hughes

I hope things are clearing. It did cross my mind, last summer, that you were under strains of an odd sort. I expect, like many another, you'll spend your life oscillating between fierce relationships that become tunnel traps, and sudden escapes into wide freedom when the whole world seems to be just there for the taking. Nobody's solved it. You solve it as you get older, when you reach the point where you've tasted so much that you can somehow sacrifice certain things more easily, and you have a more tolerant view of things like possessiveness (your own) and a broader acceptance of the pains and the losses. I came to America, when I was 27, and lived there three years as if I were living inside a damart sock—I lived in there with your mother. We made hardly any friends, no close ones, and neither of us ever did anything the other didn't want wholeheartedly to do. (It meant, Nicholas, that meeting any female between 17 and 39 was out. Your mother banished all her old friends, girl friends, in case one of them set eyes on me—presumably. And if she saw me talking with a girl student, I was in court. Foolish of her, and foolish of me to encourage her to think her laws were reasonable. But most people are the same. I was quite happy to live like that, for some years.) Since the only thing we both wanted to do was write, our lives disappeared into the blank page. My three years in America disappeared like a Rip Van Winkle snooze. Why didn't I explore America then? I wanted to. I knew it was there. Ten years later we could have done it, because by then we would have learned, maybe, that one person cannot live within another's magic circle, as an enchanted prisoner.

So take this new opportunity to look about and fill your lungs with that fantastic land, while it and you are still there. That was a most curious and interesting remark you made about feeling, occasionally, very childish, in certain situations. Nicholas, don't you know about people this first and most crucial fact: every single one is, and is painfully every moment aware of it, still a child. To get beyond the age of about eight is not permitted to this primate—except in a very special way, which I'll try to explain. When I came to Lake Victoria, it was quite obvious to me that in some of the most important ways you are much more mature than I am. And your self-reliance, your independance, your general boldness in exposing yourself to new and to-most-people-very-alarming situations, and your phenomenal ability to carry through your plans to the last practical detail (I know it probably doesn't feel like that to you, but that's how it looks to the rest of us, who simply look on in envy), is the sort of real maturity that not one in a thousand ever come near. As you know. But in many other ways obviously you are still childish—how could you not be, you alone among mankind? It's something people don't discuss, because it's something most people are aware of only as a general crisis of sense of inadequacy, or helpless dependance, or pointless loneliness, or a sense of not having a strong enough ego to meet and master inner storms that come from an unexpected angle. But not many people realise that it is, in fact, the suffering of the child inside them. Everybody tries to protect this vulnerable two three four five six seven eight year old inside, and to acquire skills and aptitudes for dealing with the situations that threaten to overwhelm it. So everybody develops a whole armour of secondary self, the artificially constructed being that deals with the outer world, and the crush of circumstances. And when we meet people this is what we usually meet. And if this is the only part of them we meet we're likely to get a rough time, and to end up making 'no contact'. But when you develop a strong divining sense for the child behind that armour, and you make your dealings and negotiations only with that child, you find that everybody becomes, in a way, like your own child. It's an intangible thing. But they too sense when that is what you are appealing to, and they respond with an impulse of real life, you get a little flash of the essential person, which is the child. Usually, that child is a wretchedly isolated undeveloped little being. It's been protected by the efficient armour, it's never participated in life, it's never been exposed to living and to managing the person's affairs, it's never been given responsibility for taking the brunt. And it's never properly lived. That's how it is in almost everybody. And that little creature is sitting there, behind the armour, peering through the slits. And in its own self, it is still unprotected, incapable, inexperienced. Every single person is vulnerable to unexpected defeat in this inmost emotional self. At every moment, behind the most efficient seeming adult exterior, the whole world of the person's childhood is being carefully held like a glass of water bulging above the brim. And in fact, that child is the only real thing in them. It's their humanity, their real individuality, the one that can't understand why it was born and that knows it will have to die, in no matter how crowded a place, quite on its own. That's the carrier of all the living qualities. It's the centre of all the possible magic and revelation. What doesn't come out of that creature isn't worth having, or it's worth having only as a tool—for that creature to use and turn to account and make meaningful. So there it is. And the sense of itself, in that little being, at its core, is what it always was. But since that artificial secondary self took over the control of life around the age of eight, and relegated the real, vulnerable, supersensitive, suffering self back into its nursery, it has lacked training, this inner prisoner. And so, wherever life takes it by surprise, and suddenly the artificial self of adaptations proves inadequate, and fails to ward off the invasion of raw experience, that inner self is thrown into the front line—unprepared, with all its childhood terrors round its ears. And yet that's the moment it wants. That's where it comes alive—even if only to be overwhelmed and bewildered and hurt. And that's where it calls up its own resources—not artificial aids, picked up outside, but real inner resources, real biological ability to cope, and to turn to account, and to enjoy. That's the paradox: the only time most people feel alive is when they're suffering, when something overwhelms their ordinary, careful armour, and the naked child is flung out onto the world. That's why the things that are worst to undergo are best to remember. But when that child gets buried away under their adaptative and protective shells—he becomes one of the walking dead, a monster. So when you realise you've gone a few weeks and haven't felt that awful struggle of your childish self—struggling to lift itself out of its inadequacy and incompetence—you'll know you've gone some weeks without meeting new challenge, and without growing, and that you've gone some weeks towards losing touch with yourself. The only calibration that counts is how much heart people invest, how much they ignore their fears of being hurt or caught out or humiliated. And the only thing people regret is that they didn't live boldly enough, that they didn't invest enough heart, didn't love enough. Nothing else really counts at all. It was a saying about noble figures in old Irish poems—he would give his hawk to any man that asked for it, yet he loved his hawk better than men nowadays love their bride of tomorrow. He would mourn a dog with more grief than men nowadays mourn their fathers.

And that's how we measure out our real respect for people—by the degree of feeling they can register, the voltage of life they can carry and tolerate—and enjoy. End of sermon. As Buddha says: live like a mighty river. And as the old Greeks said: live as though all your ancestors were living again through you.

Undated by TH, but placed here in the light of an omitted reference to his work on a 60th birthday poem for the Queen, presumably 'The Crown of the Kingdom', which was printed by *The Times* on 21 April.

To Anne Stevenson

[Autumn 1986]   Ts   Cambridge

When you told me of your plan to write about Sylvia I felt the usual dismay. I damped it by the thought—better Anne than some other, assuming the series will include the title somehow.

Still, these biographies are a perpetual smouldering in the cellar for us. There's always one or two smoking away. A month ago, on a day when my sister was lunching with the fellow who wrote the latest biography of Hemingway, and who is now contemplating Sylvia, she received two letters from different writers, wanting to open negotiations for a biography—on the very same day! All these threaten the same ordeal for all of us who are (as Aurelia put it) trapped into Sylvia's past. The ordeal has various refinements. There are all kinds of ways in which the natural healing processes are repeatedly torn up the roots. And a thousand varieties and degrees of agitation, having to see our own motives and feelings and thoughts of that time, and Sylvia's relationship to us, blandly displaced, and negated, by what a biographer—a perfect stranger—constructs out of a few hearsay legendary bits and pieces. And having to suffer watching that free style street theatre presented (and accepted and discussed) as the final truth about our lives with Sylvia. And having to realise, over the years, that no mistake can be corrected, no fantasy or lie can be extinguished, and that any attempt to correct the record only gives a weirder energy to the lies. And that nobody can hear anything but their own preoccupations or see any aspect of any fact that does not confirm their own prejudice. Having the monkey world of all this play among one's nerves for twenty five years induces a stupor of horror—it finally affects your judgement of mankind.

And for some—for my wife, for instance, and for S's children insofar as they are made aware of it—these rehearsals actually spoil life from day to day. You'll be able to imagine, Anne, my wife's role as shadow curator (and prisoner) of Sylvia's mausoleum—besieged in what she regards as her own home, where she's lived for 16 years (and where Sylvia lived for 14 months) by the Plath cultists and all the righteous photo-fit animosities that come with them. (One of them, an especially daft and voluble specimen who supplies biographers with fantasias by the yard, occasionally lets it be known that this house is really hers 'because Sylvia gave it to me'.) (People can say absolutely anything that comes into their heads!) And when I visit my son, who at thirteen was a gifted writer and natural very original poet, now living on a lonely stream in the Alaska wilderness, burrowing miles deep into his scientific data on an Arctic fish, and evading any attempt I might make to bring up Sylvia, I wonder if he hasn't searched out too perfect a removal from what the literary documentary dramatists have made of his mother.

Forgive me for all this Anne. You probably feel it's a bit graceless of me, saying this to you now after your obviously painstaking labours to be tentative and tactful in your account of everything that touches Sylvia's life. But then again I'll let it stand to help justify the one or two slight changes I'd like you to make in your text. I don't imagine for one minute that the changes will correct what you say insofar as others gave you the errors and will surely go on giving them to whatever public wants them.

First, though, a simpler detail: in your introduction page iii where you talk of Hall and Bly, I think your confining your reference here to Hall's Anthology and Bly's principles suggests that S's familiarity with the larger context of modern poetry was narrower than in fact it was. As far as she was concerned, the ground had already been pretty well broken by a number of people. I expect you remember, there was at that time a general surge of curiosity about modern poetry outside the US/English tradition. Bly was one of the earliest and most gifted transmitters sure enough, but so was Bill Merwin (whom she knew well. She had sheafs of translations by him—some of his first-rate Neruda among others). In a way, we collected that sort of thing and by 1960–61 we had a good deal—Italian, Spanish, French, German, South American, Czech & Polish (Sylvia grasped the point of Zbigniew Herbert straight off). (All this pushed eventually with Danny Weissbort's initiative into Modern Poetry In Translation). We translated some things ourselves—French, Spanish and German. She was saturated with Rilke, of course—she was perpetually studying German and used Rilke as a text. She regarded Rilke and Herbert as much more her 'fellow-countrymen' than other US poets. She really didn't need the deep image talk to tune her in to what she felt was hers anyway—hers by right rather than by belated adoption. She didn't in fact espouse those notions of the 'deep image'— though in a general sense she approved of what Bly was trying to promote and welcomed everything he did. But her sense of language was top to bottom logical and specific. And to anyone who knows the source and context of every image and reference in her poems—as in most of them I do—they are as coherent and lucid as an inspired legal argument. I don't think there is a single image that does not relate directly to a definite object—and that does not use the provenance, the whole live context in which she encountered the object, as part of her poem's argument. That is why the poems are so much more inescapably affecting, why they involve a reader with so much more immediacy, than the 'surreal' work of Lorca or Neruda or other practitioners of that style of 'deep image'. Sylvia's always carries—along with the specific reference—the urgency of specific feeling. By comparison, the 'deep image' is a rhetorical hit or miss thing, a generalised effect. In her poems there are no 'deep images' in Bly's sense. There is only psychological depth, very lucidly focused and lit. At the same time, I think the 'movement' to break down the parochial confinements of fifties verse   academic verse basically—which was also one aspect of England and America returning to an awareness of the rest of the world, after the locked doors of the war, and which Bly agitated for so effectively, did help her, give her courage and confidence, and general permission, to take the steps natural to her.

Page 88: The account of Sylvia's residence at Court Green has to be mine, or guesswork. I think what you have here is on the whole misleading. For instance, I can see the need to point up the dramatic aspect of the situation, but it falsifies Sylvia's position, let alone mine, to contrast what seems to be Sylvia's dissatisfaction with what seems to be my satisfaction. You'll not be surprised to hear me say the story was more complicated. I was enthralled by many things about our new life in Devon, but then, so was she. In many ways, she was a good deal more enthralled than I was. But we were both fairly easily enthralled, wherever we were. And she was never disenthralled. The Devon house was as precious to her at the end as the beginning of this last phase of her life. She missed easy access to films, & to a rich mix of excited and maybe talented people, but not any more than I did. We both missed it greatly. Only we had high tolerance for doing without some things, if it served our main plan. However she may have expressed it to Ruth Sillitoe, in her passionate, exaggerated sort of way, you'll easily understand that our restlessness (and the strains of confining it to the life we had for the moment chosen) was no simple thing. We knew we had created more problems than we'd solved, and the awareness made itself felt in bizarre and alarming ways, in both of us. But at least we had life on our own terms in our own place. Sylvia also wanted passionately to live in Italy, on a Greek island, in France, in Ireland, on Cape Cod, in San Francisco— and could announce how much she craved for these places, with tears in her eyes, when she met somebody who shared the taste.

Mainly we wanted somewhere to write, somewhere we could afford (which meant—free of the burden of rent), somewhere good for Frieda and whatever other children we might have, but we didn't greatly mind where it was. And in Devon, we'd found this. I had an attic, as you say, and Sylvia—you should say—had the biggest upstairs room with wall to wall red-carpetting to work in. House help was easy to find, and cheap. We intended to grow as much as we could of our own food. Sylvia worked till one oclock, while I looked after Frieda. I worked after that. In the evenings, usually, I read to her while she sewed or did something with her hands, made a rug etc. She never sat simply doing nothing. And she never read in a leisurely way. That's when we missed films, a wider range of friends etc. At that time, of course, we had no local friends, though Sylvia was good at making necessary acquaintances—with mothers of other children Frieda's age etc. And we got to know one or two interesting eccentrics. But the meetings were brief and sparse.

You should know, too, how we ended up in Devon, rather than somewhere else. Your remarks suggest that you suppose we went there because I liked the rural life. In those days, all I wanted was circumstances in which I could write and follow my own schemes, and not be forced by financial demands into some job. Sylvia too was sacrificing a lot simply to see what she could do if she did nothing but write for a few years. So Devon was partly, almost mainly, the flight from the heavy financial demands of living in a city. Our idea was to mobilise what talents we had, for living off our wits, until we could afford to take next steps.

My own simple notion, which Sylvia adopted too, was to secure two bases—one in London and one well out of it, then move to one as we got sick of the other, and back again. This would mean that all the recurrent need for upheaval change, which we both recognised, could be contained between two familiar rooted homes and not dissipated in an endless drifting from novelty to novelty, endlessly setting up new homes, improvising all the way and trailing the kids in the dust. Frieda, and the plan of more children, had imposed this idea. I still think it's a fair idea. And if Sylvia had lived I'm sure that's what we would have done. In fact, if she'd lived a little longer it might have dawned on us that we had done it. We had thought of buying the house in London first. But in 60–61 we were too physically and nervously exhausted to face the price, the mortgage etc, fear of what the debt might do to our plan. We debated buying number 9 (I think it was) Fitzroy Road—then £9,000, probably now 3 or 4 hundred thousand. A biggish house. We debated buying a house in Yorks. We actually looked across at Lumb Bank thinking that might be just about right. But Yorks in those days was eight hours by rail and full of my relatives. So we thought of going West. What decided us was that in 1961 the world seemed closer to nuclear war than ever since—and the panic was greater because the threat was really coming up for the first time. Nuclear business pre-occupied us a good deal. I collected material about this too. In 1960 we had a map, for instance, of the relationship between the nuclear waste dumps and the incidence of Leukaemia in England, Southern Scotland, Northern Ireland and Wales—a map that didn't become public till two or three years ago. (When some friends and I tried to publicise it in 1969 we were stopped by the Official Secrets Act). Fall-out was a preoccupation. With all this in the air, we thought that if we were going to move we might as well be upwind of likely accidents—which brought us to Devon. Once we were here, we were as I say well aware of the possible mistake of our move—isolating ourselves too far and finally, narrowing the children's options of good schools, losing easy access to libraries & lively friends. But we did want the isolation. We wanted to block off all other ways out except by writing. And S. defended our isolation. When two US professors visited us, offering me quite a lucrative teaching job in the US, that could have eased us fairly soon into our second base, Sylvia was outraged. She regarded it as an attempt to sabotage our experiment.

This isn't material to be used, Anne. It's simply background to what Ruth Fainlight said concerning S's remark about being homesick for the city.

P 90   I was startled to learn that for a long time after his birth I would not touch my baby son. Maybe I'm mistaken, but I remember it otherwise. I wonder what dear friend of mine came up with this particular subtlety in their careful analysis of our decomposed remains. I know that for most exemplars of the literary mentality we do not exist, or rather exist only in a book, but that's no reason to let them say anything they like, so please delete this, Anne. This is what I mean by having our real lives displaced by other people's inventions.

P 90   I know the Sillitoes are very sensitive, but evidently not sensitive enough—or at least whoever conveyed the approaching thunderstorm detail to you was not very perceptive. It's no secret that one of Sylvia's dominant moods was impending thunderstorm. A fair proportion of the observers eventually received the thunderbolt one way or another. Unless you grasp this side of Sylvia you'll misunderstand many things about her. Some people never saw any other side.

P. 90   I feel you oversimplify the circumstances of our separation, even though you grant the complexity of it. For instance, when you speak of my instinctive primitivism needing to escape from the media gloss of urban fame, I feel you are wanting to do me a favour but you make three mistakes. I've explained something of the actual nature of our 'escape'—not 'my' escape. It's a mistake to attribute the need to escape solely to me, and my instinctive etc. In this term 'instinctive primitivism' I feel you concede too much to the crude image of me set up by the earliest reviewers of my first book, and purveyed ever since by all those who find it convenient to use a sensationalised sort of logo for me. In all the letters I get from schoolchildren it's evident that teachers use nothing else—even use the very phrases from those first reviews etc. Anything about me that you might call 'instinctive primitivism' was far keener to stay near the London Libraries than deprive itself in Devon. Third mistake is that you imply that I felt persecuted by the media gloss of urban fame. I truly wasn't aware of any particular urban fame or media attention. My reviews were neither better nor worse than many anothers. I eagerly accepted the one invitation I had to appear on TV—a little piece about a children's book on Woman's Hour or something such. My picture once appeared in Vogue, together with some other writers etc. What time I managed to get on radio wasn't a fraction of what I wanted. The only literary gatherings I was ever invited to were at

Fabers. Nobody sought me out. The only Journalist who ever came to see me, an Italian woman from some Italian glossy, was expecting to find the Fox In The Attic novelist and was disappointed. Though I was in the generation of the Angry Young Men, and felt I had better barbarian credentials than any of them except maybe Alan Sillitoe, I was never noticed even among their hindermost baggage train. I would have liked a bit of fame in those days, but it seemed far off. I was far more aware of being abused, by people I'd never met, for using the 'affected, proletarian familiar abbreviation' of my first name, and for 'using language above my station'. The Cultural Church, whose high priests were the Evelyn Waughs, didn't fall on its face to the North until the Beatles came along.

What you say of my bedazzlement with this and that about Sylvia reads rather strangely to me. It's hard to say. But mainly I was aware of her helplessness, the sort of gallantry of her immense struggle to cope, simply to cope, and as for her mastery of Literature I was mainly astounded—and I mean astounded—by what she had not read. I was dazzled, perhaps, by what I saw through her of the American world, and by her mastery of it when we got there. But I think your use of 'civilisation' is a bit too inclusive, and again makes me seem more of a pathetic barbarian than I was in relation to her—though we were both pathetic enough.

Also, I think you do me some wrong by saying I was unready for fatherhood. I'm sure I was still a great deal of a child. I'm probably even more of a child now. But if I wasn't the right kind of father, it was because I was too much of a surrogate mother, quite ready to carry the children round most of the day, and some of the night too. All that was a happy time for me. And after Sylvia died I simply carried on doing the same.

Again, your image of what I might have preferred as my ideal life is a little wide of the mark. It's true I was always looking for the ideal place to write in. But I was aware enough to have realised that the perfect conditions can't be rigged—I was aware, for instance, that for me the very best place is a railway compartment, and next to that a Hotel room. One of the best places I ever had was the hallway of our flat in Chalcot Square—a windowless cubicle just big enough for a chair. Other people's flats have always been good places. Anywhere near fishing, I think, is no good—because the whole motive of writing finds perfect and satisfying expression in fishing. Fishing is a substitute symbolic activity that simply short-circuits the need to write. Also, I knew by 1960, after the experience of Yaddo, that an isolated hut is no good for me. Writing in a house where I can hear family activity at a distance is not too bad. Writing in the house when it's empty is good. Working in the same house as Sylvia was always very good. What you call the house beautiful, you know, was a passion with me too. You know those lines of Plutzik:

> Beautiful the sleeping of wife, and children,
> In a house, on a field, lit by the morning star.

They were never out of my head in those days.

P 91:   The 'jailor' and the 'nazi' in Sylvia's mythology are an intriguing curiosity to me, too. If you imagine that these were fixed figures, aspects of Sylvia's superego, you'll understand, maybe, in what form and on what occasions I might have become aware of them. Jung's theory of the animus fitted the case fairly closely, in some ways.

p 91:   You should not assume that I have felt guilt for involving Sylvia in my own occult hankerings. I feel you must underestimate the place the Moon had in her symbolic world—I mean the real, spontaneous role that image played in the dynamics of her make up. It had nothing to do with any ideas of mine. There was a quite separate entity in her, a true daemon, an independant energised Centre, of which the Moon was the totem, and which had gathered into itself the story and all the pains of her early life, and which made it at times very difficult for her to live. It provided all the illuminations of her poetry, and it threatened period-ically to kill her. It always signified impending death. This light in dark-ness certainty of impending death was the bell jar inside which she lived, and inside which I too came to live, in the end. The moment she died it evaporated instantly. Her curiosity about occult business, Tarot, other bits and pieces of hermetic arcana, were really no more than incidental bits of rubbish magnetised to that real inner knowledge. I taught her some simple procedures of meditation—but only because whatever was going on inside her made it for quite long periods very difficult for her to think, or to follow deliberately an imaginative train of thought. Quite a few of her early poems are about this tormented state. The meditations at least brought her a temporary freedom where she could write some-thing, and she did develop this. Once she got her mind freed she had as her analyst had noted quite abnormal access to her subconscious—abnormally direct, lucid, and emotionally complete. My responsibility, if anything, is for having held her so hard to the prolonged concentrated effort to get there, to come into possession of herself, whatever it might be, and to do it in writing. Would we have been better to ease off. Or would she have got there anyway. And was that final confrontation so dangerous? It wasn't the confrontation, the controlled eruption of all that primal material that killed her. It was something that ran up, when she was completely exhausted after it, when she'd actually won and had lowered her guard. It's too facile to regard her death as some inevitable culmination of her inspiration. Her death was the remotest fluke, an unbelievably freakish sequence of unlucky coincidences. Alvarez has itemised some, but he doesn't know a quarter of it.

I feel you're a little hard on me, too, where you say I expected her to be like my mother. That suggests an image of me as some crass chauvinistic working class ape lounging with my beer while she slaves at the sink. Actually, my father regularly washed up—he liked it. And I didn't mind it. We had planned schemes of sharing such things between us. I wasn't averse to cooking. I made her her morning coffee every morning we lived together, and that was what she took into her room to start writing. I can't remember that she sewed buttons on. Maybe she did. I was a fairly expert button sewer myself. I attended her fairly closely. Except for the short spell she had in hospital, we were never apart for more than two or three hours at a time in seven years—say five or six hours when we were teaching in the US. We went everywhere together.

[. . .]

I'm no expert in Plath biographies, but it has been stated (I've mentionned it, I think, somewhere) that the key factor in Sylvia's death, the mechanical factor, was the tranquilliser drug that was being administered to her by Dr Horder. Accounts of her death regularly find no place for this detail, which seems to me fairly important. In the diaries, which she wrote during her last days, she describes the terrible interval that came regularly between the point where one pill lost its effect and the next pill took hold—a matter of two hours which fell in the early morning. After her death, I learned from her mother that this particular drug had been tried on S, during her recovery from her first suicide attempt, and that it induced such an extreme suicidal reaction, in the gap between doses, that S's mother was warned never to allow it to be given to S under any circumstances. Dr Horder knew nothing about this. In her diary entry, she feared that she wouldn't get through this gap.

The poet Anne Stevenson (b.1933) had been commissioned by Penguin to produce a life of Plath for its 'Modern Women' series of mini-biographies. Stevenson had sent TH a draft of the chapters concerning him, for inspection and comment. She later withdrew from the Penguin commission and wrote the full-length biography that appeared in 1989 as *Bitter Fame*.

The term 'deep image', derived from the Spanish '*canto jondo*' (deep song), was fashionable in literary discussion and implied, among other things, reliance on the image as a conveyor of poetic meaning. Robert Bly (b.1926), one of the US poets who took the phrase up, has translated from the work of Spanish, German and Swedish poets.

Richard Hughes (1900–76), no relation, wrote *The Fox in the Attic* (1961).

To Brenda and Charles Tomlinson

5 November 1986 Ms Texas

Since April, I've been blowing along like that old tumbleweed in the song. U.S. law, mainly. Case was to have been tried in July. In June— after two months' slow-motion revelation—I realised I had the wrong lawyer. Heaven intervened, & the trial was put back to January. Finally, I managed to involve Harper (from certain angles, they carry some liability), who produced "the best libel lawyer in New York". So I met him. He's like the Samurai war-lord villain in a Kurosawa film. A quite alarming tigerish individual—a jewish Genghis Khan, with the right name: Victor Kovner! I've laid all my fortunes into his hands (or at his feet). So though in a sense I'm now travelling at close to the speed of light, well above the gravity field of earth, I'm relaxed. If he can't bring me safely to land, I don't think it can be done.

The title of the US legal action to which TH refers was 'Jane Anderson v. Avco Embassy Pictures Corp., [various other defendants affiliated with that motion picture company] and Edward James Hughes'. Applying to the US District Court for the District of Massachusetts in 1982, Dr Jane V. Anderson, a psychiatrist, had claimed that in the 1979 film *The Bell Jar*, based on Sylvia Plath's novel, a character who makes a lesbian pass at the heroine was identifiably based on her. Dr Anderson asserted that she had been defamed, and her right to privacy violated. Having signed a standard indemnity clause in the film rights contract, TH, as executor of Plath's Estate, found himself among the defendants.

TH's lawyer, Victor Kovner, was at that time practising as a member of the New York firm Lankenau Kovner & Bickford.

To Nicholas Hughes

[Late 1986]   Ts (carbon copy)   Hughes

The Fisheries Minister was down in Brixham today, a fellow called Gummer who looks like a tax clerk. By which I suppose I mean he looks somehow like a paper clip, a bit like a going out tray loosely jammed into a coming in tray, a bit like a cold cup of instant coffee at 10-20, a bit like a neon light in a windowless office etc etc. Anyway there he was, orating to the assembled fishmen of Brixham who looked more like an army of ex shot-putters. And they were very hostile, because the boat licensing laws, evidently, had a big rip in their net, which enabled a smart Irishman to buy up small boats, remove their licences and attatch them to big boats of his own, or of some conniving foreigner's, and sell off the small boats, shorn of their licence, cheap. Evidently the licensing law by limiting the number of these small local boats had intended to confine the fishing to just so much capacity and to just such a range, as a way of controlling predation. Also, it meant that the fish caught came back to England—unless the crafty small craft sold it at sea, which of course some do. But this Irishman's big boat, same licence, can fill a big hold and away with it to Spain. The whole tribe were in arms, to have this stopped. Though of course their brothers and fathers were the traitors selling the boats. However, Gummer stopped it, on the spot.

Another Brixham skipper was there—all on TV—complaining that 100, neither more nor less, very big boats were sweeping up and down this coast night and day, then away to Spain. Gummer, he said, had done nothing to sink them. Though not another EEC country permitted anything like it. 'He looks sick' said Carol. Then a shot of Gummer in his raincoat picking wretched little flatties out of the boxes. His glorious purpose in coming down here was to open a spanking new long dock in Brixham harbour, which he did in the pouring rain. Or what looked like pouring rain. Maybe it was just gloom. Gummer's probably quite a good chap. He just can't move mountains like he ought to be able to do.

I can see why those Spaniards need to comb the seven seas for their fish. Our trip was more or less an orgy of ichthyophagy.

Dated by reference, in subsequent paragraphs, to the trip made to Spain in October 1986 by TH, Carol Hughes and their friends Simon and Hilary Day. TH had been invited by the Spanish Sherry Institute to select for himself 700 bottles of sherry, in token of the 'butt of sack' that was traditionally the payment offered to the Poet Laureate.

John Selwyn Gummer was at that time Minister for Agriculture in the Conservative government. Brixham is in Devon.

To Gerald and Joan Hughes

16 December 1986   Ms   Emory

Did you like the casual bit, Gerald, about Squadron Leaders & Air Vice Marshalls? I think I've told you about the Squadron Leader. Strange world—a world of social revelations, Xrays of England's anatomy, encephelograms of England's brain, this world of retired high ranking servicemen. But I get on with them. Apart from the W.D. issue voices & N.W. frontier speech systems, many of them are remarkable chaps, naturally enough. Also, without them, I fancy there'd be no Salmon rivers left at all. The shooting—in which I seem to have lost all interest—belongs to the Bankers, Landed Rich, & Company directors—plus a few rich farmers. We have a whole gang of them that we sometimes play with—I've got to know them mainly through one of them who invited me to join his consortium when he made a bid for the S.W. T.V. franchise. I must have told you all that at the time. He owns the best & most beautiful bit of the river Dart—and that was his bribe. So we became fishing pals—then his wife & Carol became close friends. And now, it seems, we're knit together with knots. Through him I got to know a whole procession of those figures you used to breed your pheasant's for. Simon's (this pal of mine) father often shot at Alphington. Also through him I've met a troop of Tory politicians. I've got to know some better, since they get tangled into our fishing trips. A scatter of Lords—Courtenay down at Powderham Castle (on the Exe, you remember) & Clinton. So it's a mighty peculiar box seat view I have of this particular theatre of play. Mainly I meet them at feasts—at Simon's—and on fishing jams. They know how to enjoy their lives, I must say. In fact, Simon introduced me to that whole army of occupation—invisible, pretty well, to the common Englander, except as Park walls and great ornate gates & stormy voices in the House of Parliament. A very fascinating education (for what?) for me, you can guess.

From the second of two airmail letter forms, bearing the same date. 'W.D. issue': issued by the War Department, normally used of weaponry.

Alphington and Powderham Castle are both in the vicinity of Exeter and would have been known to Gerald Hughes, whose first job on leaving home had been as a gamekeeper in Devon.

1987

To János Csokits

6 January 1987   Ms Emory

Peter Jay. Yes, I did send them off. I made a huge effort, & typed the whole thing out—not all that much (the altered passages). But the gear-change on my machinery is getting stickier and stickier.

I really don't know what to think about the apparatus. I can't remember how it became attached in the first place. Actually, thinking about it, now, it seems to me out of place. Danny's book is the place for it. In the book of poems don't you think it injects too much confusion of commentary and incidental chat—as if the pianist & violinist in a duet should introduce their performance with strenuous talk about their rehearsals & studies & finger problems & then at the end engage the audience in a whole debate etc. After all, what matters is the poems simply, & the more simply the poems can sit in solitude the more clearly, it seems to me, they're going to speak.

The mystery of a book is that every item within the covers becomes a part of every other item within the covers. General contamination by osmosis. Introductions etc revolt me—though I do like to get to know about the poet from somewhere.

Scholars etc have hijacked the convention of publishing poems by the dead—or by foreigners. Like Russia—your guide, and host, is your police surveillance.

In the case of our book, there seems to me a danger it will be overwhelmed by international cultural flummery. If I recall it rightly, we stuck on those extra bits and pieces because Peter wanted a bigger—fatter—book. I can't think why we didn't question it. Well, if he now wants them out, very good. Better for Pilinszky.

I dislike my introduction too. It's a pity he can't have a simple table of events in Pilinszky's life, then the poems.

Actually, I suppose the truth is, most readers prefer chat. They might look at the poems with a peering sort of curiosity, but they settle to the preface, introduction and afterword with a smile of satisfaction—even

528

if only to smirk & be critical. That would explain why they usually review—if at all—the introduction. It's the only part they respond to in a communicable way.

If I can bring myself to ring Peter, & plug myself into that circuit of agitation, I will tell him all this.

[. . .]

U.S. Lawsuit imminent. I'm studying for this strange exam. I'm poised to fly out there, at my lawyer's signal, from Saturday onwards.

Several dramatic developments. The plaintiff is on her 3rd lawyer. In summer I also changed lawyers. Left my first one with $60,000 hanging in his jaws. Luckily, my new one ("the best in New York") prised from my Co-Defendants Insurance coverage for me of $90,000—which is just about what it had cost me up to that moment. I keep remembering:

> "Before ill chances men are ever merry,
> But heaviness fore-runs the good event."

Am I merry or heavy? A blend, I'd say.

TH absent-mindedly dates this 1986. The earlier paragraphs are part of a prolonged discussion, in letters and meetings, about the publication of János Pilinszky's *Selected Poems* by Peter Jay at the Anvil Press. After delays, the book appeared in 1989, with TH's introduction unaltered. 'Danny's book', in progress, was *Translating Poetry: The Double Labyrinth* (1989), which, edited by Daniel Weissbort, was to contain essays on Pilinszky by TH and Csokits, as well as pieces by other specialists.

The lines from Shakespeare's *Henry IV, Part 2* actually begin, 'Against ill chances . . .'.

To Jack Brown

5 February 1987   Ts   Emory

Dear Jack,

I'm always glad to hear from you, and your last letter was truly thoughtful. No, I wasn't offended.

It interests me to hear how other people regard the Laureateship business. I'm impressed, very much, by the way almost everybody takes it seriously. It's extremely peculiar that people who have no interest in poetry nevertheless have strong instinctive feelings about this. (Recently a woman near here, wife of an ex-fighter pilot, county type but very pleasant, who I know fairly well, whispered to another friend of mine: "But do you think he's the right one to be <u>our</u> Laureate?"—she having never read a poem in her life!)

I'm very aware, too, of its (ghostly) political dimensions. It did occur to me, for instance, that in the sub-committee debate about who for Laureate somebody might well have totted up my happy years in Mexborough. I doubt if anybody did. But if I'd been on that committee, I would have. I would have thought it a possibly useful qualification. A feint of sympathy for the North, whereas Philip L. might have seemed like too obvious an unfurling of the banner over the far right. I thought Charles Causley would have been a good choice.

But the political adjuncts are irrelevant, really—in fact, they're obstructive, like daft great flywheels they simply make the job more awkward to steer. The whole operation (insofar as it has any activity) has to be kept somewhere beneath Party Politics. At the level of Party debate nobody knows better than you this country is split like a schizo with nine minds. But at the level of the Monarchy—and that's the primitive, instinctive level—it seems to me we still manage to be one. And I think that image of the Monarchy, the ritualised dream-symbol made real, helps us to stay one. Something like that.

Monarchy wasn't invented by power-maniacs after all. It was extruded by that instinctive, primitive need—interesting to read Frazer's Golden Bough or Freud's Totemism and Taboo on the psychology of it.

And that's the level, it seems to me, on which Monarchy not only works but is absolutely vital, like a biological necessity. And insofar as I'm for unity above all, I'm all for Monarchy. In England, anyway.

I've just spent 3 weeks disengaging myself from a lawsuit in the U.S. that's been vampirising me for five years. So I'm feeling like a new man.

I'm intrigued by Cordelia's Way. I like it. Are you making any reference to the mythical ancestry of Cordelia? In the Welsh myth, from which the Lear story came, as the bride—the third of the triple goddess—she was Creidylad, the heron. Creidylad still means heron in welsh. And in the Irish myth, from which the Welsh myth descended, she was banished out onto the sea, as a heron, for three hundred years. So there's your margin and ditch world, of the first part, and your open ocean of the second.

How are things up there? Are they as bad as they looked to be last year?

Keep well, Jack
All the best
Ted

Brown's most recent letter to TH had been written in a state of depression after the failure of the 1984–5 Miners' Strike, and bewilderment at TH's acceptance of the Laureateship. 'Cordelia's Way' is described by Brown himself as 'a suicide poem', for which he had 'copiously researched the myths'.

To Victor Kovner

7 February 1987   Ms   Kovner

Dear Victor,

I'm feeling quite strong withdrawal symptoms—knowing I'm not going to be seeing you tomorrow, or the day after, or for many a day.

In spite of everything, that 3 weeks was one of the richest experiences I've had for a long time. The threat, the dramatic tension, etc, but above all the sense of being defended & fought for, by you, on such a momentous stage that really was something. Since you're always the defender, I suppose you've never experienced it—but I began to have strange, strange transference illusions. For instance (you'll smile) I found myself identifying you with my son & my elder brother. I kept feeling, when I was with you, that I was with them. Is that sort of thing common with clients? I didn't mention it to you, but you are so like my brother, & my son, that it's uncanny. It startled us, when we first met you in Harper's. For me, it added a whole weird dimension to our collaboration especially since I was in such an emotional turmoil generally.

I avoided coming to stay with you, partly because John & Julienne really did make me feel they wanted me, but partly too because I feared to risk damaging the relationship between you & me (by being a confounded guest under your feet) before we know each other better. I sensed that your private space is even more complicated than my own—so it meant a great deal to me when you invited me.

If there is one person as grateful to you as I am, it's Carol. Sarah, when she heard about all the garden greenery in your window, & your garden on Fire Island, she went straight out & came straight back with what I'm posting off to you—"That's only the beginning" she says.

The whole 24 year chronic malaise of Sylvia's biographical problem seems to have come to some sort of crisis. I'd say the trial forced it, but in fact the simultaneity—of trial, & of biographies (now 6 of them!)—was fortuitous (there's that word, English sense). Perhaps the trial & the newspaper response to it (especially in England) has given the biographies new point & dramatic purpose. I've a feeling the days of protecting Aurelia—and Frieda & Nick too, I suppose—are over. Since most of the abuse I've had, over the years, about my rôle in S's life, has fed on my own silence about it, suddenly these 'old friends' seem to feel I've overdone it. They're spilling the beans. I expect everybody else will jump on the great opportunity (publishing opportunity) for "new appraisal in the light of"—and the whole thing will start a revised production of the whole drama.

Wasn't La Clemenza a sensational memory! I keep remembering it. At the time I got concerned 'who's paid for me.' Well, obviously you had. I shall remember that. But what a brilliant sort of evening—that great luminous coach, in the snow, & that insane soft controlled explosion of voices in the great womb of it. I always feel there is something insane about opera—beautifully & magnificently insane.

The idiot grimacing of these English tabloids, on the other hand, is simply idiot, simply that, imbecile. I really can't get worked up about it, or go fighting those windmills, even where it's a more or less deliberate lie. As in that description of me in the court reading a book while Plaintiff accused me of 'sadism' (the best-loved word in the English Press). You know the journalist who wrote that arrived only on the 29th—he came in while we were waiting for the judge, after we'd signed the settlement.

He introduced himself, then said "I'm terribly sorry, but you know how it is, I've been asked by the paper to ask you a question." He asked his question,—I referred him to you. Then he shuffled a bit, & finally came out with "It's embarrassing l know (he actually did say that) but do you mind if I ask you another question. The paper asked me to ask you." Then he asked me about Assia etc. Again I referred him to you.

Amazing (inevitable) how all that crawling, shamefaced apology came out in the papers as heroic revelation of my unspeakable secrets.

I regard it all as a sort of popular cartoon—cretinous twin of that incredibly stupid T.V. programme we have 'Spitting image.' We shall ask them simply to correct false facts (not the trivia about me, but details of the earlier history—one or two). If they won't (and I can't imagine them giving space to such non-news) I shall drop it.

All their 'now it can be told' stuff is what ignorant journalists bought from fantasising self-publicists of matters that are quite open & on public record in several places.

They call it 'investigative journalism'. Case recently of burglars raping a vicar's daughter—this touched the fantasy of my countrymen (the wild national dream of raping the Vicar's daughter, of being the Vicar's daughter and getting raped by burglars, of being the Vicar and having your daughter raped by burglars, of being a Vicar & raping your daughter & blaming it on burglars etc etc). It became a popular event, papers full of it for weeks. But it didn't achieve the ultimate touch of artistry, the apotheosis, the highest inspiration of our National soul, till the journalists began to lower midget microphones through the vicarage letterboxes!

Much love to you both. The moment you have a date for touch-down in England, let us know. A scratch for the dogs.

love

Ted

The action brought by Dr Anderson (see letter to Charles Tomlinson of 5 November 1986) had finally come to trial in January. Before that, Avco's insurers had offered to settle out of court, but Dr Anderson's lawyers turned the offer down. No such offer was made by Victor Kovner, representing TH. After Dr Anderson had given her testimony, however, and before her cross-examination by Kovner, Avco made another offer, which was accepted. TH paid nothing.

John Scanlon was the public relations expert who had agreed to deal with press enquiries about the case. He had invited TH to stay with him and his wife, Julienne, in their New York apartment, while preparing for the case. 'Sarah' is Kovner's wife.

Spitting Image, the topically satirical show using grotesque puppets to caricature politicians and celebrities, ran on British television from 1984 to 1996.

To Mark Purdey

7 February 1987   Ms   Estate of Mark Purdey

Dear Mark Purdey,

Yes, I'm honoured to be asked, I'd love to write a foreword to your book.

I've just found in the U.S. a fascinating recent book called The Poisoned Womb. Very detailed account of the effect of agricultural/industrial toxins on the reproductive system. Horrifying. Do you know it?

But I do think this is the essential stuff to publicise—the effect of the chemicals on the cellular life & processes within us.

There was an article recently in The Times titled Return Of The Otter—optimistic survey, sliding over at one point the continued decline of Otters in East Anglia, & rejoicing, quietly, that artificially bred litters are being released there. I wrote them a letter pointing out that East Anglian otters were declining for a very good reason—then I quoted the Scientists report, on the bodies of dead otters, which made up the bulk of an article in The New Scientist (Aug 19, 1986). Ghastly descriptions of physical disintegration, tumerous, haemophiliac, ulcerated corpses—and all related, via the organochlorine in their livers etc, to the deadly sequence: toxins⟶effect on endocrine system⟶breakdown of immune system.

The Times Letters Editor rang up & asked me to shorten my letter. I asked him how he thought it could be done, so he suggested 'cutting out all the grisly stuff about the corpses & details of the poison's effects.' I said, but thats the whole point of the letter. He answered, I'm sorry then, but "we have to think of our reader's stomachs at breakfast"

The one thing he wasn't thinking of!

They refused to publish it.

I'll look forward to hearing from you again.

Yours sincerely
Ted Hughes

Farmer and environmental campaigner Mark Purdey (1953–2006) had recently heard that TH shared his concerns about the damaging and deadly effects of pesticides commonly used in agriculture. John Ellkington's *The Poisoned Womb* (1985) exposes the effects of chemicals on human fertility.

To Lucas Myers

14 February 1987   Ms   Emory

Dear Luke,

I've delayed writing to you, because I wanted to write at length &

534

with all details about the extraordinary adventure I've just had in the wilder parts of U.S. Law. Five years, it's taken.

However, I'm suddenly—against all my expectations—freed of it, returned from it, & too stunned by the surprise escape to say much about it.

The physiological effects are a curious piece of experience.

In some way, it's been just what I needed. Each day I was over there, in NY & Boston, with my Attorney (a wonderful chap, a great find) I woke from one revelation to another—great thunderflashes (of gasping horror, mainly) of enlightenment—about what has been happening to me since 1963, but more particularly since 1969, the way those events have worked on me, & what my defensive strategies have actually entailed. It's one thing to have revelations—another to turn them to account!

But let me defer all that—while I drop you a quick note about the "Ah, Youth" piece. It's a startling account—you recall so precisely things I'd forgotten utterly. You conjured whole chunks of life—from under my amnesia. And you're just, I think. I suppose.

Strange business seeing myself through your eyes. Dido Merwin recently wrote some letters (to one of Sylvia's new biographers)—savage stating of her case against Sylvia. Horribly accurate. But—laws of thermodynamics—to every force, one equal but opposite. The animus is a mirror-image of Sylvia's own. Still, in that account, the same me appears as in yours. Lamentable history of the human calf!

There are only one or two places I'd ask you to revise, if it's possible.

'Bite on the neck . . .' This most visible act of our union appears in biographical writings as 'on the face'—which is accurate, alas.

On Page 9, you quote my letter, where I liken myself to an Iago, & in the following paragraph generally transmit a critical view of American hospitality & life. God knows, it was probably true to my feelings. But Luke I have grown so paranoic about the consequences of my every petty remark—magnified, amplified, spectrally analysed & crazily polemicised in the auditoriums & laboratories & court-houses of the U.S. National Plath Investigations Committee & Patriotic Publications Inc, that I see too many dire possibilities for the words of mine that you quote here. Please delete them.

Sylvia's legend is now so out of hand, my casual words are whole new adventures, new ogres & catastrophes, for the bards of the cult. And as I say, they reappear everywhere. And much as I send it all to hell, it is startling to see rumours & speculations about my secret life of thirty years ago appear in the hands of a cross-questionner, in a U.S. court-room, authenticated as 'published, serious scholarship', & used (poised) to carve hundreds of thousands of dollars out of my very entrails. Actual dollars.

And startling to see the casual anecdotes of old acquaintance adapted by the genius of tabloid journalists—to gothicise an episode in their Sunday comic strip papers. New lives for old, with a great deal of unmotivated vengeance, general malignity, zoological basic behaviour-ism etc.

This Poet Laureatism is revealing its ghastly potential! To be Mickey Mouse!

However, to hell with all that, but—

There's another similar seed of confusion on your page 10. No doubt Sylvia & I plundered each other merrily—but if you say it, in my words—God, what new theses of accusation, what Job-loads of right-eous wrath! If you say that, our generous readers will multiply it by ten. Your balancing statement, that she profited a little from me, will be reduced to one tenth. That's the biological 1st law of human malice in action. It's no good for me to say I designed prototypes, which she put into full Germanic production—though there's truth in it. I would never be believed. But to say I stole from her—that would be an instant religion of verification, & my wretched undated efforts would reveal the new gospel, under compulsion.

Small detail of fact: she wrote The Bell Jar between Feb. & May 1961, in Bill Merwin's study on Primrose Hill. You seem to imply that she was writing it in Devon.

And the Flat where she died was in Fitzroy Road, not Place.

One slightly sour realisation I've come to, this last few revelatory weeks, is just what my long defence of Aurelia's feelings (and I sup-pose to some extent of F. & N.'s image of their mother) actually amounts to. Maybe I did help her to keep up her self-delusion, and her sustained effort to delude the public too, about Sylvia's diabolical side. When she published Letters Home, she re-invented Sylvia as the ideal & angelic daughter—and consecrated her death as a martyrdom. This was all of a piece with her colossal effort to apologise for her daughter, & to persuade herself that the novel & the poems were screams extorted on the rack, & that all Sylvia's difficulties had been implanted in her somehow, by somebody else—mainly (in Aurelia's own mind) by her analyst Dr Beutscher, who first gave Sylvia—after her attempted suicide—the resurrection mantra "I hate my mother." This image—sugar idol—of Sylvia became a divine icon, as you know. But of course it's a lie. And I colluded in the creation & propagation of it. What Aurelia saw—recognised—in the novel & poems as the voice of Sylvia's diabolical streak, she managed to represent as the voice of her suffering & martyrdom. And protecting Aurelia, I colluded—and promoted the cult which interpreted my continued silence in the blazing martyr-light shed by Sylvia's consecrated image. In which light I could only appear as a demon, the villain, the cause of all Sylvia's pains.

And now this view of me—as all the upsurge surrounding this Court-case has revealed—is the basic, unexamined, natural assumption for everybody who turns their thoughts to Sylvia or indeed to me. Even people who ought to know me better fall into the cliché when—for instance—they talk to biographers.

Because I've kept my head down, under the bellies of the cows etc, & deliberately closed my mind to the world of Sylvia's publicity, I've been fairly unaware of the human face of all this. But this Trial—where I've had to look at it all close & hard—revealed it.

I see now the explanation for many things. And I see that my poor books have led a strange kidnapped life—in the world of this Almighty pious lie.

So, now that a few voices pipe up here & there suggesting that, after all, Sylvia was a whole lot more complicated, & in no small measure a deal more perverse, than the popular saintly doll purveyed to students & literary tourists, I find myself disinclined to obstruct them. As far as I'm concerned, I'd like to see the whole truth told, down to the last word. The lie has poisonned everything to do with Sylvia, & everywhere I turn I have to drink it—since her fame ensures that she's everywhere, even in the houses of my neighbours here.

Almost. Among the 16 Boston jurors, from which we picked our 8 for the Trial, not a single one had ever heard of her.

Or so they said.

I've gone on a bit. But I'm so full of it all at the moment. I wake every morning now at 3 or 4, in a kind of horrible rage at how I've let my life be hijacked by all this sanctimonious righteous lying cant.

Poor old Sylvia! If only I hadn't humoured her, & nursed her like a patient, & coddled her like a child—if only I'd had the guts to carry on just as I was, instead of wrapping my life up in a cupboard, while I tended her. Then maybe she'd have emerged in better shape. And me too.

The whole thing's a mystery to me, except—for the logicality of it.

Luke, I miss seeing you. Will you never come over here with Agy? We're very well. Carol in great shape. Frieda blossoming with talent & high spirits, Nick happy & doing well. Olwyn OK too.

Love to you both from us
Ted

P.S. I haven't yet read the play. But I'll write again soon.

Myers's 'Ah, Youth . . . Ted Hughes and Sylvia Plath at Cambridge and After' was published in *Grand Street*, and later included in Anne Stevenson's *Bitter Fame* as the first of three appendices, the second and third being memoirs by Dido Merwin and Richard Murphy, respectively. Myers had shown his piece to TH for approval, and subsequently made the changes asked for.

TH's description of himself as an Iago has not been traced.

To Michael Hamburger

12 September 1987   Ms   Leeds

Dear Michael,

Thank you for the note—about the ecological dialogue of the Twins in the womb.

It was a note, really, after reading The Poisonned Womb, by John Elkington—(Penguin). Read it, & gain a head of perfectly white hair.

It seems, Dennis Thatcher is involved in the waste disposal business.

Margaret is no ordinary woman. If she were, she might have some conscience about cleaning up—some sense of responsibility for it.

In the various Children's Poetry Competitions, which I help to judge, the new preoccupation is pollution—poisonning of earth & people. Even with six & seven year olds. Very aware, & very frightened—depressed.

Something new!

Problem, maybe, is that Margaret can't be frightened. She's like the general who says "we can afford 25% casualties."

Her job, as an analytical chemist, was researching the maximum number of bubbles that can be pumped into ice-cream, before it disillusions the customers.

If only it were her priority, she's one person who could really clean the place up.

But I don't think she grasps the reality, & the real horror of what is happening. As a trained chemist, she naturally listens to the hired experts, the professional consultants, who lie according to the fee, & say what she wants to hear.

I've had dealings with one or two of these, as I suppose you have—in the shadow of your power-station.

I keep thinking I'll have no more to do with it—it poisons the whole of life, & all enjoyment. And in the end, it's an imposed & artificial circumstance—even though it's a matter of life & death.

Love to Anne & yourself

Ted

The Times printed 'First Things First', TH's 'ecological dialogue', on 4 June 1987. A topical piece, subtitled 'An Election Duet, performed in the Womb by foetal Twins', it was not included by TH in any subsequent collection.

As a research chemist, Margaret Thatcher – at the time of this letter Conservative Prime Minister – had been a member of the team at J. Lyons and Co that developed the first soft frozen ice cream. Her husband, Denis, was, together with his many other business appointments, deputy chairman of a waste removal firm.

Hamburger's house in Suffolk was close to Sizewell B, the nuclear power station. He was married to the poet Anne Beresford.

To Nicholas Hughes

29 October 1987   Ts (carbon copy)   Hughes

Dear Nick,

Well, I idled my way back, dozing and reading. I felt the strain of carrying my bags at this end, but not too badly. And now I can't feel anything of the operation at all, and the scar is hardly visible. So I'm feeling very foolproof without appendix. What a liability! Also, I'm hoping that saturation with antibiotics has cleared up whatever other little bugs were hanging around me all this year. Ever since I was in New York, where I had a horrendous sore-throat for about a week, I've had some funny tenant.

So now we know definitely what sort of trip not to have. The rule must be: once you've handed control of the trip to somebody else, i.e.

once you've accepted the role of guest, it won't work. At least, it won't work for you. And if it isn't working for you, obviously it fails for me. Still, it was nice having some time. I only wish we'd had a few more talks. After I left, I felt very badly we hadn't managed to separate ourselves from our generous hosts a bit more. But what I've realised is that I've been very doped: the general anaesthetic, and the general physical shock, I can see, only began to wear off this last few days. I hadn't realised what an invalid I was. What a zombie. What a triple zombie—as distinct from my average condition of single zombie.

[. . .]

What we should do, maybe, is raft down the Dean. I'd love you to meet those steelhead as I did. And we'd be free of social treacle. But what I'd like to do is fix a programme of trips next year, so I can stay clear of Scottish entanglements with a good conscience. I'd like to raft down the Gilcana—or somewhere like end of June early July, and then maybe do that Kulak River trip in October. Now that would just fit me up, and wouldn't cost more than the Scottish fantasies. And we could combine the June one with two days getting some Halibut (taking our own hooks). Also, in the October, we could combine it with maybe getting a Caribou or a Moose—since I never miss. What I mean is, if as you suggested you might consider trying to shoot your own meat I'll offer myself as a marksman for no fee. But when you come in January—supposing you do—we'll spend a lot of time on target practice, and shoot off all this ammunition.

I see this morning a headline in the Financial Section of the Times—Pressure To Open Alaskan Wildlife Refuge: Necessary To Bolster BP Shares. You know that BP has just been, or is just about to be, privatised—at the very moment the share-price collapsed. So now there will be enormous pressure to do anything that might lever the shares back up. And evidently the NE Alaskan Oilfield is the great hope—in other words, virtually the great hope of the international Share market, which needs some big good news.

There was a film on last night about Grizzlies. Lots of good sightings. A sequence naturally from Brooks Camp. It gave me a great pang to see it, and that long arm of Naknek lake. I suppose the Bears were some of them the very ones we watched there.

I'm sending off some more books.

Lovely October day today. All the leaves gone off the churchyard trees except the ash. All the leaves still on the cherries and the Walnut.

I'll walk along the Taw later and see if there are any salmon in that pool there by the Mill.

Otherwise I'm sitting in my room and just working away happily. That appendicitis and operation put various things into perspective. Salutary.

On a fishing holiday with friends in Canada, TH had undergone an emergency operation on his appendix. In June the next year, he joined Nicholas to fish in Alaska.

To Keith Sagar

14 November 1987   Ms   British Library

Once again I'm trying to get the old airplane down the runway. It's one of those climacterics—when it suddenly seems as if only now do I know what I ought to be doing, & how I ought to be doing it.

I have what I suppose is a book—excluding most things. My only hesitation about it is—it's moulted feathers, rather than new flight. So it seems. Elegiac—obsequies over a state of mind that is to me, now, defunct. It is actually, I suppose, the funeral, & the mourning. So it's sad.

The book is *Wolfwatching* (1989).

1988

To William Scammell

2 February 1988   Ts   Jan Scammell

Dear William Scammell,

Thank you for the letter. I greatly look forward to seeing the book.

What you say jolts my conscience, from several directions. I returned to writing that Introduction against strong inner resistance. I realised there must be an awful lot of commentary about Douglas of which I've seen nothing (I've really only seen Grahame's) and I paused somewhat at the apprehensions of hacking out my own ingrown observations only to find later they were everybody's current cliches. On the other hand, with Oxford pressing their deadline I didn't want to tangle with new (to me) opinions, knowing how long it takes me to disentangle myself and settle to an adjusted viewpoint. In the end I went ahead with the closest things to hand, intending of course to be brief.

I'd be interested to know what's been said about the relationship between Owen and Douglas. That symmetrical inversion of some of their salient features, which I chew over, seems to exist (maybe it's a current cliche!), yet I can see why it presented itself to me as it did. After I'd written that piece I realised I'd drawn something from my father and brother. When my elder brother joined up in 1939 my permanent pre-occupation became—praying that he wouldn't be dragged into what our father had been dragged through from 1914 to -18. I expect he contemplated it even more fatefully than I did. Owen, when I came to know his poems, grew to represent my father's experience, and later on Douglas my brother's (who was in North Africa through the same period). So that pattern of antithetical succession was prefigured, for me, and quite highly charged.

As a character in my piece, Owen offered himself as the familiar ground to set off the less familiar (?) contrasting article.

I'm sure you're right about Rosenberg. Douglas must have recognised the less dated, more serviceable components in his attitude to the business.

What you say about Art Artifice and distancing makes me feel I must have left bigger holes in my fabric than I thought. If I seem to neglect that aspect, it must be because I took it so naturally for granted as the starting point of whatever I wanted to say. I didn't go into detail, but for me the question that circumscribes all my thoughts about Douglas is—how did he manage to make such final and in their way archetypal and manifestly indestructible designs sound so spontaneous, so much like the thought of a moment?

My whole piece is striving to define something slightly different—something which in the end it fails, maybe, even to suggest. This something is whatever it is that inhabits the curious electrified inflection of his each line. It's that imprint of intimate presence—a naked activism of a very essential, irreducible self. It's not the unique identity that makes every line of Auden's obviously an Auden line and so on. Most poets don't have any suggestion of it. So it's obviously not a very necessary quality—Milton none, Wordsworth none, Eliot none. The only poet who seems to have something of the same is Wyatt. I'm always feeling I might find it in R.S. Thomas. It's personal, because it bears the tones of private anguish and struggle, but mainly it is a unique sort of essence, spiritual and hard to come by. Less a talent, or faculty, than a quality of being—that's what brought me to Gourdjieff. It's rare and different the way instant healing flows from the hands of just the odd rare individual, while nobody else, even celebrated doctors, has any touch of it. Or if one could believe in mediums, it's rare and different the way one or two of them, here and there, produce a real foxglove in January—something of that sort. I'm not going to define it here either. This is what I meant by the poetry being somehow the naked presence of the inmost being of the man—the innermost creature, the decisive, most truthful spirit control of his nature. The poems formulate the terms this creature comes to with his predicament—with its unpredictable jagged edges and reality.

Do I suggest that this formulation was an easy business? This essence I'm failing to pin down doesn't emerge in the drafts till the very last moment. I agree with you, the poems come from far down—from some place of final resolutions. So the documentary bent, and opportunity, and as I say motivation, provided the external means. So Vergissmeinicht moves from being a sharp journal entry, through psychic turmoil, to the crystalline poem—reconciling every phase of its transformation, never alltogether ceasing to be documentary.

The versified journal entries or diary jottings that I know (like my

543

pieces about my farm animals) seem to me to confine themselves to a far lower order of poetic possibility. His journal, I suppose, shows what he wrote when he wrote vivid diary jottings.

Yes, I hope the typography is the last straw. They printed it small, then shrank it. My Introduction, which had been quite hard to read, vanished before my eyes.

Faber have seen the light. Having noticed that all or nearly all the Collected Works published in the last ten years without magnifying glass have reduced their authors to graphic designer's 'hatching' and made absolutely certain that they will never now be read, they—Faber's—are getting a new designer who will be first and foremost a typographer. I wonder if he'll be able to resist designer's fashion, designer's four oclock shadow over every page.

Thank you for the suggestion about the reading. But I've been avoiding readings lately.

Do you know how Douglas' collected poems slipped from Faber to Oxford? It seems nobody does. Frank Pike told me Faber's don't.

All the best

yours

Ted Hughes

William Scammell (1939–2000) had already corresponded with TH, while putting the finishing touches to his critical study *Keith Douglas*. TH had sent Scammell a revised version of his introduction to Douglas's *Collected Poems*, for which Desmond Graham, who had written Douglas's biography (1974), had supplied a preface. A passage from the present letter is included as 'Postscript I' to TH's piece 'Keith Douglas', in *Winter Pollen*, which Scammell edited.

Wilfred Owen (1893–1918) and Isaac Rosenberg (1890–1918) are the First World War poets with whom TH contrasts and compares Douglas.

G. I. Gurdjieff (1872?–1949), mystic and teacher, was concerned to inculcate disciplines of self-transformation and self-awareness.

To W. S. Merwin

9 June 1988   Ms   Merwin

Dear Bill,

The Rain In The Trees arrived here. It stirred me a lot—always finer, ever more piercing & eerie. A book of marvels. And a marvel to see how you go on always farther into your own charts.

After all these years, how are you? You're looking pretty good in the picture. Danny Weissbort was here & saw your book—"Good God, he's beginning to look at least forty."

Funny old life we've been leading in the world, since when was it—1962.

I've had a double sort of existence—one as typecast in the Plath drama, one trying to ghost along somewhere close to the life I might have had. Problem with the Plath drama, it has gradually infiltrated the collegiate generations with its genetic bits and pieces, till now everybody under 40 carries all the assumptions as hereditary law, & this new Walpurgisnacht of biographies arrives as Holy Writ. The dogs in the street seem to have more ideas about me than I have.

It's served one purpose—made the literary life, especially the U.S. territories, enemy country. Too bad my own verses have to creep about out there.

This other life has been satisfactory more than enough. My wife Carol is a wonder—after 18 years marriage (and I've known her since she was 17) I'd do anything again to marry her tomorrow. We have a farm—about 110 acres. Used to run cattle & sheep, now I leave it all to her—she's a farmer's daughter—and she sells the grazing. Makes more than we ever made on stock. We kept our bull—he's now 18 Still weighs about a ton. He follows my wife around like a puppy.

Frieda led a tempestuous adolescence—divorced at 23, stormed through a couple of bizarre, long affairs, & is now just finishing Art School. She has a great fund of nightmare/comic fantasy—at present divides it between weird children's stories & straight mythical terrors. Natural story teller & inventor—but sheered off literary sophistication as she approached her mother's public glare. Paints little intense primitive Indian Miniature style paintings which seem wonderful to me. Has a blend of her mother & Olwyn (!!) general storminess—but better able to enjoy herself, & in the end, I think, more canny sense. I hope so.

Nicholas is my mentor. Tough concentrated sort of person, rather bright—finishing a PHD as a Fish Biologist, in Alaska. I go to stay with him, & we wander about in that fantastic land, catching the fish.

I often think about you, Bill. And with Dido's extraordinary memoir of S.P.—with which she tried to help a recent Plath biographer—just lately you're a constant thought. And now comes your book. The very best from me—as ever, & with love

Ted

The Rain in the Trees (1988) was Merwin's most recent book of poems. Dido Merwin's 'Vessel of Wrath: A Memoir of Sylvia Plath', a fiercely demythologising portrait, was included as an appendix to Anne Stevenson's *Bitter Fame*.

To Kenneth Baker

20 November 1988   Ms (photocopy)   Emory

Last week at the Observer I gave the prizes to the winners of their Children's Poetry Competition—and to each prize I added a copy of The Rattle Bag. In my little speech I described to them how I learned Latin—after all my Grammar lessons, what made sense of it all was knowing by heart the first book of the Aeneid. That gave me the keys to most of my problems. I did the same with French. My French vocabulary & hoard of locutions is still basically—and usually consciously, when I'm writing or speaking—Baudelaire & Ronsard from the pieces I learned. I did the same with Spanish—wholly by learning Lorca—and spoke it adequately (within 6 weeks) just adapting Lorca's vocabulary & grammar.

In English, students are at sea—awash in the rubbish incoherence of the jabber in the sound-waves—unless they have some internal sort of anchor of standards. Classroom grammar kits & teachers' prayers can't conjure the guardian angel/duenna of English, for kids who have no other access to it but T.V., their pals, & their parents who had only T.V. & their pals & some mysterious gulf where the natural eloquence of the illiterate age was lost. What kids need, say I, is a headfull of songs that are not songs but blocks of achieved & exemplary language. When they know by heart fifteen pages of Robert Frost, a page of Swift's Modest Proposal, Animula etc etc, they have the guardian angel installed behind the tongue. They have reefs, for the life of language to build & breed around. A 'globe of precepts' and a great sheet anchor in the maelstrom linguistic turbulence—(now we're really at sea!)

Apologies for all these metaphorical fragments—I'm in the middle of an Arvon Meeting.

I went on, in my little chat, to point out that a very ordinary actor would learn by heart, say, half The Rattle Bag for a single week of performances, & think nothing of it. So I urged them to learn the whole book—a page a day. Or even a page per week. Or even a page each month.

I said a few more things about language—that it's an artificial, human invention, and doesn't simply grow, like hair or nails, but has to be learned—like skill at tennis. And I told some curious tales from research into this sort of thing—how language is always trying to leave us, how we keep it only by constant practice, & improve it only by deliberate training—exactly like running or playing an instrument, or any sport.

My Modest Proposal: that some learning by rote of poetry be built into the exam requirements.

Extract from a letter to Kenneth Baker, then the Conservative government's Secretary of State for Education. TH's proposal involved adaptation of *The Rattle Bag* for school use, and another volume along the lines of *The School Bag*, which he and Seamus Heaney were already planning. Six poems by Frost and six by Eliot, though not 'Animula', would be included in *By Heart* (1997), the anthology that TH eventually devoted wholly to memory training.

To Frieda Hughes

6 December 1988   Ms   Emory

Dearest Frieda,

This is a quick letter, so that Clive can bring it. We received both your letters. I'm very glad you wrote the first one. It's important to say things like that, even though you have to go to Australia to find the airspace to say them. You know I've always felt you had something very special to give. Your only problem will be—finding the peculiar technical means of giving it. For instance, in your Waldorf story, the original thing is there—you only need quite slight technical adjustments (mainly simple cutting) to let that original thing emerge in its own shape, unblurred. In "The Waxman", the original thing is also there—but the technical adjustments, the artful shifts, the cuttings & changings of emphasis, that are needed to let that original thing emerge will be, in that case, much harder to find—because, as we discussed, the central idea is so ugly. I'm not sure 'ugly' is the right word. To make a reader accept a central image—even though it might be an important truth—of that 'ugly' kind, you need great tact & cunning, and diplomacy of a sort, in the way you present it to him.

The central image of Shakespeare's tragedies (and quite a few of his other plays) is 'ugly' in this sense. Same in Dostoevsky's novels. And many other examples. All Greek Tragedy. In fact, if I go on, I shall be suggesting that the precondition of a great imaginative work is that the author has some kind of obsessive concern with those truths that are 'ugly'. Well, it may be true.

Setting aside just how those 'truths' are made fascinating by those authors, the basic law of all fiction/drama, the absolute basic law, is: that the author must, at bottom, <u>be fond of</u> all his/her characters. Must be fascinated by each & every one of them & must, finally & positively, <u>love</u> each one as much as any other. I know this is God's eye view. The whole power & appeal of those horrendous Greek tragedies is that they are written from God's eye view—they are manipulated by the gods, explained by the gods, justified by the gods, & forgiven by the gods. The people—the tragic ferocious characters—are helpless, or at least pathetic puppets in the hands of the gods. The attitude of those dramatists towards their characters is a grieving one, a protective one, that knows, nevertheless, that these people have to accept the consequences of their actions, and their fates. The author makes no judgement against any one of them: he shows them as the puppets—suffering & possessed—of good & evil, the playthings of the gods.

The attitude comes quite automatically when we are writing from something inside us that is outside our own ego.

If we write from the ego, the petty prejudices of the ego become the stuff of the writing—and it is simply boring, & claustrophobic, to read of another ego dealing out judgements & punishments according to their own prejudices. We recoil from it just as we recoil from anybody's display of prejudice and dislike. Most writing is boring for no other reason than this—that it is ego-writing. Flattering its own prejudices, imposing its own attitudes in righteous scorn, & having a monologue.

A great deal of writing—some of the best—is simply (complicatedly) a projection of the fight—within the writer—between his/her ego and all that other hidden mainly subconscious part of the writer which the ego excludes from its idea of itself, & which lives its life beyond and in spite of the ego.

But even when this conflict—between ego & the hidden inner world— is the basic plot of the work (as it nearly always is, in one form or another) the view of the writer must be from outside the ego. It must be a sort of hovering 3rd eye, neither the ego nor the non-ego, but some referee which <u>mediates</u> (important word) between them.

With 'The Waxman' the viewpoint of the author is very often, I think, impure—in that ego voice (a sense of ego-prejudice) keeps intruding, with its wish to judge & punish, as the evident attitude of the writer.

But the final viewpoint must be one that watches these unforgiving, loathsome, dishonest, punitive characters, in their assaults on each other, and hears their case to the absolute limit, but finally understands—constantly understands—that all these people actually are pitiful animals, a type of bewildered ape, each one trying to hold its corner. On their own, in their most private, secret knowledge of themselves, they are little furry tree-shrews in the primaeval dark. Even though they are preoccupied by their terrible brains and voices & weapons. Yes, I know you know this better than most.

But we'll talk about The Waxman. It is full of things very important for you, and a lot can be salvaged from it.

It could be that by approaching the theme so point-blank—as an event developing from the ordinary miseries of lonely Flat-land—you gave yourself a colossal <u>artistic</u> problem of trudging over miles of the commonplace marital-problem suburban tarmac which it would need God knows what to make new & interesting—you gave yourself a mountain of roughage for the handful of protein and vitamins.

It could be, the real power of the fable, the image, that you're circling here might be released more effectively (more easily) by a more fantastic treatment. It's a thought.

Otherwise, possibly a major problem with the present shape is that it is <u>too long</u>—a more compressed, almost short-hand form of it, brief scenes jammed together, might jump the reader through it, from essential to essential.

But I'll read it all closely by the time you come back.

Meanwhile, forget about everything but enjoying yourself, as I'm sure you will.

And <u>take care.</u>

Nothing is happening here. Rain & falling leaves.

I want to get this to the post today.

Love

Daddy

'Clive' was Clive Anderson, who would become Frieda Hughes's second husband in 1991.

Some pages of Frieda Hughes's story 'The Waxman', with editorial notes by TH, are at Emory.

1989

To Craig Raine

24 January 1989   Ts   Raine

Thanks for the Eliot Essay and The Prophetic Book. In the essay, it seems to me you approach the poem along Eliot's own tracks. And you put your finger very convincingly on the main design—the one that unlocks the pattern of the poem and all the relationships and therefore the meaning of the parts. I've no doubt at all that you've hit it bull's eye. The piece is marvellous, really, in the simple, lucid way it does such a big thing, such a comprehensive thing. And unarguable too—like an engineering manual. Point-blank, no mandarin, sticks to essentials and takes them apart screw by screw.

It reminded me a little of a QC I watched at a Public Enquiry in North Devon. His evidence wasn't to be questioned. But the way he delivered it was the surprising thing. He didn't orate, or ingratiate or solemnly browbeat or morally orchestrate or flood us with the usual courtly cant. He simply gave each piece of evidence, one piece at a time, each piece in a great silence. He would lay the piece out, without any interpretation, in a clean sentence, and then wait. He'd wait about ten or fifteen seconds—a very long time in an electrified court. The effect, the real dramatic kinetic impact of each piece was quite stunning. And the argument that rose out of the whole sequence was irresistible. This struck me—because I was on the opposite side.

Isn't it peculiar, though, that the international exegetes of The Waste Land have never made anything of this before? Or is it that I'm not acquainted with the right essays. But I assume you've ranged the whole field. Are these professional oracles missing as much in other places? I was always puzzled by the way they ignored or dismissed (even Elmann it seems to me is a bit reductio ad absurd about it) Yeats' Hermetic Magic and spiritualism. Just before I read your piece I'd looked at the Eliot issue of the Southern Review. (It contains an interesting piece about Eliot's actual dealings with the paintings of St Narcissus and his attempts in those early uncollected verses to write about the figure directly or appropriate him in some way.) Not one of the more than thirty contributors does more than refer to his Buddhism. And I can't recall that I ever saw any essay that identified it as the ground of the poem's attitudes and unity—of the bottomless sort of coherence of the feelings and the 'fragments'. Your point about 'travesty' splits an arrow in the bull's eye.

I'm going on about it. Was there ever any link made by one of those New York Review Of Books style of overviewers between Eliot's Buddhism and the subsidence into Buddhism of Ginsberg's armies? Did anybody in those days point out that the great Western Buddhist poem had already been written—by the one they regarded as on the whole a figurehead of the enemy and the 'academics'? Or that there must be some level on which those Beats were Eliot's epigoni—and that W.C. Williams was, in comparison, the 'academic'.

You've established the key so self-evidently, it makes me wonder how Eliot scholars will respond. Their disadvantage (which they can't recognise) is that they don't have your instinct for knowing just what the relationship was between Eliot and his material.

In passing—the 'fit' between Buddhism and the phase of disintegration in the shamanic biography must be something like an organic one between the understanding of the experience and the experience: the one has found the terms by which the other becomes expressible. In a chaotic way, this must have been how the Beats came to Buddhism. (The great historic work that incarnates the holy/unholy marriage of the two is the Bardo Thodol —which became a bible for Timothy Leary's wing of that movement.)

Raine's essay, 'The Waste Land as a Buddhist Poem', of which he had sent a copy to TH, revealed T. S. Eliot's poetic debt to Buddhist thought. The lawyer whose succinct performance the essay had brought to mind was Michael Fitzgerald, QC.
    Richard Ellmann (1918–87) was the author of Yeats: The Man and the Masks, among other books.
    'Beat' poet Allen Ginsberg (1926–1997) had espoused a form of Zen Buddhism.

To HM Queen Elizabeth, The Queen Mother

24 March 1989   Ms   Windsor

Your Majesty,
    Thank you for our magical weekend at Royal Lodge. From start to finish it was a delight.

My sense of the honour, which does overawe me rather as we drive in through the gates, was swallowed up again, just as before, in that intense pleasure. Though I do feel that we guests glow, also, in Your Majesty's enjoyment of every moment.

I shall not forget how at the end of that video (of the Covent Garden show for Her Majesty's 60th Birthday) you still seemed as awake and as full of go as any of the performers!

The Sunday Evening Concert was extremely charming and amusing, but Her Majesty The Queen's presence there made it an historic event. Just the week before I had read about a Welsh Harpist performing before Queen Elizabeth the First. What an ancient event that had seemed—a survivor of prehistoric Celtic Britain playing to the Queen of England. And on Sunday Evening—here he still was, still playing! Strangest of all to think that four hundred years ago he was probably playing that same melody—David of The White Rock! Perhaps history is still very young!

It was a particular honour and pleasure, too, to meet for the first time Her Royal Highness Princess Margaret.

Thank you, Your Majesty, once again, for those very special hours and conversations.

Your humble and obedient servant

Ted Hughes

TH and Carol Hughes had stayed at the Royal Lodge, Windsor, from 18 to 20 March.

To the Editor of the *Guardian*

20 April 1989 [date of printing]

May I say a word or two about the letter (April 7) from Ms Parnaby and Wingfield? It has not received the response that might have been expected.

Their statement that Sylvia Plath and I signed divorce papers is false. It is difficult to imagine how they could have been unaware of this. I presume, from their addresses and the contents of their letter, that they are scholars of some kind, possibly Plath scholars, who presumably know the basic texts. A little more inquiry on their part would have made their imputations against me—that I do not respect the literary tradition, that I have failed to honour the memory of Sylvia Plath—quite unnecessary. As it stands, I believe their letter is libellous.

Whether Sylvia Plath was divorced or not was naturally one of the first questions to be asked after her death. Various legal arrangements hung on the answer, which was established without difficulty. Sylvia Plath was not divorced. If she had been divorced, my life and her children's lives would have been utterly different. I can add to that. Whatever she may have said to the advisers who were urging her on, she never touched divorce papers, and had no plan to do so. I am able to say that because she and I discussed our future quite freely up to the end.

I am no great student in the Fantasia which has obscured the life and death of Sylvia Plath, but so far as I am aware Ms Parnaby and Wingfield are the first in 26 years to decide that this bit of her history needs to be rewritten. As is well enough known, she is one of the most closely studied and widely taught writers in the Western world, and has been so for many years. By late 1986 there existed some 700 publications about her. If Ms Parnaby and Wingfield's imputations against me are to be seen for what they are, it has to be spelled out: any scholars who can assert, in 1989, that Sylvia Plath was divorced, show small respect for the truth about her, or for her memory, or for the literary tradition of which she is part. They are living in some kind of Fantasia.

There is rather more to it. Perhaps Ms Parnaby and Wingfield will plead that they did not invent this bit of apocrypha, but that certain other people have been accepting it as gospel for some time. If that is so, perhaps it would explain why Sylvia Plath's grave has been so repeatedly vandalised. Ms Parnaby and Wingfield's wording of their mischievous falsehood can be read, to my mind, very like an incitement for other misguided enthusiasts to desecrate the grave afresh. But whether they invented it or only adopted it, the fact is wrong and they have asserted it.

Guardian readers might wonder why it has been left to me to set this crucial and fundamental fact right. Among all those who are said to be so concerned about the fading of her memory, didn't anybody notice it? The situation is typified, really, by that first response to Ms Parnaby and Wingfield's letter. It was signed by eight names, all well versed in Plath. Several of them have written about her at length, have taught her work and lectured about her in universities. All have shown respect for the literary tradition. Presumably they were asked to sign only because their

553

credentials are so good. Some of them are extremely well known, and one is a greatly respected Nobel Prize Winning Poet. Their names appear under a letter which presents them as impatient guardians of the truth about Sylvia Plath, demanding to know the real facts about recent doings in Heptonstall graveyard, and fantasising a peculiar role for me. This letter is by way of being a continuation of the earlier one by Ms Parnaby and Wingfield. It is a surprise, though, to see these normally sensible names being sucked into the same delusion. Or perhaps it is not a surprise. Guardian readers can here observe the Plath Fantasia in action. These perfectly well-meaning signatories call strenuously for more truth about Sylvia Plath and commend Ms Parnaby and Wingfield for the "valid and important points" made in their letter. But at the same time they find no difficulty whatsoever in swallowing the staring historical untruth around which that whole letter revolves.

They find no difficulty, either, in countersigning what any reader might think are insinuations against Sylvia Plath's family. This too has to be spelled out. Given the choice of the truth and the lie, Ms Parnaby and Wingfield choose, with absolute confidence, the lie. Presented with the lie (in a context which develops the implications of the lie through almost every sentence) the committee of eight jurors not only swallow it, they wash it down with commendations for those who handed it to them.

I don't know whether readers find this carry-on as incomprehensible as I do. One can only suppose that some of these names, at least, never knew anything about the first letter, and so didn't catch the real implications of the second, which they were asked to sign, when it was read to them over the phone. I assume it was done over the phone, since they were conjured so quickly. In a way, that only makes their letter more typical of the genre, where morally strident demands for the truth about this or that aspect of Sylvia Plath's life are blended with incredible yet glaringly obvious evidence that at bottom nobody really gives a damn.

In the years soon after her death, when scholars approached me, I tried to take their apparently serious concern for the truth about Sylvia Plath seriously. But I learned my lesson early. The honourable few who have justified my trust have been few indeed. With others, if I tried too hard to tell them exactly how something happened, in the hope of correcting some fantasy, I was quite likely to be accused of trying to suppress Free Speech. In general, my refusal to have anything to do with the Plath Fantasia has been regarded as an attempt to suppress Free Speech.

Where my correction was accepted, it rarely displaced a fantasy. More often, it was added to the repertoire, as a variant hypothesis. It would then become itself a source of new speculations which sooner or later, somewhere or other, would be preferred to it. The truth simply tends to produce more lies. Just as this plain, self-evident truth, that Sylvia Plath was not divorced, can rest unquestioned for 26 years and then, quite suddenly, be violently displaced—by an absolute denial of it. Which has been accepted—as the present, prevailing silence confirms— without a murmur, by all who claim to be concerned about Sylvia Plath's memory.

A rational observer might conclude (correctly in my opinion) that the Fantasia about Sylvia Plath is more needed than the facts. Where that leaves respect for the truth of her life (and of mine), or for her memory, or for the literary tradition, I do not know.

In spite of that, and in acknowledgement of the awkward position of the eight signatories of that letter, or rather of the seven who did not compose it, I would like to assure them that what has been happening to Sylvia Plath's gravestone concerns me. Here is what I know about it. If I had followed custom, the gravestone would have borne the name Sylvia Hughes, which was her legal name, the name of her children's mother. Avoiding the more cumbersome form of indicating the maiden name of the deceased, I took it into my head to insert the Plath after Sylvia because I knew well enough in 1963 what she had brought off in that name, and I wished to honour it. That was the beginning and end of my thoughts about the name. I added the sentence from Sanskrit because that was what I used to tell her when she was low, and because she had fulfilled it in such a way. I got the granite from Dartmoor because of her special feeling for the place.

The mason persuaded me that riveted lead letters were more practical than letters engraved, though they seemed to me too vulnerable and temporary (as they have proved).

One day he informed me that the letters of her married name had been levered off. I asked him to replace them, which he did. They were removed again, and again he replaced them. They were removed a third time and again I asked him to replace them. Each time he had to take the stone back to his workshop, while I considered what to do next.

When the name was violated a fourth time, last year, I asked him to keep the stone in his workshop, while I considered what to do next. In November I visited him, intending to have a new kind of gravestone cut, of a shape that could not easily be shattered, in which the letters would be deeply incised. I found he had already repaired the old stone. It stood in his workshop, waiting for my decision. I asked him to give it another go and set it up. If he has not yet done so, I'm sure I agree with him that there is no hurry.

As for the matter of the signpost to the grave, I can only ask the signatories of that letter to try and see it from the ordinary human point of view, which regards graves and graveyards as sacred places, and not from the point of view of tourist associations, theme park development syndicates and cultural tour promoters. Naturally, Hebden Bridge Council have to take note of the demands of tourism, which in that region are heavy. But as they have proved, they possess normal human feeling and know where to draw the line, and to their blessed credit they drew it here.

Among those signatories are one or two, at least, who should be able to feel the horror of what it will be when Sylvia Plath's grave becomes one more trampled Disneyland toy in the Northern Cultural Theme Park, hawked on brochures. That is not so unlikely. It has already all but happened to one or two places not far off. Even as things are, visitors to the grave have not given me any reason to feel that they should be encouraged. Their record is poor. Occasionally relatives of mine up there tend the grave, but visitors merely take from it. The big North Devon beach pebbles that I set around it at one time soon disappeared. The shells with which I covered it went in no time, etc. Even so, any reasonable person with a straightforward motive for visiting the spot can find it without too much trouble, when the stone is in place, and I cannot believe they don't prefer to have it this way. When I asked the Council not to put up a signpost, I knew I wasn't stopping the future. I simply wished to preserve for a while longer something of the private remnant valued by her living family—and I trust by some others too.

Ted Hughes

Julia Parnaby and Rachel Wingfield, academics, had written jointly to the *Guardian*, complaining that Sylvia Plath's grave in Heptonstall was both hard to find and poorly looked after, and suggesting that the Plath Estate had been neglecting its duty of care. The signatories of the letter supporting them were A. Alvarez, Joseph Brodsky, Helga Graham, Ronald Hayman, Jill Neville, Peter Orr, Peter Porter and John Carey. The address on the letter was Hayman's.

The inscription on Plath's grave reads: 'Even amidst fierce flames the golden lotus can be planted'.

To the Editor of the *Independent*

22 April 1989 [date of printing]

Dear Sir,

In his piece on Sylvia Plath's grave (19 April) Ronald Hayman makes 15 factual errors or distortions of facts. I would like to correct some of them and give *Independent* readers a bearing on his drift.

He says she lived in Cornwall. Her letters, some of her poems, hundreds of commentaries about her, make a great deal of where she did live. Mr Hayman gets it wrong.

His assertion for my moving away in 1962 is wrong, though his confidence here as everywhere else, is flawless.

At least he does not go as far as two scholars in another newspaper a fortnight ago, who hung an official complaint on their false revelation that Sylvia Plath and I had signed divorce papers. But Ronald Hayman is just as mistaken to assert that divorce proceedings were under way when Sylvia Plath died.

Whatever she may have said to those who were urging her on (one of these, the most authoritative influence on her adult life, admitted to me, later, that she herself at the time had been embroiled in her own divorce), this was never part of our discussions, which moved, in fact, in the opposite direction.

Mr Hayman wishes to make some point by saying that I chose for her to be buried in Yorkshire, which his oracle tells him she hated, instead of behind the "wall of old corpses" beside our garden, which in one of her poems she says she loved.

In the classroom, his literal reading of that poem would be laughable. One wonders if it is any better in *The Independent*.

He has, of course, no idea what she felt about that graveyard next to our house, which has been (and had been then) closed to new burials for many years. My understanding was that she was fond of West Yorkshire. I know she told many different people many different things, and different things at different times, but I had to act on what I knew. Remembering her children too, who are also my family.

If Mr Hayman, or his gossip, found nothing on her grave but a few flowers in containers, that is because everything has been repeatedly stripped off it. His verbal picture of desolation omits a rose bush which is trying to grow there. I find it hard to understand how that rose has survived.

Daffodil bulbs that I planted there, over the years, from our garden in the South-west, have been removed. The big North Devon beach pebbles which I once set round the grave soon vanished. The shells with which I covered it went in no time. I rooted a cutting from the Yew Tree that appears in some of her poems, but did not transplant it to her grave when I began to realise what would happen to a hostage of that sort.

There have been three "successful" assaults on her gravestone, as Mr Hayman puts it. Each time the stone had to go back to the mason's workshop. After the fourth "unsuccessful" one, I asked the mason to keep the stone while I considered what to do next.

Last November I visited him, intending to have a new kind of gravestone cut, of a shape that could not easily be shattered, in which the letters would be deeply incised. I found he had already repaired the old stone. It stood in his workshop waiting for my decision. I asked him to give it another go and set it up. He has not yet done so, but like me he probably feels there is no hurry.

Mr Hayman colludes with the desecrators far enough to imply that I might be thinking the inscription ought to be changed. When I first had the lettering set into the stone that I had brought from Dartmoor, the only question in my mind was how to get the name "Plath" on to it. If I had followed custom, the stone would be inscribed Sylvia Hughes, which was her legal name. For her children, it was their mother's name, their own name. Avoiding the conventional style of indicating the maiden name, I inserted the Plath after Sylvia because I was already well aware, in 1963, of what she had achieved under that name, and I wished to honour it.

One other question did occur to me, but I dismissed it. Might the "Plath", coming immediately after the "Sylvia", inspire some dealer to carry off the removeable letters, or indeed the whole stone, for some collector?

Mr Hayman next offers a one-paragraph crash course in the "otherworld" of her first collection, *The Colossus*, in which, he tells us, she hurtled "painfully about a hard and hostile male universe".

People can say anything, I know, but it fits the evidence somewhat better, and suggests that the speaker actually has read the poems, to say that in *The Colossus* she seems to edge rather tentatively about a universe in which the most important (almost the only) male figure, her father, has disappeared into water or ghostliness (hard?) and the hostile elements tend to be, in fact, female—a tendency which strengthened greatly in her later poems.

Male figures excited her rage, in her later poems as throughout her life, chiefly when they exposed her to those she feared and hated who (the evidence is distasteful but it cannot be denied, it makes up a considerable part of her work) were almost exclusively women. Only Sylvia Plath can explain why that was so. Obviously it does not mean that she failed to form friendships with some women.

Mr Hayman observes that her readers "feel personally involved, almost as if she were a member of the family" (meaning "their family", which makes her own family a bit of a nuisance) and that they "care passionately about the way she is commemorated".

Her many sensible readers, I am sure, do care. But from my (admittedly rather exposed) point of view, those who make themselves most audible seem to care in a strange way. They certainly care that they should be heard to be caring, in the Hayman mode of morally outraged demand for "the facts of her life", but too often they show astonishing contempt for the facts that lie in front of them, again just as Mr Hayman does.

He tells us that I have "kept a firm grip on biographers". According to him, Sylvia Plath's first "biographer", Edward Butscher, "was threatened that permission to quote from copyright material would be refused unless he cut out 'any negative reference to the Hughes family' ". The confident Mr Hayman here adopts Mr Butscher's credibility as his own.

What I have to say will possibly not affect the fantasia, or Mr Hayman's infatuation with it, but the facts about this episode are soon told yet again. Mr Butscher collected all that he could persuade people to say about Sylvia Plath. When my agent refused permission for his quoted material he went ahead and published anyway. The unpublished early Plath poems that he quoted are now under his personal copyright in the Library of Congress. When my agent pointed out this was illegal, Mr Butscher remained unperturbed. Sylvia Plath's publisher in the US declined to sue Butscher's publisher. I considered initiating a transatlantic lawsuit, but then thought better of it.

Unfortunately for me, this very omission boomeranged some time later when the mischief included in his book involved me, via one of the many people casually aligned in that fantasia, in a US lawsuit that consumed five years and cost several people—but not Butscher—many hundreds of thousands of dollars. The charge against me, note this, was that I had failed to control what Mr Butscher wrote about the plaintiff, and had failed to take action when he published it. This is one of the "biographers" who, Mr Hayman assures us, have been gagged with a "firm grip".

Mr Hayman then recounts the trials of Linda Wagner-Martin who, apparently, complains that she would have had to forgo 15,000 words of her suppositions if she had allowed my facts to displace them. She too went ahead confident that nobody in their right mind would carry a lawsuit across the Atlantic into the US.

Two or three of her stubborn absurdities reappeared, surprisingly to me, in *The Independent*, where Mr Hayman himself was reviewing the English edition of her book. What was interesting—and comical—was the instant confidence, the evangelical dash, with which Mr Hayman found himself reciting them. He was patiently corrected at the time, and knows perfectly well how Linda Wagner-Martin published her book, but for some reason keeps the information from the readers of his article.

Obviously there is no way of getting any kind of grip on such "biographers" as these (the only two so far) without endless multiple lawsuits and a large force of secretaries, consultant scholars, specialist lawyers, etc. At the same time, and just as obviously, the lawsuits can come anyway.

Finally Mr Hayman tells us that an "official" biography by Anne Stevenson has been announced, and emphasises what he seems to believe, that I agreed to a biography of that kind. He is confident that I agreed to it. He needs to say that I agreed to it because the point he wishes to make is that I was then inconsistent to discuss my dead wife with the biographer.

May I state it quite clearly here, as far as I am concerned this biography is not "official" or authorised. It is simply another "biography". It is true that Anne Stevenson asked me whether I would mind, when she was first thinking of accepting the commission to write it. I made no objection, but I took care to explain that I would take no part beyond checking the limited number of facts, as produced by others, which are scattered through the limited period in which I knew Sylvia Plath.

Mr Hayman tells us that "nobody owns fact". I hope each of us owns the facts of his or her own life. Otherwise you, reader, might suddenly find yourself reinvented by a Mr Hayman who had decided that he owns your facts and can do what he likes with them, and you could then, I assure you, spend years struggling in court with some stranger for not having restrained the new "owner". In so far as the facts of Sylvia Plath's life are the facts of my life (this is a complication, I realise, but there it is, it can't be helped), or were facts that I happened to know that were documented somewhere, I have checked Anne Stevenson's book. I even volunteered one or two facts that she particularly asked for. Beyond that I did not go. I contributed nothing more. Nor can I take responsibility for the impressions and opinions of others, whatever I may feel about them. I ask the reader to remember this, because it may not alter in the slightest what Mr Hayman, or some others who have now absorbed his misapprehension, will say about it in the future.

Yours sincerely,
TED HUGHES

Ronald Hayman had followed up the eight-signature *Guardian* letter mentioned in TH's 20 April letter to the editor of that paper with an article in the *Independent*, enlarging on 'the battle over the memory of Sylvia Plath'. TH's reply appeared under the heading 'Sylvia Plath: the facts of her life and the desecration of her grave'.

Hayman's own biography, *The Life and Death of Sylvia Plath*, was published in 1991.

To Charles and Brenda Tomlinson

5 July 1989   Ms   Texas

Here's my 'Phaeton' piece. It was—remarks for Roy Davids' lecture on poetic manuscripts, the use thereof. I tried to smarten it up but I think I might have hardened it off. Needs unscrewing & putting together again. My description of the 'mood' of Ariel—in contrast to mood of Sheep In Fog—not quite right, is it.

Also, I didn't get to my main point, in the second part, the da capo with variations. My main point—though not really relevant—was how the writing of a poem evokes other versions of the same poem—that try to get in on the act, steal the show, put on their own performance. The feeling that version is coming up behind version—each one from some different level of simplification or the opposite—like Banquo's descendants rising out of the cauldron. Or maybe that's only an impression, rarely proved.

The 'Phaeton' piece took its final form when it appeared as 'Sylvia Plath: The Evolution of "Sheep in Fog" ', in *Winter Pollen*. Roy Davids was then Head of the Department of Printed Books at Sotheby's in London. In the following letter to Tomlinson, TH goes beyond the scope of his essay in elaborating on the myths inherent in Plath's poem.

To Charles Tomlinson

15 August 1989   Ms   Texas

Dear Charles,

What you say is the whole point, I agree.

I can't think what made me grudge the half-divine—hard to believe I was grudging anything. But who knows.

Maybe I ought to include a whole digression on the mythology. It sidetracks a lecture on poem drafts in general—but belongs to a lecture on these drafts in particular, absolutely.

The other connections are just as interesting as the Phaeton branch. The Ma'aseh Merkabah—'the work of the Chariot' (that Ezekiel saw) was the glory of God. Meditation on the Merkabah brought up Jehovah in person—the contemplative was robed in flames. So it was forbidden— the most awful of the mysteries—except to the select. Sylvia read the Bible a good deal, especially the more poetic books. [*Marginal addition:* especially that last year, underlined it a lot etc] Ariel is Jerusalem, the 'hearth of God' but mainly the Lion of God. Which is presumably how she came to 'God's Lioness'. The Cherubs of the chariot wheel— the four—have animal feet, angel wings, human faces. As if she made the connection—cherubs to babies. Sacred beast-angels to patriarchal prophets in sheep's clothing. They were both the Powers of the wheel— which carried God's chariot throne—and the Guardians. Hence— maybe—'old as the tors, and furious'. The chariot had crashed—she hoped the cherubs were still hanging around.

Whoever involved themselves with it imprudently was blasted with lightning. The initiates who ascend in it tour the dazzling heavens, & see the innermost secrets.

These cherubs also guarded the Paradises—as whirling fire-wheels— swastikas.

This chariot is fused with the chariot of the Persian Mithra, & so comes out behind the Greek Helios. (As 'God's lioness'—in Ariel—is not Greek).

562

Phaeton was a type of ritual royal victim—Hippolytus etc.—identified with the God-King for the duration of his fatal chariot ride as royal substitute.

Though as you say—the main point in Ariel is the divine paternity—the divine right to make the attempt, the knowledge of the divine fate.

Apollo as sun-god of Poetry & learning has a link with the Celtic god Lugh, who has a link with Lir. Two daughters love the same man. Complications. The father promises his blessing if both will give the man up. When one refuses he banishes her as a <u>crane</u>—out onto the Atlantic, hundreds of years. Many variants of this—to one end: the sea-god Mananan makes a bag of her skin. This is the crane bag in which the God Lir (Llud etc) carries the alphabet. [*Marginal addition:* She knew something of this—the sea-god & the banished girl turned into a bagful of letters.]

In the Welsh version of the myth—more intact—this daughter is Creiddylad (Welsh: creyr = heron)

So Cordelia is direct line of descent from the cranes that formed the Greek alphabet via the crane-skin bagful of letters, the treasures of learning. Ariel is a code—of a kind—for Cordelia.

Edgar & Edmund are Shakespeare's way of restoring Geoffrey Monmouth's anecdote to the original myth behind the version in the Mabinogion, fitting Gwion and Gwithur back into their cyclic battle for Creiddylad—behind which is the Egyptian Horus & Set cyclic battle for the Eye which is—wait for it—the Daughter (and Wisdom) of the Sun God. When she is separated from her father (torn out by Set) she becomes a raging lioness—the kingdom falls into confusion. The original 'God's Lioness' (Israelites stole it in Egypt). So Ariel = Phaeton = Cordelia = raging lioness = the Eye of divine wisdom = the crane-skin bagful of the alphabet etc etc give or take a few negative capability factors. [*Marginal addition:* She knew something of this—what she didn't know I did] 'Medusa' was the fright mask that covered the bag of the alphabet when it was Greek—the Gorgon to scare off the uninitiated.

If I insert any maybe I should mention the whole web—in which case, in a note, you should share some blame.

Love to all   Ted

To Seamus Heaney

8 October 1989   Ms   Emory

Dear Seamus,

The Quartet arrived just as I was leaving for the Isle of Lewis. So I read it over a week of blowing about on Lochs—the most NWesterly in the Hebrides, the lochs of the Grimersta which has the most astounding run of salmon in Europe. Normally. This year they were a bit scarce. Your dastardly sea-rovers & reavers ambushed them—evidently—with nets 30 miles long, somewhere west of the Islands.

I read them through & through & wandered about in them, without distraction, in a perfect light. They are brimful of a ripe, easy beauty. As you close your hand round each one, it comes away clean & whole—perfect moment for picking. Your image about the lace-webs on the back of the wave—they all do ride on the full sea of something else, some tiding. Propitious.

I read them as a reclaiming—of your own Lares & Penates. A quiet numbering & retaking possession of your house-gods—which with your father's death now come under your sole care. You handle them, salute them, & settle them into their new niches—in the new you, (the new head of the family). A ritual sort of investiture—in absolute, adult responsibility for yourself, which can never really happen while your father's alive. 'Just old truth dawning.'

The motive for it, maybe—the fear of losing the home-ground, if you don't very deliberately do something of the sort. (The day of my mother's funeral, I bought Lumb Bank.) (Or rather I walked in on the owners and offered them a price—which they accepted).

Maybe this reading narrows the occasion—but I feel sure something of it is there. Quite openly & directly in some poems—the marvellous one about the latch, the one about St Bridget's girdle, the fir-tree gauntlet, and about your father's house. Special beauties, those. Also, the Vietnam-bound face, the Giant's Causeway, the clay floor, sand beds & gravel beds, the gaunt ones, our ones—enviable, easy wealth.

Made me think of The Prelude, in the ranging self-reassessment, the lifting of sacred moments, with ordinary gestures, into the pattern of the liturgy, and in the way the whole thing is a self-rededication, a realigning of yourself, to 'the vows made for you'.

I like the way the form avoids the closure of the sonnet—less

564

ceremonious, more open on every side—yet suggests a formal music, a chosen measure, just as compact.

Obviously Glanmore is happy to have you back. It will shift the balances of power, help them to shift.

I'm looking forward to seeing how you seize the Oxford opportunity. It is an opportunity. Any operation you can perform there will be like an operation on the pituitary gland—of England. It will soon affect the whole country. Rightly used, it must be the most visible, audible forum. Has there ever been a successful advocate, in England, for Ireland's side of all the cases? As an opportunity, given your standing with Oxford students, it's maybe unique. Inject a whole new understanding, to the right audience at the right age.

Yes, definitely, let's work for a Conference, Oct/Nov cusp. [*Marginal addition:* Or mid-November—whatever suits you.] It would be pleasant if you could slip between the hands of the clock & take a breather down here. Or some little half-way house.

I was thinking I might come to Ireland some time this winter—but that gadabout Cooke is away to New Zealand <u>again</u>—the third time! It has to be a woman!

Love to Marie & the family. Is Katey pining for the U.S.? Be well—
                                                    Ted

The thought of what you might be able to do, as <u>the</u> voice of Irishness, at Oxford, gives me a shock of real excitement. I don't think that's naive.

For 'Squarings', his poem-sequence in four sections, twelve poems per section, Heaney had devised a form by which twelve unrhymed lines were arranged in three-line stanzas. It was to be included in his 1991 volume, *Seeing Things*. 'Just old truth dawning' is a phrase from the first poem in the sequence. Heaney had a cottage where he worked in Glanmore, County Wicklow. He had recently been voted to the Chair of Poetry at Oxford University. 'Katey' is his daughter, Catherine Ann.

To Lucas Myers

9 October 1989   Ms Emory

Dear Luke,

I got the Magazine with the Attila. I thought they looked marvellous. They're much the best I've seen.

What happened to Turkey? Can't forget that one you showed me. It's a Unique world. Hundreds wouldn't be nearly too many.

I raked together what I had around, in the enclosed.

Macaw is "Iago's punishment—to be reborn as Malvolio in the form of a Macaw."

The Sparrow Hawk is 'Yeats' poetic self as Cuchulain reincarnated in a bird.'

The first part of the Rhino is seen through the movie camera being charged (cameramen get so spellbound they go on photographing till the animal hits them—fact). The third part is the Rhino beset by all the maladies that require his horn—nearly every human sickness. Maladies which materialise as the poacher's bullet and the horn-trader's rake-off.

The Reservations are the now superfluous Northern proletarian millions—released from the slavery of the lives that created them (their heroic labours to stay alive) but with nowhere to go, nothing to do etc, in a land occupied by 'the enemy'. That's how they feel & that's more or less how they are. Paid by the State//to evaporate.

Everything rolls along.

Agi, How does it feel to see the Great Empire crumbling—and Hungary picking up where it left off? As if the whole thing truly had been nothing but a ghastly mistake. That Universe of hot air & mania & baboonery!

Love, & Carol sends hers too
Ted

Myers and his wife Ágnes Vadas had translated poems by Attila József for the *Hungarian Quarterly*, no. 134.

'A Sparrow Hawk', 'Macaw', 'The Black Rhino' and 'On the Reservations' are in *Wolfwatching*, published the previous month.

The 'Great Empire' was that of the USSR, showing signs of 'crumbling' even before the Berlin Wall began to be knocked down the following month.

To William Cookson

5 November 1989   Ts and ms (photocopy)   Emory

I was tempted to add a gloss on the skunk. Insofar as what we write comes out of facing in ourselves what we do not want to face, merely talking about it evolves a language (this is superstition on my part) which evades the confrontation, and which thereafter always steps in to negotiate between us and what needs, in there, to be confronted. It makes confrontation more difficult, less likely. As I say, this is my superstition, but it seems to me I have watched it in writers and particularly in very talented students. One learns how not to skin the skunk, how to leave the skunk unskinned. A form of substitute activity—which thereafter is incorporated into the pattern of the activity. Where what has to be confronted, the unskinned skunk, is positively our own failings, obviously the evasion has bad consequences—it corrupts the conscious, it stupefies us because the bad conscience has to be suppressed, the sensitivity/intelligence of the bad conscience has to be suppressed. The unskinned skunk simply rots. More superstition, but that outcome becomes acute, I tell myself, when the confrontation takes the form of self-criticism, which in all writing it obviously must if what is to be confronted is a painful failing, and that self-criticism (which, for a painful failing, must be somewhat negative or severe self-criticism) is deflected onto somebody else—to save ourselves from the worse pain of confronting our painful failing with a severe self-criticism:— then the evasion is catastrophic, so I tell myself. There the skunk is the size of a bear, with musk-glands in proportion. What we have done in deflecting negative self-criticism onto somebody else is—shove somebody else into the path of an aggressive corrective act that was incurred by and meant for (inside our own skin) our own painful failing. So our own painful failing gets away with it, under that sly reflex of suppressive (self-stupefying) anaesthesia, while out there in public we enjoy a gladiatorial triumph (negative criticism is always winning) over some other poor sod. Meanwhile, the unskinned skunk-bear rots, the miasma rises—and there we have it, the breath of the campus. At least, that is my superstitious delusion of it. All very convoluted. And I am not saying any of it because it is, after all, deflected self-criticism. On the other hand, I can't help suspecting that we do have some critical ideas that are not implanted, as natural correctives, by our own painful failings.

As a superstition—that those evasions are more or less self-destructive—maybe it is just my way of keeping my eye on the ball—skinning my own skunk. (You see what a useful concept it is).

[. . .]

To go back to the skunk—you cannot tell another person how to skin his (i.e. you cannot skin it for him), and nobody can tell you how to skin yours. That's not quite right. More like—you cannot hope to help another man skin his, because your own is more than enough. Still not right.

That is why I thought better of adding a gloss: the proverb alone says most.

Volume 27 number 3 of William Cookson's magazine *Agenda* was to be a 'Special Issue on the State of Poetry'. Of the many contributions, TH's, which read simply, 'Every man skin his own skunk,' in quotation marks and with attribution to the Sioux, was the tersest.

To Craig Raine

13 November 1989   Ts   Raine

I've also written two very short pieces about Sylvia—the DNA of her poetic metabolism. One of them came out of an argument I was preparing for the last ditch battle at my U.S. Trial—where all my missiles would have gone invisibly over the heads of my listeners. It is based on a psychic map—an actual drawing, which is also a sort of calibrated register between the two extreme poles of her system—of her double personality. Each of her poems can be placed pretty well exactly on the register by simply reading off the evident psychic components—her very systematised and consistent hieroglyphs, and fitting them to the calibration. At one extreme are the frigidly brittle self-protective, At the other extreme, the rawest of Ariel. At each extreme, the poems carry an image of the other extreme—as a remote, self-contained condition. As the poem moves from one extreme towards the other (in practice nearly all are moving from cold to hot), that self-contained image of the other grows more active and obvious. At a certain midway point, the balance is precarious. Beyond that point, the image of the extreme which is being approached becomes dominant, and enveloping, while the image of the extreme which has been left becomes self-enclosed and submerged. And so on. The map is also an anatomy of her psychic organism—the deployment of her internalised father and mother in the forms that her history had given them. So it seems very clear, for instance, that as she moved towards the liberation of her real voice, she moved towards the liberation of her child self, which was actually in the grave with her dead father. When she liberated her dead father which was also her real/her child self in the grave, she raised her own death. It

568

doesn't mean she had to die. There must have been many ways she could have extricated her child self from its death communion in her dead father's embrace. But it meant she was in real danger—that she couldn't afford to make a mistake. Or to have mistakes made for her—which they were. So the map is a kind of chart of her descent into the underworld where her dead father lies (her child/real self tight in his arms) ready to be awakened. The poems tell the story of the descent, the awakening, of her turning to make the re-ascent—having taken her child self from her dead father. What happened then? She had made the first steps upward when whatever happened happened. That's what the poems say—when they're fitted to the map. There's nothing new in the general outline. But the map makes it literal, somehow. The other piece came out of a letter I wrote to Roy Davids as notes for a talk on the rough drafts of Sheep In Fog. It dawned on me that the drafts tell the story of ARIEL as the story of Phaeton. The drafts begin by trying to take off on the near sheer vertical Ariel climb. Then gradually, very lucidly, realise that the rider lies dead on the earth—which is the ruins of a chariot. (Sheep In Fog is the only other poem about riding that same horse ARIEL.) The early drafts, which she finalised in a fashion, made the last of the Ariel poems. For two months she wrote nothing (except a bagatelle about a neighbour) then rewrote Sheep In Fog as it now stands. Went on to write two more poems that day, then the last few before she died a few days later. The whole myth—chariot, dead sun-child who is also the Sun the Father—ghost ride into the underworld—is literally there in the drafts. The details are transformed and concealed in the final version, but all still there. So the poem is the cortege of the funeral of the whole Ariel enterprise.

Both pieces are about how temperament, sensibility, inheritance, accidental history, turn into an organism of imagination within which the real person lives—it both expresses the essential life and traps it within that form, and has its own evolution, and secretes, at each stage, images of itself and in general poetry.

So I had the idea of putting these pieces, the Eliot Piece and the Shakespeare letters together. A book about three mythic poets. I don't think the disproportion in some aspects of stature matter: my point is that all three are exclusively mythical poets, writing only out of their myth (once it has evolved and become active) or rather only within their myth—being unable, actually, to write outside it. The nuclear cell of the Shakespeare myth is assembled in the sonnets, gestated foetal stage in the two long poems, kept in the dark for six years, then with crabby muted labours crawls out onto the stage in All's Well.

What do you think? I'll let you see it all when I have it typed up.

Part of a letter in which TH announces to his editor his intention to present him with essays on Shakespeare, Eliot and Plath. The omitted Shakespeare paragraphs contain material treated in other letters in this selection. (See also letters to Charles Tomlinson of 5 July and 15 August, above.)

To Nick Gammage

29 November 1989   Ts   Gammage

Dear Nick Gammage,

You're asking me questions impossible to answer.

Q.1. First sentence: it's true, I do think a good deal about the whole complication of the re-alignment of human life to the natural world which created him, and on which he depends—. It's obvious that the original alignment was lost long ago. It's also obvious that some small groups in fairly primitive cultures have managed to maintain an alignment that seems to us enviable. But the whole thing is a modern pre-occupation, isn't it. Second Question: it's commonplace since Nietsche to accuse Christianity on many counts, and blame it for this and that. And it isn't to be denied that Christian teachings, especially Reformation puritan-based Christian teachings, can be blamed for attitudes to women and to the natural world which have been destructive. Any re-alignment of man to the Natural World and to woman, any restoration of the Natural world and woman to their rightful sanctity, must entail rejection of many attitudes formulated and reinforced by puritan Christianity (I say puritan rather than protestant because there is obviously a puritan-like activity in some Catholicism). Your third sentence: if there is any consistent and clearly identifiable rejection, in what I've written, of the 'harmful doctrines in this particular religion', it is incidental.

Q 2: The story behind that poem: As a young man my father lived for football, was a professional for a brief time (my mother stopped him, she wanted him home at weekends), and went on into his thirties. I never saw him play.

During my twenties, my parents lived in the southernmost house on

Heptonstall Slack, which is a small village strung very sparsely along a road that runs along the spine of a ridge between two deep valleys. The football field lay (no longer does) on the West side of this road, about 150 yards from our house. The field slopes slightly, but beyond (i.e. West of) its lower wall the land falls steeply to the trees above Lumb Bank (now the Arvon Foundation's Northern Centre). From our house, and from the football field, the depth of the valley is far below and out of sight. The opposite slope rises as a sort of near cliff, heathery, rocky, with trees, to a skyline of rock outcrops, walls and a few trees. All around, the horizons are glaciated moorland at various depths of perspective. It is the ridge of the Pennines at that latitude and so exposed to full weather.

On one occasion I watched—for a while—a football match through the windows of that house, during a stormy gale day of the sort I describe. In other words—at a distance of 150 yards, through glass. For some reason, I found myself just very stirred. Something to do with the time-warp—my father's boyhood, his time on the war (nearly all his football friends killed)—and simply with the joyful, heroic sort of pathos, I suppose, of these little dressed up, brief figures, in that gigantic, archaic landscape. And so I tried to put my feelings into a poem. What I ended up with—at the time—was the piece entitled WIND in my first book. I lost the drafts long ago. But I didn't forget the occasion. So writing those pieces for Elmet I returned to it. If solemn readers find 'absurdity' there I'm sure it's their own contribution. My notion was a primitive painting, half-living half-puppet figures, painted with love.

Q3: The original idea of What Is The Truth was—that God's Son should learn about Man by hearing man's account of the creatures he loves best i.e. the creatures he oppresses, mythologises, misuses, kills, eats. (What he depends on for his livelihood he kills and eats.) In spite of this lesson, God's son descends into the world to be killed and eaten. But in writing I relaxed this scheme. I simply let the creatures blossom and obscured the first theme with another: that each person has his/her own idea of what any particular creature is, but none of them know that each one is actually God, implying that none of them will recognise God's Son either—each will have only a cockeyed, comfortable, private idea of him, wholly inadequate.

And so I floated the notion of a fable about the true divinity of creatures and man's inability to see that truth, but I didn't push it hard. I merely wanted a carrier wave for transmissions about creatures on a farm (I intended it for Farms For City Children—at Iddesleigh, which is run by friends of mine. Eventually I tried again, poems less complicated, less sophisticated, more juvenile, with The Cat And The Cuckoo.)

If there is a note of 'despair' it must leak through from the underlying first idea—that the fate of God on earth is to be killed and eaten, or at least killed. Though some pieces stay clear of that, perhaps.

Mainly I wanted to write pieces that would make it easier (even easier?) for readers—urban readers—to like these creatures. Or to share my liking. Or to make something pleasurable out of describing that liking. (I'm enclosing a book, so you can see how it works in schools).

Yes, I do believe it is possible to rediscover that relationship—though I don't know how many would want to.

Q4. What Is The Truth was almost a commission. The Cat And The Cuckoo was a correction of that same aim. Tales Of The Early World followed a commission to write a children's story for The Guardian on the theme of The Guardian. I wrote the Tiger story—liked it, so wrote the rest to complete a book. Ffangs also came about by accident. I wanted to demonstrate (to a close friend) what seem to me the basic simple laws of a narrative—and so wrote the first chapter. Later on, it occurred to me that if one could write an irresistible (to a child) story beginning with a very simple vocabulary and syntax but ending in more intricate sophisticated style, one might be able to force reading ability as you 'force' celery. In other words, the book was designed as a sort of gymnasium—for reading ability in the very young. Maybe it's a daft impractical theory. But that's how Ffangs came about. There wasn't much deliberation, you see, about the direction in which I aimed these books—it was decided pretty well by the occasion.

Q5. I see you have a point. Maybe I automatically draw on religion—the ultimate field of hypocrisy—as an analogy for the dissembling, hoodwinking and general self-misrepresentation by which so much of the organic world survives and even makes its living. In the organic world, what seems divinely ordained is also unscrupulously bent to take advantage of others, to seize every advantage, with a kind of grim or sly laughter implicit.

After all, this same 'natural' law is behind the suspect nature of verbal language itself. Its credentials for stating the case clearly are seized on by the animal need to manipulate, outwit, circumvent and gain power over its evolutionary (social) competitors or potential mates. The (dumb) animal in us understands this perfectly well, but how long it has taken the verbal intelligence to confess (as it did in Shakespeare) or to become a philosophical preoccupation (the crisis of modern thought).

I'm sorry if this seems brief. I hope it helps.
Yours sincerely
Ted Hughes

Nick Gammage (b.1958) had first made contact with TH while a student of English at Bristol University. He then took up a career in journalism and public relations, but continued to write about TH in his spare time. Preparing an article for the magazine *Acumen*, he had fired off questions, one of which was why so much of TH's writing in the mid-1980s had been for children. The football poem is 'Football at Slack', in *Remains of Elmet*. The Sunstone Press edition of *The Cat and the Cuckoo* (1987) had illustrations by R. J. Lloyd. *Tales of the Early World* was published in 1988; *Ffangs the Vampire Bat and the Kiss of Truth*, in 1986.

Gammage had discerned, in *The Cat and the Cuckoo*, a tendency to equate religion with hypocrisy.

1990

TH's 1990/91 correspondence was overwhelmingly concerned with Shakespeare. In a letter to his fishing friend Dermot Wilson, of 11 June, not included here, he reports: 'I have no news, as you see. Only strange tales from the depths of the Shakespearean caves, which no man wants to hear.' Also omitted from this selection is any specimen of the correspondence with the Swedish theatre director Donya Feuer that began, symbolically, on 23 April, and accumulated day by day until it grew to be the text that, in 1991, TH presented to his publishers as *Shakespeare and the Goddess of Complete Being*. Those letters are not identical to the published book, but they would be redundant here, as would many others in which he rehearsed arguments given more cogent form in the book.

To Seamus Heaney

20 January 1990   Ms Emory

Dear Seamus—

Just to make a start. Is this a method? You add (and delete?) some names & poems to [*added above:* (from)] this list, and let me have a copy of your result. Then I'll add others (maybe)—and send back to you the result. Then you, again, with 3rd thoughts, adjust the figures, & send the results back to me. So on, till we're happy. So, if we work downwards & outwards—we'll gradually find the tree-line, where mortal begins to contaminate immortal. How's that?

Actually, it struck me, just jotting down this list, that I inwardly make a clean division (fairly clean) between the poets I think of as truly great (spiritually great—voices of the whole tribe at a moment of crisis) (or at a highly-defined moment of consensus, or major polarised conflict) and those who are obviously equally-gifted, as far as poetic means goes,—but who are simply never picked up by the national gods.

So Wordsworth is obviously (to me & you too I fancy) in the first group—and Hopkins, to my mind very much in the second.

For me, the problem with Browning & Tennyson is that they were (at least, I think Tennyson was, I'm not sure about Browning—I'm simply repelled by Browning) poets of the first kind—but spoke for a national moment that was self-deluded, hypocritical, diffuse, and saturated with ideals that have gone bad). His jesuitry kept Hopkins from that sickness, immunised him—but it also deprived him of the tribal vote.

Maybe he's about like Wyatt, in that. & Donne.

Is there a policy by which we can stick to the truly great, but include the lone riders, such as Wyatt & Hopkins, by arbitrary choice?

Or is there a case for an imperious ruling: 3 vols.

Vol I: School Bag: the first team.

Vol II School Bag: the second team.

Vol III School Bag: the third team.

All boxed together?

The third team would include Browning, Tennyson etc.

Or would that be the end of us? But Vol I (with Vol II as an appendix) would be a handy book. [*This sentence linked by arrow and curly bracket to paragraph beginning 'Is there a policy . . .'*]

That was a grand, restorative evening—great to see you both looking so well, & in such resilient morale.

Love

Ted

[*Following afterthoughts are scattered at foot of page, possibly in the order proposed below*]

As you see, it tired me a little doing the Shakespeare but I recovered with Yeats. I suppose Faber could afford Yeats now he's out of copyright.

Who fits after Owen?

McDiarmid? Lawrence?

Best to begin with much too much.

P.S. I'm remembering your first idea of including everybody but only 2 poems each. Maybe we do both? Keep both going together?

Faber and Faber wanted TH and Heaney to follow up the huge success of *The Rattle Bag* with a second anthology. Ideas about the book passed through a number of mutations before it appeared as *The School Bag* (1997). In the list of major English poets from the Middle Ages to the early twentieth century accompanying this letter, the latter is represented in its entirety by the Irishman Yeats, the US-born Eliot, and the partly Welsh Owen. Titles of poems – generally two or three – are put next to some names, while the pair TH favours most highly, Shakespeare and Yeats, are allowed 33 and 27 respectively. Owen's single entry is 'Strange Meeting'. Milton's

'On the Late Massacre in Piedmont', proposed in the following letter to Heaney (as 'Avenge O Lord'), is missing from the list.

To Seamus Heaney

7 February 1990   Ts   Emory

Let's do this really quickly, off the top of our heads—THE KIT BAG. The handy vol for carrying into the frightful battles of the next century (the famine battles, the Greenhouse flood-out battles, the refugee migration battles, the general devilry battles, the democratic mutual abuse battles, the roaming bands of hand-to-mouth warrior battles. A book to deflect the bullet, the bayonet, and the long hours in the damp fox-hole.

Just the best poems—not too long, maybe Lycidas a limit for length. But the poems a person might like to learn when locked under the ice-cap for three months.

They flee from me
The Second Coming
Gerontion
The Phoenix and the Turtle
Avenge O Lord—

a new Palgrave. Send me a quick list of fifty and I'll bat it back at thee. Nothing 'representative'—only essentials.
[. . .]

Back to the KIT BAG. It's like your original idea—two poems from each author. But with no idea of a compendium or pantechnicon for the schoolroom. A book for the lonely soldier surviving on essentials. A book for the twenty second century.

To Matthew Evans

7 February 1990   Ts   Faber

Dear Matthew,

Just a note about my phone-call.

Martin Palmer will tell you all. The idea cropped up at an ideas dinner, in the Palace, where the Duke of E goaded a number of his guests to think up ways of getting environmental awareness—awareness of the issues—urgency of the issues—past the barrier that everybody now puts up against the incessant flood of chat about it.

The most memorable and stirring drama I ever saw, apart from Brook's Mahabharata, was a series of very short—15 to 20 minutes at most—plays for children, invented and put on by 2nd year drama students in Exeter. Made out of folk-tales etc.

So it was a natural extension to put together (a) a competition of plays, about that length, written by anybody, for children, based on religious stories, myths, folktales (which lifts everything out of the drearily social, into symbolic drama and big, direct statements, automatically) for children; (b) plays that would revolve around themes of environmental concern; (c) the huge lack of plays suitable for performance in schools by schoolchildren, imaginative, cross-cultural plays, and the huge hunger of teachers for plays of any sort to bring all their pupils into action on real issues; (e) the susceptibility of children to concern for the natural world (actually, as I know from my deep immersion in children's writing competition, nearly all children are in despair about the plight of the natural world); (f) the universal search for forms in which to express and better communicate the general concern, in a united and public yet not didactic and boring way; (g) the strange fact that adults are more affected and moved by children's drama, which they watch through the eyes of their children, than they are by adult drama, which they watch through their visors; (h) the easy possibility, having called a number of dramas of this sort into being, of publishing them, in acting texts, throughout schools.

First, the idea was to have simply a national competition, gather the ten or dozen best, and publish them—and with the help of some benevolent donor distribute them throughout schools.

Then, because acting companies all over the world are so enterprising and are also in general such an altruistic or idealistic breed, it occurred to us that it would be just as easy to make it international—in the sense that each country would run its own Competition separately, and simultaneously.

By the time all the winners, however many in each country, are ready to be performed, publicity, the electrical wave of timeliness, pushed around the world by Gaia herself, will make it inevitable that each country will hold its own festival performing the winners and then, just as inevitable, that national governments will fund their champions to an International Olympiad of children's drama (acted by adults or whatever), maybe in Glasgow, or some grand venue.

Then an orgy of translation. And we end up with 50 or 60 or 200 imaginative, original children's plays—to be published and distributed throughout schools <u>in each country</u>.

What an empire gapes before thee, Matthew!

I know two or three directors in other countries who are straining on the leash to get going on this competition. I can't believe it won't take off in a way that will surprise us.

Leap aboard!

They were thinking of giving it to Harper Collins—but I stood in the gap for Faber. I thought, if world rights are to handled etc etc etc

A split to the rainforests, to the washers of the water and the air, and to beleaguered beasts.

And the whole world will be performing these plays, and their teeming variants—so they'll become sacred texts of a new children's religion.

A penny a copy to me for the idea, maybe.

Martin, as you'll see, is a most remarkable chap. Ask him about the religious series of publications he's organising. [*Marginal addition in ms:* Ask him about the means he has—for publicising etc. !!]

Thank you again, Matthew, for the rattlebags etc. And for the flowers!

Yours ever
Ted

P.S. Did you meet Paul Henderson—the American proprietor of Gidleigh Park. He wants a hardback Rattle Bag for each of his guest-rooms. He's such an entrepreneur, in the world of hoteliers, I'll try & get him to promote it throughout all hotels—since the Gideon bible seems to have left so many gaps. (He's suddenly smitten with poetry.)

Matthew Evans (b.1941) was both Chairman and Managing Director of Faber and Faber. This letter to him records the genesis of the Sacred Earth Drama Trust. In 1993, Faber would publish *Sacred Earth Dramas*, a collection of the winners of a competition held in 1990.

Martin Palmer is Director of the International Consultancy on Religion, Education and Culture.

The restaurant at Gidleigh Park was a favourite with TH, who, this same year, wrote an introduction to a book of recipes by its head chef, Shaun Hill.

To Moelwyn Merchant

29 June 1990   Ms   Paul Merchant

Dear Moelwyn,

Thank you for your letters. It seems to me (from what little, admittedly, that I've glimpsed) that your conception of Christ and mine are probably quite close. We have simply come to it from opposite directions. You have come to it from within the Church, I have come to it from outside the Church. But all that means, perhaps, is that we have looked for the evidence—the reassurances that our basic, private intuition is valid—in different places.

It occurred to me—fairly recently—that my preoccupation with animal life, which was obsessively there waiting for me when I became conscious, was a natural gravitation towards whatever life had escaped the cultural imprint. Because everybody else ignored it (in those days, I couldn't have felt the same now) I felt I had the animal world absolutely to myself. I could indulge a total self-identification with all wild-life. That was the first step.

As a sort of ritual—for keeping in touch—my entire boyhood, up to about 18, was spent shooting & fishing. And trapping, I'm ashamed to say. Am I ashamed? What puzzles me now is how, while I was so obsessed with these creatures, I thought of little but getting my hands on them by killing them—which I did, in vast numbers.

About the age of 12 or so, I became infatuated with folklore. That became a craze which still comes in waves. At University, I spent 3 years sitting in the University Library reading folklore & mythology. Collecting it too.

Also at University, I discovered the literature of Shamanism.

So then these separate things—my wild life, my mythology, and a series of dreams which had recurred since I was quite young (two of them are my first memories)—showed me that something about Shamanism explained or incorporated everything that concerned me.

I can't go into details without boring you, but it began to dawn on me why from early days I had always dreaded Sunday as a day of psychological torment, and why the whole business of Sunday in the Calder Valley (Fanatic blend of Methodism and Chartism) had always seemed to me a performance <u>at the expense of the real thing</u>.

I made the association, somehow, between the world of animals, which is excluded by culture, & persecuted (killed & eaten) & the "real thing" in human beings—the part which our own culture tortures, i.e. sacrifices, crucifies. I identified, you see, the sacrificed God, the divine self which has to die to come into life, with the whole animal & vegetable kingdom, which culture tortures & destroys.

This was a very primitive thing to do, but I did it in a completely literal sense. Somehow animal life (the whole of life outside the human ego, perhaps) became identified with Christ in particular, but with the divine world in general (the world from which ego has separated us.)

At the same time, with what I had absorbed of mythology, literatures of religions etc, I fitted this into a Universal sort of system. I didn't fit it—it simply fitted itself.

So an odd sort of synthesis began to form itself—where all mythologies & religions fitted themselves into what I conceived of as the spiritual crisis of the human animal.

The basis of the system is that creation, the processes of creation & created life are 'divine'—in the sense that wherever human life (for instance) becomes in some way united to those processes, the experience is felt to be 'divine', a subjective, inexpressible state, a condition of a different order of 'awareness' than our usual human one, & an infinitely desirable one.

The animals, who were created exactly as they are by this Creation, and have never been detached from it, are therefore in a state of 'bliss'—they live a divine life in a divine world. They live in perpetual 'Samadhi', and have never fallen from it into ego-consciousness, into the acculturating, detatched cerebration which removes us from it—separates us from the 'bliss' of our animal/spiritual being, & from the 'divine' world in which we ought to be living but cannot even become aware of except under special conditions, for short spells.

In this system I explain 'ego-consciousness' as the result of the brain-transformation—following on the last mutation of our species 40,000 years ago, which produced culture as an antidote to the strange new sense of alienation from the world into which we are born, & the strange new sense of alienation from the 'divine' experience of our animal/spiritual nature. (The palaeological/biological evidence for the mutation includes the strange fact that according to the mitochondria in our cells, which we inherit only from our mother, and which—in all living human groups so far studied—have the same DNA i.e. all come from the same woman, we all come from the same woman, perhaps a very pretty mutant (not like an ugly Neanderthal, but with a dainty little chin, a handsome high brow, and instead of coarse hair all over her body a delicate lanugo) who was probably only about 4'6" high, had several daughters, & was eventually eaten by lions. But her mutant gene, in all her daughters, was dominant, & bred true).

Once, by ego consciousness i.e. free intelligence, the ability to manipulate abstract ideas & direct our behaviour <u>against</u> instinct, we had lost the divine world, and internal identity with the divine self, culture appeared, as I say, as a substitute for what we had lost—religion appeared as a technology to regain it.

Shamanism appeared (the man in the guise of a divine animal, or inspired by a divine animal or a Queen of the animals) as a spontaneous collapse of the cultural ego—in some individual—and a simultaneous 'organised' internal plunge back into the animal/spiritual consciousness that had been lost.

From this lost 'divine' consciousness, the Shaman returns with all kinds of things that the alienated 'exiled' ego consciousness of his group needs. In some way, he plunges not into his own animal/spiritual consciousness, but into that of the whole group. This is how the great ones become Holy Men, Prophets, Healers, spiritual leaders. In this sense, Shamans become, briefly, incarnations of the sacrificed God. If they can institutionalise their experience (usually some other does that) they found religions. In this sense, Tertullian's (?) "The soul is naturally Christian" states my sense of the 'biological' truth—and a life deprived of that constant revelation of the sacrificed God—is no life. This last sentence must encapsulate your faith as it does mine.

Love   Ted

[*Vertical addition in left margin:* Read: The Ghost Dance Religion by Weston La Barre—a classic.]

On 24 April, TH had sent Merchant a copy of his previous day's letter to Donya Feuer. Merchant replied with comments on that and on subsequent instalments of the work in progress. The letters to Merchant above and below represent a small part of the discussion thus generated.

The early Christian theologian Tertullian (*c.*155–230) writes about the soul in his *De anima*. The full title of Weston La Barre's book is *The Ghost Dance: Origins of Religion* (1970).

To Moelwyn Merchant

2 July 1990   Ms   Paul Merchant

Dear Moelwyn,

I expect my note describing my primitive approach to the nature of Christ will have mightily obscured all issues.

But your letter today makes me feel I should try and make some simple clarification of what must be confusions in my letters to Donya.

1ˢᵗ "Collision of Jehova Christ & Catholic Goddess"—relates only to those historic times & places where it occurs. Calvin's Christ. The Christ of Cromwell's troopers. The Christ of Paisley?

But I believe it always carries, in Shakespeare, the general psychological opposition of those extremes as they exist, for instance, in the polarised plots of Tolstoy's Kreutzer Sonata, Anna Karenina, 'Resurrection', or in the generalised puritanism of the human mind as it expresses itself in trying to close Theatres, in burning witches, in bizarre physical operations on girls, primitive societies, degradation of women, etc. Is any Protestantism as 'Puritan' as some Catholicism—i.e. Irish? As some Literary Criticism (the playground of Iago).

As you will see, (after my last letters,) in the perspective of the whole tragic cycle, the Jehova Christ is the metaphysical soul-murderer who has to be destroyed, then reconstructed as a Christ of 'the understanding heart'—the Gnostic <u>Gnosis Kardias</u>, whom, I imagine, you would claim to be the Christ of Anglo-Catholicism.

In this way, you could argue, Shakespeare in his last plays becomes the Prophet of the Anglo-Catholic synthesis.

The 'work' of these last plays is the 'successful' effort of the tragic hero (the Puritan Goddess-rejector, the Puritan Goddess-destroyer) to understand his error (in which he rejected—tried to murder—his soul, the Divine Love). He is able to do this because both he & the female in question <u>survive</u> his earlier attempt to destroy her.

Understanding his error amounts to understanding what is wrong with the extreme Puritan attitude—the Angelo/Iago attitude, & repudiating it.

The Jehovan Christ therefore—as I say in the letter about Iago—is, intellectually, the opposite of Christ. The redeemed Gnostic Christ— 'the understanding heart'—understands this absolutely, rejects that intellectuality, (hence the brainwashed Lear) and is therefore enabled to re-unite with the soul (Divine Love) in whatever female form—Cordelia, Hermione, Thaisa, Imogen—he formerly rejected it.

I think you would agree that it can be argued:—though Anglo-Catholicism, like Shakes in the last plays, has devised a third phase—a synthesis beyond the Thesis of the Goddess and the Antithesis of the Jehovan Christ—even so, that synthesis has not been effective. It has lost its grip on the imagination of the people. Individuals can make the synthesis for themselves—as you can (and as I try to, for myself). But in its simpler followers, I imagine you would concede it fails to reconcile the primaeval antagonisms of Goddess & her enemy. I imagine, because it is not inclusive enough, & therefore it induces, or encourages, or fails to enlighten, the Puritanism which clings to pragmatic reason, & for which the Iago-mentality institutionalised in materialist philosophy, & in the political philosophy of technological progress, provides the real sacraments. In this sense, I think, the Tragedies proper tell the real story of modern spiritual life—even though the late plays evolve beyond them and it. For all its evolution in that same direction, don't you think Anglo-Catholicism has failed to incorporate the female?

Love   Ted

To Ann Pasternak Slater and Craig Raine

14 August 1990   Ms   Pasternak Slater and Raine

Dear Li & Craig,

Thank you for the painstaking notes. They have been really useful. They give me the essential thing—a view from outside my own noddle, from somebody who not only knows the plays better than I do, but knows what has been written about them.

I will give full outlines of the myths (full outlines?)—wherever the first mention comes. In that context, in themselves, they would be very suggestive, especially the Sophia myth.

Maybe some things could be cut.

I've made the Rival-Brother link much clearer, much earlier.

In the last letter, the last 4 plays, I felt I had already written too much—so hurried them off. The Tempest should be several letters, each one more carefully aimed. At present, all the cross-currents confuse each other. The equation runs into difficulties there—because each character is such a summation of a long lineage, or of two lineages simultaneously.

Maybe the whole thing needs a final letter—a view of the whole monument.

In the enclosed "Introduction" [*marginal addition:* For a new edition—slightly enlarged. The introd. Without any tangling with the mythic equation.] (another blob of the tar-baby) I go into 'catastrophe & heel of pastime', & the passage around it, in a slightly different direction. Maybe add some of this to what's in the letter? Also, one or two more sentences about the 3rd language—(I had meant to write a whole letter about it, as about the All's Well 2nd language).

I still think the pairing begins—as an expression of structural thematic doubling—in All's Well. But I was interested to see your derogatory comments on the padded shoulders of Hamlet's nouns. Some of it, I agree, is a habit of stateliness—like a style of acting. Only I feel the stateliness has a purpose—to lift the speech into a higher order, a non-ordinary order, & to induce a meditative wavelength in what is, essentially, the speech of action. I wonder if it doesn't represent—very directly—the balanced participation of both left & right brains. Normally, in a verbal communication, the mode would be left brain—linear & latinate (in an educated chap like Shakes). But the effect always is of two words emerging <u>simultaneously</u>—side by side. "Sensible" (left brain acknowledging right brain—latinism acknowledging world of sense) and "true" (right acknowledging left—Anglo-Saxon mother-tongue acknowledging world of moral concepts). The effect on the reader is to balance—by mimicry—left & right brain, & this is felt as pleasure, enlargement of mental engagement, a momentary 'satori'—as they used to say in the Sixties. 'Squeak & gibber' does not really work as a marriage, more as sparrow chasing sparrow. 'Gross' & 'scope' again works as left brain & right brain—'Gross', being the full bodily presence (right brain) of 'opinion' (latinate, conceptual left brain) & the spacial dimension (right brain) of, again, 'opinion' (ditto). The means of balancing the 2 brains are slightly different—but the effect (using all 3 words) is the same.

'extravagant & erring'—same way, balances the 2 brains, where 'extravagant' (left, latinate) gives a conceptual, moral, defining ('seen to be wandering outside its limits') view of the 'spirit', while erring (right, Gothic enough to be mother-tongue) mimics the sensation & tongue-curling whimper of going wrong.

'impotent & bedrid'—same, balances the two brains, same way, & adds other suggestions (in bed not because he's potent, but impotent.

584

Once having done all he could to get into bed, now cannot get out of it—is ridden by it, as by a hag etc)

I think when you look at these couplets from this encephalic point of view, & taking account of the meditative explosion—more than that, the Koan effect, of these near but never quite tautologous synonyms, and concede that the 'poetic' response created in the reader's or listener's brain, by this effect, is important—is, artistically, Shakespeare's mature signature, then—

Boris was losing a lot. As you do say.

The metaphoric mode—maybe the same. The two in one—unite the two brains. Result (even in bad metaphors) a burst of giddy pleasure & wild relief, & a sense that a superior mental act has been performed (superior to singular precision—which is always accompanied by a sense of prohibition, imprisonment, deprivation etc.) A more human act, maybe.

I didn't mean to get on to this.

I would like to hear your analysis of my perverse rendering of Sonnet 25—do you think I find something that isn't there?

Generally, I suspect the whole collection is like a language course—in each letter you pick up a bit more of the vocabulary. So you can't understand the beginning, till you get to the end—by which time you're worn out. Like going over a mural with a pocket lens and a pencil torch.

I tried to excuse my revamping of other people's (to me unknown) clichés. But where can I find anything about Cordelia's dumbness, and the dumbness of truth, as the centrepin of the works. I need that—but I'd like to know what I'm rephrasing.

Have a good time in Italy.

Love
Ted

Raine's wife, Ann Pasternak Slater, is the author of *Shakespeare the Director* (1980). TH had asked her to comment on passages from his own Shakespeare book in the making. In her letter to him, she had mentioned that Boris Pasternak, her uncle, when translating Shakespeare, had also noticed the playwright's habit of pairing adjectives and had dealt with it by cutting. One of the epigraphs to *Shakespeare and the Goddess of Complete Being* is taken from a passage in *Shakespeare the Director*, where Slater considers 'Cordelia's dumbness'.

To Ben Sonnenberg

[Undated 1990]   Ts   Emory

Dear Ben,

Your book stirred me more than I can say. That crystalline, facetted sort of concentration you always had—prismatic disclosures. Your prose is always associated in my mind with Bartok's music—for some reason. Some essential link—in my mind. I remember those stories of yours, and the dialogue in the plays.

I was touched by your memory of our earlier times together. I remember very clearly that first meeting at the Merwins. Yes, you asked me about the handkerchief. I remember lots of details from our later meetings too. One always thinks (at least, in those days one always thought)—"our friendship's real season is still to come." And the season gradually came while we were geographically far asunder. When I visited you, three years ago, I knew I was with one of my closest friends, closest, oldest, dearest friends.

The anecdote you tell of the fly and my poem about the Jaguar exists here and there in various versions. I don't know that you should alter your memory, but just for curiosity here is what happened.

In January 1955 I was visiting a girl friend (a nurse) in Cambridge, and staying with her. She had a ground-floor flat, unheated. Each morning I sat in her front room, in a deep chair she had, and wrote. Cambridge in Winter is the coldest place in England, as a rule—open to East winds from the Baltic. (Nothing higher than a reed till you get to the Urals.) So I was wearing (as I sat there) my first world war leather greatcoat. (I was a trend-setter: that was the first leather greatcoat I ever saw being actually worn. A marvellous coat, but a bit battered. It was eventually burned in a housefire.) So: first point: the room was very cold.

During the autumn of 1954 I'd worked in Regent's park Zoo, and got to know a particular Jaguar. It lived in a 'transit' cage near the kitchen window at which I stood for most of the day washing up. (That was my job. Zoo visitors spend most of their day in the restaurant eating.) This animal connected itself, inside my head, with a jaguar I'd seen in a very small cage in a Zoo at Morecambe (on the Lancashire coast), when I was about five years old, which I remembered at regular intervals (still do). When I was that age, my toys were lead animals—a kind you could

586

get in those days, very fine detailed models. Those, and plasticene, were the only toys I ever had. (My brother, ten years older, filled the house with his model galleons and schooners that would plough up and down the canal below our house, his steamboats that turned propellors and puffed out steam, his aeroplanes that would fly—he was clever in that line, became an aircraft engineer. I suppose I worshipped him and his skills too much to think I could ever compete, so I stuck to animals and plasticene, which I turned into more animals, and drawing animals. But because (I expect) of the memory of that first Jaguar, and because its legs are thick enough to support it in plasticene, whenever I got hold of plasticene, clay or wax, a Jaguar was what I automatically modelled. So: second point: I had been modelling one Jaguar since I was about five.

Sitting in that flat, that cold morning, I was trying to write the equivalent of modelling my Jaguar. I was about halfway down a page (I didn't stop tinkering with it till 18 months later, after I'd met Sylvia. I remember places all over England where I got the final version of various lines) and was trying to find words for that irritated, black-lipped half-snarl that Jaguars (big cats generally) can have when they're going to and fro in cages feeling pent-up. They snarl slightly sideways, twisting their heads slightly as if they were making a feint at biting, lifting their side-lip in a sneering almost, you could imagine, the beginning of a crashing full-anger snarl, that never does get that far—just simmers and lifts and twists slightly. The image that came into my head, to give the idea, was—memory of a fly landing on a dog's nose (a farm sheepdog, asleep in very hot sun) and the dog trying to bite the fly by twisting its mouth and teeth right round the side of its face (the fly clung on a while, and later on there was blood where it had been). To intensify my idea and make the point of irritation more of an impossible, inaccessible fixture, I thought—better if the fly is right up there inside its nostril, so I wrote words to that effect. Probably: as if it had a fly up its nostril. While I was actually writing the words, an average size bluefly came straight across that very cold room—where no fly could have moved since November at the latest—and went straight up my nostril, where it lodged. I extracted it, and pressed it in my Shakespeare.

Close to a repeat, a few years ago: I was writing, with a fountain pen, on a table in the orchard. I wrote—can't recall how I came to the image—words to the effect: 'the flow of the script suddenly foundered— as if copulating flies had dropped from the air onto the point of the nib'. I would normally think, too fancy! But as I wrote the words, a pair of tiny copulating flies fell onto my nib, the very point, clogged the flow and blotted the word I was writing.

I've never at any other time had a bluefly go up my nostril. Never at any other time has a fly of any kind got itself fouled up in my nib. But two flies together—to order, on cue, giddily fucking.

I don't know if you remember your comment on a story I wrote called The Suitor. I wrote it sitting with Sylvia the day before and the day after Nicholas was born. Your comment was, Death and the Maiden. It hit me like a flash. The roles, Death Sylvia and Me are identified as if quite intentionally. The 'I' in the story is the other me that somehow made the interpretation.

One or two other even more overt predictions turned up as stories and radio plays. I got the idea that my fictional imagination was either drawing exclusively on my future life, or was somehow creating it. So I stopped writing either stories or plays. That is why I stopped. Two or three of the later ones are so literal I couldn't ask anybody to believe them. Maybe something to do with lead poisoning from my lead animals!

Now I write about the past. I'm sending you a couple of little books. You may have seen them. The English one is a re-issue of a sort of farming journal I kept—but I thought you might like to read the bits of prose I've added. The other is just the tidying up of a closed phase.

Pity that Bill took it badly. I haven't seen him for twenty years. We occasionally exchange a letter. How does the US regard his poems. I have lost all sense of the dramatis personae on the US poetry scene at the moment. Except that a powerful sweeping beam of blinding glare issues from the feminine component of every English faculty in the land. Getting to be the same here. Susan Schaeffer, teaches in Brooklyn, tells me her students daren't write anything any more, they won't permit each other to get away with a word. 'If it makes sense, it infringes somebody's rights'.

I imagine my fly story is too complicated for your text—but you now have it as it happened.

Love to Dorothy and yourself
Ted.

Sonnenberg had sent TH his *Lost Property: Memoirs and Confessions of a Bad Boy* (1991), whether in typescript or proof, he cannot now remember, but it was evidently too late for the jaguar-and-fly story to be amended.

TH's trend-setting leather greatcoat was a gift from his uncle Thomas Farrar, an officer in the First World War.

'The Suitor' is one of the prose stories in *Wodwo* (and, later, in *Difficulties of a Bridegroom*).

'Bill' was W. S. Merwin, another of Sonnenberg's acquaintances recollected in *Lost Property*.

1991

Just before Christmas 1990, TH had contracted shingles, which kept him in pain and in bed well into the new year. Nonetheless, he continued to work on his Shakespeare book and to exchange letters on that subject and others.

To Ann Pasternak Slater and Craig Raine

18 January 1991   Ms   Pasternak Slater and Raine

Dear Li and Craig—

Li, it is really too generous of you to send me what I expect is your next to last copy of your book. I shall go on trying to find a copy, and then I will let you have it back.

Can't you persuade Faber to do it?

Since I started writing my Shakespeare piece, I've been taking arms-fulls of Shakes. commentary from the library—simply to check whether I'm rehashing somebody else's ideas. It is fairly incredible how little I've found that seems to have even the remotest hint of relevance to my argument. The only books where I suddenly did find something were yours—your whole thesis about Shakespeare's language of action, which is of a piece with his language of imagery, which is of a piece with his idea of the ineffability of the truth, I would ideally like to have written that myself as a gigantic note to the few suggestions I do try to formulate and point in that direction. And the other is a book by Peter Milward—'Shakes' Religious Background', which I expect you know. Marvellously detailed Catholicisation of the man. Milward's a Jesuit.

The shock of seeing my letters through both your eyes (all four eyes, I mean!) roused me a little. So I took it more seriously, cut a lot of the gabble (where I was groping my way, usually), laid out the essential mythology very clearly, (I hope), as you suggested, and then went into Macbeth, Ant & Cleo & the later plays more deeply. Ideas that had just floated into the eye-corner first-time round, really opened up. I got quite excited about Macb. & Ant & Cleo. I had wanted to make the link between the Egyptian background of King Lear & the same in Ant & Cleo—and of course it opened up all kinds of things. I was always curious to know why Ant & Cleo was my favourite play—now I know. Also, it seems to me I really found the combination between the growing point in each play (the death-rebirth moment), the storm, the flower, the Boar, Caliban & Ariel. The whole thing became wonderfully lucid to me—am I kidding myself? I must be. Anyway—it's a sort of prose poem, if nothing else.

I contracted shingles, so I've been lying very low, & reciting the whole thing (except for the letters I kept) onto tapes—to be typed. Every time I fall asleep I start rewriting new letters—wonderful new ideas. Last night I analysed the whole language (the relationship between the 2 languages of the 2 myths of the equation, & the 3rd language, which is that of the inclusive greater myth of the Goddess undivided, the transcendental language) as the 3 different elements of the prickling pains in my eye—it seemed so clear & strong I knew I had to fit it into the sequence somewhere. But then when I woke it faded.

Donya Feuer is rather wonderful—intense, tireless worker. She sent me tapes of Bergman's King Lear & Hamlet—I'll send them on. Videos of the stage performance.

I'm also sending your book, Li, to Peter Brook. He doesn't read Academic books about S (or about anything) but yours is a real Director's handbook—it will fascinate him.

I hear you've all been waylaid by colds—always worse when you catch them from children. World's in terrible shape.

Anything happening to 1951?

Let some good things happen 1991.

Love

Ted

Craig—yes, I'm putting together the Shake's selection, slightly longer, with the Introduction shorter.

Shakespeare's Religious Background, by Peter Milward, SJ, was published in 1973.
Raine had recently translated Racine's *Andromaque* as 1953.

To Nick Gammage

15 March 1991   Ts   Gammage

It's dawned on me gradually, over the last few years, that for most readers of verse (people under 45?) the First World War is remote history. They know about the trenches as they know about the squares at Waterloo or the archers at Agincourt—as curious fact about other people's excitements and woes. Rather as they know about that wipe-out on the Kuwait Basra road last month. They know about it, but it doesn't mean much to them.

They are (I suppose you probably are) offspring of men who fought in the second World War. And they know that the second World War also had its sensational aspects—London Blitz, firestorm bombing of Germany, Dunkirk, atom-bomb. But because that war escaped (as far as the English were concerned) the feared repeat performance of the First World War, and because it kept light and mobile, it had almost no traumatic effect—for the English I don't think it had any. No psychological effect in that it did not ever feel like a disaster. I know, because I was expecting to be in it, had a brother in it, and was very conscious when it ended—have known since a great many who were in it. In fact, rather than shock, there was a general feeling of relief—that it had not been like the first World War. For us. And even though certain groups had a frightful time—prisoners of the Japanese etc—the country as a whole registered no impact. And from the moment it was over everybody was talking about other things—cold war, threat of the real (nuclear) war, Russia Russia Russia, Communism and in England the victory of the Left and the Welfare State. As we became aware of the effects of the war in Eastern Europe, the holocaust, the Nuclear terror etc, they became just more news. It became clear that the world had entered a whole new, lower circle of frightfulness, but it had happened according to expectations—it induced a general climate of depression and dinginess, but there was no shock. Not in England.

Now after the First World War the whole country was traumatised. A narrow band of middle and upper classes produced the hysterical gaiety of the twenties [*marginal addition at top-right corner of paragraph*: and by those too young to serve in the war, & too old to be traumatised by the news of it.], but beneath that the physical mass of the country, the body of it, the masses that had produced the infantry, was in a coma. When I came to consciousness I never heard of anything but the First World War (and it had been over, say, fifteen years). Those towns in West Yorks were still stunned. So I passed my early days in a kind of Mental Hospital of the survivors, widowers etc. And it wasn't simply the horrible mud struggle in a terrain more or less composed of liquefied corpses, the stories of how this or that village lost all its men in one day, one attack. It was something much more inclusive—the shock suffered by a species that had thought the world was quite different, and that war was quite different. The old understanding that war was fought by regular, professional armies had just blown away like a wisp. War, it turned out, was fought by whole populations. The old basic rules of cavalry style open assault on fixed positions, that had worked perfectly well for two thou sand years, had suddenly come up against machine guns—industrialised slaughter, mass-production of corpses. Those who met the shock in person never got over it, they never were able to assimilate it. My father's whole life was posthumous in some way, after that.

In the fifties, when I began publishing my first poems, to me the First World War was my most intimate experience, my mythology. But then I realised all my own generation were writing about the same thing— their Fathers' war. During the Fifties, for several years, that was a dominant theme of writers then in their twenties. They had no interest in the second world war, that they'd lived through. And what they wrote struck a deep chord—not only in their own age-group, but in the survivors of that War, the First one, the age-group of their fathers, who were still under sixty, many of them. So writing about the secret inner world of my childhood, I was using automatically a mythology shared and lived and felt by everybody under seventy—the whole country.

As the actual survivors of that war have died off, and as their children grew older (there can't be many now under fifty, and most are sixty or more), and as generations arrived that could not share that mythology and the living feeling of it—all generations after about 1936 or so (to me they feel like a different species), the country has changed to an incredible degree. What was a shared, single, sacred sort of mythology has simply gone—and nothing has taken its place.

To get back to your question: in that context, (my early background, the pervasive presence of that war,) Owen seemed to be expressing the drama of the shared mythology. In that way, he seemed contemporary. (Maybe you've noticed how he still obsesses writers such as Jon Silkin—born 1930, John Stallworthy, born about the same time). He gave form to our childhood nightmares and preoccupations. The second part of your question ('Did your reading of him swing your thinking on to the effect of the Great War etc') would be unimaginable to those two. It illustrates what I've been saying—you're too young to realise that our problem was not to get our minds to consider the Great War, but to get our minds off it.

In my own case, though I suppose I swallowed Owen as deeply as anybody well could, and have never lost my taste for his best poems (and would defend his weaker poems for what I think are good reasons), I did have a reservation about him: first, he was an officer. Throughout the war my father as an infantryman and obviously an effective soldier— being very strong physically, very combative and rather bright—refused promotion. And told strange stories about some officers (when he told any). Second, Owen did not get into the war until late 1916— Octoberish, when the Somme had been going four months or so (24,000 killed on the first day). I know he made up for it, and that men grew old in two days out there, but as I say somehow I held it against him. I've never quite been able to reconcile my liking for his poems with the fact that he was still pursuing the cultivated life in France quite late in 1915. (That gives some idea of the old-fashioned outlook that would never get over the SHOCK). It's a foolish reservation, and I disown it—but I know it's there.

Part of a letter answering further questions from Gammage.

To Christopher Reid

27 May 1991   Ts   Faber

I will ring about the other things—presentation etc. Any improvements will be gratefully incorporated. But semi-colons give me a slipped disc feeling, a broken snake feeling. Where ff might think I need them, I shall probably feel the sentence is too long. As I know my impulse is to write the entire chapter as one sentence—phrases linked by dashes (which everybody hates).

From a letter promising his new Faber editor imminent delivery of the typescript of *Shakespeare and the Goddess of Complete Being*.
    'ff': Faber and Faber, after the firm's logo.

To Gillian Bate

21 June 1991   Ts   Bate

Hello. I'm very grateful for your positive interest in The Goddess—and I already feel immense relief at having access to a pair of eyes different from my own. My eyesight has been in a way refashioned, writing this book—I'm now totally adapted to this peculiar world, like one of those shrimps living in the sulphur and fantastic temperatures of deep-sea volcanoes, and I no longer feel to have any confident idea of just how the final thing will appear in the old world where I used to live.

A difficulty, perhaps, is that in some ways my terms and concepts are like philosophical or even mathematical terms, and ought to be fully defined at the beginning and stable throughout. But the book grew as an imaginative work, or like an imaginative work, and so bears all the stages of its gestation and birth, infancy and adolescence. This is a plus in some ways, but a negative in others. In a sense, the whole book is nothing else but a prolonged full process of defining certain terms—so the terms are given in simple or rudimentary form at the beginning and then with each illustrative example become a little more complicated, and in fact do actually themselves evolve. This gave me headaches in the rewriting, since I had to re-adapt, in each chapter, to the phase of definition that the terms had reached at that point. Or the whole book is like a language course, where the simple terms and grammar given in the first lesson are necessary for the slightly fuller development in the second, and so on, till the whole system is perfectly clear and the student is a fluent speaker—but one cannot disrupt any of the earlier lessons with a sudden burst of explanations that assume an understanding only to be gained in the later lessons.

As freelance copy editor, Gillian Bate was to guide the constantly ramifying and shape-shifting text of *Shakespeare and the Goddess of Complete Being* towards publication. This is from TH's first letter to her.

To Gillian Bate

21 July 1991   Ts   Bate

I'm sorry to be so long returning this, but I wanted to clear up one thing that has been a difficulty from the beginning. The business of Occult Neoplatonism. One can't just refer to this and assume that even Shakespearean scholars will understand and supply the rest. 400 years of cultural suppressive dismissal aren't going to be lifted willingly simply to indulge me. I wanted to give a compact, concrete, vivid idea of it—as it might have impinged on Shakespeare's operation—(without it, in my opinion, there would have been no Shakespeare operation), stopping short of any assumptions about Shakespeare's actual involvement with it. It was a case of finding the adequate links (which do exist, through Sidney, Essex, Southampton, Love's Labours Lost and The Tempest) and emphasising the right aspects. What has always been lacking, even in Frances Yates' accounts of Hermetic Occult Neoplatonism, is any actual working knowledge of traditional Hermetic magic—and its relationship to products of imagination. Long, scholarly, exhaustive accounts of John Dee end up giving absolutely no idea of how he actually went about conjuring up an 'Angel'—in which he seems to have spent about three quarters of his waking time. So I thought it was worth working at a simple, comprehensible account of what exactly fascinated Chapman, Marlowe and the rest, in all that business. I think what I've done is more or less as I need it—for background to my arguments later. But I'll be grateful for your comments.

Please don't be too appalled by the mess I've made of these pages. Taken inch by inch, I think everything is clear. As you see, I accept pretty well all your suggestions—or at least try to do something about your doubts.

Frances Yates (1899–1981), Renaissance scholar, was the author of *Giordano Bruno and the Hermetic Tradition* (1964) and *The Art of Memory* (1966).

  John Dee (1527–1608) advised Elizabeth I on astrological and scientific matters, and wrote the Hermetic work *Monas Hieroglyphica*.

To Ohna and Terence McCaughey

9 September 1991   Ms   British Library

Dear Oona and Terence—

  Wasn't it worth it? It was the richest day I've had for ages. Sorley is a complete marvel. I heard him the other day again on the radio—'Poet of the Month'—and there he was, clambering & crawling through his subterranean wonderland, coming up into amazing lit caverns, or coming against dead-ends & feeling his way back out and around. Totally himself and unselfconscious. Well, if only one could live long enough to be like that! Though he was never different, I'm sure.

You both looked wonderfully well. It really made me determined to renew my visits to Ireland. It's 3 or 4 years, maybe more, since I was over there.

Now that I'm released from my struggle with Shakespeare, which has been, more or less, a 2 year sentence dangling in a cage on the walls of the Tower of London—making what I could of the odd remark floating up off the street on the general Thames miasma, or the odd comment spat out through the arrowslits by such as Wriothesley & Raleigh (You'll be appalled when you see it, buckle at the knees when you try to lift it)—however, as I say, now that I'm released, it seems I might be free to do something else. Such as write this letter—to begin with.

I didn't catch many salmon. The collapse in UK (and Irish, except for the mysteriously blessed Moy) migratory fish stocks is finally here. Hardly any fish at all in these Devon rivers.

Carol is well & sends her love. Our house, which you've never seen, is now turned around—like the witch's house on its chicken leg. Our kitchen, where we live, instead of being a trench under walls 4 feet thick, with a dark prison window at chest height, looking East, opens directly into our garden, great windows, French doors, looking West. But today, the thatcher started. When he finishes, I shall have paid him 6 × what I paid for the whole house!

Love to all

Ted

TH and the McCaugheys had been in Edinburgh when the Queen presented Sorley MacLean with her Medal for Poetry at Holyroodhouse, in a ceremony that usually takes place at Buckingham Palace (see letter to Frieda Hughes of 23 November 1974).

To Christopher Reid

27 September 1991   Ts   Faber

Thank you for the Shakespeare Choice. I like it. But. The degeneration of the art of book design and printing between 1593 and 1609 is illustrated, sometimes, by the difference between the first Edition of Venus And Adonis and the first 1609 edition of the Sonnets. V & A was printed in beautiful bold typeface, the Sonnets in the dead flies picked off the tips of scribbler's quills, collected, dried and aligned. Now between you and me Christopher, handling the 1970 Shakespeare's paperback Choice and the 1991, leafing through them as a reader might, aren't you startled at the change—typeface half the size, book twice the thickness and weight. Instead of a subtle, elegant, bold typeface that enfolds the whole nervous system like a bedful of Geisha girls—a hard spattering of gravel from under the back wheels of an articulated truck on a dark night.

It's the old right and left hemisphere business. Unless the individual letters achieve the status of shapely images, the whole page falls into the vacuous lecture hall of the left hemisphere. The poem doesn't just happen, it has to be dug for—rescued. There's something in that. With other kinds of book, it doesn't matter so much.

Back wheels of an articulated truck wouldn't spatter, would they. Back wheels of an Autobahn bus maybe, the reader a sort of racing cyclist tucked in behind, gulping the carbon monoxide, and all these gravelly letters coming up between his teeth and under his eyelids.

The new design man seems very nice though, sympathetic. Maybe he'll change the trend.

A *Choice of Shakespeare's Verse* had been revised and reissued, in an edition that TH describes quite fairly.

The 'new design man' was Ron Costley.

To Seamus Heaney

28 November 1991   Ms   Emory

Dear Seamus—

Your letter came. I'm responding immediately—to hearten you (I hope) in this business of 'fibrillation'.

In 1959, I was sitting with Sylvia's 2 Uncles—one of them (a salesman) just recovering from a near-fatal heart-attack (at age 45 about) [*arrow to marginal addition:* (He's still alive)], the other—one of the big-chief Blood-Analysts in the U.S. They were talking hearts, & the big chief asks the convalescent: 'Do you ever get any twinges of it?" Whereupon the convalescent, holding his hand slightly curved as he might be stroking the head of a baby, stroked his left lapel with his finger-tips in a peculiar gesture (—I still feel that stroking movement, almost like the memory of a burn). 'Sometimes" he said "something, down here." As he said it, I had the sensation of a sword being pushed vertically down beside my neck into that hollow behind the left clavicle & so on down through my chest. I had such a precise idea because I used to stare at a sword in the University Anthropology Museum which had been used by the Chinese for ceremonial executions, using that method. (But first (worst) a tuft of wool was placed on the point of entry, & the sword point then pushed down through the wool—which was held in place by the fingers of the executioner's left hand. The sword was then withdrawn through the wool—which presumably cleaned the blade & took the first blood).

The point is: from that moment the beating of my heart was in chaos. I couldn't lie with my ear to the pillow, because the wild syncopations of the beat—sounding in the pillow—scared me too much. It seemed genuinely physical, because at times I would suddenly feel utterly strengthless, trembling etc. Gradually, it developed into real pains & aches—especially back ache (behind the heart, as if my ribs were bruised). I started a diary of the 'episodes'. Generally, I expected to drop dead every moment. Most of the time, I couldn't feel it—though I could hear it, if I listened, or feel it in my pulse. Once or twice I blacked out—for 2 or 3 seconds. (Once with George Macbeth—just after I'd agreed to serve on his Critic's Panel—discussing Bacon's paintings. I recovered before I hit the floor (though I hit it). Then I told him: 'I've changed my mind. Count me out.')

I went to a doctor (in England) in 1960, & he called it Tachycardia or something such, & gave me a tranquilliser—which didn't affect it. About a year later, another doctor called it something else, gave me another tranquilliser, & told me it was 'not uncommon'. I never told Sylvia.

Then I read in Scientific American an account by some medic in the American Civil War. He had commented on the number of disordered hearts that were reporting to him. These became so numerous that he made a survey, & discovered that $1/3$ of the soldiers between 25 & 35 complained of irregular, staggering, stumbling, jittery heart-beats. The commentary widened this and concluded that this sort of heart disorder is almost general among males above 25/30, up to 45, who are leading stressful lives.

That convinced me (as I had already tried to convince myself) that my ailment was purely psychological. So I hypnotised myself, over a week, asking for 'instructions'—to correct whatever, in my life, was wrong. Finally, I got them—blindingly clear!! (The whole business—about 3 years up to that point—was tangled with sinister dreams).

Very strange, that following the instructions—though it smashed up everything—was effortless and in spite of the general psychological cataclysm absolutely resolute. And from the moment that I understood the 'instructions'—my heart righted itself. From the very moment. After 3 years.

After that—not a murmur from it, in spite of no lack of big upheavals & 4th degree stress, until about 1975. I had settled happily into my routine (and our farm), and—as is now painfully clear to me—I had just found the thread-end of what I ought to have spent the next 5 years following up, when I set out to take part in the Ilkley Festival (for which I'd written various things) and after that the Cambridge Festival. The morning we set out, my heart started—very strong, alarming, obtrusive. I remember thinking, as I ploughed through my act at Cambridge 'I don't see how the organ can possibly keep it up—it's got to break down, & I shall collapse here like an idiot.' I panicked so badly, I dashed about like a squirrel & a tree-weasel combination—trying everything to 'correct' whatever my error was. But my heart didn't settle till I sank back (sheer exhaustion) and tried to take up that thread-end of writing, & more or less locked myself up, two or three years later.

Since then, it recurs as a sort of warning. The moment I agree to do something it doesn't want me to do—it starts. Now (I imagine—61st year) it's presumably more serious. But usually I can stop it by figuring out what my mistake is, & undoing that. I had a bad day (first for some time) last week. In general, what sets it off is—agreeing to do something that will put me in what I feel to be a false situation, literally, involving myself in anything that I can't put my heart into, yet where I will have to lay myself on the line.

God knows, ordinary cowardice, idleness, etc could get to controlling me in that way. But my feeling is, my sensation is, during 'attacks', that I've somehow been drawn 'out of myself', that I'm flapping about somewhere above myself, and if only I could get deeply back into myself, into my own body & private self, I'd be O.K.

Something to do, maybe, with allowing myself to be lured too far from the bolt-hole back into mother's womb—you know, your own bodily being as a mobile mother's womb substitute. I've sometimes thought that maybe if I smoked (cigarettes) that might help—substitute mother's breast. Maybe that's why the tough guy only looks really dangerous and tough when he's smoking—you know, instinctively, that he's intact, he has his total security there at his lips, inhaling the womb-drug (unborn babies drink constantly). After mother's death, we're all more precarious, too, exposed.

On the other hand, I recently read (I'll try & find the reference) irregularity of the heart-rhythm is entirely dictated by signals from the frontal lobes—simultaneous contradictory signals, peremptory commands that clash. [*Marginal addition connected to underlined passage:* Shakespeare obviously suffered from it badly—it frightens Lear (OH, how this mother swells up towards my heart: Hysterica passio etc) and Leontes, whose heart 'dances' 'but not with joy'. etc.] If these signals are neutralised (some drug will do it), the heart instantly returns to normal. Evidently. (Or lobotomy will do it!!)

So—what are your simultaneous contradictory signals, permanently at full klaxon reveille?

From the right frontal lobe "Write Poems" and simultaneously, from the left frontal lobe (the lobe of rational, well-adjusted behaviour, logic & moral control) "Do this for so & so, right now, and also for so & so do that, and go here (don't shirk it) for this one, and go there (always be as good as your word) for that one, and—and—and. These are your duties. Your duties. Your duties. Your duties." (As old Basil Bunting used to say "To hell with it.")

You know the 3 'temptations' that the King of this world, the Lord of Delusion, presented to Buddha. First, Kama—the world of desire. Second, Mara—the world of the terrors of death. Third, Dharma—the world of social duties & domestic obligations. Buddha ignored them all. He had a note printed: "Shamash, the Lord Buddha, hereby cancels all appointments." Everybody carried on perfectly happily without him. Their festival programmes instantly found another name, the event organisers simply wrote to the next person on their list, the administrators quickly found a replacement, the booked-up arrangements were simply cancelled, as in war, blizzard, power-cut, or strike of transport-workers. The Antagonist, the great King of Delusion, curled up into a writhing homunculous the size of an ant, & fell raging through a crack in a dried-out cow-clap.

My words are suspect. I remember, years ago, advising you not to 'waste your time' doing a series of lectures. I have just spent 2 years—total gap—writing a 'lecture' that nobody will ever read (nobody will be able to read). Just when I'd got to something I really wanted to write. This left brain is a tyrant. And this blaming of the left brain for these distracting substitute labours is probably another example of its tyranny. [*Marginal addition by last sentence:* You know Yeats 'greatest temptation of the Artist'. ('Creation without toil')]

School-Bag: I'll go ahead making a selection—then if you like come in late on with a few corrective amplifications. It's really to be as we discussed, the golden oldies—but presented as the apparatus in a memory gymnasium. We'll see how it goes. (Another 'substitute' activity!)

Meanwhile—well, remember Buddha. In my case, whenever this heart-dither touches me, I think of the Arab Proverb: "Wherever you go—go with your whole heart. If you can't go with your whole heart—don't go." And I've noticed, when I get into hectic high-stress situations where I'm on the attack—i.e. where I want to be (my Court business, my local Govt skirmishes)—never any problem. But if I agree to "grace" a public event, especially a semi-literary event, or where I'm to appear as "that curiosity"—that will finish me off, one day, probably.

Some medic in the Andes noticed that the Incas carried little pouches of Kelp—dried obviously—that they chewed. When he asked why, they told him: "For the heart" (at those high altitudes). So he investigated. That's how kelp came to be first-line medicament for all heart problems. [*Arrow to marginal addition:* Sea-water concentrate!] Kelp tablets. Note that.

And Vitamin E.

But first & foremost: cut out one of the contradictory imperatives from the old (new, rather) forebrain. Here endyth ye firste lesson.

I wouldn't dream of leaking this tokay essenzia of fungoid advice—if it weren't that I consider myself a freakish far-into-posthumous life survivor of a delinquent heart, yea, against all odds. Only periapts & distillations, sleight of mind & telekinesis have got me this far.

But forgive me if it's wearied you, all this—love from us to you all.   Ted   Keep in touch.

1992

Shakespeare and the Goddess of Complete Being was published in March. Its critical reception was strikingly polarised: most academics and Shakespeare specialists were hostile, while such poets and intellectually free spirits as had the opportunity to write about it – e.g. Marina Warner (see letter to Ben Sonnenberg of 17 May) – greeted it as a major work.

To Wendy Cope

26 March 1992   Ms   Cope

Dear Wendy—

   I've had a lot of real pleasure out of 'Serious Concerns'—laughed out loud here and there. I like your deadpan fearless sort of way of whacking the nail on the head—when everybody else is trying to hang pictures on it.
   I miss our judgings.
        Keep well

                          Ted

Congratulations, also, on getting the best typeface out of Fabers for 14 years. It means they expect your poems to be read.

Serious Concerns, Wendy Cope's second collection of poems, had just appeared. TH and Cope had been judges of the *Observer* Poetry Competition for Children for several consecutive years

To Derwent May

10 April 1992   Ts   May

Dear Derwent,

   What a pity The Times didn't give my book to somebody who wasn't straightjacketted inside the English Tripos. Trouble with the dominant Gauleiters in that world is they don't know a thing outside their handful of disciplinary texts and nothing has ever happened to them. Those who know more and have learned otherwise keep their mouths shut and creep about, like estate workers among the gentry. The whole outfit stinks of pusillanimity and intellectual disgrace. They exactly correspond to those brave souls who ran Stalin's Writer's Union, and no doubt would have rushed to the same securitate jobs if ever that illusion had got here. They know this too and smile weakly at each other.

When I was at University these fellows tried their damndest to frighten and discourage me, and destroy what few free brain cells I tried to keep from them. Ever since, forty years, they've kept it up. And for forty years I've watched them destroying wave after wave of talented students.

When you hear the English Faculty and these Guardians of the Humanities praised remember this: for the last thirty years, each year I've seen the work of the selected geniuses among 10 to 17 year olds from the whole UK—in fact I've helped select it. More natural talent than you could believe could exist in one country. Every year I watch the march past of these little stars, all bursting with hope—hurrying excitedly off to read English according to their natural bent and their utter ignorance of what is waiting for them in those abattoirs. We used to follow their careers—after about ten years we relaxed. Now we just notice and remember names. In 30 years not a single one has survived to reappear the other side of University as something unusual—one or two children's writers, a girl wrote a novel. The whole lot are annihilated. (The pick out of fifty thousand entries). The oldest of our one-time winners now 50. I know how it happens because I know what I went through scrambling through the barbed wire and the camp searchlights. Regularly I receive letters from students in their second or third year— in absolute despair, sending me their poems, begging for some direction out of the nightmare they've got themselves into. Brian Cox, at Manchester, a few years ago, said he couldn't bear to go on doing it. Every year they come rushing over no-man's-land towards us (these are his words) faces shining with youth—and we just mow them down. But who ever hears about this? Only half a dozen competition judges know it's happening. And here is Griffiths flexing his knees to review my little line up of prisoners.

And yet, Derwent, you shared his opinion. I can't quite believe that, a man who delights in the blooming of the thousand flowers. I'd have hoped to find some solidarity in you. I would ask you my boring question but I fear it might sound impertinent. Still you could try it on others—you'll get some surprises. I'm sure you're as familiar with The Complete Works as old faithfuls used to be with the Prayer Book. But next time you're in an amiable group of honest folk just try: how many of Shakespeare's plays have you read? How many more than once? Have you ever read the two long poems? Just try it, sneakily and casually. Among ordinary folk, who tell you more or less the truth, I have yet to find anybody—other than English Professors and Peter Redgrove—who have read more than twelve more than twice. The average—read even once—I find to be eight. (I've been popping this question now and again for years. I know lots of my friends are not very literate, but I ask writers too). Sylvia Plath had read six. Nor did she read any more while I knew her. Years spent on run of the mill garbage and the old boy left quite unregarded, murmured about and yawned over—like a mountain up half the sky. So my book's real problem isn't that nobody knows the religious background.

No, I lie, I might have found two or three who have read more—crankish souls.

I was surprised to see you winking at the media cameras and sticking yourself on that bit of fly-paper about the bore.

You take care, in your kind (well, almost kind. I expect you were brought in as a poultice to repair some of Griffith's mugging damage, and you felt poultices should be (a) very hot—'it can't heal if it doesn't hurt a bit', and (b) with ginger). (Also, I know you snipers out there have to protect your flanks.)—you take care in your note of qualified kindness to isolate my verses of observation a la May from anything that might be so intellectually chaotic as Griffith's idea of what he dis-approves of, myth, metamorphosis etc, as if you were removing the rainforest to reveal the thin one-season illusion of excellent soil. As if the rainforest had somehow overwhelmed and hijacked and wholly infested the one good thing.

Even poor old Crow, you have him trudge out on your parade-ground as a salt of the earth half-literate scouse, rough as hell of course but a good chap in a tight corner on occasions, a bit of a thistle.

Derwent, a secret: Before he became pseudo history King Lear was the Llud who was Bran, the god-king of early Britain, who was a com-bination—to cut short a long story that would bore you—of Apollo and his son the Healer Asclepius (by the Crow Goddess Coronis—the White Crow). Well, I don't suppose that sounds very relevant.

Apollo, Asclepius and Bran were Crow Gods. (Bran's 'sister', Branwen, who was the cause of the great mythic battle with Ireland in which Bran received his mortal wound, was a White Crow—Branwen means: White Crow). Llud as I say was Lear: Lear was the high-priest-king of a Crow God, a representative of the Bran who was the Llud who gave his name to London, though it was Bran whose head was buried in his shrine on Tower Hill, which gave us his Ravens to protect Britain—i.e. the little chaps hopping about there at this moment. If you follow the line of association you see that King Lear, at the centre of Shakespeare, and the earliest totem of Britain, Bran's Crow—well, make of it what you like. I daresay it's all rubbish to you. But not to me, Derwent. So my Crow is Apollo the Sun God the Mighty Archer and Asclepius the Healer who are Bran, fallen like King Lear destitute and naked on evil modern times. That's where I got him. Without all that mish mash you wouldn't have been able to say a thing about him in your piece because he wouldn't have existed, he would never have emerged without that big funny egg.

My Hawk, as would occur to anybody who had any interest in the symbols that made the West, is Horus. But Horus as the nobler of the two brothers in the fight over Cordelia—Gwyn (the White One), who was the spiritual son of Bran (as, in spite of Griffiths, Edgar is the spiritual son of Lear). Edgar in Llyr's myth is Gwyn. Gwyn, as a British Hero, bequeathed all his legends to Arthur. Yea, it was so. My Hawk is the sleeping, deathless spirit of Arthur/Edgar/Gwyn/Horus—the sacrificed and reborn self of the great god Ra. Hence the line: 'The sun is behind me'. Hence, indeed, all the other lines. I don't just jot these things down, you know. If I can't bring them out of the pit I don't get them.

I could bore you further. In the first drafts of my poem Pike, which I daresay you'd class with my snowdrops, in some University Archive, the Pike is Michael, the Archangel nearest to God (Michael means like God)—the creature that 'will come from the water' (he is the Angel of Water) 'With a fish tail and talk' (in Yeats). The advocate of Israel (the imprisoned and dispossessed). Who brought the dust from which God made man. Who planted the reed in the sea around which Rome's hills accumulated. Who fought all night with Jacob at the Ford. I had him (my pike Michael) hanging—almost but not quite motionless, in the great glory (the blinding dazzle) that radiates from the throne. He is the personal chaperon of the Shekinah—the female aspect of God, and wherever he appears, she is there.

Balderdash of course. Silly business about God and such. Good heavens, what would Griffiths and the other taught starlings say. Well, we know, don't we.

So it goes.

Retournions a nos goutte-neiges.

Yours
Ted

All this sort of thing was far more current, the chatter of the excited flock, in the 1580s 90s etc, than it is now—or ever has been since. Shakespeare, untouched by the frosty breath of the Griffiths of this land, cannot have not known it—and much, much more, but whether he used it according to Griffiths and his kind or according to me and my kind is up for grabs. No doubt Griffiths would vote, with a pitying smile, for himself. He knows that Shakespeare was allowed to know and think only what Griffiths decrees he shall be allowed to have known and thought—there's a tortuous sentence for a torture chamber.

As European Arts Editor on *The Times*, Derwent May had seen Eric Griffiths's contemptuous review of *Shakespeare and the Goddess of Complete Being* before it went to press. May, who also wrote a column of nature notes for the paper, persuaded its Literary Editor to let him write a complementary article on TH as an outstanding 'poet of nature', to be printed alongside Griffiths's, on 9 April. Griffiths is a Fellow of Trinity College, Cambridge. TH also sent a letter of rebuttal to Simon Jenkins, the Editor of *The Times*, who printed it under the heading, 'Shakespeare and the Goddess: A Reply to Eric Griffiths', on 16 April 1992. An extract from the letter that TH addressed to 'Simon Jenkins personally' is given below.

Brian Cox is C. B. Cox (1928–2008), formerly John Edward Taylor Professor of English at Manchester University. His book *The Great Betrayal: Memoirs of a Life in Education* was published in 1992.

'My Hawk' is the hawk whose voice is heard in 'Hawk Roosting' (*Lupercal*).

In Yeats's 'The Happy Land', in which the Archangel Michael is invoked, it is in fact Gabriel who 'will come from the water / With a fish-tail, and talk / Of wonders . . .'.

'Retournions a nos goutte-neiges': 'Let's get back to our snowdrops', in Franglais.

To Simon Jenkins

11 April 1992   Ts (photocopy)   Emory

Any discussion of the book is not about Shakespeare or me—it's about importance of spiritual tradition versus unimportance of it, importance of imaginative life or censorship of same, sterility of artistic life versus abundance of artistic life, the survival of group culture versus the suicide of group culture, depth and reality of psychological life versus Academic orthodoxy etc etc etc. The issues seem to me important, general.

Whether the Civil War is still being fought or isn't.

Whether two historical demonic forces are at large in Northern Ireland or whether it's a matter of job competition and group loyalties at football team or neighbouring streets level, and petty tribal warfare kept astir by demagogues.

Whether the Tory party revolves round the old Norman/Anglo Saxon axis and Labour round the Celtic Fringe. Or perhaps that's going a bit fine.

To A. L. Rowse

15 April 1992   Ts (photocopy)   Emory

Common sense. I enclose a response I wrote to a malicious and incredibly superficial article in The Sunday Times by John Carey. I hope he isn't a friend of yours. I make the distinction, as you see, between great realistic poets, and great mythic poets—and define Shakespeare as a unique combination of the two. Since nobody in England recognises the psychological vitality of myth, in poetic imagination, any more than they recognise the meaning of their own dreams, this hasn't been much thought about—and comes as a most unwelcome intrusion: that such a thing as a mythic poet can exist. But see my piece.

But—common sense. Whenever was the plot and poetic logic of Macbeth or King Lear common sense? Or recognisable to common sense as anything but a language different from common sense?

Eliot as a scarecrow in The Hollow Men, Yeats' 'Woman's beauty is like a white frail bird, like a white sea-bird . . . blown between dark furrows upon the ploughed land' or himself as a bird made by a Grecian goldsmith, Keats as a grain of wheat rotting in South Devon under the rain, Blake dining with Isaiah and Ezekiel etc make it as simple as can be for Shakespeare to be a salamander (actually, to be fair, I say his 'art' was a salamander) where spiritual life is an inferno. Surely I can be allowed this in a work that closes the door to scholars?

In my introduction I tell my reader this work is a Song. When you come to a sea, and there are such things, you have to swim or sail, but you can't just go on walking across the bottom saying 'I insist that all this foolish water be removed.'

My book is logical in the way that algebra is logical, which is to say in a way that scholarship is not. As you will see, logical like a detective novel, if you could ever get to like it.

[. . .]

Yes, I agree about down to earth fact. What English scholars (I never include you in my disparaging sense of that term, as I've said, and I don't mind if it sounds like flattery, I read your scholarship with actual excitement, a very rare experience. I think because you find the same kinds of thing interesting—the same as I do, that is. Though I suppose my scope in English history is very very much narrower.) What English scholars cannot concede is that myth is a collection of facts—in any of its specific usages. Myth in Keats Lamia is a series of 'facts'—psychologically hard data. At large, the myth of the Lamia returns to fluidity—the infinite possibility, till somebody else seizes it and fastens it into a shape of fact by making it the 'word' of a psychological condition that is as 'real' as anything in life can be. In that sense, myth in Shakespeare becomes a kind of hard fact. So I can deal with the elements of it exactly as if they were the components of an algebra—hard values, but at every point susceptible to modification by other hard values. This is the strangeness of my book to those scholars who are incapable of thinking off that tightrope between the word on the page and its source point in some literature or publication. Scholarship seems to me important in that all mythical data are based on what I know as reliable, consistent materials in the vast literature of myth and its associated fields. Lit. Scholars deny me, simply, a different kind of scholarship. Because I haven't cocked my leg at every reference, as Goethe says, and piddled a little scholarly note, to reassure the next dog along. What my book has revealed to me among scholars (which I suppose I knew anyway) is their galactic ignorance of anything outside their specialised corner in their University library. And their incapacity of seeing any problem unless they already know the answer. Reading their reviews is like watching somebody scan a crossword puzzle commenting instantly only on those clues to which somebody just a few hours ago told them the answer. Then they throw the paper aside and go off yawning. I know you're as familiar with it as I am. I have ten thousand anecdotes of their typical behaviour.

Again, I except the real ones—some of the most interesting men and minds that I know.

In omitted sections of this letter, TH makes clear to the historian A. L. Rowse (1903–97) that he admires him as a Shakespeare scholar and is indebted to him for such insights as his identification of the poet Aemilia Lanier with Shakespeare's 'Dark Lady'. Rowse had, however, in the *Financial Times* of 11 April, treated *Shakespeare and the Goddess of Complete Being* as haughtily as any other academic – including John Carey, whose review in the *Sunday Times* led to a long falling-out (see letter to Carey of 6 October 1998).

The opening lines of Yeats's play *The Only Jealousy of Emer* are slightly misquoted. The Keats reference is to his letter to George and Georgina Keats of 19 March 1819. Blake writes of dining with the prophets in *The Marriage of Heaven and Hell*.

To Mrs Wylie

[1992]   Ts (photocopy)   Emory

Dear Mrs Wylie,

I'm sorry my Shakespeare book disagreed with you.

After thirty five years in the writing business, I can say—believe me—that not one reader in fifty will accept the meaning of the simplest sentence. Almost without exception, they will be reminded of something, by the sentence, and assume that's the meaning. A strange fact that you may have noticed in others.

I don't expect you can bear to face my book again, but please take my word for it—you have misunderstood it hopelessly.

Everything that I say about the 'rationality' of man and the nature of woman, in the plays—misunderstood hopelessly.

Everything about the Boar—!

I took pains to make my argument clear—and some have understood it well enough to convince me that I didn't make a total mess of it.

But in you, all I've released is an avalanche of—preconceptions (you even have preconceptions about me!), assumptions etc.

Well, I apologise, for upsetting you.

But I can't help asking: you mention the 'man/woman in the street from Finchley to Fiji who marry, live in a semi, have 2½ children' and don't concern themselves with 'abstractions' or 'things of the soul and mind' which, according to you, are of interest only to 'mystics, creative artists, scholars etc'. Supposing these people actually do exist (immune to the 'things of the soul and mind' that are driving Northern Ireland, Jugoslavia and in fact much of the world crazy), how do you suppose they look across at you (from their tourist bus, presumably), seeing you sitting there on the grass outside Stratford Theatre, as you wait in glorious anticipation for King Lear or Macbeth or Timon etc. You tell me I'm wrong (you accuse me of worse things, if you recall) for wanting my cake and eating it. But this lady on the grass—

If I would be better not to write my book, out of respect for those Finchleyite Fijians and their unconcern for 'things of the soul and mind'—and yet this Party Official seems to have—well, one doesn't know what to think.

You must agree, you wrote me a strange letter.

Yours
Ted Hughes

Mrs Wylie has not been identified.

To Ben Sonnenberg

17 May 1992   Ts Emory

I had anticipated that scholarly howl of indignation of course. Having utterly ignored my idea for twenty years (since I first sketched it in the Introduction of the Shakespeare Verse Anthology that I did in 1970) they could hardly, I thought, suddenly welcome it with open arms. Also, I could not expect our humanist post-Anglican secular orthodoxy suddenly to agree that their four hundred year censorship and prohibition of what I am trying to unearth was, as I most emphatically argue that it was, a calamitous mistake—and in fact a human crime that has by now virtually destroyed English Society, English Education, English individual life (all with the most rigourous and concerted application of the best minds in each generation).

Absolutely in character, they took on themselves the role, they identified absolutely with the tragic hero in my book, the Adonis who rejects everything outside his puritan routine of fixed ideas, and in particular the spiritual, emotional and imaginative life (embodied for him in woman)—in other words rejects in every situation the human factor, the subjective factor. They have dealt with my book precisely as Adonis

611

dealt with Venus in the long poem that is the DNA of my argument. And my book of course is the full statement of his crime, and his punishment. So that screech from the dock was inevitable.

[. . .]

Marina Warner's review is extraordinarily canny and sensitive about my own unspoken feelings [*marginal insertion:* (about several things)]—about the strange business of The Tempest, where, after the final perfect redemption of his Female in the Winter's Tale, that culmination of the whole series, he suddenly goes right back to the beginning, and deals with Sycorax (and as I say, with Dido) more savagely than in any previous play except Lear. I say nothing about this in the book, or not much. But I explain it as: after his ideal, ritual correction of the real situation, his reparation of the actual disaster (the puritan triumph, the destruction of woman, nature and the wholeness of existence) in The Winter's Tale, he dropped back into realism and simply stated the case: made a straight portrait of the historical moment and everything latent within it. A play of fundamental despair, fundamental bafflement with the given elements of mankind, fundamental tolerance of what has to be hideous, contradictory and ultimately self-destructive. At the same time, paradoxical delight in the perverse beauty of it all.

It did occur to me, as I got to the end—hacked my way through the thicket forest at last, and found the sleeping beauty—that I now need a whole other book to formulate woman's experience not only of the male's duality (his divided self and the tragic consequences for him and her) but of her own double nature. I get to it on the very last page. Now that would be something much bigger.

But no more prose.

Marina Warner (b.1946), novelist and cultural historian, had reviewed *Shakespeare and the Goddess of Complete Being* for the *Times Literary Supplement*. TH sent her a grateful letter on 12 June.

To Christopher Reid

21 June 1992   Ts   Faber

Dry Fly Fishing is a psychologically determined activity—making slight understatements at the surface in the hope of interesting the organic mysteries and terrors in the depth: attitude of detatchment, actually the concession of a basic reluctance to get involved. The English Art—which explains why it became identified with the class stratification that it did. On the most elite trout streams, in Hampshire etc, fishing with a lure (an imitation nymph or something of the sort) beneath the surface is actually forbidden. It is <u>not done</u>. It corresponds quite closely (culturally) to typical attitudes to poetic form, this regime of the Dry Fly. On the other hand, when it works it can be the most fun. For trout it is definitely more fun.

The opposite approach (poacher's approach) comes up in the next poem: Stealing Trout. There, ideally, you get down into the river bed and grab them with your bare hands.

An all-rounder has to be master of all the methods that produce the goods and the thrill.

TH's lesson to his editor is incidental to a discussion of the revised text of *River*, as it was to appear in *Three Books*, the 1993 volume that also included *Cave Birds* and *Remains of Elmet*. 'Stealing Trout on a May Morning', not in the 1983 edition of *River*, was transplanted from *Recklings*.

To Tom Paulin

13 August 1992   Ms   Emory

You know the story (from a German Tank Commander, pal of my brother's—Was a Russian prisoner): he claimed—the Russian offensive, correction, the German offensive against Russia would have been a walkover except for one detail. The German automatic weaponry was precision engineering, clearances of a millionth in the working parts—trade-fair masterpieces. The Russian automatic weaponry was crude, approximately filed, hammered & bent into place. But the Russian guns, buried in mud, dug out, would carry on killing happily, spitting grit out of their gaps. One smear of coloured water & the German guns seized up, ceased to be guns, became lumber. The end of every battle out there, he said, was the Germans overwhelmed, 'using their jammed guns as clubs'. Or with their tanks helpless as old taxis. A pitiful tale. In the black Russian mud.

Now what the German weapons lacked—was what prose should look for. Yes? Once had.

And what verse finds in 'negative capability'.

But what it all needs is—readers who, basically, share your mythos. (Don't need every word precision workshop engineering).

Now what my Shakes book runs into is—readers who don't share my mythos (let alone Shakespeare's).

All this is to give you a perspective on the enclosed—and on my rejigging of a few old polarities (into a single working model).

And why I could never hope to get past Ayer's Island—let alone land on it. A.J. Ayer's—the Caliban* whose mother was Max Muller ("myth is a disease of language".) And all those higher other noises his Isle is full of. (England, actually.)

* The Polyphemus, I mean.

The poet and critic Tom Paulin (b.1949) had reviewed *Shakespeare and the Goddess of Complete Being* in the *London Review of Books* of 9 April. The review was warmly enthusiastic, but questioned the 'batty syncretism' that allowed TH to suppose that Shakespeare might have known 'through the Occult Neoplatonist route, the legend of Buddha's enlightenment'. This is the postscript to a letter which TH had written 'just to be tenacious', and which accompanied a revised introduction to the book.

A. J. Ayer (1910–89), Oxford philosopher, was a thoroughgoing religious sceptic. Max Müller (1823–1900), German Orientalist, pioneered the study of comparative religion.

To Daniel Weissbort

18 October 1992   Ms   Emory

At least you're being spared the general joy at the publication of Larkin's letters. Faber ought to be paying compensation to all their other authors. Understand all forgive all etc—but that modest, unassuming, unnoticeable little flower (as he describes his own poetry somewhere in some poem) peers from the crown of one of those stinking bile-green weeds that use all their energy concocting poisons to spray all around them— trying to kill everything, basically, that shares the same plot & bit of light. All that self-loathing, at full spurt, bubble, ooze & drip. His tribe laps it up. What a phenomenon. Well, as they say, the underwear's in the open.

Selected Letters of Philip Larkin 1940–1985 (1992), edited by Anthony Thwaite, revealed unsuspected, or hitherto uncorroborated, aspects of Larkin's personality, including his loathing of most contemporary poets – TH pre-eminently. In his remark on 'that modest, unassuming, unnoticeable little flower', TH may be thinking of Larkin's early poem 'Modesties', where the flowers in question are, in fact, produced by weeds.

To Ohna and Terence McCaughey

19 October 1992 Ms British Library

Anyway, what this visit did was re-open my rabbit run to Ireland. It's about 6 years, maybe 7, since I was over there. I was mightily relieved to see how little had changed—in some ways, things are better. At least around Lough Arrow, in Sligo they are. We crawled into one of the passage graves on that height South of Lough Arrow. Very good. Barrie Cooke has a new place—on the site of the 2nd battle of Moytura. I'd never realised before that the apocalyptic congress of the Dagda and the Morrigu took place astride the Unshin—a little river (flows out of Lough Arrow) I dearly love (holds huge trout, dropped back into it out of the Lough).

Also, visited Clonmacnois and—what do you think?—was a bit dismayed to find it more or less encapsulated in designer fresh masonry, the ghastly raw carapace of an 'interpretative centre'. St Kieran's cell was powerful stuff, even so.

All my old craving to live over there revived with a bang. As we drove up into the town, off the boat, Nicholas said: "What a relief to be out of suffocating England and twisty Wales." He feels about England much as I do. It's not only freedom from the English psycho-social control system (as that's coded into voices, faces, the general look of things). It's a matter, I think, of inner space. Ireland has inner space—which England almost wholly lacks. To my feeling, Ireland is a bit like muslim countries, and Spain, in that way.

The passage graves, dating from the Megalithic era, are at Carrowkeel, in County Sligo.
St Kieran was the sixth-century founder and first Abbot of Clonmacnois.

To Nick Gammage

21 October 1992   Ms   Gammage

Dear Nick—

I haven't forgotten the manuscript.

Answering your earlier letter, about Eliot—I don't feel the contradiction as much as you do. It's certain he's a very complicated case. If one were to regard his poetry as a performance of 'healing power'—that continues to operate with effect—I don't think one can assume that when he ceased to write poetry, he ceased to be a 'healer'. It could be—only at that point did he become fully-fledged, & performed his rôle thereafter on a less evident wavelength. One can't really say anything about it—too little is known.

Or it could be that his poetic healing career lasted only so long as he was struggling out of his own sickness. The Shamanic state of mind is—in many ways—unconditioned, non-adapted, infantile or even pre-birth, half animal. Or can be. That is a great part of its 'affliction'—schizophrenia, even psychosis, are fairies at that cradle, bearing their magic mushrooms. One can live a life struggling with the successive crises of that—or, with exceptional character, one can actually 'heal' it, & become, if only precariously, fully adult, wholly human. In our society, the pressures to force the individual to heal him or her self & go through the whole psychic transformation, becoming 'adult' and so to speak 'normal', are immense. Ideally, the result should be—a saint, a sage.

Shakespeare, too, after all, completed the work—and stopped producing. But both Eliot & Shakes were—in biological terms—quite old, when they stopped, and ill too. Did they become saintly, or sages? I think so.

As for your projected work—the truth is, Nick, I would prefer to know as little as possible about what is written about my writing. As far as I'm concerned, I hang on tooth and nail to my own view of what I do—which is a view from the inside. It is fatally easy to acquire, through other people, a view of one's own work from the outside. As when a child is admired, in its hearing, for something it does naturally. Ever after—that something is corrupted with self-consciousness. It does not need admiration to do this—half-true description & analysis is quite enough. I have seen many talented people ruined by just this. It sounds silly—but there it is. Human beings are composed of silliness—very few are incorruptible at any point. But I'll answer questions for you, now & again.

Was that your Lupercal?

Keep well

Yours

Ted H.

After reading TH's collected writings on T. S. Eliot, *A Dancer to God*, published in September, Gammage had expressed his doubts about Eliot's credentials as a shamanic healer. He had also thanked TH for signing his copy of *Lupercal* at the Cheltenham Literary Festival. His own 'projected work' was a study of the genesis of *Crow*, interrupted during the 1990s but lately resumed.

To Nick Gammage

15 December 1992   Ts   Gammage

Dear Nick,

Four questions are to the point. Song—yes. Well—of all the verse in my books that is the one piece I got hold of <u>before</u> I stepped into the actual psychological space of contemporary literature, smogged as that is by the critical exhalations and toxic smokestacks and power stations of Academe. So it is the one song I sang in Arcadia—that came to me literally out of the air, utterly unaware of all that lay ahead, like Aphrodite blowing ashore, eager for a blissful life of endless pro-creation. Next thing, I stumbled into the smog—gasmasks, protective clothing, armour, weaponry, survival by the skin of the teeth, earth-quaking of ignorant armies, the general ninth circle of life among our colleagues and culture police. So—I just wonder how it would have been if this age had been, like all previous ages, without professionalised criticism elevated into an educational system. It would have been different.

Most of my colleagues, after all, didn't survive at all. In 1951 the University paper *Varsity* asked the 400 odd first year English students why they wanted to read English. All wanted to be novelists, poets, playwrights etc. Only a handful wanted to be teachers—I'm not sure any wanted to be 'critics' (those were very early days). Yet of that year, I don't know any who have since become novelists, poets, playwrights. Maybe there's the odd one here or there. Some very talented people—disappeared in the 'psychic cleansing'. The only well known poet from my year is Peter Redgrove—and he read Physics. On the other hand—

would they all have become novelists, poets etc—if there had been no Leavis spearheading the New Criticism? I suppose not. Still, it makes you think. There's an interesting sociology paper to be written on the contrast between what first year students reading English hope for—and what they have to settle for and why. Brian Cox—the Chairman of the National Curriculum English Working Group—told me some years back that he couldn't bear to go on with it: seeing the brilliant hopeful young flooding onto the battlefield, all hoping to be shown how to write novels and plays and poems, and year after year (he said) 'we just mow them down'.

Well, it's a strange business. I feel to know what it's like because of the effects on me of my first two years reading English. It was another three years (six years after 'Song') that I got hold of my next intact verses. No, another two years—a year after I left University. But I never again made contact with that natural music of Song.

2. Yes, I translated Seneca's Oedipus in among writing the Crow pieces in the book. Main influence was—the stylistic release of finding a simple language and tone for a supercharged theme. The sheer day after day practice of striving for that. Affected the style of Crow. Though a good many of them I wrote before I touched Oedipus.

3. My connection with the Palaeolithic world and earlier dates from my childhood. All my early years were lived in a dream of being such a hunter (with my brother—whose imaginative world that was: he was much older (ten years), and had large hunting territories all to himself which became mine). I didn't read Inheritors until my mid thirties—a while after I'd read Lord Of The Flies and Pincher Martin. My essay about The Inheritors in John Carey's book of essays about Golding was my way of writing an essay remotely connected with that world without touching Lit Crit, or indeed Golding.

4. That poem is the hieros gamos moment in the alchemical resuscitation of the protagonist. Like the 'soul' in the Bardo Thodol, having won his way to rebirth (the Bardo Thodol would say, having lost the opportunity of escaping from the cycle of death and rebirth), he 'sees' his parents begetting him: he sees the psychic reunion that then manifests itself in his rebirth as a new 'soul'—on a transcendent plane. So the marriage is (a) the ritual reassembly of the shattered fragments of his total being (b) his reunion with his lost 'life'—with the divine renewing healing life of his natural being (his 'bride'), and (c) the conception or

begetting of his 'rebirth'. Having died as a jumble of things, he is reborn (as in Egypt) as a Falcon. There are two principal actors in the drama: him—his trial, death, punishment, redemption and rebirth—and his 'bride' whose fate is parallel and contrapuntal.

5. No, these vacanas were written in and around and only gradually suggested themselves as a solution. The imagery of the story came out of the story. I always thought of another simultaneous parallel story—Lumb's experiences in the underworld, which do break through here and there into the written story. I did toy with the idea of actually writing it. I wish I had.

6. Except for the Rain Charm itself, the laureate pieces are written under the peculiar conditions in which the Royal Family themselves have to live. I mean, the extraordinary public Theatre into which they have been dragged and compelled to perform (by the tabloid media, as a drama serial) a moneyraiser for the media proprietors who (centred on the Republican Australian Murdoch) have located an inexhaustible vein of resentments in the great disaster of our times—the great English disaster of our English times—the disintegration of the union, the resurgence of old tribal differences. In this strange Theatre, the only people who raise their voices are the enemies of the Union. It is a peculiar thing: though the mass of the country feels much as it always did about the Royal family, they have no voices to say so. All the courage is with the vocable Republicans. It's like a gang tyranny: everybody wants it to be seen they're members of the gang—so they jeer and hoot and throw tomatoes from the back like the boldest. Nobody else dare raise a peep. It's a great national funk. So, believing as I do that the Monarchy has deep psychological significance for the union, and that the Republicans don't know what they're actually doing, what misery and worse they're howling for, I suppose I do in those later pieces affirm a kind of 'defence' of Monarchy in a pedagogic way, as you say, perhaps even a didactic way. Especially in the last piece which was written in the thick of the most indescribably mob howl. One paper even asked several poets to write Laureate poems since I didn't seem to be bestirring myself—and the clowns actually did submit their offerings. Together with little huffs and puffs about what I jolly well ought to be doing. Great solidarity in this trade. Then, when I actually did publish that last piece, it was pirated in a tabloid—who then rang round asking various writers for their opinion about it. And some actually replied. But even the Times wrote to various people

(various poets) asking for their opinion of it. That's Lit Crit in drag for you, or in sequins, or in Gary Glitter sparklesuit.

This last antic demonstrates one thing: culturally the country is now several utterly different groups, or sub-groups—all basically hating each other. Like the break up of Jugoslavia. The next thing, perhaps, will be regional 'protection rackets'—the country carved up into Mafia-type districts. I'm exaggerating of course. A poetical image got a bit out of hand there.

The main point: Laureate pieces can be of only two kinds. Ordinary poems that are incidentally dedicated to some royal person or occasion, (like The Rain Charm poem). Or verses written after the occasion as you might write verses for a masque or drama. Quite different.

In the book Crow the Oedipus Song was written to be sung by a gigantified African voice as accompaniment to a mime burlesque performed around the Phallus statue that stood centre stage at the end of the play. I still think it could have been good. Instead, we simply had 'Wot, no bananas' and the cast jiving about the stage and into the auditorium. Since my feeling about that sort of music is mainly sadness at its ersatz and pseudo thinness—it's pathetic nostalgia for what it so utterly lacks (real, primitive joy), I wasn't persuaded that we did solve the problem of what to do at the end. The shocking end.

I think Oedipus affected Crow thematically hardly at all—that's my sense of it. It dipped in more as an image for what was a central theme of Crow anyway—his relationship to his Creator who turns out to be a creatress.

I'm sending you a page of MS. It's a piece I rewrite about every four years. The first three sentences change. The rest stays pretty much as is. Also, I'm sending you the sequence of short jokes that in a way surround the point and infiltrate. The background I suppose is my Goddess book.

Thank you for Skakkebak's paper. You're telepathic. When your letter arrived I had just (an hour before) posted a letter to some Pathologist in Scotland who wanted to know about the dire fact (how could he not have heard—but I'm always amazed how little it concerns anybody, except Sakakkedbak and maybe Elkington), and I'd sent him a copy of the article in The Independent earlier this year. So now I'll send him a copy of this that you've sent me.

I got a copy of a book the other day by Nick Bishop. A very intelligent book, I think. Just published. He's read something of what I've read, and has a fellow feeling for it.

Keep well
Ted

'Song' is the poem so titled in *The Hawk in the Rain* – first line: 'O lady, when the tipped cup of the moon blessed you'.

TH's essay on *The Inheritors* (1955), 'Baboons and Neanderthals: A Rereading of *The Inheritors*', is in *William Golding: The Man and His Books* (1986), edited by John Carey.

'Bride and groom lie hidden for three days' is the 'hieros gamos moment' – i.e. where the sacred marriage ritual is performed – in *Cave Birds*. The 'vacanas' are Lumb's songs, collected in the 'Epilogue' of *Gaudete*. The last poem in *Rain-Charm for the Duchy* is 'A Masque for Three Voices', written for the Queen Mother's 90th birthday and dated 4 August 1990.

In 1992, the Danish doctor Niels Skakkebaek caused a stir when he published his analysis of data confirming a decline in the fertility of Western European males. John Elkington, chairman of SustainAbility and authority on sustainable development, had expressed the view that 'The sperm may yet prove to be the Trojan horse of reproductive toxicology' (*The Age*, 8 July 1985).

Nicholas Bishop's 'very intelligent' book was *Re-Making Poetry: Ted Hughes and a New Critical Psychology* (1991).

To Anne-Lorraine Bujon

16 December 1992   Ts   Bujon

Dear Anne-Lorraine Bujon—

I am enclosing one or two pieces that I had cause to look at recently, and that are remotely linked to your questions.

Your question 1: I will break it into parts.

a.   'you choose subjects outside yourself'. At my age, you can look back on what you've written as if—much of it—it was written almost by somebody else. In the letter I enclose to 'Nick'—you will see what I say about what I now see as a total change between the earliest 'song' in my collections and everything after. One difference between that piece and everything later (there's a five year gap between it—no a six year gap— and what comes next), is a shift from totally subjective statement to: as near as I could get to totally objective statement.

On the other hand, as you see from what I wrote, in that note 'two answers', I always regarded the beasts etc as subjective elements, incidentally given objective expression—or an objective form. The point is, I have never really felt much interest in objective descriptive writing for its own sake—or in writing about anything that I couldn't regard as the 'dramatisation' of a purely internal psychodrama. The nearest I have come to that is in the diary pieces about farming, that I collected in a Volume titled Moortown, and in some of the pieces in River. And in some of the portraits about relatives.

In that sense then, with just those exceptions, I have in fact chosen almost exclusively subjects from 'inside' myself—but only in that very earliest piece of Juvenilia did I give it a purely non-objective expression.

b.   Though you 'clearly have an intricate metaphysical system'. I suppose it is true, all my verses are part of the expression of what makes internal coherent sense to me: everything is related to a structure of basic attitudes and ideas about the world and life. But I have never really formulated it in discoursive terms.

Roughly, I suppose it is based on an attitude to the natural world (including the natural world—the psychobiology—of human beings) that I came to very early, when I was a child. I had an older brother who by the time I came along had a highly evolved world—a large tract of country in West Yorks which was exclusively his hunting territory. And he had a precocious imaginative view of it, fed by adventure magazines and books (he was a great reader of such things). He was (is) a very brilliantly dramatic person. He was the one-man theatre in our family—but obsessed by the world of the primaeval hunters. He also had a great turn of phrase: he had one phrase in particular that became my mantra. Until I was well into my twenties I could freeze myself to ice just repeating it once. I picked it up when I was four. When I began to write, in my teens—or maybe when I was eleven (when I first went to Grammar school)—I think I was trying to get at the magical world behind that phrase—find other routes into it. When I finally did get there—in my twenties, with my first successful poems—the phrase began to lose its drug power over me. Though it still works slightly: it still seems to me a miraculously beautiful structure of vowels and consonants. So that phrase at an early age—four or five—connected my life in my brother's palaeolithic paradise to a verbal expression.

So my early life—first consciousness to age nine—revolved around my brother's world and the animals that we searched for in it. I had a peculiar, obsessive relationship to wild creatures—simply their near presence. Not unique to me—both my son and daughter had the same, I noticed. It's a physical reaction: like a kind of ecstasy. We lived in a mill-town, where everybody—all our family—was absorbed in the life of the mills. (Our father built portable wooden buildings.) Neither of our parents, and nobody else, had any interest whatsoever in wild life or the wild countryside. In those first say six years of consciousness, in which I shared in my brother's Eden, we never met one other soul walking out there—except the farmers, who had adopted my brother anyway. So you can see, it was not only real, but—as far as our ordinary home and school life was concerned—secret and internalised. Naturally, I extended that feeling of private possession to the entire natural world and all the creatures in it. Nobody else seemed to have the faintest interest in it. And I should mention—that stretch of country, which climbed to empty moorland—was within an hour of several million people. It was in the geographical middle of the Northern industrial belt between Hull and Liverpool.

When I was nine the whole thing, by a fluke, was intensified. We moved to South Yorkshire, where my parents bought a newsagent's and tobacconist's shop, in a mining town, right in the thick of the coal and steel belt. So from that moment I had all the comics and boy's magazines published at that time. Until I was about thirteen, I read every one—before they were sold in the shop. Simultaneously, the war started and my brother went off into the RAF: we hardly saw him again until 1945, six years later. But before he went he located, right next to the town we lived in, and divided from it by a poisonous river, a completely wild stretch of farms: these became his new kingdom, which I entered with him. When he went off, they became mine. So for the next five years I had to keep our palaeolithic Eden going on my own, and I did that. The farmers adopted me. But again, and now this territory was even more tightly surrounded by industrial towns—and, within an hour, about eight million people—not once in all my years roaming that territory did I see one other soul except the farmers. Unimaginable nowadays. But that's how it was. I had the whole thing to myself.

When I was eleven I got to Grammar School, and discovered that what I wrote amused my classmates and my English teacher. That focused my interest I suppose. But with my brother gone, I came under the influence of my sister. She was ahead of me at school, and an academic star. She also has a very forceful personality. Also, as it happened, she had a sophisticated taste in poetry. Our mother, who having seen our very talented brother slip through her fingers wasn't going to let the same happen to us, bought a whole library of collected poets—I think in response to the news that the English teacher was interested in me. It was an old library, ancient editions. I can't remember reading it at the time—but it was a sign of her intent, of her desire. I can't remember that I had any interest in poetry as such until I was about fourteen. What I did like was the Bible—a good deal of the Bible was like my brother's magic phrase. I often read bits of it—Job, Song of Songs, Ezekiel, Isaiah—simply for more of that, whatever it was.

The real jolt was my discovery of folklore. Nowadays it's unthinkable that any child with an attentive mother who told incessant stories to us when we were younger (she made them up, mostly—I remember only one actual children's book with pictures) should remain unaware of folklore until thirteen years old. I came across a small group of folktales in a Children's Encyclopedia that I was borrowing out of our parent's shop. That was my first literary shock: I could not believe such treasures could exist. Again, I became totally preoccupied—a mania—in collecting them. There were not many to be found—none in shops, and only a few collections in the town library. That mania has continued ever since, I might say—in cyclic waves of renewed realisation that these things are the great treasures of the world. As I see it now, the result of that mania was, that by the time I was fifteen or sixteen I was familiar with the mythic and metaphysical systems of all the old civilisations, and was deep into their common life through the folklore. I didn't think of it in that way. To me, it was the imaginative world that fitted into the natural world. In one of the pieces I'm enclosing I call it the metaphysics of the palaeolithic world—vague and inclusive phrase, but it suggests how I felt the animal kingdom, the undisrupted paradise of the natural world, and the worlds of mythology and folklore all hung together in a wonderful single thing. Also, never did I find anybody who had the slightest interest in folklore and mythology. So it was in a way my own and <u>unspoiled</u>.

When I was about fourteen I read Kipling's poems. I think, because our English teacher had read us Mowgli, the story of the boy among the animals, in class. I fell completely under the spell of his rhythms. The stories etc that I wrote to amuse a gang of classmates from that point went into those pounding rhythms and rhymes. Here's one of my lines from those days:

And the curling lips of the five gouged rips in the bark of the pine
were the mark of the bear.

My pieces were all set in the American North West, far West, the
Brazilian jungle, or Africa.

I was looking one day in the School library for more poems in those
same long rhythms, when I came across the last part of The Wanderings
Of Oisin, by Yeats. It so happened, my particular craze, in folklore and
mythology, was the Irish (very rich, as you know). So here was an Irish
myth and my special verse metre all in one. I then read the whole
poem—for the legend. Then I searched Yeats for more—not tramping
rhythms but—folklore made into poems. So I was swallowed alive by
Yeats. From that point, my animal kingdom, the natural world, the
world of folktales and myth, and poetry, became a single thing—and
Yeats was my model for how the whole thing could be given poetic
expression. It all happened pretty quickly. I simply tried to learn the
whole of Yeats (and eventually did learn the complete poems). That
Wanderings of Oisin gave me some of the most brilliant dreams I've ever
had. My own writing jumped a whole notch in sophistication (all this
time under the close constant influence of my sister, who had become
interested in my writing, but was also constantly trying to get me to
work at school: she was a terrific worker). Soon after the Yeats trauma
(my second big literary shock—no my third, Kipling's rhythms were my
second), I was writing the odd line that I still would quite like to get into
a poem. One was:

The otter comes here in the winter but even the shells are empty.

You see how my rhythms had improved. Although in fact that is a
perfect classic hexameter. (Our latin master used to pace up and down
the classroom reciting Virgil in a strong Edinburgh accent. Had a great
permanent effect on my ear).

However, does that give you a rough idea of the topography of my
'system'? The final touch—the next big literary shock—was a book of
my sister's: Jung's Psychological types. Through Jung I made the con-
nection between my own ramshackle 'system'—and intellectual systems,
psychological and some philosophical systems. But only as other deities'
statues on the temple. The whole insides remained wholly intact, went
on amusing itself, and kept the animals and the natural world—the
occult world and the biological world—at the centre.

In among, I had become infatuated by Shakespeare and the music of Beethoven. For many years, these two immunised me in a way from any other literary or musical experiences. Blake was admitted, Keats, Eliot, Wordsworth up to a point, Dante, Hopkins, Dylan Thomas—but others, Auden for instance, were kept waiting in Customs. All other music except Mozart, Bach, Handel and Haydn were excluded—until I discovered the melodies of the old ballads, which I did at University in 1952. (An Irish friend introduced me) (In those days, those things too were rarely heard, and unobtainable on records).

So, when I got to University, I was incapable of responding to the demands of the English Course. You can see why, maybe. I was 'pre-occupied'. It was not until after University, when I discovered modern US poetry, that I came out of my magic tower.

You'll see how infatuated I was with Shakespeare and Beethoven. At home we had no gramaphone, only a radio. My girl-friend's parents, quite well off, had a magnificent gramaphone, and her mother had a taste for classical music. So I bought her (the mother) one by one the symphonies and the concertos and a few other things—so that I could hear them when I visited my girl friend. My mind boggles when I remember that. At their house, too, I had the next big literary shock since discovering Yeats: this mother of my girl friend owned a Shakespeare with the apocryphal plays included. I already knew all the plays pretty well, and the poems. I read at them constantly. But in her book I found The Two Noble Kinsmen. The passages of verse in Act I of that play had an effect on me very like the effect of Wanderings Of Oisin formerly: very brilliant and special dreams came out of it somehow. That puzzles me slightly, now—how I could have reacted so strongly to such a slight novelty in the verse. Anyway, I did. I was 18 then.

That's a passing autobiographical detail, to help you give some reality to the rest of the tale.

c. 'a Wordsworthian introspection doesn't interest you'. I take it that by this you mean 'a Wordsworthian rumination over my own auto-biography'. I suppose that has been true. But I fancy that it is true only in the sense that it apparently hasn't interested me to write in that way. I could believe, I might well have written much more in that way if I hadn't come into a literary climate (mid-fifties, Lit Crit just entering its first 'psychic cleansing operation' throughout the Academies of the West) in which the secrets of the private life needed total protection—

from the gladiatorial public demonstrations of the critics who would inevitably be your first audience, the audience which, in those days, there seemed no way to circumvent. I think that inhibited our whole generation—crippled, I think, one or two fine talents. (It might be true to say it destroyed hundreds in the egg—while still students at University).

Gradually, that State Police system of orthodox critical attitudes was not so much broken down as bypassed—in the sixties, with the flood of literature from other languages. Even then it was a bloody struggle, as I think most poetic careers that spanned those years demonstrate. If SP and I managed to get through it at all, it was because for crucial years we defended each other, we were a sufficient world to each other: our poetic folie à deux saved us from being isolated, surrounded and eliminated. In England, this external negative was far more oppressive than in the US—since it was fortified by a more intact system of socially suppressive attitudes. I think, too, in the Sixties the sudden flight into the pop world of the Academic securitate men greatly eased the constraints. (In 1965 I visited Cambridge and was amazed to find all the boys in the fancier colleges talking in broad Liverpool accents: I was then told, they were Eton boys, and boys from other grand public schools, who had gone to elocution class to learn to speak 'like the Beatles'. I don't know how much you are aware of these English games of ours.)

My introspection is not the Wordsworthian ruminative kind. But I have always been interested in systems of meditation and introspection, in fact. From the Mythology and its associated religious systems, I inevitably learned something about hermetic occultism—which is nothing if not systems of introspection, even strenuous regimes of introspection when followed up seriously.

d.   Your sentence culminating in 'points of view'. Definitely I do think, yes, that point of view is everything in bringing any literary work to expressive focus. As for the dramatic use of the first person: in general, all poems can be divided into the two groups. Those poems in which the author as author seems to speak for himself, taking responsibility for the point of view in the poem, make up one group. Obviously the 'point' of view of the authorial ego can fluctuate a good deal, from the assumed 'average voice of our culture, speaking as if our whole culture were speaking in its most intelligent mode', through the eccentric ego of a recognisable regular persona, to the mantic pronouncement of an ego suffused with some larger inspiration. This group would include Wordsworth, Shakespeare in his sonnets, Dryden. The other group are the monologues, or the poems written from a sub-personality, a dramatically assumed role, poems written in a funny voice, any poem ventriloquised in some 'point of view' other than the author's usual ego's own. So that group would include everything in Shakespeare's plays, almost all of Eliot, much of Yeats.

Speaking for myself, I have always found (in retrospect usually) that adopting another persona is in fact an immense liberation for me. I only wish I had adopted that approach more systematically, more regularly, with more of my efforts to write.

My definition of 'poetry', almost, excludes anything coming from the ego under the ego's control. I would include Shakespeare's ego sonnets as poetry in so far as they are written under the pressure of a state of mind that was, in fact, out of his ego's control, somewhat against his ego's will, and to the mortification of his ego. And you can see lots of other examples of something similar.

But to return to your point: I do feel there has to be some kind of ego in control to give that point of view, and its focus. The distinction I'm making is between the author's regular workaday ego—the one that writes his critical essays—and the attendant masks, the crowd of spirits that can each assume a kind of ego, and pronounce itself I, to tell a tale very different from anything in ken of the authorial official ego. Different kinds of points of view, but all 'points of view'.

2.   I think the shamanistic phenomenon is basically the same as the phenomenon behind artistic creation of any kind. It is a universal human way of dealing with the difficulties of experience, the damages and pains of life. That being said, I think the following illustrates the basic psychological 'dynamics'. In Rasmusson's books about his exploration across the Arctic belt, he somewhere tells of a great shaman, Isjugarjuk, who gives Rasmussen a description of Shamanic training, practice etc. Interesting. When there is a problem to be solved <u>in the group</u> to which Isjugarjuk belongs, he leaves the group. He goes far out into the wilderness—isolates himself, and shuts himself in an improvised shelter to concentrate internally <u>on making contact with the problem (and its solution)</u>. He, Isjugarjuk, explained this, saying 'I have to go far away from my people if I am to see deeply into them.' In other words, the further he goes <u>into himself</u>, the closer he comes to what is truly going

628

on in his group or tribe. The deeper he goes <u>inside</u>, the more profoundly and clearly and truly he grasps what is <u>outside</u>—i.e. in his companions. That journey inward is an escape from the limitations of the social (and divisive) ego but a penetration into what is—as it turns out—the reality that everybody shares.

What Isjugarjuk is saying here is: while we are all together, chattering away with each other, responding to every bit of news, interested in every next thing, countering every argument with an argument, while we are here in intimate contact, excited together, watching every motion of each other's face, hearing every inflection of each other's voice—we are living on an utterly superficial plane that shuts us out from what is truly happening to us. Only when we get away from this, inwards, so that instead of being fully preoccupied by that minute by minute flux of reactions to reactions, only then do we become preoccupied with sifted, clarified, understandings from that depth which—because we are telepathic members of a group—we all share, understandings that arise from the level on which we suffer the consequences and gather the big revelations of what this all amounts to, only then are we open to the intuitions that propose a solution to the big problems, the total problems.

That's what he meant, and that's how it is. When Wordsworth spoke about the psychologically blinding effects of 'too much business with the passing hour', he spoke from experience: this is what he meant. And Isjugarjuk described the 'dynamics' of the only procedure that will produce the goods. And that is how TV and the new forms of the media are destroying Europe: the leaders are overwhelmed with superficiality and instant response to instant impression: they cannot get inwards to the place that Isjugarjuk knew had to be found—if the solutions were to be seen. And so there seem to be 'no leaders'. [*Last two sentences bracketed and connected by arrow to ms insertion:* Well, no, this can't be true, can it?]

So I think.

The scabby foal was a way of finding a mount outside my own self-respecting socially responsible ego.

My whole writing career sometimes presents itself to me as a search for not one style in particular, but the style for this crisis or that. In my first book I simply wrote—trying to write poems for the way I read them. And my ideal way of reading a poem was to leave myself at the end of it strengthless and shattered, totally wrung out, utterly expended. As I say, that was an unattainable ideal—towards which I strained. But it determined the 'style' of such things as Wind, Jaguar. And it meant that occasionally I could enjoy the beautiful experience of breaking through a sound barrier and floating at a speed beyond sound, effortless: that happened in the little poem Thought-Fox.

Publishing that book, I encountered the critical world: the alien minds of all the sub-groups of our multicultural civilisation none of which—no sub-group of which—shared my understandings: at least, that's how I felt. Publishing a first book of poems is one of the most traumatic experiences that ever happens to the people who do such a thing.

I was aware, as I went on writing, that above all I wanted to rid my language of the penumbra of abstractions that to my way of thinking cluttered the writing of all other poetry being written by post-auden poets. These abstractions were not to my taste in that they seemed to me, in those days, second hand, rancid—unexamined, inauthentic in the experience to which they laid easy claim. [*Marginal addition:* All young writers are fanatics of intolerance.] So I squirmed and weaseled a way towards a language that would be wholly my own. Not my own by being exotic or eccentric in some way characteristic of me. But my own in that it would be an ABC of the simplest terms that I could feel rooted into my own life, my own feelings about quite definite things. So this conscious search for a 'solid' irrefutably defined basic (and therefore 'limited') kit of words drew me inevitably towards the solid irrefutably defined basic kit of my experiences—drew me towards animals, basic-ally: my childhood and adolescent pantheon of wild creatures, which were saturated by first hand intense feeling that went back to my infancy. Those particular subjects, in a sense, were the models on which I fashioned my workable language.

The essential series begins with View Of A Pig. The actuality of that pig was (in a sense that was almost conscious to me) the image of what I wanted each word in the poem to be. The fact that the pig is dead is also true to this. Or rather, the pig is not dead. It is like a dead Osiris, dead only to be resurrected as a falcon. It is 'like a sack of wheat' and it is 'a doorstep'. In setting these figures down I was aware in a gleeful sort of way that I was making a spell: I was conjuring into being an order of words, a density and (for me) essential simplicity of vocabulary that was inseperable from the substance of my life (the pig) and yet was life suspended—life in a kind of death-like coma. In other words, the vocabulary, in its substantiality a dead pig (a sacred pig—my pig was a holy beast), actually shuts out the life that I would want this vocabulary to express—shuts out the sacred life that I am designing it to live. These are a jumble of superstitious ideas, but it's the sort of thing does go on in my head. So I had found a language—only by locating it in its lifeless (or comatose, anaesthetised) obedience. Nevertheless, it is a language, in this operational spell, that will spring—like the pig—totally to a new kind of life. So the poem is a kind of prayer to itself—a stylist's prayer. I wrote it actually at top speed—just the other side of that sound barrier. It can take—as a language—absolute maximum force of vocal thrust, in recitation (not many poems can). It is a plain little poem, but was very important for me (and for SP)

Soon after, I got to Pike. The link is, a little bit, in the title, believe it or not. Here again I wanted a creature magically solid as the pig, sacred to me (pike obsessed great stretches of my adolescence and were central to my recurrent dream life until salmon replaced them), an angel in my heaven of heavens, and yet—coming to life, to real actual ordinary life. So this is the same language as the pig, the same ABC, the same velocity (again I got it just the other side of the sound barrier—this poem too can take maximum pressure of delivery)—but alive and on the move. Also, I wanted to evoke into it, without losing solidity and rootedness, colour—five-dimensional being. I realised what the internal link was, with pig, and I was happy about it.

Then, a few months later, I got Hawk Roosting. Here the same language has taken off. Writing this was one of the truly best moments of my life. But internally it is emerging from the two earlier poems. All three, as I've often thought about since, grow out of a complex of Egyptian and Christian mythology—the complex in which Egyptian underlies early Christian. And another contributor to the same group was The Bull Moses—though stylistically that is not one of the essential stages of the prototype. What I was also trying to find, from the first point—behind the pig—was the greatest possible musical shift between one inflexion and the next. My ultimate or furthest phase—in that line of development—was in the last one, Hawk Roosting.

All the other poems in that book dangle at various angles and in various degrees of impurity within that stylistic field—which radiates from those three pieces.

The problem is, of course, having found a language under those peculiar conditions, how do you turn it to other uses. Well, you just have to go on writing and hope that—if it can—the style will find its own way to a wider life. But even so, my vocabulary after Hawk Roosting was very different from anything before. I had a much sharper sense, after that, of what was my own and what was not.

Wodwo, in that way, was the fall-out of that effort. It was broken up by autobiographical events. But stylistically, the next conscious real step was Crow.

In Crow, my notion was, again to re-simplify my language but simultaneously to break it out of dependence on a sacred object for subject—to make it narrative and in a way lyrical-dramatic. I set about quite deliberately to relax the focus of the beam but amplify the momentum of the total input. Sometimes, writing in the Pig-pike-Hawk Roosting vein I got into such a state of fixated concentration that I felt myself sinking like a sort of stone beyond words—had to pull myself back into the physical shape of the subject. As if I had narrowed my concentration to the point where it excluded the world I was trying to write about, and then went into a sort of lock. I wanted to relax that, to find a different kind of concentration: a broad inclusive concentration—where you can take in a whole scene and simply hold it, with all its parts in their real relationships, no part under sharper focus than any other. I was also aware that the former kind of concentration excluded my freely subjective life—or included it only after it had been melted and recast as a figurine. I wanted to include a broader play of a more liberated music.

So, my notion was: to simplify the language and find that open but full-frontal sort of music and then, having got that far, to begin to include other elements, the colours and solidities and more intricate musics of that earlier form of simplicity and concentration. So my ideal was to somehow first get hold of this open, larger, inclusive but still top pressure simplicity—and then, complicate and solidify it with all the experience (all my grasp of the actual world, that I'd managed handsful of in those earlier pieces) that it excluded. In other words, to bring all I'd gained into a poetry about life in general. I only got as far as the end of the simplification stage—the actual poems are When Water Began to Play, and Horrible Religious error. Then autobiographical things knocked it all to bits, as before.

I started again at the beginning, with ABC language, in my diary pieces. As I wrote them, I began to write others simply about my life— yes Wordsworthian style. I've only printed the odd one, but maybe that was the most fertile vein, finally, for me, of all my experiments. That has gone on, with little shifts in successive models, ever since, though I've printed as I say very little of it.

In Remains Of Elmet I began first of all thinking: this is my chance to write the autobiography of my childhood, in easy descriptive little verses. I started with two no three pieces: The Canal's Drowning Black, The Long Tunnel Ceiling, and Mount Zion. Then it struck me—this is a book of photographs about a region that belongs to everybody who lives or has lived in it, not only to me. I was suddenly struck, you see, by the embarrassing egotism of my plan to convert the whole region into my childhood stage. So I abandoned my project. After that, I aimed for a blurred focus, generalised mood-evocation in each piece—something that would harmonise with Fay Godwin's photographs, but would avoid that painful collision of sharp visual image and sharp specific verbal image, in which the verbal image, after a moment of psychological distress, always loses. I expect you've noticed that. So again, that book was an exercise in a deliberately designed style. In retrospect, I missed the real opportunity: I should have written portraits, sharp and detailed, of the people I knew there: populated the photographs without challenging their images.

In Cave Birds, I was making poems to go with drawings. Here again, I saw the solution in stylistic terms. First, there were I think twelve drawings. The idea was for me to make poems, a poem to each drawing, to be published with the drawings in a limited edition. So to make the thing meaningful for me, I arranged the drawings in a sequence, and wrote the poems as the tableaux of a bird-drama (all the drawings were of birds—some fanciful, some recognisably known species). Each poem had to contain the various elements of a whole scene—and rather than aim for a 'dramatic' manner, I aimed for a static, hieratic hieroglyphic manner: as if each poem might be a cartouche of hieroglyphic signs, each incorporating some aspect of the drama of that scene. The whole plot was the crime, conviction, execution and suggested rebirth of the protagonist. The artist saw these and promptly drew twelve more drawings. (Or was it ten and ten. Shocking to have forgotten that.) Faced with another ten, I extended my drama into the underworld, where, as in the Bardo Thodol, the soul is judged, is considered for this or that or the other fate, but then is finally reborn.

I continued this second part in partly the same style, but now felt the style was, taken at such length, too cryptic and exclusive. Also, I wanted to incorporate the simultaneous drama of a man losing his soul (by a crime against it), falling (convicted, condemned because of the crime) into the underworld where, after judgements, he is reunited with his 'soul' and reborn.

I also wanted to set this in the suggested form of an alchemical disintegration and rebirth—which takes the form of a relationship between male and female, from whose union the transcendental new being is born.

Accordingly, I now wrote some pieces to interleave with the others—not quite alternate though that might have been ideal—in which the relationship between male and female in this world (this ordinary and daily, outer world, non-bird but human) appears brokenly through the goings on in the cave—or in the crucible. These pieces I wanted to be in simpler, direct, more open style—shaped by the flow of their music rather than by the cryptoglyph patterning of their cartouche. The artist had to provide a few extra drawings, to accompany extra poems.

In Gaudete, I wanted a style, for the narrative, in which a headlong rough kind of simple language, that could carry immediacy of a suspenseful narrative telling (i.e. did not get bogged down in fine writing, but remained rough and baggy enough for anything piled in) slammed head on, repeatedly, into the obstinate actuality of objects, of point-blank situations, of things being simply as they are. My governing idea was of a story coiling up on itself with increasing narrative velocity—but having to break through, in every paragraph, the resistance of an irreducibly blockish actuality. The ideal sensation, in the writing of each line (the sensation I tried to find) was of rushing at a brick wall—and breaking through it.

At the same time, I wanted everything to have a slight edge of puppet unreality, a slightly unnatural light—as in a primitive painting but not so garishly obvious. Just a slight alienation. I felt I could get this by concentrating on a certain sharpness of focus—a voyeur's deafened, slightly mystified view of events. Or like a film that has lost seven yards of footage in every ten. Lost all the dialogue for instance. It was an indescribable complex—the precise notion I had of the effect I wanted to get. But it determined the whole thing, in every detail. And overall, I wanted to keep narrative pressure—the ratchetting tightening of the tension. My image of the story was of an express train going through a tunnel and bursting out into the light at the other end.

The poems I wrote in and around that time, as vacanas (an Indian

634

form of prayer poem, specifically Tamil, I think). Again I wrote them as an attempt to reach a more direct, flexible, simpler expression of things that would be compromised by a more studied or 'literary' form. Each one jumps out of its own impulse, then shapes itself, extempore fashion, as it goes along—as you shape your remarks when you feel you have to get something over to somebody in a quarrel, or when you're trying to explain why you did something incomprehensible, or when you're pleading with somebody to do something.

4.   I imagine I have already said as much about these as I can say. Another way of looking at 'changes in stylistic approach' in any particular writer is to regard the sequence of styles simply as a record of the means preferred, or the means inwardly permitted, by the writer's feeling self, at each phase of that inward 'development' (it may be disintegration, but at least it is a process of change through time) which is the writer simply growing older—growing in and out of situations, gaining control of inner confusions or losing control, overcoming inner resistances or succumbing to them, exploring more of inner darkness and appropriating it as 'personality' or actually losing some personality to encroaching darkness. All these things are going on constantly. One example of a distinct and striking stylistic change, which corresponded to a distinct and striking inner development, was the change from objective, rigidly formed, artificial-feeling examinations of disturbing material, to a subjective, free, overwhelmingly real-feeling first-hand first-person dramatic utterance by the disturbing material itself—in SP's work. Throughout, it is the same 'material'. But in the first phase, she was only permitted—inwardly permitted—to deal with it at a distance in the first manner. In the second phase, she was inwardly permitted to let it speak for itself in its own terms. Then again, it's possible to imagine later phases, in which she might have dealt with it in still other ways—but those ways were impossible to her, because not yet inwardly permitted.

In any of these phases, the stylistic manner of one of the other phases would have been—mere academic exercise, artistically meaningless. And any style is meaningless, or makes its material artistically meaningless, makes it 'not-art' I suppose, in so far as it lacks that stamp of a compulsory necessity: as the author's only real option at that time.

But at any moment, in any phase, the option, the style chosen by the material at that moment, can be fluffed—can be poorly approximated, smothered in alien influences. The difficult thing—most writers find this—is to get the purest most essential character of the style that belongs to the material at that moment. The 'material' always being the subjectivity of the writer seen as a whole developing mass of things, the corpus of internal experience and impulse that is pushing for expression—that makes the writer want to write or need to write in the first place.

The most common phenomenon, I think, is for the writer to lose contact with the real nature of that material. It usually happens early thirties. If they don't lose contact, that's where the big change comes. In very visible authors its a clear point—it's where Shakes writes Hamlet, Joyce writes Ulysses, Eliot writes The Waste Land, Beethoven writes the 3rd Symphony. It's a sort of quantum leap. Critical point. Mozart's last Symphonies. But more usually, it's where the artist's lose internal contact simply because the material makes demands—stylistic demands, that the artist can't meet.

Sorry for rambling. But that's all illustration of what I see as the incessant shifting of the internal requirements. So, in a sense, the deadliest thing is for a writer to develope too fixed a 'style'. The ultimate, to my mind, must be the naked voice of that inner being—unimaginable, because the moment it hits the paper it becomes 'another style'. Still, I think you can see some of it in some authors—more of it in some than in others. So there's always the feeling that you can get closer to that living nerve.

In my own case, I sometimes think, I'm having to come right round the world to get back to where I started in that first little poem Song. Maybe not. Different, I hope.

Apologies for the chaotic syntax of these pages. If I had stopped to be careful, or if I started now rewriting, the little that is almost here might no longer be.

Not knowing you, and knowing you would read it with un-English eyes, has made it easier to say all this unself-consciously. I hope you will find it useful. There's nothing very original here—and nothing that hasn't occurred to me only in relation to my own writing and SP's.

Best wishes
Ted Hughes

A French MA student at Oxford, writing her thesis under the title 'An Eye for an I: Visions and Voices in Ted Hughes's Poetry', Anne-Lorraine Bujon had sent TH a number of questions. The 'one or two pieces' supplied with this letter were the interviews with TH that formed Appendix II of *Ted Hughes: The Unaccommodated Universe* (1980), by Ekbert Faas. The 'letter to "Nick" ' is the one to Nick Gammage preceding this.

The phrase of Gerald Hughes's that became TH's 'mantra' was 'The Blesbok are changing ground'. In a radio broadcast of 1980, *Crossing Lines*, a programme of poetry by schoolchildren, TH attributes the phrase to H. Rider Haggard, but in fact it is from John Buchan's *Prester John*.

The metrical pattern of Book III of Yeats's 'The Wanderings of Oisin' (1889) is set by the first line: 'Fled foam underneath us, and round us, a wandering and milky smoke' – not exactly TH's 'special verse metre', if the Kiplingesque – or Service-like – line about the ripped tree is typical. Also, the one about the otter is not a 'perfect' hexameter, as it has an extra syllable at the beginning and a misplaced caesura.

H. Godwyn Baines's translation of Jung's *Psychological Types* (1921) was published in 1923. Shakespeare and John Fletcher collaborated on *The Two Noble Kinsmen* in 1613.

Igjugarjuk was a Caribou Inuit shaman whom Knud Rasmussen (1879–1933), Danish explorer of the Arctic regions, interviewed and wrote about in *Across Arctic America* (1927).

'That scabby foal' was TH's own metaphor for the style of *Crow* (see *Ted Hughes: The Unaccommodated Universe*).

1993

To Iris Gillespie

17 February 1993   Ms (photocopy)   Emory

Your essays have just about convinced me that the time has come for me to surrender to Wagner. They were/are a feast. If you could direct me to anything more of yours like these in journals etc, I would be grateful. (My contact with libraries is laboriously long-distance.)

Because of what is I suppose an innate inclination to be aware of the 'mythic dimension' of each stage of my own efforts to grow up (I'm not sure that it helped the efforts much—but maybe it lit up my lack), I've been acutely aware of my failure, at each stage, to live up to the various requirements of the 'heroic mystique'—where often it felt that my inner survival depended on my not failing—so I can say, or I feel I can say, that essay of yours has some uncanny insights (that I would have thought were of the male subjective secrets kind—the sort that boys hear nothing about until it is too late). Maybe only a woman can see them from outside the goggle-blinding weather of trying to get through them inside a male ego.

I don't know where I've seen the portrait of the whole complex portrayed so lucidly, wholly, surely—suggestively—succinctly.

The Goddess essay drew me directly into Wagner. I'm one of those who believe that Wagner must be a magnificent experience in the flesh—but are unwilling to find a way in via radio or recorded performance. In my case, I don't think Wagnerphobia can be blamed. At least, not the generalised kind. One of my early loves was Norse mythology—that world is like an attic in my own home. And my children are ½ German (—½ German, ¾ Germanic).

Early infatuation with Beethoven, exclusive, idolatrous & fanatic, was the culprit. I have never managed to smuggle through any glimmer of liking for anything later. Wagner, in particular (but Brahms too) seemed like Beethoven in dissolution—Beethoven being disintegrated by alien sensibilities. I have never managed to get over that.

But I'm sure that if I now subjected myself to the mythic event as a

638

spectator—I would be overwhelmed. You have decided me to make the effort.

TH was an admirer of Dr Iris Gillespie's critical method, whether her topics were literary or – as here – musical. He tried, in vain, to persuade Faber and Faber to publish her essays on Wagner, which had appeared in issues of the magazine *Wagner*, under such titles as 'The Death-devoted Heart' and 'Richard Wagner and the Heroic Mystique', in the 1980s and early 1990s.

To Julie Murray

24 April 1993   Ms   Murray

Dear Julie Murray—

I expect you're quite sure I'm the most terrible person—swallowing your cake without a murmur of thanks.

Opening my mouth for your masterpiece—shutting it for your request.

Well, after studying your face, and inspecting your daughter's Portrait Of Mum & Dad (or is it your son's) propped up there by the Kleenex, and again after sure enough devouring your quite incredibly delicious cake (I rate it in the best 3 I've ever judged), how can I sidle off into everlasting silence?

The trouble is— time. I know your trouble is time, too. And cakes take time (all the time spent learning how to make a perfect cake must be there, compressed in the cake). But your time is only 28 year old time. (That's reckoning between 5 and 8 years for the artist, 17 years for the expertise patisserie, three years to get past the dark forest around my verse, and 60 years for the extreme wisdom and generosity of your approach—that's 85 to 88 years. From your photograph you're obviously not much beyond a quarter way to that. So I guess 28.)

Now my time, to my amazement, is 62 year old time. And to my absolute horror, God seems to have far fewer spare 62 year old days than he had, as I recall, 28 year old days. It should be the other way round.

Forgive me, Julie, for my unforgivable no-response to the nicest request I think I've ever had.

The truth is, I couldn't have done it—I was under a juggernaut of not requests but demands.

I will do almost anything for you (I had better say 'almost') but please don't ask me for a day. (It's not so much the day, as the day before & the day after.)

If you had been within an hour, I would have done it, I think.

I feel, though, that your letter and gift come from such a grand spirit, I feel—well, I feel very badly.

So I'm sending you something. Where it misses the mark, give it away.

The circumstances of your cake arriving, & then of it being eaten, were unique—like the cake. You would be amused.

As you see, I don't know how to thank you.

Your husband's a lucky lad. Does he know it? I'm sure he does.

Yours ever

Ted Hughes

Julie Murray, a mature student, had invited TH to visit her college seminar group, and had sent a cake she had baked as inducement. TH's reply was delivered with a box of inscribed books.

To Nick Gammage

28 July 1993   Ts   Gammage

Dear Nick,

Congratulations on your son.

Brief answers, I'm afraid. Yes, I wrote most of Oedipus during rehearsal time—I wrote the text as it now stands. My feeling was, as I got to know the actors (and I watched them all the time), that I drew everything out of them, out of the possibilities their voices and temperaments suggested. I drew it particularly out of Irene.

Early on I developed the feeling that the play is really about Jocasta. That may have been because Oedipus as Sir John described himself had to be not exactly passive but Hamlet-like in the suffering, sensitive, soul-searching vein. Olivier's Oedipus would obviously (as again Sir John pointed out) have been far more aggressively monopolist—of the feeling in the play. Irene, as it happened, did have a kind of aggressive, tigerish, elemental approach. She gripped my imagination, I suppose. Also, I was strongly attracted to her personally though our friendship, which did become quite close later, remained slightly formal. Then in Persia, through my fault, it somehow went wrong—and though

I've always intended to make efforts to repair it, I've never had the opportunity. Except by writing to her, which as it happens (coincidence) I did just the other day. (She had written to me.)

Fairly early on in the revisions (there were (I think still are) ten or fifteen slightly or radically different texts—all printed up in those actors copies) I was stuck at the crucial moment on the crucial phrase: the point at which Jocasta tries to grasp what has happened (before she kills herself—which she did by squatting on a vertical spike and forcing herself down onto it). I wanted something very brief (as you know, most of the statements in the play are minimally brief). Suddenly, Irene supplied it: 'Nothing in me moves.'

That gave me the tuning for the key in which I then tried to recast the whole play—nudging and inching and trimming each moment to that wavelength, as far as I could.

While I was trimming the play (trimming out all the latinism, all the rhetorical figures, all the formal style) I had a hankering—which had to be suppressed, to be writing the opposite kind of play, the old-fashioned kind in which everybody could be eloquent, speeches could lengthen a bit, the actors could really have their say. The longish speech for Jocasta is where I tried it. Also, I felt her part, as I was writing it, needed to be more openly declared in some way: her case needed to be stated more fully. That speech is I think the only passage which isn't based directly on the Seneca. It was the germinal point at which I began to make an adaptation instead of a 'translation' with a difference.

Also, I wanted to give Irene a chance to let rip.

In a different theatre i.e. a different theatrical culture, or if I'd had the motive to form my own company and write my own kind of play that's where I could easily have happily become a dramatist.

After a few rehearsals, I was aware of orchestrating the whole thing for the amazing instrument that Irene proved to be. That's why Brook picked her: he knew she could come out with something utterly out of bounds, she could open herself to depths. Her death scene, in the performance, was one of the most staggering things I've ever seen an actor do.

But I drew a lot out of Sir John too. There was a curious, protean, clairvoyant sort of quality about him. An inner world. Between rehearsal activities, while the others milled around, he would withdraw and sit in meditation of some kind. But he was an anchorman too.

For instance: early on, I realised I would get nowhere unless I rid my concept of every conventional notion of the classical world. I re-imagined the whole thing as an event in some broken down Afro/Egyptian kingdom. Specifically, I imagined a giant ruined temple, in a desert, surrounded by a hovel city of survivors. The royal house lived in the catacombs under the temple ruins. And were a species of troglodyte—squat, primitive, hanging on to scraps of a lost culture. But bursting with furious energy. I imagined them as spiders—who were also people. Moving at terrific scuttling speed, with alarming leaps, like spiders.

That made it easier to strip every phrase of 'style'. It also led, inevitably, to what Sir John called the smallest vocabulary he'd ever performed with.

My idea was also to strip the basic rhythm of the language to two or three fundamentals—as those last quartets of Beethoven are constructed out of very simple phrases, very short simple figures. That was helped along by the way Peter produced the choruses: actors were posted all over the theatre, and every phrase given to a different actor, so the chorus bounced all over the theatre, from voice to voice, like musical phrases being tossed among the different instruments in an orchestra. Very thrilling on the night. So my spider language was [added below: rhythms were] also adapted to that.

Also, I wanted to escape (in the version I was trying to bring to a focus) any tendency of the actors to 'speak'—i.e. to make a speech. I wanted every statement to be a cry torn out. A yell or a gasp. At the same time, I didn't want to settle into reflective debate. My idea was to keep the thing headlong, starting at full speed and accelerating the whole way—till it disintegrated at the sound barrier or burst through it, every material part worn out or melted or vapourised.

Back to Sir John. Half way through the rehearsals, Peter gathered all the actors around him. A lot could be said about these conversations of his, when he draws everybody to him and speaks in that near-whisper. On this occasion, he asked them how they imagined the world of the play.

So one by one, as he went round the group, they told him—all, without exception, describing some variant of the noble columns and toga type of conventional classical setting. Until it came to Sir John. Apologising slightly for it (apologising to me, I think), he then floated off on that musical carpet of his and described a gigantic, ruined temple in the desert, surrounded by wretched hovels, with the royal court as a kind of mad troglodyte (he used the very word) people living in caves and cellars under the temple, scuttling about like dreadful insects, going through these dreadful insect torments.

Strange business, working with actors.

In spite of my efforts to reduce the language to particles of howl, one sentence fell into a shapely rhetorical cadence, formal and balanced. For some reason I kept it. I would have to look through the play to find it. What surprised me, startled me, dismayed me, intrigued me was—in the performance that sentence suddenly, briefly, opened a whole other world of possible theatre: it rang out like a marvellous bell, opened a magical casement etc. A curiosity. A lesson. If I'd gone on with plays I would have looked further into that. But the rest of my work with Peter threw language out altogether. (Which had the effect, for me, of teaching me far more about essential theatre.)

Curiously enough, in her death scene Irene went into an extraordinary posture and crabbed across the stage, slowly, like a huge spider—a big part of the astonishing effect.

Stories: If I were to interpret now, I would say that the Horse and the Greyhounds are the same entity. The horse wants something. The Greyhounds take it by force. When they take it, whatever it is enters a new existence: the state of having been captured, or overtaken, by the entity that appeared first as a horse then as greyhounds, is the new existence. It is entered through the body of a hare and a simultaneous death. The narrator goes through this 'death'. When it pursues him and frightens him it is a horse. When it overtakes him and seizes him it is greyhounds. When it transforms him (by seizing and overpowering him) it becomes his own metamorphosis into a hare, which is simultaneously sacrificially killed. His new existence is within the hare, which is within the hounds, which are within the horse. The horse, the hounds, the hare, and himself, have become one. [*Ms insertion:* In both stories the setting is the same hill, on the same farm, in S. Yorks]

So what existence is that? Well, you please yourself.

It, that action, is related to the other series, Snow, The Suitor and The Wound. I dreamed The Wound as a full length film with a parallel long poem—many scenes, far more detail and complexity. I woke and was aggrieved that a theme so absolutely my own should have been written, and made into a film, by John Arden—which is what I had understood in my dream. But I was awake enough to realise that it was my own dream (I think it's connection with John Arden was maybe that I had recently read Sergeant Musgrave's Dance.) I then fell asleep and dreamed the whole film again, and the whole text of the poem, exactly the same, without one detail different.

But then the usual Person from Porlock arrived. I'd arranged to go to the Old Bailey with a friend, to watch a case. He arrived soon after I got up. I scribbled about five lines of the key plot, just to keep hold of it—though when I woke much of the verse was still very clear and the film utterly clear (much of it is still utterly clear). By the time I got back from the Court, in the afternoon, I was thinking I would adapt it as a radio play—which I started to do. But by then the verse had gone.

Snow, The Suitor and The Wound are prophecies about my own life. One or two others I wrote a bit later made this so clear, I stopped writing stories. That's why I have never written any more. I became convinced that everything I wrote would somehow come true—as if the only subject I had was my own future life. That stopped me, as you can imagine.

At the time of The Wound I was making an oratorio of the Bardo Thodol. In my dream was also the idea that this was a Celticised Bardo Thodol. (In the film, far more dreadful things happened in the chateau). Simultaneously, Sylvia was writing The Bell Jar (though I did not know that.)

Norman N. My English Master, John Fisher, went to school with Norman. So when I was (I think) seventeen, he sent Norman some of my verses. N. was very encouraging, as I recall. Maybe my English master's daughter still has the letter. He told me to beware of the influence of Dylan Thomas. One of the poems appeared in the School Mag about that time, it began:

> O lean dry man with your thin withered feet,
> Feet like old rain-worn weasels, like old roots
> Frost-warped and shrunken on the cold sea beach etc

There were one or two good bits later.
Congratulations again

Yours ever
Ted

Gammage had already questioned Irene Worth about her working with TH, Peter Brook and Sir John Gielgud on *Seneca's Oedipus*. Sir Laurence (later Lord) Olivier (1907–89) had been Artistic Director of the National Theatre at the time of Brook's production.

The stories and play TH discusses are all in *Wodwo*.

'Norman N' is the Cumbrian poet Norman Nicholson (1914–87). The school-magazine poem, 'The Recluse', which TH misquotes slightly, can be found under 'Early Poems and Juvenilia' in the *Collected Poems*.

To William Scammell

15 August 1993   Ms   Jan Scammell

Dear Bill—

Yes, it's all tucked up. Last I heard (2 weeks ago) it was with Ron Costley, the designer.

I thought better of inserting the epigraph:

> "Every man skin his own skunk"
>
> (Sioux proverb)

Interested to hear about your Eliot essay. In the various accounts of him, I've never seen mention of the two things about his physical presence that most struck me. First—when he spoke, I had the impression of a slicing, advancing, undeflectible force of terrific mass. My image for it was—like the bows of the Queen Mary. Second—he had the most enormous and powerfully built hands. Equalled (in my observation) only by those on my wife's Father—which were a sort of local legend. A whole class larger than the ordinary sort of 'large hands'. Thick, long, massive fingers.

And he ate extremely slowly.

Danny Weissbort just sent me a Collected Sidney Keyes. He was larval, where Douglas was the full flying insect. But he's good—in his cold, strange, private world way.

> Keep well—
> Ted

Winter Pollen was now in production. For light on the 'Sioux proverb', see TH's letter to William Cookson of 5 November 1989.

Scammell's essay 'Eliot's Extremities' remains unpublished.

Sidney Keyes (1922–43) had been included, with Keith Douglas, in *Eight Oxford Poets* (1941) and, like him, was killed in the Second World War.

To Frieda Hughes

10 September 1993   Ms   Emory

Dear Frieda—

You will now be sitting feasting, after your show. I've been thinking of you on and off all evening.

Seeing all your pieces together was really something. You have no idea how joyful I felt. I had absolute confidence that you are getting hold of the real thing. The best of them could not be more beautiful, or more strong.

What I like is the terrific full-face blaze of feeling coming out of the flower-painting—as if you were pushing yourself into a furnace of your real feeling. Frieda, that is so rare. And they are so beautifully grasped—completely and strongly grasped. So complete in themselves.

They might be too much for some people, you know. Ignore those people.

The ancient trees & the egg-rocks are images of everything to come. The terrific strength and richness of the ancient trees are what will hatch the rocks. The whole show is like a nest of a terrific bird.

You mustn't think I don't react. Some of your paintings really amaze me—they're so crammed with fearless, large-scale potential. As well as being such lovely things in themselves.

That's why I'm not so enthusiastic about wilting sticks, the depressed, low spirited remote pieces—only one or two of those, fortunately. You set yourself a high standard.

I was surprised to see how strong and interesting the abstract stone-pattern paintings were—in the company of the others.

Don't be depressed if none sold. Your best paintings are unforgettable and absolutely your own. People will come back to them—and gradually pluck up the courage to buy them.

They are so free of the slick tricks, evasions, easy options, impersonal stylishness of 'accepted' art. They are purely your own & absolutely true to you. That's a guarantee, Frieda.

All you have to go is straight on—further & deeper in to what you've got hold of. Not in some other direction—but deeper in to what you've brought into focus. They will lead you where you need to go.

I shall get back just before you go—in London on the Sunday. I

646

just rang Carol and she said you both had a really good time together at lunch.

Read that book I gave you.

Big hug and love

Daddy

And you've done it all on your own—following nobody, you've dug it out of yourself. Remember that. That show is a terrific psychological <u>victory</u>.

Frieda Hughes's first one-woman exhibition was at the Anna-Mei Chadwick Gallery in London.

To William Scammell

2 October 1993   Ms   Jan Scammell

Dear Bill—

Here's the Ironess.

You have to detach yourself from the gruesome pollutions of all adult reactions—pro & con—to the mention of 'Green issues'. Then read it like a ten year old.

I wrote it as a ten year old.

Not sure how the book will get past those reactions, to the ten year olds.

The cover of Winter Pollen is pretty good. I'll ask Jane to send you a copy. It's an ancient Turkish painting of a Shaman dancing among his demons. Though you'd never know.

Some day I'll tell you how I came to 'Winter Pollen'—mainly because it was so curious, comical, weird, irresistible, oracular.

If I'd written the Coleridge Essay first, I'd have been tempted to call it 'The Snake In The Oak'. So glad I was saved from that.

Every book I pick up, since that essay, brings in that Snake, who is a woman, who is a river, who lives in the chief Tree of Trees—which can become a mountain. Just reading a book I've had here unread for a long time—'The Catalpa Bow' by Carmen Blacker—about female Shaman-ism in modern Japan. I hadn't realised quite how thoroughly Japanese psychic life is suffused with the shamanic mythos. Shintoism is sha-manic in its first origins & has been revitalised throughout its history by episodes of full-blown shamanic revelation. And at the middle of it all—the Snake, originally from water, who now lives in the Tree, or in the sacred mountain, & who is female.

Carmen Blacker also makes the connection, which I make in my Coleridge piece and which I've never seen made anywhere else, between that Snake Tree vision, as a Shamanic staple, and the Yogi's Kundalini Serpent which is also the great Mother & bride. Similar in its transformative effects etc.

She spent years in Japan studying these people (the modern vestiges of a more or less organised Shamanic priesthood—in various sects, sometimes more Buddhist, sometimes more Shinto, sometimes straight primitive). It's quite a book, first-hand throughout and very detailed.

Yes, interesting what you say about the boomerang of reviewing your colleagues. It's not only the named and known targets of your negative remarks that pursue you vengefully (and as you say secretly) throughout the rest of your life—it's all those unidentified others, who extrapolate your remarks to apply, conjecturally, to their own productions, and so feel you've injured them 'by implication'. You must have received many an unexpected arrow from some shower shot at somebody else.

But everything one writes upsets somebody—to some degree. In that P.B.S. anth. you assembled there is a poem by Charles Tomlinson about a corridor in a house. Carol instantly—she's clairvoyant—found it and recognised Charles' true opinion (which he'd concealed at the time) about our putting a right angle diversion in the corridor that formerly went straight through this house from front door to back!   !!!

When I think how various remarks, attitudes, opinions etc in that prose book of ours will stir sleeping dogs—how that piece on metre will upset the Queen's English etc not to speak of John Fuller (suddenly finding my painted arrow sticking in his garden path)—well, my shadow down there heaves a kind of sigh. (Not that I haven't found John Fuller's stray smooth arrows sticking in my pillow). And the bowmen amazed to see where their misses ended up. They thought they were having fun at the butts.

Must get Mandeville on the Bees.

I'm trying to get back to verse—as I do, I expect all the symptoms of age to disappear. I've been mired in prose on and off for nigh on four years. Very unhealthy.

I've noticed, the closer you get to the real thing in any bout of writing, the more formidable are the perverse interruptions, the deflections, tempting diversions and sheer obstacular accidents. The Alchemists were so familiar with it, they gave it a name—Ophiucos i.e. the Great Snake (no less!)

Keep well

yours ever
Ted

The 'Ironess' was *The Iron Woman*, TH's environmentalist sequel to *The Iron Man*. The cover of *Winter Pollen* showed a painting by the fifteenth-century Turkish artist Siyah Qalem, alias 'Mohamed of the Black Pen'. The title of the book came out of a dream.

'Jane' was Jane Feaver, then Assistant to the Poetry Editor at Faber and Faber.

Carmen Blacker's *The Catalpa Bow: A Study of Shamanistic Practices in Japan* was first published in 1975.

Scammell, a poet himself, was at this time a regular reviewer of poetry books for the *Independent on Sunday*. Charles Tomlinson's poem about the Court Green corridor, 'The Improvement', was in *Poetry Book Society Anthology 3*, which Scammell had edited. John Fuller (b.1937), poet and Oxford don, was the son of Roy Fuller, who had found the last line of TH's 'The Horses' 'unsayable'.

The Fable of the Bees (1714) by Bernard de Mandeville (1670–1733) was a riposte to the argument that human society could be founded on benevolence.

In Greek mythology, the constellation Ophiucus is associated with Asklepius, the first surgeon, whose skills were sometimes said to include revival of the dead.

To Mrs Yates

2 October 1993   Ms (photocopy)   Emory

Dear Mrs Yates—

I'm sorry to be so late answering your letter—I've been away throughout September.

I read Gerrard's poems with real interest. As you can imagine, I see a good deal of verse written by young people—maybe the work of two or three hundred each year (in Competitions, etc). So I fancy I can see straight off if there is anything worth reading twice.

I was immediately arrested by something in Gerrard's writing.

The most important things are not technical virtuosity or ability to find apt, surprising images (almost anybody, with enough motivation, and with guidance, can learn to produce those—and they are important eventually).

The most important things in the 16 year old writer are

(a) an authentic, subjective grasp of his (or her) own sensibility—or at least a strong tendency towards that, towards trusting their own feelings, their own view of things, towards taking responsibility for their own differentness from other people.

(b) a strong instinct for the <u>musical priority</u> in verse—not just for the sequence of sounds, vowels and consonants, in the line, but for the <u>cadence</u> of each line, and the contrast of each line's cadence with what went before and what comes after it. This is crucial because the musical component of verse is an expression of body, and of the deeper ¾ of the nervous system, and without the cooperation, the full cooperation, of all that, then real writing cannot develop.

(c) a feeling—hard to analyse—that verse is the natural, perhaps <u>only</u>, expression for that person. (If that person is going to express themself at all).

(d) a sense of compulsion—behind what is written. This is maybe the most important of all. A sense that a real situation (a real psychological predicament) is insisting on finding expression, is demanding the means.

It seems to me, Gerrard's poems have these four essentials, quite strongly.

All that he needs is <u>patience</u>—to defend his corner on his own terms through the next few years. I did it by ignoring my contemporaries (though I had no pop world to contend with I did have the jazz world—which I ignored) and digging my foxhole in the works of a few great figures of the past, and in folklore. My figures were Yeats, Blake, Shakespeare & Beethoven. But I also devoured, whole, Tolstoy, Dostoevsky, Hardy, Eliot, Keats, Wordsworth, Shelley, Owen. By the age of 21 I knew all Yeats' lyrics by heart and a great deal of Shakespeare—some whole plays.

I did this not only because I became addicted to them, but to defend myself—as people enter a religion to defend themselves. <u>I read a lot aloud</u>.

All that time, I had no idea what I would do—except that I would somehow write. My mother despaired—but she also supported me. So did my father. I just hacked away at my own path! Can Gerrard make anything of this? Well, my blessings on him. Yours sincerely
                                        Ted Hughes

P.S. Nearly all 16 year olds write a lot about death—part of their new craving for ultimate experience, & for grasping reality.

Neither Mrs Yates nor her son Gerrard has been identified.

To HRH Prince Charles

9 November 1993   Ms   Clarence House

Your Royal Highness—

May I thank you for the most superb evening. The fox that led us in through the farmyard must have been the Folktale Fox—the one that opens the story and leads directly to marvels.

Several things in The Tempest were better done than I have ever seen—particularly the Masque and Caliban. If I were asked at the moment for my most favourite Shakespeare performance I think I might well say David Troughton's Caliban. One of the most difficult, most complicated, of all parts, I always feel. And the key to so much in Shakespeare.

I hope the evening laid a magic finger on His Royal Highness Prince William. It cannot have failed. At the time, one can rarely recognise what gradually turns out to have been a crucial encounter.

But altogether it was a memorable party. Next morning, Paddy took Lady Cawdor, Carol and me through the garden. At every few steps, Lady Cawdor and Carol fizzed and brimmed with learned exclamations. We all became intense with satisfaction about the yew enclosure, the long vista with the new fountain, the little paradises opening out of paradises—each one gently startling, with deeper perspectives striking through, from odd angles, like sunbeams.

I loved the sense of every square yard being crammed with hidden thought, affectionate surprises—like hidden gifts, hidden Easter eggs. And the overall <u>imagination</u> of it.

Well, we came away like fruit soaked in mingled licqueurs—saturated with the million flavours & delight of everything.

Since then, in Devon, we have been driving after dark three times, and have each time seen a fox. Not leading anywhere—just leaping across. But we don't need reminding.

Thank you again, Sir, for the most unforgettable of lovely occasions, sincerely

Your loyal and humble servant

Ted Hughes

TH refers to a visit to see *The Tempest* done by the Royal Shakespeare Company at Stratford-upon-Avon – Prince William's first taste of Shakespeare.

To Thom Gunn

16 December 1993   Ms   Estate of Thom Gunn

Dear Thom—

I wonder if you're the first to have declined.

Thom, you mistake the matter completely. To begin with, if you don't want it, we don't simply give it to somebody else. My own feeling is, at the moment we would not give it at all—maybe for another couple of years. Till somebody's overwhelming performance knocks another out of us.

Secondly, however special it may be, as an honour, it raises amazingly little dust. Never more than a bald ½″ announcement on some page 11 in some unlikely newspaper. It has that singular virtue—it is almost invisible.

Thirdly, if you don't want ever to come to England again—we'll send it to you. Or, maybe, if the Queen comes to the States, she'll give it to you there. (She gave it to Alan Curnow, in New Zealand. He didn't suppose he'd ever come to England again. Also, I fancy he has a strong case against many things English. No matter.) Or you let it stay here.

MacCaig may not loathe England as much as MacDiarmid did, but he's no great affection for it. So she gave it to him in Scotland.

Same with Sorley McClean. Are you less of an English person than Sorley? He doesn't even write in English! He loathes the Sassenach hierarchy. But he agreed to accept it from the Queen in Scotland. (I got the pipers to strike up as he walked across the Courtyard toward Holyrood—and all the guards of the castle presented arms to him, with a great yell and a crash. Gaels saluting a Gael.)

It has nothing to do with you living & breathing here. It has to do with English poetry's claim on your poetry. The life your poetry leads as a vital organ of English poetry. Or British poetry rather. Or poetry among the Queen's subjects rather. i.e. among us.

So we're giving it to you because we want to.

Cash is different, I agree—cash refused will always go somewhere else. Cash is tricky. You have to pay for cash.

652

How do you compare, as an old islander, with Derek Walcott? I imagine he's spent about $\frac{1}{10,000}$th of the time in England that you have. No roots here, no education, no stratification. We just wanted to give it to him, & acknowledge the sacred link—and he accepted. He happened to be coming to England—otherwise we'd have sent it. Or waited until he did come—simply saved it for him, with his name on it.

It's no part of that Honours business. It exists on a completely different level. (That's why it's so quiet.)

As for resentment of you—if you were to accept it! Thom, don't you remember? The British (generally speaking) resent every breath you draw. Every good word they have—is a kind of curse. You cannot publish a word over here without making a thousand enemies. Your only friends are those who hate your enemies worse. You can't be serious, fearing that you might be incurring resentment, by accepting.

On the other hand, we've all (and they've all) learned to live with this, like hedgehogs with fleas.

The truth is, because you live where you do, and visit so rarely—people don't feel the pressure of your presence, they're not constantly having to see your presence stealing their stage space, magnetising the attention that might otherwise stray to them. You're out of mind—you exist only as a book, that magically propagates a new volume every now and again while you, as author, achieve that British ideal (for others) of total holy self-effacement, the brilliant modesty of physical absence. So every admirable quality can be projected onto you—untainted by the sweat & stink of the crèche, the Private Eye-d bile contest.

As a fully active poet, at the peak of your productive powers, you are therefore unique—resentment-proof. Whatever you do, whatever you receive in the way of prizes, everybody can enjoy the full rush of crying—'wonderful', without it twisting in their throat to the old broken bread-knife.

Mind you, if you get the MCarther Prize—then you might be in trouble. But possibly even more with U.S. poets than British, no?

I don't think we should live our lives watching the bile ducts or any other secretions in our colleagues—(God bless them, we're two of them).

'Accept what gifts God gives' etc . . . and since the Queen as God's rep. in Britain is giving you this . . . on our request, I admit.

Thom, if you still feel you must refuse, I shall go into a tiny round graveyard on a cliff over the River Thurso in the NE of Scotland, where about thirty Gunns, under variously elaborate, marvellously lichen-patched gravestones and crumbling monuments, defend your ancestral bit of body-garden, behind a 6 foot high whistling stone-wall—out on the blasted heath there, not a visible roof in any direction—and I shall shout: "He says No!"

I can understand if it makes you feel uneasy. Takes a bit of your freedom maybe. Inner wild anonymity. A domesticating touch.

Still, if it's possible for a man to change his mind, I shall be glad to hear from you that you have. I haven't mentioned your reply to anybody. My Committee is still very happy.

You could accept and let it lie in the Palace—with the other national treasures. An ear.

Just in case you heard about my Shakespeare book, and some day meet somebody who can't make sense of it—here's an item.

Some Theatre directors are talking about making a massive historical pageant out of the reincarnations (from play to play) of the 4 main roles, embedding that in an epic background of events & personalities of that Century between Henry VIII casting away Katherine and the beheading of Cromwell. They asked me for a brief guide (a busy man's way in) to the main circuitry of my theme. Christopher Reid thought the enclosed piece would make it unnecessary to buy and bother with the book. Maybe he's right. Still—the idea's the main thing. The opening & closing bits are just general rambling to the fellow who's pushing it.

Sorry for all this. I'll understand absolutely if you want to stay with 'no'.

Love from us
Ted

Gunn, a British citizen who had lived most of his life in California, had written to give his reasons for refusing the Queen's Medal for Poetry. Despite TH's attempt to meet every imaginable objection, Gunn did not change his mind. The New Zealand poet Allen Curnow (1911–2001), and the Scots Norman MacCaig and Sorley MacLean, had all received the Medal since TH's appointment as Poet Laureate.

The John D. and Catherine T. MacArthur Foundation awarded a Fellowship – or grant – to Gunn in 1993.

654

1994

The rock musician and lead guitarist of The Who, Pete Townshend (b.1945), had adapted TH's *The Iron Man* as a stage musical. Opening on 25 November 1993, it was presented at the Young Vic, in London, as a Christmas show for children, and played to full houses, but a hoped-for transfer to the West End never came about. The part of the Space-Bat-Angel-Dragon was taken by Josette Bushell-Mingo, whose performance TH praises in the letter to Nicholas Hughes immediately below.

To Nicholas Hughes

9 January 1994   Ts (photocopy)   Hughes

Pete Townshend finally made his musical of The Iron Man, but so far it's been a successful flop, or a nosediving success, not sure which. A director at the Young Vic, a theatre which runs on a low budget, asked him for his musical Tommy—as a Christmas show for kids. You've probably heard that in the US he's just revived Tommy: it's a booming rave over there, and he's high in the Heavens, more or less living over there, hoovering up the adulation and glitzy glory, especially as he's spent the last few years more or less in Pop's dog-house fighting for air among the has-beens. Pete informed this director that Tommy was tied up but suggested the Iron Man. The Director knew the book so took it on. Pete then dug out those songs, do you remember, that he composed about three no four or five years ago and took around the US on his tour with the resurrected WHO. He hoped then they might attract some billionaire's attention and shake down big financial backing to make a full musical. They weren't well received. We have all the reviews, and the abuse he got for them is hard to credit. Pop world criticism has an arsenal all its own. So Pete lost interest in his creations, presumably shoved them into some bottom drawer—and the whole idea of an Iron Man musical went into deep freeze. Until this Director comes asking for something and Pete—four years recovered from his mauling—dusts off his old songs and hands them over.

They put together a show very quickly (it was almost Christmas)—
by taking bits of the narrative and setting it up as recitative. They
hoped that would make the story-line clear. The Director, one David
Thacker—who is quite a well known and respected Shakespeare dir-
ector—shaped it all into what he hoped would be effective dramatic
scenes in an effective sequence. Pete wrote some more music for the
recitative and connecting bits between the songs—which are sung of
course at the high moments, or whenever the chance presents itself.
Since financial backing was still wholly absent Pete put in £100,000
himself. The cast was the Young Vic company—who do mainly shows
'for young people' (not quite sure what that means). So they and the
theatre had to be paid. The cash also produced a rather magnificent
set—a complete scrap metal yard. In the cliff at the back of this yard
was embedded—perfectly camouflaged, what suddenly appears at a
dramatic moment as the twenty foot Iron Man, a mobile puppet of
scrap metal—he emerges with a great crash, very good moment. The
best moment. The Space Bat Angel Dragon can't really compete: that's a
black girl who actually does have a most spectacular voice and is a good
mover, good actress. But there isn't cash in that £100,000 to provide her
with wings and stupefying emergence from a great star—as there might
be in a full-scale production. So good as she is, she's outclassed by the
Iron Monster Man.

The whole take-off of the show was a little odd, from my point
of view. I knew nothing about it till newspapers began to ring me up
asking for interviews about how I felt, working with the great Pete
on this great new musical etc. I had to tell them I knew nothing
about it alas. So it was pretty well mid-rehearsal before I grasped
what was going on. Pete of course is in great demand, in the media,
as the recreator of Tommy—so news of this Iron Man put his Fame
into full pyrotechnic loop the loop. He obliged with interviews on
all sides. In interviews he talks freely—you have to understand what
that can mean, you know, remembering Pete's star turn of smashing
guitars. He had a good time with his limelight. But managed to give
the impression, one way and another, that the Iron Man was going
to be a very glitzy glossy grand Rock Opera. Of course, I've no idea
what his reputation is with reviewers or the Pop world in which they're
all experts.

The rehearsals were so short, at the first night everything was still a bit
rough. But the cast were in great shape and full of go. Our party—Robert

and Ainslie, Steph and her boy-friend, Carol me and Roy—thought it was wonderful. But the reviewers—without exception—panned it flat. They truly did hit Pete with everything, from every direction.

What went wrong, I think, was their expectations. Somehow they'd come along expecting the usual grand musical. But also, they'd come along with some fixed sort of attitude to Pete, let alone to his music. He must have upset them all somehow by his self-revelatory long interviews of the previous weeks. Why, he raged later, couldn't they see that it was a 'workshop (i.e. work in progress) Christmas show for kids'? But alas he'd neglected to tell them that. And the theatre itself, wanting to assume a smash and glossy hit, had produced a programme like the most expensive international opera brochure.

Another shortcoming, of the show, was that unless you were me or a child who'd just read the book you could have no idea what was going on. Our old story is actually very dramatic—I was startled just how much stage potential it has. But it isn't the most obvious kind of tale, unless you're told very clearly. Those bits of narrative recitative were simply not enough to make the story blindingly clear—as it is in the book. They got lost in the rock, and the whirlabout of actors on their scrap heap. So nobody had the faintest idea what was going on. Either the spectacular dazzle of one peculiar moment following another kept you enthralled, or you were bewildered. In every opera, of course, you have a full synopsis of the plot in the programme. The £100,000, having stretched to that sumptuously glazed brochure of actor's biographies and advertisements, had failed to go that bit further and put in ten sentences about the plot.

Result of those reviews was that Pete's great gamble came to nothing. On those reviews depended all his chances of finding his big money backing, to lift this 'workshop' production into a full-scale professional show. His agent approached 200 angels and every one refused to touch it, on account of those reviews.

However, the reviews haven't affected the audience—mainly of schoolchildren. Every performance is full, booked up well ahead. All the kids love it. And various friends of ours who've been think it is either wonderful or absolutely sensational—only of course they can't quite make out what's going on. What everybody sees is the fantastic potential. Everybody except those first reviewers.

To Terry Gifford

16 January 1994   Ts   Gifford

Dear Terry,

Thank you for the note and the cuttings.

[. . .]

Your questions are not really possible to answer. Do you know Jung's description of his therapy as—a way of putting the human being back in contact with the primitive human animal? Meaning—most neuroses, of individuals and of cultures—result from the loss of that contact. It's a metaphor we recognise, if nothing else. To that loss of contact he attributes wars etc.

Think of the many extreme ways in which 'civilised' individuals do keep something of that contact? Or in which they remake that contact. Having a child, hectic bout of adultery, immersion in pop-music and raves, physically violent sport, high-power predatory behaviour in business, farming stock animals, immersing consciousness in the sexual and killing freedoms of Video and TV etc etc, petty terrorism of some kind, crime generally etc etc

According to Jung's metaphor, every individual has to have one way or another of solving the problem—otherwise, neurosis, psychosis etc.

Which would you say is most harmless—among the activities that do fill the bill?

After sixty years of experience it seems to me that rod and line fishing in fairly wild places is a perfect hold-all substitute for every other kind of aberrant primitive impulse. Moreover, it doesn't interfere with the lives of others and is not limited to any one period of life. Nor is it self-destructive—in every way the opposite.

It interferes with the fish you say. Well, I suppose in some cases that's true. I can't lay my hand on a collection of accounts by survivors of attacks by big predatory animals. Two kinds of experience. When the victim was jumped, surprised, all said the same: they felt nothing, except in some cases (while the lion or whatever was chewing at an arm) euphoria—a sort of drunken happiness. When the victim had been hunted, in full apprehension of what was coming, then they felt the pain, terror etc. Even so, in battle, the most terrible wounds are often not felt. Strange thing, the old nervous system. I've read of shark attacks where the victim was as frightened as one could be in the sea surrounded by sharks, yet the shearing off of a leg under water was felt simply as a bump. Horses that break their legs at jumps will hobble aside and start grazing.

When fish are hooked say on long lines or snagged in gill nets they struggle naturally enough and then at some point begin to produce the chemicals corresponding to physical pain in human beings: presumably the whole body goes into some fear shock—fighting for its last gasp. At least, I've seen a paper where that was so in a fish that was hooked and let struggle until it began to drown. As must be the case with most fish commercially caught on long lines or in gill nets.

In rod and line fishing things are different, in my own observation. What do you make of this: friend of mine flyfishing on the Lyd was using a barbless hook, and having hooked a pound trout (a big fish for the very light gear he was using, it took a while to get under control) he finally brought it alongside his boot in about a foot of water, slid his fingers down the nylon and slipped out the hook. The fish swam off into deep water but he stayed bent over, rinsing the fly between his thumb and forefinger. Suddenly the fish came back out of the deep water, swam right up to his fingers 'within inches', examined them for a few seconds then swam off. So what was going on in that fish's head? Conrad Voss Bark whose wife runs the Arundel Arms at Lifton was the fisherman, if you want to check the story. Even worse: in a river I occasionally fish in British Columbia the Steelhead run up I think about thirty miles of river (there's another thirty miles above that) past I think about a hundred rod fishermen (quite tightly controlled, the numbers, by wardens). On two or three occasions down near the sea I've helped to catch fish for the Fish And Game Wardens who were tagging the fish and releasing them. Every fish caught in that river is recorded and the details of any tagged fish caught are also recorded—again the supervision is tight. Many of those tagged fish are caught again but some of them are caught up to seven times while they're running up that thirty miles—(in other words during a few days). Similar statistics on other catch and release rivers. Those are tremendously active and strong big fish—no joke to get in. Do you suppose the ones that keep getting recaught are hooked on the buzz? Whatever they go through, it doesn't seem to be aversion therapy.

When I want to kill and eat a salmon I sink myself up to the fontanelle in evolution's mutual predation system within which every animal cell has been fashioned and tap it on the head knowing that at least it is not—like the vast exterminatory tonnage of fish that feeds the world on fish fingers—dangling for a day on a long line or cut to ribbons in a gill net or hauled out en masse to die of suffocation under a heap of its own juveniles. When I'm not going to eat it I put it back. This won't help you to read my verses alas.

By putting the individual back in contact with the primitive being Jung means obviously back in contact that both satisfies and <u>contains</u> its requirements—contains is the crucial word. Once contact is lost—he argues—the requirements will exact satisfaction, in the end, in an uncontained i.e. uncontrolled way. [*Inserted by hand*: the petty terrorism, crime etc?] That's his argument. First the deadness and misery of alienation—then the explosion. Does it fit the evidence, do you think?

Keep well
Ted H.

Gifford had written to TH asking for his ethical justification for fishing, and whether he thought the sport caused pain in fish.

To Seamus Heaney

24 January 1994   Ts   Emory

Thank you for the lovely little book, the Merriman and the Ovid. In the Merriman you've invented a new alloy, in that general mix of your tones and tempers—the poem comes marvellously alive into the present. Have you done the whole thing? No need, I suppose, condensed that way. It was a cult object for a few friends and me at University. But to my ear your translation really proves or realises the possibility I dimly divined then—that as a mode, a genre, the piece holds a whole lot still to be developed. That combination of baggy popular doggerel, Swift-style outrageous parable, music-hall surreal political lampoon, miracle-play poster-paint imaginative licence, unbreached lyrical scurrile manners, cartoon immunity etc. Looking at Coleridge's doggerel, witch-dance howl The Raven, and Fire, Famine and Slaughter (which set Shelley off on the Masque Of Anarchy), I was thinking recently what a marvellous swerve they were—towards a whole literature that never followed. Yet not that far from Merriman, no? A literature that ought to exist but doesn't—sort of Hogarth tradition in verse. These are just the buds of it, like thalidomide fingers on a shoulder stump. The crucial essential must be that doggerel—elastic and hold all, the contrabasso belly laugh

660

throughout. Dream world of Bottom. I once made an attempt or two—following Merriman actually, and I regret not having kept it up. I'd have been happy to write nothing else, if I'd had the single mindedness and the savvy (and the guts, I suppose). It must slip awfully easily sideways, also, into drama. I'm sure there's no lack of the audience—once you've smashed through the perimeter electrified barbed wire, and scampered clear of the Academy tower machine-gunners. As in this piece you have.

The 'lovely little book' was *The Midnight Verdict* (1993), in which Heaney's rendering of a pair of passages from Brian Merriman's *Cúirt an Mheán Oíche* was flanked by translations from Ovid's *Metamorphoses*. Merriman (*c.*1750–1805), who wrote in Irish and lived and died in County Clare, was almost certainly unknown to either Coleridge (1772–1834) or Shelley (1792–1822).

To Christopher Reid

7 February 1994   Ts   Faber

We had an old Scots poet near here, Sean Rafferty. I've known him well since the seventies. Used to write plays in the forties. Was at Edinburgh with Sorley Maclean. Managed to get PN Review to publish a lot of his poems early eighties. He led a severely curtailed life since the war—a powerful little wife, and a busy pub. Started to write again when he retired at seventy odd. I used to take him books. He was immune to translations—a great formal stylist, on principle. Until, about five years ago, when he was approximately 78/9, I unloaded on him about six of Yehuda's books. Back in the seventies he'd found it impenetrable. But now—it was like a religious revelation. It liberated him completely. So in these last five years—80 and over—he's written quite different poems (different from his earlier work) that are infinitely far his best. Quite a phenomenon. About three days before he died—he was pretty fit—I visited him with Yehuda. Carcanet is going to do his Collected Works (Sean's) this next year. He was sitting there in his kitchen surrounded by piles of his typescripts. Then three nights later, as he came back from locking up the chickens, he dropped dead—according to the doctor was dead before he hit the ground. Timing!

Think of it—eighty years more or less total neglect by any reading public, a frustrating seemingly wasted life, toiling away at his rare verses, then at eighty a sudden really wonderful musical inspiration, what he'd been looking for all his life, then sudden recognition by a good publisher, Collected Works all prepared for the Press, and— bang. Exit before one critical squeak can be raised against him. There he fell, dart-free, not an arrow. (And lay in the lane all night.) Sweetest fellow.

The *Collected Poems* of Seán Rafferty (1909–93) were brought out by Carcanet in 1996. Until late in life, he and his wife ran the Duke of York pub in Iddesleigh, North Devon.

To Nick Gammage

2 March 1994   Ms   Gammage

Dear Nick—

Thank you for your generous remarks about W.P.

Interesting, your anecdotes about 'music'. It was the accumulated realisation of just how <u>deaf</u> to my verse most readers are, especially speakers of 'received English', how deaf, also, they are to everything in verse that is to me the real music, that I felt I had to write metres & rhythms, simply for the sake of my own verse. That led me into Coleridge.

But it isn't only the matter of metres (though that is a colossal amount). It is something to do with the 'personality' of the rhythmic ensemble and <u>tone</u> (which is a matter of echoic weave of vowel & consonant)—they find it non-English, alien, disturbing, as they find, say, a thick dialect disturbing. [*Marginal addition:* I wanted to make clear the historic 'fear' of that attitude. Sad for me.] Long ago, before I'd published anything, a rather refined girl rejected my poems saying: "it's all grs and -gles & hurts my throat." How's that for criticism? But she heard a <u>difference</u>.

Keep well   Ted

Gammage had written appreciatively of *Winter Pollen*, in particular of the essay 'Metres, Rhythms, Myths', and had passed on remarks by certain Cambridge academics faulting TH's musicality.

To Nicholas Hagger

19 March 1994   Ts and ms   Hagger

Dear Nicholas Hagger,

I've been thinking the note I dropped you the other day might seem rudely abrupt. I would not want it to have that effect.

I expect your mail is a tremendous volume, but possibly a bit more interesting than most of mine. Also, I expect that admirable infrastructure—or is it an extrastructure—you've created to deal with your school etc, might help you to filter out the bulk of the toxins. Since I deal with my own I find I'm always improvising new methods—of freeing myself from it, metabolising the awful chemicals of incessantly having to say no, etc. My fall-back strategy (exhaustion style) is to ignore it for weeks then try to overpower it in a hectic day or two of brief notes.

Then it dawns on me that here and there a brief note was quite misplaced.

I do find I have a great deal to ask you about. I read your books with a sort of automatic assent. You are saying what I have always believed— and I mean always.

What is extraordinary about you (and I'm not sure what the implications are, for what you want to do) is that you have learned the language of the opposition in which to persuade them. That is quite new. It means, I suppose, that they will listen to you. The historical moment is right too, obviously—you too are simply one more sign of that. But when it comes to convincing them, I do wonder if 'their language' is of any use at all—in doing the trick, taking them the ultimate step to a transfigured outlook. To do that, it seems to me, you will have to do as you do at your Meditation meetings—lift them right out of the mentality to which 'their language' and all its concepts belongs, and somehow bring them to experience in their own way 'the light'. In that case, your mastery of 'their language' becomes a means of persuading them, just briefly, to play your game—as a sort of concession to you. [*Marginal insertion:* And maybe—all the physicists old enough to listen to that language and feel it is their own are <u>too old</u> to be changed. No, how can anybody be too old.] Then, with luck, it will hit them—with luck, strongly enough to hook and finally transform them [*marginal insertion:* i.e. pass from rational 'understanding' to direct experience]. i.e. 'it' being the Light.

My own approach (though obviously far less clear than yours) has been to ignore them. My view has always been, that science has been laboriously groping back, through provisional language (sets of terms) after provisional language, error after error, to the point where there will be only one answer: consciousness must be changed, if the true nature of reality (as it is accessible to us) is to be grasped [*marginal insertion:* and lived in]. Physics, modern philosophy, even dear old Lit Crit and its contortions, have always appeared to me as the synthetically constituted poisonous Water Supply that the whole Public is compelled to purchase (for real cash) and drink in one form or another, while the simple, pure sources of real water, in the wells, have been sealed and must remain sealed, and that water untouched, on pain of dreadful punishment (ostracism, enforced hospitalisation in mental prisons etc). Not that I think physics has been wasting its time.

As I saw it, I found my own little trickle, and tried to make little earthenware bottles of it for whoever came by and felt thirsty enough to pick up what I set out at the roadside. Meanwhile I led my own life. (Trying to see through human eyes and dowsing twig rather than any other kind of lens or stellar probe.)

By contrast, you've made a raid on the Kremlin Kapital with a storm of thunderbolts and monsoonal swampings.

One reason, I must say, I hesitated to write to you at any length was: in your autobiography you not only tell an immense amount about yourself—you quote what everybody else said to you. My life, I should say, would have been ruined by what other people have said about what they thought I said or did, on occasions,—if I had let it be. So I am simply wary of saying anything to anybody: it ends up publicly hung round my neck. You know what Rilke said about poetic fame. He was right.

I was struck, reading your autobiography, by small things in which your thoughts coincide with mine: I mean very small things—that Shakespeare was commissioned to write the Sonnets (or to begin writing the Sonnets) by Wriothesley's mother, for instance. But what do you think of the deep scar on Shake's left temple (in the Chandos, & on the mask). And of his 'lameness'?

But I was also struck (it occurred to me when I first encountered you in The Fire And The Stones—in which I'm sure you've seen a genuine historical pattern and law) by the exclusive 'masculinity' of your vision. I wonder what your thoughts are about that: the almost total absence from your scheme of the Feminine Matrix—out of which the fire-bringing God rises, and against which he performs his drama of self-separation, total triumph, and then—inevitable withering decline, as the fire is first rationalised, then secularised and lost (as the civilisation disintegrates—or rather, whereupon the civilisation finally disintegrates).

In one sense, the 'tragic' trajectory of religions projects this (relationship of Light to Matrix) into the 'tragedy' of the relationship between man and woman. This is how my 'vision' differs radically, as I see it, from yours. You chart the life of the Fire as a 'gift' (to some founding visionary), which then blazes up, in priestly and political armour, to some triumphant career, but soon nursing its own 'heresy' and so one way or another tumbling to fireless extinction (absorption in a younger other). You fit history to your (much to be admired detailed analysis of it) description of this process. But from my point of view, the 'fire' in first rising to political power separates itself from its actual source, (by a severing violent suppression—even mythic 'murder'), which in religions was the preceding Goddess (maternal) phase. From then on, it is the story of Sophia. Or the story of Shakespeare's tragic heroes. At some point, that is, the triumph of the 'fire' (as civilisations embody and concretise it) becomes 'self-destructive'—the rational, secularising intelligence is then what destroys the civilisation (having destroyed the 'source' of the fire [*marginal insertion:* from the Gnostic—'depth' & 'silence'—the 'gnosis cardias'; *subsidiary insertion:* which was both male & female, as in Cabala]—the underlying female darkness: having separated itself from it, then denied it, forbidden access to it etc). Till we end up, as now in England, where any gathering of the land's most intelligent men, to solve any problem, will inevitably turn it, with the greatest care, into a disaster [*marginal insertion:* the image, in the stuff of reality, of the intelligence's own nature] (our educational system, for instance). Perhaps you will say that I am simply psychologising the various shifts in consciousness within the electromagnetic spectrum, or between the luminous bands & the biological sense-darkness of the animal body. Yes, perhaps I am. But my point, I suppose, is that man born of woman has to take the consequences of that kind of birth, and that whatever may be accessible to us, in the way of the Light, or the Fire,—and I mean the Light or Fire as you describe it, which I accept as a very lucid description of what it is in reality—has to be reconciled with our biological machinery and fate. I expect you will say 'of course'. But

665

your scheme is centred on the Fire, nevertheless, and as I say to my mind excludes its equal but opposite: our biological machinery and Fate—from which the experience of the Fire rises (from which our function as an aerial and receiver of the Fire rises) and into which it eventually descends. In other words, I cannot find in your system the human (mainly female) <u>cost</u> of the Fire, and the inevitable dynamics of man's inability to hang onto the Fire (the revenge of what had to be sacrificed).

I say, it seems to me that your system excludes this. You've thought about so much I'm sure you've thought about it all.

But that is my limitation: my allegiance to the pathos of the mother's child and the Mother in the crucible of the Fire.

I'm sure my 'begging to differ' is only a question of emphasis.

So the question that occurs to me is: how is that original experience of the Fire to be kept alive and fresh generation after generation. Every 'scrap of Fire' has always fallen into the hands of a priesthood, creating a dogmatic tyranny that excludes the people from first-hand experience of the Fire—then everything else follows. (Intelligence goes 'mad', vision dies, relationships & hierarchies crumble).

The founding visionary has it as a gift. The first enthusiasts catch it like a disease, and also have it—as a real experience: but it needs some powerful hypnoidal sort of event to transmit the disease, and to induce the subsequent regular fevers. How do you create that effective event without a ritual—which inevitably ossifies etc.

How do you remove from the Guides, the pontiffs, <u>the secret prejudice</u> —the lust for Power, which inevitably turns into dogma etc.

I believe an enormous amount can be done, enormous changes can be made, just by groups, as you describe. But my own experience is—the problems with the ego of the group leaders, the trivialisation of the mystery by those (the majority) who so easily persuade themselves that they have seen something holy. The problems of Ashrams. The problem of the mythic level—which is the laboratory [*marginal insertion:* Parliament] of the instincts, & which always controls (secretly) conscious behaviour: an enclave of wise Powers, or a Mafia of tyrants.

These are just rambling thoughts as I try to send you a brief letter.

Just for curiosity I'm sending you a cutting from The Times of some day this last week. The truth behind it (as you probably know) is that one known common chemical is quite sufficient to produce the observed effects (the 50% drop in fifty years): surfactants in industrial detergents—still a booming line in production. What she doesn't say, either, is that it is linked with a 4% annual increase in breast cancer in women. A recent programme on TV stated (actually, rather under-stated) the situation pretty clearly, in horrifying terms. It coincided with the first part of Middlemarch. Thousands of column inches were poured over Middlemarch. Not a single word, in any newspaper, reached out a cooling hand to the shocker. The public doesn't want to know about the Light. Or the Darkness. But what do you think? While this 1% per year fall in sperm count goes on being ignored, and while the causes go on being nursed and subsidised, everything else in newspapers looks pretty silly to me. Our Govt has had inklings since 1979. I sent the details, as they were known at the time, to Margaret Thatcher in 1986, and she acknowledged them. (The conference in Washington, that she mentions, a few weeks ago, has made it a big public issue in the U.S. $^1/_3$ the people attending were lawyers—preparing for the Insurance Wars)

I asked if you knew Tony Buzan—rather assuming that you would have heard of him. He began as a teacher, did some startling work with backward kids, moved on to the martial arts of the mind, now master-minds what he calls the Brain Olympics—memory feats etc. Writes books about Mind-mapping, How to study etc. Is now pretty big busi-ness. I got (very lightly) involved with him because we both had the same notion that Memory Training (through mnemonic games) ought to become part of the school curriculum from primary age onwards. We had a go at Eton, Radley and their Prep Schools, to tempt them with this magic herb. They were interested (we went up to a gathering of the masters for a day)—but finally rejected it 'due to pressure of work for exams'. Over the years, wherever I've suggested it to teachers, or given a little demonstration in class (of how twenty ten year olds can be trained in fifteen minutes) the teacher's reaction has always been the same: "but if they learned everything so fast, what would we do with the empty time?" Terror.

Now Japan, China, Eastern Europe are buying up Tony's books at a fierce rate, (and shall we still be stuck with our old rote-learning aver-sion-therapy long past phase 60?) (Supposing children are still being born)

However, evidently just this last six months students themselves have started taking it up, forming Brain Clubs, as Tony calls them, and it looks as if this lower-case fire has taken hold of the underbrush.

Would you be interested in meeting him? He writes verse, and like you thinks the poet should be absolutely the centrepin of culture (the ideal poet: everybody has an ideal poet, even I have). He would certainly want to meet you. Maybe your school—laboratory—well, maybe it's all old hat to you. Main thing is, it puts the actual 'learning' of school-work into its place—and leaves huge time for other things now wholly neglected. He has W.H. Smith behind him too.

If we occasionally exchange a letter, can we keep it to ourselves?

All the very best, believe me—

Yours

Ted Hughes

Re-reading: it strikes me, the Goddess cultures did not produce what you could call civilisations: maybe 'civilisations' began when the critical numbers reached the point of rule by warriors—who took (as according to mythologies in each case they did, and did in West Africa within living memory) political control from the women (where political power was magical power, fecundity power). So 'civilisations' would be based on the 'tragic crime'—the conquest of a 'natural Goddess religion', centred on women, by a religion of the Fire, always a misogyny insofar as it is a religion of the Fire, centred on men. Is this last phrase blasphemy? It's only a fleeting thought.

Nicholas Hagger (b.1939), British man of letters, philosopher, cultural historian and educationalist, had sent TH a number of his books, including *A Mystic Way: A Spiritual Autobiography* (1994) and an early volume of his epic poem *Overlord: The Triumph of Light 1944–1945*. His *The Fire and the Stones* (1991) is subtitled *A Grand Unified Theory of World History and Religion*.

Hagger had quoted, as an epigraph in *A Mystic Way*, 'what Rilke said about poetic fame' from *Malte Laurids Brigge* (1910): 'Young man everywhere, profit from the fact that nobody knows you.'

Whilst acknowledging 'a great similarity between us', when writing back to TH on 28 March, Hagger disputed aspects of TH's commentary, in particular his remark about the 'exclusive "masculinity" ' of Hagger's vision, which he regards rather as recognising the equal balance of masculine and feminine, light and darkness. In a letter to the editor, Hagger adds that he 'nevertheless sees the early civilisations as maturing when worship of a matriarchal Earth Goddess historically gave way to worship of a patriarchal Sky Father'.

Tony Buzan (b.1942) is the founder of the World Memory Championships.

To Moelwyn Merchant

16 May 1994   Ms   Paul Merchant

Dear Moelwyn—

Thank you for the poems. Enjoyable as always—such a surprising, subtle, varied movement to them.

To my mind, they 'translate' a more intimate complexity of structure. And it occurred to me, reading the very good poem about Aneurin, that something in you is yearning for a Cynghannedd-like intricacy of pattern, line by line. As if—were these (your poems in English) to be translated back into Welsh,—they might be in Cynghanned-like sequences of sound.

It kept occurring to me, when I was writing about Shakespeare's verse, to argue that he <u>deliberately</u> adapted something of Welsh technique.

<u>Our dreadful marches to delightful measures</u> etc. Later on, there are whole passages that permutate and counterpoint two or three sound-clusters—in the tightest possible way. Like Owen's <u>None shall break ranks though nations trek from progress</u> but far subtler, & more dramatically urgent.

He would hear about it from his Welsh schoolmaster, as a mnemonic device—then, when it came to writing verse that would be <u>easy for his actors to remember</u>, he would requisition it deliberately—and then recognise the whole realm of incidental poetic beauties that it opened.

No other Elizabethan/Jacobean uses it so as-if deliberately. In fact, no other English poet except Hopkins & Owen seems aware of it as a <u>means</u>. Perhaps the Puritan instinct rejects it.

But then again—maybe he re-invented it out of Elizabethan wordplay.

Love to all, as ever

Ted

P.S. Is there a book that describes Welsh verse forms & patterns? The technical laws etc.

Cynghanedd is the general term for the various systems of patterning stress, alliteration and rhyme in Welsh verse. Thomas Jenkins was headmaster of King Edward VI Grammar School in Stratford-upon-Avon, and so may have taught Shakespeare. The Shakespeare line is from *Richard III*; the Owen, slightly misquoted, is from 'Strange Meeting'.

To Peter Brook

19 May 1994   Ms (Photocopy)   Emory

Dear Peter—

'The Man Who' is your masterpiece. It must be. It is so far beyond anything I've ever seen in a theatre—it must be. I thought Mahabharata was the ultimate, and so it was, I think. But this, as the antithesis, completed the sphere—like the centre to the circumference.

It was like the ultimate interior analysis of a single gesture and word from the deepest moment of the Mahabharata.

The performance we saw gave the impression of flawless intensity and solidity—like a big dark mysterious jewel showing its facets one by one and finally the full glow of its wholeness. That sense of a gradually constructed completeness was very very strong. With every movement and moment so intensely focused, and so perfectly in place—each one seemed to magnify as it happened. The waves of resonance expanded from each one—like ripples from the rise of a fish in a dead still lake. Like slow motion, enlarging.

The amazing thing was the way these moments accumulated—as if each contained all that had gone before. Before I saw it, I felt your difficulty would be—to create a sense of the many-layered, massively working, suspenseful accompaniment of complex consciousness, which in Shakespeare, or any good play, is supplied by the situation and human containment of the story, like the yolk & white round the germ of the egg. I thought—the situations & instances in Sacks' book are so de-mythologised, so exposed and stripped right down to the chemical automatisms of the synapses in crisis, that any dramatisation might seem merely illustrative. Well, how pointless my fears were. Sack's anecdotes truly were exactly what you've been looking for. They simply provided an absolutely clear transparent lens into the depth of naked being—

So instead of life mediated through a parable, or an image, you got the sense of the bottomless cosmic dimension, the helplessly atomic dimension, behind life itself, which the poor faces have to endure & come to terms with. Really the thing itself.

My sense of this was so overpowering, I did not see how this same 'vision' could ever be contained in a play that was shaped by an image, or a 'story'—or a documentary subject.

Somehow here you staged the plasm itself.

The 'musical' construction of it, the way episode melted into episode, was simply perfect—and at each moment astonishing. Each of the actors, like one of the four necessary elements, or one of the instruments in a quartet, gradually became quite overpowering. That sense of cumulative power to affect & signify. Finally entering that holy of holies— those visionary dissolves of the creator & destroyer itself. Literally stunning.

I've only ever felt that sensation of being drawn deeper & deeper into some wholly beautiful wholly terrifying & utterly concentrated state of awareness by Beethoven's late quartets. (Four!?)

Not the story—but the <u>quality</u> of every moment. With all the other moments behind it.

Well, Peter, I can't express what I feel about it. But how strangely this work draws together the converging <u>internal</u> tracks of what you've been doing all along—the birds, the Ik, Caspar Hauser etc. Finally—the perfect lexicon for that statement.

The language passed all the tests. From the perfectly simple—Yoshi's "the music has gone away" scene, to Bruce's virtuoso tourettomania. That was quite something. The tiniest touch of literary cleverness—or even Becketian timbre—would have collapsed the web. The truest, the most minimal—vast!

The ultimate poetic drama!

I've been thinking ever since—it will be lost! How can it be scored, like a piece of music. Because the real expressive form is—the nature of those 4 actors. And actors aren't like violins—Stradivarius can't churn them out, computer technology can't simulate Yoshi & Bruce & the other two.

Could there be a whole type of theatre like that. As Noh is like Noh.

Well, you'd say—ultimate points are in themselves dead ends, or transit camps.

I can't wait to see how what you've done here will be infused into something utterly different. It inevitably will. You lose nothing.

Disastrous, in a way, that English theatre life got such a small dose of it. You should have your own theatre over here. Or some theatre centred on your productions. Maybe not. Your itinerant 'unhoused free condition' is that much less lumbered. Still, Paris has it.

I attended the 'opening' of Sam Wanamaker's Globe. 500 New Zealand embroiderers had made a giant tapestry of "Venus And

Adonis" to hang across the back of the stage. It was presented and 'dedicated'. They asked me to write verses (just to amuse you—I enclose them. For the New Zealand embroiderers, remember!!!)

Have you been there? It's still only ½ done, still unenclosed, but the minute I got on that stage I realised: that shape of theatre is a whispering gallery, & the echo chamber. And the audience are <u>in the play</u>, precariously hanging over it, all but toppling into it, as exposed as the actors.

There must be imitation Globe's elsewhere—have you ever tried one? Soon after, I gave a reading in Wren's Sheldonian, in Oxford—and of course there it was again. He must have based it on the design of the Elizabethan theatre—for its acoustics & its in-built drama. Marvellous place. Last year, I saw Walcotts Odysseus—the best things in the production were straight Mahabharata. But he had a sensational black actress—superb-looking & a marvellous speaker. She played Circe. ('The real thing') Look forward to when we can meet—Carol sends love too

Ted

Brook's *The Man Who Mistook His Wife for a Hat* was a theatrical treatment of the neurological case studies by Oliver Sacks (b.1933) published under that title in 1985. Yoshi Oida and Bruce Myers were members of the cast who had also performed in *Orghast* (1971) and *The Conference of the Birds* (1973). Other Brook productions referred to by TH are *The Ik* (1975) and *The Mahabharata* (1985).

The phrase 'unhoused free condition' is Othello's.

The rebuilding of the Elizabethan Globe Theatre in Southwark, London, had come about largely through the inspiration and hard work of US actor and impresario Sam Wanamaker (1919–93).

In Derek Walcott's stage adaptation of *The Odyssey*, mounted by the Royal Shakespeare Company in 1993, Bella Enahoro played Circe.

To Beryl Graves

9 July 1994   Ts   Graves Trust

Dear Mrs Graves,

We met once with Robert at the Sillitoes, in London.

I'm writing to you because a man by name of Strang wrote to me asking if I would be interested in helping to start some sort of Fund to pay for a grander monument at Robert's grave.

672

Evidently he wrote a biography about Robert, at one time, and so feels involved. And recently, when he visited the grave, he heard Germans deploring the fact that the English allow such a great writer to lie under such a local and modest piece of cemetary architecture. Strang's national pride was piqued—hence his letter to me.

I don't know what to think about it. As it happens, I have had to accept years of public (in newspapers) abusive criticism, because lovers of my first wife's poetry disapprove of the fact that her grave is not kept like a sacred shrine, that it is no more than a single stone, that its soil grows weeds faster than anybody can pull them out (two hundred miles from where I live). And so on. So I more than sympathise with any resentment you may feel against anybody who makes any comment about Robert's grave.

It did occur to me, reading Strang's letter and looking at the photograph he sent me, that was probably exactly the kind of monument Robert would have wanted—simple, local, part of the place. And that he would have loathed any grander effort designed by some Committee of protectors of National Pride.

I asked the Sillitoes what they thought, [*marginal insertion:* Haven't heard back, yet.] and now I am asking you. It could just be that you would like something not rhetorically grand but something—different Not that I have any ideas whatsoever. My own preference would be an unmarked stretch of wilderness—the sea perhaps.

However, I shan't do more till I hear from you.

Yours ever

Ted H.

The stone marking Robert Graves's burial-place in the churchyard at Deya, on Mallorca, is an incised concrete slab, in the local style, and remains unchanged to this day.

To Stephen Stuart-Smith

20 August 1994   Ms   Leeds

Dear Stephen—

No, I would welcome any comments.

I should say—I'm not concerned to improve it as a translation, but always keen to make more of it in other ways. If I had any conscience—

twinges of—while I worked on the pieces, they (the twinges) sprang from my craven cringing within too narrow a licence, too many servile straightenings & re-alignments of my behaviour.

I read the literal & the latin for hints rather than for guidance.

But I see all kinds of plain awkwardnesses & ineptitudes and so—as I say—I'll be glad of comments.

Yours,   Ted

Stephen Stuart-Smith's Enitharmon Press was to publish *Shakespeare's Ovid* in 1995. In this limited edition, the 'Venus and Adonis' section of TH's translation of Ovid's *Metamorphoses* – first seen in *After Ovid* (1994), edited by James Lasdun and Michael Hofmann – was matched with drawings and an etching by Christopher Le Brun (b.1951). Stuart-Smith had asked whether TH would accept editing. The following letter shows how he did.

To Stephen Stuart-Smith

31 August 1994   Ts   Leeds

Yes, all you say is true. But something is needed to suggest Herm's prudishness—his sexual shyness—and so justify his absolute no. So promptly delivered. A slightly over-the-top off-register second-hand salacity seemed like one means. A colloquialism that sits uneasily. As a prude's attempts at a sexual colloquialism always do.
[. . .]
Odd you flinch at this. Believe it or not, I once snagged my nipple on a bit of ripped metal—not to be forgotten. And a friend of mine slashed her thigh on the tip of a scalpel that had worked through her satchel. I won cups with a bow and arrow in my early days, and I've seen enough of hunting arrow tips coming through quivers to imagine just how dangerous they could be swinging around on the back of a boy in the arms of a naked big-breasted woman. 'Snagged' is dead right, believe me—when you get used to it.
[. . .]
'goyles'—westcountry common word for the deep cleaves, usually full of scrub and trees with maybe a stream in the bottom, that divide the roundy hills: where the wildlife collects.
[. . .]
Yes, fenced enclosure in African style early world: actually a fence of heaped cut thorns. All Classic mythol has more life, for me, if I set it in

a kind of Africa. 'Bomas' for me keeps that setting—dusty, thorny, spirit- and god-infested. Filters out the deadening overlay of togas and pure columns.

[. . .]

In character, I felt—also, true: a psychological world in a moment that 'non movet' does not touch. Have you never had the experience—not necessarily a lion: without the beauty, the youth etc, but with plenty of idiot confidence I've had it with a bear—quite a small black bear. And with a bull. And with a horse.

[. . .]

I wanted Turkish, because—simply—Turkish bows are famously the most powerfully built of all bows: horn, backed with sinew. The record long-shot of an arrow was from a Turkish bow—700 yards or so. So it's worth the anachronistic use of the word: same technology I'm sure—but Scythian would be more or less meaningless (tasteless) in the great classic stew boiled out of the bullion cube 'Scythian'.

[. . .]

Yes, scry for haruspicate. Technically scry is divine by peering into water or crystal, I know, and, logical extension, by peering into blood (or ink, held in the palm of a pre-adolescent boy). But haruspicate is too fancy a word for my wavelength, and I wanted entrails to locate the text firmly within the opened bodies of the suitors. So I go for 'scry' in its general meaning of peer into with intent to discover something, and in its family-link with haruspicate which is technically divining by peering into entrails. Suspended my usage between two stools—guiltily.

[. . .]

yes, I mean 'nape'—the barley bowing, hair tresses flowing forward and downward under the wind, and the wind running therefore over the nape of its neck—the nape of every ear, to tangle things trickier. At the same time, when you smooth the nap of velvet, with a finger, you get the same or a similar effect of a changed catspaw of colour-tone, and texture, gloss and matt, as when a push of wind goes over barley— only more static. So 'nap' also serves, though it only stands in the wings.

[. . .]

No longer sure of what I omitted, but I did chop this stanza quite a bit, one way or another. The face of the Cybele in Rome was a black meteorite. Earlier, here and there, the Goddess was simply a black meteorite.

Take time to locate the references. I used it simply to lift her out of the stock image of late classical statues in flowing drapery—and set her back where she belongs, in an aboriginal world.

[. . .]

Literal translation doesn't account adequately for what happened here—only suggests it remotely. As if you chalked on a blank wall: 'Picture here of a couple overcome with sexual lust'.

[. . .]

'sweating'—because the phase of their sacriledgous act needs to be registered in a condition we recognise. 'Gargoyle' because (quite apart from derivation of Gargoyle as the demonic form of a gaping mouth and gullet which is also a dizzy whirlpool etc) gargoyles often enough are lion-demon faced, and because these perverted (demon-ised) faces are physically now lions but psychically demons, the accursed of the Goddess, and finally yes because these transformed faces are indeed in a church, in the temple of the Goddess who became, after shedding a skin or two, the goddess of the Catholic Church (the Vatican is built on the site of the temple to Cybele): so to have these outcasts, lion-faced, demon-natured, clinging to the temple as they continue to copulate insatiably i.e. all gullet, seemed to me apt enough, where their only likeness would be gargoyles—faces set in a permanent rictus of appetite and damnation. Gargoyles is good, Polonius might say.

[. . .]

yes, slight blur. What I wanted was the image of a single swan's plume—floating with its curl upward, like a luxurious sort of sky-barge. 'Swan's plume' could suggest a big horny pinion—as for a quill pen. 'Swan's down-feather' is Shakespeare. My difficulty is to suggest a single plume of down in some way that would not look like a Chesterfield on a donkey—in the trot of the words. Actually, I don't find your image of a flying eiderdown so bad. I've already made it clear (I hope) that swans are pulling it along.

[. . .]

Yes, aware of this too. More serious. The 'sprawled' I defended, as a proper reminder of st 5 page 6. I considered 'Grovelling', instead of 'wallowing'—but something in that is at the wrong angle to 'sprawled', and though I adore alliteration I know when it tickles the toes of the comic, which here it would. Also, this is one of my favourite lines in the whole piece. Going back to the hog's wallow, maybe I could skip over a comic effect—a semi-comic effect might be sheathed, like a hog in mud, in the general straightforwardness of

His hounds woke a wild-boar in its mud-bath

A wallow is nothing if not a mud bath: mud-bathing for Boars is the whole point of the 'wallow'. Also, that smears mud liberally over everything that follows—the horrible wounds, the swansdown in the high blue, the cirrus, Venus' garments, her clawed hair her torn breasts etc etc. To good effect.

Maybe, better than mud-bath, would be mud-pit. Avoids the comedy, deepens the black hole—for sensitive souls the mouth of the underworld. Emerges again under my flower, later.

[. . .]

In general, I tried to pare off the Classical encrustations, familiar and pleasurable only to classicists—confusing and deadening to those who might read this. Yes, to keep things simple. Adonis and Venus are going to be more than enough (you know, for the 'myth-kitty' allergics).

'Herm's prudishness': Stuart-Smith had wondered if, in the account of Salmacis and Hermaphroditus, the phrase 'basket of tricks' didn't 'sit rather uneasily'.

'Odd you flinch at this' relates to the lines, 'Venus plucking kisses from her Cupid / Snagged her nipple on an unnoticed arrow / Sticking from his quiver.'

TH had used the Swahili word 'boma', in the plural.

'non movet': TH had amplified this to 'Feel silly and go blank'.

Atalanta's speed is likened to an arrow from a Turkish bow in the published text, which also retains, later, the 'silky nape of a field of barley'.

Stuart-Smith had queried both the image of 'Venus, afloat on swansdown in the high blue', which he said gave him 'an unfortunate picture of a flying eiderdown, rather than someone in a chariot pulled by flying swans', and the closeness of the 'wild boar in a wallow' to the line, a few stanzas later, describing wounded Adonis 'Wallowing in a mire of gluey scarlet'. In the published text, TH allowed 'mud-bath' to become 'mud-pit'.

'Myth-kitty' was a scornful phrase of Philip Larkin's.

1995

To Frieda Hughes

12 February 1995   Ms   Emory

You seem to be writing a good deal. Don't be too dashed by my criticisms—everything you write is, if it's not good, a rough map for a later exploration. You will know yourself when you hit on a piece of writing that can stand up to more work and intensification.

The problem about writing directly of recent experiences is—the memory is simply too unfinished. And the feelings—as in Insomniac—are still too engaged in the real situation. They are too painful & unresolved to say anything about. You can try—but they, your attempts to express those feelings, will always seem shallow, one-sided, exaggerated, false etc.

At the same time, they will find expression through some image that seems to have nothing to do with them—i.e. where you can deal with them because they are disguised. So your attempts to express the feeling of an experience directly, in the terms of the experience, will be blocked, false, cramped etc, and yet if at the time you wrote a story about witches & demons, or mechanical dogs, it would be full of wild feelings & you would feel the release. The emotions of a real situation are shy, but if they can find a mask they are shameless exhibitionists. So—look for the right masks. Cast about & experiment. A feeling is always looking for a metaphor of itself in which it can reveal itself <u>unrecognised</u>.

When you find yourself writing directly about something that preoccupies you with rage etc—just remember that. A metaphor provides the escape route.

These remarks follow three and a half pages of critical comment on poems that Frieda Hughes had shown her father while assembling her first collection, *Wooraloo* (1998).

To Nick Gammage

7 April 1995   Ts   Gammage

Dear Nick,

Not sure how I can help.

I first met The White Goddess September 1951—my English teacher gave it to me as a present when I went up to Cambridge. I remember my first impressions of it, because it was the first thing of Graves that I had read (I had not been attracted by his poetry at that point), and I recall my slight resentment to find him taking possession of what I considered to be my secret patch. I was familiar with all but the more arcane bits of the mythology—had known The Middle Eastern and Egyptian material since I was fifteen, plus the Mabinogion and the Irish. I regarded all that as my specialty. And in particular, I suppose, what really interested me were those supernatural women. Especially the underworld women—I had a turmoiling sort of baffled constant meditation going on all that, with various tunnels of special effects, Indian, Chinese and Japanese. And I suppose I'd worked out a kind of relationship to it all. That piece titled Song, beginning of the Selected vol, arrived in June 1949.

But once I got used to Graves, and realised that he shared some of my obsessions, I suppose I more or less soaked the book up. It was there all through my three university years, to hand. Eventually I imagine it had a big effect on me. (And on SP when I got her into it, later on). I suppose through Graves I began to see the whole thing had roots in biology—rather than in the fantasies of different or related nations. I began to see it more as a language in itself. Also, by chance I had started to read Jung before I did my National Service. My sister (my pathfinder) had bought Psychological Types and that was one book I knew backwards—the theory of it—by the time I went to University. So I read Graves through Jung.

I began reading myths and folklore when I was thirteen or fourteen, and for years, apart from poetry, that was pretty well all I read. So I got to University not having read a single English novel except two or three of Hardy's, and most of Lawrence. (But I had read all Dostoevsky in translation [*marginal insertion:* No, I was reading it.] and all the Tolstoy that could be found.) (Boast.)

[. . .]

Yes, Full Moon and Little F. I think what I resented about Graves was the way he took the Moon, and all the reflections of its properties and its possessions, without ever convincing me that he has done more than perceive their poetic significance. Even a very fine poem like Juan at the Winter Solstice seems to me to be slightly inventorising the demonic properties. I can't ever feel that he experiences them first hand and recreates them in their own occult terms. Some kind of witty dry distance always comes between him and the sacred event. I did always feel that. And still do, I suppose. His good poems are good for other reasons. And the good ones are perfect, undated, solid, irreducible. At the same time—I claim a source for my understanding of all that business very far from Graves. It could be—I've felt this on other occasions—that odd moments in his books did strike me as a clue to raw material of my own. I hope this hasn't upset an apple cart.

You also ask about—whether TWG was my 'first exposure to . . . the religious context in which Shakespeare's imagination was formed.' Impossible to say how clearly or consciously I conceived all that at the time. The overall pattern of Goddess-centred matriarchy being overthrown by a God-centred patriarchy was most likely something I first really grasped in the Graves. Yes, I think that's quite likely. But I already had the material, so to speak—and one of my obsessions, first year at Univ, was the hideous destructiveness of everything post-Restoration in Eng Lit, in Architecture, interior design, furniture etc and, after Handel, in music. I was made to feel all this as a personal sort of torment because, it is a fact, undergraduate life seemed to me modelled, in its exhibitionist manners and styles, and especially in its speech, the exaggeration of its vocal displays, on the Restoration fop. An undergraduate played a Congreve fop more naturally, more as his own true style of self-expression, more enthusiastically, than any other type of stage character. Gradually, I came to think of the aesthetic mode of modern England—really the public school aesthetic mode but also the mode glorified and embellished by such lecturers as Rylands (whom I actually liked a lot, he was wonderfully entertaining)—as a state of psychologically arrested post-Restoration attitudes. From that, I did eventually—and quite quickly—come to regard all post-Restoration English psychic life as something cut off from its true source and grafted onto other supply lines, alien ones. Except for the generation of Blake, Wordsworth, Coleridge, Keats.

I then translated this overthrow of pre-Restoration England by post-Restoration England into Blake's terms of the battle between Los and Urizen. I bought my Complete Blake in March 1948 (a few days from the day my wife was born) and from that day I read it constantly. At University I tried to model my prose on a combination of Swift and Blake's Island in the Moon. [*Marginal addition:* I exempted Swift from the Post-Restoration crime—regarded him (like Smart) as a victim of it, a casualty.] The 'Creative Writing' option (a voluntary submission you could make—it could lift your degree but not lower it) for Part I of the English tripos received from me a sort of imitation of The Island In The Moon. I dont know if it helped me to my 2:1. I never saw it again.

Gradually, after Graves [*ms insertion:*—plus Blake,], I began to see the religious aspect of that Civil War division. Again, I had that all in my locker—because of my early experience of methodist puritanism in the Calder Valley (which cost my brother and I dear, my brother more than me—I understood the enemy fairly early). So once the big picture was there—from Blake, Jung, Graves and my own experience of what the conflict cost me in modern England, everything else I read gradually filled in the detail. In the end I began to see Shakespeare's works as the magnetic field where the whole disaster was given a wonderfully complete descriptive and prophetic pattern. So, when—by accident—I came to write The Goddess book, it did literally write itself. I simply panted along behind, trying to make it readable. So it seemed.

But in giving me that big picture fairly early, yes, The White Goddess had a big part—and it was the Graves maybe that made the link directly to that lineage in English poetry—from the Sycorax figure to La Belle Dame and the Nightmare Life in Death. Made it conscious and obvious.

Sorry for the typing.

All the best

Ted

Gammage had sent TH a paper he had written for a conference on Robert Graves.

For fuller comment on the 'piece titled Song', see TH's letter to Gammage of 15 December 1992. The single omitted paragraph concerns TH's poem 'The Lamentable History of the Human Calf' – first seen in the magazine *New Departures* in 1975; classified under 'Uncollected (1974–75)' in *Collected Poems* – which TH dismisses as a 'bagatelle'. 'Full Moon and Little Frieda' (*Wodwo*) is the other poem of his own that he mentions.

Graves's 'To Juan at the Winter Solstice' was written in 1948.

Blake's 'An Island in the Moon' (c.1784), a fragmentary prose satire scattered with verses, was not published in the author's own lifetime.

To Simon Armitage

7 April 1995   Ms   Armitage

Dear Simon—

If I'm here next week, I'll look you up in Totleigh. But I would prefer not to give an interview (the idiocies I hung around my own neck—said in a moment, a yoke for life). Never written any article. Etc. I suppose I'm the age now when I should formulate my wise sayings for young writers. That would be another article, another wall-full of chains for the neck. Maybe it could be boiled down to 'Speak, poems, for me'—as Casca did not say.

The Tyre story is very good. The vanishing of it! A bit like the way it got to be where you found it.

But don't peculiar objects turn up on moors? What always puzzled me was the number of shoes you found up there—just one odd shoe at a time, quite light sorts of shoes sometimes. If they turned up anywhere else you wouldn't have to think they'd fallen from space. But what happened to the shoeless foot—if it lost its shoe out there? Who would carry shoes there, to lose one inadvertently? Poltergeists hopping for fun. Abducted wretches being violently stripped in flying saucers— shoes flung out through the portholes at 9 miles high.

But a big tyre? Makes you think.

Very good story—that wild sort of glee suddenly waking up into wild guilt, then nothing—

We once got a really good fire going—and kept it going for about three hours till we heard a yell. We'd burned the entire fence around some man's chicken pen—board by board, just one more, then two at a time, then what the hell. Then a yell! We ran a detour of about 3 miles then hid under my bed.

I hope we meet down here. Meanwhile, here's my piece about 'football'—just a note about my father really, & his craze (lifelong).

Keep it going & keep well
Ted

682

The poet Simon Armitage (b.1963) had hoped, on his way to tutoring an Arvon course at Totleigh Barton, to interview TH for *Stanza*, the radio programme of which he was then presenter.

'Speak, hands for me!' are Casca's words before the assassination of Caesar, in Shakespeare's *Julius Caesar*.

Moorland is the setting for the events of 'The Tyre', a poem that Armitage had written as a contribution to *A Parcel of Poems*, the privately printed anthology of poetic tributes with which Faber was to surprise TH on his 65th birthday; but he failed to finish it on time.

To Seamus Heaney

8 October 1995   Ms   Emory

Dear Seamus—

Well—there it is. And it's there forever.

Like a sea-god on a great wave you emerged and inevitably took it, by sovereignty of nature.

It's struck me—was there ever such an undisturbed undistorted full development of the possibilities—so timely, so prepared for the part. So wholeheartedly grasped.

So perfectly ripe at just the right historical moment.

Well—congratulations is a poor tame word, for what seems so naturally right, & mysteriously meant.

I was circling writing to you about the Oxford Lectures. Your ultimate statement on what it's all about—I simply marvel at the fullness, patience and subtle thoroughness with which you alter the genetic structure of things thought too long. And of the all-enfolding Welfare State of psychic accomodations, that keeps our intelligence in a good conceit of itself, and everything else—our general infantilised neediness or pathology—in a worse & worse plight.

I thought the crown of the collection was the last—'Frontiers of Writing'. By addressing it to an English audience, you were able to speak all the more clearly and urgently to the other audience, that will hear it more deeply—the Irish. Wouldn't be surprised if that lecture has a big effect—bit by bit. I mean political effect. Again—coming just at the right moment, with just the right mesmeric divine accompaniment!

Well—the whole business is wonderful, Seamus—love from us to all the rejoicers there.

Ted

683

[*Addition in left-hand margin of second page:* The School Bag!]

Written on hearing that Heaney had been awarded the Nobel Prize in Literature. Heaney's lectures as Professor of Poetry at Oxford were published in 1995 as *The Redress of Poetry*.

1996

To Renée Wilson

14 January 1996   Ms   Wilson

Dear Renée—

Anne Voss Bark gave me the news. She tells me that Fergus is there with you. I never realised his illness might be so acute—always expecting a recovery and fishing again somewhere.

I am terribly sorry. All that coming to an end. Carol joins me sending our deepest sympathy.

My friendship with him was quite recent and brief, I suppose. But with such a lovable man, so fascinating in so many ways, time makes no difference. I felt very close to him. And now, of course, I feel badly that such a long time has passed since I last saw him. I thought I was always deferring it to the time I would bring back the box of books he lent me—next month, the month after. So it goes.

A lot of people will have a lot to say about him, I'm sure. He always provided a lot of memorable moments—or he made ordinary moments memorable by his humour and wit and special attitude. So painstaking to make everything special. All my time with him is very vivid.

Much supportive love to you, Renee, in these bad moments.

Ted

Dermot Wilson had died on 10 January 1996. TH had borrowed the 'box of books' from Wilson's library to research an anthology of fishing literature that he and a Canadian friend, Ehor Boyanowsky, had been commissioned to edit. More pressing tasks had overwhelmed him and TH had held on to the books for years, until it became an apologetic theme of his letters to Wilson. The anthology never happened.

To Mark Hinchliffe

12 August 1996   Ms   Hinchliffe

Dear Mark—

Thank you for Tarka. The typeface brings it all back. I still recognise every sentence.

When I first came to live here, on the River Taw, the first morning I went fishing—1ˢᵗ day of the 1962 season—an otter jumped out of a ditch and ran ahead of me to the river. It was a shock to realise what I'd done—ended up in my childhood dream, on Tarka's river. He was actually born on the Torridge—which shares the same estuary, but he roamed over both. I ended up—later—with the fishing on the Torridge, which included the trees under one of which he was born—and spent all the eighties fighting one way or another to save that river.

I never saw another otter, down here, till four or five years ago, when they started to release artificially bred otters into the Torridge.

Have a good time in Cornwall. When Keith Sagar went down there, he asked at the farm-house whether they still had any souvenir of Lawrence—and they gave him his jacket, still hanging behind the door.

All the best—

Ted

Knowing TH's love for the book, Hinchliffe had sent a first general edition of Henry Williamson's *Tarka the Otter*.

TH simplifies and distorts the story of D. H. Lawrence's jacket, which was given to Keith Sagar by the puppeteer and author of *The Peep Show*, Walter Wilkinson, who had received it from Lawrence in Tuscany, when he, Wilkinson, paid a visit there, sweltering in a worsted suit.

To Ann Vaughan-Williams

26 August 1996   Ms   Vaughan-Williams

Dear Ann Vaughan-Williams—

Thank you for your most thoughtful and generous letter. If only all readers were as sensitive to the movement of verse as you are. Or even a tenth as sensitive.

You are perfectly right—there is as you say 'a backbone of iambic and anapaestic metre'. The only law, in dramatic narrative poems, is a musical one—since the whole point is to control pace, pitch, restraint and release, all forms of contrast, urgency and relaxation, within a single, broad, headlong current of inevitability. Ideally, one tries to feel the thing as a whole—so the whole thing is somehow there behind each word. Then very simple words begin to communicate the charge and psychological complexity of the whole. It is Chaucer's secret. And when that begins to happen one finds a curious thing—the piece begins to invent its own language. The words within any line, or sentence, become bonded in an odd way, as if they were all made out of bits of each other. That effect can be faked (assonance, alliteration, rudimentary Cynganned) but it never works when you fake it—it blocks the current rather than transmits it. Funny business, but very satisfying when it comes off—and even more satisfying when it finds a reader who understands it.

Also, all the verbal & musical detail has to disappear in the main purpose—which is to <u>tell the tale</u>. But thank you again for your rather wonderful letter.

Yours   Ted Hughes

Ann Vaughan-Williams had read the 'Actaeon' section of *Tales from Ovid* when it was printed in *The Times*. Her letter asking permission to photocopy it, for use in a creative writing class, was forwarded to TH, who at first replied suspiciously. Vaughan-Williams then wrote back to make clear her admiration for the piece, and to comment on aspects of its imagery and versification, both of which had put her in mind of Sylvia Plath's poetry.

For TH's thoughts on cynghanedd and its possible influence on Shakespeare and other English poets, see his letter to Moelwyn Merchant of 16 May 1994.

To Leonard Baskin

13 October 1996   Ms   British Library

Dear Leonard—

Yes, I'm a miserable correspondent. All silence or excuses. This time, my excuse is—for the last year or two I've hardly communicated with myself. Two years since I wrote a connected page of my own verse. Translations got me off my own rails—with a feeling of going somewhere. But they went on too long. Perhaps they've taken more in time than they've given in mind-broadening travel. Other confusions & crises. A sort of desperation accumulating—at 66. Perhaps.

Meanwhile, there are you ploughing on through the icecaps, undeflected and undeflectable.

It's true, the skull project did give me pause. The good thing about Cappricios, for me, was the programme. i.e. the fact that there was no programme. We then simply combined what I'd written with what you'd drawn. With the skulls—each skull comes as a cell, a bit of a prison. At least, that's the danger. Each one invited me to compose its story—in some way. That could have been done, no doubt—but I still want more freedom. Finally I was thinking—some sequence of pieces on which the skulls would make an oblique, suggestive comment. But then—what sequence while (a) I'm wound up in translations, and (b) I'm not writing even one couplet of my own. As if I'd forgotten how.

It did occur to me—some of those Ovid stories might have supplied a rich, suggestive kind of setting. But when you made no comment on the pieces I sent, I thought—better not push it. Also, I was aware of the setting-up costs, of such lengthy tales.

So I was stewing along supposing that some day when I get out of this post-shingles confusion, if ever, I'll just happen to write what suits me as much as it suits the skulls. That's about where I was sitting, am sitting. But what I can't guarantee is when it will happen. It's not writer's block, it's just some horrible huge restlessness that I'm failing to pin down.

So Leonard—please do use another writer for the Skulls. What we'll then do is—I simply send you whatever I write, & if it fits anything you've drawn, we make a book.

I did about 25 Ovid stories, in the end.

Also, the Oresteia—I quite like what I've done with it. But it's a huge block of typescript. If you feel up to ploughing through it—I'll send it.

Devon autumn rain, at the moment. You remember.

Nicholas is still commuting between Vancouver and Alaska—deep in his fish and toying (!) with property development. Frieda is getting married, again, to an Australian/Hungarian—very nice fellow, a painter. Her best paintings get better—very intense. She's started writing surprising poems—sold some to The New Yorker, so you'll see them. Both seem to be in good shape.

I translated Wedekind's 'Spring Awakening' for a director, friend of mine, which came off quite well, and Lorca's Blood Wedding—on at the moment, hell of a tricky play to produce. I translated it very simple & literal. No fancy business. English actors find it difficult. Still, I bet Spanish ones do too.

I hope all goes well, & that the election business isn't boiling over onto your bare feet.

Love to Lisa and everybody, from us both.

Ted

As Lisa Baskin has told the editor: 'Ted and Leonard often invented books when they were together . . . some did come to fruition'; but the 'skull project', conjured up in just this way, had no such result. *Capriccio* – which includes the poem 'Capriccios' – appeared in 1990, as a limited edition by the Gehenna Press. Although TH here denies a 'programme', the undeclared theme was his relationship with Assia Wevill.

TH's translation of the *Oresteia* had been suggested by John Durnin, director of the Northcott Theatre in Exeter, but was not in the end produced there, but at the National Theatre in London, with Katie Mitchell directing, in 1999. His version of Frank Wedekind's *Spring Awakening* had been staged by the Royal Shakespeare Company in 1995.

To Arren Sagar

15 November 1996   Ms   Melissa and Keith Sagar

Dear Arren—

I thought you'd like a rattlesnake tail, to scare your mother.

Keep happy

Ted

Arren is Keith and Melissa Sagar's son.

1997

In April 1997, TH was diagnosed with cancer. Surgery and chemotherapy were to follow.

To Keith Sagar

15 August 1997   Ms   British Library

Dear Keith—

I woke this morning thinking—I must write to Keith, must do something about that cataloguing he did, must send a skull or two (I found the fox in the car—not a brilliant specimen) to Aaron, must think of an equaliser for Ursula, etc. So I get up and here's your letter.

Yes, I know what you mean about the library piece. etc. [*In left-hand margin:* 2 different Oxford editions give 2 different readings—I changed that line, in proof, to fit one of them]

Two different attitudes to poems, aren't there. There's the making of stylistic artefacts—where the subject matter is simply usable material, and there's the truth-seeking exploration of the subject matter, where you're simply searching out the electrical life and the circuits. Shakes' sonnets are the first—wrought-doublets and costly codpieces. The big speeches in the plays the second. I suppose the ideal desirable thing is the first—using material which has been put through the process of the second internally and exhaustively. Is the best of Yeats like that? The best of Frost? The first is entertainment, creating beauty objects. The second religion/science.

The Hunt piece was making a real point. That protection does work in the West Country. Partly because we're an island. Poaching from outside is heavy—and very nasty—but not yet heavy enough to affect numbers (of deer, obviously).

But imagine what would happen to any stag or hind that wandered into Heptonstall Crags—or onto Manor Farm opposite Mexborough. Wouldn't last two days. Never would have, in 200 years.

And where are the foxes in the wild Calder Valley? When I first went

690

into Lumb Bank, one day I met 3 or 4 men halfway up the Lane, with dogs. They were Savile's gamekeepers. A fox had been seen going into that valley, (week or two before) and they'd traced it to a pile of rocks in the wood down towards Hebden. They'd come miles to get it (they were way off Savile's land—though I think he owns the hill-face opposite L.B. and the green strip at the top of L.B. lane.) All the time my brother and I roamed those hillsides, we never saw a fox or heard of one—except that one in Crimsworth Dene. When I went to Mexborough, the first time I walked on Manor Farm (across the river) I saw a dead fox—then saw others, all dead, later. I saw one living cub, caught it—and the farmer killed it. I got hold of another fox-cub in Holderness and my landlord—he kept chickens—killed it.

But I know these West Country farmers—and these West Country boyos too. One of the reasons I came to Devon, thinking of living on Exmoor, was the possibility of knocking over the occasional deer—subsistence.

On the other hand—yes, the Hunt! That horse culture! When a man/woman gets up on a horse in his/her hunting kit he/she becomes something quite awful, as a rule. It has something to do with the nervous fear of what your horse might do if you relax your despotic control of its every move. But also to do with (a) being mounted & therefore ⅔ big powerful animal (b) being in a uniform (out of your normal self) with a rigid funny hat (the hat crucial to attitude—as cavalry and commanding officers have always known) and (c) suddenly being in the rôle of King William's barons. Decent folk become instantly dreadful. I've been in some scenes!

Also, I've known for some years what a hunted deer goes through physically. And a hunted fox. And a fish being caught, for that matter.

For years I've kept having an idea that I daren't quite formulate: why aren't wild animals simply given the legal status of 'fellow citizens".

As you say—there is a big mass change. But West Country farmers —!!! Deprived of the Hunt by Blair & Prescott. That puts Blair in the role of William the Conq. God help the deer then! You know, when the Tories wouldn't give public libraries increased index-linked funding, those mild, civilised, responsible citizens <u>began to sell off the books</u>—beginning with the rarest & oldest. For some years now some book-sellers (one in Museum St) have operated almost wholly on library sell-offs. I expect you know about that. But the motive was only secondarily to raise cash—primarily it was good old human nature, bureaucratic spite. Oh, well, if they wont etc etc they mustn't expect us etc etc. That's how it went. That's well known, in the business.

There's been a catastrophic quiet destruction of the libraries throughout Britain that few people seem to know about it. (Hence my rhymes.)

Too bad about the Gouldians. Can't you isolate the males?

I'm putting together a vast pile of pieces about S.P. & me—Those few at the end of New Selected were picked from them, or some of those few. Very much the second kind of verse—rough. Not even that. Basically, my model was 'a letter'. Poetical effects incidental. Very self-exposing, I suppose, unguarded—my attempt to write about those things without aesthetic exploitation or concern for my artistic reputation. I no longer give much thought to that. Except to write clearly and expressively. Simply. No style. Plain.

It will bring the sky down on my head, if I publish it—about 90–100 pieces. But so what. The sky's fallen anyway.

One notion was—to set down something for F & N. Written at odd times since the early seventies. Now I've had enough of it. The whole business has sat on me too long—done me no good at all.

Anyway, love to you all, Ted

P.S. Manchester is off. I just don't feel like that sort of jamboree at the moment.

Ursula is the Sagars' daughter.
'the library piece': in his letter of 15 July 1997, Sagar had suggested that one of the lines from Chaucer's *The Parlement of Foules* that TH had used as epigraph to 'Hear It Again', his poem against the destruction of books, contained an error.

The remark about Gouldians refers to Keith Sagar's frustrated attempts to breed that species of finch.

To Terry Gifford

6 October 1997   Ts and ms   Gifford

Dear Terry,
    Very odd for me to think of your literary tour.
    However, answers of a kind to your questions:

1.   We went to Mexborough on 13th September 1938, when I was

692

just 8. We left—my parents left the shop and returned to the Calder Valley—on 13th September 1951. Thirteen years.

2.   The Crossing to Old Denaby was made by ferry—bottom of the little road that turned off (Old Church St was it) the long street past the old church. The Ferryman was a little crippled fellow I never knew as anything but Limpy. He had a stone hut at the top of the ramp down to the ferry (a bridge there, now, I think), where he used to sit with his cronies waiting for a passenger—or waiting for two or three passengers to gather. Heard some odd stories in that hut. The old Mexborough men were a very distinctive type—mainly old colliers.

The ferry was a flat open barge, with a worn iron rail round the edge. Limpy pulled it across by heaving on a thick twisted wire hauser that ran behind a vertical seven or eight foot high steel roller standing up from the blunt rounded prow. Penny was the fare. A low dam had been built just below the crossing to give a bit of depth. The road or lane then ran up the other bank to the railway crossing, on down after that past the old oxbow pond on the right and up into the village. Everything to the right of that lane, from the railway crossing and up behind the houses on the right of the lane, up the deep ditch to Manor Farm, was mine. When you look right from the lane where it passes the oxbow (supposing things are roughly the same), you see the land rising to a crest that runs with a slight dip between its two high points. That was the middle of my kingdom. From each of those higher points a copse hung down the slope facing Mexborough just across the river. The near one had been some sort of quarry—probably produced the stone that built the farm, encircled by and full of thorns, where I first met the local foxes. The further copse was more of a wood—quite close small oaks in the top half. That's where I had the experience that turned into my story about the rain horse. Though I was once hunted by a horse for a rather horrible ten minutes in the long stretch of rough scrubby land that used to lie between canal and the river, just opposite those two woods, and just before you got to the ferry via the canal tow-path. The canal tow-path was my usual route—bicycle. I got onto that at the point where the road out towards Swinton comes close to the canal—near the old Working Men's Club which was still there a few years ago, marooned among the new building developments.

I knew that land—the whole of Manor Farm and some two or three extra fields and bits of ground all of a piece with it—better than any place I've ever known. I think I knew every inch. I had trap-lines of various kinds all over it. I crawled over most of it. I knew every rat-hole, let alone every rabbit hole. From 1939—when my brother discovered it delivering newspapers (Old Denaby was part of our paper round)—to 1944/45, when my big love-affair with Crookhill and the Wholey family began (my pal John's father was the Head Gardener up at the house—then a TB Sanatorium). (John was as obsessed by guns and fishing as I was.)

Over Old Denaby I was always alone. I used to deliver the newspaper to the right of that lane where it met the main east-west road through the village—presumably still meets it in the same place—and turn in at Manor Farm (where I also delivered a newspaper) to inspect my traps (they began with a line of dozens of mouse traps all over the farm buildings: I used to sell the mouse-skins at school), or just wander about a bit. Sometimes I'd be delivering the newspapers on the East side of the village late in the afternoon, if it were a weekend.

During all the time I roamed over that ground I never met one other person strayed over from the town. Except for the farmer, old Oats, and his one man, and the extra labour at harvesting, I never met another soul there. And that was through the war years when a rabbit was a desirable object, and a partridge precious. There were always plenty of rabbits, partridges in every field pretty well, and a few hares.

When I went back there in 1982 for my old English teacher's funeral, the entire farm was one field, the copses had been ploughed out along with all the hedges. Even the quarry had been smoothed over and ploughed as required: might have been a bit of outcrop there still visible.

A year or two ago I went back to the farm-house itself and got one of the devastating shocks of my life.

To get to Crookhill—always by bicycle—I went round past the Power Station and through Denaby, on to Conisborough.

I wonder what fish are in the Don now. I remember reading a few years ago of a salmon seen 'splashing in distress' upstream of Doncaster. In the old days the Don seemed to me more or less solid chemicals— bubbling, fuming, multicoloured.

3. The pond of my pike poem is still classified secret, though we did catch pike in quite a few places. There were big pike in that tiny pond at Crookhill. Another bit of soul-damage there, the last time I saw that. [. . .]

After leaving Mytholmroyd the first school I went to (first day in Mexborough) was Schofield Street—about 150 yards down the Barnsley road from the shop, on the right. Probably gone. My best pal, till I went to Grammar School, was a lad called Gilbert Swift: his parents had a Greengrocer's shop quite near the school—mother kept the shop, father was a miner. Wonderful playmate he was. No idea what happened to him.

Opposite our shop stood a big brick church—now gone, I believe. As has Mt Zion's in Mytholmroyd. Behind the shop we had what was left of an old printing works. We used the ground floor as a general repository for junk, pets etc. Upstairs—odd to think of it now—we never entered. We built on a bathroom that sealed off the upstairs entrance—and after that, nothing. The size of a couple of flats—wasted. Some of the smarter customers knew that we printed the newspapers up there.

In those days, there was a permanent fairground down near the station: so Mexborough was perpetually bathed in fairground music. So it seemed. Though I suppose it was only weekends. I spent a good deal of time there, too, in the early years.

Well, there it is.

When I last saw Mexborough, far more seemed to have been razed or replaced than remained. Denaby—once like the darkest badlands, narrow streets full of black miners & their wives (and racing cyclists—the craze of the whole region, during my teens, was bicycle clubs & bicycle racing. I never raced, but we were forever upgrading our bikes (the desirable parts couldn't be obtained by human means—only by sub or superhuman means) and forever "training", as we called it.) Anyway, Denaby is now unimaginably other than it was. Unreal. What species does it produce these days, I wonder.

Keep well
Ted

Gifford's 'literary tour' was one that he had organised, with Dave Sissons, for Sheffield Libraries' 'Off the Shelf' festival on 19 October 1997. The 'Ted Hughes Ramble' visited sites around Mexborough associated with TH and his writings: Swinton Straight Mile (for 'The Motorbike'), St Peter's Church at Barnburgh ('Esther's Tomcat'), Old Denaby ('Old Oats', 'The Rain Horse'), Crookhill Golf Course and Roche Abbey ('Pike'), etc.

To Jutta and Wolfgang Kaussen

19 November 1997   Ts   Kaussen

Dear Jutta and Wolfgang,

Taking your points in order:

1. Shibboleth: 'something pinioned'. The ethos, of this weekend
Country House party, is somewhere between an Officer's mess in the
Raj and a shooting Party Dinner in Hampshire. The guests are a parti-
cular middle-class to fringe-aristocracy mixture who inherit the basically
public school but heightened by Military Officer's Mess Tradition of—
addiction to a unique form of social banter of incredible mutual cruelty,
used almost as the norm for dinner party conversation. It is a masculine
thing, but their women imitate it—and by family or school tradition are
usually bred to it. You must have noticed them often on their noisy
travels. They are the English the world hates. (There is some passage
somewhere in Jung where he remarks in amazement on their behaviour
in some German Hotel). At bottom, of course, they are often very good
chaps—but trapped in the style. The black sheep and dark horses
among them are always good value. Well, quite often. (As you know we
have other types maybe more amazing.) (But which country hasn't?)
But these (mid-1950s) aforementioned Country House guests tend to
affect—almost as a sort of defiant perversity if not political correct-
ness—violently racist and often quite anti-semitic attitudes. Defence
of the attitudes of colonial times. On this occasion I was not present,
but I know exactly what was going on. The 'you' was an exotic and
by fashionable standards very beautiful foreigner whose mother tongue
was German but who now spoke (left Germany in 1935, though her
mother was Prussian) an elocutioner's English rather more lofty than
the élite English who sat around her (German behind English can
sound super-echt English). True to type, all were disturbed by her. They
were out of their depth with her, of course, and at some point their
attentions turned nasty. She had no defences, being a born refugee:
a jew born in Hitler's Germany (Father a Russian Jew); later, a German
in Israel (Mother as I said Prussian); later, in Western Canada, a con-
tinental freak (married to an English ex-Army officer); later, cosmo-
politan beauty and wife of a wandering Canadian student in the far
East, eventually settling in England—but never forgetting for a moment

that she was <u>on the run</u> and belonged nowhere. But a big personality. Passionate about Tolstoy.

So I can draw on both English meanings of pinioned—one a bird winged and unable to fly; two a prisoner immobilised by his/her arms being twisted up their back or bound there. Two situations are simultaneously present: one is an incident on a 'rough shoot'—in which hunters with double-barreled shotguns are 'walking up', i.e. flushing from rough cover as they walk through it, various items of game, using dogs; the other is an incident involving British Officers of the Raj on some North-West frontier post (Afghan frontier or the like). In the first situation all the other (English) guests are simultaneously the hunters, their dogs, their double-barreled guns. The whole company (dog-phase) halts to 'point'. When hunting hounds 'point' they halt, stop waving their tails, and go into a characteristic tense pose, body extended, one forefoot curled, while the whole spinal assembly, from tail tip to nose end ideally, aims unmoving at the game (they have scented it) still hidden ahead—wounded or as yet unflushed. At the same time, the double-barreled guns are readied and the hunters stare fixedly towards what is going to move and be instantly killed. Slight private joke in there. She (the refugee now detected) would do an imitation of that particular English type which required her to lift the tip of her nose (with her finger) till her nostrils flared as if opening straight forward—like shotgun muzzles—and then speak in their commanding officer tones. Bizarre, that must sound, but it was actually so accurately expressive of the way those types stare down their noses as they investigate some wretch so to speak in the dust that it was very funny.

The 'game'—her—it now becomes clear, has been winged (hit on the wing), has fallen, and has been seized, and is now held, by one of the dogs. Held in that fashion—broken-winged (pinioned) and held trussed (pinioned), she is both held to be killed (as the game bird) but also held, arm-pinioned, for cruel interrogation, as a human alien. So she floatingly exists in my lines simultaneously as the wounded about to be killed bird held in the mouth of the dog, as all the hunters stare down, and as a foreign fugitive suddenly dragged upright, arms screwed up her back, to face these dusty officers of the Raj on some North-West frontier. Double exposure of the two locations and events. It has now dawned on the whole table that they have here not only a disturbingly exotic woman who is <u>faking her English manners</u> (like a spy) but who is also actually a savage Tartar probably begotten by some big black geni out of the Arabian Nights. Hence the coup-de-grace—the Englishman's ultimate social skull-crusher: 'Lick of the tar-brush?'—a phrase from colonial days meaning 'tainted with native (Indian or African) blood'.

I expect I've made everything more complicated.

Cannot find the Tolstoy reference to the wolf. Somewhere—a description of hunters returning with a wolf bound across the saddle of a horse. The point of the image, in the story, as Tolstoy focuses it, is that the wolf, having willed itself to death (it was alive when they bound it on), is infinitely superior to the men who are standing round it staring at it— it's a Hadji Murad in wolf's clothing. She often mentioned it and I guess identified with it. I can't for the life of me find the page.

2. Apple Dumps: 'wet star melting the gland'. Depicts that moment in the orchard, the blossom at full, when the creative life in matter itself, in cosmos-stuff, star-stuff, becomes tissue and plasm of the blossom just at the point where nectar has to flow and the perfume pour out, melting the sexual operation of the flower for impregnation, for fertilisation—a moment 'unearthly' in its deep-space sources and actual substance and in the 'holiness' of its out-of-nothing actuality, and 'staggering' in that the density and richness of this blossoming moment in the orchard literally staggers you, because it is too much for you to take, it heaps over you far more than you can conceive on every level—

All that revolving in my sense of the phrase. When the God-flame of star-stuff descends into earthly beauty, blossom of nectar and perfume, at the moment of living (sexual, wet) ecstatic (gland of all hormones) impregnation (and orgasm). Something like that. Literal.

3. Sheep: 'chopping off hopelessness'. Lambs have as you know a peculiarly despairing cry at best, but as they panic—as in events like the one being described—the cry is shortened—a sense of it being cut off, swallowed, half way through. Simply a descriptive phrase in that sense. As though they couldn't bear to let their distress out except in short little blips that don't hurt too much.

4. Gaudete. 'pony's eye'. No, not little. In fact, precisely and intentionally the opposite. Nor the genitive in that sense. She had extremely large, very frank, bold, clear eyes that were spaced—widely—in her face somehow to give me strongly the impression of a pony—a childlike face in some ways, big prominent brow, upturned nose, very heavy eyelashes. Like a pony when that pony has a big, innocent, bold

eye. I hoped I was guiding my reader (and expressing my sense of) towards the right kind of pony's eye, not the wrong kind—ie the little wicked sort.

5. 'wait under blackened backs'. Backs simply blackened by soaking rain. After long rain, red cattle (as these were) begin to look black along their backs, necks, heads.

6. 'in her feathers'. I'm sending you a story (The Deadfall) where this is explained.

'through the brick wall'. Figurative as follows: my mother was a passionately romantic sort of person. She was born and grew up in a valley in the Pennine Moors not far from Haworth and had Bronte-esque dreams of spectacular freedom—of riding across the moors on a horse. But in fact from her early days led a hardworking confined life—as a weaver when she was a girl, later in her brothers' clothing factory (all in that moorland valley). Later on when she and my father eventually escaped that world they bought a Newsagents and Tobacconist's shop in a Mining Town in the heart of the South Yorks coal belt, about as far as you can climb down into Hell without actually losing sight of the stars. (Hell for her, Paradise for me). So her dreams of wild freedom intensified and she poured them (i.e. only her dreams broke through the brick wall) into my sister and me. My brother, ten years older than me, was away in the war, then emigrated to Australia. So he was the absent god in our family and my mother and I had a shared cult. At the end of that poem, of that little event, I sat down beside her on the garden seat (we lived back on the moor-edge by then, on top of a high ridge) and we just wept together.

7. 'puckering amputations'. Sylvia dreaded passing the beggars who exposed the healed up ends of amputated limbs. The healed-up end was puckered, like lips puckered for a kiss, or a purse mouth, draw-string tightened close. Her greatest single terror, maybe, as a single image, was an amputated limb, as you will know if you are familiar with her work. Her father died of diabetic gangrene—successive amputation of foot, lower leg etc. When she was eight.

8. 'Seven treasures of Asia'. A Folktalism—intended to suggest the essential (biological) treasures of the seven (meaning 'all') races or cultures or whatever of Asia. The hair from here, the eyes from there etc

etc. She was racially mixed all right. But then, within three generations, my own children belong to at least 8 different—biologically distinct in the sense of coming from ancient stocks indigenous to each region—peoples.

9. Descent: the 'waterproof' is not literally a garment, but a whole provisional persona, assumed under duress—working in the North West Pacific Coast British Columbian salmon canneries, rough places in those days and far out. But converted, by her, into something very rich and fascinating, along with all the Tlingit and whatnot familiarities she'd collected, though in fact it was deeply entangled with a disastrous and harrowing relationship that she never managed to escape completely and that resurfaced during her bad times right to the end.

10: 'lammed our holly billets'. Refers to an old North Country game. A club, long-handled like a golf-club, had for head a heavy ten inch long cylinder of thicker wood, aligned with the shaft i.e. not across it like a T but prolonging its length. In one side of this cylinder, a couple of inches from the end, was cut a deepish notch, inch across. That was the club. The 'billet' was a curved piece of wood, thick as a thumb and a half, maybe four inches long, almost always cut from holly (Christmas holly) which is tough and very heavy, (but exotic heavier woods were prized). Everybody carved their own billets so all were slightly different. The idea was to lay the billet in the notch, with the club extended—the stance as for golf but with the club end a foot or so from the ground. You then flipped the billet into the air and at the right moment as it turned or came down hit it with all your strength and the full swing of the club. All for distance. No other refinements. A craze that would come and go.

Banksfields—was a slope of pastures above the village where we used to play the game.

11. Holly—always Christmas prickly holly.

12. October dawn: 'whistling'—full of singing birds.

13: Casualty: This was description of one especially striking install-ment of a recurrent dream that I have had on and off most of my life.
  The sense goes: Smoke beckons (i.e. by its rising presence) some (people) who saw (something) fall. So those people are the human sub-ject of all the 'they'—understood or present—sentences that follow.

I thought that if I wrote about it I might stop having it—and did for some years. Then it crept back in various guises. I'm told it's a dream image of the return into the body after an out-of-the-body flight. Or, by Jungians, that it's an image of some new psychic material breaking in from beyond ego—arriving as an 'accident' because the ego doesn't know what to make of it, how to accept it or catch it 'safely'. But who knows. I knew a young fellow who had never had any other kind of dream since he was a boy—crashing in aeroplanes, falling from aeroplanes etc. So he told me when he came back after the war from being a prisoner in Germany where he'd been shot down as a bomber pilot.

Let me know if there's anything else.

All the best meanwhile

Ted (Hughes)

Please excuse the hasty syntax!

Jutta and Wolfgang Kaussen were preparing a selection of TH's poems for translation into German. Their *Der Tiger tötet nicht* came out from Insel Verlag in the autumn of 1998.

'Shibboleth' is from *Capriccio*, as are 'Folktale', where the 'seven treasures of Asia' are spoken of, and 'Descent'. Assia Wevill's experiences are the subject of all three poems.

Tolstoy gives an account of the capture of a wolf in Chapter 5, Part VII, of *War and Peace*.

'Apple Dumps' and 'Sheep' are from *Season Songs*. In 'Rain', from *Moortown*, cattle 'wait under blackened backs'. 'Anniversary', in the 'Uncollected 1992–1997' section of *Collected Poems*, is about TH's mother and contains the phrases about the feathers and the brick wall. 'You Hated Spain', which had been in both TH's *Selected Poems* and his *New Selected Poems*, and was to be incorporated into *Birthday Letters*, has the 'puckering amputations'. 'He [an uncle of TH's] and I / Lammed our holly billets' in 'Sacrifice', from *Wolfwatching*. 'October Dawn', from *The Hawk in the Rain*, has the 'whistling green shrubbery'. 'The Casualty' is from the same book.

To Andrew Motion

7 December 1997   Ms Motion

Dear Andrew—

Just read, in the paragraph about your Keats in The Sunday Times book section, that the reviewer (would be interesting to know how her background fits into the equation) "was never entirely convinced by his presentation of Keats as a political poet" but, a little later, "I did wish he had written more to explain why Keats' poetry was so repugnant to his contemporaries."

This is a perfect specimen example of just how your complete evocation of Keats as a social/political animal has <u>provoked</u> exactly the same opposition (to your account in general & of him in particular) to the same factors, from the same embattled English attitudes (so little changed, at bottom!) that he himself, & his poetry, provoked during his life.

Some day I ought to set down my own experience of having come into Southern England (age 18 when I first heard & met a boy from a public school, & first met King's English spoken live) out of the Calder Valley (1930s vintage) via the South Yorks coal belt. Though I never associated myself or aligned myself so openly rather with any political extreme as Keats did, I experienced exactly the same mortifying pressures of exactly the same attitudes not just here & there—but constantly, in every possible situation. And when I began to write, whatever positive reactions might have stirred here & there, mainly I was aware of—well. It's a thick book.

Your account of exactly what put the screws on Keats seems to me so familiar, exact & profound—but, the attitudes that were unaware of it (because they twisted the screws) then, are still in place, as I say, and are still unaware because they are still twisting the same screws. At the moment into your resurrected Keats, poor chap. Different model plastic screws—powered (automated) screwdrivers.

I slipped sideways, via Scotland & Ireland, into the U.S., for literary survival—otherwise, I would have gone to ground in Australia, like a wombat. As my brother did.

Anyway—how interesting, this response to your brilliant book.

Love to you both
Ted

TH had already (24 August) written to the poet Andrew Motion (b.1952) to tell him how 'overwhelmed' he had been by Motion's biography *Keats*, which he had read in proof, adding particularly: 'the cumulative effect in those last chapters, is annihilating. Tolstoyan'.

1998

The publication of *Birthday Letters*, TH's intimate account, in poems, of his life with Sylvia Plath – and his first public declaration on a subject on which innumerable biographers, literary critics and journalists had freely commented for thirty-five years – had been prepared with the utmost secrecy. The first the public knew of it was a two-page spread in *The Times* of 17 January, including a selection of poems from the book and an account of their background. The book was an immediate best-seller. Before publication, copies had already gone to close friends, Seamus Heaney (see letter below) among them.

To Seamus Heaney

1 January 1998   Ms Emory

Your letter overwhelmed me. I dearly wanted to know what you would feel about all those pieces, and about the niceties and not-so-niceties of publishing them—your opinion above everybody's, (as a veteran of ticklish declarations). In a way, my final decision was 3 parts blind—a gamble. I'd come to the point where there seemed no alternative. Given the funny old physical corner I've got myself into, and the mysterious rôle in my life that SP's posthumous life has played—and that our posthumous marriage has played—publication came to seem not altogether a literary matter, more a physical operation that just might change the psychic odds crucially for me, and clear a route. Though I did wonder whether my very sudden determination to ignore every kind of reaction to them, and every possible impropriety of revealing them, didn't signify some diminution of brain—since all these 25 years or so I've lived under a regime that found every reason to hide them like the family idiot, perhaps quietly do away with them someday if I could find the courage. Do away with them or—I suppose this was my working justification— absorb their vital suggestions into some more objective properly creative other work. I always had some idea that the real accounting for my dealings with Sylvia would have to emerge inadvertently, in some oblique fashion, through some piece only symbolically related to it—the authentic creative way. But there they are. I hit on the direct letter as an illegal private transaction between her & me—then simply followed the clues, and they piled up.

The realisation that I had to rid myself of the whole log-jam pile-up— as a matter of urgency—dawned as I was doing the Shakespeare book. I sometimes wondered if that Shakes tome wasn't the poem I should have written—decoded, hugely deflected and dumped on shoulders that could carry it. Then when I assembled my New & Selected (mainly to displace the bilious physical appearence and illegible typeface of the earlier one) I thought of adding a good heap of these pieces—30 or 40 maybe—and started grooming & trimming the most ragged of the more attractive. But Carol's sister was dying, & nursing her daily Carol was in no shape to deal with these extras. I managed to clear those few— with the pieces about Assia (written very differently)—that I did include. The rest I stuffed back into the sack. But they wouldn't stay. So I brought them back up & wrote at them en masse for some time—not knowing what I'd end up with or where I'd end. Till suddenly—between one day & the next—I realised that was it. I couldn't grasp the wholeness of it but I had the sensation of the whole load of long preoccupation dropping away—separating itself and dropping away like a complete piece of fruit. The sense of being released from it very strong & weird. I had huge quantities of little germinal notes—all suddenly obsolete.

When TH's *New Selected Poems* (1957–1994) appeared in 1995, the inclusion of poems about Sylvia Plath and Assia Wevill passed without comment from most reviewers. The poems about Wevill were collected, with others, in *Capriccio*, published less sensationally than *Birthday Letters* in 1990.

To Jack Brown

3 February 1998   Ms   British Library

Dear Jack—

Good to hear from you as always. Yes, I got a bit off colour—pulling myself together again now.

Interesting to compare our snaring histories. I wonder if I was the last of a breed. I doubt it. But it was easier in the 30s and 40s to preserve the hunting & trapping sensibility intact—especially if you'd grown up inside it, as I did, by a fluke. Right up into the fifties, I shot hares and partridges (in E. Yorks, with a rifle, on my RAF station) and sent the dressed corpses through the post to friends (who were still on meat-rationing.)

It was S.P. who transformed me actually—in one flash, one particular moment. But I still see why country people need to get hold of meat. Less so now, I suppose. It's all become so confused with diseases and Civil War petty tyrannies, & welfare.

Your rabbit was probably dragged out of its snare by a fox or a dog. I can't imagine a rabbit would have the weight/strength to do what you describe. But who knows.

Snares are horrible things, alright. I once caught a fox-cub in a snare and it was sitting there like a dog in a kennel—pretty healthy. I had a trapline: I sold the skins.

Curious fact: when I stopped shooting, which I did in 1956, I lost a whole faculty of vision & awareness. Before then, whatever landscape I looked into, I saw every living thing—every tiniest trace. It never occurred to me, what I had lost, till about 15 years ago a friend down here invited me on a farmer's shoot—walking up pheasants in these deep 'goyles' as they call them. I'd agreed to go on as a 'beater'—but he shoved a gun into my hands. My heart began to pound and instantly, I realised, I could see absolutely everything—just as when I was a boy. I had a clairvoyant, dream sort of day, shot my pheasants, then gave back the gun. Instantly—the vision went, the old, marvellous alertness simply went. I've never touched a gun since. And now shingles has blurred my best eye, anyway—too late.

But there's more to that business than filling a pot. In salmon fishing, it's a whole different array of faculties, but similar—I've managed to hang on to that. Look after yourself, Jack

love

Ted

The incident recounted by TH in his *Birthday Letters* poem 'The Rabbit Catcher' had prompted Brown to write. 'Your rabbit' refers to a passage from Brown's unpublished novel *Genesis*, which Brown had shown TH.

To Matthew Sweeney

5 February 1998   Ms   Sweeney

Dear Matthew—

I'm a long time responding to your Bridal Suite book—but that's good, I've got to know it better, & got to like it more & more. So pure and sustained—so all of a piece.

I read through the whole thing, the other day, and was struck—every line, every word, is surprising, seems absolutely right, & stays solid, even where the whole narrative stays utterly mysterious. These narratives must be to you what Kafka's brief narratives were to Kafka—they're what your natural muse produces naturally. And I've wondered—if Matthew were to go on writing, or launching himself into, a fresh one of these say every 3 days, they would gradually become the real Sweeney autobiography: Sweeney's mythic life. They seem so unstudied, so spontaneous, yet so real—and comprehensive.

I remember when I was doing those Crow pieces, every time I wrote down "Once upon a time there was a—" inevitably I got a kind of story, a metaphoric Tale, a spiel of some kind, that I could never alter much & that always came out of nowhere, total surprise. And I remember thinking: if I write one of these every other day, and stick at it, after a few years what would I have? A whole autobiography of my mythic life, at some level. Ah, God, why didn't I stick at it? Is it too late to try again? Those are my thoughts now.

So it would be interesting to see what your pieces would become—written in exactly that playful free but really open to any mood fantasia flight, dream flight, that you've discovered. I really believe it would become something big. Everything in you would gather to it, maybe, to take the opportunity for a total statement.

Like the effect of Jung's 'active imagination'—or like the effect Jung claims for it. Gradual integration of the whole mind. If that does happen, what develops must be—bigger & deeper & really more intimately you. Nothing prohibited.

Every other day, an hour's experiment—doesn't work if consciously steered or in any way controlled. Am I telling myself?

It's a more purposeful form of free-association (which Schiller invented to 'loosen his imagination" before settling down to work.) (I wonder if he got it from Yoga—some forms of meditation are similar)

706

What's wonderful about the Bridal Suite narratives is that they're so 'complete'. Seem centred on something serious—not arbitrary.

Anyway, I shall look out for what follows.

All the best Matthew & keep well.

Ted

Good to keep these secret schemes to yourself. Funny thing, the way our colleagues are so quick to check & trip up every new step we try to take. Nobody else can do what only you can do—and nobody else is going to do it. It's half the game—to ignore them.

Matthew Sweeney (b.1952) records that, although this letter bears the date 5 February, it arrived on 6 October, his birthday. Receiving it, he says, 'was the most important thing that happened in my professional life, worth any number of reviews'. *The Bridal Suite*, a collection of poems, had been published the previous year.

In speaking of the 'active imagination', Jung was concerned with the beneficial mutual accessibility of conscious and subconscious. An account of his own experience of it is given in *Memories, Dreams and Reflections* (1961).

To Nicholas Hughes

20 February 1998   Ms (photocopy)   Hughes

I've been thinking about your kiln. Do you remember, when you were at Bedales, you read that book about the Primal Scream. However cock-eyed that whole book and therapy, riding its wave of fashion, may have been—it stirred up one giant Truth. At the time, when you were telling me about what you thought of it, you described a dream—that I immediately connected to what the book had wakened up in you. You were walking up a garden path towards a building with a glass door. A frog was jumping up the path behind you. You entered the building and closed the glass door, shutting out the frog. The frog then jumped against the glass of the door. Do you remember it?

If I had had that dream it would have seemed immensely important to me. In fact, at times, I have had several dreams very like it—especially in my late twenties and thirties when I was trying might and main to make contact with my real resources—doing all kinds of things to conjure them up, summon them, [*words missing from photocopy*] of them and incorporate them and become <u>whole</u>—instead of being two minds, one having all the clever ideas, the other having all the real knowledge, the real truths, and my own real nature, whatever it might be. Being a writer was in a way a side-issue, a by-product, of wanting to do that. Writing was merely a way of formulating how I was getting on with it. And because when it worked—there was nothing like it, nothing else mattered, by comparison, because everything fell into perspective, for a while, at a big depth.

One series of dreams I had, from my teens on. Occasionally still have. Were versions of your frog. Instead of a frog, mine, in these dreams, is an aeroplane. Sometimes I'm in it. More often, it goes over—in <u>trouble</u>. On fire, or driving out of control. It crashes—usually just out of sight. (But about a month ago, it crashed on the building I was in—a huge troop-transport carrier. I was trying to smash the windows of the office I was in—blast proof glass, military building—when a friend suddenly managed to open one by simply turning the handle. As we got out I was expecting the whole building to go up in flames.)

When it crashes, I go towards it and always find somebody who either fell out of it or is crawling from the wreck. I wrote a poem once about one of these dreams—thought it might stop me having them, but it didn't.

That plane is the frog hitting the glass. Something from the other side of my conscious mind—something mighty important, i.e. the news from my whole body and its understandings, is trying to get through to me. What gets through (smashes through the glass) is burned and horribly mutilated and usually dead. (In the poem, the fallen man is just dying). In other words, these dreams record how—whatever is trying to reach me out of myself—I am somehow rejecting it, evading it, not accepting it.

Another occasion (I even remember the date) I was at a writer's resort in Upper New York State, Yaddo, with your mother. That's where she really began to write. Each day, we went to a separate cabin in the woods, with a packed lunch, and wrote all day. Wonderful stove, masses of pine cones as fuel. For about an hour each day I would read Dante's Divine Comedy to myself—aloud, in the Italian. The sound of Dante's language is unique, and ties his words together in the most powerful and incisive way. His whole mentality is wonderful to sink yourself into. Anyway, after I finished the Paradiso—the 3rd of the 3 parts—I had a dream. I was in a vast quarry, like the Grand Canyon (which we'd visited earlier that summer). I was suddenly aware of something moving in the depths of the quarry, then saw it was a colossal ape, coming up towards me at great speed. I was very alarmed, and scrambled away up the quarry side. On the brink was a flimsy building—a sort of builder's caravan. Just ahead of the Gorilla (the frog) I got into the caravan, and dragged in after me my old leather first world war trench coat (which was my big link to authentic life, I suppose). But the ape grabbed the hem of the coat. I tried to shut the door, but the coat, halfway in, halfway out, prevented that. So I stared at the ape through the gap of the partly open door. As our eyes met, he let go of the coat, and very gently, with a sort of amused expression in his eyes, lifted his hands and put a forefinger tip into each of his ears. As if to say (I've thought later) "No more Italian please!" But to me, the main point was, I'd made a contact that stayed open and was friendly (I'm writing this bit on the train).

Just before that, I had a series of animal confrontation dreams that all ended badly. These dreams came up so vividly, I expect, because I had isolated myself to do nothing else but make contact with the other side. (I think this effort has to be constantly renewed, because what is pressing towards you, to enlighten you with the truth about yourself, is always developing, always different from the truth which you did manage to admit and integrate with your conscious self, a while ago.) In one of these dreams I fought a bear—and actually seemed to be winning. First it stood over me, breathing into my face, then I was on top of it and crushing its throat with an iron bar. (Next morning, there was a new New Yorker in the breakfast room, and the first page I opened was a cartoon of a hunter lying under a bear.) Another dream, night or two later, I saw a wolf under a tree, watching me from behind the trunk. Next thing, it was loping towards me at great speed. All I had in my hand was a spade. As it came towards me, I became blind. I tried desperately to strain some chink of sight through the fog in my eyes, and hit the wolf with the spade, as hard as I could. I then went on battering it to death. Suddenly my eyes cleared, and I had killed—a kitten. (That's called—that dream—'Slamming the door on the frog'.)

The most disturbing to remember was another version—years later.

When I began to write, I began to dream about Crookhill pond—you remember, where we caught that perch in the last puddle of water. In my dreams, that pond was always different. When I was in good contact with myself, the pond would be full of big pike. Once or twice, the pike were big water-leopards. I might be just seeing these—or [*words missing*] them. Other occasions it would be empty of any except one or two very tiny pike. That meant—a general state of being in very poor contact with myself. Once or twice, it was lined with tiles and empty—that meant, total breakdown of communication between me and myself. (So you see, when I saw the actual pond drained and converted to a sort of rubbish dump, it gave me a big shock.)

But before then, when we first went to Ireland in 1965, to live, I had switched from pike in Crookhill pond to salmon in rivers. Influence of the Taw. Before we went to Ireland, after living in Court Green for 2 years with Olwyn, my writing was at a very low ebb. I was at a dead end, that I could not get past. Then I made the break-out, to Ireland: fixed the house to go to, Doonreagan House you remember [*words missing*] Cleggan. The night before we left I had an amazingly vivid dream. I was walking down the upper Taw stream—on Dartmoor, thin acidy pools, with skinny dark tiny trout. The moor ended at a cliff, and the Taw stream fell over it—as a thin waterfall, joining a big fast river that flowed along the bottom of the cliff, rather as the Gulcana flows under that bluff. (But flowing right to left.) As I got to the bottom of the cliff, and stood beside this big river, I saw that masses of huge salmon were rushing up it. As they went, they leapt clear of the water, writhing their bodies as they do going up a weir, and this shaking snaking movement of their flanks hurled milt and roe out of their bodies and plastered me head to foot. So I stood there being showered and drenched with salmon milt and roe, as they went up crashing past me. What it meant—as turned out to be true—was that going to Ireland broke me out of that arid sterile alienation from myself that my life at C.G. had trapped me into, and with a single stride plunged me right into the productive, fruitful thick of my best chances. And in Ireland I did make a big breakthrough—in my writing and in everything to do with myself.

After that—ever since—my 'frog' has been salmon, mainly. But sometimes other creatures.

But in that fish series the most disturbing as I say was in about 1975—when we had the farm, and the Baskins had moved to Devon. My fishing those days was reduced to Reservoirs (I didn't really start salmon fishing till about 78) and fiddling with the trout in the Taw now and again. By 1975, we had got into a regular social life with the Baskins—as they taught us about wine. So we dined about 3 nights a week with them, or more, and drank a lot of fine wine. Also bought wine for C.G. I was noticing how one of those evenings would clobber me mentally for

2 or 3 days, by which time we had another. Also, reservoir fishing—a bit of a mania, as you'll recall.

Meanwhile, the farm. And all the time trying to get time in my hut to get back to the flow of good inspiration that I'd found in Ireland and hung on to till about 1969—(when death of Assia and my mother and general struggles to solve how I could look after Frieda and you had brought it to a close.) I was then 45 or so, and full of ideas and visions of what I wanted to write, but clobbered by the life I was living—concentration battered, social life etc etc. All very clear to me now.

In the middle of that I had a visionary dream. I was beside an estuary, near a harbour. A ship was coming in—quite a large ship. Brilliantly coloured. Then I noticed it was loaded way above the gunwales with enormous salmon, piled high, a floating small mountain of giant salmon, and on top them, scattered like cloths or carpets, many jaguars, as if they were asleep. As it came in towards me, at the wharfe—another dream superimposed itself. A theatre stage—onto which I wandered (to perform my part?) totally drunk, so drunk I had to sit in a chair. From that position, I somehow fished the whole scene of the dream—the estuary, the ship loaded with salmon and jaguars—drunkenly, with one of those wretched reservoir rods, and a Grouse and Claret Fly. I then got up and simply—wandered away, drunkenly, dazed. That was the dream.

So that boatload of truths, insights, wisdoms from the other side, inspirations, my 'frog' turned into a huge, laden treasure boat gift from the gods, I simply abandoned. I wasn't up to it. I was so hopelessly mentally scrambled by the stupid life I was leading—I couldn't grasp it. So I lost it—just as surely as if I'd slammed the glass door on it.

That was probably the best opportunity of my life—to enter a wholly richer, more productive, more complete existence, as a person and a writer. And I muffed it.

Instead—I took up <u>real</u> salmon fishing. I dug out, with your help, the <u>real</u> rivers of big salmon. But I should have done it internally, through my work on myself, rather than simply gathered happy outer experiences. I should have done both, perhaps, simultaneously.

What I was needing to do, all those years, was deal with what had happened to your mother and me. That was the big unmanageable event in my life, that had somehow to be managed—internally—by me. Somehow through my writing—because that's the method I've developed to deal with myself. In Ireland, I did find a way of dealing with it—not by writing about it directly, but dealing with the deep emotional tangle of it <u>indirectly</u>, through other symbols, which is the best and most natural way.

When I lost that grasp of those things, which I'd achieved in Ireland and kept as I say until 1969, I also lost contact with myself—and with my writing. When I started trying to get it back—in other words in 1972 when we got back from working with Peter Brook, and started living at C.G. again—I had tremendous difficulty finding my writing again. I was writing ABC nursery writing exercises. As if I had to start again right back at the start, trying to rediscover the keys to open the glass door. But because of the life I was living, I never did find them. Hence—the ship of salmon and Jaguars had to sail away again. The best I could do, through all those following years, to deal with that giant psychological log-jam of your mother and me, was write, as if to her, quite privately, simple little attempts to communicate with her about our time together. They were what accumulated, over the years, to this Birthday Letters. Most of them I never dreamed of publishing—they expose too much, I always thought. But they were inadequate to break up the log-jam. That thickening thickening glass window between me and that real self of mine which was trapped in the unmanageable experience of what had happened with her and me. And so—because I could never break up the log-jam—except for those 3 or 4 years in Ireland after—never open the giant plate glass door of it, <u>that real self of mine could never get on with its life</u>, could never join me and help me get on with my life.

So all I wrote, through all those years, contained nothing of what I really needed to say. And nothing in my way of life contained the real me—I <u>was living on the wrong side</u> of the glass door. All I was aware of, all that time, was the desperate need to break the glass door, and blow up the log jam, but I <u>didn't dare</u> because it was—the business of your mother and me. The incessant interference of the feminists and every-thing to do with your mother's public fame made it impossible for me—it seems—to deal with it naturally, and express it indirectly, obliquely, through other symbols, because everything I did was examined so minutely for signs of it. Also, I was not allowed ever to forget it enough to let it sink into imagination and be changed there subconsciously. Which is the natural process for dealing with unmanageable experiences.

So my daily feeling that I could write nothing and hardly even live until I freed myself from the log-jam was blocked and frustrated all those years—till I got ill.

It was when I realised that my only chance of getting past 1963 was to blow up that log-jam, and assemble whatever I had written about your mother and me, and simply make it public—like a confession—that I decided to publish those Birthday Letters as I've called them. I thought, let the feminists do what they like, let people think what they like about me, let critics demolish and tear to bits these simple, unguarded, quite private for the most part, unsophisticated bits of writing, let the heavens fall, let your mother's Academic armies of support demolish me, let Carol go bananas, let Frieda and Nick bolt for their bomb-shelters—I can't care any more, I can't lock myself in behind this glass door one more week.

So I did it, and now I'm getting the surprise of my life. What I've been hiding all my life, from myself and everybody else, is not terrible at all. Though you didn't want to read it.

And the effect on me, Nicky, the sense of gigantic, upheaval transformation in my mind, is quite bewildering. It's as though I have completely new different brains. I can think thoughts I never could think. I have a freedom of imagination I've not felt since 1962. Just to have got rid of all that.

Well, let's hope it wasn't all just a bit too late.

But I tell you all this, with a hope that it will let you understand a lot of things. Also, that it will make you think about the frog, and the kiln. Don't laugh it off. In 1963 you were hit even harder than me. But you will have to deal with it, just as I have had to. And as Frieda has had to. You were given the means—if you use them, everything about you will be changed, by what follows the frog through the door. Slowly. Like a leakage. Bit by bit.

Nicholas Hughes was a skilled maker of ceramic animals.
    The poem about the plane crash must be 'The Casualty', from *The Hawk in the Rain*.

To Siv Arb

16 March 1998   Ms Arb

Dear Siv—
    After all these years!
    I remember you so vividly—so tall and slim, on this lawn. I remember

you saying—maybe it's a good thing living outside your own country and language, because it reduces your vocabulary to the poetic essentials—and cleanses it of the daily pollution of newspaper speech etc. You are very vivid to me. 36 years!

I hope you are well and happy.

Yours ever

Ted

See letter to Siv Arb of 10 February 1964.

To Gerald and Joan Hughes

25 April 1998   Ms   Emory

Couldn't help seeing your note to Carol. I know you must be wanting to know what's going on with me.

When I first got ill, I was very happy to stop attending any literary business, to cancel all those engagements—playing other people's games with other people's toys—that this career of mine had tended to side-slip into, and that simply waste my time, & that at bottom I detest. Suddenly I had an excuse that excused me from their resentment—which is often the price I have to pay for a straightforward declining of their invitation. So I tended to use it. I could say 'doctor's orders'.

Instantly, rumours blew it up. Somebody was told in Belgrade that I had been having chemotherapy for two years at a special clinic in the US, etc. I know everybody thought the worst, who heard at all that I was in some way ill—because everybody jumps so promptly and with such relief to hear that a colleague is out of the running. And since I'm anybody's table chat, any rumour about me goes the whole way in every direction.

I don't know whether other people feel it, but my instinct about letting people know that you're ill is like the antelope's instinct that doesn't want the leopards and hyenas to notice its limp. My instinct also tells me, every person who believes I'm ill is—for me—a real, living obstacle to my getting better. They don't want to change their idea, they want it to be as dramatic as possible i.e. as bad as possible (except for the few who are closest to me—and how many is that?). Every person who says, 'I've heard you're ill (though they've all heard it, not

714

everybody says it)—feels to be putting a brick in my escape route &
cementing it into place. I'm only telling you how it affects me. God
knows what their thoughts amount to inside their own heads beyond
'thank God it's him & not me'.

So I simply tell nobody. Inevitably, I've told one or two—very close
confidentes. And inevitably they've told one or two—very close con-
fidentes. And inevitably etc etc etc.

If I'd been an anonymous citizen, I would never have let a soul know
that I was even worried about myself. So it's quite a load, having to
meet friends—whom I've told nothing, who I know are full of goggling
curiosity and the rumours they've heard. Humiliating.

I'm too impressionable—or maybe I know too well what it all really
means, for them & for me, what's in their heads.

So, dearest & nearest, please don't let that steam come screaming out
of your ears—and remember that whatever you say to your closest old
pal about me is quite likely to appear on the front page of one of these
newspapers in our English Collosseum—where the lions are hungry and
the mob roaring for the next.

My doctor says I'm safe, I'm trickling along at a very low order of
malign activity, I'm not really aware that I'm ill at all—except just a day
or two after the treatment. And except when I try to walk hard for a
couple of hours   but I've never been right that way since I had shingles.
My spirits are good, I'm feeling eager for all sorts of projects & trips,
which I certainly wasn't a year ago. I have a lot to do. I feel perfectly
happy, actually—or I would do, if I didn't have the horrible problem of
'other people's reactions'.

If I suddenly got really ill, don't worry I'd tell you.

At this time, it seemed that chemotherapy was successfully controlling TH's illness.

To Nick Gammage

11 May 1998   Ms (photocopy)   Emory

Have you noticed that you write quite different prose on your word
processor than when you're writing by hand? You do. The reason:
because handwriting is basically drawing of images (that's how graphol-
ogists read it—they decode the images in the various letters—read them
as 'pictures') it engages not only the whole record of your psychological

history (as your unique handwriting does) but it engages from word to word all the preverbal activities of your brain (as drawing images does), which then bring the (non-verbal) associative contribution to bear on what is being written about, and therefore help to determine the sequence of ideas and expressions, tones & rhythms etc. That is why handwritten letters give you the impression of dealing with the real, i.e. the whole person. And why you feel a formality about a typed letter. And why a word-processed letter from a friend (word-processors are a whole range further removed from that preverbal engagement than typewriters, as typewriters are removed further than handwriting) can seem to be from an unknown person, or even from a robot, and why the writer feels the need to apologise for it (as you did.)

So beware. I'm going to get all that proved if I can get some brain-scanning specialist to do the experiments.

Just observe it in yourself & in others, as I have. It is very strange. Some curious consequences. As entries for School Writing Competitions have gone over to wordprocessors, the poetic quality has disappeared. The psychological, subjectively-naked quality has disappeared. Catastrophic, actually. But there we are, so much for Blair and his computer on every desk.

What is really strange—you cannot prevent yourself succumbing to the change, between one mode & the other. On word processors everybody writes wordprocessorese. They cannot even fake their handwritten style. Their attempts look self-conscious, faked.

One of the problems with getting anybody to see what is happening, is that almost nobody can see the difference between a clever poem written on a wordprocessor (by a clever 16 year old, or 10 year old) and a clever poem composed by hand. So nobody—virtually—sees it as a problem. Everybody is happy or even enraptured with the fake. But that's no news. Still it is an obstacle to doing anything about this latest educational disaster.

When the preverbal brain is suppressed—i.e. is not somehow brought into the mental activity—the IQ falls by 10% or 15%. In the U.S., at some large Scientific Institutes, the scientists are encouraged to spend at least an hour a day drawing, modelling, composing music etc—because they've discovered that even that enhances all their other abilities, i.e. raises their general IQ.

Just as Blair & Blunkett remove drawing & music from the school curriculum, these strange facts are being acknowledged throughout the world of scientists.

End of complaint.

Nick Gammage never received this letter, so it may not have been sent.

'A computer on every school desk' had been an early slogan of Tony Blair, when the Labour Party that he led came to government in 1997. David Blunkett was Blair's first Secretary of State for Education and Employment.

To Marie and Seamus Heaney

27 June 1998   Ms   Emory

That was a magical dip into Dublin, for us. And the impression of your house becoming the control tower of a ship—definitely a tower. Once a house has lost its foursquare plan, and acquired even one slant wall—on the astral plane it is perceived as a hexagon, and therefore a tower, as one mailed glove is perceived as a warrior. I dare say. Anyway, it has left me with a very distinct impression of a tower—almost a conning tower. So much better to have grown it out of the old, in a natural way—than to have started afresh transplanted, 'emerging as he goes'.

Though I must say, transplanting does occasionally tempt me. Just reading how Euripides got away finally to Macedon, age 76 or thereabouts, and wrote Iphigenia in Aulis, Alcmaeon & The Bacchae before he was torn to pieces by the King's hounds (as he sat meditating in woodland). (So they say.) [*Marginal addition:* Did I say tempting?!]
[. . .]

I've a horrible feeling I never spoke to you since you sent me the fax of the Beowulf Section poem to the hotel. When I spoke to you on the phone, of course, you hadn't sent it. Honour apart, it seems to me a rather wonderful piece, many-textured and a whole cat's cradle of subtle counterbalances. A very memorable clarity and deep-toned music to it. And one of your very best bits of Beowulf. God knows what that book of mine is, but I know in my heart it sets a problem for readers (who don't respond in a purely sentimental way, or a 'well this isn't quite our idea of the leading edge' way) and your poem seems to acknowledge the problem with the wise humane comprehending solution—which made certain aspects of what I've done there seem clearer to me too. So I was/am very grateful that you've written this piece.

The weird effects of having got rid of it all (and maybe, especially of staying absolutely clear of public response to it) are still making themselves felt. Strange euphorias of what I can only call 'freedom' or a sense of self-determination, internally, that are quite new to me. Sometimes I have a mad waft of how I felt in 1955, before I met S.P. I wouldn't want a thing different. But a pity I left that unburdening (even if it was mainly symbolic unburdening) so late!

Strange business, confession.

'On His Work in the English Tongue', with the epigraph 'in memory of Ted Hughes', is included in Seamus Heaney's 2001 volume *Electric Light*. Heaney had recently been working on a translation of *Beowulf*, a passage from which is incorporated into the poem.

To Keith Sagar

18 July 1998   Ms   British Library

Dear Keith—

Got your letter and chapter—which I've read. Your account of the cooperation between S.P. & me is pretty much as I see it—so far as it goes. Obviously, I could add a vast amount of detail. And even something more of her influence on me. But it is clear as you've done it, and supports what you say about my changing attitude to the whole event, and my failure, in the end, to turn it positive—which makes BL just the book you describe.

I have wondered—some justification I think—if an all-out attempt [*insertion*: much much earlier] to complete a full account, in the manner of those BL, of that part of my life, would not have liberated me to deal with it on deeper, more creative levels—i.e. where the very worst things can be made positive, where the whole point of the operation is to turn deadly negatives into triumphant positives, in the total picture. On the autobiographical level, that can be difficult, because—if things cannot be got off that level, and onto the creative level (i.e. a bit forgotten, maybe), then they simply stay as if they were a recurrent stuck dream that simply goes on delivering its inescapable blow. Two things kept me stuck on the autobiographical level. One—a moral reluctance to deal with the episode directly, as material for an artistic work. As I might— or as one might—find a close metaphor in some dramatic action &

718

make a play of it or bury the main features of it in the plot of a novel. As even Tolstoy did—quite deliberately. That seemed to me reprehensible, not truly creative. When poets did it—as Snodgrass, then Lowell, then Sexton did—picking it up from each other—I despised it. In poetry, I believed, if the experience was to be dealt with creatively, it would have to emerge obliquely, through a symbol, inadvertently—as in Shakes. Venus & Adonis, or Ancient Mariner, or Christabel, or Lamia, or Eve of St Agnes, or something of that sort. And in fact, with me, in retrospect, I can see that it began to emerge in exactly this fashion in Crow—which I started in 1965, just after coming from Ireland, where I'd found a way out of a 3 year impasse, with Skylarks. But I was still too close to the experience, maybe, to deal with it quickly enough, and those years were devoured too by other preoccupations, mainly centred round the children & my mother, who died in 69, after Assia.

This revival, in A's death, of S's, and in my mother's death a big psychological melt-down with accidental complicating factors, knocked Crow off his perch. (I wrote the last of them a week before A's death—on my way to take her looking for a new home in Northumberland, returning from which, she died.) Then I escaped from it all into working with Peter Brook—total suspension of my own writing except for that little myth of sinister import and total inner stasis, Prometheus on his Crag, which I was tinkering with in Iran.

But I was pulled inescapably back onto the autobiographical level of S's death by the huge outcry that flushed me from my thicket in 1970-71-72 when Sylvia's poems & novel hit the first militant wave of Feminism as a divine revelation from their Patron Saint. And never gave me another moment to let it all sink away to the levels on which I might deal with it naturally & creatively. Nor to escape constantly more hectic involvement with it—on that autobiographical level.

This arrest, of what I might have made of Crow, and of that material in other truly creative works, held me till I more or less abandoned the effort—and from the piece about Baskin (took a year, almost), the piece about Eliot (a few months), the new introduction to Ecco Press' republication of the Selected Shakes, which turned into Shakespeare & the Goddess (2 years, staying up till 3 & 4 a.m.—destroying my immune system), I took refuge in prose. Oh, yes, & the Coleridge essay & revisions of the Winter Pollen pieces, maybe the best part of a year, though it was all done by early 1994. Still—5 or 6 years nothing but prose—nothing but burning the foxes. (That fox was telling—prose is destroying you physically, literally: maybe not others, but you, yes.) Finally, I cracked. I got together all the BL letters, wrote some more—with mighty relief, and did what Carol could never have borne 3 years before (when I did put some into the New Selected) published them. A thing that I too had always thought unthinkable—so raw, so vulnerable, so unprocessed, so naive, so self-exposing & unguarded, so without any of the niceties that any poetry workshop student could have helped me to. And so dead against my near-inborn conviction that you never talk about yourself in this way—in poetry. So at bottom, somewhere, I do now have the feeling of having committed some kind of obscure crime, publishing them. But there is no way I could have gone on letting all that business gag me, knowing, with Sylvia's reputation as my environment, I could never escape with her onto the other levels. There simply was no more time, and I was feeling pretty low, physically. Once I'd determined to do it, & put them together, & started repairing them wherever I could, & writing the few last ones, I suddenly had free energy I hadn't known since Crow. Which went into Ovid, then the Oresteia, Phèdre maybe—and parts of Alcestis, (which I haven't done anything with yet).

Hence the tone, etc, of B.L. God knows what sort of book it is, but at least none of it is faked, innocent as it is. And I must take some uplift from the consistency of the interconnections—though I wrote them over such a long time, rarely re-reading them, merely adding another now & again, never regarding them as a single structure—in fact the book has a structure, intricate, & accurate so far as I can judge. Solidly of a piece, somehow. So I can't care what people say. It has worked for me—better than I'd thought possible. Though I see now that any traumatic event—if writing is your method—has to be dealt with deliberately. An image has to be looked for—consciously—and then mined to the limit: but not in autobiographical terms. My high-minded principal was simply wrong—for my own psychological & physical health. It was stupid. The public interference, later, was just bad luck. Though it deflected me into Season Songs, Moortown, Gaudete, River, Elmet, Cave-birds etc—lots of little things I'm glad to have got down.

I'd written almost all the Wodwo poems before S.P. died. After I left her, she kept typescripts of Out, Green Wolf, New Moon in January, Heptonstall, Full Moon & Frieda & a few little experimental improvisations & versions of Lorca that I'd made, on her desk. They were there when she died. I think she got certain things from them. Also a piece I never collected—The Road to Easington, to which her reply was

The Bee Meeting, mocking the rhythms with a different meaning i.e. your escape is my funeral. That's how she read it, I think, eventually, though she was excited by it when I wrote it.

After her death—2 or 3 weeks later, I wrote The Howling of Wolves, & finished Gnat-Psalm, I think. (Might have finished that earlier—or much later. Drafted it before she died.) After the Wolves, the Song of the Rat. Then nothing till I went to Ireland—and eventually got to Skylarks. About 3 years, of rubbishy efforts, radio plays, prose, in there.

About Otter: Yes, Pan asked me to write it, whereupon I dutifully wrote Part I. Felt I had got somewhere, but nowhere like far enough. Later on—days, couple of weeks—I was writing something else, (forget what) when I became aware of a written scroll hanging somewhere in the air just to my right. It was verses, not perfectly distinct but just legible—rather like the retinal distortions you can experience sometimes in a slight migraine. I copied the words down—and the whole poem came out as it is in Part II, exactly as it is, I think. Very odd experience, but so involuntary—so oddly pushed onto me—that I assumed that Pan was presenting his version of Otter as a mild hallucination. It recapitulates most of the themes of the first—but in visual close-up, with more subjectivity, more delicately, far better.

About the 2 levels, in that essay on the poems & the Bell Jar. I believe that the lower level, the unalterable experience, can be changed—if the ritual is strong enough, or if the 'experience' is weak and malleable enough. With her, the experience was hellish strong, and her ritual— The Bell Jar—not strong enough. And the Ariel poems were not so much triumphant ritual—as double-tongued, triumph & doom. The most triumphant—Ariel itself, the poem—is a prophecy of suicide. If we had got back together mid-Ariel, or even any time before she died, maybe, the ritual could have been confirmed. New experience would have re-enforced it. She would probably have been able to hang on to all her new energy & enlarged personality. But accidents accelerated that last week to free fall 32 ft per sec per sec. We ran out of time—by days, I think. So I shall always believe. The horrors visited on us that last week, by well-meaning busybodies, brought her to that state where she was helpless. At that most dangerous moment—when a neurosis overcome suddenly makes a last effort and stabs its victim in the back. Evidently a well-known regular occurrence, in similar cases. So I have to think.

But don't let this complicate your account, which is true on this point, in essentials.

And yes, it's true—because I accepted her temperament & its apparent needs as a given set of facts, to be tended, humoured, cared for, cured if possible in the long-term, and did not impose on her a whole new pattern of behaviour, more actively extraverted & organised towards a disciplined engagement with the world,—I surrendered the chance to change her in other ways than by inward concentrated search for the essential voice of an essential self. If she had married a lawyer, a banker—as her mother wanted her to—well, God knows, maybe that would have been hopeless. God knows what way of life would have been better than the one we followed. Though in retrospect, it does read like the scenario written by her father, that she had to perform—and which I unwittingly directed so vigourously, with such fixed ideas, making such sacrifices, thinking we had all time ahead.

The landscape at Mex. was Manor Farm, old Denaby—the land you see immediately across the river (Don, not Dearne) from Mexborough Station. Now one big ploughed field. A copse hanging down the near face of the right hand hill was the setting for my story the Rain Horse. Across the river you can see the dips & hollows in the high earthen river bank. I know that farm, as it was in the late thirties early forties, better than any place on earth. A year or two ago I went back to look at the farm building itself. Shock of my life. It would shock you too, if you saw it.

First to take an interest in my writing was our form mistress in my first class—a Miss Mcleod, who was also the Headmistress. Fine looking woman—I fell in love with her, somewhat. Next was Pauline Mayne—then about 23. She touched off my passion to write poetry. I used to write long lolloping Kiplingesque sagas, about all kinds of things. She pointed to a phrase—describing the hammer of a wildfowlers' gun breaking in the cold 'with frost-chilled snap'. 'That's poetry' she said. And I thought, well if that's poetry that's the way I think so I can give you no end of it. She became a close friend of my family's—still is I suppose. Then came John Fisher—demobbed. For a while it was Pauline and John together. I was in love with both, so they could teach me anything. John F. had only to exclaim about the unearthly mightiness of Beethoven—whom I had never knowingly listened to—for me to become such a sotted addict of Beethoven that his music dominated my life till I left University & lost my gramaphone & radio. Even so, ever since, it has preoccupied me at some level. I still listen to it in preference to anything else. That's education, I suppose.

The Pike we caught was big—very big—but not 40 lb. Nicholas' 1st Pike, in Ireland, was twice as big. [*Marginal insertion:* (He's never caught one bigger—caught it on his mother's birthday, at Six-mile Bridge, home town of Edna O'Brien).]

No, the night fishing did not involve trespassing. We just liked fishing on into the dark. I've always liked fishing at night. Although, it's true, poaching is more exciting than legal fishing—night or day.

I climbed to the top of Scout Rock <u>first</u> when I was about six—yes, that was late. But our side of the valley I'd been climbing as long as I could remember, certainly from 3 or 4. And the moors there were higher than Scout Rock—level with the moors behind & beyond Scout Rock. My mother's mother's family—Smiths—farmed above Scout Rock. I used to go up to that farm, occasionally, with her—but only along the top edge of Scout Rock, much later, with my brother. There's a path, at the brink. Impressive outlook—moreso than from the moorline opposite (above Height's Road—behind the Skip Inn and the Golf course). Impressive outlook into the valley, that is. Ewood—the home of my mother's father's family, the Farrars—is opposite, big house gone, but many of the outbuildings still there. Crowded now by housing developments.

Moorland had an effect on me—still has. The moment I get to heather, everything feels better. I shall live in Caithness yet. (Like the top of the Pennine Moors, but in fact a plain, with the most marvellous wild, neglected rivers going through it. The whole area a bit neglected—too flat & desolate for tourists, too poor for the old crofting population: a landscape of little ruins, alive with Northern birds.) But I felt it very early, very strong, the feeling for heather.

Orpheus was the first story that occurred to me after S.P.s death. I rejected it: I thought it would be too obvious an attempt to exploit my situation—I was too conscious of that obviousness. I saw my little note about it, the other day. The shock twist was that Pluto answered: No, of course you can't have her back. She's dead, you idiot. Too close to it, you see.

I wrote the musical play in 1971, same time as the Max Nicholson essay, in a farmhouse in North Devon that I'd escaped to [*insertion:* After A's & my mother's death.] trying to sort out marriage dilemmas etc. Wrote it in the spirit of a bagatelle. Should have gone on and written lots more things in that vein—but life intervened, production lines were destroyed, I had to start afresh elsewhere, in time. (In fact, I got married and went off with Peter Brook.)

I'm babbling on. I'd intended to make this succinct—(less of my scrawl to test you.)

Crag Jack was my grandfather—Dad's father, Irish. A dyer, died age about 40 from pneumonia. He's the subject of my piece 'Familiar'. Came down out of Crag Vale (leads up through the deep gorge opening South from Mytholmroyd). Family legend makes him a local sage— solved people's problems, wrote their letters, closest friends the local Catholic and Wesleyan Ministers, though he spent a lot of time in pubs. Said to be a great singer. No photo, left my Dad a 3 year old orphan (and his younger brother—and older sister). Mystery man. A geneologist up there—a Hughes—tried to trace his origins, but failed, though there are other Hughes' about. Probably came from Manchester or Liverpool. My Dad's mother's father was a regular soldier, surnamed Major, rank of Major, known in the family legend as Major Major of the Rock—permanently stationed at Gibraltar, where he married a Spaniard, small very dark woman, Arab-looking, high thin nose like Olwyn's. Often thought I'd like to learn more about them—should be possible through Army records on Gibraltar. Granny died age 92 or so in the mid-forties. My brother's nose is like a comic Julius Caesar—he had blue-black straight hair.

The 'magic landscape' behind the Old Denaby landscape was Tarka the Otter's N. Devon. In 38, when we moved to Mex. my brother went off to Devon as a Gamekeeper's assistant—age 18, his last free year before the war. My life over old Denaby was a dream life—keeping going alone the life I'd lived with him. Made doubly so by Williamson's Tarka the Otter—which I found in the School library in 1941, and kept out, on & off, for 2 years—till I knew it by heart pretty well. By then, my brother was gone right away, into North Africa—where he stayed till the war ended, and after. So his paradisal life as a Gamekeeper (he still calls it the happiest year of his life) in Devon, made more actual by Williamson's book, became the inner life I simply went on living—but alone. I lived it in that double vision—the real manor farm over Old Denaby, & the imagined world of Tarka. He was like my surrogate father—old enough for that.

Later on, I teamed up with a boy in my sister's class—whose father was the gardener on Crookhill Estate above Conisborough. The big house was a Sanatorium for miners with T.B. The 100 acre park & woodlands were ours. He shared my obsessions. I became a member of that family, pretty well, till I went into the RAF. He married my girl friend of the day—no rancour or problems—and went on to become Head of Parks in Hong Kong for 18 years. We spent all weekends, and all long summer evenings together, fishing, shooting. Bicycle crazed too: we rode all over South Yorks, Derbyshire & into Nottinghamshire, fishing.

The Devon dream must have stayed with me. When S.P. and I moved down here in 1961, we looked at quite a few houses. I wanted a place up on Exmoor—near deer, sea-bass & sea-trout. Idea was to be self-sufficient. But I ended up here. First morning of the 1962 trout season, I went out at dawn (to get back by 9 am—for Sylvia's writing stint) and was walking across the meadow towards the river when an otter jumped out of the ditch in front of me, and went bobbing along toward the river—into which it vanished. I suddenly realised what I'd done. The Taw is one of Tarka's two rivers. I never again saw an otter on the Taw—in thousands of hours night & day. Saw plenty on the Torridge—Tarka's birth-river—later on, when it became an otter sanctuary, for nursing the otters released from hand-rearing.

So my Mytholmroyd landscape, my Old Denaby landscape, & North Devon, all flowed into one—through my inner life with my brother—present the first 7 years, absent ever after. (When he left the RAF, he went to Australia).

His absence left me to my sister—who took his place as my mentor. She was the prodigy at School—and I see now she had marvellously precocious taste in poetry. When my teacher began to make remarks about my writing, my mother went out and bought a whole library—2nd hand—of classic poets. All the Warwick Shakespeares, & everything after. Eventually Olwyn got me into the Shakespeare. They coached me, somehow—perpetual expectations. And Olwyn as you know is a formidable force. So all that started up alongside my shooting & fishing obsession. The later teachers—Pauline Mayne & John F.—became close friends of my mother's & Olwyn's, & of mine, of course. So, I was in that cooker from age of about eleven—and totally confident that I belonged in it, so by 16 I had no thought of becoming anything but a writer of some kind, certainly writing verse. When I sat my entrance exam to Pembroke, John F sent a notebook of my poems to the College Master—S.C. Roberts. When I got back, our latin master, Neil, had composed a latin epigram on my ignominious failure. If it had been decided by my answer papers, he would have been right—but Roberts liked my poems. He persuaded them to take me on as a 'dark horse'. So I heard later.

That's pretty much how I got to Grammar School too. My mother had made a close friend of the headmaster at the Junior School—Schofield St. He bought his tobacco in the shop. When I failed the preliminary for the 11 plus, she persuaded him to let me sit the actual exam. I wrote a long essay on how I wanted to be a gamekeeper, spent all my exam time on it. And got through, with 2 others. So I had some funny luck, in those days.

Babbling on again. It's too easy, writing about yourself. I hope it helps.

Yes, do give us a card or call when you're coming this way.

Interested in what you say about the audiobook commentary on Crow—yes, publish it as an appendix by all means.

I only ever mention the 3 answers to the ogress because they are the only three I've published. Each one was a big thing for me—it's not easy to find that pitch. And not be repetitive—from piece to piece. Others are in chaotic draft. But I have all the questions—which I would never disclose, for fear of disrupting what might be getting itself ready. Tiger-psalm was originally one—but took off on a different plane. It's that headlong huddle of first lines, crowding towards the right conclusion—with the authentic feeling of the plight identified by the question: somehow, absolutely everything in me has to be in on it—I've made too many attempts at them that just skid over the top. I should have tried again, maybe, when I was doing the Oresteia. I certainly had all the right material white-hot, that year, maybe still have.

You must be proud of Ursula & Arren—you've got that right, whatever you might think you've got less than right.

Having a foolish struggle to set brief prose intros to the U.S. editions of Phèdre & Oresteia. Farrar Straus want me to do something like the piece I did for the Ovid. [*Marginal insertion:* To make a series—of 3—for Schools!] What can you say about the Oresteia in 3 or 4 pages? There's a review in today's Times by Fredrick Raphael, of a reissue of Burckhard's Rise & fall of Democracy in Greece, that I wouldn't mind stealing complete. Better than burning the foxes.

This is too long.

Love to you all
Ted

Have you read Tom Paulin's marvellous book about Hazlitt?

Dated 18 June by TH, its date corrected by Sagar, this letter was a response to the chapter 'From Prospero to Orpheus', in Sagar's *The Laughter of Foxes*.

W. D. Snodgrass (1926–2009), whose books of poems include *Heart's Needle* (1959) and *After Experience* (1968), was associated with Lowell and Sexton in discussions of so-called 'confessional' poetry.

'The Road to Easington' was printed in the *Listener* of 23 August 1962', 'The Bee Meeting' in *Ariel*.

Pan was TH's ouija spirit. The ouija session that stimulated part I of 'An Otter' took place on 3 July 1958.

The 'essay on the poems & the Bell Jar' is 'Publishing Sylvia Plath'.

TH wrote two poems with the title 'Familiar': the one referred to here appeared first in the *Times Literary Supplement*, in 1984, and was later gathered into *Elmet*.

On 15 July, Sagar had written to TH: 'I have always felt that it was a mistake publishing those Crow poems without any indication of their larger context.' And: 'Incidentally, I wonder why, in all the many versions I have heard from you of the ogress episode you only ever mention the same three of the seven questions. Do you not want to disclose what the other four questions are, and which poems are the answers to them?'

Frederic Raphael (b.1931), novelist and journalist, had reviewed *The Greeks and Greek Civilisation* by Jakob Burckhardt (1818–97).

To Tom Paulin

6 August 1998   Ms Emory

Dear Tom—

I just got back from Scotland where I've been reading your Hazlitt book—what a threshing out of sensibilities in the wars of the proses! It's a great book about the psycho-genetics (is there such a word?) of English prose—(and, am I right, by extension of American prose— where it struck new roots in the Tennessee oaks etc, or is that too general a leap?). You almost get to—what do they call it, 'photophore-sis'—reading the fine blending of the psychic DNA that determines the vital difference between one prose and another. Translating the prose rhythms etc back into the electrograph of the writer's whole sensibility. Reading the chemical components of a star by analysing the colour-bands of its light. I'm sure you're right—the method you develop so brilliantly with Hazlitt (and Burke) is the real way in to distinguish any one prose or verse from another.

Each of the horizontal lines—a quality of sensibility or temperament. The vertical line calibrated—like the atomic weight code of the elements—into the fixed components of human sensibility—from deepest primal at bottom to most superficial imitative at top. Then you fit your writer to it.

I'm sure with practice you could (one could) develop a solid intuitive analysis of just what it is a particular writer has, and what he/she hasn't. Or a particular piece of writing—more fairly. Different works can define different wave-bands, by the same writer.

A way of finding a subtler language for intuition, maybe.

I don't know any other book that touches that method—though I expect you do. But you really make it live. I'd never have believed it could be done so radically—following the nerve roots back into every twist of religious & social influence. Yet presenting the whole combine as a vital personality, a historical force, in a situation.

Your letter about the programme (and another letter from the Lion T.V. producer who hopes to make it)—were waiting for me here. Tom— I would impose only one difficulty, refusal to stand sit silent or vocal in front of that camera. I've only one bare little rag of anonymity left—but I know that T.V. camera would snatch it.

Is there a way of doing it? There must be—since KD & AC aren't going to be offering any more smiles.

Let me know what you think.

My rusty old translation of Phèdre trundles into action tonight. Rusty & old in that it's straight (near literal) and as plain as Racine—

without the clangour, or any equivalent. Main thing I wanted was the express pace—and the howl. But that's up to Dame Diana, Toby Stephens et al.

Keep well, Tom
yours ever
Ted

Tom Paulin's 'Hazlitt book' was *The Day-Star of Liberty*, with its radically political approach to the analysis of prose style.

Some years earlier, TH had turned down the opportunity to translate *Medea*, by Euripides, for a production, with Diana Rigg in the title role, that went on to be a hit. So when the director Jonathan Kent asked TH to work on Racine's *Phèdre*, in which Rigg would also star, he seized the opportunity. Toby Stephens played Hippolyte. The play opened at the Festival Theatre, Malvern.

To Marina Warner

19 August 1998   Ms   Warner

Dear Marina—

The Insomniac Princess is a magical piece—it reads like a single hypnotic sentence—a single scroll of embroidered silk being unrolled. And the last paragraph made my eyes prickle. I don't know anything quite like it.

Makes me even more impatient than I was with what I'm tangled in— a 2 (3) page introduction of the Oresteia (for the U.S. market—where they hope it will be taken up by schools along with the Ovid.) "Oh" they said "do something like what you did for the Ovid." !! I know both too much and too little. In the end, it's like welding a 5 bar gate out of municipal cast iron. They want me to do the same for a translation I did of Racine's Phèdre. For some reason I'm telling myself that will be easier (—i.e. not impossible).

An idea has kept recurring to me that—in my case—writing critical prose actually damages my immune system. Is it possible? Maybe that's how writing certain books seems to make people ill—or as they say themselves kills them. Your immune system bounces up and down awfully easily. Missing the sleep between 12 and 3 a.m. drops it to the bottom for 24 hours. Failing an exam, losing a fight, being humiliated in any way, drops it very low, almost immediately. Laughing real laughter, passing an exam, winning a fight, etc, puts it right up, etc. So maybe in some people, whatever that critical overview separated part of the brain does to the poor old pre-verbal body of life, when it's drilling its squads, actually can collapse the immune system. Maybe that explains a lot about (Eng. Lit) Academic life. Something about the nucleus of our sense of the tragic:—in the world of rational, suppressive moral order, the pre-verbal body of individuality, subjectivity, must die. At least must suffer a form of death. It struck me that might explain the Fox dream I tell in my book Winter Pollen. I've had so many experiences like it. I tackle these little 'critical' jobs—not 'critical', 'intellectualised commentary'? Yes? No?—with such physical dread, I swear I'll never do any more—but then you get dragged back in. Lectures worst of all. I'll stand and answer questions on a platform all day—but a lecture! I think my Eliot lecture, followed by my Shakespeare book, were what dumped me into shingles—in bed blind in my right eye when I was writing the chapters about the Eye in King Lear—then on down lower. Not sure I've ever got over it. Soon as I get back to my own verse or anything freely imaginative, I begin to get better. Marina, do you experience anything like this? I think of it in your case, because you write such powerfully intellectual surveys and critical pieces—then come out with this story in such a beautiful flow of feeling and music—so natural and flawless, like the opening of an orchid. Not a jagged crackle of intellectual interference anywhere in it. 'A balm poured out.' (Sorry for the misquote).

Not sure I've ever heard a nightingale—or seen one. I've always lived beyond the bird's pale. Thousands of hours in woods at night—never heard a note. Once in S. Yorks rumour went through the school that there was a nightingale in some woodland near Conisborough. (Rather as you now hear the 'beast' has been sighted in some copse round here). Groups of enthusiasts were going out there. Eventually, I sat in there for a couple of hours and finally heard 3 piercing notes—but I could swear they were the squeals of dry brakes in the shunting yard down below the wood. That's as close as I've been.

I see there are only 4,000 nightingales left. But then. Friend of mine, 20 years in Australia, came back last week—visited me yesterday and almost his first words were 'Where are all the birds?' Then "I was 3 days in London before I saw my first sparrow." I've sat all afternoon in the orchard near a fountain that used to be crowded all day with birds. I didn't see a single bird till about 7 p.m. then a magpie flew across. Strange? Thanks for the address. Must get together. Greetings to Nick.

Love, Ted

'Lullaby for an Insomniac Princess' is a story from Marina Warner's collection *Murderers I Have Known* (1997). She had sent it to TH after he had given her a bottle of the sherry from the 700-odd 'Laureate' bottles he had received from the Sherry Institute of Spain. The label bore TH's own drawing of a hoopoe, reminding Warner of the myth of Tereus, changed to a hoopoe after raping and cutting out the tongue of Philomel, who then became a nightingale. Ovid's account lies behind her story.

The 'Eliot lecture' was the address given by TH at the dinner to celebrate T. S. Eliot's centenary (1988) and published as 'A Dancer to God'. '*King Lear* as a reactivation of its mythic sources' is a section of Chapter 3 of *Shakespeare and the Goddess of Complete Being*, and touches on the Egyptian myth of the sun god, Re, and his daughter, the Eye.

TH mixes the phrases 'in embalmed darkness' and 'pouring forth thy soul', from Keats's 'Ode to a Nightingale', to get his misquotation. Compare what he says next with 'Once I heard three notes of a nightingale in a dark wood' – line 6 of 'Era of Giant Lizards', first printed in *Poetry (Chicago)*, December 1963, and included in *Collected Poems*, in the section 'Uncollected (1960–67)'.

To Herbert Lomas

1 October 1998   Ms Lomas

Dear Herbert—

I've been tumbling along the bed of various rocky rivers since I brought out BL. I reversed the assumption—that arrived with the first of those pieces, about 1972—that I would never publish them. The assumption went on hardening with every one I added to them until— well until I'd grown old enough to realise that the big logjam holding back any inside story of my first wife's death had gagged my whole life, arrested me, essentially, right back there at that point. Like those first World War survivors who never climbed entirely out of the trench.

Well, a whole literary, psychological junk-heap of theories, with other goblins, kept me trying to deflect some trickle of the current into other things—metaphors of some kind. It never happened—or only as a kind of sweat. Small beads on pores. In the end, I tried releasing a few (in my selected poems) that my wife could cope with. But then simply cracked. And let the bulk of them go. I expected the heavens to fall, one way or another. I was amazed by what did happen. My wife coped pretty well. My feeling of release is marvellous.

That is why: (a) I set your book aside so I could write to you at length,

(b) I was chastened—to see you do what I didn't have the wisdom (or guts) to do back in the sixties.

I've read A Useless Passion through twice—each time one sitting, and dipped into it a lot, lately. As I read the first part I kept thinking—did he write these at the time, one or two a day, then select the best? If only I'd kept a diary of just this kind of poem—or my attempt at this kind of poem, because they are among your best, I think. Absolutely solid, surprising, beautifully compressed and shaped—and presenting a life-size living portrait of you. That humour—vital part of the whole impact—very congenial to me. Then as I went on through Parts II and III, I began to recognise the weird parallels between your experience and mine. In that setting, with that maturing story behind them, the poems of Part III become genuine symbolic events. You make some marvellous, prismatic, penetrating, visionary talismans. Those things can so easily be faked. But I see all sorts of parallels in this part too. And that both our books should end as they do, on that particular poem is a bit uncanny, isn't it?

I really can't tell you how much I like it. I keep being drawn back to it. You've made a very real thing. Every poem seems to resonate with all the others, the tones deepen & multiply as you go on. So solid and actual.

Did you write the 1st book at the time—back in the 40s? Or all, all of a piece, since your wife's death?

Yes, I do like the cover—if I were asked for my favourite painter I think I might say Cranach. Calder Valley foliage always seems to me the model for Cranach's. And those sly dames—Luther's Venus, (mail-order section)

All the very best

Ted

Herbert Lomas's book of poems *A Useless Passion* (1998) has two sections devoted to his late wife, Mary, who had died of a heart attack while out riding. 'Blue Rose', the last poem in the book, ends with the lines:

and you were the blue rose,

the unattainable, the impossible.

'Red', the last poem in *Birthday Letters*, concludes, 'But the jewel you lost was blue'.

To John Carey

6 October 1998   Ms   Carey

Dear John—

I regret our misunderstandings. Something keeps prompting me to tell you so.

Do you know this visual riddle—where you have to divine the other distinctly different image hidden within and behind the surface image—three dimensional and just as real. (Because it's 3 dimensional it seems <u>more</u> real).

Do you think—asking viewers to divine this hidden image is a good metaphor for what I was asking readers to do in my Shakespeare book (and in my Coleridge Essay)?

I suppose it's a metaphor for any act of literary interpretation—and therefore should be natural—easy, familiar. Even so, looking at these visual riddles, you find it's not at all natural, or easy or familiar.

For some people it seems to be impossible. For most, it's difficult. And even when most have divined it, and gloated on it in all its 3-dimensional glaring obviousness, the moment they glance away they've lost it again.

Yet that is really what I'm expecting every reader to do—divine the 'Equation' myth in the Shakespeare plays, & the other myth in the Coleridge poems, then hold on to it.

And just as with these riddle pictures, there is only one hidden image in each, no alternatives, none to be unearthed by ingenuity—simply that complete, single, implanted thing,—so in the Shakes & the Coleridge.

But just as viewers have difficulties with the riddle pictures—they have (worse?) difficulties with the Shakes & the Coleridge. Yet until they see through to that hidden image, they can't begin to hear my argument. I wonder if that just isn't a problem I underestimated: the difficulty of acquiring the double vision, then holding on to it, as I make my comments.

Again & again I've thought of sending you the book enclosed.

Please don't write back. Let's just leave things to heal over—as for me they have done.

Best wishes
Ted

John Carey, an admirer of TH's poetry, had dismissed *Shakespeare and the Goddess of Complete Being* as critically worthless in a review in the *Sunday Times*. When TH replied angrily, the paper's literary editor printed what he had written, together with a further put-down by Carey. TH and Carey never spoke again. Touched by the letter of 6 October, Carey wrote to thank TH, but suspects he died before receiving his reply.

The 'visual riddle' consisted of two optical puzzles, in colour, torn from a newspaper.

To Mark Hinchliffe

6 October 1998   Ms   Hinchliffe

Dear Mark—

There's a lovely lyrical completeness about your poems, you know. So natural & full—they just float out. Something perfect about them. So whole-hearted & affectionate. (So rare!)

Thanks for the Lawrentian granite.

Is anybody publishing your poems?

All the best

Ted

Hinchliffe had sent TH a stone he had picked up from the track by the cottage in Zennor, Cornwall, where D. H. Lawrence had stayed. Hinchliffe's poems remain unpublished.

To Nick Gammage

10 October 1998   Ms   Gammage

Dear Nick—

Very clearly written piece about The Gulcana. Are there truly 150 ms pages!!

'We'—my fishing party—were just two of us: my son and myself.

The Main River there is the Copper—a big <u>glacial</u> river—the colour of cement. We fished the Gulkana—one of its bigger tributaries, which was not fully glacial (if at all) and ran pretty clear. We fished just above the junction—so fish we couldn't handle went back (usually) downstream, into the glacial Copper, where we lost them, as a rule.

That's why—when we did manage to land them and release them into the <u>Gulkana</u>, we could <u>see</u> them melting away into the <u>clearish</u> water.

The glacial Copper was about 2 feet visibility—if that: we could never have seen them in it.

Pre-dreamed: I stopped writing stories and radio plays etc in the 60ˢ because I began to realise that each one foretold an episode in my life—sometimes in quite unbelievable physical detail.

I did wonder if my writing such pieces actually brought them into existence.

I had thought—and dreamed—about the Pacific North West all my life. That's where my brother & I were going to emigrate and set up as hunters/trappers: that was our dream, when I was a boy.

Years after stopping the writing of stories and plays (I stopped in 1963) I wrote a fairy tale for Bananas—edited by Emma Tennant—titled "The Head". It's in "Difficulties of a Bridegroom"—those 9 narrative pieces I published a few years ago.

I thought no more about it till about 3 years later (1980) I first went to Alaska. Nicholas & I tramped off, flew off, canoed off, generally removed ourselves, to explore various remote spots—for about a month. One day I found myself in the setting of The Head—exact & in detail. (Not the Gulkana). I was astonished—and realised that I had done it again. But nothing dreadful happened, fortunately.

A few years later, when Nicholas had moved to Alaska perman-ently—he's still there—I started visiting him. I think we found the Gul-kana about 1983. That was the time & place I fell in love with Alaska. The poem—which I wrote at over the next years—was an attempt to get all my feeling about it into that one experience. But I never, that I remember, connected it with 'The Head'—I suppose because the place and the details were so utterly different. Still, I see the connections now.

Better not look at them—they'll drag you into deeper complications. I saw the connections when I wrote—2 or 3 years ago—a semi-children's story (what's that?) for an Anthology of strange experiences (ghostly) in places belonging to the National Trust. And then through that I glimpsed some peculiar secrets of 'The Head'—and of 'The Gulkana'. That latest story is also in 'Difficulties of a Bridegroom'.

Chronology. I've a good memory for where & when I wrote any of my verses. "Remembering Teheran" began to come together after our Orghast in Persepolis year—but before the Shah's downfall. I loved Persia, & got fairly deeply involved in the whole Sufi aspect of Islam—passion shared by Peter Brook. But was aware of the explosion coming, the catastrophe. Very fond of that poem. Nearly as many drafts as The Gulkana.

'Littleblood' came in the first flush of confident Crow pieces, about 1967. Interesting to me. Only a page or two of manuscript. First part is just free-fall flip-flapping effort to find I'm not quite sure what. Then I made the deliberate conscious decision to 'listen' instead of to 'invent'. Without any change in the speed of the writing—but with a noticeable change in the form of the handwriting—I then wrote out the whole poem exactly as it is.

The Gulkana has been ruined. The old road that made it fairly accessible (but still pretty arduous to get to) is a high grade motorway jammed with Winnebagos & Tourist Buses. In our day, no fishing lodges brought their guests in to fish the run: now there are guide boats in every pool, & helicopter-loads of anglers along the banks. Pretty well the whole of Alaska has gone the same way. Thanks to a fishing guide book written by the editor of 'Alaska Sportfish'—a magazine—and that film 'A River runs through it', which converted ²/₃ of U.S. males to macho fly-fishers. Happened in 12 or so years.

All the best
Ted

One manuscript draft of 'The Gulkana' had mentioned that TH had 'pre-dreamed' the event that inspired the poem.

Gammage had asked about the dates of certain poems chosen for discussion by contributors to *The Epic Poise*, which he was editing as a celebration of TH's life and work, and which should have been published on his 70th birthday. When TH died before reaching that age, it was brought out as a memorial volume. In it, Michael Hofmann wrote about TH's 'Remembering Teheran', Seamus Heaney about 'Littleblood'.

To Hilda Farrar

19 October 1998   Ms   Vicky Watling

Dear Aunt Hilda—

Well—there you go! Still, if you're anything like others we know, you'll be wanting your other hip done now.

Brother-in-Law Ian is always complaining about his unrepaired one.

The Order of Merit came as a big surprise. It's the one <u>every</u>body wants. 24 of us in all. Not a political appointment—entirely the gift of the Monarch. So it has no social effect on you—except to make you very grand, and envied, I suppose.

T.S. Eliot, Bernard Crick (who discovered DNA) etc.

First came a letter, asking whether I would accept it, from the Queen's Secretary. I answered with enthusiasm, and a solemn acknowledgement of the great honour. Then came the date of the private appointment. Together with an invitation to Lunch with the Royal Household afterwards.

The date was fixed for last Friday—following a meeting with the Indian Ambassador.

Usual astonished disbelief from the taxi-driver. Crowd of Bucks Palace gates, taking photographs of us as we went in. Right in on to the red carpet.

Met by her old Equerry—Sir Edward Somebody (forget his name). Then the message that the Queen wanted Carol to join us. So after 15 minutes we were led in to her little room, and there she was beaming at us from a group of people who turned out to be a photographer (woman) and some flunkeys. I'd agreed to be photographed receiving the Award from the Queen—(after some reluctance I might say. But then I thought it rather churlish to refuse what the Queen herself approved of.) A couple of flashey shots, as the Queen opened the magnificent box to hand me the superb & beautiful Cross—red and blue enamel, deeply translucent, a ring of enamel oak-leaves, a crown of ivory tiny balls & gold balls, very beautiful, intense object, as below:

Actual medal a bit bigger, chunkier. Wouldn't it have pleased Ma!

Then I gave her a copy of Birthday Letters—and she was fascinated. I told her how I had come to write it, & even moreso how I had come to publish it. I felt to make contact with her as never before. She was extremely vivacious & happy-spirited—more so than ever before. I suppose, talking about those poems, I was able to open my heart more than ever before—and so she responded in kind.

She looked extraordinary well & happy—after 3 months holiday maybe.

Like Charles & the Queen Mum she is extremely easy to speak to quite intimately.

Afterwards, we had a lovely jolly lunch with Sir Robert Fellowes & the Household, where Carol was a great hit. She's wonderfully good in those situations. (Queen was absent).

Then we came home. Recovering ever since. I suppose these visits are a bit arduous. Love from us, Hilda—

> take it easy. Ted & Carol

Hilda Farrar had fallen and broken her hip. After complications, she was moved into intensive care. During that time, TH and Carol Hughes were in almost daily contact with Hilda's daughter, Vicky Watling, who was not told that TH himself was seriously ill. The penmanship of this letter, with its many crossings-out, may show signs either of haste or of failing strength, but the medal is drawn vigorously.

The Queen had presented TH with the Order of Merit, her highest award, at Buckingham Palace on 16 October. Francis (not Bernard) Crick (1916–2004) had received it in 1991.

TH was to die nine days after writing this.

Illustration Credits

Index

743

Index of Works

For thematic entries on poetry collections, *see* main index.

Index of Recipients

I

INSOMNIA

'Stephen King brings his usual chilly touch to *Insomnia*, the story of a small town gripped by a creeping evil . . . This is not a horror story in the classic mould; it is a supernatural adventure romp on the fringes of the imagination, popular fiction at its best' – *The Times*

'A supreme page-turner and a plot that will keep you awake at night' – *GQ*

'As accomplished as ever' – *Interzone*

CELL

Anyone using their mobile cellphones at the time of The Pulse is infected. Artist Clayton Riddell embarks on a terrifying journey though the 'crazies' to reach his son before the young boy switches on his phone. And time is running out . . .

DESPERATION

A group of unsuspecting travellers is stopped in the middle of the Nevada desert and lured to the abandoned mining town of Desperation where a terrifying transformation is taking place.

DREAMCATCHER

Four lifelong friends gather in the woods of western Maine for their annual hunting trip. Before long, the friends are plunged into a terrifying confrontation. Their only hope of survival is locked in their shared past . . .

IT

A promise made twenty-eight years before calls seven adults to reunite in Derry, Maine, where as teenagers they battled an evil presence that preyed on the city's children. Now, Derry's children are being murdered again and they must confront It once more . . .

NEEDFUL THINGS

There is a new shop in Castle Rock called Needful Things, run by a stranger. There's something here for everyone. At a price you can just about afford. But there is another price. There always is when your heart's most secret desire is for sale . . .

THE STAND

One man escapes from a biological weapons facility after an accident, carrying with him a rapidly mutating flu that wipes out most of the world's population. In the aftermath, survivors must choose between two factions and prepare for a confrontation between the forces of good and evil.

UNDER THE DOME

The small town of Chester's Mill, Maine, is sealed off from the rest of the world by an invisible force field. War veteran Dale Barbara must discover the source of the Dome before it's too late . . .

ABOUT THE AUTHOR

STEPHEN KING Photograph © Dick Dickinson

There is a reason why Stephen King is one of the bestselling writers in the world, *ever*. Described by John Connolly as 'utterly compelling' and by the *Daily Express* as an author 'who can create an entire world and make the reader live in it', Stephen King writes stories that draw you in and are *impossible to put down*.

King is the author of more than fifty books, all of them worldwide bestsellers, including the epic thrillers *IT*, *The Stand* and *Under the Dome*. Many of his books and novellas have been turned into celebrated films, including *The Green Mile*, *Stand By Me* and *The Shawshank Redemption*.

King was the recipient of the 2003 National Book Foundation Medal for Distinguished Contribution to American Letters. He lives with his wife, novelist Tabitha King, in Maine.

By Stephen King and published by Hodder & Stoughton

NOVELS:

Carrie
'Salem's Lot
The Shining
The Stand
The Dead Zone
Firestarter
Cujo
Cycle of the Werewolf
Christine
The Talisman (with Peter Straub)
Pet Sematary
IT
The Eyes of the Dragon
Misery
The Tommyknockers
The Dark Half
Needful Things
Gerald's Game
Dolores Claiborne
Insomnia
Rose Madder
Desperation
Bag of Bones
The Girl Who Loved Tom Gordon
Dreamcatcher
From a Buick 8
Cell
Lisey's Story
Duma Key
Under the Dome
Blockade Billy

The Dark Tower I: The Gunslinger
The Dark Tower II: The Drawing of
the Three
The Dark Tower III: The Waste Lands
The Dark Tower IV: Wizard and Glass
The Dark Tower V: Wolves of the Calla
The Dark Tower VI: Song of Susannah
The Dark Tower VII: The Dark Tower

As Richard Bachman
Thinner
The Running Man
The Bachman Books
The Regulators
Blaze

STORY COLLECTIONS:

Night Shift
Different Seasons
Skeleton Crew
Four Past Midnight
Nightmares and Dreamscapes
Hearts in Atlantis
Everything's Eventual
Just After Sunset
Stephen King Goes to the Movies
Full Dark, No Stars

NON-FICTION

Danse Macabre
On Writing (A Memoir of the Craft)

STEPHEN KING
INSOMNIA

HODDER

Grateful acknowledgement is made for permission to reprint excerpts from the
following copyrighted material:

'White Rabbit' lyrics and music by Grace Slick. © 1967 Irving Music, Inc. (BMI).
All rights reserved. International copyright secured.
'The Pursuit' from Cemetery Nights by Stephen Dobyns. Copyright © Stephen Dobyns, 1987. By
permission of the author and Viking Penguin, a division of Penguin Books USA Inc.
'You Can't Sit Down' by Delecta Clark, Cornell Muldrow, and Kal Mann. © 1960 (renewed), 1968
Conrad Music, a division of Arc Music Corp. All rights reserved. Used by permission.
The Lord of the Rings by J. R. R. Tolkien, Copyright © 1965 by J. R. R. Tolkien
© renewed 1993 by Christopher R. Tolkien, John F. R. Tolkien, and Priscilla M. A. R. Tolkien. Reprinted
by permission of Houghton Mifflin Co. and HarperCollins Publishers Limited.
All rights reserved.
'Your Baby,' words and music by P. F. Sloan and Steve Barri. © Copyright 1965 by
MCA Music Publishing, a Division of MCA Inc. All rights reserved.
International copyright secured. Used by permission.
'Lantern' by Michael McDermott © 1993 EMI Blackwood Music, Inc., and Wanted Mann Music. All
rights reserved for Wanted Man Music controlled and administered by EMI Blackwood Music, Inc. All
rights reserved. International copyright secured. Used by permission

First published in Great Britain in 1994 by Hodder and Stoughton
A division of Hodder Headline

This paperback edition published in 2011

A Hodder Paperback

4

British Library Cataloguing in Publication Data
King, Stephen
Insomnia
I. Title
813.54[F]

ISBN 978 1 444 70785 4

Typeset in Bembo by Palimpsest Book Production Limited,
Falkirk, Stirlingshire
Printed and bound in Great Britain by
Clays Ltd, St Ives plc

Hodder & Stoughton
338 Euston Road
London NW1 3BH

www.hodder.co.uk

For Tabby . . . and for Al Kooper,
who knows the playing-field.
No fault of mine.

PROLOGUE

WINDING THE DEATHWATCH (I)

Old age is an island surrounded by death.

Juan Montalvo

'On Beauty'

1

No one – least of all Dr Litchfield – came right out and told Ralph Roberts that his wife was going to die, but there came a time when Ralph understood without needing to be told. The months between March and June were a jangling, screaming time inside his head – a time of conferences with doctors, of evening runs to the hospital with Carolyn, of trips to other hospitals in other states for special tests (Ralph spent much of his travel time on these trips thanking God for Carolyn's Blue Cross/Major Medical coverage), of personal research in the Derry Public Library, at first looking for answers the specialists might have overlooked, later on just looking for hope and grasping at straws.

Those four months were like being dragged drunk through some malign carnival where the people on the rides were really screaming, the people lost in the mirror maze were really lost, and the denizens of Freak Alley looked at you with false smiles on their lips and terror in their eyes. Ralph began to see these things by the middle of May, and as June set in, he began to understand that the pitchmen along the medical midway had only quack remedies to sell, and the cheery quickstep of the calliope could no longer quite hide the fact that the tune spilling out of the loudspeakers was 'The Funeral March'. It was a carnival, all right; the carnival of lost souls.

Ralph continued to deny these terrible images – and the even more terrible idea lurking behind them – all through the early summer of 1992, but as June gave way to July, this finally became impossible. The worst midsummer heatwave since 1971 rolled over central Maine, and Derry simmered in a bath of hazy sun, humidity, and daily temperatures in the mid-nineties. The city – hardly a bustling metropolis at the best of times – fell into a complete stupor, and it was in this hot silence that Ralph Roberts first heard the ticking of the deathwatch and understood that in the passage from June's cool damp greens to the baked stillness of July, Carolyn's slim chances had become no chances at all. She was going to die. Not this summer, probably – the doctors claimed to have quite a few tricks up their sleeves yet, and Ralph was sure they did – but this fall or this winter. His longtime companion, the only woman he had ever loved, was going to die. He tried to deny the idea, scolding himself for being a morbid old fool, but in the gasping silences of those long hot days, Ralph heard that ticking everywhere – it even seemed to be in the walls.

Yet it was loudest from within Carolyn herself, and when she turned her calm white face toward him – perhaps to ask him to turn on the radio so she could listen while she shelled some beans for their supper, or to ask him if he would go across to the Red Apple and get her an ice-cream on a stick – he would see that she heard it, too. He would see it in her dark eyes, at first only when she was straight, but later even when her eyes were hazed by the pain medication she took. By then the ticking had grown very loud, and when Ralph lay in bed beside her on those hot summer nights when even a single sheet seemed to weigh ten pounds and he believed every dog in Derry was barking at the moon, he listened to it, to the deathwatch ticking inside Carolyn, and it seemed to him that his heart would break with sorrow and terror. How much would she be required to suffer before the end came? How much would *he* be required to suffer? And how could he possibly live without her?

It was during this strange, fraught period that Ralph began to go for increasingly long walks through the hot summer afternoons and slow, twilit evenings, returning on many occasions too exhausted to eat. He kept expecting Carolyn to scold him for these outings, to say, *Why don't you stop it, you stupid old man? You'll kill yourself if you keep walking in this heat!* But she never did, and he gradually realized she didn't even know. That he went out, yes – she knew that. But not all the miles he went, or that when he came home he was often trembling with exhaustion and near sunstroke. Once upon a time it had seemed to Ralph she saw everything, even a change of half an inch in where he parted his hair. No more; the tumor in her brain had stolen her powers of observation, as it would soon steal her life.

So he walked, relishing the heat in spite of the way it sometimes made his head swim and his ears ring, relishing it mostly *because* of the way it made his ears ring; sometimes there were whole hours when they rang so loudly and his head pounded so fiercely that he couldn't hear the tick of Carolyn's deathwatch.

He walked over much of Derry that hot July, a narrow-shouldered old man with thinning white hair and big hands that still looked capable of hard work. He walked from Witcham Street to the Barrens, from Kansas Street to Neibolt Street, from Main Street to the Kissing Bridge, but his feet took him most frequently west along Harris Avenue, where the still beautiful and much beloved Carolyn Roberts was now spending her last year in a haze of headaches and morphine, to the Harris Avenue Extension and Derry County Airport. He would walk out the Extension – which was treeless and completely exposed to the pitiless sun – until he felt his legs threatening to cave in beneath him, and then double back.

He often paused to catch his second wind in a shady picnic area close to the airport's service entrance. At night this place was a teenage drinking and makeout spot, alive with the sounds of rap coming from boombox radios, but during the days it was the more-or-less exclusive domain of a group Ralph's friend Bill McGovern called the Harris Avenue Old Crocks. The Old Crocks gathered to play chess, to play gin, or just to shoot the shit. Ralph had known many of them for years (had, in fact, gone to grammar school with Stan Eberly), and was comfortable with them . . . as long as they didn't get too nosy. Most didn't. They were old-school Yankees, for the most part, raised to believe that what a man doesn't choose to talk about is no one's business but his own.

It was on one of these walks that he first became aware that something had gone very wrong with Ed Deepneau, his neighbor from up the street.

2

Ralph had walked much farther out the Harris Avenue Extension than usual that day, possibly because thunderheads had blotted out the sun and a cool, if still sporadic, breeze had begun to blow. He had fallen into a kind of trance, not thinking of anything, not watching anything but the dusty toes of his sneakers, when the four forty-five United Airlines flight from Boston swooped low overhead, startling him back to where he was with the teeth-rattling whine of its jet engines.

He watched it cross above the old GS&WM railroad tracks and the Cyclone fence that marked the edge of the airport, watched it settle toward the runway, marked the blue puffs of smoke as its wheels touched down. Then he glanced at his watch, saw how late it was getting, and looked up with wide eyes at the orange roof of the Howard Johnson's just up the road. He had been in a trance, all right; he had walked more than five miles without the slightest sense of time passing.

Carolyn's time, a voice deep inside his head muttered.

Yes, yes; Carolyn's time. She would be back in the apartment, counting the minutes until she could have another Darvon Complex, and he was out on the far side of the airport . . . halfway to Newport, in fact.

Ralph looked up at the sky and for the first time really saw the bruise-purple thunderheads which were stacking up over the airport. They did not mean rain, not for sure, not yet, but if it *did* rain, he was almost surely going to be caught in it; there was nowhere to shelter between here and the little picnic area back by Runway

3, and there was nothing there but a ratty little gazebo that always smelled faintly of beer.

He took another look at the orange roof, then reached into his right-hand pocket and felt the little sheaf of bills held by the silver money-clip Carolyn had given him for his sixty-fifth. There was nothing to prevent him walking up to HoJo's and calling a cab . . . except maybe for the thought of how the driver might look at him. *Stupid old man,* the eyes in the rear-view mirror might say. *Stupid old man, walked a lot further than you should on a hot day. If you'd been swimming, you woulda drownded.*

Paranoid, Ralph, the voice in his head told him, and now its clucky, slightly patronizing tone reminded him of Bill McGovern.

Well, maybe it was and maybe it wasn't. Either way, he thought he would chance the rain and walk back.

What if it doesn't just rain? Last summer it hailed so hard that one time in August it broke windows all over the west side.

'Let it hail, then,' he said. 'I don't bruise that easy.'

Ralph began to walk slowly back toward town along the shoulder of the Extension, his old high-tops raising small, parched puffs of dust as he went. He could hear the first rumbles of thunder in the west, where the clouds were stacking up. The sun, although blotted out, was refusing to quit without a fight; it edged the thunderheads with bands of brilliant gold and shone through occasional rifts in the clouds like the fragmented beam of some huge movie-projector. Ralph found himself feeling glad he had decided to walk, in spite of the ache in his legs and the steady nagging pain in the small of his back.

One thing, at least, he thought. *I'll sleep tonight. I'll sleep like a damn rock.*

The verge of the airport — acres of dead brown grass with the rusty railroad tracks sunk in them like the remains of some old wreck — was now on his left. Far in the distance beyond the Cyclone fence he could see the United 747, now the size of a child's toy plane, taxiing toward the small terminal which United and Delta shared.

Ralph's gaze was caught by another vehicle, this one a car, leaving the General Aviation terminal, which stood at this end of the airport. It was heading across the tarmac toward the small service entrance which gave on the Harris Avenue Extension. Ralph had watched a lot of vehicles come and go through that entrance just lately; it was only seventy yards or so from the picnic area where the Harris Avenue Old Crocks gathered. As the car approached the gate, Ralph recognized it as Ed and Helen Deepneau's Datsun . . . and it was really moving.

Ralph stopped on the shoulder, unaware that his hands had curled into anxious fists as the small brown car bore down on the closed gate. You needed a key-card to open the gate from the outside; from the inside an electric-eye beam did the job. But the beam was set close to the gate, very close, and at the speed the Datsun was going . . .

At the last moment (or so it seemed to Ralph), the small brown car scrunched to a stop, the tires sending up puffs of blue smoke that made Ralph think of the 747 touching down, and the gate began to trundle slowly open on its track. Ralph's fisted hands relaxed.

An arm emerged from the driver's side window of

the Datsun and began to wave up and down, apparently haranguing the gate, urging it to hurry it up. There was something so absurd about this that Ralph began to smile. The smile died before it had exposed even a gleam of teeth, however. The wind was still freshening from the west, where the thunderheads were, and it carried the screaming voice of the Datsun's driver.

'*You son of a bitch fucker! You bastard! Eat my cock! Hurry up! Hurry up and lick shit, you fucking asshole cuntlapper! Fucking booger! Ratdick ringmeat! Suckhole!*'

'That can't be Ed Deepneau,' Ralph murmured. He began to walk again without realizing it. '*Can't* be.'

Ed was a research chemist at the Hawking Laboratories research facility in Fresh Harbor, one of the kindest, most civil young men Ralph had ever met. Both he and Carolyn were very fond of Ed's wife, Helen, and their new baby, Natalie, as well. A visit from Natalie was one of the few things with the power to lift Carolyn out of her own life these days, and, sensing this, Helen brought her over frequently. Ed never complained. There were men, he knew, who wouldn't have cared to have the missus running to the old folks down the street every time the baby did some new and entrancing thing, especially when the granny-figure in the picture was ill. Ralph had an idea that Ed wouldn't be able to tell someone to go to hell without suffering a sleepless night in consequence, but—

'*You fucking whoremaster! Move your sour shit-caked ass, you hear me? Butt-fucker! Cunt-rammer!*'

But it sure *sounded* like Ed. Even from two or three hundred yards away, it certainly *sounded* like him.

Now the driver of the Datsun was revving his engine like a kid in a muscle-car waiting for the light to turn green. Clouds of exhaust smoke farted up from the tailpipe. As soon as the gate had retracted enough to allow the Datsun passage, the car leaped forward, squirting through the gap with its engine roaring, and when it did, Ralph got a clear look at the driver. He was close enough now for there to be no doubt: it was Ed, all right.

The Datsun bounced along the short unpaved stretch of lane between the gate and the Harris Street Extension. A horn blared suddenly, and Ralph saw a blue Ford Ranger, heading west on the Extension, swerve to avoid the oncoming Datsun. The driver of the pickup saw the danger too late, and Ed apparently never saw it at all (it was only later that Ralph came to consider Ed might have rammed the Ranger on purpose). There was a brief scream of tires followed by the hollow bang of the Datsun's fender driving into the Ford's sidewall. The pickup was driven halfway across the yellow line. The Datsun's hood crumpled, came unlatched, and popped up a little; headlight glass tinkled into the street. A moment later both vehicles were dead in the middle of the road, tangled together like some weird sculpture.

Ralph stood where he was for the time being, watching as oil spread beneath the Datsun's front end. He had seen several road accidents in his almost-seventy years, most of them minor, one or two serious, and he was always stunned by how quickly they happened and how little drama there was. It wasn't like in the movies, where the camera could slow things down, or on a videotape, where you could watch the car go off the cliff again and again if you so chose; there was usually just a series of converging blurs, followed by that quick and toneless combination of sounds: the cry of the tires, the hollow bang of metal crimping metal, the tinkle of glass. Then, *voilà – tout finis*.

There was even a kind of protocol for this sort of thing: How One Should Behave When Involved in a Low-Speed Collision. Of course there was, Ralph mused. There were probably a dozen two-bit collisions in Derry every day, and maybe twice that number in the wintertime, when there was snow and the roads got slippery. You got out, you met your opposite number at the point where the two vehicles had come together (and where, quite often, they were still entwined), you looked, you shook your heads. Sometimes – often, actually – this phase of the encounter was marked with angry words: fault was assigned (often rashly), driving skills impugned, legal action threatened. Ralph supposed what the drivers were really trying to say without coming right out and saying it was, *Listen, fool, you scared the living hell out of me!*

The final step in this unhappy little dance was the Exchange of the Sacred Insurance Screeds, and it was at this point that the drivers usually began to get control of their galloping emotions . . . always assuming that no one had been hurt, as appeared to be the case here. Sometimes the drivers involved even finished up by shaking hands.

Ralph prepared to watch all this from his vantage point less than a hundred and fifty yards away, but as soon as the driver's door of the Datsun opened he understood that things were going to go differently here – that the accident was maybe not over but still happening. It certainly did not seem that anyone was going to shake at the end of *these* festivities.

The door did not *swing* open; it *flew* open. Ed Deepneau leaped out, then simply stood stock-still beside his car, his slim shoulders squared against a background of deepening clouds. He was wearing faded jeans and a tee-shirt, and Ralph realized he had never seen Ed in a shirt that didn't button up the front. And there was something around his neck: a long white something. A scarf? It *looked* like a scarf, but why would anyone be wearing a scarf on a day as hot as this one had been?

Ed stood beside his wounded car for a moment, seeming to look in every direction but the right one. The fierce little pokes of his narrow head reminded Ralph of the way roosters studied their barnyard turf, looking for invaders and interlopers. Something about that similarity made Ralph feel uneasy. He had never seen Ed look that way before, and he supposed that was part of it, but it wasn't *all* of it. The truth of the matter was simply this: he had never seen *anyone* look exactly like that.

Thunder rumbled in the west, louder now. And closer.

The man getting out of the Ranger would have made two of Ed Deepneau, possibly three. His vast, deep belly hung over the rolled waistband of his green chino work-pants; there were sweatstains the size of dinner-plates under the arms of his open-throated white shirt. He tipped back the bill of the West Side Gardeners gimme-cap he was wearing to get a better look at the man who had broad-sided him. His heavy-jowled face was dead pale except for bright patches of color like rouge high on his cheekbones,

13

and Ralph thought: *There's a man who's a prime candidate for a heart attack. If I was closer I bet I'd be able to see the creases in his earlobes.*

'Hey!' the heavyset guy yelled at Ed. The voice coming out of that broad chest and deep gut was absurdly thin, almost reedy. 'Where'd you get your license? Fuckin Sears n Roebuck?'

Ed's wandering, jabbing head swung immediately toward the sound of the big man's voice – seemed almost to home in, like a jet guided by radar – and Ralph got his first good look at Ed's eyes. He felt a bolt of alarm light up in his chest and suddenly began to run toward the accident. Ed, meanwhile, had started toward the man in the sweat-soaked white shirt and gimme-cap. He was walking in a stiff-legged, high-shouldered strut that was nothing at all like his usual easygoing amble.

'Ed!' Ralph shouted, but the freshening breeze – cold now with the promise of rain – seemed to snatch the words away before they could even get out of his mouth. Certainly Ed never turned. Ralph made himself run faster, the ache in his legs and the throbbing in the small of his back forgotten. It was murder he had seen in Ed Deepneau's wide, unblinking eyes. He had absolutely no previous experience upon which to base such an assessment, but he didn't think you could mistake such a naked glare; it was the look fighting cocks must wear when they launch themselves at each other, spurs up and slashing. 'Ed! Hey, Ed, hold up! It's Ralph!'

Not so much as a glance around, although Ralph was now so close that Ed must have heard, wind or no wind. Certainly the heavyset man glanced around, and Ralph

14

could see both fear and uncertainty in his look. Then Heavyset turned back to Ed and raised his hands placatingly.

'Look,' he said. 'We can talk—'

That was as far as he got. Ed took another quick step forward, reached up with one slim hand – it was very white in the rapidly darkening day – and slapped Heavyset across his far from inconsiderable jowls. The sound was like the report of a kid's air rifle.

'How many have you killed?' Ed asked.

Heavyset pressed back against the side of his pickup, his mouth open, his eyes wide. Ed's queer, stiff strut never faltered. He walked into the other man and stood belly to belly with him, seemingly oblivious of the fact that the pickup's driver was four inches taller and outweighed him by a hundred pounds or more. Ed reached up and slapped him again. 'Come on! Fess up, brave boy – *how many have you killed?*' His voice rose to a shriek that was lost in the coming storm's first really authoritative clap of thunder.

Heavyset pushed him away – a gesture not of aggression but of simple fright – and Ed went reeling backward against the crumpled nose of his Datsun. He bounced back at once, fists clenched, gathering himself to leap at Heavyset, who was cringing against the side of his truck with his gimme-cap now askew and his shirt untucked in the back and at the sides. A memory flashed across Ralph's mind – a Three Stooges short he'd seen years ago, Larry, Curly, and Moe playing painters without a clue – and he felt a sudden surge of sympathy for Heavyset, who looked absurd as well as scared to death.

15

Ed Deepneau did not look absurd. With his yanked-back lips and wide, unblinking eyes, Ed looked more like a fighting cock than ever. 'I know what you've been doing,' he whispered to Heavyset. 'What kind of comedy did you think this was? Did you think you and your butcher friends could get away with it forev—'

At that moment Ralph arrived, puffing and gasping like an old carthorse, and put an arm around Ed's shoulders. The heat beneath the thin tee-shirt was unnerving; it was like putting an arm around an oven, and when Ed turned to look at him, Ralph had the momentary (but unforgettable) impression that that was exactly what he was looking into. He had never seen such utter, unreasoning fury in a pair of human eyes; had never even suspected such fury might exist.

Ralph's immediate impulse was to recoil, but he suppressed it and stood firm. He had an idea that if he pulled back, Ed would fall on him like a rogue dog, biting and clawing. It was absurd, of course; Ed was a research chemist, Ed was a member of the Book of the Month Club (the kind who took the twenty-pound histories of the Crimean War they always seemed to offer as alternates to the main selection), Ed was Helen's husband and Natalie's dad. Hell, Ed was a friend.

. . . except this wasn't that Ed, and Ralph knew it.

Instead of pulling back, Ralph leaned forward, grasped Ed's shoulders (so hot under the tee-shirt, so incredibly, throbbingly hot), and moved his face until it blocked Heavyset from Ed's creepy fixed gaze.

'Ed, quit it!' Ralph said. He used the loud but steadily firm voice he assumed one used with people who were having hysterics. 'You're all right! Just quit it!'

For a moment Ed's fixed gaze didn't waver, and then his eyes moved over Ralph's face. It wasn't much, but Ralph felt a small surge of relief just the same.

'What's the matter with him?' Heavyset asked from behind Ralph. 'He crazy, do you think?'

'He's fine, I'm sure,' Ralph said, although he was sure of no such thing. He spoke out of the corner of his mouth, and didn't take his eyes from Ed. He didn't *dare* take his eyes from Ed — that contact felt like the only hold he had over the man, and tenuous at best. 'Just shaken up from the crash. He needs a few seconds to calm d—'

'Ask him what he's got under that tarp!' Ed yelled suddenly, and pointed over Ralph's shoulder. Lightning flashed, and for a moment the pitted scars of Ed's adolescent acne were thrown into sharp relief, like some strange organic treasure map. Thunder rolled. 'Hey, hey, Susan Day! he chanted in a high, childlike voice that made Ralph's forearms break out in goosebumps. 'How many kids did you kill today?'

'He ain't shook up,' Heavyset said. 'He's crazy. And when the cops get here, I'm gonna see he gets tooken in.'

Ralph glanced around and saw a blue tarpaulin stretched across the bed of the pickup. It had been tied down with bright yellow hanks of rope. Round shapes bulked beneath it.

'Ralph?' a timid voice asked.

He glanced to his left and saw Dorrance Marstellar — at ninety-something easily the oldest of the Harris Avenue Old Crocks — standing just beyond Heavyset's pickup truck. There was a paperback book in his waxy, liver-spotted hands, and Dorrance was bending it anxiously back and forth, giving the spine a real workout. Ralph supposed it was a book of poetry, which was all he had ever seen old Dorrance read. Or maybe he didn't really read at all; maybe he just liked to hold the books and look at the artfully stacked words.

'Ralph, what's wrong? What's happening?'

More lightning flashed overhead, a purple-white snarl of electricity. Dorrance looked up at it as if unsure of where he was, who he was, or what he was seeing. Ralph groaned inside.

'Dorrance —' he began, and then Ed lunged beneath him, like some wild animal which has only lain quiet to regain its strength. Ralph staggered, then pushed Ed back against the crumpled hood of his Datsun. He felt panicky – unsure of what to do next or how to do it. There were too many things going on at once. He could feel the muscles in Ed's arms humming fiercely just below his grip; it was almost as if the man had somehow swallowed a bolt of the lightning now loose in the sky.

'Ralph?' Dorrance asked in that same calm but worried voice. 'I wouldn't touch him anymore, if I were you. I can't see your hands.'

Oh, good. Another lunatic to deal with. Just what he needed.

Ralph glanced down at his hands, then looked at the old man. 'What are you talking about, Dorrance?'

'Your hands,' Dorrance said patiently. 'I can't see your—'

'This is no place for you, Dor – why don't you get lost?'

The old man brightened a little at that. 'Yes!' he said

in the tone of one who has just stumbled over a great truth. 'That's just what I oughtta do!' He began to back up, and when the thunder cracked again, he cringed and put his book on top of his head. Ralph was able to read the bright red letters of the title: *Buckdancer's Choice*. 'It's what *you* ought to do, too, Ralph. You don't want to mess in with long-time business. It's a good way to get hurt.'

'What are you—'

But before Ralph could finish, Dorrance turned his back and went lumbering off in the direction of the picnic area with his fringe of white hair – as gossamer as the hair on a new baby's head – rippling in the breeze of the oncoming storm.

One problem solved, but Ralph's relief was short-lived. Ed had been temporarily distracted by Dorrance, but now he was looking daggers at Heavyset again. 'Cuntlicker!' he spat. 'Fucked your mother and licked her cunt!'

Heavyset's enormous brow drew down. *'What?'*

Ed's eyes shifted back to Ralph, whom he now seemed to recognize. 'Ask him what's under that tarp!' he cried. 'Better yet, get the murdering cocksucker to show you!'

Ralph looked at the heavyset man. 'What have you got under there?'

'What's it to you?' Heavyset asked, perhaps trying to sound truculent. He sampled the look in Ed Deepneau's eyes and took two more sidling steps away.

'Nothing to me, something to him,' Ralph said, lifting his chin in Ed's direction. 'Just help me cool him out, okay?'

'You know him?'

'Murderer!' Ed repeated, and this time he lunged hard enough under Ralph's hands to drive him back a step. Yet something was happening, wasn't it? Ralph thought the scary, vacant look was seeping out of Ed's eyes. There seemed to be a little more *Ed* in there than there had been before . . . or perhaps that was only wishful thinking. 'Murderer, *baby* murderer!'

'Jesus, what a loony tune,' Heavyset said, but he went to the rear of the truckbed, yanked one of the ropes free, and peeled back a corner of the tarpaulin. Beneath it were four pressboard barrels, each marked WEED-GO. 'Organic fertilizer,' Heavyset said, his eyes flicking from Ed to Ralph and then back to Ed again. He touched the bill of his West Side Gardeners cap. 'I spent the day workin on a set of new flower-beds outside the Derry Psych Wing . . . where *you* could stand a short vacation, friend.'

'Fertilizer?' Ed asked. It was himself he seemed to be speaking to. His left hand rose slowly to his temple and began to rub there. *'Fertilizer?'* He sounded like a man questioning some simple yet staggering scientific development.

'Fertilizer,' Heavyset agreed. He glanced back at Ralph and said, 'This guy is sick in the head. You know it?'

'He's confused, that's all,' Ralph answered uneasily. He leaned over the side of the truck and rapped a barrel-top. Then he turned back to Ed. 'Barrels of fertilizer,' he said. 'Okay?'

No response. Ed's right hand rose and began to rub at his other temple. He looked like a man sinking into a terrible migraine.

'Okay?' Ralph repeated gently.

Ed closed his eyes for a moment, and when they opened again, Ralph observed a sheen in them he thought was probably tears. Ed's tongue slipped out and dabbed delicately first at one corner of his mouth and then the other. He took the end of his silk scarf and wiped his forehead, and as he did, Ralph saw there were Chinese figures embroidered on it in red, just above the fringe.

'I guess maybe –' he began, and then broke off. His eyes widened again in that look Ralph didn't like. 'Babies!' he rasped. 'You hear me? *Babies!*'

Ralph shoved him back against his car for the third or fourth time – he'd lost count. 'What are you talking about, Ed?' An idea suddenly occurred to him. 'Is it Natalie? Are you worried about Natalie?'

A small, crafty smile touched Ed's lips. He looked past Ralph at the heavyset man. 'Fertilizer, huh? Well, if that's all it is, you won't mind opening one of them, will you?'

Heavyset looked at Ralph uneasily. 'Man needs a doctor,' he said.

'Maybe he does. But he was calming down, I thought . . . *could* you open one of those barrels? It might make him feel better.'

'Yeah, sure, what the heck. In for a penny, in for a pound.'

There was another flash of lightning, another heavy blast of thunder – one that seemed to go rolling all the way across the sky this time – and a cold spackle of rain struck the back of Ralph's sweaty neck. He glanced to his left and saw Dorrance Marstellar standing at the entrance to the picnic area, book in hand, watching the three of them anxiously.

'It's gonna rain a pretty bitch, looks like,' Heavyset

said, 'and I can't let this stuff get wet. It starts a chemical reaction. So look fast.' He felt around between one of the barrels and the sidewall of his truck for a moment, then came up with a crowbar. 'I must be as nutty as he is, doin this,' he said to Ralph. 'I mean, I was just goin along home, mindin my business. He hit *me*.'

'Go on,' Ralph said. 'It'll only take a second.'

'Yeah,' Heavyset replied sourly, turning and setting the flat end of the crowbar under the lid of the nearest barrel, 'but the memories will last a lifetime.'

Another thunderclap rocked the day just then, and Heavyset did not hear what Ed Deepneau said next. Ralph did, however, and it chilled the pit of his stomach.

'Those barrels are full of dead babies,' Ed said. 'You'll see.'

Heavyset popped the lid on the end barrel, and such was the conviction in Ed's voice that Ralph almost expected to see tangles of arms and legs and bundles of small hairless heads. Instead, he saw a mixture of fine blue crystals and brown stuff. The smell which rose from the barrel was rich and peaty, with a thin chemical undertone.

'See? Satisfied?' Heavyset asked, speaking directly to Ed again. 'I ain't Ray Joubert or that guy Dahmer after all. How 'bout that!'

The look of confusion was back on Ed's face, and when the thunder cracked overhead again, he cringed a little. He leaned over, reached a hand toward the barrel, then looked a question at Heavyset.

The big man nodded to him, almost sympathetically, Ralph thought. 'Sure, touch it, fine by me. But if it rains

22

while you're holdin a fistful, you'll dance like John Travolta. It burns.'

Ed reached into the barrel, grabbed some of the mix, and let it run through his fingers. He shot Ralph a perplexed look (*there was an element of embarrassment in that look as well,* Ralph thought), and then sank his arm into the barrel all the way to the elbow.

'Hey!' Heavyset cried, startled. 'That ain't a box of Cracker Jack!'

For a moment the crafty grin resurfaced on Ed's face – a look that said *I know a trick worth two of that* – and then it subsided into puzzlement again as he found nothing further down but more fertilizer. When he drew his arm out of the barrel, it was dusty and aromatic with the mix. Another flash of lightning exploded above the airport. The thunder which followed was almost deafening.

'Get that off your skin before it rains, I'm warning you,' Heavyset said. He reached through the Ranger's open passenger window and produced a McDonald's take-out sack. He rummaged in it, came out with a couple of napkins, and handed them to Ed, who began to wipe the fertilizer dust from his forearm like a man in a dream. While he did this, Heavyset replaced the lid on the barrel, tamping it into place with one large, freckled fist and taking quick glances up at the darkening sky. When Ed touched the shoulder of his white shirt, the man stiffened and pulled away, looking at Ed warily.

'I think I owe you an apology,' Ed said, and to Ralph his voice sounded completely clear and sane for the first time.

'You're damn tooting,' Heavyset said, but he sounded

relieved. He stretched the plastic-coated tarpaulin back into place and tied it in a series of quick, efficient gestures. Watching him, Ralph was struck by what a sly thief time was. Once he could have tied that same sheetbend with that same dextrous ease. Today he could still tie it, but it would take him at least two minutes and maybe three of his best curse-words.

Heavyset patted the tarp and then turned to them, folding his arms across the substantial expanse of his chest. 'Did you see the accident?' he asked Ralph.

'No,' Ralph said at once. He had no idea why he was lying, but the decision to do it was instantaneous. 'I was watching the plane land. The United.'

To his complete surprise, the flushed patches on Heavyset's cheeks began to spread. *You were watching it, too!* Ralph thought suddenly. *And not just watching it land, either, or you wouldn't be blushing like that . . . you were watching it taxi!*

This thought was followed by a complete revelation: Heavyset thought the accident had been his fault, or that the cop or cops who showed up to investigate might read it that way. He had been watching the plane and hadn't seen Ed's reckless charge through the service gate and out to the Extension.

'Look, I'm *really* sorry,' Ed was saying earnestly, but he actually looked more than sorry; he looked dismayed. Ralph suddenly found himself wondering how much he trusted that expression, and if he really had even the slightest idea of

(*Hey, hey, Susan Day*)

what had just happened here . . . and who the hell *was* Susan Day, anyhow?

'I bumped my head on the steering wheel,' Ed was saying, 'and I guess it . . . you know, it rattled my cage pretty good.'

'Yeah, I guess it did,' Heavyset said. He scratched his head, looked up at the dark and convoluted sky, then looked back at Ed again. 'Want to make you a deal, friend.'

'Oh? What deal is that?'

'Let's just exchange names and phone numbers instead of going through all that insurance shit. Then you go your way and I go mine.'

Ed looked uncertainly at Ralph, who shrugged, and then back at the man in the West Side Gardeners cap.

'If we get into it with the cops,' Heavyset went on, 'I'm in for a ration of shit. First thing they're going to find out when they call it in is I had an Operating Under the Influence last winter, and I'm drivin on a provisional license. They're apt to make problems for me even though I was on the main drag and had the right-of-way. See what I mean?'

'Yes,' Ed said, 'I guess so, but the accident was entirely my fault. I was going much too fast—'

'The accident part is maybe not so important,' Heavyset said, then looked mistrustfully around at an approaching panel truck that was pulling over onto the shoulder. He looked back at Ed again and spoke with some urgency. 'You lost some oil, but it's stopped leakin now. I bet you could drive her home . . . if you live here in town. You live here in town?'

'Yes,' Ed said.

'And I'd stand you good on repairs, up to fifty bucks or so.'

25

Another revelation struck Ralph; it was the only thing he could think of to explain the man's sudden change from truculence to something close to wheedling. An OUI last winter? Yes, probably. But Ralph had never heard of such a thing as a provisional license, and thought it was almost certainly bullshit. Old Mr West Side Gardeners had been driving without a license. What complicated the situation was this: Ed was telling the truth – the accident *had* been entirely his fault.

'If we just drive away and call it good,' Heavyset was going on, 'I don't have to explain all over again about my OUI and *you* don't have to explain why you jumped out of your car and started slapping me and yelling about how I had a truckload of dead bodies.'

'Did I actually say that?' Ed asked, sounding bewildered.

'You know you did,' Heavyset told him grimly.

A voice with a wispy French-Canadian accent asked, 'Everyt'ing okay here, fellers? Nobody urt? . . . Eyyy, Ralph! Dat you?'

The truck which had pulled over had Derry Dry Cleaners printed on the side, and Ralph recognized the driver as one of the Vachon brothers from Old Cape. Probably Trigger, the youngest.

'That's me,' Ralph said, and without knowing or asking himself why – he was operating purely on instinct at this point – he went to Trigger, put an arm around his shoulders, and led him back in the direction of the laundry truck.

'Dem guys okay?'

'Fine, fine,' Ralph said. He glanced back and saw that

Ed and Heavyset were standing by the truckbed with their heads together. Another cold spatter of rain fell, drumming on the blue tarpaulin like impatient fingers. 'A little fender-bender, that's all. They're working it out.'

'Beauty, beauty,' Trigger Vachon said complacently. 'Howdat pretty little wife of yours, Ralph?'

Ralph twitched, suddenly feeling like a man who remembers at lunch that he has forgotten to turn off the stove before leaving for work. 'Jesus!' he said, and looked at his watch, hoping for five-fifteen, five-thirty at the latest. Instead he saw it was ten minutes of six. Already twenty minutes past the time Carolyn expected him to bring her a bowl of soup and half a sandwich. She would be worried. In fact, with the lightning and the thunder booming through the empty apartment, she might be downright scared. And if it *did* rain, she would not be able to close the windows; she had almost no strength left in her hands.

'Ralph?' Trigger asked. 'What's wrong?'

'Nothing,' he said. 'It's just that I got walking and lost all track of time. Then this accident happened, and . . . could you give me a ride home, Trig? I'll pay you.'

'No need to pay nuttin,' Trigger said. 'It's on my way. Hop in, Ralph. You t'ink dose guys gonna be all right? Ain't gonna take after each udder or nuttin?'

'No,' Ralph said. 'I don't think so. Just one second.'

'Sure.'

Ralph walked over to Ed. 'Are you okay with this? Are you getting it worked out?'

'Yes,' Ed replied. 'We're going to settle it privately. Why not? A little broken glass is all it really comes down to.'

27

He sounded completely like his old self now, and the big man in the white shirt was looking at him with something that was almost respect. Ralph still felt perplexed and uneasy about what had happened here, but he decided he was going to let it go. He liked Ed Deepneau a lot, but Ed was not his business this July; Carolyn was. Carolyn and the thing which had started ticking in the walls of their bedroom — and inside her — late at night.

'Great,' he told Ed. 'I'm headed home. I make Carolyn her supper these days, and I'm running way late.'

He started to turn away. The heavyset man stopped him with an outstretched hand. 'John Tandy,' he said.

He shook it. 'Ralph Roberts. Pleased to meet you.'

Tandy smiled. 'Under the circumstances, I kinda doubt that . . . but I'm real glad you showed up when you did. For a few seconds there I really thought him and me was gonna tango.'

So did I, Ralph thought but didn't say. He looked at Ed, his troubled eye taking in the unfamiliar tee-shirt clinging to Ed's stalk-thin midriff and the white silk scarf with the Chinese-red figures embroidered on it. He didn't entirely like the look in Ed's eyes when they met his; Ed was perhaps not all the way back after all.

'Sure you're okay?' Ralph asked him. He wanted to go, wanted to get back to Carolyn, and yet he was somehow reluctant. The feeling that this situation was about nine miles from right persisted.

'Yes, fine,' Ed said quickly, and gave him a big smile which did not reach his dark green eyes. They studied Ralph carefully, as if asking how much he had seen . . . and how much

(*hey hey Susan Day*)
he would remember later on.

3

The interior of Trigger Vachon's truck smelled of clean, freshly pressed clothes, an aroma which for some reason always reminded Ralph of fresh bread. There was no passenger seat, so he stood with one hand wrapped around the doorhandle and the other gripping the edge of a Dandux laundry basket.

'Man, dat look like some strange go-on back dere,' Trigger said, glancing into his outside mirror.

'You don't know the half of it,' Ralph replied.

'I know the guy drivin the rice-burner – Deepneau, his name is. He got a pretty little wife, send stuff out sometime. Seem like a nice fella, mos usually.'

'He sure wasn't himself today,' Ralph said.

'Had a bug up his ass, did he?'

'Had a whole damn ant-farm up there, I think.'

Trigger laughed hard at that, pounding the worn black plastic of the big steering wheel. 'Whole damn ant-farm! Beauty! Beauty! I'm savin dat one, me!' Trigger wiped his streaming eyes with a handkerchief almost the size of a tablecloth. 'Look to me like Mr Deepneau come out dat airport service gate, him.'

'That's right, he did.'

'You need a pass to use dat way,' Trigger said. 'How Mr D get a pass, you tink?'

Ralph thought it over, frowning, then shook his head. 'I don't know. It never even occurred to me. I'll have to ask him next time I see him.'

'You do dat,' Trigger said. 'And ask him how dem ants doin.' This stimulated a fresh throe of laughter, which in turn occasioned more flourishes of the comic-opera handkerchief.

As they turned off the Extension and onto Harris Avenue proper, the storm finally broke. There was no hail, but the rain came in an extravagant summer flood, so heavy at first that Trigger had to slow the panel truck to a crawl. 'Wow!' he said respectfully. 'Dis remine me of the big storm back in '85, when haffa downtown fell inna damn Canal! Member dat, Ralph?'

'Yes,' Ralph said. 'Let's hope it doesn't happen again.'

'Nah,' Trigger said, grinning and peering past his extravagantly flapping windshield wipers, 'dey got the drainage system all fixed up now. Beauty!'

The combination of the cold rain and the warm cab caused the bottom half of the windshield to steam up. Without thinking, Ralph reached out a finger and drew a figure in the steam:

'What's dat?' Trigger asked.

'I don't really know. Looks Chinese, doesn't it? It was on the scarf Ed Deepneau was wearing.'

'Look a little familiar to me,' Trigger said, glancing at it again. Then he snorted and flapped a hand. 'Listen to me, wouldja? On'y t'ing I can say in Chinese is *moo-goo-gai-pan*!'

Ralph smiled, but didn't seem to have a laugh in him. It was Carolyn. Now that he had remembered her, he couldn't stop thinking about her – couldn't stop imagining the windows open, and the curtains streaming like Edward Gorey ghost arms as the rain poured in.

'You still live in dat two-storey across from the Red Apple?'

'Yes.'

Trigger pulled in to the curb, the wheels of the truck spraying up big fans of water. The rain was still pouring down in sheets. Lightning raced across the sky; thunder cracked.

'You better stay right here wit me for a little bit,' Trigger said. 'She let up in a minute or two.'

'I'll be all right.' Ralph didn't think anything could keep him in the truck a second longer, not even handcuffs. 'Thanks, Trig.'

'Wait a sec! Let me give you a piece of plastic – you can puddit over your head like a rainhat!'

'No, that's okay, no problem, thanks, I'll just—'

There seemed to be no way of finishing whatever it was he was trying to say, and now what he felt was close to panic. He shoved the truck's passenger door back on its track and jumped out, landing ankle-deep in the cold water racing down the gutter. He gave Trigger a final wave without looking back, then hurried up the walk to the house he and Carolyn shared with Bill McGovern, feeling in his pocket for his latchkey as he went. When he reached the porch steps he saw he wouldn't need it – the door was standing ajar. Bill, who lived downstairs, often forgot to lock it, and Ralph would rather think it had been him than think that Carolyn had wandered out to look for him and been caught in the storm. That was a possibility Ralph did not even want to consider.

He hurried into the shadowy foyer, wincing as thunder banged deafeningly overhead, and crossed to the foot of the stairs. He paused there a moment, hand on the newel post of the banister, listening to rainwater drip from his soaked pants and shirt onto the hardwood floor. Then he started up, wanting to run but no longer able to find the next gear up from a fast walk. His heart was beating hard and fast in his chest, his soaked sneakers were clammy anchors dragging at his feet, and for some reason he kept seeing the way Ed Deepneau's head had moved when he got out of his Datsun — those stiff, quick jabs that made him look like a rooster spoiling for a fight.

The third riser creaked loudly, as it always did, and the sound provoked hurried footsteps from above. They were no relief because they weren't Carolyn's, he knew that at once, and when Bill McGovern leaned over the rail, his face pale and worried beneath his Panama hat, Ralph wasn't really surprised. All the way back from the Extension he had felt that something was wrong, hadn't he? Yes. But under the circumstances, that hardly qualified as precognition. When things reached a certain degree of wrongness, he was discovering, they could no longer be redeemed or turned around; they just kept going wronger and wronger. He supposed that on some level or other he'd always known that. What he had never suspected was how long that wrong road could be.

'Ralph!' Bill called down. 'Thank God! Carolyn's

having . . . well, I guess it's some sort of seizure. I just dialed 911, asked them to send an ambulance.'

Ralph discovered he could run up the rest of the stairs, after all.

4

She was lying half in and half out of the kitchen with her hair in her face. Ralph thought there was something particularly horrible about that; it looked sloppy, and if there was one thing Carolyn refused to be, it was sloppy. He knelt beside her and brushed the hair away from her eyes and forehead. The skin beneath his fingers felt as chilly as his feet inside his soaked sneakers.

'I wanted to put her on the couch, but she's too heavy for me,' Bill said nervously. He had taken off his Panama and was fiddling nervously with the band. 'My back, you know—'

'I know, Bill, it's okay,' Ralph said. He slid his arms under Carolyn and picked her up. She did not feel heavy to him at all, but light – almost as light as a milkweed pod which is ready to burst open and disgorge its filaments into the wind. 'Thank God you were here.'

'I almost wasn't,' Bill replied, following Ralph into the living room and still fiddling with his hat. He made Ralph think of old Dorrance Marstellar with his book of poems. *I wouldn't touch him anymore, if I were you,* old Dorrance had said. *I can't see your hands.* 'I was on my way out when I heard a hell of a thud . . . it must have been her falling . . .' Bill looked around the storm-darkened living room, his face somehow distraught and avid at the

33

same time, his eyes seeming to search for something that wasn't there. Then they brightened. 'The door!' he said. 'I'll bet it's still open! It'll be raining in! I'll be right back, Ralph.'

He hurried out. Ralph barely noticed; the day had taken on the surreal aspects of a nightmare. The ticking was the worst. He could hear it in the walls, so loud now that even the thunder could not blot it out.

He put Carolyn on the couch and knelt beside her. Her respiration was fast and shallow, and her breath was terrible. Ralph did not turn away from it, however. 'Hang in there, sweetheart,' he said. He picked up one of her hands – it was almost as clammy as her brow had been – and kissed it gently. 'You just hang in there. It's fine, everything's fine.'

But it wasn't fine, the ticking sound meant that *nothing* was fine. It wasn't in the walls, either – it had never been in the walls, but only in his wife. In Carolyn. It was in his dear one, she was slipping away from him, and what would he ever do without her?

'You just hang on,' he said. 'Hang on, you hear me?' He kissed her hand again, and held it against his cheek, and when he heard the warble of the approaching ambulance, he began to cry.

5

She came around in the ambulance as it sped across Derry (the sun was already out again, the wet streets steaming), and at first she talked such gibberish that Ralph was sure she had suffered a stroke. Then, just as she began to clear up and speak coherently, a second convulsion struck, and it took both Ralph and one of the paramedics who had answered the call to hold her down.

It wasn't Dr Litchfield who came to see Ralph in the third-floor waiting room early that evening but Dr Jamal, the neurologist. Jamal talked to him in a low, soothing voice, telling him that Carolyn was now stabilized, that they were going to keep her overnight, just to be safe, but that she would be able to go home in the morning. There were going to be some new medications – drugs that were expensive, yes, but also quite wonderful.

'We must not be losing the hope, Mr Roberts,' Dr Jamal said.

'No,' Ralph said, 'I suppose not. Will there be more of these, Dr Jamal?'

Dr Jamal smiled. He spoke in a quiet voice that was rendered somehow even more comforting by his soft Indian accent. And although Dr Jamal did not come right out and tell him that Carolyn was going to die, he came as close as anyone ever did during that long year in which she battled to stay alive. The new medications, Jamal said, would probably prevent any further seizures, but things had reached a stage where all predictions had to be taken 'with the grains of salt'. The tumor was spreading in spite of everything they had tried, unfortunately.

'The motor-control problems may show up next,' Dr Jamal said in his comforting voice. 'And I am seeing some deterioration in the eyesight, I am afraid.'

'Can I spend the night with her?' Ralph asked quietly. 'She'll sleep better if I do.' He paused, then added: 'So will I.'

'Of gorse!' Dr Jamal said, brightening. 'That is a fine idea!'

'Yes,' Ralph said heavily. 'I think so, too.'

6

So he sat beside his sleeping wife, and he listened to the ticking that was not in the walls, and he thought: *Some day soon — maybe this fall, maybe this winter — I will be back in this room with her.* It had the feel not of speculation but of prophecy, and he leaned over and put his head on the white sheet that covered his wife's breast. He didn't want to cry again, but did a little anyway.

That ticking. So loud and so steady.

I'd like to get hold of what's making that sound, he thought. *I'd stamp it until it was so many pieces scattered across the floor. With God as my witness I would.*

He fell asleep in his chair a little after midnight, and when he woke the next morning the air was cooler than it had been in weeks, and Carolyn was wide awake, coherent, and bright-eyed. She seemed, in fact, hardly to be sick at all. Ralph took her home and began the not-inconsiderable job of making her last months as comfortable as possible. It was a long while before he thought of Ed Deepneau again; even after he began to see the bruises on Helen Deepneau's face, it was a long time before he thought of Ed again.

As that summer became fall, and as that fall darkened down toward Carolyn's final winter, Ralph's thoughts were occupied more and more by the deathwatch, which seemed to tick louder and louder even as it slowed down.

But he had no trouble sleeping.

That came later.

PART 1

LITTLE BALD DOCTORS

There is a gulf fixed between those who can sleep and those who cannot. It is one of the great divisions of the human race.

Iris Murdoch
Nuns and Soldiers

CHAPTER ONE

1

About a month after the death of his wife, Ralph Roberts began to suffer from insomnia for the first time in his life.

The problem was mild to begin with, but it grew steadily worse. Six months after the first interruptions in his heretofore unremarkable sleep cycle, Ralph had reached a state of misery he could hardly credit, let alone accept. Toward the end of the summer of 1993 he began to wonder what it would be like to spend his remaining years on earth in a starey-eyed daze of wakefulness. *Of course it wouldn't come to that,* he told himself, *it never does.*

But was that true? He didn't really know, that was the devil of it, and the books on the subject Mike Hanlon steered him to down at the Derry Public Library weren't much help. There were several on sleep disorders, but they seemed to contradict one another. Some called insomnia a symptom, others called it a disease, and at least one called it a myth. The problem went further than that, however; so far as Ralph could tell from the books, no one seemed exactly sure what sleep itself was, how it worked, or what it did.

He knew he should quit playing amateur researcher and go to the doctor, but he found that surprisingly hard to do. He supposed he still bore Dr Litchfield a grudge. It was Litchfield, after all, who had originally diagnosed Carolyn's brain tumor as tension headaches (except Ralph had an idea that Litchfield, a lifelong bachelor, might actually have believed that Carolyn was suffering from nothing but a moderate case of the vapors), and Litchfield who had made himself as scarce as medically possible once Carolyn *was* diagnosed. Ralph was positive that if he had asked the man about that point-blank, Litchfield would have said he had handed the case off to Jamal, the specialist . . . all quite proper and aboveboard. Yes. Except Ralph had made it his business to get a good look into Litchfield's eyes on the few occasions he had seen him between Carolyn's first convulsions last July and her death this March, and Ralph thought that what he'd seen in those eyes was a mixture of unease and guilt. It was the look of a man trying very hard to forget he has fucked up. Ralph believed the only reason he could still look at Litchfield without wanting to knock his block off was that Dr Jamal had told him that an earlier diagnosis probably would have made no difference; by the time Carolyn's headaches started, the tumor was already well entrenched, and no doubt sending out little bursts of bad cells to other areas of the brain like malignant CARE packages.

In late April Dr Jamal had left to establish a practice in southern Connecticut, and Ralph missed him. He thought that he could have talked about his sleeplessness to Dr Jamal, and he had an idea that Jamal would have listened in a way Litchfield wouldn't . . . or couldn't.

By late summer Ralph had read enough about insomnia to know that the type with which he was afflicted, while not rare, was a lot less common than the usual slow-sleep insomnia. People unaffected by insomnia are usually in first-stage sleep seven to twenty minutes after turning in. Slow-sleepers, on the other hand, sometimes take as long as three hours to slip below the surface, and while normal sleepers begin to ramp down into third-stage sleep (what some of the old books called theta sleep, Ralph had discovered) forty-five minutes or so after drifting off, slow-sleepers usually took an additional hour or two to get down there . . . and on many nights they did not get all the way down at all. They awoke unrefreshed, sometimes with unfocused memories of unpleasant, tangled dreams, more often with the mistaken impression that they had been awake all night.

Following Carolyn's death, Ralph began to suffer from premature waking. He continued to go to bed most nights following the conclusion of the eleven o'clock news, and he continued to pop off to sleep almost at once, but instead of waking promptly at six-fifty-five, five minutes before the clock-radio alarm buzzed, he began to wake at six. At first he dismissed this as no more than the price of living with a slightly enlarged prostate and a seventy-year-old set of kidneys, but he never seemed to have to go *that* badly when he woke up, and he found it impossible to get back to sleep even after he'd emptied what *had* accumulated. He simply lay in the bed he'd shared with Carolyn for so many years, waiting for it to be five of seven (quarter till, anyway) so he could get up. Eventually he gave up even trying to drop off again; he simply lay there with his long-fingered, slightly swollen hands laced together on his chest and stared up at the shadowy ceiling with eyes that felt as big as door-knobs. Sometimes he thought of Dr Jamal down there in Westport, talking in his soft and comforting Indian accent, building up his little piece of the American dream. Sometimes he thought of places he and Carolyn had gone in the old days, and the one he kept coming back to was a hot afternoon at Sand Beach in Bar Harbor, the two of them sitting at a picnic table in their bathing suits, sitting under a big bright umbrella, eating sweet fried clams and drinking Bud from longneck bottles as they watched the sailboats scudding across the dark-blue ocean. When had that been? 1964? 1967? Did it matter? Probably not.

The alterations in his sleep schedule wouldn't have mattered, either, if they had ended there; Ralph would have adapted to the changes not just with ease but with grati-tude. All the books he hunted through that summer seemed to confirm one bit of folk wisdom he'd heard all his life – people slept less as they got older. If losing an hour or so a night was the only fee he had to pay for the dubious pleasure of being 'seventy years young', he would pay it gladly, and consider himself well off.

But it *didn't* end there. By the first week of May, Ralph was waking up to birdsong at 5:15 a.m. He tried earplugs for a few nights, although he doubted from the outset that they would work. It wasn't the newly returned birds that were waking him up, nor the occasional delivery-truck backfire out on Harris Avenue. He had always been the sort of guy who could sleep in the middle of a brass marching band, and he didn't think that had changed. What had changed was inside his head. There was a switch in there, something was turning it on a little earlier every day, and Ralph hadn't the slightest idea of how to keep it from happening.

By June he was popping out of sleep like Jack out of his box at 4:30 a.m., 4:45 at the latest. And by the middle of July – not quite as hot as July of '92, but bad enough, thanks very much – he was snapping to at around four o'clock. It was during those long hot nights, taking up too little of the bed where he and Carolyn had made love on so many hot nights (and cold ones), that he began to consider what a hell his life would become if sleep departed entirely. In daylight he was still able to scoff at the notion, but he was discovering certain dismal truths about F. Scott Fitzgerald's dark night of the soul, and the grand-prize winner was this: at 4:15 a.m., anything seems possible. *Anything.*

During the days he was able to go on telling himself that he was simply experiencing a readjustment of his sleep-cycle, that his body was responding in perfectly normal fashion to a number of big changes in his life, retirement and the loss of his wife being the two biggest. He sometimes used the word 'loneliness' when he thought about his new life, but he shied away from The Dreaded D-Word, stuffing it back into the deep closet of his subconscious whenever it happened to glimmer for a moment in his thoughts. Loneliness was okay. Depression most certainly was not.

Maybe you need to get more exercise, he thought. *Do some walking, like you used to last summer. After all, you've been leading a pretty sedentary life – get up, eat toast, read a book, watch some TV, get a sandwich across the street in the Red Apple for lunch, potter around in the garden a little, maybe go to the library or visit with Helen and the baby if they happen to be out, eat supper, maybe sit on the porch and visit with McGovern or Lois Chasse for a while. Then what? Read a little more, watch a little more TV, wash up, go to bed. Sedentary.* Boring. *No wonder you wake up early.*

Except that was crap. His life *sounded* sedentary, yes, no doubt, but it really wasn't. The garden was a good example. What he did out there was never going to win him any prizes, but it was a hell of a long way from 'pottering around'. Most afternoons he weeded until sweat made a dark tree-shape down the back of his shirt and spread damp circles at his armpits, and he was often trembling with exhaustion by the time he let himself go back inside. 'Punishment' probably would have been closer to the mark than 'pottering', but punishment for what? Waking up before dawn?

Ralph didn't know and didn't care. Working in the garden filled up a large piece of the afternoon, it took his mind off things he didn't really care to think of, and that was enough to justify the aching muscles and the occasional flights of black spots in front of his eyes. He began his extended visits to the garden shortly after the Fourth of July and continued all through August, long after the early crops had been harvested and the later ones had been hopelessly stunted by the lack of rain.

'You ought to quit that,' Bill McGovern told him one night as they sat on the porch, drinking lemonade. This was in mid-August, and Ralph had begun to wake up around three-thirty each morning. 'It's got to be hazardous to your health. Worse, you look like a lunatic.'

'Maybe I *am* a lunatic,' Ralph responded shortly, and either his tone or the look in his eyes must have been convincing, because McGovern changed the subject.

2

He did begin walking again – nothing like the Marathons of '92, but he managed two miles a day if it wasn't raining. His usual route took him down the perversely named Up-Mile Hill, to the Derry Public Library, and then on to Back Pages, a used bookstore and newsstand on the corner of Witcham and Main.

Back Pages stood next to a jumbled junkatorium called Secondhand Rose, Secondhand Clothes, and as he passed this store one day during the August of his discontent, Ralph saw a new poster among the announcements of outdated bean suppers and ancient church socials, placed so it covered roughly half of a yellowing PAT BUCHANAN FOR PRESIDENT placard.

The woman in the two photographs at the top of the poster was a pretty blonde in her late thirties or early forties, but the style of the photos – unsmiling full face on the left, unsmiling profile on the right, plain white background in both was unsettling enough to stop Ralph in his tracks. The photos made the woman look as if she belonged on a post office wall or in a TV docudrama . . . and that, the poster's printed matter made clear, was no accident.

The photos were what stopped him, but it was the woman's name that held him.

WANTED FOR MURDER
SUSAN EDWINA DAY

was printed across the top in big black letters. And below the simulated mug-shots, in red:

STAY OUT OF OUR CITY!

There was a small line of print at the very bottom of the poster. Ralph's close vision had deteriorated quite a bit since Carolyn's death – gone to hell in a handbasket might actually have been a more accurate way of putting it – and he had to lean forward until his brow was pressed against the dirty show window of Secondhand Rose, Secondhand Clothes before he could decipher it:

Paid for by the Maine LifeWatch Committee

Far down in his mind a voice whispered: *Hey, hey, Susan Day! How many kids did you kill today?*

Susan Day, Ralph recalled, was a political activist from either New York or Washington, the sort of fast-speaking woman who regularly drove taxi-drivers, barbers, and hardhat construction workers into foaming frenzies. Why that particular little jangle of doggerel had come into his mind, however, he couldn't say; it was tagged to some memory that wouldn't quite come. Maybe his tired old brains were just cross-referencing that sixties Vietnam protest chant, the one which had gone *Hey, hey, LBJ! How many kids did you kill today?*

No, that's not it, he thought. *Close, but no cigar. It was—*

Just before his mind could cough up Ed Deepneau's name and face, a voice spoke from almost beside him. 'Earth to Ralph, earth to Ralph, come in, Ralphie-baby!'

Roused out of his thoughts, Ralph turned toward the voice. He was both shocked and amused to find he had almost been asleep on his feet. *Christ,* he thought, *you never know how important sleep is until you miss a little. Then all the floors start to tilt and all the corners on things start to round off.*

It was Hamilton Davenport, the proprietor of Back Pages, who had spoken to him. He was stocking the library cart he kept in front of his shop with brightly jacketed paperbacks. His old corncob pipe — to Ralph it always looked like the stack of a model steamship — jutted from the corner of his mouth, sending little puffs of blue smoke into the hot, bright air. Winston Smith, his old gray tomcat, sat in the open doorway of the shop with his tail curled around his paws. He looked at Ralph with yellow eyed indifference, as if to say, *You think you know old, my friend? I'm here to testify you don't know* dick *about getting old.*

'Sheesh, Ralph,' Davenport said. 'I must have called your name at least three times.'

'I guess I was woolgathering,' Ralph said. He stepped past the library cart, leaned in the doorway (Winston Smith held his place with regal indifference), and grabbed the two papers he bought every day: a Boston *Globe* and a *USA Today.* The Derry *News* came right to the house, courtesy of Pete the paperboy. Ralph sometimes told people that he was sure one of the three papers was comic relief, but he had never been able to make up his mind which one it was. 'I haven't—'

He broke off as Ed Deepneau's face came into his mind. It was Ed he'd heard that nasty little chant from, last summer, out by the airport, and it really wasn't any wonder it had taken him a little while to retrieve the memory. Ed Deepneau was the last person in the world from whom you'd expect to hear something like that.

'Ralphie?' Davenport said. 'You just shut down on me.'

Ralph blinked. 'Oh, sorry. I haven't been sleeping very well, that's what I started to say.'

'Bummer . . . but there are worse problems. Just drink a glass of warm milk and listen to some quiet music half an hour before bed.'

Ralph had begun to discover this summer that everyone in America apparently had a pet remedy for insomnia, some bit of bedtime magic that had been handed down through the generations like the family Bible.

'Bach's good, also Beethoven, and William Ackerman ain't bad. But the real trick' – Davenport raised one finger impressively to emphasize this – 'is *not to get up from your chair* during that half hour. Not for anything. Don't answer the phone, don't wind up the dog and put out the alarm-clock, don't decide to brush your teeth . . . *nothing*! Then, when you *do* go to bed . . . bam! Out like a light!'

'What if you're sitting there in your favorite easy-chair and all at once you realize you have a call of nature?' Ralph asked. 'These things can come on pretty suddenly when you get to be my age.'

'Do it in your pants,' Davenport said promptly, and burst out laughing. Ralph smiled, but it had a dutiful feel. His insomnia was rapidly losing whatever marginal humor value it might once have had. 'In your *pants*!' Ham chortled. He slapped the library cart and wagged his head back and forth.

Ralph happened to glance down at the cat. Winston

Smith looked blandly back at him, and to Ralph his calm yellow gaze seemed to say, *Yes, that's right, he's a fool, but he's my fool.*

'Not bad, huh? Hamilton Davenport, master of the snappy comeback. Do it in your . . .' He snorted laughter, shook his head, then took the two dollar bills Ralph was holding out. He slipped them into the pocket of his short red apron and came out with some change. 'That about right?'

'You bet. Thanks, Ham.'

'Uh-huh. And all joking aside, try the music. It really works. Mellows out your brain-waves, or something.'

'I will.' And the devil of it was, he probably would, as he had already tried Mrs Rapaport's lemon and hot water recipe, and Shawna McClure's advice on how to clear his mind by slowing his respiration and concentrating on the word *cool* (except when Shawna said it, the word came out *cuhhhh-ooooooooooool*). When you were trying to deal with a slow but relentless erosion of your good sleep-time, any folk remedy started to look good.

Ralph began to turn away, then turned back. 'What's with that poster next door?'

Ham Davenport wrinkled his nose. 'Dan Dalton's place? I don't look in there at all, if I can help it. Screws up my appetite. Has he got something new and disgusting in the window?'

'I *guess* it's new – it's not as yellow as the rest of them, and there's a notable lack of flydirt on it. Looks like a wanted poster, only it's Susan Day in the photos.'

'Susan Day on a – son of a bitch!' He cast a dark and humorless look at the shop next door.

'What is she, President of the National Organization of Women, or something?'

'Ex-President and co-founder of Sisters in Arms. Author of *My Mother's Shadow* and *Lilies of the Valley* – that one's a study of battered women and why so many of them refuse to blow the whistle on the men that batter them. She won a Pulitzer Prize for it. Susie Day's one of the three or four most politically influential women in America right now, and she can really write as well as think. That clown *knows* I've got one of her petitions sitting right by my cash register.'

'What petitions?'

'We're trying to get her up here to speak,' Davenport said. 'You know the right-to-lifers tried to firebomb WomanCare last Christmas, right?'

Ralph cast his mind cautiously back into the black pit he'd been living in at the end of 1992 and said, 'Well, I remember that the cops caught some guy in the hospital's long-term parking lot with a can of gasoline, but I didn't know—'

'That was Charlie Pickering. He's a member of Daily Bread, one of the right-to-life groups that keep the pickets marching out there,' Davenport said. 'They put him up to it, too – take my word. This year they're not bothering with gasoline, though; they're going to try to get the City Council to change the zoning regulations and squeeze WomanCare right out of existence. They just might do it, too. You know Derry, Ralph – it's not exactly a hotbed of liberalism.'

'No,' Ralph said with a wan smile. 'It's never been that. And WomanCare *is* an abortion clinic, isn't it?'

Davenport gave him an out-of-patience look and jerked his head in the direction of Secondhand Rose. 'That's what assholes like *him* call it,' he said, 'only they like to use the word *mill* instead of *clinic*. They ignore all the other stuff WomanCare does.' To Ralph, Davenport had begun to sound a little like the TV announcer who hawked run-free pantyhose during the Sunday afternoon movie. 'They're involved in family counselling, they deal with spouse and child abuse, and they run a shelter for abused women over by the Newport town line. They have a rape crisis center at the in-town building by the hospital, and a twenty-four-hour hotline for women who've been raped or beaten. In short, they stand for all the things that make Marlboro Men like Dalton shit bullets.'

'But they *do* perform abortions,' Ralph said. 'That's what the pickets are about, right?'

There had been sign-carrying demonstrators in front of the low-slung, unobtrusive brick building that housed WomanCare for years, it seemed to Ralph. They always looked too pale to him, too intense, too skinny or too fat, too utterly sure that God was on their side. The signs they carried said things like THE UNBORN HAVE RIGHTS, TOO and LIFE, WHAT A BEAUTIFUL CHOICE and that old standby, ABORTION IS MURDER! On several occasions women using the clinic – which was near Derry Home but not actually associated with it, Ralph thought – had been spat upon.

'Yeah, they perform abortions,' Ham said. 'You got a problem with that?'

Ralph thought of all the years he and Carolyn had tried to have a baby – years that had produced nothing but several false alarms and a single messy five-months miscarriage – and shrugged. Suddenly the day seemed too hot and his legs too tired. The thought of his return journey – the Up-Mile Hill leg of it in particular – hung in the back of his mind like something strung from a line of fish-hooks. 'Christ, I don't know,' he said. 'I just wish people didn't have to get so . . . so shrill.'

Davenport grunted, walked over to his neighbor's display window, and peered at the bogus wanted poster. While he was looking at it, a tall, pallid man with a goatee – the absolute antithesis of the Marlboro Man, Ralph would have said – materialized from the gloomy depths of Secondhand Rose like a vaudeville spook that has gotten a bit mouldy around the edges. He saw what Davenport was looking at, and a tiny disdainful smile dimpled the corners of his mouth. Ralph thought it was the kind of smile that could cost a man a couple of teeth, or a broken nose. Especially on a dog-hot day like this one.

Davenport pointed to the poster and shook his head violently.

Dalton's smile deepened. He flapped his hands at Davenport – *Who gives a shit what you think?* the gesture said – and then disappeared back into the depths of his store.

Davenport returned to Ralph, bright spots of color burning in his cheeks. 'That man's picture should be next to the word *prick* in the dictionary,' he said.

Exactly what he thinks about you, I imagine, Ralph thought, but of course did not say.

Davenport stood in front of the library cart full of paperbacks, hands stuffed into his pockets beneath his red change apron, brooding at the poster of

(hey hey)

Susan Day.

'Well,' Ralph said, 'I suppose I better—'

Davenport shook himself out of his brown study. 'Don't go yet,' he said. 'Sign my petition first, will you? Put a little shine back on my morning.'

Ralph shifted his feet uncomfortably. 'I usually don't get involved in confrontational stuff like—'

'Come on, Ralph,' Davenport said in a let's-be-reasonable voice. 'We're not talking confrontation here; we're talking about making sure that the fruits and nuts like the ones who run Daily Bread – and political Neanderthals like Dalton – don't shut down a really useful women's resource center. It's not like I'm asking you to endorse testing chemical warfare weapons on dolphins.'

'No,' Ralph said. 'I suppose not.'

'We're hoping to send five thousand signatures to Susan Day by the first of September. Probably won't do any good – Derry's really not much more than a wide place in the road, and she's probably booked into the next century anyhow – but it can't hurt to try.'

Ralph thought about telling Ham that the only petition he wanted to sign was one asking the gods of sleep to give him back the three hours or so of good rest a night they had stolen away, but then he took another look at the man's face and decided against it.

Carolyn would have signed his damned petition, he thought. *She was no fan of abortion, but she was also no fan of men coming home after the bars close and mistaking their wives and kids for soccer balls.*

True enough, but that wouldn't have been her main

reason for signing; she would have done it on the off-chance that she might get to hear an authentic firebrand like Susan Day up close and in person. She would have done it out of the ingrained curiosity which had perhaps been her dominating characteristic – something so strong not even the brain tumor had been able to kill it. Two days before she died she had pulled the movie ticket he'd been using as a bookmark out of the paperback novel he'd left on her bedside table because she had wanted to know what he'd been to see. It had been *A Few Good Men,* as a matter of fact, and he was both surprised and dismayed to discover how much it hurt to remember that. Even now it hurt like hell.

'Sure,' he told Ham. 'I'll be happy to sign it.'

'My man!' Davenport exclaimed, and clapped him on the shoulder. The broody look was replaced by a grin, but Ralph didn't think the change much of an improvement. The grin was hard and not especially charming. 'Step into my den of iniquity!'

Ralph followed him into the tobacco-smelling shop, which did not seem particularly iniquitous at nine-thirty in the morning. Winston Smith fled before them, pausing just once to look back with his ancient yellow eyes. *He's a fool and you're another,* that parting stare might have said. Under the circumstances, it wasn't a conclusion Ralph felt much inclined to dispute. He tucked his newspapers under his arm, leaned over the ruled sheet on the counter beside the cash register, and signed the petition asking Susan Day to come to Derry and speak in defense of WomanCare.

3

He did better climbing Up–Mile Hill than he had expected, and crossed the X-shaped intersection of Witcham and Jackson thinking, *There, that wasn't so bad, was—*

He suddenly realized that his ears were ringing and his legs had begun to tremble beneath him. He stopped on the far side of Witcham and placed one hand against his shirt. He could feel his heart beating just beneath it, pumping away with a ragged fierceness that was scary. He heard a papery rustle and saw an advertising supplement slip out of the Boston *Globe* and go seesawing down into the gutter. He started to bend over and get it, then stopped.

Not a good idea, Ralph – if you bend over, you're more than likely going to fall over. I suggest you leave that one for the sweeper.

'Yeah, okay, good idea,' he muttered, and straightened up. Black dots surged across his vision like a surreal flock of crows, and for a moment Ralph was almost positive he was going to wind up lying on top of the ad supplement no matter what he did or didn't do.

'Ralph? You all right?'

He looked up cautiously and saw Lois Chasse, who lived on the other side of Harris Avenue and half a block down from the house he shared with Bill McGovern. She was sitting on one of the benches just outside Strawford Park, probably waiting for the Canal Street bus to come along and take her downtown.

'Sure, fine,' he said, and made his legs move. He felt as if he were walking through syrup, but he thought he

57

got over to the bench without looking too bad. He could not, however, suppress a grateful little gasp as he sat down next to her.

Lois Chasse had large dark eyes − the kind that had been called Spanish eyes when Ralph was a kid − and he bet they had danced through the minds of dozens of boys during Lois's high school years. They were still her best feature, but Ralph didn't much care for the worry he saw in them now. It was . . . what? *A little too neighborly for comfort* was the first thought to occur to him, but he wasn't sure it was the *right* thought.

'Fine,' Lois echoed.

'You betcha.' He took his handkerchief from his back pocket, checked to make sure it was clean, and then wiped his brow with it.

'I hope you don't mind me saying it, Ralph, but you don't *look* fine.'

Ralph *did* mind her saying it, but didn't know how to say so.

'You're pale, you're sweating, and you're a litterbug.'

Ralph looked at her, startled.

'Something fell out of your paper. I think it was an ad circular.'

'Did it?'

'You know perfectly well it did. Excuse me a second.'

She got up, crossed the sidewalk, bent (Ralph noticed that, while her hips were fairly broad, her legs were still admirably trim for a woman who had to be sixty-eight), and picked up the circular. She came back to the bench with it and sat down.

'There,' she said. 'Now you're not a litterbug anymore.'

He smiled in spite of himself. 'Thank you.'

'Don't mention it. I can use the Maxwell House coupon, also the Hamburger Helper and the Diet Coke. I've gotten so *fat* since Mr Chasse died.'

'You're not fat, Lois.'

'Thank you, Ralph, you're a perfect gentleman, but let's not change the subject. You had a dizzy spell, didn't you? In fact, you almost passed out.'

'I was just catching my breath,' he said stiffly, and turned to watch a bunch of kids playing scrub baseball just inside the park. They were going at it hard, laughing and grab-assing around. Ralph envied the efficiency of their air-conditioning systems.

'Catching your breath, were you?'

'Yes.'

'Just catching your breath.'

'Lois, you're starting to sound like a broken record.'

'Well, the broken record's going to tell you something, okay? You're *nuts* to be trying Up-Mile Hill in this heat. If you want to walk, why not go out the Extension, where it's flat, like you used to?'

'Because it makes me think of Carolyn,' he said, not liking the stiff, almost rude way that sounded but unable to help it.

'Oh shit,' she said, and touched his hand briefly. 'Sorry.'

'It's okay.'

'No, it's not. I should have known better. But the way you looked just now, that's not okay, either. You're not twenty anymore, Ralph. Not even forty. I don't mean you're not in good shape — anyone can see you're in great shape for a guy your age — but you ought to take better care of yourself. Carolyn would want you to take care of yourself.'

'I know,' he said, 'but I'm really—'

— *all right,* he meant to finish, and then he looked up from his hands, looked into her dark eyes again, and what he saw there made it impossible to finish for a moment. There was a weary sadness in her eyes . . . or was it loneliness? Maybe both. In any case, those were not the only things he saw in them. He also saw himself.

You're being silly, the eyes looking into his said. *Maybe we both are. You're seventy and a widower, Ralph. I'm sixty-eight and a widow. How long are we going to sit on your porch in the evenings with Bill McGovern as the world's oldest chaperone? Not too long, I hope, because neither of us is exactly fresh off the showroom lot.*

'Ralph?' Lois asked, suddenly concerned. 'Are you okay?'

'Yes,' he said, looking down at his hands again. 'Yes, sure.'

'You had a look on your face like . . . well, I don't know.'

Ralph wondered if maybe the combination of the heat and the walk up Up-Mile Hill *had* scrambled his brains a little. Because this was *Lois,* after all, whom McGovern always referred to (with a small, satiric lift of his left eyebrow) as 'Our Lois'. And okay, yes, she was still in good shape — trim legs, nice bust, and those remarkable eyes — and maybe he wouldn't mind taking her to bed, and maybe she wouldn't mind being taken. But what would there be after that? If she happened to see a ticket-stub poking out of the book he was reading, would she pull it out, too curious about

60

what movie he'd been to see to think about how she was losing his place?

Ralph thought not. Lois's eyes were remarkable, and he had found his own eyes wandering down the V of her blouse more than once as the three of them sat on the front porch, drinking iced tea in the cool of the evening, but he had an idea that your little head could get your big head in trouble even at seventy. Getting old was no excuse to get careless.

He got to his feet, aware of Lois looking at him and making an extra effort not to stoop. 'Thanks for your concern,' he said. 'Want to walk an old feller up the street?'

'Thanks, but I'm going downtown. They've got some beautiful rose-colored yarn in at The Sewing Circle, and I'm thinking afghan. Meanwhile, I'll just wait for the bus and gloat over my coupons.'

Ralph grinned. 'You do that.' He glanced over at the kids on the scrub ballfield. As he watched, a boy with an extravagant mop of red hair broke from third, threw himself down in a headfirst slide . . . and fetched up against one of the catcher's shinguards with an audible *thonk*. Ralph winced, envisioning ambulances with flashing lights and screaming sirens, but the carrot-top bounced to his feet laughing.

'Missed the tag, you hoser!' he shouted.

'The hell I did!' the catcher responded indignantly, but then he began to laugh, too.

'Ever wish you were that age again, Ralph?' Lois asked.

He thought it over. 'Sometimes,' he said. 'Mostly it

just looks too strenuous. Come on over tonight, Lois – sit with us awhile.'

'I might just do that,' she said, and Ralph started up Harris Avenue, feeling the weight of her remarkable eyes on him and trying hard to keep his back straight. He thought he managed fairly well, but it was hard work. He had never felt so tired in his life.

CHAPTER TWO

1

Ralph made the appointment to see Dr Litchfield less than an hour after his conversation with Lois on the park bench; the receptionist with the cool, sexy voice told him she could fit him in next Tuesday morning at ten, if that was okay, and Ralph told her that was fine as paint. Then he hung up, went into the living room, sat in the wing-chair that overlooked Harris Avenue, and thought about how Dr Litchfield had initially treated his wife's brain tumor with Tylenol-3 and pamphlets explaining various relaxation techniques. From there he moved on to the look he'd seen in Litchfield's eyes after the magnetic resonance imaging tests had confirmed the CAT scan's bad news . . . that look of guilt and unease.

Across the street, a bunch of kids who would soon be back in school came out of the Red Apple armed with candy bars and Slurpies. As Ralph watched them mount their bikes and tear away into the bright eleven o'clock heat, he thought what he always did when the memory of Dr Litchfield's eyes surfaced: that it was most likely a false memory.

The thing is, old buddy, you wanted *Litchfield to look uneasy . . . but even more than that, you wanted him to look guilty.*

Quite possibly true, quite possibly Carl Litchfield was a peach of a guy and a helluva doctor, but Ralph still found himself calling Litchfield's office again half an hour later. He told the receptionist with the sexy voice that he'd just rechecked his calendar and discovered next Tuesday at ten wasn't so fine after all. He'd made an appointment with the podiatrist for that day and forgotten all about it.

'My memory's not what it used to be,' Ralph told her.

The receptionist suggested next Thursday at two.

Ralph countered by promising to call back.

Liar, liar, pants on fire, he thought as he hung up the phone, walked slowly back to the wing-chair, and lowered himself into it. *You're done with him, aren't you?*

He supposed he was. Not that Dr Litchfield was apt to lose any sleep over it; if he thought about Ralph at all, it would be as one less old geezer to fart in his face during the prostate exam.

All right, so what are you going to do about the insomnia, Ralph?

'Sit quiet for half an hour before bedtime and listen to classical music,' he said out loud. 'Buy some Depends for those troublesome calls of nature.'

He startled himself by laughing at the image. The laughter had a hysterical edge he didn't much care for – it was damned creepy, as a matter of fact – but it was still a little while before he could make himself stop.

Yet he supposed he would try Hamilton Davenport's suggestion (although he would skip the diapers, thank you), as he had tried most of the folk remedies well-meaning people had passed on to him. This made him think of his first *bona fide* folk remedy, and that raised another grin.

It had been McGovern's idea. He had been sitting on the porch one evening when Ralph came back from the Red Apple with some noodles and spaghetti sauce, had taken one look at his upstairs neighbor and made a *tsk-tsk* sound, shaking his head dolefully.

'What's that supposed to mean?' Ralph asked, taking the seat next to him. A little farther down the street, a little girl in jeans and an oversized white tee-shirt had been skipping rope and chanting in the growing gloom.

'It means you're looking folded, spindled, and mutilated,' McGovern said. He used one thumb to tilt the Panama back on his head and looked more closely at Ralph. 'Still not sleeping?'

'Still not sleeping,' Ralph agreed.

McGovern was quiet for a few seconds. When he spoke again, he did so in a tone of absolute — almost apocalyptic, in fact — finality. 'Whiskey is the answer,' he said.

'I beg your pardon?'

'To your insomnia, Ralph. I don't mean you should take a bath in it — there's no need of that. Just mix a tablespoon of honey with half a shot of whiskey and hook it down fifteen or twenty minutes before you hit the hay.'

'You think?' Ralph had asked hopefully.

'All I can say is it worked for me, and I had some real problems sleeping around the time I turned forty. Looking back on it, I guess that was my midlife crisis — six months of insomnia and a year-long depression over my bald spot.'

Although the books he'd been consulting all said that booze was a vastly overrated cure for sleeplessness – that it often made the problem worse instead of better, in fact – Ralph had tried it just the same. He had never been much of a drinker, so he began by adjusting McGovern's recommended half-shot dosage down to a quarter of a shot, but after a week of no relief he had upped the ante to a full shot . . . then to two. He woke up one morning at four-twenty-two with a nasty little headache to accompany the dull brown taste of Early Times on the roof of his mouth, and realized he was suffering his first hangover in fifteen years.

'Life's too short for this shit,' he had announced to his empty apartment, and that had been the end of the great whiskey experiment.

2

Okay, Ralph thought now as he watched the desultory mid-morning flow of customers in and out of the Red Apple across the street. *Here's the situation: McGovern says you look like shit, you almost fainted at Lois Chasse's feet this morning, and you just cancelled the appointment you made with Ye Olde Family Physician. So what next? Just let it go? Accept the situation and let it go?*

The idea had a certain Oriental charm – fate, karma, and all that – but he was going to need more than charm to get him through the long hours of early morning. The books said there were people in the world, quite a lot of them, who managed very well on no more than three or four hours of sleep a night. There were even some who got along on only two. They were an extremely small minority, but they *did* exist. Ralph Roberts, however, was not among their number.

How he looked wasn't very important to him – he had a feeling that his matinee-idol days were well behind him – but how he felt was, and it was no longer just a matter of not feeling good; he felt horrible. The insomnia had begun to pervade every aspect of his life, the way the smell of frying garlic on the fifth floor will eventually pervade an entire apartment building. The color had started to drain out of things; the world had begun to take on the dull, grainy quality of a newspaper photograph.

Simple decisions – whether to heat up a frozen dinner for his evening meal or grab a sandwich at the Red Apple and go up to the picnic area by Runway 3, for example – had become difficult, almost agonizing. In the last couple of weeks he had found himself coming back to the apartment from Dave's Video Stop empty-handed more and more often, not because there was nothing at Dave's he wanted to watch but because there was too much – he couldn't decide if he wanted one of the *Dirty Harry* movies or a Billy Crystal comedy or maybe a few old *Star Trek* episodes. After a couple of these unsuccessful trips, he had plopped himself down in this very wing-chair, almost crying with frustration . . . and, he supposed, fear.

That creeping sensory numbness and the erosion of his decision-making capabilities were not the only problems he had come to associate with the insomnia; his short-term memory had also begun to slip. It had been his practice to go to the movies at least once and sometimes twice a week ever since his retirement from the printshop where he had finished his working life as the bookkeeper and general supervisor. He had taken Carolyn until last year, when she had gotten too sick to enjoy going out anywhere. After her death he had mostly gone alone, although Helen Deepneau had accompanied him once or twice when Ed was home to mind the baby (Ed himself almost never went, claiming he got headaches at the movies). Ralph had gotten so used to calling the cinema center's answering machine to check showtimes that he had the number by heart. As the summer went on, however, he found himself having to look it up in the Yellow Pages more and more often – he could no longer be sure if the last four digits were 1317 or 1713.

'It's 1713,' he said now. 'I *know* it is.' But *did* he know it? Did he really?

Call Litchfield back. Go on, Ralph – stop sifting through the wreckage. Do something constructive. And if Litchfield really sticks in your craw, call somebody else. The phone book's as full of doctors as it ever was.

Probably true, but seventy was maybe a little old to be picking a new sawbones by the eenie-meenie-minie-moe method. And he wasn't going to call Litchfield back. Period.

Okay, so what's next, you stubborn old goat? A few more folk remedies? I hope not, because at the rate you're going you'll be down to eye of newt and tongue of toad in no time.

The answer that came was like a cool breeze on a hot day . . . and it was an absurdly simple answer. All his book-research this summer had been aimed at understanding the problem rather than finding a solution. When it came to answers, he had relied almost solely on back-fence remedies like whiskey and honey, even when the books had already assured him they probably wouldn't work or would only work for a while. Although the books *did* offer some presumably reliable methods for coping with insomnia, the only one Ralph had actually tried was the simplest and most obvious: going to bed earlier in the evening. That solution hadn't worked – he had simply lain awake until eleven-thirty or so, then dropped off to wake at his new, earlier time – but something else might.

It was worth a try, anyway.

3

Instead of spending the afternoon in his usual frenzy of backyard pottering, Ralph went down to the library and skimmed through some of the books he had already looked at. The general consensus seemed to be that if going to bed earlier didn't work, going later might. Ralph went home (mindful of his previous adventures, he took the bus) filled with cautious hope. It might work. If it didn't, he always had Bach, Beethoven and William Ackerman to fall back on.

His first attempt at this technique, which one of the texts called 'delayed sleep', was comic. He awoke at his now-usual time (3:45 by the digital clock on the living-room mantel) with a sore back, an aching neck, no immediate idea of how he had gotten into the wing-chair by the window, or why the TV was on, broadcasting nothing but snow and a soft, surflike roar of static.

It was only as he allowed his head to roll cautiously back, supporting the nape of his neck with a cupped palm, that he realized what had happened. He had intended to sit up until at least three o'clock and possibly four. He would then stroll off to bed and sleep the sleep of the just. That had been the plan, anyway. Instead, The Incredible Insomniac of Harris Avenue had dropped off during Jay Leno's opening monologue, like a kid who's trying to stay up all night long just to see what it's like. And then, of course, he had finished the adventure by waking up in the damned chair. The problem was the same, Joe Friday might have said; only the location had changed.

Ralph strolled off to bed anyway, hoping against hope, but the urge (if not the need) to sleep had passed. After an hour of lying awake, he had gone back to the wing-chair again, this time with a pillow propped behind his stiff neck and a rueful grin on his face.

4

There was nothing funny about his second try, which took place the following night. Sleepiness began to steal over him at its usual time – eleven-twenty, just as Pete Cherney was giving the following day's weather forecast. This time Ralph fought it successfully, making it all the way through *Whoopi* (although he almost nodded off during Whoopi's conversation with Roseanne Arnold, that evening's guest) and the late-night movie that came on after that. It was an old Audie Murphy flick in which Audie appeared to be winning the war in the Pacific pretty much single-handed.

It sometimes seemed to Ralph that there was an unspoken rule among local TV broadcasters which stated that movies telecast in the small hours of the morning could only star Audie Murphy or James Brolin.

After the last Japanese pillbox had been blown up, Channel 2 signed off. Ralph dialed around, looking for another movie, and found nothing but snow. He supposed he could have watched movies all night if he had the cable, like Bill downstairs or Lois down the street; he remembered having put that on his list of things to do in the new year. But then Carolyn had died and cable TV – with or without Home Box Office – had no longer seemed very important.

He found a copy of *Sports Illustrated* and began to slog through an article on women's tennis he'd missed the first time through, glancing up at the clock every now and then as the hands began to close in on 3:00 a.m. He had become all but convinced that this was going to work. His eyelids were so heavy they felt as if they had been dipped in concrete, and although he was reading the tennis article carefully, word for word, he had no idea of what the writer was driving at. Whole sentences zipped across his brain without sticking, like cosmic rays.

I'm going to sleep tonight – I really think I am. For the first time in months the sun is going to have to come up without my help, and that isn't just good, friends and neighbors; that is great.

Then, shortly after three o'clock, that pleasant drowsiness began to disappear. It did not go with a champagne-cork pop but rather seemed to ooze away, like sand through a fine sieve or water down a partially clogged drain. When Ralph realized what was happening, it wasn't panic he felt, but sick dismay. It was a feeling he had come to recognize as the true opposite of hope, and when he slipper-scuffed his way into the bedroom at quarter past three, he couldn't remember a depression as deep as the one which now enveloped him. He felt as if he were suffocating in it.

'Please, God, just forty winks,' he muttered as he turned off the light, but he strongly suspected that this was one prayer which was not going to be answered.

It wasn't. Although he had been awake for twenty-four hours by then, every trace of sleepiness had left his mind and body by quarter of four. He was tired, yes — more deeply and fundamentally tired than he had ever been in his life — but being tired and being sleepy, he had discovered, were sometimes poles apart. Sleep, that undiscriminating friend, humankind's best and most reliable nurse since the dawn of time, had abandoned him again.

By four o'clock Ralph's bed had become hateful to him, as it always did when he realized he could put it to no good use. He swung his feet back onto the floor, scratching the mat of hair — almost entirely gray now — which curled through his mostly unbuttoned pajama top. He slid on his slippers again and scuffed back to the living room, where he dropped into the wing-back chair and looked down at Harris Avenue. It was laid out like a stage set where the only actor currently on view wasn't even human: it was a stray dog moving slowly down Harris Avenue in the direction of Strawford Park and Up-Mile Hill. It held its right rear leg up as much as possible, limping along as best it could on the other three.

'Hi there, Rosalie,' Ralph muttered, and rubbed a hand across his eyes.

It was a Thursday morning, garbage-pickup day on Harris Avenue, so he wasn't surprised to see Rosalie, who'd been a wandering, here-and-there fixture in the neighborhood for the last year or so. She made her way down the street in leisurely fashion, investigating the rows and clusters of cans with the discrimination of a jaded flea-market shopper.

Now Rosalie – who was limping worse than ever this morning, and looked as tired as Ralph felt – found what looked like a good-sized beef bone and trotted away with it in her mouth. Ralph watched her out of sight, then simply sat with his hands folded in his lap, gazing out on the silent neighborhood, where the orange hi-intensity lamps added to the illusion that Harris Avenue was nothing but a stage set standing deserted after the evening performance had ended and the actors had gone home; they shone down like spotlights in a perfect diminishing perspective that was surreal and hallucinatory.

Ralph Roberts sat in the wing-chair where he had spent so many early-morning hours lately and waited for light and movement to invest the lifeless world below him. Finally the first human actor – Pete the paperboy – entered stage right, riding his Raleigh. He biked his way up the street, tossing rolled newspapers from the bag slung over his shoulder and hitting the porches he aimed at with a fair degree of accuracy.

Ralph watched him awhile, then heaved a sigh which felt as if it had come all the way from the basement, and got up to make tea.

'I don't remember *ever* reading about this shit in my horoscope,' he said hollowly, and then turned on the kitchen tap and began to fill the kettle.

5

That long Thursday morning and even longer Thursday afternoon taught Ralph Roberts a valuable lesson: not to sneer at three or four hours' sleep a night simply because he had spent his entire life under the mistaken impression that he had a right to at least six and usually seven. It also served as a hideous preview: if things didn't improve, he could look forward to feeling like this most of the time. Hell, *all* of the time. He went into the bedroom at ten o'clock and again at one, hoping for a little nap – even a catnap would do, and half an hour would be a life-saver – but he could not so much as drowse. He was miserably tired but not in the least bit sleepy.

Around three o'clock he decided to make himself a Lipton Cup-A-Soup. He filled the teakettle with fresh water, put it on to boil, and opened the cupboard over the counter where he kept condiments, spices, and various envelopes containing foods which only astronauts and old men actually seem to eat – powders to which the consumer need only add hot water.

He pushed cans and bottles around in aimless fashion and then simply stared into the cupboard for awhile, as if expecting the box of soup packets to magically appear in the space he had made. When they didn't, he repeated the process, only this time moving things back to their original positions before staring in again with the look of distant

74

perplexity which was becoming (Ralph, mercifully, did not know this) his dominant expression.

When the teakettle shrieked, he put it on one of the rear burners and went back to staring into the cupboard. It dawned on him – very, very slowly – that he must have drunk his last packet of Cup-A-Soup yesterday or the day before, although he could not for the life of him remember doing so.

'That's a surprise?' he asked the boxes and bottles in the open cupboard. 'I'm so tired I can't remember my own name.'

Yes, I can, he thought. *It's Leon Redbone. So there!*

It wasn't much of a joke, but he felt a small smile – it felt as light as a feather – touch his lips. He stepped into the bathroom, combed his hair, and then went downstairs. *Here's Audie Murphy, heading out into enemy territory in search of supplies,* he thought. *Primary target: one box of Lipton Chicken and Rice Cup-A-Soup packets. If locating and securing this target should prove impossible, I'll divert to my secondary: Noodles 'n Beef. I know this is a risky mission, but—*

'– but I work best alone,' he finished as he came out on the porch.

Old Mrs Perrine happened to be passing, and she favored Ralph with a sharp look but said nothing. He waited for her to get a little way up the sidewalk – he did not feel capable of conversation with anyone this afternoon, least of all Mrs Perrine, who at eighty-two could still have found stimulating and useful work among the Marines at Parris Island. He pretended to be examining the spider-plant which hung from the hook under the porch eave until she had reached what he deemed a safe distance, then crossed Harris Avenue to the Red Apple. Which was where the day's real troubles began.

6

He entered the convenience store once again mulling over the spectacular failure of the delayed-sleep experiment and wondering if the advice in the library texts was no more than an uptown version of the folk remedies his acquaintances seemed so eager to press upon him. It was an unpleasant idea, but he thought his mind (or the force below his mind which was actually in charge of this slow torture) had sent him a message which was even more unpleasant: *You have a sleep-window, Ralph. It's not as big as it once was, and it seems to be getting smaller with every passing week, but you better be grateful for what you've got, because a small window is better than no window at all. You see that now, don't you?*

'Yes,' Ralph mumbled as he walked down the center aisle to the bright red Cup-A-Soup boxes. 'I see that very well.'

Sue, the afternoon counter-girl, laughed cheerfully. 'You must have money in the bank, Ralph,' she said.

'Beg pardon?' Ralph didn't turn; he was inventorying the red boxes. Here was onion . . . split pea . . . the beef-and-noodles combo . . . but where the hell was the Chicken and Rice?

'My mom always said people who talk to themselves have *Oh my God!*'

For a moment Ralph thought she had simply made a statement a little too complex for his tired mind to immediately grasp, something about how people who talked to themselves had found God, and then she screamed. He had hunkered down to check the boxes on the bottom shelf, and the scream shot him to his feet so hard and fast that his knees popped. He wheeled toward the front of the store, bumping the top shelf of the soup display with his elbow and knocking half a dozen red boxes into the aisle.

'Sue? What's wrong?'

Sue paid no attention. She was looking out through the door with her fisted hands pressed against her lips and her brown eyes huge above them. 'God, look at the blood!' she cried in a choked voice.

Ralph turned further, knocking a few more Lipton boxes into the aisle, and looked through the Red Apple's dirty show window. What he saw drew a gasp from him, and it took him a space of seconds — five, maybe — to realize that the bloody, beaten woman staggering toward the Red Apple was Helen Deepneau. Ralph had always thought Helen the prettiest woman on the west side of town, but there was nothing pretty about her today. One of her eyes was puffed shut; there was a gash at her left temple that was soon going to be lost in the gaudy swelling of a fresh bruise; her puffy lips and her cheeks were covered with blood. The blood had come from her nose, which was still leaking. She wove through the Red Apple's little parking lot toward the door like a drunk, her one good eye seeming to see nothing; it simply stared.

More frightening than the way she looked was the way she was handling Natalie. She had the squalling, frightened baby slung casually on one hip, carrying her as she might have carried her books to high school ten or twelve years before.

'*Oh Jesus, she's gonna drop the kid!*' Sue screamed, but although she was ten steps closer to the door than he was, she made no move – simply stood where she was with her hands pressed to her mouth and her eyes gobbling up her face.

Ralph didn't feel tired anymore. He sprinted up the aisle, tore open the door, and ran outside. He was just in time to catch Helen by the shoulders as she banged a hip against the ice cabinet – mercifully not the hip with Natalie on it – and went veering off in a new direction.

'Helen!' he yelled. 'Jesus, Helen, what happened?'

'Hun?' she asked, her voice dully curious, totally unlike the voice of the lively young woman who sometimes accompanied him to the movies and moaned over Mel Gibson. Her good eye rolled toward him and he saw that same dull curiosity in it, a look that said she didn't know who she was, let alone where she was, or what had happened, or when. 'Hun? Ral? Wha?'

The baby slipped. Ralph let go of Helen, grabbed for Natalie, and managed to snag one of her jumper straps. Nat screamed, waved her hands, and stared at him with huge dark-blue eyes. He got his other hand between Nat's legs an instant before the strap he was holding tore free. For a moment the howling baby balanced on his hand like a gymnast on a balance beam, and Ralph could feel the damp bulge of her diapers through the overall she was wearing. Then he slipped his other hand around her back and hoisted her up against his chest. His heart was pounding hard, and even with the baby safe in his arms he kept seeing her slip away, kept seeing her head with its cap of fine hair slamming against the butt-littered pavement with a sickening crack.

'Hum? Ar? Ral?' Helen asked. She saw Natalie in Ralph's arms, and some of the dullness went out of her good eye. She raised her hands toward the child, and in Ralph's arms, Natalie mimicked the gesture with her own chubby hands. Then Helen staggered, struck the side of the building, and reeled backward a step. One foot tangled in the other (Ralph saw splatters of blood on her small white sneakers, and it was amazing how bright everything was all of a sudden; the color had come back into the world, at least temporarily), and she would have fallen if Sue hadn't picked that moment to finally venture out. Instead of going down, Helen landed against the opening door and just leaned there, like a drunk against a lamp-post.

'Ral?' The expression in her eyes was a little sharper now, and Ralph saw it wasn't so much curiosity as incredulity. She drew in a deep breath and made an effort to force intelligible words past her swelled lips. 'Gih. Gih me my bay-ee. *Bay*-be. Gih me . . . Nah-lie.'

'Not just yet, Helen,' Ralph said. 'You're not too steady on your feet right now.'

Sue was still on the other side of the door, holding it so Helen wouldn't fall. The girl's cheeks and forehead were ashy pale, her eyes filled with tears.

'Get out here,' Ralph told her. 'Hold her up.'

'I can't!' she blubbered. 'She's all bluh-bluh-*bloody*!'

'Oh for God's sake, quit it! It's Helen! Helen Deepneau from up the street!'

And although Sue must have known that, actually hearing the name seemed to turn the trick. She slipped around the open door, and when Helen staggered backward again, Sue curled an arm around her shoulders and braced her firmly. That expression of incredulous surprise remained on Helen's face. Ralph found it harder and harder to look at. It made him feel sick to his stomach.

'Ralph? What happened? Was it an accident?'

He turned his head and saw Bill McGovern standing at the edge of the parking lot. He was wearing one of his natty blue shirts with the iron's creases still in the sleeves and holding one of his long-fingered, oddly delicate hands up to shade his eyes. He looked strange, somehow naked that way, but Ralph had no time to think about why; too much was happening.

'It was no accident,' he said. 'She's been beaten up. Here, take the kid.'

He held Natalie out to McGovern, who at first shrank back and then took the baby. Natalie immediately began to shriek again. McGovern, looking like someone who has just been handed an overfilled airsick bag, held her out at arm's length with her feet dangling. Behind him a small crowd was beginning to gather, many of them teenage kids in baseball uniforms on their way home from an afternoon game at the field around the corner. They were staring at Helen's puffed and bloody face with an unpleasant avidity, and Ralph found himself thinking of the Bible story about the time Noah had gotten drunk – the good sons who had looked away from the naked old man lying in his tent, the bad one who had looked . . .

Gently, he replaced Sue's arm with his own. Helen's

good eye rolled back to him. She said his name more clearly this time, more positively, and the gratitude Ralph heard in her blurry voice made him feel like crying.

'Sue – take the baby. Bill doesn't have a clue.'

She did, folding Nat gently and expertly into her arms. McGovern gave her a grateful smile, and Ralph suddenly realized what was wrong with the way he looked. McGovern wasn't wearing the Panama hat which seemed as much a part of him (in the summertime, at least) as the wen on the bridge of his nose.

'Hey, mister, what happened?' one of the baseball kids asked.

'Nothing that's any of your business,' Ralph said.

'Looks like she went a few rounds with Riddick Bowe.'

'Nah, Tyson,' one of the other baseball kids said, and incredibly, there was laughter.

'Get out of here!' Ralph shouted at them, suddenly furious. 'Go peddle your papers! Mind your business!'

They shuffled back a few steps, but no one left. It was blood they were looking at, and not on a movie screen.

'Helen, can you walk?'

'Yeff,' she said. 'Fink . . . *Think* so.'

He led her carefully around the open door and into the Red Apple. She moved slowly, shuffling from foot to foot like an old woman. The smell of sweat and spent adrenaline was baking out of her pores in a sour reek, and Ralph felt his stomach turn over again. It wasn't the smell, not really; it was the effort to reconcile this Helen with the pert and pleasantly sexy woman he had spoken to yesterday while she worked in her flower-beds.

81

Ralph suddenly remembered something else about yesterday. Helen had been wearing blue shorts, cut quite high, and he had noticed a couple of bruises on her legs – a large yellow blotch far up on the left thigh, a fresher, darker smudge on the right calf.

He walked Helen toward the little office area behind the cash register. He glanced up into the convex anti-theft mirror mounted in the corner and saw McGovern holding the door for Sue.

'Lock the door,' he said over his shoulder.

'Gee, Ralph, I'm not supposed to—'

'Just for a couple of minutes,' Ralph said. 'Please.'

'Well . . . okay. I guess.'

Ralph heard the snick of the bolt being turned as he eased Helen into the hard plastic contour chair behind the littery desk. He picked up the telephone and punched the button marked 911. Before the phone could ring on the other end, a blood-streaked hand reached out and pushed down the gray disconnect button.

'Dough . . . Ral.' She swallowed with an obvious effort, and tried again. '*Don't.*'

'Yes,' Ralph said. 'I'm going to.'

Now it was fear he saw in her one good eye, and nothing dull about it.

'No,' she said. 'Please, Ralph. Don't.' She looked past him and held out her hands again. The humble, pleading look on her beaten face made Ralph wince with dismay.

'Ralph?' Sue asked. 'She wants the baby.'

'I know. Go ahead.'

Sue handed Natalie to Helen, and Ralph watched as the baby – a little over a year old now, he was pretty sure — put her arms around her mother's neck and her face against her mother's shoulder. Helen kissed the top of Nat's head. It clearly hurt her to do this, but she did it again. And then again. Looking down at her, Ralph could see blood grimed into the faint creases on the nape of Helen's neck like dirt. As he looked at this, he felt the anger begin to pulse again.

'It was Ed, wasn't it?' he asked. Of course it was — you didn't hit the cutoff button on the phone when someone tried to call 911 if you had been beaten up by a total stranger — but he had to ask.

'Yes,' she said. Her voice was no more than a whisper, the answer a secret imparted into the fine cloud of her baby daughter's hair. 'Yes, it was Ed. But you can't call the police.' She looked up now, the good eye full of fear and misery. 'Please don't call the police, Ralph. I can't bear to think of Natalie's dad in jail for . . . for . . .'

Helen burst into tears. Natalie goggled at her mother for a moment in comic surprise, and then joined her.

7

'Ralph?' McGovern asked hesitantly. 'Do you want me to get her some Tylenol or something?'

'Better not,' he said. 'We don't know what's wrong with her, how bad she might be hurt.' His eyes shifted to the show window, not wanting to see what was out there, hoping not to, and seeing it anyway: avid faces lined up all the way down to the place where the beer cooler cut off the view. Some of them were cupping their hands to the sides of their faces to cut the glare.

'What should we do, you guys?' Sue asked. She was looking at the gawkers and picking nervously at the hem of the Red Apple duster employees had to wear. 'If the company finds out I locked the door during business hours, I'm apt to lose my job.'

Helen tugged at his hand. 'Please, Ralph,' she repeated, only it came out *Peese, Raff* through her swollen lips. 'Don't call anybody.'

Ralph looked at her uncertainly. He had seen a lot of women wearing a lot of bruises over the course of his life, and a couple (although not many, in all honesty) who had been beaten much more severely than Helen. It hadn't always seemed this grim, though. His mind and morals had been formed at a time when people believed that what went on between a husband and wife behind the closed doors of their marriage was their business, and that included the man who hit with his fists and the woman who cut with her tongue. You couldn't make people behave, and meddling into their affairs – even with the best of intentions – all too often turned friends into enemies.

But then he thought of the way she had been carrying Natalie as she staggered across the parking lot: held casually on one hip like a textbook. If she had dropped the baby in the lot, or crossing Harris Avenue, she probably wouldn't have known it; Ralph guessed that it was nothing but instinct that had caused Helen to take the baby in the first place. She hadn't wanted to leave Nat in the care of the man who had beaten her so badly she could only see out of one eye and talk in mushy, rounded syllables.

He thought of something else, as well, something that had to do with the days following Carolyn's death earlier in the year. He had been surprised at the depth of his grief – it had been an expected death, after all; he had believed he had taken care of most of his grieving while Carolyn was still alive – and it had rendered him awkward and ineffective about the final arrangements which needed to be made. He had managed the call to the Brookings-Smith funeral home, but it was Helen who had gotten the obit form from the Derry *News* and helped him to fill it out, Helen who had gone with him to pick out a coffin (McGovern, who hated death and the trappings which surrounded it, had made himself scarce), and Helen who had helped him choose a floral centerpiece – the one which said *Beloved Wife*. And it had been Helen, of course, who had orchestrated the little party afterward, providing sandwiches from Frank's Catering and soft drinks and beer from the Red Apple.

These were things Helen had done for him when he could not do them for himself. Did he not have an obligation to repay her kindness, even if Helen might not see it as kindness right now?

'Bill?' he asked. 'What do you think?'

McGovern looked from Ralph to Helen, sitting in the red plastic chair with her battered face lowered, and then back to Ralph again. He produced a handkerchief and wiped his lips nervously. 'I don't know. I like Helen a lot, and I want to do the right thing – you *know* I do – but something like this . . . who knows what the right thing is?'

Ralph suddenly remembered what Carolyn used to say whenever he started moaning and bitching about some chore he didn't want to do, some errand he didn't want to run, or some duty call he didn't want to make: *It's a long walk back to Eden, sweetheart, so don't sweat the small stuff.*

He reached for the phone again, and this time when Helen reached for his wrist, he pushed it away.

'You have reached the Derry Police Department,' a recorded voice told him. 'Push one for emergency services. Push two for police services. Push three for information.'

Ralph, who suddenly understood he needed all three, hesitated for a second and then pushed two. The telephone buzzed and a woman's voice said, 'This is Police 911, how may I help you?'

He took a deep breath and said, 'This is Ralph Roberts. I'm at the Red Apple Store on Harris Avenue, with my neighbor from up the street. Her name is Helen Deepneau. She's been beaten up pretty badly.' He put his hand gently on the side of Helen's face and she pressed her forehead against his side. He could feel the heat of her skin through his shirt. 'Please come as fast as you can.'

He hung up the telephone, then squatted down next to Helen. Natalie saw him, crowed with delight, and reached out to give his nose a friendly honk. Ralph smiled, kissed her tiny palm, then looked into Helen's face.

'I'm sorry, Helen,' he said, 'but I had to. I couldn't not do it. Do you understand that? I couldn't not do it.'

'I don't understand *anyfing*!' she said. Her nose had stopped bleeding, but when she reached up to swipe at it, she winced back from the touch of her own fingers.

'Helen, why did he do it? Why would Ed beat you up like this?' He found himself remembering the other bruises – a pattern of them, perhaps. If there *had* been a pattern, he had missed it until now. Because of Carolyn's death. And because of the insomnia which had come afterward. In any case, he did not believe this was the first time Ed had put his hands on his wife. Today might have been a drastic escalation, but it hadn't been the first time. He could grasp that idea and admit its logic, but he discovered he still couldn't see Ed *doing* it. He could see Ed's quick grin, his lively eyes, the way his hands moved restlessly when he talked . . . but he couldn't see Ed using those hands to beat the crap out of his wife, no matter how hard he tried.

Then a memory resurfaced, a memory of Ed walking stiff-legged toward the man who had been driving the blue pickup – it had been a Ford Ranger, hadn't it? – and then flicking the flat of his hand across the heavyset man's jowls. Remembering that was like opening the door of Fibber McGee's closet in that old radio show – only what came falling out wasn't an avalanche of old stored junk but a series of vivid images from that day last July. The thunderheads building over the airport. Ed's arm popping out of the Datsun's window and waving up and down, as if he could make the gate slide open faster that way. The scarf with the Chinese symbols on it.

Hey, hey, Susan Day, how many kids did you kill today? Ralph thought, only it was Ed's voice he heard, and he pretty well knew what Helen was going to say before she even opened her mouth.

'So stupid,' she said dully. 'He hit me because I signed a *petition* – that's all it was. They're circulating all over town. Someone pushed it into my face when I was going into the supermarket day before yesterday. He said something about a benefit for WomanCare, and that seemed all right. Besides, the baby was fussing, so I just . . .'

'You just signed it,' Ralph finished softly.

She nodded and began to cry again.

'What petition?' McGovern asked.

'To bring Susan Day to Derry,' Ralph told him. 'She's a feminist—'

'I know who Susan Day is,' McGovern said irritably.

'Anyway, a bunch of people are trying to get her here to speak. On behalf of WomanCare.'

'When Ed came home today he was in a great mood,' Helen said through her tears. 'He almost always is on Thursdays, because it's his half day. He was talking about how he was going to spend the afternoon pretending to read a book and actually just watching the sprinkler go around . . . you know how he is . . .'

'Yes,' Ralph said, remembering how Ed had plunged his arm into one of the heavyset man's barrels, and the crafty grin

(*I know a trick worth two of that*)

on his face. 'Yes, I know how he is.'

'I sent him out to get some baby food . . .' Her voice was rising, becoming fretful and frightened. '*I* didn't know he'd be upset . . . I'd all but forgotten about signing the damned thing, to tell the truth . . . and I still don't know exactly *why* he was so upset . . . but . . . but when he came back . . .' She hugged Natalie to her, trembling.

'Shhh, Helen, take it easy, everything's okay.'

'No, it's *not*!' She looked up at him, tears streaming from one eye and seeping out from beneath the swelled lid of the other. 'It's nuh-nuh-*not*! Why didn't he stop this time? And what's going to happen to me and the baby? Where will we go? I don't have any money except for what's in the joint checking account . . . I don't have a *job* . . . oh Ralph, why did you call the police? You shouldn't have done that!' And she hit his forearm with a strengthless little fist.

'You're going to get through this just fine,' he said. 'You've got a lot of friends in the neighborhood.'

But he barely heard what he was saying and hadn't felt her small punch at all. The anger was thudding away in his chest and at his temples like a second heartbeat.

Not *Why didn't he stop*; that wasn't what she had said. What she had said was *Why didn't he stop this time?*

This time.

'Helen, where's Ed now?'

'Home, I guess,' she said dully.

Ralph patted her on the shoulder, then turned and started for the door.

'Ralph?' Bill McGovern asked. He sounded alarmed. 'Where you going?'

'Lock the door after me,' Ralph told Sue.

'Jeez, I don't know if I can do that.' Sue looked doubtfully at the line of gawkers peering in through the dirty window. There were more of them now.

'You can,' he said, then cocked his head, catching the first faint wail of an approaching siren. 'Hear that?'

'Yes, but—'

'The cops will tell you what to do, and your boss won't be mad at you, either – he'll probably give you a medal for handling everything just right.'

'If he does, I'll split it with you,' she said, then glanced at Helen again. A little color had come back into Sue's cheeks, but not much. 'Jeepers, Ralph, look at her! Did he really beat her up because she signed some stupid paper in the S and S?'

'I guess so,' Ralph said. The conversation made perfect sense to him, but it was coming in long distance. His rage was closer; it had its hot arms locked around his neck, it seemed. He wished he were forty again, even fifty, so he could give Ed a taste of his own medicine. And he had an idea he might try doing that anyway.

He was turning the thumb-bolt of the door when McGovern grabbed his shoulder. 'What do you think you're doing?'

'Going to see Ed.'

'Are you kidding? He'll take you apart if you get in his face. Didn't you see what he did to her?'

'You bet I did,' Ralph replied. The words weren't quite a snarl, but close enough to make McGovern drop his hand.

'You're seventy fucking years old, Ralph, in case you forgot. And Helen needs a friend right now, not some busted-up antique she can visit because his hospital room is three doors down from hers.'

Bill was right, of course, but that only made Ralph angrier. He supposed the insomnia was at work in this, too, stoking his anger and blurring his judgement, but that made no difference. In a way, the anger was a relief. It was better, certainly, than drifting through a world where every-thing had turned shades of dark gray.

'If he beats me up bad enough, they'll give me some

Demerol and I can get a decent night's sleep,' he said. 'Now leave me alone, Bill.'

He crossed the Red Apple parking lot at a brisk walk. A police car was approaching with its blue grille flashers pulsing. Questions – *What happened? She okay?* – were thrown at him, but Ralph ignored them. He paused on the sidewalk, waited for the police car to swing into the parking lot, then crossed Harris Avenue at that same brisk walk with McGovern trailing anxiously after him at a prudent distance.

CHAPTER THREE

1

Ed and Helen Deepneau lived in a small Cape Cod —
chocolate brown, whipped-cream trim, the kind of house
which older women often call 'darling' — four houses up
from the one Ralph and Bill McGovern shared. Carolyn
had liked to say the Deepneaus belonged to 'the Church
of the Latter-Day Yuppies', although her genuine liking for
them had robbed the phrase of any real bite. They were
laissez-faire vegetarians who considered both fish and dairy
products okay, they had worked for Clinton in the last
election, and the car in the driveway — not a Datsun now
but one of the new mini-vans — was wearing bumper
stickers which said SPLIT WOOD, NOT ATOMS and FUR
ON ANIMALS, NOT PEOPLE.

The Deepneaus had also apparently kept every
album they had ever purchased during the sixties —
Carolyn had found this one of their most endearing
characteristics — and now, as Ralph approached the Cape
Cod with his hands curled into fists at his sides, he heard
Grace Slick wailing one of those old San Francisco
anthems:

INSOMNIA

One pill makes you bigger,
One pill makes you small,
And the ones that Mother gives you
Don't do anything at all,
Go ask Alice, when she's ten feet tall.

The music was coming from a boombox on the Cape Cod's postage stamp-sized porch. A sprinkler twirled on the lawn, making a *hisha-hisha-hisha* sound as it cast rainbows in the air and deposited a shiny wet patch on the sidewalk. Ed Deepneau, shirtless, was sitting in a lawn-chair to the left of the concrete walk with his legs crossed, looking up at the sky with the bemused expression of a man trying to decide if the cloud passing overhead looks more like a horse or a unicorn. One bare foot bopped up and down in time to the music. The book lying open and face-down in his lap went perfectly with the music pouring from the boombox: *Even Cowgirls Get the Blues,* by Tom Robbins.

An all but perfect summer vignette; a scene of small-town serenity Norman Rockwell might have painted and then titled *Afternoon Off.* All you had to overlook was the blood on Ed's knuckles and the drop on the left lens of his round John Lennon specs.

'Ralph, for God's sake don't get into a fight with him!' McGovern hissed as Ralph left the sidewalk and cut across the lawn. He walked through the lawn sprinkler's fine cold spray almost without feeling it.

Ed turned, saw him, and broke into a sunny grin. 'Hey, Ralph!' he said. 'Good to see you, man!'

In his mind's eye, Ralph saw himself reaching out and shoving Ed's chair, pushing him over and spilling him onto his lawn. He saw Ed's eyes widen with shock and surprise behind the lenses of his glasses. This vision was so real he even saw the way the sun reflected on the face of Ed's watch as he tried to sit up.

'Grab yourself a beer and drag up a rock,' Ed was saying. 'If you feel like a game of chess—'

'Beer? A game of *chess*? Christ Jesus, Ed, what's wrong with you?'

Ed didn't answer immediately, only looked at Ralph with an expression that was both frightening and infuriating. It was a mixture of amusement and shame, the look of a man who's getting ready to say, *Aw, shit, honey — did I forget to put out the trash* again?

Ralph pointed down the hill, past McGovern, who was standing — he would have been lurking, if there had been something to lurk behind — near the wet patch the sprinkler had put on the sidewalk, watching them nervously. The first police car had been joined by a second, and Ralph could faintly hear the crackle of radio calls through the open windows. The crowd had gotten quite a bit bigger.

'The police are there because of *Helen*!' he said, telling himself not to shout, it would do no good to shout, and shouting anyway. 'They're there because you beat up your *wife*, is that getting through to you?'

'Oh,' Ed said, and rubbed his cheek ruefully. '*That.*'

'Yes, *that*,' Ralph said. He now felt almost stupefied with rage.

Ed peered past him at the police cars, at the crowd standing around the Red Apple . . . and then he saw McGovern.

'Bill!' he cried. McGovern recoiled. Ed either didn't notice or pretended not to. 'Hey, man! Drag up a rock! Want a beer?'

That was when Ralph knew he was going to hit Ed, break his stupid little round-lensed spectacles, drive a splinter of glass into his eye, maybe. He was going to do it, nothing on earth could stop him from doing it, except at the last moment something did. It was Carolyn's voice he heard inside his head most frequently these days – when he wasn't just muttering along to himself, that was – but this wasn't Carolyn's voice; this one, as unlikely as it seemed, belonged to Trigger Vachon, whom he'd seen only once or twice since the day Trig had saved him from the thunderstorm, the day Carolyn had had her first seizure.

Ayy, Ralph! Be damn careful, you! Dis one crazy like a fox! Maybe he want you to hit im!

Yes, he decided. Maybe that was *just* what Ed wanted. Why? Who knew? Maybe to muddy the waters up a little bit, maybe just because he was crazy.

'Cut the shit,' he said, dropping his voice almost to a whisper. He was gratified to see Ed's attention snap back to him in a hurry, and even more pleased to see Ed's pleasantly vague expression of rueful amusement disappear. It was replaced by a narrow, watchful expression. *It was,* Ralph thought, *the look of a dangerous animal with its wind up.*

Ralph hunkered down so he could look directly at Ed. 'Was it Susan Day?' he asked in the same soft voice. 'Susan Day and the abortion business? Something about dead babies? Is that why you unloaded on Helen?'

There was another question on his mind – *Who are you really, Ed?* – but before he could ask it, Ed reached out,

95

placed a hand in the center of Ralph's chest, and pushed. Ralph fell backward onto the damp grass, catching himself on his elbows and shoulders. He lay there with his feet flat on the ground and his knees up, watching as Ed suddenly sprang out of his lawn-chair.

'Ralph, don't mess with him!' McGovern called from his place of relative safety on the sidewalk.

Ralph paid no attention. He simply remained where he was, propped on his elbows and looking attentively up at Ed. He was still angry and afraid, but these emotions had begun to be overshadowed by a strange, chilly fascination. This was madness he was looking at – the genuine article. No comicbook super-villain here, no Norman Bates, no Captain Ahab. It was just Ed Deepneau who worked down the coast at Hawking Labs – one of those eggheads, the old guys who played chess at the picnic area out on the Extension would have said, but still a nice enough fella for a Democrat. Now the nice enough fella had gone totally bonkers, and it hadn't just happened this afternoon, when Ed had seen his wife's name on a petition hanging from the Community Bulletin Board in the Shop 'n Save. Ralph now understood that Ed's madness was at least a year old, and that made him wonder what secrets Helen had been keeping behind her normal cheery demeanor and sunny smile, and what small, desperate signals – besides the bruises, that was – he might have missed.

And then there's Natalie, he thought. *What's she seen? What's she experienced? Besides, of course, being carried across Harris Avenue and the Red Apple parking lot on her staggering, bleeding mother's hip?*

Ralph's arms broke out in goosebumps.

Ed had begun to pace, meanwhile, crossing and recrossing the cement path, trampling the zinnias Helen had planted along it as a border. He had returned to the Ed Ralph had encountered out by the airport the year before, right down to the fierce little pokes of the head and the sharp, jabbing glances at nothing.

This is what the gee-whiz act was supposed to hide, Ralph thought. *He looks the same now as he did when he took after the guy driving that pickup truck. Like a rooster protecting his little piece of the barnyard.*

'None of this is strictly her fault, I admit that.' Ed spoke rapidly, pounding his right fist into his open left palm as he walked through the cloud of spray thrown by the sprinkler. Ralph realized he could see every rib in Ed's chest; the man looked as if he hadn't had a decent meal in months.

'Still, once stupidity reaches a certain level, it becomes hard to live with,' Ed went on. 'She's like the Magi, actually coming to *King Herod* for information. I mean, how dumb can you get? "Where is he that is born King of the Jews?" To *Herod* they say this. I mean, wise men my ass! Right, Ralph?'

Ralph nodded. Sure, Ed. Whatever you say, Ed.

Ed returned the nod and went on tramping back and forth through the spray and the ghostly interlocking rainbows, smacking his fist into his palm. 'It's like that Rolling Stones song – "Look at that, look at that, look at that stupid girl". You probably don't remember that one, do you?' Ed laughed, a jagged little sound that made Ralph think of rats dancing on broken glass.

McGovern knelt beside him. 'Let's get out of here,'

he muttered. Ralph shook his head, and when Ed swung back in their direction, McGovern quickly got up and retreated to the sidewalk again.

'She thought she could fool you, is that it?' Ralph asked. He was still lying on the lawn, propped up on his elbows. 'She thought you wouldn't find out she signed the petition.'

Ed leaped over the walk, bent over Ralph, and shook his clenched fists over his head like the bad guy in a silent movie. 'No-no-no-*no*!' he cried.

The Jefferson Airplane had been replaced by the Animals, Eric Burdon growling out the gospel according to John Lee Hooker: Boom-boom-boom-boom, gonna shoot ya right down. McGovern uttered a thin cry, apparently thinking Ed meant to attack Ralph, but instead Ed sank down with the knuckles of his left hand pressed into the grass, assuming the position of a sprinter who waits for the starter's gun to explode him out of the blocks. His face was covered with beads of what Ralph at first took for sweat before remembering the way Ed had paced back and forth through the spray from the sprinkler. Ralph kept looking at the spot of blood on the left lens of Ed's glasses. It had smeared a little, and now the pupil of his left eye looked as if it had filled up with blood.

'Finding out that she signed the petition was fate! Simple fate! Do you mean to tell me you don't see that? Don't insult my intelligence, Ralph! You may be getting on in years, but you're far from stupid. The thing is, I go down to the supermarket to buy baby-food, how's that for irony — and find out she's signed on with the baby-*killers*!

The Centurions! With the Crimson King himself! And do you know what? I . . . just . . . saw . . . *red!*'

'The Crimson King, Ed? Who's he?'

'Oh, please.' Ed gave Ralph a cunning look. '"Then Herod, when he saw that he was mocked, was exceeding wroth, and sent forth, and slew all the children that were in Bethlehem, and in all the coasts thereof, from two years old and under, according to the time which he had diligently enquired of the wise men." It's in the Bible, Ralph. Matthew, chapter 2, verse 16. Do you doubt it? Do you have *any fucking question* that it says that?'

'No. If you say so, I believe it.'

Ed nodded. His eyes, a deep and startling shade of green, darted here and there. Then he slowly leaned forward over Ralph, planting one hand on either side of Ralph's arms. It was as if he meant to kiss him. Ralph could smell sweat, and some sort of aftershave that had almost completely faded away now, and something else – something that smelled like old curdled milk. He wondered if it might be the smell of Ed's madness.

An ambulance was coming up Harris Avenue, running its flashers but not its siren. It turned into the Red Apple's parking lot.

'You *better*,' Ed breathed into his face. 'You just *better* believe it.'

His eyes stopped wandering and centered on Ralph's.

'They are killing the babies wholesale,' he said in a low voice which was not quite steady. 'Ripping them from the wombs of their mothers and carrying them out of town in covered trucks. Flatbeds for the most part. Ask yourself this, Ralph: how many times a week do you see one of those big flatbeds tooling down the road? A flatbed with a tarp stretched across the back? Ever ask yourself what those trucks were carrying? Ever wonder what was under most of those tarps?'

Ed grinned. His eyes rolled.

'They burn most of the fetuses over in Newport. The sign says *landfill,* but it's really a crematorium. They send some of them out of state, though. In trucks, in light planes. Because fetal tissue is extremely valuable. I tell you that not just as a concerned citizen, Ralph, but as an employee of Hawking Laboratories. Fetal tissue is . . . more . . . valuable . . . than gold.'

He turned his head suddenly and stared at Bill McGovern, who had crept a little closer again in order to hear what Ed was saying.

'*YEA, MORE VALUABLE THAN GOLD AND MORE PRECIOUS THAN RUBIES!*' he screamed, and McGovern leaped back, eyes widening in fear and dismay. '*DO YOU KNOW THAT, YOU OLD FAGGOT?*'

'Yes,' McGovern said. 'I . . . I guess I did.' He shot a quick glance down the street, where one of the police cars was now backing out of the Red Apple lot and turning in their direction. 'I might have read it somewhere. In *Scientific American,* perhaps.'

'*Scientific American!*' Ed laughed with gentle contempt and rolled his eyes at Ralph again, as if to say *You see what I have to deal with.* Then his face grew sober again. 'Wholesale murder,' he said, 'just as in the time of Christ. Only now it's the murder of the unborn. Not just here, but all over the world. They've been slaughtering them by their thousands, Ralph, by their *millions,* and do you know why? Do you know why we've re-entered the Court of the Crimson King in this new age of darkness?'

Ralph knew. It wasn't that hard to put together, if you had enough pieces to work with. If you had seen Ed with his arm buried in a barrel of chemical fertilizer, fishing around for the dead babies he had been sure he would find.

'King Herod got a little advance word this time around,' Ralph said. 'That's what you're telling me, isn't it? It's the old Messiah thing, right?'

He sat up, half expecting Ed to shove him down again, almost hoping he would. His anger was coming back. It was surely wrong to critique a madman's delusional fantasies the way you might a play or a movie – maybe even blasphemous – but Ralph found the idea that Helen had been beaten because of such hackneyed old shit as this infuriating.

Ed didn't touch him, merely got to his feet and dusted his hands off in businesslike fashion. He seemed to be cooling down again. Radio calls crackled louder as the police cruiser which had backed out of the Red Apple's lot now glided up to the curb. Ed looked at the cruiser, then back at Ralph, who was getting up himself.

'You can mock, but it's true,' he said quietly. 'It's not King Herod, though – it's the Crimson King. Herod was merely one of his incarnations. The Crimson King jumps from body to body and generation to generation like a kid using stepping-stones to cross a brook, Ralph, always looking for the Messiah. He's always missed him, but this time it could be different. Because *Derry's* different. All lines of force have begun to converge here. I know how difficult that is to believe, but it's true.'

The Crimson King, Ralph thought. *Oh Helen, I'm so sorry. What a sad thing this is.*

Two men – one in uniform, one in streetclothes, both presumably cops – got out of the police car and approached McGovern. Behind them, down at the store, Ralph spotted two more men, these dressed in white pants and white short-sleeved shirts, coming out of the Red Apple. One had his arm around Helen, who was walking with the fragile care of a post-op patient. The other was holding Natalie.

The paramedics helped Helen into the back of the ambulance. The one with the baby got in after her while the other moved toward the driver's seat. What Ralph sensed in their movements was competency rather than urgency, and he thought that was good news for Helen. Maybe Ed hadn't hurt her too badly . . . this time, at least.

The plainclothes cop – burly, broad-shouldered, and wearing his blond mustache and sideburns in a style Ralph thought of as Early American Singles Bar – had approached McGovern, whom he seemed to recognize. There was a big grin on the plainclothes cop's face.

Ed put an arm over Ralph's shoulders and pulled him a few steps away from the men on the sidewalk. He also dropped his voice to a bare murmur. 'Don't want them to hear us,' he said.

'I'm sure you don't.'

'These creatures . . . Centurions . . . servants of the Crimson King . . . will stop at nothing. They are relentless.'

'I'll bet.' Ralph glanced over his shoulder in time to see McGovern point at Ed. The burly man nodded calmly.

His hands were stuffed in the pockets of his chinos. He was still wearing a small, benign smile.

'This isn't just about abortion, don't get that idea! Not anymore. They're taking the unborn from all kinds of mothers, not just the junkies and the whores – eight days, eight weeks, eight months, it's all the same to the Centurions. The harvest goes on day and night. The slaughter. I've seen the corpses of infants on roofs, Ralph . . . under hedges . . . they're in the sewers . . . floating in the sewers and in the Kenduskeag down in the Barrens . . .'

His eyes, huge and green, as bright as trumpery emeralds, stared off into the distance.

'Ralph,' he whispered, 'sometimes the world is full of colors. I've seen them since *he* came and told me. But now all the colors are turning black.'

'Since who came and told you, Ed?'

'We'll talk about it later,' Ed replied, speaking out of the corner of his mouth like a con in a prison movie. Under other circumstances it would have been funny.

A big game-show host grin dawned on his face, banishing the madness as convincingly as sunrise banishes night. The change was almost tropical in its suddenness, and creepy as hell, but Ralph found something comforting about it, just the same. Perhaps they – he, McGovern, Lois, all the others on this little stretch of Harris Avenue who knew Ed – would not have to blame themselves too much for not seeing his madness sooner, after all. Because Ed was good; Ed really had his act down. That grin was an Academy Award winner. Even in a bizarre situation like this, it practically demanded that you respond to it.

'Hey, hi!' he told the two cops. The burly one had

finished his conversation with McGovern, and both of them were advancing across the lawn. 'Drag up a rock, you guys!' Ed stepped around Ralph with his hand held out.

The burly plainclothes cop shook it, still smiling his small, benign smile. 'Edward Deepneau?' he asked.

'Right.' Ed shook hands with the uniformed cop, who looked a trifle bemused, and then returned his attention to the burly man.

'I'm Detective Sergeant John Leydecker,' the burly man said. 'This is Officer Chris Nell. Understand you had a little trouble here, sir.'

'Well, yes. I guess that's right. A little trouble. Or, if you want to call a spade a spade, I behaved like a horse's ass.' Ed's embarrassed little chuckle was alarmingly normal. Ralph thought of all the charming psychopaths he'd seen in the movies – George Sanders had always been particularly good at that sort of role – and wondered if it was possible for a smart research chemist to snow a small-city detective who looked as if he had never completely outgrown his *Saturday Night Fever* phase. Ralph was terribly afraid it might be.

'Helen and I got into an argument about a petition she'd signed,' Ed was saying, 'and one thing just led to another. Man, I just can't believe I hit her.'

He flapped his arms, as if to convey how flustered he was – not to mention confused and ashamed. Leydecker smiled in return. Ralph's mind returned to the confrontation last summer between Ed and the man in the blue pickup. Ed had called the heavyset man a murderer, had even stroked him one across the face, and still the guy had ended up looking at Ed almost with respect. It had been like a kind of hypnosis, and Ralph thought he was seeing the same force at work here.

'Things just kinda got out of hand a little, is that what you're telling me?' Leydecker asked sympathetically.

'That's about the size of it, yeah.' Ed had to be at least thirty-two, but his wide eyes and innocent expression made him look barely old enough to buy beer.

'Wait a minute,' Ralph blurted. 'You can't believe him, he's nuts. And dangerous. He just told me—'

'This is Mr Roberts, right?' Leydecker asked McGovern, ignoring Ralph completely.

'Yes,' McGovern said, and to Ralph he sounded insufferably pompous. 'That is Ralph Roberts.'

'Uh-huh.' Leydecker at last looked at Ralph. 'I'll want to speak to you in a couple of minutes, Mr Roberts, but for the time being I'd like you to stand over there beside your friend and keep quiet. Okay?'

'But—'

'*Okay?*'

Angrier than ever, Ralph stalked over to where McGovern was standing. This did not seem to upset Leydecker in the least. He turned to Officer Nell. 'You want to turn off the music, Chris, so we can hear ourselves think?'

'Yo.' The uniformed cop went to the boombox, inspected the various knobs and switches, then killed The Who halfway through the song about the blind pinball wizard.

'I guess I *did* have it cranked a little.' Ed looked sheepish. 'Wonder the neighbors didn't complain.'

'Oh, well, life goes on,' Leydecker said. He tilted his

small, serene smile up toward the clouds drifting across the blue summer sky.

Wonderful, Ralph thought. *This guy is a regular Will Rogers.* Ed, however, was nodding as if the detective had produced not just a single pearl of wisdom but a whole string of them.

Leydecker rummaged in his pocket and came out with a little tube of toothpicks. He offered them to Ed, who declined, then shook one out and stuck it in the corner of his mouth. 'So,' he said. 'Little family argument. Is that what I'm hearing?'

Ed nodded eagerly. He was still smiling his sincere, slightly puzzled smile. 'More of a discussion, actually. A political—'

'Uh-huh, uh-huh,' Leydecker said, nodding and smiling, 'but before you go any further, Mr Deepneau—'

'Ed. Please.'

'Before we go any further, Mr Deepneau, I just kind of want to tell you that anything you say could be used against you – you know, in a court of law. Also that you have a right to an attorney.'

Ed's friendly but puzzled smile – *Gosh, what did I do? Can you help me figure it out?* – faltered for a moment. The narrow, appraising look replaced it. Ralph glanced at McGovern, and the relief he saw in Bill's eyes mirrored what he was feeling himself. Leydecker was maybe not such a hick after all.

'What in God's name would I want an attorney for?' Ed asked. He made a half-turn and tried the puzzled smile out on Chris Nell, who was still standing beside the boombox on the porch.

'I don't know, and maybe you don't,' Leydecker said, still smiling. 'I'm just telling you that you can have one. And that if you can't afford one, the City of Derry will provide you with one.'

'But I don't—'

Leydecker was nodding and smiling. 'That's okay, sure, whatever. But those are your rights. Do you understand your rights as I've explained them to you, Mr Deepneau?'

Ed stood stock-still for a moment, his eyes suddenly wide and blank again. To Ralph he looked like a human computer trying to process a huge and complicated wad of input. Then the fact that the snow-job wasn't working seemed to get through to him. His shoulders sagged. The blankness was replaced by a look of unhappiness too real to doubt . . . but Ralph doubted it, anyway. He *had* to doubt it; he had seen the madness on Ed's face before Leydecker and Nell arrived. So had Bill McGovern. Yet doubt was not quite the same as disbelief, and Ralph had an idea that on some level Ed honestly regretted beating Helen up.

Yes, he thought, *just as on some level he honestly believes that these Centurions of his are driving truckloads of fetuses out to the Newport landfill. And that the forces of good and evil are gathering in Derry to play out some drama that's going on in his mind. Call it* Omen V: In the Court of the Crimson King.

Still, he could not help feeling a reluctant sympathy for Ed Deepneau, who had visited Carolyn faithfully three times a week during her final confinement at Derry Home, who always brought flowers, and always kissed her on the cheek when he left. He had continued giving her that kiss even when the smell of death had begun to surround her, and Carolyn had never failed to clasp his hand and give him a smile of gratitude. *Thank you for remembering that I'm still a human being,* that smile had said. *And thank you for treating me like one.* That was the Ed Ralph had thought of as his friend, and he thought – or maybe only hoped – that that Ed was still in there.

'I'm in trouble here, aren't I?' he asked Leydecker softly.

'Well, let's see,' Leydecker said, still smiling. 'You knocked out two of your wife's teeth. Looks like you fractured her cheekbone. I'd bet you my grandfather's watch she's got a concussion. Plus selected short subjects – cuts, bruises, and this funny bare patch over her right temple. What'd you try to do? Snatch her bald-headed?'

Ed was silent, his green eyes fixed on Leydecker's face.

'She's going to spend the night in the hospital under observation because some asshole pounded the hell out of her, and everybody seems in agreement that the asshole was you, Mr Deepneau. I look at the blood on your hands and the blood on your glasses, and I got to say I also think it was probably you. So what do *you* think? You look like a bright guy. Do *you* think you're in trouble?'

'I'm very sorry I hit her,' Ed said. 'I didn't mean to.'

'Uh-huh, and if I had a quarter for every time I've heard that, I'd never have to buy another drink out of my paycheck. I'm arresting you on a charge of second-degree assault, Mr Deepneau, also known as domestic assault. This charge falls under Maine's Domestic Violence law. I'd like you to confirm once more that I've informed you of your rights.'

'Yes.' Ed spoke in a small, unhappy voice. The smile – puzzled or otherwise – was gone. 'Yes, you did.'

'We're going to take you down to the police station and book you,' Leydecker said. 'Following that, you can make a telephone call and arrange bail. Chris, put him in the car, would you?'

Nell approached Ed. 'Are you going to be a problem, Mr Deepneau?'

'No,' Ed said in that same small voice, and Ralph saw a tear slip from Ed's right eye. He wiped it away absently with the heel of his hand. 'No problem.'

'Great!' Nell said heartily, and walked with him to the cruiser.

Ed glanced at Ralph as he crossed the sidewalk. 'I'm sorry, old boy,' he said, then got into the back of the car. Before Officer Nell closed the door, Ralph saw there was no handle on the inside of it.

2

'Okay,' Leydecker said, turning to Ralph and holding out his hand. 'I'm sorry if I seemed a little brusque, Mr Roberts, but sometimes these guys can be volatile. I especially worry about the ones who look sober, because you can never tell what they'll do. John Leydecker.'

'I had Johnny as a student when I was teaching at the Community College,' McGovern said. Now that Ed Deepneau was safely tucked away in the back of the cruiser, he sounded almost giddy with relief. 'Good student. Did an excellent term paper on the Children's Crusade.'

'It's a pleasure to meet you,' Ralph said, shaking Leydecker's hand. 'And don't worry. No offense taken.'

'You were insane to come up here and confront him, you know,' Leydecker said cheerfully.

'I was pissed off. I'm *still* pissed off.'

'I can understand that. And you got away with it – that's the important thing.'

'No. *Helen's* the important thing. Helen and the baby.'

'I can ride with that. Tell me what you and Mr Deepneau talked about before we got up here, Mr Roberts . . . or can I call you Ralph?'

'Ralph, please.' He ran through his conversation with Ed, trying to keep it brief. McGovern, who had heard some of it but not all of it, listened in round-eyed silence. Every time Ralph looked at him, he found himself wishing Bill had worn his Panama. He looked older without it. Almost ancient.

'Well, that certainly sounds pretty weird, doesn't it?' Leydecker remarked when Ralph had finished.

'What will happen? Will he go to jail? He shouldn't go to jail; he should be committed.'

'Probably should be,' Leydecker agreed, 'but there's a lot of distance between should be and will be. He won't go to jail, and he isn't going to be carted off to Sunnyvale Sanitarium, either – that sort of thing only happens in old movies. The best we can hope for is some court-ordered therapy.'

'But didn't Helen tell you—'

'The lady didn't tell us anything, and we didn't try to question her in the store. She was in a lot of pain, both physical and emotional.'

'Yes, of course she was,' Ralph said. 'Stupid of me.'

'She might corroborate your stuff later on . . . but she

might not. Domestic abuse victims have a way of turning into clams, you know. Luckily, it doesn't really matter one way or the other under the new law. We got him nailed to the wall. You and the lady in the little store down the street can testify to Mrs Deepneau's condition, and to who she said put her in that condition. I can testify to the fact that the victim's husband had blood on his hands. Best of all, he said the magic words: "Man, I just can't believe I hit her." I'd like you to come in – probably tomorrow morning, if that works for you – so I can take a complete statement from you, Ralph, but that's just filling in the blanks. Basically, this one's a done deal.'

Leydecker took the toothpick out of his mouth, broke it, tossed it in the gutter, and produced his tube again. 'Pick?'

'No thanks,' Ralph said, smiling faintly.

'Don't blame you. Lousy habit, but I'm trying to quit smoking, which is an even worse one. The thing about guys like Deepneau is that they're too goddam smart for their own good. They go over the high side, hurt someone . . . and then they pull back. If you get there soon enough after the blow-up – like you did, Ralph – you can almost see them standing there with their heads cocked, listening to the music and trying to get back on the beat.'

'That's just how it was,' Ralph said. '*Exactly* how it was.'

'It's a trick the bright ones manage for quite awhile – they appear remorseful, appalled by their own actions, determined to make amends. They're persuasive, they're charming, and it's often all but impossible to see that underneath the sugar coating they're as nutty as Christmas fruitcakes. Even extreme cases like Ted Bundy sometimes manage to look normal for years. The good news is that there aren't many guys like Ted Bundy out there, in spite of all the psycho-killer books and movies.'

Ralph sighed deeply. 'What a mess.'

'Yeah. But look on the bright side: we're gonna be able to keep him away from her, at least for a while. He'll be out by suppertime on twenty-five dollars bail, but—'

'Twenty-five dollars?' McGovern asked. He sounded simultaneously shocked and cynical. 'That's *all*?'

'Yup,' Leydecker said. 'I gave Deepneau the second-degree assault stuff because it do sound fearsome, but in the state of Maine, lumping up your wife is only a misdemeanor.'

'Still, there's a nifty new wrinkle in the law,' Chris Nell said, joining them. 'If Deepneau wants bail, he has to agree that he'll have absolutely no contact with his wife until the case is settled in court – he can't come to the house, approach her on the street, or even call her on the phone. If he doesn't agree, he sits in jail.'

'Suppose he agrees and then comes back, anyway?' Ralph asked.

'Then we slam-dunk him,' Nell said, 'because that one *is* a felony . . . or can be, if the district attorney wants to play hardball. In any case, violators of the Domestic Violence bail agreement usually spend a lot more than just the afternoon in jail.'

'And hopefully the spouse he breaks the agreement to visit will still be alive when he comes to trial,' McGovern said.

'Yeah,' Leydecker said heavily. 'Sometimes that's a problem.'

3

Ralph went home and sat staring not at the TV but through it for an hour or so. He got up during a commercial to see if there was a cold Coke in the refrigerator, staggered on his feet, and had to put a hand on the wall to steady himself. He was trembling all over and felt unpleasantly close to vomiting. He understood that this was nothing but delayed reaction, but the weakness and nausea still frightened him.

He sat down again, took a minute's worth of deep breaths with his head down and his eyes closed, then got up and walked slowly into the bathroom. He filled the tub with warm water and soaked until he heard *Night Court,* the first of the afternoon sitcoms, starting up on the TV in the living room. By then the water in the tub had become almost chilly, and Ralph was glad to get out. He dried off, dressed in fresh clothes, and decided that a light supper was at least in the realm of possibility. He called downstairs, thinking McGovern might like to join him for a bite to eat, but there was no answer.

Ralph put on water in which to boil a couple of eggs and called Derry Home Hospital from the phone by the stove. His call was shunted to a woman in Patient Services who checked her computer and told him yes, he was correct, Helen Deepneau *had* been admitted to the hospital. Her condition was listed as fair. No, she had no idea who was taking care of Mrs Deepneau's baby; all she knew was that she did not have a Natalie Deepneau on her admissions list. No, Ralph could not visit Mrs Deepneau that evening, but not because her doctor had established a no-visitors policy; Mrs Deepneau had left that order herself.

Why would she do that? Ralph started to ask, then didn't bother. The woman in Patient Services would probably tell him she was sorry, she didn't have that information in her computer, but Ralph decided he had it in *his* computer, the one between his giant economy-size ears. Helen didn't want visitors because she was ashamed. None of what had happened was her fault, but Ralph doubted if that changed the way she felt. She had been seen by half of Harris Avenue staggering around like a badly beaten boxer after the ref has stopped the fight, she had been taken to the hospital in an ambulance, and her husband – the father of her daughter – was responsible. Ralph hoped they would give her something that would help her sleep through the night; he had an idea things might look a little better to her in the morning. God knew they couldn't look much worse.

Hell, I wish someone would give me something to help me sleep through the night, he thought.

Then go see Dr Litchfield, you idiot, another part of his mind responded immediately.

The woman in Patient Services was asking Ralph if she could do anything else for him. Ralph said no and was starting to thank her when the line clicked in his ear.

'Nice,' Ralph said. 'Very nice.' He hung up himself, got a tablespoon, and gently lowered his eggs into the water. Ten minutes later, as he was sitting down with the boiled eggs sliding around on a plate and looking like the world's biggest pearls, the phone rang. He put his supper on the table and grabbed it off the wall. 'Hello?'

Silence, broken only by breathing.

'Hello?' Ralph repeated.

There was one more breath, this one almost loud enough to be an aspirated sob, and then another click in his ear. Ralph hung up the telephone and stood looking at it for a moment, his frown putting three ascending wave-lines on his brow.

'Come on, Helen,' he said. 'Call me back. Please.' Then he returned to the table, sat down, and began to eat his small bachelor's supper.

4

He was washing up his few dishes fifteen minutes later when the phone rang again. *That won't be her*, he thought, wiping his hands on a dishtowel and then flipping it over his shoulder as he went to the phone. *No way it'll be her. It's probably Lois or Bill*. But another part of him knew differently.

'Hi, Ralph.'

'Hello, Helen.'

'That was me a few minutes ago.' Her voice was husky, as if she had been drinking or crying, and Ralph didn't think they allowed booze in the hospital.

'I kind of figured that.'

'I heard your voice and I . . . I couldn't . . .'

'That's okay. I understand.'

'Do you?' She gave a long, watery sniff.

'I think so, yes.'

'The nurse came by and gave me a pain-pill. I can use it, too — my face really hurts. But I wouldn't let myself

115

take it until I called you again and said what I had to say. Pain sucks, but it's a hell of an incentive.'

'Helen, you don't have to say anything.' But he was afraid that she did, and he was afraid of what it might be . . . afraid of finding out that she had decided to be angry at him because she couldn't be angry with Ed.

'Yes I do. I have to say thank you.'

Ralph leaned against the side of the door and closed his eyes for a moment. He was relieved but unsure how to reply. He had been ready to say *I'm sorry you feel that way, Helen* in the calmest voice he could manage, that was how sure he'd been that she was going to start off by asking him why he couldn't mind his own business.

And, as if she had read his mind and wanted to let him know he wasn't entirely off the hook, Helen said, 'I spent most of the ride here, and the check-in, and the first hour or so in the room, being terribly angry at you. I called Candy Shoemaker, my friend from over on Kansas Street, and she came and got Nat. She's keeping her for the night. She wanted to know what had happened, but I wouldn't tell her. I just wanted to lie here and be mad that you called 911 even though I told you not to.'

'Helen—'

'Let me finish so I can take my pill and go to sleep. Okay?'

'Okay.'

'Just after Candy left with the baby – Nat didn't cry, thank God, I don't know if I could have handled that – a woman came in. At first I thought she must have gotten the wrong room because I didn't know her from Eve, and when I got it through my head that she was here to see me, I told her I didn't want any visitors. She didn't pay any attention. She closed the door and lifted her skirt up so I could see her left thigh. There was a deep scar running down it, almost all the way from her hip to her knee.

'She said her name was Gretchen Tillbury, that she was a family-abuse counsellor at WomanCare, and that her husband had cut her leg open with a kitchen knife in 1978. She said if the man in the downstairs apartment hadn't gotten a tourniquet on it, she would have bled to death. I said I was very sorry to hear that, but I didn't want to talk about my own situation until I'd had a chance to think it over.' Helen paused and then said, 'But that was a lie, you know. I've had plenty of time to think it over, because Ed first hit me two years ago, just before I got pregnant with Nat. I just kept . . . pushing it away.'

'I can see how a person would do that,' Ralph said.

'This lady . . . well, they must give people like her lessons on how to get through people's defenses.'

Ralph smiled. 'I believe that's about half their training.'

'She said I couldn't put it off, that I had a bad situation on my hands and I had to start dealing with it right away. I said that whatever I did, I didn't have to consult her before I did it, or listen to her line of bullshit just because her husband had cut her once. I almost said he probably did it because she wouldn't shut up and go away and give him some peace, can you believe that? But I was really pissed, Ralph. Hurting . . . confused . . . ashamed . . . but mostly just PO'd.'

'I think that's probably a pretty normal reaction.'

'She asked me how I'd feel about myself – not about Ed but about *myself* – if I went back into the relationship

117

and Ed beat me up again. Then she asked how I'd feel if I went back in and Ed did it to Nat. That made me furious. It *still* makes me furious. Ed has never laid so much as a finger on her, and I said so. She nodded and said, "That doesn't mean he *won't,* Helen. I know you don't want to think about that, but you have to. Still, suppose you're right? Suppose he never so much as slaps her on the wrist? Do you want her to grow up watching him hit *you*? Do you want her to grow up seeing the things she saw today?" And that stopped me. Stopped me cold. I remembered how Ed looked when he came back in . . . how I knew as soon as I saw how white his face was . . . the way his head was moving . . .'

'Like a rooster,' Ralph murmured.

'What?'

'Nothing. Go on.'

'I don't know what set him off . . . I never do anymore, but I knew he was going to start in on me. There's nothing you can do or say to stop it once he gets to a certain point. I ran for the bedroom, but he grabbed me by the hair . . . he pulled out a great big bunch of it . . . I screamed . . . and Natalie was sitting there in her highchair . . . sitting there watching us . . . and when *I* screamed, *she* screamed . . .'

Helen broke down then, crying hard. Ralph waited with his forehead leaning against the side of the doorway between the kitchen and the living room. He used the end of the dishtowel he'd slung over his shoulder to wipe away his own tears almost without thinking about it.

'Anyway,' Helen said when she was capable of speaking again, 'I ended up talking to this woman for almost an hour. It's called Victim Counselling and she does it for a living, can you believe it?'

'Yes,' Ralph said. 'I can. It's a good thing, Helen.'

'I'm going to see her again tomorrow, at WomanCare. It's ironic, you know, that I should be going there. I mean, if I hadn't signed that petition . . .'

'If it hadn't been the petition, it would have been something else.'

She sighed. 'Yes, I guess that might be true. *Is* true. Anyway, Gretchen says I can't solve Ed's problems, but I can start solving some of my own.' Helen started to cry again and then took a deep breath. 'I'm sorry – I've cried so much today I never want to cry again. I told her I loved him. I felt ashamed to say it, and I'm not even sure it's true, but it *feels* true. I said I wanted to give him another chance. She said that meant I was committing Natalie to give him another chance, too, and that made me think of how she looked sitting there in the kitchen, with pureed spinach all over her face, screaming her head off while Ed hit me. God, I hate the way people like her drive you into a corner and won't let you out.'

'She's trying to help, that's all.'

'I hate that, too. I'm very confused, Ralph. Probably you didn't know that, but I am.' A wan chuckle drifted down the telephone line.

'That's okay, Helen. It's natural for you to be confused.'

'Just before she left, she told me about High Ridge. Right now that sounds like just the place for me.'

'What is it?'

'A kind of halfway house – she kept explaining that it was a *house,* not a shelter – for battered women. Which

119

is what I guess I now officially am.' This time the wan
chuckle sounded perilously close to a sob. 'I can have Nat
with me if I go, and that's a major part of the attraction.'

'Where is this place?'

'In the country. Out toward Newport, I think.'

'Yeah, I guess I knew that.'

Of course he did; Ham Davenport had told him
during his WomanCare spiel. *They're involved in family coun-
selling . . . spouse and child abuse . . . they run a shelter for abused
women over by the Newport town line.* All at once WomanCare
seemed to be everywhere in his life. Ed would undoubt-
edly have seen sinister implications in this.

'That Gretchen Tillbury is one hard sugarbun,' Helen
was saying. 'Just before she left she told me it was all
right for me to love Ed – "It *has* to be all right," she
said, "because love doesn't come out of a faucet you can
turn on and off whenever you want to" – but that I had
to remember my love couldn't fix him, that not even
Ed's love for Natalie could fix him, and that no amount
of love changed my responsibility to take care of my
child. I've been lying in bed, thinking about that. I think
I liked lying in bed and being mad better. It was certainly
easier.'

'Yes,' he said, 'I can see how it might be. Helen, why
don't you just take your pill and let it all go for awhile?'

'I will, but first I wanted to say thanks.'

'You know you don't have to do that.'

'I don't think I know any such thing,' she said, and
Ralph was glad to hear the flash of emotion in her voice.
It meant the essential Helen Deepneau was still there. 'I
haven't quit being mad at you, Ralph, but I'm glad you

didn't listen when I told you not to call the police. It's just that I was afraid, you know? Afraid.'

'Helen, I —' His voice was thick, close to cracking. He cleared his throat and tried again. 'I just didn't want to see you hurt any more than you already were. When I saw you coming across the parking lot with blood all over your face, I was so afraid . . .'

'Don't talk about that part. Please. I'll cry if you do, and I can't stand to cry anymore.'

'Okay.' He had a thousand questions about Ed, but this was clearly not the time to ask them. 'Can I come see you tomorrow?'

There was a short hesitation and then Helen said, 'I don't think so. Not for a little while. I have a lot of thinking to do, a lot of things to sort out, and it's going to be hard. I'll be in touch, Ralph. Okay?'

'Of course. That's fine. What are you doing about the house?'

'Candy's husband is going to go over and lock it up. I gave him my keys. Gretchen Tillbury said that Ed isn't supposed to go back for anything, not even his check-book or a change of underwear. If there's stuff he needs, he gives a list and his housekey to a policeman, and the policeman goes to get it. I suppose he'll go to Fresh Harbor. There's plenty of housing there for lab employees. These little cottages. They're actually sort of cute . . .' The brief flash of fire he'd heard in her voice was long gone. Helen now sounded depressed, forlorn, and very, very tired.

'Helen, I'm delighted that you called. And relieved, I won't kid you about that. Now get some sleep.'

121

'What about you, Ralph?' she asked unexpectedly. 'Are *you* getting any sleep these days?'

The switch in focus startled him into an honesty he might not otherwise have managed. 'Some . . . but maybe not as much as I need. Probably not as much as I need.'

'Well, take care of yourself. You were very brave today, like a knight in a story about King Arthur, but I think even Sir Lancelot had to fall out every now and then.'

He was touched by this, and also amused. A momentary picture, very vivid, arose in his mind: Ralph Roberts dressed in armor and mounted on a snow-white steed while Bill McGovern, his faithful squire, rode behind him on his pony, dressed in a leather jerkin and his snappy Panama hat.

'Thank you, dear,' he said. 'I think that's the sweetest thing anyone's said to me since Lyndon Johnson was President. Have the best night you can, okay?'

'Okay. You too.'

She hung up. Ralph stood looking at the phone thoughtfully for a moment or two, then put it back in its cradle. Perhaps he *would* have a good night. After everything that had happened today, he certainly deserved one. For the time being he thought he might go downstairs, sit on the porch, watch the sun go down, and let later take care of itself.

5

McGovern was back, slouched in his favorite chair on the porch. He was looking at something up the street and didn't immediately turn when his upstairs neighbor stepped outside. Ralph followed his gaze and saw a blue step-van parked at the curb half a block up Harris Avenue, on the Red Apple side of the street. DERRY MEDICAL SERVICES was printed across the rear doors in large white letters.

'Hi, Bill,' Ralph said, and dropped into his own chair. The rocker where Lois Chasse always sat when she came over stood between them. A little twilight breeze had sprung up, delightfully cool after the heat of the afternoon, and the empty rocker moved lazily back and forth at its whim.

'Hi,' McGovern said, glancing over at Ralph. He started to look away, then did a doubletake. 'Man, you better start pinning up the bags under your eyes. You're going to be stepping on them pretty soon if you don't.' Ralph thought this was supposed to come out sounding like one of the caustic little *bons mots* for which McGovern was famous along the street, but the look in his eyes was one of genuine concern.

'It's been a bitch of a day,' he said. He told McGovern about Helen's call, editing out the things he thought she might be uncomfortable with McGovern's knowing. Bill had never been one of her favorite people.

'Glad she's okay,' McGovern said. 'I'll tell you something, Ralph – you impressed me today, marching up the street that way, like Gary Cooper in *High Noon*. Maybe it was insane, but it was also pretty cool.' He paused. 'To tell the truth, I was a little in awe of you.'

This was the second time in fifteen minutes that someone had come close to calling Ralph a hero. It made him uncomfortable. 'I was too mad at him to realize how dumb I was being until later. Where you been, Bill? I tried to call you a little while ago.'

'I took a walk out to the Extension,' McGovern said. 'Trying to cool my engine off a little, I guess. I've felt headachey and sick to my stomach ever since Johnny Leydecker and that other one took Ed away.'

Ralph nodded. 'Me, too.'

'Really?' McGovern looked surprised, and a little skeptical.

'Really,' Ralph said with a faint smile.

'Anyway, Faye Chapin was at the picnic area where those old lags usually hang out during the hot weather, and he coaxed me into a game of chess. What a piece of work that guy is, Ralph – he thinks he's the reincarnation of Ruy López, but he plays chess more like Soupy Sales . . . and he *never* shuts up.'

'Faye's all right, though,' Ralph said quietly.

McGovern seemed not to have heard him. 'And that creepy Dorrance Marstellar was out there,' he went on. 'If we're old, he's a fossil. He just stands there by the fence between the picnic area and the airport with a book of poetry in his hands, watching the planes take off and land. Does he really read those books he carries around, do you think, or are they just props?'

'Good question,' Ralph said, but he was thinking about the word McGovern had employed to describe Dorrance – *creepy*. It wasn't one he would have used himself, but there could be no doubt that old Dor was one of life's originals. He wasn't senile (at least Ralph didn't *think* he was); it was more as if the few things he said were the product of a mind that was slightly skewed and perceptions that were slightly bent.

He remembered that Dorrance had been there that

day last summer when Ed ran into the guy in the pickup truck. At the time he'd thought that Dorrance's arrival had added the final screwy touch to the festivities. And Dorrance had said something funny. Ralph tried to recall what it was and couldn't.

McGovern was gazing back up the street, where a whistling young man in a gray coverall had just come out of the house in front of which the Medical Services step-van was parked. This young man, looking all of twenty-four and as if he hadn't needed a single medical service in his entire life, was rolling a dolly with a long green tank strapped to it.

'That's the empty,' McGovern said. 'You missed them taking in the full one.'

A second young man, also dressed in a coverall, stepped out through the front door of the small house, which combined yellow paint and deep pink trim in an unfortunate manner. He stood on the stoop for a moment, hand on the doorknob, apparently speaking to someone inside. Then he pulled the door shut and ran lithely down the walk. He was in time to help his colleague lift the dolly, with the tank still strapped to it, into the back of the van.

'Oxygen?' Ralph asked.

McGovern nodded.

'For Mrs Locher?'

McGovern nodded again, watching as the Medical Services workers slammed the doors of the step-van and then stood behind them, talking quietly in the fading light. 'I went to grammar school and junior high with May Locher. Way out in Cardville, home of the brave and land of the cows. There were only five of us in our graduating class. Back in those days she was known as a hot ticket and fellows like me were known as "a wee bit lavender". In that amusingly antique era, gay was how you described your Christmas tree after it was decorated.'

Ralph looked down at his hands, uncomfortable and tongue-tied. Of course he knew that McGovern was a homosexual, had known it for years, but Bill had never spoken of it out loud until this evening. Ralph wished he could have saved it for another day . . . preferably one when Ralph himself wasn't feeling as if most of his brains had been replaced with goosedown.

'That was about a thousand years ago,' McGovern said. 'Who'd've thought we'd both wash up on the shores of Harris Avenue.'

'It's emphysema she has, isn't that right? I think that's what I heard.'

'Yep. One of those diseases that keep on giving. Getting old is certainly no job for sissies, is it?'

'No, it's not,' Ralph said, and then his mind brought the truth of it home with sudden force. It was Carolyn he thought of, and the terror he had felt when he came squelching into the apartment in his soaked sneakers and had seen her lying half in and half out of the kitchen . . . exactly where he had stood during most of his conversation with Helen, in fact. Facing Ed Deepneau had been nothing compared to the terror he had felt at that moment, when he had been sure Carolyn was dead.

'I can remember when they just brought May oxygen once every two weeks or so,' McGovern said. 'Now they come every Monday and Thursday evening, like clockwork. I go over and see her when I can. Sometimes I read to her – the most boring women's magazine bullshit you can imagine – and sometimes we just sit and talk. She says it feels as if her lungs are filling up with seaweed. It won't be long now. They'll come one day, and instead of loading an empty oxy tank into the back of that wagon, they'll load May in. They'll take her off to Derry Home, and that'll be the end.'

'Was it cigarettes?' Ralph asked.

McGovern favored him with a look so alien to that lean, mild face that it took Ralph several moments to realize it was contempt. 'May Perrault never smoked a cigarette in her whole life. What she's paying off is twenty years in the dyehouse at a mill in Corinna and another twenty working the picker at a mill in Newport. It's cotton, wool, and nylon she's trying to breathe through, not seaweed.'

The two young men from Derry Medical Services got into their van and drove away.

'Maine's the north-eastern anchor of Appalachia, Ralph – a lot of people don't realize that, but it's true – and May's dying of an Appalachian disease. The doctors call it Textile Lung.'

'That's a shame. I guess she means a lot to you.'

McGovern laughed ruefully. 'Nah. I visit her because she happens to be the last visible piece of my misspent youth. Sometimes I read to her and I always manage to get down one or two of her dry old oatmeal cookies, but that's about as far as it goes. My concern is safely selfish, I assure you.'

Safely selfish, Ralph thought. *What a really odd phrase. What a really* McGovern *phrase.*

'Never mind May,' McGovern said. 'The question on

the lips of Americans everywhere is what we're going to do about *you,* Ralph. The whiskey didn't work, did it?'

'No,' Ralph said. 'I'm afraid it didn't.'

'To make a particularly apropos pun, did you give it a fair shot?'

Ralph nodded.

'Well, you have to do *something* about the bags under your eyes or you'll never land the lovely Lois.' McGovern studied Ralph's facial response to this and sighed. 'Not that funny, huh?'

'Nope. It's been a long day.'

'Sorry.'

'It's okay.'

They sat in companionable silence for a while, watching the comings and goings on their part of Harris Avenue. Three little girls were playing hopscotch in the Red Apple's parking lot across the street. Mrs Perrine stood nearby, straight as a sentry, watching them. A boy with his Red Sox cap turned around backward went past, bopping to the beat of his Walkman headset. Two kids were tossing a Frisbee back and forth in front of Lois's house. A dog barked. Somewhere a woman was yelling for Sam to get his sister and come inside. It was just the usual streetlife serenade, no more and no less, but to Ralph it all seemed strangely false. He supposed it was because he had gotten so used to seeing Harris Avenue empty lately.

He turned to McGovern and said, 'You know what was just about the first thing I thought of when I saw you in the Red Apple parking lot this afternoon? In spite of everything else that was going on?'

McGovern shook his head.

'I wondered where the hell your hat was. The Panama. You looked very strange to me without it. Naked, almost. So come clean – where'd you stash the lid, son?'

McGovern touched the top of his head, where the remaining strands of his baby-fine white hair were combed carefully left to right across his pink skull. 'I don't know,' he said. 'I missed it this morning. I almost always remember to drop it on the table by the front door when I come in, but it's not there. I suppose I put it down somewhere else this time and the exact locale has slipped my mind for the nonce. Give me another few years and I'll be wandering around in my underwear because I can't remember where I left my pants. All part of the wonderful aging experience, right, Ralph?'

Ralph nodded and smiled, thinking to himself that of all the elderly people he knew – and he knew at least three dozen on a casual walk-in-the-park, hi-how-ya-doin basis – Bill McGovern bitched the most about getting on in years. He seemed to regard his vanished youth and recently departed middle age as a general would regard a couple of soldiers who desert on the eve of a big battle. He wasn't about to say such a thing, however. Everyone had their little eccentricities; being theatrically morbid about growing old was simply one of McGovern's.

'Did I say something funny?' McGovern asked.

'Pardon?'

'You were smiling, so I thought I must have said something funny.' He sounded a bit touchy, especially for a man so fond of ribbing his upstairs neighbor about the pretty widow down the street, but Ralph reminded himself it had been a long day for McGovern, too.

129

'I wasn't thinking about you at all,' Ralph said. 'I was thinking about how Carolyn used to say practically the same thing – that getting old was like getting a bad dessert at the end of a really fine meal.'

This was at least half a lie. Carolyn *had* made the simile, but she had used it to describe the brain tumor that was killing her, not her life as a senior citizen. She hadn't been all that senior, anyway, just sixty-four when she died, and until the last six or eight weeks of her life, she had claimed to feel only half of that on most days.

Across from them, the three girls who had been playing hopscotch approached the curb, looked both ways for traffic, then joined hands and ran across the street, laughing. For just a moment they looked to him as if they were surrounded by a gray glow – a nimbus that illuminated their cheeks and brows and laughing eyes like some strange, clarifying Saint Elmo's fire. A little frightened, Ralph squeezed his eyes shut and then popped them open again. The gray envelope he'd imagined around the trio of girls was gone, which was a relief, but he *had* to get some sleep soon. He *had* to.

'Ralph?' McGovern's voice seemed to be coming from the far end of the porch, although he hadn't moved. 'You all right?'

'Sure,' Ralph said. 'Thinking about Ed and Helen, that's all. Did you have any idea how screwy he was getting, Bill?'

McGovern shook his head decisively. 'None whatsoever,' he said. 'And although I saw bruises on Helen from time to time, I always believed her stories about them. I don't like to consider myself a tremendously gullible person, but I may have to reassess my thinking on that score.'

130

'What do you think will happen with them? Any predictions?'

McGovern sighed and touched the top of his head with his fingertips, feeling for the missing Panama without realizing it. 'You know me, Ralph – I'm a cynic from a long line of them. I think it's very rare for ordinary human conflicts to resolve themselves the way they do on TV. In reality they just keep coming back, turning in diminishing circles until they finally disappear. Except disappearing isn't really what they do; they dry up, like mudpuddles in the sun.' McGovern paused and then added: 'And most of them leave the same scummy residue behind.'

'Jesus,' Ralph said. 'That *is* cynical.'

McGovern shrugged. 'Most retired teachers *are* cynical, Ralph. We see them come in, so young and so strong, so convinced that it's going to be different for them, and we see them make their messes and then paddle around in them, just as their parents and grandparents did. What I think is that Helen will go back to him, and Ed will do okay for awhile, and then he'll beat her up again and she'll leave again. It's like one of those sappy country-western songs they have on the juke out at Nicky's Lunch, and some people have to listen to that song a long, long time before they decide they don't want to hear it anymore. Helen's a bright young woman, though. I think one more verse is all she'll need.'

'One more verse might be all she'll ever get,' Ralph said quietly. 'We're not talking about some drunk husband coming home on Friday night and beating his wife up because he lost his paycheck in a poker game and she dared to bitch about it.'

'I know,' McGovern said, 'but you asked for my opinion and I gave it to you. I think Helen's going to need one more go-round before she can bring herself to call it off. And even then they're apt to keep on bumping up against each other. It's still a pretty small town.' He paused, squinting down the street. 'Oh, look,' he said, hoisting his left brow. 'Our Lois. She walks in beauty, like the night.'

Ralph gave him an impatient look which McGovern either did not see or pretended not to. He got up, once again touching the tips of his fingers to the place where the Panama wasn't, and then went down the steps to meet her on the walk.

'Lois!' McGovern cried, dropping to one knee before her and extending his hands theatrically. 'Would that our lives might be united by the starry bonds of love! Wed your fate to mine and let me whirl you away to climes various in the golden car of my affections!'

'Gee, are you talking about a honeymoon or a one-night stand?' Lois asked, smiling uncertainly.

Ralph poked McGovern in the back. 'Get up, fool,' he said, and took the small bag Lois was carrying. He looked inside and saw three cans of beer.

McGovern got to his feet. 'Sorry, Lois,' he said. 'It was a combination of summer twilight and your beauty. I plead temporary insanity, in other words.'

Lois smiled at him, then turned to Ralph. 'I just heard what happened,' she said, 'and I hurried over as fast as I could. I was in Ludlow all afternoon, playing nickel–dime poker with the girls.' Ralph didn't have to look at McGovern to know his left eyebrow – the one that said *Poker with the girls! How wonderfully, perfectly Our Lois!* – would be hoisted to its maximum altitude. 'Is Helen all right?'

'Yes,' Ralph said. 'Well, maybe not exactly all right – they're keeping her in the hospital overnight – but she's not in any danger.'

'And the baby?'

'Fine. Staying with a friend of Helen's.'

'Well, come on up on the porch, you two, and tell me all about it.' She linked one arm through McGovern's, the other through Ralph's, and led them back up the walk. They mounted the porch steps that way, like two elderly musketeers with the woman whose affections they had vied for in the days of their youth held safely between them, and as Lois sat down in her rocking chair, the streetlights went on along Harris Avenue, glimmering in the dusk like a double rope of pearls.

6

Ralph fell asleep that night bare instants after his head hit the pillow, and came wide awake again at 3:30 a.m. on Friday morning. He knew immediately there was no question of going back to sleep; he might as well proceed directly to the wing-chair in the living room.

He lay there a moment longer anyway, looking up into the dark and trying to catch the tail of the dream he'd been having. He couldn't do it. He could only remember that Ed had been in it . . . and Helen . . . and Rosalie, the dog he sometimes saw limping up or down Harris Avenue before Pete the paperboy showed up.

Dorrance was in it, too. Don't forget him.

Yes, right. And as if a key had turned in a lock, Ralph suddenly remembered the strange thing Dorrance had said during the confrontation between Ed and the heavyset man last year . . . the thing Ralph hadn't been able to remember earlier this evening. He, Ralph, had been holding Ed back, trying to keep him pinned against the bent hood of his car long enough for reason to reassert itself, and Dorrance had said

(*I wouldn't*)

that Ralph ought to stop touching him.

'He said he couldn't see my hands anymore,' Ralph muttered, swinging his feet out of bed. 'That was it.'

He sat where he was for a little while, head down, hair frizzed up wildly in back, his fingers laced loosely together between his thighs. At last he stepped into his slippers and shuffled into the living room. It was time to start waiting for the sun to come up.

CHAPTER FOUR

1

Although cynics always sounded more plausible than the cock-eyed optimists of the world, Ralph's experience had been that they were wrong at least as much of the time, if not more, and he was delighted to find that McGovern was wrong about Helen Deepneau – in her case, a single verse of 'The Beaten Up, Broken-Hearted Blues' seemed to have been enough.

On Wednesday of the following week, just as Ralph was deciding he'd better track down the woman Helen had spoken with in the hospital (Tillbury, her name had been – Gretchen Tillbury) and try to make sure Helen was okay, he received a letter from her. The return address was simple – just *Helen and Nat, High Ridge* – but it was enough to relieve Ralph's mind considerably. He sat down in his chair on the porch, tore the end off the envelope, and shook out two sheets of lined paper crammed with Helen's back-slanted handwriting.

Dear Ralph, [the letter began],
I suppose by now you must be thinking I decided to be mad at you after all, but I really didn't. It's just that we're supposed

*to stay out of contact with everyone – by phone and letter
– for the first few days. Rules of the house. I like this place
very much, and so does Nat. Of course she does; there are
at least six kids her age to crawl around with. As for me, I
am finding more women who know what I've been through
than I ever would have believed. I mean, you see the TV
shows –* Oprah Talks With Women Who Love Men
Who Use Them For Punching Bags *– but when it
happens to you, you can't help feeling that it's happening in
a way it's never happened to anyone else, in a way that's
brand-new to the world. The relief of knowing that's not true
is the best thing that's happened to me in a long, long time . . .*

She talked about the chores to which she had been assigned
– working in the garden, helping to repaint an equipment
shed, washing the storm windows with vinegar and water
– and about Nat's adventures in learning to walk. The rest
of the letter was about what had happened and what she
intended to do about it, and it was here that Ralph for
the first time really sensed the emotional turmoil Helen
must be feeling, her worries about the future, and, counter-
balancing these things, a formidable determination to do
what was right for Nat . . . and for herself, too. Helen
seemed to be just discovering that she also had a right to
the right thing. Ralph was happy she had found out, but
sad when he thought of all the dark times she must have
trudged through in order to reach that simple insight.

I'm going to divorce him, [she wrote.] *Part of my mind
(it sounds like my mother when it talks) just about howls
when I put it that bluntly, but I'm tired of fooling myself*

about my situation. There's a lot of therapy out here, the kind of thing where people sit around in a circle and use up about four boxes of Kleenex an hour, but it all seems to come back to seeing things plain. In my case, the plain fact is that the man I married has been replaced by a dangerous paranoid. That he can sometimes be loving and sweet isn't the point but a distraction. I need to remember that the man who used to bring me hand-picked flowers now sometimes sits on the porch and talks to someone who isn't there, a man he calls 'the little bald doctor.' Isn't that a beaut? I think I have an idea of how all this started, Ralph, and when I see you I'll tell you, if you really want to hear.

I should be back at the house on Harris Avenue (for awhile, anyway) by mid-September, if only to look for a job . . . but no more about that now, the whole subject scares me to death! I had a note from Ed — just a paragraph, but a great relief just the same — saying that he was staying at one of the cottages at the Hawking Labs compound in Fresh Harbor, and that he would honor the non-contact clause in the bail agreement. He said he was sorry for everything, but I didn't get any real sense of it, if he was. It's not that I was expecting tear-stains on the letter or a package with his ear in it, but . . . I don't know. It was as if he wasn't really apologizing at all, but just getting on the record. Does that make sense? He also included a $750 check, which seems to indicate he understands his responsibilities. That's good, but I think I'd have been happier to hear he was getting help with his mental problems. That should be his sentence, you know: eighteen months at hard therapy. I said that in group and several people laughed as if they thought I was joking. I wasn't.

Sometimes I get these scary pictures in my head when I try to think of the future. I see us standing in line at Manna for a free meal, or me walking into the Third Street homeless shelter with Nat in my arms, wrapped in a blanket. When I think of that stuff I start to shake, and sometimes I cry. I know it's stupid; I've got a graduate degree in Library Science, for God's sake, but I can't help it. And do you know what I hold onto when those bad pictures come? What you said after you took me behind the counter in the Red Apple and sat me down. You told me that I had a lot of friends in the neighborhood, and I was going to get through this. I know I have one friend, at least. One very true friend.

The letter was signed *Love, Helen.*

Ralph wiped tears from the corners of his eyes – he cried at the drop of a hat just lately, it seemed; it probably came from being so goddam tired – and read the PS she had crammed in at the bottom of the sheet and up the right-hand margin:

I'd love to have you come and visit, but men are off limits out here for reasons I'm sure you will understand. They even want us to be quiet about the exact location! H.

Ralph sat for a minute or two with Helen's letter in his lap, looking out over Harris Avenue. It was the tag end of August now, still summer but the leaves of the poplars had begun to gleam silver when the wind stroked them and there was the first touch of coolness in the air. The sign in the window of the Red Apple said SCHOOL SUPPLIES OF ALL TYPES! CHECK HERE FIRST! And, out by the Newport town line, in some big old farmhouse where

138

battered women went to try and start putting their lives back together, Helen Deepneau was washing storm windows, getting them ready for another long winter.

He slid the letter carefully back into its envelope, trying to remember how long Ed and Helen had been married. Six or seven years, he thought. Carolyn would have known for sure. *How much courage does it take to fire up your tractor and plow under a crop you spent six or seven years growing?* he asked himself. *How much courage to go on and do that after you've spent all that time finding out how to prepare the soil and when to plant and how much to water and when to reap? How much to just say, 'I have to quit these peas, peas are no good for me, I better try corn or beans.'*

'A lot,' he said, wiping at the corners of his eyes again. 'A damn lot, that's what I think.'

Suddenly he wanted very badly to see Helen, to repeat what she so well remembered hearing and what he could barely remember saying: *You'll be okay, you'll get through this, you have a lot of friends in the neighborhood.*

'Take it to the bank,' Ralph said. Hearing from Helen seemed to have taken a great weight off his shoulders. He got up, put her letter in his back pocket, and started up Harris Avenue toward the picnic area on the Extension. If he was lucky, he could find Faye Chapin or Don Veazie and play a little chess.

2

His relief at hearing from Helen did nothing to alleviate Ralph's insomnia; the premature waking continued, and by Labor Day he was opening his eyes around 2:45 a.m. By the tenth of September – the day when Ed Deepneau was arrested again, this time along with fifteen others – Ralph's average night's sleep had shrunk to roughly three hours and he had begun to feel quite a little bit like something on a slide under a microscope. *Just a lonely l'il protozoa, that's me,* he thought as he sat in the wing-back chair, staring out at Harris Avenue, and wished he could laugh.

His list of sure-fire, never-miss folk remedies continued to grow, and it had occurred to him more than once that he could write an amusing little book on the subject . . . if, that was, he ever got enough sleep to make organized thinking possible again. This late summer he was doing well to slide into matching socks each day, and his mind kept returning to his purgatorial efforts to find a Cup-A-Soup in the kitchen cabinet on the day Helen had been beaten. There had been no return to that level since, because he had managed at least *some* sleep every night, but Ralph was terribly afraid he would arrive there again – and perhaps places beyond there – if things didn't improve. There were times (usually sitting in the wing-back chair at four-thirty in the morning) when he swore he could actually feel his brains draining.

The remedies ranged from the sublime to the ridiculous. The best example of the former was a full-color brochure advertising the wonders of the Minnesota Institute for Sleep Studies in St Paul. A fair example of the latter was the Magic Eye, an all-purpose amulet sold through supermarket tabloids like the *National Enquirer* and *Inside View*. Sue, the counter-girl at the Red Apple, bought one of these and presented it to him one afternoon. Ralph looked down at the badly painted blue eye staring up at him from the medallion (which he believed had probably started life as a poker-chip) and felt wild laughter bubbling up inside him. He somehow managed to suppress it until he had regained the safety of his own upstairs apartment across the street, and for that he was very grateful. The gravity with which Sue had given it to him – and the expensive-looking gold chain she had threaded through the eyelet on top – suggested it had cost her a fair amount of money. She had regarded Ralph with something close to awe since the day the two of them had rescued Helen. This made Ralph uncomfortable, but he had no idea what to do about it. In the meantime, he supposed it didn't hurt to wear the medallion so she could see the shape of it under his shirt. It didn't help him sleep, though.

After taking his statement on Ralph's part in the Deepneaus' domestic problems, Detective John Leydecker had pushed back his desk chair, laced his fingers together behind his not inconsiderable breadth of neck, and said that McGovern had told him Ralph suffered from insomnia. Ralph allowed that he did. Leydecker nodded, rolled his chair forward again, clasped his hands atop the litter of paperwork beneath which the surface of his desk was mostly buried, and looked at Ralph seriously.

'Honeycomb,' he said. His tone of voice reminded Ralph of McGovern's tone when he had suggested that whiskey was the answer, and his reply now was exactly the same.

'I beg your pardon?'

'My grandfather swore by it,' Leydecker said. 'Little piece of honeycomb just before bedtime. Suck the honey out of the comb, chew the wax a little – like you would a wad of gum – then spit it out. Bees secrete some sort

141

of natural sedative when they make honey. Put you right out.'

'No kidding,' Ralph said, simultaneously believing it was utter crap and believing every word. 'Where would a person get honeycomb, do you think?'

'Nutra – the health food store out at the mall. Try it. By next week this time your troubles are going to be over.'

Ralph enjoyed the experiment – the comb honey was so sweetly powerful it seemed to suffuse his whole being – but he still woke at 3:10 a.m. after the first dosage, at 3:08 after the second, and at 3:07 after the third. By then the small piece of honeycomb he'd purchased was gone, and he went out to Nutra right away for another one. Its value as a sedative might be nil, but it made a wonderful snack; he only wished he had discovered it earlier.

He tried putting his feet in warm water. Lois bought him something called an All-Purpose Gel Wrap from a catalogue – you put it around your neck and it was supposed to take care of your arthritis as well as help you sleep (it did neither for Ralph, but he had only the mildest case of arthritis to begin with). Following a chance meeting with Trigger Vachon at the counter of Nicky's Lunch, he tried camomile tea. 'That cammy's a beaut,' Trig told him. 'You gonna sleep great, Ralphie.' And Ralph did . . . right up until 2:58 a.m., that was.

Those were the folk cures and homeopathic remedies he tried. Ones he didn't included mega-vitamin packages which cost much more than Ralph could afford to spend on his fixed income, a yoga position called The Dreamer (as described by the postman, The Dreamer sounded to Ralph like a fine way to get a look at your own hemorrhoids), and marijuana. Ralph considered this last one very carefully before deciding it would very likely turn out to be an illegal version of the whiskey and honeycomb and the camomile tea. Besides, if McGovern found out Ralph was smoking pot, he would never hear the end of it.

And through all these experiments a voice in his brain kept asking him if he really *was* going to have to get down to eye of newt and tongue of toad before he gave up and went to the doctor. That voice was not so much critical as genuinely curious. Ralph had become fairly curious himself.

On September 10th, the day of the first Friends of Life demonstration at WomanCare, Ralph decided that he would try something from the drugstore . . . but not the Rexall downtown where he'd gotten Carolyn's prescriptions filled. They knew him down there, knew him well, and he didn't want Paul Durgin, the Rexall druggist, to see him buying sleeping-pills. It was probably stupid – like going across town to buy rubbers – but that didn't change the way he felt. He had never traded at the Rite Aid across from Strawford Park, so that was where he meant to go. And if the drugstore version of newt's eye and toad's tongue didn't work, he really *would* go to the doctor.

Is that true, Ralph? Do you really mean it?

'I do,' he said out loud as he walked slowly down Harris Avenue in the bright September sunshine. 'Be damned if I'll put up with this much longer.'

Big talk, Ralph, the voice replied skeptically.

Bill McGovern and Lois Chasse were standing outside

the park, having what looked like an animated discussion. Bill looked up, saw him, and motioned for him to come over. Ralph went, not liking the combination of their expressions: bright-eyed interest on McGovern's face, distress and worry on Lois's.

'Have you heard about the thing out at the hospital?' she asked as Ralph joined them.

'It wasn't at the hospital, and it wasn't a "thing",' McGovern said testily. 'It was a demonstration – that's what they called it, anyway – and it was at WomanCare, which is actually *behind* the hospital. They took a bunch of people to jail – somewhere between six and two dozen, nobody really seems to know yet.'

'One of them was Ed Deepneau!' Lois said breathlessly, and McGovern shot her a disgusted glance. He clearly believed that handling this piece of news had been his job.

'Ed!' Ralph said, startled. 'Ed's in Fresh Harbor!'

'Wrong,' McGovern said. The battered brown fedora he was wearing today gave him a slightly rakish look, like a newspaperman in a forties crime drama. Ralph wondered if the Panama was still lost or had merely been retired for the fall. 'Today he's once more cooling his heels in our picturesque city jail.'

'What exactly happened?'

But neither of them really knew. At that point the story was little more than a rumor which had spread through the park like a contagious headcold, a rumor which was of particular interest in this part of town because Ed Deepneau's name was attached to it. Marie Callan had told Lois that there had been rock-throwing involved, and that was why the demonstrators had been arrested. According to Stan Eberly, who had passed the story on to McGovern shortly before McGovern ran into Lois, someone – it might have been Ed, but it might well have been one of the others – had Maced a couple of doctors as they used the walkway between WomanCare and the back entrance to the hospital. This walkway was technically public property, and had become a favorite haunt of anti-abortion demonstrators during the seven years that WomanCare had been providing abortions on demand.

The two versions of the story were so vague and conflicting that Ralph felt he could reasonably hope neither was true, that perhaps it was just a case of a few over-enthusiastic people who'd been arrested for trespassing, or something. In places like Derry, that kind of thing happened; stories had a way of inflating like beachballs as they were passed from mouth to mouth.

Yet he couldn't shake the feeling that this time it would turn out to be more serious, mostly because both the Bill version and the Lois version included Ed Deepneau, and Ed was not your average anti-abortion protestor. This was, after all, the guy who had pulled a clump of his wife's hair right out of her scalp, rearranged her dental work, and fractured her cheekbone simply because he had seen her name on a petition which mentioned WomanCare. This was the guy who seemed honestly convinced that someone calling himself the Crimson King – *it would be a great name for a pro wrestler,* Ralph thought – was running around Derry, and that his minions were hauling their unborn victims out of town on flatbed trucks (plus a few pickups with the fetuses stuffed into barrels marked WEED-GO). No, he had an idea that if Ed had been there, it had probably not been just a case of someone accidentally bonked on the head with a protest sign.

'Let's go up to my house,' Lois proposed suddenly. 'I'll call Simone Castonguay. Her niece is the day receptionist at WomanCare. If anyone knows exactly what happened up there this morning, it'll be Simone – she'll have called Barbara.'

'I was just on my way down to the supermarket,' Ralph said. It was a lie, of course, but surely a very small one; the market stood next to the Rite Aid in the stripmall half a block down from the park. 'Why don't I stop in on my way back?'

'All right,' Lois said, smiling at him. 'We'll expect you in a few minutes, won't we, Bill?'

'Yes,' McGovern said, and suddenly swept her into his arms. It was a bit of a reach, but he managed. 'In the meantime, I'll have you all to myself. Oh, Lois, how those sweet minutes will fly!'

Just inside the park, a group of young women with babies in strollers (*a gossip of mothers,* Ralph thought) had been watching them, probably attracted by Lois's gestures, which had a tendency to become grandiose when she was excited. Now, as McGovern bent Lois backward, looking down at her with the counterfeit ardor of a bad actor at the end of a stage tango, one of the mothers spoke to another and both laughed. It was a shrill, unkind sound that made Ralph think of chalk squealing on blackboards and forks dragged across porcelain sinks. *Look at the funny old people,* the laughter said. *Look at the funny old people, pretending to be young again.*

'Stop that, Bill!' Lois said. She was blushing, and maybe

not just because Bill was up to his usual tricks. She'd also heard the laughter from the park. McGovern undoubtedly had, too, but McGovern would believe they were laughing with him, not at him. *Sometimes,* Ralph thought wearily, *a slightly inflated ego could be a protection.*

McGovern let her go, then removed his fedora and swept it across his waist as he made an exaggerated bow. Lois was too busy making sure that her silk blouse was still tucked into the waistband of her skirt all the way around to pay him much notice. Her blush was already fading, and Ralph saw she looked rather pale and not particularly well. He hoped she wasn't coming down with something.

'Come by, if you can,' she told Ralph quietly.

'I will, Lois.'

McGovern slipped an arm around her waist, the gesture of affection both friendly and sincere this time, and they started up the street together. Watching them, Ralph was suddenly gripped by a strong sense of *déjà vu,* as if he had seen them like that in some other place. Or some other life. Then, just as McGovern dropped his arm, breaking the illusion, it came to him: Fred Astaire leading a dark-haired and rather plump Ginger Rogers out onto a small-town movie set, where they would dance together to some tune by Jerome Kern or maybe Irving Berlin.

That's weird, he thought, turning back toward the little strip-mall halfway down Up-Mile Hill. *That's very weird, Ralph. Bill McGovern and Lois Chasse are about as far from Fred Astaire and Ginger Rogers as you can g—*

'Ralph?' Lois called, and he turned back. There was one intersection and about a block's worth of distance between them now. Cars zipped back and forth on Elizabeth Street, turning Ralph's view of them into a moderate stutter.

'What?' he called back.

'You look better! More rested! Are you finally getting some sleep?'

'Yes!' he returned, thinking, *Just another small lie, in another good cause.*

'Didn't I say you'd feel better once the seasons changed? See you in a little while!'

Lois wiggled her fingers at him, and Ralph was amazed to see bright blue diagonal lines stream back from the short but carefully shaped nails. They looked like contrails.

What the fuck—?

He shut his eyes tight, then popped them open again. Nothing. Only Bill and Lois once again walking up the street toward Lois's house, their backs to him. No bright blue diagonals in the air, nothing like that—

Ralph's eyes dropped to the sidewalk and he saw that Lois and Bill were leaving tracks behind them on the concrete, tracks that looked exactly like the footprints in the old Arthur Murray learn-to-dance instructions you used to be able to get by mail-order. Lois's were gray. McGovern's – larger but still oddly delicate – were a dark shade of olive green. They glowed on the sidewalk, and Ralph, who was standing on the far side of Elizabeth Street with his jaw hanging almost down to his breastbone, suddenly realized he could see little ribbands of colored smoke rising from them. Or perhaps it was steam.

A city bus bound for Old Cape snored by, momentarily blocking his view, and when it passed the tracks were gone. There was nothing on the sidewalk but a message chalked inside a fading pink heart: SAM + DEANIE 4-EVER.

Those tracks are not gone, Ralph; they were never there in the first place. You know that, don't you?

Yes, he knew. The idea that Bill and Lois looked like Fred Astaire and Ginger Rogers had gotten into his head; progressing from that idea to a hallucination of phantom footprints leading up the sidewalk like tracks in an Arthur Murray dance-diagram had a certain bizarre logic. Still, it was scary. His heart was beating too fast, and when he closed his eyes for a moment to try and calm down, he saw those marks trailing up from Lois's waving fingers like bright blue jet contrails.

I've got to get more sleep, Ralph thought. *I've got to. If I don't, I'm apt to start seeing anything.*

'That's right,' he muttered under his breath as he turned toward the drugstore again. 'Anything at all.'

3

Ten minutes later, Ralph was standing at the front of the Rite Aid Pharmacy and looking at a sign which hung on chains from the ceiling. FEEL BETTER AT RITE AID! it said, seeming to suggest that feeling better was a goal attainable by any reasonable, hard-working consumer. Ralph had his doubts about that.

This, Ralph decided, was retail drug-dealing on a grand scale – it made the Rexall where he usually traded look like a tenement apartment by comparison. The fluorescent-lit aisles seemed as long as bowling alleys and displayed everything from toaster ovens to jigsaw puzzles. After a little study,

Ralph decided Aisle 3 contained most of the patent medicines and was probably his best bet. He made his way slowly through the area marked STOMACH REMEDIES, sojourned briefly in the kingdom of ANALGESICS, and quickly crossed the land of LAXATIVES. And there, between LAXATIVES and DECONGESTANTS, he stopped.

This is it, folks – my last shot. After this there's only Dr Litchfield, and if he suggests chewing honeycomb or drinking camomile tea, I'll probably snap and it'll take both nurses and the receptionist to pull me off him.

SLEEPING AIDS, the sign over this section of Aisle 3 read.

Ralph, never much of a patent medicine user (he would otherwise have arrived here much sooner, no doubt), didn't know exactly what he'd expected, but it surely had not been this wild, almost indecent profusion of products. His eye slipped across the boxes (the majority were a soothing blue), reading the names. Most seemed strange and slightly ominous: Compoz, Nytol, Sleepinal, Z-Power, Sominex, Sleepinex, Drow-Zee. There was even a generic brand.

You have to be kidding, he thought. None of these things are going to work for you. It's time to quit fucking around, don't you know that? When you start to see colored footprints on the sidewalk, it's time to quit fucking around and go to the doctor.

But on the heels of this he heard Dr Litchfield, heard him so clearly it was as if a tape recorder had turned on in the middle of his head: *Your wife is suffering from tension headaches, Ralph – unpleasant and painful, but not life-threatening. I think we can take care of the problem.*

Unpleasant and painful, but not life-threatening – yes,

right, that was what the man had said. And then he had reached for his prescription pad and written out the order for the first bunch of useless pills while the tiny clump of alien cells in Carolyn's head continued to send out its microbursts of destruction, and maybe Dr Jamal had been right, maybe it was too late even then, but maybe Jamal was full of shit, maybe Jamal was just a stranger in a strange land, trying to get along, trying not to make waves. Maybe this and maybe that; Ralph didn't know for sure and never would. All he really knew was that Litchfield hadn't been around when the final two tasks of their marriage had been set before them: her job to die, his job to watch her do it.

Is that what I want to do? Go to Litchfield and watch him reach for his prescription pad again?

Maybe this time it would work, he argued to – *with* himself. At the same time his hand stole out, seemingly of its own volition, and took a box of Sleepinex from the shelf. He turned it over, held it slightly away from his eyes so he could read the small print on the side panel, and ran his eye slowly down the list of active ingredients. He had no idea of how to pronounce most of the jawbreaking words, and even less of what they were or how they were supposed to help you sleep.

Yes, he answered the voice. *Maybe this time it* would *work. But maybe the real answer would be just to find another doc—*

'Help you?' a voice asked from directly behind Ralph's shoulder.

He was in the act of returning the box of Sleepinex to its place, meaning to take something that sounded a little less like a sinister drug in a Robin Cook novel, when the voice spoke. Ralph jumped and knocked a dozen assorted boxes of synthetic sleep onto the floor.

'Oh, sorry – clumsy!' Ralph said, and looked over his shoulder.

'Not at all. My fault entirely.' And before Ralph could do more than pick up two boxes of Sleepinex and one box of Drow-Zee gel capsules, the man in the white smock who had spoken to him had swept up the rest and was redistributing them with the speed of a riverboat gambler dealing a hand of poker. According to the gold ID bar pinned to his breast, this was JOE WYZER, RITE AID PHARMACIST.

'Now,' Wyzer said, dusting off his hands and turning to Ralph with a friendly grin, 'let's start over. Can I help you? You look a little lost.'

Ralph's initial response – annoyance at being disturbed while having a deep and meaningful conversation with himself – was being replaced with guarded interest. 'Well, I don't know,' he said, and gestured to the array of sleeping potions. 'Do any of these actually work?'

Wyzer's grin widened. He was a tall, middle-aged man with fair skin and thinning brown hair which he parted in the middle. He stuck out his hand, and Ralph had barely begun the polite reciprocatory gesture when his own hand was swallowed. 'I'm Joe,' the pharmacist said, and tapped the gold tunic-pin with his free hand. 'I used to be Joe Wyze, but now I'm older and Wyzer.'

This was almost certainly an ancient joke, but it had lost none of its savor for Joe Wyzer, who laughed uproariously. Ralph smiled a polite little smile with just the smallest touch of anxiety around its edges. The hand which had enfolded his was clearly a strong one, and he was afraid if the pharmacist squeezed hard, his hand might finish the day in a cast. He found himself wishing, at least momentarily, that he'd taken his problem to Paul Durgin downtown after all. Then Wyzer gave his hand two energetic pumps and let go.

'I'm Ralph Roberts. Nice to meet you, Mr Wyzer.'

'Mutual. Now, concerning the efficacy of these fine products. Let me answer your question with one of my own, to wit, does a bear shit in a telephone booth?'

Ralph burst out laughing. 'Rarely, I'd think,' he said when he could say anything again.

'Correct. And I rest my case.' Wyzer glanced at the sleeping aids, a wall done in shades of blue. 'Thank God I'm a pharmacist and not a salesman, Mr Roberts; I'd starve trying to peddle stuff door to door. Are you an insomniac? I'm asking partly because you're investigating the sleeping aids, but mostly because you have that lean and hollow-eyed look.'

Ralph said, 'Mr Wyzer, I'd be the happiest man on earth if I could get five hours' sleep some night, and I'd settle for four.'

'How long's it been going on, Mr Roberts? Or do you prefer Ralph?'

'Ralph's fine.'

'Good. And I'm Joe.'

'It started in April, I think. A month or six weeks after my wife died, anyway.'

'Gee, I'm sorry to hear you lost your wife. My sympathies.'

'Thank you,' Ralph said, then repeated the old formula. 'I miss her a lot, but I was glad when her suffering was over.'

'Except now *you're* suffering. For . . . let's see.' Wyzer counted quickly on his big fingers. 'Going on half a year now.'

Ralph suddenly found himself fascinated by those fingers. No jet contrails this time, but the tip of each one appeared to be wrapped in a bright silvery haze, like tinfoil you could somehow look right through. He suddenly found himself thinking of Carolyn again, and remembering the phantom smells she had sometimes complained of last fall – cloves, sewage, burning ham. Maybe this was the male equivalent, and the onset of his own brain tumor had been signaled not by headaches but by insomnia.

Self-diagnosis is a fool's game, Ralph, so why don't you just quit it?

He moved his eyes resolutely back to Wyzer's big, pleasant face. No silvery haze there; not so much as a hint of a haze. He was almost sure of it.

'That's right,' he said. 'Going on half a year. It seems longer. A lot longer, actually.'

'Any noticeable pattern? There usually is. I mean, do you toss and turn before you go to sleep, or—'

'I'm a premature waker.'

Wyzer's eyebrows went up. 'And read a book or three about the problem too, I deduce.' If Litchfield had made a remark of this sort, Ralph would have read condescension into it. From Joe Wyzer he sensed not condescension but genuine admiration.

'I read what the library had, but there wasn't much,

and none of it has helped much.' Ralph paused, then added: 'The truth is none of it has helped at all.'

'Well, let me tell you what I know on the subject, and you just kind of flop your hand when I start heading into territory you've already explored. Who's your doctor, by the way?'

'Litchfield.'

'Uh-huh. And you usually trade at . . . where? The People's Drug out at the mall? The Rexall downtown?'

'The Rexall.'

'You're incognito today, I take it.'

Ralph blushed . . . then grinned. 'Yeah, something like that.'

'Uh-huh. And I don't need to ask if you've been to see Litchfield about your problem, do I? If you had, you wouldn't be exploring the wonderful world of patent medicines.'

'Is that what these are? Patent medicines?'

'Put it this way — I'd feel a helluva lot more comfortable selling most of this crap off the back of a big red wagon with fancy yellow wheels.'

Ralph laughed, and the bright silvery cloud which had been gathering in front of Joe Wyzer's tunic blew away when he did.

'That kind of salesmanship I might be able to get into,' Wyzer said with a misty little grin. 'I'd get a sweet little honeybun to do a dance in a sequined bra and a pair of harem pants . . . call her Little Egypt, like in that old Coasters song . . . she'd be my warm-up act. Plus I'd have a banjo-picker. In my experience, there's nothing like a good dose of banjo music to put people in a buying mood.'

155

Wyzer looked off past the laxatives and analgesics, enjoying this gaudy daydream. Then he looked back at Ralph again.

'For a premature waker like you, Ralph, this stuff is entirely useless. You'd be better off with a shot of booze or one of those wave machines they sell through the catalogues, and looking at you, I'd guess you probably tried em both.'

'Yes.'

'Along with about two dozen other oldtimer-tested home remedies.'

Ralph laughed again. He was coming to like this guy a lot. 'Try four dozen and you'll be in the ballpark.'

'Well, you're an industrious bugger, I'll give you that,' Wyzer said, and waved a hand at the blue boxes. 'These things are nothing but antihistamines. Essentially they're trading on a side-effect – antihistamines make people sleepy. Check out a box of Comtrex or Benadryl down there in Decongestants and it'll say you shouldn't take it if you're going to be driving or operating heavy machinery. For people who suffer from occasional sleeplessness, a Sominex every now and then may work. It gives them a nudge. But they wouldn't work for you in any case, because your problem isn't *getting* to sleep, it's *staying* asleep . . . correct?'

'Correct.'

'Can I ask you a delicate question?'

'Sure. I guess so.'

'Do you have a problem with Dr Litchfield regarding this? Maybe have some doubts about his ability to understand how really pissy your insomnia is making you feel?'

'Yes,' Ralph said gratefully. 'Do you think I should

go see him? Try to explain that to him so he'll under-stand?' To this question Wyzer would of course respond in the affirmative, and Ralph would finally make the call. And it would be, *should* be Litchfield – he saw that now. It was madness to think of hooking up with a new doctor at his age.

Can you tell Dr Litchfield you're seeing things? Can you tell him about the blue marks you saw shooting up from the tips of Lois Chasse's fingers? The footprints on the sidewalk, like the footprints in an Arthur Murray dance-diagram? The silvery stuff around the tips of Joe Wyzer's fingers? Are you really going to tell Litchfield that stuff? And if you're not, if you can't, why are you going to see him in the first place, no matter what this guy recommends?

Wyzer, however, surprised him by going in an entirely different direction. 'Are you still dreaming?'

'Yes. Quite a lot, in fact, considering that I'm down to about three hours' sleep a night.'

'Are they coherent dreams – dreams that consist of perceivable events and have some kind of narrative flow, no matter how kooky – or are they just jumbled images?'

Ralph remembered a dream he'd had the night before. He and Helen Deepneau and Bill McGovern had been having a three-sided game of Frisbee in the middle of Harris Avenue. Helen had a pair of huge, clunky saddle shoes on her feet; McGovern was wearing a sweatshirt with a vodka bottle on it. ABSOLUT-LY THE BEST, the sweatshirt proclaimed. The Frisbee had been bright red with fluorescent green stripes. Then Rosalie the dog had shown up. The faded blue bandanna someone had hung around her neck was flapping as she limped toward them.

All at once she had leaped into the air, snatched the Frisbee, and gone running off with it in her mouth. Ralph wanted to give chase, but McGovern said, *Relax, Ralph, we're getting a whole case of them for Christmas*. Ralph turned to him, intending to point out that Christmas was over three months away and to ask what the hell they were going to do if they wanted to play Frisbee between then and now, but before he could, the dream had either ended or gone on to some other, less vivid, mind-movie.

'If I understand what you're saying,' Ralph replied, 'my dreams are coherent.'

'Good. I also want to know if they're *lucid* dreams. Lucid dreams fulfill two requirements. First, you know you're dreaming. Second, you can often influence the course the dream takes – you're more than just a passive observer.'

Ralph nodded. 'Sure, I have those, too. In fact, I seem to have a lot of them lately. I was just thinking of one I had last night. In it this stray dog I see on the street from time to time ran off with a Frisbee some friends of mine and I were playing with. I was mad that she broke up the game, and I tried to make her drop the Frisbee just by sending her the thought. Sort of a telepathic command, you know?'

He uttered a small, embarrassed chuckle, but Wyzer only nodded matter-of-factly. 'Did it work?'

'Not this time,' Ralph said, 'but I think I *have* made that sort of thing work in other dreams. Only I can't be sure, because most of the dreams I have seem to fade away almost as soon as I wake up.'

'That's the case with everyone,' Wyzer said. 'The brain

158

treats most dreams as disposable matter, storing them in extreme short-term memory.'

'You know a lot about this, don't you?'

'Insomnia interests me very much. I did two research papers on the link between dreams and sleep disorders when I was in college.' Wyzer glanced at his watch. 'It's my break-time. Would you like to have a cup of coffee and a piece of apple pie with me? There's a place just two doors down, and the pie is fantastic.'

'Sounds good, but maybe I'll settle for an orange soda. I've been trying to cut down on my coffee intake.'

'Understandable but completely useless,' Wyzer said cheerfully. 'Caffeine is not your problem, Ralph.'

'No, I suppose not . . . but what is?' To this point Ralph had been quite successful at keeping the misery out of his voice, but now it crept back in.

Wyzer clapped him on the shoulder and looked at him kindly. 'That,' he said, 'is what we're going to talk about. Come on.'

CHAPTER FIVE

1

'Think of it this way,' Wyzer recommenced five minutes later. They were in a New Age-y sort of diner called Day Break, Sun Down. The place was a little too ferny for Ralph, who believed in old-fashioned diners that gleamed with chrome and smelled of grease, but the pie was good, and while the coffee was not up to Lois Chasse's standards – Lois made the best cup he had ever tasted – it was hot and strong.

'Which way is that?' Ralph asked.

'There are certain things mankind – womankind, too – keeps striving for. Not the stuff that gets written up in the history and civics books, either, at least for the most part; I'm talking fundamentals here. A roof to keep the rain out. Three hots and a cot. A decent sex-life. Healthy bowels. But maybe the most fundamental thing of all is what you've been missing, my friend. Because there's really nothing in the world that can measure up to a good night's sleep, is there?'

'Boy, you got that right,' Ralph said.

Wyzer nodded. 'Sleep is the overlooked hero and

the poor man's physician. Shakespeare said it's the thread that knits up the ravelled sleeve of care, Napoleon called it the blessed end of night, and Winston Churchill — one of the great insomniacs of the twentieth century — said it was the only relief he ever got from his deep depressions. I put all that stuff in my papers, but what all the quotes come down to is what I just said: nothing in the whole wide world can measure up to a good night's sleep.'

'You've had the problem yourself, haven't you?' Ralph asked suddenly. 'Is that why you . . . well . . . why you're taking me under your wing?'

Joe Wyzer grinned. 'Is that what I'm doing?'

'I think so, yes.'

'Hey, I can live with that. The answer is yes. I've suffered from slow-sleep insomnia ever since I was thirteen. It's why I ended up doing not just one research paper on the subject but two.'

'How are you doing with it these days?'

Wyzer shrugged. 'So far it's been a pretty good year. Not the best, but I'll take it. For a couple of years in my early twenties, the problem was acute — I'd go to bed at ten, fall asleep around four, get up at seven, and drag myself through the day feeling like a bit player in someone else's nightmare.'

This was so familiar to Ralph that his back and upper arms broke out in goosebumps.

'Here comes the most important thing I can tell you, Ralph, so listen up.'

'I am.'

'The thing you have to hang onto is that you're

still basically okay, even though you feel like shit a lot of the time. All sleep is not created equal, you see – there's good sleep and bad sleep. If you're still having coherent dreams, and, maybe even more importantly, *lucid* dreams, you're still having good sleep. And because of that, a scrip for sleeping pills could be about the worst thing in the world for you right now. And I know Litchfield. He's a nice enough guy, but he loves that prescription pad.'

'Say it twice,' Ralph told him, thinking of Carolyn.

'If you tell Litchfield what you told me while we were walking down here, he's going to prescribe a benzo-diazepine – probably Dalmane or Restoril, maybe Halcion or even Valium. You'll sleep, but you'll pay a price. Benzodiazepines are habit-forming, they're respiratory depressants, and worst of all, for guys like you and me, they significantly reduce REM sleep. Dreaming sleep, in other words.

'How's your pie? I only ask because you've hardly touched it.'

Ralph took a big bite and swallowed it without tasting. 'Good,' he said. 'Now tell me why you have to have dreams to make your sleep good sleep.'

'If I could answer that, I'd retire from the pill-pushing business and go into business as a sleep guru.' Wyzer had finished his pie and was now using the pad of his index finger to pick up the larger crumbs left on his plate. 'REM stands for rapid eye movements, of course, and the terms REM sleep and dreaming sleep have become synonymous in the public mind, but nobody really knows just how the eye movements of sleepers relate to the dreams they are having. It seems unlikely that the eye movements indicate "watching" or "tracking", because sleep researchers see a lot of it even in dreams test subjects later describe as fairly static – dreams of conversations, for instance, like the one we're having now. Similarly, no one really knows why there seems to be a clear relationship between lucid, coherent dreams and overall mental health: the more dreams of that sort a person has, the better off he seems to be, the less he has, the worse. There's a real scale there.'

'Mental health's a pretty general phrase,' Ralph said skeptically.

'Yeah.' Wyzer grinned. 'Makes me think of a bumper sticker I saw a few years back – SUPPORT MENTAL HEALTH OR I'LL KILL YOU. Anyway, we're talking about some basic, measurable components: cognitive ability, problem-solving ability, by both inductive and deductive methods, ability to grasp relationships, memory—'

'My memory is lousy these days,' Ralph said. He was thinking of his inability to remember the number of the cinema complex and his long hunt through the kitchen cabinet for the last Cup-A-Soup envelope.

'Yeah, you're probably suffering some short-term memory loss, but your fly is zipped, your shirt is on right-side out, and I bet if I asked you what your middle name is, you could tell me. I'm not belittling your problem – I'd be the last person in the world to do that – but I *am* asking you to change your point of view for a minute or two. To think of all the areas in your life where you're still perfectly functional.'

'All right. These lucid and coherent dreams – do they

just indicate how well you're functioning, like a gas gauge in a car, or do they actually help you function?'

'No one knows for sure, but the most likely answer is a little of both. In the late fifties, around the time the doctors were phasing out the barbiturates – the last really popular one was a fun drug called Thalidomide – a few scientists even tried to suggest that the good sleep we've been beating our gums about and dreams aren't related.'

'And?'

'The tests don't support the hypothesis. People who stop dreaming or suffer from constant dream interruptions have all sorts of problems, including loss of cognitive ability and emotional stability. They also start to suffer perceptual problems like hyper-reality.'

Beyond Wyzer, at the far end of the counter, sat a fellow reading a copy of the Derry *News*. Only his hands and the top of his head were visible. He was wearing a rather ostentatious pinky-ring on his left hand. The head-line at the top of the front page read ABORTION RIGHTS ADVOCATE AGREES TO SPEAK IN DERRY NEXT MONTH. Below it, in slightly smaller type, was a subhead: *Pro-Life Groups Promise Organized Protests*. In the center of the page was a color picture of Susan Day, one that did her much more justice than the flat photographs on the poster he had seen in the window of Secondhand Rose, Secondhand Clothes. In those she had looked ordinary, perhaps even a bit sinister; in this one she was radiant. Her long, honey-blonde hair had been pulled back from her face. Her eyes were dark, intelligent, arresting. Hamilton Davenport's pessimism had been misplaced, it seemed. Susan Day was coming after all.

Then Ralph saw something which made him forget all about Ham Davenport and Susan Day.

A gray-blue aura had begun to gather around the hands of the man reading the newspaper, and around the just-visible crown of his head. It seemed particularly bright around the onyx pinky-ring he wore. It did not obscure but seemed to *clarify*, turning the ringstone into something that looked like an asteroid in a really realistic science-fiction movie—

'What did you say, Ralph?'

'Hmm?' Ralph drew his gaze away from the newspaper reader's pinky-ring with an effort. 'I don't know . . . was I talking? I guess I asked you what hyper-reality is.'

'Heightened sensory awareness,' Wyzer said. 'Like taking an LSD trip without having to ingest any chemicals.'

'Oh,' Ralph said, watching as the bright gray blue aura began to form complicated, runic patterns on the nail of the finger Wyzer was using to mash up crumbs. At first they looked like letters written in frost . . . then sentences written in fog . . . then odd, gasping faces.

He blinked and they were gone.

'Ralph? You still there?'

'Sure, you bet. But listen, Joe — if the folk remedies don't work and the stuff in Aisle 3 doesn't work and the prescription drugs could actually make things worse instead of better, what does that leave? Nothing, right?'

'You going to eat the rest of that?' Wyzer said, pointing at Ralph's plate. Chilly gray-blue light drifted off the tip of his finger like Arabic letters written in dry ice vapor.

'Nope. I'm full. Be my guest.'

Wyzer pulled Ralph's plate to him. 'Don't give up so fast,' he said. 'I want you to come back to the pharm with me so I can give you a couple of business cards. My advice, as your friendly neighborhood drug-pusher, is that you give these guys a try.'

'What guys?' Ralph watched, fascinated, as Wyzer opened his mouth to receive the last bite of pie. Each of his teeth was lit with a fierce gray glow. The fillings in his molars glowed like tiny suns. The fragments of crust and apple filling on his tongue crawled with

(*lucid Ralph lucid*)

light. Then Wyzer closed his mouth to chew, and the glow was gone.

'James Roy Hong and Anthony Forbes. Hong is an acupuncturist with offices on Kansas Street. Forbes is a hypnotist with a place over on the east side – Hesser Street, I think. And before you yell quack—'

'I'm not going to yell quack,' Ralph said quietly. His hand rose to touch the Magic Eye, which he was still wearing under his shirt. 'Believe me, I'm not.'

'Okay, good. My advice is that you try Hong first. The needles look scary, but they only hurt a little, and he's got something going there. I don't know what the hell it is or how it works, but I do know that when I went through a bad patch two winters ago, he helped me a lot. Forbes is also good – so I've heard – but Hong's my pick. He's busy as hell, but I might be able to help you there. What do you say?'

Ralph saw a bright gray glow, no thicker than a thread, slip from the corner of Wyzer's eye and slide down his cheek like a supernatural tear. It decided him. 'I say let's go.'

Wyzer clapped him on the shoulder. 'Good man! Let's pay up and get out of here.' He produced a quarter. 'Flip you for the check?'

2

Halfway back to the pharmacy, Wyzer stopped to look at a poster which had been put up in the window of an empty storefront between the Rite Aid and the diner. Ralph only glanced at it. He had seen it before, in the window of Secondhand Rose, Secondhand Clothes.

'Wanted for murder,' Wyzer marvelled. 'People have lost all goddam sense of perspective, do you know it?'

'Yes,' Ralph said. 'If we had tails, I think most of us would spend all day chasing them and trying to bite them off.'

'The poster's bad enough,' Wyzer said indignantly, 'but look at this!'

He was pointing at something beside the poster, something which had been written in the dirt which coated the outside of the empty display window. Ralph leaned close to read the short message. KILL THIS CUNT, it said. Below the words was an arrow pointing at the left-hand photo of Susan Day.

'Jesus,' Ralph said quietly.

'Yeah,' Wyzer agreed. He pulled a handkerchief from his back pocket and wiped away the message, leaving in place of the words a bright silvery fan-shape which Ralph knew only he could see.

3

He followed Wyzer to the rear of the pharmacy and stood in the doorway of an office not much bigger than a public-toilet cubicle while Wyzer sat on the only piece of furniture – a high stool that would have looked at home in Ebenezer Scrooge's counting-house – and phoned the office of James Roy Hong, acupuncturist. Wyzer pushed the phone's speaker button so Ralph could follow the conversation.

Hong's receptionist (someone named Audra who seemed to know Wyzer on a basis a good deal warmer than a merely professional one) at first said Dr Hong could not possibly see a new patient until after Thanksgiving. Ralph's shoulders slumped. Wyzer raised an open palm in his direction – *Wait a minute, Ralph* – and then proceeded to talk Audra into finding (or perhaps creating) an opening for Ralph in early October. That was almost a month away, but a lot better than Thanksgiving.

'Thanks, Audra,' Wyzer said. 'We still on for dinner Friday night?'

'Yes,' she said. 'Now turn off the damned speaker, Joe – I have something that's for your ears only.'

Wyzer did it, listened, laughed until tears – to Ralph they looked like gorgeous liquid pearls – stood in his eyes. Then he smooched twice into the phone and hung up.

'You're all set,' he said, handing Ralph a small white card with the time and date of the appointment written on the back. 'October fourth, not great, but really the best she could do. Audra's good people.'

'It's fine.'

'Here's Anthony Forbes's card, in case you want to call him in the interim.'

'Thanks,' Ralph said, taking the second card. 'I owe you.'

'The only thing you owe me is a return visit so I can find out how it went. I'm concerned. There are doctors who won't prescribe *anything* for insomnia, you know. They like to say that no one ever died from lack of sleep, but I'm here to tell you that's crap.'

Ralph supposed this news should have frightened him, but he felt pretty steady, at least for the time being. The auras had gone away – the bright gray gleams in Wyzer's eyes as he'd laughed at whatever Hong's receptionist had said had been the last. He was starting to think they had just been a mental fugue brought on by a combination of extreme tiredness and Wyzer's mention of hyper-reality. There was another reason for feeling good – he now had an appointment with a man who had helped *this* man through a similar bad patch. Ralph thought he'd let Hong stick needles into him until he looked like a porcupine, if the treatment allowed him to sleep until the sun came up.

And there was a third thing: the gray auras hadn't actually been *scary*. They had been sort of . . . interesting.

'People die from lack of sleep all the time,' Wyzer was saying, 'although the medical examiner usually ends up writing *suicide* on the cause-of-death line, rather than *insomnia*. Insomnia and alcoholism have a lot in common, but the major thing is this: they're both diseases of the heart and mind, and when they're allowed to run their course they usually gut the spirit long before they're able to destroy the body. So yeah – people *do* die from lack of sleep. This is a dangerous time for you, and you have to take care of yourself. If you start to feel really wonky, *call Litchfield*. Do you hear me? Don't stand on ceremony.'

Ralph grimaced. 'I think I'd be more apt to call you.'

Wyzer nodded as if he had absolutely expected this. 'The number under Hong's is mine,' he said.

Surprised, Ralph looked down at the card again. There *was* a second number there, marked J.W.

'Day or night,' Wyzer said. 'Really. You won't disturb my wife; we've been divorced since 1983.'

Ralph tried to speak and found he couldn't. All that came out was a choked, meaningless little sound. He swallowed hard, trying to clear the obstruction in his throat.

Wyzer saw he was struggling and clapped him on the back. 'No bawling in the store, Ralph – it scares away the big spenders. You want a Kleenex?'

'No, I'm okay.' His voice was slightly watery, but audible and mostly under control.

Wyzer cast a critical eye on him. 'Not yet, but you will be.' Wyzer's big hand swallowed Ralph's once more, and this time Ralph didn't worry about it. 'For the time being, try to relax. And remember to be grateful for the sleep you *do* get.'

'Okay. Thanks again.'

Wyzer nodded and walked back to the prescription counter.

4

Ralph walked back down Aisle 3, turned left at the formidable condom display, and went out through a door with THANK YOU FOR SHOPPING AT RITE AID declared above the push-bar. At first he thought there was nothing unusual about the fierce brightness that made him squint his eyes almost shut — it was midday, after all, and perhaps the drugstore had been a little darker than he had realized. Then he opened his eyes wide again, and his breath came to a dead stop in his throat.

A look of thunderstruck amazement spread over his face. It was the expression an explorer might wear when, after pushing his way through just one more nondescript tangle of bushes, he finds himself looking at some fabulous lost city or brain-busting geological feature — a cliff of diamonds, perhaps, or a spiral waterfall.

Ralph shrank back against the blue mailbox standing to one side of the drugstore's entrance, still not breathing, his eyes shuttling jerkily from left to right as the brain behind them tried to understand the wonderful and terrible news it was receiving.

The auras were back, but that was a little like saying Hawaii was a place where you didn't have to wear your overcoat. This time the light was everywhere, fierce and flowing, strange and beautiful.

Ralph had had only one experience in his entire life which was remotely similar to this. During the summer of 1941, the year he'd turned eighteen, he'd been riding his thumb from Derry to his uncle's place in Poughkeepsie, New York, a distance of about four hundred miles. An early evening thunderstorm at the end of his second day on the road had sent him scurrying for the nearest available shelter — a decrepit barn swaying drunkenly at the end of a long hayfield. He had spent more of that day walking than riding, and had fallen soundly asleep in one of the barn's long-abandoned horse stalls even before the thunder had stopped blasting the sky overhead.

He'd awakened at mid-morning the next day after a solid fourteen hours of sleep and had looked around in utter wonder, not even sure, in those first few moments, where he was. He only knew it was some dark, sweet-smelling place, and that the world above and on all sides of him had been split open with brilliant seams of light. Then he had remembered taking shelter in the barn, and it came to him that this strange vision had been caused by the cracks in the barn's walls and roof combined with the bright summer sunlight . . . only that, and nothing more. Yet he'd sat there in mute wonder for at least five minutes just the same, a wide-eyed teenage boy with hay in his hair and his arms dusted with chaff; he sat there looking up at the tidal gold of dust-motes spinning lazily in the slanting, crosshatching rays of the sun. He remembered thinking it had been like being in church.

This was that experience to the tenth power. And the hell of it was simply this: he could not describe exactly what had happened, and how the world had changed, to make it so wonderful. Things and people, particularly the people, had auras, yes, but that was only where this amazing phenomenon began. Things had never been so *brilliant,* so utterly and completely *there.* The cars, the telephone poles, the shopping carts in the Kart Korral in front of the supermarket, the frame apartment buildings across the street — all these things seemed to pop out at him like 3-D images in an old film. All at once this dingy little strip-mall on Witcham Street had become wonderland, and although Ralph was looking right at it, he was not sure what he was looking at, only that it was rich and gorgeous and fabulously strange.

The only things he *could* isolate were the auras surrounding the people going in and out of stores, stowing packages in their trunks, or getting in their cars and driving away. Some of these auras were brighter than others, but even the dimmest were a hundred times brighter than his first glimpses of the phenomenon.

But it's what Wyzer was talking about, no doubt of that. It's hyper-reality, and what you're looking at is no more there than the hallucinations of people who are under the influence of LSD. What you're seeing is just another symptom of your insomnia, no more and no less. Look at it, Ralph, and marvel over it as much as you want – it is marvellous – just don't believe it.

He didn't need to tell himself to marvel, however – there were marvels everywhere. A bakery truck was backing out of a slot in front of Day Break, Sun Down, and a bright maroon substance – it was almost the color of dried blood – came from its tailpipe. It was neither smoke nor vapor but had some of the characteristics of each. This brightness rose in gradually attenuating spikes, like the lines of an EEG read-out. Ralph looked down at the pavement and saw the tread of the van's tires printed on the concrete in that same maroon shade. The van speeded up as it left the parking lot, and the ghostly graph-trail emerging with its exhaust turned the bright red of arterial blood as it did.

There were similar oddities everywhere, phenomena which intersected in slanting paths and made Ralph think again of how the light had come slanting through the cracks in the roof and walls of that long-ago barn. But the real wonder was the people, and it was around them that the auras seemed most clearly defined and real.

A bagboy came out of the supermarket, pushing a cartload of groceries and walking in a nimbus of such brilliant white that it was like a travelling spotlight. The aura of the woman beside him was dingy by comparison, the gray-green of cheese which has begun to mould.

A young girl called to the bagboy from the open window of a Subaru and waved; her left hand left bright contrails, as pink as cotton candy, in the air as it moved. They began to fade almost as soon as they appeared. The bagboy grinned and waved back; his hand left a fantail of yellowish-white behind. To Ralph it looked like the fin of a tropical fish. This also began to fade, but more slowly.

Ralph's fear at this confused, shining vision was considerable, but for the time being, at least, fear had taken a back seat to wonder, awe, and simple amazement. It was more beautiful than anything he had ever seen in his life. *But it's not real,* he cautioned himself. *Remember that, Ralph.* He promised himself he would try, but for the time being that cautioning voice seemed very far away.

Now he noticed something else: there was a line of that lucid brightness emerging from the head of every person he could see. It trailed upward like a ribbon of bunting or brightly colored crepe paper until it attenuated and disappeared. For some people the point of disappearance was five feet above the head; for others it was ten or fifteen. In most cases the color of the bright, ascending line matched the rest of the aura — bright white for the bagboy, gray-green in the case of the female customer beside him, for instance — but there were some striking exceptions.

Ralph saw a rust-red line rising from a middle-aged man who was striding along in the middle of a dark-blue aura, and a woman with a light-gray aura whose ascending line was an amazing (and slightly alarming) shade of magenta. In some cases – two or three, not a lot – the rising lines were almost black. Ralph didn't like those, and he noticed that the people to whom these 'balloon-strings' (they were named just that simply and quickly in his mind) belonged invariably looked unwell.

Of course they do. The balloon-strings are an indicator of health . . . and ill-health, in some cases. Like the Kirlian auras people were so fascinated with back in the late sixties and early seventies.

Ralph, another voice warned, *you are not really seeing these things, okay? I mean, I hate to be a bore, but—*

But wasn't it at least possible that the phenomenon *was* real? That his persistent insomnia, coupled with the stabilizing influence of his lucid, coherent dreams, had afforded him a glimpse of a fabulous dimension just beyond the reach of ordinary perception?

Quit it, Ralph, and right now. You have to do better than that, or you'll end up in the same boat as poor old Ed Deepneau.

Thinking of Ed kicked off some association – something he'd said on the day he'd been arrested for beating his wife – but before Ralph could isolate it, a voice spoke almost at his left elbow.

'Mom? Mommy? Can we get the Honey Nut Cheerios again?'

'We'll see once we get inside, hon.'

A young woman and a little boy passed in front of him, walking hand-in-hand. It was the boy, who looked to be four or five, who had spoken. His mother was walking in an envelope of almost blinding white. The 'balloon-string' rising out of her blonde hair was also white and very wide – more like the ribbon on a fancy gift box than a string. It rose to a height of at least twenty feet and floated out slightly behind her as she walked. It made Ralph think of things bridal – trains, veils, gauzy billows of skirt.

Her son's aura was a healthy dark blue verging on violet, and as the two of them walked past, Ralph saw a fascinating thing. Tendrils of aura were also rising from their clasped hands: white from the woman, dark blue from the boy. They twined in a pigtail as they rose, faded, and disappeared.

Mother-and-son, mother-and-son, Ralph thought. There was something perfectly, simply symbolic about those bands, which were wrapped around each other like woodbine climbing a garden stake. Looking at them made his heart rejoice – corny, but it was exactly how he felt. *Mother-and-son, white-and-blue, mother-and—*

'Mom, what's that man looking at?'

The blonde woman's glance at Ralph was brief, but he saw the way her lips thinned down and pressed together before she turned away. More importantly, he saw the brilliant aura which surrounded her suddenly darken, close in, and pick up spiraling tints of dark red.

That's the color of fright, Ralph thought. *Or maybe anger.*

'I don't know, Tim. Come on, stop dawdling.' She began to move him along faster, her ponytailed hair flipping back and forth and leaving small fans of gray tinged with red in the air. To Ralph they looked like the arcs that wipers sometimes left on dirty windshields.

'Hey, Mom, get a life! Quit *pull*-ing!' The little boy had to trot in order to keep up.

That's my fault, Ralph thought, and an image of how he must have looked to the young mother flashed into his mind: old guy, tired face, big purplish pouches under his eyes. He's standing – *hunching* – by the mailbox outside the Rite Aid Pharmacy, staring at her and her little boy as if they were the most remarkable things in the world.

Which you just about are, ma'am, if you but knew it.

To her he must have looked like the biggest pervo of all time. He had to get rid of this. Real or hallucination, it didn't matter – he had to make it quit. If he didn't somebody was going to call either the cops or the men with the butterfly nets. For all he knew, the pretty mother could be making the bank of pay-phones just inside the market's main doors her first stop.

He was just asking himself how one thought away something which was all in one's mind to begin with when he realized it had already happened. Psychic phenomenon or sensory hallucination, it had simply disappeared while he'd been thinking about how awful he must have looked to the pretty young mother. The day had gone back to its previous Indian summery brilliance, which was wonderful but still a long way from that pellucid, all-pervading glow. The people crisscrossing the parking lot of the strip-mall were just people again: no auras, no balloon-strings, no fireworks. Just people on their way to buy groceries in the Shop 'n Save, or to pick up their last batch of summer pictures at Photo-Mat, or to grab a take-out coffee from Day Break, Sun Down. Some of them might even be ducking into the

Rite Aid for a box of Trojans or, God bless us and keep us, a SLEEPING AID.

Just your ordinary, everyday citizens of Derry going about their ordinary, everyday business.

Ralph released pent-up breath in a gusty sigh and braced himself for a wave of relief. Relief *did* come, but not in the tidal wave he had expected. There was no sense of having drawn back from the brink of madness in the nick of time; no sense of having been close to *any* sort of brink. Yet he understood perfectly well that he couldn't live for long in a world that bright and wonderful without endangering his sanity; it would be like having an orgasm which lasted for hours. That might be how geniuses and great artists experienced things, but it was not for him; so much juice would blow his fuses in short order, and when the men with the butterfly nets rolled up to give him a shot and take him away, he would probably be happy to go.

The most readily identifiable emotion he was feeling just now wasn't relief but a species of pleasant melancholy which he remembered sometimes experiencing after sex when he was a very young man. This melancholy was not deep but it was wide, seeming to fill the empty places of his body and mind the way a receding flood leaves a scrim of loose, rich topsoil. He wondered if he would ever have such an alarming, exhilarating moment of epiphany again. He thought the chances were fairly good . . . at least until next month, when James Roy Hong got his needles into him, or perhaps until Anthony Forbes started swinging his gold pocket watch in front of his eyes and telling him he was getting . . . very . . . sleepy. It was possible that neither

Hong nor Forbes would have any success in curing his insomnia, but if one of them did, Ralph guessed he would stop seeing auras and balloon-strings after his first good night's sleep. And, after a month or so of restful nights, he would probably forget this had ever happened. As far as he was concerned, that was a perfectly good reason to feel a touch of melancholy.

You better get moving, buddy – if your new friend happens to look out the drugstore window and sees you still standing here like a dope, he'll probably send for the men with the nets himself.

'Call Dr Litchfield, more like it,' Ralph muttered, and cut across the parking lot toward Harris Avenue.

5

He poked his head through Lois's front door and called, 'Yo! Anybody home?'

'Come on in, Ralph!' Lois called back. 'We're in the living room!'

Ralph had always imagined a hobbit-hole would be a lot like Lois Chasse's little house half a block or so down the hill from the Red Apple – neat and crowded, a little too dark, perhaps, but scrupulously clean. And he guessed a hobbit like Bilbo Baggins, whose interest in his ancestors was eclipsed only by his interest in what might be for dinner, would have been enchanted by the tiny living room, where relatives looked down from every wall. The place of honor, on top of the television, was held by a tinted studio photograph of the man Lois always referred to as 'Mr Chasse'.

McGovern was sitting hunched forward on the couch

with a plate of macaroni and cheese balanced on his bony knees. The television was on and a game-show was clattering through the bonus round.

'What does she mean, *we're* in the living room?' Ralph asked, but before McGovern could answer, Lois came in with a steaming plate in her hands.

'Here,' she said. 'Sit down, eat. I talked with Simone, and she said it'll probably be on *News at Noon*.'

'Gee, Lois, you didn't have to do this,' he said, taking the plate, but his stomach demurred strongly when he got his first smell of onions and mellow cheddar. He glanced at the clock on the wall – just visible between photos of a man in a raccoon coat and a woman who looked as if *vo-do-dee-oh-do* might have been in her vocabulary – and was astounded to see it was five minutes of twelve.

'I didn't do anything but stick some leftovers into the microwave,' she said. 'Someday, Ralph, I'll *cook* for you. Now sit down.'

'Not on my hat, though,' McGovern said, without taking his eyes from the bonus round. He picked the fedora up off the couch, dropped it on the floor beside him, and went back to his own portion of the casserole, which was disappearing rapidly. 'This is very tasty, Lois.'

'Thank you.' She paused long enough to watch one of the contestants bag a trip to Barbados and a new car, then hurried back into the kitchen. The screaming winner faded out and was replaced by a man in wrinkled pajamas, tossing and turning in bed. He sat up and looked at the clock on the nightstand. It said 3:18 a.m., a time of day with which Ralph had become very familiar.

'Can't sleep?' an announcer asked sympathetically.

'Tired of lying awake night after night?' A small glowing pill came gliding in through the insomniac's bedroom window. To Ralph it looked like the world's smallest flying saucer, and he wasn't surprised to see that it was blue.

Ralph sat down beside McGovern. Although both men were quite slim (*scrawny* might actually have described Bill better), between them they used up most of the couch.

Lois came in with her own plate and sat down in the rocker by the window. Over the canned music and studio applause that marked the end of the game-show, a woman's voice said, "This is Lisette Benson. Topping our *News at Noon,* a well-known women's rights advocate agrees to speak in Derry, sparking a protest – and six arrests – at a local clinic. We'll also have Chris Altoberg's weather and Bob McClanahan on sports. Stay tuned.'

Ralph forked a bite of macaroni and cheese into his mouth, looked up, and saw Lois watching him. 'All right?' she asked.

'Delicious,' he said, and it was, but he thought that right now a big helping of Franco-American spaghetti served cold right out of the can would have tasted just as good. He wasn't just hungry; he was ravenous. Seeing auras apparently burned a lot of calories.

'What happened, very briefly, was this,' McGovern said, swallowing the last of his own lunch and putting the plate down next to his hat. 'About eighteen people showed up outside WomanCare at eight-thirty this morning, while people were arriving for work. Lois's friend Simone says they're calling themselves The Friends of Life, but the core group are the assorted fruits and nuts that used to go by the name of Daily Bread. She said one of them was Charles

Pickering, the guy the cops caught apparently getting ready to firebomb the joint late last year. Simone's niece said the police only arrested four people. It looks like she was a little low.'

'Was Ed really with them?' Ralph asked.

'Yes,' Lois said, 'and he got arrested, too. At least no one got Maced. That was just a rumor. No one got hurt at all.'

'*This* time,' McGovern added darkly.

The *News at Noon* logo appeared on Lois's hobbit-sized color TV, then dissolved into Lisette Benson. 'Good afternoon,' she said. 'Topping our news on this beautiful late-summer day, prominent writer and controversial women's rights advocate Susan Day agrees to speak at the Civic Center next month, and the announcement of her speech sparks a demonstration at WomanCare, the Derry women's resource center and abortion clinic which has so polarized—'

'There they go with that abortion clinic stuff again!' McGovern exclaimed. 'Jesus!'

'Hush!' Lois said in a peremptory tone not much like her usual tentative murmur. McGovern gave her a surprised look and hushed.

'– John Kirkland at WomanCare, with the first of two reports,' Lisette Benson was finishing, and the picture switched to a reporter doing a stand-up outside a long, low brick building. A super at the bottom of the screen informed viewers that this was a LIVE-EYE REPORT. A strip of windows ran along one side of WomanCare. Two of them were broken, and several others were smeared with red stuff that looked like blood. Yellow police-line tape had been strung between the reporter and the building; three uniformed Derry cops and one plainclothesman stood in a little group on the far side of it. Ralph was not very surprised to recognize the detective as John Leydecker.

'They call themselves The Friends of Life, Lisette, and they claim their demonstration this morning was a spontaneous outpouring of indignation prompted by the news that Susan Day — the woman radical pro-life groups nationwide call "America's Number One Baby-Killer" — is coming to Derry next month to speak at the Civic Center. At least one Derry police officer believes that's not quite the way it was, however.'

Kirkland's report went to tape, beginning with a close-up of Leydecker, who seemed resigned to the microphone in his face.

'There was no spontaneity about this,' he said. 'Clearly a lot of preparation went into it. They've probably been sitting on advance word of Susan Day's decision to come here and speak for most of the week, just getting ready and waiting for the news to break in the paper, which it did this morning.'

The camera went to a two-shot. Kirkland was giving Leydecker his most penetrating Geraldo look. 'What do you mean "a lot of preparation"?' he asked.

'Most of the signs they were carrying had Ms Day's name on them. Also, there were over a dozen of *these*.'

A surprisingly human emotion slipped through Leydecker's policeman-being-interviewed mask; Ralph thought it was distaste. He raised a large plastic evidence bag, and for one horrified instant Ralph was positive that there was a mangled and bloody baby inside. Then he realized that, whatever the red stuff might be, the body in the evidence bag was a doll's body.

'They didn't buy these at Kmart,' Leydecker told the TV reporter. 'I guarantee you that.'

The next shot was a long-lens close-up of the smeared and broken windows. The camera panned them slowly. The stuff on the smeared ones looked more like blood than ever, and Ralph decided he didn't want the last two or three bites of his macaroni and cheese.

'The demonstrators came with baby-dolls whose soft bodies had been injected with what police believe to be a mixture of Karo syrup and red food-coloring,' Kirkland said in voice-over. 'They flung the dolls at the side of the building as they chanted anti-Susan Day slogans. Two windows were broken, but there was no major damage.'

The camera stopped, centering on a gruesomely smeared pane of glass.

'Most of the dolls split open,' Kirkland was saying, 'splattering a substance that looked enough like blood to badly frighten the employees who witnessed the bombardment.'

The shot of the red-smeared window was replaced by one of a lovely dark-haired woman in slacks and a pullover.

'Oooh, look, it's Barbie!' Lois cried. 'Golly, I hope Simone's watching! Maybe I ought to—'

It was McGovern's turn to say hush.

'I was terrified,' Barbara Richards told Kirkland. 'At first I thought they were really throwing dead babies, or maybe fetuses they'd gotten hold of somehow. Even after

Dr Warper ran through, yelling they were only dolls, I still wasn't sure.'

'You said they were chanting?' Kirkland asked.

'Yes. What I heard most clearly was "Keep the Angel of Death out of Derry."'

The report now reverted to Kirkland in his live stand-up mode. 'The demonstrators were ferried from WomanCare to Derry Police Headquarters on Main Street around nine o'clock this morning, Lisette. I understand that twelve were questioned and released; six others were arrested on charges of malicious mischief, a misdemeanor. So it seems that another shot in Derry's continuing war over abortion has been fired. This is John Kirkland, Channel Four news.'

'"Another shot in —"' McGovern began, and threw up his hands.

Lisette Benson was back on the screen. 'We now go to Anne Rivers, who talked less than an hour ago to two of the so-called Friends of Life who *were* arrested in this morning's demonstration.'

Anne Rivers was standing on the steps of the Main Street cop-shop with Ed Deepneau on one side and a tall, sallow, goateed individual on the other. Ed was looking natty and downright handsome in a gray tweed jacket and navy slacks. The tall man with the goatee was dressed as only a liberal with daydreams of what he might think of as 'the Maine proletariat' could dress: faded jeans, faded blue workshirt, wide red fireman's suspenders. It took Ralph only a second to place him. It was Dan Dalton, owner of Secondhand Rose, Secondhand Clothes. The last time Ralph had seen him, he had been standing behind the hanging guitars and bird-cages in his shop window, flapping his

185

hands at Ham Davenport in a gesture that said *Who gives a shit what you think?*

But it was Ed his eyes were drawn back to, of course, Ed who looked natty and put together in more ways than one.

McGovern apparently felt the same. 'My God, I can't believe it's the same man,' he murmured.

'Lisette,' the good-looking blonde was saying, 'with me I have Edward Deepneau and Daniel Dalton, both of Derry, two of those arrested in this morning's demonstration. That's correct, gentlemen? You were arrested?'

They nodded, Ed with the barest twinkle of humor, Dalton with dour, jut-jawed determination. The gaze the latter fixed on Anne Rivers made him look − to Ralph, at least − as if he were trying to remember which abortion clinic he had seen her hurrying into, head down and shoulders hunched.

'Have you been released on bail?'

'We were released on our own recognizance,' Ed answered. 'The charges were minor. It was not our intention to hurt anyone, and no one *was* hurt.'

'We were arrested only because the Godless entrenched power-structure in this town wants to make an example of us,' Dalton said, and Ralph thought he saw a minute wince momentarily tighten Ed's face. A there-he-goes-again expression.

Anne Rivers swung the mike back to Ed.

'The major issue here isn't philosophical but practical,' he said. 'Although the people who run WomanCare like to concentrate on their counselling services, therapy services, free mammograms and other such admirable functions, there's another side to the place. Rivers of blood run out of WomanCare—'

'*Innocent* blood!' Dalton cried. His eyes glowed in his long, lean face, and Ralph had a disturbing insight: all over eastern Maine, people were watching this and deciding that the man in the red suspenders was crazy, while his partner seemed like a pretty reasonable fellow. It was almost funny.

Ed treated Dalton's interjection as the pro-life equivalent of *Hallelujah,* giving it a single respectful beat before speaking again.

'The slaughter at WomanCare has been going on for nearly eight years now,' Ed told her. 'Many people – especially radical feminists like Dr Roberta Warper, WomanCare's chief administrator – like to gild the lily with phrases like "early termination", but what she's talking about is abortion, the ultimate act of abuse against women by a sexist society.'

'But is lobbing dolls loaded with fake blood against the windows of a private clinic the way to put your views before the public, Mr Deepneau?'

For a moment – just a moment, there and gone – the twinkle of good humor in Ed's eyes was replaced by a flash of something much harder and colder. For that one moment Ralph was again looking at the Ed Deepneau who had been ready to take on a truck-driver who outweighed him by a hundred pounds. Ralph forgot that what he was watching had been taped an hour ago and was afraid for the slim blonde, who was almost as pretty as the woman to whom her interview subject was still married. *Be careful, young lady,* Ralph thought. *Be careful and be afraid. You're standing next to a very dangerous man.*

Then the flash was gone and the man in the tweed coat was once more just an earnest young fellow who had followed his conscience to jail. Once more it was Dalton, now nervously snapping his suspenders like big red rubber bands, who looked a few sandwiches shy of a picnic.

'What we're doing is what the so-called good Germans failed to do in the thirties,' Ed was saying. He spoke in the patient, lecturely tones of a man who has been forced to point this out over and over . . . mostly to those who should already know it. 'They were silent and six million Jews died. In this country a similar holocaust—'

'Over a thousand babies every day,' Dalton said. His former shrillness had departed. He sounded horrified and desperately tired. 'Many of them are ripped from the wombs of their mothers in pieces, with their little arms waving in protest even as they die.'

'Oh good God,' McGovern said. 'That's the most ridiculous thing I have ever—'

'Hush, Bill!' Lois said.

'– purpose of this protest?' Rivers was asking Dalton.

'As you probably know,' Dalton said, 'the City Council has agreed to re-examine the zoning regulations that allow WomanCare to operate where it does and how it does. They could vote on the issue as early as November. The abortion rights people are afraid the Council might throw sand in the gears of their death-machine, so they've summoned Susan Day, this country's most notorious pro-abortion advocate, to try and keep the machine running. We are marshalling our forces—'

The pendulum of the microphone swung back to

Ed. 'Will there be more protests, Mr Deepneau?' she asked, and Ralph suddenly had an idea she might be interested in him in a way which was not strictly professional. Hey, why not? Ed was a good-looking guy, and Ms Rivers could hardly know that he believed the Crimson King and his Centurions were in Derry, joining forces with the baby-killers at WomanCare.

'Until the legal aberration which opened the door to this slaughter has been corrected, the protests will continue,' Ed replied. 'And we'll go on hoping that the histories of the next century will record that not all Americans were good Nazis during this dark period of our history.'

'*Violent* protests?'

'It's violence we oppose.' The two of them were now maintaining strong eye contact, and Ralph thought Anne Rivers had what Carolyn would have called a case of hot thighs. Dan Dalton was standing off to one side of the screen, all but forgotten.

'And when Susan Day comes to Derry next month, can you guarantee her safety?'

Ed smiled, and in his mind's eye Ralph saw him as he had been on that hot August afternoon less than a month ago – kneeling with one hand planted on either side of Ralph's shoulders and breathing *They burn the fetuses over in Newport* into his face. Ralph shivered.

'In a country where thousands of children are sucked from the wombs of their mothers by the medical equivalent of industrial vacuum cleaners, I don't believe anyone can guarantee anything,' Ed replied.

Anne Rivers looked at him uncertainly for a moment,

as if deciding whether or not she wanted to ask another question (maybe for his telephone number), and then turned back to face the camera. 'This is Anne Rivers, at Derry Police Headquarters,' she said.

Lisette Benson reappeared, and something in the bemused cast of her mouth made Ralph think that perhaps he hadn't been the only one to sense the attraction between interviewer and interviewee. 'We'll be following this story all day,' she said. 'Be sure to tune in at six for further updates. In Augusta, Governor Greta Powers responded to charges that she may have—'

Lois got up and pushed the Off button on the TV. She simply stared at the darkening screen for a moment, then sighed heavily and sat down. 'I have blueberry compote,' she said, 'but after that, do either of you want any?'

Both men shook their heads. McGovern looked at Ralph and said, 'That was scary.'

Ralph nodded. He kept thinking of how Ed had gone striding back and forth through the spray thrown by the lawn-sprinkler, breaking the rainbows with his body, pounding his fist into his open palm.

'How could they let him out on bail and then inter-view him on the news as if he was a normal human being?' Lois asked indignantly. 'After what he did to poor Helen? My God, that Anne Rivers looked ready to invite him home to dinner!'

'Or to eat crackers in bed with her,' Ralph said dryly.

'The assault charge and this stuff today are entirely different matters,' McGovern said, 'and you can bet your boots the lawyer or lawyers these yo-yos have got on retainer will be sure to keep it that way.'

'And even the assault charge was only a misdemeanor,' Ralph reminded her.

'How can assault be a misdemeanor?' Lois asked. 'I'm sorry, but I never *did* understand that part.'

'It's a misdemeanor when you only do it to your wife,' McGovern said, hoisting his satiric eyebrow. 'It's the American way, Lo.'

She twisted her hands together restlessly, took Mr Chasse down from the television, looked at him for a moment, then put him back and resumed twisting her hands. 'Well, the law's one thing,' she said, 'and I'd be the first to admit that I don't understand it all. But somebody ought to tell them he's crazy. That he's a wife-beater and he's crazy.'

'You don't know *how* crazy,' Ralph said, and for the first time he told them the story of what had happened the previous summer, out by the airport. It took about ten minutes. When he finished, neither of them said anything – they only looked at him with wide eyes.

'What?' Ralph asked uneasily. 'You don't believe me? You think I imagined it?'

'Of course I believe it,' Lois said. 'I was just . . . well . . . stunned. And frightened.'

'Ralph, I think maybe you ought to pass that story on to John Leydecker,' McGovern said. 'I don't think he can do a goddam thing with it, but considering Ed's new playmates, I think it's information he should have.'

Ralph thought it over carefully, then nodded and pushed himself to his feet. 'No time like the present,' he said. 'Want to come, Lois?'

She thought it over, then shook her head. 'I'm tired

out,' she said. 'And a little – what do the kids call it these days? – a little freaked. I think I'll put my feet up for a bit. Take a nap.'

'You do that,' Ralph said. 'You do look a little tuckered. And thanks for feeding us.' Impulsively, he bent over her and kissed the corner of her mouth. Lois looked up at him with startled gratitude.

6

Ralph turned off his own television a little over six hours later, as Lisette Benson finished the evening news and handed off to the sports guy. The demonstration at WomanCare had been bumped to the number two slot – the evening's big story was the continuing allegations that Governor Greta Powers had used cocaine as a grad student – and there was nothing new, except that Dan Dalton was now being identified as the head of the Friends of Life. Ralph thought *figurehead* was probably a better word. Was Ed actually in charge yet? If he wasn't, Ralph guessed he would be before long – Christmas at the latest. A potentially more interesting question was what Ed's employers thought about Ed's legal adventures up the road in Derry. Ralph had an idea they would be a lot less comfortable with what had gone on today than with last month's domestic abuse charge; he had read only recently that Hawking Labs would soon become the fifth such research center in the Northeast to be working with fetal tissue. They probably wouldn't applaud the information that one of their research chemists had been arrested for chucking dolls filled with fake blood at the side of a clinic that did abortions. And if they knew how crazy he really was—

Who's going to tell them, Ralph? You?

No. That was a step further than he was willing to go, at least for the time being. Unlike going down to the police station with McGovern to talk to John Leydecker about the incident last summer, it felt like persecution. Like writing KILL THIS CUNT beside a picture of a woman with whose views you didn't agree.

That's bullshit, and you know it.

'I don't know anything,' he said, getting up and going to the window. 'I'm too *tired* to know anything.' But as he stood there, looking across the street at two men coming out of the Red Apple with a six-pack apiece, he suddenly *did* know something, remembered something that drew a cold line up his back.

This morning, when he had come out of the Rite Aid and been overwhelmed by the auras – and a sense of having stepped up to some new level of awareness – he had reminded himself again and again to enjoy but not to believe; that if he failed to make that crucial distinction, he was apt to end up in the same boat as Ed Deepneau. That thought had almost opened the door on some associative memory, but the shifting auras in the parking lot had pulled him away from it before it had been able to kick all the way in. Now it came to him: *Ed* had said something about seeing auras, hadn't he?

No – he might have meant *auras, but the word he actually used was* colors. *I'm almost positive of that. It was right after he talked about seeing the corpses of babies everyplace, even on the roofs. He said—*

193

Ralph watched the two men get into a beat-up old van and thought that he would never be able to remember Ed's words exactly; he was just too tired. Then, as the van drove off trailing a cloud of exhaust that reminded him of the bright maroon stuff he'd seen coming from the tailpipe of the bakery truck that noon, another door opened and the memory *did* come.

'He said that sometimes the world is full of colors,' Ralph told his empty apartment, 'but that at some point they all started turning black. I *think* that was it.'

It was close, but was it everything? Ralph thought there had been at least a little more to Ed's spiel, but he couldn't remember what. And did it matter, anyway? His nerves suggested strongly that it did – the cold line up his back had both widened and deepened.

Behind him, the telephone rang. Ralph turned and saw it sitting in a bath of baleful red light, dark red, the color of nosebleeds and

(*cocks fighting cocks*)

rooster-combs.

No, part of his mind moaned. *Oh no, Ralph, don't get going on this again—*

Each time the phone rang, the envelope of light got brighter. During the intervals of silence, it darkened. It was like looking at a ghostly heart with a telephone inside it.

Ralph closed his eyes tightly, and when he opened them again, the red aura around the telephone was gone.

No, you just can't see it right now. I'm not sure, but I think you might have willed it away. Like something in a lucid dream.

As he crossed the room to the telephone, he told

194

himself – and in no uncertain terms – that that idea was as crazy as seeing the auras in the first place. Except it wasn't, and he *knew* it wasn't. Because if it was crazy, how come it had taken only one look at that rooster-red halo of light to make him sure that it was Ed Deepneau calling?

That's crap, Ralph. You think it's Ed because Ed's on your mind . . . and because you're so tired your head's getting funny. Go on, pick it up, you'll see. It's not the tell-tale heart, not even the tell-tale phone. It's probably some guy wanting to sell you subscriptions or the lady at the blood-bank, wondering why you haven't been in lately.

Except he knew better.

Ralph picked up the phone and said hello.

7

No answer. But *someone* was there; Ralph could hear breathing.

'Hello?' he asked again.

There was still no immediate answer, and he was about to say *I'm hanging up now* when Ed Deepneau said, 'I called about your mouth, Ralph. It's trying to get you in trouble.'

The line of cold between his shoulderblades was no longer a line; now it was a thin plate of ice covering him from the nape of his neck to the small of his back.

'Hello, Ed. I saw you on the news today.' It was the only thing he could think of to say. His hand did not seem to be holding the phone so much as to be cramped around it.

'Never mind that, old boy. Just pay attention. I've had

195

a visit from that wide detective who arrested me last month – Leydecker. He just left, in fact.'

Ralph's heart sank, but not as far as he might have feared. After all, Leydecker's going to see Ed wasn't that surprising, was it? He had been very interested in Ralph's story of the airport confrontation in the summer of '92. Very interested indeed.

'Did he?' Ralph asked evenly.

'Detective Leydecker has the idea that I think people – or possibly supernatural beings of some sort – are trucking fetuses out of town in flatbeds and pickup trucks. What a scream, huh?'

Ralph stood beside the sofa, pulling the telephone cord restlessly through his fingers and realizing that he could see dull red light creeping out of the wire like sweat. The light pulsed with the rhythms of Ed's speech.

'You've been telling tales out of school, old boy.'

Ralph was silent.

'Calling the police after I gave that bitch the lesson she so richly deserved didn't bother me,' Ed told him. 'I put it down to . . . well, grandfatherly concern. Or maybe you thought that if she was grateful enough, she might actually spare you a mercy-fuck. After all, you're old but not exactly ready for Jurassic Park yet. You might have thought she'd let you get a finger into her at the very least.'

Ralph said nothing.

'Right, old boy?'

Ralph said nothing.

'You think you're going to rattle me with the silent treatment? Forget it.' But Ed *did* sound rattled, thrown off

196

his stride. It was as if he had made the call with a certain script in his head and Ralph was refusing to read his lines. 'You can't . . . you better not . . .'

'My calling the police after you beat Helen didn't upset you, but your conversation with Leydecker today obviously did. Why's that, Ed? Are you finally starting to have some questions about your behavior? And your thinking, maybe?'

It was Ed's turn to be silent. At last he whispered harshly, 'If you don't take this seriously, Ralph, it would be the worst mistake—'

'Oh, I take it seriously,' Ralph said. 'I saw what you did today, I saw what you did to your wife last month . . . and I saw what you did out by the airport a year ago. Now the police know. I listened to you, Ed, now you listen to me. You're ill. You've had some sort of mental breakdown, you're having delusions—'

'*I don't have to listen to your crap!*' Ed nearly screamed.

'No, you don't. You can hang up. It's your dime, after all. But until you do, I'm going to keep hammering away. Because I liked you, Ed, and I want to like you again. You're a bright guy, delusions or no delusions, and I think you can understand me: Leydecker knows, and Leydecker is going to be watching y—'

'Are you seeing the colors yet?' Ed asked. His voice had become calm again. At the same instant, the red glow around the telephone wire popped out of existence.

'What colors?' Ralph asked at last.

Ed ignored the question. 'You said you liked me. Well, I like you, too. I've *always* liked you. So I'm going to give you some very valuable advice. You're drifting into deep water, and there are things swimming around in the undertow you can't even *conceive* of. You think I'm crazy, but I want to tell you that you don't know what madness is. You don't have the slightest idea. You will, though, if you keep on meddling in things that don't concern you. Take my word for it.'

'What things?' Ralph asked. He tried to keep his voice light, but he was still squeezing the telephone receiver tight enough to make his fingers throb.

'Forces,' Ed replied. 'There are forces at work in Derry that you don't want to know about. There are . . . well, let's just say there are *entities*. They haven't really noticed you yet, but if you keep fooling with me, they will. And you don't want that. Believe me, you don't.'

Forces. Entities.

'You asked me how I found out about all this stuff. Who brought me into the picture. Do you remember that, Ralph?'

'Yes.' He did, too. Now. That had been the last thing Ed had said to him before turning on the big game-show grin and going over to greet the cops. *I've seen the colors since* he *came and told me . . . we'll talk about it later.*

'The doctor told me. The little bald doctor. I think it's him you'll have to answer to if you try to mind my business again. And then God help you.'

'The little bald doctor, uh-huh,' Ralph said. 'Yes, I see. First the Crimson King and the Centurions, now the little bald doctor. I suppose next it'll be—'

'Spare me your sarcasm, Ralph. Just stay away from me and my interests, do you hear? *Stay away.*'

There was a click and Ed was gone. Ralph looked

at the telephone in his hand for a long time, then slowly hung it up.

Just stay away from me and my interests.

Yes, and why not? He had plenty of his own fish to fry.

Ralph walked slowly into the kitchen, stuck a TV dinner (filet of haddock, as a matter of fact) into the oven, and tried to put abortion protests, auras, Ed Deepneau, and the Crimson King out of his mind.

It was easier than he would have expected.

CHAPTER SIX

1

Summer slipped away as it does in Maine, almost unnoticed. Ralph's premature waking continued, and by the time the fall colors had begun to burn in the trees along Harris Avenue, he was opening his eyes around two-fifteen each morning. That was lousy, but he had his appointment with James Roy Hong to look forward to and there had been no repeat of the weird fireworks show he had been treated to after his first meeting with Joe Wyzer. There were occasional flickers around the edges of things, but Ralph found that if he squeezed his eyes shut and counted to five, the flickers were gone when he opened them again.

Well . . . *usually* gone.

Susan Day's speech was scheduled for Friday, the eighth of October, and as September drew toward its conclusion, the protests and the public abortion-on-demand debate sharpened and began to focus more and more on her appearance. Ralph saw Ed on the TV news many times, sometimes in the company of Dan Dalton but more and more frequently on his own, speaking swiftly, cogently, and often with that little gleam of humor not only in his eyes but in his voice.

People liked him, and The Friends of Life was apparently attracting the large membership to which Daily Bread, its political progenitor, had only been able to aspire. There were no more doll-throwing parties or other violent demonstrations, but there were plenty of marches and counter-marches, plenty of name-calling and fist-shaking and angry letters to the editor. Preachers promised damnation; teachers urged moderation and education; half a dozen young women calling themselves The Gay Lesbo Babes for Jesus were arrested for parading in front of The First Baptist Church of Derry with signs which read GET THE FUCK OUT OF MY BODY. A nameless policeman was quoted in the Derry *News* as saying that he hoped Susan Day would come down with the flu or something and have to cancel her appearance.

Ralph received no further communications from Ed, but on September twenty-first he received a postcard from Helen with fourteen jubilant words scrawled across the back: '*Hooray, a job! Derry Public Library! I start next month! See you soon – Helen.*'

Feeling more cheered than he had since the night Helen had called him from the hospital, Ralph went downstairs to show the card to McGovern, but the door of the downstairs apartment was shut and locked.

Lois, then . . . except that Lois was also gone, probably off to one of her card-parties or maybe downtown shopping for yarn and plotting another afghan.

Mildly chagrined and musing on how the people you most wanted to share good news with were hardly ever

201

around when you were all but bursting with it, Ralph wandered down to Strawford Park. And it was there that he found Bill McGovern, sitting on a bench near the soft-ball field and crying.

2

Crying was perhaps too strong a word; *leaking* might have been better. McGovern sat with a handkerchief sticking out of one gnarled fist, watching a mother and her young son play roll-toss along the first-base line of the diamond where the last big softball event of the season — the Intramural City Tournament — had concluded just two days before.

Every now and then he would raise the fist with the handkerchief in it to his face and swipe at his eyes. Ralph, who had never seen McGovern weep — not even at Carolyn's funeral — loitered near the playground for a few moments, wondering if he should approach McGovern or just go back the way he had come.

At last he gathered up his courage and walked over to the park bench. ''Lo, Bill,' he said.

McGovern looked up with eyes that were red, watery, and a trifle embarrassed. He wiped them again and tried a smile. 'Hi, Ralph. You caught me snivelling. Sorry.'

'It's okay,' Ralph said, sitting down. 'I've done my share of it. What's wrong?'

McGovern shrugged, then dabbed at his eyes again. 'Nothing much. I'm suffering the effects of a paradox, that's all.'

'What paradox is that?'

'Something good is happening to one of my oldest friends – the man who hired me for my first teaching position, in fact. He's dying.'

Ralph raised his eyebrows but said nothing.

'He's got pneumonia. His niece will probably haul him off to the hospital today or tomorrow, and they'll put him on a ventilator, at least for awhile, but he's almost certainly dying. I'll celebrate his death when it comes, and I suppose it's that more than anything else that's depressing the shit out of me.' McGovern paused. 'You don't understand a thing I'm saying, do you?'

'Nope,' Ralph said. 'But that's all right.'

McGovern looked into his face, did a doubletake, then snorted. The sound was harsh and thick with his tears, but Ralph thought it was a real laugh just the same, and risked a small return smile.

'Did I say something funny?'

'No,' McGovern said, and clapped him lightly on the shoulder. 'I was just looking at your face, so earnest and sincere – you're really an open book, Ralph – and thinking how much I like you. Sometimes I wish I could *be* you.'

'Not at three in the morning, you wouldn't,' Ralph said quietly.

McGovern sighed and nodded. 'The insomnia.'

'That's right. The insomnia.'

'I'm sorry I laughed, but—'

'No apology necessary, Bill.'

'– but please believe me when I say it was an *admiring* laugh.'

'Who's your friend, and why's it a good thing that he's dying?' Ralph asked. He already had a guess as to what lay at the root of McGovern's paradox; he was not quite as goodheartedly dense as Bill sometimes seemed to think.

'His name's Bob Polhurst, and his pneumonia is good news because he's suffered from Alzheimer's since the summer of '88.'

It was what Ralph had thought . . . although AIDS had crossed his mind, as well. He wondered if that would shock McGovern, and felt a small ripple of amusement at the idea. Then he looked at the man and felt ashamed of his amusement. He knew that when it came to gloom McGovern was at least a semi-pro, but he didn't believe that made his obvious grief over his old friend any less genuine.

'Bob was head of the History Department at Derry High from 1948, when he couldn't have been more than twenty-five, until 1981 or '82. He was a great teacher, one of those fiercely bright people you sometimes find out in the sticks, hiding their lights under bushels. They usually end up heading their departments and running half a dozen extra-curricular activities on the side because they simply don't know how to say no. Bob sure didn't.'

The mother was now leading her little boy past them and toward the little snackbar that would be closing up for the season very soon now. The kid's face had an extra-ordinary translucence, a beauty that was enhanced by the rose-colored aura Ralph saw revolving about his head and moving across his small, lively face in calm waves.

'Can we go home, Mommy?' he asked. 'I want to use my Play-Doh now. I want to make the Clay Family.'

'Let's get something to eat first, big boy – 'kay? Mommy's hungry.'

'Okay.'

There was a hook-shaped scar across the bridge of the boy's nose, and here the rosy glow of his aura deepened to scarlet.

Fell out of his crib when he was eight months old, Ralph thought. *Reaching for the butterflies on the mobile his mom hung from the ceiling. It scared her to death when she ran in and saw all the blood; she thought the poor kid was dying. Patrick, that's his name. She calls him Pat. He's named after his grandfather, and—*

He closed his eyes tightly for a moment. His stomach was fluttering lightly just below his Adam's apple and he was suddenly sure he was going to vomit.

'Ralph?' McGovern asked. 'Are you all right?'

He opened his eyes. No aura, rose-colored or otherwise; just a mother and son heading over to the snackbar for a cold drink, and there was no way, absolutely no way that he could tell she didn't want to take Pat home because Pat's father was drinking again after almost six months on the wagon, and when he drank he got mean—

Stop it, for God's sake stop it.

'I'm okay,' he told McGovern. 'Got a speck in my eye is all. Go on. Finish telling me about your friend.'

'Not much to tell. He was a genius, but over the years I've become convinced that genius is a vastly overrated commodity. I think this country is *full* of geniuses, guys and gals so bright they make your average card-carrying MENSA member look like Fucko the Clown. And I think that most of them are teachers, living and working in small-town obscurity because that's the way they like it. It was certainly the way Bob Polhurst liked it.

'He saw into people in a way that seemed scary to me . . . at first, anyway. After awhile you found out you didn't have to be scared, because Bob was kind, but at first he inspired a sense of dread. You sometimes wondered if it was an ordinary pair of eyes he was using to look at you, or some kind of X-ray machine.'

At the snackbar, the woman was bending down with a small paper cup of soda. The kid reached up for it with both hands, grinning, and took it. He drank thirstily. The rosy glow pulsed briefly into existence around him again as he did, and Ralph knew he had been right: the kid's name was Patrick, and his mother didn't want to take him home. There was no way he could know such things, but he did just the same.

'In those days,' McGovern said, 'if you were from central Maine and not one hundred per cent heterosexual, you tried like hell to *pass* for it. That was the only choice there was, outside of moving to Greenwich Village and wearing a beret and spending Saturday nights in the kind of jazz clubs where they used to applaud by snapping their fingers. Back then, the idea of "coming out of the closet" was ridiculous. For most of us the closet was all there was. Unless you wanted a pack of liquored-up fraternity boys sitting on you in an alley and trying to pull your face off, the *world* was your closet.'

Pat finished his drink and tossed his paper cup on the ground. His mother told him to pick it up and put it in the litter basket, a task he performed with immense good cheer. Then she took his hand and they began to walk slowly out of the park. Ralph watched them go with a feeling of trepidation, hoping the woman's fears and worries would turn out to be unjustified, fearing that they wouldn't be.

'When I applied for a job in the Derry High history department – this was in 1951 – I was fresh from two years teaching in the sticks, way to hell and gone in Lubec, and I figured if I could get along up there with no questions being asked, I could get along anywhere. But Bob took one look at me – hell, *inside* me – with those X-ray eyes of his and just knew. And he wasn't shy, either. "If I decide to offer you this job and you decide to take it, Mr McGovern, may I be assured that there will never be so much as an iota of trouble over the matter of your sexual preference?"

'*Sexual preference,* Ralph! Man, oh man! I'd never even *dreamed* of such a phrase before that day, but it came sliding out of his mouth slicker than a ball-bearing coated with Crisco. I started to get up on my high horse, tell him I didn't have the slightest idea what he was talking about but I resented the hell out of it just the same – on general principles, you might say – and then I took another look at him and decided to save my energy. I might have fooled some people up in Lubec, but I wasn't fooling Bob Polhurst. He wasn't thirty himself yet, probably hadn't been south of Kittery more than a dozen times in his whole life, but he knew everything that mattered about me, and all it had taken him to find it out was one twenty-minute interview.

'"No, sir, not an iota," I said, just as meek as Mary's little lamb.'

McGovern dabbed at his eyes with the handkerchief again, but Ralph had an idea that this time the gesture was mostly theatrical.

'In the twenty-three years before I went off to teach at Derry Community College, Bob taught me everything I know about teaching history and playing chess. He was a brilliant player . . . he certainly would have given that windbag Faye Chapin some hard bark to chew on, I can tell you that. I only beat him once, and that was after the Alzheimer's started to take hold. I never played him again after that.

'And there were other things. He never forgot a joke. He never forgot the birthdays or anniversaries of the people who were close to him – he didn't send cards or give gifts, but he always offered congratulations and good wishes, and no one ever doubted his sincerity. He published over sixty articles on teaching history and on the Civil War, which was his specialty. In 1967 and 1968 he wrote a book called *Later That Summer*, about what happened in the months following Gettysburg. He let me read the manuscript ten years ago, and I think it's the best book on the Civil War I've ever read – the only one that even comes close is a novel called *The Killer Angels*, by Michael Shaara. Bob wouldn't hear of publishing it, though. When I asked him why, he said that I of all people should understand his reasons.'

McGovern paused briefly, looking out across the park, which was filled with green-gold light and black interlacings of shadow which moved and shifted with each breath of wind.

'He said he had a fear of exposure.'

'Okay,' Ralph said. 'I get it.'

'Maybe this sums him up best of all: he used to do the big *Sunday New York Times* crossword puzzle in ink.

I poked him about that once – accused him of *hubris*. He gave me a grin and said, "There's a big difference between pride and optimism, Bill – I'm an optimist, that's all."

'Anyway, you get the picture. A kind man, a good teacher, a brilliant mind. His specialty was the Civil War, and now he doesn't even know what a civil war is, let alone who won ours. Hell, he doesn't even know his own name, and at some point soon – the sooner the better, actually – he's going to die without any idea that he ever lived.'

A middle-aged man in a University of Maine tee-shirt and a pair of ragged blue jeans came shuffling through the playground, carrying a crumpled paper shopping bag under one arm. He stopped beside the snackbar to examine the contents of the waste-barrel, hoping for a returnable or two. As he bent over, Ralph saw the dark green envelope which surrounded him and the lighter green balloon-string which rose, wavering, from the crown of his head. And suddenly he was too tired to close his eyes, too tired to wish it away.

He turned to McGovern and said, 'Ever since last month I've been seeing stuff that –'

'I guess I'm in mourning,' McGovern said, giving his eyes another theatrical wipe, 'although I don't know if it's for Bob or for me. Isn't that a hoot? But if you could have seen how bright he was in those days . . . how goddam scary-bright . . .'

'Bill? You see that guy over there by the snackbar? The one rooting through the trash barrel? I see—'

'Yeah, those guys are all over the place now,' McGovern said, giving the wino (who had found two empty Budweiser cans and tucked them into his bag) a cursory glance before turning to Ralph again. 'I hate being old – I guess maybe that's all it really comes down to. I mean big-time.'

The wino approached their bench in a bent-kneed shuffle, the breeze heralding his arrival with a smell which was not English Leather. His aura – a sprightly and energetic green that made Ralph think of Saint Patrick's Day decorations – went oddly with his subservient posture and sickly grin.

'Say, you guys! How you doon?'

'We've been better,' McGovern said, hoisting the satiric eyebrow, 'and I expect we'll be better again once you shove off.'

The wino looked at McGovern uncertainly, seemed to decide he was a lost cause, and shifted his gaze to Ralph. 'You got a bitta spare change, mister? I gotta get to Dexter. My uncle call me out dere at the Shelter on Neibolt Street, say I can have my old job back at the mill, but only if I—'

'Get lost, chum,' McGovern said.

The wino gave him a brief, anxious glance, and then his bloodshot brown eyes rolled back to Ralph again. 'Dass a good job, you know? I could have it back, but on'y if I get dere today. Dere's a bus—'

Ralph reached into his pocket, found a quarter and a dime, and dropped them into the outstretched hand. The wino grinned. The aura surrounding him brightened, then suddenly disappeared. Ralph found that a great relief.

'Hey, great! Thank you, mister!'

'Don't mention it,' Ralph said.

The wino lurched off in the direction of the Shop 'n

Save, where such brands as Night Train, Old Duke, and Silver Satin were always on sale.

Oh shit, Ralph, would it hurt you to be a little charitable in your head, as well? he asked himself. *Go another half a mile in that direction, you come to the bus station.*

True, but Ralph had lived long enough to know there was a world of difference between charitable thinking and illusions. If the wino with the dark green aura was going to the bus station, then Ralph was going to Washington to be Secretary of State.

'You shouldn't do that, Ralph,' McGovern said reprovingly. 'It just encourages them.'

'I suppose,' Ralph said wearily.

'What were you saying when we were so rudely interrupted?'

The idea of telling McGovern about the auras now seemed an incredibly bad one, and he could not for the life of him imagine how he had gotten so close to doing it. The insomnia, of course – that was the only answer. It had done a number on his judgement as well as his short-term memory and sense of perception.

'That I got something in the mail this morning,' Ralph said. 'I thought it might cheer you up.' He passed Helen's postcard over to McGovern, who read it and then reread it. The second time through, his long, horsey face broke into a broad grin. The combination of relief and honest pleasure in that expression made Ralph forgive McGovern his self-indulgent bathos at once. It was easy to forget that Bill could be generous as well as pompous.

'Say, this is great, isn't it? A job!'

'It sure is. Want to celebrate with some lunch? There's

211

a nice little diner two doors down from the Rite Aid – Day Break, Sun Down, it's called. Maybe a little ferny, but—'

'Thanks, but I promised Bob's niece I'd go over and sit with him awhile. Of course he's doesn't have the slightest idea of who I am, but that doesn't matter, because *I* know who *he* is. You *capisce*?'

'Yep,' Ralph said. 'A raincheck, then?'

'You got it.' McGovern scanned the message on the postcard again, still grinning. 'This is the berries – the absolute berries!'

Ralph laughed at this winsome old expression. 'I thought so, too.'

'I would have bet you five bucks she was going to walk right back into her marriage to that weirdo, and pushing the baby in front of her in its damn stroller . . . but I would have been glad to lose the money. I suppose that sounds crazy.'

'A little,' Ralph said, but only because he knew it was what McGovern expected to hear. What he really thought was that Bill McGovern had just summed up his own character and world-view more succinctly than Ralph ever could have done himself.

'Nice to know someone's getting better instead of worse, huh?'

'You bet.'

'Has Lois seen that yet?'

Ralph shook his head. 'She's not home. I'll show it to her when I see her, though.'

'You do that. Are you sleeping any better, Ralph?'

'I'm doing okay, I guess.'

'Good. You look a little better. A little stronger. We can't give in, Ralph, that's the important thing. Am I right?'

'I guess you are,' Ralph said, and sighed. 'I guess you are, at that.'

3

Two days later Ralph sat at his kitchen table, slowly eating a bowl of bran flakes he didn't really want (but supposed in some vague way to be good for him) and looking at the front page of the Derry *News*. He had skimmed the lead story quickly, but it was the photo that kept drawing his eye back; it seemed to express all the bad feelings he had been living with over the last month without really explaining any of them.

Ralph thought the headline over the photograph – WOMANCARE DEMONSTRATION SPARKS VIOLENCE – didn't reflect the story which followed, but that didn't surprise him; he had been reading the *News* for years and had gotten used to its biases, which included a firm anti-abortion stance. Still, the paper had been careful to distance itself from The Friends of Life in that day's tut-tut, now-you-boys-just-stop-it editorial, and Ralph wasn't surprised. The Friends had gathered in the parking lot adjacent to both WomanCare and Derry Home Hospital, waiting for a group of about two hundred pro-choice marchers who were walking across town from the Civic Center. Most of the marchers were carrying signs with pictures of Susan Day and the slogan CHOICE, NOT FEAR on them.

The marchers' idea was to gather supporters as they went, like a snowball rolling downhill. At WomanCare there would be a short rally – intended to pump people up for the coming Susan Day speech – followed by refreshments. The rally never happened. As the pro-choice marchers approached the parking lot, the Friends of Life people rushed out and blocked the road, holding their own signs (MURDER IS MURDER, SUSAN DAY STAY AWAY, STOP THE SLAUGHTER OF THE INNOCENTS) in front of them like shields.

The marchers had been escorted by police, but no one had been prepared for the speed with which the heckling and angry words escalated into kicks and punches. It had begun with one of The Friends of Life recognizing her own daughter among the pro-choice people. The older woman had dropped her sign and charged the younger. The daughter's boyfriend had caught the older woman and tried to restrain her. When Mom opened his face with her fingernails, the young man had thrown her to the ground. That had ignited a ten-minute mêlée and provoked more than thirty arrests, split roughly half and half between the two groups.

The picture on the front page of this morning's *News* featured Hamilton Davenport and Dan Dalton. The photographer had caught Davenport in a snarl which was entirely unlike his usual look of calm self-satisfaction. One fist was raised over his head in a primitive gesture of triumph. Facing him – and wearing Ham's CHOICE, NOT FEAR sign around the top of his head like a surreal cardboard halo – was The Friends of Life's *grand fromage*. Dalton's eyes were dazed, his mouth slack. The high-contrast black and white photo made the blood flowing from his nostrils look like chocolate sauce.

Ralph would look away from this for awhile, try to concentrate on finishing his cereal, and then he would remember the day last summer when he had first seen one of the pseudo 'wanted' posters that were now pasted up all over Derry – the day he had nearly fainted outside Strawford Park. Mostly it was their faces his mind fixed on: Davenport's full of angry intensity as he peered into the dusty show window of Secondhand Rose, Secondhand Clothes, Dalton's wearing a small, disdainful smile that seemed to suggest that an ape like Hamilton Davenport could not be expected to understand the higher morality of the abortion issue, and they both knew it.

Ralph would think of those two expressions and the distance between the men who wore them, and after awhile his dismayed eyes would wander back to the news photo. Two men stood close behind Dalton, both carrying pro-life signs and watching the confrontation intently. Ralph didn't recognize the skinny man with the hornrimmed glasses and the cloud of receding gray hair, but he knew the man beside him. It was Ed Deepneau. Yet in this context, Ed seemed almost not to matter. What drew Ralph – and frightened him – were the faces of the two men who had done business next door to each other on Lower Witcham Street for years – Davenport with his caveman's snarl and clenched fist, Dalton with his dazed eyes and bloody nose.

He thought, *If you're not careful with your passions, this is where they get you. But this is where things had better stop, because—*

'Because if those two had had guns, they'd've shot each other,' he muttered, and at that moment the doorbell rang – the one down on the front porch. Ralph got up, looked at the picture again, and felt a kind of vertigo sweep through him. With it came an odd, dismal surety: it was Ed down there, and God knew what he might want.

Don't answer it then, Ralph!

He stood by the kitchen table for a long undecided moment, wishing bitterly that he could cut through the fog that seemed to have taken up permanent residence in his head this year. Then the doorbell chimed again and he found he *had* decided. It didn't matter if that was Saddam Hussein down there; this was *his* place, and he wasn't going to cower in it like a whipped cur.

Ralph crossed the living room, opened the door to the hall, and went down the shadowy front stairs.

4

Halfway down he relaxed a little. The top half of the door which gave on the front porch was composed of heavy glass panes. They distorted the view, but not so much that Ralph could not see that his two visitors were both women. He guessed at once who one of them must be and hurried the rest of the way down, running one hand lightly over the banister. He threw the door open and there was Helen Deepneau with a tote-bag (BABY FIRST-AID STATION was printed on the side) slung over one shoulder and Natalie peering over the other, her eyes as bright as the eyes of a cartoon mouse. Helen was smiling hopefully and a little nervously.

Natalie's face suddenly lit up and she began to bounce up and down in the Papoose carrier Helen was wearing, waving her arms excitedly in Ralph's direction.

She remembers me, Ralph thought. *How about that.* And as he reached out and let one of the waving hands grasp his right index finger, his eyes flooded with tears.

'Ralph?' Helen asked. 'Are you okay?'

He smiled, nodded, stepped forward, and hugged her. He felt Helen lock her own arms around his neck. For a moment he was dizzy with the smell of her perfume, mingled with the milky smell of healthy baby, and then she gave his ear a dazzling smack and let him go.

'You *are* okay, aren't you?' she asked. There were tears in her eyes, too, but Ralph barely noticed them; he was too busy taking inventory, wanting to make sure that no signs of the beating remained. So far as he could see, none did. She looked flawless.

'Better right now than in weeks,' he said. 'You are *such* a sight for sore eyes. You too, Nat.' He kissed the small, chubby hand that was still wrapped around his finger, and was not entirely surprised to see the ghostly gray-blue lip-print his mouth left behind. It faded almost as soon as he had noted it and he hugged Helen again, mostly to make sure that she was really there.

'Dear Ralph,' she murmured in his ear. 'Dear, sweet Ralph.'

He felt a stirring in his groin, apparently brought on by the combination of her light perfume and the gentle puffs her words made against the cup of his ear . . . and then he remembered another voice in his ear. Ed's voice. *I called about your mouth, Ralph. It's trying to get you in trouble.*

Ralph let her go and held her at arm's length, still smiling. 'You're a sight for sore eyes, Helen. I'll be damned if you're not.'

'You are, too. I'd like you to meet a friend of mine. Ralph Roberts, Gretchen Tillbury. Gretchen, Ralph.'

Ralph turned toward the other woman and took his first good look at her as he carefully folded his large, gnarled hand over her slim white one. She was the kind of woman that made a man (even one who had left his sixties behind) want to stand up straight and suck in his gut. She was very tall, perhaps six feet, and she was blonde, but that wasn't it. There was something else – something that was like a smell, or a vibration, or

(*an aura*)

yes, all right, like an aura. She was, quite simply, a woman you couldn't not look at, couldn't not think about, couldn't not speculate about.

Ralph remembered Helen's telling him that Gretchen's husband had cut her leg open with a kitchen knife and left her to bleed to death. He wondered how any man could do such a thing; how any man could touch a creature such as this with anything but awe.

Also a little lust, maybe, once he got beyond the 'She walks in beauty like the night' stage. And just by the way, Ralph, this might be a really good time to reel your eyes back into their sockets.

'Very pleased to meet you,' he said, letting go of her hand. 'Helen told me about how you came to see her in the hospital. Thank you for helping her.'

'Helen was a pleasure to help,' Gretchen said, and gave him a dazzling smile. 'She's the kind of woman that makes it all worthwhile, actually . . . but I have an idea you already know that.'

'I guess I might at that,' Ralph said. 'Have you got time for a cup of coffee? Please say yes.'

Gretchen glanced at Helen, who nodded.

'That would be fine,' Helen said. 'Because . . . well . . .'

'This isn't entirely a social call, is it?' Ralph asked, looking from Helen to Gretchen Tillbury and then back to Helen again.

'No,' Helen said. 'There's something we need to talk to you about, Ralph.'

5

As soon as they had reached the top of the gloomy front stairs, Natalie began to wriggle impatiently around in the Papoose carrier and to talk in that imperious baby pig Latin that would all too soon be replaced by actual words.

'Can I hold her?' Ralph asked.

'All right,' Helen said. 'If she cries, I'll take her right back. Promise.'

'Deal.'

But the Exalted & Revered Baby didn't cry. As soon as Ralph had hoisted her out of the Papoose, she slung an arm companionably around his neck and cozied her bottom into the crook of his right arm as if it were her own private easy-chair.

'Wow,' Gretchen said. 'I'm impressed.'

'Blig!' Natalie said, seizing Ralph's lower lip and pulling it out like a windowshade. 'Ganna-wig! Andoo-sis!'

'I think she just said something about the Andrews Sisters,' Ralph said. Helen threw her head back and laughed her hearty laugh, the one that seemed to come all the way up from her heels. Ralph didn't realize how much he had missed it until he heard it.

219

Natalie let Ralph's lower lip snap back as he led them into the kitchen, the sunniest room of the house at this time of day. He saw Helen looking around curiously as he turned on the Bunn, and realized she hadn't been here for a long time. Too long. She picked up the picture of Carolyn that stood on the kitchen table and looked at it closely, a little smile playing about the corners of her lips. The sun lit the tips of her hair, which had been cropped short, making a kind of corona around her head, and Ralph had a sudden revelation: he loved Helen in large part because Carolyn had loved her – they had both been allowed into the deeper ranges of Carolyn's heart and mind.

'She was so pretty,' Helen murmured. 'Wasn't she, Ralph?'

'Yes,' he said, putting out cups (and being careful to set them beyond the reach of Natalie's restless, interested hands). 'That was taken just a month or two before the headaches started. I suppose it's eccentric to keep a framed studio portrait on the kitchen table in front of the sugar-bowl, but this is the room where I seem to spend most of my time lately, so . . .'

'I think it's a lovely place for it,' Gretchen said. Her voice was low, sweetly husky. Ralph thought, *If she'd been the one to whisper in my ear, I bet the old trouser-mouse would have done a little more than just turn over in its sleep.*

'I do, too,' Helen said. She gave him a fragile, not-quite-eye-contact smile, then slipped the pink tote-bag off her shoulder and set it on the counter. Natalie began to gabble impatiently and hold her hands out again as soon as she saw the plastic shell of the Playtex Nurser. Ralph had a vivid but mercifully brief flash of memory: Helen staggering toward the Red Apple, one eye puffed shut, her cheek lashed with beads of blood, carrying Nat on one hip, the way a teenager might carry a textbook.

'Want to give it a try, old fella?' Helen asked. Her smile had strengthened a little and she was meeting his eye again.

'Sure, why not? But the coffee—'

'I'll take care of the coffee, Daddy-O,' Gretchen said. 'Made a million cups in my time. Is there half-and-half?'

'In the fridge.' Ralph sat down at the table, letting Natalie rest the back of her head in the hollow of his shoulder and grasp the bottle with her tiny, fascinating hands. This she did with complete assurance, guiding the nipple into her mouth and beginning to suck at once. Ralph grinned up at Helen and pretended not to see that she had begun to cry a little again. 'They learn fast, don't they?'

'Yes,' she said, and pulled a paper towel off the roll mounted on the wall by the sink. She wiped her eyes with it. 'I can't get over how easy she is with you, Ralph – she wasn't that way before, was she?'

'I don't really remember,' he lied. She hadn't been. Not standoffish, no, but a long way from this comfortable.

'Keep pushing up on the plastic liner inside the bottle, okay? Otherwise she'll swallow a lot of air and get all gassy.'

'Roger.' He glanced over at Gretchen. 'Doing okay?'

'Fine. How do you take it, Ralph?'

'Just in a cup's fine.'

She laughed and put the cup on the table out of Natalie's reach. When she sat down and crossed her legs,

Ralph checked – he was helpless not to. When he looked up again, Gretchen was wearing a small, ironic smile.

What the hell, Ralph thought. No goat like an old goat, I guess. Even an old goat that can't manage much more than two or two and a half hours' worth of sleep a night.

'Tell me about your job,' he said as Helen sat down and sipped her coffee.

'Well, I think they ought to make Mike Hanlon's birthday a national holiday – does that tell you anything?'

'A little, yes,' Ralph said, smiling.

'I was all but positive I'd have to leave Derry. I sent away for applications to libraries as far south as Portsmouth, but I felt sick doing it. I'm going on thirty-one and I've only lived here for six of those years, but Derry feels like home – I can't explain it, but it's the truth.'

'You don't have to explain it, Helen. I think home's just one of those things that happens to a person, like their complexion or the color of their eyes.'

Gretchen was nodding. 'Yes,' she said. 'Just like that.'

'Mike called Monday and told me the assistant's position in the Children's Library had opened up. I could hardly believe it. I mean, I've been walking around all week just pinching myself. Haven't I, Gretchen?'

'Well, you've been very happy,' Gretchen said, 'and that's been very good to see.'

She smiled at Helen, and for Ralph that smile was a revelation. He suddenly understood that he could look at Gretchen Tillbury all he wanted, and it wouldn't make any difference. If the only man in this room had been Tom Cruise, it still would have made no difference. He wondered if Helen knew, and then scolded himself for his foolishness. Helen was many things, but stupid wasn't one of them.

'When do you start?' he asked her.

'Columbus Day week,' she said. 'The twelfth. Afternoons and evenings. The salary's not exactly a king's ransom, but it'll be enough to keep us through the winter no matter how the . . . the rest of my situation works out. Isn't it great, Ralph?'

'Yes,' he said. 'Very great.'

The baby had drunk half the bottle and now showed signs of losing interest. The nipple popped halfway out of her mouth, and a little rill of milk ran down from the corner of her lips toward her chin. Ralph reached to wipe it away, and his fingers left a series of delicate gray-blue lines in the air.

Baby Natalie snatched at them, then laughed as they dissolved in her fist. Ralph's breath caught in his throat.

She sees. The baby sees what I see.

That's nuts, Ralph. That's nuts and you know it.

Except he knew no such thing. He had just *seen* it – had seen Nat try to grab the aural contrails his fingers left behind.

'Ralph?' Helen asked. 'Are you all right?'

'Sure.' He looked up and saw that Helen was now surrounded by a luxurious ivory-colored aura. It had the satiny look of an expensive slip. The balloon-string floating up from it was an identical shade of ivory, and as broad and flat as the ribbon on a wedding present. The aura surrounding Gretchen Tillbury was a dark orange shading to yellow at the edges. 'Will you be moving back into the house?'

223

Helen and Gretchen exchanged another of those glances, but Ralph barely noticed. He didn't need to observe their faces or gestures or body language to read their feelings, he discovered; he only had to look at their auras. The lemony tints at the edges of Gretchen's now darkened, so that the whole was a uniform orange. Helen's, meanwhile, simultaneously pulled in and brightened until it was hard to look at. Helen was afraid to go back. Gretchen knew it, and was infuriated by it.

And her own helplessness, Ralph thought. *That infuriates her even more.*

'I'm going to stay at High Ridge awhile longer,' Helen was saying. 'Maybe until winter. Nat and I will move back into town eventually, I imagine, but the house is going up for sale. If someone actually buys it — and with the real estate market the way it is that looks like a pretty big question mark — the money goes into an escrow account. That account will be divided according to the decree. You know — the divorce decree.'

Her lower lip was trembling. Her aura had grown still tighter; it now fit her body almost like a second skin, and Ralph could see minute red flashes skimming through it. They looked like sparks dancing over an incinerator. He reached out across the table, took her hand, squeezed it. She smiled at him gratefully.

'You're telling me two things,' he said. 'That you're going ahead with the divorce and that you're still scared of him.'

'She's been regularly battered and abused for the last two years of her marriage,' Gretchen said. 'Of *course* she's still scared of him.' She spoke quietly, calmly, reasonably, but looking at her aura now was like looking through the small isinglass window you used to find in the doors of coal-furnaces.

He looked down at the baby and saw her now surrounded in her own gauzy, brilliant cloud of wedding-satin. It was smaller than her mother's, but otherwise identical . . . like her blue eyes and auburn hair. Natalie's balloon-string rose from the top of her head in a pure white ribbon that floated all the way to the ceiling and then actually coiled there in an ethereal heap beside the light-fixture. When a breath of breeze puffed in through the open window by the stove, he saw the wide white band bell and ripple. He glanced up and saw Helen's and Gretchen's balloon-strings were also rippling.

And if I could see my own, it would be doing the same thing, he thought. *It's real — whatever that two-and-two-make-four part of my mind may think, the auras are real. They're real and I'm seeing them.*

He waited for the inevitable demurral, but this time none came.

'I feel like I'm spending most of my time in an emotional washing-machine these days,' Helen said. 'My mom's mad at me . . . she's done everything but call me a quitter outright . . . and sometimes I *feel* like a quitter . . . ashamed . . .'

'You have nothing to be ashamed of,' Ralph said. He glanced up at Natalie's balloon-string again, wavering in the breeze. It was beautiful, but he felt no urge to touch it; some deep instinct told him that might be dangerous for both of them.

'I guess I know that,' Helen said, 'but girls go through

a lot of indoctrination. It's like, "Here's your Barbie, here's your Ken, here's your Hostess Play Kitchen. Learn well, because when the real stuff comes along it'll be your job to take care of it, and if any of it gets broken, you'll get the blame." And I think I could have gone down the line with that – I really do. Except no one told me that in some marriages Ken goes nuts. Does that sound self-indulgent?'

'No. That's pretty much what happened, so far as I can see.'

Helen laughed – a jagged, bitter, guilty sound. 'Don't try to tell my mother that. She refuses to believe Ed ever did anything more than give me a husbandly swat on the fanny once in awhile . . . just to get me moving in the right direction again if I happened to slip off-course. She thinks I imagined the rest. She doesn't come right out and say it, but I hear it in her voice every time we talk on the phone.'

'*I* don't think you imagined it,' Ralph said. 'I saw you, remember? And I was there when you begged me not to call the police.'

He felt his thigh squeezed beneath the table and looked up, startled. Gretchen Tillbury gave him a very slight nod and another squeeze – this one more emphatic.

'Yes,' Helen said. 'You *were* there, weren't you?' She smiled a little, which was good, but what was happening to her aura was better – those tiny red flickers were fading, and the aura itself was spreading out again.

No, he thought. *Not spreading out. Loosening. Relaxing.*

Helen got up and came around the table. 'Nat's bailing out on you – better let me take her.'

Ralph looked down and saw Nat looking across the room with heavy, fascinated eyes. He followed her gaze and saw the little vase standing on the windowsill beside the sink. He had filled it with fall flowers less than two hours ago and now a low green mist was sizzling off the stems and surrounding the blooms with a faint, misty glow.

I'm watching them breathe their last, Ralph thought. *Oh my God, I'm never going to pick another flower in my life. I promise.*

Helen took the baby gently from his arms. Nat went tractably enough, although her eyes never left the sizzling flowers as her mother went back around the table, sat down, and nestled her in the crook of her arm.

Gretchen tapped the face of her watch lightly. 'If we're going to make that meeting at noon—'

'Yes, of course,' Helen said, a little apologetically. 'We're on the official Susan Day Welcoming Committee,' she told Ralph, 'and in this case that's not quite as Junior League as it sounds. Our main job really isn't to welcome her but to help protect her.'

'Is that going to be a problem, do you think?'

'It'll be tense, let's put it that way,' Gretchen said. 'She's got half a dozen of her own security people, and they've been sending us turn-around faxes of all the Derry-related threats she's received. It's standard operating procedure with them – she's been in a lot of people's faces for a lot of years. They're keeping us in the picture, but they're also making sure we understand that, because we're the inviting group, her safety is WomanCare's responsibility as well as theirs.'

Ralph opened his mouth to ask if there had been

many threats, but he supposed he already knew the answer to that question. He'd lived in Derry for seventy years, off and on, and he knew it was a dangerous machine – there were a lot of sharp points and cutting edges just below the surface. That was true of a lot of cities, of course, but in Derry there had always seemed to be an extra dimension to the ugliness. Helen had called it home, and it was his home, too, but—

He found himself remembering something which had happened almost ten years ago, shortly after the annual Canal Days Festival had ended. Three boys had thrown an unassuming and inoffensive young gay man named Adrian Mellon into the Kenduskeag after repeatedly biting and stabbing him; it was rumored they had stood there on the bridge behind the Falcon Tavern and watched him die. They'd told the police they hadn't liked the hat he was wearing. That was also Derry, and only a fool would ignore the fact.

As if this memory had led him to it (perhaps it had), Ralph looked at the photo on the front page of today's paper again – Ham Davenport with his upraised fist, Dan Dalton with his bloody nose and dazed eyes, wearing Ham's sign on his head.

'How many threats?' he asked. 'Over a dozen?'

'About thirty,' Gretchen said. 'Of those, her security people take half a dozen seriously. Two are threats to blow up the Civic Center if she doesn't cancel. One – this is a real honey – is from someone who says he's got a Big Squirt water-gun filled with battery acid. "If I make a direct hit, not even your dyke friends will be able to look at you without throwing up," that one says.'

'Nice,' Ralph said.

'It brings us to the point, anyway,' Gretchen said. She rummaged in her bag, brought out a small can with a red top, and put it on the table. 'A little present from all your grateful friends at WomanCare.'

Ralph picked the can up. On one side was a picture of a woman spraying a cloud of gas at a man wearing a slouch hat and a Beagle Boys-type eye-mask. On the other was a single word in bright red capital letters:

BODYGUARD

'What is this?' he asked, shocked in spite of himself. 'Mace?'

'No,' Gretchen said. 'Mace is a risky proposition in Maine, legally speaking. This stuff is much milder . . . but if you give somebody a faceful, they won't even think of hassling you for at least a couple of minutes. It numbs the skin, irritates the eyes, and causes nausea.'

Ralph took the cap off the can, looked at the red aerosol nozzle beneath, then replaced the cap. 'Good Christ, woman, why would I want to lug around a can of this stuff?'

'Because you've been officially designated a Centurion,' Gretchen said.

'A *what*?' Ralph asked.

'A Centurion,' Helen repeated. Nat was fast asleep in her arms, and Ralph realized the auras were gone again. 'It's what The Friends of Life call their major enemies – the ringleaders of the opposition.'

'Okay,' Ralph said, 'I've got it now. Ed talked about

people he called Centurions on the day he . . . assaulted you. He talked about a lot of things that day, though, and all of them were crazy.'

'Yes, Ed's at the bottom of it, and he *is* crazy,' Helen said. 'We don't think he's mentioned this Centurion business except to a small inner circle – people who are almost as gonzo as he is. The rest of The Friends of Life . . . I don't think they have any idea. I mean, did you? Until last month, did *you* have any idea that he was crazy?'

Ralph shook his head.

'Hawking Labs finally fired him,' Helen said. 'Yesterday. They held onto him as long as they could – he's great at what he does, and they had a lot invested in him – but in the end they had to let him go. Three months' severance pay in lieu of notice . . . not bad for a guy who beats up his wife and throws dolls loaded with fake blood at the windows of the local women's clinic.' She tapped the newspaper. 'This last demonstration was the final straw. It's the third or fourth time he's been arrested since he got involved with The Friends of Life.'

'You have someone inside, don't you?' Ralph said. 'That's how you know all this.'

Gretchen smiled. 'We're not the only ones who've got someone at least partway inside; we have a running joke that there really *are* no Friends of Life, just a bunch of double agents. Derry PD's got someone; the State Police do, too. And those are just the ones our . . . our *person* . . . knows about. Hell, the FBI could be monitoring them, as well. The Friends of Life are eminently infiltratable, Ralph, because they're convinced that, deep down, *everyone* is on their side. But we believe that our person is the only one who's gotten in toward the middle, and this person says that Dan Dalton is just the tail Ed Deepneau wags.'

'I guessed that the first time I saw them together on the TV news,' Ralph said.

Gretchen got up, gathered the coffee cups, took them over to the sink, and began to rinse them. 'I've been active in the women's movement for thirteen years now, and I've seen a lot of crazy shit, but I've never seen anything like this. He's got these dopes believing that women in Derry are undergoing involuntary abortions, that half of them haven't even realized they're pregnant before the Centurions come in the night and take their babies.'

'Has he told them about the incinerator over in Newport?' Ralph asked 'The one that's really a baby crematorium?'

Gretchen turned from the sink, her eyes wide. 'How did *you* know about that?'

'Oh, I got the lowdown from Ed himself, up close and in person. Starting in July of '92.' He hesitated for just a moment, then gave them an account of the day he had met Ed out by the airport, and how Ed had accused the man in the pickup of hauling dead babies in the barrels marked WEED-GO. Helen listened silently, her eyes growing steadily wider and rounder. 'He was going on about the same stuff on the day he beat you up,' Ralph finished, 'but he'd embellished it considerably by then.'

'That probably explains why he's fixated on you,' Gretchen said, 'but in a very real sense, the why doesn't matter. The fact is, he's given his nuttier friends a list of these so-called Centurions. We don't know everyone who's

231

on it, but I am, and Helen is, and Susan Day, of course . . . and you.'

Why me? Ralph almost asked, then recognized it as another pointless question. Maybe Ed had targeted him because he had called the cops after Ed had beaten Helen; more likely it had happened for no understandable reason at all. Ralph remembered reading somewhere that David Berkowitz — also known as the Son of Sam — claimed to have killed on some occasions under instructions from his dog.

'What do you expect them to try?' Ralph asked. 'Armed assault, like in a Chuck Norris movie?'

He smiled, but Gretchen did not answer it. 'The thing is, we don't know *what* they might try,' she said. 'The most likely answer is nothing at all. Then again, Ed or one of the others might take it into his head to try and push you out your own kitchen window. The spray is basically nothing but watered-down teargas. A little insurance policy, that's all.'

'Insurance,' he said thoughtfully.

'You're in very select company,' Helen said with a wan smile. 'The only other male Centurion on their list — that we know about, anyway — is Mayor Cohen.'

'Did you give him one of these?' Ralph asked, picking up the aerosol can. It looked no more dangerous than the free samples of shaving cream he got in the mail from time to time.

'We didn't need to,' Gretchen said. She looked at her watch again. Helen saw the gesture and stood up with the sleeping baby in her arms. 'He's got a license to carry a concealed weapon.'

'How would you know a thing like that?' Ralph asked.

'We checked the files at City Hall,' she said, and grinned. 'Gun permits are a matter of public record.'

'Oh.' A thought occurred to him. 'What about Ed? Did you check on him? Does he have one?'

'Nope,' she said. 'But guys like Ed don't necessarily apply for weapons permits once they get past a certain point . . . you know that, don't you?'

'Yes,' Ralph replied, also getting up. 'I suppose I do. What about you guys? Are you watching out?'

'You bet, Daddy-O. You bet we are.'

He nodded, but wasn't entirely satisfied. There was a faintly patronizing tone in her voice that he didn't like, as if the very question were a silly one. But it *wasn't* silly, and if she didn't know that, she and her friends could be in trouble down the line. Bad trouble.

'I hope so,' he said. 'I really do. Can I carry Nat downstairs for you, Helen?'

'Better not − you'd wake her.' She looked at him gravely. 'Would you carry that spray for me, Ralph? I can't stand the thought of you being hurt just because you tried to help me and he's got some crazy bee in his bonnet.'

'I'll think about it very seriously. Will that do?'

'I guess it will have to.' She looked at him closely, her eyes searching his face. 'You look much better than the last time I saw you − you're sleeping again, aren't you?'

He grinned. 'Well, to tell you the truth, I'm still having my problems, but I *must* be getting better, because people keep telling me that.'

She stood on tiptoe and kissed the corner of his

mouth. 'We'll be in touch, won't we? I mean, we'll *stay* in touch.'

'I'll do my part if you'll do yours, sweetie.'

She smiled. 'You can count on that, Ralph – you're the nicest male Centurion I know.'

They all laughed at that, so hard that Natalie woke up and looked around at them in sleepy surprise.

6

After he had seen the women off (I'M PRO-CHOICE, AND I *VOTE!* read the sticker on the rear bumper of Gretchen Tillbury's Accord fastback), Ralph climbed slowly up to the second floor again. Weariness dragged at his heels like invisible weights. Once in the kitchen he looked first at the vase of flowers, trying to see that strange and gorgeous green mist rising from the stems. Nothing. Then he picked up the aerosol and re-examined the cartoon on the side of the can. One Menaced Woman, heroically warding off her attacker; one Bad Man, complete with eye-mask and slouch hat. No shades of gray here; just a case of go ahead, punk, make my day.

It occurred to Ralph that Ed's madness was catching. There were women all over Derry – Gretchen Tillbury and his own sweet Helen among them – walking around with these little spray-cans in their purses, and all the cans really said the same thing: *I'm afraid. The bad men in the masks and the slouch hats have arrived in Derry and I'm afraid.*

Ralph wanted no part of it. Standing on tiptoe, he put the can of Bodyguard on top of the kitchen cabinet beside the sink, then shrugged into his old gray leather jacket. He would go up to the picnic area near the airport and see if he could find a game of chess. Lacking that, maybe a few rounds of cribbage.

He paused in the kitchen doorway, looking fixedly at the flowers, trying to *make* that sizzling green mist come. Nothing happened.

But it was there. You saw it; Natalie did, too.

But had she? Had she really? Babies were always goggling at stuff, *everything* amazed them, so how could he know for sure?

'I just do,' he said to the empty apartment. Correct. The green mist rising from the stems of the flowers had been there, *all* the auras had been there, and . . .

'And they're *still* there,' he said, and did not know if he should be relieved or appalled by the firmness he heard in his own voice.

For right now, why don't you try being neither, sweetheart?

His thought, Carolyn's voice, good advice.

Ralph locked up his apartment and went out into the Derry of the Old Crocks, looking for a game of chess.

CHAPTER SEVEN

1

When Ralph came walking up Harris Avenue to his apartment on October 2nd, with a couple of recycled Elmer Kelton Westerns from Back Pages in one hand, he saw that someone was sitting on the porch steps with his own book. The visitor wasn't reading, however; he was watching with dreamy intensity as the warm wind which had been blowing all day harvested the yellow and gold leaves from the oaks and the three surviving elms across the street.

Ralph came closer, observing the thin white hair flying around the skull of the man on the porch, and the way all his bulk seemed to have run into his belly, hips, and bottom. That wide center section, coupled with the scrawny neck, narrow chest, and spindly legs clad in old green flannel pants, gave him the look of a man wearing an inner tube beneath his clothes. Even from a hundred and fifty yards away, there was really no question about who the visitor was: Dorrance Marstellar.

Sighing, Ralph walked the rest of the way up to his building. Dorrance, seemingly hypnotized by the bright falling leaves, did not look around until Ralph's shadow dropped across him. Then he turned, craned his neck, and smiled his sweet, strangely vulnerable smile.

Faye Chapin, Don Veazie, and some of the other oldtimers who hung out at the picnic area up by Runway 3 (they would retire to the Jackson Street Billiard Emporium once Indian summer broke and the weather turned cold) saw that smile as just another indicator that Old Dor, poetry books or no poetry books, was essentially brainless. Don Veazie, nobody's idea of Mr Sensitivity, had fallen into the habit of calling Dorrance Old Chief Dumbhead, and Faye had once told Ralph that he, Faye, wasn't in the least surprised that Old Dor had lived to the age of half-past ninety. 'People who don't have any furniture on their upper storey *always* live the longest,' he had explained to Ralph earlier that year. 'They don't have anything to worry about. That keeps their blood-pressure down and they ain't so likely to blow a valve or throw a rod.'

Ralph, however, was not so sure. The sweetness in Dorrance's smile did not make the old man look empty-headed to him; it made him look somehow ethereal and knowing at the same time . . . sort of like a small-town Merlin. None the less, he could have done without a visit from Dor today; this morning he had set a new record, waking at 1:58 a.m., and he was exhausted. He only wanted to sit in his own living room, drink coffee, and try to read one of the Westerns he had picked up downtown. Maybe later on he would take another stab at napping.

'Hello,' Dorrance said. The book he was holding was a paperback – *Cemetery Nights,* by a man named Stephen Dobyns.

'Hello, Dor,' he said. 'Good book?'

237

Dorrance looked down at the book as if he'd forgotten he had one, then smiled and nodded. 'Yes, very good. He writes poems that are like stories. I don't always like that, but sometimes I do.'

'That's good. Listen, Dor, it's great to see you, but the walk up the hill kind of tired me out, so maybe we could visit another t—'

'Oh, that's all right,' Dorrance said, standing up. There was a faint cinnamony smell about him that always made Ralph think of Egyptian mummies kept behind red velvet ropes in shadowy museums. His face was almost without lines except for the tiny sprays of crow's feet around his eyes, but his age was unmistakable (and a little scary): his blue eyes were faded to the watery gray of an April sky and his skin had a translucent clarity that reminded Ralph of Nat's skin. His lips were loose and almost lavender in color. They made little smacking sounds when he spoke. 'That's all right, I didn't come to visit; I came to give you a message.'

'What message? From who?'

'I don't know who it's *from,*' Dorrance said, giving Ralph a look that suggested he thought Ralph was either being foolish or playing dumb. 'I don't mess in with long-time business. I told *you* not to, either, don't you remember?'

Ralph *did* remember something, but he was damned if he knew exactly what. Nor did he care. He was tired, and he had already had to listen to a fair amount of tiresome proselytizing on the subject of Susan Day from Ham Davenport. He had no urge to go round and round with Dorrance Marstellar on top of that, no matter how beautiful this Saturday morning was. 'Well then, just give me the message,' he said, 'and I'll toddle along upstairs – how would that be?'

'Oh, sure, good, fine.' But then Dorrance stopped, looking across the street as a fresh gust of wind sent a funnel of leaves storming into the bright October sky. His faded eyes were wide, and something in them made Ralph think of the Exalted & Revered Baby again – of the way she had snatched at the gray-blue marks left by his fingers, and the way she had looked at the flowers sizzling in the vase by the sink. Ralph had seen Dor stand watching airplanes take off and land on Runway 3 with that same slack-jawed expression, sometimes for an hour or more.

'Dor?' he prompted.

Dorrance's sparse eyelashes fluttered. 'Oh! Right! The message! The message is . . .' He frowned slightly and looked down at the book which he was now bending back and forth in his hands. Then his face cleared and he looked up at Ralph again. 'The message is, "Cancel the appointment."'

It was Ralph's turn to frown. 'What appointment?'

'You shouldn't have messed in,' Dorrance repeated, then heaved a big sigh. 'But it's too late now. Done-bun-can't-be-undone. Just cancel the appointment. Don't let that fellow stick any pins in you.'

Ralph had been turning to the porch steps; now he turned back to Dorrance. 'Hong? Are you talking about *Hong?*'

'How would I know?' Dorrance asked in an irritated tone of voice. 'I don't mess in, I told you that. Every now and then I carry a message, is all, like now. I was supposed to tell you to cancel the appointment with the pin-sticker man, and I done it. The rest is up to you.'

Dorrance was looking up at the trees across the street again, his odd, lineless face wearing an expression of mild exaltation. The strong fall wind rippled his hair like seaweed. When Ralph touched his shoulder the old man turned to him willingly enough, and Ralph suddenly realized that what Faye Chapin and the others saw as foolishness might actually be joy. If so, the mistake probably said more about them than it did about Old Dor.

'Dorrance?'

'What, Ralph?'

'This message – who gave it to you?'

Dorrance thought it over – or perhaps only appeared to think it over – and then held out his copy of *Cemetery Nights*. 'Take it.'

'No, I'll pass,' Ralph said. 'I'm not much on poetry, Dor.'

'You'll like these. They're like stories—'

Ralph restrained a strong urge to reach out and shake the old man until his bones rattled like castanets. 'I just picked up a couple oat operas downtown, at Back Pages. What I want to know is who gave you the message about—'

Dorrance thrust the book of poems into Ralph's right hand – the one not holding the Westerns – with surprising force. 'One of them starts, "Each thing I do I rush through so I can do something else."'

And before Ralph could say another word, Old Dor cut across the lawn to the sidewalk. He turned left and started toward the Extension with his face turned dreamily up to the blue sky where the leaves flew wildly, as if to some rendezvous over the horizon.

'Dorrance!' Ralph shouted, suddenly infuriated. Across the street at the Red Apple, Sue was sweeping fallen leaves off the hot-top in front of the door. At the sound of Ralph's voice she stopped and looked curiously over at him. Feeling stupid — feeling *old* — Ralph manufactured what he hoped looked like a big, cheerful grin and waved to her. Sue waved back and resumed her sweeping. Dorrance, meanwhile, had continued serenely on his way. He was now almost half a block up the street.

Ralph decided to let him go.

2

He climbed the steps to the porch, switching the book Dorrance had given him to his left hand so he could grope for his key-ring, and then saw he didn't have to bother — the door was not only unlocked but standing ajar. Ralph had scolded McGovern repeatedly for his carelessness about locking the front door, and had thought he was finally having some success in getting the message through his downstairs tenant's thick skull. Now, however, it seemed that McGovern had backslid.

'Dammit, Bill,' he said under his breath, pushing his way into the shadowy lower hall and looking nervously up the stairs. It was all too easy to imagine Ed Deepneau lurking up there, broad daylight or not. Still, he could not stay here in the foyer all day. He turned the thumb-bolt on the front door and started up the stairs.

There was nothing to worry about, of course. He had one bad moment when he thought he saw someone standing in the far corner of the living room, but it was only his own old gray jacket. He had actually hung it on the coat-tree for a change instead of just slinging it onto a chair or draping it over the arm of the sofa; no wonder it had given him a turn.

He went into the kitchen and, with his hands poked into his back pockets, stood looking at the calendar. Monday was circled, and within the circle he had scrawled HONG – 10:00.

I was supposed to tell you to cancel the appointment with the pin-sticker man, and I done it. The rest is up to you.

For a moment Ralph felt himself step back from his life so he was able to look at the latest section of the mural it made instead of just the detail which was this day. What he saw frightened him: an unknown road heading into a lightless tunnel where anything might be waiting. Anything at all.

Then turn back, Ralph!

But he had an idea he couldn't do that. He had an idea he was for the tunnel, whether he wanted to go in there or not. The feeling was not one of being led so much as it was one of being shoved forward by powerful, invisible hands.

'Never mind,' he muttered, rubbing his temples nervously with the tips of his fingers and still looking at the circled date – two days from now – on the calendar. 'It's the insomnia. That's when things really started to . . .'

Really started to *what*?

'To get weird,' he told the empty apartment. 'That's when things started to get really weird.'

Yes, weird. Lots of weird things, but the auras he was seeing were clearly the weirdest of them all. Cold gray light – it had looked like living frost – creeping over the man reading the paper in Day Break, Sun Down. The mother and son walking toward the supermarket, their entwined auras rising from their clasped hands like a pigtail. Helen and Nat buried in gorgeous clouds of ivory light; Natalie snatching at the marks left by his moving fingers, ghostly contrails which only she and Ralph had been able to see.

And now Old Dor, turning up on his doorstep like some peculiar Old Testament prophet . . . only instead of telling him to repent, Dor had told him to cancel his appointment with the acupuncturist Joe Wyzer had recommended. It should have been funny, but it wasn't.

The mouth of that tunnel. Looming closer every day. *Was* there really a tunnel? And if so, where did it lead?

I'm more interested in what might be waiting for me in there, Ralph thought. *Waiting in the dark.*

You shouldn't have messed in, Dorrance had said. *Anyway, it's too late now.*

'Done-bun-can't-be-undone,' Ralph murmured, and suddenly decided he didn't want to take the wide view anymore; it was unsettling. Better to move in close again and consider things a detail at a time, beginning with his appointment for acupuncture treatment. Was he going to keep it, or follow the advice of Old Dor, alias the Ghost of Hamlet's Father?

It really wasn't a question that needed much thought, Ralph decided. Joe Wyzer had sweet-talked Hong's secretary into finding him an appointment in early October, and Ralph intended to keep it. If there was a path out of this thicket, starting to sleep through the night was probably it. And that made Hong the next logical step.

'Done-bun-can't-be-undone,' he repeated, and went into the living room to read one of his Westerns.

Instead he found himself paging through the book of poetry Dorrance had given him – *Cemetery Nights,* by Stephen Dobyns. Dorrance had been right on both counts: the majority of the poems *were* like stories, and Ralph discovered that he liked them just fine. The poem from which Old Dor had quoted was called 'Pursuit', and it began:

> *Each thing I do I rush through so I can do*
> *something else. In such a way do the days pass –*
> *a blend of stock car racing and the never*
> *ending building of a gothic cathedral.*
> *Through the windows of my speeding car, I see*
> *all that I love falling away: books unread,*
> *jokes untold, landscapes unvisited . . .*

Ralph read the poem twice, completely absorbed, thinking he would have to read it to Carolyn. Carolyn would like it, which was good, and she would like him (who usually stuck to Westerns and historical novels) even more for finding it and bringing it to her like a bouquet of flowers. He was actually getting up to find a scrap of paper he could mark the page with when he remembered that Carolyn had been dead for half a year now and burst into tears. He sat in the wing-chair for almost fifteen minutes, holding *Cemetery Nights* in his lap and wiping at his eyes with the heel of his left hand. At last he went into the bedroom, lay down, and tried to sleep. After an hour of staring at the ceiling, he got up, made himself a cup of coffee, and found a college football game on TV.

3

The Public Library was open on Sunday afternoons from one until six, and on the day after Dorrance's visit, Ralph went down there, mostly because he had nothing better to do. The high-ceilinged reading room would ordinarily have contained a scattering of other old men like himself, most of them leafing through the various Sunday papers they now had time to read, but when Ralph emerged from the stacks where he had spent forty minutes browsing, he discovered he had the whole room to himself. Yesterday's gorgeous blue skies had been replaced by driving rain that pasted the new-fallen leaves to the sidewalks or sent them flooding down the gutters and into Derry's peculiar and unpleasantly tangled system of storm-drains. The wind was still blowing, but it had shifted into the north and now had a nasty cutting edge. Old folks with any sense (or any luck) were at home where it was warm, possibly watching the last game of another dismal Red Sox season, possibly playing Old Maid or Candyland with the grandkids, possibly napping off a big chicken dinner.

Ralph, on the other hand, did not care for the Red Sox, had no children or grandchildren, and seemed to have completely lost any capacity for napping he might once have had. So he had taken the one o'clock Green Route bus down to the library, and here he was, wishing he had worn something heavier than his old scuffed gray jacket – the reading room was chilly. Gloomy, as well. The fireplace was empty, and the clankless radiators strongly suggested that the furnace had yet to be fired up. The Sunday librarian hadn't bothered flipping the switches that turned on the hanging overhead globes, either. The light which did manage to find its way in here seemed to fall dead on the floor, and the corners were full of shadows. The loggers and soldiers and drummers and Indians in the old paintings on the walls looked like malevolent ghosts. Cold rain sighed and gusted against the windows.

I should have stayed home, Ralph thought, but didn't really believe it; these days the apartment was even worse. Besides, he had found an interesting new book in what he had come to think of as the Mr Sandman Section of the stacks: *Patterns of Dreaming,* by James A. Hall, MD. He turned on the overheads, rendering the room marginally less grue-some, sat down at one of the four long, empty tables, and was soon absorbed in his reading.

> *Prior to the realization that REM sleep and NREM sleep were distinct states* [Hall wrote], *studies concerned with total deprivation of a particular stage of sleep led to Dement's suggestion (1960) that deprivation . . . causes disorganiza-tion of the waking personality . . .*

Boy, you got that right, my friend, Ralph thought. *Can't even find a fucking Cup-A-Soup packet when you want one.*

> *. . . early dream-deprivation studies also raised the exciting speculation that schizophrenia might be a disorder in which*

deprivation of dreaming at night led to a breakthrough of the dream process into everyday waking life.

Ralph hunched over the book, elbows on the table, fisted hands pressed against his temples, forehead lined and eyebrows drawn together in a clench of concentration. He wondered if Hall could be talking about the auras, maybe without even knowing it. Except he was still *having* dreams, dammit – very vivid ones, for the most part. Just last night he'd had one in which he was dancing at the old Derry Pavilion (gone now; destroyed in the big storm which had wiped out most of the downtown area eight years before) with Lois Chasse. He seemed to have taken her out with the intention of proposing to her, but Trigger Vachon, of all people, had kept trying to cut in.

He rubbed his eyes with his knuckles, tried to focus his attention, and began to read again. He did not see the man in the baggy gray sweatshirt materialize in the doorway of the reading room and stand there, silently watching him. After about three minutes of this, the man reached beneath the sweatshirt (Charlie Brown's dog Snoopy was on the front, wearing his Joe Cool glasses) and produced a hunting knife from the scabbard on his belt. The hanging overhead globes threw a thread of light along the knife's serrated blade as the man turned it this way and that, admiring the edge. Then he moved forward toward the table where Ralph was sitting with his head propped on his hands. He sat down beside Ralph, who noticed that someone was there only in the faintest, most distant way.

Tolerance to sleep loss varies somewhat with the age of the subject. Younger subjects show an earlier onset of disturbance and more physical reactions, while older subjects—

A hand closed lightly on Ralph's shoulder, startling him out of the book.

'I wonder what they'll look like?' an ecstatic voice whispered in his ear, the words flowing on a tide of what smelled like spoiled bacon cooking slowly in a bath of garlic and rancid butter. 'Your guts, I mean. I wonder what they'll look like when I let them out all over the floor. What do you think, you Godless baby-killing Centurion? Do you think they'll be yellow or black or red or what?'

Something hard and sharp pressed into Ralph's left side and then slowly traced its way down along his ribs.

'I can't wait to find out,' the ecstatic voice whispered. 'I can't *wait.*'

4

Ralph turned his head very slowly, hearing the tendons in his neck creak. He didn't know the name of the man with the bad breath – the man who was sticking something that felt too much like a knife not to be one into his side – but he recognized him at once. The hornrimmed glasses helped, but the zany gray hair, standing up in clumps that reminded Ralph simultaneously of Don King and Albert Einstein, was the clincher. It was the man who had been standing with Ed Deepneau in the background of the newspaper photo that had showed Ham Davenport with his fist raised and Dan Dalton wearing Davenport's

CHOICE, NOT FEAR sign for a hat. Ralph thought he had seen this same guy in some of the TV news stories about the continuing abortion demonstrations. Just another sign-waving, chanting face in the crowd; just another spear-carrier. Except it now seemed that this particular spear-carrier intended to kill him.

'What do you think?' the man in the Snoopy sweat-shirt asked, still in that ecstatic whisper. The sound of his voice frightened Ralph more than the blade as it slid slowly up and then back down his leather jacket, seeming to map the vulnerable organs on the left side of his body: lung, heart, kidney, intestines. 'What color?'

His breath was nauseating, but Ralph was afraid to pull back or turn his head, afraid that any gesture might cause the knife to stop tracking and plunge. Now it was moving back up his side again. Behind the thick lenses of his hornrims, the man's brown eyes floated like strange fish. The expression in them was disconnected and oddly fright-ened, Ralph thought. The eyes of a man who would see signs in the sky and perhaps hear voices whispering from deep in the closet late at night.

'I don't know,' Ralph said. 'I don't know why you'd want to hurt me in the first place.' He shot his eyes quickly around, still not moving his head, hoping to see someone, anyone, but the reading room remained empty. Outside, the wind gusted and rain racketed against the windows.

'Because you're a fucking *Centurion*!' the gray-haired man spat. 'A fucking *baby-killer*! Stealing the *fetal unborn*! Selling them to the *highest bidder*! I know all about you!'

Ralph dropped his right hand slowly from the side of his head. He was right-handed, and all the stuff he

249

happened to pick up in the course of the day generally went into the handiest righthand pocket of whatever he was wearing. The old gray jacket had big flap pockets, but he was afraid that even if he could sneak his hand in there unnoticed, the most lethal thing he would find was apt to be a crumpled-up Dentyne wrapper. He doubted that he even had a nail-clipper.

'Ed Deepneau told you that, didn't he?' Ralph asked, then grunted as the knife poked painfully into his side just below the place where his ribs stopped.

'Don't speak his name,' the man in the Snoopy sweatshirt whispered. 'Don't you even speak his *name* ! Stealer of infants! Cowardly murderer! *Centurion!*' He thrust forward with the blade again, and this time there was real pain as the tip punched through the leather jacket. Ralph didn't think he was cut – yet, anyway – but he was quite sure the nut had already applied enough pressure to leave a nasty bruise. That was okay, though; if he got out of this with no more than a bruise, he would count himself lucky.

'All right,' he said. 'I won't mention his name.'

'Say you're sorry!' the man in the Snoopy sweatshirt hissed, prodding with the knife again. This time it went through Ralph's shirt, and he felt the first warm trickle of blood down his side. *What's under the point of the blade right now?* he wondered. *Liver? Gall bladder? What's under there on the lefthand side?*

He either couldn't remember or didn't want to. A picture had come into his mind, and it was trying to get in the way of any organized thought – a deer hung head-down from a set of scales outside some country store during hunting season. Glazed eyes, lolling tongue, and a dark slit up the belly where a man with a knife – a knife just like this one – had opened it up and yanked its works out, leaving just head, meat, and hide.

'I'm sorry,' Ralph said in a voice which was no longer steady. 'I am, really.'

'Yeah, right! You ought to be, but you aren't! You *aren't!*'

Another prod. A bright lance of pain. More wet heat trickling down his side. And suddenly the room was brighter, as if two or three of the camera crews which had been wandering around Derry since the abortion protests began had crowded in here and turned on the floods they mounted over their videocams. There were no cameras, of course; the lights had gone on inside of *him*.

He turned toward the man with the knife – the man who was actually pressing the blade into him now – and saw he was surrounded by a shifting green and black aura that made Ralph think of

(*swampfire*)

the dim phosphorescence he had sometimes seen in marshy woods after dark. Twisting through it were spiky brambles of purest black. He looked at his assailant's aura with mounting dismay, hardly feeling the tip of the knife sink a sixteenth of an inch deeper into him. He was distantly aware that blood was puddling at the bottom of his shirt, along the line of his belt, but that was all.

He's crazy, and he really does mean to kill me – it isn't just talk. He's not quite ready to do it yet, he hasn't quite worked himself up to it, but he's almost there. And if I try to run – if I try to move even an inch away from the knife he's got in me – he'll do it right away. I think he's hoping I will decide to move . . . then he can tell himself I brought it on myself, that it was my own fault.

'You and your kind, oh boy,' the man with the zany shock of gray hair was saying. 'We know all about *you.*'

Ralph's hand had reached the right pocket . . . and felt a largish something inside he didn't recognize or remember putting there. Not that that meant much; when you could no longer remember if the last four digits of the cinema center phone number were 1317 or 1713, anything was possible.

'You guys, oh boy!' the man with the zany hair said. 'Ohboy ohboy *ohBOY*!' This time Ralph had no trouble feeling the pain when the man pushed with the knife; the tip spread a thin red net all the way across the curve of his chest wall and up the nape of his neck. He uttered a low moan, and his right hand clamped tight on the gray jacket's right-hand pocket, moulding the leather to the curved side of the object inside.

'Don't scream,' the man with the zany hair said in that low, ecstatic whisper. 'Oh jeepers jeezly crow, you don't want to do *that*!' His brown eyes peered at Ralph's face, and the lenses of his glasses so magnified them that the tiny flakes of dandruff caught in his lashes looked almost as big as pebbles. Ralph could see the man's aura even in his eyes – it went sliding across his pupils like green smoke across black water. The snakelike twists running through the green light were thicker now, twining together, and Ralph understood that when the knife sank all the way in, the part of this man's personality which was generating those black swirls would be what pushed it. The green was confusion and paranoia; the black was something else. Something

(*from outside*)
much worse.

'No,' he gasped. 'I won't. I won't scream.'

'Good. I can feel your heart, you know. It's coming right up the blade of the knife and into the palm of my hand. It must be beating really hard.' The man's mouth pulled up in a jerky, humorless smile. Flecks of spittle clung to the corners of his lips. 'Maybe you'll just keel over and die of a heart attack, save me the trouble of killing you.' Another gust of that sickening breath washed over Ralph's face. 'You're awful old.'

Blood was now running down his side in what felt like two streams, maybe even three. The pain of the knife-point gouging into him was maddening – like the stinger of a gigantic bee.

Or a pin, Ralph thought, and discovered that this idea was funny in spite of the fix he was in . . . or perhaps because of it. This was the *real* pin-sticker man; James Roy Hong could be only a pale imitation.

And I never had a chance to cancel this appointment, Ralph thought. But then again, he had an idea that nuts like the guy in the Snoopy sweatshirt didn't take cancellations. Nuts like this had their own agenda and they stuck to it, come hell or high water.

Whatever else might happen, Ralph knew he couldn't stand that knife-tip boring into him much longer. He used his thumb to lift the flap of his coat pocket and slipped his hand inside. He knew what the object was the minute his fingertips touched it: the aerosol can Gretchen had taken out of her purse and put on his kitchen table. *A little present from all your grateful friends at WomanCare,* she had said.

Ralph had no idea how it had gotten from the top of the kitchen cabinet where he had put it into the pocket of his battered old fall jacket, and he didn't care. His hand closed around it, and he used his thumb again, this time to pop off the can's plastic top. He never took his eyes away from the twitching, frightened, exhilarated face of the man with the zany hair as he did this.

'I know something,' Ralph said. 'If you promise not to kill me, I'll tell you.'

'What?' the man with the zany hair asked. 'Jeepers, what could a scum like *you* know?'

What could *a scum like me know?* Ralph asked himself, and the answer came at once, popping into his mind like jackpot bars in the windows of a slot machine. He forced himself to lean into the green aura swirling around the man, into the terrible cloud of stink coming from his disturbed guts. At the same time he eased the small can from his pocket, held it against his thigh, and settled his index finger on the button which triggered the spray.

'I know who the Crimson King is,' he murmured.

The eyes widened behind the dirty hornrims – not just in surprise but in shock – and the man with the zany hair recoiled a little. For a moment the terrible pressure high on Ralph's left side eased. It was his chance, the only one he was apt to have, and he took it, throwing himself to the right, falling off his chair and tumbling to the floor. The back of his head smacked the tiles, but the pain seemed distant and unimportant compared to the relief at the removal of the knife-point.

The man with the zany hair squawked – a sound of mingled rage and resignation, as if he had become used to such setbacks over his long and difficult life. He leaned over Ralph's now-empty chair, his twitching face thrust forward, his eyes looking like the sort of fantastic, glowing creatures which live in the ocean's deepest trenches. Ralph raised the spray-can and had just a moment to realize he hadn't had time to check which direction the pinhole in the nozzle was pointing – he might very well succeed only in giving himself a faceful of Bodyguard.

No time to worry about that now.

He pressed the nozzle as the man with the zany hair thrust his knife forward. The man's face was enveloped in a thin haze of droplets that looked like the stuff that came out of the pine-scented air-freshener Ralph kept on the bathroom toilet tank. The lenses of his glasses fogged over.

The result was immediate and all Ralph could have wished for. The man with the zany hair screamed in pain, dropped his knife (it landed on Ralph's left knee and came to rest between his legs), and clutched at his face, pulling his glasses off. They landed on the table. At the same time the thin, somehow greasy aura around him flashed a brilliant red and then winked out – out of Ralph's view, at least.

'*I'm blind!*' the man with the zany hair cried in a high, shrieky voice. '*I'm blind, I'm blind!*'

'No, you're not,' Ralph said, getting shakily to his feet. 'You're just—'

The man with the zany hair screamed again and fell to the floor. He rolled back and forth on the black and white tiles with his hands over his face, howling like a child who has gotten his hand caught in a door. Ralph could see little pie-wedges of cheeks between his splayed fingers. The skin there was turning an alarming shade of red.

Ralph told himself to leave the guy alone, that he was crazy as a loon and dangerous as a rattlesnake, but he found himself too horrified and ashamed of what he had done to take this no doubt excellent advice. The idea that it had been a matter of survival, of disabling his assailant or dying, had already begun to seem unreal. He bent down and put a tentative hand on the man's arm. The nut rolled away from him and began to drum his dirty low-top sneakers on the floor like a child having a tantrum. '*Oh you son of a bitch!*' he was screaming. '*You shot me with something!*' And then, incredibly: '*I'll sue the pants off you!*'

'You'll have to explain about the knife before you're able to progress much with your lawsuit, I think,' Ralph said. He saw the knife lying on the floor, reached for it, then thought again. It would be better if his fingerprints weren't on it. As he straightened, a wave of dizziness rushed through his head and for a moment the rain beating against the window sounded hollow and distant. He kicked the knife away, then tottered on his feet and had to grab the back of the chair he'd been sitting in to keep from falling over. Things steadied again. He heard approaching footsteps from the main lobby and murmuring, questioning voices.

Now you come, Ralph thought wearily. *Where were you three minutes ago, when this guy was on the verge of popping my left lung like a balloon?*

Mike Hanlon, looking slim and no more than thirty despite his tight cap of gray hair, appeared in the doorway. Behind him was the teenage boy Ralph recognized as the weekend desk assistant, and behind the teenager were four or five gawkers, probably from the periodicals room.

'Mr Roberts!' Mike exclaimed. 'Christ, how bad are you hurt?'

'I'm fine, it's *him* that's hurt,' Ralph said. But he happened to look down at himself as he pointed at the man on the floor and saw he *wasn't* fine. His coat had pulled up when he pointed, and the left side of the plaid shirt beneath had gone a deep, sodden red in a teardrop shape that started just below the armpit and spread out from there. 'Shit,' he said faintly, and sat down in his chair again. He bumped the hornrimmed glasses with his elbow and they skittered almost all the way across the table. The mist of droplets on their lenses made them look like eyes which had been blinded by cataracts.

'He shot me with acid!' the man on the floor screamed. *'I can't see and my skin is melting! I can feel it melting!'* To Ralph, he sounded like an almost conscious parody of the Wicked Witch of the West.

Mike tossed a quick glance at the man on the floor, then sat down in the chair next to Ralph. 'What happened?'

'Well, it sure wasn't acid,' Ralph said, and held up the can of Bodyguard. He set it on the table beside *Patterns of Dreaming*. 'The lady who gave it to me said it's not as strong as Mace, it just irritates your eyes and makes you sick to your—'

'It's not what's wrong with *him* that I'm worried about,' Mike said impatiently. 'Anyone who can yell that loud probably isn't going to die in the next three minutes. It's you I'm worried about, Mr Roberts – any idea how bad he stabbed you?'

'He didn't actually stab me at all,' Ralph said. 'He . . . sort of poked me. With that.' He pointed at the knife lying on the tile floor. At the sight of the red tip, he felt another wave of faintness track through his head. It felt like an express train made of feather pillows. That was stupid, of course, made no sense at all, but he wasn't in a very sensible frame of mind.

The assistant was looking cautiously down at the man on the floor. 'Uh-oh,' he said. 'We know this guy, Mike — it's Charlie Pickering.'

'Goodness-gracious, great balls of fire,' Mike said. 'Now why aren't I surprised?' He looked at the teenage assistant and sighed. 'Better call the cops, Justin. It looks like we've got us a situation here.'

5

'Am I in trouble for using that?' Ralph asked an hour later, and pointed to one of the two sealed plastic bags sitting on the cluttered surface of the desk in Mike Hanlon's office. A strip of yellow tape, marked EVIDENCE *Aerosol can* DATE *3 October 93* and SITE *Derry Public Library* ran across the front.

'Not as much as our old pal Charlie's going to be in for using this,' John Leydecker said, and pointed to the other sealed bag. The hunting knife was inside, the blood on the tip now dried to a tacky maroon. Leydecker was wearing a University of Maine football sweater today. It made him look approximately the size of a dairy barn. 'We still pretty much believe in the concept of self-defense out here in the sticks. We don't talk it up much, though – it's sort of like admitting you believe the world is flat.'

Mike Hanlon, who was leaning in the doorway, laughed.

Ralph hoped his face didn't show how deeply relieved he felt. As a paramedic (one of the guys who had run Helen Deepneau to the hospital back in August, for all he knew) worked on him – first photographing, then disinfecting, finally butterfly-clamping and bandaging – he had sat with his teeth gritted, imagining a judge sentencing him to six months in the county clink for assault with a semi-deadly weapon. *Hopefully, Mr Roberts, this will serve as an example and a warning to any other old farts in this vicinity who may feel justified in carrying around spray-cans of disabling nerve gas . . .*

Leydecker looked once more at the six Polaroid photographs lined up along the side of Hanlon's computer terminal. The fresh-faced emergency medical technician had taken the first three before patching Ralph up. These showed a small dark circle – it looked like the sort of oversized period made by children just learning to print – low down on Ralph's side. The EMT had taken the second set of three after applying the butterfly clamp and getting Ralph's signature on a form attesting to the fact that he had been offered hospital service and had refused it. In this latter group of photographs, the beginnings of what was going to be an absolutely spectacular bruise could be seen.

'God bless Edwin Land and Richard Polaroid,' Leydecker said, putting the photographs into another EVIDENCE Baggie.

'I don't think there ever was a Richard Polaroid,' Mike Hanlon said from his spot in the doorway.

'Probably not, but God bless him just the same. No jury who got a look at these photos would do anything but give you a medal, Ralph, and not even Clarence Darrow could keep em out of evidence.' He looked back at Mike. 'Charlie Pickering.'

Mike nodded. 'Charlie Pickering.'

'Fuckhead.'

Mike nodded again. 'Fuckhead deluxe.'

The two of them looked at each other solemnly, then burst into gales of laughter at the same moment. Ralph understood exactly how they felt — it was funny because it was awful and awful because it was funny — and he had to bite his lips savagely to keep from joining them. The last thing in the world he wanted to do right now was get laughing; it would hurt like a bastard.

Leydecker took a handkerchief out of his back pocket, mopped his streaming eyes with it, and began to get himself under control.

'Pickering's one of the right-to-lifers, isn't he?' Ralph asked. He was remembering how Pickering had looked when Hanlon's teenage assistant had helped him sit up. Without his glasses, the man had looked about as dangerous as a bunny in a petshop window.

'You could say that,' Mike agreed dryly. 'He's the one they caught last year in the parking garage that services the hospital and WomanCare. He had a can of gasoline in his hand and a knapsack filled with empty bottles on his back.'

'Also strips of sheeting, don't forget those,' Leydecker

said. 'Those were going to be his fuses. That was back when Charlie was a member in good standing of Daily Bread.'

'How close did he come to lighting the place up?' Ralph asked curiously.

Leydecker shrugged. 'Not very. Someone in the group apparently decided firebombing the local women's clinic might be a little closer to terrorism than politics and made an anonymous phone call to your local police authority.'

'Good deal,' Mike said. He snorted another little chuckle, then crossed his arms as if to hold any further outburst inside.

'Yeah,' Leydecker said. He laced his fingers together, stretched out his arms, and popped his knuckles. 'Instead of prison, a thoughtful, caring Judge sent Charlie to Juniper Hill for six months' worth of treatment and therapy, and they must have decided he was okay, because he's been back in town since July or so.'

'Yep,' Mike agreed. 'He's down here just about every day. Kind of improving the tone of the place. Buttonholes everyone who comes in, practically, and gives them his little peptalk on how any woman who has an abortion is going to perish in brimstone, and how the real baddies like Susan Day are going to burn forever in a lake of fire. But I can't figure out why he'd take after you, Mr Roberts.'

'Just lucky, I guess.'

'Are you okay, Ralph?' Leydecker asked. 'You look pale.'

'I'm fine,' Ralph said, although he did not feel fine; in fact, he had begun to feel very queasy.

'I don't know about fine, but you're sure lucky. Lucky those women gave you that can of pepper-gas, lucky you had it with you, and luckiest of all that Pickering didn't just walk up behind you and stick that knife of his into the nape of your neck. Do you feel like coming down to the station and making a formal statement now, or—'

Ralph abruptly lunged out of Mike Hanlon's ancient swivel chair, bolted across the room with his left hand over his mouth, and clawed open the door in the rear right corner of the office, praying it wasn't a closet. If it was, he was probably going to fill up Mike's galoshes with a partially processed grilled cheese sandwich and some slightly used tomato soup.

It turned out to be the room he needed. Ralph dropped to his knees in front of the toilet and vomited with his eyes closed and his left arm clamped tightly against the hole Pickering had made in his side. The pain as his muscles first locked and then pushed was still enormous.

'I take it that's a no,' Mike Hanlon said from behind him, and then put a comforting hand on the back of Ralph's neck. 'Are you okay? Did you get that thing bleeding again?'

'I don't think so,' Ralph said. He started to unbutton his shirt, then paused and clamped his arm tight against his side again as his stomach gave another lurch before quieting once more. He raised his arm and looked at the dressing. It was pristine. 'I appear to be okay.'

'Good,' Leydecker said. He was standing just behind the librarian. 'You done?'

'I think so, yes.' Ralph looked at Mike shamefacedly. 'I apologize for that.'

'Don't be a goof.' Mike helped Ralph to his feet.

'Come on,' Leydecker said, 'I'll give you a ride home. Tomorrow will be time enough for the statement. What you need is to put your feet up the rest of today, and a good night's sleep tonight.'

'Nothing like a good night's sleep,' Ralph agreed. They had reached the office door. 'You want to let go of my arm now, Detective Leydecker? We're not going steady just yet, are we?'

Leydecker looked startled, then dropped Ralph's arm. Mike started to laugh again. '"Not going –" That's pretty good, Mr Roberts.'

Leydecker was smiling. 'I guess we're not, but you can call me Jack, if you want. Or John. Just not Johnny. Since my mother died, the only one who calls me Johnny is old Prof McGovern.'

Old Prof McGovern, Ralph thought. *How strange that sounds.*

'Okay – John it is. And both of you guys can call me Ralph. As far as I'm concerned, *Mr Roberts* is always going to be a Broadway play starring Henry Fonda.'

'You got it,' Mike Hanlon said. 'And take care of yourself.'

'I'll try,' he said, then stopped in his tracks. 'Listen, I have something to thank you for, quite apart from your help today.'

Mike raised his eyebrows. 'Oh?'

'Yes. You hired Helen Deepneau. She's one of my favorite people, and she desperately needed the job. So thanks.'

Mike smiled and nodded. 'I'll be happy to accept the bouquets, but she's the one who did me the favor, really. She's actually over-qualified for the job, but I think she wants to stay in town.'

'So do I, and you've helped make it possible. So thanks again.'

Mike grinned. 'My pleasure.'

6

As Ralph and Leydecker stepped out behind the circulation desk, Leydecker said: 'I guess that honeycomb must have really turned the trick, huh?'

Ralph at first had absolutely no idea what the big detective was talking about – he might as well have asked a question in Esperanto.

'Your insomnia,' Leydecker said patiently. 'You got past it, right? Must have – you look a gajillion times better than on the day I first met you.'

'I was a little stressed that day,' Ralph said. He found himself remembering the old Billy Crystal routine about Fernando – the one that went, *Listen, dahling, don't be a schnook; it's not how you feel, it's how you* look! *And you . . . look . . . MAHVELLOUS!*

'And you're not today? C'mon, Ralph, this is me. So give – was it the honeycomb?'

Ralph appeared to think this over, then nodded. 'Yes, I guess that must have been what did it.'

'Fantastic! Didn't I tell you?' Leydecker said cheerfully as they pushed their way out into the rainy afternoon.

7

They were waiting for the light at the top of Up-Mile Hill when Ralph turned to Leydecker and asked what the chances were of nailing Ed as Charlie Pickering's accomplice. 'Because Ed put him up to it,' he said. 'I know that as well as I know that's Strawford Park over there.'

'You're probably right,' Leydecker replied, 'but don't kid yourself – the chances of nailing him as an accomplice are shitty. They wouldn't be very good even if the County Prosecutor wasn't as conservative as Dale Cox.'

'Why not?'

'First of all, I doubt if we'll be able to show any deep connection between the two men. Second, guys like Pickering tend to be fiercely loyal to the people they identify as "friends", because they have so few of them – their worlds are mostly made up of enemies. Under interrogation I don't think Pickering will repeat much or any of what he told you while he was tickling your ribs with his hunting knife. Third, Ed Deepneau is no fool. Crazy, yes – maybe crazier than Pickering, when you get right down to it – but not a fool. He won't admit anything.'

Ralph nodded. It was exactly his opinion of Ed.

'If Pickering *did* say that Deepneau ordered him to find you and waste you – on the grounds that you were one of these baby-killing, fetus-snatching Centurions – Ed would just smile at us and nod and say he was sure that poor Charlie had told us that, that poor Charlie might even *believe* that, but that didn't make it true.'

The light turned green. Leydecker drove through the intersection, then bent left onto Harris Avenue. The windshield wipers thumped and flapped. Strawford Park, on Ralph's right, looked like a wavery mirage through the rain streaming down the passenger window.

'And what could we say to that?' Leydecker asked. 'The fact is, Charlie Pickering has got a *long* history of mental instability – when it comes to nuthatches, he's made the grand tour: Juniper Hill, Acadia Hospital, Bangor Mental Health Institute . . . if it's a place where they have free electrical treatments and jackets that button up the back, Charlie's most likely been there. These days his hobbyhorse is abortion. Back in the late sixties he had a bug up his ass about Margaret Chase Smith. He wrote letters to everyone – Derry PD, the State Police, the FBI – claiming she was a Russian spy. He had the evidence, he said.'

'Good God, that's incredible.'

'Nope; that's Charlie Pickering, and I bet there's a dozen like him in every city this size in the United States. Hell, all over the world.'

Ralph's hand crept to his left side and touched the square of bandage there. His fingers traced the butterfly shape beneath the gauze. What he kept remembering was Pickering's magnified brown eyes – how they had looked terrified and ecstatic at the same time. He was already having trouble believing the man to whom those eyes belonged had almost killed him, and he was afraid that by tomorrow the whole thing would seem like one of the so-called 'breakthrough dreams' James A. Hall's book talked about.

'The bitch of it is, Ralph, a nut like Charlie Pickering makes the perfect tool for a guy like Deepneau. Right now our little wife-beating buddy has got about a ton of deniability.'

Leydecker turned into the driveway next to Ralph's building and parked behind a large Oldsmobile with

blotches of rust on the trunk lid and a very old sticker –
DUKAKIS '88 – on the bumper.

'Who's *that* brontosaurus belong to? The Prof?'

'No,' Ralph said. 'That's my brontosaurus.'

Leydecker gave him an unbelieving look as he shoved
the gearshift lever of his stripped-to-the-bone Police
Department Chevy into Park. 'If you own a car, how come
you're out standing around the bus stop in the pouring
rain? Doesn't it run?'

'It runs,' Ralph said a little stiffly, not wanting to add
that he could be wrong about that; he hadn't had the Olds
on the road in over two months. 'And I wasn't standing
around in the pouring rain; it's a bus *shelter*, not a bus *stop*.
It has a roof. Even a bench inside. No cable TV, true, but
wait till next year.'

'Still . . .' Leydecker said, gazing doubtfully at the Olds.

'I spent the last fifteen years of my working life driving
a desk, but before that I was a salesman. For twenty-five
years or so I averaged eight hundred miles a week. By the
time I settled in at the printshop, I didn't care if I ever sat
behind the wheel of a car again. And since my wife died,
there hardly ever seems to be any reason to drive. The bus
does me just fine for most things.'

All true enough; Ralph saw no need to add that he
had increasingly come to mistrust both his reflexes and his
short vision. A year ago, a kid of about seven had chased
his football out into Harris Avenue as Ralph was coming
back from the movies, and although he had been going
only twenty miles an hour, Ralph had thought for two
endless, horrifying seconds that he was going to run the
little boy down. He hadn't, of course – it hadn't even been

close, not really – but since then he thought he could count the number of times he'd driven the Olds on both hands.

He saw no need to tell John that, either.

'Well, whatever does it for you,' Leydecker said, giving the Olds a vague wave. 'How does one o'clock tomorrow afternoon sound for that statement, Ralph? I come on at noon, so I could kind of look over your shoulder. Buy you a coffee, if you wanted one.'

'That sounds fine. And thanks for the ride home.'

'No problem. One other thing . . .'

Ralph had started to open the car door. Now he closed it again and turned back to Leydecker, eyebrows raised.

Leydecker looked down at his hands, shifted uncomfortably behind the wheel, cleared his throat, then looked up again. 'I just wanted to say that I think you're a class act,' Leydecker said. 'Lots of guys forty years younger than you would have finished today's little adventure in the hospital. Or the morgue.'

'My guardian angel was looking out for me, I guess,' Ralph said, thinking of how surprised he had been when he realized what the round shape in his jacket pocket was.

'Well, maybe that was it, but you still want to be sure to lock your door tonight. You hear what I'm saying?'

Ralph smiled and nodded. Warranted or not, Leydecker's praise had made a warm spot in his chest. 'I will, and if I can just get McGovern to cooperate, everything will be hunky-dory.'

Also, he thought, *I can always go down and double-check the lock myself when I wake up. That should be just about two and a half hours after I fall asleep, the way things are going.*

'Everything *is* going to be hunky-dory,' Leydecker said. 'No one down where I work was very pleased when Deepneau more or less co-opted The Friends of Life, but I can't say we were surprised – he's an attractive, charismatic guy. If, that is, you happen to catch him on a day when he hasn't been using his wife for a punching-bag.'

Ralph nodded.

'On the other hand, we've seen guys like him before, and they have a way of self-destructing. That process has already started with Deepneau. He's lost his wife, he's lost his job . . . did you know that?'

'Uh-huh. Helen told me.'

'Now he's losing his more moderate followers. They're peeling off like jet fighters heading back to base because they're running out of fuel. Not Ed, though – he's going on come hell or high water. I imagine he'll keep at least some of them with him until the Susan Day speech, but after that I think it's gonna be a case of the cheese stands alone.'

'Has it occurred to you that he might try something Friday? That he might try to hurt Susan Day?'

'Oh yes,' Leydecker said. 'It's occurred to us, all right. It certainly has.'

8

Ralph was extremely happy to find the porch door locked this time. He unlocked it just long enough to let himself in, then trudged up the front stairs, which seemed longer and gloomier than ever this afternoon.

The apartment seemed too silent in spite of the steady beat of the rain on the roof, and the air seemed to smell of too many sleepless nights. Ralph took one of the chairs from the kitchen table over to the counter, stood on it, and looked at the top of the cabinet closest to the sink. It was as if he expected to find another can of Bodyguard – the *original* can, the one he'd put up here after seeing Helen and her friend Gretchen off – on top of that cabinet, and part of him actually did expect that. There was nothing up there, however, but a toothpick, an old Buss fuse, and a lot of dust.

He got carefully down off the chair, saw he had left muddy footprints on the seat, and used a swatch of paper towels to wipe them away. Then he replaced the chair at the table and went into the living room. He stood there, letting his eyes run from the couch with its dingy floral coverlet to the wing-chair to the old television sitting on its oak table between the two windows looking out on Harris Avenue. From the TV his gaze moved into the far corner. When he had come into the apartment yesterday, still a little on edge from finding the porch door unlatched, Ralph had briefly mistaken his jacket hanging on the coat-tree in that corner for an intruder. Well, no need to be coy; he had thought for a moment that Ed had decided to pay him a visit.

I never hang my coat up, though. It was one of the things about me – one of the few, I think – that used to genuinely irritate Carolyn. And if I never managed to get in the habit of hanging it up when she was alive, I sure as shit haven't since she died. No, I'm not the one who hung this jacket up.

Ralph crossed the room, rummaging in the pockets of the gray leather jacket and putting the stuff he found on top of the television. Nothing in the left but an old roll of Life Savers with lint clinging to the top one, but the righthand pocket was a treasure-trove even with the aerosol can gone. There was a lemon Tootsie Pop, still in its wrapper; a crumpled advertising circular from the Derry House of Pizza; a double-A battery; a small empty carton that had once contained an apple pie from McDonald's; his discount card from Dave's Video Stop, just four punches away from a free rental (the card had been MIA for over two weeks and Ralph had been sure it was lost); a book of matches; various scraps of tinfoil . . . and a folded piece of lined blue paper.

Ralph unfolded it and read a single sentence, written in a scrawling, slightly unsteady old man's script: *Each thing I do I rush through so I can do something else.*

That was all there was, but it was enough to confirm for his brain what his heart already knew: Dorrance Marstellar had been on the porch steps when Ralph had returned from Back Pages with his paperbacks, but he'd had other stuff to do before sitting down to wait. He had gone up to Ralph's apartment, taken the aerosol can from the top of the kitchen shelf, and put it in the righthand pocket of Ralph's old gray jacket. He had even left his calling-card: a bit of poetry scrawled on a piece of paper probably torn from the battered notebook in which he sometimes recorded arrivals and departures along Runway 3. Then, instead of returning the jacket to wherever Ralph had left it, Old Dor had hung it neatly on the coat-tree. With that accomplished

(done-bun-can't-be-undone)

he had returned to the porch to wait.

Last night Ralph had given McGovern a scolding for leaving the front door unlocked again, and McGovern had borne it as patiently as Ralph himself had borne Carolyn's scoldings about tossing his jacket onto the nearest chair when he came in instead of hanging it up, but now Ralph found himself wondering if he hadn't accused Bill unjustly. Perhaps Old Dor had picked the lock . . . or witched it. Under the circumstances, witchery seemed the more likely choice. Because . . .

'Because look,' Ralph said in a low voice, mechanically scooping his pocket litter up from the top of the TV and dumping it back into his pockets. 'It isn't just like he knew I'd need the stuff; he knew where to find it, and *he knew where to put it.*'

A chill zig-zagged up his back at that, and his mind tried to gavel the whole idea down – to label it mad, illogical, just the sort of thing a man with a grade-A case of insomnia would think up. Maybe so. But that didn't explain the scrap of paper, did it?

He looked at the scrawled words on the blue-lined sheet again – *Each thing I do I rush through so I can do something else.* That wasn't his handwriting any more than *Cemetery Nights* was his book.

'Except it is now; Dor gave it to me,' Ralph said, and the chill raced up his back again, jagged as a crack in a windshield.

And what other explanation comes to mind? That can didn't just fly into your pocket. The sheet of notepaper, either.

That sense of being pushed by invisible hands toward the maw of some dark tunnel had returned. Feeling like a man in a dream, Ralph walked back toward the kitchen. On the way he slipped out of the gray jacket and tossed it over the arm of the couch without even thinking about it. He stood in the doorway for some time, looking fixedly at the calendar with its picture of two laughing boys carving a jack-o-lantern. Looking at tomorrow's date, which was circled.

Cancel the appointment with the pin-sticker man, Dorrance had said; that was the message, and today the knife-sticker man had more or less underlined it. Hell, lit it in neon.

Ralph hunted out a number in the Yellow Pages and dialed it.

'You have reached the office of Dr James Roy Hong,' a pleasant female voice informed him. 'There is no one available to take your call right now, so please leave a message at the sound of the tone. We will get back to you just as soon as possible.'

The answering machine beeped. In a voice which surprised him with its steadiness, Ralph said: 'This is Ralph Roberts. I'm scheduled to come in tomorrow at ten o'clock. I'm sorry, but I won't be able to make it. Something has come up. Thank you.' He paused, then added: 'I'll pay for the appointment, of course.'

He shut his eyes and groped the phone back into the cradle. Then he leaned his forehead against the wall.

What are you doing, Ralph? What in God's name do you think you're doing?

'It's a long walk back to Eden, sweetheart.'

You can't seriously think whatever you're thinking . . . can you?

'. . . a long walk, so don't sweat the small stuff.'

What exactly are you thinking, Ralph?

He didn't know; he didn't have the slightest idea. Something about fate, he supposed, and appointments in

Samarra. He only knew for sure that rings of pain were spreading out from the little hole in his left side, the hole the knife-sticker man had made. The EMT had given him half a dozen pain-pills and he supposed he should take one, but just now he felt too tired to go to the sink and draw a glass of water . . . and if he was too tired to cross one shitty little room, how the hell would he ever make the long walk back to Eden?

Ralph didn't know, and for the time being he didn't care. He only wanted to stand where he was, with his forehead against the wall and his eyes shut so he wouldn't have to look at anything.

CHAPTER EIGHT

1

The beach was a long white edging, like a flirt of silk slip at the hem of the bright blue sea, and it was totally empty except for a round object about seventy yards away. This round object was about the size of a basketball, and it filled Ralph with a fear that was both deep and – for the moment, at least – groundless.

Don't go near it, he told himself. *There's something bad about it. Something* really *bad. It's a black dog barking at a blue moon, blood in the sink, a raven perched on a bust of Pallas just inside my chamber door. You don't want to go near it, Ralph, and you don't need to go near it, because this is one of Joe Wyzer's lucid dreams. You can just turn and cruise away, if you want.*

Except his feet began to carry him forward anyway, so maybe this wasn't a lucid dream. Not pleasant, either, not at all. Because the closer he got to that object on the beach, the less it looked like a basketball.

It was by far the most realistic dream Ralph had ever experienced, and the fact that he knew he was dreaming actually seemed to heighten that sense of realism. Of lucidity. He could feel the fine, loose sand under his bare feet, warm but not hot; he could hear the grinding, rock-throated roar of the incoming waves as they lost their balance and sprawled their way up the lower beach, where the sand glistened like wet tanned skin; could smell salt and drying seaweed, a strong and tearful smell that reminded him of summer vacations spent at Old Orchard Beach when he was a child.

Hey, old buddy, if you can't change this dream, I think maybe you ought to hit the ejection switch and bail out of it — wake yourself up, in other words, and right away.

He had closed half the distance to the object on the beach and there was no longer any question about what it was — not a basketball but a head. Someone had buried a human being up to the chin in the sand . . . and, Ralph suddenly realized, the tide was coming in.

He didn't bail out; he began to run. As he did, the frothy edge of a wave touched the head. It opened its mouth and began to scream. Even raised in a shriek, Ralph knew that voice at once. It was Carolyn's voice.

The froth of another wave ran up the beach and back-washed the hair which had been clinging to the head's wet cheeks. Ralph began to run faster, knowing he was almost certainly going to be too late. The tide was coming in fast. It would drown her long before he could free her buried body from the sand.

You don't have to save her, Ralph. Carolyn's already dead, and it didn't happen on some deserted beach. It happened in Room 317 of Derry Home Hospital. You were with her at the end, and the sound you heard wasn't surf but sleet hitting the window. Remember?

He remembered, but he ran faster nevertheless, sending puffs of sugary sand out behind him.

You won't ever get to her, though; you know how it is in dreams, don't you? Each thing you rush toward turns into something else.

No, *that* wasn't how the poem went . . . or was it? Ralph couldn't be sure. All he clearly remembered now was that it had ended with the narrator running blindly from something deadly

(Glancing over my shoulder I see its shape)

which was hunting him through the woods . . . hunting him and closing in.

Yet he *was* getting closer to the dark shape on the sand. It wasn't changing into anything else, either, and when he fell on his knees before Carolyn, he understood at once why he had not been able to recognize his wife of forty-five years, even from a distance: something was terribly wrong with her aura. It clung to her skin like a filthy dry-cleaning bag. When Ralph's shadow fell on her, Carolyn's eyes rolled up like the eyes of a horse that has shattered its leg going over a high fence. She was breathing in rapid, frightened gasps, and each expulsion of air sent jets of gray-black aura from her nostrils.

The tattered balloon-string straggling up from the crown of her head was the purple-black of a festering wound. When she opened her mouth to scream again, an unpleasant glowing substance flew from her lips in gummy strings which disappeared almost as soon as his eyes had registered their existence.

I'll save you, Carol! he shouted. He fell on his knees and began digging at the sand around her like a dog digging up a bone . . . and as the thought occurred to him, he realized that Rosalie, the early morning scavenger of

277

Harris Avenue, was sitting tiredly behind his screaming wife. It was as if the dog had been summoned by the thought. Rosalie, he saw, was also surrounded by one of those filthy black auras. She had Bill McGovern's missing Panama hat between her paws, and it looked as though she had enjoyed many a good chew on it since it had come into her possession.

So that's where the damn hat went, Ralph thought, then turned back to Carolyn and began to dig even faster. So far he hadn't managed to uncover so much as a single shoulder.

Never mind me! Carolyn screamed at him. *I'm already dead, remember? Watch for the white-man tracks, Ralph! The—*

A wave, glassy green on the bottom and the curdled white of soapsuds on top, broke less than ten feet from the beach. It ran up the sand toward them, freezing Ralph's balls with cold water and burying Carolyn's head momentarily in a grit-filled surge of foam. When the wave retreated, Ralph raised his own horror-filled shriek to the indifferent blue sky. The retreating wave had done in seconds what it had taken the radiation treatments almost a month to do; took her hair, washed her bald. And the crown of her head had begun to bulge at the spot where the blackish balloon-string was attached.

Carolyn, no! he howled, digging even faster. The sand was now dank and unpleasantly heavy.

Never mind, she said. Gray-black puffs came from her mouth with each word, like dirty vapor from an industrial smokestack. *It's just the tumor, and it's inoperable, so don't lose any sleep over that part of the show. What the hell, it's a long walk back to Eden, so don't sweat the small stuff, right? But you have to keep an eye out for those tracks . . .*

Carolyn, I don't know what you're talking about!

Another wave came, wetting Ralph to the waist and inundating Carolyn again. When it withdrew, the swelling on the crown of her head was beginning to split open.

You'll find out soon enough, Carolyn replied, and then the swelling on her head popped with a sound like a hammer striking a slab of meat. A haze of blood flew into the clear, salt-smelling air, and a horde of black bugs the size of cockroaches were pouring out of her. Ralph had never seen anything like them before – not even in a dream – and they filled him with an almost hysterical loathing. He would have fled, Carolyn or not, but he was frozen in place, too stunned to move a single finger, let alone get up and run.

Some of the black bugs ran back into Carolyn by way of her screaming mouth, but most of them hurried down her cheek and shoulder to the wet sand. Their accusing, alien eyes never left Ralph as they went. *All this is your fault,* the eyes seemed to say. *You could have saved her, Ralph, and a better man* would *have saved her.*

Carolyn! he screamed. He put his hands out to her, then pulled them back, terrified of the black bugs, which were still spewing out of her head. Behind her, Rosalie sat in her own small pocket of darkness, looking gravely at him and now holding McGovern's misplaced *chapeau* in her mouth.

One of Carolyn's eyes popped out and lay on the

wet sand like a blob of blueberry jelly. Bugs vomited from the now-empty socket.

Carolyn! he screamed. *Carolyn! Carolyn! Car—*

2

'– olyn! Carolyn! Car—'

Suddenly, in the same instant that he knew the dream was over, Ralph was falling. He barely registered the fact before he thumped to the bedroom floor. He managed to break his fall with one outstretched hand, probably saving himself a nasty rap on the head but provoking a howl of pain from beneath the butterfly bandage taped high up on his left side. For the moment, at least, he barely registered the pain. What he felt was fear, revulsion, a horrible, aching grief . . . and most of all an overwhelming sense of gratitude. The bad dream – surely the worst dream he'd ever had – was over, and he was in the world of real things again.

He pulled back his mostly unbuttoned pajama top, checked the bandage for bleeding, saw none, and then sat up. Just doing that much seemed to exhaust him; the thought of getting up, even long enough to fall back into bed, seemed out of the question for the time being. Maybe after his panicky, racing heart slowed down a little.

Can people die of bad dreams? he wondered, and in answer he heard Joe Wyzer's voice: *You bet they can, Ralph, although the medical examiner usually ends up writing* suicide *on the cause-of-death line.*

In the shaky aftermath of his nightmare, sitting on the floor and hugging his knees with his right arm, Ralph had no real doubt that some dreams *were* powerful enough to kill. The details of this one were fading out now, but he could still remember the climax all too well: that thudding sound, like a hammer hitting a thick cut of beef, and the vile spew of bugs from Carolyn's head. Plump they had been, plump and lively, and why not? They had been feasting on his dead wife's brain.

Ralph uttered a low, watery moan and swiped at his face with his left hand, provoking another jolt from beneath the bandage. His palm came away slick with sweat.

What, exactly, had she been telling him to watch out for? White-man traps? No — *tracks,* not traps. White-man *tracks,* whatever they were. Had there been more? Maybe, maybe not. He couldn't remember for sure, and so what? It had been a dream, for Christ's sake, just a *dream,* and outside of the fantasy world described in the tabloid newspapers, dreams meant nothing and proved nothing. When a person went to sleep, his mind seemed to turn into a kind of rathouse bargain hunter, sifting through the discount bins of mostly worthless short-term memories, looking not for items which were valuable or even useful but only for things that were still bright and shiny. These it put together in freakshow collages which were often striking but had, for the most part, all the sense of Natalie Deepneau's conversation. Rosalie the dog had turned up, even Bill's missing Panama had made a cameo appearance, but it all meant nothing . . . except tomorrow night he would not take one of the pain-pills the EMT had given him even if his arm felt like it was falling off. Not only had the one he'd taken during the late news failed to keep him under, as he had hoped and half-expected; it had probably played its own part in causing the nightmare.

Ralph managed to get up off the floor and sit on the edge of the bed. A wave of faintness floated through his head like parachute silk, and he shut his eyes until the feeling passed. While he was sitting there with his head down and his eyes closed, he groped for the lamp on the bedside table and turned it on. When he opened his eyes, the area of the bedroom lit by its warm yellow glow looked very bright and very real.

He looked at the clock beside the lamp: 1:48 a.m., and he felt totally awake and totally alert, pain-pill or no pain-pill. He got up, walked slowly into the kitchen, and put on the teakettle. Then he leaned against the counter, absently massaging the bandage beneath his left armpit, trying to quiet the throbbing his most recent adventures had awakened there. When the kettle steamed, he poured hot water over a bag of Sleepytime – *there* was a joke for you – and then took the cup into the living room. He plopped into the wing-back chair without bothering to turn on a light; the streetlamps and the dim glow coming from the bedroom provided all he needed.

Well, he thought, *here I am again, front row center. Let the play begin.*

Time passed, just how much he could not have said, but the throbbing beneath his arm had eased and the tea had gone from hot to barely lukewarm when he registered movement at the corner of his eye. Ralph turned his head, expecting to see Rosalie, but it wasn't Rosalie. It was two men stepping out onto the stoop of a house on the other side of Harris Avenue. Ralph couldn't make out the colors of the house – the orange arc-sodiums the city had installed several years ago provided great visibility but made any perception of true colors almost impossible – yet he could see that the color of the trim was radically different from the color of the rest. That, coupled with its location, made Ralph almost positive it was May Locher's house.

The two men on May Locher's stoop were very short, probably no more than four feet tall. They appeared to be surrounded by greenish auras. They were dressed in identical white smocks, which looked to Ralph like the ones worn by actors in those old TV doc-operas – black and white melodramas like *Ben Casey* and *Dr Kildare*. One of them had something in his hand. Ralph squinted. He couldn't make it out, but it had a sharp and hungry look. He could not have sworn under oath that it was a knife, but he thought it might be. Yes, it might very well be a knife.

His first clear evaluative thought about this experience was that the men over there looked like aliens in a movie about UFO abductions – *Communion*, perhaps, or *Fire in the Sky*. His second was that he had fallen asleep again, right here in his wing-chair, without even noticing.

That's right, Ralph – it's just a little more rummage-sale action, probably brought on by the stress of being stabbed and helped along by that frigging pain-pill.

He sensed nothing frightening about the two figures on May Locher's stoop other than the long, sharp-looking thing one of them was holding. Ralph supposed that not even your dreaming mind could do much with a couple of short bald guys wearing white tunics which looked left over from Central Casting. Also, there was nothing frightening about their behaviour – nothing furtive, nothing menacing. They stood on the stoop as if they had every right to be there in the darkest, stillest hour of the morning.

They were facing each other, the attitudes of their bodies and large bald heads suggesting two old friends having a sober, civilized conversation. They looked thoughtful and intelligent – the kind of space-travellers who would be more apt to say 'We come in peace' than kidnap you, stick a probe up your ass, and then take notes on your reaction.

All right, so maybe this new dream's not an out-and-out nightmare. After the last one, are you complaining?

No, of course he wasn't. Winding up on the floor once a night was plenty, thanks. Yet there was something very disquieting about this dream just the same; it felt real in a way that his dream of Carolyn had not. This was his own living room, after all, not some weird, deserted beach he had never seen before. He was sitting in the same wing-back chair where he sat every morning, holding a cup of tea which was now almost cold in his left hand, and when he raised the fingers of his right hand to his nose, as he was doing now, he could still smell a faint whiff of soap beneath the nails . . . the Irish Spring he liked to use in the shower . . .

Ralph suddenly reached beneath his left armpit and pressed his fingers to the bandage there. The pain was immediate and intense . . . but the two small bald men in the white tunics stayed right where they were, on May Locher's doorstep.

It doesn't matter what you think you feel, Ralph. It can't matter, because—

'Fuck you!' Ralph said in a hoarse, low voice. He rose from the wing-chair, putting his cup down on the little table beside it as he did. Sleepytime slopped onto the *TV Guide* there. 'Fuck you, *this is no dream!*'

3

He hurried across the living room to the kitchen, pajamas flapping, old worn slippers scuffing and thumping, the place where Charlie Pickering had stuck him sending out hot little bursts of pain. He grabbed a chair and took it into the apartment's small foyer. There was a closet here. Ralph opened its door, snapped on the light just inside, positioned the chair so he would be able to reach the closet's top shelf, and then stood on it.

The shelf was a clutter of lost or forgotten items, most of which had belonged to Carolyn. These were small things, little more than scraps, but looking at them drove away the last lingering conviction that this had to be a dream. There was an ancient bag of M&M's – her secret snack-food, her comfort-food. There was a lace heart, a single discarded white satin pump with a broken heel, a photo album. These things hurt a lot more than the knife-prick under his arm, but he had no time to hurt just now.

Ralph leaned forward, placing his left hand on the high, dusty shelf to balance his weight, then began to shuffle through the junk with his right hand, all the while praying that the kitchen chair wouldn't take a notion to scoot out from under him. The wound below his armpit was now throbbing outrageously, and he knew he was going to get it bleeding again if he didn't stop the athletics soon, but . . .

I'm sure they're up here somewhere . . . well . . . almost *sure . . .*

He pushed aside his old fly-box and his wicker creel. There was a stack of magazines behind the creel. The one on top was an issue of *Look* with Andy Williams on the cover. Ralph shoved them aside with the heel of his hand, sending up a flurry of dust. The old bag of M&M's fell to the floor and split open, spraying brightly colored bits of candy in every direction. Ralph leaned even farther forward, now almost on his toes. He supposed it was his imagination, but he thought he could sense the kitchen chair he was on getting ready to be evil.

The thought had no more than crossed his mind when the chair squawked and began to slide slowly backward on the hardwood floor. Ralph ignored that, ignored his throbbing side, and ignored the voice telling him he ought to stop this, he really ought to, because he was dreaming awake, just as the Hall book said many insomniacs eventually did, and although those little fellows across the street didn't really exist, he could really be standing here on this slowly sliding chair, and he could really break his hip when it went out from under him, and just how the hell was he going to explain what had happened when some smartass doctor in the Emergency Room of Derry Home asked him?

Grunting, he reached all the way back, pushed aside a carton from which half a Christmas tree star protruded like a strange spiky periscope (knocking the heel-less evening pump to the floor in the process), and saw what he wanted in the far lefthand corner of the shelf: the case which contained his old Zeiss-Ikon binoculars.

Ralph stepped off the chair just before it could slide all the way out from under him, moved it closer in, then got up on it again. He couldn't reach all the way into the corner where the binocular case stood, so he grabbed the trout-net which had been lying up here next to his creel and fly-box for lo these many years and succeeded in bagging the case on his second try. He dragged it forward until he could grab the strap, stepped off the chair, and came down on the fallen evening pump. His ankle twisted painfully. Ralph staggered, flailed his arms for balance, and managed to avoid going face-first into the wall. As he started back into the living room, however, he felt liquid warmth beneath the bandage on his side. He had managed to open the knife-wound again after all. Wonderful. Just a wonderful night *chez* Roberts . . . and how long had he been away from the window? He didn't know, but it felt like a long time, and he was sure the little bald doctors would be gone when he got back there. The street would be empty, and—

He stopped dead, the binocular case dangling at the end of its strap and tracking a long slow trapezoidal shadow back and forth across the floor where the orange glow of the streetlights lay like an ugly coat of paint.

Little bald doctors? Was that how he had just thought of them? Yes, of course, because that was what *they* called them – the folks who claimed to have been abducted by them . . . examined by them . . . operated on by them in some cases. They were physicians from space, proctologists from the great beyond. But that wasn't the big deal. The big deal was—

Ed used the phrase, Ralph thought. *He used it the night he called me and warned me to stay away from him and his interests. He said it was the doctor who told him about the Crimson King and the Centurions and all the rest.*

'Yes,' Ralph whispered. His back was prickling madly with gooseflesh. 'Yes, that's what he said. "The doctor told me. The little bald doctor."'

When he reached the window, he saw that the strangers were still out there, although they had moved from May Locher's stoop to the sidewalk while he had been fishing for the binoculars. They were standing directly beneath one of those damned orange streetlights, in fact. Ralph's feeling that Harris Avenue looked like a deserted stage set after the evening performance returned with weird, declamatory force . . . but with a different significance. For one thing, the set was no longer deserted, was it? Some ominous, long-past-midnight play had commenced in what the two odd creatures below no doubt assumed was a totally empty theater.

What would they do if they knew they had an audience? Ralph wondered. *What would they do to me?*

The bald doctors now had the shared demeanor of men who have nearly reached agreement. In that instant they did not look like doctors at all to Ralph, in spite of their smocks – they looked like blue-collar workers coming offshift at some plant or factory. These two guys, clearly buddies, have stopped outside the main gate for a moment or two to finish off some subject that can't wait even long enough for them to walk down the block to the nearest bar, knowing it will only take a minute or so in any case; total agreement is only a conversational exchange or two away.

Ralph uncased the binoculars, raised them to his eyes, and wasted a moment or two in puzzled fiddling with the focus knob before realizing he had forgotten to take off the lens caps. He did so, then raised the glasses again. This time the two figures standing under the streetlamp jumped into his field of vision at once, large and perfectly lit, but fuzzed out. He turned the little knob between the barrels again, and the two men popped into focus almost immediately. Ralph's breath stopped in his throat.

The look he got was extremely brief; no more than three seconds passed before one of the men (if they were men) nodded and clapped a hand on his companion's shoulder. Then they both turned away, leaving Ralph with nothing to look at but their bald heads and smooth, white-clad backs. Only three seconds at most, but Ralph saw enough in that brief space of time to make him profoundly uneasy.

He had run to get the binoculars for two reasons, both predicated on his inability to go on believing that this was a dream. First, he wanted to be sure he could identify the two men if he was ever called upon to do so. Second (this one was less admissible to his conscious mind but every bit as urgent), he had wanted to dispel the unsettling notion that he was having his own close encounter of the third kind.

Instead of dispelling it, his brief look through the binoculars intensified it. The little bald doctors did not actually seem to *have* features. They had *faces,* yes – eyes, noses, mouths – but they seemed as interchangeable as the chrome trim on the same make and model of a car. They could have been identical twins, but that wasn't the impression Ralph got, either. To him they looked more like department store mannequins with their Arnel wigs whisked off for the night, their eerie resemblance not the result of genetics but of mass production.

The only peculiar quality he could isolate and name was the preternaturally smooth quality of their skin – neither of them had so much as a single visible line or wrinkle. No moles, blotches, or scars, either, although Ralph supposed those were things you might miss with even a great pair of binoculars. Beyond the smooth and strangely line-free quality of their skin, everything became subjective. And his only look had been so goddam *brief*! If he had been able to get to the binoculars more quickly, without the rigmarole of the chair and the fishing net, and if he had realized that the lens caps were on right away instead of wasting more time fiddling with the focusing knob, he might have saved himself some or all of the unease he was now feeling.

They look sketched, he thought in the instant before they turned their backs on him. *That's what's really bothering me, I think. Not the identical bald heads, the identical white smocks, or even the lack of wrinkles. It's how they look sketched — the eyes just circles, the small pink ears just squiggles made with a felt-tip pen, the mouths a pair of quick, almost careless strokes of pale pink watercolor. They don't really look like either people or aliens; they look like hasty representations of . . . well, of I don't know what.*

He was sure of one thing: Docs #1 and #2 were both immersed in bright auras which in the binoculars appeared to be green-gold and filled with deep reddish-orange flecks that looked like sparks swirling up from a campfire. These auras conveyed a feeling of power and vitality to Ralph that their featureless, uninteresting faces did not.

The faces? I'm not sure I could pick them out again even if someone held a gun to my head. It's as if they were made to be forgotten. If they were still bald, sure — no problem. But if they were wearing wigs and maybe sitting down, so I couldn't see how short they are? Maybe . . . the lack of lines might do the trick . . . but then again, maybe not. The auras, though . . . those green-gold auras with the red flecks swirling through them . . . I'd know them anywhere. But there's something wrong with them, isn't there? What is it?

The answer popped into Ralph's mind as suddenly and easily as the two creatures had popped into view when he had finally remembered to remove the lens caps from the binoculars. Both of the little doctors were swaddled in brilliant auras . . . but neither had a balloon-string floating up from his hairless head. Not even a sign of one.

They went strolling down Harris Avenue in the direction of Strawford Park, moving with the ease of two friends out for a Sunday stroll. Just before they left the bright circle of light thrown by the streetlamp in front of May Locher's house, Ralph dropped the angle of the binoculars so they picked up the item in Doc #1's right hand. It wasn't a knife, as he had surmised, but it still wasn't the sort of object you felt comfortable seeing in the hand of a departing stranger in the wee hours of the morning.

It was a pair of long-bladed, stainless-steel scissors.

4

That sense of being pushed relentlessly toward the mouth of a tunnel where all sorts of unpleasant things were waiting was with him again, only now it was accompanied by a feeling of panic, because it seemed that the latest big shove had taken place while he had been asleep and dreaming of his dead wife. Something inside him wanted to shriek with terror, and Ralph understood that if he didn't do something to soothe it immediately, he would soon be shrieking out loud. He closed his eyes and began to take deep breaths, trying to picture a different item of food with each one: a tomato, a potato, an ice-cream sandwich, a Brussels sprout. Dr Jamal had taught Carolyn this simple relaxation technique, and it had frequently staved off her headaches before they could get up a full head of steam – even in the last six weeks, when the tumor had been out of control, the technique had sometimes worked, and it controlled Ralph's panic now. His heartbeat began to slow, and that feeling that he needed to scream began to pass.

Continuing to take deep breaths and to think

(*apple   pear   slice of lemon pie*)

of food, Ralph carefully snapped the lens caps back on the binoculars. His hands were still trembling, but not so badly he couldn't use them. Once the binoculars were capped and returned to their case, Ralph gingerly raised his left arm and looked at the bandage. There was a red spot in the center of it the size of an aspirin tablet, but it did not appear to be spreading. Good.

There isn't anything good about this, Ralph.

Fair enough, but that wasn't going to help him decide exactly what had happened, or what he was going to do about it. Step one was to push his dreadful dream of Carolyn to one side for the time being and decide what had actually happened.

'I've been awake ever since I hit the floor,' Ralph told the empty room. 'I know that, and I know I saw those men.'

Yes. He had really seen them, and the green-gold auras around them. He wasn't alone, either; Ed Deepneau had seen at least one of them, too. Ralph would have bet the farm on it, if he'd had a farm to bet. It didn't ease his mind much, however, to know that he and the wife-beating paranoid from up the street were seeing the same little bald guys.

And the auras, Ralph — didn't he say something about those, too?

Well, he hadn't used that exact word, but Ralph was quite sure he had spoken of the auras at least twice, just the same. *Ralph, sometimes the world is full of colors.* That had been August, shortly before John Leydecker had arrested Ed on a charge of domestic abuse, a misdemeanor. Then, almost a month later, when he had called Ralph on the phone. *Are you seeing the colors yet?*

First the colors, now the little bald doctors; surely the Crimson King himself would be along any time. And all that aside, what was he supposed to do about what he had just seen?

The answer came in an unexpected but welcome burst of clarity. The issue, he saw, was not his own sanity, not the auras, not the little bald doctors, but May Locher. He had just seen two strangers step out of Mrs Locher's house in the dead of night . . . and one of them had been carrying a potentially lethal weapon.

Ralph reached past the cased binoculars, took the telephone, and dialed 911.

5

'This is Officer Hagen.' A woman's voice. 'How may I help you?'

'By listening carefully and acting fast,' Ralph said crisply. The look of dazed indecision which he had worn so frequently since midsummer was gone now; sitting erect in the wing-back chair with the phone in his lap he looked not seventy but a healthy and capable fifty-five. 'You may be able to save a woman's life.'

'Sir, would you please give me your name and—'

'Don't interrupt me, please, Officer Hagen,' said the man who could no longer remember the last four digits of the Derry Cinema Center. 'I woke up a short time ago, couldn't go back to sleep, and decided to sit up for a while. My living room looks out on upper Harris Avenue. I just saw—'

Here Ralph paused for the barest moment, thinking not about what he had seen but what he wanted to tell Officer Hagen he had seen. The answer came as quickly and effortlessly as the decision to call 911 in the first place.

'I saw two men coming out of a house up the street from the Red Apple store. The house belongs to a woman named May Locher. That's L-O-C-H-E-R, first letter L as in Lexington. Mrs Locher is severely ill. I've never seen these two men before.' He paused again, but this time consciously, wanting to achieve maximum effect. 'One of them had a pair of scissors in his hand.'

'Site address?' Officer Hagen asked. She was calm enough, but Ralph sensed he had turned on a lot of her lights.

'I don't know,' he said. 'Get it out of the phone book, Officer Hagen, or just tell the responding officers to look for the yellow house with the pink trim half a block or so up from the Red Apple. They'll probably have to use a flashlight to pick it out because of the damned orange streetlights, but they'll find it.'

'Yes, sir, I'm sure they will, but I still need your name and telephone number for our rec—'

Ralph replaced the phone gently in its cradle. He sat looking at it for almost a full minute, expecting it to ring. When it didn't, he decided they either didn't have the fancy traceback equipment he saw on the TV true-crime shows, or it hadn't been turned on. That was good. It didn't solve the problem of what he was going to do or say if they hauled May Locher out of her hideous yellow-and-pink house in pieces, but it *did* buy a little more thinking time.

Below, Harris Avenue remained still and silent, lit only by the hi-intensity lamps which marched off in both directions like some surrealist dream of perspective. The play – short, but full of drama appeared to be over. The stage was empty again. It—

No, not quite empty after all. Rosalie came limping out of the alley between the Red Apple and the True-Value Hardware next door. The faded bandanna flapped around her neck. This wasn't a Thursday, there were no garbage cans set out for Rosalie to investigate, and she moved briskly up the sidewalk until she got to May Locher's house. There she stopped and lowered her nose (looking at that long and rather pretty nose, Ralph had thought on occasion that there must be a collie somewhere in Rosalie's woodpile).

Something was glimmering there, Ralph realized.

He got the binoculars out of their case once more and trained them on Rosalie. As he did, he found his mind returning to September 10th again – this time to his meeting with Bill and Lois just outside the entrance to Strawford Park. He remembered how Bill had put his arm around Lois's waist and led her up the street; how the two of them together had made Ralph think of Ginger Rogers and Fred Astaire. Most of all he remembered the spectral tracks the two of them had left behind. Lois's had been gray; Bill's olive green. Hallucinations, he had thought them at the time, back in the good old days before he'd started attracting the attention of nuts like Charlie Pickering and seeing little bald doctors in the middle of the night.

Rosalie was sniffing at a similar track. It was the same green-gold as the auras which had surrounded Bald Doc #1 and Bald Doc #2. Ralph panned the binoculars slowly away from the dog and saw more tracks, two sets of them, leading down the sidewalk in the direction of the park. They were fading – he could almost see them fading as he looked at them – but they were there.

Ralph panned the binoculars back to Rosalie, suddenly feeling an enormous wave of affection for the mangy old stray . . . and why not? If he had needed final, absolute proof that he had actually seen the things he *thought* he had seen, Rosalie was it.

If baby Natalie was here, she'd see them too, Ralph thought . . . and then all his doubts tried to crowd back in. Would she? Would she really? He thought he had seen the baby grab at the faint auras left by his fingers, and he had been sure she was gawking at the spectral green smoke sizzling off the flowers in the kitchen, but how could he be sure? How could anyone be sure what a baby was looking at or reaching for?

But Rosalie . . . look, right down there, see her?

The only trouble with that, Ralph realized, was that he hadn't seen the tracks until Rosalie had begun to sniff the sidewalk. Maybe she was sniffing at an entrancing remnant of leftover postman, and what he was seeing had been created by nothing more than his tired, sleep-starved mind . . . like the little bald doctors themselves.

In the magnified field of the binoculars, Rosalie now began to make her way down Harris Avenue with her nose to the sidewalk and her ragged tail waving slowly back and forth. She was moving from the green-gold tracks left by Doc #1 to those left by Doc #2, and then back to Doc #1's trail again.

So now why don't you tell me what that stray bitch is following, Ralph? Do you think it's possible for a dog to track a fucking hallucination? It's not a hallucination; it's tracks. Real tracks. The white-man tracks that Carolyn told you to watch out for. You know that. You see that.

'It's crazy, though,' he told himself. 'Crazy!'

But was it? Was it really? The dream might have been more than a dream. If there was such a thing as hyper-reality – and he could now testify that there was – then maybe there was such a thing as precognition, too. Or ghosts which came in dreams and foretold the future. Who knew? It was as if a door in the wall of reality had come ajar . . . and now all sorts of unwelcome things were flying through.

Of one thing he was sure: the tracks *were* really there. He saw them, Rosalie smelled them, and that was all there was to it. Ralph had discovered a number of strange and interesting things during his six months of premature waking, and one of them was that a human being's capacity for self-deception seemed to be at its lowest ebb between three and six in the morning, and it was now . . .

Ralph leaned forward so he could see the clock on the kitchen wall. Just past three-thirty. Uh-huh.

He raised the binoculars again and saw Rosalie still moving up the bald docs' backtrail. If someone came strolling along Harris Avenue right now – unlikely, given the hour, but not impossible – they would see nothing but a stray mutt with a dirty coat, sniffing at the sidewalk in the aimless fashion of untrained, unowned dogs everywhere. But Ralph could see what Rosalie was sniffing *at,* and had finally given himself permission to believe his eyes. It was a permission he might revoke once the sun was up, but for now he knew exactly what he was seeing.

Rosalie's head came up suddenly. Her ears cocked forward. For one moment she was almost beautiful, the way a hunting dog on point is beautiful. Then, moments before the headlights of a car approaching the Harris Avenue-Witcham Street intersection splashed the street, she was gone back the way she had come, running in a corkscrewing, limping gait that made Ralph feel sorry for her. When you came right down to it, what was Rosalie but another Harris Avenue Old Crock, one that didn't even have the comfort of the occasional game of gin rummy or penny-ante poker with others of her kind? She darted back into the alley between the Red Apple and the hardware store an instant before a Derry police cruiser turned the corner and floated slowly up the street. Its siren was off, but the revolving flashers were on. They painted the sleeping houses and small businesses ranged along this part of Harris Avenue with alternating pulses of red and blue light.

Ralph put the binoculars back in his lap and leaned forward in the wing-chair, forearms on his thighs, watching intently. His heart was beating hard enough for him to be able to feel it in his temples.

The cruiser slowed to a crawl as it passed the Red Apple. The spotlight mounted on its righthand side snapped on, and the beam began to slide across the fronts of the sleeping houses on the far side of the street. In most cases it also slid across the street numbers mounted beside doors or on porch columns. When it lit on the number of May Locher's house (86, Ralph saw, and he didn't need the binoculars to read it, either), the cruiser's tail-lights flashed and the car came to a stop.

Two uniformed policemen got out and approached the walk leading up to the house, oblivious of both the man watching from a darkened second-floor window across the street and the fading green-gold footprints over which they were walking. They conferred, and Ralph raised the binoculars again to get a closer look. He was almost positive that the younger of the two men was the uniformed cop who had shown up with Leydecker at Ed's house on the day Ed had been arrested. Knoll? Had that been his name?

'No,' Ralph murmured. 'Nell. Chris Nell. Or maybe it was Jess.'

Nell and his partner seemed to be having a serious discussion about something – much more serious than the one the little bald doctors had been having before they strolled away. This one ended with the cops drawing their sidearms and then climbing the narrow steps to Mrs Locher's stoop in single file, with Nell in front. He pressed

299

the doorbell, waited, then pressed it again. This time he leaned on the button for a good five seconds. They waited a little more, and then the second cop brushed past Nell and had a go at the button himself.

Maybe that one knows The Secret Art of Doorbell-Ringing, Ralph thought. *Probably learned it by answering a Rosicrucians ad.*

If so, the technique failed him this time. There was still no response, and Ralph wasn't surprised. Strange bald men with scissors notwithstanding, he doubted May Locher could even get out of bed.

But if she's bedridden, she might have a companion, someone to get her her meals, help her to the toilet or give her the bedpan—

Chris Nell – or maybe it was Jess – stepped up to the plate again. This time he forwent the doorbell in favor of the old wham-wham-wham, open-in-the-name-of-the-law technique. He used his left fist to do this. He was still holding his gun in his right, the barrel pressed against the leg of his uniform pants.

A terrible image, every bit as clear and persuasive as the auras he had been seeing, suddenly filled Ralph's mind. He saw a woman with a clear plastic oxygen mask over her mouth and nose lying in bed. Above the mask, her glazed eyes bulged sightlessly from their sockets. Below it, her throat had been opened in a wide, ragged smile. The bedclothes and the bosom of the woman's nightgown were drenched with blood. Not far away, lying on the floor, was the facedown corpse of another woman – the companion. Marching up the back of this second woman's pink flannel nightgown were half a dozen stab-wounds made by the points of Doc #1's scissors. And, Ralph knew, if you raised the nightgown for a closer look, each would look a lot like the wound under his own arm . . . like the sort of oversized period made by children just learning to print.

Ralph tried to blink the grisly vision away. It wouldn't go. He felt dull pain in his hands and saw he had closed them into tight fists; the nails were digging into his palms. He forced his hands open and clamped them on his thighs. Now the eye in his mind saw the woman in the pink nightgown twitching slightly – she was still alive. But maybe not for long. Almost certainly not for long unless these two oafs decided to try something a little more productive than just standing on the stoop and taking turns knocking or jazzing the doorbell.

'Come on, you guys,' Ralph said, squeezing at his thighs. 'Come on, come on, let's get with it, what do you say?'

You know the things you're seeing are all in your head, don't you? he asked himself uneasily. *I mean, there might be a couple of women lying dead over there, sure, there might be, but you don't* know *that, right? It's not like the auras, or the tracks . . .*

No, it wasn't like the auras or the tracks, and yes, he *did* know that. He also knew that no one was answering the door over there at 86 Harris Avenue, and that did not bode well for Bill McGovern's old Cardville schoolmate. He hadn't seen any blood on the scissors in Doc #1's hand, but given the iffy quality of the old Zeiss-Ikon binocs, that didn't prove much. Also, the guy could have wiped them clean before leaving the house. The thought had no more than crossed Ralph's mind before his imagination added a bloody handtowel lying beside the dead companion in the pink nightgown.

'Come *on,* you two!' Ralph cried in a low voice. 'Jesus Christ, you gonna stand there all *night*?'

More headlights splashed up Harris Avenue. The new arrival was an unmarked Ford sedan with a flashing red dashboard bubble. The man who got out was wearing plain clothes – gray poplin windbreaker and blue knitted watchcap. Ralph had maintained momentary hopes that the newcomer would turn out to be John Leydecker, even though Leydecker had told him he wouldn't be coming on until noon, but he didn't have to check with the binoculars to make sure it wasn't. This man was much slimmer, and wearing a dark mustache. Cop #2 went down the walk to meet him while Chris-or-Jess Nell went around the corner of Mrs Locher's house.

One of those pauses which the movies so conveniently edit out then ensued. Cop #2 reholstered his gun. He and the newly arrived detective stood at the foot of Mrs Locher's stoop, apparently talking and glancing at the closed door every now and then. Once the uniformed cop took a step or two in the direction Nell had gone. The detective reached out, grasped his arm, detained him. They talked some more. Ralph clutched his upper thighs tighter and made a small, frustrated noise in his throat.

A few minutes crawled by, and then everything happened at once in that confusing, overlapping, inconclusive way with which emergency situations seem to develop. Another police car arrived (Mrs Locher's house and those neighboring it on the right and left were now bathed in streaks of conflicting red and yellow light). Two more uniformed cops got out of it, opened the trunk, and removed a bulky contraption that looked to Ralph like a portable torture device. He believed this gadget was known as the Jaws of Life. Following the huge storm in the spring of 1985, a storm which had resulted in the deaths of more than two hundred people – many of whom had been trapped and drowned in their cars – Derry's schoolchildren had mounted a penny-drive to buy one.

As the two new cops were carrying the Jaws of Life across the sidewalk, the front door of the house on the uphill side of Mrs Locher's opened and the Eberlys, Stan and Georgina, stepped out onto *their* stoop. They wore matching his 'n hers bathrobes, and Stan's gray hair was standing up in wild tufts that made Ralph think of Charlie Pickering. He raised the binoculars, scanned their curious, excited faces briefly, then put them back in his lap again.

The next vehicle to appear was an ambulance from Derry Home Hospital. Like the police cars which had already arrived, its howler was off in deference to the hour, but it had a full roofrack of red lights, and they were strobing wildly. To Ralph, the developments across the street looked like a scene from one of his beloved *Dirty Harry* movies, only with the sound turned off.

The two cops got the Jaws of Life halfway across the lawn and then dropped it. The detective in the windbreaker and the watchcap turned to them and raised his hands to shoulder-level, palms out, as if to say *What did you think you were going to do with that thing? Break down the goddam door with it?* At the same second, Officer Nell came back around the house. He was shaking his head.

The detective in the watchcap abruptly turned, brushed past Nell and his partner, mounted the steps, raised one foot, and kicked in May Locher's front door. He paused to unzip his jacket, probably to free access to his gun, and then walked in without looking back.

Ralph felt like applauding.

Nell and his partner looked at each other uncertainly, then followed the detective up the steps and through the door. Ralph leaned forward even farther in his chair, now close enough to the window for his nostrils to make little fog-roses on the glass. Three men, their white hospital pants looking orange in the glare of the hi-intensity streetlamps, got out of the ambulance. One of them opened the rear doors and then all three of them simply stood there, hands in jacket pockets, waiting to see if they would be needed. The two cops who had carried the Jaws of Life halfway across Mrs Locher's lawn looked at each other, shrugged, picked it up, and began carrying it back toward their cruiser again. There were several large divots in the lawn where they had dropped it.

Just let her be okay, that's all, Ralph thought. *Just let her — and anyone who was in the house with her — be okay.*

The detective appeared in the doorway again, and Ralph's heart sank as he motioned to the men standing at the rear of the ambulance. Two of them removed a stretcher with a collapsible undercarriage; the third remained where he was. The men with the stretcher went up the walk and into the house at a smart pace, but they did not run, and when the orderly who had remained behind produced a pack of cigarettes and lit one, Ralph knew — suddenly, completely, and with no doubts — that May Locher was dead.

6

Stan and Georgina Eberly walked to the low line of hedge which separated their front yard from Mrs Locher's. They had put their arms around each other's waists, and to Ralph they looked like the Bobbsey Twins grown old and fat and frightened.

Other neighbors were also coming out, either awakened by the silent convergence of emergency lights or because the telephone network along this little stretch of Harris Avenue was already beginning to operate. Most of the people Ralph saw were old ('We golden-agers', Bill McGovern liked to call them . . . always with that small satirical lift of the eyebrow, of course), men and women whose rest was fragile and easily broken at the best of times. He suddenly realized that Ed, Helen, and Baby Natalie had been the youngest people between here and the Extension . . . and now the Deepneaus were gone.

I could go down there, he thought. *I'd fit right in. Just another one of Bill's golden-agers.*

Except he couldn't. His legs felt like bunches of teabags held together by weak twists of string, and he was quite sure that if he tried to get up, he would go flopping bonelessly to the floor. So he sat and watched from his window, watched the play develop below him on the stage which had always been empty at this hour before . . . except for the occasional walk-through by Rosalie, that was. It was a play he had produced himself, with a single anonymous telephone call. He watched the orderlies re-emerge with the stretcher, this time moving more slowly because of the sheeted figure which had been strapped to it. Warring streaks of blue and red light flickered over that sheet, and the shapes of legs, hips, arms, neck, and head beneath it.

Ralph was suddenly plunged back into his dream. He saw his wife under the sheet – not May Locher but Carolyn Roberts, and at any moment her head would split open and the black bugs, the ones which had grown fat on the meat of her diseased brain, would begin to boil out.

Ralph raised the heels of his palms to his eyes. Some sound – some inarticulate sound of grief and rage, horror and weariness – escaped him. He sat that way for a long time, wishing he had never seen any of this and hoping blindly that if there really *was* a tunnel, he would not be required to enter it after all. The auras were strange and beautiful, but there was not enough beauty in all of them to make up for one moment of that terrible dream in which he had discovered his wife buried below the high-tide line, not enough beauty to make up for the dreary horror of his lost, wakeful nights, or the sight of that sheeted figure being rolled out of the house across the street.

It was a lot more than just wishing that the play was over; as he sat there with the heels of his palms pressing against the lids of his closed eyes, he wanted *all* of it to be over – all of it. For the first time in his twenty-five thousand days of life, Ralph Roberts found himself wishing he were dead.

CHAPTER NINE

1

There was a movie poster, probably picked up at one of the local video stores for a buck or three, on the wall of the cubbyhole which served Detective John Leydecker as an office. It showed Dumbo the elephant cruising along with his magical ears outstretched. A headshot of Susan Day had been pasted over Dumbo's face, carefully cut to allow for the trunk. On the cartoon landscape below, someone had drawn a signpost which read DERRY 250.

'Oh, charming,' Ralph said.

Leydecker laughed. 'Not very politically correct, is it?'

'I think that's an understatement,' Ralph said, wondering what Carolyn would have made of the poster – wondering what Helen would make of it, for that matter. It was quarter of two on an overcast, chilly Monday afternoon, and he and Leydecker had just come across from the Derry County Courthouse, where Ralph had given his statement about his encounter with Charlie Pickering the day before. He had been questioned by an assistant district attorney who looked to Ralph as if he might be ready to start shaving in another year or two.

Leydecker had accompanied him as promised, sitting in the corner of the assistant DA's office and saying nothing. His promise to buy Ralph a cup of coffee turned out to be mostly a figure of speech – the evil-looking brew had come from the Silex in the corner of the cluttered second-floor Police Department dayroom. Ralph sipped cautiously at his and was relieved to find it tasted a little better than it looked.

'Sugar? Cream?' Leydecker asked. 'Gun to shoot it with?'

Ralph smiled and shook his head. 'Tastes fine . . . although it'd probably be a mistake to trust my judgement. I cut back to two cups a day last summer, and now it all tastes pretty good to me.'

'Like me with cigarettes – the less I smoke, the better they taste. Sin's a bitch.' Leydecker took out his little tube of toothpicks, shook one out, and stuck it in the corner of his mouth. Then he put his own cup on top of his computer terminal, went over to the Dumbo poster, and began to lever out the thumbtacks which held the corners.

'Don't do it on my account,' Ralph said. 'It's *your* office.'

'Wrong.' Leydecker pulled the carefully scissored photo of Susan Day off the poster, balled it up, tossed it in the wastebasket. Then he began to roll the poster itself into a tight little cylinder.

'Oh? Then how come your name's on the door?'

'It's my name, but the office belongs to you and your fellow taxpayers, Ralph. Also to any news vidiot with a Minicam who happens to wander in here, and if this poster happened to show up on *News at Noon,* I'd be in a world

308

of hurt. I forgot to take it down when I left Friday night, and I had most of the weekend off – a rare occurrence around here, let me tell you.'

'You didn't put it up, I take it.' Ralph moved some papers off the tiny office's one extra chair and sat down.

'Nope. Some of the fellows had a party for me Friday afternoon. Complete with cake, ice cream, and presents.' Leydecker rummaged in his desk and came up with a rubber band. He slipped it around the poster so it wouldn't spring open again, peeked one amused eye through it at Ralph, then tossed it into the wastebasket. 'I got a set of those days-of-the-week panties with the crotches snipped out, a can of strawberry-scented vaginal douche, a packet of Friends of Life anti–abortion literature – said literature including a comic-book called *Denise's Unwanted Pregnancy* – and that poster.'

'I guess it wasn't a birthday party, huh?'

'Nope.' Leydecker cracked his knuckles and sighed at the ceiling. 'The boys were celebrating my appointment to a special detail.'

Ralph could see faint flickers of blue aura around Leydecker's face and shoulders, but in this case he didn't have to try and read them. 'It's Susan Day, isn't it? You got the job of protecting her while she's in town.'

'Hole in one. Of course the State Police will be around, but they stick pretty much to traffic control in situations like this. There may be some FBI, too, but what they do mostly is hang back, take pictures, and give each other the secret Club Sign.'

'She's got her own security people, doesn't she?'

'Yes, but I don't know how many or how good. I

talked to the head guy this morning and he's at least coherent, but we have to put in our own guys. Five of them, according to the orders I got on Friday. That's me plus four guys who'll volunteer as soon as I tell em to. The object is . . . wait a minute . . . you'll like this . . .' Leydecker shuffled through the papers on his desk, found the one he was looking for, and held it up. ' ". . . to maintain a strong presence and high visibility".'

He dropped the paper again and grinned at Ralph. The grin did not have a lot of humor in it.

'In other words, if someone tries to shoot the bitch or give her an acid shampoo, we want Lisette Benson and the other vidiots to at least record the fact that we were there.' Leydecker looked at the rolled-up poster leaning in his wastebasket and flipped it the bird.

'How can you dislike someone so much when you've never even met her?'

'I don't just *dislike* her, Ralph; I fucking *hate* her. Listen – I'm a Catholic, my lovin mother was a Catholic, my kids – if I ever have any – are all gonna be altarboys at St Joe's. Great. Being a Catholic's great. They even let you eat meat on Fridays now. But if you think being Catholic means I'm in favor of making abortions illegal again, you got the wrong puppy. See, I'm the Catholic who gets to question the guys who beat their kids with rubber hoses or push them downstairs after a night of drinking good Irish whiskey and getting all sentimental about their mothers.'

Leydecker fished inside his shirt and brought out a small gold medallion. He placed it on his fingers and tilted it toward Ralph.

'Mary, mother of Jesus. I've worn this since I was thirteen. Five years ago I arrested a man wearing one just like it. He had just boiled his two-year-old stepson. This is a true thing I'm telling you. Guy put on a great big pot of water, and when it was boiling, he picked the kid up by the ankles and dropped him into the pot like he was a lobster. Why? Because the kid wouldn't stop wetting the bed, he told us. I saw the body, and I'll tell you what, after you've seen something like that, the photos the right-to-life assholes like to show of vacuum abortions don't look so bad.'

Leydecker's voice had picked up a slight tremor.

'What I remember most of all is how the guy was crying, and how he kept holding onto that Mary medallion around his neck and saying he wanted to go to confession. Made me proud to be a Catholic, Ralph, let me tell you . . . and as far as the Pope goes, I don't think he should be allowed to have an opinion until he's had a kid himself, or at least spent a year or so taking care of crack-babies.'

'Okay,' Ralph said. 'What's your problem with Susan Day?'

'She's stirring the motherfucking *pot!*' Leydecker cried. 'She comes into my town and I have to protect her. Fine. I've got good men, and with just a pinch of luck, I think we can probably see her out of town with her head still on and her tits pointing the right way, but what about what happens before? And what happens after? Do you think she cares about any of that? Do you think the people who run WomanCare give much of a shit about the side-effects, as far as that goes?'

'I don't know.'

311

'The WomanCare advocates are a little less prone to violence than The Friends of Life, but in terms of the all-important ass-ache quotient, they're not much different. Do you know what this was all about when it started?'

Ralph cast his memory back to his first conversation about Susan Day, the one he'd had with Ham Davenport. For a moment he almost had it, but then it squiggled away. The insomnia had won again. He shook his head.

'Zoning,' Leydecker said, and laughed with disgusted amazement. 'Plain old garden-variety zoning regulations. Great, huh? Early this summer, two of our more conservative City Councillors, George Tandy and Emma Wheaton, petitioned the Zoning Committee to reconsider the zone with WomanCare in it, the idea being to kind of gerrymander the place out of existence. I doubt if that's exactly the right word, but you get the gist, don't you?'

'Sure.'

'Uh-huh. So the pro-choicers ask Susan Day to come to town and make a speech, help them to raise a war-chest to combat the pro-life grinches. The only problem is, the grinches never had a chance of rezoning District 7, *and the WomanCare people knew it!* Hell, one of their directors, June Halliday, is *on* the City Council. She and the Wheaton bitch just about spit at each other when they pass in the hall.

'Rezoning District 7 was a pipe-dream from the start, because WomanCare is technically a hospital, just like Derry Home, which is only a stone's throw away. If you change the zoning laws to make WomanCare illegal, you do the same to one of only three hospitals in Derry County – the third-largest county in the state of Maine. So it was never going to happen, but that's okay, because it was never about that in the first place. It was about being pissy and in-your-face. About being an ass-ache. And for most of the pro-choicers – one of the guys I work with calls em the Whale People – it's about being *right*.'

'Right? I don't get you.'

'It isn't enough that a woman can walk in there and get rid of the troublesome little fishie growing inside her any time she wants; the pro-choicers want the argument to *end*. What they want, down deep, is for people like Dan Dalton to admit they're right, and that'll never happen. It's more likely that the Arabs and the Jews will decide it was all a mistake and throw down their weapons. I support the right of a woman to have an abortion if she really needs to have one, but the pro-choicers' holier-than-thou attitude makes me want to puke. They're the new Puritans, as far as I'm concerned, people who believe that if you don't think the way they do, you're going to hell . . . only their version is a place where all you get on the radio is hillbilly music and all you can find to eat is chicken-fried steak.'

'You sound pretty bitter.'

'Try sitting on a powderkeg for three months and see how it makes *you* feel. Tell me this – do you think Pickering would have stuck a knife in your armpit yesterday if it hadn't been for WomanCare, The Friends of Life, and Susan Leave-My-Sacred-Twat-Alone Day?'

Ralph appeared to give the question serious thought, but what he was really doing was watching John Leydecker's aura. It was a healthy dark blue, but the edges were tinged with rapidly shifting greenish light. It was this edging which interested Ralph; he had an idea he knew what it meant.

313

Finally he said, 'No. I guess not.'

'Me either. You got wounded in a war that's already been decided, Ralph, and you won't be the last. But if you went to the Whale People – or to Susan Day – and opened your shirt and pointed at the bandage and said "This is partly your fault, so own the part that's yours," they'd raise their hands and say, "Oh no, goodness no, we're sorry you got hurt, Ralph, we whale watchers *abhor* violence, but it wasn't *our* fault, we have to keep WomanCare open, we have to man and woman the barricades, and if a little spilled blood is what it takes to do that, then so be it." But it's not *about* WomanCare, and that's what drives me absolutely bugfuck. It's about—'

'– abortion.'

'Shit, no! Abortion rights are safe in Maine and in Derry, no matter what Susan Day says at the Civic Center Friday night. This is about whose team is the best team. About whose side God's on. It's about who's *right*. I wish they'd all just sing "We Are the Champions" and go get drunk.'

Ralph threw back his head and laughed. Leydecker laughed with him.

'So they're assholes,' he finished with a shrug. 'But they're *our* assholes. Does that sounds like I'm joking? I'm not. WomanCare, Friends of Life, Body Watch, Daily Bread . . . they're *our* assholes, *Derry* assholes, and I really don't mind watching out for our own. That's why I took this job, and why I stay with it. But you'll have to forgive me if I'm less than crazy about being tapped to watch out for some long-stemmed American Beauty from New York who's going to fly in here and give an incendiary speech and then fly out with a few more press-clippings and enough material for chapter five of her new book.

'To our faces she'll talk about what a wonderful little grassroots community we are, and when she gets back to her duplex on Park Avenue, she'll tell her friends about how she hasn't managed to shampoo the stink of our paper mills out of her hair yet. She is woman; hear her roar . . . and if we're lucky, the whole thing will quiet down with no one dead or disabled.'

Ralph had become sure of what those greenish flickers meant. 'But you're scared, aren't you?' he asked.

Leydecker looked at him, surprised. 'Shows, does it?'

'Only a little,' Ralph said, and thought: *Just in your aura, John, that's all. Just in your aura.*

'Yeah, I'm scared. On a personal level I'm scared of fucking up the assignment, which has absolutely no upside to compensate for all the things that can go wrong. On a professional level I'm scared of something happening to her on my watch. On a community level I'm fucking *terrified* of what happens if there's some sort of confrontation and the genie comes out of the bottle . . . more coffee, Ralph?'

'I'll pass. I ought to be going soon, anyway. What's going to happen to Pickering?'

He didn't actually care much about Charlie Pickering's fate, but the big cop would probably think it strange if he asked about May Locher before he asked about Pickering. Suspicious, maybe.

'Steve Anderson – the ADA who questioned you – and Pickering's court-appointed attorney are probably horse-trading even as we speak. Pickering's guy will be saying he might be able to get his client – the thought of Charlie Pickering being *anyone's* client – for *anything,* sort of blows my mind, by the way – to plead out to second-degree assault. Anderson will say the time has come to put Pickering away for good and he's going for attempted murder. Pickering's lawyer will pretend to be shocked, and tomorrow your buddy is going to be charged with first-degree assault with a deadly weapon and bound over for trial. Then, possibly in December but more likely early next year, you'll be called as the star witness.'

'Bail?'

'It'll probably be set in the forty-thousand-dollar range. You can get out on ten per cent if the rest can be secured in event of flight, but Charlie Pickering doesn't have a house, a car, or even a Timex watch. In the end, he's liable to go back to Juniper Hill, but that's really not the object of the game. We're going to be able to keep him off the street for quite a while this time, and with people like Charlie, *that's* the object of the game.'

'Any chance The Friends of Life might go his bail?'

'Nah. Ed Deepneau spent a lot of last week with him, the two of them drinking coffee in the Bagel Shop. I imagine Ed was giving Charlie the lowdown on the Centurions and the King of Diamonds—'

'Crimson King is what Ed—'

'Whatever,' Leydecker agreed, waving a hand. 'But most of all I imagine he spent the time explaining how you were the devil's righthand man and how only a smart, brave, and dedicated fellow like Charlie Pickering could take you out of the picture.'

'You make him sound like such a calculating shit,'

Ralph said. He was remembering the Ed Deepneau he'd played chess with before Carolyn had fallen ill. That Ed had been an intelligent, well-spoken, civilized man with a deep capacity for kindness. Ralph still found it all but impossible to reconcile that Ed with the one he'd first glimpsed in July of 1992. He had come to think of the more recent arrival as 'rooster Ed'.

'Not just a calculating shit, a *dangerous* calculating shit,' Leydecker said. 'For him Charlie was just a tool, like a paring knife you'd use to peel an apple with. If the blade snaps off a paring knife, you don't run to the knife-grinder's to get a new one put on; that's too much trouble. You toss it in the wastebasket and get a new paring knife instead. That's the way guys like Ed treat guys like Charlie, and since Ed *is* The Friends of Life – for the time being, at least – I don't think you have to worry about Charlie making bail. In the next few days, he's going to be lonelier than a Maytag repairman. Okay?'

'Okay,' Ralph said. He was a little appalled to realize he felt sorry for Pickering. 'I want to thank you for keeping my name out of the paper, too . . . if you were the one who did it, that is.'

There had been a brief mention of the incident in the Derry *News*'s Police Beat column, but it said only that Charles H. Pickering had been arrested on 'a weapons charge' at the Derry Public Library.

'Sometimes we ask them for a favor, sometimes they ask us for one,' Leydecker said, standing up. 'It's how things work in the real world. If the nuts in The Friends of Life and the prigs in The Friends of WomanCare ever discover that, my job is going to get a lot easier.'

317

Ralph plucked the rolled-up Dumbo poster from the wastebasket, then stood up on his side of Leydecker's desk. 'Could I have this? I know a little girl who might really like it, in a year or so.'

Leydecker held out his hands expansively. 'Be my guest – think of it as a little premium for being a good citizen. Just don't ask for my crotchless panties.'

Ralph laughed. 'Wouldn't think of it.'

'Seriously, I appreciate you coming in. Thanks, Ralph.'

'No problem.' He reached across the desk, shook Leydecker's hand, then headed for the door. He felt absurdly like Lieutenant Columbo on TV – all he needed was the cigar and the ratty trenchcoat. He put his hand on the knob, then paused and turned back. 'Can I ask you about something totally unrelated to Charlie Pickering?'

'Fire away.'

'This morning in the Red Apple Store I heard that Mrs Locher, my neighbor up the street, died in the night. Nothing so surprising about that; she had emphysema. But there are police-line tapes up between the sidewalk and her front yard, plus a sign on the door saying the site has been sealed by the Derry PD. Do you know what it's about?'

Leydecker looked at him so long and hard that Ralph would have felt acutely uncomfortable . . . if not for the man's aura. There was nothing in it which communicated suspicion.

God, Ralph, you're taking these things a little too seriously, aren't you?

Well, maybe yes and maybe no. Either way he was glad that the green flickers at the edges of Leydecker's aura had not reappeared.

318

'Why are you looking at me that way?' Ralph asked. 'If I presumed or spoke out of turn, I'm sorry.'

'Not at all,' Leydecker said. 'It's a little weird, that's all. If I tell you about it, can you keep it quiet?'

'Yes.'

'It's your downstairs tenant I'm chiefly worried about. When the word discretion is mentioned, it's *not* the Prof I think of.'

Ralph laughed heartily. 'I won't say a word to him — Scout's Honor — but it's interesting you'd mention him; Bill went to school with Mrs Locher, way back when. *Grammar* school.'

'Man, I can't imagine the Prof in grammar school,' Leydecker said. 'Can you?'

'Sort of,' Ralph said, but the picture which rose in his mind was an exceedingly peculiar one: Bill McGovern looking like a cross between Little Lord Fauntleroy and Tom Sawyer in a pair of knickers, long white socks . . . and a Panama hat.

'We're not sure *what* happened to Mrs Locher,' Leydecker said. 'What we do know is that shortly after three a.m., 911 logged an anonymous call from someone — a male — who claimed to have just seen two men, one carrying a pair of scissors, come out of Mrs Locher's house.'

'She was killed?' Ralph exclaimed, realizing two things simultaneously: that he sounded more believable than he ever would have expected, and that he had just crossed a bridge. He hadn't burned it behind him — not yet, anyway — but he would not be able to go back to the other side without a lot of explanations.

Leydecker turned his hands palms up and shrugged.

319

'If she was, it wasn't with a pair of scissors or any other sharp object. There wasn't a mark on her.'

That, at least, was something of a relief.

'On the other hand, it's possible to scare someone to death — especially someone who's old and sick — during the commission of a crime,' Leydecker said. 'Anyway, this'll be easier to explain if you let me just tell you what I know. It won't take long, believe me.'

'Of course. Sorry.'

'Want to hear something funny? The first person I thought of when I looked over the 911 call-sheet was you.'

'Because of the insomnia, right?' Ralph asked. His voice was steady.

'That and the fact that the caller claimed to have seen these men from his living room. *Your* living room looks out on the Avenue, doesn't it?'

'Yes.'

'Uh-huh. I even thought of listening to the tape, then I remembered that you were coming in today . . . and that you're sleeping through again. That's right, isn't it?'

Without an instant of pause or consideration, Ralph set fire to the bridge he had just crossed. 'Well, I'm not sleeping like I did when I was sixteen and working two after-school jobs, I won't kid you about that, but if I was the guy who called 911 last night, I did it in my sleep.'

'Exactly what I figured. Besides, if you saw something a little off-kilter on the street, why would you make the call anonymously?'

'I don't know,' Ralph said, and thought, *But suppose*

it was a little more than off-kilter, John? Suppose it was completely unbelievable?

'Me, neither,' Leydecker said. 'Your place has a view of Harris Avenue, yes, but so do about three dozen others . . . and just because the guy who made the call *said* he was inside, that doesn't mean he really was, does it?'

'I guess not. There's a pay-phone outside the Red Apple he could have called from, plus one outside the liquor store. A couple in Strawford Park, too, if they work.'

'Actually there are four in the park, and they all work. We checked.'

'Why would he lie about where he was calling from?'

'The most likely reason is because he was lying about the rest of what he had to say, too. Anyway, Donna Hagen said the guy sounded very young and sure of himself.' The words were barely out of his mouth before Leydecker winced and put a hand on top of his head. 'That didn't come out just the way I meant it, Ralph. Sorry.'

'It's okay – the idea that I sound like an old fart on a pension is not exactly a new concept to me. I *am* an old fart on a pension. Go on.'

'Chris Nell was the responding officer – first on the scene. Do you remember him from the day we arrested Ed?'

'I remember the name.'

'Uh-huh. Steve Utterback was the responding detective and the OIC – officer in charge. He's a good man.'

The guy in the watchcap, Ralph thought.

'The lady was dead in bed, but there was no sign of violence. Nothing obvious taken, either, although old ladies like May Locher aren't usually into a lot of real hockable stuff – no VCR, no big fancy stereo, nothing like that.

321

She *did* have one of those Bose Waves, though, and two or three pretty nice pieces of jewelry. This is not to say that there wasn't other jewelry as nice or nicer, but—'

'But why would a burglar take some and not all?'

'Exactly. What's more interesting in this case is that the front door – the one the 911 caller said he saw the two men coming out of – was locked from the inside. Not just a spring-lock, either; there was a thumb-bolt and a chain. Same with the back door, by the way. So if the 911 caller was on the up and up, and if May Locher was dead when the two guys left, who locked the doors?'

Maybe it was the Crimson King, Ralph thought . . . and to his horror, almost said aloud.

'I don't know. What about the windows?'

'Locked. Thumb-latches turned. And, just in case that's not Agatha Christie enough for you, Steve says the storms were on. One of the neighbors told him Mrs Locher hired a kid to put them on just last week.'

'Sure she did,' Ralph said. 'Pete Sullivan, the same kid who delivers the newspaper. Now that I think of it, I saw him doing it.'

'Mystery-novel bullshit,' Leydecker said, but Ralph thought Leydecker would have swapped Susan Day for May Locher in about three seconds. 'The prelim medical came in just before I left for the courthouse to meet you. I had a glance at it. Myocardial this, thrombosis that . . . heart-failure's what it comes down to. Right now we're treating the 911 call as a crank – we get em all the time, all cities do – and the lady's death as a heart-attack brought on by her emphysema.'

'Just a coincidence, in other words.' That conclusion

might save him a lot of trouble – if it flew, that was – but Ralph could hear the disbelief in his own voice.

'Yeah, I don't like it, either. Neither does Steve, which is why the house has been sealed. State Forensics will give it a complete top-to-bottom, probably starting tomorrow morning. Meanwhile, Mrs Locher has taken a little ride down to Augusta for a more comprehensive postmortem. Who knows what it'll show? Sometimes they *do* show things. You'd be surprised.'

'I suppose I would,' Ralph said.

Leydecker tossed his toothpick into the trash, appeared to brood for a moment, then brightened up. 'Hey, here's an idea – maybe I'll get someone in clerical to make a dupe of that 911 call. I could bring it over and play it for you. Maybe you'll recognize the voice. Who knows? Stranger things have happened.'

'I suppose they have,' Ralph said, smiling uneasily.

'Anyway, it's Utterback's case. Come on, I'll see you out.'

In the hall, Leydecker gave Ralph another searching look. This one made Ralph feel a good deal more uncomfortable, because he had no idea what it meant. The auras had disappeared again.

He tried on a smile that felt lame. 'Something hanging out of my nose that shouldn't be?'

'Nope. I'm just amazed at how good you look for someone who went through what you did yesterday. And compared to how you looked last summer . . . if that's what honeycomb can do, I'm going to buy myself a beehive.'

Ralph laughed as though this were the funniest thing he had ever heard.

2

1:42 a.m., Tuesday morning.

Ralph sat in the wing-chair, watching wheels of fine mist revolve around the streetlights. Up the street, the police-line tapes hung dispiritedly in front of May Locher's house.

Barely two hours' sleep tonight, and he found himself again thinking that dead might be better. No more insomnia then. No more long waits for dawn in this hateful chair. No more days when he seemed to be looking at the world through the Gardol Invisible Shield they used to prattle about on the toothpaste commercials. Back when TV had been almost brand-new, that had been, in the days when he had yet to find the first strands of gray in his hair and he was always asleep five minutes after he and Carol had finished making love.

And people keep talking about how good I look. That's the weirdest part of it.

Except it wasn't. Considering some of the things he'd seen just lately, a few people saying he looked like a new man was far, far down on his list of oddities.

Ralph's eyes returned to May Locher's house. The place had been locked up, according to Leydecker, but Ralph had seen the two little bald doctors come out the front door, he had *seen* them, goddammit—

But had he?

Had he really?

Ralph cast his mind back to the previous morning. Sitting down in this same chair with a cup of tea and thinking *Let the play begin.* And then he had seen those two little bald bastards come out, damn it, *he had seen them come out of May Locher's house!*

Except maybe that was wrong, because he hadn't really been looking at Mrs Locher's house; he had been pointed more in the direction of the Red Apple. He'd thought the flicker of movement in the corner of his eye was probably Rosalie, and had turned his head to check. *That* was when he'd seen the little bald doctors on the stoop of May Locher's house. He was no longer entirely sure he had seen the front door open; maybe he had just assumed that part, and why not? They sure as hell hadn't come up Mrs Locher's walk.

You can't be sure of that, Ralph.

Except he could. At three in the morning, Harris Avenue was as still as the mountains of the moon – the slightest movement anywhere within the range of his vision registered.

Had Doc #1 and Doc #2 come out the front door? The longer Ralph thought about it, the more he doubted it.

Then what happened, Ralph? Did they maybe step out from behind the Gardol Invisible Shield? Or – how's this? – maybe they walked through *the door, like those ghosts that used to haunt Cosmo Topper in that old TV show!*

And the craziest thing of all was that felt just about right.

What? That they walked through the fucking DOOR? *Oh, Ralph, you need help. You need to talk to someone about what's happening to you.*

Yes. That was the one thing of which he was sure: he needed to spill all this to someone before it drove him crazy. But who? Carolyn would have been best, but she was dead. Leydecker? The problem there was that Ralph had already lied to him about the 911 call. Why? Because the truth would have sounded insane. It would have sounded, in fact, as if he had caught Ed Deepneau's paranoia like a cold. And wasn't that really the most likely explanation, when you looked at the situation dead on?

'But that's not it,' he whispered. 'They were real. The auras, too.'

It's a long walk back to Eden, sweetheart . . . and watch out for those green-gold white-man tracks while you're on the way.

Tell someone. Lay it all out. Yes. And he ought to do it before John Leydecker listened to that 911 tape and showed up asking for an explanation. Wanting to know, basically, why Ralph had lied, and what Ralph actually knew about the death of May Locher.

Tell someone. Lay it all out.

But Carolyn was dead, Leydecker was still too new, Helen was lying low at the WomanCare shelter somewhere out in the willywags, and Lois Chasse might gossip to her girlfriends. Who did that leave?

The answer became clear once he put it to himself that way, but Ralph still felt a surprising reluctance to talk to McGovern about the things which had been happening to him. He remembered the day he had found Bill sitting on a bench by the softball field, crying over his old friend and mentor, Bob Polhurst. Ralph had tried to tell Bill about the auras, and it had been as if McGovern couldn't hear him; he had been too busy running through his well-thumbed script on the subject of how shitty it was to grow old.

Ralph thought of the satiric raised eyebrow. The

unfailing cynicism. The long face, always so gloomy. The literary allusions, which usually made Ralph smile but often left him feeling a tad inferior, as well. And then there was McGovern's attitude toward Lois: condescending, even a touch cruel.

Yet this was a long way from being fair, and Ralph knew it. Bill McGovern *was* capable of kindness, and — perhaps far more important in this case — understanding. He and Ralph had known each other for over twenty years; for the last ten of those years they had lived in the same building. He had been one of Carolyn's pallbearers, and if Ralph couldn't talk to Bill about what had been happening to him, who *could* he talk to?

The answer seemed to be no one.

CHAPTER TEN

1

The misty rings around the streetlamps were gone by the time daylight began to brighten the sky in the east, and by nine o'clock the day was clear and warm – the beginning of Indian summer's final brief passage, perhaps. Ralph went downstairs as soon as *Good Morning America* was over, determined to tell McGovern what had been happening to him (or as much as he dared, anyway) before he could lose his nerve. Standing outside the door of the downstairs apartment, however, he could hear the shower running and the mercifully distant sound of William D. McGovern singing 'I Left My Heart in San Francisco'.

Ralph went out to the porch, stuck his hands in his back pockets, and read the day like a catalogue. There was nothing, he reflected, really nothing in the world like October sunshine; he could almost feel his night-miseries draining away. They would undoubtedly be back, but for now he felt all right – tired and muzzy-headed, yes, but still pretty much all right. The day was more than pretty; it was downright gorgeous, and Ralph doubted if there would be another as good before next May. He decided he would be a fool not to take advantage of it. A walk up to the Harris Avenue Extension and back again would take half an hour, forty-five minutes if there happened to be someone up there worth batting a little breeze with, and by then Bill would be showered, shaved, combed, and dressed. Also ready to lend a sympathetic ear, if Ralph was lucky.

He walked as far as the picnic area outside the County Airport fence without quite admitting to himself that he was hoping to come across Old Dor. If he did, perhaps the two of them could talk a little poetry – Stephen Dobyns, for instance – or maybe even a bit of philosophy. They might start that part of their conversation with Dorrance explaining what 'long-time business' was, and why he believed Ralph shouldn't 'mess in' with it.

Except Dorrance wasn't at the picnic area; no one was there but Don Veazie, who wanted to explain to Ralph why Bill Clinton was doing such a horrible job as President, and why it would have been better for the good old US of A if the American people had elected that fiscal genius Ross Perot. Ralph (who had voted for Clinton and actually thought the man was doing a pretty good job) listened long enough to be polite, then said he had an appointment to have his hair cut. It was the only thing he could think of on short notice.

'Something else, too!' Don blared after him. 'That uppity wife of his! Woman's a lesbian! I can always tell! You know how? I look at their shoes! Shoes is like a secret code with em! They always wear those ones with the square toes and—'

'See you, Don!' Ralph called back, and beat a hasty retreat.

He had gone about a quarter of a mile back down the hill when the day exploded silently all around him.

2

He was opposite May Locher's house when it happened. He stopped dead in his tracks, staring down Harris Avenue with wide, unbelieving eyes. His right hand was pressed against the base of his throat and his mouth hung open. He looked like a man having a heart attack, and while his heart seemed all right — for the time being, anyway — he certainly felt as if he were having *some* kind of an attack. Nothing he had seen this fall had prepared him for this. Ralph didn't think *anything* could have prepared him for this.

That other world — the secret world of auras — had come into view again, and this time there was more of it than Ralph had ever dreamed . . . so much that he wondered fleetingly if it was possible for a person to die of perceptual overload. Upper Harris Avenue was a fiercely glowing wonderland filled with overlapping spheres and cones and crescents of color. The trees, which were still a week or more away from the climax of their fall transformation, none the less burned like torches in Ralph's eyes and mind. The sky had gone past color; it was a vast blue sonic boom.

The telephone lines on Derry's west side were still above ground, and Ralph stared fixedly at them, vaguely aware that he had stopped breathing and should probably start again soon if he didn't want to pass out. Jagged yellow spirals were running briskly up and down the black wires, reminding Ralph of how barber-poles had looked when he was a kid. Every now and then this bumblebee pattern was broken by a spiky red vertical stroke or a green flash that seemed to spread both ways at once, obliterating the yellow rings for a moment before fading out.

You're watching people talk, he thought numbly. *Do you know that, Ralph? Aunt Sadie in Dallas is chatting with her favorite nephew, who lives in Derry; a farmer in Haven is jawing with the dealer he buys his tractor parts from; a minister is trying to help a troubled parishioner. Those are* voices, *and I think the bright strokes and flashes are coming from people in the grip of some strong emotion — love or hate, happiness or jealousy.*

And Ralph sensed that all he was seeing and all he was feeling was *not* all; that there was a whole world still waiting just beyond the current reach of his senses. Enough, perhaps, to make even what he was seeing now seem faint and faded. And if there *was* more, how could he possibly bear it without going mad? Not even putting his eyes out would help; he understood somehow that his sense of 'seeing' these things came mostly from his lifelong acceptance of sight as his primary sense. But there was, in fact, a lot more than seeing going on here.

In order to prove this to himself he closed his eyes . . . and went right on seeing Harris Avenue. It was as if his eyelids had turned to glass. The only difference was that all the usual colors had reversed themselves, creating a world that looked like the negative of a color photograph. The trees were no longer orange and yellow but the bright, unnatural green of lime Gatorade. The surface of Harris Avenue, repaved with fresh asphalt in June, had become a great white way, and the sky was an amazing red lake. He opened his eyes again, almost positive that the auras would be gone, but they weren't; the world still boomed and rolled with color and movement and deep, resonating sound.

When do I start seeing them? Ralph wondered as he began to walk slowly down the hill again. *When do the little bald doctors start coming out of the woodwork?*

There were no doctors in evidence, however, bald or otherwise; no angels in the architecture; no devils peering up from the sewer gratings. There was only—

'Look out, Roberts, watch where you're going, can't you?'

The words, harsh and a little alarmed, seemed to have actual physical texture; it was like running a hand over oak panelling in some ancient abbey or ancestral hall. Ralph stopped short and saw Mrs Perrine from down the street. She had stepped off the sidewalk into the gutter to keep from being bowled over like a tenpin, and now she stood ankle-deep in fallen leaves, holding her net shopping bag in one hand and glaring at Ralph from beneath her thick salt-and-pepper eyebrows. The aura which surrounded her was the firm, no-nonsense gray of a West Point uniform.

'Are you drunk, Roberts?' she asked in a clipped voice, and suddenly the riot of color and sensation fell out of the world and it was just Harris Avenue again, drowsing its way through a lovely weekday morning in mid-autumn.

'Drunk? Me? Not at all. Sober as a judge, honest.'

He held out his hand to her. Mrs Perrine, over eighty but not giving in to it so much as a single inch, looked at it as if she believed Ralph might have a joy-buzzer hidden in his palm. *Wouldn't put it past you, Roberts,* her cool gray eyes said. *Wouldn't put it past you at all.* She stepped back onto the sidewalk without Ralph's aid.

'I'm sorry, Mrs Perrine. I wasn't watching where I was going.'

'No, you certainly weren't. Lollygagging along with your mouth hanging open is what you were doing. You looked like the village idiot.'

'Sorry,' he repeated, and then had to bite his tongue to stifle a bray of laughter.

'Hmmp.' Mrs Perrine looked him slowly up and down, like a Marine drill-sergeant inspecting a raw recruit. 'There's a rip under the arm of that shirt, Roberts.'

Ralph raised his left arm and looked. There was indeed a large rip in his favorite plaid shirt. He could look through it and see the bandage with its dried spot of blood; also an unsightly tangle of old-man armpit hair. He lowered his arm hurriedly, feeling a blush rising in his cheeks.

'Hmmp,' Mrs Perrine said again, expressing everything she needed to express on the subject of Ralph Roberts without recourse to a single vowel. 'Drop it off at the house, if you like. Any other mending you might have, as well. I can still run a needle, you know.'

'Oh yes, I'll bet you can, Mrs Perrine.'

Mrs Perrine now gave him a look which said, *You're a dried-up old asskisser, Ralph Roberts, but I suppose you can't help it.*

'Not in the afternoon,' she said. 'I help make dinner at the homeless shelter in the afternoons, and help serve it out at five. It's God's work.'

'Yes, I'm sure it—'

'There'll be no homeless in heaven, Roberts. You can count on that. No ripped shirts, either, I'm sure. But while

333

we're here, we have to get along and make do. It's our job.' *And I, for one, am doing spectacularly well at it,* Mrs Perrine's face proclaimed. 'Bring your mending in the morning or in the evening, Roberts. Don't stand on ceremony, but don't you show up on my doorstep after eight-thirty. I go to bed at nine.'

'That's very kind of you, Mrs Perrine,' Ralph said, and had to bite his tongue again. He was aware that very soon this trick would cease to work; soon it was going to be a case of laugh or die.

'Not at all. Christian duty. Also, Carolyn was a friend of mine.'

'Thank you,' Ralph said. 'Terrible about May Locher, wasn't it?'

'No,' Mrs Perrine said. 'God's mercy.' And she glided upon her way before Ralph could say another word. Her spine was so excruciatingly straight that it hurt him to look at it.

He walked on a dozen steps, then could hold it no longer. He leaned a forearm against a telephone pole, pressed his mouth to his arm, and laughed as quietly as he could – laughed until tears poured down his cheeks. When the fit (and that was what it really felt like; a kind of hysterical seizure) had passed, Ralph raised his head and looked around with attentive, curious, slightly teary eyes. He saw nothing that anyone else couldn't see as well, and that was a relief.

But it will come back, Ralph. You know it will. All of it.

Yes, he supposed he *did* know it, but that was for later. Right now he had some talking to do.

3

When Ralph finally arrived back from his amazing journey up the street, McGovern was sitting in his chair on the porch and idling through the morning paper. As Ralph turned up the walk, he came to a sudden decision. He would tell Bill a lot, but not everything. One of the things he would definitely leave out was how much the two guys he'd seen coming out of Mrs Locher's house had looked like the aliens in the tabloids for sale at the Red Apple.

McGovern looked up as he climbed the steps. 'Hello, Ralph.'

'Hi, Bill. Can I talk to you about something?'

'Of course.' He closed the paper and folded it carefully. 'They finally took my old friend Bob Polhurst to the hospital yesterday.'

'Oh? I thought you expected that to happen sooner.'

'I did. *Everybody* did. He fooled us. In fact, he seemed to be getting better – of the pneumonia, at least – and then he relapsed. He had a breathing arrest yesterday around noon, and his niece thought he was going to die before the ambulance got there. He didn't, though, and now he seems to have stabilized again.' McGovern looked up the street and sighed. 'May Locher pops off in the middle of the night and Bob just keeps chugging along. What a world, huh?'

'I guess so.'

'What did you want to talk about? Have you finally decided to pop the question to Lois? Want a little fatherly advice on how to handle it?'

'I need advice, all right, but not about my love-life.'

'Spill it,' McGovern said tersely.

Ralph did, gratified and more than a little relieved by McGovern's silent attentiveness. He began by sketching in things Bill already knew about – the incident between Ed and the truck-driver in the summer of '92, and how similar Ed's rantings on that occasion had been to the things he had said on the day he had beaten Helen for signing the petition. As Ralph spoke, he began to feel more strongly than ever that there were connections between all the odd things which had been happening to him, connections he could almost see.

He told McGovern about the auras, although not about the silent cataclysm he had experienced less than half an hour before – that was also further than he was willing to go, at least for the time being. McGovern knew about Charlie Pickering's attack on Ralph, of course, and that Ralph had averted a much more serious injury by using the spray Helen and her friend had given him, but now Ralph told him something he had held back on Sunday night, when he'd told McGovern about the attack over a scratch dinner: how the spray-can had magically appeared in his jacket pocket. Except, he said, he suspected that the magician had been Old Dor.

'Holy shit!' McGovern exclaimed. 'You've been living dangerously, Ralph!'

'I guess so.'

'How much of this have you told Johnny Leydecker?'

Very little, Ralph started to say, then realized that even that would be an exaggeration. 'Almost none of it. And there's something else I haven't told him. Something a lot more . . . well, a lot more substantive, I guess. To do with what happened up there.' He pointed toward May Locher's house, where a couple of blue and white vans had just pulled up. MAINE STATE POLICE was written on the sides. Ralph assumed they were the forensics people Leydecker had mentioned.

'May?' McGovern leaned a little further forward in his chair. 'You know something about what happened to May?'

'I think I do.' Speaking carefully, moving from word to word like a man using stepping-stones to cross a treacherous brook, Ralph told McGovern about waking up, going into the living room, and seeing two men come out of Mrs Locher's house. He recounted his successful rummage for the binoculars, and told McGovern about the scissors he had seen one of the men carrying. He did not mention his nightmare of Carolyn or the glowing tracks, and he most certainly did not mention his belated impression that the two men might have come right through the door; that would have finished off any remaining tatters of credibility he might still possess. He ended with his anonymous call to 911 and then sat in his chair, looking at McGovern anxiously.

McGovern shook his head as if to clear it. 'Auras, oracles, mysterious housebreakers with scissors . . . you *have* been living dangerously.'

'What do you think, Bill?'

McGovern sat quietly for several moments. He had rolled his newspaper up while Ralph was talking, and now he began to tap it absently against his leg. Ralph felt an urge to phrase his question even more bluntly – *Do you think I'm crazy, Bill?* – and quashed it. Did he really believe that was the sort of question to which people gave honest answers . . . at least without a healthy shot of sodium pentothal first? That Bill might say *Oh yes, I think you're just as crazy as a bedbug, Ralphie-baby, so why don't we call Juniper Hill right away and see if they have a bed for you*? Not very likely . . . and since any answer Bill gave would mean nothing, it was better to forgo the question.

'I don't exactly *know* what I think,' Bill said at last. 'Not yet, at least. What did they look like?'

'Their faces were hard to make out, even with the binoculars,' Ralph said. His voice was as steady as it had been yesterday, when he had denied making the 911 call.

'You probably don't have any idea of how old they were, either?'

'No.'

'Could either of them have been our old pal from up the street?'

'Ed Deepneau?' Ralph looked at McGovern in surprise. 'No, neither one was Ed.'

'What about Pickering?'

'No. Not Ed, not Charlie Pickering. I would have known either of them. What are you driving at? That my mind just sort of buckled and put the two guys who've caused me the most stress in the last few months on May Locher's front stoop?'

'Of course not,' McGovern replied, but the steady tap-tap-tap of the newspaper against his leg paused and his eyes flickered. Ralph felt a sinking in the pit of his stomach. Yes; that was in fact *exactly* what McGovern had been driving at, and it wasn't really so surprising, was it?

Maybe not, but it didn't change that sinking feeling.

'And Johnny said all the doors were locked.'

'Yes.'

'From the inside.'

'Uh-huh, but—'

McGovern got up from his chair so suddenly that for one crazy moment Ralph had the idea that he was going to run away, perhaps screaming *Watch out for Roberts! He's gone crazy!* as he went. But instead of bolting down the steps, he turned toward the door leading back into the house. In some ways Ralph found this even more alarming.

'What are you going to do?'

'Call Larry Perrault,' McGovern said. 'May's younger brother. He still lives out in Cardville. She'll be buried in Cardville, I imagine.' McGovern gave Ralph a strange, speculative look. 'What did you *think* I was going to do?'

'I don't know,' Ralph said uneasily. 'For a second there I thought you were going to run away like the Gingerbread Man.'

'Nope.' McGovern reached out and patted him on the shoulder, but to Ralph the gesture felt cold and comfortless. Perfunctory.

'What does Mrs Locher's brother have to do with any of this?'

'Johnny said they sent May's body down to Augusta for a more comprehensive autopsy, right?'

'Well, I think the word he actually used was post-mortem—'

McGovern waved this away. 'Same difference, believe me. If anything odd *does* crop up – anything suggesting that she was murdered – Larry would have to be informed. He's her only close living relative.'

'Yes, but won't he wonder what your interest is?'

'Oh, I don't think we have to worry about that,' McGovern said, speaking in a soothing tone Ralph didn't care for at all. 'I'll say the police have sealed off the house and that the old Harris Avenue rumor mill is turning briskly. He knows May and I were school chums, and that I visited her regularly over the last couple of years. Larry and I aren't crazy about each other, but we get along reasonably well. He'll tell me what I want to know if for no other reason than that we're both Cardville survivors. Get it?'

'I guess so, but—'

'I *hope* so,' McGovern said, and suddenly he looked like a very old and very ugly reptile – a gila monster, or perhaps a basilisk lizard. He pointed a finger at Ralph. 'I'm not a stupid man, and I *do* know how to respect a confidence. Your face just now said you weren't sure about that, and I resent it. I resent the hell out of it.'

'I'm sorry,' Ralph said. He was stunned by McGovern's outburst.

McGovern looked at him a moment longer with his leathery lips pulled back against his too-large dentures, then nodded. 'Yeah, okay, apology accepted. You've been sleeping like shit, I have to factor that into the equation, and as for me, I can't seem to get Bob Polhurst off my mind.' He heaved one of his weightiest poor-old-Bill sighs. 'Listen – if you'd prefer me not to try calling May's brother—'

'No, no,' Ralph said, thinking that what he'd like to do was roll the clock back ten minutes or so and cancel this entire conversation. And then a sentiment he was sure Bill McGovern would appreciate floated into his mind, fully constructed and ready for use. 'I'm sorry if I impugned your discretion.'

McGovern smiled, reluctantly at first and then with his whole face. 'Now I know what keeps you awake – thinking up crap like that. Sit still, Ralph, and think good thoughts about a hippopotamus, as my mother used to say. I'll be right back. Probably won't even catch him in, you know; funeral arrangements and all that. Want to look at the paper while you wait?'

'Sure. Thanks.'

McGovern handed him the paper, which still retained the tube shape into which it had been rolled, then went inside. Ralph glanced at the front page. The headline read PRO-CHOICE, PRO-LIFE ADVOCATES READY FOR ACTIVIST'S ARRIVAL. The story was flanked by two news photographs. One showed half a dozen young women making signs which said things like OUR BODIES, OUR CHOICE and IT'S A BRAND-NEW DAY IN DERRY! The other showed picketers marching in front of WomanCare. They carried no signs and needed none; the hooded black robes they wore and the scythes they carried said it all.

Ralph heaved a sigh of his own, dropped the paper onto the seat of the rocking chair beside him, and watched Tuesday morning unfold along Harris Avenue. It occurred to him that McGovern might well be on the phone with John Leydecker rather than Larry Perrault, and that the two of them might at this very moment be having a little student-teacher conference about that nutty old insomniac Ralph Roberts.

Just thought you'd like to know who really made that 911 call, Johnny.

Thanks, Prof. We were pretty sure, anyway, but it's good to get confirmation. I imagine he's harmless. I actually sort of like him.

Ralph pushed away his speculations about who Bill might or might not be calling. It was easier just to sit here and not think at all, not even good thoughts about a hippopotamus. Easier to watch the Budweiser truck lumber into the Red Apple parking lot, pausing to give courtesy to the Magazines Incorporated van which had dropped off this week's ration of tabloids, magazines, and paperbacks and was now leaving. Easier to watch old Harriet Bennigan, who made Mrs Perrine look like a spring chicken, bent over her walker in her bright red fall coat, out for her morning lurch. Easier to watch the young girl, who was wearing jeans, an oversized white tee-shirt, and a man's hat about four sizes too big for her, jumping rope in the weedy vacant lot between Frank's Bakery and Vicky Moon's Tanning Saloon (Body Wraps Our Specialty). Easier to watch the girl's small hands penduluming up and down. Easier to listen as she chanted her endless, shuttling rhyme.

Three-six-nine, the goose drank wine . . .

Some distant part of Ralph's mind realized, with great astonishment, that he was on the verge of going to sleep as he sat here on the porch steps. At the same time this was happening, the auras were creeping into the world again, filling it with fabulous colors and motions. It was wonderful, but . . .

. . . but something was wrong with it. *Something.* What?

The girl jumping rope in the vacant lot. *She* was wrong. Her denim-clad legs pumped up and down like the bobbin of a sewing machine. Her shadow jumped next to her on the jumbled pavement of an ancient alley over-grown with weeds and sunflowers. The rope whirled up and down . . . all around . . . up and down and all around . . .

Not an oversized tee-shirt, though, he'd been wrong about that. The figure was wearing a smock. A white smock, like the kind worn by actors in the old TV doc-operas.

Three-six-nine, hon, the goose drank wine,
The monkey chewed tobacco on the streetcar line . . .

A cloud blocked the sun and a grim green light sailed across the day, driving it underwater. Ralph's skin first chilled, then broke out in goosebumps. The girl's pumping shadow disappeared. She looked up at Ralph and he saw she wasn't a little girl at all. The creature looking at him was a man about four feet tall. Ralph had first taken the hat-shadowed face for that of a child because it was utterly smooth, unmarked by so much as a single line. And yet despite that, it conveyed a clear feeling to Ralph – a sense of evil, of malignity beyond the comprehension of a sane mind.

That's it, Ralph thought numbly, staring at the skipping creature. *That's exactly it. Whatever the thing over there is, it's insane. Totally gone.*

The creature might have read Ralph's thought, for at that moment its lips skinned back in a grin that was both coy and nasty, as if the two of them shared some unpleasant secret. And he was sure – yes, quite sure, almost positive – that it was somehow chanting through its grin, doing it without moving its lips in the slightest:

[*The line BROKE! The monkey got CHOKED! And they all died together in a little row-BOAT!*]

It was neither of the two little bald doctors Ralph had seen coming out of Mrs Locher's, he was almost positive of that. *Related* to them, maybe, but not the same. It was—

The creature threw its jump-rope away. The rope turned first yellow and then red, seeming to give off sparks as it flew through the air. The small figure – Doc #3 – stared at Ralph, grinning, and Ralph suddenly realized something else, something which filled him with horror. He finally recognized the hat the creature was wearing.

It was Bill McGovern's missing Panama.

4

Again it was as if the creature had read his mind. It dragged the hat from its head, revealing the round, hairless skull beneath, and waved McGovern's Panama in the air as if it were a cowpoke astride a bucking bronco. It continued to grin its unspeakable grin as it waved the hat.

Suddenly it pointed at Ralph, as if marking him. Then it clapped the hat back on its head and darted into the narrow, weed-choked opening between the tanning salon and the bakery. The sun sailed free of the cloud which had covered it, and the shifting brightness of the auras began to fade once more. A moment or two after the creature had disappeared it was just Harris Avenue in front of him again – boring old Harris Avenue, the same as always.

Ralph pulled a shuddering breath, remembering the madness in that small, grinning face. Remembering the way it had pointed

(*the monkey got* CHOKED)

at him, as if

(*they all died together in a little row-BOAT!*)

marking him.

'Tell me I fell asleep,' he whispered hoarsely. 'Tell me I fell asleep and dreamed that little bugger.'

The door opened behind him. 'Oh my, talking to yourself,' McGovern said. 'Must have money in the bank, Ralphie.'

'Yeah, about enough to cover my burial expenses,' Ralph said. To himself he sounded like a man who has just suffered a terrible shock and is still trying to cope with the residual fright; he half expected Bill to dart forward, face filling with concern (or maybe just suspicion), to ask what was wrong.

McGovern did nothing of the sort. He plumped into the rocking chair, crossed his arms over his narrow chest in a brooding X, and looked out at Harris Avenue, the stage upon which he and Ralph and Lois and Dorrance Marstellar and so many other old folks – we golden-agers, in McGovern-ese – were destined to play out their often boring and sometimes painful last acts.

Suppose I told him about his hat? Ralph thought. *Suppose I just opened the conversation by saying, 'Bill, I also know what happened to your Panama. Some badass relation to the guys I saw last night has got it. He wears it when he jumps rope between the bakery and the tanning salon.'*

If Bill had any lingering doubts about his sanity, *that* little newsflash would certainly set them to rest. Yep.

Ralph kept his mouth shut.

'Sorry I was gone so long,' McGovern said. 'Larry claimed I just caught him going out the door to the funeral

345

parlor, but before I could ask my questions and get away he'd rehashed half of May's life and damned near all of his own. Talked nonstop for forty-five minutes.'

Positive this was an exaggeration – McGovern had surely been gone five minutes, tops – Ralph glanced at his watch and was astounded to see it was eleven-fifteen. He looked up the street and saw that Mrs Bennigan had disappeared. So had the Budweiser truck. *Had* he been asleep? It seemed that he must have been . . . but he could not for the life of him find the break in his conscious perceptions.

Oh, come on, don't be dense. You were sleeping when you saw the little bald guy. Dreamed *the little bald guy.*

That made perfect sense. Even the fact that it had been wearing Bill's Panama made sense. The same hat had shown up in his nightmare about Carolyn. It had been between Rosalie's paws in that one.

Except this time he hadn't been dreaming. He was sure of it.

Well . . . *almost* sure.

'Aren't you going to ask me what May's brother said?' McGovern sounded slightly piqued.

'Sorry,' Ralph said. 'I was woolgathering, I guess.'

'Forgiven, my son . . . provided you listen closely from here on out, that is. The detective in charge of the case, Funderburke—'

'I'm pretty sure it's Utterback. Steve Utterback.'

McGovern waved his hand airily, his most common response to being corrected on some point. 'Whatever. Anyway, he called Larry and said the autopsy showed nothing but natural causes. The thing they were most concerned about, in light of your call, was that May had been scared into a heart attack – literally frightened to death – by housebreakers. The doors being locked from the inside and the lack of missing valuables militated against that, of course, but they took your call seriously enough to investigate the possibility.'

His half-reproachful tone – as if Ralph had wantonly poured glue into the gears of some usually smooth-running machine – made Ralph feel impatient. 'Of *course* they took it seriously. I saw two guys leaving her house and reported it to the authorities. When they got there, they found the lady dead. How could they *not* take it seriously?'

'Why didn't you give your name when you made the call?'

'I don't know. What difference does it make? And how in God's name can they be sure she *wasn't* scared into a heart attack?'

'I don't know if they *can* be a hundred per cent sure,' McGovern said, now sounding a bit testy himself, 'but I guess it must be close to that if they're turning May's body over to her brother for burial. It's probably a blood-test of some kind. All I know is that this guy Funderburke—'

'Utterback—'

'—told Larry that May probably died in her sleep.'

McGovern crossed his legs, fiddled with the creases in his blue slacks, then gave Ralph a clear and piercing look.

'I'm going to give you some advice, so listen up. Go to the doctor. Now. Today. Do not pass Go, do not collect two hundred dollars, go directly to Litchfield. This is getting heavy.'

The ones I saw coming out of Mrs Locher's didn't see me,

but this one did, Ralph thought. *It saw me and it pointed at me. For all I know, it might actually have been looking for me.*

Now *there* was a nice paranoid thought.

'Ralph? Did you hear what I said?'

'Yes. I take it you don't believe I actually saw anyone coming out of Mrs Locher's house.'

'You take it right. I saw the look on your face just now when I told you I'd been gone forty-five minutes, and I also saw the way you looked at your watch. You didn't believe so much time had passed, did you? And the *reason* you didn't believe it is because you dozed off without even being aware of it. Had yourself a little pocket nap. That's probably what happened to you the other night, Ralph. Only the other night you dreamed up those two guys, and the dream was so real you called 911 when you woke up. Doesn't that make sense?'

Three-six-nine, Ralph thought. *The goose drank wine.*

'What about the binoculars?' he asked. 'They're still sitting on the table beside my chair in the living room. Don't they prove I was awake?'

'I don't see how. Maybe you were sleepwalking, have you thought of that? You say you saw these intruders, but you can't really describe them.'

'Those orange hi–intensity lights—'

'All the doors locked from the inside—'

'Just the same I—'

'And these auras you talked about. The insomnia is causing them – I'm almost sure of it. Still, it *could* be more serious than that.'

Ralph got up, walked down the porch steps, and stood at the head of the walk with his back to McGovern. There was a throbbing at his temples and his heart was beating hard. Too hard.

He didn't just point. I was right the first time, the little sonofabitch marked me. And he was no dream. Neither were the ones I saw coming out of Mrs Locher's. I'm sure of it.

Of course you are, Ralph, another voice replied. *Crazy people are always sure of the crazy things they see and hear. That's what makes them crazy, not the hallucinations themselves. If you really saw what you saw, what happened to Mrs Bennigan? What happened to the Budweiser truck? How did you lose the forty-five minutes McGovern spent on the phone with Larry Perrault?*

'You're experiencing very serious symptoms,' McGovern said from behind him, and Ralph thought he heard something terrible in the man's voice. Satisfaction? Could it possibly be satisfaction?

'One of them had a pair of scissors,' Ralph said without turning around. 'I saw them.'

'Oh, come on, Ralph! Think! Use that brain of yours and *think*! On Sunday afternoon, less than twenty-four hours before you're due to have acupuncture treatment, a lunatic nearly sticks a knife into you. Is it any wonder that your mind serves up a nightmare featuring a sharp object that night? Hong's pins and Pickering's hunting knife become scissors, that's all. Don't you see that this hypothesis covers all the bases while what you claim to have seen covers none of them?'

'And I was sleepwalking when I got the binoculars? That's what you think?'

'It's possible. Even likely.'

'Same thing with the spray-can in my jacket pocket, right? Old Dor didn't have a thing to do with it.'

'I don't care about the spray-can or Old Dor!' McGovern cried. 'I care about *you*! You've been suffering from insomnia since April or May, you've been depressed and disturbed ever since Carolyn died—'

'I have *not* been depressed!' Ralph shouted. Across the street, the mailman paused and looked in their direction before going on down the block toward the park.

'Have it your own way,' McGovern said. 'You haven't been depressed. You also haven't been sleeping, you're seeing auras, guys creeping out of locked houses in the middle of the night . . .' And then, in a deceptively light voice, McGovern said the thing Ralph had been dreading all along: 'You want to watch out, old son. You're starting to sound too much like Ed Deepneau for comfort.'

Ralph turned around. Dull hot blood pounded behind his face. 'Why are you being this way? Why are you taking after me this way?'

'I'm not taking after you, Ralph, I'm trying to *help* you. To be your friend.'

'That's not how it feels.'

'Well, sometimes the truth hurts a little,' McGovern said calmly. 'You need to at least consider the idea that your mind and body are trying to tell you something. Let me ask you a question – is this the *only* disturbing dream you've had lately?'

Ralph thought fleetingly of Carol, buried up to her neck in the sand and screaming about white-man tracks. Thought of the bugs which had flooded out of her head. 'I haven't had *any* bad dreams lately,' he said stiffly. 'I suppose you don't believe that because it doesn't fit into the little scenario you've created.'

'Ralph—'

'Let me ask *you* something. Do you really believe that my seeing those two men and May Locher turning up dead was just a coincidence?'

'Maybe not. Maybe your physical and emotional upset created conditions favorable to a brief but perfectly genuine psychic event.'

Ralph was silenced.

'I believe such things do happen from time to time,' McGovern said, standing up. 'Probably sounds funny, coming from a rational old bird like me, but I do. I'm not out-and-out saying that *is* what happened here, but it *could* have been. What I *am* sure of is that the two men you think you saw did not in fact exist in the real world.'

Ralph stood looking up at McGovern with his hands jammed deep into his pockets and clenched into fists so hard and tight they felt like rocks. He could feel the muscles in his arms thrumming.

McGovern came down the porch steps and took him by the arm, gently, just above the elbow. 'I only think—'

Ralph pulled his arm away so sharply that McGovern grunted with surprise and stumbled a little on his feet. 'I *know* what you think.'

'You're not hearing what I—'

'Oh, I've heard plenty. More than enough. Believe me. And excuse me – I think I'm going for another walk. I need to clear my head.' He could feel dull hot blood pounding away in his cheeks and brow. He tried to throw his brain into some forward gear that would allow it to leave this senseless, impotent rage behind and couldn't do it. He felt a lot as he had when he had awakened from the dream of Carolyn; his thoughts roared with terror and confusion, and as he started his legs moving the sense he got was not one of walking but of falling, as he had fallen out of bed yesterday morning. Still, he kept going. Sometimes that was all you could do.

'Ralph, you need to see a doctor!' McGovern called after him, and Ralph could no longer tell himself that he didn't hear a weird, shrewish pleasure in McGovern's voice. The concern which overlaid it was probably genuine enough but it was like sweet icing on a sour cake.

'Not a pharmacist, not a hypnotist, not an acupuncturist! You need to see *your own family doctor!*'

Yeah, the guy who buried my wife below the high-tide line! he thought in a kind of mental scream. *The guy who stuck her in sand up to her neck and then told her she didn't have to worry about drowning as long as she kept taking her Valium and Tylenol-3!*

Aloud he said, 'I need to take a *walk!* That's what I need and that's *all* I need.' His heartbeat was now slamming into his temples like the short, hard blows of a sledge-hammer, and it occurred to him that this was how strokes must happen; if he didn't control himself soon, he was apt to fall down with what his father had called 'a bad-temper apoplexy'.

He could hear McGovern coming down the walk after him. *Don't touch me, Bill,* Ralph thought. *Don't even put your hand on my shoulder, because I'm probably going to turn around and slug you if you do.*

'I'm trying to *help* you, don't you see that?' McGovern shouted. The mailman on the other side of the street had stopped again to watch them, and outside the Red Apple,

Karl, the guy who worked mornings, and Sue, the young woman who worked afternoons, were gawking frankly across the street at them. Karl, he saw, had a bag of hamburger buns in one hand. It was really sort of amazing, the things you saw at a time like this . . . although not as amazing as some of the things he had already seen that morning.

The things you thought *you saw, Ralph,* a traitor voice whispered softly from deep inside his head.

'Walk,' Ralph muttered desperately. 'Just a damn *walk.*' A mind-movie had begun to play in his head. It was an unpleasant one, the sort of film he rarely went to see even if he had seen everything else that was playing at the cinema center. The soundtrack to this mental horror flick seemed to be 'Pop Goes the Weasel', of all things.

'Let me tell you something, Ralph — at our age, mental illness is common! At our age it's common as hell, so GO SEE YOUR DOCTOR*!'*

Mrs Bennigan was now standing on her stoop, her walker abandoned at the foot of the front steps. She was still wearing her bright red fall coat, and her mouth appeared to be hanging open as she stared down the street at them.

'Do you hear me, Ralph? I hope you do! I just hope you do!'

Ralph walked faster, hunching his shoulders as if against a cold wind. *Suppose he just keeps on yelling, louder and louder? Suppose he follows me right up the street?*

If he does that, people will think he's *the one who's gone crazy,* he told himself, but this idea had no power to soothe him. In his mind he continued to hear a piano playing a children's tune — no, not really *playing*; picking it out in nursery-school plinks and plonks:

All around the mulberry bush
The monkey chased the weasel,
The monkey thought 'twas all in fun,
Pop! Goes the weasel!

And now Ralph began to see the old people of Harris Avenue, the ones who bought their insurance from companies that advertised on cable TV, the ones with the gallstones and the skin tumors, the ones whose memories were diminishing even as their prostates enlarged, the ones who were living on Social Security and peering at the world through thickening cataracts instead of rose-colored glasses. These were the people who now read all the mail which came addressed to Occupant and scanned the supermarket advertising circulars for specials on canned goods and generic frozen dinners. He saw them dressed in grotesque short pants and fluffy short skirts, saw them wearing beanies and tee-shirts which showcased such characters as Beavis and Butt-Head and Rude Dog. He saw them, in short, as the world's oldest pre-schoolers. They were marching around a double row of chairs as a small bald man in a white smock played 'Pop Goes the Weasel' on the piano. Another baldy filched the chairs one by one, and when the music stopped and everyone sat down, one person – this time it had been May Locher, next time it would probably be McGovern's old department head – was left standing. That person would have to leave the room, of course. And Ralph heard McGovern laughing. Laughing because *he'd* found a seat again. Maybe May Locher was dead, Bob Polhurst dying, Ralph Roberts losing his marbles, but *he* was still all right, William D. McGovern, Esq was still fine, still dandy, still vertical and taking nourishment, still able to find a chair when the music stopped.

Ralph walked faster still, shoulders hunched even higher, anticipating another fusillade of advice and admonition. He thought it unlikely that McGovern would actually follow him up the street, but not entirely out of the question. If McGovern was angry enough he might do just that – remonstrating, telling Ralph to stop fooling around and go to the doctor, reminding him that the piano could stop anytime, any old time at all, and if he didn't find a chair while the finding was good, he might be out of luck forever.

No more shouts came, however. He thought of looking back to see where McGovern was, then thought better of it. If he saw Ralph looking back, it might set him off all over again. Best to just keep going. So Ralph lengthened his stride, heading back in the direction of the airport again without even thinking about it, walking with his head down, trying not to hear the relentless piano, trying not to see the old children marching around the chairs, trying not to see the terrified eyes above their make-believe smiles.

It came to him as he walked that his hopes had been denied. He had been pushed into the tunnel after all, and the dark was all around him.

PART 2

THE SECRET CITY

Old men ought to be explorers.
T.S. Eliot
Four Quartets

CHAPTER ELEVEN

1

The Derry of the Old Crocks was not the only secret city existing quietly within the place Ralph Roberts had always thought of as home; as a boy growing up in Mary Mead, where the various Old Cape housing developments stood today, Ralph had discovered there was, in addition to the Derry that belonged to the grownups, one that belonged strictly to the children. There were the abandoned hobo jungles near the railroad depot on Neibolt Street, where one could sometimes find tomato soup cans half-full of mulligatawny stew and bottles with a swallow or two of beer left in them; there was the alley behind the Aladdin Theater, where Bull Durham cigarettes were smoked and Black Cat firecrackers sometimes set off; there was the big old elm which overhung the river, where scores of boys and girls had learned to dive; there were the hundred (or perhaps it was closer to two hundred) tangled trails winding through the Barrens, an overgrown valley which slashed through the center of town like a badly healed scar.

These secret streets and highways in hiding were all below the adult plane of vision and were consequently overlooked by them . . . although there *had* been exceptions. One of them had been a cop named Aloysius Nell – Mr Nell to generations of Derry children – and it was only now, as he walked up toward the picnic area near the place where Harris Avenue became the Harris Avenue Extension, that it occurred to Ralph that Chris Nell was probably old Mr Nell's son . . . except that couldn't be quite right, because the cop Ralph had first seen in the company of John Leydecker wasn't old enough to be old Mr Nell's son. Grandson, more like it.

Ralph had become aware of a second secret city – one that belonged to the old folks – around the time he retired, but he hadn't fully realized that he himself was a citizen of it until after Carol's death. What he had discovered then was a submerged geography eerily similar to the one he had known as a child, a place largely ignored by the hurry-to-work, hurry-to-play world which thumped and hustled all around it. The Derry of the Old Crocks overlapped yet a third secret city: the Derry of the Damned, a terrible place inhabited mostly by winos, runaways, and lunatics who could not be kept locked up.

It was in the picnic area that Lafayette Chapin had introduced Ralph to one of life's most important considerations . . . once you'd become a bona fide Old Crock, that was. This consideration had to do with one's 'real life'. The subject had come up while the two men were just getting to know one another. Ralph had asked Faye what he had done before he started coming out to the picnic area.

'Well, in my real life I was a carpenter n fancy cabinetmaker,' Chapin had replied, exposing his remaining teeth in a wide grin, 'but all that ended almost ten year ago.' As if, Ralph remembered thinking, retirement was something like a vampire's kiss, pulling those who survived it into the world of the undead. And when you got right down to cases, was that really so far off the mark?

2

Now, with McGovern safely behind him (at least he hoped so), Ralph stepped through the screen of mixed oak and maple which shielded the picnic area from the Extension. He saw that eight or nine people had drifted in since his earlier walk, most with bag lunches or Coffee Pot sandwiches. The Eberlys and Zells were playing hearts with the greasy deck of Top Hole cards which was kept stashed in a knothole of a nearby oak; Faye and Doc Mulhare, a retired vet, were playing chess; a couple of kibbitzers wandered back and forth between the two games.

Games were what the picnic area was about – what *most* of the places in the Derry of the Old Crocks were about – but Ralph thought the games were really just framework. What people actually came here for was to touch base, to report in, to confirm (if only to themselves) that they were still living *some* kind of life, real or otherwise.

Ralph sat on an empty bench near the Cyclone fence and traced one finger absently over the engraved carvings – names, initials, lots of FUCKS YOUS – as he watched planes land at orderly two-minute intervals: a Cessna, a Piper, an Apache, a Twin Bonanza, the eleven forty-five Air Express out of Boston. He kept one ear cocked to the ebb and flow of conversation behind him. May Locher's name was mentioned more than once. She had been known by several of these people, and the general opinion seemed to be Mrs Perrine's – that God had finally shown mercy and ended her suffering. Most of the talk today, however, concerned the impending visit of Susan Day. As a rule, politics wasn't much of a conversational draw with the Old Crocks, who preferred a good bowel cancer or stroke any day, but even out here the abortion issue exercised its singular ability to engage, inflame, and divide.

'She picked a bad town to come to, and the hell of it is, I doubt she knows it,' Doc Mulhare said, watching the chessboard with glum concentration as Faye Chapin blitzkrieged his king's remaining defenders. 'Things have a way of happening here. Remember the fire at the Black Spot, Faye?'

Faye grunted and captured the doc's remaining bishop.

'What *I* don't understand is *these* cootie-bugs,' Lisa Zell said, picking up the front section of the *News* from the picnic table and slapping the photograph of the hooded figures marching in front of WomanCare. 'It's like they want to go back to the days when women gave themselves abortions with coathangers.'

'That's what they *do* want,' Georgina Eberly said. 'They figure if a woman's scared enough of dying, she'll have the baby. It never seems to cross their minds that a woman can be more scared of having a kid than using a coathanger to get rid of it.'

'What does bein afraid have to do with it?' one of the kibbitzers – a shovel-faced oldster named Pedersen – asked truculently. 'Murder is murder whether the baby's inside or outside, that's the way I look at it. Even when they're so small you need a microscope to see em, it's still murder. Because they'd *be* kids if you let em alone.'

'I guess that just about makes you Adolf Eichmann every time you jerk off,' Faye said, and moved his queen. 'Check.'

'La-fay-*ette Cha*-pin!' Lisa Zell cried.

'Playin with yourself ain't the same at all,' Pedersen said, glowering.

'Oh no? Wasn't there some guy in the Bible got cursed by God for hammerin the old haddock?' the other kibbitzer asked.

'You're probably thinking of Onan,' said a voice from behind Ralph. He turned, startled, and saw Old Dor standing there. In one hand he held a paperback with a large number 5 on the cover. *Where the hell did* you *come from?* Ralph wondered. He could almost have sworn there had been no one standing behind him a minute or so before.

'Onan, Shmonan,' Pedersen said. 'Those sperms aren't the same as a baby —'

'No?' Faye asked. 'Then why ain't the Catholic Church sellin rubbers at Bingo games? Tell me that.'

'That's just ignorant,' Pedersen said. 'And if you don't see—'

'But it wasn't masturbation Onan was punished for,' Dorrance said in his high, penetrating old man's voice. 'He was punished for refusing to impregnate his brother's widow, so his brother's line could continue. There's a poem, by Allen Ginsberg, I think—'

'Shut up, you old fool!' Pedersen yelled, and then glowered at Faye Chapin. 'And if you don't see that there's a big difference between a man beating his meat and a woman flushing the baby God put in her belly down the toilet, you're as big a fool as he is.'

'This is a *disgusting* conversation,' Lisa Zell said, sounding more fascinated than disgusted. Ralph looked over her shoulder and saw a section of chainlink fencing had been torn loose from its post and bent backward, probably by the kids who took this place over at night. That solved one mystery, anyway. He hadn't noticed Dorrance because the old man hadn't been in the picnic area at all; he'd been wandering around the airport grounds.

It occurred to Ralph that this was his chance to grab Dorrance and maybe get some answers out of him . . . except that Ralph would likely end up more confused than ever. Old Dor was too much like the Cheshire Cat in *Alice in Wonderland* – more smile than substance.

'Big difference, huh?' Faye was asking Pedersen.

'Yeah!' Red patches glowered in Pedersen's chapped cheeks.

Doc Mulhare shifted uneasily on his seat. 'Look, let's just forget it and finish the game, Faye, all right?'

Faye took no notice; his attention was still fixed on Pedersen. 'Maybe you ought to think again about all the little spermies that died in the palm of your hand every time you sat on the toilet seat thinkin about how nice it'd be to have Marilyn Monroe cop your—'

Pedersen reached out and slapped the remaining chesspieces off the board. Doc Mulhare winced backward, mouth trembling, eyes wide and frightened behind pink-rimmed glasses which had been mended in two places with electrical tape.

'Yeah, good!' Faye shouted. 'That's a very reasonable fuckin argument, you geek!'

Pedersen raised his fists in an exaggerated John L. Sullivan pose. 'Want to do somethin about it?' he asked. 'Come on, let's go!'

Faye got slowly to his feet. He stood easily a foot taller than the shovel-faced Pedersen and outweighed him by at least sixty pounds.

Ralph could hardly believe what he was seeing. And if the poison had seeped this far, what about the rest of the city? It seemed to him that Doc Mulhare was right; Susan Day must not have the slightest idea of how bad an idea bringing her act to Derry really was. In some ways — in a lot of ways, actually — Derry wasn't like other places.

He was moving before he was consciously aware of what he meant to do, and he was relieved to see Stan Eberly doing the same thing. They exchanged a glance as they approached the two men standing nose to nose, and Stan nodded slightly. Ralph slipped an arm around Faye's shoulders a bare second before Stan gripped Pedersen's upper left arm.

'You ain't doing none of that,' Stan said, speaking directly into one of Pedersen's tufted ears. 'We'll end up taking the both of you over to Derry Home with heart attacks, and you don't need another one of those, Harley — you had two already. Or is it three?'

'I ain't letting him make jokes about wimmin murderin babies!' Pedersen said, and Ralph saw there were tears rolling down the man's cheeks. 'My wife *died* havin our second daughter! Sepsis carried her off back in '46! So I ain't havin that talk about murderin babies!'

'Christ,' Faye said in a different voice. 'I didn't know that, Harley. I'm sorry—'

'Ah, *frig* your sorry!' Pedersen cried, and ripped his arm out of Stan Eberly's grip. He lunged toward Faye, who raised his fists and then lowered them again as Pedersen went blundering past without looking at him. He took the path through the trees which led back out to the Extension and was gone. What followed his departure was thirty seconds of pure shocked silence, broken only by the wasp-whine of an incoming Piper Cub.

3

'Jesus,' Faye said at last. 'You see a guy every few days over five, ten years, and you start to think you know everything. Christ, Ralphie, *I* didn't know how his wife died. I feel like a fool.'

'Don't let it get you down,' Stan said. 'He's prob'ly just havin his monthlies.'

'Shut up,' Georgina said. 'We've had enough dirty talk for one morning.'

'I'll be glad when that Day woman comes n goes n things can get back to normal,' Fred Zell said.

Doc Mulhare was down on his hands and knees, collecting chess-pieces. 'Do you want to finish, Faye?' he asked. 'I think I remember where they all were.'

'No,' Faye said. His voice, which had remained steady during the confrontation with Pedersen, now sounded trembly. 'Think I've had enough for awhile. Maybe Ralph'll give you a little tourney prelim.'

'Think I'm going to pass,' Ralph said. He was looking

around for Dorrance, and at last spotted him. He had gone back through the hole in the fence. He was standing in knee-high grass at the edge of the service road over there, bending his book back and forth in his hands as he watched the Piper Cub taxi toward the General Aviation terminal. Ralph found himself remembering how Ed had come tearing along that service road in his old brown Datsun, and how he had sworn

(*Hurry up! Hurry up and lick shit!*)

at the slowness of the gate. For the first time in over a year he found himself wondering what Ed had been doing in there to begin with.

'– than you did.'

'Huh?' He made an effort and focused on Faye again.

'I said you must be sleepin again, because you look a hell of a lot better than you did. But now your hearin's goin to hell, I guess.'

'I guess so,' Ralph said, and tried a little smile. 'Think I'll go grab myself a little lunch. You want to come, Faye? My treat.'

'Nah, I already had a Coffee Pot,' Faye said. 'It's sittin in my gut like a piece of lead right now, to tell you the truth. Cheez, Ralph, the old fart was *crying*, did you see that?'

'Yes, but I wouldn't make it into a big deal if I were you,' Ralph said. He started walking toward the Extension, and Faye ambled along beside him. With his broad shoulders slumped and his head lowered, Faye looked quite a lot like a trained bear in a man–suit. 'Guys our age cry over just about anything. You know that.'

'I spose.' He gave Ralph a grateful smile. 'Anyway,

thanks for stoppin me before I could make it worse. You know how I am, sometimes.'

I only wish someone had been there when Bill and I got into it, Ralph thought. Out loud he said, 'No problem. It's me that should be thanking you, actually. It's something else to put on my résumé when I apply for that high-paying job at the UN.'

Faye laughed, delighted, and clapped Ralph on the shoulder. 'Yeah, Secretary-General! Peacemaker Number One! You could do it, Ralph, no shit!'

'No question about it. Take care of yourself, Faye.'

He started to turn away and Faye touched his arm. 'You're still up for the tournament next week, aren't you? The Runway 3 Classic?'

It took a moment for Ralph to figure out what he was talking about, although it had been the retired carpenter's main topic of conversation ever since the leaves had begun to show color. Faye had been putting on the chess tournament he called The Runway 3 Classic ever since the end of his 'real life' in 1984. The trophy was an oversized chrome hubcap with a fancy crown and scepter engraved on it. Faye, easily the best player among the Old Crocks (on the west side of town, at least), had awarded the trophy to himself on six of the nine occasions it had been given out, and Ralph had a suspicion that he had gone in the tank the other three times, just to keep the rest of the tourney participants interested. Ralph hadn't thought much about chess this fall; he'd had other things on his mind.

'Sure,' he said, 'I guess I'll be playing.'

Faye grinned. 'Good. We should have had it last weekend – that was the schedule – but I was hopin that if I put it off, Jimmy V would be able to play. He's still in the hospital, though, and if I put it off much longer it'll be too cold to play outdoor and we'll end up in the back of Duffy Sprague's barber shop, like we did in '90.'

'What's wrong with Jimmy V?'

'Cancer come back on him again,' Faye said, then added in a lower tone: 'I don't think he's got a snowball's chance in hell of beatin it this time.'

Ralph felt a sudden and surprisingly sharp pang of sorrow at this news. He and Jimmy Vandermeer had known each other well during their own 'real lives'. Both had been on the road back then, Jimmy in candy and greeting cards, Ralph in printing supplies and paper products, and the two of them had gotten on well enough to team up on several New England tours, splitting the driving and sharing rather more luxurious accommodations than either could have afforded alone.

They had also shared the lonely, unremarkable secrets of travelling men. Jimmy told Ralph about the whore who'd stolen his wallet in 1958, and how he'd lied to his wife about it, telling her that a hitchhiker had robbed him. Ralph told Jimmy about his realization, at the age of forty-three, that he had become a terpin hydrate junkie, and about his painful, ultimately successful struggle to kick the habit. He had no more told Carolyn about his bizarre cough-syrup addiction than Jimmy V had told his wife about his last B-girl.

A lot of trips; a lot of changed tires; a lot of jokes about the travelling salesman and the farmer's beautiful daughter; a lot of late-night talks which had gone on until the small hours of the morning. Sometimes it was God they had talked about, sometimes the IRS. All in all, Jimmy

Vandermeer had been a damned good pal. Then Ralph had gotten his desk-job with the printing company and fallen out of touch with Jimmy. He'd only begun to reconnect out here, and at a few of the other dim landmarks which dotted the Derry of the Old Crocks – the library, the pool-hall, the back room of Duffy Sprague's barber shop, four or five others. When Jimmy told him shortly after Carolyn's death that he had come through a bout with cancer a lung shy but otherwise okay, what Ralph had remembered was the man talking baseball or fishing as he fed smoldering Camel stubs into the slipstream rushing by the wing-window of the car, one after another.

I got lucky was what he had said. *Me and the Duke, we both got lucky.* Except neither of them had stayed lucky, it seemed. Not that anyone did, in the end.

'Oh, man,' Ralph said. 'I'm sorry to hear that.'

'He's been in Derry Home almost three weeks now,' Faye said. 'Havin those radiation treatments and gettin injects of poison that's supposed to kill the cancer while it's half killing you. I'm surprised you didn't know, Ralph.'

I suppose you are, but I'm not. The insomnia keeps swallowing stuff, you see. One day it's the last Cup-A-Soup envelope you lose track of; next day it's your sense of time; the day after that it's your old friends.

Faye shook his head. 'Fucking cancer. It's spooky, how it waits.'

Ralph nodded, now thinking of Carolyn. 'What room's Jimmy in, do you know? Maybe I'll go visit him.'

'Just so happens I do. 315. Think you can remember it?'

Ralph grinned. 'For awhile, anyway.'

'Go see him if you can, sure – they got him pretty

doped up, but he still knows who comes in, and I bet he'd love to see you. Him and you had a lot of high old times together, he told me once.'

'Well, you know,' Ralph said. 'Couple of guys on the road, that's all. If we flipped for the check in some diner, Jimmy V always called tails.' Suddenly he felt like crying.

'Lousy, isn't it?' Faye said quietly.

'Yes.'

'Well, you go see him. He'll be glad, and you'll feel better. That's how it's supposed to work, anyway. And don't you go and forget the damn chess tournament!' Faye finished, straightening up and making a heroic effort to look and sound cheerful. 'If you step out now you'll fuck up the seedings.'

'I'll do my best.'

'Yeah, I know you will.' He made a fist and punched Ralph's upper arm lightly. 'And thanks again for stopping me before I could do something I'd, you know, feel bad about later.'

'Sure. Peacemaker Number One, that's me.' Ralph started down the path which led to the Extension, then turned back. 'You see that service road over there? The one that goes from General Aviation out to the street?' He pointed. A catering truck was currently driving away from the private terminal, its windshield reflecting bright darts of sunlight into their eyes. The truck stopped just short of the gate, breaking the electric-eye beam. The gate began to trundle open.

'Sure I do,' Faye said.

'Last summer I saw Ed Deepneau using that road, which means he had a key-card to the gate. Any idea how he would have come by a thing like that?'

'You mean The Friends of Life guy? Lab scientist who did a little research in wife-beating last summer?'

Ralph nodded. 'But it's the summer of '92 I'm talking about. He was driving an old brown Datsun.'

Faye laughed. 'I wouldn't know a Datsun from a Toyota from a Honda, Ralph – I stopped bein able to tell cars apart around the time Chevrolet gave up the gullwing tail-fins. But I can tell you who mostly uses that road: caterers, mechanics, pilots, crew, and flight controllers. Some passengers have key-cards, I think, if they fly private a lot. The only scientists over there are the ones who work at the air-testing station. Is that the kind of scientist he is?'

'Nope, a chemist. He worked at Hawking Labs until just a little while ago.'

'Played with the white rats, did he? Well there aren't any rats over at the airport – that I know of, anyway – but now that I think of it, there is one other bunch of people who use that gate.'

'Oh? Who?'

Faye pointed at a prefab building with a corrugated roof standing about seventy yards from the General Aviation terminal. 'See that building? That's SoloTech.'

'What's SoloTech?'

'A school,' Faye said. 'They teach people to fly.'

4

Ralph walked back down Harris Avenue with his big hands stuffed into his pockets and his head lowered so he did not see much more than the cracks in the sidewalk passing beneath his sneakers. His mind was fixed on Ed Deepneau again . . . and on SoloTech. He had no way of knowing if SoloTech was the reason Ed had been out at the airport on the day he had run into Mr West Side Gardeners, but all of a sudden that was a question to which Ralph very much wanted an answer. He was also curious as to just where Ed was living these days. He wondered if John Leydecker might share his curiosity on these two points, and decided to find out.

He was passing the unpretentious double storefront which housed George Lyford, CPA, on one side and Maritime Jewelry (WE BUY YOUR OLD GOLD AT TOP PRICES) on the other, when he was pulled out of his thoughts by a short, strangled bark. He looked up and saw Rosalie sitting on the sidewalk just outside the upper entrance to Strawford Park. The old dog was panting rapidly; saliva drizzled off her lolling tongue, building up a dark puddle on the concrete between her paws. Her fur was stuck together in dark clumps, as if she had been running, and the faded blue bandanna around her neck seemed to shiver with her rapid respiration. As Ralph looked at her, she gave another bark, this one closer to a yelp.

He glanced across the street to see what she was barking at and saw nothing but the Buffy-Buffy Laundromat. There were a few women moving around inside, but Ralph found it impossible to believe Rosalie was barking at them. No one at all was currently passing on the sidewalk in front of the coin-op laundry.

Ralph looked back and suddenly realized that Rosalie wasn't just sitting on the sidewalk but crouching there . . . *cowering* there. She looked scared almost to death.

Until that moment, Ralph had never thought much

about how eerily human the expressions and body language of dogs were: they grinned when they were happy, hung their heads when they were ashamed, registered anxiety in their eyes and tension in the set of their shoulders – all things that people did. And, like people, they registered abject, total fear in every quivering line of the body.

He looked across the street again, at the spot where Rosalie's attention seemed focused, and once again saw nothing but the laundry and the empty sidewalk in front of it. Then, suddenly, he remembered Natalie, the Exalted & Revered Baby, snatching at the gray-blue contrails his fingers left behind as he reached out with them to wipe the milk from her chin. To anyone else she would have looked as if she were grabbing at nothing, the way babies always appeared to be grabbing at nothing . . . but Ralph had known better.

He had *seen* better.

Rosalie uttered a string of panicky yelps that grated on Ralph's ear like the sound of unoiled hinges.

So far it's only happened on its own . . . but maybe I can make it happen. Maybe I can make myself see—

See what?

Well, the auras. Them, of course. And maybe whatever Rosalie

(*three-six-nine hon*)

was looking at, as well. Ralph already had a pretty good idea

(*the goose drank wine*)

of what it was, but he wanted to be sure. The question was how to do it.

How does a person see in the first place?

By looking, of course.

Ralph looked at Rosalie. Looked at her carefully, trying to see everything there was to see: the faded pattern on the blue bandanna which served as her collar, the dusty clumps and tangles in her uncared-for coat, the sprinkle of gray around her long muzzle. After a few moments of this she seemed to feel his gaze, for she turned, looked at him, and whined uneasily.

As she did, Ralph felt something turn over in his mind – it felt like the starter-motor of a car. There was a brief but very clear sense of being suddenly *lighter*, and then brightness flooded into the day. He had found his way back into that more vivid, more deeply textured world. He saw a murky membrane – it made him think of spoiled eggwhite – swim into existence around Rosalie, and saw a dark gray balloon-string rising from her. Its point of origin wasn't the skull, however, as had been the case in all the people Ralph had seen while in this heightened state of awareness; Rosalie's balloon-string rose from her muzzle.

Now you know the most essential difference between dogs and men, he thought. *Their souls reside in different places.*

[*Doggy! Here, doggy, c'mere!*]

Ralph winced and drew back from that voice, which was like chalk squeaking on a blackboard. The heels of his palms rose most of the way to his ears before he realized that wouldn't help; he wasn't really hearing it with his ears, and the part that the voice hurt the worst was deep inside his head, where his hands couldn't reach.

[*Hey, you fucking flea suitcase! You think I've got all day? Get your raggedy ass over here!*]

Rosalie whined and switched her gaze from Ralph back toward whatever she had been looking at before. She started to get up, then shrank back down on her haunches again. The bandanna she wore was shaking harder than ever, and Ralph saw a dark crescent begin to spread around her left flank as her bladder let go.

He looked across the street and there was Doc #3, standing between the laundromat and the elderly apartment house next door, Doc #3 in his white smock (it was badly stained, Ralph noticed, as if he had been wearing it for a long time) and his midget-sized blue jeans. He still had McGovern's Panama on his head. The hat now appeared to balance on the creature's ears; it was so big for him that the top half of his head seemed submerged in it. He was grinning ferociously at the dog, and Ralph saw a double row of pointed white teeth − the teeth of a cannibal. In his left hand he was holding something which was either an old scalpel or a straight-razor. Part of Ralph's mind tried to convince him that it was blood he saw on the blade, but he was pretty sure it was just rust.

Doc #3 slipped the first two fingers of his right hand into the corners of his mouth and blew a piercing whistle that went through Ralph's head like a drillbit. Down the sidewalk, Rosalie flinched backward and then voiced a brief howl.

[*Get your fucking ass over, Rover! Do it now!*]

Rosalie got up, tail between her legs, and began to slink toward the street. She whined as she went, and her fear had worsened her limp to the point where she was barely able to stagger; her hindquarters threatened to slide out from under her at each reluctant, lurching step.

[*'Hey!'*]

Ralph only realized that he had yelled when he saw the small blue cloud float up in front of his face. It was etched with gossamer silver lines that made it look like a snowflake.

The bald dwarf wheeled toward the sound of Ralph's shout, instinctively raising the weapon he held as he did. His expression was one of snarling surprise. Rosalie had stopped with her front paws in the gutter and was looking at Ralph with wide, anxious brown eyes.

[*What do you want, Shorts?*]

There was fury at being interrupted in that voice, fury at being challenged . . . but Ralph thought there were other emotions underneath. Fear? He wished he could believe it. Perplexity and surprise seemed surer bets. Whatever this creature was, it wasn't used to being seen by the likes of Ralph, let alone challenged.

[*What's the matter, Short-Time, cat got your tongue? Or have you already forgotten what you wanted?*]

[*'I want you to leave that dog alone!'*]

Ralph heard himself in two different ways. He was fairly sure he was speaking aloud, but the sound of his actual voice was distant and tinny, like music drifting up from a pair of Walkman headphones which have been temporarily laid aside. Someone standing right beside him might have heard what he said, but Ralph knew the words would have sounded like a weak, out-of-breath gasp – talk from a man who has just been gutpunched. Inside his head, however, he sounded as he hadn't in years – young, strong, and confident.

Doc #3 must have heard it that second way, for he

recoiled momentarily, again raising his weapon (Ralph was now almost certain it was a scalpel) for a moment, as if in self-defense. Then he seemed to regroup. He left the sidewalk and strode to the edge of Harris Avenue, standing on the leaf-drifted strip of grass between the sidewalk and the street. He hitched at the waistband of his jeans, yanking it through the dirty smock, and stared grimly at Ralph for several moments. Then he raised the rusty scalpel in the air and made an unpleasantly suggestive sawing gesture with it.

[*You can see me — big deal! Don't poke your nose into what doesn't concern you, Short-Time! The mutt belongs to me!*]

The bald doc turned back to the cringing dog.

[*I'm done fooling with you, Rover! Get over here! Right now!*]

Rosalie gave Ralph a beseeching, despairing look and then began to cross the street.

I don't mess in with long-time business, Old Dor had told him on the day he'd given him the book of Stephen Dobyns poems. *I told* you *not to, either.*

Yes, he had, yes indeed, but Ralph had a feeling it was too late now. Even if it wasn't, he had no intention of leaving Rosalie to the unpleasant little gnome standing in front of the coin-op laundry across the street. Not if he could help it, that was.

[*'Rosalie! Over here, girl! Heel!'*]

Rosalie gave a single bark and trotted over to where Ralph stood. She placed herself behind his right leg and then sat down, panting and looking up at him. And here was another expression Ralph found he could read with ease: one part relief, two parts gratitude.

The face of Doc #3 was twisted into a grimace of hate so severe it was almost a cartoon.

[*Better send her across, Shorts! I'm warning you!*]

[*'No.'*]

[*I'll fuck you over, Shorts. I'll fuck you over big-time. And I'll fuck your friends over. Do you get me? Do you—*]

Ralph suddenly raised one hand to shoulder height with the palm turned inward toward the side of his head, as if he meant to administer a karate chop. He brought it down and watched, amazed, as a tight blue wedge of light flew off the tips of his fingers and sliced across the street like a thrown spear. Doc #3 ducked just in time, clapping one hand to McGovern's Panama to keep it from flying off. The blue wedge skimmed two or three inches over that small, clutching hand and struck the front window of the Buffy-Buffy. There it spread like some supernatural liquid, and for a moment the dusty glass became the brilliant, perfect blue of today's sky. It faded after only a moment and Ralph could see the women inside the laundromat again, folding their clothes and loading their washers exactly as if nothing had happened.

The bald dwarf straightened, rolled his hands into fists, and shook them at Ralph. Then he snatched McGovern's hat off his head, stuck the brim in his mouth, and tore a bite out of it. As he performed this bizarre equivalent of a child's tantrum, the sun struck splinters of fire from the lobes of his small, neatly made ears. He spat out the chunk of splintery straw and then clapped the hat back on his head.

[*That dog was mine, Shorts! I was gonna play with her! I guess maybe I'll have to play with you instead, huh? You and your asshole friends!*]

['*Get out of here.*']

[*Cuntlicker! Fucked your mother and licked her cunt!*]

Ralph knew where he had heard *that* charming senti-
ment before: Ed Deepneau, out at the airport, in the summer
of '92. It wasn't the sort of thing you forgot, and all at
once he was terrified. What in God's name had he stum-
bled into?

5

Ralph lifted his hand to the side of his head again, but
something inside had changed. He could bring it down in
that chopping gesture again, but he was almost positive that
this time no bright blue flying wedge would result.

The doc apparently didn't know he was being threat-
ened with an empty gun, however. He shrank back, raising
the hand holding the scalpel in a shielding gesture. The
grotesquely bitten hat slipped down over his eyes, and for
a moment he looked like a stage-melodrama version of
Jack the Ripper . . . one who might have been working
out pathologic inadequacies caused by extreme shortness.

[*Gonna get you for this, Shorts! You wait! You just wait!
No Short-Timer runs the game on me!*]

But for the time being, the little bald doctor had had
enough. He wheeled around and ran into the weedy lane
between the laundromat and the apartment house with his
dirty, too-long smock flapping and snapping at the legs of
his jeans. The brightness slipped out of the day with him.
Ralph marked its passage to a large extent with senses he
had never before even suspected. He felt totally awake, totally
energized, and almost exploding with delighted excitement.

I drove it off, by God! I drove the little sonofawhore off!

He had no idea what the creature in the white smock really was, but he knew he had saved Rosalie from it, and for now that was enough. Nagging questions about his sanity might creep back tomorrow morning as he sat in the wing-chair looking down at the deserted street below . . . but for the time being, he felt like a million bucks.

'You saw him, didn't you, Rosalie? You saw the nasty little—'

He looked down, saw that Rosalie was no longer sitting by his heel, and looked up in time to see her limping into the park, head down, right leg slueing stiffly off to the side with every pained stride.

'Rosalie!' he shouted. 'Hey, girl!' And, without really knowing why – except that they had just gone through something extraordinary together – Ralph started after her, first just jogging, then running, finally sprinting all out.

He didn't sprint for long. A stitch that felt like a hot chrome needle buried itself in his left side, then spread rapidly across the left half of his chest wall. He stopped just inside the park, standing bent over at the intersection of two paths, hands clamped on his legs just above the knees. Sweat ran into his eyes and stung like tears. He panted harshly, wondering if it was just the ordinary sort of stitch he remembered from the last lap of the mile run in high-school track, or if this was how the onset of a fatal heart attack felt.

After thirty or forty seconds the pain began to abate, so maybe it had just been a stitch, after all. Still, it went a good piece toward supporting McGovern's thesis, didn't it?

Let me tell you something, Ralph – at our age, mental illness is common! At our age it's common as hell! Ralph didn't know if that was true or not, but he did know that the year he had made All-State Track was now over half a century in the past, and sprinting after Rosalie the way he'd done was stupid and probably dangerous. If his heart *had* seized up, he supposed he wouldn't have been the first old guy to be punished with a coronary thrombosis for getting excited and forgetting that when eighteen went, it went forever.

The pain was almost gone and he was getting his wind back, but his legs still felt untrustworthy, as if they might unlock at the knees and spill him onto the gravel path without the slightest warning. Ralph lifted his head, looking for the nearest park bench, and saw something that made him forget stray dogs, shaky legs, even possible heart attacks. The nearest bench was forty feet farther along the left-hand path, at the top of a gentle, sloping hill. Lois Chasse was sitting on that bench in her good blue fall coat. Her gloved hands were folded together in her lap, and she was sobbing as if her heart would break.

CHAPTER TWELVE

1

'What's wrong, Lois?'

She looked up at him, and the first thought to cross Ralph's mind was actually a memory: a play he had taken Carolyn to see at the Penobscot Theater in Bangor eight or nine years ago. Some of the characters in it had supposedly been dead, and their makeup had consisted of clown-white greasepaint with dark circles around the eyes to give the impression of huge empty sockets.

His second thought was much simpler: *Raccoon.*

She either saw some of his thoughts on his face or simply realized how she must look, because she turned away, fumbled briefly at the clasp of her purse, then simply raised her hands and used them to shield her face from his view.

'Go away, Ralph, would you?' she asked in a thick, choked voice. 'I don't feel very well today.'

Under ordinary circumstances, Ralph would have done as she asked, hurrying away without looking back, feeling nothing but a vague shame at having come across her with her mascara smeared and her defenses down. But these weren't ordinary circumstances, and Ralph decided he wasn't leaving – not yet, anyway. He still retained some of that strange lightness, and still felt that other world, that other Derry, was very close. And there was something else, something perfectly simple and straightforward. He hated to see Lois, whose happy nature he had never even questioned, sitting here by herself and bawling her eyes out.

'What's the matter, Lois?'

'I just don't feel well!' she cried. 'Can't you leave me alone?'

Lois buried her face in her gloved hands. Her back shook, the sleeves of her blue coat trembled, and Ralph thought of how Rosalie had looked when the bald doctor had been yelling at her to get her ass across the street: miserable, scared to death.

Ralph sat down next to Lois on the bench, slipped an arm around her, and pulled her to him. She came, but stiffly . . . as if her body were full of wires.

'Don't you look at me!' she cried in that same wild voice. 'Don't you *dare*! My makeup's a mess! I put it on special for my son and daughter-in-law . . . they came for breakfast . . . we were going to spend the morning . . . "We'll have a nice time, Ma," Harold said . . . but the *reason* they came . . . you see, the real reason . . .'

Communication broke down in a fresh spate of weeping. Ralph groped in his back pocket, came up with a handkerchief which was wrinkled but clean, and put it in one of Lois's hands. She took it without looking at him.

'Go on,' he said. 'Scrub up a little if you want, although you don't look bad, Lois; honest you don't.'

A *little raccoony* is all, he thought. He began to smile,

and then the smile died. He remembered the day in September when he had set off for the Rite Aid to check out the over-the-counter sleep aids and had encountered Bill and Lois standing outside the park, talking about the doll-throwing demonstration which Ed had orchestrated at WomanCare. She had been clearly distressed that day – Ralph remembered thinking that she looked tired in spite of her excitement and concern – but she had also been close to beautiful: her considerable bosom heaving, her eyes flashing, her cheeks flushed with a maid's high color. That all but irresistible beauty was hardly more than a memory today; in her melting mascara Lois Chasse looked like a sad and elderly clown, and Ralph felt a quick hot spark of fury for whatever or whoever had wrought the change.

'I look *horrible!*' Lois said, applying Ralph's handkerchief vigorously. 'I'm a *fright!*'

'No, ma'am. Just a little smeary.'

Lois at last turned to face him. It clearly took a lot of effort with her rouge and eye makeup now mostly on Ralph's handkerchief. 'How bad am I?' she breathed. 'Tell the truth, Ralph Roberts, or your eyes'll cross.'

He bent forward and kissed one moist cheek. 'Only lovely, Lois. You'll have to save ethereal for another day, I guess.'

She gave him an uncertain smile, and the upward movement of her face caused two fresh tears to spill from her eyes. Ralph took the crumpled handkerchief from her and gently wiped them away.

'I'm so glad it was you who came along and not Bill,' she told him. 'I would have died of shame if Bill had seen me crying in public.'

Ralph looked around. He saw Rosalie, safe and sound at the bottom of the hill – she was lying between the two Portosans that stood down there, her muzzle resting on one paw – but otherwise this part of the park was empty. 'I think we've got the place pretty much to ourselves, at least for now,' he said.

'Thank God for small favors.' Lois took the handkerchief back and went to work on her makeup again, this time in a rather more businesslike manner. 'Speaking of Bill, I stopped into the Red Apple on my way down here – that was before I got feeling sorry for myself and started to bawl my silly head off – and Sue said you two had a big argument just a little while ago. Yelling and everything, right out in your front yard.'

'Nah, not that big,' Ralph said, smiling uneasily.

'Can I be nosy and ask what it was about?'

'Chess,' Ralph said. It was the first thing to pop into his mind. 'The Runway 3 Tournament Faye Chapin has every year. Only it really wasn't about anything. You know how it is – sometimes people get out of bed on the wrong side and just grab the first excuse.'

'I wish that was all it was with me,' Lois said. She opened her purse, managing the clasp effortlessly this time, and took out her compact. Then she sighed and stuffed it back into the bag again without opening it. 'I can't. I know I'm being a baby, but I just *can't*.'

Ralph darted his hand into her purse before she could close it, removed the compact, opened it, and held the mirror up in front of her. 'See? That's not so bad, is it?'

She averted her face like a vampire turning away from a crucifix. 'Ugh,' she said. 'Put it away.'

386

'If you promise to tell me what happened.'

'Anything, just put it away.'

He did. For a little while Lois said nothing but only sat and watched her hands fiddle restlessly with the clasp of her purse. He was about to prod her when she looked up at him with a pitiful expression of defiance.

'It just so happens you're not the *only* one who can't get a decent night's sleep, Ralph.'

'What are you talking ab——'

'*Insomnia!*' she snapped. 'I go to sleep at about the same time I always did, but I don't sleep through anymore. And it's worse than that. I wake up earlier every morning, it seems.'

Ralph tried to remember if he had told Lois about that aspect of his own problem. He didn't think he had.

'Why are you looking so surprised?' Lois asked. 'You didn't really think you were the only person in the world to ever have a sleepless night, did you?'

'Of course not!' Ralph responded with some indignation . . . but hadn't it often felt as if he were the only person in the world to have that particular *kind* of sleepless night? Standing helplessly by as his good sleep-time was eroded minute by minute and quarter hour by quarter hour? It was like a weird variant of the Chinese water-torture.

'When did yours start?' he asked.

'A month or two before Carol died.'

'How much sleep are you getting?'

'Barely an hour a night since the start of October.' Her voice was calm, but Ralph heard a tremor which might have been panic just below the surface. 'The way things are going, I'll have entirely quit sleeping by Christmas, and if that really happens, I don't know how I'll survive it. I'm barely surviving now.'

Ralph struggled for speech and asked the first question to come into his mind: 'How come I've never seen your light?'

'For the same reason I hardly ever see yours, I imagine,' she said. 'I've been living in the same place for almost thirty-five years, and I don't need to turn on the lights to find my way around. Also, I like to keep my troubles to myself. You keep turning on the lights at two in the morning and sooner or later someone sees them. It gets around, and then the nosybirds start asking questions. I don't like nosybird questions, and I'm not one of those people who feel like they have to take an ad out in the paper every time they have a little constipation.'

Ralph burst out laughing. Lois looked at him in round-eyed perplexity for a moment, then joined in. His arm was still around her (or had it crept back on its own after he had taken it away? Ralph didn't know and didn't really care), and he hugged her tightly. This time she pressed against him easily; those stiff little wires had gone out of her body. Ralph was glad.

'You're not laughing at me, are you, Ralph?'

'Nope. Absolutely not.'

She nodded, still smiling. '*That's* all right, then. You never even saw me moving around in my living room, did you?'

'No.'

'That's because there's no streetlamp in front of my house. But there's one in front of *yours*. I've seen you in that ratty old wing-chair of yours many times, sitting and looking out and drinking tea.'

I always assumed I was the only one, he thought, and suddenly a question – both comic and embarrassing – popped into his head. How many times had she seen him sitting there and picking his nose? Or picking at his crotch?

Either reading his mind or the color in his cheeks, Lois said, 'I really couldn't make out much more than your shape, you know, and you were always wearing your robe, perfectly decent. So you don't have to worry about *that.* Also, I hope you know that if you'd ever started doing anything you wouldn't want people to *see* you doing, I wouldn't have looked. I wasn't exactly raised in a barn, you know.'

He smiled and patted her hand. 'I *do* know that, Lois. It's just . . . you know, a surprise. To find out that while I was sitting there and watching the street, somebody was watching *me.*'

She fixed him with an enigmatic smile that might have said, *Don't worry, Ralph – you were just another part of the scenery to me.*

He considered this smile for a moment, then groped his way back to the main point. 'So what happened, Lois? Why were you sitting here and crying? Just sleeplessness? If that's what it was, I certainly sympathize. There's really no just about it, is there?'

Her smile slipped away. Her gloved hands folded together again in her lap and she looked somberly down at them. 'There are worse things than insomnia. Betrayal, for instance. Especially when the people doing the betraying are the people you love.'

2

She fell quiet. Ralph didn't prompt her. He was looking down the hill at Rosalie, who appeared to be looking up at him. At both of them, maybe.

'Did you know we share the same doctor as well as the same problem, Ralph?'

'You go to Litchfield, too?'

'*Used* to go to Litchfield. He was Carolyn's recommendation. I'll never go to him again, though. He and I are quits.' Her upper lip drew back. 'Double-crossing son of a *bitch*!'

'What happened?'

'I went along for the best part of a year, waiting for things to get better by themselves – for nature to take her course, as they say. Not that I didn't try to help nature along every now and then. We probably tried a lot of the same things.'

'Honeycomb?' Ralph asked, smiling again. He couldn't help it. *What an amazing day this has been,* he thought. *What a perfectly amazing day . . . and it's not even one in the afternoon yet.*

'Honeycomb? What about it? Does that help?'

'No,' Ralph said, grinning more widely than ever, 'doesn't help a bit, but it tastes *wonderful*.'

She laughed and squeezed his bare left hand in both of her gloved ones. Ralph squeezed back.

'You never went to see Dr Litchfield about it, did you, Ralph?'

'Nope. Made an appointment once, but cancelled it.'

'Did you put it off because you didn't trust him? Because you felt he missed the boat on Carolyn?'

Ralph looked at her, surprised.

'Never mind,' Lois said. 'I had no right to ask that.'

'No, it's okay. I guess I'm just surprised to hear the idea from someone else. That he . . . you know . . . that he might have misdiagnosed her.'

'Huh!' Lois's pretty eyes flashed. 'It crossed *all* our minds! Bill used to say he couldn't believe you didn't have that fumble-fingered bastard in district court the day after Carolyn's funeral. Of course back then I was on the other side of the fence, defending Litchfield like mad. *Did* you ever think of suing him?'

'No. I'm seventy, and I don't want to spend whatever time I have left flogging a malpractice suit. Besides – would it bring Carol back?'

She shook her head.

Ralph said, 'What happened to Carolyn *was* the reason I didn't go see him, though. I guess it was, at least. I just couldn't seem to trust him, or maybe . . . I don't know . . .'

No, he didn't really know, that was the devil of it. All he knew for sure was that he had cancelled the appointment with Dr Litchfield, as he had cancelled his appointment with James Roy Hong, known in some quarters as the pinsticker man. That latter appointment had been scratched on the advice of a ninety-two- or -three-year-old man who could probably no longer remember his own middle name. His mind slipped to the book Old Dor had given him, and to the poem Old Dor had quoted from – 'Pursuit', it had been called, and Ralph couldn't seem to get it out of his head . . . especially the part where the poet talked about all the things he saw falling away behind him: the unread books, the untold jokes, the trips that would never be taken.

'Ralph? Are you there?'

'Yeah – just thinking about Litchfield. Wondering why I cancelled that appointment.'

She patted his hand. 'Just be glad you did. I kept mine.'

'Tell me.'

Lois shrugged. 'When it got so bad I felt I couldn't stand it anymore, I went to him and told him everything. I thought he'd give me a prescription for sleeping pills, but he said he couldn't even do that – I sometimes have an irregular heartbeat, and sleeping pills can make that worse.'

'When did you see him?'

'Early last week. Then, yesterday, my son Harold called me out of a clear blue sky and said he and Janet wanted to take me out to breakfast. Nonsense, I said. I can still get around the kitchen. If you're coming all the way down from Bangor, I said, I'll get up a nice little feed for you, and that's the end of it. Then, after, if you want to take me out – I was thinking of the mall, because I always like to go out there – why, that would be fine. That's just what I said.'

She turned to Ralph with a smile that was small and bitter and fierce.

'It never occurred to me to wonder why *both* of them were coming to see me on a weekday, when both of them have jobs – and they must really love those jobs, because they're about all they ever talk about. I just thought how *sweet* of them it was . . . how *thoughtful* . . . and I put out a special effort to look nice and do everything right so Janet wouldn't suspect I was having a problem. I think *that* rankles most of all. Silly old Lois, "Our Lois", as Bill always says . . . don't look so surprised, Ralph! Of course I knew about that; did you think I fell off a stump just yesterday? And he's right. I *am* foolish, I *am* silly, but that doesn't mean I don't hurt just like anyone else when I'm taken advantage of . . .' She was beginning to cry again.

'Of course it doesn't,' Ralph said, and patted her hand.

'You would have laughed if you'd seen me,' she said, 'baking fresh squash muffins at four o'clock in the morning and slicing mushrooms for an Italian omelette at four-fifteen and starting in with the makeup at four-thirty just to be *sure,* absolutely *sure* that Jan wouldn't get going with that "Are you sure you feel all right, Mother Lois?" stuff. I *hate* it when she starts in with that crap. And do you know what, Ralph? She knew what was wrong with me all the time. They *both* did. So I guess the laugh was on me, wasn't it?'

Ralph thought he had been following closely, but apparently he had lost her on one of the turns. 'Knew? How could they know?'

'*Because Litchfield told them!*' she shouted. Her face twisted again, but this time it was not hurt or sorrow Ralph saw there but a terrible rueful rage. '*That tattling son of a bitch called my son on the telephone and* TOLD HIM EVERY-THING!'

Ralph was dumbfounded.

'Lois, they can't do that,' he said when he finally found his voice again. 'The doctor-patient relationship is . . . well, it's privileged. Your son would know all about it, because he's a lawyer, and the same thing applies to them. Doctors can't tell *anyone* what their patients tell them unless the patient—'

'Oh Jesus,' Lois said, rolling her eyes. 'Crippled wheelchair Jesus. What world are you living in, Ralph? Fellows like Litchfield do whatever they think is right. I guess I knew that all along, which makes me double-stupid for going to him at all. Carl Litchfield is a vain, arrogant man who cares more about how he looks in his suspenders and designer shirts than he does about his patients.'

'That's awfully cynical.'

'And awfully true, that's the sad part. You know what? He's thirty-five or thirty-six, and he's somehow gotten the idea that when he hits forty, he's just going to . . . stop. Stay forty for as long as he wants to. He's got an idea that people are old once they get to be sixty, and that even the best of them are pretty much in their dotage by the age of sixty-eight or so, and that once you're past eighty, it'd be a mercy if your relatives would turn you over to that Dr Kevorkian. Children don't have any rights of confidentiality from their parents, and as far as Litchfield is concerned, old poops like us don't have any rights of confidentiality from our kids. It wouldn't be in our best interests, you see.

'What Carl Litchfield did practically the minute I was out of his examining room was to phone Harold in Bangor. He said I wasn't sleeping, that I was suffering from depression, and that I was having the sort of sensory problems that accompany a premature decline in cognition. And then he said, "You have to remember that your mother is getting on in years, Mr Chasse, and if I were you I'd think very seriously about her situation down here in Derry."'

'He didn't!' Ralph cried, amazed and horrified. 'I mean . . . did he?'

Lois was nodding grimly. 'He said it to Harold and Harold said it to me and now I'm saying it to you. Silly old me, I didn't even know what "a premature decline in cognition" meant, and neither of them wanted to tell me. I looked up "cognition" in the dictionary, and do you know what it means?'

'Thinking,' Ralph said. 'Cognition is thinking.'

'Right. My doctor called my son to tell him I was going senile!' Lois laughed angrily and used Ralph's handkerchief to wipe fresh tears off her cheeks.

'I can't believe it,' Ralph said, but the hell of it was he could. Ever since Carolyn's death he had been aware that the naïveté with which he had regarded the world up until the age of eighteen or so had apparently not departed forever when he crossed the threshold between childhood and manhood; that peculiar innocence seemed to be returning as he stepped over the threshold between manhood and *old* manhood. Things kept surprising him . . . except surprise was really too mild a word. What a lot of them did was knock him ass over teakettle.

The little bottles under the Kissing Bridge, for instance. He had taken a long walk out to Bassey Park one day in July and had gone under the bridge to rest out of the afternoon sun for awhile. He had barely gotten comfortable before noticing a little pile of broken glass in the weeds by the stream that trickled beneath the bridge. He had swept at the high grass with a length of broken branch and discovered six or eight small bottles. One had some crusty white stuff in the bottom. Ralph had picked it up, and as he turned it curiously before his eyes, he realized he was looking at the remains of a crack-party. He had dropped the bottle as if it were hot. He could still remember the numbed shock he had felt, his unsuccessful attempt to convince himself that he was nuts, that it *couldn't* be what he thought it was, not in this hick town two hundred and fifty miles north of Boston. It was that emerging naïf which had been shocked, of course; that part of him seemed to believe (or had until he had discovered the little bottles under the Kissing Bridge) that all those news stories about the cocaine epidemic had just been make-believe, no more real than a TV crime show or a Jean-Claude Van Damme movie.

He felt a similar sensation of shock now.

'Harold said they wanted to "run me up to Bangor" and show me the place,' Lois was saying. 'He never takes me for rides these days; he just runs me places. Like I'm an errand. They had lots of brochures, and when Harold gave Janet the nod, she whipped them out so fast—'

'Whoa, slow down. What place? What brochures?'

'I'm sorry, I'm getting ahead of myself, aren't I? It's a place in Bangor called Riverview Estates.'

Ralph knew the name; had gotten a brochure himself, as a matter of fact. One of those mass mailing things, this one targeted at people sixty-five and over. He and McGovern had shared a laugh about it . . . but the laugh had been just a touch uneasy – like kids whistling past the graveyard.

'Shit, Lois – that's a retirement home, isn't it?'

'No, *sir!*' she said, widening her eyes innocently. 'That's what *I* said, but Harold and Janet set me straight. No, Ralph, Riverview Estates is *a condominium development site for community-oriented senior citizens!* When Harold said that I said, "Is that so? Well, let me tell you both something — you can put a fruit pie from McDonald's in a sterling-silver chafing dish and call it a French tart, but it's still just a fruit pie from McDonald's, as far as I am concerned."

'When I said that, Harold started to sputter and get red in the face, but Jan just gave me that sweet little smile of hers, the one she saves up for special occasions because she knows it drives me crazy. She says, "Well, why don't we look at the brochures anyway. Mother Lois? You'll do *that* much, won't you, after we both took Personal Days from work and drove all the way down here to see you?"'

'Like Derry was in the heart of Africa,' Ralph muttered.

Lois took his hand and said something that made him laugh. 'Oh, to her it is!'

'Was this before or after you found out Litchfield had tattled?' Ralph asked. He used the same word Lois had on purpose; it seemed to fit this situation better than a fancier word or phrase would have done. 'Committed a breach of confidentiality' was far too dignified for this nasty bit of work. Litchfield had run and tattled, simple as that.

'Before. I thought I might as well look at the brochures; after all, they'd come forty miles, and it wouldn't exactly kill me. So I looked while they ate the food I'd fixed — there wasn't any that had to be scraped into the swill later on, either — and drank coffee.

'That's quite a place, that Riverview. They have their

own medical staff on duty twenty-four hours a day, and their own kitchen. When you move in they give you a complete physical and decide what you can have to eat. There's a Red Diet Plan, a Blue Diet Plan, a Green Diet Plan, and a Yellow Diet Plan. There were three or four other colors as well. I can't remember what all of them were, but Yellow is for diabetics and Blue is for fatties.'

Ralph thought of eating three scientifically balanced meals a day for the rest of his life – no more sausage pizzas from Gambino's, no more Coffee Pot sandwiches, no more chiliburgers from Mexico Milt's – and found the prospect almost unbearably grim.

'Also,' Lois said brightly, 'they have a pneumatic-tube system that delivers your daily pills right to your kitchen. Isn't that a marvellous idea, Ralph?'

'I guess so,' Ralph said.

'Oh, yes, it is. It's marvellous, the wave of the future. There's a computer to oversee everything, and I bet it never has a decline in cognition. There's a special bus that takes the Riverview people to places of scenic or cultural interest twice a week, and it also takes them shopping. You have to take the bus, because Riverview people aren't allowed to have cars.'

'Good idea,' he said, giving her hand a little squeeze. 'What are a few drunks on Saturday night compared to an old fogey with a slippery cognition on the loose in a Buick sedan?'

She didn't smile, as he had hoped she would. 'The pictures in those brochures turned my blood. Old ladies playing canasta. Old men throwing horseshoes. Both flavors together in this big pine-panelled room they call the River

Hall, square-dancing. Although that *is* sort of a nice name, don't you think? River Hall?'

'I guess it's okay.'

'I think it sounds like the kind of room you'd find in an enchanted castle. But I've visited quite a few old friends in Strawberry Fields — that's the geriatrics' home in Skowhegan — and I know an old folks' rec room when I see one. It doesn't matter how pretty a name you give it, there's still a cabinet full of board games in the corner and jigsaw puzzles with five or six pieces missing from each one and the TV's always tuned to something like *Family Feud* and never to the kind of movies where good-looking young people take off their clothes and roll around on the floor together in front of the fireplace. Those rooms always smell of paste . . . and piss . . . and the five-and-dime watercolors that come in a long tin box . . . and despair.'

Lois looked at him with her dark eyes.

'I'm only sixty-eight, Ralph. I know that sixty-eight doesn't seem like only *anything* to Dr Fountain of Youth, but it does to me, because my mother was ninety-two when she died last year and my dad lived to be eighty-six. In my family, dying at eighty is dying young . . . and if I had to spend twelve years living in a place where they announce dinner over the loudspeaker, I'd go crazy.'

'I would, too.'

'I looked, though. I wanted to be polite. When I was finished, I made a neat little pile of them and handed them back to Jan. I said they were very interesting and thanked her. She nodded and smiled and put them back in her purse. I thought that was going to be the end of it and good riddance, but then Harold said, "Put your coat on, Ma."

'For a second I was so scared I couldn't breathe. I thought they'd already signed me up! And I had an idea that if I said I wasn't going, Harold would open the door and there would be two or three men in white coats outside, and one of them would smile and say, "Don't worry, Mrs Chasse; once you get that first handful of pills delivered direct to your kitchen, you'll never want to live anywhere else."

'"I don't *want* to put my coat on," I told Harold, and I tried to sound the way I used to when he was only ten and always tracking mud into the kitchen, but my heart was beating so hard I could hear it tapping in my voice. "I've changed my mind about going out. I forgot how much I had to do today." And then Jan gave the laugh I hate even more than her syrupy little smile and said, "Why, Mother Lois, what would you have to do that's so important you can't go up to Bangor with *us* after we've taken time off to come down to Derry and see *you?*"

'That woman always gets my back hair up, and I guess I do the same to her. I must, because I've never in my life known one woman to smile that much at another without hating her guts. Anyway, I told her I had to wash the kitchen floor, to start with. "Just look at it," I said. "Dirty as the devil."

'"Huh!" Harold says. "I can't believe you're going to send us back to the city empty-handed after we came all the way down here, Ma."

'"Well I'm not moving into that place no matter how far you came," I said back, "so you can get *that* idea right out of your head. I've been living in Derry for thirty-five years, half my life. All my friends are here, and I'm not moving."

'They looked at each other the way parents do when they've got a kid who's stopped being cute and started being a pain in the tail. Janet patted my shoulder and said, "Now don't get all upset, Mother Lois — we only want you to come and *look*." Like it was the brochures again, and all I had to do was be polite. Just the same, her saying it was just to look set my mind at ease a little. I should have known they couldn't *make* me live there, or even afford it on their own. It's Mr Chasse's money they're counting on to swing it — his pension and the railroad insurance I got because he died on the job.

'It turned out they had an appointment all made for eleven o'clock, and a man lined up to show me around and give me the whole pitch. I was mostly over being scared by the time I got all that straight in my mind, but I was hurt by the high-handed way they were treating me, and mad at how every other thing out of Janet's mouth was Personal Days this and Personal Days that. It was pretty clear that she could think of a lot better ways to spend a day off than coming to Derry to see her fat old bag of a mother-in-law.

'"Stop fluttering and come on, Mother," she says after a little more back-and-forth, like I was so pleased with the whole idea I couldn't even decide which hat to wear. "Hop into your coat. I'll help you clean up the breakfast things when we get back."

'"You didn't hear me," I said. "I'm not going anywhere. Why waste a beautiful fall day like this touring a place I'll never live in? And what gives you the right to drive down here and give me this kind of bum's rush in the first place? Why didn't one of you at least call and say, 'We have an idea, Mom, want to hear it?' Isn't that how you would have treated one of your friends?"

'And when I said that, they traded another glance . . .'

Lois sighed, wiped her eyes a final time, and gave back Ralph's handkerchief, damper but otherwise none the worse for wear.

'Well, I knew from that look that we hadn't reached bottom yet. Mostly it was the way Harold looked – like he did when he'd just hooked a handful of chocolate bits out of the bag in the pantry. And Janet . . . she gave him back the expression I dislike most of all. Her bulldozer look, I call it. And then she asked him if he wanted to tell me what the doctor had said, or if she should do it.

'In the end they both told it, and by the time they were done I was so mad and scared that I felt like yanking my hair out by the roots. The thing I just couldn't seem to get over no matter how hard I tried was the thought of Carl Litchfield telling Harold all the things I thought were private. Just calling him up and *telling* him, like there was nothing in the world wrong with it.

'"So you think I'm senile?" I asked Harold. "Is that what it comes down to? You and Jan think I've gone soft in the attic at the advanced age of sixty-eight?"

'Harold got red in the face and started shuffling his feet under his chair and muttering under his breath. Something about how he didn't think any such thing, but he had to consider my safety, just like I'd always consid- ered his when he was growing up. And all the time Janet was sitting at the counter, nibbling a muffin and giving him a look I could have killed her for – as if she thought he was just a cockroach that had learned to talk like a lawyer. Then she got up and asked if she could "use the facility". I told her to go ahead, and managed to keep from saying it would be a relief to have her out of the room for two minutes.

'"Thanks, Mother Lois," she says. "I won't be long. Harry and I have to leave soon. If you feel you can't come with us and keep your appointment, then I guess there's nothing more to say."'

'What a peach,' Ralph said.

'Well, that was the end of it for me; I'd had enough. "I keep my appointments, Janet Chasse," I said, "but only the ones I make for myself. I don't give a fart in a high wind for the ones other people make for me."

'She tossed up her hands like I was the most unreasonable woman who ever walked the face of the earth, and left me with Harold. He was looking at me with those big brown eyes of his, like he expected me to apologize. I almost felt like I *should* apologize, too, if only to get that cocker spaniel look off his face, but I didn't. *I wouldn't.* I just looked back at him, and after awhile he couldn't stand it anymore and told me I ought to stop being mad. He said he was just worried about me down here all by myself, that he was only trying to be a good son and Janet was only trying to be a good daughter.

'"I guess I understand that," I said, "but you should know that sneaking around behind a person's back is no way to express love and concern." He got all stiff then, and said he and Jan didn't see it as sneaking around. He cut his eyes toward the bathroom for a second or two when he said it, and I pretty much got the idea that what he meant was *Jan* didn't see it as sneaking around. Then he

403

told me it wasn't the way I was making it out to be – that *Litchfield* had called *him,* not the other way around.

'"All right," I said back, "but what kept you from hanging up once you realized what he'd called to talk to you *about*? That was just plain *wrong,* Harry. What in God's good name got into you?"

'He started to flutter and flap around – I think he might even have been starting to apologize – when Jan came back and the you-know-what really hit the fan. She asked where my diamond earrings were, the ones they'd given me for Christmas. It was such a change of direction that at first I could only sputter, and I suppose I sounded like I *was* going senile. But finally I managed to say they were in the little china dish on my bedroom bureau, same as always. I have a jewelry box, but I keep those earrings and two or three other nice pieces out because they are so pretty that looking at them always cheers me up. Besides, they're only clusters of diamond chips – it's not like anyone would want to break in just to steal *those*. Same with my engagement ring and my ivory cameo, which are the other two pieces I keep in that dish.'

Lois gave Ralph an intense, pleading look. He squeezed her hand again.

She smiled and took a deep breath. 'This is very hard for me.'

'If you want to stop—'

'No, I want to finish . . . except that, past a certain point, I can't remember what happened, anyway. It was all so horrible. You see, Janet said she *knew* where I kept them, but they weren't there. My engagement ring was, and the cameo, but not my Christmas earrings. I went in to check myself, and she was right. We turned the place upside down, looked everywhere, but we didn't find them. They're *gone.*'

Lois was now gripping Ralph's hands in both of her own, and seemed to be talking mostly to the zipper of his jacket.

'We took all the clothes out of the bureau . . . Harold pulled the bureau itself out from the wall and looked behind it . . . under the bed and the sofa cushions . . . and it seemed like every time I looked at Janet, she was looking back at *me,* giving me that sweet, wide-eyed look of hers. Sweet as melting butter, it is – except in the eyes, anyway – and she didn't have to come right out and say what she was thinking, because I already knew. "You see? You see how right Dr Litchfield was to call us, and how right *we* were to make that appointment? And how pigheaded *you're* being? Because you *need* to be in a place like Riverview Estates, and this just proves it. You've lost the lovely earrings we gave you for Christmas, you're having a *serious* decline in cognition, and this just proves it. It won't be long before you're leaving the stove-burners on . . . or the bathroom heater . . ."'

She began to cry again, and these tears made Ralph's heart hurt – they were the deep, scouring sobs of someone who has been shamed to the deepest level of her being. Lois hid her face against his jacket. He tightened his arm around her. *Lois,* he thought. *Our Lois.* But no; he didn't like the sound of that anymore, if he ever had.

My Lois, he thought, and at that instant, as if some greater power had approved, the day began to fill with light again. Sounds took on a new resonance. He looked down at his hands and Lois's, entwined on her lap, and saw a lovely blue-gray nimbus around them, the color of cigarette smoke. The auras had returned.

3

'You should have sent them away the minute you realized the earrings were gone,' he heard himself say, and each word was separate and gorgeously unique, like a crystal thunderclap. 'The very second.'

'Oh, I know that now,' Lois said. 'She was just waiting for me to stick my foot in my mouth, and of course I obliged. But I was so *upset* — first the argument about whether or not I was going to Bangor with them to look at Riverview Estates, then hearing my doctor had told them things he had no right to tell them, and on top of all that, finding out I'd lost one of my most treasured possessions. And do you know what the cherry on top was? Having *her* be the one to discover those earrings were gone! Do you blame me for not knowing what to do?'

'No,' he said, and lifted her gloved hands to his mouth. The sound of them passing through the air was like the hoarse whisper of a palm sliding down a wool blanket, and for a moment he clearly saw the shape of his lips on the back of her right glove, printed there in a blue kiss.

Lois smiled. 'Thank you, Ralph.'

'Welcome.'

'I suppose you have a pretty good idea of how things turned out, don't you? Jan said, "You really *should* take better care, Mother Lois, only Dr Litchfield says you've come to a time of life when you really *can't* take better care, and that's why we've been thinking about Riverview Estates. I'm sorry we ruffled your feathers, but it seemed important to move quickly. Now you see why."'

Ralph looked up. Overhead, the sky was a cataract of green-blue fire filled with clouds that looked like chrome airboats. He looked down the hill and saw Rosalie still lying between the Portosans. The dark gray balloon-string rose from her snout, wavering in the cool October breeze.

'I got really mad, then –' She broke off and smiled. Ralph thought it was the first smile he'd seen from her today which expressed real humor instead of some less pleasant and more complicated emotion. 'No – that's not right. I did more than just get mad. If my great-nephew had been there, he would have said, "Nana went nuclear."'

Ralph laughed and Lois laughed with him, but her half sounded a trifle forced.

'What galls me is that Janet knew I would,' she said. 'She *wanted* me to go nuclear, I think, because she knew how guilty I'd feel later on. And God knows I *do*. I screamed at them to get the hell out. Harold looked like he wanted to sink right through the floorboards – shouting has always made him so embarrassed – but Jan just sat there with her hands folded in her lap, smiling and actually *nodding her head,* as if to say "That's right, Mother Lois, you go on and get all that nasty old poison out of your system, and when it's gone, maybe you'll be ready to hear sense."'

Lois took a deep breath.

'Then something happened. I'm not sure just what. This wasn't the first time, either, but it was the *worst* time. I'm afraid it was some kind of . . . well . . . some kind of seizure. Anyway, I started to see Janet in a really funny way . . . a really *scary* way. And I said something that finally got to her. I can't remember what it was, and I'm not sure I want to know, but it certainly wiped that sweety-sweety-sweet smile I hate so much off her face. In fact, she just about *dragged* Harold out. The last thing I remember her saying is that one of them would call me when I wasn't so hysterical that I couldn't help making ugly accusations about the people who loved me.

'I stayed in my house for a little while after they were gone, and then I came out to sit in the park. Sometimes just sitting in the sun makes a body feel better. I stopped in the Red Apple for a snack, and that's when I heard you and Bill had a fight. Are you and he really on the outs, do you think?'

Ralph shook his head. 'Nah – we'll make it up. I really like Bill, but—'

'– but you have to be careful what you say with him,' she finished. 'Also, Ralph, may I add that you can't take what he says back to you too seriously?'

This time it was Ralph who gave their linked hands a squeeze. 'That might be good advice for you, too, Lois – you shouldn't take what happened this morning too seriously.'

She sighed. 'Maybe, but it's hard not to. I said some terrible things at the end, Ralph. *Terrible.* That awful smile of hers . . .'

A rainbow of understanding suddenly hit Ralph's consciousness. In its glow he saw a very large thing, so large it seemed both unquestionable and preordained. He fully faced Lois for the first time since the auras had returned to him . . . or since he had returned to them. She sat in a capsule of translucent gray light as bright as fog on a summer morning which is about to turn sunny. It transformed the woman Bill McGovern called 'Our Lois' into a creature of great dignity . . . and almost unbearable beauty.

She looks like Eos, he thought. *Goddess of the dawn.*

Lois stirred uneasily on the bench. 'Ralph? Why are you looking at me that way?'

Because you're beautiful, and because I've fallen in love with you, Ralph thought, amazed. *Right now I'm so in love with you that I feel as if I'm drowning, and the dying's fine.*

'Because you remember *exactly* what you said.'

She began to play nervously with the clasp of her purse again. 'No, I—'

'Yes you do. You told your daughter-in-law that *she* took your earrings. She did it because she realized you were going to stick to your guns about not going with them, and not getting what she wants makes your daughter-in-law crazy . . . it makes her go nuclear. She did it because you pissed her off. Isn't that about the size of it?'

Lois was looking at him with round, frightened eyes. 'How do you know that, Ralph? *How do you know that about her?*'

'I know it because *you* know it, and you know it because you saw it.'

'Oh, no,' she whispered. 'No, I didn't see anything. I was in the kitchen with Harold the whole time.'

'Not *then,* not when she did it, but when she came back. You saw it in her and all around her.'

As he himself now saw Harold Chasse's wife in Lois, as if the woman sitting beside him on the bench had become a lens. Janet Chasse was tall, fair-skinned, and long-waisted.

Her cheeks were spattered with freckles she covered with makeup, and her hair was a vivid, gingery shade of red. This morning she had come to Derry with that fabulous hair lying over one shoulder in a bulky braid like a sheaf of copper wire. What else did he know about this woman he had never met?

Everything, everything.

She covers her freckles with pancake because she thinks they make her look childish; that people don't take women with freckles seriously. Her legs are beautiful and she knows it. She wears short skirts to work, but today when she came to see

(the old bitch)

Mother Lois, she was wearing a cardigan and an old pair of jeans. Derry dress-downs. Her period is overdue. She's reached that time of life when it doesn't come as regular as clockwork anymore, and during that uneasy two- or three-day pause she suffers through every month, a pause when the whole world seems made of glass and everyone in it seems either stupid or wicked, her behavior and her moods have become erratic. That's probably the real reason she did what she did.

Ralph saw her coming out of Lois's tiny bathroom. Saw her shoot an intense, furious glance toward the kitchen door – there is no sign of the sweety-sweety-sweet smile on that narrow, intense face now – and then scoop the earrings out of the china dish. Saw her cram them into the left front pocket of her jeans.

No, Lois had not actually witnessed this small, ugly theft, but it had changed the color of Jan Chasse's aura from pale green to a complex, layered pattern of browns and reds which Lois had seen and understood at once, probably without the slightest idea of what was really happening to her.

'She took them, all right,' Ralph said. He could see a gray mist drifting dreamily across the pupils of Lois's wide eyes. He could have looked at it for the rest of the day.

'Yes, but—'

'If you'd agreed to keep the appointment at Riverview Estates after all, I bet you would have found them again after her next visit . . . or *she* would have found them, I guess that's more likely. Just a lucky accident – "Oh, Mother Lois, come see what *I* found!" Under the bathroom sink, or in a closet, or lying in some dark corner.'

'Yes.' She was looking into his face now, fascinated, almost hypnotized. 'She must feel terrible . . . and she won't dare bring them back, will she? Not after the things I said. Ralph, how did you *know*?'

'The same way you did. How long have you been seeing the auras, Lois?'

4

'Auras? I don't know what you mean.' Except she did.

'Litchfield told your son about the insomnia, but I doubt if that alone would have been enough to get even Litchfield to . . . you know, tattle. The other thing – what you said he called sensory problems – went right by me. I was too amazed by the idea of anyone thinking you could possibly be prematurely senile, I guess, even though I've been having my own sensory problems lately.'

'*You!*'

'Yes, ma'am. Then, just a little bit ago, you said something even more interesting. You said you started to see Janet in a really funny way. A really *scary* way. You couldn't remember what you *said* just before the two of them walked out, but you knew exactly how you *felt*. You're seeing the other part of the world – the *rest* of the world. Shapes around things, shapes *inside* things, sounds within sounds. I call it the world of auras, and that's what you're experiencing. Isn't it, Lois?'

She looked at him silently for a moment, then put her hands over her face. 'I thought I was losing my mind,' she said, and then said it again: 'Oh Ralph, I thought I was losing my mind.'

5

He hugged her, then let her go and tilted her chin up. 'No more tears,' he said. 'I didn't bring a spare hanky.'

'No more tears,' she agreed, but her eyes were already brimming again. 'Ralph, if you only knew how awful it's been—'

'I *do* know.'

She smiled radiantly. 'Yes . . . you do, don't you?'

'What made that idiot Litchfield decide you were slipping into senility – except Alzheimer's is probably what he had in mind – wasn't just insomnia but insomnia accompanied by something else . . . something he decided were hallucinations. Right?'

'I guess, but he didn't say anything like that at the time. When I told him about the things I'd been seeing – the colors and all – he seemed very understanding.'

'Uh-huh, and the minute you were out the door he called your son and told him to get the hell down to Derry and do something about old Mom, who's started seeing people walking around in colored envelopes with long balloon-strings floating up from their heads.'

'You see those, too? Ralph, *you see those, too?*'

'Me too,' he said, and laughed. It sounded a bit loon-like, and he wasn't surprised. There were a hundred things he wanted to ask her; he felt crazed with impatience. And there was something else, something so unexpected he hadn't even been able to identify it at first: he was horny. Not just interested; actually horny.

Lois was crying again. Her tears were the color of mist on a still lake, and they smoked a little as they slipped down her cheeks. Ralph knew they would taste dark and mossy, like fiddleheads in spring.

'Ralph . . . this . . . this is . . . oh *my!*'

'Bigger than Michael Jackson at the SuperBowl, isn't it?'

She laughed weakly. 'Well, just . . . you know, just a little.'

'There's a name for what's happening to us, Lois, and it's not insomnia or senility or Alzheimer's Disease. It's hyper-reality.'

'Hyper-reality,' she murmured. 'God, what an exotic word!'

'Yes, it is. A pharmacist down the street at Rite Aid, Joe Wyzer, told it to me. Only there's a lot more to it than he knew. More than anyone in their right minds would guess.'

'Yes, like telepathy . . . if it's really happening, that is. Ralph, *are* we in our right minds?'

'Did your daughter-in-law take your earrings?'

'I . . . she . . . yes.' Lois straightened. 'Yes, she did.'

'No doubts?'

'No.'

'Then you've answered your own question. We're sane, all right . . . but I think you're wrong about the telepathy part. It isn't *minds* we read, but *auras*. Listen, Lois, there's all sorts of things I want to ask you, but I have an idea that right now there's only one thing I really have to know. Have you seen –' He stopped abruptly, wondering if he really wanted to say what was on the tip of his tongue.

'Have I seen what?'

'Okay. This is going to sound crazier than anything you've told me, but I'm not crazy. Do you believe that? I'm *not*.'

'I believe you,' she said simply, and Ralph felt a vast weight slip from his heart. She was telling the truth. There was no question about it; her belief shone all around her.

'Okay, listen. Since this started happening to you, have you seen certain people who don't look like they belong on Harris Avenue? People who don't look like they belong *anywhere* in the ordinary world?'

Lois was looking at him with puzzled incomprehension.

'They're bald, they're very short, they wear white smock tops, and what they look like more than anything are the drawings of space aliens they sometimes have on the front pages of those tabloid newspapers they sell in the Red Apple. You haven't seen anyone like that when you've been having one of these hyper-reality attacks?'

'No, no one.'

He banged a fist on his leg in frustration, thought for a moment, then looked up again. 'Monday morning,' he said. 'Before the cops showed up at Mrs Locher's . . . did you see me?'

Very slowly, Lois nodded her head. Her aura had darkened slightly, and spirals of scarlet, thin as threads, began to twist slowly up through it on a diagonal.

'I imagine you have a pretty good idea of who called the police, then,' Ralph said. 'Don't you?'

'Oh, I know it was you,' Lois said in a small voice. 'I suspected before, but I wasn't sure until just now. Until I saw it . . . you know, in your colors.'

In my colors, he thought. It was what Ed had called them, too.

'But you didn't see two pint-sized versions of Mr Clean come out of her house?'

'No,' she said, 'but that doesn't mean anything. I can't even *see* Mrs Locher's house from my bedroom window. The Red Apple's roof is in the way.'

Ralph laced his hands together on top of his head. Of *course* it was, and he should have known it.

'The reason I thought you called the police is that just before I went to take a shower, I saw you looking at something through a pair of binoculars. I never saw you do that before, but I thought maybe you just wanted a better look at the stray dog who raids the garbage cans on Thursday mornings.' She pointed down the hill. '*Him.*'

Ralph grinned. 'That's no him, that's the gorgeous Rosalie.'

'Oh. Anyway, I was in the shower a long time, because there's a special rinse I put in my hair. Not *color,*' she said sharply, as if he had accused her of this, 'just proteins and things that are supposed to keep it looking a little thicker.

When I came out, the police were flocking all around. I looked over your way once, but I couldn't see you anymore. You'd either gone into a different room or kind of scrunched back in your chair. You do that, sometimes.'

Ralph shook his head as if to clear it. He hadn't been in an empty theater on all those nights, after all; someone else had been there, too. They had just been in separate boxes.

'Lois, the fight Bill and I had wasn't really about chess. It—'

Down the hill, Rosalie voiced a rusty bark and began struggling to her feet. Ralph looked in that direction and felt an icicle slip into his belly. Although the two of them had been sitting here for going on half an hour and no one had even come near the comfort stations at the bottom of the hill, the pressed plastic door of the Portosan marked MEN was now slowly opening.

Doc #3 emerged from it. McGovern's hat, the Panama with the crescent bitten in the brim, was cocked back on his head, making him look weirdly as McGovern had on the day Ralph had first seen him in his brown fedora – like an enquiring newshawk in a forties crime drama.

Upraised in one hand the bald stranger held the rusty scalpel.

CHAPTER THIRTEEN

1

'Lois?' To Ralph's own ears, his voice seemed to be an echo winding down a long, deep canyon. 'Lois, do you see that?'

'I don't—' Her voice broke off. 'Did the wind blow that bathroom door open? It didn't, did it? Is someone there? Is that why the dog's making that racket?'

Rosalie backed slowly away from the bald man, her ragged ears laid back, her muzzle wrinkled to expose teeth so badly eroded that they were not much more menacing than hard rubber pegs. She uttered a cracked volley of barks, then began to whine desperately.

'Yes! Don't you *see* him, Lois? Look! He's *right there*!'

Ralph got to his feet. Lois got up with him, shielding her eyes with one hand. She peered down the slope with desperate intensity. 'I see a shimmer, that's all. Like the air over an incinerator.'

'*I told you to leave her alone!*' Ralph shouted down the hill. '*Quit it! Get the hell out!*'

The bald man looked in Ralph's direction, but there was no surprise in the glance this time; it was casual, dismissive. He raised the middle finger of his right hand, flicked it at Ralph in the ancient salute, then bared his own teeth – much sharper and much more menacing than Rosalie's – in a silent laugh.

Rosalie cringed as the little man in the dirty smock began to walk toward her again, then actually raised a paw and put it on her own head, a cartoonish gesture that should have been funny and was horribly expressive of her terror instead.

'What can't I see, Ralph?' Lois moaned. 'I see *something,* but—'

'*Get AWAY from her!*' Ralph shouted, and raised his hand in that karate-chop gesture again. The hand inside – the hand which earlier had produced that wedge of tight blue light – still felt like an unloaded gun, however, and this time the bald doc seemed to know it. He glanced in Ralph's direction and offered a small, jeering wave.

[*Aw, quit it. Shorts – sit back, shut up, and enjoy the show.*]

The creature at the foot of the hill returned his attention to Rosalie, who sat huddled at the base of an old pine. The tree was emitting a thin green fog from the cracks in its bark. The bald doctor bent over Rosalie, one hand outstretched in a gesture of solicitude that went very badly with the scalpel curled into his left fist.

Rosalie whined . . . then stretched her neck forward and humbly licked the bald creature's palm.

Ralph looked down at his own hands, sensing something in them – not the power he'd had before, nothing like that, but *something.* Suddenly there were snaps of clear white light dancing just above his nails. It was as if his fingers had been turned into sparkplugs.

Lois was grabbing frantically at him now. 'What's wrong with the dog? *Ralph, what's wrong with it?*'

With no thought about what he was doing or why, Ralph put his hands over Lois's eyes, like someone playing Guess Who with a loved one. His fingers flashed a momentary white so bright it was almost blinding. *Must be the white they're always talking about in the detergent commercials,* he thought.

Lois screamed. Her hands flew to his wrists, clamped on them, then loosened. 'My God, Ralph, what did you do to me?'

He took his hands away and saw a glowing figure-eight surrounding her eyes; it was as if she had just taken off a pair of goggles which had been dipped in confectioner's sugar. The white began to dim almost as soon as his hands were gone . . . except . . .

It's not dimming, he thought. *It's sinking in.*

'Never mind,' he said, and pointed. 'Look!'

The widening of her eyes told him what he needed to know. Doc #3, completely unmoved by Rosalie's desperate effort to make friends, shoved her muzzle aside with the hand holding the scalpel. He seized the old bandanna hanging around her neck in his other hand and yanked her head up. Rosalie howled miserably. Slobber ran back along the sides of her face. The bald man voiced a scabrous chuckle that made Ralph's flesh crawl.

[*'Hi! Leave off! Leave off teasing that dog!'*]

The bald man's head snapped around. The grin ran off his face and he snarled at Lois, sounding a little like a dog himself.

[*Yahh, go fuck yourself, you fat old Short-Time cunt! Dog's mine, just like I already told your limpdick boyfriend!*]

The bald man had let go of the blue bandanna when Lois shouted at him, and Rosalie was now cringing back against the pine again, her eyes rolling, curds of foam dripping from the sides of her muzzle. Ralph had never seen such a completely terrified creature in his life.

'*Run!*' Ralph screamed. '*Get away!*'

She seemed not to hear him, and after a moment Ralph realized she *wasn't* hearing him, because Rosalie was no longer entirely *there*. The bald doctor had done something to her already – had pulled her at least partway out of ordinary reality like a farmer using his tractor and a length of chain to pull a stump.

Ralph tried once more, anyway.

['*Run, Rosalie! Run away!*']

This time her laid-back ears cocked forward and her head began to turn in Ralph's direction. He didn't know if she would have obeyed him or not, because the bald man renewed his hold on the bandanna before she could even begin to move. He yanked her head up again.

'*He's going to kill it!*' Lois screamed. '*He's going to cut its throat with that thing he has! Don't let him, Ralph! Make him stop!*'

'I can't! Maybe you can! Shoot him! Shoot your hand at him!'

She looked at him, not understanding. Ralph made frantic wood-chopping gestures with his right hand, but before Lois could respond, Rosalie gave a dreadful lost howl. The bald doc raised the scalpel and brought it down, but it wasn't Rosalie's throat he cut.

He cut her balloon-string.

2

A thread emerged from each of Rosalie's nostrils and floated upward. They twined together about six inches above her snout, making a delicate pigtail, and it was at this point that Baldy #3's scalpel did its work. Ralph watched, frozen with horror, as the severed pigtail rose into the sky like the string of a released helium balloon. It was unravelling as it went. He thought it would tangle in the branches of the old pine, but it didn't. When the ascending balloon-string finally did meet one of the branches, it simply passed through.

Of course, Ralph thought. *The same way this guy's buddies walked through May Locher's locked front door after they finished doing the same thing to her.*

This idea was followed by a thought too simple and gruesomely logical not to be believed: not space-aliens, not little bald doctors, but Centurions. Ed Deepneau's Centurions. They didn't look like the Roman soldiers you saw in tin-pants epics like *Spartacus* and *Ben Hur,* true, but they *had* to be Centurions . . . didn't they?

Sixteen or twenty feet above the ground, Rosalie's balloon-string simply faded away to nothingness.

Ralph looked back down in time to see the bald dwarf pull the faded blue bandanna off over the dog's head and then push her down at the base of the tree. Ralph looked at her more closely and felt all his flesh shrink closer to his bones. His dream of Carolyn recurred with cruel intensity, and he found himself struggling to bottle up a shriek of terror.

That's right, Ralph, don't scream. You don't want to do

421

that because once you start, you might not be able to stop — you might just go on doing it until your throat bursts. Remember Lois, because she's in this now, too. Remember Lois and don't start screaming.

Ah, but it was hard not to, because the dream-bugs which had come spewing out of Carolyn's head were now pouring from Rosalie's nostrils in writhing black streams.

Those aren't bugs. I don't know what they are, but they are not bugs.

No, not bugs — just another kind of aura. Nightmarish black stuff, neither liquid nor gas, was pumping out of Rosalie with each exhaled breath. It did not float away but instead began to surround her in slow, nasty coils of anti-light. That blackness should have hidden her from view, but it didn't. Ralph could see her pleading, terrified eyes as the darkness gathered around her head and then began to ooze down her back and sides and legs.

It was a deathbag, a *real* deathbag this time, and he was watching as Rosalie, her balloon-string now cut, wove it relentlessly about herself like a poisonous placental sac. This metaphor triggered the voice of Ed Deepneau inside his head, Ed saying that the Centurions were ripping babies from the wombs of their mothers and taking them away in covered trucks.

Ever wonder what was under most of those tarps? Ed had asked.

Doc #3 stood grinning down at Rosalie. Then he united the knot in her bandanna and put it around his own neck, tying it in a big, loose knot, making it look like a bohemian artist's necktie. This done, he looked up at Ralph and Lois with an expression of loathsome complacency. *There!* his look said. *I took care of my business after all, and there wasn't a damned thing you could do about it, was there?*

[*'Do something, Ralph! Please do something! Make him stop!'*]

Too late for that, but maybe not too late to send him packing before he could enjoy the sight of Rosalie dropping dead at the foot of the tree. He was pretty sure Lois couldn't produce a karate-chop of blue light as he had done, but maybe she could do something else.

Yes — she can shoot him in her own way.

He didn't know why he was so sure of that, but suddenly he was. He grabbed Lois by the shoulders to make her look at him, then raised his right hand. He cocked his thumb and pointed his forefinger at the bald man. He looked like a small child playing cops and robbers.

Lois responded with a look of dismay and incomprehension. Ralph grabbed her hand and stripped off her glove.

[*'You! You, Lois!'*]

She got the idea, raised her own hand, extended her forefinger, and made the child's shooting gesture: Pow! Pow!

Two compact lozenge shapes, their gray-blue shade identical to Lois's aura but much brighter, flew from the end of her finger and streaked down the hill.

Doc #3 screeched and leaped upward, fisted hands held at shoulder height, the heels of his black shoes clipping against his buttocks, as the first of these 'bullets' went under him. It struck the ground, rebounded like a flat stone skipped across the surface of a pond, and hit the Portosan marked WOMEN. For a moment the entire front of it glowed fiercely, as the window of the Buffy-Buffy had done.

The second blue-gray pellet clipped the baldy's left hip and ricocheted up into the sky. He screamed – a high, chattery sound that seemed to twist like a worm in the middle of Ralph's head. Ralph raised his hands to his ears even though it could do no good, and saw Lois doing the same thing. He felt sure that if that scream went on for long, it would burst his head open just as surely as high C shatters fine crystal.

Doc #3 fell to the needle-carpeted ground beside Rosalie and rolled back and forth, howling and holding his hip the way a small child will hold the place he banged when he tumbled off his tricycle. After a few moments of this, his cries began to diminish and he scrambled to his feet. His eyes blazed at them from below the white expanse of his brow. Bill's Panama was tilted far back on his head now, and the left side of his smock was black and smoking.

[*I'll get you! I'll get you both! Goddam interfering Short-Time fucks! I'LL GET YOU BOTH!*]

He whirled and bounded down the path which led to the playground and the tennis courts, running in big flying leaps like an astronaut on the moon. Lois's shot didn't appear to have done any real damage, judging by his speed afoot.

Lois seized Ralph's shoulder and shook him. As she did, the auras began to fade again.

[*'The children! It's going toward the chi*]

She was fading out, and that seemed to make perfect sense, because he suddenly saw that Lois wasn't really talking at all, only staring at him fixedly with her dark eyes as she clutched his shoulder.

'I can't hear you!' he yelled. 'Lois, I can't hear you!'

'What's wrong, are you deaf? It's going toward the play-ground! Toward the children! *We can't let it hurt the children!*'

Ralph let out a deep, shuddering sigh. 'It won't.'

'How can you be sure?'

'I don't know. I just am.'

'I shot it.' She turned her finger toward her face, for a moment looking like a woman who mimes suicide. 'I shot it with my finger.'

'Uh-huh. It stung him, too. Hard, from the way he looked.'

'I can't see the colors anymore, Ralph.'

He nodded. 'They come and go, like radio stations at night.'

'I don't know how I feel . . . I don't even know how I *want* to feel!' She wailed this last, and Ralph folded her into his arms. In spite of everything that was going on in his life right now, one fact registered very clearly: it was wonderful to be holding a woman again.

'That's okay,' he told her, and pressed his face against the top of her head. Her hair smelled sweet, with none of the underlying murk of beauty-shop chemicals he'd gotten used to in Carolyn's hair over the last ten or fifteen years of their life together. 'Let go of it for now, okay?'

She looked at him. He could no longer see the faint mist drifting across her pupils, but felt sure it was still there. And besides, they were very pretty eyes even without the extra added attraction. 'What's it for, Ralph? Do you know what it's *for*?'

He shook his head. His mind was whirling with jigsaw pieces – hats, docs, bugs, protest signs, dolls that exploded in splatters of fake blood – that would not fit together. And for the time being, at least, the thing that seemed to recur with the most resonance was Old Dor's nonsense saying: *Done-bun-can't-be-undone.*

Ralph had an idea that was nothing but the truth.

3

A sad little whine came to his ears and Ralph looked down the hill. Rosalie was lying at the base of the big pine, trying to get up. Ralph could no longer see the black bag around her, but he was sure it was still there.

'Oh Ralph, the poor thing! What can we do?'

There was nothing they could do. Ralph was sure of it. He took Lois's right hand in both of his and waited for Rosalie to lie back and die.

Instead of that, she gave a whole-body lurch that sent her so strongly to her feet that she almost toppled over the other way. She stood still for a moment, her head held so low her muzzle was almost on the ground, and then sneezed three or four times. With that out of the way, she shook herself and looked up at Ralph and Lois. She yapped at them once, a short, brisk sound. To Ralph it sounded as if she were telling them to quit worrying. Then she turned and made off through a little grove of pine trees toward the park's lower entrance. Before Ralph lost sight of her, she had achieved the limping yet insouciant trot which was her trademark. The bum leg was no better than it had been before Doc #3's interference, but it seemed no worse.

Clearly old but seemingly a long way from dead (*Just like the rest of the Harris Avenue Old Crocks,* Ralph thought), she disappeared into the trees.

'I thought that thing was going to kill her,' Lois said. 'In fact, I thought it *had* killed her.'

'Me too,' Ralph said.

'Ralph, did all that really happen? It did, didn't it?'

'Yes.'

'The balloon-strings ... do you think they're life-lines?'

He nodded slowly. 'Yes. Like umbilical cords. And Rosalie ...'

He thought back to his first real experience with the auras, of how he'd stood outside the Rite Aid with his back to the blue mailbox and his jaw hanging down almost to his breastbone. Of the sixty or seventy people he had observed before the auras faded again, only a few had been walking inside the dark envelopes he now thought of as deathbags, and the one Rosalie had knitted around herself just now had been blacker by far than any he had seen that day. Still, those people in the parking lot whose auras had been dingy-dark had invariably looked unwell ... like Rosalie, whose aura had been the color of old sweatsocks even before Baldy #3 started messing with her.

Maybe he just hurried up what may otherwise be a perfectly natural process, he thought.

'Ralph?' Lois asked. 'What about Rosalie?'

'I think my old friend Rosalie is living on borrowed time now,' Ralph said.

Lois considered this, looking down the hill and into the sun-dusty grove where Rosalie had disappeared. At last

427

she turned to Ralph again. 'That midget with the scalpel was one of the men you saw coming out of May Locher's house, wasn't he?'

'No. Those were two other ones.'

'Have you seen more?'

'No.'

'Do you think there *are* more?'

'I don't know.'

He had an idea that next she'd ask if Ralph had noticed that the creature had been wearing Bill's Panama, but she didn't. Ralph supposed it was possible she hadn't recognized it. Too much weirdness swirling around, and besides, there hadn't been a chunk bitten out of the brim the last time she'd seen Bill wearing it. *Retired history teachers just aren't the hat-biting type,* he reflected, and grinned.

'This has been quite a morning, Ralph.' Lois met his gaze frankly, eye to eye. 'I think we need to talk about this, don't you? I really need to know what's going on.'

Ralph remembered this morning – a thousand years ago, now – walking back down the street from the picnic area, running over his short list of acquaintances, trying to decide whom he should talk to. He had crossed Lois off that mental list on the grounds that she might gossip to her girlfriends, and he was now embarrassed by that facile judgement, which had been based more on McGovern's picture of Lois than on his own. It turned out that the only person Lois had spoken to about the auras before today was the one person she should have been able to trust to keep her secret.

He nodded at her. 'You're right. We need to talk.'

'Would you like to come back to my house for a

little late lunch? I make a pretty mean stir-fry for an old gal who can't keep track of her earrings.'

'I'd love to. I'll tell you what I know, but it's going to take awhile. When I talked to Bill this morning, I gave him the *Reader's Digest* version.'

'So,' Lois said. 'The fight was about chess, was it?'

'Well, maybe not,' Ralph said, smiling down at his hands. 'Maybe it was actually more like the fight you had with your son and your daughter-in-law. And I didn't even tell him the craziest parts.'

'But you'll tell me?'

'Yes,' he said, and started to get up. 'I'll bet you're a hell of a good cook, too. In fact—' He stopped suddenly and clapped one hand to his chest. He sat back down on the bench, heavily, his eyes wide and his mouth ajar.

'Ralph? Are you all right?'

Her alarmed voice seemed to be coming from a great distance. In his mind's eye he was seeing Baldy #3 again, standing between the Buffy-Buffy and the apartment house next door. Baldy #3 trying to get Rosalie to cross Harris Avenue so he could cut her balloon-string. He'd failed then, but he'd gotten the job done

(*I was gonna play with her!*)

before the morning was out.

Maybe the fact that Bill McGovern isn't the hat-biting type wasn't the only reason Lois didn't notice whose hat Baldy #3 was wearing, Ralph old buddy. Maybe she didn't notice because she didn't want to notice. Maybe there are a couple of pieces here that fit together, and if you're right about that, the implications are wide-ranging. You see that, don't you?

'Ralph? What's wrong?'

He saw the dwarf snatching a bite from the brim of the Panama and then clapping it back on his head. Heard him saying he guessed he would have to play with Ralph instead.

But not just me. Me and my friends, he said. Me and my asshole friends.

Now, thinking back on it, he saw something else, as well. He saw the sun striking splinters of fire from the lobes of Doc #3's ears as he − or it − chomped into the brim of McGovern's hat. The memory was too clear to deny, and so were those implications.

Those wide-ranging implications.

Take it easy − you don't know a thing for sure, and the funny-farm is just over the horizon, my friend. I think you need to remember that, maybe use it as an anchor. I don't care if Lois is also seeing all this stuff or not. The other men in the white coats, not the pint-sized baldies but the muscular guys with the butterfly nets and the Thorazine shots, can show up at any time. Any old time at all.

But still.

Still.

'Ralph! Jesus Christ, *talk* to me!' Lois was shaking him now and shaking hard, like a wife trying to rouse a husband who is going to be late for work.

He looked around at her and tried to manufacture a smile. It felt false from the inside but must have looked all right to Lois, because she relaxed. A little, anyway. 'Sorry,' he said. 'For a few seconds there it all just sort of . . . you know, ganged up on me.'

'Don't you scare me like that! The way you grabbed your chest, my God!'

'I'm fine,' Ralph said, and forced his false smile even wider. He felt like a kid pulling a wad of Silly Putty, seeing how far he could stretch it before it thinned enough to tear. 'And if you're still cookin, I'm still eatin.'

Three-six-nine, hon, the goose drank wine.

Lois took a close look at him and then relaxed. 'Good. That would be fun. I haven't cooked for anyone but Simone and Mina – they're my girlfriends, you know – in a long time.' Then she laughed. 'Except that isn't what I mean. That isn't why it would be, you know, fun.'

'What *do* you mean?'

'That I haven't cooked for a *man* in a long time. I hope I haven't forgotten how.'

'Well, there was the day Bill and I came in to watch the news with you – we had macaroni and cheese. It was good, too.'

She made a dismissive gesture. 'Reheated. Not the same.'

The monkey chewed tobacco on the streetcar line. The line broke—

Smiling wider than ever. Waiting for the rips to start. 'I'm sure you haven't forgotten how, Lois.'

'Mr Chasse had a *very* hearty appetite. All sorts of hearty appetites, in fact. But then he started having his liver trouble, and . . .' She sighed, then reached for Ralph's arm and took it with a mixture of timidity and resolution he found completely endearing. 'Never mind. I'm tired of snivelling and moaning about the past. I'll leave that to Bill. Let's go.'

He stood up, linked his arm through hers, and walked her down the hill and toward the lower entrance to the park. Lois beamed blindingly at the young mothers in the playground as she and Ralph passed them. Ralph was glad for the distraction. He could tell himself to withhold judgement, he could remind himself over and over again that he didn't know enough about what was happening to him and Lois to even kid himself that he could think logically about it, but he kept jumping at that conclusion anyway. The conclusion felt right to his heart, and he had already come a long way toward believing that, in the world of auras, feeling and knowing were close to identical.

I don't know about the other two, but #3 is one crazy medic . . . and he takes souvenirs. Takes them the way some of the crazies in Vietnam took ears.

That Lois's daughter-in-law had given in to an evil impulse, scooping the diamond earrings from the china dish and putting them in the pocket of her jeans, he had no doubt. But Janet Chasse no longer had them; even now she was no doubt reproaching herself bitterly for having lost them and wondering why she had ever taken them in the first place.

Ralph knew the shrimp with the scalpel had McGovern's hat even if Lois had failed to recognize it, and they had both seen him take Rosalie's bandanna. What Ralph had realized as he started to get up from the bench was that those splinters of light he had seen reflected from the bald creature's earlobes almost certainly meant that Doc #3 had Lois's earrings, as well.

4

The late Mr Chasse's rocking chair stood on faded linoleum by the door to the back porch. Lois led Ralph to it and admonished him to 'stay out from underfoot'. Ralph thought this was an assignment he could handle. Strong light, mid-afternoon light, fell across his lap as he sat and rocked. Ralph wasn't sure how it had gotten so late so fast, but somehow it had. *Maybe I fell asleep,* he thought. *Maybe I'm asleep right now, and dreaming all this.* He watched as Lois took down a wok (definitely hobbit-sized) from an over-head cupboard. Five minutes later, savory smells began to fill the kitchen.

'I *told* you I'd cook for you someday,' Lois said, adding vegetables from the fridge crisper and spices from one of the overhead cabinets. 'That was the same day I gave you and Bill the leftover macaroni and cheese. Do you remember?'

'I believe I do,' Ralph said, smiling.

'There's a jug of fresh cider in the milk-box on the front porch – cider always keeps best outside. Would you get it? You can pour out, too. My good glasses are in the cupboard over the sink, the one I can't reach without drag-ging over a chair. You're tall enough to do without the chair, I judge. What are you, Ralph, about six-two?'

'Six-three. At least I was; I guess maybe I've lost an inch or two in the last ten years. Your spine settles, or some-thing. And you don't have to go putting on the dog just for me. Honest.'

She looked at him levelly, hands on hips, the spoon with which she had been stirring the contents of the wok jutting from one of them. Her severity was offset by a trace of a smile. 'I said my *good* glasses, Ralph Roberts, not my *best* glasses.'

'Yes, ma'am,' he said, grinning, then added: 'From the

way that smells, I guess you still remember how to cook for a man.'

'The proof of the pudding is in the eating,' Lois replied, but Ralph thought she looked pleased as she turned back to the wok.

5

The food was good, and they didn't talk about what had happened in the park as they applied themselves to it. Ralph's appetite had become uncertain, out more often than in, since his insomnia had really begun to bite, but today he ate heartily and chased Lois's spicy stir-fry with three glasses of apple cider (hoping uneasily as he finished the last one that the rest of the day's activities wouldn't take him too far from a toilet). When they had finished, Lois got up, went to the sink, and began to draw hot water for dishes. As she did, she resumed their earlier conversation as if it were a half-finished piece of knitting which had been temporarily laid aside for some other, more pressing, chore.

'What did you do to me?' she asked him. 'What did you do to make the colors come back?'

'I don't know.'

'It was as if I was on the edge of that world, and when you put your hands over my eyes, you pushed me into it.'

He nodded, remembering how she'd looked in the first few seconds after he'd removed his hands — as if she'd just taken off a pair of goggles which had been dipped in powdered sugar. 'It was pure instinct. And you're right, it *is* like a world. I keep thinking of it just that way, as the world of auras.'

'It's wonderful, isn't it? I mean, it's scary, and when it first started to happen to me – back in late July or early August, this was – I was sure I was going crazy, but even then I liked it, too. I couldn't help liking it.'

Ralph gazed at her, startled. Had he once upon a time thought of Lois as transparent? Gossipy? Unable to keep a secret?

No, I'm afraid it was a little worse than that, old buddy. You thought she was shallow. You saw her pretty much through Bill's eyes, as a matter of fact: as 'our Lois'. No less . . . but not much more.

'What?' she asked, a little uneasily. 'Why are you looking at me like that?'

'You've been seeing these auras since *summer*? That long?'

'Yes – brighter and brighter. Also more often. That's why I finally went to see the tattletale. Did I really shoot that thing with my finger, Ralph? The more time goes by, the less I can believe that part of it.'

'You did. I did something like it myself shortly before I ran into you.'

He told her about his earlier confrontation with Doc #3, and about how he had banished the dwarf . . . temporarily, at least. He raised his hand to his shoulder and brought it swiftly down. 'That's all I did – like a kid pretending to be Chuck Norris or Steven Seagal. But it sent this incredible bolt of blue light at him, and he scurried in a hurry. Which was probably for the best, because I couldn't have done it again. I don't know how I did *that*, either. Could you have shot your finger again?'

Lois giggled, turned toward him, and cocked her finger in his general direction. 'Want to find out? Kapow! Kablam!'

'Don't point dat ding at me, lady,' Ralph told her. He smiled as he said it, but wasn't entirely sure he was joking.

Lois lowered her finger and squirted Joy into the sink. As she began to stir the water around with one hand, puffing up the suds, she asked what Ralph thought of as the Big Questions: 'Where did this power come from, Ralph? And what's it for?'

He shook his head as he got up and walked over to the dish-drainer. 'I don't know and I don't know. How's that for helpful? Where do you keep your dish-wipers, Lois?'

'Never mind where I keep my dish-wipers. Go sit down. Please tell me you're not one of these modern men, Ralph – the ones that are always hugging each other and bawling.'

Ralph laughed and shook his head. 'Nope. I was just well trained, that's all.'

'Okay. As long as you don't start going on about how sensitive you are. There are *some* things a girl likes to find out for herself.' She opened the cupboard under the sink and tossed him a faded but scrupulously clean dishtowel. 'Just dry them and put them on the counter. I'll put them away myself. While you're working, you can tell me your story. The unabridged version.'

'You got a deal.'

He was still wondering where to begin when his mouth opened, seemingly of its own accord, and began for him. 'When I finally started to get it through my head that

Carolyn was going to die, I went for a lot of walks. And one day, while I was out on the Extension . . .'

6

He told her everything, beginning with his intervention between Ed and the fat man wearing the West Side Gardeners gimme-cap and ending with Bill telling him that he'd better go see his doctor, because at their age mental illness was common, at their age it was common as hell. He had to double back several times to pick up dropped stitches – the way Old Dor had showed up in the middle of his efforts to keep Ed from going at the man from West Side Gardeners, for instance – but he didn't mind doing that, and Lois didn't seem to have any trouble keeping his narrative straight, either. The overall feeling Ralph was conscious of as he wound his way through his tale was a relief so deep it was nearly painful. It was as if someone had stacked bricks on his heart and mind and he was now removing them, one by one.

By the time he was finished, the dishes were done and they had left the kitchen in favor of the living room with its dozens of framed photographs, presided over by Mr Chasse from his place on the TV.

'So?' Ralph said. 'How much of it do you believe?'

'All of it, of course,' she said, and either did not notice the expression of relief of Ralph's face or chose to ignore it. 'After what we saw this morning – not to mention what you knew about my wonderful daughter-in-law – I can't very well not believe. That's my advantage over Bill.'

Not your only one, Ralph thought but didn't say.

'None of this stuff is coincidental, is it?' she asked him.

Ralph shook his head. 'No, I don't think so.'

'When I was seventeen,' she said, 'my mother hired this boy from down the road – Richard Henderson, his name was – to do chores around our place. There were a lot of boys she could have hired, but she hired Richie because she liked him . . . and she liked him for *me,* if you understand what I mean.'

'Of course I do. She was matchmaking.'

'Uh-huh, but at least she wasn't doing it in a big, gruesome, embarrassing way. Thank God, because I didn't care a fig for Richie – at least not like that. Still, Mother gave it her very best. If I was studying my books at the kitchen table, she'd have him loading the woodbox even though it was May and already hot. If I was feeding the chickens, she'd have Richie cutting side-hay next to the dooryard. She wanted me to see him around . . . to get used to him . . . and if we got to like each other's company and he asked me to a dance or the town fair, that would have been just fine with her. It was gentle, but it was there. A push. And that's what this is like.'

'The pushes don't feel all that gentle to me,' Ralph said. His hand went involuntarily to the place where Charlie Pickering had pricked him with the point of his knife.

'No, of course they don't. Having a man stick a knife in your ribs like that must have been horrible. Thank God you had that spray-can. Do you suppose Old Dor sees the auras, too? That something from that world *told* him to put the can in your pocket?'

Ralph gave a helpless shrug. What she was suggesting

had crossed his mind, but once you got beyond it, the ground really started to slope away. Because if Dorrance had done that, it suggested that some

((*entity*)

force or being had known that Ralph would need help. Nor was that all. That force – or being – would also have had to know that (a) Ralph would be going out on Sunday afternoon, that (b) the weather, quite nice up until then, would turn nasty enough to require a jacket, and (c) which jacket he would wear. You were talking, in other words, about something that could foretell the future. The idea that he had been noticed by such a force frankly scared the hell out of him. He recognized that in the case of the aerosol can, at least, the intervention had probably saved his life, but it still scared the hell out of him.

'Maybe,' he said. 'Maybe something *did* use Dorrance as an errand-boy. But why?'

'And what do we do now?' she added.

Ralph could only shake his head.

She glanced up at the clock squeezed in between the picture of the man in the raccoon coat and the young woman who looked ready to say *Twenty-three skidoo* any old time, then reached for the phone. 'Almost three-thirty! My goodness!'

Ralph touched her hand. 'Who are you calling?'

'Simone Castonguay. I'd made plans to go over to Ludlow with her and Mina this afternoon – there's a card-party at the Grange – but I can't go after all this. I'd lose my shirt.' She laughed, then colored prettily. 'Just a figure of speech.'

Ralph put his hand over hers before she could lift the receiver. 'Go on to your card-party, Lois.'

'Really?' She looked both doubtful and a little disappointed.

'Yes.' He was still unclear about what was going on here, but he sensed that was about to change. Lois had spoken of being pushed, but to Ralph it felt more as if he were being *carried,* the way a river carries a man in a small boat. But he couldn't see where he was going; heavy mist shrouded the banks, and now, as the current began to grow swifter, he could hear the rumble of rapids somewhere up ahead.

Still, there are shapes, Ralph. Shapes in the mist.

Yes. Not very comforting ones, either. They might be trees that only looked like clutching fingers . . . but on the other hand, they might be clutching fingers trying to look like trees. Until Ralph knew which was the case, he liked the idea of Lois being out of town just fine. He had a strong intuition – or perhaps it was only hope masquerading as intuition – that Doc #3 couldn't follow her to Ludlow, that he might not even be able to follow her across the Barrens to the east side.

You can't know any such thing, Ralph.

Maybe not, but it *felt* right, and he was still convinced that in the world of the auras, feeling and knowing were pretty nearly the same thing. One thing he *did* know was that Doc #3 hadn't cut Lois's balloon-string yet; that Ralph had seen for himself, along with the joyously healthy gray glow of her aura. Yet Ralph could not escape a growing certainty that Doc #3 – Crazy Doc – *intended* to cut it, and that, no matter how lively Rosalie had looked when she went trotting away from Strawford Park, the severing of that cord was a mortal, murderous act.

Let's say you're right, Ralph; let's say he can't get at her this afternoon if she's playing nickel-in, dime-or-out in Ludlow. What about tonight? Tomorrow? Next week? What's the solution? Does she call up her son and her bitch of a daughter-in-law, tell them she's changed her mind about Riverview Estates and wants to go there after all?

He didn't know. But he knew he needed time to think, and he also knew that constructive thinking would be hard to do until he was fairly sure that Lois was safe, at least for awhile.

'Ralph? You're getting that moogy look again.'

'That *what* look?'

'Moogy.' She tossed her hair pertly. 'That's a word I made up to describe how Mr Chasse looked when he was pretending to listen to me but was actually thinking about his coin collection. I know a moogy look when I see one, Ralph. What are you thinking about?'

'I was wondering what time you think you'll get back from your card-game.'

'That depends.'

'On what?'

'On whether or not we stop at Tubby's for chocolate frappés.' She spoke with the air of a woman revealing a secret vice.

'Suppose you come straight back.'

'Seven o'clock. Maybe seven-thirty.'

'Call me as soon as you get home. Would you do that?'

441

'Yes. You *want* me out of town, don't you? That's what that moogy look really means.'

'Well . . .'

'You think that nasty bald thing means to hurt me, don't you?'

'I think it's a possibility.'

'Well, he might hurt you, too!'

'Yes, but . . .'

But so far as I can tell, Lois, he's not wearing any of my fashion accessories.

'But *what*?'

'I'm going to be okay until you get back, that's all.' He remembered her deprecating remark about modern men hugging each other and bawling and tried for a masterful frown. 'Go play cards and leave this business to me, at least for the time being. That's an order.'

Carolyn would have either laughed or gotten angry at such comic-opera macho posturing. Lois, who belonged to an entirely different school of feminine thought, only nodded and looked grateful to have the decision taken out of her hands. 'All right.' She tilted his chin down so she could look directly into his eyes. 'Do you know what you're doing, Ralph?'

'Nope. Not yet, anyway.'

'All right. Just as long as you admit it.' She placed a hand on his forearm and a soft, open-mouthed kiss on the corner of his mouth. Ralph felt an entirely welcome prickle of heat in his groin. 'I'll go to Ludlow and win five dollars playing poker with those silly women who are always trying to fill their inside straights. Tonight we'll talk about what to do next. Okay?'

'Yes.'

Her small smile – a thing more in the eyes than of the mouth – suggested that they might do a little more than just talk, if Ralph was bold . . . and at that moment he felt quite bold, indeed. Not even Mr Chasse's stern gaze from his place atop the TV affected that feeling very much.

CHAPTER FOURTEEN

1

It was quarter to four by the time Ralph crossed the street and walked the short distance back up the hill to his own building. Weariness was stealing over him again; he felt as if he had been up for roughly three centuries. Yet at the same time he felt better than he had since Carolyn had died. More together. More *himself.*

Or is that maybe just what you want to believe? That a person can't feel this miserable without some sort of positive payback? It's a lovely idea, Ralph, but not very realistic.

All right, he thought, *so maybe I'm a little confused right now.*

Indeed he was. Also frightened, exhilarated, disoriented, and a touch horny. Yet one clear idea came through this mix of emotions, one thing he needed to do before he did anything else: he had to make up with Bill. If that meant apologizing, he could do that. Maybe an apology was even in order. Bill, after all, hadn't come to *him,* saying, 'Gee, old buddy, you look terrible, tell me all about it.' No, *he* had gone to *Bill.* He had done so with misgivings, true, but that didn't change the fact, and—

444

Ah, Ralph, jeez, what am I going to do with you? It was Carolyn's amused voice, speaking to him as clearly as it had during the weeks following her death, when he'd handled the worst of his grief by discussing everything with her inside his head . . . and sometimes aloud, if he happened to be alone in the apartment. *Bill was the one who blew his top, sweetie, not you. I see you're just as determined to be hard on yourself now as you were when I was alive. I guess some things never change.*

Ralph smiled a little. Yeah, okay, maybe some things never *did* change, and maybe the argument *had* been more Bill's fault than his. The question was whether or not he wanted to cut himself off from Bill's companionship over a stupid quarrel and a lot of stiff-necked horseshit about who had been right and who had been wrong. Ralph didn't think he did, and if that meant making an apology Bill didn't really deserve, what was so awful about that? So far as he knew, there were no bones in the three little syllables that made up *I'm sorry.*

The Carolyn inside his head responded to this idea with wordless incredulity.

Never mind, he told her as he started up the walk. *I'm doing this for me, not for him. Or for you, as far as that goes.*

He was amazed and amused to discover how guilty that last thought made him feel – almost as if he had committed an act of sacrilege. But that didn't make the thought any less true.

He was feeling around in his pocket for his latchkey when he saw a note thumbtacked to the door. Ralph felt for his glasses, but he had left them upstairs on the kitchen table. He leaned back, squinting to read Bill's scrawling hand:

> *Dear Ralph/Lois/Faye/Whoever,*
>
> *I expect to be spending most of the day at Derry Home. Bob Polhurst's niece called and told me that this time it's almost certainly the real thing; the poor man has almost finished his struggle. Room 313 in Derry Home ICU is about the last place on earth I want to be on a beautiful day in October, but I guess I'd better see this through to the end.*
>
> *Ralph, I'm sorry I gave you such a hard time this morning. You came to me for help and I damned near clawed your face off instead. All I can say by way of apology is that this thing with Bob has completely wrecked my nerves. Okay? I think I owe you a dinner . . . if you still want to eat with the likes of me, that is.*
>
> *Faye, please please PLEASE quit bugging me about your damned chess tournament. I promised I'd play, and I keep my promises.*
>
> Goodbye, cruel world,
Bill

Ralph straightened up with a feeling of relief and gratitude. If only everything else that had been happening to him lately could straighten itself out as easily as this part had done!

He went upstairs, shook the teakettle, and was filling it at the sink when the telephone rang. It was John Leydecker. 'Boy, I'm glad I finally got hold of you,' he said. 'I was getting a little worried, old buddy.'

'Why?' Ralph asked. 'What's wrong?'

'Maybe nothing, maybe something. Charlie Pickering made bail after all.'

'You told me that wouldn't happen.'

'I was wrong, okay?' Leydecker said, clearly irritated. 'It wasn't the only thing I was wrong about, either. I told you the judge'd probably set bail in the forty-thousand-dollar range, but I didn't know Pickering was going to draw Judge Steadman, who has been known to say that he doesn't even *believe* in insanity. Steadman set bail at eighty grand. Pickering's court-appointed bellowed like a calf in the moonlight, but it didn't make any difference.'

Ralph looked down and saw he was still holding the teakettle in one hand. He put it on the table. 'And he *still* made bail?'

'Yep. Remember me telling you that Ed would throw him away like a paring knife with a broken blade?'

'Yes.'

'Well, score it as another strikeout for John Leydecker. Ed marched into the bailiff's office at eleven o'clock this morning with a briefcase full of money.'

'Eight thousand dollars?' Ralph asked.

'I said briefcase, not envelope,' Leydecker replied. 'Not eight but eighty. They're still buzzing down at the court-house. Hell, they'll be buzzing about it even after the Christmas tinsel comes down.'

Ralph tried to imagine Ed Deepneau in one of his baggy old sweaters and a pair of worn corduroys – Ed's mad-scientist outfits, Carolyn had called them – pulling banded stacks of twenties and fifties out of his briefcase and couldn't do it. 'I thought you said ten per cent was enough to get out.'

'It is, if you can also escrow something – a house or a piece of property, for instance – that stacks up somewhere near the total bail amount. Apparently Ed couldn't do that, but he *did* have a little rainy-day cash under the mattress. Either that or he gave the tooth-fairy one hell of a blowjob.'

Ralph found himself remembering the letter he had gotten from Helen about a week after she had left the hospital and moved out to High Ridge. She had mentioned a check she'd gotten from Ed – seven hundred and fifty dollars. *It seems to indicate he understands his responsibilities,* she had written. Ralph wondered if Helen would still feel that way if she knew that Ed had walked into the Derry County Courthouse with enough money to send his daughter sailing through the first fifteen years of her life . . . and pledged it to free a crazy guy who liked to play with knives and Molotov cocktails.

'Where in God's name *did* he get it?' he asked Leydecker.

'Don't know.'

'And he isn't required to say?'

'Nope. It's a free country. I understand he said something about cashing in some stocks.'

Ralph thought back to the old days – the good old days before Carolyn had gotten sick and died and Ed had just gotten sick. Thought back to meals the four of them had had together once every two weeks or so, take-out pizza at the Deepneaus' or maybe Carol's chicken pot-pie in the Robertses' kitchen, and remembered Ed saying on one occasion that he was going to treat them all to prime rib at the Red Lion in Bangor when his stock accounts matured. *That's right,* Helen had replied, smiling at Ed fondly.

She had been pregnant then, just beginning to show, and looking all of fourteen with her hair pulled back in a pony-tail and wearing a checkered smock that was still yards too big for her. *Which do you think will mature first, Edward? The two thousand shares of United Toejam or the six thousand of Amalgamated Sourballs?* And he had growled at her, a growl that had made them all laugh because Ed Deepneau didn't have a mean bone in his body, anyone who had known him more than two weeks knew that Ed wouldn't hurt a fly. Except Helen might have known a little different – even back then Helen had almost surely known a little different, fond look or no fond look.

'Ralph?' Leydecker asked. 'Are you still there?'

'Ed didn't have any stocks,' Ralph said. 'He was a research chemist, for Christ's sake, and his father was foreman in a bottling plant in some crazy place like Plaster Rock, Pennsylvania. No dough there.'

'Well, he got it somewhere, and I'd be lying if I said I liked it.'

'From the other Friends of Life, do you think?'

'No, I don't. First, we're not talking rich folks here – most of the people who belong to The Friends are blue-collar types, working-class heroes. They give what they can, but this much? No. They could have gotten together enough property deeds among them to spring Pickering, I suppose, but they didn't. Most of them wouldn't, even if Ed had asked. Ed's all but *persona non grata* with them now, and I imagine they wish they'd never heard of Charlie Pickering. Dan Dalton's taken back the leadership of The Friends of Life, and to most of them, that's a big relief. Ed and Charlie and two other people – a man named Frank Felton and a woman named Sandra McKay — seem to be operating very much on their own hook now. Felton I don't know anything about and there's no jacket on him, but the McKay woman has toured some of the same fine institutions as Charlie. She's unmissable, too — pasty complexion, lots of acne, glasses so thick they make her eyes look like poached eggs, goes about three hundred pounds.'

'You joking?'

'No. She favors stretch pants from Kmart and can usually be observed travelling in the company of assorted Ding-Dongs, Funny Bones, and Hostess Twinkies. She often wears a big sweatshirt with the words BABY FACTORY on the front. Claims to have given birth to fifteen children. She's never actually had any, and probably can't.'

'Why are you telling me all this?'

'Because I want you to watch out for these people,' Leydecker said. He spoke patiently, as if to a child. 'They may be dangerous. Charlie is for sure, that you know without me telling you, and Charlie is out. Where Ed got the money to spring him is secondary — he got it, that's what matters. I wouldn't be a bit surprised if he came after you again. Him, or Ed, or the others.'

'What about Helen and Natalie?'

'They're with their friends — friends who are very hip to the dangers posed by screwloose hubbies. I filled Mike Hanlon in, and he'll also keep an eye on her. The library is being watched very closely by our men. We don't think Helen's in any real danger at the present time — she's still staying at High Ridge — but we're doing what we can.'

'Thank you, John. I appreciate that, and I appreciate the call.'

'I appreciate that you appreciate it, but I'm not quite done yet. You need to remember who Ed called and threatened, my friend – not Helen but *you*. She doesn't seem to be much of a concern to him anymore, but you linger on his mind, Ralph. I asked Chief Johnson if I could assign a man – Chris Nell would be my pick – to keep an eye on you, at least until after WomanCare's Rent-A-Bitch has come and gone. I was turned down. Too much going on this week, he said . . . but the *way* I was turned down suggests to me that if *you* asked, you'd get someone to watch your back. So what do you say?'

Police protection, Ralph thought. *That's what they call it on the TV cop shows and that's what he's talking about – police protection.*

He tried to consider the idea, but too many other things got in the way; they danced in his head like weird sugarplums. Hats, docs, smocks, spray-cans. Not to mention knives, scalpels, and a pair of scissors glimpsed in the dusty lenses of his old binoculars. *Each thing I do I rush through so I can do something else,* Ralph thought, and on the heels of that: *It's a long walk back to Eden, sweetheart, so don't sweat the small stuff.*

'No,' he said.

'What?'

Ralph closed his eyes and saw himself picking up this same phone and calling to cancel his appointment with the pin-sticker man. This was the same thing all over again, wasn't it? Yes. He could get police protection from the Pickerings and the McKays and the Feltons, but that wasn't the way this was supposed to go. He knew that, felt it in every beat of his heart and pulse of his blood.

'You heard me,' he said. 'I don't want police protection.'

'For God's sake, *why*?'

'I can take care of myself,' Ralph said, and grimaced a little at the pompous absurdity of this sentiment, which he had heard expressed in John Wayne Westerns without number.

'Ralph, I hate to be the one to break the news to you, but you're old. You got lucky on Sunday. You might not get lucky again.'

I didn't just get lucky, Ralph thought. *I've got friends in high places. Or maybe I should say entities in high places.*

'I'll be okay,' he said.

Leydecker sighed. 'If you change your mind, will you call me?'

'Yes.'

'And if you see either Pickering or a large lady with thick glasses and stringy blonde hair hanging around—'

'I'll call you.'

'Ralph, please think this over. Just a guy parked down the street is all I'm talking about.'

'Done-bun-can't-be-undone,' Ralph said.

'Huh?'

'I said I appreciate it, but no. I'll be talking to you.'

Ralph gently replaced the telephone in its cradle. Probably John was right, he thought, probably he was crazy, yet he had never felt so completely sane in his life.

'Tired,' he told his sunny, empty kitchen, 'but sane.' He paused, then added: 'Also halfway to being in love, maybe.'

That made him grin, and he was still grinning when he finally put the kettle on to heat.

2

He was on his second cup of tea when he remembered what Bill had said in his note about owing him a meal. He decided on the spur of the moment to ask Bill to meet him at Day Break, Sun Down for a little supper. They could start over.

I think we have to start over, he thought, *because that little psycho has got his hat, and I'm pretty sure that means he's in trouble.*

Well, no time like the present. He picked up the phone and dialed a number he had no trouble remembering: 941–5000. The number of Derry Home Hospital.

3

The hospital receptionist connected him with Room 313. The clearly tired woman who answered the phone was Denise Polhurst, the dying man's niece. Bill wasn't there, she told him. Four other teachers from what she termed 'Unc's glory days' had shown up around one, and Bill had proposed lunch. Ralph even knew how his downstairs tenant would have put it: better belated than never. It was one of his favorites. When Ralph asked her if she expected him back soon, Denise Polhurst said she did.

'He's been so faithful. I don't know what I would have done without him, Mr Robbins.'

'Roberts,' he said. 'Bill made Mr Polhurst sound like a wonderful man.'

'Yes, they all feel that way. But of course the bills won't be coming to his *fan club,* will they?'

453

'No,' Ralph said uncomfortably. 'I suppose not. Bill's note said your uncle is very low.'

'Yes. The doctor says he probably won't last the day, let alone the night, but I've heard *that* song before. God forgive me, but sometimes it's like Uncle Bob's one of those ads from Publishers Clearing House – always promising, never delivering. I suppose that sounds awful, but I'm too tired to care. They turned off the life-support stuff this morning – I couldn't have taken the responsibility all by myself, but I called Bill and he said it was what Unc would have wanted. "It's time for Bob to explore the next world," he said. "He's mapped this one to a nicety." Isn't that poetic, Mr Robbins?'

'Yes. It's *Roberts,* Ms Polhurst. Will you tell Bill that Ralph Roberts called and would like him to call ba—'

'So we turned it off and I was all prepared – nerved up, I guess you'd say – and then he didn't die. I can't understand it. He's ready, *I'm* ready, his life's work is done . . . so why won't he die?'

'I don't know.'

'Death is very stupid,' she said, speaking in the nagging and unlovely voice which only the very tired and the deeply heartsick seem to employ. 'An obstetrician this slow in cutting a baby's umbilical cord would be fired for malpractice.'

Ralph's mind had a tendency to drift these days, but this time it snapped back in a hurry. 'What did you say?'

'Beg your pardon?' She sounded startled, as if her own mind had been drifting.

'You said something about cutting the cord.'

'I didn't *mean* anything,' she said. That nagging tone had grown stronger . . . except it wasn't nagging, Ralph realized; it was whining, and it was frightened. Something was wrong here. His heartbeat suddenly speeded up. 'I didn't mean anything at *all*,' she insisted, and suddenly the phone Ralph was holding turned a deep and sinister shade of blue in his hand.

She's been thinking about killing him, and not just idly, either − she's been thinking about putting a pillow over his face and smothering him with it. It wouldn't take long, *she thinks.* A mercy, *she thinks.* Over at last, *she thinks.*

Ralph pulled the phone away from his ear. Blue light, cold as a February sky, rose in pencil-thin rays from the holes in the earpiece.

Murder is blue, Ralph thought, holding the phone at arm's length and staring with wide-eyed unbelief as the blue rays began to bend and drip toward the floor. He could hear, very faintly, the quacking, anxious voice of Denise Polhurst. *It wasn't anything I ever wanted to know, but I guess I know it anyway: murder is blue.*

He brought the handset toward his mouth again, cocking it to keep the top half, with its freight of icicle aura, away from him. He was afraid that if that end of the handset got too close to his ear, it might deafen him with her cold and furious desperation.

'Tell Bill that Ralph called,' he said. '*Roberts,* not Robbins.' He hung up without waiting for a reply. The blue rays shattered away from the phone's earpiece and tumbled toward the floor. Ralph was again reminded of icicles; this time of how they fell in a neat row when you ran your gloved hand along the underside of an eave after a warm winter day. They disappeared before they hit the linoleum. He glanced around. Nothing in the room glowed, shimmered, or vibrated. The auras were gone again. He began to let out a sigh of relief and then, from outside on Harris Avenue, a car backfired.

In the empty second-floor apartment, Ralph Roberts screamed.

4

He didn't want any more tea, but he was still thirsty. He found half a Diet Pepsi – flat but wet – in the back of the fridge, poured it into a plastic cup with a faded Red Apple logo on it, and took it outside. He could no longer stand to be in the apartment, which seemed to smell of unhappy wakefulness. Especially not after what had happened with the phone.

The day had become even more beautiful, if that was possible; a strong, mild wind had developed, rolling bands of light and shadow across the west side of Derry and combing the leaves from the trees. These the wind sent hurrying along the sidewalks in rattling dervishes of orange and yellow and red.

Ralph turned left not because he had any conscious desire to revisit the picnic area up by the airport but only because he wanted the wind at his back. Nevertheless, he found himself entering the little clearing again some ten minutes later. This time it was empty, and he wasn't surprised. There was no edge in the wind that had sprung up, nothing to make old men and women scurry indoors, but it was hard work keeping cards on the table or chess-pieces on the board when the puckish wind kept trying to snatch them away. As Ralph approached the small trestle table where Faye Chapin usually held court, he was not exactly surprised to see a note held down by a rock, and he had a good idea what the subject would be even before he put down his plastic Red Apple cup and picked it up.

Two walks; two sightings of the bald doc with the scalpel; two old people suffering insomnia and seeing brightly colored visions; two notes. It's like Noah leading the animals onto the ark, not one by one but in pairs . . . and is another hard rain going to fall? Well, what do you think, old man?

He didn't know what he thought . . . but Bill's note had been a kind of obituary-in-progress, and he had absolutely no doubt that Faye's was the same thing. That sense of being carried forward, effortlessly and without hesitation, was simply too strong to doubt; it was like awakening on some alien stage to find oneself speaking lines (or stumbling through them, anyway) in a drama for which one could not remember having rehearsed, or seeing a coherent shape in what had up until then looked like complete nonsense, or discovering . . .

Discovering what?

'Another secret city, that's what,' he murmured. 'The Derry of Auras.' Then he bent over Faye's note and read it while the wind played prankishly with his thinning hair.

5

Those of you who want to pay your final respects to Jimmy Vandermeer are advised to do so by tomorrow at the very latest. Father Coughlin came by this noon and told me the poor old guy is sinking fast. He CAN have visitors, tho. He is in Derry Home ICU, Room 315.

Faye

PS Remember that time is short.

Ralph read the note twice, put it back on the table with the rock on top to weight it down for the next Old Crock to happen along, then simply stood there with his hands in his pockets and his head down, gazing out at Runway 3 from beneath the bushy tangle of his brows. A crisp leaf, orange as one of the Halloween pumpkins which would soon decorate the street, came flipping down from the deep blue sky and landed in his sparse hair. Ralph brushed it away absently and thought of two hospital rooms on Home's ICU floor, two rooms side by side. Bob Polhurst in one, Jimmy V in the other. And the next room up the hall? That one was 317, the room in which his wife had died.

'This is not a coincidence,' he said softly.

But what was it? Shapes in the mist? A secret city? Evocative phrases, both of them, but they answered no questions.

Ralph sat on top of the picnic table next to the one upon which Faye had left his note, took off his shoes, and crossed his legs. The wind gusted, ruffling his hair. He sat there amid the falling leaves with his head slightly bent and his brow furrowed in thought. He looked like a Winslow Homer version of Buddha as he meditated with his hands cupping his kneecaps, carefully reviewing his impressions of Doc #1 and Doc #2 . . . and then contrasting these impressions with those he'd gotten of Doc #3.

First impression: all three docs had reminded him of the aliens in tabloids like *Inside View,* and pictures which were always labelled 'artist's conceptions'. Ralph knew that these bald-headed, dark-eyed images of mysterious visitors from space went back a good many years; people had been reporting contacts with short baldies – the so-called little doctors – for a long time, maybe for as long as people had been reporting UFOs. He was quite sure that he had read at least one such account way back in the sixties.

'Okay, so say there are quite a few of these fellows around,' Ralph told a sparrow which had just lit on the picnic area's litter barrel. 'Not just three docs but three hundred. Or three thousand. Lois and I aren't the only ones who've seen them. And . . .'

And didn't most of the people who gave accounts of such meetings also mention sharp objects?

Yes, but not scissors or scalpels – at least Ralph didn't think so. Most of the people who claimed to have been abducted by the little bald doctors talked about probes, didn't they?

The sparrow flew off. Ralph didn't notice. He was thinking about the little bald docs who had visited May Locher on the night of her death. What else did he know of them? What else had he seen? They had been dressed in white smocks, like the ones worn by TV-show doctors in the fifties and sixties, like the ones pharmacists still wore. Only *their* smocks, unlike the one worn by Doc #3, had been clean. #3 had been toting a rusty scalpel; if there had been any rust on the scissors Doc #1 had been holding in his right hand, Ralph hadn't noticed it. Not even after he'd trained the binoculars on them.

Something else – probably not important, but at least you noticed it. Scissors-Toting Doc was right-handed, at least judging from the way he held his weapon. Scalpel-Wielding Doc is a southpaw.

No, probably not important, but something about it – another of those shapes in the mist, this a small one – tugged at him just the same. Something about the dichotomy of left and right.

'Go to the left and you'll be right,' Ralph muttered, repeating the punchline of some joke he no longer even remembered. 'Go to the right and you'll be left.'

Never mind. What else did he know about the docs?

Well, they had been surrounded by auras, of course – rather lovely greenish-gold ones – and they had left those

(*white-man tracks*)

Arthur Murray dance-diagrams behind them. And although their features had struck him as perfectly anonymous, their auras had conveyed feelings of power . . . and sobriety . . . and . . .

'And *dignity*, goddammit,' Ralph said. The wind gusted again and more leaves blew down from the trees. Some fifty yards from the picnic area, not far from the old train tracks, a twisted, half-uprooted tree seemed to reach in Ralph's direction, stretching branches that actually *did* look a little like clutching hands.

It suddenly occurred to Ralph that he had seen quite a lot that night for an old guy who was supposed to be living on the edge of the last age of man, the one Shakespeare (and Bill McGovern) called 'the slippered pantaloon'. And none of it – not one single thing – suggested danger or evil intent. That Ralph had *inferred* evil intent wasn't very surprising. They were physically freakish strangers; he had observed them coming out of a sick woman's house at a time of night when visitors seldom if ever called; he had seen them only minutes after waking from a nightmare of epic proportions.

Now, however, recollecting what he had seen, other things recurred. The way they had stood on Mrs Locher's stoop, for instance, as if they had every right to be there; the sense he had gotten of two old friends indulging themselves in a bit of conversation before going on their way. Two old buddies talking it over one more time before heading home after a long night's work.

That was your impression, yes, but that doesn't mean you can trust it, Ralph.

But Ralph thought he *could* trust it. Old friends, long-time colleagues, done for the night. May Locher's had been their last stop.

All right, so Docs #1 and #2 were as different from the third one as day is from night. They were clean while he was dirty, they were invested with auras while he had none (none that Ralph had seen, at least), they carried scissors while he carried a scalpel, they seemed as sane and sober as a couple of respected village elders while #3 seemed as crazy as a shithouse rat.

One thing is perfectly clear, though, isn't it? Your playmates are supernatural beings, and other than Lois, the only person who seems to know they're there is Ed Deepneau. Want to bet on how much sleep Ed is getting just lately?

'No,' Ralph said. He raised his hands from his knees

and held them in front of his eyes. They were shaking a little. Ed had mentioned bald docs, and there *were* bald docs. Was it the docs he'd been talking about when he talked about Centurions? Ralph didn't know. He almost hoped so, because that word – Centurions – had begun to call up a much more terrible image in his mind each time it occurred to him: the Ringwraiths from Tolkien's fantasy trilogy. Hooded figures astride skeletal, red-eyed horses, bearing down on a small party of cowering hobbits outside the Prancing Pony Tavern in Bree.

Thinking of hobbits made him think of Lois, and the trembling in his hands grew worse.

Carolyn: *It's a long walk back to Eden, sweetheart, so don't sweat the small stuff.*

Lois: *In my family, dying at eighty is dying young.*

Joe Wyzer: *The medical examiner usually ends up writing* suicide *on the cause-of-death line rather than insomnia.*

Bill: *His specialty was the Civil War, and now he doesn't even know what a civil war is, let alone who won ours.*

Denise Polhurst: *Death is very stupid. An obstetrician this slow in cutting a baby's umbilical cord—*

It was as if someone had suddenly clicked on a bright searchlight inside his head, and Ralph cried out into the sunny autumn afternoon. Not even the Delta 727 settling in for a landing on Runway 3 could entirely drown that cry.

6

He spent the rest of the afternoon sitting on the porch of the house he shared with McGovern, waiting impatiently for Lois to come back from her card-game. He could have tried McGovern again at the hospital, but didn't. The need to speak to McGovern had passed. Ralph didn't understand everything yet, but he thought he understood a great deal more than he had, and if his sudden flash of insight at the picnic area had any validity at all, telling McGovern what had happened to his Panama would serve absolutely no purpose even if Bill believed him.

I have to get the hat back, Ralph thought. *And I have to get Lois's earrings back, too.*

It was an amazing late afternoon and early evening. On the one hand, nothing happened. On the other hand, *everything* happened. The world of auras came and went around him like the stately progression of cloud-shadows across the west side. Ralph sat and watched, rapt, breaking off only to eat a little and make a trip to the bathroom. He saw old Mrs Bennigan standing on her front porch in her bright red coat, clutching her walker and taking inventory of her fall flowers. He saw the aura surrounding her − the scrubbed and healthy pink of a freshly bathed infant − and hoped Mrs B didn't have a lot of relatives waiting around for her to die. He saw a young man of no more than twenty bopping along the other side of the street toward the Red Apple. He was the picture of health in his faded jeans and sleeveless Celtics jersey, but Ralph could see a deathbag clinging to him like an oilslick, and a balloon-string rising from the crown of his head that looked like a decaying drape-pull in a haunted house.

He saw no little bald doctors, but shortly after five-thirty he observed a startling shaft of purple light erupt from a manhole cover in the middle of Harris Avenue; it rose into the sky like a special effect in a Cecil B. DeMille

Bible epic for perhaps three minutes, then simply winked out. He also saw a huge bird that looked like a prehistoric hawk go floating between the chimneys of the old dairy building around the corner on Howard Street, and alternating red and blue thermals twisting over Strawford Park in long, lazy ribbons.

When soccer practice at Fairmount Grammar let out at quarter to six, a dozen or so kids came swarming into the parking lot of the Red Apple, where they would buy tons of pre-supper candy and bales of trading cards – football cards by this time of year, Ralph supposed. Two of them stopped to argue about something, and their auras, one green and the other a vibrant shade of burnt orange, intensified, drew in, and began to gleam with rising spirals of scarlet thread.

Look out! Ralph shouted mentally at the boy within the orange envelope of light, just a moment before Green Boy dropped his schoolbooks and socked the other in the mouth. The two of them grappled, spun around in a clumsy, aggressive dance, then tumbled to the sidewalk. A little circle of yelling, cheering kids formed around them. A purplish-red dome like a thunderhead began to build up around and above the fight. Ralph found this shape, which was circulating in a slow counter-clockwise movement, both terrible and beautiful, and he wondered what the aura above a full-scale military battle would look like. He decided that was a question to which he didn't really want an answer. Just as Orange Boy climbed on top of Green Boy and began to pummel him in earnest, Sue came out of the store and hollered at them to quit fighting in the damned parking lot.

Orange Boy dismounted reluctantly. The combatants rose to their feet, looking at each other warily. Then Green Boy, trying to appear nonchalant, turned and went into the store. Only his quick glance back over his shoulder to make sure his opponent was not pursuing, spoiled the effect.

The spectators were either following Green Boy into the store for their post-practice supplies or clustered around Orange Boy, congratulating him. Above them, unseen, that virulent red-purple toadstool was breaking up like a cloud-bank before a strong wind. Pieces of it tattered, unravelled, and disappeared.

The street is a carnival of energy, Ralph thought. *The juice thrown off by those two boys during the ninety seconds they were mixing it up looked like enough to light Derry for a week, and if a person could tap the energy the* watchers *generated — the energy inside that mushroom cloud — you could probably light the whole state of Maine for a month. Can you imagine what it would be like to enter the world of auras in Times Square at two minutes to midnight on New Year's Eve?*

He couldn't and didn't want to. He suspected he had glimpsed the leading edge of a force so huge and so vital that it made all the nuclear weapons created since 1945 seem about as powerful as a child's cap-pistol fired into an empty peach can. Enough force to destroy the universe, perhaps . . . or to create a new one.

7

Ralph went upstairs, dumped a can of beans into one pot and a couple of hotdogs into another, and walked impatiently back and forth through the flat, snapping his fingers and occasionally running his fingers through his hair, as he waited for this impromptu bachelor's supper to cook. The bone-deep weariness which had hung on him like invisible weights ever since midsummer was, for the time being, at least, entirely gone; he felt filled with manic, antic energy, absolutely *stuffed* with it. He supposed this was why people liked Benzedrine and cocaine, only he had an idea that this was a much better high, that when it departed it would not leave him feeling plundered and mistreated, more used than user.

Ralph Roberts, unaware that the hair his fingers were combing through had grown thicker, and that threads of black were visible in it for the first time in five years, jive-toured his apartment, walking on the balls of his feet, first humming and then singing an old rock-and-roll tune from the early sixties: 'Hey, pretty bay-bee, you can't sit down . . . you gotta slop, bop, slip, slop, flip top *alll* about . . .'

The beans were bubbling in their pot, the hotdogs boiling in theirs – only it looked to Ralph almost as if they were *dancing* in there, doing the Bristol Stomp to the old Dovells tune. Still singing at the top of his lungs ('When you hear the hippie with the backbeat, you can't sit down'), Ralph cut the hotdogs into the beans, dumped in half a pint of ketchup, added some chili sauce, then stirred everything vigorously together and headed for the door. He carried his supper, still in the pot, in one hand. He ran down the stairs as nimbly as a kid who's running late on the first day of school. He hooked a baggy old cardigan sweater – McGovern's, but what the hell – out of the front hall closet, and then went back out on the porch.

The auras were gone, but Ralph wasn't dismayed; for

the time being he was more interested in the smell of food. He couldn't remember the last time he'd felt as flat-out hungry as he did at that moment. He sat on the top step with his long thighs and bony knees sticking out on either side of him, looking decidedly Ichabod Crane-ish, and began to eat. The first few bites burned his lips and tongue, but instead of being deterred, Ralph ate faster, almost gobbling.

He paused with half the pot of beans and franks consumed. The animal in his stomach hadn't gone back to sleep – not yet – but it had been pacified a bit. Ralph belched unselfconsciously and looked out at Harris Avenue with a feeling of contentment he hadn't known in years. Under the current circumstances, that feeling made no sense at all, but that didn't change it in the slightest. When was the last time he had felt this good? Maybe not since the morning he'd awakened in that barn somewhere between Derry, Maine and Poughkeepsie, New York, amazed by the conflicting rays of light – thousands of them, it had seemed – which crisscrossed the warm, sweet-smelling place where he lay.

Or maybe never.

Yes, or maybe never.

He spied Mrs Perrine coming up the street, probably returning from A Safe Place, the combination soup-kitchen and homeless shelter down by the canal. Ralph once again found himself fascinated by her strange, gliding walk, which she achieved without the aid of a cane and seemingly without any side-to-side movement of her hips. Her hair, still more black than gray, was now held – or perhaps subdued was the word – by the hairnet she wore on the serving line. Thick support hose the color of cotton candy rose from her spotless white nurse's shoes . . . not that Ralph could see much of either them or the legs they covered; this evening Mrs Perrine wore a man's wool overcoat, and the hem came almost to her ankles. She seemed to depend almost entirely on her upper legs to move her along – a sign of some chronic back problem, Ralph guessed – and this mode of locomotion, coupled with the overcoat, gave Esther Perrine a somewhat surreal aspect as she approached. She looked like the black queen on a chessboard, a piece that was either being guided by an invisible hand or moving all by itself.

As she neared the place where Ralph sat – still wearing the ripped shirt and now eating his supper directly from the pot in the bargain – the auras began to steal back into the world again. The streetlights had already come on, and now Ralph saw delicate lavender arcs hung over each. He could also see a red haze hovering above some roofs, a yellow haze above others, a pale cerise above still others. In the east, where night was now gathering itself, the horizon flocked with dim green speckles.

Closer to hand, he watched as Mrs Perrine's aura sprang to life around her – that firm gray that reminded him of a West Point cadet's uniform. A few darker spots, like phantom buttons, shimmered above her bosom (Ralph assumed there *was* a bosom hidden somewhere beneath the overcoat). He was not sure, but thought these might be signs of impending ill health.

'Good evening, Mrs Perrine,' he said politely, and watched as the words rose in front of his eyes in snowflake shapes.

She gave him a penetrating glance, flicking her eyes up and down, seeming to simultaneously sum him up and dismiss him in a single look. 'I see you're still wearing that same shirt, Roberts,' she said.

What she didn't say – but what Ralph was sure she was thinking – was *I also see you sitting there and eating beans right out of the pot, like some ragged street-person who never learned any better . . . and I have a way of* remembering *what I see, Roberts.*

'So I am,' Ralph said. 'I guess I forgot to change it.'

'Hmmp,' said Mrs Perrine, and now he thought it was his underwear she was considering. *When was the last time it occurred to you to change that? I shudder to think, Roberts.*

'Lovely evening, isn't it, Mrs Perrine?'

Another of those quick, birdlike glances, this time up at the sky. Then back to Ralph. 'It's going to turn cold.'

'Do you think so?'

'Oh, yes – Indian summer's over. My back isn't good for much besides weather forecasting these days, but at that it does very well.' She paused. 'I believe that's Bill McGovern's sweater.'

'I guess it is,' Ralph agreed, wondering if she would ask him next if Bill knew he had it. He wouldn't have put it past her.

Instead, she told him to button it up. 'You don't want to be a candidate for pneumonia, do you?' she asked, and the tucked set of her mouth added, *As well as for the nuthouse?*

'Absolutely not,' Ralph said. He set the pot aside, reached for the sweater buttons, then stopped. He was still wearing a quilted stove-glove on his left hand. He hadn't noticed it until now.

'It will be easier if you take that off,' Mrs Perrine said. There might have been the faintest gleam in her eyes.

'I suppose so,' Ralph said humbly. He shook off the glove and buttoned McGovern's sweater.

'My offer holds good, Roberts.'

'Beg your pardon?'

'My offer to mend your shirt. If you can bring yourself to part with it for a day or so, that is.' She paused. 'You *do* have another shirt, I assume? One you could wear while I mend the one you have on?'

'Oh, yes,' Ralph said. 'You bet. Quite a few of them.'

'Choosing among them each day must be challenging for you. There's bean juice on your chin, Roberts.' With this pronouncement, Mrs Perrine's eyes flicked forward and she began to march once more.

What Ralph did then he did with no forethought or understanding; it was as instinctive as the chopping gesture he had made earlier to scare Doc #3 away from Rosalie. He raised the hand which had been wearing the thermal glove and curled it into a tube around his mouth. Then he inhaled sharply, producing a faint, whispery whistle.

The results were amazing. A pencil of gray light poked out of Mrs Perrine's aura like the quill of a porcupine. It lengthened rapidly, angling backward as the lady herself moved forward, until it had crossed the leaf-littered lawn and darted into the tube formed by Ralph's curled fingers. He felt it enter him as he inhaled and it was like swallowing pure energy. He suddenly felt lit up, like a neon sign or the marquee of a big-city movie theater. An explosive sense of force – a feeling of *Pow!* – ran through his chest and stomach, then raced down his legs all the way

470

to the tips of his toes. At the same time it rocketed upward into his head, threatening to blow off the top of his skull as if it were the thin concrete roof of a missile silo.

He could see rays of light, as gray as electrified fog, smoking out from between his fingers. A terrible, joyous sense of power lit up his thoughts, but only for a moment. It was followed by shame and amazed horror.

What are you doing, Ralph? Whatever that stuff is, it doesn't belong to you. Would you reach into her purse and take some of her money while she wasn't looking?

He felt his face flush. He lowered his cupped hand and shut his mouth. As his lips and teeth came together, he clearly heard – and actually *felt* – something crunch crisply inside. It was the sound you heard when you were chomping off a bite of fresh rhubarb.

Mrs Perrine stopped, and Ralph watched apprehensively as she made a half-turn and looked out at Harris Avenue. *I didn't mean to,* he thought at her. *Honest I didn't, Mrs P – I'm still learning my way around this thing.*

'Roberts?'

'Yes?'

'Did you hear something? It sounded almost like a gunshot.'

Ralph could feel his ears throbbing with hot blood as he shook his head. 'No . . . but my ears aren't what they—'

'Probably just a backfire over on Kansas Street,' she said, dismissing his weak-sister excuses out of hand. 'It made my heart miss a beat, though, I can tell you.'

She started off again in her odd, gliding, chess-queen walk, then stopped once more and looked back at him. Her aura had begun to fade out of Ralph's view, but he had no trouble seeing her eyes — they were as sharp as a kestrel's.

'You look different, Roberts,' she said. 'Younger, somehow.'

Ralph, who had expected something else (*Give me back what you stole, Roberts, and right this minute,* for instance), could only flounder. 'Do you think . . . that's very . . . I mean to say thank y—'

She flapped an impatient oh–shut–up hand at him. 'Probably the light. I advise you not to dribble on that sweater, Roberts. My impression of Mr McGovern is that he is a man who takes care of his things.'

'He should have taken better care of his hat,' Ralph said.

Those bright eyes, which had begun once more to shift away from him, shifted back. 'I beg your pardon?'

'His Panama,' Ralph said. 'He lost it somewhere.'

Mrs Perrine held this up to the light of her intellect for a moment, then cast it aside with another *Hmmp*. 'Go inside, Roberts. If you stay out here much longer, you'll catch your death of cold.' And then she slid upon her way, not visibly the worse for wear as a result of Ralph's thoughtless act of thievery.

Thievery? I'm pretty sure that's the wrong word, Ralph. What you did just now was a lot closer to—

'Vampirism,' Ralph said bleakly. He put the pot of beans aside and began to slowly rub his hands together. He felt ashamed . . . guilty . . . and all but exploding with energy.

You stole some of her life-force instead of her blood, but a vampire is a vampire, Ralph.

Yes indeed. And it suddenly occurred to Ralph that this must not have been the first time he had done such a thing.

You look different, Roberts. Younger, somehow. That was what Mrs Perrine had said tonight, but people had been making similar comments to him ever since the end of the summer, hadn't they? The main reason his friends hadn't hectored him into going to the doctor was because he didn't *look* like anything was wrong with him. He complained of insomnia, but he apparently looked like the picture of health. *I guess that honeycomb must have really turned the trick,* Johnny Leydecker had said just before the two of them had left the library on Sunday – back in the Iron Age, that felt like now. And when Ralph had asked him what he was talking about, Leydecker had said he was talking about Ralph's insomnia. *You look a gajillion times better than on the day I first met you.*

And Leydecker hadn't been the only one. Ralph had been more or less dragging himself through the days, feeling folded, spindled, and mutilated . . . but people kept telling him how *good* he looked, how *refreshed* he looked, how *young* he looked. Helen . . . McGovern . . . even Faye Chapin had said something a week or two ago, although Ralph couldn't remember exactly what—

'Sure I do,' he said in a low, dismayed voice. 'He asked me if I was using wrinkle cream. *Wrinkle* cream, for God's sake!'

Had he been stealing from the life-force of others even back then? Stealing without even knowing it?

'I must have been,' he said in that same low voice. 'Dear Jesus, I'm a vampire.'

But was that the right word? he wondered suddenly. Wasn't it at least possible that, in the world of auras, a life-stealer was called a Centurion?

Ed's pallid, frantic face rose before him like a ghost which returns to accuse its murderer, and Ralph, suddenly terrified, wrapped his arms around his knees and lowered his head to rest upon them.

CHAPTER FIFTEEN

1

At twenty minutes past seven, a perfectly maintained Lincoln Town Car of late seventies vintage drew up to the curb in front of Lois's house. Ralph – who had spent the last hour showering, shaving, and trying to get himself calmed down – stood on the porch and watched Lois get out of the back seat. Goodbyes were said and girlish, sprightly laughter drifted across to him on the breeze.

The Lincoln pulled away and Lois started up her walk. Halfway along it, she stopped and turned. For a long moment the two of them regarded each other from their opposite sides of Harris Avenue, seeing perfectly well in spite of the deepening darkness and the two hundred yards which separated them. They burned for each other in that darkness like secret torches.

Lois pointed a finger at him. It was very close to the hand gesture she'd made before shooting at Doc #3, but this didn't upset Ralph in the least.

Intent, he thought. *Everything lies in intent. There are few mistakes in this world . . . and once you get to know your way around, maybe there are no mistakes at all.*

A narrow, gray-glistening beam of force appeared at the end of Lois's finger and began to extend itself across the deepening shadows of Harris Avenue. A passing car drove blithely through it. The car's windows flashed a momentary bright, blind gray and its headlights seemed to flicker briefly, but that was all.

Ralph raised his own finger, and a blue beam grew from it. These two narrowcasts of light met in the center of Harris Avenue and twined together like woodbine. Higher and higher the interwoven pigtail rose, paling slightly as it went. Then Ralph curled his finger, and his half of the love-knot in the middle of Harris Avenue winked out of existence. A moment later, Lois's half also disappeared. Ralph slowly descended the porch steps and began to cross his lawn. Lois came toward him. They met in the middle of the street . . . where, in a very real sense, they had met already.

Ralph put his arms around her waist and kissed her.

2

You look different, Roberts. Younger, somehow.

Those words kept running through his head — recycling themselves like an endless tape-loop — as Ralph sat in Lois's kitchen, drinking coffee. He was unable to take his eyes off her. She looked easily ten years younger and ten pounds lighter than the Lois he'd gotten used to seeing over the last few years. Had she looked this young and pretty in the park this morning? Ralph didn't think so, but of course she had been upset this morning, upset and crying, and he supposed that made a difference.

Still . . .

Yes, still. The tiny networks of wrinkles around the corners of her mouth were gone. So were the incipient turkey-wattles beneath her neck and the sag of flesh which had begun to hang from her upper arms. She had been crying this morning and was radiantly happy tonight, but Ralph knew that couldn't account for all the changes he saw.

'I know what you're looking at,' Lois said. 'It's spooky, isn't it? I mean, it solves the question of whether or not all this has just been in our minds, but it's still spooky. We've found the Fountain of Youth. Forget Florida; it was right here in Derry, all along.'

'*We've* found it?'

For a moment she only looked surprised . . . and a little wary, as if she suspected he was teasing her, having her on. Of treating her as 'our Lois'. Then she reached across the table and squeezed his hand. 'Go in the bathroom. Take a look at yourself.'

'I know what I look like. Hell, I just finished shaving. Took my time over it, too.'

She nodded. 'You did a fine job, Ralph . . . but this isn't about your five o'clock shadow. Just *look* at yourself.'

'Are you serious?'

'Yes,' she said firmly. 'I am.'

He had almost gotten to the door when she said, 'You didn't just shave; you changed your shirt, too. That's good. I didn't like to say anything, but that plaid one was ripped.'

'Was it?' Ralph asked. His back was to her, so she couldn't see his smile. 'I didn't notice.'

3

He stood with his hands braced on the bathroom sink, looking into his own face, for a good two minutes. It took him that long to admit to himself that he was really seeing what he thought he was seeing. The streaks of black, lustrous as crow feathers, which had returned to his hair were amazing, and so was the disappearance of the ugly pouches beneath his eyes, but the thing he could not seem to take his eyes away from was the way the lines and deep cracks had disappeared from his lips. It was a small thing . . . but it was also an enormous thing. It was the mouth of a young man. And . . .

Abruptly, Ralph ran a finger into his mouth, along the righthand line of his lower teeth. He couldn't be entirely positive, but it seemed to him that they were longer, as if some of the wear had been rolled back.

'Holy shit,' Ralph murmured, and his mind returned to that sweltering day last summer when he had confronted Ed Deepneau on his lawn. Ed had first told him to drag up a rock and then confided in him that Derry had been invaded by sinister, baby-killing creatures. *Life-stealing* creatures. *All lines of force have begun to converge here,* Ed had told him. *I know how difficult that is to believe, but it's true.*

Ralph was finding it less difficult to believe all the time. What was getting harder to believe was the idea that Ed was mad.

'If this doesn't stop,' Lois said from the doorway, startling him, 'we're going to have to get married and leave town, Ralph. Simone and Mina could not — literally *could not* — take their eyes off me. I made a lot of glib talk about some new makeup I'd gotten out at the mall, but they didn't swallow it. A man would, but a woman knows what makeup can do. And what it can't.'

They walked back to the kitchen, and although the auras were gone again for the time being, Ralph discovered he could see one anyway: a blush rising out of the collar of Lois's white silk blouse.

'Finally I told them the only thing they *would* believe.'

'What was that?' Ralph asked.

'I said I'd met a man.' She hesitated, and then, as the rising blood reached her cheeks and stained them pink, she plunged. 'And had fallen in love with him.'

He touched her arm and turned her toward him. He looked at the small, clean crease in the bend of her elbow and thought how much he would like to touch it with his mouth. Or the tip of his tongue, perhaps. Then he raised his eyes to look at her. 'And was it true?'

She looked back with eyes that were all hope and candor. 'I *think* so,' she said in a small, clear voice, 'but everything's so strange now. All I know for sure is that I *want* it to be true. I want a friend. I've been frightened and unhappy and lonely for quite awhile now. The loneliness is the worst part of getting old, I think – not the aches and pains, not the cranky bowels or the way you lose your breath after climbing a flight of stairs you could have just about *flown* up when you were twenty – but being lonely.'

'Yes,' Ralph said. 'That *is* the worst.'

'No one talks to you anymore – oh, they talk *at* you, sometimes, but that's not the same – and mostly it's like people don't even *see* you. Have you ever felt that way?'

Ralph thought of the Derry of the Old Crocks, a city mostly ignored by the hurry-to-work, hurry-to-play world which surrounded it, and nodded.

'Ralph, would you hug me?'

'My pleasure,' he said, and pulled her gently into the circle of his arms.

4

Some time later, rumpled and dazed but happy, Ralph and Lois sat together on the living-room couch, a piece of furniture so stringently hobbit-sized it was really not much more than a love-seat. Neither of them minded. Ralph's arm was around Lois's shoulders. She had let her hair down and he twined a lock of it in his fingers, musing upon how easy it was to forget the feel of a woman's hair, so marvellously different from the feel of a man's. She had told him about her card-game and Ralph had listened closely, amazed but not, he discovered, much surprised.

There were a dozen or so of them who played every week or so at the Ludlow Grange for small stakes. It was possible to go home a five-buck loser or a ten-buck winner, but the most likely result was finishing a dollar ahead or a handful of change behind. Although there were a couple of good players and a couple of *shlumps* (Lois counted herself among the former), it was mostly just a fun way to spend an afternoon – the Lady Old Crock version of chess tournaments and marathon gin-rummy games.

'Only this afternoon I just couldn't lose. I should have come home completely broke, what with all of them asking what kind of vitamins I was taking and where I'd gotten my last facial and all the rest of it. Who can concentrate on a silly game like Deuces and Jacks, Man with the Axe, Natural Sevens Take All when you have to keep telling new lies and trying not to trip over the ones you've already told?'

'Must have been hard,' Ralph said, trying not to grin.

'It *was. Very* hard! But instead of losing, I just kept raking it in. And do you know why, Ralph?'

He did, but shook his head so she would tell him. He liked listening to her.

'It was their auras. I didn't always know the exact cards they were holding, but a lot of times I did. Even when I didn't, I could get a pretty clear idea of how good their hands were. The auras weren't always there, you know how they come and go, but even when they were gone I played better than I ever have in my life. During the last hour, I began to lose on purpose just so they wouldn't all *hate* me. And do you know something? Even *losing on purpose* was hard.' She looked down at her hands, which had begun to twine together nervously in her lap. 'And on the way back, I did something I'm ashamed of.'

Ralph began to glimpse her aura again, a dim gray ghost in which unformed blobs of dark blue swirled. 'Before you tell me,' he said, 'listen to this and see if it sounds familiar.'

He related how Mrs Perrine had approached while he was sitting on the porch, eating and waiting for Lois to get back. As he told her what he had done to the old lady, he dropped his eyes and felt his ears heating up again.

'Yes,' she said when he was finished. 'It's the same thing *I* did . . . but I didn't *mean* to, Ralph . . . at least, I don't *think* I meant to. I was sitting in the back seat with Mina, and she was starting to go on and on again about how *different* I looked, how *young* I looked, and I thought – I'm embarrassed to say it right out loud, but I guess I better – I thought, I'll shut you up, you snoopy, envious old thing. Because it *was* envy, Ralph. I could see it in her aura. Big, jagged spikes the exact color of a cat's eyes. No wonder they call jealousy the green–eyed monster! Anyway, I pointed out the window and said "Oooh, Mina, isn't that the *dearest* little house?" And when she turned to look, I . . . I did what you did, Ralph. Only I didn't curl up my hand. I just kind of puckered my lips . . . like this . . .' She demonstrated, looking so kissable that Ralph felt moved (almost compelled, in fact) to take advantage of the expression. '. . . and I breathed in a big cloud of her stuff.'

'What happened?' Ralph asked, fascinated and afraid.

Lois laughed ruefully. 'To me or her?'

'Both of you.'

'Mina jumped and slapped the back of her neck. "There's a bug on me!" she said. "It bit me! Get it off, Lo! Please get it off!" Of course there was no bug on her – *I* was the bug – but I brushed at her neck just the same, then opened the window and told her it was gone, it flew away. She was lucky I didn't knock her brains out instead of just brushing her neck – that's how full of pep I was. I felt like I could have opened the car door and run all the way home.'

Ralph nodded.

'It was wonderful . . . *too* wonderful. It's like the stories about drugs you see on TV, how they take you to heaven at first and then lock you in hell. What if we start doing this and can't stop?'

'Yeah,' Ralph said. 'And what if it hurts people? I keep thinking about vampires.'

'Do you know what *I* keep thinking about?' Lois's voice had dropped to a whisper. 'Those things you said Ed Deepneau talked about. Those Centurions. What if they're us, Ralph? What if they're *us*?'

He hugged her and kissed the top of her head. Hearing his worst fear coming from her mouth made it less heavy on his own heart, and that made him think of what Lois had said about loneliness being the worst part of getting old.

'I know,' he said. 'And what I did to Mrs Perrine was totally spur-of-the-moment – I don't remember thinking about it at all, just doing it. Was it that way with you?'

'Yes. Just like that.' She laid her head against his shoulder.

'We can't do it anymore,' he said. 'Because it really might be addictive. Anything that feels that good just about *has* to be addictive, don't you think? We've got to try and build up some safeguards against doing it unconsciously, too. Because I think I have been. That could be why—'

A scream of brakes and sliding, wailing tires cut him off. They stared at each other, wide-eyed, as outside on the street that sound went on and on, grief seeming to search for a point of impact.

There was a muffled thud from the street as the scream of the brakes and tires silenced. It was followed by a brief cry uttered by either a woman or a child, Ralph could not tell which. Someone else shouted, 'What happened?' and then, 'Oh, *cripe*!' There was a rattle of running footsteps on pavement.

'Stay on the couch,' Ralph said, and hurried to the living room window. When he ran up the shade Lois was standing right beside him, and Ralph felt a flash of approval. It was what Carolyn would have done under similar circumstances.

They looked out on a night-time world that pulsed with strange color and fabulous motion. Ralph knew it was Bill they were going to see, *knew* it – Bill hit by a car and lying dead in the street, his Panama with the crescent bitten out of the brim lying near one outstretched hand. He slipped an arm around Lois and she gripped his hand.

But it wasn't McGovern in the fan of headlights thrown by the Ford which was slued around in the middle of Harris Avenue; it was Rosalie. Her early-morning shopping expeditions were at an end. She lay on her side in a spreading pool of blood, her back bunched and twisted in several places. As the driver of the car which had struck her knelt beside the old stray, the pitiless glare of the nearest streetlamp illuminated his face. It was Joe Wyzer, the Rite Aid druggist, his orange-yellow aura now swirling with confused eddies of red and blue. He stroked the old dog's side, and each time his hand slipped into the vile black aura which clung to Rosalie, it disappeared.

Dreams of terror washed through Ralph, dropping his temperature and shrivelling his testicles until they felt like hard little peach-pits. Suddenly it was July of 1992 again, Carolyn dying, the deathwatch ticking, and something weird had happened to Ed Deepneau. Ed had freaked out, and Ralph had found himself trying to keep Helen's normally good-natured husband from springing at the man in the West Side Gardeners cap and attempting to rip his throat out. Then – the cherry on the *Charlotte russe,* Carol would have said – Dorrance Marstellar had arrived. Old Dor. And what had he said?

I wouldn't touch him anymore . . . I can't see your hands. I can't see your hands.

'Oh my God,' Ralph whispered.

5

He was brought back to the here and now by the feeling of Lois swaying against him, as if she were on the edge of a faint.

'Lois!' he said sharply, gripping her arm. 'Lois, are you okay?'

'I think so . . . but Ralph . . . do you see . . .'

'Yes, it's Rosalie. I guess she—'

'I don't mean *her;* I mean *him!*' She pointed to the right.

Doc #3 was leaning against the trunk of Joe Wyzer's Ford, McGovern's Panama tipped jauntily back on his bald skull. He looked toward Ralph and Lois, grinned insolently, then slowly raised his thumb to his nose and waggled his small fingers at them.

'*You bastard!*' Ralph bellowed, and slammed his fist against the wall beside the window in frustration.

Half a dozen people were running toward the scene of the accident, but there was nothing they could do; Rosalie would be dead before even the closest of them arrived at the place where she lay in the glare of the car's headlights. The black aura was solidifying, becoming something which looked almost like soot-darkened brick. It

485

encased her like a form-fitting shroud, and Wyzer's hand disappeared up to the wrist every time it slipped through that terrible garment.

Now Doc #3 raised his hand with the forefinger sticking up and cocked his head – a teacherly pantomime so good that it almost said *Pay attention, please!* right out loud. He tiptoed forward – unnecessary, as he couldn't be seen by the people out there, but good theater – and reached toward Joe Wyzer's back pocket. He glanced around at Ralph and Lois, as if to ask them if they were still paying attention. Then he began to tiptoe forward again, reaching out with his left hand.

'Stop him, Ralph,' Lois moaned. 'Oh please stop him.'

Slowly, like a man who has been drugged, Ralph raised his hand and then chopped it down. A blue wedge of light flew from his fingertips, but it diffused as it passed through the windowglass. A pastel fog spread out a little distance from Lois's house and then disappeared. The bald doctor shook his finger in an infuriating pantomime – *Oh, you naughty boy,* it said.

Doc #3 reached out again, and plucked something from Wyzer's back pocket as he knelt in the street, mourning the dog. Ralph couldn't tell for sure what it was until the creature in the dirty smock swept McGovern's hat from his head and pretended to use it on his own nonexistent hair. He had taken a black pocket-comb, the kind you could buy in any convenience store for a buck twenty-nine. Then he leaped into the air, clicking his heels like a malignant elf.

Rosalie had raised her head at the bald doctor's approach. Now she lowered it back to the pavement and died. The aura surrounding her disappeared at once, not fading but simply winking out of existence like a soap-bubble. Wyzer got to his feet, turned to a man standing on the curb, and began to tell him what had happened, gesturing with his hands to indicate how the dog had run out in front of his car. Ralph found he could actually read a string of six words as they came off Wyzer's lips: *seemed to come out of nowhere.*

And when Ralph shifted his gaze back down to the side of Wyzer's car, he saw that was the place to which the little bald doctor had returned.

CHAPTER SIXTEEN

1

Ralph was able to get his rustbucket Oldsmobile started, but it still took him twenty minutes to get them across town to Derry Home on the east side. Carolyn had understood his increasing worries about his driving and had tried to be sympathetic, but she'd had an impatient, hurry-up streak in her nature, and the years had not mellowed it much. On trips longer than half a mile or so, she was almost always unable to keep from lapsing into reproof. She would stew in silence for awhile, thinking, then begin her critique. If she was particularly exasperated with their progress – or lack of it – she might ask him if he thought an enema would help him get the lead out of his ass. She was a sweetheart, but there had always been an edge to her tongue.

Following such remarks, Ralph would always offer – and always without rancor – to pull over and let her drive. Such offers Carol had always declined. Her belief was that, on short hops, at least, it was the husband's job to drive and the wife's to offer constructive criticism.

He kept waiting for Lois to comment on either his

speed or his sloppy driving habits (he didn't think he would be able to remember his blinkers with any consistency these days even if someone put a gun to his head), but she said nothing — only sat where Carolyn had sat on five thousand rides or more, holding her purse on her lap exactly as Carolyn had always held hers. Wedges of light — store neon, traffic signals, streetlights — ran like rainbows across Lois's cheeks and brows. Her dark eyes were distant and thoughtful. She had cried after Rosalie died, cried hard, and made Ralph pull down the shade again.

Ralph almost hadn't done that. His first impulse had been to bolt out into the street before Joe Wyzer could get away. To tell Joe he had to be very careful. To tell him that when he emptied his pants pockets tonight, he was going to be missing a cheap comb, no big deal, people were always losing combs, except this time it *was* a big deal, and next time it might be Rite Aid pharmacist Joe Wyzer lying at the end of the skid. *Listen to me, Joe, and listen closely. You have to be very careful, because there's all sorts of news from the Hyper-Reality Zone, and in your case all of it comes inside black borders.*

There were problems with that, however. The biggest was that Joe Wyzer, sympathetic as he had been on the day he had gotten Ralph an appointment with the acupuncturist, would think Ralph was crazy. Besides, how did one defend oneself against a creature one couldn't even see?

So he had pulled the shade . . . but before he did, he took one last hard look at the man who had told him he used to be Joe Wyze but was now older and Wyzer. The auras were still there, and he could see Wyzer's balloon-string, a bright orange-yellow, rising intact from the top of his head. So he was still all right.

For now, at least.

Ralph had led Lois into the kitchen and poured her another cup of coffee – black, with lots of sugar.

'He killed her, didn't he?' she asked as she raised the cup to her lips with both hands. 'The little beast killed her.'

'Yes. But I don't think he did it tonight. I think he really did it this morning.'

'Why? *Why?*'

'Because he could,' Ralph said grimly. 'I think that's the only reason he needs. Just because he could.'

Lois had given him a long, appraising look, and an expression of relief had slowly crept into her eyes. 'You've figured it out, haven't you? I should have known it the minute I saw you this evening. I *would* have known, if I hadn't had so many other things rolling around in what passes for my mind.'

'Figured it out? I'm miles from that, but I have had some ideas. Lois, do you feel up to a trip to Derry Home with me?'

'I suppose so. Do you want to see Bill?'

'I'm not sure exactly *who* I want to see. It *might* be Bill, but it might be Bill's friend, Bob Polhurst. Maybe even Jimmy Vandermeer – do you know him?'

'Jimmy V? Of *course* I know him! I knew his wife even better. In fact, she used to play poker with us until she died. It was a heart attack, and so sudden –' She broke off suddenly, looking at Ralph with her dark Spanish eyes. 'Jimmy's in the hospital? Oh God, it's the cancer, isn't it? The cancer came back.'

490

'Yes. He's in the room right next to Bill's friend.' Ralph told her about the conversation he'd had with Faye that morning and the note he'd found on the picnic table that afternoon. He pointed out the odd conjunction of rooms and residents – Polhurst, Jimmy V, Carolyn – and asked Lois if she thought it was just a coincidence.

'No. I'm sure it isn't.' She had glanced at the clock. 'Come on – regular visiting hours over there finish at nine-thirty, I think. If we're going to get there before then, we'd better wiggle.'

2

Now, as he turned onto Hospital Drive (*Forgot your damned turnblinker again, sweetheart,* Carolyn commented), he glanced at Lois – Lois sitting there with her hands clasped on her purse and her aura invisible for the time being – and asked if she was all right.

She nodded. 'Yes. Not great, but okay. Don't worry about me.'

But I do worry, Lois, Ralph thought. *A lot. And by the way, did you see Doc #3 take the comb out of Joe Wyzer's pocket?*

That was a stupid question. Of course she'd seen. The bald midget had *wanted* her to see. Had wanted *both* of them to see. The real question was how much significance she had attached to it.

How much do you really know, Lois? How many connections have you made? I have to wonder, because they're not really that hard to see. I wonder . . . but I'm afraid to ask.

There was a low brick building about a quarter of a mile farther down the feeder road – WomanCare. A number of spotlights (new additions, he was quite sure) threw fans of illumination across its lawn, and Ralph could see two men walking back and forth at the end of grotesquely elongated shadows . . . rent-a-cops, he supposed. Another new wrinkle; another straw flying in an evil wind.

He turned left (this time remembering the blinker, at least) and eased the Olds carefully up the chute which led into the multilevel hospital parking garage. At the top, an orange barrier-arm blocked the way. PLEASE STOP & TAKE TICKET, read the sign next to it. Ralph could recall a time when there used to be actual people in places like this, rendering them a little less eerie. *Those were the days, my friend, we thought they'd never end,* he thought as he unrolled his window and took a ticket from the automated dispenser.

'Ralph?'

'Hmmm?' He was concentrating on avoiding the back bumpers of the cars slant-parked on both sides of the ascending aisles. He knew that the aisles were much too wide for the bumpers of those other cars to be an actual impediment to his progress – *intellectually* he knew it – but what his guts knew was something else. *How Carolyn would bitch and moan about the way I'm driving,* he thought with a certain distracted fondness.

'*Do* you know what we're doing here, or are we just winging it?'

'Just another minute – let me get this damned thing parked.'

He passed several slots big enough for the Olds on the first level, but none with enough buffer-zone to make him feel comfortable. On the third level he found three spaces side by side (together they were big enough to hold a Sherman tank comfortably) and babied the Olds into the one in the middle. He killed the motor and turned to face Lois. Other engines idled above and below them, their locations impossible to pinpoint because of the echo. Orange light – that persistent, penetrating tone-glow now common to all such facilities as this, it seemed – lay upon their skins like thin toxic paint. Lois looked back at him steadily. He could see traces of the tears she had cried for Rosalie in her puffy, swollen lids, but the eyes themselves were calm and sure. He was struck by how much she had changed just since that morning, when he had found her sitting slump-shouldered on a park bench and weeping. *Lois,* he thought, *if your son and daughter-in-law could see you tonight, I think they might run away screaming at the top of their lungs. Not because you look scary, but because the woman they came to bulldoze into moving to Riverview Estates is gone.*

'Well?' she asked with just a hint of a smile. 'Are you going to talk to me or just look at me?'

Ralph, ordinarily a cautious sort of man, recklessly said the first thing to come into his head. 'What I'd *like* to do, I think, is eat you like ice-cream.'

Her smile deepened enough to make dimples at the corners of her mouth. 'Maybe later we'll see how much of an appetite for ice-cream you really have, Ralph. For now, just tell me why you brought me here. And don't tell me you don't know, because I think you do.'

Ralph closed his eyes, drew in a deep breath, and opened them again. 'I guess we're here to find the other two bald guys. The ones I saw coming out of May Locher's. If anyone can explain what's going on, it'll be them.'

'What makes you think you'll find them here?'

'I think they've got work to do . . . two men, Jimmy V and Bill's friend, dying side by side. I should have known what the bald doctors are – what they *do* – from the minute I saw the ambulance guys bring Mrs Locher out strapped to a stretcher and with a sheet over her face. I *would* have known, if I hadn't been so damned tired. The scissors should have been enough. Instead, it took me until this afternoon, and I only got it then because of something Mr Polhurst's niece said.'

'What was it?'

'That death was stupid. That if an obstetrician took as much time cutting the umbilical cord, he'd be sued for malpractice. It made me think of a myth I read when I was in grade-school and couldn't get enough of gods and goddesses and Trojan horses. The story was about three sisters – the Greek Sisters, maybe, or maybe it was the Weird Sisters. Shit, don't ask me; I can't even remember to use my damned turnblinkers half the time. Anyway, these sisters were responsible for the course of all human life. One of them spun the thread, one of them decided how long it would be . . . is any of this ringing a bell, Lois?'

'Of course it is!' she nearly shouted. 'The balloon-strings!'

Ralph nodded. 'Yes. The balloon-strings. I don't remember the names of the first two sisters, but I never forgot the name of the last one – Atropos. And according to the story, her job is to cut the thread the first one spins and the second one measures. You could argue with her, you could beg, but it never made any difference. When she decided it was time to cut, she cut.'

Lois was nodding. 'Yes, I remember that story. I don't know if I read it or someone told it to me when I was a kid. You believe it's actually true, Ralph, don't you? Only it turns out to be the Bald Brothers instead of the Weird Sisters.'

'Yes and no. As I remember the story, the sisters were all on the same side – a team. And that's the feeling I got about the two men who came out of Mrs Locher's house, that they were long-time partners with *immense* respect for each other. But the other guy, the one we saw again tonight, isn't like them. I think Doc #3's a rogue.'

Lois shivered, a theatrical gesture that became real at the last moment. 'He's awful, Ralph. I hate him.'

'I don't blame you.'

He reached for the doorhandle, but Lois stopped him with a touch. 'I saw him do something.'

Ralph turned and looked at her. The tendons in his neck creaked rustily. He had a pretty good idea what she was going to say.

'He picked the pocket of the man who hit Rosalie,' she said. 'While he was kneeling beside her in the street, the bald man picked his pocket. Except all he took was a comb. And the hat that bald man was wearing . . . I'm pretty sure I recognized it.'

Ralph went on looking at her, fervently hoping that Lois's memory of Doc #3's apparel did not extend any further.

'It was Bill's, wasn't it? Bill's Panama.'

Ralph nodded. 'Sure it was.'

Lois closed her eyes. 'Oh, Lord.'

'What do you say, Lois? Are you still game?'

495

'Yes.' She opened her door and swung her legs out. 'But let's get going right away, before I lose my nerve.'

'Tell me about it,' said Ralph Roberts.

3

As they approached the main doors of Derry Home, Ralph leaned toward Lois's ear and murmured, 'Is it happening to you?'

'Yes.' Her eyes were very wide. 'God, yes. It's strong this time, isn't it?'

As they broke the electric-eye beam and the doors to the hospital lobby swung open before them, the surface of the world suddenly peeled back, disclosing another world, one that simmered with unseen colors and shifted with unseen shapes. Overhead, on the wall-to-wall mural depicting Derry as it had been during its halcyon lumbering days at the turn of the century, dark brown arrow-shapes chased each other, growing closer and closer together until they touched. When that happened, they flashed a momentary dark green and changed direction. A bright silver funnel that looked like either a waterspout or a toy cyclone was descending the curved staircase which led up to the second-floor meeting rooms, cafeteria, and auditorium. Its wide top end nodded back and forth as it moved from step to step, and to Ralph it felt distinctly *friendly*, like an anthropomorphic character in a Disney cartoon. As Ralph watched, two men with briefcases hurried up the stairs, and one of them passed directly through the silver funnel. He never paused in what he was saying to his companion, but when he emerged on the other side, Ralph saw he was absently using his free hand to smooth back his hair . . . although not a strand was out of place.

The funnel reached the bottom of the stairs, raced around the center of the lobby in a tight, exuberant figure-eight, and then popped out of existence, leaving only a faint, rosy mist behind. This quickly dissipated.

Lois dug her elbow into Ralph's side, started to point toward an area beyond the Central Information booth, realized there were people all around them, and settled for lifting her chin in that direction instead. Earlier, Ralph had seen a shape in the sky which had looked like a prehistoric bird. Now he saw something which looked like a long translucent snake. It was essing its way across the ceiling above a sign which read PLEASE WAIT HERE FOR BLOOD-TESTING.

'Is it *alive*?' Lois whispered with some alarm.

Ralph looked more closely and realized the thing had no head . . . no discernible tail, either. It was all body. He supposed it *was* alive − he had an idea *all* the auras were alive in some fashion − but he didn't think it was really a snake, and he doubted that it was dangerous, at least to the likes of them.

'Don't sweat the small stuff, sweetheart,' he whispered back to her as they joined the short line at Central Information, and as he said it, the snake-thing seemed to melt into the ceiling and disappear.

Ralph didn't know how important such things as the bird and the cyclone were in the secret world's scheme of things, but he was positive that people were still the main show. The lobby of Derry Home Hospital was like a gorgeous Fourth of July fireworks display, a display in which the parts of the Roman candles and Chinese fountains were being played by human beings.

Lois hooked a finger into his collar to make him bend his head toward her. 'You'll have to do the talking, Ralph,' she said in a strengthless, amazed little voice. 'I'm having all I can do not to wee in my pants.'

The man ahead of them left the booth and Ralph stepped forward. As he did, a clear, sweetly nostalgic memory of Jimmy V surfaced in his mind. They'd been on the road someplace in Rhode Island – Kingston, maybe – and had decided on the spur of the moment that they wanted to attend the tent revival going on in a nearby hayfield. They had both been drunk as fleas in a gin-bottle, of course. A pair of well-scrubbed young ladies had been standing outside the turned-back flaps of the tent, handing out tracts, and as he and Jimmy neared them, they began to admonish each other in aromatic whispers to act sober, dammit, to just act sober. Had they gotten in that day? Or—

'Help you?' the woman in the Central Information booth asked, her tone saying she was doing Ralph a real favor just by speaking to him. He looked through the glass at her and saw a woman buried inside a troubled orange aura that looked like a burning bramble-bush. *Here's a lady who loves the fine print and stands on all the ceremony she can,* he thought, and on the heels of that, Ralph remembered that the two young women flanking the entrance to the tent had gotten one whiff of him and Jimmy V and turned them politely but firmly away. They had ended up spending the evening in a Central Falls juke-joint, as he recalled, and had probably been lucky not to get rolled when they staggered out after last call.

'Sir?' the woman in the glass booth asked impatiently. 'Can I *help* you?'

Ralph came back to the present with a thud he could almost feel. 'Yes, ma'am. My wife and I would like to visit Jimmy Vandermeer on the third floor, if—'

'That's ICU!' she snapped. 'Can't go up to ICU without a special pass.' Orange hooks began to poke their way out of the glow around her head, and her aura began to look like barbed wire strung across some ghostly no-man's-land.

'I know,' Ralph said, more humbly than ever, 'but my friend, Lafayette Chapin, he said—'

'Gosh!' the woman in the booth interrupted. 'It's wonderful, the way everyone's got a friend. Really *wonderful*.' She rolled a satiric eye toward the ceiling.

'Faye said Jimmy could have visitors, though. You see, he has cancer and he's not expected to live much l—'

'Well, I'll check the files,' the woman in the booth said with the grudging air of one who knows she is being sent upon a fool's errand, 'but the computer is very slow tonight, so it's going to take awhile. Give me your name, then you and your wife go sit over there. I'll page you as soon as—'

Ralph decided that he had eaten enough humble pie in front of this bureaucratic guard dog. It wasn't as if he wanted an exit visa from Albania, after all; just a goddam ICU pass would do.

There was a slot in the base of the glass booth. Ralph reached through it and grasped the woman's wrist before she could pull it away. There was a sensation, painless but very clear, of those orange hooks passing directly through his flesh without finding anything to catch on. Ralph squeezed gently and felt a small burst of force — something that would have been no bigger than a pellet if it had been seen — pass from him to the woman. Suddenly the officious orange aura around her left arm and side turned the faded turquoise of Ralph's aura. She gasped and jerked forward on her chair, as if someone had just dumped a paper cup filled with ice-cubes down the back of her uniform.

[*Never mind the computer. Just give me a couple of passes, please. Right away.*]

'Yes, sir,' she said at once, and Ralph let go of her wrist so she could reach beneath her desk. The turquoise glow around her arm was turning orange again, the change in color creeping down from her shoulder toward her wrist.

But I could have turned her all blue, Ralph thought. *Taken her over. Run her around the room like a wind-up toy.*

He suddenly remembered Ed quoting Matthew's Gospel — *Then Herod, when he saw that he was mocked, was exceeding wroth* — and a mixture of fright and shame filled him. Thoughts of vampirism recurred as well, and a snatch from a famous old Pogo comic strip: *We have met the enemy and he is us.* Yes, he could probably do almost anything he wanted with this orange-haloed grump; his batteries were fully charged. The only problem was that the juice in those batteries — and in Lois's, as well — was stolen goods.

When the information-lady's hand emerged from beneath the desk, it was holding two pink laminated badges marked INTENSIVE CARE/VISITOR. 'Here you are, sir,' she said in a courteous voice utterly unlike the tone in which she had first addressed him. 'Enjoy your visit and thank you for waiting.'

'Thank *you*,' Ralph said. He took the badges and grasped Lois's hand. 'Come on, dear. We ought to

[*'Ralph, what did you* DO *to her?'*]

[*'Nothing, I guess — I think she's all right.'*]

get upstairs and make our visit before it gets too late.'

Lois glanced back at the woman in the information booth. She was dealing with her next customer, but slowly, as if she'd just been granted some moderately amazing revelation and had to think it over. The blue glow was now visible only at the very tips of her fingers, and as Lois watched, that disappeared as well.

Lois looked up at Ralph again and smiled.

[*'Yes . . . she is all right. So stop beating up on yourself.'*]

[*'Was that what I was doing?'*]

[*'I think so, yes . . . we're talking that way again, Ralph.'*]

[*'I know.'*]

[*'Ralph?'*]

[*'Yes?'*]

[*'This is all pretty wonderful, isn't it?'*]

[*'Yes.'*]

Ralph tried to hide the rest of what he was thinking from her: that when the price for something which felt this wonderful came due, they were apt to discover it was very high.

4

[*'Stop staring at that baby, Ralph. You're making its mother nervous.'*]

Ralph glanced at the woman in whose arms the baby slept and saw that Lois was right . . . but it was hard *not* to look. The baby, no more than three months old, lay within a capsule of violently shifting yellow-gray aura. This powerful but disquieting thunderlight circled the tiny body with the idiot speed of the atmosphere surrounding a gas giant – Jupiter, say, or Saturn.

[*Jesus, Lois, that's brain-damage, isn't it?*]

[*'Yes. The woman says there was a car accident.'*]

[*'Says? Have you been talking to her?'*]

[*'No. It's - - - - -.'*]

[*'I don't understand.'*]

[*'Join the club.'*]

The oversized hospital elevator labored slowly upward. Those inside – the lame, the halt, the guilty few in good health – didn't speak but either turned their eyes up to the floor-indicator over the doors or down to inspect their own shoes. The only exception to this was the woman with the thunderstruck baby. She was watching Ralph with distrust and alarm, as if she expected him to leap forward at any moment and try to rip her infant from her arms.

It's not just that I was looking, Ralph thought. *At least I don't think so. She felt me thinking about her baby. Felt me . . . sensed me . . . heard me . . . some damned thing, anyway.*

The elevator stopped on the second floor and the doors wheezed open. The woman with the baby turned to Ralph. The infant shifted slightly as she did, and Ralph got a look at the crown of its head. There was a deep crease in the tiny skull. A red scar ran the length of it. To Ralph it looked like a rill of tainted water standing at the bottom of a ditch. The ugly and confused yellow-gray aura which surrounded the baby was emerging from this scar like steam from a crack in the earth. The baby's balloon-string was the same color as its aura, and it was unlike any other balloon-string Ralph had seen so far — not unhealthy in appearance but short, ugly, and no more than a stub.

'Didn't your mother ever teach you any manners?' the baby's mother asked Ralph, and what cut him wasn't so much the admonition as the way she made it. He had scared her badly.

'Madam, I assure you—'

'Yeah, go on and assure my fanny,' she said, and stepped out of the car. The elevator doors started to slide closed. Ralph glanced at Lois and the two of them exchanged a moment of brief but total understanding. Lois shook her finger at the doors as if scolding them, and a gray, mesh-like substance fanned out from its tip. The doors struck this and then slid back into their slots, as they were programmed to do upon encountering any barrier to their progress.

[*'Madam!'*]

The woman stopped and turned around, clearly confused. She shot suspicious glances about her, trying to identify who had spoken. Her aura was a dark, buttery yellow with faint tints of orange spoking out from its inner edges. Ralph fixed her eyes with his.

[*I'm sorry if I offended you. This is all very new to my friend and me. We're like children at a formal dinner. I apologize.*]

['- - - - - - - - - - -.']

He didn't know just what she was trying to communicate — it was like watching someone talk inside a soundproof booth — but he sensed relief and deep unease . . . the sort of unease people feel when they think they may have been observed doing something they shouldn't. Her doubtful eyes remained on his face a moment or two longer, then she turned and began to walk rapidly down the corridor in the direction of a sign reading NEUROLOGICAL SURVEY. The gray mesh Lois had cast at the door was thinning, and when the doors tried to close again, they cut neatly through it. The car continued its slow upward journey.

[*'Ralph . . . Ralph, I think I know what happened to that baby.'*]

She reached toward his face with her right hand and slipped it between his nose and mouth with her palm down. She pressed the pad of her thumb lightly against one of his cheekbones and the pad of her index finger lightly against the other. It was done so quickly and confidently that no one else in the elevator noticed. If one of the three other riders *had* noticed, he or she would have seen something that looked like a neatness-minded wife smoothing away a blot of skin lotion or a dollop of left-over shaving cream.

Ralph felt as if someone had pulled a high-voltage switch inside his brain, one that turned on whole banks of blazing stadium lights. In their raw, momentary glow, he saw a terrible image: hands clad in a violent brownish-purple aura reaching into a crib and snatching up the baby they had just seen. He was shaken back and forth, head snapping and rolling on the thin stalk of neck like the head of a Raggedy Andy doll—

– and *thrown*—

The lights in his head went black then, and Ralph let out a harsh, shuddery sigh of relief. He thought of the pro-life protestors he'd seen on the evening news just last night, men and women waving signs with Susan Day's picture and WANTED FOR MURDER on them, men and women in Grim Reaper robes, men and women carrying a banner which read LIFE, WHAT A BEAUTIFUL CHOICE.

He wondered if the thunderstruck baby might have a differing opinion on that last one. He met Lois's amazed, agonized eyes with his own, and groped out to take her hands.

[*Father did it, right? Threw the kid against the wall?*]

[*Yes. The baby wouldn't stop crying.*]

[*And she knows. She knows, but she hasn't told anyone.*]

[*No . . . but she might, Ralph. She's thinking about it.*]

[*She might also wait until he does it again. And next time he might finish the job.*]

A terrible thought occurred to Ralph then; it shot across his mind like a meteor scratching momentary fire across a midnight summer sky: it might be better if he *did* finish the job. The thunderstruck baby's balloon-string had only been a stump, but it had been a *healthy* stump. The child might live for years, not knowing who he was or where he was, let alone *why* he was, watching people come and go like trees in the mist . . .

Lois was standing with her shoulders slumped, looking at the floor of the elevator car and radiating a sadness that squeezed Ralph's heart. He reached out, put a finger under her chin, and watched a delicate blue rose spin itself out of the place where his aura touched hers. He tilted her head up and was not surprised to see tears in her eyes.

'Do you still think it's all pretty wonderful, Lois?' he asked softly, and to this he received no answer, either with his ears or in his mind.

5

They were the only two to get out on the third floor, where the silence was as thick as the dust under library shelves. A pair of nurses stood halfway up the hall, clipboards held to white-clad bosoms, talking in low whispers. Anyone else standing by the elevators might have looked at them and surmised a conversation dealing with life, death, and heroic measures; Ralph and Lois, however, took one look at their overlapping auras and knew that the subject currently under discussion was where to go for a drink when their shift ended.

Ralph saw this and at the same time he didn't, the way a deeply preoccupied man sees and obeys traffic signals without really seeing them. Most of his mind was occupied with a deadly sense of *déjà vu* which had washed over him the moment he and Lois stepped out of the elevator and into this world where the faint squeak of the nurses' shoes on the linoleum sounded almost exactly like the faint beep of the life-support equipment.

Even-numbered rooms on your left; odd-numbered rooms on your right, he thought, and 317, where Carolyn died, is up by the nurses' station. It was 317, all right — I remember. Now that I'm here I remember everything. *How someone was always sticking her chart in the little pocket on the back of the door upside down. How the light from the window fell across the bed in a kind of crooked rectangle on sunny days. How you could sit in the visitor's chair and look out at the desk-nurse, whose job it is to monitor vital signs, incoming telephone calls, and outgoing pizza orders.*

The same. All the same. It was early March again, the

gloomy end of a leaden, overcast day, sleet beginning to spick-spack off the one window of Room 317, and he had been sitting in the visitor's chair with an unopened copy of Shirer's *Rise and Fall of the Third Reich* in his lap since early morning. Sitting there, not wanting to get up even long enough to use the bathroom because the deathwatch had almost run down by then, each tick was a lurch and the gap between each tick and the next was a lifetime; his long-time companion had a train to catch and he wanted to be on the platform to see her off. There would only be one chance to do it right.

It was very easy to hear the sleet as it picked up speed and velocity, because the life support equipment had been turned off. Ralph had given up during the last week of February; it had taken Carolyn, who had never given up in her life, a little longer to get the message. And what, exactly, was that message? Why that, in a hard-fought ten-round match pitting Carolyn Roberts against Cancer, the winner was Cancer, that all-time heavyweight champeen, by a TKO.

He had sat in the visitor's chair, watching and waiting as her respiration grew more and more pronounced – the long, sighing exhale, the flat, moveless chest, the growing certainty that the last breath had indeed been the last breath, that the watch had run down, the train arrived in the station to take on its single passenger . . . and then another huge, unconscious gasp would come as she tore the next lungful out of the unfriendly air, no longer breathing in any normal sense but only lunging reflexively along from one gasp to the next like a drunk lurching down a long dark corridor in a cheap hotel.

Spickle-spickle-spackle-spackle: the sleet had gone on rapping invisible fingernails against the window as the dirty March day drew down to dirty March dark and Carolyn went on fighting the last half of her last round. By then she had been running completely on autopilot, of course; the brain which had once existed within that finely made skull was gone. It had been replaced by a mutant – a stupid gray-black delinquent that could not think or feel but only eat and eat and eat until it had gorged itself to death.

Spickle-spickle-spackle-spackle, and he had seen that the T-shaped breathing apparatus in her nose had come askew. He waited for her to tear one of her awful, labored breaths out of the air and then, as she exhaled, he had leaned forward and replaced the small plastic nosepiece. He had gotten a little mucus on his fingers, he remembered, and had wiped it off on a tissue from the box on the bedside table. He had sat back, waiting for the next breath, wanting to make sure the nosepiece didn't come askew again, but there *wasn't* any next breath, and he realized that the ticking sound he had heard coming from everywhere since the previous summer seemed to have stopped.

He remembered waiting as the minutes passed – one, then three, then six – unable to believe that all the good years and good times (not to mention the few bad ones) had ended in this flat and toneless fashion. Her radio, tuned to the local easy-listening station, was playing softly in the corner and he listened to Simon and Garfunkel sing 'Scarborough Fair'. They sang it all the way to the end. Wayne Newton came on next, and began to sing 'Danke Shoen'. He sang it all the way to the end. The weather report came next, but before the disc jockey could finish telling about how the weather was going to be on Ralph Roberts's first full day as a widower, all that stuff about clearing and colder and winds shifting around to the north-east, Ralph finally got it through his head. The watch had stopped ticking, the train had come, the boxing match was over. All the metaphors had fallen down, leaving only the woman in the room, silent at last. Ralph began to cry. Still crying, he had blundered over into the corner and turned off the radio. He remembered the summer they had taken a fingerpaint class, and the night they had ended up fingerpainting each other's naked bodies. This memory made him cry harder. He went to the window and leaned his head against the cold glass and cried. In that first terrible minute of understanding, he had wanted only one thing: to be dead himself. A nurse heard him crying and came in. She tried to take Carolyn's pulse. Ralph told her to stop being a goddam fool. She came over to Ralph and for a moment he thought she was going to try to take *his* pulse. Instead, she had put her arms around him. She—

[*'Ralph? Ralph, are you all right?'*]

He looked around at Lois, started to say he was fine, and then remembered there was precious little he could hide from her while they were in this state.

[*'Feeling sad. Too many memories in here. Not good ones.'*]

[*'I understand . . . but look down, Ralph! Look on the floor!'*]

He did, and his eyes widened. The floor was covered with an overlay of multicolored tracks, some fresh, most fading to invisibility. Two sets stood out clearly from the rest, as brilliant as diamonds in a litter of paste imitations.

They were a deep green-gold in which a few tiny reddish flecks still swam.

[*Do they belong to the ones we're looking for, Ralph?*]

[*Yes – the docs are here.*]

Ralph took Lois's hand – it felt very cold – and began to lead her slowly up the hall.

CHAPTER SEVENTEEN

1

They hadn't gone far when something very strange and rather frightening happened. For a moment the world bled white in front of them. The doors to the rooms ranged along the hall, barely visible in this bright white haze, expanded to the size of warehouse loading bays. The corridor itself seemed to simultaneously elongate and grow taller. Ralph felt the bottom go out of his stomach the way it often had back when he was a teenager, and a frequent customer on the Dust Devil roller coaster at Old Orchard Beach. He heard Lois moan, and she squeezed his hand with panicky tightness.

The whiteout lasted only a second, and when the colors swarmed back into the world, they were brighter and crisper than they had been a moment before. Normal perspective returned, but objects looked *thicker*, somehow. The auras were still there, but they appeared both thinner and paler – pastel coronas instead of spray-painted primary colors. At the same time Ralph realized he could see every crack and pore in the Sheetrocked wall to his left . . . and then he realized he could see the pipes, wires, and insulation *behind* the walls, if he wanted to; all he had to do was look.

Oh my God, he thought. *Is this really happening? Can this really be happening?*

Sounds were everywhere: hushed bells, a toilet being flushed, muted laughter. Sounds a person normally took for granted, as part of everyday life, but not now. Not here. Like the visible reality of things, the sounds seemed to have an extraordinarily sensuous texture, like thin overlapping scallops of silk and steel.

Nor were all the sounds ordinary; there were a great many exotic ones weaving their way through the mix. He heard a fly buzzing deep in a heating duct. The fine-grain sandpaper sound of a nurse adjusting her pantyhose in the staff bathroom. Beating hearts. Circulating blood. The soft tidal flow of respiration. Each sound was perfect on its own; fitted into the others, they made a beautiful and complicated auditory ballet – a hidden *Swan Lake* of gurgling stomachs, humming power outlets, hurricane hairdryers, whispering wheels on hospital gurneys. Ralph could hear a TV at the end of the hall beyond the nurses' station. It was coming from Room 340, where Mr Thomas Wren, a kidney patient, was watching Kirk Douglas and Lana Turner in *The Bad and the Beautiful.* 'If you team up with me, baby, we'll turn this town on its ear,' Kirk was saying, and Ralph knew from the aura which surrounded the words that Mr Douglas had been suffering a toothache on the day that particular scene was filmed. Nor was that all; he knew he could go

(*higher? deeper? wider?*)

if he wanted. Ralph most definitely did *not* want. This

was the forest of Arden, and a man could get lost in its thickets.

Or eaten by tigers.

[*'Jesus! It's another level — it must be, Lois! A whole other level!'*]

[*'I know.'*]

[*'Are you okay with this?'*]

[*'I think I am, Ralph . . . are you?'*]

[*'I guess so, for now . . . but if the bottom drops out again, I don't know. Come on.'*]

But before they could begin following the green-gold tracks again, Bill McGovern and a man Ralph didn't know came out of Room 313. They were in deep conversation.

Lois turned a horror-struck face toward Ralph.

[*'Oh, no! Oh God, no! Do you see, Ralph? Do you see?'*]

Ralph gripped her hand more tightly. He saw, all right. McGovern's friend was surrounded by a plum-colored aura. It didn't look especially healthy, but Ralph didn't think the man was seriously ill, either; it was just a lot of chronic stuff like rheumatism and kidney gravel. A balloon-string of the same mottled purple shade rose from the top of the man's aura, wavering hesitantly back and forth like a diver's air-hose in a mild current.

McGovern's aura, however, was totally black. The stump of what had once been a balloon-string jutted stiffly up from it. The thunderstruck baby's balloon-string had been short but healthy; what they were looking at now was the decaying remnant of a crude amputation. Ralph had a momentary image, so strong it was almost a hallucination, of McGovern's eyes first bulging and then popping out of their sockets, knocked loose by a flood of black bugs. He had to close his own eyes for a moment to keep from screaming, and when he opened them again, Lois was no longer at his side.

2

McGovern and his friend were walking in the direction of the nurses' station, probably bound for the water-fountain. Lois was in hot pursuit, trotting up the corridor, bosom heaving. Her aura flashed with twizzling pinkish sparks that looked like neon-flavored asterisks. Ralph bolted after her. He didn't know what would happen if she caught McGovern's attention, and didn't really want to find out. He thought he was probably going to, however.

[*Lois! Lois, don't do that!*]

She ignored him.

[*Bill, stop! You have to listen to me! Something's wrong with you!*]

McGovern paid no attention to her; he was talking about Bob Polhurst's manuscript, *Later That Summer*. 'Best damned book on the Civil War I ever read,' he told the man inside the plum-colored aura, 'but when I suggested that he publish, he told me that was out of the question. Can you believe it? A possible Pulitzer Prize winner, but—'

[*Lois, come back! Don't go near him!*]

[*Bill! Bill! B—*]

Lois reached McGovern just before Ralph was able to reach her. She put out her hand to grab his shoulder. Ralph saw her fingers plunge into the murk which surrounded him . . . and then slide *into* him.

Her aura changed at once, from a gray-blue shot with those pinkish sparks to a red as bright as the side of a fire engine. Jagged flocks of black shot through it like clouds of tiny swarming insects. Lois screamed and pulled her hand back. The expression on her face was a mixture of terror and loathing. She held her hand up in front of her eyes and screamed again, although Ralph could see nothing on it. Narrow black stripes were now whirring giddily around the outer edges of her aura; to Ralph they looked like planetary orbits marked on a map of the solar system. She turned to flee. Ralph grabbed her by the upper arms and she beat at him blindly.

McGovern and his friend, meanwhile, continued their placid amble up the hall to the drinking fountain, completely unaware of the shrieking, struggling woman not ten feet behind them. 'When I asked Bob why he wouldn't publish the book,' McGovern was continuing, 'he said that I of all people should understand his reasons. I told him . . .'

Lois drowned him out, shrieking like a firebell.

[*'!!! - - - - - - !!! - - - - - - - - - - !!!'*]

[*'Quit it, Lois! Quit it right now! Whatever happened to you is over now! It's over and you're all right!'*]

But Lois continued to struggle, dinning those inarticulate screams into his head, trying to tell him how awful it had been, how he'd been *rotting,* that there were things inside him, *eating him alive,* and that was bad enough, but it wasn't the worst. Those things were *aware,* she said, they were *bad,* and *they had known she was there.*

[*'Lois, you're with me! You're with me and it's all r—'*]

One of her flying fists clipped the side of his jaw and Ralph saw stars. He understood that they had passed to a

515

plane of reality where physical contact with others was impossible – hadn't he seen Lois's hand pass directly into McGovern, like the hand of a ghost? – but they were obviously still real enough to each other; he had the bruised jaw to prove it.

He slipped his arms around her and hugged her against him, imprisoning her fists between her breasts and his chest. Her cries

[*'!!! - - - - - - - - !!! - - - - - - - !!!'*]

continued to rant and blast in his head, however. He locked his hands together between her shoulderblades and squeezed. He felt the power leap out of him again, as it had that morning, only this time it felt entirely different. Blue light spilled through Lois's turbulent red-black aura, soothing it. Her struggles slowed and then ceased. He felt her draw a shuddering breath. Above and around her, the blue glow was expanding and fading. The black bands disappeared from her aura, one after the other, from the bottom up, and then that alarming shade of infected red also began to fade. She put her head against his arm.

[*'I'm sorry, Ralph – I went nuclear again, didn't I?'*]

[*'I suppose so, but never mind. You're okay now. That's the important thing.'*]

[*'If you knew how horrible that was . . . touching him that way . . .'*]

[*'You put it across very well, Lois.'*]

She glanced down the corridor, where McGovern's friend was now getting a drink. McGovern lounged against the wall next to him, talking about how the Exalted & Revered Bob Polhurst had always done the *Sunday New*

York Times crossword puzzle in ink. 'He used to tell me that wasn't pride but optimism,' McGovern said, and the deathbag swirled sluggishly around him as he spoke, flowing in and out of his mouth and between the fingers of his gesturing, eloquent hand.

[*'We can't help him, can we, Ralph? There's not a thing in the world we can do.'*]

Ralph gave her a brief, strong hug. Her aura, he saw, had entirely returned to normal.

McGovern and his friend were walking back down the corridor toward them. Acting on impulse, Ralph disengaged himself from Lois and stepped directly in front of Mr Plum, who was listening to McGovern hold forth on the tragedy of old age and nodding in the right places.

[*'Ralph, don't do that!'*]

[*'It's okay, don't worry.'*]

But all at once he wasn't so sure it *was* okay. He might have stepped back, given another second. Before he could, however, Mr Plum glanced unseeingly into his face and walked right through him. The sensation that swept through Ralph's body at his passage was perfectly familiar; it was the pins-and-needles feeling one gets when a sleeping limb starts to wake up. For one moment his aura and Mr Plum's mingled, and Ralph knew everything about the man that there was to know, including the dreams he'd had in his mother's womb.

Mr Plum stopped short.

'Something wrong?' McGovern asked.

'I guess not, but . . . did you hear a bang someplace? Like a firecracker, or a car backfire?'

'Can't say I did, but my hearing isn't what it used to

be.' McGovern chuckled. 'If something *did* blow up, I certainly hope it wasn't in one of the radiation labs.'

'I don't hear anything now. Probably just my imagination.' They turned into Bob Polhurst's room.

Ralph thought, *Mrs Perrine said it sounded like a gunshot. Lois's friend thought there was a bug on her, maybe biting her. Just a difference in touch, maybe, the way different piano-players have different touches. Either way, they feel it when we mess with them. They may not know what it is, but they sure do feel it.*

Lois took his hand and led him to the door of Room 313. They stood in the hall, looking in as McGovern seated himself in a plastic contour chair at the foot of the bed. There were at least eight people crammed into the room and Ralph couldn't see Bob Polhurst clearly, but he could see one thing: although he was deep within his own deathbag, Polhurst's balloon-string was still intact. It was as filthy as a rusty exhaust pipe, peeling in some places and cracked in others . . . but it was still intact. He turned to Lois.

[*'These people may have longer to wait than they think.'*]

Lois nodded, then pointed down at the greeny-gold footprints – the white-man tracks. They bypassed 313, Ralph saw, but turned in at the next doorway – 315, Jimmy V's room.

He and Lois walked up together and stood looking in. Jimmy V had three visitors, and the one sitting beside the bed thought he was all alone. That one was Faye Chapin, idly looking through the double stack of get-well cards on Jimmy's bedside table. The other two were the little bald doctors Ralph had seen for the first time on May Locher's stoop. They stood at the foot of Jimmy V's bed, solemn in their clean white tunics, and now that he stood close to them, Ralph could see that there were worlds of character in those unlined, almost identical faces; it just wasn't the sort of thing one could see through a pair of binoculars – or maybe not until you slid up the ladder of perception a little way. Most of it was in the eyes, which were dark, pupil-less, and flecked with deep golden glints. Those eyes shone with intelligence and lively awareness. Their auras gleamed and flashed around them like the robes of emperors . . .

. . . or perhaps of Centurions on a visit of state.

They looked over at Ralph and Lois, who stood holding hands in the doorway like children who have lost their way in a fairy-tale wood, and smiled at them.

[*Hello, woman.*]

That was Doc #1. He was holding the scissors in his right hand. The blades were very long, and the points looked very sharp. Doc #2 took a step toward them and made a funny little half-bow.

[*Hello, man. We've been waiting for you.*]

3

Ralph felt Lois's hand tighten on his own, then loosen as she decided they were in no immediate danger. She took a small step forward, looking from Doc #1 to Doc #2 and then back to #1 again.

[*'Who are you?'*]

Doc #1 crossed his arms over his small chest. The long blades of his scissors lay the entire length of his white-clad left forearm.

[*We don't have names, not the way Short-Timers do — but you may call us after the fates in the story this man has already told you. That these names originally belonged to women means little to us, since we are creatures with no sexual dimension. I will be Clotho, although I spin no thread, and my colleague and old friend will be Lachesis, although he shakes no rods and has never thrown the coins. Come in, both of you — please!*]

They came in and stood warily between the visitor's chair and the bed. Ralph didn't think the docs meant them any harm — for now, at least — but he still didn't want to get too close. Their auras, so bright and fabulous compared to those of ordinary people, intimidated him, and he could see from Lois's wide eyes and half-open mouth that she felt the same. She sensed him looking at her, turned toward him, and tried to smile. *My Lois,* Ralph thought. He put an arm around her shoulders and hugged her briefly.

Lachesis: [*We've given you our names — names you may use, at any rate; won't you give us yours?*]

Lois: [*'You mean you don't already know? Pardon me, but I find that hard to believe.'*]

Lachesis: [*We* could *know, but choose not to. We like to observe the rules of common Short-Time politeness wherever we can. We find them lovely, for they are passed on by your kind from large hand to small and create the illusion of long lives.*]

[*'I don't understand.'*]

Ralph didn't, either, and wasn't sure he wanted to. He found something faintly patronizing in the tone of the one who called himself Lachesis, something that reminded him of McGovern when he was in a mood to lecture or pontificate.

Lachesis: [*It doesn't matter. We felt sure you would come. We know that you were watching us on Monday morning, man, at the home of*]

At this point there was a queer overlapping in Lachesis's speech. He seemed to say two things at exactly the same time, the terms rolling together like a snake with its own tail in its mouth:

[*May Locher.*]   [*the finished woman.*]

Lois took a hesitant step forward.

[*'My name is Lois Chasse. My friend is Ralph Roberts. And now that we've all been properly introduced, maybe you two fellows will tell us what's going on around here.'*]

Lachesis: [*There is another to be named.*]

Clotho: [*Ralph Roberts has already named him.*]

Lois looked at Ralph, who was nodding his head.

[*'They're talking about Doc #3. Right, guys?'*]

Clotho and Lachesis nodded. They were wearing identical approving smiles. Ralph supposed he should have been flattered, but he wasn't. Instead he was afraid, and very angry – they had been neatly manipulated, every step down the line. This was no chance meeting; it had been a setup from the word go. Clotho and Lachesis, just a couple of little bald doctors with time on their hands, standing around in Jimmy V's room waiting for the Short-Timers to arrive, ho-hum.

Ralph glanced over at Faye and saw he had taken a book called *50 Classic Chess Problems* out of his back pocket. He was reading and picking his nose in ruminative fashion as he did so. After a few preliminary explorations, Faye dove deep and hooked a big one. He examined it, then parked it on the underside of the bedside table. Ralph

521

looked away, embarrassed, and a saying of his grandmother's popped into his mind: *Peek not through a keyhole, lest ye be vexed.* He had lived to be seventy without fully understanding that; at last he thought he did. Meanwhile, another question had occurred to him.

[*'Why doesn't Faye see us? Why didn't Bill and his friend see us, for that matter? And how could that man walk right through me? Or did I just imagine that?'*]

Clotho smiled.

[*You didn't imagine it. Try to think of life as a kind of building, Ralph – what you would call a skyscraper.*]

Except that wasn't quite what Clotho was thinking of, Ralph discovered. For one flickering moment he seemed to catch an image from the mind of the other, one he found both exciting and disturbing: an enormous tower constructed of dark and sooty stone, standing in a field of red roses. Slit windows twisted up its sides in a brooding spiral.

Then it was gone.

[*You and Lois and all the other Short-Time creatures live on the first two floors of this structure. Of course there are elevators—*]

No, Ralph thought. *Not in the tower I saw in your mind, my little friend. In that building – if such a building actually exists – there are no elevators, only a narrow staircase festooned with cobwebs and doorways leading to God knows what.*

Lachesis was looking at him with a strange, almost suspicious curiosity, and Ralph decided he didn't much care for that look. He turned back to Clotho and motioned for him to go on.

Clotho: [*As I was saying, there are elevators, but Short-Timers are not allowed to use them under ordinary circumstances. You are not*

[*ready*]   [*prepared*]   [- - - - - - - - -.]

The last explanation was clearly the best, but it danced away from Ralph just before he could grasp it. He looked at Lois, who shook her head, and then back at Clotho and Lachesis again. He was beginning to feel angrier than ever. All the long, endless nights sitting in the wing-chair and waiting for dawn; all the days he'd spent feeling like a ghost inside his own skin; the inability to remember a sentence unless he read it three times; the phone numbers, once carried in his head, which he now had to look up—

A memory came then, one which simultaneously summed up and justified the anger he felt as he looked at these bald creatures with their darkly golden eyes and almost blinding auras. He saw himself peering into the cupboard over his kitchen counter, looking for the powdered soup his tired, overstrained mind insisted must be in there someplace. He saw himself poking, pausing, then poking some more. He saw the expression on his face – a look of distant perplexity that could easily have been mistaken for mild mental retardation but which was really simple exhaustion. Then he saw himself drop his hands and simply stand there, as if he expected the packet to jump out on its own.

Not until now, at this moment and at this memory, did he realize how totally horrible the last few months had been. Looking back at them was like looking into a wasteland painted in desolate maroons and grays.

[*'So you took us onto the elevator . . . or maybe that wasn't good enough for the likes of us and you just trotted us up the fire stairs. Got us acclimated a little at a time so we wouldn't strip*

523

our gears completely, I imagine. And it was easy. All you had to do was rob us of our sleep until we were half-crazy. Lois's son and daughter-in-law want to put her in a theme-park for geriatrics, did you know that? And my friend Bill McGovern thinks I'm ready for Juniper Hill. Meanwhile, you little angels—']

Clotho offered just a trace of his former wide smile.

[*We're no angels, Ralph.*]

[*'Ralph, please don't shout at them.'*]

Yes, he *had* been shouting, and at least some of it seemed to have gotten through to Faye; he had closed his chess book, stopped picking his nose, and was now sitting bolt upright in his chair, looking uneasily about the room.

Ralph looked from Clotho (who took a step backward, losing what was left of his smile) to Lachesis.

[*'Your friend says you're not angels. So where are they? Playing poker six or eight floors farther up? And I suppose God's in the penthouse and the devil's stoking coal in the boiler room.'*]

No reply. Clotho and Lachesis glanced doubtfully at each other. Lois plucked at Ralph's sleeve, but he ignored her.

[*'So what are we supposed to do, guys? Track down your little bald version of Hannibal Lecter and take his scalpel away? Well, fuck you.'*]

Ralph would have turned on his heel and walked out then (he had seen a lot of movies, and he knew a good exit-line when he heard one), but Lois burst into shocked, frightened tears, and that held him where he was. The look of bewildered reproach in her eyes made him regret his outburst at least a little. He slipped his arm back around Lois's shoulders, and looked at the two bald men defiantly.

They exchanged another glance and something – some

communication just above his and Lois's ability to hear or understand – passed between them. When Lachesis turned to them again, he was smiling . . . but his eyes were grave.

[*I hear your anger, Ralph, but it is not justified. You do not believe that now, but perhaps you may. For the time being, we must set your questions and our answers – such answers as we may give – aside.*]

[*'Why?'*]

[*Because the time of severing has come for this man. Watch closely, that you may learn and know.*]

Clotho stepped to the left side of the bed. Lachesis approached from the right, walking through Faye Chapin as he went. Faye bent over, afflicted with a sudden coughing-fit, and then opened his book of chess problems again as it eased.

[*'Ralph, I can't watch this! I can't watch them do it!'*]

But Ralph thought she would. He thought they both would. He held her tighter as Clotho and Lachesis bent over Jimmy V. Their faces were lit with love and caring and gentleness; they made Ralph think of the faces he had once seen in a Rembrandt painting – *The Night Watch,* he thought it had been called. Their auras mingled and over-lapped above Jimmy's chest, and suddenly the man in the bed opened his eyes. He looked through the two little bald doctors at the ceiling for a moment, his expression vague and puzzled, and then his gaze shifted toward the door and he smiled.

'Hey! Look who's here!' Jimmy V exclaimed. His voice was rusty and choked, but Ralph could still hear his South Boston wiseguy accent, where *here* came out *heah.* Faye jumped. The book of chess problems tumbled out of his lap and fell on the floor. He leaned over and took Jimmy's hand, but Jimmy ignored him and kept looking across the room at Ralph and Lois. 'It's Ralph Roberts! And Paul Chasse's wife widdim! Say, Ralphie, do you remember the day we tried to get into that tent revival so we could hear em sing "Amazing Grace"?'

[*'I remember, Jimmy.'*]

Jimmy appeared to smile, and then his eyes slipped closed again. Lachesis placed his hands against the dying man's cheeks and moved his head a bit, like a barber getting ready to shave a customer. At the same moment Clotho leaned even closer, opened his scissors, and slid them forward so that the long blades held Jimmy V's black balloon-string. As Clotho closed the scissors, Lachesis leaned forward and kissed Jimmy's forehead.

[*Go in peace, friend.*]

There was a small, unimportant *snick!* sound. The segment of the balloon-string above the scissors drifted up toward the ceiling and disappeared. The deathbag in which Jimmy V lay turned a momentary bright white, then winked out of existence just as Rosalie's had done earlier that evening. Jimmy opened his eyes again and looked at Faye. He started to smile, Ralph thought, and then his gaze turned fixed and distant. The dimples which had begun to form at the corners of his mouth smoothed out.

'Jimmy?' Faye shook Jimmy V's shoulder, running his hand through Lachesis's side to do it. 'You all right, Jimmy? . . . Oh shit.'

Faye got up and left the room, not quite running.

Clotho: [*Do you see and understand that what we do we do with love and respect? That we are, in fact, the physicians of last resort? It is vital to our dealings with you, Ralph and Lois, that you understand that.*]

[*'Yes.'*]

[*'Yes.'*]

Ralph hadn't intended to agree with anything either one of them said, but that phrase — the physicians of last resort — sliced cleanly and effortlessly through his anger. It felt true. They had freed Jimmy V from a world where there was nothing left for him but pain. Yes, they had undoubtedly stood in Room 317 with Ralph on a sleety afternoon some seven months ago and given Carolyn the same release. And yes, they went about their work with love and respect — any doubts he might have had on that score had been laid to rest when Lachesis kissed Jimmy V's forehead. But did love and respect give them the right to put him — and Lois, too — through hell and then send them after a supernatural being that had gone off the rails? Did it give them the right to even *dream* that two ordinary people, neither of them young anymore, could deal with such a creature?

Lachesis: [*Let us move on from this place. It's going to fill up with people, and we need to talk.*]

[*'Do we have any choice?'*]

Their answers

[*Yes, of course!*]   [*There is always a choice!*]

came back quickly, colored with overtones of surprise.

Clotho and Lachesis walked toward the door; Ralph and Lois shrank back to let them pass. The auras of the little bald doctors swept over them for a moment, however, and Ralph registered them in taste and texture: the taste of sweet apples, the texture of dry, light bark.

527

As they left, side by side, speaking gravely and respect-fully to each other, Faye came back in, now accompanied by a pair of nurses. These newcomers passed through Lachesis and Clotho, then through Ralph and Lois, without slowing or seeming to notice anything untoward.

In the hall outside, life went on at its usual muted pace. No buzzers went off, no lights flashed, no orderlies came sprinting down the hallway, pushing the crash-wagon ahead of them. No one cried 'Stat!' over the loudspeaker. Death was too common a visitor here for such things. Ralph guessed that it was not welcome, even under such circumstances as these, but it was familiar and accepted. He also guessed that Jimmy V would have been happy enough with his exit from the third floor of Derry Home – he had done it with no fuss or bother, and he hadn't had to show anyone either his driver's license or his Blue Cross Major Medical card. He had died with the dignity that simple, expected things often hold. One or two moments of consciousness, accompanied by a slightly wider perception of what was going on around him, and then poof. Pack up all my care and woe, black-bird, bye-bye.

4

They joined the bald docs in the hallway outside Bob Polhurst's room. Through the open door, they could see the deathwatch continuing around the old teacher's bed.

Lois: ['*The man closest to the bed is Bill McGovern, a friend of ours. There's something wrong with him. Something awful. If we do what you want, could you—?*']

But Lachesis and Clotho were shaking their heads in unison.

Clotho: [*Nothing can be changed.*]

Yes, Ralph thought. *Dorrance knew: done-bun-can't-be-undone.*

Lois: [*'When will it happen?'*]

Clotho: [*Your friend belongs to the other, to the third. To the one Ralph has already named Atropos. But Atropos could tell you the exact hour of the man's death no more than we could. He cannot even tell whom he will take next. Atropos is an agent of the Random.*]

This phrase sent a chill through Ralph's heart.

Lachesis: [*But this is no place for us to talk. Come.*]

Lachesis took one of Clotho's hands, then held out his free hand to Ralph. At the same time, Clotho reached toward Lois. She hesitated, then looked at Ralph.

Ralph, in his turn, looked grimly at Lachesis.

[*'You better not hurt her.'*]

[*Neither of you will be hurt, Ralph. Take my hand.*]

I'm a stranger in paradise, Ralph's mind finished. Then he sighed through his teeth, nodded to Lois, and gripped Lachesis's outstretched hand. That shock of recognition, as deep and pleasant as an unexpected encounter with an old and valued friend, washed over him again. Apples and bark; memories of orchards he had walked through as a kid. He was somehow aware, without actually seeing it, that his aura had changed color and become – at least for a little while – the gold–flecked green of Clotho and Lachesis.

Lois took Clotho's hand, inhaled a sharp little gasp over her teeth, then smiled hesitantly.

Clotho: [*Complete the circle, Ralph and Lois. Don't be afraid. All is well.*]

Boy, do I ever disagree with that, Ralph thought, but when Lois reached for his hand, he grasped her fingers. The taste of apples and the texture of dry bark was joined by some dark and unknowable spice. Ralph inhaled its aroma deeply and then smiled at Lois. She smiled back — no hesitation in that smile — and Ralph felt a dim, far-off confusion. How *could* you be afraid? How could you even hesitate when what they brought felt this good and seemed this right?

I sympathize, Ralph, but hesitate anyway, a voice counseled.

[*'Ralph? Ralph!'*]

She sounded alarmed and giddy at the same time. Ralph looked around just in time to see the top of the door of Room 315 descending past her shoulders . . . except it wasn't the door going down; it was Lois going up. *All* of them going up, still holding hands in a circle.

Ralph had just gotten this through his head when momentary darkness, sharp as a knife-edge, crossed his vision like a shadow thrown by the slat of a venetian blind. He had a brief glimpse of narrow pipes that were probably part of the hospital's sprinkler system, surrounded by tufted pink pads of insulation. Then he was looking down a long tiled corridor. A gurney cart was rolling straight at his head . . . which, he suddenly realized, had surfaced like a periscope in one of the fourth-floor corridors.

He heard Lois cry out and felt her grip on his hand tighten. Ralph closed his eyes instinctively and waited for the approaching gurney to flatten his skull.

Clotho: [*Be calm! Please, be calm! Remember that these things exist on a different level of reality from the one where you are now!*]

Ralph opened his eyes. The gurney was gone, although he could hear its receding wheels. The sound was coming from behind him now. The gurney, like McGovern's friend, had passed right through him. The four of them were now levitating slowly into the corridor of what had to be the pediatrics wing — fairy-tale creatures pranced and gambolled up and down the walls, and characters from Disney's *Aladdin* and *The Little Mermaid* were decaled onto the windows of a large, brightly lighted play area. A doctor and a nurse strolled toward them, discussing a case.

'— further tests seem indicated, but only if we can make at least ninety per cent sure that—'

The doctor walked through Ralph and as he did Ralph understood that he had started smoking again on the sly after five years off the weed and was feeling guilty as hell about it. Then they were gone. Ralph looked down just in time to see his feet emerge from the tiled floor. He turned to Lois, smiling tentatively.

[*'It sure beats the elevator, doesn't it?'*]

She nodded. Her grip on his hand was still very tight.

They rose through the fifth floor, surfaced in a doctor's lounge on the sixth (two doctors — the full-sized kind — present, one watching an old *F Troop* rerun and the other snoring on the hideous Swedish Modern sofa), and then they were on the roof.

The night was clear, moonless, gorgeous. Stars glittered across the arc of the sky in an extravagant, misty sprawl of light. The wind was blowing hard, and he thought of Mrs Perrine saying Indian summer was over, he could mark her words. Ralph could hear the wind but not feel it . . . although he had an idea he *could* feel it, if he wanted to. It was just a matter of concentrating in the right way . . .

Even as this thought came, he sensed some minor, momentary change in his body, something that felt like a blink. Suddenly his hair was blowing back from his forehead, and he could hear his pants cuffs flapping around his shins. He shivered. Mrs Perrine's back had been right about the weather changing. Ralph gave another interior blink and the push of the wind was gone. He looked over at Lachesis.

[*'Can I let go of your hand now?'*]

Lachesis nodded and dropped his own grip. Clotho released Lois's hand. Ralph looked across town to the west and saw the pulsing blue runway lights of the airport. Beyond them was the gridwork of orange arc sodiums that marked Cape Green, one of the new housing developments on the far side of the Barrens. And someplace, in the sprinkle of lights just east of the airport, was Harris Avenue.

[*'It's beautiful, isn't it, Ralph?'*]

He nodded and thought that standing there and seeing the city spread out in the dark like this was worth everything he had been through since the insomnia had started. Everything and then some. But that wasn't a thought he entirely trusted.

He turned to Lachesis and Clotho.

[*'All right, explain. Who are you, who is he, and what do you want us to do?'*]

The two bald docs were standing between two rapidly

turning heat ventilators which were spraying brownish-
purple fans of effluent into the air. They glanced nervously
at each other, and Lachesis gave Clotho an almost imper-
ceptible nod. Clotho stepped forward, looked from Ralph
to Lois, and seemed to gather his thoughts.

[*Very well. First, you must understand that the things which
are happening, while unexpected and distressing, are not precisely
unnatural. My colleague and I do what we were made to do;
Atropos does what he was made to do; and you, my Short-Time
friends, will do what you were made to do.*]

Ralph favored him with a bright, bitter smile.

[*'There goes freedom of choice, I guess.'*]

Lachesis: [*You mustn't think so! It's simply that what you
call freedom of choice is part of what we call ka, the great wheel
of being.*]

Lois: [*'We see now through a glass darkly . . . is that what
you mean?'*]

Clotho, smiling his somehow youthful smile: [*The
Bible, I believe. And a very good way of putting it.*]

Ralph: [*'Also pretty convenient for guys like you, but let's
pass on that for now. We have a saying that isn't from the Bible,
gentlemen, but it's a pretty good one, just the same: Don't gild
the lily. I hope you'll keep it in mind.'*]

Ralph had an idea, however, that that might be a
little too much to ask.

5

Clotho began to speak then, and he went on for a fair
length of time. Ralph had no idea how long, exactly, because
time was different on this level – compressed, somehow.

At times there were no words at all in what he said; verbal
terms were replaced with simple bright images like those
in a child's rebus puzzle. Ralph supposed this was telepathy,
and thus pretty amazing, but while it was happening it felt
as natural as breath.

Sometimes both words and images were lost, inter-
rupted by puzzling breaks

[- - - - - - - - - - - -]

in communication. Yet even then Ralph was usually able
to get some idea of what Clotho was trying to convey, and
he had an idea Lois was understanding what was hidden
in those lapses even more clearly than he was himself.

[*First, know that there are only four constants in that area
of existence where your lives and ours, the lives of the*

[- - - - - - - - - -

[*overlap. These four constants are Life, Death, the Purpose,
and the Random. All these words have meaning for you, but you
now have a slightly different concept of Life and Death, do you
not?*]

Ralph and Lois nodded hesitantly.

[*Lachesis and I are agents of Death. This makes us figures
of dread to most Short-Timers; even those who pretend to accept
us and our function are usually afraid. In pictures we are some-
times shown as a fearsome skeleton or a hooded figure whose face
cannot be seen.*]

Clotho put his tiny hands on his white-clad shoul-
ders and pretended to shudder. The burlesque was good
enough to make Ralph grin.

[*But we are not only agents of death, Ralph and Lois; we
are also agents of the Purpose. And now you must listen closely,
for I would not be misunderstood. There are those of your kind*

who feel that everything happens by design, and there are those who feel all events are simply a matter of luck or chance. The truth is that life is both random and on purpose, although not in equal measure. Life is like]

Here Clotho formed a circle with his arms, like a small child trying to show the shape of the earth, and within it Ralph saw a brilliant and evocative image: thousands (or perhaps it was millions) of playing cards fanned out in a flickering rainbow of hearts and spades and clubs and diamonds. He also saw a great many jokers in this huge pack; not so many as to make up a suit of their own, but clearly a lot more, proportionally speaking, than the two or three found in the usual deck. Every one of them was grinning, and every one was wearing a battered Panama with a crescent bitten out of the brim.

Every one carried a rusty scalpel.

Ralph looked at Clotho with widening eyes. Clotho nodded.

[*Yes. I don't know exactly what you saw, but I know you saw what I was trying to convey. Lois? What about you?*]

Lois, who loved playing cards nodded palely.

[*'Atropos is the joker in the deck — that's what you mean.'*]

[*He is an agent of the Random. We, Lachesis and I, serve that other force, the one which accounts for most events in both individual lives and in life's wider stream. On your level of the building, Ralph and Lois, every creature is a Short-Time creature, and has an appointed span. This isn't to say that a child pops out of its mother's womb with a sign around its neck reading* CUT CORD@84 YEARS, 11 MONTHS, 9 DAYS, 6 HOURS, 4 MINUTES, AND 21 SECONDS. *That idea is ridiculous. Yet time passages are usually set, and as both of you have*] *seen, one of the many functions the Short-Time aura serves is as a clock.*]

Lois stirred, and as Ralph turned to look at her, he saw an amazing thing: the sky overhead was growing pale. He guessed it must be five in the morning. They had arrived at the hospital at around nine o'clock on Tuesday evening, and now all at once it was Wednesday, October 6th. Ralph had heard of time flying, but this was ridiculous.

Lois: [*'Your job is what we call natural death, isn't it?'*]

Her aura flickered with confused, incomplete images. A man (the late Mr Chasse, Ralph was quite sure) lying in an oxygen tent. Jimmy V opening his eyes to look at Ralph and Lois in the instant before Clotho cut his balloon-string. The obituary page from the Derry *News,* peppered with photographs, most not much bigger than postage stamps, of the weekly harvest from the local hospitals and nursing homes.

Both Clotho and Lachesis shook their heads.

Lachesis: [*There is no such thing as natural death, not really. Our job is purposeful death. We take the old and the sick, but we take others, as well. Just yesterday, for instance, we took a young man of twenty-eight. A carpenter. Two Short-Time weeks ago, he fell from a scaffold and fractured his skull. During those two weeks his aura was*]

Ralph got a fractured image of a thunderstruck aura like the one which had surrounded the baby in the elevator.

Clotho: [*At last the change came — the turning of the aura. We knew it would come, but not when it would come. When it did, we went to him and sent him on.*]

[*'Sent him on to where?'*]

It was Lois who asked the question, broaching the

touchy subject of the afterlife almost by accident. Ralph grabbed for his mental safety belt, almost hoping for one of those peculiar blanks, but when their overlapped answers came, they were perfectly clear.

Clotho: [*To everywhere.*]

Lachesis: [*To other worlds than these.*]

Ralph felt a mixture of relief and disappointment.

[*'That sounds very poetic, but I think what it means — correct me if I'm wrong — is that the afterlife is as much a mystery to you guys as it is to us.'*]

Lachesis, sounding a bit stiff: [*On another occasion we might have time to discuss such things, but not now — as you have no doubt already noticed, time passes faster on this level of the building.*]

Ralph looked around and saw the morning had already brightened considerably.

[*'Sorry.'*]

Clotho, smiling: [*Not at all — we enjoy your questions, and find them refreshing. Curiosity exists everywhere along life's continuum, but nowhere is it as abundant as here. But what you call the afterlife has no place in the four constants — Life and Death, the Random and the Purpose — which concern us now.*

[*The approach of almost every death which serves the Purpose takes a course with which we are very familiar. The auras of those who will die Purposeful deaths turn gray as the time of finishing approaches. This gray deepens steadily to black. We are called when the aura*

[- - - - - - - - - - - -,

[*and we come exactly as you saw last night. We give release to those who suffer, peace to those in terror, rest to those who cannot find rest. Most Purposeful deaths are expected, even welcomed, but not all. We are sometimes called to take men, women, and children who are in the best of health . . . yet their auras turn suddenly and their time of finishing has come.*]

Ralph remembered the young man in the sleeveless Celtics jersey he'd seen bopping into the Red Apple yesterday afternoon. He had been the picture of health and vitality . . . except for the spectral oil–slick surrounding him, that was.

Ralph opened his mouth, perhaps to mention this young man (or to ask about his fate), then closed it again. The sun was directly overhead now, and a bizarre certainty suddenly came to him: that he and Lois had become the subject of lecherous discussion in the secret city of the Old Crocks.

Anybody seen em? . . . No? . . . Think they run off together? . . . Eloped, maybe? . . . Naw, not at their age, but they might be shacked up . . . I dunno if Ralphie's got any live rounds left in the old ammo dump, but she's always looked like a hot ticket to me . . . Yeah, walks like she knows what to do with it, don't she?

The image of his oversized rustbucket waiting patiently behind one of the ivy-covered units of the Derry Cabins while the springs boinged and sproinged salaciously inside came to Ralph, and he grinned. He couldn't help it. A moment later the alarming idea that he might be broadcasting his thoughts on his aura came to him, and he slammed the door on the picture at once. Yet wasn't Lois looking at him with a certain amused speculation?

Ralph turned his attention hastily back to Clotho.

[*Atropos serves the Random. Not all deaths of the sort Short-Timers call 'senseless' and 'unnecessary' and 'tragic' are his work, but most are. When a dozen old men and women die in a fire at a retirement hotel, the chances are good that Atropos has been there, taking souvenirs and cutting cords. When an infant dies in his crib for no apparent reason, the cause, more often than not, is Atropos and his rusty scalpel. When a dog — yes, even a dog, for the destinies of almost all living things in the Short-Time world fall among either the Random or the Purpose — is run over in the road because the driver of the car that hit him picked the wrong moment to glance at his watch—]*

Lois: [*'Is that what happened to Rosalie?'*]

Clotho: [Atropos *is what happened to Rosalie, Ralph's friend Joe Wyzer was only what we call 'fulfilling circumstance'.*]

Lachesis: [*And Atropos is also what happened to your friend, the late Mr McGovern.*]

Lois looked the way Ralph felt: dismayed but not really surprised. It was now late afternoon, perhaps as many as eighteen Short-Time hours had passed since they had last seen Bill, and Ralph had known the man's time was extremely short even last night. Lois, who had inadvertently put her hand inside him, probably knew it even better.

Ralph: [*'When did it happen? How long after we saw him?'*]

Lachesis: [*Not long. While he was leaving the hospital. I'm sorry for your loss, and for giving you the news in such clumsy fashion. We speak to Short-Timers so infrequently that we forget how. I didn't mean to hurt you, Ralph and Lois.*]

Lois told him it was all right, that she quite understood, but tears were trickling down her cheeks, and Ralph felt them burning in his own eyes. The idea that Bill could be gone — that the little shithead in the dirty smock had gotten him – was hard to grasp. Was he to believe McGovern would never hoist that satiric, bristly eyebrow of his again? Never bitch about how cruddy it was to get old again? Impossible. He turned suddenly to Clotho.

[*Show us.*]

Clotho, surprised, almost dithering: [*I . . . I don't think*—]

Ralph: [*'Seeing is believing to us Short-Time schmoes. Didn't you guys ever hear that one?'*]

Lois spoke up unexpectedly.

[*'Yes – show us. But only enough so we can know it and accept it. Try not to make us feel any worse than we already do.'*]

Clotho and Lachesis looked at each other, then seemed to shrug without actually moving their narrow shoulders. Lachesis flicked the first two fingers of his right hand upward, creating a blue-green peacock's fan of light. In it Ralph saw a small, eerily perfect representation of the ICU corridor. A nurse pushing a pharmacy cart came into this arc and crossed it. At the far side of the viewing area, she actually seemed to *curve* for a moment before passing out of view.

Lois, delighted in spite of the circumstances: [*'It's like watching a movie in a soapbubble!'*]

Now McGovern and Mr Plum stepped out of Bob Polhurst's room. McGovern had put on an old Derry High letter sweater and his friend was zipping up a jacket; they were clearly giving up the deathwatch for another night. McGovern was walking slowly, lagging behind Mr Plum. Ralph could see that his downstairs neighbor and some-time friend didn't look good at all.

He felt Lois's hand slip into his upper arm and grip hard. He put his hand over hers.

Halfway to the elevator, McGovern stopped, braced himself against the wall with one hand, and lowered his head. He looked like a totally blown runner at the end of a marathon. For a moment Mr Plum went on walking. Ralph could see his mouth moving and thought, *He doesn't know he's talking to thin air – not yet, at least.*

Suddenly Ralph didn't want to see any more.

Inside the blue-green arc, McGovern put one hand to his chest. The other went to his throat and began to rub, as if he were checking for wattles. Ralph couldn't tell for sure, but he thought his downstairs neighbor's eyes looked frightened. He remembered the grimace of hate on Doc #3's face when he realized a Short-Timer had presumed to step into his business with one of the local strays. What had he said?

[*I'll fuck you over, Shorts. I'll fuck you over big-time. And I'll fuck your friends over. Do you get me?*]

A terrible idea, almost a certainty, dawned in Ralph's mind as he watched Bill McGovern crumple slowly to the floor.

Lois: [*'Make it go away – please make it go away!'*]

She buried her face against Ralph's shoulder. Clotho and Lachesis exchanged uneasy looks, and Ralph realized he had already begun to revise his mental picture of them as omniscient and all-powerful. They might be supernatural creatures, but Dr Joyce Brothers they were not. He had an idea they weren't much shakes at predicting the future, either; fellows with really efficient crystal balls probably wouldn't have a look like that in their entire repertoire.

They're feeling their way along, just like the rest of us,

Ralph thought, and he felt a certain reluctant sympathy for Mr C and Mr L.

The blue-green arc of light floating in front of Lachesis – and the images trapped inside it – suddenly disappeared.

Clotho, sounding defensive: [*Please remember that it was your choice to see, Ralph and Lois. We did not show you that willingly.*]

Ralph barely heard this. His terrible idea was still developing, like a photograph one does not wish to see but cannot turn away from. He was thinking of Bill's hat . . . Rosalie's faded blue bandanna . . . and Lois's missing diamond earrings.

[*I'll fuck your friends over, Shorts – do you get me? I hope so. I most certainly do.*]

He looked from Clotho to Lachesis, his sympathy for them disappearing. What replaced it was a dull pulse of anger. Lachesis had said there was no such thing as accidental death, and that included McGovern's. Ralph had no doubt that Atropos had taken McGovern when he had for one simple reason: he'd wanted to hurt Ralph, to punish Ralph for messing into . . . what had Dorrance called it? Long-time business.

Old Dor had suggested he not do that – a good policy, no doubt, but he, Ralph, had really had no choice . . . because these two bald half-pints had messed in with *him*. They had, in a very real sense, gotten Bill McGovern killed.

Clotho and Lachesis saw his anger and took a step backward (although they seemed to do it without actually moving their feet), their faces becoming more uneasy than ever.

[*'You two are the reason Bill McGovern's dead. That's the truth of it, isn't it?'*]

Clotho: [*Please . . . if you'll just let us finish explaining—*]
Lois was staring at Ralph, worried and scared.
[*'Ralph? What's wrong? Why are you angry?'*]
[*'Don't you get it? This little setup of theirs cost Bill
McGovern his life. We're here because Atropos has either done
something these guys don't like or is getting ready to—'*]
Lachesis: [*You're jumping to conclusions, Ralph—*]
[*'— but there's one very basic problem: he* knows *we see
him!* Atropos KNOWS we see him!'*]
Lois's eyes widened with terror . . . and with under-
standing.

CHAPTER EIGHTEEN

1

A small white hand fell on Ralph's shoulder and lay there like smoke.

[*Please . . . if you'll only let us explain—*]

He felt that change – that *blink* – happen in his body even before he was fully aware he had willed it. He could feel the wind again, coming out of the dark like the blade of a cold knife, and shivered. The touch of Clotho's hand was now no more than a phantom vibration just below the surface of his skin. He could see all three of them, but now they were milky and faint. Now they were ghosts.

I've stepped down. Not all the way back down to where we started, but at least down to a level where they can have almost no physical contact with me. My aura, my balloon-string . . . yes, I'm sure they could get at those things, but the physical part of me that lives my real life in the Short-Time world? No way, José.

Lois's voice, as distant as a fading echo: ['*Ralph! What are you doing to your*   ]

He looked at the ghostly images of Clotho and Lachesis. Now they looked not just uneasy or slightly guilty but downright scared. Their faces were distorted and hard to see, but their fear was none the less unmistakable.

Clotho, his voice distant but audible: [*Come back, Ralph! Please come back!*]

'If I do, will you quit playing games and be straight with us?'

Lachesis, fading, disappearing: [*Yes! Yes!*]

Ralph made that interior blink happen again. The three of them came back into focus. At the same time, color once more filled up the spaces of the world and time resumed its former sprint – he observed the waning moon sliding down the far side of the sky like a dollop of glowing mercury. Lois threw her arms around his neck, and for a moment he wasn't sure if she was hugging him or trying to strangle him.

[*'Thank God! I thought you were going to leave me!'*]

Ralph kissed her and for a moment his head was filled with a pleasant jumble of sensory input: the taste of fresh honey, a texture like combed wool, and the smell of apples. A thought blipped across his mind

(*what would it be like to make love up here?*)

and he banished it at once. He needed to think and speak very carefully in the next few

(*minutes? hours? days?*)

and thinking about stuff like that would only make it that much harder. He turned to the little bald doctors and measured them with his eyes.

[*'I hope you mean it. Because if you don't, I think we'd better call this horserace off right now and go our separate ways.'*]

Clotho and Lachesis didn't bother with the exchanged glance this time; they both nodded eagerly. Lachesis spoke, and he did so in a defensive tone of voice. These fellows, Ralph suspected, were a lot more pleasant to deal with than Atropos, but no more used to being questioned – to being put on their mettle, Ralph's mother would have said – than he was.

[*Everything we told you was true, Ralph and Lois. We may have left out the possibility that Atropos has a slightly greater understanding of the situation than we would really like, but—*]

Ralph: [*'What if we refuse to listen to any more of this nonsense? What if we just turn and walk away?'*]

Neither replied, but Ralph thought he saw a dismaying thing in their eyes: they knew that Atropos had Lois's earrings, and they knew *he* knew. The only one who didn't know – he hoped – was Lois herself.

She was now tugging his arm.

[*'Don't do that, Ralph – please don't. We need to hear them out.'*]

He turned back to them and made a curt motion for them to go on.

Lachesis: [*Under ordinary circumstances, we don't interfere with Atropos, nor he with us. We couldn't interfere with him even if we wanted to; the Random and the Purpose are like the red and black squares on a checkerboard, defining each other by contrast. But Atropos does want to interfere with the way things operate – interfering is, in a very real sense, what he was made to do – and on rare occasions, the opportunity to do so in a really big way presents itself. Efforts to stop his meddling are rare—*]

Clotho: [*The truth is actually a little stronger, Ralph and Lois; never in our experience has an effort been made to check or bar him.*]

Lachesis: [– *and are made only if the situation into which he intends to meddle is a very delicate one, where many serious matters are balanced and counterbalanced. This is one of those situations. Atropos has severed a life-cord he would have done well to leave alone. This will cause terrible problems on all levels, not to mention a serious imbalance between the Random and the Purpose, unless the situation is rectified. We cannot deal with what's happening; the situation has passed far beyond our skills. We can no longer see clearly, let alone act. Yet in this case our inability to see hardly matters, because in the end, only Short-Timers can oppose the will of Atropos. That is why you two are here.*]

Ralph: [*'Are you saying that Atropos cut the cord of someone who was supposed to die a natural death . . . or a Purposeful death?'*]

Clotho: [*Not exactly. Some lives – a very few – bear no clear designation. When Atropos touches such lives, trouble is always likely. 'All bets are off,' you say. Such undesignated lives are like—*]

Clotho drew his hands apart and an image – playing cards again – flashed between them. A row of seven cards that were swiftly turned over, one after another, by an unseen hand. An ace; a deuce; a joker; a trey; a seven; a queen. The last card the invisible hand flipped over was blank.

Clotho: [*Does this picture help?*]

Ralph's brow furrowed. He didn't know if it did or not. Somewhere out there was a person who was neither a regular playing card nor a joker in the deck. A person who was perfectly blank, up for grabs by either side. Atropos had slashed this guy's metaphysical air-hose, and now somebody – or some*thing* – had called a time-out.

Lois: [*'It's Ed you're talking about, isn't it?'*]

Ralph wheeled around and stared at her sharply, but she was looking at Lachesis.

[*'Ed Deepneau is the blank card.'*]

Lachesis was nodding.

[*'How did you know that, Lois?'*]

[*'Who else could it be?'*]

She wasn't smiling at him, precisely, but Ralph felt the *sense* of a smile. He turned back to Clotho and Lachesis.

[*'Okay, at last we're getting somewhere. So who flashed the red light on this deal? I don't think it was you guys – I have an idea that on this one, at least, you two aren't much more than the hired help.'*]

They put their heads together for a moment and murmured, but Ralph saw a faint ocher tinge appear like a seam at the place where their green-gold auras overlapped and knew he was right. At last the two of them faced Ralph and Lois again.

Lachesis: [*Yes, that is basically the case. You have a way of putting things in perspective, Ralph. We haven't had a conversation like this in a thousand years—*]

Clotho: [*If ever.*]

Ralph: [*'All you have to do is tell the truth, boys.'*]

Lachesis, as plaintively as a child: [*We have been!*]

Ralph: [*'The whole truth.'*]

Lachesis: [*All right; the whole truth. Yes, it is Ed Deepneau's cord Atropos cut. We don't know this because we have seen it – we've passed beyond our ability to see clearly, as I said – but because it is the only logical conclusion. Deepneau is undesignated, neither of the Random nor of the Purpose, that we do know, and his must have been some sort of master-cord to have*] *caused all this uproar and concern. The very fact that he has lived so long after his life-cord was severed indicates his power and importance. When Atropos severed this cord, he set a terrible chain of events in motion.*]

Lois shivered and stepped closer to Ralph.

Lachesis: [*You called us hired help. You were more right than you knew. We are, in this case, simply messengers. Our job is to make you and Lois aware of what has happened and what is expected of you, and that job is now almost done. As to who 'flashed the red light', we can't answer that question because we don't really know.*]

[*'I don't believe you.'*]

But he heard the lack of conviction in his own voice (if it *was* a voice).

Clotho: [*Don't be silly — of course you do! Would you expect the directors of a large automobile company to invite a lowly worker up to the boardroom so they could explain the reasons behind all the company's policies? Or perhaps give him the details on why they decided to close one plant and leave another one open?*]

Lachesis: [*We're a little more highly placed than the men who work on automobile assembly lines, but we're still what you would call 'working joes', Ralph — no more and no less.*]

Clotho: [*Be content with this: beyond the Short-Time levels of existence and the Long-Time levels on which Lachesis, Atropos, and I exist, there are yet other levels. These are inhabited by creatures we could call All-Timers, beings which are either eternal or so close to it as to make no difference. Short-Timers and Long-Timers live in overlapping spheres of existence — on connected floors of the same building, if you like — ruled by the Random and the Purpose. Above these floors, inaccessible to us*] *but very much a part of the same tower of existence, live other beings. Some of them are marvellous and wonderful; others are hideous beyond our ability to comprehend, let alone yours. These beings might be called the Higher Purpose and the Higher Random . . . or perhaps there is no Random beyond a certain level; we suspect that may be the case, but we have no real way of telling. We* do *know that it is something from one of these higher levels that has interested itself in Ed, and that something else from up there made a countermove. That countermove is you, Ralph and Lois.*]

Lois gave Ralph a dismayed look that he hardly noticed. The idea that something was moving them around like chess-pieces in Faye Chapin's beloved Runway 3 Classic – an idea that would have infuriated him under other circumstances – went right by him for the time being. He was remembering the night Ed had called him on the telephone. *You're drifting into deep water,* he'd said, *and there are things swimming around in the undertow you can't even* conceive *of.*

Entities, in other words.

Beings too hideous to comprehend, according to Mr C, and Mr C was a gentleman who dealt death for a living.

They haven't really noticed you yet, Ed had told him that night, *but if you keep fooling with me, they will. And you don't want that. Believe me, you don't.*

Lois: [*'How did you get us up to this level in the first place? It was the insomnia, wasn't it?'*]

Lachesis, cautiously: [*Essentially, yes. We're able to make certain small changes in Short-Time auras. These adjustments caused a rather special form of insomnia that altered the way you dream and the way you perceive the waking world. Adjusting*

Short-Term auras is delicate, frightening work. Madness is always a danger.]

Clotho: [*At times you may have felt that you were going mad, but neither of you was ever even close. You're much tougher, both of you, than you give yourself credit for.*]

These assholes actually think they're being comforting, Ralph marvelled, and then pushed his anger away again. He simply had no time to be angry now. Later, maybe, he could make up for that. He hoped so. For now he simply patted Lois's hands, then turned to Clotho and Lachesis again.

[*'Last summer, after he beat his wife up, Ed spoke to me of a being he called the Crimson King. Does that mean anything to you fellows?'*]

Clotho and Lachesis exchanged another look, one which Ralph at first mistook for solemnity.

Clotho: [*Ralph, you must remember that Ed is insane, existing in a delusional state—*]

[*'Yeah, tell me about it.'*]

[*- but we believe that his 'Crimson King' does exist in one form or another, and that when Atropos cut his life-cord, Ed Deepneau fell directly under this being's influence.*]

The two little bald doctors looked at each other again, and this time Ralph saw the shared expression for what it really was: not solemnity but terror.

2

A new day had dawned – Thursday – and was now brightening its way toward noon. Ralph couldn't tell for sure, but he thought the speed with which the hours were passing down there on the Short-Time level was increasing; if they didn't wrap this thing up soon, Bill McGovern wouldn't be the only one of their friends they outlived.

Clotho: [*Atropos knew that the Higher Purpose would send* someone *to try to change what he has set in motion, and now he knows who. But you must not allow yourselves to be sidetracked by Atropos; you must remember that he is little more than a pawn on this board. It is not Atropos who really opposes you.*]

He paused and looked doubtfully at his colleague. Lachesis nodded for him to go on, and he did so confidently enough, but Ralph felt his heart sink a little, just the same. He was sure the two bald doctors had the best of intentions, but they were pretty clearly flying on instruments, just the same.

Clotho: [*You must not approach Atropos directly, either. I cannot emphasize that enough. He has been surrounded by forces much greater than himself, forces that are malignant and powerful, forces that are* conscious *and will stop at nothing to stop you. Yet we think that, if you stay away from Atropos, you may be able to block the terrible thing which is about to happen . . . which is, in a very real sense, happening already.*]

Ralph didn't much care for the unspoken assumption that he and Lois were going to do whatever it was these two happy gauchos wanted, but this didn't seem like exactly the right time to say so.

Lois: [*'What is about to happen? What is it you want from us? Are we supposed to find Ed and talk him out of doing something bad?'*]

Clotho and Lachesis looked at her with identical expressions of shocked horror.

[*Haven't you been listening to*—]

[— *you mustn't even think of*—]

They stopped, and Clotho motioned Lachesis to go ahead.

[*If you didn't hear us before, Lois, hear us now:* stay away from Ed Deepneau! *Like Atropos, this unusual situation has temporarily invested him with great power. To even go near him would be to risk a visit from the entity he thinks of as the Crimson King . . . and besides, he is no longer in Derry.*]

Lachesis glanced out over the roof, where lights were coming on in the dusk of Thursday evening, then looked back at Ralph and Lois again.

[*He has left for*

[- - - - - - - - - - - - - - - - - - -.]

No words, but Ralph caught a clear sensory impression which was part smell (oil, grease, exhaust, sea-salt), part feel and sound (the wind snapping at something – perhaps a flag), and part sight (a large rusty building with a huge door standing open on a steel track).

[*'He's on the coast, isn't he? Or going there.'*]

Clotho and Lachesis nodded, and their faces suggested that the coast, eighty miles from Derry, was a very good place for Ed Deepneau.

Lois tugged his hand again, and Ralph glanced at her.

[*'Did you see the building, Ralph?'*]

He nodded.

Lois: [*'It's not Hawking Labs, but it's near there. I think it might even be a place I know*—']

Lachesis, speaking rapidly, as if to change the subject: [*Where he is or what he might be planning really doesn't matter. Your task lies elsewhere, in safer waters, but you still may need to use all of your considerable Short-Time powers to accomplish it, and there still may be great danger.*]

Lois looked nervously at Ralph.

[*'Tell them we won't hurt anybody, Ralph – we might agree to help them if we can, but we won't hurt anybody, no matter what.'*]

Ralph, however, told them no such thing. He was thinking of how the diamond chips had glittered at Atropos's earlobes, and meditating on how perfectly he had been trapped – and Lois along with him, of course. Yes, he would hurt someone to get the earrings back. That wasn't even a question. But just how far would he go? Would he perhaps kill to get them back?

Not wanting to tackle that issue – not wanting to even look at Lois, at least for the time being – Ralph turned back to Clotho and Lachesis. He opened his mouth to speak, but she got there first.

[*'There's one other thing I want to know before we go any further.'*]

It was Clotho who replied, sounding slightly amused – sounding, in fact, remarkably like Bill McGovern. Ralph didn't care for it much.

[*What is that, Lois?*]

[*'Is Ralph in danger, too? Does Atropos have something of Ralph's we need to take back later on? Something like Bill's hat?'*]

Lachesis and Clotho exchanged a quick, apprehensive glance. Ralph didn't think Lois caught it, but he did. *She's getting too close for comfort,* that look said. Then it was gone. Their faces were smooth again as they turned their attention back to Lois.

Lachesis: [*No. Atropos has taken nothing from Ralph because, up until now, doing so would not help him in any way.*]

Ralph: [*'What do you mean, "up until now"?'*]

Clotho: [*You have spent your life as part of the Purpose, Ralph, but that has changed.*]

Lois: [*'When did it change? It happened when we started seeing the auras, didn't it?'*]

They looked at each other, then at Lois, then – nervously – at Ralph. They said nothing, and an interesting idea occurred to Ralph: like the boy George Washington of the cherry tree myth, Clotho and Lachesis could not tell a lie . . . and at moments like this they probably regretted it. The only alternative was the one they were employing: keeping their lips zipped and hoping the conversation would move on to safer areas. Ralph decided he didn't want it to move on – at least not yet – even though they were dangerously close to allowing Lois to find out where her earrings had gone . . . always assuming she didn't know that already, a possibility that did not strike him as at all remote. An old carny pitchman's line occurred to him: *Step right up, gentlemen . . . but if you want to* play, *you have to pay.*

[*'Oh no, Lois – the change didn't happen when I started to see the auras. I think a lot of people catch a glimpse into the Long-Time world of auras every now and again, and nothing bad happens to them. I don't think I got knocked out of my nice safe place in the Purpose until we started to talk to these two fine fellows. What do you say, fine fellows? You did everything but leave a trail of breadcrumbs, even though you knew perfectly well what was going to happen. Isn't that about the size of it?'*]

They looked down at their feet, then slowly, reluctantly, back up at Ralph. It was Lachesis who answered.

[*Yes, Ralph. We drew you to us even though we knew it would alter your* ka. *It's unfortunate, but the situation demanded it.*]

Now Lois will ask about herself, Ralph thought. *Now she must ask.*

But she didn't. She only looked at the two little bald doctors with an inscrutable expression completely unlike any of her usual *Our Lois* looks. Ralph wondered again how much she knew or guessed, marvelled again that he didn't have the slightest clue . . . and then these speculations were swallowed in a fresh wave of anger.

[*'You guys . . . man oh man, you guys . . .'*]

He didn't finish, although he might have, if Lois hadn't been standing beside him: *You guys have done quite a bit more than just mess with our sleep, haven't you? I don't know about Lois, but I had a nice little niche in the Purpose . . . which means that you deliberately made me an exception to the very rules you've spent your whole lives upholding. In a way, I've become as much a blank as this guy we're supposed to find. How did Clotho put it? 'All bets are off.' How very fucking true.*

Lois: [*'You talked about using our powers. What* powers?*'*]

Lachesis turned to her, clearly delighted at the change of subject. He pressed his hands together, palm to palm, then opened them in a curiously Oriental gesture. What appeared between them were two swift images: Ralph's hand producing a bolt of cold blue fire as it cut the air in a karate chop, and Lois's forefinger producing bright blue-gray pellets of light that looked like nuclear cough-drops.

Ralph: [*'Yes, all right, we have* something, *but it isn't reliable. It's like—'*]

He concentrated and created an image of his own: hands opening the back of a radio and removing a pair of

AA batteries encrusted with blue-gray crud. Clotho and Lachesis frowned at him, not getting it.

Lois: ['He's trying to say we can't always do that, and when we can, we can't do it for long. Our batteries go flat, you see.']

Understanding mixed with amused incredulity broke over their features.

Ralph: ['What's so damned funny?']

Clotho: [Nothing . . . everything. You have no concept of how strange you and Lois seem to us — incredibly wise and perceptive at one moment, incredibly naïve at the next. Your batteries, as you call them, need never go flat, because the two of you are standing next to a bottomless reservoir of power. We assumed that, since you have both already drunk from it, you must surely know about it.]

Ralph: ['What in the world are you talking about?']

Lachesis made that curiously Oriental hand-opening gesture again. This time Ralph saw Mrs Perrine, walking stiffly upright within an aura the color of a West Pointer's dress uniform. Saw a shaft of gray brilliance, as thin and straight as the quill of a porcupine, poke out of this aura.

This image was overlaid by one of a skinny woman encased in a smoggy brown aura. She was looking out a car window. A voice — Lois's — spoke: Oooh, Mina, isn't that the dearest little house? A moment later there was a soft, indrawn whistle and a narrow ray of the woman's aura poked out from behind her neck.

This was followed by a third image, brief but strong: Ralph reaching through the slot in the bottom of the information booth and gripping the wrist of the woman with the brambly orange aura . . . except that all at once the

557

aura around her left arm no longer *was* orange. All at once it was the faded turquoise he now thought of as Ralph Roberts Blue.

The image faded. Lachesis and Clotho stared at Ralph and Lois; they stared back, shocked.

Lois: [*'Oh, no! We can't do that! It's like—'*]

Image: Two men in striped prison suits and little black masks tiptoeing out of a bank vault, carrying bulging sacks with the $ symbol printed on the sides.

Ralph: [*'No, even worse. It's like—'*]

Image: A bat flies in through an open casement window, makes two swooping circles in a silvery shaft of moonlight, then turns into Ralph Lugosi in a cape and old-fashioned tuxedo. He approaches a sleeping woman – not a young, rosy virgin but old Mrs Perrine in a sensible flannel nightgown – and bends over to suck her aura.

When Ralph looked back at Clotho and Lachesis, both of them were shaking their heads vehemently.

Lachesis: [*No! No, no, no! You couldn't be more wrong! Have you not wondered why you are Short-Timers, marking the spans of your lives in decades rather than in centuries? Your lives are short because you burn like bonfires! When you draw energy from your fellow Short-Timers, it's like—*]

Image: A child at the seashore, a lovely little girl with golden ringlets bouncing on her shoulders, runs down the beach to where the waves break. In one hand she carries a red plastic bucket. She kneels and fills it from the vast gray-blue Atlantic.

Clotho: [*You are like that child, Ralph and Lois – your fellow Short-Timers are like the sea. Do you understand now?*]

Ralph: [*'There's really that much of this aural energy in the human race?'*]

Lachesis: [*You still don't understand. That's how much there is—*]

Lois broke in. Her voice was trembling, although whether with fear or ecstasy, Ralph could not tell.

[*'That's how much there is in* each one of us, Ralph. *That's how much there is in* every human being on the face of the earth!*']

Ralph whistled softly and looked from Lachesis to Clotho. They were nodding confirmation.

[*'You're saying we can stock up on this energy from whoever happens to be handy? That it's safe for the people we take it from?'*]

Clotho: [*Yes. You could no more hurt them than you could empty the Atlantic with a child's beach-pail.*]

Ralph hoped that was so, because he had an idea that he and Lois had been unconsciously borrowing energy like mad – it was the only explanation he could think of for all the compliments he had been getting. People telling him that he looked great. People telling him that he must be over his insomnia, had to be, because he looked so rested and healthy. That he looked younger.

Hell, he thought, *I* am *younger.*

The moon had set again, and Ralph realized with a start that the sun would soon be coming up on Friday morning. It was high time they got back to the central issue of this discussion.

[*'Let's cut to the chase here, fellows. Why have you gone to all this trouble? What is it we're supposed to stop?'*]

And then, before either of them could reply, he was

struck by a flash of insight too strong and bright to be questioned or denied.

[*It's Susan Day, isn't it? He means to kill Susan Day. To assassinate her.*]

Clotho: [*Yes, but—*]

Lachesis: [*– but that isn't what matters—*]

Ralph: [*'Come on, you guys – don't you think the time has come to lay the rest of your cards on the table?'*]

Lachesis: [*Yes, Ralph. That time has come.*]

There had been little or no touching among them since they had formed the circle and risen through the intervening hospital floors to the roof, but now Lachesis put a gentle, feather-light arm around Ralph's shoulders and Clotho took Lois by the arm, as a gentleman of a bygone age might have led a lady onto a dance-floor.

Scent of apples, taste of honey, texture of wool . . . but this time Ralph's delight in that mingled sensory input could not mask the deep disquiet he felt as Lachesis turned him to the left and then walked with him toward the edge of the flat hospital roof.

Like many larger and more important cities, Derry seemed to have been built in the most geographically unsuitable place the original settlers could find. The downtown area existed on the steep sides of a valley; the Kenduskeag River flowed sluggishly through the over-grown tangle of the Barrens at this valley's lowest level. From their vantage point atop the hospital, Derry looked like a town whose heart had been pierced by a narrow green dagger . . . except in the darkness, the dagger was black.

One side of the valley was Old Cape, site of a seedy postwar housing development and a glossy, flossy new mall.

The other side contained most of what people meant when they talked about 'downtown'. Derry's downtown centered around Up-Mile Hill. Witcham Street took the most direct course up this hill, rising steeply before branching off into the tangle of streets (Harris Avenue was one of them) that made up the west side. Main Street diverged from Witcham halfway up the hill and headed southwest along the valley's shallower side. This area of town was known both as Main Street Hill and as Bassey Park. And, near the very top of Main Street's rise—

Lois, almost moaning: [*'Dear God, what is it?'*]

Ralph tried to say something comforting and produced nothing but a feeble croak. Near the top of Main Street Hill, a huge black umbrella-shape floated above the ground, blotting out stars which had begun to pale toward morning. Ralph tried to tell himself at first that it was only smoke, that one of the warehouses out that way had caught on fire . . . perhaps even the abandoned railroad depot at the end of Neibolt Street. But the warehouses were farther south, the old depot was farther west, and if that evil-looking toadstool had really been smoke, the prevailing wind would be driving it across the sky in plumes and banners. That wasn't happening. Instead of dissipating, the silent blotch in the sky simply hung there, darker than the darkness.

And no one sees it, Ralph thought. *No one but me . . . and Lois . . . and the little bald doctors. The goddam little bald doctors.*

He squinted to make out the shape within the giant deathbag, although he didn't really need to; he had lived in Derry most of his life, and could almost have navigated its streets with his eyes closed (as long as he did not have to do so behind the wheel of his car, that was). Nevertheless, he *could* make out the building inside the deathbag, especially now that daylight was beginning to seep over the horizon. The flat circular roof which sat atop the curving glass-and-brick façade was a dead giveaway. This throwback to the 1950s, designed very much tongue-in-cheek by the famous architect (and one-time Derry resident) Benjamin Hanscom, was the new Derry Civic Center, a replacement for the one destroyed in the flood of '85.

Clotho turned Ralph to look at him.

[*You see, Ralph, you were right — he does mean to assassinate Susan Day . . . but not just Susan Day.*]

He paused, glanced at Lois, then turned his grave face back to Ralph.

[*That cloud — what you two quite correctly call a death bag — means that in a sense he has already done what Atropos has set him on to do. There will be more than two thousand people there tonight . . . and Ed Deepneau means to kill them all. If the course of events is not changed, he* will *kill them all.*]

Lachesis stepped forward to join his colleague.

[*You, Ralph and Lois, are the only ones who can stop that from happening.*]

3

In his mind's eye Ralph saw the poster of Susan Day which had been propped in the empty storefront between the Rite Aid Pharmacy and Day Break, Sun Down. He remembered the words written in the dust on the outside of the window: KILL THIS CUNT. And something like that might well happen in Derry, that was the thing. Derry was not precisely *like* other places. It seemed to Ralph that the city's atmosphere had improved a great deal since the big flood eight years before, but it was still not precisely like other places. There was a mean streak in Derry, and when its residents got wrought up, they had been known to do some exceedingly ugly things.

He wiped at his lips and was momentarily distracted by the silky, distant feel of his hand on his mouth. He kept being reminded in different ways that his state of being had changed radically.

Lois, horrified: [*'How are we supposed to do it? If we can't go near Atropos or Ed, how are we supposed to stop it from happening?'*]

Ralph realized he could see her face quite clearly now; the day was brightening with the speed of stop-motion photography in an old Disney nature film.

[*'We'll phone in a bomb-threat, Lois. That should work.'*]

Clotho looked dismayed at this; Lachesis actually smacked his forehead with the heel of his hand before glancing nervously at the brightening sky. When he looked back at Ralph, his small face was full of something that might have been carefully muzzled panic.

[*That* won't *work, Ralph. Now listen to me, both of you, and listen carefully: whatever you do in the next fourteen hours or so, you must not underestimate the power of the forces Atropos unleashed when he first discovered Ed and then slashed his life-cord.*]

Ralph: [*'Why won't it work?'*]

Lachesis, sounding both angry and frightened: [*We can't just go on and on answering your questions, Ralph — from*

563

here on you're going to have to take things on trust. You know how fast time passes on this level; if we stay up here much longer, your chance to stop what is going to happen tonight at the Civic Center will be lost. You and Lois must step down again. You must!]

Clotho held up a hand to his colleague, then turned back to Ralph and Lois.

[I'll answer this one last question, although I'm sure that with a little thought you could answer it yourself. There have already been twenty-three bomb-threats regarding Susan Day's speech tonight. The police have explosives-sniffing dogs at the Civic Center, for the last forty-eight hours they have been X-raying all packages and deliveries which have come into the building, and they have been conducting spot searches, as well. They expected bomb-threats, and they take them seriously, but their assumption in this case is that they are being made by pro-life advocates who are trying to keep Ms Day from speaking.]

Lois, dully: ['Oh God – the little boy who cried wolf.']

Clotho: [Correct, Lois.]

Ralph: ['Has he planted a bomb? He has, hasn't he?']

Bright light washed across the roof, stretching the shadows of the twirling heat-ventilators like taffy. Clotho and Lachesis looked at these shadows and then to the east, where the sun's top arc had broken over the horizon, with identical expressions of dismay.

Lachesis: [We don't know, and it doesn't matter. You must stop the speech from happening, and there is only one way to do that: you must convince the women in charge to cancel Susan Day's appearance. Do you understand? She must not appear in the Civic Center tonight! You can't stop Ed, and you daren't try to approach Atropos, so you must stop Susan Day.]

Ralph: [*'But—'*]

It wasn't the strengthening sunlight that shut his mouth, or the growing look of harried fear on the faces of the little bald docs. It was Lois. She put a hand on his cheek and gave a small but decisive shake of the head.

[*'No more. We have to go down, Ralph. Now.'*]

Questions were circling in his mind like mosquitoes, but if she said there was no more time, there was no more time. He glanced at the sun, saw it had entirely cleared the horizon, and nodded. He slipped his arm around her waist.

Clotho, anxiously: [*Do not fail us, Ralph and Lois.*]

Ralph: [*'Save the pep-talk, short stuff. This isn't a football game.'*]

Before either of them could reply, Ralph closed his eyes and concentrated on dropping back down to the Short-Time world.

CHAPTER NINETEEN

1

There was that sensation of *blink!* and a chill morning breeze struck his face. Ralph opened his eyes and looked at the woman beside him. For just a moment he could see her aura wisping away behind her like the gauzy overskirt of a lady's ball-gown and then it was just Lois, looking twenty years younger than she had the week before . . . and also looking extremely out of place, in her light fall coat and good visiting-the-sick dress, here on the tar-and-gravel hospital roof.

Ralph hugged her tighter as she began to shiver. Of Lachesis and Clotho there was no sign.

Although they could be standing right beside us, Ralph thought. *Probably are, as a matter of fact.*

He suddenly thought of that old carny pitchman's line again, the one about how you had to pay if you wanted to play, so step right up, gentlemen, and lay your money down. But more often than not you were played instead of playing. Played for what? A sucker, of course. And why did he have that feeling now?

Because there were a lot of things you never found out,

Carolyn said from inside his head. *They led you down a lot of interesting sidetracks and kept you away from the main point until it was too late for you to ask the questions they might not have wanted to answer . . . and I don't think something like that happens by accident, do you?*

No. He didn't.

That feeling of being pushed by invisible hands into some dark tunnel where anything might be waiting was stronger now. That sense of being manipulated. He felt small . . . and vulnerable . . . and pissed off.

'W Well, we're b-b-back,' Lois said through her briskly chattering teeth. 'What time is it, do you think?'

It felt like about six o'clock, but when Ralph glanced down at his watch, he wasn't surprised to see it had stopped. He couldn't remember when he had last wound it. Tuesday morning, probably.

He followed Lois's gaze to the southwest and saw the Civic Center standing like an island in the middle of a parking-lot ocean. With the early morning sunlight kicking bright sheets of reflection from its curved banks of windows, it looked like an oversized version of the office building George Jetson worked in. The vast deathbag which had surrounded it only moments before was gone.

Oh, no it's not. Don't kid yourself, buddy. You may not be able to see it right now, but it's there, all right.

'Early,' he said, pulling her more tightly against him as the wind gusted, blowing his hair — hair that now had almost as much black in it as white — back from his forehead. 'But it's going to get late fast, I think.'

She took his meaning and nodded. 'Where are L-Lachesis and C-C—'

567

'On a level where the wind doesn't freeze your ass off, I imagine. Come on. Let's find a door and get the hell off this roof.'

She stayed where she was a moment longer, though, shivering and looking across town. 'What has he done?' she asked in a small voice. 'If he hasn't planted a bomb in there, what *can* he have done?'

'Maybe he *has* planted a bomb and the dogs with the educated noses just haven't found it yet. Or maybe it's something the dogs aren't trained to find. A canister stuck up in the rafters, say – a little something nasty Ed whipped up in the bathtub. Chemistry is what he did for a living, after all . . . at least until he gave up his job to become a full-time psycho. He could be planning to gas them like rats.'

'Oh Jesus, Ralph!' She put her hand to her chest just above the swell of her bosom and looked at him with wide, dismayed eyes.

'Come on, Lois. Let's get off this damned roof.'

This time she came willingly enough. Ralph led her toward the roof door . . . which, he fervently hoped, they would find unlocked.

'Two thousand people,' she almost moaned as they reached the door. Ralph was relieved when the knob turned under his hand, but Lois seized his wrist with chilly fingers before he could pull the door open. Her uptilted face was full of frantic hope. 'Maybe those little men were lying, Ralph – maybe they've got their own axe to grind, some-thing we couldn't even *hope* to understand, and they were lying.'

'I don't think they *can* lie,' he said slowly. 'That's the

hell of it, Lois − I don't think they *can*. And then there's that.' He pointed at the Civic Center, at the dirty membrane they couldn't see but which both knew was still there. Lois would not turn to look at it. She put her cold hand over his instead, pulled the roof door open, and started down the stairs.

2

Ralph opened the door at the foot of the stairs, peeped into the sixth-floor corridor, saw that it was empty, and drew Lois out of the stairwell. They headed for the elevators, then stopped together outside an open door with DOCTOR'S LOUNGE printed on the wall beside it in bright red letters. Inside was the room they had seen on their way up to the roof with Clotho and Lachesis − Winslow Homer prints hanging crooked on the walls, a Silex standing on a hotplate, hideous Swedish Modern furniture. No one was in the room right now, but the TV bolted to the wall was playing nevertheless, and their old friend Lisette Benson was reading the morning news. Ralph remembered the day he and Lois and Bill had sat in Lois's living room, eating macaroni and cheese as they watched Lisette Benson report on the doll-throwing incident at WomanCare. Less than a month ago that had been. He suddenly remembered that Bill McGovern would never watch Lisette Benson again, or forget to lock the front door, and a sense of loss as fierce as a November gale swept through him. He could not completely believe it, at least not yet. How could Bill have died so quickly and so unceremoniously? *He would have hated it,* Ralph thought, *and not just because he would have considered dying of a heart attack in a hospital corridor in bad taste. He would've considered it bad theater, as well.*

But he had seen it happen, and Lois had actually felt it eating away at Bill's insides. That made Ralph think of the deathbag surrounding the Civic Center, and what was going to happen there if they didn't stop the speech. He started toward the elevator again, but Lois pulled him back. She was looking at the TV, fascinated.

'– will feel a lot of relief when tonight's speech by feminist abortion-rights advocate Susan Day is history,' Lisette Benson was saying, 'but the police aren't the *only* ones who will feel that way. Apparently both pro-life and pro-choice advocates are beginning to feel the strain of living on the edge of confrontation. John Kirkland is live at the Derry Civic Center this morning, and he has more. John?'

The pallid, unsmiling man standing next to Kirkland was Dan Dalton. The button on his shirt showed a scalpel descending toward an infant with its knees drawn up in the fetal position. This was surrounded by a red circle with a diagonal red line slashed across it. Ralph could see half a dozen police cars and two news trucks, one with the NBC logo on its side, in the background of the shot. A uniformed cop strolled across the lawn leading two dogs – a bloodhound and a German Shepherd – on leashes.

'That's right, Lisette, I'm here at the Civic Center, where the mood could be termed one of worry and quiet determination. With me is Dan Dalton, President of The Friends of Life organization which has been so vehemently opposed to Ms Day's speech. Mr Dalton, would you agree with that assessment of the situation?'

'That there's a lot of worry and determination in the air?' Dalton asked. To Ralph his smile looked both nervous and disdainful. 'Yes, I suppose you could put it that way. We're *worried* that Susan Day, one of this country's greatest unindicted criminals, will succeed in her efforts to confuse the central issue here in Derry: the murder of twelve to fourteen helpless unborn children each and every day.'

'But Mr Dalton—'

'And,' Dalton overrode him, 'we are *determined* to show a watching nation that we are not willing to be good Nazis, that we are not all cowed by the religion of political correctness – the dreaded pee-cee.'

'Mr Dalton—'

'We are also determined to show a watching nation that some of us are still capable of standing up for our beliefs, and to fulfill the sacred responsibility which a loving God has—'

'Mr Dalton, are The Friends of Life planning any sort of violent protest here?'

That shut him up for a moment and at least temporarily drained all the canned vitality from his face. With it gone, Ralph saw a dismaying thing: underneath his bluster, Dalton was scared to death.

'Violence?' he said at last. He brought the word out carefully, like something that could give his mouth a bad cut if mishandled. 'Good Lord, no. The Friends of Life reject the idea that two wrongs can ever make a right. We intend to mount a massive demonstration – we are being joined in this fight by pro-life advocates from Augusta, Portland, Portsmouth, and even Boston – but there will be no violence.'

'What about Ed Deepneau? Can you speak for him?'

Dalton's lips, already thinned down to little more than a seam, now seemed to disappear altogether. 'Mr Deepneau is no longer associated with The Friends of Life,' he said. Ralph thought he detected both fear and anger in Dalton's tone. 'Neither are Frank Felton, Sandra McKay, and Charles Pickering, in case you intended to ask.'

John Kirkland's glance at the camera was brief but telling. It said that he thought Dan Dalton was as nutty as a bag of trail-mix.

'Are you saying that Ed Deepneau and these other individuals – I'm sorry, I don't know who they are – have formed their own anti-abortion group? A kind of offshoot?'

'We are not anti-abortion, we are *pro-life!*' Dalton cried. 'There's a big difference, but you reporters seem to keep missing it!'

'So you don't know Ed Deepneau's whereabouts, or what – if anything – he might be planning?'

'I don't know where he is, I don't *care* where he is, and I don't care about his . . . *offshoots,* either.'

You're afraid, though, Ralph thought. *And if a self-righteous little prick like you is afraid, I think I'm terrified.*

Dalton started off. Kirkland, apparently deciding he wasn't wrung completely dry yet, walked after him, shaking out his microphone cord as he went.

'But isn't it true, Mr Dalton, that while he was a member of The Friends of Life, Ed Deepneau instigated *several* violence-oriented protests, including one last month where dolls soaked with artificial blood were thrown—'

'You're all the same, aren't you?' Dan Dalton asked. 'I'll pray for you, my friend.' He stalked off.

Kirkland looked after him for a moment, bemused,

then turned back to the camera. 'We tried to get hold of Mr Dalton's opposite number – Gretchen Tillbury, who has taken on the formidable job of coordinating this event for WomanCare – but she was unavailable for comment. We've heard that Ms Tillbury is at High Ridge, a women's shelter and halfway house which is owned and operated by WomanCare. Presumably, she and her associates are out there putting the finishing touches on plans for what they hope will be a safe, violence-free rally and speech at the Civic Center tonight.'

Ralph glanced at Lois and said, 'Okay – now we know where we're going, at least.'

The TV picture switched to Lisette Benson, in the studio. 'John, are there any real signs of possible violence at the Civic Center?'

Back to Kirkland, who had returned to his original location in front of the cop cars. He was holding up a small white rectangle with some printing on it in front of his tie. 'Well, the private security police on duty here found hundreds of these file-cards scattered on the Civic Center's front lawn this morning just after first light. One of the guards claims to have seen the vehicle they were dumped from. He says it was a Cadillac from the late sixties, either brown or black. He didn't get the license number, but says there was a sticker on the back bumper reading ABORTION IS MURDER, NOT CHOICE.'

Back to the studio, where Lisette Benson was looking mighty interested. 'What's on those cards, John?'

Back to Kirkland.

'I guess you'd have to say it's sort of a riddle.' He glanced down at the card. '"If you have a gun loaded with only two bullets and you're in a room with Hitler, Stalin, and an abortionist, what do you do?"' Kirkland looked back up into the camera and said, 'The answer printed on the other side, Lisette, is "Shoot the abortionist twice."

'This is John Kirkland, reporting live from the Derry Civic Center.'

3

'I'm starving,' Lois said as Ralph carefully guided the Oldsmobile down the series of parking-garage ramps which would presumably set them free . . . if Ralph didn't miss any of the exit signs, that was. 'And if I'm exaggerating, I'm not doing it by much.'

'Me too,' Ralph said. 'And considering that we haven't eaten since Tuesday, I guess that's to be expected. We'll grab a good sit-down breakfast on the way out to High Ridge.'

'Do we have time?'

'We'll *make* time. After all, an army fights on its stomach.'

'I suppose so, although I don't feel very army-ish. Do you know where—'

'Hush a second, Lois.'

He stopped the Oldsmobile short, put the gearshift lever in Park, and listened. There was a clacking sound from under the hood that he didn't like very much. Of course the concrete walls of places like this tended to magnify sounds, but still . . .

'Ralph?' she asked nervously. 'Don't tell me something's wrong with the car. Just don't tell me that, okay?'

'I think it's fine,' he said, and began creeping toward

daylight again. 'I've just kind of fallen out of touch with old Nellie here since Carol died. Forgotten what kinds of sounds she makes. You were going to ask me something, weren't you?'

'If you know where that shelter is. High Ridge.'

Ralph shook his head. 'Somewhere out near the Newport town line is all I know. I don't think they're supposed to tell men where it is. I was kind of hoping you might have heard.'

Lois shook her head. 'I never had to use a place like that, thank God. We'll have to call her. The Tillbury woman. You've met her with Helen, so you can talk to her. She'll listen to you.'

She gave him a brief glance, one that warmed his heart – *Anyone with any sense would listen to you, Ralph,* it said – but Ralph shook his head. 'I bet the only calls she's taking today are ones that come from the Civic Center or from wherever Susan Day is.' He shot her a glance. 'You know, that woman's got a lot of guts, coming here. Either that or she's donkey-dumb.'

'Probably a little of both. If Gretchen Tillbury won't take a call, how will we get in touch with her?'

'Well, I tell you what. I was a salesman for a lot of what Faye Chapin would call my real life, and I bet I can still be inventive when I need to be.' He thought of the information-lady with the orange aura and grinned. 'Persuasive, too, maybe.'

'Ralph?' Her voice was small.

'What, Lois?'

'This feels like real life to me.'

He patted her hand. 'I know what you mean.'

575

4

A familiar skinny face poked out of the pay-booth of the hospital parking garage; a familiar grin – one from which at least half a dozen teeth had gone AWOL – brightened it.

'Eyyyy, Ralph, dat you? Goddam if it ain't! Beauty! Beauty!'

'Trigger?' Ralph asked slowly. 'Trigger Vachon?'

'None udder!' Trigger flipped his lank brown hair out of his eyes so he could get a better look at Lois. 'And who's dis marigold here? I know her from somewhere, goddam if I don't!'

'Lois Chasse,' Ralph said, taking his parking ticket from its place over the sun-visor. 'You might have known her husband, Paul—'

'Goddam right I did!' Trigger cried. 'We was weekend warriors togedder, back in nineteen-seb'ny, maybe seb'ny-one! Closed down Nan's Tavern more'n once! My suds n body! How is Paul dese days, ma'am?'

'Mr Chasse passed on a little over two years ago,' Lois said.

'Oh, damn! I'm sorry to hear it. He was a champ of a guy, Paul Chasse. Just an all-around champ of a guy. Everybody liked him.' Trigger looked as distressed as he might have done if she had told him it had happened only that morning.

'Thank you, Mr Vachon.' Lois glanced at her watch, then looked up at Ralph. Her stomach rumbled, as if to add one final point to the argument.

Ralph handed his parking ticket through the open window of the car, and as Trigger took it, Ralph suddenly

576

realized the stamp would show that he and Lois had been here since Tuesday night. Almost sixty hours.

'What happened to the dry-cleaning business, Trig?' he asked hastily.

'Ahhh, dey laid me off,' Trigger said. 'Didn't I tell you? Laid almos everybody off. I was downhearted at first, but I caught on here last April, and . . . eyyy! I like dis all kindsa better. I got my little TV for when it's slow, and there ain't nobody beepin their horns at me if I don't go the firs second a traffic-light turns green, or cuttin me off out dere on the Extension. Everyone in a hurry to get to the nex place, dey are, jus why I dunno. Also, I tell you what, Ralph: dat damn van was colder'n a witch's tit in the winter. Pardon me, ma'am.'

Lois did not reply. She seemed to be studying the backs of her hands with great interest. Ralph, meanwhile, watched with relief as Trigger crumpled up the parking ticket and tossed it into his wastebasket without so much as a glance at the time-and-date stamp. He punched one of the buttons on his cash-register, and $0.00 popped up on the screen in the booth's window.

'Jeez, Trig, that's really nice of you,' Ralph said.

'Eyyy, don't mention it,' Trigger said, and grandly punched another button. This one raised the barrier in front of the booth. 'Good to see you. Say, you member dat time out by the airport? Gosh! Hotter'n hell, it was, and dose two fella almos got in a punchup? Den it rained like a bugger. Hailed some, too. You was walkin and I give you a ride home. Oney seen you once or twice since den.' He took a closer look at Ralph. 'You look a hell of a lot better today than you did den, Ralphie, I'll tell you dat. Hell, you don't look a day over fifty-five. Beauty!'

Beside him, Lois's stomach rumbled again, louder this time. She went on studying the backs of her hands.

'I feel a little older than that, though,' Ralph said. 'Listen, Trig, it was good to see you, but we ought to—'

'Damn,' Trigger said, and his eyes had gone distant. 'I had sumpin to tell you, Ralph. At least I *t'ink* I did. Bout dat day. Gosh, ain't I got a dumb old head!'

Ralph waited a moment longer, uncomfortably poised between impatience and curiosity. 'Well, don't feel bad about it, Trig. That was a long time ago.'

'What the *hell* . . . ?' Trigger asked himself. He gazed up at the ceiling of his little booth, as if the answer might be written there.

'Ralph, we ought to go,' Lois said. 'It's not just wanting breakfast, either.'

'Yes. You're right.' He got the Oldsmobile rolling slowly again. 'If you think of it, Trig, give me a call. I'm in the book. It was good to see you.'

Trigger Vachon ignored this completely; he no longer seemed aware of Ralph at all, in fact. 'Was it sumpin we *saw*?' he enquired of the ceiling. 'Or sumpin we *did*? Gosh!'

He was still looking up there and scratching the frizz of hair on the nape of his neck when Ralph turned left and, with a final wave, guided his Oldsmobile down Hospital Drive toward the low brick building which housed WomanCare.

5

Now that the sun was up, there was only a single security guard, and no demonstrators at all. Their absence made

Ralph remember all the jungle epics he'd seen as a young man, especially the part where the native drums would stop and the hero – Jon Hall or Frank Buck – would turn to his head bearer and say he didn't like it, it was too quiet. The guard took a clipboard from under his arm, squinted at Ralph's Olds, and wrote something down – the plate number, Ralph supposed. Then he came ambling toward them along the leaf-strewn walk.

At this hour of the morning, Ralph had his pick of the ten-minute spaces across from the building. He parked, got out, then came around to open Lois's door, as he had been trained.

'How do you want to handle this?' she asked as he took her hand and helped her out.

'We'll probably have to be a little cute, but let's not get carried away. Right?'

'Right.' She ran a nervous, patting hand down the front of her coat as they crossed, then flashed a megawatt smile at the security guard. 'Good morning, officer.'

'Morning.' He glanced at his watch. 'I don't think there's anyone in there just yet but the receptionist and the cleaning woman.'

'The receptionist is who we want to see,' Lois said cheerfully. It was news to Ralph. 'Barbie Richards. Her aunt Simone has a message for her to pass along. Very important. Just say it's Lois Chasse.'

The security guard thought this over, then nodded toward the door. 'That won't be necessary. You go on right ahead, ma'am.'

Lois said, smiling more brilliantly than ever, 'We won't be two shakes, will we, Norton?'

'Shake and a half, more like it,' Ralph agreed. As they approached the building and left the security man behind he leaned toward her and murmured: 'Norton? Good God, Lois, *Norton?*'

'It was the first name that came into my head,' she replied. 'I guess I was thinking of *The Honeymooners* – Ralph and Norton, remember?'

'Yes,' he said. 'One of these days, Alice . . . pow! Right to da moon!'

Two of the three doors were locked, but the one on the far left opened and they went in. Ralph squeezed Lois's hand and felt her answering squeeze. He sensed a strong focusing of his concentration at the same moment, a narrowing and brightening of will and awareness. All around him the eye of the world seemed to first blink and then open wide. All around them both.

The reception area was almost ostentatiously plain. The posters on the walls were mostly the sort foreign tourist agencies send out for the price of postage. The only exception was to the right of the receptionist's desk: a large black-and-white photo of a young woman in a maternity smock. She was sitting on a barstool with a martini glass in one hand. WHEN YOU'RE PREGNANT, YOU NEVER DRINK ALONE, the copy beneath the photo read. There was no indication that in a room or rooms behind this pleasant, unremarkable business space, abortions were done on demand.

Well, Ralph thought, *what did you expect? An advertisement? A poster of aborted fetuses in a galvanized garbage pail between the one showing the Isle of Capri and the one of the Italian Alps? Get real, Ralph.*

To their left, a heavyset woman in her late forties or early fifties was washing the top of a glass coffee-table; there was a little cart filled with various cleaning implements parked beside her. She was buried in a dark blue aura speckled with unhealthy-looking black dots which swarmed like queer insects over the places where her heart and lungs were, and she was looking at the newcomers with undisguised suspicion.

Straight ahead, another woman was watching them carefully, although without the janitor's suspicion. Ralph recognized her from the TV news report on the day of the doll-throwing incident. Simone Castonguay's niece was dark haired, about thirty-five, and close to gorgeous even at this hour of the morning. She sat behind a severe gray metal desk that perfectly complemented her looks and within a forest-green aura which looked much healthier than the cleaning woman's. A cut-glass vase filled with fall flowers stood on one corner of her desk.

She smiled tentatively at them, showing no immediate recognition of Lois, then wiggled the tip of one finger at the clock on the wall. 'We don't open until eight,' she said, 'and I don't think we could help you today in any case. The doctors are all off – I mean, Dr Hamilton is technically covering, but I'm not even sure I could get to her. There's a lot going on – this is a big day for us.'

'I know,' Lois said, and gave Ralph's hand another squeeze before letting it go. He heard her voice in his mind for a moment, very faint – like a bad overseas telephone conversation – but audible:

['*Stay where you are, Ralph. She's got*—']

Lois sent him a picture which was even fainter than

the thought, and gone almost as soon as Ralph glimpsed it. This sort of communication was a lot easier on the upper levels, but what he got was enough. The hand with which Barbara Richards had pointed at the clock was now resting easily on top of the desk, but the other was underneath it, where a small white button was mounted on one side of the kneehole. If either of them showed the slightest sign of odd behavior, she would push the button, summoning first their friend with the clipboard who was posted outside, and then most of the private security cops in Derry.

And I'm the one she's watching most carefully, because I'm the man, Ralph thought.

As Lois approached the reception desk, Ralph had an unsettling thought: given the current atmosphere in Derry, that sort of sex-discrimination — unconscious but very real — could get this pretty black-haired woman hurt . . . maybe even killed. He remembered Leydecker telling him that one of Ed's small cadre of co-crazies was a woman. *Pasty complexion,* he'd said, *lots of acne, glasses so thick they make her eyes look like poached eggs.* Sandra something, her name was. And if Sandra Something had approached Ms Richards's desk as Lois was approaching it now, first opening her purse and then reaching into it, would the woman dressed in the forest-green aura have pushed the hidden alarm button?

'You probably don't remember me, Barbara,' Lois was saying, 'because I haven't seen you much since you were in college, when you were going with the Sparkmeyer boy—'

'Oh my God, Lennie Sparkmeyer, I haven't thought of him in years,' Barbara Richards said, and gave an embarrassed little laugh. 'But I remember you. Lois Delancey. Aunt Simone's poker buddy. Do you guys still play?'

'It's Chasse, not Delancey, and we still do.' Lois sounded delighted that Barbara had remembered her, and Ralph hoped she wouldn't lose track of what they were supposed to be doing here. He needn't have worried. 'Anyway, Simone sent me with a message for Gretchen Tillbury.' She brought a piece of paper out of her purse. 'I wonder if you could give it to her?'

'I doubt very much if I'll even talk to Gretchen on the phone today,' Richards said. 'She's as busy as the rest of us. Busier.'

'I'll bet.' Lois tinkled an amazingly genuine little laugh. 'I guess there's no real hurry about this, though. Gretchen has got a niece who's been granted a full scholarship at the University of New Hampshire. Have you ever noticed how much harder people try to get in touch when it's bad news they have to pass on? Strange, isn't it?'

'I suppose so,' Richards said, reaching for the folded slip of paper. 'Anyway, I'll be happy to put this in Gretchen's—'

Lois seized her wrist, and a flash of gray light – so bright Ralph had to squint his eyes against it to keep from being dazzled – leaped up the woman's arm, shoulder, and neck. It spun around her head in a brief halo, then disappeared.

No, it didn't, Ralph thought. *It didn't disappear, it sank in.*

'What was that?' the cleaning woman asked suspiciously. 'What was that bang?'

'A car backfired,' Ralph said. 'That's all.'

583

'Huh,' she said. 'Goshdarn men think they know everything. Did you hear that, Barbie?'

'Yes,' Richards said. She sounded entirely normal to Ralph, and he knew that the cleaning woman would not be able to see the pearl gray mist which had now filled her eyes. 'I think he's right, but would you check with Peter outside? We can't be too careful.'

'You goshdarn *bet*,' the cleaning woman said. She set her Windex bottle down, crossed to the doors (sparing Ralph a final dark look which said *You're old but I just goshdarn bet you still have a penis down there somewhere*), and went out.

As soon as she was gone, Lois leaned over the desk. 'Barbara, my friend and I have to talk to Gretchen this morning,' she said. 'Face to face.'

'She's not here. She's at High Ridge.'

'Tell us how to get there.'

Richards's gaze drifted to Ralph. He found her gray, pupil-less eye sockets profoundly unsettling. It was like looking at a piece of classic statuary which had somehow come to life. Her dark green aura had paled considerably as well.

No, he thought. *It's been temporarily overlaid by Lois's gray, that's all.*

Lois glanced briefly around, followed Barbara Richards's gaze to Ralph, then turned back to her again. 'Yes, he's a man, but this time it's okay. I promise you that. Neither one of us means any harm to Gretchen Tillbury or any of the women at High Ridge, but we have to talk to her, *so tell us how to get there.*' She touched Richards's hand again, and more gray flashed up Richards's arm.

'Don't hurt her,' Ralph said.

'I won't, but she's going to talk.' She bent closer to Richards. 'Where is it? Come on, Barbara.'

'You take Route 33 out of Derry,' she said. 'The old Newport Road. After you've gone about ten miles, there'll be a big red farmhouse on your left. There are two barns behind it. You take your first left after that—'

The cleaning woman came back in. 'Peter didn't hear –' She stopped abruptly, perhaps not liking the way Lois was bent over her friend's desk, perhaps not liking the blank look in her friend's eyes.

'Barbara? Are you all ri—'

'Be quiet,' Ralph said in a low, friendly voice. 'They're talking.' He took the cleaning woman's arm just above the elbow, feeling a brief but powerful pulse of energy as he did so. For a moment all the colors in the world brightened further. The cleaning woman's name was Rachel Anderson. She'd been married once, to a man who'd beaten her hard and often until he disappeared eight years ago. Now she had a dog and her friends at WomanCare, and that was enough.

'Oh sure,' Rachel Anderson said in a dreamy, thoughtful voice. 'They're talking, and Peter says everything's okay, so I guess I better just be quiet.'

'What a good idea,' Ralph said, still holding her upper arm lightly.

Lois took a quick look around to confirm Ralph had the situation under control, then turned back to Barbara Richards once again. 'Take a left after the red farmhouse with the two barns. Okay, I've got that. What then?'

'You'll be on a dirt road. It goes up a long hill – about

a mile and a half – and then ends at a white farmhouse. That's High Ridge. It's got the most lovely view—'

'I'll bet,' Lois said. 'Barbara, it was great to see you again. Now my friend and I—'

'Great to see you, too, Lois,' Richards said in a distant, uninterested voice.

'Now my friend and I are going to leave. Everything is all right.'

'Good.'

'You won't need to remember any of this,' Lois said.

'Absolutely not.'

Lois started to turn away, then turned back and plucked up the piece of paper she had taken from her purse. It had fallen to the desk when Lois grabbed the woman's wrist.

'Why don't you go back to work, Rachel?' Ralph asked the cleaning lady. He let go of her arm carefully, ready to grab it again at once if she showed signs of needing reinforcement.

'Yes, I better go back to work,' she said, sounding much more friendly. 'I want to be done here by noon, so I can go out to High Ridge and help make signs.'

Lois joined Ralph as Rachel Anderson drifted back to her cart of cleaning supplies. Lois looked both amazed and a little shaky. 'They'll be okay, won't they, Ralph?'

'Yes, I'm sure they will be. Are *you* all right? Not going to faint or anything like that?'

'I'm okay. Can you remember the directions?'

'Of course – she's talking about the place that used to be Barrett's Orchards. Carolyn and I used to go out there every fall to pick apples and buy cider until they sold out in the early eighties. To think *that's* High Ridge.'

'Be amazed later, Ralph – I really *am* starving to death.'

'All right. What was the note, by the way? The note about the niece with the full scholarship at UNH?'

She flashed him a little smile and handed it to him. It was her light-bill for the month of September.

6

'Were you able to leave your message?' the security guard asked as they came out and started down the walk.

'Yes, thanks,' Lois said, turning on the megawatt smile again. She kept moving, though, and her hand was gripping Ralph's very tightly. He knew how she felt; he hadn't the slightest idea how long the suggestions they had given the two women would hold.

'Good,' the guard said, following them to the end of the walk. 'This is gonna be a long, long day. I'll be glad when it's over. You know how many security people we're gonna have here from noon until midnight? A dozen. And that's just *here*. They're gonna have over forty at the Civic Center – that's in addition to the local cops.'

And it won't do a damned bit of good, Ralph thought.

'And what for? So one blonde with an attitude can run her mouth.' He looked at Lois as if he expected her to accuse him of being a male sexist oinker, but Lois only renewed her smile.

'I hope everything goes well for you, officer,' Ralph said, and then led Lois back across the street to the Oldsmobile. He started it up and turned laboriously around in the WomanCare driveway, expecting either Barbara

587

Richards, Rachel Anderson, or maybe both of them to come rushing out through the front door, eyes wild and fingers pointing. He finally got the Olds headed in the right direction and let out a long sigh of relief. Lois looked over at him and nodded in sympathy.

'I thought I was the salesman,' Ralph said, 'but man, I've *never* seen a selling job like that.'

Lois smiled demurely and clasped her hands in her lap.

They were approaching the hospital parking garage when Trigger came rushing out of his little booth, waving his arms. Ralph's first thought was that they weren't going to make a clean getaway after all – the security guard with the clipboard had tipped to something suspicious and phoned or radioed Trigger to stop them. Then he saw the look – out of breath but happy – and what Trigger had in his right hand. It was a very old and very battered black wallet. It flapped open and closed like a toothless mouth with each wave of his right arm.

'Don't worry,' Ralph said, slowing the Olds down. 'I don't know what he wants, but I'm pretty sure it's not trouble. At least not yet.'

'I don't care *what* he wants. All *I* want is to get out of here and eat some food. If he starts to show you his fishing pictures, Ralph, I'll step on the gas pedal myself.'

'Amen,' Ralph said, knowing perfectly well that it wasn't fishing pictures Trigger Vachon had in mind. He still wasn't clear on everything, but one thing he knew for sure: nothing was happening by chance. Not anymore. This was the Purpose with a vengeance. He pulled up beside Trigger and pushed the button that lowered his window. It went down with an ill-tempered whine.

'Eyyy, Ralph!' Trigger cried. 'I t'ought I missed you!'

'What is it, Trig? We're in kind of a hurry—'

'Yeah, yeah, dis won't take but a secon. I got it right here in my wallet, Ralph. Man, I keep all my paperwork in here, and I never lose a t'ing out of it.'

He spread the old billfold's limp jaws, revealing a few crumpled bills, a celluloid accordion of pictures (and damned if Ralph didn't catch a glimpse of Trigger holding up a big bass in one of them), and what looked like at least forty business cards, most of them creased and limber with age. Trigger began to go through these with the speed of a veteran bank-teller counting currency.

'I never t'row dese t'ings out, me,' Trigger said. 'They're great to write stuff on, better'n a notebook, and free. Now just a secon . . . just a secon, oh you damn t'ing, where you be?'

Lois gave Ralph an impatient, worried look and pointed up the road. Ralph ignored both the look and the gesture. He had begun to feel a strange tingling in his chest. In his mind's eye he saw himself reaching out with his index finger and drawing something in the foggy condensate that had appeared on the windshield of Trigger's van as a result of a summer storm fifteen months ago – cold rain on a hot day.

'Ralph, you 'member the scarf Deepneau was wearin dat day? White, wit some kind of red marks on it?'

'Yes, I remember,' Ralph said. *Cuntlicker,* Ed had told the heavyset guy. *Fucked your mother and licked her cunt.* And yes, he remembered the scarf – of course he did. But the red thing hadn't been just marks or a splotch or a meaningless bit of pattern; it had been an ideogram or ideograms.

The sudden sinking in the pit of his stomach told Ralph that Trigger could quit rummaging through his old business cards right now. He knew what this was about. He knew.

'Was you in da war, Ralph?' Trigger asked. 'The big one? Number Two?'

'In a way, I guess,' Ralph said. 'I fought most of it in Texas. I went overseas in early '45, but I was rear-echelon all the way.'

Trigger nodded. 'Dat means Europe,' he said. '*Wasn't* no rear-echelon in the Pacific, not by the end.'

'England,' Ralph said. 'Then Germany.'

Trigger was still nodding, pleased. 'If you'd been in da Pacific, you woulda known the stuff on that scarf wasn't Chinese.'

'It was *Japanese,* wasn't it? Wasn't it, Trig?'

Trigger nodded. In one hand he held a business card plucked from among many. On the blank side, Ralph saw a rough approximation of the double symbol they had seen on Ed's scarf, the double symbol he himself had drawn in the windshield mist.

'What are you talking about?' Lois asked, now sounding not impatient but just plain scared.

'I should have known,' Ralph heard himself say in a faint, horrified voice. 'I still should have *known.*'

'Known *what*?' She grabbed his shoulder and shook it. 'Known *what*?'

He didn't answer. Feeling like a man in a dream, he reached out and took the card. Trigger Vachon was no longer smiling, and his dark eyes studied Ralph's face with grave consideration. 'I copied it before it could melt offa da windshield,' Trigger said, 'cause I knew I seen it before, and by the time I got home dat night, I knew where. My big brother, Marcel, fought dar las year of the war in the Pacific. One of the t'ings he brought back was a scarf with dat same two marks on it, in dat same red. I ast him, jus to be sure, and he wrote it on dat card.' Trigger pointed to the card Ralph was holding between his fingers. 'I meant to tell you as soon as I saw you again, only I forgot until today. I was glad I finally remembered, but lookin at you now, I guess it woulda been better if I'd stayed forgetful.'

'No, it's okay.'

Lois took the card from him. 'What is it? What does it mean?'

'Tell you later.' Ralph reached for the gearshift. His heart felt like a stone in his chest. Lois was looking at the symbols on the blank side of the card, allowing Ralph to see the printed side. R.H. FOSTER, WELLS & DRY-WALLS, it said. Below this, Trigger's big brother had printed a single word in black capital letters.

KAMIKAZE.

PART 3

THE CRIMSON KING

We are old-timers,
each of us holds a locked razor.
Robert Lowell
'Walking in the Blue'

CHAPTER TWENTY

1

There was only one conversational exchange between them as the Oldsmobile rolled up Hospital Drive, and it was a brief one.

'Ralph?'

He glanced over at her, then quickly back at the road. That clacking sound under the hood had begun again, but Lois hadn't mentioned it yet. He hoped she wasn't going to do so now.

'I think I know where he is. Ed, I mean. I was pretty sure, even up on the roof, that I recognized that ramshackle old building they showed us.'

'What is it? And where?'

'It's an airplane garage. A whatdoyoucallit. Hangar.'

'Oh my God,' Ralph said. 'Coastal Air, on the Bar Harbor Road?'

Lois nodded. 'They have charter flights, seaplane rides, things like that. One Saturday when we were out for a drive, Mr Chasse went in and asked a man who worked there how much he'd charge to take us for a sightseeing hop over the islands. The man said forty dollars, which was much more than we could have afforded to spend on something like that, and in the summer I'm sure the man would've stuck to his guns, but it was only April, and Mr Chasse was able to dicker him down to twenty. I thought that was still too much to spend on a ride that didn't even last an hour, but I'm glad we went. It was scary, but it was beautiful.'

'Like the auras,' Ralph said.

'Yes, like . . .' Her voice wavered. Ralph looked over and saw tears trickling down her plump cheeks. '. . . like the auras.'

'Don't cry, Lois.'

She found a Kleenex in her purse and wiped her eyes. 'I can't help it. That Japanese word on the card means kamikaze, doesn't it, Ralph? Divine Wind.' She paused, lips trembling. 'Suicide pilot.'

Ralph nodded. He was gripping the wheel very tightly. 'Yes,' he said. 'That's what it means. Suicide pilot.'

2

Route 33 – known as Newport Avenue in town – passed within four blocks of Harris Avenue, but Ralph had absolutely no intention of breaking their long fast over on the west side. The reason was as simple as it was compelling: he and Lois couldn't afford to be seen by any of their old friends, not looking fifteen or twenty years younger than they had on Monday.

Had any of those old friends reported them missing to the police yet? Ralph knew it was possible, but felt he could reasonably hope that so far they had escaped much notice and concern, at least from his circle; Faye and the rest of the folks who hung out in the picnic area near the Extension would be in too much of a dither over the passing of not just one Old Crock colleague but a pair of them to spend much time wondering about where Ralph Roberts had gotten his skinny old ass off to.

Both Bill and Jimmy could have been waked, funeralled, and buried by now, he thought.

'If we've got time for breakfast, Ralph, find a place as quick as you can — I'm so hungry I could eat a horse with the hide still on!'

They were almost a mile west of the hospital now — far enough away to allow Ralph to feel reasonably safe — and he saw the Derry Diner up ahead. As he signalled and turned into the parking lot, he realized he hadn't been here since Carol had gotten sick . . . a year at least, maybe more.

'Here we are,' he told Lois. 'And we're not just going to eat, we're going to eat all we can. We may not get another chance today.'

She grinned like a schoolkid. 'You've just put your finger on one of my great talents, Ralph.' She wriggled a little on the seat. 'Also, I have to spend a penny.'

Ralph nodded. No food since Tuesday, and no bathroom stops, either. Lois could spend her penny; he intended to pop into the men's room and let go of a couple of dollars.

'Come on,' he said, turning off the motor and silencing that troublesome clacking under the hood. 'First the bathroom, then the foodquake.'

On the way to the door she told him (speaking in a voice Ralph found just a trifle too casual) that she didn't think either Mina or Simone would have reported her missing, at least not yet. When Ralph turned his head to ask her why, he was amazed and amused to see she was blushing rosy-red.

'They both know I've had a crush on you for years.'

'Are you kidding?'

'Of course not,' she said, sounding a bit put out. 'Carolyn knew, too. Some women would have minded, but she understood how harmless it was. How harmless *I* was. She was such a dear, Ralph.'

'Yes. She was.'

'Anyway, they'll probably assume that we've . . . you know . . .'

'Gone off on a little French leave?'

Lois laughed. 'Something like that.'

'Would you *like* to go off on a little French leave, Lois?'

She stood on tiptoe and nibbled briefly at his earlobe. 'If we get out of this alive, you just ask me.'

He kissed the corner of her mouth before pushing open the door. 'You can count on it, lady.'

They made for the bathrooms, and when Ralph rejoined her, Lois looked both thoughtful and a little shaken. 'I can't believe it's me,' she said in a low voice. 'I mean, I must have spent at least two minutes staring at myself in the mirror, and I still can't believe it. The crow's-feet around my eyes are all gone, and Ralph . . . my *hair* . . .' Those dark Spanish eyes of hers looked up at him, filled with brilliance and wonder. 'And *you*! My God, I doubt if you looked this good when you were forty.'

'I didn't, but you should have seen me when I was thirty. I was an *animal*.'

She giggled. 'Come on, fool, let's sit down and murder some calories.'

3

'Lois?'

She glanced up from the menu she'd plucked from a little collection of them filed between the salt and pepper shakers.

'When I was in the bathroom, I tried to make the auras come back. This time I couldn't do it.'

'Why would you *want* to, Ralph?'

He shrugged, not wanting to tell her about the feeling of paranoia that had dropped over him as he stood at the basin in the little bathroom, washing his hands and looking into his own strangely young face in the water-spotted mirror. It had suddenly occurred to him that he might not be alone in there. Worse, Lois might not be alone next door in the women's room. Atropos might be creeping up behind her, completely unseen, diamond-cluster earrings glittering from his tiny lobes . . . scalpel outstretched . . .

Then, instead of Lois's earrings or McGovern's Panama, his mind's eye had conjured the jump-rope Atropos had been using when Ralph had spotted him

(*three-six-nine, hon, the goose drank wine*)

in the vacant lot between the bakery and the tanning salon, the jump-rope which had once been the prized possession of a little girl who had stumbled during a game of apartment-tag, fallen out of a second-storey window, and died of a broken neck (*what a dreadful accident, she had her whole life ahead of her, if there's a God why does He let things like that happen,* and so on and so on, not to mention blah–blah–blah).

He had told himself to stop it, that things were bad enough without his indulging in gruesome fantasies of Atropos slashing Lois's balloon-string, but it didn't help much . . . mostly because he knew Atropos might really be here with them in the restaurant, and Atropos could do anything to them he liked. Anything at all.

Lois reached across the table and touched the back of his hand. 'Don't worry. The colors will come back. They always do.'

'I suppose.' He took a menu of his own, opened it, and cast an eye down the breakfast bill of fare. His initial impression was that he wanted one of everything.

'The first time you saw Ed acting crazy, he was coming out of the Derry Airport,' Lois said. 'Now we know why. He was taking flying lessons, wasn't he?'

'Of course. While Trig was giving me a lift back to Harris Avenue, he even mentioned that you need a pass to come out that way, through the service gate. He asked me if I knew how Ed had gotten one, and I said I didn't. Now I do. They must give them to all the General Aviation flying students.'

'Do you think Helen knew about his hobby?' Lois asked. 'She probably didn't, did she?'

'I'm sure she didn't. I'll bet he switched over to Coastal Air right after he ran into the guy from West Side Gardeners, too. That little episode could have convinced him he was losing control, and he might do well to move his lessons a little farther away from home.'

'Or maybe it was Atropos who convinced him,' Lois said bleakly. 'Atropos or someone from even higher up.'

Ralph didn't care for the idea, but it felt right, just the same. *Entities,* he thought, and shivered. *The Crimson King.*

'They're dancing him around like a puppet on a string, aren't they?' Lois asked.

'Atropos, you mean?'

'No. Atropos is a nasty little bugger, but otherwise I think he's not much different from Mr C and Mr L – low-level help, maybe only a step above unskilled labor in the grand scheme of things.'

'Janitors.'

'Well, yes, maybe,' Lois agreed. 'Janitors and gofers. Atropos is probably the one who's done most of the actual work on Ed, and I'd bet a cookie it's work he loves, but I'd bet my *house* that his orders come from higher up. Does that sound more or less on the beam to you?'

'Yes. We'll probably never know exactly how nuts he was before this started, or exactly when Atropos cut his balloon-string, but the thing I'm most curious about at this moment is pretty mundane. I'd like to know how in the hell he went Charlie Pickering's bail and how he paid for his damned flying lessons.'

Before Lois could reply, a waitress approached them, digging an order-pad and a ballpoint pen out of the pocket of her apron. 'Help you guys?'

'I'd like a cheese and mushroom omelet,' Ralph said.

'Uh-huh.' She switched her cud from one side of her jaw to the other. 'Two-egg or three-egg, hon?'

'Four, if that's okay.'

601

She raised her eyebrows slightly and jotted on the pad. 'Okay by me if it's okay by you. Anything with that?'

'Yes, please. A glass of OJ, large, an order of bacon, an order of sausage, and an order of home fries. Better make that a *double* order of home fries.' He paused, thinking, then grinned. 'Oh, and do you have any Danish left?'

'I think I might have one cheese and one apple.' She glanced up at him. 'You a little hungry, hon?'

'Feel like I haven't eaten for a week,' Ralph said. 'I'll have the cheese Danish. And coffee to start. Lots of black coffee. Did you get all that?'

'Oh, I got it, hon. I just want to see what you look like when you leave.' She looked at Lois. 'How 'bout you, ma'am?'

Lois smiled sweetly. 'I'll have what he's having. *Hon.*'

4

Ralph looked past the retreating waitress to the clock on the wall. It was only ten past seven, and that was good. They could be out at Barrett's Orchards in less than half an hour, and with their mental lasers trained on Gretchen Tillbury, it was possible that the Susan Day speech could be called off – aborted, if you liked – as early as 9:00 a.m. Yet instead of relief he felt relentless, gnawing anxiety. It was like having an itch in a place your fingers cannot quite reach.

'All right,' he said. 'Let's put it together. I think we can assume that Ed's been concerned about abortion for a long time, that he's probably been a pro-life supporter for years. Then he starts to lose sleep . . . hear voices . . .'

'. . . see little bald men . . .'

'Well, one in particular,' Ralph agreed. 'Atropos becomes his guru, filling him in on the Crimson King, the Centurions, the whole nine yards. When Ed talked to me about King Herod—'

'—he was *thinking* about Susan Day,' Lois finished. 'Atropos has been . . . what do they say on TV? . . . psyching him up. Turning him into a guided missile. Where did Ed get that scarf, do you think?'

'Atropos,' Ralph said. 'Atropos has got a lot of stuff like that, I'll bet.'

'And what do you suppose he's got in the plane he'll be flying tonight?' Lois's voice was trembling. 'Explosives or poison gas?'

'Explosives would seem the more likely bet if he really is planning to get everyone; a strong wind could create problems for him if it's gas.' Ralph took a sip of his water and was interested to see that his hand was not quite steady. 'On the other hand, we don't know what goodies he might have been cooking up in his laboratory, do we?'

'No,' Lois said in a small voice.

Ralph put his water-glass down. 'What he's planning to use doesn't interest me very much.'

'What does?'

The waitress came back with fresh coffee, and the smell alone seemed to light up Ralph's nerves like neon. He and Lois grabbed their cups and began to sip as soon as she had started away. The coffee was strong and hot enough to burn Ralph's lips, but it was heaven. When he set his cup back in its saucer again, it was half empty and there was a very warm place in his midsection, as if he had swallowed a live ember. Lois was looking at him somberly over the rim of her own cup.

'What interests me,' Ralph told her, 'is *us*. You said Atropos has turned Ed into a guided missile. That's right; that's exactly what the World War II kamikaze pilots were. Hitler had his V–2s; Hirohito had his Divine Wind. The disturbing thing is that *Clotho and Lachesis have done the same thing to us.* We've been loaded up with a lot of special powers and programmed to fly out to High Ridge in my Oldsmobile and stop Susan Day. I'd just like to know why.'

'But we *do* know,' she protested. 'If we don't step in, Ed Deepneau is going to commit suicide tonight during that woman's speech and take two thousand people with him.'

'Yeah,' Ralph said, 'and we're going to do whatever we can to stop him, Lois, don't worry about that.' He finished his coffee and set the cup down again. His stomach was fully awake now, and raving for food. 'I could no more stand aside and let Ed kill all those people than I could stand in one place and not duck if someone threw a base-ball at my head. It's just that we never got a chance to read the fine print at the bottom of the contract, and that scares me.' He hesitated a moment. 'It also pisses me off.'

'What are you talking about?'

'About being played for a couple of patsies. We know why we're going to try and stop Susan Day's speech; we can't stand the thought of a lunatic killing a couple of thousand innocent people. *But we don't know why they want us to do it.* That's the part that scares me.'

'We have a chance to save two thousand lives,' she said. 'Are you telling me that's enough for us but not for them?'

'That's what I'm telling you. I don't think numbers impress these fellows very much; they clean us up not just by the tens or hundreds of thousands but by the millions. And they're used to seeing the Random or the Purpose swat us in job lots.'

'Disasters like the fire at the Cocoanut Grove,' Lois said. 'Or the flood here in Derry eight years ago.'

'Yes, but even things like that are pretty small beans compared to what can and does go on in the world every year. The Flood of '85 here in Derry killed two hundred and twenty people, something like that, but last spring there was a flood in Pakistan that killed thirty-five hundred, and the last big earthquake in Turkey killed over four thousand. And how about that nuclear reactor accident in Russia? I read someplace that you can put the floor on that one at seventy thousand dead. That's a lot of Panama hats and jump-ropes and pairs of . . . of eyeglasses, Lois.' He was horrified at how close he had come to saying *pairs of earrings*.

'Don't,' she said, and shuddered.

'I don't like thinking about it any more than you do,' he said, 'but we *have* to, if only because those two guys were so goddam anxious to keep us from doing just that. Do you see what I'm getting at yet? You must. Big tragedies have always been a part of the Random; why is this so different?'

'I don't know,' Lois said, 'but it was important enough for them to draft us, and I have an idea that was a pretty big step.'

Ralph nodded. He could feel the caffeine hitting him now, jiving up his head, jittering his fingers the tiniest bit. 'I'm sure it was. Now think back to the hospital roof. Did

605

you ever in your entire life hear two guys explain so much without explaining anything?'

'I don't get what you mean,' Lois said, but her face suggested something else: that she didn't *want* to get what he meant.

'What I mean goes back to one central idea: *maybe they can't lie.* Suppose they can't. If you have certain information you don't want to give out but you can't tell a lie, what do you do?'

'Keep dancing away from the danger zone,' Lois said. 'Or zones.'

'Bingo. And isn't that what they did?'

'Well,' she said, 'I guess it was a dance, all right, but I thought you did a fair amount of leading, Ralph. In fact, I was impressed by all the questions you asked. I think I spent most of the time we were on that roof just trying to convince myself it was all really happening.'

'Sure, I asked questions, lots of them, but . . .' He stopped, not sure how to express the concept in his head, a concept which seemed simultaneously complex and baby-simple to him. He made another effort to go up a little, searching inside his head for that sensation of *blink,* knowing that if he could reach her mind, he could show her a picture that would be crystal clear. Nothing happened, and he drummed his fingers on the tablecloth in frustration.

'I was just as amazed as you were,' he said finally. 'If my amazement came out as questions, it's because men — those from my generation, anyway — are taught that it's very bad form to ooh and aah. That's for women who are picking out the drapes.'

'Sexist.' She smiled as she said it, but it was a smile

Ralph couldn't return. He was remembering Barbie Richards. If Ralph had moved toward her, she would almost certainly have pushed the alarm button beneath her desk, but she had allowed Lois to approach because she had swallowed a little too much of the old sister-sister-sister crap.

'Yes,' he said quietly, 'I'm sexist, I'm old-fashioned, and sometimes it gets me in trouble.'

'Ralph, I didn't mean—'

'I know what you meant, and it's okay. What I'm trying to get across to you is that I was as amazed . . . as knocked out . . . as you were. So I asked questions, so what? Were they good questions? *Useful* questions?'

'I guess not, huh?'

'Well, maybe I didn't start out so badly. As I remember, the first thing I asked when we finally made it to the roof was who they were and what they wanted. They slipped those questions with a lot of philosophical blather, but I imagine they got a little sweaty on the backs of their necks for awhile, just the same. Next we got all that background on the Purpose and the Random – fascinating, but nothing we exactly needed in order to drive out to High Ridge and persuade Gretchen Tillbury to cancel Susan Day's speech. Hell, we would have done better – saved time – getting the road directions from them that we ended up getting from Simone's niece.'

Lois looked startled. 'That's true, isn't it?'

'Yeah. And all the time we were talking, time was flying by the way it does when you go up a couple of levels. They were *watching* it fly, too, you can believe that. They were timing the whole scene so that when they finished telling us the things we *did* need to know, there would be no time left to ask the questions they didn't want to answer. I think they wanted to leave us with the idea that this whole thing was a public service, that saving all those lives is what it's all about, but they couldn't come right out and say so, because—'

'Because that would be a lie, and maybe they can't lie.'

'Right. Maybe they can't lie.'

'So what *do* they want, Ralph?'

He shook his head. 'I don't have a clue, Lois. Not even a hint.'

She finished her own coffee, set the cup carefully back down in its saucer, studied her fingertips for a moment, then looked up at him. Again he was forcibly struck by her beauty — almost levelled by it.

'They were good,' she said. 'They *are* good. I felt that very strongly. Didn't you?'

'Yes,' he said, almost reluctantly. Of course he had felt it. They were everything Atropos was not.

'And you're going to try to stop Ed regardless – you said you could no more *not* try than you could not try to duck a baseball someone chucked at your head. Isn't that so?'

'Yes,' he said, more reluctantly still.

'Then you should let the rest of it go,' she said calmly, meeting his blue eyes with her dark ones. 'It's just taking up space inside your head, Ralph. Making clutter.'

He saw the truth of what she said, but still doubted if he could simply open his hand and let that part of it fly free. Maybe you had to live to be seventy before you could fully appreciate how hard it was to escape your upbringing.

He was a man whose education on how to *be* a man had begun before Adolf Hitler's rise to power, and he was still a prisoner of a generation that had listened to H.V. Kaltenborn and the Andrews Sisters on the radio – a generation of men that believed in moonlight cocktails and walking a mile for a Camel. Such an upbringing almost negated such nice moral questions as who was working for the good and who was working for the bad; the important thing was not to let the bullies kick sand in your face. Not to be led by the nose.

Is that so? Carolyn asked, coolly amused. *How fascinating. But let me be the first to let you in on a little secret, Ralph: that's crap. It was crap back before Glenn Miller disappeared over the horizon and it's crap now. The idea that a man's got to do what a man's got to do, now . . . there might be a little truth to that, even in this day and age. It's a long walk back to Eden in any case, isn't it, sweetheart?*

Yes. A very long walk back to Eden.

'What are you smiling about, Ralph?'

He was saved the need to reply by the arrival of the waitress and a huge tray of food. He noticed for the first time that there was a button pinned to the frill of her apron. LIFE IS NOT A CHOICE, it read.

'Are you going to the rally at the Civic Center tonight?' Ralph asked her.

'I'll be there,' she said, setting her tray down on the unoccupied table next to theirs in order to free her hands. 'Outside. Carrying a sign. Walking roundy-round.'

'Are you a Friend of Life?' Lois asked as the waitress began to deal out omelets and side-dishes.

'Am I livin?' the waitress asked.

'Yes, you certainly appear to be,' Lois said politely.

'Well, I guess that makes me a Friend of Life, doesn't it? Killing something that could someday write a great poem or invent a drug that cures AIDS or cancer, in my book that's just flat wrong. So I'll wave my sign around and make sure the Norma Kamali feminists and Volvo liberals can see that the word on it is MURDER. They hate that word. They don't use it at their cocktail parties and fundraisers. You folks need ketchup?'

'No,' Ralph said. He could not take his eyes off her. A faint green glow had begun to spread around her – it almost seemed to come wisping up from her pores. The auras were coming back, cycling up to full brilliance.

''D I grow a second head or somethin while I wasn't lookin?' the waitress asked. She popped her gum and switched it to the other side of her mouth.

'I was staring, wasn't I?' Ralph asked. He felt blood heating his cheeks. 'Sorry.'

The waitress shrugged her beefy shoulders, setting the upper part of her aura into lazy, fascinating motion. 'I try not to get carried away with this stuff, you know? Most days I just do my job and keep my mouth shut. But I ain't no quitter, either. Do you know how long I've been marchin around in front of that brick slaughterin pen, on days hot enough to fry my butt and nights cold enough to freeze it off?'

Ralph and Lois shook their heads.

'Since 1984. Nine long years. You know what gets me the most about the choicers?'

'What?' Lois asked quietly.

'They're the same people who want to see guns

610

outlawed so people won't shoot each other with them, the same ones who say the electric chair and the gas chamber are unconstitutional because they're cruel and unusual punishment. They say those things, then go out and support laws that allow doctors – *doctors!* – to stick vacuum tubes into women's wombs and pull their unborn sons and daughters to pieces. *That's* what gets me the most.'

The waitress said all this – it had the feel of a speech she had made many times before – without raising her voice or displaying the slightest outward sign of anger. Ralph only listened with half an ear; most of his attention was fixed on the pale green aura which surrounded her. Except it wasn't *all* pale green. A yellowish-black blotch revolved slowly over her lower right side like a dirty wagon wheel.

Her liver, Ralph thought. *Something wrong with her liver.*

'You wouldn't *really* want anything to happen to Susan Day, would you?' Lois asked, looking at the waitress with troubled eyes. 'You seem like a very nice person, and I'm sure you wouldn't want that.'

The waitress sighed through her nose, producing two jets of fine green mist. 'I ain't as nice as I look, hon. If *God* did something to her, I'd be the first wavin my hands around in the air and sayin "Thy will be done," believe me. But if you're talking about some nut, I guess that's different. Things like that drag us all down, put us on the same level as the people we're trying to stop. The nuts don't see it that way, though. They're the jokers in the deck.'

'Yes,' Ralph said. 'Jokers in the deck is just what they are.'

'I guess I really don't want anything bad to happen

to that woman,' the waitress said, 'but something could. It really could. And the way I look at it, if something *does,* she's got no one to blame but herself. She's running with the wolves . . . and women who run with wolves shouldn't go acting too surprised if they get bitten.'

5

Ralph wasn't sure how much he would want to eat after that, but his appetite turned out to have survived the waitress's views on abortion and Susan Day quite nicely. The auras helped; food had never tasted this good to him, not even as a teenager, when he'd eaten five and even six meals a day, if he could get them.

Lois matched him bite for bite, at least for awhile. At last she pushed the remains of her home fries and her last two strips of bacon aside. Ralph plugged gamely on down the home stretch alone. He wrapped the last bite of toast around the last bit of sausage, pushed it into his mouth, swallowed, and sat back in his chair with a vast sigh.

'Your aura has gone two shades darker, Ralph. I don't know if that means you finally got enough to eat or that you're going to die of indigestion.'

'Could be both,' he said. 'You see them again too, huh?'

She nodded.

'You know something?' he asked. 'Of all the things in the world, the one I'd like most right now is a nap.' Yes indeed. Now that he was warm and fed, the last four months of largely sleepless nights seemed to have fallen on him like a bag filled with sashweights. His eyelids felt as if they had been dipped in cement.

'I think that would be a bad idea right now,' Lois said, sounding alarmed. 'A *very* bad idea.'

'I suppose so,' Ralph agreed.

Lois started to raise her hand for the check, then lowered it again. 'What about calling your policeman friend? Leydecker, isn't that his name? Could he help us? Would he?'

Ralph considered this as carefully as his muzzy head would allow, then reluctantly shook his head. 'I don't quite dare try it. What could we tell him that wouldn't get us committed? And that's only part of the problem. If he *did* get involved . . . but in the wrong way . . . he might make things worse instead of better.'

'Okay.' Lois waved to the waitress. 'We're going to ride out there with all the windows open, and we're going to stop at the Dunkin' Donuts out in the Old Cape for giant economy-sized coffees. My treat.'

Ralph smiled. It felt large and dopey and discon-nected on his face – almost a drunken smile. 'Yes, ma'am.'

When the waitress came over and slid their check face-down in front of him, Ralph noticed that the button reading LIFE IS NOT A CHOICE was no longer pinned to the frill of her apron.

'Listen,' she said with an earnestness Ralph found almost painfully touching, 'I'm sorry if I offended you folks. You came in for breakfast, not a lecture.'

'You didn't offend us,' Ralph said. He glanced across the table at Lois, who nodded agreement.

The waitress smiled briefly. 'Thanks for saying so,

but I still kinda zoomed on you. Any other day I wouldn'ta, but we're having our own rally this afternoon at four, and I'm introducing Mr Dalton. They told me I could have three minutes, and I guess that's about what I gave you.'

'That's all right,' Lois said, and patted her hand. 'Really.'

The waitress's smile was warmer and more genuine this time, but as she started to turn away, Ralph saw Lois's pleasant expression falter. She was looking at the yellow-black blob floating just above the waitress's right hip.

Ralph pulled out the pen he kept clipped to his breast pocket, turned over his paper placemat, and printed quickly on the back. When he was done, he took out his wallet and placed a five-dollar bill carefully below what he had written. When the waitress reached for the tip, she would hardly be able to avoid seeing the message.

He picked up the check and flapped it at Lois. 'Our first real date and I guess it'll have to be dutch,' he said. 'I'm three bucks short if I leave her the five. Please tell me you're not broke.'

'Who, the poker queen of Ludlow Grange? Don't be seely, dollink.' She handed him a helter-skelter fistful of bills from her purse. While he sorted through them for what he needed, she read what he had written on the placemat:

Madam:
> *You are suffering from reduced liver function and should see your doctor immediately. And I strongly advise you to stay away from the Civic Center tonight.*

'Pretty stupid, I know,' Ralph said.

She kissed the tip of his nose. 'Trying to help other people is never stupid.'

'Thanks. She won't believe it, though. She'll think we were pissed off about her button and her little speech in spite of what we said. That what I wrote is just our weird way of trying to get our own back on her.'

'Maybe there's a way to convince her otherwise.'

Lois fixed the waitress – who was standing hipshot by the kitchen pass-through and talking to the short-order cook while she drank a cup of coffee – with a look of dark concentration. As she did, Ralph saw Lois's normal blue-gray aura deepen in color and draw inward, becoming a kind of body-hugging capsule.

He wasn't exactly sure what was going on . . . but he could feel it. The hairs on the back of his neck stood at attention; his forearms broke out in gooseflesh. *She's powering up,* he thought, *flipping all the switches, turning on all the turbines, and doing it on behalf of a woman she never saw before and will probably never see again.*

After a moment the waitress felt it, too. She turned to look at them as if she had heard her name called. Lois smiled casually and twiddled her fingers in a small wave, but when she spoke to Ralph, her voice was trembling with effort. 'I've almost . . . almost got it.'

'Almost got *what?*'

'I don't know. Whatever it is I need. It'll come in a second. Her name is Zoë, with two dots over the e. Go pay the check. Distract her. Try to keep her from looking at me. It makes it harder.'

615

He did as she asked and was fairly successful in spite of the way Zoë kept trying to look over his shoulder at Lois. The first time she attempted to ring the check into the register, Zoë came up with a total of $234.20. She cleared the numbers with an impatient poke of her finger, and when she looked up at Ralph, her face was pale and her eyes were upset.

'What's with your wife?' she asked Ralph. 'I apologized, didn't I? So why does she keep looking at me like that?'

Ralph knew Zoë couldn't see Lois, because he was all but tap-dancing in an effort to keep his body between the two of them, but he also knew she was right – Lois *was* staring.

He attempted to smile. 'I don't know what—'

The waitress jumped and shot a startled, irritated glance back at the short-order cook. '*Quit banging those pots around!*' she shouted, although the only thing Ralph had heard from the kitchen was a radio playing elevator-music. Zoë looked back at Ralph. 'Christ, it sounds like Vietnam back there. Now if you could just tell your wife it's not polite to—'

'To stare? She's not. She's really not.' Ralph stood aside. Lois had gone to the door and was looking out at the street with her back to them. 'See?'

Zoë didn't reply for several seconds, although she kept looking at Lois. At last she turned back to Ralph. 'Sure. I see. Now why don't you and her just make yourselves scarce?'

'All right – still friends?'

'Whatever you want,' Zoë said, but she wouldn't look at him.

When Ralph rejoined Lois, he saw that her aura had gone back to its former, more diffuse state, but it was much brighter than it had been.

'Still tired, Lois?' he asked her softly.

'No. As a matter of fact, I feel fine now. Let's go.'

He started to open the door for her, then stopped. 'Got my pen?'

'Gee, no – I guess it's still on the table.'

Ralph went over to pick it up. Below his note, Lois had added a PS in rolling Palmer-method script:

In 1989 you had a baby and gave him up for adoption. Saint Anne's, in Providence, RI. Go and see your doctor before it's too late, Zoë. No joke. No trick. We know what we're talking about.

'Oh boy,' Ralph said as he rejoined her. 'That's going to scare the bejesus out of her.'

'If she gets to her doctor before her liver goes belly-up, I don't care.'

He nodded and they went out.

6

'Did you get that stuff about her kid when you dipped into her aura?' Ralph asked as they crossed the leaf-strewn parking lot.

Lois nodded. Beyond the lot, the entire east side of Derry was shimmering with bright, kaleidoscopic light. It was coming back hard now, very hard, that secret light cycling up and up. Ralph reached out and put his hand

617

on the side of his car. Touching it was like tasting a slick, licorice-flavored cough-drop.

'I don't think I took very much of her . . . her stuff,' Lois said, 'but it was as if I swallowed *all* of her.'

Ralph remembered something he'd read in a science magazine not long ago. 'If every cell in our bodies contains a complete blueprint of how we're made,' he said, 'why shouldn't every bit of a person's aura contain a complete blueprint of what we *are*?'

'That doesn't sound very scientific, Ralph.'

'I suppose not.'

She squeezed his arm and grinned up at him. 'It *does* sound about right, though.'

He grinned back at her.

'You need to take some more, too,' she told him. 'It still feels wrong to me – like stealing – but if you don't, I think you're going to pass right out on your feet.'

'As soon as I can. Right now all I want to do is get out to High Ridge.' Yet once he got behind the wheel, his hand faltered away from the ignition key almost as soon as he touched it.

'Ralph? What is it?'

'Nothing . . . everything. I can't drive like this. I'll wrap us around a telephone pole or drive us into somebody's living room.'

He looked up at the sky and saw one of those huge birds, this one transparent, roosting atop a satellite dish on the roof of an apartment house across the way. A thin, lemon-colored haze drifted up from its folded prehistoric wings.

Are *you seeing it?* a part of his mind asked doubtfully. *Are you sure of that, Ralph? Are you really, really sure?*

I'm seeing it, all right. Fortunately or unfortunately, I'm seeing it all . . . but if there was ever a right time to see such things, this isn't it.

He concentrated, and felt that interior blink happen deep within his mind. The bird faded away like a ghost-image on a TV screen. The warmly glowing palette of colors spread out across the morning lost their vibrancy. He went on perceiving that other part of the world long enough to see the colors run into one another, creating the bright gray-blue haze which he'd begun seeing on the day he'd gone into Day Break, Sun Down for coffee and pie with Joe Wyzer – and then that was gone, too. Ralph felt an almost crushing need to curl up, pillow his head on his arm, and go to sleep. He began taking long, slow breaths instead, pulling each one a little deeper into his lungs, and then turned the ignition key. The engine roared into life, accompanied by that clacking sound. It was much louder now.

'What's that?' Lois asked.

'I don't know,' Ralph said, but he thought he did – either a tie-rod or a piston. In either case they would be in trouble if it let go. At last the sound began to diminish, and Ralph dropped the transmission into Drive. 'Just poke me hard if you see me starting to nod off, Lois.'

'You can count on it,' she said. 'Now let's go.'

CHAPTER TWENTY-ONE

1

The Dunkin' Donuts on Newport Avenue was a jolly pink sugarchurch in a drab neighborhood of tract houses. Most had been built in a single year, 1946, and were now crumbling. This was Derry's Old Cape, where elderly cars with wired-up mufflers and cracked windshields wore bumper stickers saying things like DON'T BLAME ME I VOTED FOR PEROT and ALL THE WAY WITH THE NRA, where no house was complete without at least one Fisher-Price Big Wheel trike standing on the listless lawn, where girls were stepping dynamite at sixteen and all too often dull-eyed, fat-bottomed mothers of three at twenty-four.

Two boys on fluorescent bikes with extravagant ape-hanger handlebars were doing wheelies in the parking lot, weaving in and out of each other's paths with a dexterity that suggested a solid background in video gaming and possible high-paying futures as air-traffic controllers . . . if they managed to stay away from coke and car accidents, that was. Both wore their hats backward. Ralph wondered briefly why they weren't in school on a Friday morning, or at least on the way, and decided he didn't care. Probably they didn't, either.

Suddenly the two bikes, which had been avoiding each other easily up until then, crashed together. Both boys fell to the pavement, then got to their feet almost immediately. Ralph was relieved to see neither was hurt; their auras did not even flicker.

'Goddam wet end!' the one in the Nirvana tee-shirt yelled indignantly at his friend. He was perhaps eleven. 'What the hell's the matter with you? You ride a bike like old people fuck!'

'I heard something,' the other said, resetting his hat carefully on his dirty-blond hair. 'Great big bang. You tellin me you didn't hear it? Boo-ya!'

'I didn't hear jack shit,' Nirvana Boy said. He held out his palms, which were now dirty (or perhaps just dirtier) and oozing blood from two or three minor scratches. 'Look at this — fuckin road-rash!'

'You'll live,' his friend said.

'Yeah, but —' Nirvana Boy noticed Ralph, leaning against his rusty whale of an Oldsmobile with his hands in his pockets, watching them. 'The fuck you lookin at?'

'You and your friend,' Ralph said. 'That's all.'

'That's all, huh?'

'Yep — the whole story.'

Nirvana Boy glanced at his friend, then back at Ralph. His eyes glowered with a purity of suspicion which, in Ralph's experience, could be found only here in the Old Cape. 'You got a problem?'

'Not me,' Ralph said. He had inhaled a great deal of Nirvana Boy's russet-colored aura and now felt quite a bit

621

like Superman on a speed trip. He also felt like a child-molester. 'I was just thinking that we didn't talk much like you and your friend when I was a kid.'

Nirvana Boy regarded him insolently. 'Yeah? What'd you talk like?'

'I can't quite remember,' Ralph said, 'but I don't think we sounded quite so much like shitheads.' He turned away from them as the screen door slammed. Lois came out of the Dunkin' Donuts with a large container of coffee in each hand. The boys, meanwhile, jumped on their fluorescent bikes and streaked off, Nirvana Boy giving Ralph one final distrustful look over his shoulder.

'Can you drink this and drive the car at the same time?' Lois asked, handing him a coffee.

'I think so,' Ralph said, 'but I don't really need it anymore. I'm fine, Lois.'

She glanced after the two boys, then nodded. 'Let's go.'

2

The world blazed all around them as they drove out Route 33 toward what had once been Barrett's Orchards, and they didn't have to slide even a single inch up the ladder of perception to see it. The city fell away and they drove through second-growth woods on fire with autumn. The sky was a blue lane above the road, and the Oldsmobile's shadow raced beside them, wavering across leaves and branches.

'God, it's so beautiful,' Lois said. 'Isn't it beautiful, Ralph?'

'Yes. It is.'

'You know what I wish? More than anything?'

He shook his head.

'That we could just pull over to the side of the road – stop the car and get out and walk into the woods a little way. Find a clearing, sit in the sun, and look up at the clouds. You'd say, "Look at that one, Lois, it looks like a horse." And I'd say, "Look over there, Ralph, it's a man with a broom." Wouldn't that be nice?'

'Yes,' Ralph said. The woods opened in a narrow aisle on their left; power-poles marched down the steep slope like soldiers. High-tension lines shone silver between them in the morning sunlight, gossamer as spiderwebs The feet of the poles were buried in brazen drifts of red sumac, and when Ralph looked up above the slash he saw a hawk riding an air-current as invisible as the world of auras. 'Yes,' he said again. 'That would be nice. Maybe we'll even get a chance to do it sometime. But . . .'

'But what?'

'"Each thing I do I rush through so I can do something else,"' Ralph said.

She looked at him, a little startled. 'What a terrible idea!'

'Yeah. I think most true ideas *are* terrible. It's from a book of poems called *Cemetery Nights*. Dorrance Marstellar gave it to me on the same day he slipped upstairs to my apartment and put the spray-can of Bodyguard into my jacket pocket.'

He glanced up into his rear-view mirror and saw at least two miles of Route 33 laid out behind them, a strip of black running through the fiery woods. Sunlight twinkled on chrome. A car. Maybe two or three. And coming fast, from the look.

'Old Dor,' she mused.

'Yes. You know, Lois, I think he's also a part of this.'

'Maybe he is,' Lois said. 'And if Ed's a special case, maybe Dorrance is, too.'

'Yes, that thought occurred to me. The most interesting thing about him – Old Dor, I mean, not Ed – is that I don't think Clotho and Lachesis know about him. It's like he's from an entirely different neighborhood.'

'What do you mean?'

'I'm not sure. But Mr C and Mr L never *mentioned* him, and that . . . that seems . . .'

He glanced back at the rear-view. Now there was a fourth car, behind the others but moving up fast, and he could see the blue flashers atop the closer three. Police cars. Headed for Newport? No, probably headed for someplace a little closer than that.

Maybe they're after us, Ralph thought. *Maybe Lois's suggestion that the Richards woman forget we were there didn't hold.*

But would the police send four cruisers after two golden-agers in a rustbucket Oldsmobile? Ralph didn't think so. Helen's face suddenly flashed into his mind. He felt a sinking in the pit of his stomach as he guided the Olds over to the side of the road.

'Ralph? What –' Then she heard the rising howl of the sirens and turned in her seat, alarm widening her eyes. The first three police cars roared past at better than eighty miles an hour, pelting Ralph's car with grit and sending crisp fallen leaves into dancing dervishes in their wake.

'Ralph!' she nearly screamed. 'What if it's High Ridge? Helen's out there! *Helen and her baby!*'

'I know,' Ralph said, and as the fourth police car slammed by them hard enough to rock the Oldsmobile on its springs, he felt that interior blink happen again. He reached for the transmission lever, and then his hand stopped in mid-air, still three inches from it. His eyes were fixed upon the horizon. The smudge there was less spectral than the obscene black umbrella they had seen hanging over the Civic Center, but Ralph knew it was the same thing: a deathbag.

3

'Faster!' Lois shouted at him. 'Go faster, Ralph!'

'I can't,' he said. His teeth were clamped together, and the words came out sounding squeezed. 'I've got it matted.' *Also,* he did not add, *this is the fastest I've gone in thirty-five years, and I'm scared to death.*

The needle quivered a hair's breadth beyond the eighty mark on the speedometer; the woods slid by in a blurred mix of reds and yellows and magentas; under the hood the engine was no longer just clacking but hammering like a platoon of blacksmiths on a binge. In spite of this, the fresh trio of police cars Ralph saw in his mirror were catching up easily.

The road curved sharply right up ahead. Denying every instinct, Ralph kept his foot away from the brake pedal. He did take it off the gas as they went into the curve . . . then mashed it back to the mat again as he felt the rear end trying to break loose on the back side. He was hunched over the wheel now, upper teeth clamped tightly on his lower lip, eyes wide open and bulging beneath the salt-and-pepper tangle of his eyebrows. The sedan's rear tires howled, and Lois fell into him, scrabbling at the back of her seat for purchase. Ralph clung to the wheel with sweaty fingers and waited for the car to flip. The Olds was one of the last true Detroit road-monsters, however, wide and heavy and low. It outlasted the curve, and on the far side Ralph saw a red farmhouse on the left. There were two barns behind it.

'Ralph, there's the turn!'

'I see.'

The new batch of police cars had caught up with them and were swinging out to pass. Ralph got as far over as he could, praying that none of them would rear-end him at this speed. None did; they zipped by in close bumper-to-bumper formation, swung left, and started up the long hill which led to High Ridge.

'Hang on, Lois.'

'Oh, I am, I am,' she said.

The Olds slid almost sideways as Ralph made the left onto what he and Carolyn had always called the Orchard Road. If the narrow country lane had been tarred, the big car probably would have rolled over like a stunt vehicle in a thrill-show. It wasn't, however, and instead of going door-over-roof the Olds just skidded extravagantly, sending up dry billows of dust. Lois gave a thin, out-of-breath shriek, and Ralph snatched a quick look at her.

'Go on!' She flapped an impatient hand at the road ahead, and in that moment she looked so eerily like Carolyn that Ralph almost felt he was seeing a ghost. He wondered what Carol, who had nearly made a career out of telling him to go faster during the last five years of her life, would have made of *this* little spin in the country. 'Never mind me, just watch the road!'

More police cars were making the turn onto Orchard Road now. How many was that in all? Ralph didn't know; he'd lost count. Maybe a dozen in all. He steered the Oldsmobile over until the right two wheels were running on the edge of a nasty-looking ditch, and the reinforcements – three with DERRY POLICE printed in gold on the sides and two State Police cruisers – blew past, throwing up fresh showers of dirt and gravel. For just a moment Ralph saw a uniformed policeman leaning out of one of the Derry police cars, waving at him, and then the Olds was buried in a yellow cloud of dust. Ralph smothered a new and even stronger urge to climb on the brake by thinking of Helen and Nat. A moment later he could see again – sort of, anyway. The newest batch of police cars was already halfway up the hill.

'That cop was waving you off, wasn't he?' Lois asked.

'You bet.'

'They're not even going to let us get close.' She was looking at the black smudge on top of the hill with wide, dismayed eyes.

'We'll get as close as we need to.' Ralph checked the rear-view for more traffic and saw nothing but hanging road-dust.

'Ralph?'

'What?'

'Are you up? Do you see the colors?'

He took a quick look at her. She still looked beautiful to him, and marvellously young, but there was no sign of her aura. 'No,' he said. 'Do you?'

'I don't know. I still see *that*.' She pointed through the windshield at the dark smudge on top of the hill. 'What is it? If it's not a deathbag, what is it?'

He opened his mouth to tell her it was smoke, and there was only one thing up there likely to be on fire, but before he could get out a single word, there was a tremendous hot bang from the Oldsmobile's engine compartment. The hood jumped and even dimpled in one place, as if an angry fist had lashed up inside. The car took a single forward snap-jerk that felt like a hiccup; the red idiot-lights came on and the engine quit.

He steered the Olds toward the soft shoulder, and when the edge gave way beneath the rightside wheels and the car canted into the ditch, Ralph had a strong, clear premonition that he had just completed his last tour of duty as a motor vehicle operator. This idea was accompanied by absolutely no regret at all.

'What happened?' Lois nearly screamed.

'We blew a rod,' he said. 'Looks like it's shank's pony the rest of the way up the hill, Lois. Come on out on my side so you don't squelch in the mud.'

4

There was a brisk westerly breeze, and once they were out of the car the smell of smoke from the top of the hill was very strong. They started the last quarter-mile without talking about it, walking hand-in-hand and walking fast. By the time they saw the State Police cruiser slued sideways across the top of the road, the smoke was rising in billows above the trees and Lois was gasping for breath.

'Lois? Are you all right?'

'I'm fine,' she gasped. 'I just weigh too—'

Crack-crack-crack: pistol-shots from beyond the car blocking the road. They were followed by a hoarse, rapid coughing sound Ralph could easily identify from TV news stories about civil wars in third-world countries and drive-by shootings in third-world American cities: an automatic weapon set to rapid-fire. There were more pistol-shots, then the louder, rougher report of a shotgun. This was followed by a shriek of pain that made Ralph wince and want to cover his ears. He thought it was a woman's scream, and he suddenly remembered something which had been eluding him: the last name of the woman John Leydecker had mentioned. McKay, it had been. Sandra McKay.

That thought coming at this time filled him with unreasoning horror. He tried to tell himself that the screamer could have been anyone – even a man, sometimes men sounded like women when they had been hurt – but he knew better. It was her. It was *them*. Ed's crazies. They had mounted an assault on High Ridge.

More sirens from behind them. The smell of the smoke, thicker now. Lois, looking at him with dismayed, frightened eyes and still gasping for breath. Ralph glanced up the hill and saw a silver R.F.D. box standing at the side of the road. There was no name on it, of course; the women who ran High Ridge had done their best to keep a low profile and maintain their anonymity, much good it had done them today. The mailbox's flag was up. Somebody had a letter for the postman. That made Ralph think of the letter Helen had sent *him* from High Ridge – a cautious letter, but full of hope nevertheless.

More gunfire. The whine of a ricochet. Breaking glass. A bellow that might have been anger but was probably pain. The hungry crackle of hot flames gobbling dry wood. Warbling sirens. And Lois's dark Spanish eyes, fixed on him because he was the man and she'd been raised to believe that men knew what to do in situations like this.

Then do something! he yelled at himself. *For Christ's sweet sake,* do *something!*

But what? What?

'*PICKERING!*' a bullhorn-amplified voice bellowed from beyond the place where the road curved into a grove of young Christmas-tree-size spruces. Ralph could now see red sparks and licks of orange flame in the thickening smoke rising above the firs. '*PICKERING, THERE ARE WOMEN IN THERE! LET US SAVE THE WOMEN!*'

'He *knows* there are women,' Lois murmured. 'Don't they understand that he *knows* that? Are they *fools*, Ralph?'

A strange, wavering shriek answered the cop with the bullhorn, and it took Ralph a second or two to realize that this response was a species of laughter. There was another chattering burst of automatic fire. It was returned by a barrage of pistol-shots and shotgun blasts.

Lois squeezed his hand with chilly fingers. 'What do we do, Ralph? What do we do now?'

He looked at the billowing gray-black smoke rising over the trees, then back down toward the police cars racing up the hill — over half a dozen of them this time — and finally back to Lois's pale, strained face. His mind had cleared a little — not much, but enough for him to realize there was really just one answer to her question.

'We go up,' he said.

5

Blink! and the flames shooting over the grove of spruces went from orange to green. The hungry crackling sound became muffled, like the sound of firecrackers going off inside a closed box. Still holding Lois's hand, Ralph led her around the front bumper of the State Police car which had been left as a roadblock.

The newly arrived police cars were pulling up behind the roadblock. Men in blue uniforms came spilling out of them almost before they had stopped. Several were carrying riot guns and most were wearing puffy black vests. One of them sprinted through Ralph like a gust of warm wind before he could dodge aside: a young man named David Wilbert who thought his wife might be having an affair with her boss at the real-estate office where she worked as a secretary. The question of his wife had taken a back seat (at least temporarily) to David Wilbert's almost overpowering need to pee, however, and to the constant, frightened chant that wove through his thoughts like a snake:

[*'You* won't *disgrace yourself, you* won't *disgrace yourself, you* won't, *you* won't, *you* won't.']

'PICKERING!' the amplified voice bellowed, and Ralph found he could actually taste the words in his mouth, like small silver pellets. *'YOUR FRIENDS ARE DEAD, PICKERING!* THROW DOWN YOUR WEAPON AND STEP OUT INTO THE YARD! *LET US SAVE THE WOMEN!'*

Ralph and Lois rounded the corner, unseen by the men running all around them, and came to a tangle of police cars parked at the place where the road became a driveway lined on both sides by pretty planter-boxes filled with bright flowers.

The woman's touch that means so much, Ralph thought.

The driveway opened into the dooryard of a rambling white farmhouse at least seventy years old. It was three storeys high, with two wings and a long porch which ran the length of the building and commanded a fabulous view toward the west, where dim blue mountains rose in the mid-morning light. This house with its peaceful view had once housed the Barrett family and their apple business and had more recently housed dozens of battered, frightened women, but one look was enough to tell Ralph that it would house no one at all come this time tomorrow morning. The south wing was in flames, and that side of the porch was catching; tongues of fire poked out the windows and licked lasciviously along the eaves, sending shingles floating upward in fiery scraps. He saw a wicker rocking chair burning at the far end of the porch. A half-knitted scarf lay over one of the rocker's arms; the needles dangling from it glowed white-hot. Somewhere a wind-chime was tinkling a mad repetitive melody.

A dead woman in green fatigues and a flak-jacket sprawled head-down on the porch steps, glaring at the sky through the blood-smeared lenses of her glasses. There was dirt in her hair, a pistol in her hand, and a ragged black hole in her midsection. A man lay draped over the railing at the north end of the porch with one booted foot propped on the lawn-glider. He was also wearing fatigues and a flak-jacket. An assault-rifle with a banana clip sticking out of it lay in a flower-bed below him. Blood ran down his fingers and dripped from his nails. To Ralph's heightened eye, the drops looked black and dead.

Felton, he thought. *If the police are still yelling at Charlie Pickering — if Pickering's inside — then that must be Frank Felton. And what about Susan Day? Ed's down the coast somewhere — Lois seemed sure of that, and I think she's right — but what if Susan Day's in there? Jesus, is that possible?*

He supposed it was, but the possibilities didn't matter — not now. Helen and Natalie were almost certainly in there, along with God knew how many other helpless, terrorized women, and that *did* matter.

There was the sound of breaking glass from inside the house, followed by a soft explosion — almost a gasp. Ralph saw new flames jump up behind the panes of the front door.

Molotov cocktails, he thought. *Charlie Pickering finally got a chance to throw a few. How wonderful for him.*

Ralph didn't know how many cops were crouched behind the cars parked at the head of the driveway — it looked like at least thirty — but he picked out the two who had busted Ed Deepneau at once. Chris Nell was crouched behind the front tire of the Derry police car closest to the house, and John Leydecker was down on one knee beside him. Nell was the one with the bullhorn, and as Ralph and Lois approached the police strongpoint, he glanced at Leydecker. Leydecker nodded, pointed at the house, then pushed his palms at Nell in a gesture Ralph read easily: *Be careful.* He read something more distressing in Chris Nell's aura — the younger man was too excited to be careful. Too stoked. And at that instant, almost as if Ralph's thought had caused it to happen, Nell's aura began changing color.

It cycled from pale blue to dark gray to dead black with gruesome speed.

'*GIVE IT UP, PICKERING!*' Nell shouted, unaware that he was a dead man breathing.

The wire stock of an assault-rifle smashed through the glass of a window on the lower floor of the north wing, then disappeared back inside. At the same instant the fanlight over the front door exploded, showering the porch with glass. Flames roared out through the hole. A second later the door itself shuddered open, as if nudged by an invisible hand. Nell leaned out farther, perhaps believing the shooter had finally seen reason and intended to give himself up.

Ralph, screaming: [*'Pull him back, Johnny!* PULL HIM BACK!*'*]

The rifle emerged again, barrel-first this time.

Leydecker reached for Nell's collar, but he was too slow. The automatic rifle hacked its series of rapid dry coughs, and Ralph heard the metallic *pank! pank! pank!* of bullets poking holes in the thin steel of the police car. Chris Nell's aura was totally black now – it had become a deathbag. He jerked sideways as a bullet caught him in the neck, breaking Leydecker's grip on his collar and sprawling into the dooryard with one foot kicking spasmodically. The bullhorn spilled from his hand with a brief squawk of feedback. A policeman behind one of the other cars cried out in surprise and horror. Lois's shriek was much louder.

More bullets stitched across the ground toward Nell and then slapped small black holes into the thighs of his blue uniform. Ralph could dimly see the man inside the deathbag which was suffocating him; he was making blind efforts to roll over and get up. There was something singularly horrible about his struggles – to Ralph it was like watching a creature caught in a net drown in shallow, filthy water.

Leydecker lunged out from behind the police car, and as his fingers disappeared into the black membrane surrounding Chris Nell, Ralph heard Old Dor say, *I wouldn't touch him anymore if I were you, Ralph – I can't see your hands.*

Lois: [*'Don't! Don't, he's dead, he's already dead!'*]

The gun poking out of the window had started to move to the right. Now it swivelled unhurriedly back toward Leydecker, the man behind it undeterred – and apparently unhurt – by the hail of bullets directed at him from the other police. Ralph raised his right hand and brought it down in the karate-chop gesture again, but this time instead of a wedge of light, his fingertips produced something that looked like a large blue teardrop. It spread across Leydecker's lemon-colored aura just as the rifle sticking out of the window opened fire. Ralph saw two slugs strike the tree just to Leydecker's right, sending chips of bark flying into the air and making black holes in the fir's yellowish-white undersurface. A third struck the blue covering which had coated Leydecker's aura – Ralph saw a momentary flicker of dark red just to the left of the detective's temple and heard a low whine as the bullet either richocheted or *skipped,* the way a flat stone will skip across the surface of a pond.

Leydecker pulled Nell back behind the car, looked at him, then tore open the driver's-side door and threw himself into the front seat. Ralph could no longer see him, but could hear him screaming at someone over the radio, asking where the fuck the rescue vehicles were.

More shattering glass, and Lois was grabbing frantically at Ralph's arm, pointing at something — at a brick tumbling end over end into the dooryard. It had come through one of the low, narrow windows at the base of the north wing. These windows were almost obscured by the flower-beds which edged the house.

'*Help us!*' a voice screamed through the broken window, even as the man with the assault-rifle fired reflexively at the tumbling brick, sending up puffs of reddish dust and then breaking it into three jagged chunks. Neither Ralph nor Lois had ever heard that voice raised in a scream, but both recognized it at once, nevertheless; it was Helen Deepneau's voice. '*Help us, please! We're in the cellar! We have children! Please don't let us burn to death, WE HAVE CHILDREN!*'

Ralph and Lois exchanged a single wide-eyed glance, then ran for the house.

6

Two uniformed figures, looking more like pro football linemen than cops in their bulky Kevlar vests, charged from behind one of the cruisers, running flat-out for the porch with their riot guns held at port arms. As they crossed the dooryard on a diagonal, Charlie Pickering leaned out of his window, still laughing wildly, his gray hair zanier than ever. The volume of fire directed at him was enormous, showering him with splinters from the sides of the window and actually knocking down the rusty gutter above his head – it struck the porch with a hollow *bonk* – but not a single bullet touched him.

How can they not be hitting him? Ralph thought as he and Lois mounted the porch toward the lime-colored flames which were now billowing through the open front door. *Christ Jesus, it's almost point-blank range, how can they possibly not be hitting him?*

But he knew how . . . and why. Clotho had told them that both Atropos and Ed Deepneau had been surrounded by forces which were malignant yet protective. Was it not likely that those same forces were now taking care of Charlie Pickering, much as Ralph himself had taken care of Leydecker when he'd left the protection of the police car to drag his dying colleague back to cover?

Pickering opened up on the charging State Troopers, his weapon switched to rapid-fire. He aimed low to negate the value of the vests they were wearing and swept their legs out from under them. One of them fell in a silent heap; the other crawled back the way he had come, shrieking that he was hit, he was hit, oh fuck, he was hit bad.

'*Barbecue!*' Pickering cried out the window in his screaming, laughing voice. '*Barbecue! Barbecue! Holy cookout! Burn the bitches! God's fire! God's holy fire!*'

There were more screams now, seemingly from right under Ralph's feet, and when he looked down he saw a terrible thing: a medley of auras was seeping up from between the porch boards like steam, the variety of their colors muted by the scarlet blood-glow which was rising with them . . . and surrounding them. This blood-red shape wasn't quite the same as the thunderhead which had formed above the fight between Green Boy and Orange Boy outside the Red Apple, but Ralph thought it was closely related; the only difference was that this one had been born of fear instead of anger and aggression.

'*Barbecue!*' Charlie Pickering was screaming, and then something about killing the devil-cunts. Suddenly Ralph hated him more than he had ever hated anyone in his life.

[*'Come on, Lois – let's go get that asshole.'*]

He took her by the hand and pulled her into the burning house.

CHAPTER TWENTY-TWO

1

The porch door opened on a central hallway that ran from the front of the house to the back, and the whole length of it was now engulfed in flames. To Ralph's eyes they were a bright green, and when he and Lois passed through them, they were cool — it was like passing through gauzy membranes which had been infused with Mentholatum. The crackle of the burning house was muffled; the gunfire had become as faint and unimportant as the sound of thunder to someone who is swimming underwater . . . and that was what this felt like more than anything, Ralph decided — being underwater. He and Lois were unseen beings swimming through a river of fire.

He pointed to a doorway on the right and looked questioningly at Lois. She nodded. He reached for the knob and grimaced with disgust as his fingers passed right through it. Just as well, of course; if he had actually been able to grab the damned thing, he would have left the top two layers of his fingers hanging off the brass knob in char-broiled strips.

[*We have to go through it, Ralph!*]

He looked at her assessingly, saw a great deal of fear and worry in her eyes but no panic, and nodded. They went through the door together just as the chandelier halfway down the hall fell to the floor with an unmusical crash of glass pendants and iron chain.

There was a parlor on the other side, and what they saw there made Ralph's stomach clench in horror. Two women were propped against the wall below a large poster of Susan Day in jeans and a Western-style shirt (DON'T LET HIM CALL YOU BABY UNLESS YOU WANT HIM TO TREAT YOU LIKE ONE, the poster advised). Both had been shot in the head at point-blank range; brains, ragged flaps of scalp, and bits of bone were splattered across the flowered wallpaper and Susan Day's fancy-stitched cowgirl boots. One of the women had been pregnant. The other had been Gretchen Tillbury.

Ralph remembered the day she had come to his home with Helen to warn him and to give him a can of something called Bodyguard; on that day he had thought her beautiful . . . but of course on that day her finely made head had still been intact and half of her pretty blonde hair hadn't been roasted off by a close-range rifle-blast. Fifteen years after she had narrowly escaped being killed by her abusive husband, another man had put a gun to Gretchen Tillbury's head and blown her right out of the world. She would never tell another woman about how she had gotten the scar on her left thigh.

For one horrible moment Ralph thought he was going to faint. He concentrated and pulled himself back by thinking of Lois. Her aura had gone a dark, shocked red. Jagged black lines raced across it and through it. They looked like the EKG readout of someone suffering a fatal heart attack.

[*'Oh Ralph! Oh Ralph, dear God!'*]

Something exploded at the south end of the house with force enough to blow open the door they had just walked through. Ralph guessed it might have been a propane tank or tanks . . . not that it mattered much at this point. Flaming scraps of wallpaper came wafting in from the hall, and he saw both the room's curtains and the remaining hair on Gretchen Tillbury's head ripple toward the doorway as the fire sucked the air out of the room to feed itself. How long would it take for the fire to turn the women and children down cellar into crispy critters? Ralph didn't know, and suspected that didn't matter much, either; the people trapped down there would be dead of suffocation or smoke inhalation long before they began to burn.

Lois was staring at the dead women in horror. Tears slipped down her cheeks. The spectral gray light which rose from the tracks they left behind looked like vapor rising from dry ice. Ralph walked her across the parlor toward the closed double doors on the far side, paused before them long enough to take a deep breath, then put his arm around Lois's waist and stepped into the wood.

There was a moment of darkness in which not just his nose but his entire body seemed suffused with the sweet aroma of sawdust, and then they were in the room beyond, the northernmost room in the house. It had perhaps once been a study, but had since been converted into a group therapy room. In the center, a dozen or so folding chairs had been set up in a circle. The walls were hung with plaques saying things like I CANNOT EXPECT RESPECT

FROM ANYONE ELSE UNTIL I RESPECT MYSELF. On a
blackboard at one end of the room someone had printed
WE ARE FAMILY, I'VE GOT ALL MY SISTERS WITH ME in
capital letters. Crouched beside it at one of the east-facing
windows that overlooked the porch, wearing his own Kevlar
vest over a Snoopy sweatshirt Ralph would have recog-
nized anywhere, was Charlie Pickering.

'*Barbecue all Godless women!*' he screamed. A bullet
whined past his shoulder; another buried itself in the
windowframe to his right and flicked a splinter against one
of the lenses of his hornrimmed glasses. The idea that he was
being protected returned to Ralph, this time with the force
of a conviction. '*Lesbian cookout! Give em a taste of their own
medicine! Teach em how it feels!*'

[*'Stay up, Lois – right up where you are now.'*]

[*'What are you going to do?'*]

[*'Take care of him.'*]

[*'Don't kill him, Ralph! Please don't kill him!'*]

Why not? Ralph thought bitterly. *I'd be doing the world
a favor.* That was undoubtedly true, but this was no time
to argue.

[*'All right, I won't kill him! Now stay put, Lois – there's
too many goddam bullets flying around for both of us to risk
going down.'*]

Before she could reply, Ralph concentrated,
summoned the blink, and dropped back to the Short-Time
level. It happened so fast and hard this time that it left him
feeling winded, as if he had jumped out of a second-storey
window onto a hard patch of concrete. Some of the color
drained out of the world and noise fell in to replace it: the
crackle of fire, no longer muffled but sharp and close; the

crump of a shotgun blast; the crack of pistol-shots fired in rapid succession. The air tasted of soot, and the room was sweltering. Something that sounded like an insect droned past Ralph's ear. He had an idea it was a .45-caliber bug.

Better hurry up, sweetheart, Carolyn advised. *When bullets hit you on this level they kill you, remember?*

He remembered.

Ralph ran bent-over toward Pickering's turned back. His feet crunched on slivers of glass and scatters of splinters, but Pickering did not turn. In addition to the automatic weapon in his hands, there was a revolver on his hip and a small green duffle-bag by his left foot. The bag was unzipped, and Ralph saw a number of wine bottles inside. Their open mouths had been stuffed with wet rags.

'*Kill the bitches!*' Pickering screamed, spraying the yard with another burst of fire. He popped the clip and raised his sweatshirt, exposing three or four more tucked under his belt. Ralph reached into the open duffel-bag, seized one of the gasoline-filled wine bottles by the neck, and swung it at the side of Pickering's head. As he did, he saw the reason Pickering hadn't heard his approach: the man was wearing shooter's plugs. Before Ralph had time to reflect upon the irony of a man on a suicide mission taking pains to protect his hearing, the bottle shattered against Pickering's temple, dousing him with amber liquid and green glass. He staggered backward, one hand going to his scalp, which was cut open in two places. Blood poured through his long fingers — *fingers that should have belonged to a pianist or a painter,* Ralph thought — and down his neck. He turned, his eyes wide and shocked behind the smeary lenses of his spectacles, his hair reaching for the sky and making him look like a cartoon of a man who has just received a huge jolt of electricity.

'*You!*' he cried. 'Devil-sent Centurion! Godless baby-killer!'

Ralph thought of the two women in the other room and was once more overwhelmed with anger . . . except that anger was too mild a word, much too mild. He felt as if his nerves were burning inside his skin. And the thought that drummed at his mind was *one of them was pregnant so who's the baby-killer, one of them was pregnant so who's the baby-killer, one of them was pregnant so who's the baby-killer.*

Another high-caliber bug droned past his face. Ralph didn't notice. Pickering was trying to lift the rifle with which he had undoubtedly killed Gretchen Tillbury and her pregnant friend. Ralph snatched it from his hands and turned it on him. Pickering shrieked with fear. The sound of it maddened Ralph even more, and he forgot the promise he had made to Lois. He raised the rifle, fully meaning to empty it into the man who was now cringing abjectly against the wall (in the heat of the moment it occurred to neither of them that there was currently no clip in the gun), but before he could pull the trigger he was distracted by a brilliant swarm of light bleeding into the air beside him. At first it was without shape, a fabulous kaleidoscope whose colors had somehow escaped the tube which was supposed to contain them, and then it took on the form of a woman with a long, gauzy gray ribbon rising from her head.

[*Don't kill him*]

Ralph, please don't kill him!'

For a moment he could see the blackboard and read

the quote chalked on it right through her, and then the colors became her clothes and hair and skin as she came all the way down. Pickering stared at her in cross-eyed terror. He shrieked again, and the crotch of his army fatigue pants darkened. He stuck his fingers into his mouth, as if to stifle the sound he was making. '*A ghose!*' he screamed through his mouthful of fingers. '*A Hennurion anna ghose!*'

Lois ignored him and grabbed the barrel of the rifle. 'Don't kill him, Ralph! Don't!'

Ralph was suddenly furious with her, too. 'Don't you understand, Lois? Don't you get it? He understood what he was doing! On some level, he *did* understand − *I saw it in his goddam aura!*'

'It doesn't matter,' she said, still holding the barrel of the rifle down so it pointed at the floor. 'It doesn't matter what he did or didn't understand. We mustn't do what they do. We mustn't be what they are.'

'But—'

'Ralph, I want to let go of this gun-barrel. It's hot. It's burning my fingers.'

'All right,' he said, and let go at the same instant she did. The gun fell to the floor between them, and Pickering, who had been sliding slowly down the wall with his fingers still in his mouth and his shining, glazed eyes still fixed on Lois, lunged for it with the speed of a striking rattlesnake.

What Ralph did then he did without forethought and certainly without anger − he acted purely on instinct, reaching out for Pickering with both hands and grasping the sides of his face. Something flashed brightly inside his mind as he did it, something that felt like the lens of a powerful magnifying glass. He slammed back up through the levels, for a split second going higher than either of them had yet been. At the height of his ascent, he felt a terrible force flash in his head and explode down his arms. Then, as he dropped back down, *he* heard the bang, a hollow but emphatic sound which was entirely different from the guns still firing outside.

Pickering's body jerked galvanically, and his legs shot out with such force that one of his shoes flew off. His buttocks rose and then thumped down. His teeth clamped shut on his lower lip, and blood squirted out of his mouth. For a moment Ralph was almost sure he saw tiny blue sparks snapping from the ends of his zany hair. Then they were gone and Pickering slumped back against the wall. He stared at Ralph and Lois with eyes from which all concern had fled.

Lois screamed. At first Ralph thought she was screaming because of what he had done to Pickering, and then he saw she was beating at the top of her head. A piece of burning wallpaper had landed there and her hair was on fire.

He swept an arm around her, beat at the flames with his own hand, then covered her body with his as a fresh gust of rifle- and shotgun-fire hit the north wing. Ralph's free hand was splayed out against the wall, and he saw a bullet-hole appear between the third and fourth fingers like a magic trick.

'*Go up, Lois! Go up*

[*right now!*']

They went up together, turning to colored smoke before Charlie Pickering's empty eyes . . . and then disappearing.

2

[*'What did you do to him, Ralph? For a second you were gone – you were up – and then . . . then he . . . what did you do?'*]

She was looking at Charlie Pickering with stunned horror. Pickering was sitting against the wall in almost exactly the same position as the two dead women in the next room. As Ralph watched, a large pinkish spit-bubble appeared between his slack lips, grew, then popped.

He turned to Lois, took her by the arms just above the elbows, and made a picture in his mind: the circuit-breaker box in the basement of his house on Harris Avenue. Hands opened the box, then quickly flipped all the switches from ON to OFF. He wasn't sure that this was right – it had all happened too fast for him to be sure of anything – but he thought it was close.

Lois's eyes widened a little, and then she nodded. She looked at Pickering, then at Ralph.

[*'He brought it on himself, didn't he? You didn't do it on purpose.'*]

Ralph nodded, and then fresh screams came up from below their feet, screams he was quite sure he was not hearing with his ears.

[*'Lois?'*]

[*'Yes, Ralph – right now.'*]

He slipped his hands down her arms and gripped her hands, as the four of them had held hands in the hospital, only this time they went down instead of up, sliding into the plank floor as if it were a pool of water. Ralph was once again aware of a knife-edge of darkness crossing his vision, and then they were in the cellar, sinking slowly down to a dirty cement floor. He saw shadowy furnace-pipes, grimy with dust, a snowblower covered with a large sheet of dirty transparent plastic, gardening equipment lined up to one side of a dim cylinder that was probably the water heater, and cartons stacked against one brick wall – soup, beans, spaghetti sauce, coffee, garbage bags, toilet-tissue. All of these things looked slightly hallucinatory, not quite there, and at first Ralph thought this was a new side-effect of having gone to the next level. Then he realized it was just smoke – the cellar was filling up with it rapidly.

There were eighteen or twenty people clustered at one end of the long, shadowy room, most of them women. Ralph also saw a little boy of about four clinging to his mother's knees (Mommy's face showed the fading bruises of what might have been an accident but was probably on purpose), a little girl a year or two older with her face pressed against her mother's stomach . . . and he saw Helen. She was holding Natalie in her arms and blowing into the baby's face, as if she could keep the air around her clear of smoke that way. Nat was coughing and screaming in choked, desperate whoops. Behind the women and children, Ralph could make out a dusty set of steps climbing up into darkness.

[*'Ralph? We have to go down now, don't we?'*]

He nodded, made that blink inside his head, and suddenly he was also coughing as he pulled acrid smoke into his lungs. They materialized directly in front of the group at the foot of the stairs, but only the little boy with his arms around his mother's knees reacted. In that moment, Ralph was positive he had seen this kid somewhere before, but he had no idea where – the day near the end of summer when he'd seen him playing roll-toss with his mother in Strawford Park was the furthest thing from his mind at that moment.

'Look, Mama!' the boy said, pointing and coughing. 'Angels!'

Inside his head Ralph heard Clotho saying *We're no angels, Ralph,* and then he pushed forward toward Helen through the thickening smoke, still holding Lois's hand. His eyes were stinging and tearing already, and he could hear Lois coughing. Helen was looking at him with dazed unrecognition − looking at him the way she had on that day in August when Ed had beaten her so badly.

'Helen!'

'*Ralph?*'

'Those stairs, Helen! Where do they go?'

'What are you doing here, Ralph? How did you get h −' She broke into a coughing spasm and doubled over. Natalie almost tumbled out of her arms and Lois took the screaming child before Helen could drop her.

Ralph looked at the woman to Helen's left, saw she seemed even less aware of what was going on, then grabbed Helen again and shook her. '*Where do the stairs go?*'

She glanced over her shoulder at them. 'Cellar bulk-head,' she told him. 'But that's no good. It's −' She bent over, coughing dryly. The sound was weirdly like the chatter of Charlie Pickering's automatic weapon. 'It's locked,' Helen finished. 'The fat woman locked it. She had the lock in her pocket. I saw her put it on. Why did she do that, Ralph? How did she know we'd come down here?'

Where else did you have to go? Ralph thought bitterly, then turned to Lois. 'See what you can do, will you?'

'Okay.' She handed him the screaming, coughing baby and pushed through the little crowd of women. Susan Day was not among them, so far as Ralph could see. At the far end of the cellar, a section of the floor fell in with a gush of sparks and a wave of baking heat. The girl with her face buried against her mother's stomach began to scream.

Lois climbed four of the stairs, then reached up with her palms held out, like a minister giving a benediction. In the light of the swirling sparks, Ralph could dimly see the slanting shadow that was the bulkhead. Lois put her hands against it. For a moment nothing happened, and then she flickered briefly out of existence in a rainbow-swirl of colors. Ralph heard a sharp explosion that sounded like an aerosol can exploding in a hot fire, and then Lois was back. At the same moment he thought he saw a pulse of white light from just above her head.

'What was that, Mama?' asked the little boy who had called Ralph and Lois angels. 'What was that?' Before she could reply, a stack of curtains on a card-table about twenty feet away whooshed into flame, painting the faces of the trapped women in stark Halloween shades of black and orange.

'Ralph!' Lois cried. 'Help me!'

He pushed through the dazed women and climbed the stairs. 'What?' His throat felt as if he had been gargling with kerosene. 'Can't you get it?'

'I got it, I felt the lock break – in my mind I felt it – but this boogery door is too heavy for me! You'll have to do that part. Give me the baby.'

He let her take Nat again, then reached up and tested the bulkhead. It was heavy, all right, but Ralph was running on pure adrenaline and when he put his shoulders into it and shoved, it flew open. A flood of bright light and fresh air swept down the narrow stairwell. In one of Ralph's beloved films, such moments were usually greeted by screams of triumph and relief, but at first none of the women who had been trapped down here made any sound at all. They only stood in silence, looking up with stunned faces at the rectangle of blue sky Ralph had conjured in the roof of the room most of them had accepted as their grave.

And what will they say later? he wondered. *If they really do survive this, what will they say later? That a skinny man with bushy eyebrows and a lady on the stout side (but with beautiful Spanish eyes) materialized in the cellar, broke the lock on the bulkhead door, and led them to safety?*

He looked down and saw the strangely familiar little boy looking back up at him with large, grave eyes. There was a hook-shaped scar across the bridge of the boy's nose. Ralph had an idea that this kid was the only one who had *really* seen them, even after they had dropped back down to the Short-Time level, and Ralph knew perfectly well what he would say: that angels had come, a man angel and a lady angel, and they had saved them. *Should make for an interesting sidebar on the news tonight,* Ralph thought. Yes indeed. Lisette Benson and John Kirkland would love it.

Lois slapped her hand against one of the support-posts. 'Come on, you guys! Get going before the fire gets to the furnace oil-tanks!'

The woman with the little girl moved first. She hoisted her crying child into her arms and staggered upstairs, coughing and weeping. The others began to follow. The

STEPHEN KING

little boy looked up at Ralph admiringly as his mother led
him past. 'Cool, man,' he said.

Ralph grinned at him – he couldn't help it – then
turned to Lois and pointed up the stairs. 'If I'm not all
turned around in my head, that comes out behind the
house. Don't let them go around to the front yet. The cops
are apt to blow half of them away before they realize they're
shooting the people they came to save.'

'All right,' she said – not a single question, not another
word, and Ralph loved her for that. She went up the stairs
at once, pausing only to shift Nat and grab one woman
by the elbow when she stumbled.

Now only Ralph and Helen Deepneau were left.
'Was that Lois?' she asked him.

'Yes.'

'She had Natalie?'

'Yes.' Another large chunk of the cellar's roof fell in,
more sparks whooshed up, and runners of fire went racing
nimbly along the overhead beams toward the furnace.

'Are you sure?' She clutched at his shirt and looked
at him with frantic, swollen eyes. 'Are you sure she had
Nat?'

'Positive. Let's go now.'

Helen looked around and seemed to count in her
head. She looked alarmed. 'Gretchen!' she exclaimed. 'And
Merrilee! We have to get Merrilee, Ralph, she's seven
months pregnant!'

'She's up there,' Ralph said, grabbing Helen's arm
when she showed signs of wanting to leave the foot of the
stairs and go back into the burning cellar. 'She and Gretchen
both. Is that everyone else?'

'Yes, I think so.'

'Good. Come on. We're getting out of here.'

3

Ralph and Helen stepped out of the bulkhead in a cloud of dark gray smoke, looking like the conclusion of a world-class illusionist's best trick. They were indeed in back of the house, near the clotheslines. Dresses, slacks, underwear, and bed-linen flapped in the freshening breeze. As Ralph watched, a flaming shingle landed on one of the sheets and set it ablaze. More flames were billowing out of the kitchen windows. The heat was intense.

Helen sagged against him, not unconscious but simply used up for the time being. Ralph had to grab her around the waist to keep her from falling to the ground. She clawed weakly at the back of his neck, trying to say something about Natalie. Then she saw her in Lois's arms and relaxed a little. Ralph got a better grip on her and half carried, half dragged her away from the bulkhead. As he did, he saw the remains of what looked like a brand-new padlock on the ground beside the open door. It was split into two pieces and oddly twisted, as if immensely powerful hands had torn it apart.

The women were about forty feet away, huddled at the corner of the house. Lois was facing them, talking to them, keeping them from going any farther. Ralph thought that with a little preparation and a little luck they would be okay when they did – the firing from the police strong-point hadn't stopped, but it had slackened off considerably.

'*PICKERING!*' It sounded like Leydecker, although the

amplification of the bullhorn made it impossible to be sure. *'WHY DON'T YOU BE SMART FOR ONCE IN YOUR LIFE AND COME OUT WHILE YOU STILL CAN?'*

More sirens were approaching, the distinctive watery warble of an ambulance among them. Ralph led Helen to the other women. Lois handed Natalie back to her, then turned in the direction of the amplified voice and cupped her hands around her mouth. '*Hello!*' she screamed. '*Hello out there, can you* –' She stopped, coughing so hard she was nearly retching, doubled over with her hands on her knees and tears squirting from her smoke-irritated eyes.

'Lois, are you okay?' Ralph asked. From the corner of his eye he saw Helen covering the face of the Exalted & Revered Baby with kisses.

'Fine,' she said, wiping her cheeks with her fingers. "S the damn smoke, that's all.' She cupped her hands around her mouth again. '*Can you hear me?*'

The firing had died down to a few isolated handgun pops. Still, Ralph thought, just one of those little pops in the wrong place might be enough to get an innocent woman killed.

'*Leydecker!*' he yelled, cupping his own hands around his mouth. '*John Leydecker!*'

There was a pause, and then the amplified voice gave a command that gladdened Ralph's heart. '*STOP FIRING!*'

One more pop, then silence except for the sound of the burning house.

'WHO'S TALKING TO ME? IDENTIFY YOURSELVES!'

But Ralph thought he had enough problems without adding that to them.

'*The women are back here!*' he yelled, now having to

fight a need to cough himself. *'I'm sending them around to the front!'*

'NO, DON'T!' Leydecker responded. *'THERE'S A MAN WITH A GUN IN THE LAST ROOM ON THE GROUND FLOOR! HE'S SHOT SEVERAL PEOPLE ALREADY!'*

One of the women moaned at this and put her hands over her face.

Ralph cleared his burning throat as best he could – at that moment he believed he would have swapped his whole retirement fund for one ice-cold bottle of Coke – and screamed back: *'Don't worry about Pickering! Pickering's—'*

But what exactly *was* Pickering? That was a damned good question, wasn't it?

'Mr Pickering is unconscious! That's why he's stopped shooting!' Lois screamed from beside him. Ralph didn't think 'unconscious' really covered it, but it would do. *'The women are coming around the side of the house with their hands up! Don't shoot! Tell us you won't shoot!'*

There was a moment of silence. Then: *'WE WON'T, BUT I HOPE YOU KNOWN WHAT YOU'RE TALKING ABOUT, LADY.'*

Ralph nodded at the mother of the little boy. 'Go on, now. You two can lead the parade.'

'Are you sure they won't hurt us?' The fading bruises on the young woman's face (a face which Ralph also found vaguely familiar) suggested that questions of who would or would not hurt her and her son formed a vital part of her life. 'Are you *sure*?'

'Yes,' Lois said, still coughing and leaking around the eyes. 'Just put your hands up. You can do that, can't you, big boy?'

The kid shot his hands up with the enthusiasm of a veteran cops-and-robbers player, but his shining eyes never left Ralph's face.

Pink roses, Ralph thought. *If I could see his aura, that's what color it would be.* He wasn't sure if that was intuition or memory, but he knew it was so.

'What about the people inside?' another woman asked. 'What if they shoot? They had guns – what if they shoot?'

'There won't be any more shooting from in there,' Ralph said. 'Go on, now.'

The little boy's mother gave Ralph another doubtful look, then looked down at her son. 'Ready, Pat?'

'Yes!' Pat said, and grinned.

His mother nodded and raised one hand. The other she curled around his shoulders in a frail gesture of protection that touched Ralph's heart. They walked around the side of the house that way. '*Don't hurt us!*' she cried. '*Our hands are up and my little boy is with me, so don't hurt us!*'

The others waited a moment, and then the woman who had put her hands to her face went. The one with the little girl joined her (the child was in her arms now, but holding her hands obediently in the air just the same). The others followed along, most coughing, all with their empty hands held high. When Helen started to fall in at the end of the parade, Ralph touched her shoulder. She looked up at him, her reddened eyes both calm and wondering.

'That's the second time you've been there when Nat and I needed you,' she said. 'Are you our guardian angel, Ralph?'

'Maybe,' he said. 'Maybe I am. Listen, Helen – there isn't much time. Gretchen is dead.'

She nodded and began to cry. 'I knew it. I didn't want to, but somehow I did, just the same.'

'I'm very sorry.'

'We were having such a good time when they came – I mean, we were nervous, but there was also a lot of laughing and a lot of chatter. We were going to spend the day getting ready for the speech tonight. The rally and Susan Day's speech.'

'It's tonight I have to ask you about,' Ralph said, speaking as gently as he could. 'Do you think they'll still—'

'We were making breakfast when they came.' She spoke as if she hadn't heard him; Ralph supposed she hadn't. Nat was peeking over Helen's shoulder, and although she was still coughing, she had stopped crying. Safe within the circle of her mother's arms, she looked from Ralph to Lois and then back to Ralph again with lively curiosity.

'Helen –' Lois began.

'Look! See there?' Helen pointed to an old brown Cadillac parked beside the ramshackle shed which had been the cider-press in the days when Ralph and Carolyn had occasionally come out here; it had probably served High Ridge as a garage. The Caddy was in bad shape – cracked windshield, dented rocker panels, one headlight crisscrossed with masking tape. The bumper was layered with pro-life stickers.

'That's the car they came in. They drove around to the back of the house as if they meant to put it in our garage. I think that's what fooled us. They drove right around to the back as if they *belonged* here.' She contemplated the car for a moment, then returned her

657

smoke-reddened, unhappy eyes to Ralph and Lois. 'Somebody should have paid attention to the stickers on the damned thing.'

Ralph suddenly thought of Barbara Richards back at WomanCare – Barbie Richards, who had relaxed when Lois approached. It hadn't mattered to her that Lois was reaching for something in her purse; what had mattered was that Lois was a woman. Sandra McKay had been driving the Cadillac; Ralph didn't need to ask Helen to know that. They had seen the woman and ignored the bumper stickers. We are family; I've got all my sisters with me.

'When Deanie said the people getting out of the car were dressed in army clothes and carrying guns, we thought it was a joke. All of us but Gretchen, that is. She told us to get downstairs as quick as we could. Then she went into the parlor. To call the police, I suppose. I should have stayed with her.'

'No,' Lois said, and slipped a lock of Natalie's fine-spun auburn hair through her fingers. 'You had this one to look out for, didn't you? And still do.'

'I suppose,' she said dully. 'I suppose I do. But she was my friend, Lois. My *friend*.'

'I know, dear.'

Helen's face twisted like a rag, and she began to cry. Natalie looked at her mother with an expression of comical astonishment for a moment, and then she began to cry, too.

'Helen,' Ralph said. 'Helen, listen to me. I have something to ask you. It's very, very important. Are you listening?'

Helen nodded, but she went on crying. Ralph had no idea if she was really hearing him or not. He glanced at the corner of the building, wondering how long it would be before the police charged around it, then took a deep breath. 'Do you think there's any chance that they'll still hold the rally tonight? Any chance at all? You were as close to Gretchen as anybody. Tell me what you think.'

Helen stopped crying and looked at him with still, wide eyes, as if she couldn't believe what she had just heard. Then those eyes began to fill with a frightening depth of anger.

'How can you ask? How can you even *ask*?'

'Well . . . because . . .' He stopped, unable to go on. Ferocity was the last thing he had expected.

'If they stop us now, they win,' Helen said. 'Don't you see that? Gretchen's dead, Merrilee's dead, High Ridge is burning to the ground with everything some of these women own inside, and if they stop us now they win.'

One part of Ralph's mind — a deep part — now made a terrible comparison. Another part, one that loved Helen, moved to block it, but it moved too late. Her eyes looked like Charlie Pickering's eyes when Pickering had been sitting next to him in the library, and there was no reasoning with a mind that could make eyes look like that.

'*If they stop us now they win!*' she screamed. In her arms, Natalie began to cry harder. '*Don't you get it? Don't you fucking GET it? We'll never let that happen! Never! Never! Never!*'

Abruptly she raised the hand she wasn't using to hold the baby and went around the corner of the building. Ralph reached for her and touched the back of her blouse with his fingertips. That was all.

'*Don't shoot me!*' Helen was crying at the police on

the other side of the house. *'Don't shoot me, I'm one of the women! I'm one of the women! I'm one of the women!'*

Ralph lunged after her – no thought, just instinct – and Lois seized him by the back of his belt. 'Better not go out there, Ralph. You're a man, and they might think—'

'Hello, Ralph! Hello, Lois!'

They both turned toward this new voice. Ralph recognized it at once, and he felt both surprised and not surprised. Standing beyond the clotheslines with their freight of flaming sheets and garments, wearing a pair of faded flannel pants and an old pair of Converse high-tops which had been mended with electrician's tape, was Dorrance Marstellar. His hair, as fine as Natalie's (but white instead of auburn), blew about his head in the October wind which combed the top of this hill. As usual, he had a book in one hand.

'Come on, you two,' he said, waving to them and smiling. 'Hurry up and hurry along. There's not much time.'

4

He led them down a weedy, little-used path that meandered away from the house in a westerly direction. It wound first through a fair-sized garden-plot from which everything had been harvested but the pumpkins and squashes, then into an orchard where the apples were just coming to full ripeness, then through a dense blackberry tangle where thorns seemed to reach out everywhere to snag their clothes. As they passed out of the blackberry brambles and into a gloomy stand of old pines and spruces, it occurred to Ralph that they must be on the Newport side of the ridge now.

Dorrance walked briskly for a man of his years, and the placid smile never left his face. The book he carried was *For Love, Poems 1950–1960,* by a man named Robert Creeley. Ralph had never heard of him, but supposed Mr Creeley had never heard of Elmore Leonard, Ernest Haycox or Louis L'Amour, either. He only tried to talk to Old Dor once, when the three of them finally reached the foot of a slope made slick and treacherous with pine-needles. Just ahead of them, a small stream foamed coldly past.

'Dorrance, what are you doing out here? How'd you *get* here, for that matter? And where the hell are we going?'

'Oh, I hardly ever answer questions,' Old Dor replied, smiling widely. He surveyed the stream, then raised one finger and pointed at the water. A small brown trout jumped into the air, flipped bright drops from its tail, and fell back into the water again. Ralph and Lois looked at each other with identical *Did I just see what I thought I saw?* expressions.

'Nope, nope,' Dor continued, stepping off the bank and onto a wet rock. 'Hardly ever. Too difficult. Too many possibilities. Too many levels . . . eh, Ralph? The world is full of levels, isn't it? How are you, Lois?'

'Fine,' she said absently, watching Dorrance cross the stream on a number of conveniently placed stones. He did it with his arms held out to either side, a posture which made him look like the world's oldest acrobat. Just as he reached the far bank, there was a violent exhalation from the ridge behind them – not quite an explosion.

There go the oil-tanks, Ralph thought.

Dor turned to face them from the other side of the brook, smiling his placid Buddha's smile. Ralph went up this time without any conscious intention of doing so, and without that sense of a blink inside his mind. Color rushed into the day, but he barely noticed; all his attention was fixed on Dorrance, and for a space of almost ten seconds, he forgot to breathe.

Ralph had seen auras of many shades in the last month or so, but none even remotely approached the splendid envelope that enclosed the old man Don Veazie had once described as 'nice as hell, but really sort of a fool'. It was as if Dorrance's aura had been strained through a prism . . . or a rainbow. He tossed off light in dazzling arcs: blue followed by magenta, magenta followed by red, red followed by pink, pink followed by the creamy yellow-white of a ripe banana.

He felt Lois's hand groping for his and enfolded it.

[*'My God, Ralph, do you see? Do you see how beautiful he is?'*]

[*'I sure do.'*]

[*'What is he? Is he even human?'*]

[*'I don't kn—'*]

[*'Stop it, both of you. Come back down.'*]

Dorrance was still smiling, but the voice they heard in their heads was commanding and not a bit vague. And before Ralph could consciously think himself down, he felt a push. The colors and the heightened quality of the sounds dropped out of the day at once.

'There's no time for that now,' Dor said. 'Why, it's noon already.'

'*Noon?*' Lois asked. 'It *can't* be! It wasn't even nine when we got here, and that can't have been half an hour ago!'

'Time goes faster when you're high,' Old Dor said. He spoke solemnly, but his eyes twinkled. 'Just ask anyone drinking beer and listening to country music on Saturday night. Come on! Hurry up! The clock is ticking! Cross the stream!'

Lois went first, stepping carefully from stone to stone with her arms held out, as Dorrance had done. Ralph followed with his hands poised to either side of her hips, ready to catch her if she showed signs of wavering, but he was the one who ended up almost tumbling in. He managed to avoid it, but only at the cost of wetting one foot all the way to the ankle. It seemed to him that someplace in the far reaches of his head, he could hear Carolyn laughing.

'Can't you tell us anything, Dor?' he asked as they reached the far side. 'We're pretty lost here.' *And not just mentally or spiritually, either,* he thought. He had never been in these woods in his life, not even hunting partridge or deer as a young man. If the path they were on petered out, or if Old Dor lost whatever passed for his bearings, what then?

'Yes,' Dor responded at once. 'I can tell you one thing, and it's absolutely for sure.'

'What?'

'These are the best poems Robert Creeley ever wrote,' Old Dor said, holding up his copy of *For Love,* and before either of them could respond to that, he turned around and once again began tracing his way along the faint path which ran west through the woods.

Ralph looked at Lois. Lois looked back at him, equally at a loss. Then she shrugged. 'Come on, old buddy,' she said. 'We better not lose him now. I forgot the breadcrumbs.'

5

They climbed another hill, and from the top of it Ralph could see that the path they were on led down to an old woods road with a strip of grass running up the middle. It dead-ended in an overgrown gravel-pit about fifty yards further along. There was a car idling just outside the entrance to the pit, a perfectly anonymous late model Ford which Ralph nevertheless felt he knew. When the door opened and the driver got out, everything fell into place. Of course he knew the car; he had last seen it from Lois's living room window on Tuesday night. Then it had been slued around in the middle of Harris Avenue with the driver kneeling in the glow of the headlights . . . kneeling beside the dying dog he had struck. Joe Wyzer heard them coming, looked up, and waved.

CHAPTER TWENTY-THREE

1

'He said he wanted me to drive,' Wyzer told them as he carefully turned his car around at the entrance to the gravel-pit.

'Where to?' Lois asked. She was sitting in the back with Dorrance. Ralph was in the front seat with Joe Wyzer, who looked as if he weren't quite sure where or even who he was. Ralph had slid up – just the tiniest bit – as he shook hands with the pharmacist, wanting to get a look at Wyzer's aura. Both it and his balloon-string were there, and both looked perfectly healthy . . . but the bright yellow-orange looked slightly muted to him. Ralph had an idea that was very likely Old Dor's influence.

'Good question,' Wyzer said. He voiced a small, confused laugh. 'I don't have the slightest idea, really. This has been the *weirdest* day of my entire life. Absolutely no doubt about it.'

The woods road ended in a T-junction with a stretch of two-lane blacktop. Wyzer stopped, looked for traffic, then turned left. They passed a sign reading TO 1–95 almost right away, and Ralph guessed that Wyzer would turn north as soon as they reached the turnpike. He knew where they were now – just about two miles south of Route 33. From here they could be back in Derry in less than half an hour, and Ralph had no doubt that was just where they were going.

He abruptly began to laugh. 'Well, here we are,' he said. 'Just three happy folks out for a midday drive. Make that four. Welcome to the wonderful world of hyper-reality, Joe.'

Joe gave him a sharp look, then relaxed into a grin. 'Is that what this is?' And before either Ralph or Lois could reply: 'Yeah, I suppose it is.'

'Did you read that poem?' Dorrance asked from behind Ralph. 'The one that starts "Each thing I do I rush through so I can do something else"?'

Ralph turned and saw that Dorrance was still smiling his wide, placid smile. 'Yes, I did. Dor—'

'Isn't it a crackerjack? It's *so* good. Stephen Dobyns reminds me of Hart Crane without the pretensions. Or maybe I mean *Stephen* Crane, but I don't think so. Of course he doesn't have the music of Dylan Thomas, but is that so bad? Probably not. Modern poetry is not about music. It's about *nerve* – who has it and who doesn't.'

'Oh boy,' Lois said. She rolled her eyes.

'He could probably tell us everything we need to know if we went up a few levels,' Ralph said, 'but you don't want that, do you, Dor? Because time goes faster when you're high.'

'Bingo,' Dorrance replied. The blue signs marking the north and south entrances to the turnpike glimmered up ahead. 'You'll have to go up later, I imagine, you and Lois both, and so it's very important to save as much time as you can now. Save . . . time.' He made a queerly evocative gesture, drawing a gnarled thumb and forefinger down in the air, bringing them together as he did, as if to indicate some narrowing passage.

Joe Wyzer put on his blinker, turned left, and headed down the northbound ramp to Derry.

'How did you get involved in this, Joe?' Ralph asked him. 'Of all the people on the west side, why did Dorrance draft you as chauffeur?'

Wyzer shook his head, and when the car reached the turnpike it drifted immediately over into the passing lane. Ralph reached out quickly and made a midcourse correction, reminding himself that Joe probably hadn't been getting much sleep himself just lately. He was very happy to see the highway was mostly deserted, at least this far out of town. It would save some anxiety, and God knew he would take whatever he could get in that department today.

'We are all bound together by the Purpose,' Dorrance said abruptly. 'That's *ka-tet*, which means one made of many. The way that many rhymes make up a single poem. You see?'

'No.' Ralph, Lois, and Joe said it at the same time, in perfect, unrehearsed chorus, and then laughed nervously together. *The Three Insomniacs of the Apocalypse,* Ralph thought. *Jesus save us.*

'That's okay,' Old Dor said, smiling his wide smile. 'Just take my word for it. You and Lois . . . Helen and her little daughter . . . Bill . . . Faye Chapin . . . Trigger Vachon . . . me! All part of the Purpose.'

'That's fine, Dor,' Lois said, 'but where's the Purpose

taking us now? And what are we supposed to do when we get there?'

Dorrance leaned forward and whispered in Joe Wyzer's ear, guarding his lips with one puffy, age-spotted hand. Then he sat back again, looking deeply satisfied with himself.

'He says we're going to the Civic Center,' Joe said.

'The *Civic* Center!' Lois exclaimed, sounding alarmed. 'No, that can't be right! Those two little men said—'

'Never mind them right now,' Dorrance said. 'Just remember what it's about — nerve. Who has it, and who doesn't.'

2

Silence in Joe Wyzer's Ford for almost the space of a mile. Dorrance opened his book of Robert Creeley poems and began to read one, tracing his way from line to line with the yellowed nail of one ancient finger. Ralph found himself remembering a game they had sometimes played as kids — not a very nice one. Snipe Hunt, it had been called. You got kids who were a little younger and a lot more gullible than you were, fed them a cock-and-bull story about the mythical snipe, then gave them towsacks and sent them out to spend a strenuous afternoon wandering around in the damps and the willywags, looking for nonexistent birds. This game was also called Wild Goose Chase, and he suddenly had the inescapable feeling that Clotho and Lachesis had been playing it with him and Lois up on the hospital roof.

He turned around in his seat and looked directly at

Old Dor. Dorrance folded over the top corner of the page he was reading, closed his book, and looked back at Ralph with polite interest.

'They told us we weren't to go near either Ed Deepneau or Doc #3,' Ralph said. He spoke slowly and with great clarity. 'They told us very specifically that we weren't even to *think* of doing that, because the situation had invested both of them with great power and we were apt to get swatted like flies. In fact, I think Lachesis said that if we tried getting near either Ed or Atropos, we might end up having a visit from one of the upper-level honchos . . . someone Ed calls the Crimson King. Not a very nice fellow, either, by all reports.'

'Yes,' Lois said in a faint voice. 'That's what they told us on the hospital roof. They said we had to convince the women in charge to cancel Susan Day's appearance. That's why we went out to High Ridge.'

'And did you succeed in convincing them?' Wyzer asked.

'No. Ed's crazy friends came before we could get there, set the place on fire, and killed at least two of the women. Shot them. One was the woman we really wanted to talk to.'

'Gretchen Tillbury,' Ralph said.

'Yes,' Lois agreed. 'But surely we don't need to do any more — I can't believe they'll go ahead with the rally now. I mean, how could they? My God, at least four people are dead! Probably more! They'll *have* to cancel her speech or at least postpone it. Isn't that so?'

Neither Dorrance nor Joe replied. Ralph didn't reply, either — he was thinking of Helen's red-rimmed, furious eyes. *How can you even ask?* she'd said. *If they stop us now, they win.*

If they stop us now, they win.

Was there any legal way the police *could* stop them? Probably not. The City Council, then? Maybe. Maybe they could hold a special meeting and revoke WomanCare's rally permit. But *would* they? If there were two thousand angry, grief-stricken women marching around the Municipal Building and yelling *If they stop us now they win* in unison, *would* the Council revoke the permit?

Ralph began to feel a deep sinking sensation in his gut.

Helen clearly considered tonight's rally more important than ever, and she wouldn't be the only one. It was no longer just about choice and who had the right to decide what a woman did with her own body; now it was about causes important enough to die for and honoring the friends who had done just that. Now they were talking not just about politics but about a kind of secular requiem mass for the dead.

Lois had grabbed his shoulder and was shaking it hard. Ralph came back to the here and now, but slowly, like a man being shaken awake in the middle of an incredibly vivid dream.

'They *will* cancel it, won't they? And even if they don't, if for some crazy reason they don't, most people will stay away, right? After what happened at High Ridge, they'll be afraid to come!'

Ralph thought about that and then shook his head. 'Most people will think the danger's over. The news reports are going to say that two of the radicals who attacked

High Ridge are dead, and the third is catatonic, or some-thing.'

'But Ed! What about Ed?' she cried. 'He's the one who got them to attack, for heaven's sake! *He's the one who sent them out there in the first place!*'

'That may be true, probably *is* true, but how would we prove it? Do you know what I think the cops will find at wherever Charlie Pickering's been hanging his hat? A note saying it was all his idea. A note exonerating Ed completely, probably in the guise of an accusation . . . how Ed deserted them in their time of greatest need. And if they don't find a note like that in Charlie's rented room, they'll find it in Frank Felton's. Or Sandra McKay's.'

'But that . . . that's . . .' Lois stopped, biting at her lower lip. Then she looked at Wyzer with hopeful eyes. 'What about Susan Day? Where is *she*? Does anybody know? Do you? Ralph and I will call her on the telephone and—'

'She's already in Derry,' Wyzer said, 'although I doubt if even the police know for sure where she is. But what I heard on the news while the old fella and I were driving out here is that the rally is going to happen tonight . . . and that's supposedly straight from the woman herself.'

Sure, Ralph thought. *Sure it is. The show's going on, the show has to go on, and she knows it. Someone who's ridden the crest of the women's movement all these years – hell, since the Chicago convention in '68 – knows a genuine watershed moment when she sees it. She's evaluated the risks and found them acceptable. Either that or she's evaluated the situation and decided that the credibility-loss involved in walking away would be unacceptable. Maybe both. In any case, she's as much a prisoner of events – of* ka-tet *– as the rest of us.*

671

They were on the outskirts of Derry again. Ralph could see the Civic Center on the horizon.

Now it was Old Dor Lois turned to. 'Where is she? Do *you* know? It doesn't matter how many security people she's got around her; Ralph and I can be invisible when we want to be . . . and we're very good at changing people's minds.'

'Oh, changing Susan Day's mind wouldn't change anything,' Dor said. He still wore that broad, maddening smile. 'They'll come to the Civic Center tonight no matter what. If they come and find the doors locked, they'll break them open and go inside and have their rally just the same. To show they're not afraid.'

'Done-bun-can't-be-undone,' Ralph said dully.

'Right, Ralph!' Dor said cheerily, and patted Ralph's arm.

3

Five minutes later, Joe drove his Ford past the hideous plastic statue of Paul Bunyan which stood in front of the Civic Center and turned in at a sign which read THERE'S ALWAYS FREE PARKING AT YOUR CIVIC CENTER!

The acre of parking lot lay between the Civic Center building itself and the Bassey Park racetrack. If the event that evening had been a rock concert or a boat-show or a wrestling card, they would have had the parking lot entirely to themselves this early, but tonight's event was clearly going to be light-years from an exhibition basketball game or a monster truck-pull. There were already sixty or seventy cars in the lot, and little groups of people standing around, looking at the building. Most of them were women. Some had picnic hampers, several were crying, and almost all wore black armbands. Ralph saw a middle-aged woman with a weary, intelligent face and a great mass of gray hair passing these out from a carrybag. She was wearing a tee-shirt with Susan Day's face on it and the words WE SHALL ♀ VERC♀ ME.

The drive-through area in front of the Civic Center's bank of entrance doors was even busier than the parking lot. No fewer than six TV newsvans were parked there, and various tech crews stood under the triangular cement canopy in little clusters, discussing how they were going to handle tonight's event. And according to the bedsheet banner which hung down from the canopy, flapping lazily in the breeze, there *was* going to be an event. RALLY IS *ON*, it read in large, blurry spray-paint letters. 8 P.M. COME SHOW YOUR SOLIDARITY EXPRESS YOUR OUTRAGE COMFORT YOUR SISTERS.

Joe put the Ford in Park, then turned to Old Dor, eyebrows raised. Dor nodded, and Joe looked at Ralph. 'I guess this is where you and Lois get out, Ralph. Good luck. I'd come with you if I could – I even asked him – but he says I'm not equipped.'

'That's all right,' Ralph said. 'We appreciate everything you've done, don't we, Lois?'

'We certainly do,' Lois said.

Ralph reached for the doorhandle, then let it go again. He turned to face Dorrance. 'What's this about? Really, I mean. It's *not* about saving the two thousand or so people Clotho and Lachesis said are going to be here tonight, that's for sure. To the kind of All-Time forces *they* talked

673

about, two thousand lives are probably just a little more grease on the bearings. So what's it all about, Alfie? Why are we here?'

Dorrance's grin had faded at last; with it gone he looked younger and strangely formidable. 'Job asked God the same question,' he said, 'and got no answer. You're not going to get one either, but I'll tell you this much: you've become the pivot-point of great events and vast forces. The work of the higher universe has almost completely come to a stop as those of both the Random and the Purpose turn to mark your progress.'

'That's great, but I don't get it,' Ralph said, more in resignation than in anger.

'Neither do I, but those two thousand lives are enough for me,' Lois said quietly. 'I could never live with myself if I didn't at least try to stop what's going to happen. I'd dream of the deathbag around that building for the rest of my life. Even if I only got an hour's sleep a night I'd dream of it.'

Ralph considered this, then nodded. He opened his door and swung one foot out. 'That's a good point. And Helen'll be there. She might even bring Nat. Maybe, for little Short-Time farts like us, that's enough.'

And maybe, he thought, *I want a rematch with Doc #3.*

Oh, Ralph, Carolyn mourned. *Clint Eastwood? Again?*

No, not Clint Eastwood. Not Sylvester Stallone or Arnold Schwarzenegger, either. Not even John Wayne. He was no big action-hero or movie-star; he was just plain old Ralph Roberts from Harris Avenue. That didn't make the grudge he bore the doc with the rusty scalpel any less real, however. And now that grudge was a lot bigger than just a stray dog and the retired history teacher who had lived downstairs for the last ten years or so. Ralph kept thinking of the parlor at High Ridge, and the women propped against the wall below the poster of Susan Day. It wasn't upon Merrilee's pregnant belly which the eye in his mind kept focusing but Gretchen Tillbury's hair – her beautiful blonde hair that had been mostly burned off by the close-range rifle-shot that had taken her life. Charlie Pickering had pulled the trigger, and maybe Ed Deepneau had put the gun in his hands, but it was Atropos Ralph blamed, Atropos the jump-rope-thief, Atropos the hat-thief, Atropos the comb-thief.

Atropos the earring-thief.

'Come on, Lois,' he said. 'Let's –'

But she put her hand on his arm and shook her head. 'Not just yet – get back in here and shut the door.'

He looked at her carefully, then did what she said. She paused, gathering her thoughts, and when she spoke, she looked directly at Old Dor.

'I still don't understand why we were sent out to High Ridge,' she said. 'They never even came right out and said that was what we were supposed to do, but we know – don't we, Ralph? – that that was what they wanted from us. *And I want to understand.* If we're supposed to be *here,* why did we have to go out *there*? I mean, we saved some lives, and I'm glad, but I think Ralph's right – a few lives don't mean much to the people running this show.'

Silence for a moment, and then Dorrance said, 'Did Clotho and Lachesis really strike you as all-wise and all-knowing, Lois?'

'Well . . . they were smart, but I guess they weren't exactly geniuses,' she said after a moment's thought. 'At one point they called themselves working joes who were a long way down the ladder from the boardroom executives who actually made the decisions.'

Old Dor was nodding and smiling. 'Clotho and Lachesis are almost Short-Timers themselves, in the big scheme of things. They have their own fears and mental blindspots. They are also capable of making bad decisions . . . but in the end, that doesn't matter, because they also serve the Purpose. And *ka-tet*.'

'They thought we'd lose if we went head-to-head with Atropos, didn't they?' Ralph asked. 'That's why they talked themselves into believing we could accomplish what they wanted to using the back door . . . the back door being High Ridge.'

'Yes,' Dor said. 'That's it.'

'Great,' Ralph said. 'I love a vote of confidence. Especially when—'

'No,' Dor said. 'That's *not* it.'

Ralph and Lois exchanged a bewildered glance.

'What are you talking about?'

'It's both things at the same time. That's very often the way things are within the Purpose. You see . . . well . . .' He sighed. 'I *hate* all these questions. I hardly *ever* answer questions, did I tell you that?'

'Yes,' Lois said. 'You did.'

'Yes. And now, bingo! All these questions. Nasty! And useless!'

Ralph looked at Lois, and she looked back at him. Neither of them made any move to get out.

Dor heaved a sigh. 'All right . . . but this is the last thing I'm going to say, so pay attention. Clotho and Lachesis may have sent you to High Ridge for the wrong reasons, but the Purpose sent you there for the right ones. You fulfilled your task there.'

'By saving the women,' Lois said.

But Dorrance was shaking his head.

'Then what *did* we do?' she nearly shouted. '*What?* Don't we have a right to know what part of the gosh-damned Purpose we fulfilled?'

'No,' Dorrance said. 'At least not yet. Because you have to do it again.'

'This is crazy,' Ralph said.

'It isn't, though,' Dorrance replied. He was holding *For Love* tightly against his chest now, bending it back and forth and looking at Ralph earnestly. '*Random* is crazy. Purpose is sane.'

All right, Ralph thought, *what did we do at High Ridge besides save the people in the cellar? And John Leydecker, of course – I think Pickering might have killed him as well as Chris Nell if I hadn't intervened. Could it be something to do with Leydecker?*

He supposed it could, but it didn't feel right.

'Dorrance,' he said, 'can't you please give us a little more information? I mean—'

'No,' Old Dor said, not unkindly. 'No more questions, no more time. We'll have a good meal together after this is over . . . if we're still around, that is.'

'You really know how to cheer a fellow up, Dor.' Ralph opened his door. Lois did the same, and they both stepped out into the parking lot. He bent down and looked at Joe Wyzer. 'Is there anything else? Anything you can think of?'

'No, I don't think—'

677

Dor leaned forward and whispered in his ear. Joe listened, frowning.

'Well?' Ralph asked when Dorrance sat back. 'What did he say?'

'He said not to forget my comb,' Joe said. 'I don't have the slightest idea what he's talking about, but what else is new?'

'That's okay,' Ralph said, and smiled a little. 'It's one of the few things I *do* understand. Come on, Lois – let's check out the crowd. Mingle a little.'

4

Halfway across the parking lot, she elbowed him so hard in the side that Ralph staggered. 'Look!' she whispered. 'Right over there! Isn't that Connie Chung?'

Ralph looked. Yes; the woman in the beige coat standing between two techs with the CBS logo on their jackets was almost certainly Connie Chung. He had admired her pretty, intelligent face and pleasant smile over too many evening meals to have much doubt about it.

'Either her or her twin sister,' he said.

Lois seemed to have forgotten all about Old Dor and High Ridge and the bald docs; in that moment she was once more the woman Bill McGovern had liked to call 'our Lois'. 'I'll be darned! What's *she* doing here?'

'Well,' Ralph began, and then covered his mouth to hide a jaw-cracking yawn, 'I guess what's going on in Derry is national news now. She must be here to do a live segment in front of the Civic Center for tonight's news. In any case—'

Suddenly, with no warning at all, the auras swam back. Ralph gasped.

'*Jesus!* Lois, are you seeing this?'

But he didn't think she was. If she *had* been, Ralph didn't think Connie Chung would have rated even an honorable mention on Lois's attention-roster. This was horrible almost beyond conceiving, and for the first time Ralph fully realized that even the bright world of auras had its dark side, one that would make an ordinary person fall on his knees and thank God for his reduced perceptions.

And this isn't even stepping up the ladder, he thought. *At least, I don't think it is. I'm only looking at that wider world, like a man looking through a window. I'm not actually in it.*

Nor did he *want* to be in it. Just looking at something like this was almost enough to make you wish you were blind.

Lois was frowning at him. 'What, the colors? No. Should I try to? Is there something wrong with them?'

He tried to answer and couldn't. A moment later he felt her hand seize his arm in a painful pincers grip above the elbow and knew that no explanation was necessary. For better or worse, Lois was now seeing for herself.

'Oh *dear,*' she whimpered in a breathless little voice that teetered on the edge of tears. 'Oh *dear,* oh *dear,* oh jeez Louise.'

From the roof of Derry Home, the aura hanging over the Civic Center had looked like a vast, saggy umbrella – the

Travelers' Insurance Company logo colored black by a child's crayon, perhaps. Standing here in the parking lot, it was like being inside a large and indescribably nasty mosquito net, one so old and badly cared-for that its gauzy walls had silted up with blackish-green mildew. The bright October sun shrank to a bleary circle of tarnished silver. The air took on a gloomy, foggy cast that made Ralph think of pictures of London at the end of the nineteenth century. They were not just looking at the Civic Center deathbag, not anymore; they were buried alive in it. Ralph could feel it pressing hungrily in on him, trying to overwhelm him with feelings of loss and despair and dismay.

Why bother? he asked himself, watching apathetically as Joe Wyzer's Ford drove back down toward Main Street with Old Dor still sitting in the back seat. *I mean hey, really, what the hell is the use? We can't change this thing, no way we can. Maybe we did something out at High Ridge, but the difference between what was going on out there and what's happening here is like the difference between a smudge and a black hole. If we try to mess in with this business, we're going to get flattened.*

He heard moaning from beside him and realized Lois was crying. Mustering his flagging energy, he slid an arm around her shoulders. 'Hold on, Lois,' he said. 'We can stand up to this.' But he wondered.

'*We're breathing it in!*' she wept. 'It's like we're sucking up death! Oh, Ralph, let's get away from here! Please let's just get away from here!'

The idea sounded as good to him as the idea of water must sound to a man dying of thirst in the desert, but he shook his head. 'Two thousand people are going to die here tonight if we don't do something. I'm pretty confused about the rest of this business but that much I can grasp with no trouble at all.'

'Okay,' she whispered. 'Just keep your arm around me so I don't crack my head open if I faint.'

It was ironic, Ralph thought. They now had the faces and bodies of people in the early years of a vigorous middle age, but they shuffled across the parking lot like a pair of old-timers whose muscles have turned to string and whose bones have turned to glass. He could hear Lois's breathing, rapid and labored, like the breathing of a woman who has just sustained some serious injury.

'I'll take you back if you want,' Ralph said, and he meant it. He would take her back to the parking lot, he would take her to the orange bus-stop bench he could see from here. And when the bus came, getting on and going back to Harris Avenue would be the simplest thing in the world.

He could feel the killer aura which surrounded this place pressing in on him, trying to smother him like a plastic dry-cleaning bag, and he found himself remembering something McGovern had said about May Locher's emphysema that it was one of those diseases that keep on giving. And now he supposed he had a pretty good idea of how May Locher had felt during her last few years. It didn't matter how hard he sucked at the black air or how deep he dragged it down; it did not satisfy. His heart and head went on pounding, making him feel as if he were suffering the worst hangover of his life.

He was opening his mouth to repeat that he'd take her back when she spoke up, talking in little out-of-breath gasps. 'I guess I can make it . . . but I hope . . . it won't take long. Ralph, how come we can feel something this bad even without being able to see the colors? Why can't *they*?' She pointed at the media people milling around the Civic Center. 'Are we Short-Timers that insensitive? I hate to think that.'

He shook his head, indicating that he didn't know, but he thought that perhaps the news crews, video technicians, and security guards clustered around the doors and beneath the spray-painted banner hanging from the canopy *did* feel something. He saw lots of hands holding styrofoam cups of coffee, but he didn't see anyone actually drinking the stuff. There was a box of doughnuts sitting on the hood of a station wagon, but the only one which had been taken out had been laid aside on a napkin with just a single bite gone. Ralph ran his eye over two dozen faces without seeing a single smile. The newspeople were going about their work – setting camera angles, marking locations from which the talking heads would do their stand-ups, laying down coaxial cable and duct-taping it to the cement – but they were doing it without the sort of excitement which Ralph would have expected to accompany a story as big as this one was turning out to be.

Connie Chung walked out from beneath the canopy with a bearded, handsome cameraman – MICHAEL ROSENBERG, the tag on his CBS jacket said – and then raised her small hands in a framing gesture, showing him how she wanted him to shoot the bedsheet banner hanging down from the canopy. Rosenberg nodded. Chung's face was pale and solemn, and at one point during her conversation with the bearded cameraman, Ralph saw her pause and raise a hand uncertainly to her temple, as if she had lost her train of thought or perhaps felt faint.

There seemed to be an underlying similarity to all the expressions he saw — a common chord — and he thought he knew what it was: they were all suffering from what had been called melancholia when he was a kid, and melancholia was just a fancy word for the blues.

Ralph found himself remembering times in his life when he'd hit the emotional equivalent of a cold spot while swimming or clear air turbulence while flying. You'd be cruising along through your day, sometimes feeling great, sometimes just feeling okay, but getting along and getting it done . . . and then, for no apparent reason at all, you'd go down in flames and crash. A sense of *What the hell's the use* would slide over you — unconnected to any real event in your life at that moment but incredibly powerful all the same — and you felt like simply creeping back to bed and pulling the covers up over your head.

Maybe this is what causes feelings like that, he thought. *Maybe it's running into something like this — some big mess of death or sorrow waiting to happen, spread out like a banquet tent made of cobwebs and tears instead of canvas and rope. We don't see it, not down on our Short-Time level, but we feel it. Oh yes, we feel it. And now . . .*

Now it was trying to suck them dry. Maybe *they* weren't vampires, as they both had feared, but *this* thing was. The deathbag had a sluggish, half-sentient life, and it would suck them dry if it could. If they let it.

Lois stumbled against him and Ralph had all he could do to keep them both from sprawling to the pavement. Then she lifted her head (slowly, as if her hair had been

683

dipped in cement), curled a hand around her mouth, and inhaled sharply. At the same time she flickered a little. Under other circumstances, Ralph might have dismissed that flicker as a momentary glitch in his own eyes, but not now. She had slid up. Just a little. Just enough to feed.

He hadn't seen Lois dip into the waitress's aura, but this time everything happened in front of him. The auras of the newspeople were like small but brightly colored Japanese lanterns glowing bravely in a vast, gloomy cavern. Now a tight beam of violet light speared out from one of them – from Michael Rosenberg, Connie Chung's bearded cameraman, in fact. It divided in two an inch or so in front of Lois's face. The upper branch divided in two again and slipped into her nostrils; the lower branch went between her parted lips and into her mouth. He could see it glowing faintly behind her cheeks, lighting her from the inside as a candle lights a jack-o'-lantern.

Her grip on him loosened, and suddenly the leaning pressure of her weight was gone. A moment later the violet beam of light disappeared. She looked around at him. Color – not a lot, but some – was returning to her leaden cheeks.

'That's better – a *lot* better. Now you, Ralph!'

He was reluctant – it still felt like stealing – but it had to be done if he didn't want to simply collapse right here; he could almost feel the last of Nirvana Boy's borrowed energy running out through his pores. He curled his hand around his mouth now as he had in the Dunkin' Donuts parking lot that morning and turned slightly to his left, seeking a target. Connie Chung had backed several steps closer to them; she was still looking up at the bedsheet banner hanging from the canopy and talking to Rosenberg (who seemed none the worse for wear as a result of Lois's borrowing) about it. With no further thought, Ralph inhaled sharply through the curled tube of his fingers.

Chung's aura was the same lovely shade of wedding-gown ivory as those which had surrounded Helen and Nat on the day they'd come to his apartment with Gretchen Tillbury. Instead of a ray of light, something like a long, straight ribbon shot from Chung's aura. Ralph felt strength begin to fill him almost at once, banishing the aching weariness in his joints and muscles. And he could think clearly again, as if a big cloud of sludge had just been washed out of his brain.

Connie Chung broke off, looked up at the sky for a moment, then began to talk to the cameraman again. Ralph glanced around and saw Lois looking at him anxiously. 'Any better?' she whispered.

'All kinds,' he said, 'but it's still like being zipped up in a body-bag.'

'I think –' Lois began, and then her eyes fixed on something to the left of the Civic Center doors. She screamed and shrank back against Ralph, her eyes so wide it seemed they must tumble from their sockets. He followed her gaze and felt his breath stop in his throat. The planners had tried to soften the building's plain brick sides by planting ever-green bushes along them. These had either been neglected or purposely allowed to grow until they interlaced and threatened to entirely hide the narrow strip of grass between them and the concrete walk which bordered the drive-through.

Giant bugs that looked like prehistoric trilobites were squirming in and out of these evergreens in droves, crawling over each other, bumping heads, sometimes rearing up and pawing each other with their front legs like stags locking horns during mating season. They weren't transparent, like the bird on the satellite dish, but there was something ghostly and unreal about them, just the same. Their auras flickered feverishly (and brainlessly, Ralph guessed) through a whole spectrum of colors; they were so bright and yet so ephemeral that it was almost possible to think of them as weird lightning-bugs.

Except that's not what they are. You know *what they are.*

'Hey!' It was Rosenberg, Chung's cameraman, who hailed them, but most of the others in front of the building were looking. 'She okay, bud?'

'Yes,' Ralph called back. He still had his hand curled around his mouth and lowered it quickly, feeling foolish. 'She just . . .'

'I saw a mouse!' Lois called, smiling a daffy, dazed smile . . . an 'our Lois' smile if Ralph had ever seen one. He was very proud of her. She pointed toward the evergreen shrubs to the left of the door with a finger that was almost steady. 'He went right in there. Gosh, but he was a fat one! Did you see him, Norton?'

'No, Alice.'

'Stick around, lady,' Michael Rosenberg called. 'You'll see all kinds of wildlife here tonight.' There was some desultory, almost forced laughter, and then they turned back to their tasks.

'God, Ralph!' Lois whispered. 'Those . . . those *things* . . .'

He took her hand and squeezed it. 'Steady, Lois.'

'They know, don't they? That's why they're here. They're like vultures.'

Ralph nodded. As he watched, several bugs emerged from the tops of the bushes and began to ooze aimlessly up the wall. They moved with dazed sluggishness – like flies buzzing against a windowpane in November – and left slimy trails of color behind them. These quickly dimmed and faded. Other bugs crawled out from beneath the bushes and onto the small strip of lawn.

One of the local news commentators began strolling toward this infested area, and when he turned his head, Ralph saw it was John Kirkland. He was talking to a good-looking woman dressed in one of those 'power look' business outfits which Ralph found – under normal circumstances, anyway – extremely sexy. He guessed she was Kirkland's producer, and wondered if Lisette Benson's aura turned green when this woman was around.

'They're going toward those bugs!' Lois whispered fiercely at him. 'We have to stop them, Ralph – we *have* to!'

'We're not going to do a damned thing.'

'But—'

'Lois, we can't start raving about bugs nobody but us can see. We'll end up in the nuthatch if we do. Besides, the bugs aren't there for them.' He paused and added: 'I hope.'

They watched as Kirkland and his good-looking colleague walked onto the lawn . . . and into a jellylike knot of the twitching, crawling trilobites. One slid onto Kirkland's highly polished loafer, paused until he stopped moving for a second, then climbed onto his pantsleg.

'I don't give much of a shit about Susan Day, one way or the other,' Kirkland was saying. 'WomanCare's the story here, not her – crying babes wearing black armbands.'

'Watch out, John,' the woman said dryly. 'Your sensitivity is showing.'

'Is it? Goddam.' The bug on his pantsleg appeared bound for his crotch. It occurred to Ralph that if Kirkland were suddenly given the power to see what was shortly going to be crawling over his balls, he would probably go right out of his mind.

'Okay, but be sure to talk to the women who run the local power-network,' the producer was saying. 'Now that Tillbury's dead, the ones that matter are Maggie Petrowsky, Barbara Richards, and Dr Roberta Warper. Warper's going to introduce the Big Kahuna tonight, I think . . . or maybe in this case it's the Big Kahunette.' The woman took a step off the sidewalk and one of her high heels skewered a lumbering color-bug. A rainbow of guts spewed out of it, and a waxy-white substance that looked like stale mashed potatoes. Ralph had an idea the white stuff had been eggs.

Lois pressed her face against his arm.

'And keep your eyes open for a lady named Helen Deepneau,' the producer said, taking a step closer to the building. The bug stuck on the heel of her shoe flopped and twisted as she walked.

'Deepneau,' Kirkland said. He tapped his knuckles against his brow. 'Somewhere, deep inside, a bell is ringing.'

'Nah, it's just your last active brain-cell rolling around in there,' the producer said. 'She's Ed Deepneau's wife. They're separated. If you want tears, she's your best bet. She and Tillbury were good friends. Maybe *special* friends, if you know what I mean.'

Kirkland leered – an expression so foreign to his

on-camera persona that Ralph felt slightly disoriented. One of the color-bugs, meanwhile, had found its way onto the toe of the woman's shoe and was working its way up her leg. Ralph watched in helpless fascination as it disappeared beneath the hem of her skirt. Watching the moving bump climb her thigh was like watching a kitten under a bath-towel. And again, it seemed that Kirkland's colleague felt *something*; as she talked to him about interviews during Day's speech, she reached down and absently scratched at the lump, which had now made it almost all the way up to her right hip. Ralph didn't hear the thick popping sound the fragile, flabby thing made when it burst, but he could imagine it. Was helpless not to, it seemed. And he could imagine its innards dripping down her nyloned leg like pus. It would remain there at least until her evening shower, unseen, unfelt, unsuspected.

Now the two of them began discussing how they should cover the scheduled pro-life rally this afternoon . . . assuming it actually happened, that was. The woman was of the opinion that not even The Friends of Life would be dumbheaded enough to show up at the Civic Center after what had happened at High Ridge. Kirkland told her it was impossible to underestimate the idiocy of fanatics; people who could wear that much polyester in public were clearly a force to be reckoned with. And all the time they were talking, exchanging quips and ideas and gossip, more of the swollen, multi-colored bugs were swarming busily up their legs and torsos. One pioneer had made it all the way up to Kirkland's red tie, and was apparently bound for his face.

Movement off to the right caught Ralph's eye. He

turned toward the doors in time to see one of the techs elbowing a buddy and pointing at him and Lois. Ralph suddenly had an all-too-clear picture of what they were seeing: two people with no visible reason for being here (neither of them was wearing a black armband and they were clearly not representatives of the media) just hanging out at the edge of the parking lot. The lady, who had already screamed once, had her face buried against the gentleman's arm . . . and the gentleman in question was gaping like a fool at nothing in particular.

Ralph spoke softly and from the corner of his mouth, like an inmate discussing escape in an old Warner Bros. jailbreak epic. 'Get your head up. We're attracting more attention than we can afford.'

For a moment he really didn't believe she was going to be able to do that . . . and then she came through and lifted her head. She glanced at the shrubs growing along the wall one final time – an involuntary, horrified little peek – and then looked resolutely back at Ralph and *only* Ralph. 'Do you see any sign of Atropos, Ralph? That *is* why we're here, isn't it . . . to pick up his trail?'

'Maybe. I suppose. Haven't even looked, to tell the truth – too many other things going on. I think we ought to get a little closer to the building.' This wasn't a thing he wanted to do, but it seemed very important to do *something*. He could feel the deathbag all around them, a gloomy, suffocating presence that was passively opposed to forward motion of any kind. *That* was what they had to fight.

'All right,' she said. 'I'm going to ask for Connie Chung's autograph, and I'm going to be all giggly and silly while I do it. Can you stand that?'

'Yes.'

'Good. Because that will mean that if they're looking at anybody, they'll be looking at me.'

'Sounds good.'

He spared one last look at John Kirkland and the woman producer. They were now discussing what events might cause them to break into the evening's network feed and go live, totally unaware of the lumbering trilobites crawling back and forth on their faces. One of them was currently squirming slowly into John Kirkland's mouth.

Ralph looked away in a hurry and let Lois pull him over to where Ms Chung stood with Rosenberg, the bearded cameraman. He saw the two of them glance first at Lois and then at each other. The shared look was one part amusement and three parts resignation – *here comes one of them* – and then Lois gave his hand a hard little squeeze that said, *Never mind me, Ralph, you take care of your business and I'll take care of mine.*

'Pardon me, but aren't you Connie Chung?' Lois asked in her gushiest isn't-this-the-living-end voice. 'I saw you over there and at first I said to Norton, "Is that the lady who's on with Dan Rather, or am I crazy?" And then—'

'I *am* Connie Chung, and it's very nice to meet you, but I'm getting ready for tonight's news, so if you could excuse me—'

'Oh, of course, I wouldn't *dream* of bothering you, I only want an autograph – just a quick little scribble would do – because I'm your number one fan, at least in Maine.'

Ms Chung glanced at Rosenberg. He was already holding a pen out in one hand, much as a good OR nurse has the instrument the doctor will want next even before

691

he calls for it. Ralph turned his attention to the area in front of the Civic Center and slid his perceptions up the tiniest bit.

What he saw in front of the doors was a semi-transparent, blackish substance that puzzled him at first. It was about two inches deep and looked almost like some sort of geological formation. That couldn't be, though . . . could it? If what he was looking at was real (the way objects in the Short-Time world were real, at least), the stuff would have blocked the doors from opening, and it wasn't doing that. As Ralph watched, two TV techs strolled ankle-deep through the stuff as if it were no more substantial than low-lying groundmist.

Ralph remembered the aural footprints people left behind – the ones that looked like Arthur Murray learn-to-dance diagrams – and suddenly thought he understood. The tracks faded away like cigarette smoke . . . except that cigarette smoke really *didn't* go away; it left a residue on walls, on windows, and in lungs. Apparently, human auras left their own residue. It probably wasn't enough to see once the colors faded if it was only one person, but this was the biggest public meetingplace in Maine's fourth-largest city. Ralph thought of all the people who had poured in and out through these doors – all the banquets, conventions, coin-shows, concerts, basketball tourneys – and understood that semi-transparent slag. It was the equivalent of the slight dip you sometimes saw in the middle of much-used steps.

Never mind that now, sweetheart – take care of your business.

Nearby, Connie Chung was scribbling her name on

the back of Lois's light-bill for September. Ralph looked at that slaggy residue on the cement apron in front of the doors, hunting for a trace of Atropos, something which might register more as smell than sight, a nasty, meaty aroma like the alley which used to run behind Mr Huston's butcher shop when Ralph was a kid.

'Thank you!' Lois was burbling. 'I said to Norton, "She looks just like she does on TV, just like a little China doll." Those were my exact words.'

'Very welcome, I'm sure,' Chung said, 'but I really have to get back to work.'

'Of course you do. Say hello to Dan Rather for me, won't you? Tell him I said "Courage!"'

'I certainly will.' Chung smiled and nodded as she handed the pen back to Rosenberg. 'Now, if you'll excuse us—'

If it's here, it's higher up than I am, Ralph thought. *I'll have to slide up a little bit farther.*

Yes, but he'd have to be careful, and not just because time had become an extremely valuable commodity. The simple fact was that if he went up too high, he would disappear from the Short-Time world, and that was the sort of occurrence which might even distract these newspeople from the impending pro-choice rally . . . at least for awhile.

Ralph concentrated, but when the painless spasm inside his head happened this time, it didn't come as a blink but as the soft lowering of a lash. Color bloomed silently into the world; everything stood forth with exclamatory brilliance. Yet the strongest of these colors, the oppressive key-chord, was the black of the deathbag, and it was a negation of all the others. Depression and that sense of debilitating weakness fell on him again, sinking into his heart like the pointed ends of a clawhammer. He realized that if he had business to do up here, he had better do it quickly and scoot back down to the Short-Time level before he was stripped clean of life-force.

He looked at the doors again. For a moment there was still nothing but the fading auras of Short-Timers like himself . . . and then what he was looking for suddenly came clear, rising into his view as a message which has been written in lemon juice rises into sight when it is held close to a candle-flame.

He had expected something which would look and smell like the rotting guts in the bins behind Mr Huston's knacker's shop, but the reality was even worse, possibly because it was so unexpected. There were fans of a bloody, mucusy substance on the doors themselves – marks made by Atropos's restless fingers, perhaps – and a revoltingly large puddle of the same stuff sinking into the hardened residue in front of the doors. There was something so terrible about this stuff – so alien – that it made the color-bugs look almost normal by comparison. It was like a pool of vomit left by a dog suffering from some new and dangerous strain of rabies. A trail of this stuff led away from the puddle, first in drying clots and splashes, then in smaller drips like spilled paint.

Of course, Ralph thought. *That's why we had to come here. The little bastard can't stay away from the place. It's like cocaine to a dope-addict.*

He could imagine Atropos standing right here where he, Ralph, was standing now, looking . . . grinning . . . then

694

stepping forward and putting his hands on the doors. Caressing them. Creating those filthy, filmy marks. Could imagine Atropos drawing strength and energy from the very blackness which was robbing Ralph of his own vitality.

He has other places to go and other things to do, of course – every day is undoubtedly a busy day when you're a supernatural psycho like him – but it must be hard for him to stay away from this place for long, no matter how busy he is. And how does it make him feel? Like a tight fuck on a summer afternoon, that's how.

Lois tugged his sleeve from behind and he turned to her. She was still smiling, but the feverish intensity in her eyes made the expression on her lips look suspiciously like a scream. Behind her, Connie Chung and Rosenberg were strolling back toward the building.

'You've got to get me out of here,' Lois whispered. 'I can't stand it anymore. I feel like I'm losing my mind.'

[*'Okay – no problem.'*]

'I can't hear you, Ralph – and I think I can see the sun shining through you. Jesus, I'm *sure* I can!'

[*'Oh – wait—'*]

He concentrated, and felt the world slide slightly around him. The colors faded; Lois's aura seemed to disappear back inside her skin.

'Better?'

'Well, *solider,* anyway.'

He smiled briefly. 'Good. Come on.'

He took her by the elbow and began guiding her back toward where Joe Wyzer had dropped them off. It was the same direction in which the bloody splashes led.

'Did you find what you were looking for?'

'Yes.'

She brightened at once. 'That's great! I saw you go up, you know — it was very odd, like watching you turn into a sepia-toned photograph. And then . . . thinking I could see the sun shining through you . . . that was *very* peculiar.' She looked at him severely.

'Bad, huh?'

'No . . . not *bad,* exactly. Just peculiar. Those bugs, now . . . *they* were bad. Ugh!'

'I know what you mean. But I think they're all back there.'

'Maybe, but we're still a long way from being out of the woods, aren't we?'

'Yeah — a long way from Eden, Carol would have said.'

'Just stick with me, Ralph Roberts, and don't get lost.'

'Ralph Roberts? Never heard of him. Norton's the name.'

And that, he was happy to see, made her laugh.

CHAPTER TWENTY-FOUR

1

They walked slowly across the asphalt parking lot with its gridwork of spray-painted yellow lines. Tonight, Ralph knew, most of these spaces would be filled. Come, look, listen, be seen . . . and, most importantly, show your city and a whole watching country beyond it that you cannot be intimidated by the Charlie Pickerings of the world. Even the minority kept away by fear would be replaced by the morbidly curious.

As they approached the racetrack, they also approached the edge of the deathbag. It was thicker here, and Ralph could see slow, swirling movement, as if the deathbag were made up of tiny specks of charred matter. It looked a bit like the air over an open incinerator, shimmering with heat and fragments of burnt paper.

And he could hear two sounds, one overlaying the other. The top one was a silvery sighing. The wind might make a sound like that, Ralph thought, if it learned how to weep. It was a creepy sound, but the one beneath it was actively unpleasant – a slobbery chewing noise, as if a gigantic toothless mouth were ingesting large amounts of soft food somewhere close by.

Lois stopped as they approached the deathbag's dark, particle-flecked skin and turned frightened, apologetic eyes up to Ralph. When she spoke, it was in a little girl's voice: 'I don't think I can go through that.' She paused, struggled, and at last brought out the rest. 'It's alive, you know. The whole thing. It sees them' – Lois jerked a thumb back over her shoulder to indicate both the people in the parking lot and the news crews closer in to the building – 'and that's bad, but it also sees *us,* and that's worse . . . because it knows that *we* see *it.* It doesn't like being seen. *Felt,* maybe, but not seen.'

Now the lower-pitched sound – the slobbery eating sound – seemed almost to be articulating words, and the longer Ralph listened, the more sure he became that that was actually the case.

[*Geddout. Fucoff. Beedit.*]

'Ralph,' Lois whispered. 'Do you hear it?'

[*Hatechew. Killyew. Eeechew.*]

He nodded and took her by the elbow again. 'Come on, Lois.'

'Come –? *Where?*'

'Down. All the way.'

For a moment she only looked at him, not understanding; then the light dawned and she nodded. Ralph felt the blink happen inside him – a little stronger than the eyelash-flutter of a few moments ago – and suddenly the day around him cleared. The swirling, smoggy barrier ahead of them melted away and was gone. Nevertheless, they closed their eyes and held their breath as they approached the place where they knew the edge of the deathbag lay. Ralph felt Lois's hand tighten on his as she hurried through the invisible barrier, and as he passed through himself, a dark node of tangled memories – the slow death of his wife, the loss of a favorite dog as a child, the sight of Bill McGovern leaning over with one hand pressed against his chest – seemed to first lightly surround his mind and then clamp down on it like a cruel hand. His ears filled with that silvery sobbing sound, so constant and so chillingly vacuous; the weeping voice of a congenital idiot.

Then they were through.

2

As soon as they had passed beneath the wooden arch on the far side of the parking lot (WE'RE OFF TO THE RACES AT BASSEY PARK! was printed along its curve), Ralph drew Lois over to a bench and made her sit down, although she insisted vehemently that she was just fine.

'Good, but I need a second or two to get myself back together.'

She brushed a lock of hair off his temple and planted a gentle kiss in the hollow beneath. 'Take all the time you need, dear heart.'

That turned out to be about five minutes. When he felt reasonably confident that he could stand up without coming unlocked at the knees, Ralph took her hand again and they stood up together.

'Did you find it, Ralph? Did you find his trail?'

He nodded. 'In order to see it, we have to go up about two jumps. I tried going up just enough to see the auras at first, because that doesn't seem to speed everything up, but it didn't work. It has to be a little more than that.'

'All right.'

'But we have to be careful. Because when we can see—'

'We can be seen. Yes. We can't lose track of the time, either.'

'Absolutely not. Are you ready?'

'Almost. I think I need another kiss first. Just a little one will do.'

Smiling, he gave it to her.

'*Now* I'm ready.'

'Okay – here we go.'

Blink!

3

The reddish splotches of spoor led them across the packed-dirt area where the midway stood during County Fair week, then to the racetrack where the pacers ran from May to September. Lois stood at the chest-high slat fence for a moment, glanced around to make sure the grandstand was empty, and then boosted herself up. She moved with the sweet litheness of a young girl at first, but once she had swung a leg over the top and straddled the fence, she paused. On her face was an expression of mingled surprise and dismay.

[*Lois? Are you all right?*]

[*Yes, fine. It's my darned old underwear! I guess I've lost weight, because it just won't stay where it belongs! For gosh sakes!*]

Ralph realized he could see not just the frilly hem of Lois's slip but three or four inches of pink nylon. He stifled a grin as she sat astride the broad plank top of the fence, yanking at the fabric. He thought of telling her she looked cuter than kitten-britches and decided that might not be such a good idea.

[*'Turn your back while I get this damned slip fixed, Ralph. And wipe the smirk off your face while you're at it.'*]

He turned his back on her and looked at the Civic Center. If there *had* been a smirk on his face (he thought it more likely that she had seen one in his aura), the sight of that dark, slowly swirling deathbag took care of it in a hurry.

[*'Lois, you might be happier if you just took it off.'*]

[*'Pardon me all to heck and back, Ralph Roberts, but I wasn't raised to take off my underwear and leave it lying around on racetracks, and if you ever knew a girl who did do things like that, I hope it was before you met Carolyn. I only wish I had a—'*]

Vague image of a gleaming steel safety-pin in Ralph's head.

[*'I don't suppose you have one, do you, Ralph?'*]

He shook his head and sent back an image of his own: sand running through an hourglass.

[*'All right, all right, I get the message. I think I've fixed it so it'll hold together at least a little longer. You can turn around now.'*]

He did. She was letting herself down the other side of the board fence, and doing it with easy confidence, but her aura had paled considerably, and Ralph could see dark circles under her eyes again. The Revolt of the Foundation

Garments had been quelled, however, at least for the time being.

Ralph boosted himself up, swung a leg over the fence, and dropped down on the other side. He liked the way doing it felt – it seemed to wake old, long memories in his bones.

[*We're going to need to power up again before long, Lois.*]
Lois, nodding wearily: [*I know. Come on, let's go.*]

4

They followed the trail across the racetrack, climbed another board fence on the other side, then descended a brushy, overgrown slope to Neibolt Street. Ralph saw Lois grimly holding her slip up through the skirt of her dress as they struggled down the hill, thought again about asking if she wouldn't be happier just ditching the damned thing, and decided again to mind his own business. If it became enough of a problem to her, she would do it without any further advice on the subject from him.

Ralph's greatest worry – that Atropos's trail would simply peter out on them – initially proved groundless. The dim pink blotches led directly down the crumbling, patched surface of Neibolt Street, between paintless tenements that should have been demolished years ago. Tattered laundry flapped on sagging lines; dirty children with snotty noses watched them pass from dusty front yards. A beautiful tow-headed boy of about three gave Ralph and Lois a deeply suspicious look from his front step, then grabbed his crotch with one hand and used the other to flash them the bird.

Neibolt Street dead-ended at the old trainyards, and

here Ralph and Lois momentarily lost the track. They stood by one of the sawhorses blocking off an ancient rectangular cellar-hole – all that remained of the old passenger depot – and looked around at a big semicircle of waste ground. Rusty-red siding tracks glowered from deep within tangles of sunflowers and thorny weeds; shards from a hundred broken bottles twinkled in the afternoon sun. Spray-painted in hot pink letters across the splintery side of the old diesel shed were the words SUZY SUCKT MY BIG FAT ONE. This sentimental declaration stood within a border of dancing swastikas.

Ralph: [*'Where the hell did it go?'*]

[*'Down there, Ralph – see?'*]

She was pointing along what had been the main line until 1963, the only line until 1983, and was now just another pair of rusty, overgrown steel tracks on the way to nowhere. Even most of the ties were gone, burned as evening campfires either by local winos or vags passing through on their way to the potato fields of Aroostook County or the apple orchards and fishing smacks of the Maritimes. On one of the few remaining crossties, Ralph saw splashes of pink spoor. They looked fresher than the ones they had followed down Neibolt Street.

He stared along the half-hidden course of the tracks, trying to recall. If memory served, this line skirted the Municipal Golf Course on its way back to . . . well, on its way back to the west side. Ralph thought this must be the same set of defunct tracks which ran along the edge of the airport and past the picnic area where Faye Chapin might even now be brooding over the seedings in the upcoming Runway 3 Classic.

It's all been one big loop, he thought. *It's taken us damned near three days, but I think in the end we're going to be right back where we started . . . not Eden, but Harris Avenue.*

'Say, you guys! How you doon?'

It was a voice Ralph almost thought he recognized, and that feeling was reinforced by his first look at the man it came from. He was standing behind them, at the point where the Neibolt Street sidewalk finally gave up the ghost. He looked fifty or so, but Ralph guessed he might actually be five or even ten years younger than that. He was wearing a sweatshirt and old ragged jeans. The aura surrounding him was as green as a glass of Saint Patrick's Day beer. That was finally what turned the trick for Ralph. It was the wino who had approached him and Bill on the day he had found Bill in Strawford Park, bawling over his old pal Bob Polhurst . . . who, as it had turned out, had outlived him. Life was funnier than Groucho Marx sometimes.

A queer sense of fatalism was creeping over Ralph, and with it an intuitive understanding of the forces which now surrounded them. It was one he could have done without. It hardly mattered if those forces were beneficent or malign, Random or Purpose; they were *gigantic,* that was what mattered, and they made the things Clotho and Lachesis had said about choice and free will seem like a joke. He felt as if he and Lois were roped to the spokes of a gigantic wheel – a wheel which kept rolling them back to where they had come from even as it took them deeper and deeper into this horrible tunnel.

'You got a bitta the old spare change, mister?'

Ralph slid down a little so the wino would be sure to hear him when he talked.

'I'll bet your uncle called you from Dexter,' Ralph said. 'Told you you could have your old job back at the mill . . . but only if you got there today. Is that about right?'

The wino blinked at him in cautious surprise. 'Well . . . yeah. Sumpin like that.' He felt for the story – one he probably believed in more fully than anyone he told it to these days – and found its tattered thread again. 'Dass a good job, you know? And I could have it back. There's a Bangor n Aroostook bus at two o'clock, but the fare's five-fifty and so far I got only toon a quarter . . .'

'Seventy-six cents is what you've got,' Lois said. 'Two quarters, two dimes, one nickel, and a penny. But considering how much you drink, your aura looks extremely healthy, I'll say that much for you. You must have the constitution of an ox.'

The wino gave her a puzzled look, then took a step backward and wiped his nose with the palm of one hand.

'Don't worry,' Ralph reassured him, 'my wife sees auras everywhere. She's a very spiritual person.'

'Izzat so, now?'

'Uh-huh. She's also very generous, and I think she'll do quite a bit better by you than a little spare change. Won't you, Alice?'

'He'll just drink it up,' she said. 'There's no job in Dexter.'

'No, probably not,' Ralph said, fixing her with his eyes, 'but his aura does look extremely healthy. *Extremely.*'

'You kinda got your own spiritual side, I guess,' the wino said. His eyes were still shifting cautiously back and forth between Ralph and Lois, but there was a guarded flicker of hope in them.

'You know, that's true,' Ralph said. 'And just lately it's really come to the fore.' He pursed his lips as if an interesting thought had just occurred to him, and inhaled. A bright green ray shot out of the panhandler's aura, crossed the ten feet separating him from Ralph and Lois, and entered Ralph's mouth. The taste was clear and at once identifiable: Boone's Farm Apple Wine. It was rough and lowdown, but sort of pleasant, just the same – it had a working man's sparkle to it. With the taste came that sense of returning strength, which was good, and a sharp-edged clarity of thought that was even better.

Lois, meanwhile, was holding out a twenty-dollar bill. The wino didn't immediately see it, however; he was scowling up into the sky. At that instant, another bright green ray quilled out of his aura. It shot across the weedy clearing beside the cellar-hole like a brilliant flashlight beam and into Lois's mouth and nose. The bill in her hand shook briefly.

[*'Oh, God, that's so good!'*]

'Goddam jet-jockeys from Charleston Air Force Base!' the wino cried disapprovingly. 'They ain't s'pozed to boom the soun-barrier til they get out over the ocean! I damn near wet my –' His eye fell on the bill between Lois's fingers, and his scowl deepened. 'Sa-aay, what kind of joke you think you pullin here? I ain't stupid, you know. Maybe I like a drink every now n then, but that don't make me stupid.'

Give it time, Ralph thought. *It will.*

'No one thinks you're stupid,' Lois said, 'and it's no joke. Take the money, sir.'

The bum tried to hold onto his suspicious glower,

but after another close look at Lois (and a quick side-glance at Ralph), it was overwhelmed by a large and winning smile. He stepped toward Lois, putting out his hand to take the money, which he had earned without even knowing it.

Lois raised her hand just before he could close his fingers on the bill. 'Just mind you get something to eat as well as something to drink. And you might ask yourself if you're happy with the way you're living.'

'You're absolutely right!' the wino cried enthusiastically. His eyes never left the bill between Lois's fingers. 'Absolutely, ma'am! They got a program other side of the river, detox and rehab, you know. I'm thinkin about it. I really am. I think about it every damn day.' But his eyes were still tacked to the twenty, and he was almost drooling. Lois gave Ralph a brief, doubtful look, then shrugged and let the bill pass from her fingers to his. 'Thanks! Thanks, lady!' His eyes shifted to Ralph. 'Dis lady a real princess! I jus hope you know dat!'

Ralph favored Lois with a fond glance. 'As a matter of fact, I do,' he said.

5

Half an hour later, the two of them were walking between the rusty steel rails as they curved gently past the Municipal Golf Course . . . except they had drifted up a little higher above the Short-Time world after their meeting with the wino (perhaps because he had been a little high himself), and walking was not exactly what they were doing. There was little or no effort involved, for one thing, and although their feet were moving, to Ralph it felt more like gliding than walking. Nor was he entirely sure they were visible to the Short-Time world; squirrels hopped unconcernedly about their feet, busy gathering supplies for the winter ahead, and once he saw Lois duck sharply as a wren almost parted her hair. The bird veered to the left and upward, as if realizing only at the last moment that there was a human in its flight-pattern. The golfers didn't pay them any mind, either. Ralph's opinion of golfers was that they were self-absorbed to the point of obsession, but he thought this lack of interest extreme even so. If *he* had seen a couple of neatly dressed adults strolling along a defunct GS&WM spur-line in the middle of the day, he thought he might have taken a brief time-out to try and guess what they were up to and where they might be going. *I think I'd be especially curious about why the lady kept on muttering 'stay where you are, you darned old thing' and hitching at her skirt,* Ralph thought, and grinned. But the golfers didn't even spare them a glance, although a foursome bound for the ninth hole passed close enough so that Ralph could hear them worrying over a developing softness in the bond market. The idea that he and Lois had become invisible again – or at least very dim – began to seem more and more plausible to Ralph. Plausible . . . and worrisome. *Time goes faster when you're high,* Old Dor had said.

The trail became fresher as they went west, and Ralph liked the drips and splashes which made it up less and less. Where the goop had fallen on the steel rails, it had eaten away the rust like corrosive acid. The weeds it had fallen on were black and dead – even the hardiest of them had died. As Ralph and Lois passed Derry Muni's third green and entered a tangle of scrawny trees and undergrowth, Lois tugged at his sleeve. She pointed ahead. Large splotches of Atropos's spoor gleamed like sick paint on the trunks of the trees now pressing in close to the tracks, and there were pools of it in some of the sunken dips between the old rails – places where crossties had once been, Ralph supposed.

[*'We're getting close to where he lives, Ralph.'*]

[*'Yes.'*]

[*'If he comes back and finds us in his place, what will we do?'*]

Ralph shrugged. He didn't know, and wasn't sure he cared. Let the forces that were moving them around like pawns on a chessboard – the ones Mr C and Mr L had called the Higher Purpose – worry about that. If Atropos showed up, Ralph would try to yank out the little bald bugger's tongue and strangle him with it. And if that upset somebody's applecart, too goddam bad. He couldn't take responsibility for grand plans and Long-Time business; his job now was to watch out for Lois, who was at risk, and try to stop the carnage that was going to occur not far from here in just a few hours. And who knew? He might even find a little extra time along the way which he could use to try and protect his own partially rejuvenated hide. This was the stuff he had to do, and if the nasty little fuck got in Ralph's way, one of them was going down. If that didn't fit in with the big boys' plans, tough titty.

Lois was picking most of this up from his aura – he could read that in her own when she touched his arm and he turned to look at her.

709

[*'What does that mean, Ralph? That you'll try to kill him if he gets in our way?'*]

He considered this, then nodded.

[*'Yeah – that's* exactly *what it means.'*]

She thought about it, then nodded.

[*'Ralph?'*]

He looked at her, eyebrows raised.

[*'If it needs to be done, I'll help you do it.'*]

He was absurdly touched by this . . . and at pains to hide the rest of his thinking from her: that the only reason she was still with him at all was so that he could keep a protective eye on her. That thought led him back toward her earrings, but he pushed the image of them away, not wanting her to see – or even suspect – them in his aura.

Lois's thoughts, meanwhile, had gone on in a different, marginally safer, direction.

[*'Even if we get in and out without meeting him, he'll know someone was there, won't he? He'll probably know who it was, too.'*]

Ralph couldn't deny it, but didn't see that it mattered much; their options had been narrowed to just this one, at least temporarily. They would take it a step at a time and just keep hoping that when the sun came up tomorrow morning, they would be around to see it. *Although, given a choice, I'd probably opt to sleep in,* Ralph thought, and a small, wistful grin touched the corners of his mouth. *God, it feels like years since I slept in.* His mind flashed from there to Carolyn's favorite saying, the one about how it was a long walk back to Eden. It seemed to him right now that Eden might simply be sleeping until noon . . . or maybe a little past.

He took Lois's hand and they started forward along Atropos's trail again.

6

Forty feet east of the cyclone fence marking the edge of the airport, the rusty tracks petered out. Atropos's trail pushed on, however, although not for long; Ralph was quite sure he could see the spot where it ended, and the image of the two of them roped to the spokes of a big wheel recurred. If he was right, Atropos's den was only a stone's throw from where Ed had run into the fat man with the barrels of fertilizer in the back of his pickup truck.

The wind gusted, bringing them a sick, rotten smell from close by, and, from a little further away, the voice of Faye Chapin, haranguing someone on his favorite subject: '. . . what I *always* say! *Mah-jongg* is like chess, chess is like life, so if you can play either of those games –' The wind dropped again. Ralph could still hear Faye's voice if he strained his ears, but he had lost the individual words. That was all right, though; he had heard the lecture often enough to know pretty much how it went.

[*Ralph, that stink is* awful! *It's him, isn't it?*]

He nodded, but didn't think Lois saw him. She held his hand tightly in hers, looking straight ahead with wide eyes. The splotchy track which had begun at the doors of the Civic Center ended at the base of a drunkenly leaning dead oak tree two hundred feet away. The cause of both the tree's death and its final leaning position was clear: one side of the venerable relic had been peeled like a banana by a glancing stroke of lightning. The cracks and

711

crenellations and bulges of its gray bark seemed to make the shapes of half-buried, silently screaming faces, and the tree spread its nude branches against the sky like grim ideograms . . . ones which bore — at least in Ralph's imagination — an uncomfortable resemblance to the Japanese ideograms which meant *kamikaze*. The bolt which had killed the tree hadn't succeeded in knocking it over, but it had certainly done its best. The part of its extensive root-system which faced the airport had been yanked right out of the ground. These roots had extended beneath the chainlink fence and pulled a section of it upward and outward in a bell shape that made Ralph think, for the first time in years, of a childhood acquaintance named Charles Engstrom.

'Don't you play with Chuckie,' Ralph's mother used to tell him. 'He's a dirty boy.' Ralph didn't know if Chuckie was a dirty boy or not, but he was fruitcrackers, no question about that. Chuckie Engstrom liked to hide behind the tree in his front yard with a long tree-branch which he called his Peekie Wand. When a woman in a full skirt passed, Chuckie would tiptoe after her, extending the Peekie Wand under the hem and then lifting. Quite often he got to check out the color of the woman's underwear (the color of ladies' underwear held great fascination for Chuckie) before she realized what was going on and chased the wildly cackling lad back to his house, threatening to tell his mother. The airport fence, pulled out and up by the old oak's roots, reminded Ralph of the way the skirts of Chuckie's victims had looked when he started to raise them with the Peekie Wand.

[*Ralph?*]

712

He looked at her.

[*'Who's Piggy Juan? And why are you thinking about him now?'*]

Ralph burst out laughing.

[*'Did you see that in my aura?'*]

[*'I guess so — I don't really know anymore. Who is he?'*]

[*'Tell you another time. Come on.'*]

He took her hand and they walked slowly toward the oak tree where Atropos's trail ended, into the thickening odor of wild decay that was his scent.

CHAPTER TWENTY-FIVE

1

They stood at the base of the oak, looking down. Lois was gnawing obsessively on her lower lip.

[*'Do we have to go down there, Ralph? Do we really?'*]

[*'Yes.'*]

[*'But why? What are we supposed to do? Take something he stole? Kill him? What?'*]

Other than retrieve Joe's comb and Lois's earrings, he didn't know . . . but he felt certain he *would* know, that they both would, when the time came.

[*'I think for now we better just keep moving, Lois.'*]

The lightning had acted like a strong hand, shoving the tree violently toward the east and opening a large hole at the bottom on its western side. To a man or woman with Short-Time vision, that hole would undoubtedly look dark – and maybe a little scary, with its crumbly sides and barely glimpsed roots squirming in the deep shadows like snakes – but otherwise not very unusual.

A kid with a good imagination might see more, Ralph thought. *That dark space at the bottom of the tree might make him think of pirate treasure . . . outlaw hideouts . . . troll-holes . . .*

But Ralph didn't think even an imaginative Short-Time kid would have been able to see the dim red glow filtering up from beneath the tree, or realize that those squirming roots were actually rough rungs leading down to some unknown (and undoubtedly unpleasant) place.

No — even an imaginative kid wouldn't see those things . . . but he or she might sense them.

Right. And after doing so, one with any brains would turn and run as if all the demons of hell were in hot pursuit. As would he and Lois, if they had any sense at all. Except for Lois's earrings. Except for Joe Wyzer's comb. Except for his own lost place in the Purpose. And, of course, except for Helen (and possibly Nat) and the two thousand other people who were going to be at the Civic Center tonight. Lois was right. They were supposed to do *something,* and if they backed out now, it was a something that would remain forever done–bun–undone.

And those are the ropes, he thought. *The ropes the powers that be use to tie us poor, muddled Short-Time creatures to their wheel.*

He now visualized Clotho and Lachesis through a bright lens of hate, and he thought that if the two of them had been here right now, they would have exchanged one of their uneasy looks and then taken a quick step or two away.

And they would be right to do that, he thought. *Very right.*

['*Ralph? What's wrong? Why are you so angry?*']

He raised her hand to his lips and kissed it.

[*'It's nothing. Come on. Let's go before we lose our nerve.'*]

She looked at him a moment longer, then nodded. And when Ralph sat down and poked his legs into the gaping, root-lined mouth at the foot of the tree, she was right beside him.

2

Ralph slid beneath the tree on his back, holding his free hand over his face to keep dirt from crumbling into his open eyes. He tried not to flinch as root-knuckles caressed the side of his neck and prodded the small of his back. The smell under the tree was a revolting monkeyhouse aroma that made his gorge rise. He was able to go on kidding himself that he would get used to it until he was all the way into the hole under the oak, and then the kidding stopped. He raised himself on one elbow, feeling smaller roots digging at his scalp and dangling flaps of bark tickling his cheeks, and ejected as much of his breakfast as still remained in the holding-tank. He could hear Lois doing the same thing on his left.

A terrible, woozy faintness went rolling through his head like a breaking wave. The stench was so thick he was almost *eating* it, and he could see the red stuff they had followed to this nightmare place under the tree all over his hands and arms. Just *looking* at this stuff had been bad; now he found himself taking a bath in it, for God's sake.

Something groped for his hand and he almost gave in to panic before realizing it was Lois. He laced his fingers through hers.

[*'Ralph, come up a little bit! It's better! You can breathe!'*]

He understood what she meant at once, and had to restrain himself, haul himself down, at the last moment. If he hadn't, he would have shot up the ladder of perception like a rocket under full thrust.

The world wavered, and suddenly there seemed to be a little more light in this stinking hole . . . and a little more room, too. The smell didn't go away, but it became bearable. Now it was like being in a small closed tent full of people with dirty feet and sweaty armpits – not nice, but something you could live with, at least for awhile.

Ralph suddenly imagined the face of a pocket-watch, complete with hands that were moving too fast. It was better without the stench trying to pour down his throat and gag him, but this was still a dangerous place to be – suppose they came out of here tomorrow morning, with nothing left of the Civic Center but a smoking hole on Main Street? And it could happen. Keeping track of time down here – short time, long time, or all-time – was impossible. He glanced at his watch, but it was meaningless. He should have set it earlier, but he had forgotten.

Let it go, Ralph – you can't do anything about it, so let it go.

He tried, and as he did it occurred to him that Old Dor had been a hundred per cent correct on the day Ed had crashed into Mr West Side Gardeners' pickup truck; it was better not to mess into Long-Time business. And yet here they were, the world's oldest Peter Pan and the world's oldest Wendy, sliding under a magic tree into some slimy underworld neither one of them wanted to see.

Lois was looking at him, her pale face lit with that sick red glow, her expressive eyes full of fright. He saw dark threads on her chin and realized it was blood. She had quit just nibbling at her lower lip and had begun taking bites out of it.

[*'Ralph, are you all right?'*]

[*'I get to crawl under an old oak tree with a pretty girl and you even have to ask? I'm fine, Lois. But I think we better hurry.'*]

[*'All right.'*]

He felt around below him and placed his foot on a gnarled root-knuckle. It took his weight and he slid down the stony slope, squeezing beneath another root and holding Lois around the waist. Her skirt skidded up to her thighs and Ralph thought again, briefly, about Chuckie Engstrom and his Peekie Wand. He was both amused and exasperated to see Lois was trying to pull the skirt back down.

[*'I know that a lady tries to keep her skirt down whenever possible, but I think the rule goes by the boards when you're sliding down troll staircases under old oak trees. Okay?'*]

She gave him an embarrassed, frightened little smile.

[*'If I'd known what we were going to be doing, I would have worn slacks. I thought we were just going to the hospital.'*]

If I'd known what we were going to be doing, Ralph thought, *I would have cashed in my bonds, developing softness in the market or not, and had us on a plane to Rio, my dear.*

He felt around with his other foot, very aware that if he fell, he was probably going to end up in a place far beyond the reach of Derry Rescue. Just above his eyes, a reddish worm poked out of the earth, dribbling little crumbles of dirt down on Ralph's forehead.

For what seemed like an eternity he felt nothing, and

INSOMNIA

then his foot found smooth wood – not a root this time,
but something like a real step. He slid down, still holding
Lois around the waist, and waited to see if the thing he
was standing on would hold or snap under their combined
weight.

It held, and it was wide enough for both of them.
Ralph looked down and saw that it was the top step of a
narrow staircase which curved down into the red-tinged
dark. It had been built for – and perhaps by – a creature
that was a lot shorter than they were, making it necessary
for them to hunch, but it was still better than the night-
mare of the last few moments.

Ralph looked at the ragged wedge of daylight above
them, his eyes gazing out of his dirt- and sweat-streaked
face with an expression of dumb longing. Daylight had
never looked so sweet or so distant. He turned back to
Lois and nodded to her. She squeezed his hand and nodded
back. Bending over, cringing each time a dangling root
touched their necks or backs, they started down the stair-
case.

3

The descent seemed endless. The red light grew brighter,
the stench of Atropos grew thicker, and Ralph was aware
that they were both 'going up' as they went down; it was
either that or be flattened by the smell. He continued telling
himself that they were doing what they had to do, and that
there must be a timekeeper on an operation this big –
someone who would give them a poke if and when the
schedule got too tight for comfort – but he kept worrying,

719

just the same. Because there might *not* be a timekeeper, or an ump, or a team of refs in zebra–striped shirts. *All bets are off,* Clotho had said.

Just as Ralph was starting to wonder if the stairs went all the way down into hell itself, they ended. A short stone-lined corridor, no more than forty inches high and twenty feet long, led to an arched doorway. Beyond it, that red glow pulsed and flared like the reflected glow of an open oven.

[*'Come on, Lois, but be ready for anything. Be ready for him.'*]

She nodded, hitched at her wayward slip again, then walked beside him up the narrow passage. Ralph kicked something that wasn't a stone and bent over to pick it up. It was a red plastic cylinder, wider at one end than at the other. After a moment he realized what it was: a jump-rope handle. *Three-six-nine, hon, the goose drank wine.*

Don't butt into what doesn't concern you, Short-Time, Atropos had said, but he had butted in, and not just because of what the little bald doctors called *ka,* either. He had gotten involved because what Atropos was up to *was* his concern, whatever the little creep might think to the contrary. Derry was his town, Lois Chasse was his friend, and Ralph found within himself a sincere desire to make Doc #3 sorry he'd ever seen Lois's diamond earrings.

He flipped the jump-rope handle away and started walking again. A moment later he and Lois passed under the arch and simply stood there, staring into Atropos's underground apartment. With their wide eyes and linked hands, they looked more like children in a fairy-tale than ever – not Peter Pan and Wendy now but Hansel and Gretel, coming upon the witch's candy house after days spent wandering in the trackless forest.

4

[*'Oh, Ralph. Oh my God, Ralph . . . do you see?'*]

[*'Shhh, Lois. Shhh.'*]

Directly ahead of them was a small, mean chamber which seemed to be a combination kitchen and bedroom. The room was simultaneously sordid and creepy. Standing in the center was a low round table which Ralph thought was the amputated top half of a barrel. The remains of a meal – some gray, rancid gruel that looked like liquefied brains congealing in a chipped soup tureen – stood on it. There was a single dirty folding chair. To the right of the table was a primitive commode which consisted of a rusty steel drum with a toilet-seat balanced on top of it. The smell rising from this was incredibly foul. The room's only decoration was a full-length brass-bordered mirror on one wall, its reflective surface so age-darkened that the Ralph and Lois captured within it looked as if they might have been floating in ten or twelve feet of water.

To the left of the mirror was a stark sleeping accommodation which consisted of a filthy mattress and a burlap sack stuffed with straw or feathers. Both pillow and mattress glowed and raved with the nightsweats of the creature who used them. *The dreams inside that burlap pillow would drive me insane,* Ralph thought.

Somewhere, God only knew how much further under the earth, water was dripping hollowly.

On the far side of the apartment was another, higher arch, through which they could see a jumbled, surreal storage area. Ralph actually blinked two or three times to try to make sure he was really seeing what he thought he was seeing.

This is the place, all right, he thought. *Whatever we came to find, it's here.*

Lois began to drift toward this second arch as if hypnotized. Her mouth was quivering with dismay, but her eyes were full of helpless curiosity – it was the expression, he was quite sure, that must have been on the face of Bluebeard's wife when she had used the key which unlocked the door to her husband's forbidden room. Ralph was suddenly sure that Atropos was lurking just inside that arch with his rusty scalpel poised. He hurried after Lois and stopped her just before she could step through. He grasped her upper arm, then put a finger to his lips and shook his head at her before she could speak.

He hunkered down with the fingers of one hand tented on the packed dirt floor, looking like a sprinter awaiting the crack of the starter's gun. Then he launched himself through the arch (relishing the eager response of his body even at this moment), hitting on his shoulder and rolling. His feet struck a cardboard box and knocked it over, spilling out a jumble of stuff: mismatched gloves and socks, a couple of old paperbacks, a pair of Bermuda shorts, a screwdriver with smears of maroon stuff – maybe paint, maybe blood – on its steel shaft.

Ralph got to his knees, looking back toward Lois, who was standing in the doorway and staring at him with her hands clasped under her chin. There was no one on either side of the archway, and really no room for anyone. More boxes were stacked on either side. Ralph read the printing on them with a kind of bemused wonder: Jack Daniel's, Gilbey's, Smirnoff, J&B. Atropos, it seemed, was as fond of liquor cartons as anyone else who couldn't bear to throw anything away.

[*'Ralph? Is it safe?'*]

The word was a joke, but he nodded his head and held out his hand. She hurried toward him, giving her slip another sharp upward yank as she came and looking about herself in growing amazement.

Standing on the other side of the arch, in Atropos's grim little apartment, this storage area had looked large. Now that they were actually in it, Ralph saw it went well beyond that; rooms this big were usually called warehouses. Aisles wandered among great, tottery piles of junk. Only the stuff by the door had actually been boxed; the rest had been piled any whichway, creating something which was two parts maze and three parts booby-trap. Ralph decided that even *warehouse* was too small a word – this was an underground suburb, and Atropos might be lurking anywhere within it . . . and if he was here, he was probably watching them.

Lois didn't ask what they were looking at; he saw by her face that she already knew. When she did speak, it was in a dreamy tone that sent a chill scampering up Ralph's back.

[*'He must be so very old, Ralph.'*]

Yes. So very old.

Twenty yards into the room, which was lit with the same sunken, sourceless red glow as the stairway, Ralph

723

could see a large spoked wheel lying atop a cane-backed chair which was, in turn, standing on top of a splintery old clothes press. Looking at that wheel brought a deeper chill; it was as if the metaphor his mind had seized to help grasp the concept of *ka* had become real. Then he noted the rusty iron strip which circled the wheel's outer circumference and realized it had probably come from one of those Gay Nineties bikes that looked like over-grown tricycles.

It's a bicycle wheel, all right, and it's a hundred years old if it's a day, he thought. That led him to wonder how many people – how many thousands or tens of thousands – had died in and around Derry since Atropos had somehow transported this wheel down here. And of those thousands, how many had been Random deaths?

And how far back does he go? How many hundreds of years?

No way of telling, of course; maybe all the way to the beginning, whenever or however that had been. And during that time, he had taken a little something from everyone he had fucked with . . . and here it all was.

Here it all was.

[*'Ralph!'*]

He looked around and saw that Lois was holding out both hands. In one was a Panama hat with a crescent bitten from the brim. In the other was a black nylon pocket-comb, the kind you could buy in any convenience store for a buck twenty-nine. A ghostly glimmer of orange-yellow still clung to it, which didn't surprise Ralph much. Each time the comb's owner had used it, it must have picked up a little of that glow from both his aura and his balloon-string, like dandruff. It also didn't surprise him that the comb should have been with McGovern's hat; the last time he'd seen those two things, they'd been together. He remembered Atropos's sarcastic grin as he swept the Panama from his head and pretended to use the comb on his own bald dome.

And then he jumped up and clicked his heels together.

Lois was pointing at an old rocking chair with a broken runner.

[*'The hat was right there, on the seat. The comb was underneath. It's Mr Wyzer's, isn't it?'*]

[*'Yes.'*]

She held it out to him immediately.

[*'You take it. I'm not as ditzy as Bill always thought, but sometimes I lose things. And if I lost this, I'd never forgive myself.'*]

He took the comb, started to put it into his back pocket, then thought how easily Atropos had plucked it from that same location. Easy as falling off a log, it had been. He put it into his front pants pocket instead, then looked back at Lois, who was gazing at McGovern's bitten hat with the sad wonder of Hamlet looking at the skull of his old pal Yorick. When she looked up, Ralph saw tears in her eyes.

[*'He loved this hat. He thought he looked very dashing and debonair when he had it on. He didn't — he just looked like Bill — but he thought he looked good, and that's the important part. Wouldn't you say so, Ralph?'*]

[*'Yes.'*]

She tossed the hat back into the seat of the old rocker and turned to examine a box of what looked like rummage-sale clothes. As soon as her back was to him, Ralph squatted down, peering beneath the chair, hoping to see a splintered double gleam in the darkness. If Bill's hat and Joe's comb were both here, then maybe Lois's earrings –

There was nothing beneath the rocker but dust and a pink knitted baby bootee.

Should have known that'd be too easy, Ralph thought, getting to his feet again. He suddenly felt exhausted. They had found Joe's comb with no trouble at all, and that was good, absolutely great, but Ralph was afraid it had also been a spectacular case of beginner's luck. They still had Lois's earrings to worry about . . . and doing whatever else it was they had been sent here to do, of course. And what was that? He didn't know, and if someone from upstairs was sending instructions, he wasn't receiving them.

[*'Lois, do you have any idea what—'*]

[*'Shhhh!'*]

[*'What is it? Lois, is it him?'*]

[*'No! Be quiet, Ralph! Be quiet and listen!'*]

He listened. At first he heard nothing, and then the clenching sensation – the blink – came inside his head again. This time it was very slow, very cautious. He slipped upward a little further, as lightly as a feather lifted in a draft of warm air. He became aware of a long, low groaning sound, like an endlessly creaking door. There was something familiar about it – not in the sound itself, but in its associations. It was like—

– a burglar alarm, or maybe a smoke-detector. It's telling us where it is. It's calling us.

Lois seized his hand with fingers that were as cold as ice.

726

[*'That's it, Ralph – that's what we're looking for. Do you hear it?'*]

Yes, of course he did. But whatever that sound was, it had nothing to do with Lois's earrings . . . and without Lois's earrings, he wasn't leaving this place.

[*'Come on, Ralph! Come on! We have to find it!'*]

He let her lead him deeper into the room. Atropos's souvenirs were piled at least three feet higher than their heads in most places. How a shrimp like him had managed this trick Ralph didn't know – levitation, maybe – but the result was that he quickly lost all sense of direction as they twisted, turned, and occasionally seemed to double back. All he knew for sure was that low groaning sound kept getting louder in his ears; as they began to draw near its source, it became an insectile buzzing which Ralph found increasingly unpleasant. He kept expecting to round a corner and find a giant locust staring at him with dull brownish-black eyes as big as grapefruits.

Although the separate auras of the objects which filled the storage vault had faded like the scent of flower-petals pressed between the pages of a book, they were still there beneath Atropos's stench – and at this level of perception, with all their senses exquisitely awake and attuned, it was impossible not to sense those auras and be affected by them. These mute reminders of the Random dead were both terrible and pathetic. The place was more than a museum or a packrat's lair, Ralph realized; it was a profane church where Atropos took his own version of Communion – grief for bread, tears for wine.

Their stumbling course through the narrow zigzag rows was a gruesome, almost shattering experience. Each

727

not–quite–aimless turn presented a hundred more objects Ralph wished he had never seen and would not have to remember; each voiced its own small cry of pain and bewilderment. He did not have to wonder if Lois shared his feelings – she was sobbing steadily and quietly beside him.

Here was a child's battered Flexible Flyer sled with the knotted towrope still draped over the steering bar. The boy to whom it had belonged had died of convulsions on a crisp January day in 1953.

Here was a majorette's baton with its shaft wrapped in purple and white spirals of crepe – the colors of Grant Academy. She had been raped and bludgeoned to death with a rock in the fall of 1967. Her killer, who had never been caught, had stuffed her body into a small cave where her bones – along with the bones of two other unlucky victims – still lay.

Here was the cameo brooch of a woman who had been struck by a falling brick while walking down Main Street to buy the new issue of *Vogue*; if she had left her home thirty seconds earlier or later, she would have been fine.

Here was the buck knife of a man who had been killed in a hunting accident in 1937.

Here was the compass of a Boy Scout who had fallen and broken his neck while hiking on Mount Katahdin.

The sneaker of a little boy named Gage Creed, run down by a speeding tanker-truck on Route 15 in Ludlow.

Rings and magazines; key-chains and umbrellas; hats and glasses; rattles and radios. They looked like different things, but Ralph thought they were really all the same thing: the faint, sorrowing voices of people who had found themselves written out of the script in the middle of the second act while they were still learning their lines for the third, people who had been unceremoniously hauled off before their work was done or their obligations fulfilled, people whose only crime had been to be born in the Random . . . and to have caught the eye of the madman with the rusty scalpel.

Lois, sobbing: [*I hate him! I hate him so much!*]

He knew what she meant. It was one thing to hear Clotho and Lachesis say that Atropos was also part of the big picture, that he might even serve some higher purpose himself, and quite another to see the faded Boston Bruins cap of a little boy who had fallen into an overgrown cellar-hole and died in the dark, died in agony, died with no voice left after six hours spent screaming for his mother.

Ralph reached out and briefly touched the cap. Its owner's name had been Billy Weatherbee. His final thought had been of ice-cream.

Ralph's hand tightened over Lois's.

[*Ralph, what is it? I can hear you thinking — I'm sure I can — but it's like listening to someone whisper under his breath.*]

[*I was thinking that I want to bust that little bastard's chops for him, Lois. Maybe we could teach him what it's like to lie awake at night. What do you think?*]

Her grip on his hand tightened. She nodded.

5

They reached a place where the narrow corridor they'd been following branched into diverging paths. That low, steady buzz was coming from the lefthand one, and not very far up it, either, by the sound. It was now impossible for them to walk side by side, and as they worked their way toward the end, the passage grew narrower still. Ralph was finally obliged to begin sidling along.

The reddish exudate Atropos left behind was very thick here, dripping down the jumbled stacks of souvenirs and making little puddles on the dirt floor. Lois was holding his hand with painful tightness now, but Ralph didn't complain.

[*It's like the Civic Center, Ralph – he spends a lot of time here.'*]

Ralph nodded. The question was, what did Mr A come down this aisle to commune with? They were coming to the end now – it was blocked by a solid wall of junk – and he still couldn't see what was making that buzzing sound. It was now starting to drive him crazy; it was like having a horsefly trapped in the middle of your head. As they approached the end of the passage, he became more and more sure that what they were looking for was on the other side of the wall of junk which blocked it – they would either have to retrace their steps and try to find a way around, or break through. Either choice might consume more time than they could afford. Ralph felt nibbles of desperation at the back of his mind.

But the corridor did not dead-end; on the left there was a crawlspace beneath a dining room table piled high with dishes and stacks of green paper and . . .

Green paper? No, not quite. Stacks of *bills*. Tens, twenties, and fifties were piled up in random profusion on the dishes. There was a choke of hundreds in a cracked gravy-boat, and a rolled-up five hundred dollar bill poking drunkenly out of a dusty wineglass.

[*Ralph! My God, it's a fortune!*]

She wasn't looking at the table but at the other wall of the passageway. The last five feet had been constructed of banded gray-green bricks of currency. They were in an alleyway which was literally made of money, and Ralph realized he could now answer another of the questions that had been troubling him: where Ed had been getting his dough. Atropos was rolling in it . . . but Ralph had an idea that the little bald-headed sonofabitch still had trouble getting dates.

He bent down a little to get a better look into the crawlspace underneath the table. There appeared to be yet another chamber on the other side, this one very small. A slow red glow waxed and waned in there like the beating of a heart. It cast uneasy pulses of light on their shoes.

Ralph pointed, then looked at Lois. She nodded. He dropped to his knees and crawled beneath the money-laden table, and into the shrine Atropos had created around the thing which lay in the middle of the floor. It *was* what they had been sent to find, he hadn't a single doubt about it, but he still had no idea what it was. The object, not much bigger than the sort of marbles children call croakers, was wrapped in a deathbag as impenetrable as the center of a black hole.

Oh, great — lovely. Now what?

[*Ralph! Do you hear singing? It's very faint.*]

He looked at her dubiously, then glanced around. He had already come to hate this cramped space, and although he was not claustrophobic by nature, he now felt a panicky desire to get away squeezing into his thoughts. A very distinct voice spoke up in his head. *It's not just what I want, Ralph; it's what I need. I'll do my best to hang in with you, but if you don't finish whatever the hell it is you're supposed to be doing in here soon, it won't make any difference what either of us want – I'm just going to take over and run like hell.*

The controlled terror in that voice didn't surprise him, because this really was a horrible place – not a room at all but the bottom of a deep shaft whose circular walls were constructed of rickrack and stolen goods: toasters, footstools, clock-radios, cameras, books, crates, shoes, rakes. Dangling almost right in front of Ralph's eyes was a battered saxophone on a frayed strap with the word JAKE printed on it in dust-dulled rhinestones. Ralph reached out to grab it, wanting to get the damned thing out of his face. Then he imagined the removal of this one object starting a landslide that would bring the walls down on them, burying them alive. He pulled his hand back. At the same time he opened his mind and senses as fully as he could. For a moment he thought he *did* hear something – a faint sigh, like the whisper of the ocean in a seashell – but then it was gone.

[*'If there are voices in here, I can't hear them, Lois – that damned thing is drowning them out.'*]

He pointed at the object in the middle of the circle – black beyond any previously held conception of black, a deathbag which was the apotheosis of all deathbags. But Lois was shaking her head.

[*'No, not drowning them out. Sucking them dry.'*]

She looked at the screaming black thing with horror and loathing.

[*'That thing is sucking the life out of all this stuff piled up around it . . . and it's trying to suck the life out of us, too.'*]

Yes, of course it was. Now that Lois had actually said it out loud, Ralph could feel the deathbag – or the object inside it – pulling at something far down in his head, yanking at it, twisting at it, shoving at it . . . trying to pull it out like a tooth from its pink socket of gum.

Trying to suck the life out of them? Close, but no cigar. Ralph didn't think it was their lives the thing inside the deathbag wanted, nor their souls . . . at least, not exactly. It was their life force it wanted. Their *ka*.

Lois's eyes widened as she picked up this thought . . . and then they shifted to a place just beyond his right shoulder. She leaned forward on her knees and reached out.

[*'Lois, I wouldn't do that – you could bring the whole place down around our—'*]

Too late. She yanked something free, looked at it with horrified understanding, and then held it out to him.

[*'It's still alive* – everything *that's in here is still alive. I don't know how that can be, but it is . . . somehow it is. But they're faint. Why are they so faint?'*]

What she was holding out to him was a small white sneaker that belonged to a woman or a child. As Ralph took it, he heard it singing softly in a distant voice. The sound was as lonely as November wind on an overcast afternoon, but incredibly sweet, as well – an antidote to the endless bray of the black thing on the floor.

And it was a voice he knew. He was sure it was.

There was a maroon splatter on the sneaker's toe. Ralph at first thought it was chocolate milk, then recognized it for what it really was: dried blood. In that instant he was outside the Red Apple again, grabbing Nat before Helen could drop her. He remembered how Helen's feet had tangled together; how she had stumbled backward, leaning against the Red Apple's door like a drunk against a lamppost, holding out her hands to him. *Gih me my bay-ee . . . Gih me Nah-lie.*

He knew the voice because it was Helen's voice. This sneaker had been on her foot that day, and the drops of blood on the toe had come either from Helen's smashed nose or from Helen's lacerated cheek.

It sang and sang, its voice not quite buried beneath the buzz of the thing in the deathbag, and now that Ralph's ears — or whatever passed for ears in the world of auras — were all the way open, he could hear all the other voices of all the other objects. They sang like a lost choir.

Alive. Singing.

They *could* sing, all the things lining these walls *could* sing, because their *owners* could still sing.

Their owners were still alive.

Ralph looked up again, this time noting that while some of the objects he saw were old — the battered alto sax, for instance — a great many of them were new; there were no wheels from Gay Nineties bicycles in this little alcove. He saw three clock-radios, all of them digital. A shaving kit that looked as if it had hardly been used. A lipstick that still had a Rite Aid pricetag on it.

[*'Lois, Atropos has taken this stuff from the people who'll be at the Civic Center tonight. Hasn't he?'*]

[*'Yes. I'm sure that's right.'*]

He pointed at the black cocoon shrieking on the

floor, almost drowning out the songs all around it . . . drowning them out as it fed on them.

[*'And whatever's inside that deathbag has something to do with what Clotho and Lachesis called the master-cord. It's the thing that ties all these different objects — all these different lives — together.'*]

[*'That makes them* ka–tet. *Yes.'*]

Ralph handed the sneaker back to Lois.

[*'This goes with us when we go. It's Helen's.'*]

[*'I know.'*]

Lois looked at it for a moment, then did something Ralph thought extremely clever: pulled out two eyelets' worth of lacing and tied the sneaker to her left wrist like a bracelet.

He crawled closer to the small deathbag and then bent over it. Getting close was hard, and staying close was harder — it was like placing your ear next to the motor-housing of a power drill shrieking at full volume or looking into a bright light without squinting. This time there seemed to be actual words buried within that buzzing, the same ones they'd heard as they approached the edge of the deathbag around the Civic Center: *Geddout. Fucoff. Beedit.*

Ralph placed his hands over his ears for a moment, but of course that did no good. The sounds weren't coming from the outside, not really. He let his hands drop again and looked at Lois.

[*'What do you think? Any ideas on what we should do next?'*]

He didn't know exactly what he had expected of her, but it wasn't the quick, positive response he got.

[*'Cut it open and take out what's inside — and do it right away. That thing's dangerous. Also, it might be calling Atropos, have you thought of that? Tattling just like the hen tattled on Jack in the story about the magic beanstalk.'*]

Ralph actually *had* considered this possibility, although not in such vivid terms. *All right,* he thought. *Cut open the bag and take the prize. Except just how are we supposed to do that?*

He remembered the bolt of lightning he'd sent at Atropos when the little bald creep had been trying to lure Rosalie across the street. A good trick, but something like that might do more harm than good here; what if he vaporized the thing they were supposed to take?

I don't think you can do that.

All right, fair enough, as a matter of fact *he* didn't think he could do it, either . . . but when you were surrounded by the possessions of people who could all be dead when the sun came up tomorrow, taking chances seemed like a very bad idea. An *insane* idea.

What I need isn't lightning but a nice sharp pair of scissors, like the ones Clotho and Lachesis use to—

He stared at Lois, startled by the clarity of the image.

[*'I don't know what you just thought of, but hurry up and do it, whatever it is.'*]

6

Ralph looked down at his right hand – a hand from which the wrinkles and the first twists of arthritis had now disappeared, a hand which lay inside a bright blue corona of light. Feeling a little foolish, he folded his last two fingers against his palm and extended the first two, thinking of a game they'd played as kids – rock breaks scissors, scissors cut paper, paper covers rock.

Be scissors, he thought. *I need a pair of scissors. Help me out.*

Nothing. He glanced at Lois and saw her looking at him with a serene calm which was somehow terrifying. *Oh Lois, if you only knew,* he thought, and then swept that out of his mind. Because he had felt something, hadn't he? Yes. *Something.*

This time he didn't make words in his mind but a picture: not the scissors Clotho had used to send on Jimmy V but the stainless-steel shears from his mother's sewing basket – long, slim blades tapering to a point almost as sharp as the tip of a knife. As he deepened his concentration, he could even see the two tiny words engraved on the metal just south of the pivot-point: SHEFFIELD STEEL. And now he could feel that thing in his mind again, not a blink this time but a muscle – an immensely powerful one – slowly flexing. He looked fixedly down at his fingers and made the shears in his mind open and close. As they did, he slowly opened and closed his fingers, creating a V that widened and narrowed.

Now he could feel the energy he had taken from Nirvana Boy and the bum out at the trainyards, first gathering in his head and then moving down his right arm to his fingers like a cramp.

The aura surrounding the extended first and second fingers of his right hand began to thicken . . . and to lengthen. To take on the slim shape of blades. Ralph waited until they had extended themselves about five inches out

737

from his nails and then worked his fingers back and forth again. The blades opened and closed.

[*'Go, Ralph! Do it!'*]

Yes – he couldn't afford to wait around and run experiments. He felt like a car battery that had been called on to crank a motor much too big for it. He could feel all his energy – the stuff he'd taken as well as his own – running down his right arm and into those blades. It wouldn't last long.

He leaned forward, fingers pressed together in a pointing gesture, and sank the tip of the scissors into the deathbag. He had been concentrating so hard on first creating and then maintaining the scissors that he had stopped hearing that steady, hoarse buzz – at least with his conscious mind – but when the scissors-point sank into its black skin, the deathbag suddenly cycled up to a new, shrieking pitch of mingled pain and alarm. Ralph saw dribbles of thick, dark goo running out of the bag and across the floor. It looked like diseased snot. At the same time he felt the power-drain inside him roughly double. He could *see* it, he realized: his own aura running down his right arm and across the back of his hand in slow, peristaltic waves. And he could sense it dimming around the rest of his body as its essential protection of him thinned out.

[*'Hurry, Ralph! Hurry!'*]

He made a tremendous effort and tore his fingers open. The shimmering blue blades also opened, making a small slit in the black egg. It screamed, and two bright, jagged flashes of red light raced across its surface. Ralph brought his fingers together and watched the shears growing from their tips snap shut, cutting through dense black stuff that was part shell and part flesh. He cried out. It was not pain he felt, exactly, but a sense of awful weariness. *This is what bleeding to death must feel like,* he thought.

Something inside the bag gleamed bright gold.

Ralph gathered all his strength and attempted to open his fingers for another cut. At first he didn't think he was going to be able to do it – they felt as if they had been stuck together with Krazy Glue – and then they drew apart, widening the slit. Now he could almost see the object inside, something small and round and shiny. *Really only one thing it can be,* he thought, and then his heart suddenly fluttered in his chest. The blue blades flickered.

[*'Lois! Help me!'*]

She seized his wrist. Ralph felt strength roar into him in big fresh volts. He watched, bemused, as the shears solidified again. Now only one of the blades was blue. The other was a pearly gray.

Lois, screaming inside his head: [*'Cut it! Cut it now!'*]

He brought his fingers together again, and this time the blades cut the deathbag wide open. It uttered one last wavering shriek, turned entirely red, and disappeared. The shears growing from the tips of Ralph's fingers flickered out of existence. He closed his eyes for a moment, suddenly aware that big warm drops of sweat were running down his cheeks like tears. In the dark field behind his eyelids he could see crazy afterimages that looked like dancing scissors-blades.

[*'Lois? Are you okay?'*]

[*'Yes . . . but drained. I don't have the slightest idea how I'm supposed to get back to those stairs under the tree, let alone climb them. I'm not sure I can even stand up.'*]

Ralph opened his eyes, put his hands on his thighs above the knees, and leaned forward again. Lying on the floor where the deathbag had been was a man's wedding ring. He could easily read what had been engraved on the wide inner curve: HD − ED 5–8–87.

Helen Deepneau and Edward Deepneau. Married on August 5th, 1987.

It was what they had come for. It was Ed's token. All that remained now was to pick it up . . . slip it into the watchpocket of his pants . . . find Lois's earrings . . . and get the hell out of here.

7

As he reached for the ring, a flicker of verse slipped through his mind − not Stephen Dobyns this time but J. R. R. Tolkien, who had invented the hobbits Ralph had last thought of in Lois's cozy, picture-filled living room. It had been almost thirty years since he had read Tolkien's story of Frodo and Gandalf and Sauron, the Dark Lord − a story which contained a token very similar to this one, now that he thought about it − but the lines were momentarily as clear as the scissors-blades had been only moments before:

One Ring to rule them all, One Ring to find them,
One Ring to bring them all and in the darkness bind them
In the Land of Mordor where the Shadows lie.

I won't be able to pick it up, he thought. *It will be as tightly bound to the wheel of* ka *as Lois and I are, and I won't be able to pick it up. Either that, or it will be like grasping a live high-tension wire, and I'll be dead before I know it's happening.*

Except he didn't really believe either of those things were going to happen. If the ring was not his for the taking, why had it been protected by the deathbag? If the ring was not his for the taking, why had the forces which stood behind Clotho and Lachesis – and Dorrance, he couldn't forget Dorrance – set him and Lois upon this journey in the first place?

One Ring to rule them all, One Ring to find them, Ralph thought, and closed his fingers around Ed's wedding ring. For a moment he felt a deep, glassy pain in his hand and wrist and forearm; at the same moment, the softly singing voices of the objects which Atropos had hoarded here rose in a great, harmonic shout.

Ralph made a sound – perhaps a scream, perhaps only a moan – and lifted the ring up, clenched tightly in his right hand. A sense of victory sang in his veins like wine, or like—

[*'Ralph.'*]

He looked at her, but Lois was looking down at where Ed's ring had been, her eyes dark with a mixture of fear and confusion.

Where Ed's ring had been; where Ed's ring still was. It lay exactly as it had lain, a glimmering gold circlet with HD – ED 5–8–87 inscribed around the inner arc.

Ralph felt an instant of dizzy disorientation and controlled it with an effort. He opened his hand, half expecting the ring to be gone in spite of what his senses told him, but it still lay in the center of his palm, neatly enclosed within the fork where his loveline and his lifeline diverged, glimmering in the baleful red light of this nasty place. HD − ED 5–8–87.

The two rings were identical.

8

One in his hand; one on the floor; absolutely no difference. At least none that Ralph could see.

Lois reached for the ring which had replaced the one Ralph had picked up, hesitated, then grasped it. As they watched, ghost-gold glowed just above the chamber's floor, then solidified into a third wedding band. Like the other two, HD − ED 5–8–87 was inscribed on the inner curve.

Ralph found himself thinking of yet another story − not Tolkien's long tale of the Ring, but a story by Dr Seuss which he had read one of Carolyn's sister's kids back in the fifties. That was a long time ago, but he had never completely forgotten the story, which had been richer and darker than Dr Seuss's usual jingle-jangle nonsense about rats and bats and troublesome cats. It was called *The Five Hundred Hats of Bartholomew Cubbins,* and Ralph supposed it really wasn't any wonder that the story had come to mind now.

Poor Bartholomew was a country hayseed who had the bad luck to be in the big city when the King happened by. You were supposed to take your hat off in the presence of that august personage, and Bartholomew had certainly tried, but without any luck; each time he took his hat off, another one, identical to the last, appeared beneath it.

[*Ralph, what's happening? What does it mean?*]

He shook his head without answering, eyes moving

from the ring on his palm to the one in Lois's hand to the one on the floor, around and around and around. Three rings, all of them identical, just like the hats Bartholomew Cubbins had kept trying to take off. The poor kid had gone on trying to make his manners to the King, Ralph remembered, even as the executioner had led him up a curving flight of stairs to the place where he would be beheaded for the crime of disrespect . . .

Except that wasn't right, because after awhile the hats on poor Bartholomew's head *did* begin to change, to grow ever more fabulous and rococo.

And are the rings the same, Ralph? Are you sure?

No, he guessed he wasn't. When he'd picked up the first one, he had felt a deep, momentary ache spread up his arm like rheumatism, but Lois had shown no signs of pain when she picked up the second one.

And the voices – I didn't hear them shout when she picked up the one she has.

Ralph leaned forward and grasped the third ring. There was no jolt of pain and no shout from the objects which formed the walls of the room – they just kept singing softly. Meanwhile, a fourth ring materialized where the other three had been, materialized exactly like another hat on the head of hapless Bartholomew Cubbins, but Ralph barely glanced at it. He looked at the first ring, lying between the fork of his lifeline and loveline on the palm of his right hand.

One Ring to rule them all, he thought. *One Ring to bind them. And I think that's you, beautiful. I think the others are just clever counterfeits.*

And maybe there was a way to check that. Ralph

held the two rings to his ears. The one in his left hand was silent; the one in his right, the one that had been inside the deathbag when he cut it open, gave off a faint, chilling echo of the deathbag's final scream.

The one in his right hand was alive.

[*'Ralph?'*]

Her hand on his arm, cold and urgent. Ralph looked at her, then tossed the ring in his left hand away. He held the other up and gazed at Lois's strained, strangely young face through it, as if through a telescope.

[*'This is the one. The others are just place-holders, I think – like zeros in a big, complicated math problem.'*]

[*'You mean they don't matter?'*]

He hesitated, unsure of how to reply . . . because they *did* matter, that was the thing. He just didn't know how to put his intuitive understanding of this into words. As long as the false rings kept appearing in this nasty little room, like hats on the head of Bartholomew Cubbins, the future represented by the deathbag around the Civic Center remained the one true future. But the first ring, the one which Atropos had actually stolen off Ed's finger (perhaps as he lay sleeping next to Helen in the little Cape Cod house which was now standing empty), could change all that.

The replicas were tokens which preserved the shape of *ka* just as spokes radiating out from a hub preserved the shape of a wheel. The original, however . . .

Ralph thought the original *was* the hub: One Ring to bind them.

He gripped the gold band tightly, feeling its hard curve bite into his palm and fingers. Then he slipped it into his watchpocket.

There was one thing about ka *they didn't tell us,* he thought. *It's slippery. Slippery as some nasty old fish that won't come off the hook but just keeps flopping around in your hand.*

And it was like climbing a sand dune, too – you slid one step back for every two you managed to lunge forward. They had gone out to High Ridge and accomplished *something* – just what Ralph didn't know, but Dorrance had assured them it was true; according to him, they had fulfilled their task there. Now they had come here and taken Ed's token, but it *still* wasn't enough, and why? Because *ka* was like a fish, *ka* was like a sand dune, *ka* was like a wheel that didn't want to stop but only to roll on and on, crushing whatever might happen to be in its path. A wheel of many spokes.

But most of all, perhaps, *ka* was like a ring.

Like a wedding ring.

He suddenly understood what all the talk on the hospital roof and all of Dorrance's efforts to explain hadn't been able to convey: Ed's undesignated status, coupled with Atropos's discovery of the poor, confused man, had conveyed a tremendous power upon him. A door had opened, and a demon called the Crimson King had strolled through, one that was stronger than Clotho, Lachesis, Atropos, any of them. And it didn't intend to be stopped by a Derry Old Crock like Ralph Roberts.

[*'Ralph?'*]

[*'One Ring to rule them all, Lois – One Ring to bind them.'*]

[*'What are you talking about? What do you mean?'*]

He patted his watchpocket, feeling the small yet momentous bulge that was Ed's ring. Then he reached out and grasped her shoulders.

745

[*The replacements — the false rings — are spokes, but this one is the hub. Take away the hub, and a wheel can't turn.*]

[*Are you sure?*]

He was sure, all right. He just didn't know how to do it.

[*Yes. Now come on — let's get out of here while we still can.*]

Ralph sent her beneath the overloaded dining room table first, then dropped to his knees and followed. He paused halfway under and looked back over his shoulder. He saw a strange and terrible thing: although the buzzing sound had not returned, the deathbag was reknitting itself around the replacement wedding ring. Already the bright gold had dimmed to a ghostly circlet.

He stared at it for several seconds, fascinated, almost hypnotized, then tore his eyes away with an effort and began to crawl after Lois.

9

Ralph was afraid they would lose valuable time trying to navigate their way back through the maze of corridors which crisscrossed Atropos's storehouse of keepsakes, but that turned out not to be a problem. Their own footprints, fading but still visible, were there to guide them.

He began to feel a little stronger as they put the terrible little room behind them, but Lois was now flagging badly. By the time they reached the archway between the storehouse and Atropos's filthy apartment, she was leaning on him. He asked if she was all right. Lois managed a shrug and a small, tired smile.

[*'Most of my problem is being in this place. It doesn't really matter how high up we go, it's still foul and I hate it. Once I get some fresh air, I think I'll be fine. Honestly.'*]

Ralph hoped she was right. As he ducked under the arch into Atropos's apartment, he was trying to think of a pretext by which he could send Lois on ahead of him. That would give him an opportunity to give the place a quick search. If that didn't turn up the earrings, he would have to assume that Atropos was still wearing them.

He noticed her slip was hanging below the hem of her dress again, opened his mouth to tell her, and saw a flicker of movement from the tail of his left eye. He realized they had been a lot less cautious on the return trip – partly because they were worn out – and now they might have to pay a high price for dropping their guard.

[*'Lois, look out!'*]

Too late. Ralph felt her arm jerked away as the snarling creature in the dirty tunic seized her about the waist and dragged her backward. Atropos's head only came to her armpit, but that was enough to allow him to hold his rusty blade over her. When Ralph made an instinctive lunge at him, Atropos brought the straight-razor down until it was touching the pearl-gray cord which drifted up from the crown of her head. He bared his teeth at Ralph in an unspeakable grin.

[*Not another step, Shorts . . . not one!*]

Well, he didn't have to worry about Lois's errant earrings anymore, at least. They glittered a murky, pinkish-red against the tiny lobes of Atropos's ears. It was more the sight of them than the shout that stopped Ralph where he was.

The scalpel drew back a little . . . but only a little.

[*Now, Shorts — you took something of mine just now, didn't you? Don't try to deny it; I know. And now you're going to give it back.*]

The scalpel returned to Lois's balloon-string; Atropos caressed it with the flat of the blade.

[*You give it back or this bitch is going to die here in front of you — you can stand there and watch the sack turn black. So what do you say, Short Stuff? Hand it over.*]

CHAPTER TWENTY-SIX

1

Atropos's smile shone out, full of repulsive triumph, and full of –

Full of fear. He caught you flat-footed, he's got his scalpel to Lois's balloon-string and his hand around her throat, but he's still scared to death. Why?

[*Come on! Quit wasting time, shithead! Give me the ring!*]

Ralph reached slowly into his watchpocket and grasped the ring, wondering why Atropos hadn't killed Lois outright. Surely he didn't intend to let her – to let either of them – go.

He's afraid I might hammer him with another one of those telepathic karate-chops. And that's just for starters. I think he's also afraid of screwing up. Afraid of the thing – the entity – that's running him. Afraid of the Crimson King. You're scared of the boss, aren't you, my filthy little friend?

He held the ring up between the thumb and forefinger of his right hand and peeked through it again.

[*'Come and get it, why don't you? Don't be shy.'*]

Atropos's face knotted with rage. The expression twisted his nervy, gloating grin into a cartoon scowl.

[*I'll kill her, Shorts, didn't you hear me? Is that what you want?*]

Ralph slowly and deliberately raised his left hand. He made a sawing gesture in the air with it, and was gratified to see Atropos wince when the edge of the palm turned momentarily toward him.

[*'If you even nick her with that blade, I'll hit you so hard you'll need a pocket-knife to dig your teeth out of the wall. And that's a promise.'*]

[*Just give me the ring, Shorts.*]

They can't lie, Ralph thought suddenly. *I can't remember if I was actually told that or just intuited it, but I'm sure it's true — they can't lie. I can, though.*

[*'I'll tell you what, Mr A — promise me it's a push and I'll give it to you.'*]

Atropos gave him a narrow look in which doubt and suspicion were mingled.

[*A push? What do you mean, a push?*]

[*'Ralph, no!'*]

He glanced at her, then back at Atropos. He raised his left hand to scratch his cheek without considering how the gesture would look to the little bald doctor. The scalpel was pressed against Lois's balloon-string again in a trice, this time hard enough to dent it and create a dark splotch at the point of contact. It looked like a blood-blister. Great beads of sweat stood out on Atropos's brow, and when he spoke, his voice was a panicky shriek.

[*Don't you go throwing any of your cut-rate thunderbolts at me! The woman dies if you do!*]

Ralph lowered his hand in a hurry, then put both of them behind his back like a penitent child. Ed's wedding ring was still folded into his hand, and now, almost without thinking about it, he tucked it into the back pocket of his pants. It was only then that he was completely sure he didn't mean to give up the ring. Even if it cost Lois her life – both of them their lives – he didn't mean to give up the ring.

But perhaps it wouldn't come to that.

[*'A push means we both walk away, Mr A – I give you the ring, you give me back my lady-friend. All you have to do is promise not to hurt her. What do you say?'*]

[*'No, Ralph, no!'*]

What Atropos said was nothing. His eyes glittered at Ralph with feary, hateful impotence. If ever in his long life he'd wished for the ability to lie, Ralph supposed he must be wishing for it at that moment. All it would take was *Okay, it's a deal,* and the ball would be right back in Ralph's court. But he couldn't say that, because he couldn't *do* that.

He knows he's in a nasty corner, Ralph thought. *It really doesn't matter if he cuts her cord or lets her go – he must think I mean to flash-fry him in either case, and he's not wrong.*

How much damage can you actually do to him, sweetheart? Carolyn asked doubtfully from the place she kept inside his head. *How much juice have you got left after cutting open the deathbag around the wedding ring?*

The answer, unfortunately, was not much. Maybe enough to singe his bald head, but probably not enough to sauté it. And—

Then Ralph saw something he didn't like: the edge-of-panic quality in Atropos's grin was being replaced by cautious confidence. And he felt those mad eyes crawling avidly over him – his face, his body, but mostly his *aura.*

Ralph had a sudden clear vision of a mechanic using a dipstick to find out how much oil was left in an automobile crankcase.

Do something, Lois begged him with her eyes. *Please, Ralph.*

But he didn't know what to do. He was completely out of ideas.

Atropos's smile took on a gloating, nasty edge.

[*You're unloaded, Short Stuff, ain'tcha? Gee, that's sad.*]

[*'Hurt her and you'll find out, you sawed-off piece of shit.'*]

Atropos's grin went on widening.

[*You couldn't give a rat a hotfoot with what you've got left. Why don't you just be a good boy and hand over the ring before I—*]

[*'Oh, you bastard!'*]

It was Lois. She was no longer looking at Ralph; she was looking across the room, into the mirror where Atropos no doubt checked the fit and tilt of his latest fashion accents – Rosalie's bandanna, say, or Bill McGovern's Panama. Her eyes were wide and full of fury, and Ralph knew exactly what she was seeing.

[*'Those are MINE, you rotten little thief!'*]

She shoved violently backward, using her greater weight to slam Atropos against the side of the archway. A startled grunt escaped him. The hand holding the scalpel flew upward; the blade dug dry scales of dirt from the wall. Lois turned toward him, her face knotted in an angry snarl – a look so un-*our Lois* that McGovern might have fainted in shock at the sight of it. Her hands clawed at the sides of his face, reaching for his ears. One of her fingers dug into his cheek. Atropos yapped like a dog whose paw has been stepped on, then grabbed her by the waist again and whirled her back around.

He turned the scalpel's blade inward, getting ready to slash. Ralph shook the forefinger of his right hand at it in a scolding gesture. A flash of light so pallid it was almost invisible shot out from the nail and struck the scalpel's tip, momentarily knocking it away from Lois's balloon-string. And that was all there was; Ralph sensed that his personal armory was now empty.

Atropos bared his teeth at him from over Lois's shoulder as she bucked and twisted in his arms. She was not trying to get away, either; she was trying to turn and attack him. Her feet flailed out as she threw all her weight against him again, trying to squash him against the wall behind them, and without having the slightest idea of what he meant to do, Ralph lunged forward and dropped to his knees with his hands out. He looked like a manic suitor making a strenuous marriage proposal, and one of Lois's thrashing feet came close to kicking him in the throat. He snatched at the hem of her slip and it came free in a slithery little rush of pink nylon. Meanwhile, Lois was still yelling.

[*Miserable little thief! Here's something for you! How do you like it?*]

Atropos uttered a squeal of pain, and when Ralph looked up, he saw that Lois had buried her teeth in his right wrist. His left hand, the one holding the scalpel, flailed blindly at her balloon-string, missing it by less than an inch. Ralph sprang to his feet and, still with no clear idea of what he was doing, pulled Lois's pink half-slip over Atropos's slashing hand . . . and his head.

[*Get away from him, Lois! Run!*]

753

She spat out the small white hand and stumbled toward the barrel-head table in the center of the room, wiping Atropos's blood from her mouth with atavistic loathing . . . but the dominant expression on her face was still one of anger. Atropos himself, for the moment just a bawling, writhing shape under the pink half-slip, groped after her with his free hand. Ralph slapped it away and shoved him back against the side of the archway.

[*'No you don't, my friend — not at all.'*]

[*Let me go! Let me go, you bastard! You can't do this!*]

And the weirdest thing of all is that he really believes that, Ralph thought. *He's had it his own way for so long that he's completely forgotten what Short-Timers can do. I can fix that, I think.*

Ralph remembered how Atropos had slashed Rosalie's balloon-string after the dog had licked his hand, and his hatred for this strutting, leering, complacently insane creature suddenly exploded in his head like a rotten-green roadflare. He grabbed one side of Lois's slip and twisted his fist twice around it in a savage winding-up gesture, pulling it so tight that Atropos's features stood out in a pink nylon deathmask.

Then, just as the blade of the scalpel popped through the fabric and began to cut it open, Ralph whirled Atropos around, using the slip as a man might use a sling to whirl a stone, and sent him flying across the archway. The damage might have been less if Atropos had fallen, but he didn't; his feet knocked against each other but never quite crossed. He hit the rock facing of the archway with a thud, voiced a muffled scream of pain, and dropped to his knees. Spots of blood bloomed on Lois's half-slip like flower-petals. The scalpel had disappeared back through the slit it had made in the cloth. Ralph sprang after Atropos just as it reappeared and lengthened the original cut, freeing the bald creature's staring, bewildered face. His nose was bleeding; so were his forehead and right temple. Before he could begin to get up, Ralph grabbed the slippery pink bulges that were his shoulders.

[*Stop it! I'm warning you, Shorts! I'll make you sorry you were ever bo—*]

Ralph ignored this pointless bluster and slammed Atropos forward, hard. The midget's arms were still tangled in the slip and he caught the floor with nothing but face. His shriek was part amazement, mostly pain. Incredibly, Ralph felt Lois in the back of his mind, telling him that enough was enough, not to really hurt him – not to hurt the pint-sized psychotic who had just tried to kill her. Atropos attempted to roll over. Ralph knee-dropped him in the middle of the back and knocked him flat again.

[*'Don't move, friend. I like you just the way you are.'*]

He looked up at Lois, and saw that her amazing fury had departed as suddenly as it had come – like some freak weather phenomenon. A tornado, perhaps, that touches down out of a clear blue sky, rips the top off a barn, and then disappears again. She was pointing at Atropos.

[*'He's got my earrings, Ralph. The nasty little thief has got my earrings. He's wearing them!'*]

[*'I know. I saw.'*]

One snarling side of Atropos's face poked out of the slit in the nylon like the face of the world's ugliest baby at the moment of its birth. Ralph could feel the muscles of the small creature's back trembling beneath his pinioning

knee, and he remembered an old proverb he'd read some-
where . . . maybe at the end of a Salada teabag string: *He
who takes a tiger by the tail dare not let go.* Now, in this
unlikely den beneath the ground and feeling like a char-
acter in a fairy-tale concocted by a lunatic, Ralph thought
he had achieved a sort of divine understanding of that
proverb. Through a combination of Lois's sudden rage and
plain old shitass luck, he had wound up at least temporarily
on top of the scuzzy little fuck. The question – and a fairly
pressing one, at that – was what to do next.

The hand holding the scalpel lashed up, but the stroke
was both weak and blind. Ralph avoided it easily. Sobbing
and cursing, not afraid even now but clearly hurting and
all but consumed with impotent rage, Atropos flailed up
at him again.

[*Let me up, you overgrown Short-Time bastard! Silly old
white-hair! Ugly wrinkle-face!*]

[*'I look a little better than that just lately, my friend.
Haven't you noticed?'*]

[*Asshole! Stupid Short-Time asshole! I'll make you sorry!
I'll make you so sorry!*]

Well, Ralph thought, *at least he's not begging. I almost
would have expected him to start begging by now.*

Atropos continued to flail weakly with the scalpel. Ralph
ducked two or three of these strokes easily, then slid one
hand toward the throat of the creature lying beneath him.

[*'Ralph! No! Don't!'*]

He shook his head at her, not knowing if he was
expressing annoyance, reassurance, or both. He touched
Atropos's skin, and felt him shudder. The bald doc uttered
a choked cry of revulsion, and Ralph knew exactly how

he felt. It was sickening for both of them, but he didn't take his hand away. Instead, he tried to close it around Atropos's throat and wasn't very surprised to find he couldn't do it. Still, hadn't Lachesis said that only Short-Timers could oppose the will of Atropos? He thought so. The question was, how?

Beneath him, Atropos laughed nastily.

[*'Please, Ralph! Please just get my earrings and we'll go!'*]

Atropos rolled his eyes in her direction, then looked back at Ralph.

[*Did you think you could kill me, Shorts? Well, guess again.*]

No, he hadn't thought it, but he'd needed to find out for sure.

[*Life's a bitch, ain't it, Shorts? Why don't you just give me back the ring? I'm going to get it sooner or later, I guarantee you that.*]

[*'Fuck you, you little weasel.'*]

Tough talk, but talk was cheap. The most pressing question was still unanswered: What the hell was he supposed to do with this monster?

Whatever it is, you won't be able to do it with Lois standing there and watching you, a cold voice that was not quite Carolyn's advised him. *She was fine when she was pissed off, but she's not pissed off now. She's too tenderhearted for whatever's going to happen next, Ralph. You have to get her out of here.*

He turned toward Lois. Her eyes were half closed. She looked ready to crumple at the base of the archway and go to sleep.

[*'Lois, I want you to get out of here. Right now. Go up the stairs and wait for me under the tr—'*]

The scalpel flashed up again, and this time it almost sliced off the end of Ralph's nose. He recoiled, and his knee slid on nylon. Atropos gave a mighty heave and came within a whisker of rolling out from under. At the last second, Ralph shoved the little man's head flat again with the heel of his hand — that, it seemed, was allowed by the rules — and replanted his knee.

[*Owww! Owww! Stop it! You're killing me!*]

Ralph ignored him and looked at Lois.

[*'Go on, Lois! Go on up! I'll be there as soon as I can!'*]

[*'I don't think I can climb out on my own — I'm too tired.'*]

[*'Yes, you can. You have to, and you can.'*]

Atropos subsided again — for the moment, at least — a small, gasping engine under Ralph's knee. But that was a long way from being enough. Time was passing topside, passing fast, and right now time was the real enemy, not Ed Deepneau.

[*'My earrings—'*]

[*'I'll bring them when I come, Lois. I promise.'*]

Making what looked like a supreme effort, Lois straightened and looked solemnly at Ralph.

[*'You shouldn't hurt him, Ralph, not if you don't have to. It's not Christian.'*]

No, not at all Christian, a capering little creature deep inside Ralph's head agreed. *Not Christian, but still . . . I can't wait to get started.*

[*'Go on, Lois. Leave him to me.'*]

She looked at him sadly.

[*'It wouldn't do me any good to ask you to promise not to hurt him, would it?'*]

He thought about it, then shook his head.

[*'No, but I'll promise you this much: it won't be any harder than he makes it. Is that good enough?'*]

Lois considered carefully, then nodded.

[*'Yes, I think that will do. And maybe I can make it back up, if I take it slow and easy . . . but what about you?'*]

[*'I'll be fine. Wait for me under the tree.'*]

[*'All right, Ralph.'*]

He watched her cross the filthy room, Helen's sneaker bobbing from one wrist. She ducked beneath the arch between the apartment and the stairway and slowly started up. Ralph waited until her feet had disappeared from view, then turned back to Atropos.

[*'Well, Chumley, here we are — two old pals reunited. What should we do? Should we play? You like to play, don't you?'*]

Atropos immediately renewed his struggles, simultaneously waving his scalpel above his head and trying to buck Ralph off.

[*Quit it! Get your hands off me, you old faggot!*]

Atropos thrashed so wildly that kneeling on him now was like kneeling on a snake. Ralph ignored the yelling, the bucking, and the blindly waving scalpel. Atropos's whole head was now sticking out of the slip, which made things a lot easier. He grabbed Lois's earrings and tugged. They stayed where they were but earned him a hearty, pained scream from Atropos. Ralph leaned forward, smiling a little.

[*'For pierced ears, aren't they, pal?'*]

[*Yes! Yes, goddammit!*]

[*'To quote you, life's a bitch, ain't it?'*]

Ralph seized the earrings again and ripped them free. There were two small fans of blood as the minute holes in the lobes of Atropos's ears became flaps. The bald man's scream was as sharp as a new drillbit. Ralph felt an uneasy mixture of pity and contempt.

Little bastard's used to hurting other people, but not being hurt himself. Maybe he's never been hurt himself. Well say hello to how the other half lives, pal.

[*Stop it! Stop it! You can't do this to me!*]

[*I've got a newsflash for you, buddy . . . I am doing it. Now why don't you just get with the program?*]

[*What do you think you're going to accomplish by this, Shorts? It'll happen anyway, you know. All those people at the Civic Center are going to go bye-bye, and taking the ring won't stop it.*]

Don't I know it, Ralph thought.

Atropos was still panting, but he had stopped thrashing. Ralph felt able to look away from him for a moment and send his eyes on a quick tour of the room. He supposed what he was really looking for was inspiration – even a small bolt would do.

[*'Can I make a suggestion, Mr A? As your new little pal and playmate? I know you're busy, but you ought to find time to do something about this place. I'm not talking about getting it in* House Beautiful *or anything like that, but sheesh! What a sty!'*]

Atropos, simultaneously sulky and wary: [*Do you think I give a fuck what you think, Shorts?*]

He could only think of one way to proceed. He didn't like it, but he was going to go ahead, just the same. He *had* to go ahead; there was a picture in his mind that guaranteed it. It was a picture of Ed Deepneau flying toward Derry from the coast in a light plane, one with either a crate of high explosive or a tank of nerve-gas stowed in the nose.

[*'What* can *I do with you, Mr A? Any ideas?'*]

The response was immediate and unequivocal.

[*Let me go. That's the answer. The* only *answer. I'll leave you alone, both of you. Leave you for the Purpose. You'll live another ten years. Hell, maybe another twenty, it's not impossible. All you and the little lady have to do is butt out. Go home. And when the big bang comes, watch it on the TV news.*]

Ralph tried to sound as if he were honestly considering this.

[*'And you'd leave us alone? You'd* promise *to leave us alone?'*]

[*Yes!*]

Atropos's face had taken on a hopeful look, and Ralph could see the first traces of an aura springing up around the little creep. It was the same low and nasty red as the pulsing glow which lit the apartment.

[*'Do you know something, Mr A?'*]

Atropos, looking more hopeful than ever: [*No, what?*]

Ralph shot one hand forward, grabbed Atropos's left wrist, and twisted it hard. Atropos shrieked in agony. His fingers loosened on the handle of the scalpel, and Ralph plucked it free with the ease of a veteran pickpocket lifting a wallet.

[*'I believe you.'*]

2

[*Give it back! Give it back! Give it back! Give it—*]

In his hysteria, Atropos might have gone on shrieking

this for hours, so Ralph put a stop to it in the most direct way he knew. He leaned forward and slashed a shallow vertical cut down the back of the big bald head poking out of the hole in Lois's half-slip. No invisible hand tried to repel him, and his own hand moved with no trouble at all. Blood – a shocking amount of it – welled out of the line-cut. The aura around Atropos had now gone to the dark and baleful red of an infected wound. He shrieked again.

Ralph rocked forward and spoke chummily into his ear.

[*'Maybe I can't kill you, but I can certainly fuck you up, can't I? And I don't need to be loaded with psychic juice to do it, either. This little honey will do just fine.'*]

He used the scalpel to cross the first cut he'd made, making a lower-case *t* on the back of Atropos's head. Atropos shrieked and began to flail wildly. Ralph was disgusted to discover that part of him – the capering gremlin – was enjoying this enormously.

[*'If you want me to go on cutting you, go on struggling. If you want me to stop, then* you *stop.'*]

Atropos became still at once.

[*'Okay. Now I'm going to ask you a few questions. I think you'll find it in your best interest to answer them.'*]

[*Ask me anything! Whatever you want! Just don't cut me anymore!*]

[*'That's a pretty good attitude, pally, but I think there's always room for improvement, don't you? Let's see.'*]

Ralph sliced down again, this time opening a long gash in the side of Atropos's skull. A flap of skin peeled loose like badly glued wallpaper. Atropos howled. Ralph felt a cramp of revulsion in the pit of his stomach and was actually relieved . . . but when he spoke/thought at Atropos, he took great pains not to let that feeling show.

[*'Okay, that's my motivational lecture, doc. If I have to repeat it, you'll need Krazy Glue to keep the top of your head from flying off in a high wind. Do you understand me?'*]

[*Yes! Yes!*]

[*'And do you believe me?'*]

[*Yes! Rotten old white-hair, YES!*]

[*'Okay, that's good. Here's my question, Mr A: if you make a promise, are you bound by it?'*]

Atropos was slow in answering, an encouraging sign. Ralph laid the flat of the scalpel's blade against his cheek to hurry him up. He was rewarded with another scream and instant cooperation.

[*Yes! Yes! Just don't cut me again! Please don't cut me again!*]

Ralph took the scalpel away. The outline of the blade burned on the little creature's unlined cheek like a birthmark.

[*'Okay, sunshine, listen up. I want you to promise you'll leave me and Lois alone until the rally at the Civic Center is over. No more chasing, no more slashing, no more bullshit. Promise me that.'*]

[*Fuck you! Take your promise and shove it up your ass!*]

Ralph was not put out of temper by this; his smile, in fact, widened. Because Atropos hadn't said *I won't,* and even more important, Atropos hadn't said *I can't.* He had just said no. Just a little backsliding, in other words, and easily remedied.

Steeling himself, Ralph ran the scalpel straight down

the middle of Atropos's back. The slip split, the dirty white tunic beneath it split, and so did the flesh beneath the tunic. Blood poured out in a sickening flood, and Atropos's tortured, wailing shriek beat at Ralph's ears.

He leaned over and murmured into the small ear again, grimacing and avoiding the blood as best he could.

[*'I don't like doing this anymore, Chumley — in fact, about two more cuts and I'm going to throw up again — but I want you to know that I can do it and I'm going to* keep on *doing it until you either give me the promise I want or until the force that stopped me from choking you stops me again. I think if you wait for that to happen, you're going to be one hurting unit. So what do you say? Do you want to promise, or do you want me to peel you like a grape?'*]

Atropos was blubbering. It was a nauseating, horrible sound.

[*You don't understand! If you succeed in stopping what's been started — the chances are slim, but it's possible that you might — I will be punished by the creature you call the Crimson King!*]

Ralph clamped his teeth together and slashed down again, his lips pressed so tightly together that his mouth looked like a long-healed scar. There was a faint tug as the scalpel's blade slid through gristle, and then Atropos's left ear tumbled to the floor. Blood poured out of the hole on the side of his bald head, and his scream this time was loud enough to hurt Ralph's ears.

They're sure a long way from being gods, aren't they? Ralph thought. He felt sick with horror and dismay. *The only real difference between them and us is that they live longer and they're a little harder to see. And I guess I'm not much of a soldier — just looking at all that blood makes me feel like passing out. Shit.*

[*All right, I promise! Just stop cutting me! No more! Please, no more!*]

['*That's a start, but you're going to have to be more specific. I want to hear you say that you promise to stay away from me and Lois, and Ed, too, until the rally at the Civic Center is over.*']

He expected more wiggling and weaseling, but Atropos surprised him.

[*I promise! I promise to stay away from you, and from the bitch you're running around with—*]

['*Lois. Say her name. Lois.*']

[*Yeah, yeah, her – Lois Chasse! I agree to stay away from her, and Deepneau, too. From all of you, just as long as you don't cut me anymore. Are you satisfied? Is it good enough, God damn you?*]

Ralph decided he *was* satisfied . . . or as satisfied as any man can be when he is deeply sickened by his own methods and actions. He didn't believe there were any trap-doors hidden in Atropos's promise; the little bald man knew he might pay a high price later for giving in now, but in the end that hadn't been able to offset the pain and terror Ralph had inflicted on him.

['*Yes, Mr A, I think it's good enough.*']

Ralph slid off his small victim with his stomach rolling and a sensation – it had to be false, didn't it? – that his throat was opening and closing like the valve of a clam. He looked at the blood-spattered scalpel for a moment, then cocked his arm back and threw it as hard as he could. It flew end-for-end through the arch and disappeared into the storeroom beyond.

Good riddance, Ralph thought. *At least I didn't get*

much on myself. There's that. He no longer felt like vomiting. Now he felt like crying.

Atropos got slowly to his knees and looked around with the dazed eyes of a man who has survived a killer storm. He saw his ear lying on the floor and picked it up. He turned it over in his small hands and looked at the strands of gristle trailing out from the back side. Then he looked up at Ralph. His eyes swam with tears of pain and humiliation, but there was something else in them as well – a rage so deep and deadly that Ralph recoiled from it. All his precautions seemed flimsy and foolish in the face of that rage. He took a blundering step backward and pointed at Atropos with an unsteady finger.

[*'Remember your promise!'*]

Atropos bared his teeth in a gruesome grin. The dangling flap of skin on the side of his face swung back and forth like a slack sail, and the raw flesh beneath it oozed and trickled.

[*Of course I'll remember it – how could I forget? In fact, I'd like to make you another. Two for the price of one, you might say.*]

Atropos made a gesture Ralph remembered well from the hospital roof, spreading the first two fingers of his right hand in a V and then flicking them upward, creating a red arc in the air. Within it, Ralph saw a human figure. Beyond it, dimly glimpsed, as if seen though a mist of blood, was the Red Apple Store. He started to ask who that was standing in the foreground, on the curb of Harris Avenue . . . and then, suddenly, he knew. He looked up at Atropos with shocked eyes.

[*'Jesus, no! No, you can't!'*]

The grin on Atropos's face continued to widen.

[*You know, that's what I kept thinking about you, Short-Time. Only I was wrong. You are, too. Watch.*]

Atropos moved his spread fingers slightly wider. Ralph saw someone wearing a Boston Red Sox baseball cap come out of the Red Apple, and this time Ralph knew immediately whom he was looking at. This person called to the one across the street, and then something terrible began to happen. Ralph turned away, sickened, from the bloody arc of the future between Atropos's small fingers.

But he heard it when it happened.

[*The one I showed you first belongs to the Random, Shorts — to me, in other words. And here's my promise to you: if you go on getting in my way, what I've just shown you is going to happen. There's nothing you can do, no warning you can give, that will stop it from happening. But if you leave off now — if you and the woman simply stand aside and let events take their course — then I will stay my hand.*]

The vulgarities which formed so large a part of Atropos's usual discourse had been left behind like a discarded costume, and for the first time Ralph had some clear sense of how truly old and malevolently wise this being was.

[*Remember what the junkies say, Shorts: dying is easy, living is hard. It's a true saying. If anyone should know, it's me. So what do you think? Having any second thoughts?*]

Ralph stood in the filthy chamber with his head down and his fists clenched. Lois's earrings burned in one of them like small hot coals. Ed's ring also seemed to burn against him, and he knew there wasn't a thing in the world to stop him from taking it out of his pocket and throwing it into the other room after the scalpel. He remembered a story he'd read in school about a thousand years ago. 'The Lady or the Tiger?' it had been called, and now he understood what it was to be given such a terrible power . . . and such a terrible choice. On the surface it seemed easy enough; what, after all, was one life against a thousand?

But that one life——!

Yet really, it isn't as if anyone would ever have to know, he thought coldly. *No one except maybe for Lois . . . and Lois would accept my decision. Carolyn might not have done, but they're very different women.*

Yes, but did he have the right?

Atropos also read this in his aura – it was spooky, how much the creature saw.

[*Of course you do, Ralph – that's what these matters of life and death are really about: who has the right. This time it's you. So what do you say?*]

[*'I don't know what I say. I don't know what I think. All I know is that I wish all three of you had* LEFT ME THE FUCK ALONE!*'*]

Ralph Roberts raised his head toward the root-riddled ceiling of Atropos's den and screamed.

CHAPTER TWENTY-SEVEN

1

Five minutes later, Ralph's head poked out of the shadows beneath the old, leaning oak. He saw Lois at once. She was kneeling in front of him, peering anxiously through the tangle of roots at his upturned face. He raised a grimy, blood-streaked hand and she took it firmly, holding him steady as he made his way up the last few steps – gnarled roots that were actually more like ladder-rungs.

Ralph wriggled his way out from under the tree and turned over on his back, taking the sweet air in great long pulls of breath. He thought air had never in his whole life tasted so good. In spite of everything else, he was enormously grateful to be out. To be free.

[*'Ralph? Are you all right?'*]

He turned her hand over, kissed her palm, then put her earrings where his lips had been.

[*'Yes. Fine. These are yours.'*]

She looked at them curiously, as if she had never seen earrings – these or any others – before, and then put them in her dress pocket.

[*'You saw them in the mirror, didn't you, Lois?'*]

[*'Yes, and it made me angry . . . but I don't think I was really surprised, not down deep.'*]

[*'Because you knew.'*]

[*'Yes. I guess I did. Maybe from when we first saw Atropos wearing Bill's hat. I just kept it . . . you know . . . in the back of my mind.'*]

She was looking at him carefully, assessingly.

[*'Never mind my earrings right now — what happened down there? How did you get away?'*]

Ralph was afraid if she looked at him in that careful way for too long, she would see too much. He also had an idea that if he didn't get moving soon, he might never move again; his weariness was now so large it was like some great encrusted object — a long-sunken ocean liner, perhaps — lying inside him, calling to him, trying to drag him down. He got to his feet. He couldn't allow either of them to be dragged down, not now. The news the sky told wasn't as bad as it could have been, but it was bad enough — it was six o'clock at least. All over Derry, people who didn't give a shit one way or the other about the abortion issue (the vast majority, in other words) were sitting down to hot dinners. At the Civic Center the doors would now be open; 10-K TV lights would be bathing them, and Minicams would be transmitting live shots of early arriving pro-choice advocates driving past Dan Dalton and his sign-waving Friends of Life. Not far from here, people were chanting that old Ed Deepneau favorite, the one that went *Hey, hey, Susan Day, how many kids did you kill today?* Whatever he and Lois did, they would have to do it in the next sixty to ninety minutes. The clock was ticking.

[*'Come on, Lois. We have to get moving.'*]

[*'Are we going back to the Civic Center?'*]

[*'No, not to start with. I think that to start with, we ought to . . .'*]

Ralph discovered that he simply couldn't wait to hear what he had to say. Where *did* he think they ought to go to start with? Back to Derry Home? The Red Apple? His house? Where did you go when you needed to find a couple of well-meaning but far from all-knowing fellows who had gotten you and your few close friends into a world of hurt and trouble? Or could you reasonably expect *them* to find *you*?

They might not want *to find you, sweetheart. In fact, they might actually be hiding from you.*

[*'Ralph, are you sure you're—'*]

He suddenly thought of Rosalie, and knew.

[*'The park, Lois. Strawford Park. That's where we have to go. But we need to make a stop on the way.'*]

He led her along the Cyclone fence, and soon they heard the lazy sound of interwoven voices. Ralph could smell roasting hotdogs as well, and after the fetid stench of Atropos's den, the smell was ambrosial. A minute or two later, he and Lois stepped to the edge of the little picnic area near Runway 3.

Dorrance was there, standing at the heart of his amazing, multicolored aura and watching as a light plane drifted down toward the runway. Behind him, Faye Chapin and Don Veazie were sitting at one of the picnic tables with a chessboard between them and a half-finished bottle of Blue Nun near to hand. Stan and Georgina Eberly were drinking beer and twiddling forks with hotdogs impaled upon them in the heat-shimmer – to Ralph that shimmer was a strangely dry pink, like coral-colored sand – above the picnic area's barbecue pit.

For a moment Ralph simply stood where he was, struck dumb by their beauty – the ephemeral, powerful beauty that was, he supposed, what Short-Time life was mostly about. A snatch of song, something at least twenty-five years old, occurred to him: *We are stardust, we are golden.* Dorrance's aura was different – fabulously different – but even the most prosaic of the others glittered like rare and infinitely desirable gemstones.

[*'Oh, Ralph, do you see? Do you see how beautiful they are?'*]

[*'Yes.'*]

[*'What a shame they don't know!'*]

But was it? In light of all that had happened, Ralph wasn't so sure. And he had an idea – a vague but strong intuition he could never have put into words – that perhaps real beauty was something unrecognized by the conscious self, a work that was always in progress, a thing of being rather than seeing.

'Come on, dumbwit, make your move,' a voice said. Ralph jerked, first thinking the voice was speaking to him, but it was Faye, talking to Don Veazie. 'You're slower'n old creepin Jesus.'

'Never mind,' Don said. 'I'm thinkin.'

'Think till hell freezes over, Slick, and it's still gonna be mate in six moves.'

Don poured some wine into a paper cup and rolled his eyes. 'Oh boogersnot!' he cried. 'I didn't realize I was playin chess with Boris Spassky! I thought it was just plain old Faye Chapin! I apologize all to hell and gone!'

'That's a riot, Don. An act like that, you could take it on the road and make a million dollars. You won't have to wait long to do it, either – you can start just six moves from now.'

'Ain't you smart,' Don said. 'You just don't know when to—'

'*Hush!*' Georgina Eberly said in a sharp tone. 'What was that? It sounded like something blew up!'

'That' was Lois, sucking a flood of vibrant rainforest green from Georgina's aura.

Ralph raised his right hand, curled it into a tube around his lips, and began to inhale a similar stream of bright blue light from Stan Eberly's aura. He felt fresh energy fill him at once; it was as if fluorescent lights were going on in his brain. But that vast sunken ship, which was really no more or less than four months' worth of mostly sleepless nights, was still there, and still trying to suck him down to the place where it was.

The decision was still right there, too – not yet made one way or the other, but only deferred.

Stan was also looking around. No matter how much of his aura Ralph took (and he had drawn off a great deal, it seemed to him), the source remained as densely bright as ever. Apparently what they had been told about the all-but-endless reservoirs of energy surrounding each human being had been the exact, literal truth.

'Well,' Stan said, 'I did hear *somethin*—'

'*I* didn't,' Faye said.

'Coss not, you're deaf as dirt,' Stan replied. 'Stop interruptin for just one minute, can'tcha? I started to say it wasn't a fuel-tank, because there ain't no fire or smoke.

Can't be that Don farted, either, cause there ain't no squirrels droppin dead out of the trees with their fur burnt off. I guess it musta been one of those big Air National Guard trucks backfirin. Don't worry, darlin, I'll pertect ya.'

'Pertect this,' Georgina said, slapping one hand into the crook of her elbow and curling her fist at him. She was smiling, however.

'Oh boy,' Faye said. 'Take a peek at Old Dor.'

They all looked at Dorrance, who was smiling and waving in the direction of the Harris Avenue Extension.

'Who do you see there, old fella?' Don Veazie asked with a grin.

'Ralph and Lois,' Dorrance said, smiling radiantly. 'I see Ralph and Lois. They just came out from under the old tree!'

'Yep,' Stan said. He shaded his eyes, then pointed directly at them. This delivered a wallop to Ralph's nervous system which only abated when he realized Stan was just pointing where Dorrance was waving. 'And look! There's Glenn Miller coming out right behind em! Goddam!'

Georgina threw an elbow and Stan stepped away nimbly, grinning.

[*'Hello, Ralph! Hello, Lois!'*]

[*'Dorrance! We're going to Strawford Park! Is that right?'*]

Dorrance, grinning happily: [*'I don't know, it's all Long-Time business now, and I'm through with it. I'm going back home soon and read Walt Whitman. It's going to be a windy night, and Whitman's always best when the wind blows.'*]

Lois, sounding nearly frantic: [*'Dorrance, help us!'*]

Dor's grin faltered, and he looked at her solemnly.

[*'I can't. It's passed out of my hands. Whatever's done will have to be done by you and Ralph now.'*]

'Ugh,' Georgina said. 'I hate it when he stares that way. You could almost believe he really does see someone.' She picked up her long-handled barbecue fork and began to toast her hotdog again. '*Has* anybody seen Ralph and Lois, by the way?'

'No,' Don said.

'They're shacked up in one of those X-rated motels down the coast with a case of beer and a bottle of Johnson's Baby Oil,' Stan said. 'The giant-economy-size bottle. I toldja that yesterday.'

'Filthy old man,' Georgina said, this time throwing the elbow with a little more force and a lot more accuracy.

Ralph: [*'Dorrance, can't you give us any help at all? At least tell us if we're on the right track?'*]

For a moment he was sure Dor was going to reply. Then there was a buzzing, approaching drone from overhead and the old man looked up. His daffy, beautiful smile resurfaced. 'Look!' he cried. 'An old Grumman Yellow Bird! And a beauty!' He jogged to the chainlink fence to watch the small yellow plane land, turning his back to them.

Ralph took Lois's arm and tried to smile himself. It was hard going – he thought he had never felt quite so frightened and confused in his entire life – but he gave it the old college try.

[*'Come on, dear. Let's go.'*]

2

Ralph remembered thinking – this while they'd been making their way along the abandoned rail-line which had eventually taken them back to the airport – that walking was not exactly what they were doing; it had seemed more like gliding. They went from the picnic area at the end of Runway 3 back to Strawford Park in that same fashion, only the glide was faster and more pronounced now. It was like being carried along by an invisible conveyor belt.

As an experiment, he stopped walking. The houses and storefronts continued to flow mildly past. He looked down at his feet to make sure, and yes, they were completely still. It seemed the sidewalk was moving, not him.

Here came Mr Dugan, head of the Derry Trust's Loan Department, decked out in his customary three-piece suit and rimless eyeglasses. As always, he looked to Ralph like the only man in the history of the world to be born without an asshole. He had once rejected Ralph's application for a Bill-Payer loan, which, Ralph supposed, might account for a few of his negative feelings about the man. Now he saw that Dugan's aura was the dull, uniform gray of a corridor in a Veterans Administration hospital, and Ralph decided that didn't surprise him much. He held his nose like a man forced to swim across a polluted canal and passed directly through the banker. Dugan did not so much as twitch.

That was sort of amusing, but when Ralph glanced at Lois, his amusement faded in a hurry. He saw the worry on her face, and the questions she wanted to ask. Questions to which he had no satisfactory answers.

Ahead was Strawford Park. As Ralph looked, the streetlights came on suddenly. The little playground where he and McGovern – Lois too, more often than not – had stood watching the children play was almost deserted. Two junior-high kids were sitting side by side on the swings, smoking cigarettes and talking, but the mothers and toddlers who came here during the daylight hours were all gone now.

Ralph thought of McGovern – of his ceaseless, morbid chatter and his self-pity, so hard to see when you first got to know him, so hard to miss once you'd been around him for awhile, both of them lightened and somehow turned into something better by his irreverent wit and his surprising, impulsive acts of kindness – and felt deep sadness steal over him. Short-Timers might be stardust, and they might be golden as well, but when they were gone they were as gone as the mothers and babies who made brief playtime visits here on sunny summer afternoons.

[*'Ralph, what are we doing here? The deathbag's over the Civic Center, not Strawford Park!'*]

Ralph guided her to the park bench where he had found her several centuries ago, crying over the argument she'd had with her son and daughter-in-law . . . and over her lost earrings. Down the hill, the two Portosans glimmered in the deepening twilight.

Ralph closed his eyes. *I am going mad,* he thought, *and I'm headed there on the express rather than the local. Which is it going to be? The lady . . . or the tiger?*

[*'Ralph, we have to do something. Those lives . . . those thousands of lives . . .'*]

In the darkness behind his closed lids, Ralph saw someone coming out of the Red Apple Store. A figure in dark corduroy pants and a Red Sox cap. Soon the terrible thing would start to happen again, and because Ralph didn't want to see it, he opened his eyes and looked at the woman beside him.

['Every *life is important, Lois, wouldn't you agree? Every single one.*']

He didn't know what she saw in his aura, but it clearly terrified her.

['*What happened down there after I left? What did he do or say to you? Tell me, Ralph! You tell me!*']

So which was it going to be? The one or the many? The lady or the tiger? If he didn't choose soon, the choice would be taken out of his hands by nothing more than the simple passage of time. So which one? *Which?*

'Neither . . . or both,' he said hoarsely, unaware in his terrible agitation that he was speaking aloud, and on several different levels at once. 'I won't choose one or the other. I *won't*. Do you hear me?'

He leaped up from the bench, looking around wildly.

'*Do you hear me?*' he shouted. '*I reject this choice! I will have* BOTH *or I will have* NEITHER!'

On one of the paths north of them, a wino who had been poking through a trash-barrel, searching for returnable cans and bottles, took one look at Ralph, then turned and ran. What he had seen was a man who appeared to be on fire.

Lois stood up and grasped his face between her hands.

['*Ralph, what is it? Who is it? Me? You? Because if it's me, if you're holding back because of me, I don't want—*']

He took a deep, steadying breath and then put his forehead against hers, looking into her eyes.

[*It's not you, Lois, and not me. If it was either of us, I might be able to choose. But it's not, and I'll be goddamned if I'm going to be a pawn anymore.*]

He shook her loose and took a step away from her. His aura flashed out so brilliantly that she had to raise her hand in front of her eyes; it was as if he were somehow exploding. And when his voice came, it reverberated in her head like thunder.

[*CLOTHO! LACHESIS! COME TO ME, DAMMIT, AND COME NOW!*]

3

He took two or three more steps and stood looking down the hill. The two junior-high-school boys sitting on the swings were looking up at him with identical expressions of startled fear. They were up and gone the moment Ralph's eyes lit on them, running flat-out toward the lights of Witcham Street like a couple of deer, leaving their cigarettes to smolder in the foot-ditches beneath the swings.

[*CLOTHO! LACHESIS!*]

He was burning like an electric arc, and suddenly all the strength ran out of Lois's legs like water. She took one step backward and collapsed onto the park bench. Her head was whirling, her heart full of terror, and below everything was that vast exhaustion. Ralph saw it as a sunken ship; Lois saw it as a pit around which she was forced to walk in a gradually tightening spiral, a pit into which she must eventually fall.

['*CLOTHO! LACHESIS! LAST CHANCE! I MEAN IT!*']

For a moment nothing happened, and then the doors of the Portosans at the foot of the hill opened in perfect unison. Clotho stepped from the one marked MEN, Lachesis from the one marked WOMEN. Their auras, the brilliant green-gold of summer dragonflies, glimmered in the ashy light of day's end. They moved together until their auras overlapped, then walked slowly toward the top of the hill that way, with their white-clad shoulders almost touching. They looked like a pair of frightened children.

Ralph turned to Lois. His aura still blazed and burned.

['*Stay here.*']

['*Yes, Ralph.*']

She let him get partway down the hill, then gathered her courage and called after him.

['*But I'll try to stop Ed if you won't. I mean it.*']

Of course she did, and his heart responded to her bravery . . . but she didn't know what he knew. Hadn't seen what he had seen.

He looked back at her for a moment, then walked down to where the two little bald doctors looked at him with their luminous, frightened eyes.

4

Lachesis, nervously: [*We didn't lie to you — we didn't.*]

Clotho, even more nervously (if that were possible): [*Deepneau is on his way. You have to stop him, Ralph — you have to at least try.*]

The fact is I don't have *to anything, and your faces show*

it, he thought. Then he turned to Lachesis, and was grat-
ified to see the small bald man flinch from his gaze and
drop his dark, pupil-less eyes.

[*'Is that so? When we were on the hospital roof you told
us to stay away from Ed, Mr L. You were very emphatic about
that.'*]

Lachesis shifted uncomfortably and fidgeted with his
hands.

[*I . . . that is to say we . . . we can be wrong. This time
we were.*]

Except Ralph knew that *wrong* wasn't the best word
for what they had been; *self-deceived* would be better. He
wanted to scold them for it – oh, tell the truth, he wanted
to scold them for getting him into this shitting mess in
the first place – and found he couldn't. Because, according
to old Dor, even their self-deception had served the
Purpose; the side-trip to High Ridge had for some reason
not been a side-trip at all. He didn't understand why or
how that was, but he intended to find out, if finding out
was possible.

[*'Let's forget that part of it for the time being, gentlemen,
and talk about why all this is happening. If you want help from
me and Lois, I think you better tell me.'*]

They looked at each other with their big, frightened
eyes, then back at Ralph.

Lachesis: [*Ralph, do you doubt that all those people are
really going to die? Because if you do—*]

[*'No, but I'm tired of having them waved in my face. If
an earthquake that served the Purpose happened to be sched-
uled for this area and the butcher's bill came to ten thousand
instead of just two thousand and change, you'd never even bat*

an eye, would you? So what's so special about this situation? Tell me!']

Clotho: [*Ralph, we don't make the rules any more than you do. We thought you understood that.*]

Ralph sighed.

[*'You're weaseling again, and not wasting anybody's time but your own.'*]

Clotho, uneasily: [*All right, perhaps the picture we gave you wasn't completely clear, but time was short and we were fright-ened. And you must see that, regardless of all else, those people will die if you can't stop Ed Deepneau!*]

[*'Never mind all of them for now; I only want to know about* one *of them — the one who belongs to the Purpose and can't be handed over just because some undesignated* pisher *comes along with a headful of loose screws and a planeful of explosive. Who is it you feel you can't give up to the Random? Who? It's Day, isn't it? Susan Day.'*]

Lachesis: [*No. Susan Day is part of the Random. She is none of our concern, none of our worry.*]

[*'Who, then?'*]

Clotho and Lachesis exchanged another glance. Clotho nodded slightly, and then they both turned back to Ralph. Once again Lachesis flicked the first two fingers of his right hand upward, creating that peacock's fan of light. It wasn't McGovern Ralph saw this time, but a little boy with blond hair cut in bangs across his forehead and a hook-shaped scar across the bridge of his nose. Ralph placed him at once — the kid from the basement of High Ridge, the one with the bruised mother. The one who had called him and Lois angels.

And a little child shall lead them, he thought, utterly

flabbergasted. *Oh my God.* He looked disbelievingly at Clotho and Lachesis.

[*'Am I understanding? All this has been about that one little boy?'*]

He expected more waffling, but the reply from Clotho was simple and direct: [*Yes, Ralph.*]

Lachesis: [*He's at the Civic Center now. His mother, whose life you and Lois also saved this morning, got a call from her babysitter less than an hour ago, saying she'd cut herself badly on a piece of glass and wouldn't be able to take care of the boy tonight after all. By then it was too late to find another sitter, of course, and this woman has been determined for weeks to see Susan Day . . . to shake her hand, even give her a hug, if possible. She idolizes the Day woman.*]

Ralph, who remembered the fading bruises on her face, supposed that was an idolatry he could understand. He understood something else even better: the babysitter's cut hand had been no accident. *Something* was determined to place the little boy with the shaggy blond bangs and the smoke-reddened eyes at the Civic Center, and was willing to move heaven and earth to do it. His mother had taken him not because she was a bad parent, but because she was as subject to human nature as anyone else. She hadn't wanted to miss her one chance at seeing Susan Day, that was all.

No, it's not all, Ralph thought. *She also took him because she thought it would be safe, with Pickering and his Daily Bread crazies all dead. It must have seemed to her that the worst she'd have to protect her son from tonight would be a bunch of sign-waving pro-lifers, that lightning couldn't possibly strike her and her son twice on the same day.*

783

Ralph had been gazing off toward Witcham Street. Now he turned back to Clotho and Lachesis.

['*You're sure he's there? Positive?*']

Clotho: [*Yes. Sitting in the upper north balcony next to his mother with a McDonald's poster to color and some storybooks. Would it surprise you to know that one of the stories is* The 500 Hats of Bartholomew Cubbins?]

Ralph shook his head. At this point, nothing would surprise him.

Lachesis: [*It's the north side of the Civic Center that Deepneau's plane will strike. This little boy will be killed instantly if steps are not taken to prevent it . . . and that can't be allowed to happen. This boy must not die before his scheduled time.*]

5

Lachesis was looking earnestly at Ralph. The fan of blue-green light between his fingers had disappeared.

[*We can't go on talking like this, Ralph – he's already in the air, less than a hundred miles from here. Soon it will be too late to stop him.*]

That made Ralph feel frantic, but he held his place just the same. Frantic, after all, was how they *wanted* him to feel. How they wanted both of them to feel.

['*I'm telling you that none of that matters until I understand what the stakes are. I won't let it matter.*']

Clotho: [*Listen, then. Every now and again a man or woman comes along whose life will affect not just those about him or her, or even all those who live in the Short-Time world, but those on many levels above and below the Short-Time world. These people are the Great Ones, and their lives always serve the Purpose.*]

If they are taken too soon, everything changes. The scales cease to balance. Can you imagine, for instance, how different the world might be today if Hitler had drowned in the bathtub as a child? You may believe the world would be better for that, but I can tell you that the world would not exist at all if it had happened. Suppose Winston Churchill had died of food-poisoning before he ever became Prime Minister? Suppose Augustus Caesar had been born dead, strangled on his own umbilicus? Yet the person we want you to save is of far greater importance than any of these.]

[*'Dammit, Lois and I already saved this kid once! Didn't that close the books, return him to the Purpose?'*]

Lachesis, patiently: [*Yes, but he is not safe from Ed Deepneau, because Deepneau has no designation in either Random or Purpose. Of all the people on earth, only Deepneau can harm him before his time comes. If Deepneau fails, the boy will be safe again – he will pass his time quietly until his moment comes and he steps upon the stage to play his brief but crucially important part.*]

[*'One life means so much, then?'*]

Lachesis: [*Yes. If the child dies, the Tower of all existence will fall, and the consequences of such a fall are beyond your comprehension. And beyond ours, as well.*]

Ralph stared down at his shoes for a moment. His head seemed to weigh a thousand pounds. There was an irony here, one he was able to grasp easily in spite of his weariness. Atropos had apparently set Ed in motion by inflaming some sort of Messiah complex which might have been pre-existing . . . a by-product of his undesignated status, perhaps. What Ed didn't see – and would never believe if told – was that Atropos and his bosses on the upper levels intended to use him not to save the Messiah but to kill him.

He looked up again into the anxious faces of the two little bald doctors.

[*'Okay, I don't know how I'm supposed to stop Ed, but I'll give it a shot.'*]

Clotho and Lachesis looked at each other and smiled identical (and very human) broad smiles of relief. Ralph raised a cautioning finger.

[*'Wait. You haven't heard all of it.'*]

Their smiles faded.

[*'I want something back from you. One life. I'll trade the life of your four-year-old boy for—'*]

6

Lois didn't hear the end of that; his voice dropped below the range of audibility for a moment, but when she saw first Clotho and then Lachesis begin shaking their heads, her heart sank.

Lachesis: [*I understand your distress, and yes, Atropos can certainly do as he threatens. Yet you must surely comprehend that this one life is hardly as important as—*]

Ralph: [*'But I think it is, don't you see? I think it is. What you two guys need to get through your heads is that to me,* both *lives are equally—'*]

She lost him again, but had no problem hearing Clotho; in the depth of his distress he was almost wailing.

[*But this is different! This boy's* life *is different!*]

Now she heard Ralph clearly, speaking (if speech was what it was) with a fearless, relentless logic that made Lois think of her father.

[*'All* lives *are different. All of them matter or none matters.*

That's only my short-sighted, Short-Time view, of course, but I guess you boys are stuck with it, since I'm the one with the hammer. The bottom line is this: I'll trade you, even-up. The life of yours for the life of mine. All you have to do is promise, and the deal's on.']

Lachesis: [*Ralph, please! Please understand that we really must not!*]

There was a long moment of silence. When Ralph spoke, his voice was soft but still audible. It was, however, the last completely audible thing Lois heard in their conversation.

[*'There's a world of difference between* cannot *and* must not, *wouldn't you say?'*]

Clotho said something, but Lois caught only an isolated

[*trade might possibly be*]

phrase. Lachesis shook his head violently. Ralph replied and Lachesis answered by making a grim little scissoring gesture with his fingers.

Surprisingly, Ralph replied to this with a laugh and a nod.

Clotho put a hand on his colleague's arm and spoke to him earnestly before turning back to Ralph.

Lois clenched her hands in her lap, willing them to reach some sort of agreement. *Any* agreement that would keep Ed Deepneau from killing all those people while they just stood here yattering.

Suddenly the side of the hill was illuminated by brilliant white light. At first Lois thought it came down from the sky, but that was only because myth and religion had taught her to believe the sky was the source of all supernatural emanations. In reality, it seemed to come from everywhere – trees, sky, ground, even from herself, streaming out of her aura like ribbons of fog.

There was a voice, then . . . or rather a Voice. It spoke only four words, but they echoed in Lois's head like iron bells.

[*IT MAY BE SO.*]

She saw Clotho, his small face a mask of terror and awe, reach into his back pocket and bring out his scissors. He fumbled and almost dropped them, a nervous blunder that made Lois feel real kinship for him. Then he was holding them up with one handle in each hand and the blades open.

Those four words came again:

[*IT MAY BE SO.*]

This time they were followed by a glare so bright that for a moment Lois believed she must be blinded. She clapped her hands over her eyes but saw – in the last instant when she could see anything – that the light had centered on the scissors Clotho was holding up like a two-pronged lightning-rod.

There was no refuge from that light; it turned her eyelids and upraised, shielding hands to glass. The glare outlined the bones of her fingers like X-ray pencils as it streamed through her flesh. From somewhere far away she heard a woman who sounded suspiciously like Lois Chasse, screaming at the top of her mental voice:

[*'Turn it off! God, please turn it off before it kills me!'*]

And at last, when it seemed to her that she could stand no more, the light did begin to fade. When it was gone – except for a fierce blue afterimage that floated in the new darkness like a pair of phantom scissors — she slowly opened her eyes. For a moment she continued to see nothing but that brilliant blue cross and thought she had indeed been blinded. Then, as dim as a developing photograph at first, the world began to resurface. She saw Ralph, Clotho, and Lachesis lowering their own hands and peering around with the blind bewilderment of a nest of moles turned up by the blade of a harrow.

Lachesis was looking at the scissors in his colleague's hands as if he had never seen them before, and Lois was willing to bet he never *had* seen them as they were now. The blades were still shining, shedding eldritch fairy-glimmers of light in misty droplets.

Lachesis: [*Ralph! That was . . .*]

She lost the rest of it, but his tone was that of a common peasant who answers a knock at the door of his hut and finds that the Pope has stopped by for a spot of prayer and a little confession.

Clotho was still staring at the blades of the scissors. Ralph was also looking, but at last he lifted his gaze to the bald doctors.

Ralph: [*'. . . the hurt?'*]

Lachesis, speaking like a man emerging from a deep dream: [*Yes . . . won't last long, but . . . agony will be intense . . . change your mind, Ralph?*]

Lois was suddenly afraid of those shining scissors. She wanted to cry out to Ralph, tell him to never mind his one, to just give them *their* one, their little boy. She wanted to tell him to do whatever it took to get them to hide those scissors again.

But no words came from either her mouth or her mind.

Ralph: ['. . . *in the least . . . just wanted to know what to expect.*']

Clotho: [. . . *ready? . . . must be . . .*]

Tell them no, Ralph! she thought at him. *Tell them NO!*

Ralph: ['. . . *ready.*']

Lachesis: [*Understand . . . terms he has . . . and the price?*]

Ralph, impatient now: [*'Yes, yes. Can we please just . . .'*]

Clotho, with immense gravity: [*Very well, Ralph. It may be so.*]

Lachesis put an arm around Ralph's shoulders; he and Clotho led him a little further down the hill, to the place where the younger children started their downhill sled-runs in the winter. There was a small flat area there, circular in shape, about the size of a nightclub stage. When they reached it, Lachesis stopped Ralph, then turned him so he and Clotho were facing each other.

Lois suddenly wanted to shut her eyes and found she couldn't. She could only watch and pray that Ralph knew what he was doing.

Clotho murmured to him. Ralph nodded and slipped out of McGovern's sweater. He folded it and laid it neatly on the leaf-strewn grass. When he straightened again, Clotho took his right wrist and held his arm out straight. He then nodded to Lachesis, who unbuttoned the cuff of Ralph's shirt and rolled the sleeve to the elbow in three quick turns. With that done, Clotho rotated Ralph's arm so it was wrist-up. The fine tracery of blue veins just beneath the skin of his forearm was poignantly clear, highlighted in delicate strokes of aura. All of this was horribly familiar to Lois: it was like watching a patient on a TV doctor-show being prepped for an operation.

Except this wasn't TV.

Lachesis leaned forward and spoke again. Although she still couldn't hear the words, Lois knew he was telling Ralph this was his last chance.

Ralph nodded, and although his aura now told her that he was terrified of what was coming, he somehow even managed a smile. When he turned to Clotho and spoke, he did not seem to be seeking reassurance but rather offering a word of comfort. Clotho tried to return Ralph's smile, but without success.

Lachesis wrapped one hand around Ralph's wrist, more to steady the arm (or so it seemed to Lois) than to actually hold it immobile. He reminded her of a nurse attending a patient who must receive a painful injection. Then he looked at his partner with frightened eyes and nodded. Clotho nodded back, took a breath, and then bent over Ralph's upturned forearm with its ghostly tree of blue veins glowing beneath the skin. He paused for a moment, then slowly opened the jaws of the scissors with which he and his old friend traded life for death.

7

Lois staggered to her feet and stood swaying back and forth on legs that felt like lumber. She meant to break the paralysis which had locked her in such a cruel silence, to shout at Ralph and tell him to stop – tell him he didn't know what they meant to *do* to him.

Except he did. It was in the pallor of his face, his

half-closed eyes, his painfully thinned lips. Most of all it was in the blotches of red and black which were flashing across his aura like meteors, and in the aura itself, which had tightened down to a hard blue shell.

Ralph nodded at Clotho, who brought the lower scissorblade down until it was touching Ralph's forearm just below the fold of the elbow. For a moment the skin only dimpled, and then a smooth dark blister of blood formed where the dimple had been. The blade slid into this blister. When Clotho squeezed his fingers, bringing the razor-sharp blades together, the skin on either side of the lengthwise cut snapped back with the suddenness of windowshades. Subcutaneous fat glimmered like melting ice in the fierce blue glow of Ralph's aura. Lachesis tightened his hold on Ralph's wrist, but so far as Lois could tell, Ralph did not make even a first instinctive effort to pull back, only lowered his head and clenched his left fist in the air like a man giving a Black Power salute. She could see the cords in his neck standing out like cables. Not a single sound escaped him.

Now that this terrible business was actually begun, Clotho proceeded with a speed which was both brutal and merciful. He cut rapidly down the middle of Ralph's forearm to his wrist, using the scissors the way a man will to open a parcel which has been heavily taped, guiding the blades with the fingers and bearing down with the thumb. Inside Ralph's arm, tendons gleamed like cuts of flank steak. Blood ran in freshets, and there was a fine scarlet spray each time an artery or a vein was severed. Soon fans of backspatter decorated the white tunics of the two small men, making them look more like little doctors than ever.

When his blades had at last severed the Bracelets of Fortune at Ralph's wrist (the 'operation' took less than three seconds but seemed to last forever to Lois), Clotho removed the dripping scissors and handed them to Lachesis. Ralph's upturned arm had been cut open from elbow to wrist in a dark furrow. Clotho clamped his hands over this furrow at its point of origination and Lois thought: *Now the other one will pick up Ralph's sweater and use it as a tourniquet.* But Lachesis made no move to do that; he merely held the scissors and watched.

For a moment the blood went on flowing between Clotho's grasping fingers, and then it stopped. He slowly drew his hands down Ralph's arm, and the flesh which emerged from his grip was whole and firm, although scarred with a thick white ridge of scar-tissue.

[*Lois . . . Lo-isssss . . .*]

This voice was not coming from inside her head, nor from down the hill; it had come from behind her. A soft voice, almost cajoling. Atropos? No, not at all. She looked down and saw green and somehow sunken light flowing all around her – it rayed through the spaces between her arms and her body, between her legs, even between her fingers. It rippled her shadow ahead of her, scrawny and somehow twisted, like the shadow of a hanged woman. It caressed her with heatless fingers the color of Spanish moss.

[*Turn around, Lo-isss . . .*]

At that moment the last thing on earth Lois Chasse wanted to do was turn around and look at the source of that green light.

[*Turn around, Lo-isss . . . see me, Lo-iss . . . come into the light, Lo-isss . . . come into the light . . . see me and come into the light . . .*]

It was not a voice which could be disobeyed. Lois turned as slowly as a toy ballerina whose cogs have grown rusty, and her eyes seemed to fill up with Saint Elmo's fire.

Lois came into the light.

CHAPTER TWENTY-EIGHT

1

Clotho: [*You have your visible sign, Ralph — are you satisfied?*]

Ralph looked down at his arm. Already the agony, which had swallowed him as the whale had swallowed Jonah, seemed like a dream to him, or a mirage. He supposed it was this same sort of distancing which allowed women to have lots of babies, forgetting the stark physical pain and effort of delivery each time the act was successfully accomplished. The scar looked like a length of ragged white string rippling its way over the bulges of his scant muscles.

[*'Yes. You were brave, and very quick. I thank you for both.'*]

Clotho smiled but said nothing.

Lachesis: [*Ralph, are you ready? Time is now very short.*]

[*'Yes, I'm—'*]

[*'Ralph! Ralph!'*]

It was Lois, standing at the top of the hill and waving to him. For a moment he thought her aura had changed from its usual dove-gray to some other, darker color, and then the idea, undoubtedly caused by shock and weariness, passed. He trudged up the hill to where she stood.

Lois's eyes were distant and dazed, as if she had just heard some amazing, life-changing word.

[*Lois, what is it? What's wrong? Is it my arm? Because if that's it, don't worry. Look! Good as new!*]

He held it out so she could see for herself, but Lois didn't look. She looked at him instead, and he saw the depth of her shock.

[*Ralph, a green man came.*]

A *green* man? He reached out and took her hands, instantly concerned.

[*Green? Are you sure? It wasn't Atropos or—*]

He didn't finish the thought. He didn't have to.

Lois shook her head slowly.

[*It was a green man. If there are sides in this, I don't know which one this . . . this person . . . is on. He felt good, but I could be wrong. I couldn't see him. His aura was too bright. He told me to give these back to you.*]

She held out her hand to him and tipped two small, glittering objects from her palm to his: her earrings. He could see a maroon speck on one, and supposed it was Atropos's blood. He started to close his hand over them, then winced at a tiny prick of pain.

[*You forgot the backs, Lois.*]

She spoke in the slow, unthoughtful tones of a woman in a dream.

[*No, I didn't – I threw them away. The green man said to. Be careful. He felt . . . warm . . . but I don't really know, do I? Mr Chasse always said I was the most gullible woman alive, always willing to believe the best of everybody. Of anybody.*]

She reached out slowly and grasped his wrists, looking earnestly into his face all the while.

'I just don't know.'

Vocalizing the thought seemed to wake her up, and she stood blinking at him. Ralph supposed it was possible – just barely – that she actually *had* been asleep, that she had dreamed this so-called 'green man'. But perhaps it would be wiser to just take the earrings. They might mean nothing, but then again, having Lois's earrings in his pocket couldn't hurt . . . unless he poked himself with them, that was.

Lachesis: [*Ralph, what is it? Is something wrong?*]

He and Clotho had lagged behind, and so had missed Ralph's conversation with Lois. Ralph shook his head, turning his hand to hide the earrings from them. Clotho had picked up McGovern's sweater and brushed away the few bright leaves which had been clinging to it. Now he held it out to Ralph, who unobtrusively slipped Lois's no-back earrings into one of its pockets before putting it on again.

Time to get going, and the line of warmth up the middle of his right arm – along the scar – told him how he was supposed to begin.

['*Lois?*']

['*Yes, dear?*']

['*I need to take from your aura, and I need to take a lot. Do you understand?*']

['*Yes.*']

['*Is it all right?*']

['*Yes, of course.*']

['*Be brave – it won't take long.*']

He put his arms on her shoulders and clasped his hands behind her neck. She copied the gesture, and they slowly leaned together until their foreheads were touching and their lips less than two inches apart. He could smell some perfume still lingering about her — coming perhaps from the dark, sweet hollows behind her ears.

[*'Ready, dear?'*]

He found what came in return both odd and comforting.

[*'Yes, Ralph. See me. Come into the light. Come into the light and take the light.'*]

Ralph pursed his lips and began to inhale. A band of smoky brilliance began to flow from her mouth and nose and into him. His aura began to brighten at once, and it continued to do so until it had become a dazzling, cloudy corona around him. And still he went on inhaling, breathing with something that was beyond breath, feeling the scar on his arm grow hotter and hotter until it was like an electric filament buried in his flesh. He could not have stopped even if he had wanted to . . . and he didn't.

She staggered once. He saw her eyes lose focus and felt her hands loosen for a moment on the back of his neck. Then her eyes, large and bright and full of trust, returned to his, and her grip firmed again. At last, as that titanic intake of breath finally began to crest, Ralph realized her aura had grown so pale he could hardly see it. Her cheeks were milk-white and the gray had come back into her hair, so much that the black was now almost gone. He had to stop it, *had* to, or he was going to kill her.

He managed to pull his left hand free of his right, and that seemed to break some sort of circuit; he was able to step back from her. Lois swayed on her feet and would have fallen, but Clotho and Lachesis, looking quite a bit like Lilliputians from *Gulliver's Travels,* grabbed her arms and lowered her carefully to the bench again.

Ralph dropped to one knee before her. He was frantic with fear and guilt, and at the same time filled with a sense of power so great that he felt as if a single hard jolt might cause him to explode, like a bottle filled with nitroglycerine. He could knock down a building with that karate-chop gesture now – maybe a whole row of them.

Still, he had hurt Lois. Perhaps badly.

[*'Lois! Lois, can you hear me? I'm sorry!'*]

She looked up at him dazedly, a woman who had blasted forward from forty to sixty in a matter of seconds . . . and then right past it and into her seventies, like a rocket overshooting its intended target. She tried a smile that didn't work very well.

[*'Lois, I'm sorry. I didn't know, and once I did, I couldn't stop.'*]

Lachesis: [*If you're to have any chance at all, Ralph, you must go now. He's almost here.*]

Lois was nodding agreement.

[*'Go on, Ralph – I'm just weak, that's all. I'll be fine. I'm just going to sit here until my strength comes back.'*]

Her eyes shifted to the left, and Ralph followed her gaze. He saw the wino they'd frightened away earlier. He had returned to inspect the litter-baskets at the top of the hill for returnable cans and bottles, and although his aura did not look as healthy as that of the fellow they had met out by the old trainyards earlier, Ralph reckoned he would do in a pinch . . . which, for Lois, this definitely was.

Clotho: [*We'll see that he wanders over this way, Ralph*

— we don't have much power over the physical aspects of the Short-Time world, but I think we can manage that much.]

[*'You're sure?'*]

[*Yes.*]

[*'Okay. Good.'*]

Ralph took a quick look at the two little men, noted their anxious, frightened eyes, and nodded. Then he bent and kissed Lois's cool, wrinkled cheek. She gave him the smile of a tired old grandmother.

I did that to her, he thought. *Me.*

Then you better make sure you didn't do it for nothing, Carolyn's voice responded tartly.

Ralph gave the three of them — Clotho and Lachesis were now flanking Lois protectively on the bench — a final glance, and then began to walk down the hill again.

When he reached the toilets, he stood between them for a moment, then leaned his head against the one marked WOMEN. He heard nothing. When he tipped his head against the blue plastic wall of MEN, however, he heard a faint, droning voice raised in song:

> *Who believes that my wildest dreams*
> *And my craziest schemes will come true?*
> *You, baby, nobody but you.*

Christ, he's nuttier than a fruitcake.

This is news, sweetheart?

Ralph supposed it wasn't. He walked around to the door of the Portosan and opened it. Now he could also hear the distant, waspy buzz of an airplane engine, but there was nothing to see that he hadn't seen dozens of times before: the cracked toilet seat resting askew over the hole in the seat, a roll of toilet paper with a strange and somehow ominous *swelled* look, and, to the left, a urinal that looked like a plastic teardrop. The walls were tangles of graffiti. The largest – and most exuberant – had been printed in foot-high red letters above the urinal: TONY BOYNTON HAS GOT THE TIGHTEST LITTLE BUNS IN DERRY! A cloying pine-scented deodorizer overlay the smells of shit, piss, and lingering wino-farts like makeup on the face of a corpse. The voice he was hearing seemed to come from the hole in the center of the Portosan's bench seat, or perhaps it was seeping out of the very walls:

> *From the time I fall asleep*
> *Until the morning comes*
> *I dream about you, baby, nobody but you.*

Where is he? Ralph wondered. *And how the hell do I get to him?*

Ralph felt sudden heat against his hip; it was as if someone had slipped a warm coal into his watchpocket. He began to frown, then remembered what was in there. He reached into the scrap of a pocket with one finger, touched the gold band he had stowed there, and hooked it out. He laid it on his palm over the place where his loveline and lifeline diverged and poked at it gingerly. It had cooled again. Ralph found he wasn't very surprised.

HD – ED 5–8–87.

'One Ring to rule them all, One Ring to bind them,' Ralph murmured, and slipped Ed's wedding band onto the third finger of his own left hand. It was a perfect fit. He pushed it up until it clinked softly against the wedding ring Carolyn had put onto his own finger some forty-five years ago. Then he looked up and saw that the back wall of the Portosan had disappeared.

2

What he saw, framed by the walls which *did* remain, was a just-past-sunset sky and a swatch of Maine countryside fading into a blue-gray twilight haze. He estimated that he was looking out from a height of about ten thousand feet. He could see glimmering lakes and ponds and vast stretches of dark green woodland scrolling down toward the Portosan's bench seat and then disappearing. Far ahead — up toward the roof of the toilet cubicle — Ralph could see a glimmering nest of lights. That was probably Derry, now no more than ten minutes away. In the lower left quadrant of this vision Ralph could see part of an instrument panel. Taped over the altimeter was a small color photograph that stopped his breath. It was Helen, looking impossibly happy and impossibly beautiful. Cradled in her arms was the Exalted & Revered Baby, fast asleep and no more than four months old.

He wants them to be the last thing he sees in this world, Ralph thought. *He's been turned into a monster, but I guess even monsters don't forget how to love.*

Something on the instrument panel began to beep. A hand came into view and flicked a switch. Before it disappeared, Ralph could see the white indentation on the third finger of that hand, faint but still visible, where the wedding ring had rested for at least six years. He saw something else, as well – the aura surrounding the hand was the same as the one which had surrounded the thunderstruck baby in the hospital elevator, a turbulent, rapidly moving membrane that seemed as alien as the atmosphere of a gas giant.

Ralph looked back once and raised his hand. Clotho and Lachesis raised theirs in return. Lois blew him a kiss. Ralph made a catching gesture, then turned and stepped into the Portosan.

3

He hesitated for a moment, wondering what to do about the bench seat, then remembered the oncoming hospital gurney, which should have crushed their skulls but hadn't, and walked toward the back of the cubicle. He clenched his teeth, preparing to bark his shin – what you knew was one thing, what you believed after seventy years of bumping into stuff quite another – and then stepped through the bench seat as if it were made of smoke . . . or as if *he* were.

There was a scary sensation of weightlessness and vertigo, and for a moment he was sure he was going to vomit. This was accompanied by a feeling of *drain,* as if much of the power he had taken in from Lois was now being siphoned off. He supposed it was. This was a form of teleportation, after all, fabulous science fiction stuff, and something like that *had* to use up a lot of energy.

The vertigo passed, but it was replaced by a perception that was even worse – a feeling that he had been split at the neck somehow. He realized he now had a completely unobstructed view of a whole sprawling section of the world.

Jesus Christ, what's happened to me? What's wrong?

His senses reluctantly reported back that there was nothing wrong, exactly, it was just that he had achieved a position which should have been impossible. He was seventy-three inches tall; the cockpit of the plane was sixty inches from floor to ceiling. This meant that any pilot much bigger than Clotho and Lachesis had to slouch his way to his seat. Ralph, however, had entered the plane not only while it was in flight but while he was standing up, and he was *still* standing up, between and slightly behind the two seats in the cockpit. The reason his view was unobstructed was both simple and horrible: his head was sticking out of the top of the plane.

Ralph had a nightmare image of his old dog, Rex, who'd liked to ride with his head out the passenger window and his raggedy ears blowing back in the slipstream. He closed his eyes.

What if I fall? If I can stick my head out through the damned roof, what's to keep me from sliding right down through the floor and falling all the way to the ground? Or maybe through the ground, and then through the very earth itself?

But that wasn't happening, and nothing like it *would* happen, not on this level – all he had to do was remember the effortless way they'd risen through the floors of the hospital and the ease with which they'd stood on the roof. If he kept those things in mind, he would be okay. Ralph tried to center on that idea, and when he felt quite sure he had himself under control, he opened his eyes again.

Sloping out just below him was the plane's windshield. Beyond it was the nose, tipped with a quicksilver blur of propeller. The nestle of lights he had observed from the door of the Portosan was closer now.

Ralph bent his knees, and his head slid smoothly through the ceiling of the cockpit. For a moment he could taste oil in his mouth and the tiny hairs in his nose seemed to bristle as if with an electric shock, and then he was kneeling between the pilot's and co-pilot's seats.

He didn't know what he had expected to feel, seeing Ed again after all this time and under such extravagantly weird circumstances, but the pang of regret — not just pity but regret — which came was a surprise. As on the day in the summer of '92 when Ed had run into the West Side Gardeners truck, he was wearing an old tee shirt instead of an Oxford or Arrow with buttons up the front and a fruit-loop on the back. He had lost a lot of weight — Ralph thought perhaps as much as forty pounds — and it had had an extraordinary effect, making him look not emaciated but somehow heroic, in a gothic/romantic way; Ralph was forcefully reminded of Carolyn's favorite poem, 'The Highwayman', by Alfred Noyes. Ed's skin was as pale as paper, his green eyes both dark and light (*like emeralds in moonlight,* Ralph thought) behind the small round John Lennon spectacles, his lips so red they looked as if they had been rouged. He had tied the white silk scarf with its red Japanese characters around his forehead so that the fringed ends trailed down his back. Within the thunder-bolt swirls of his aura, Ed's intelligent, mobile face was filled with terrible regret and fierce determination. He was beautiful — beautiful — and Ralph felt a sense of *déjà vu* twist through him. Now he knew what he had glimpsed on the day he'd stepped between Ed and the man from West Side

Gardeners; he was seeing it again. Looking at Ed, lost inside a typhoon aura from which no balloon-string floated, was like looking at a priceless Ming vase which had been thrown against a wall and shattered.

At least he can't see me, not on this level. At least, I don't think he can.

As if in response to this thought, Ed turned and glanced directly at Ralph. His eyes were wide and full of mad caution; the corners of his finely molded mouth quivered and gleamed with buds of saliva. Ralph recoiled, momentarily positive that he *was* being seen, but Ed didn't react to Ralph's sudden backward movement. He threw a suspicious glance into the empty four-seat passenger cabin behind him instead, as if he had heard the stealthy movements of a stowaway. At the same time he reached past Ralph and put his right hand on a cardboard carton which had been seatbelted into the co-pilot's chair. The hand caressed the box briefly, then went to his forehead and made some tiny adjustment to the scarf serving him as a headband. That done, he resumed singing . . . only this time it was a different song, one that sent a tremor zigzagging up Ralph's back:

> *One pill makes you bigger,*
> *One pill makes you small,*
> *And the ones that Mother gives you*
> *Don't do anything at all . . .*

Right, Ralph thought. *Go ask Alice, when she's ten feet tall.*

His heart was trip-hammering in his chest − having Ed suddenly turn around like that had scared him in a way even finding himself riding along at ten thousand feet with his head sticking out of the top of the plane hadn't been able to do. Ed didn't see him, Ralph was almost positive of that, but whoever had said that the senses of lunatics were more acute than those of the sane must have known what he was talking about, because Ed sure had an idea that *something* had changed.

The radio squawked, making both men jump. 'This is for the Cherokee over South Haven. You are on the edge of Derry airspace at an altitude which requires a filed flight-plan. Repeat, *you are about to enter controlled airspace over a municipal area.* Get your hot-dogging butt up to sixteen thousand feet, Cherokee, and come to one seventy, that's one-seven-oh. While you're doing it, please identify yourself and state—'

Ed closed his hand into a fist and began to hammer the radio with it. Glass flew; soon blood also began to fly. It spattered the instrument panel, the picture of Helen and Natalie, and Ed's clean gray tee-shirt. He went on hammering until the voice on the radio first began to fade into a rising roar of static and then quit altogether.

'Good,' he said in the low, sighing voice of a man who talks to himself a lot. '*Lots* better. I hate all those questions. They just—'

He caught sight of his bloody hand and broke off. He held it up, looked at it more closely, and then rolled it into a fist again. A large sliver of glass was sticking out of his pinky just below the third knuckle. Ed pulled it free with his teeth, spat it casually aside, then did something which chilled Ralph's heart: drew the side of his bloody fist first down his left cheek and then his right, leaving a pair of red marks. He reached into the elasticized pocket built into the wall on his left, pulled out a hand-mirror, and used it to check his makeshift warpaint. What he saw seemed to please him, because he smiled and nodded before returning the mirror to the pocket.

'Just remember what the dormouse said,' Ed advised himself in his low, sighing voice, and then pushed in on the control wheel. The Cherokee's nose dropped and the altimeter slowly began to unwind. Ralph could see Derry straight ahead now. The city looked like a handful of opals scattered across dark blue velvet.

There was a hole in the side of the carton in the co-pilot's seat. Two wires came out of it. They led into the back of a doorbell taped to the arm of Ed's seat. Ralph supposed that as soon as he had a visual on the Civic Center and actually began his kamikaze run, Ed would settle one finger on the raised white button in the middle of the plastic rectangle. And just before the plane hit, he would push it. Ding-dong, Avon calling.

Break those wires, Ralph! Break them!

An excellent idea with only one drawback: he couldn't break so much as a strand of cobweb while he was on this level. That meant dropping back down to Short-Time country, and he was preparing to do just that when a soft, familiar voice on his right spoke his name.

[*Ralph.*]

To his *right*? That was impossible. There was *nothing* on his right but the co-pilot's seat, the side of the aircraft, and leagues of twilit New England air.

The scar along his arm had begun to tingle like a filament in an electric heater.

[*Ralph!*]

Don't look. Don't pay any attention at all. Ignore it.

But he couldn't. Some great, bricklike force had come to bear on him, and his head began to turn. He fought it, aware that the airplane's angle of descent was growing steeper, but it did no good.

[*Ralph, look at me — don't be afraid.*]

He made one last effort to disobey the voice and was unable. His head went on turning, and Ralph suddenly found himself looking at his mother, who had died of lung cancer twenty-five years ago.

4

Bertha Roberts sat in her bentwood rocker about five feet beyond where the sidewall of the Cherokee's cockpit had been, knitting and rocking back and forth on thin air a mile or more above the ground. The slippers Ralph had given her for her fiftieth birthday — lined with real mink, they had been, how goofy — were on her feet. A pink shawl was thrown around her shoulders. An old political button — WIN WITH WILLKIE! it said — held the shawl closed.

That's right, Ralph thought. *She wore them as jewelry — it was her little affectation. I'd forgotten that.*

The only thing that struck a wrong note (other than that she was dead and currently rocking at six thousand feet) was the bright red piece of afghan in her lap. Ralph had never seen his mother knit, wasn't even sure she knew how, but she was knitting furiously just the same. The needles gleamed and winked as they shuttled through the stitches.

['Mother? Mom? Is it really you?']

The needles paused as she looked up from the crimson blanket in her lap. Yes, it was his mother – the version Ralph remembered from his teens, anyway. Narrow face, high scholar's brow, brown eyes, and a bun of salt-and-pepper hair rolled tightly at the nape of the neck. It was her small mouth, which looked mean and ungenerous . . . until it smiled, that was.

[Why, Ralph Roberts! I'm surprised that you even have to ask!]

That's not really an answer, though, is it? Ralph thought. He opened his mouth to say so and then decided it might be wiser – for the time being, at least – to keep quiet. A milky shape was now swimming in the air to her right. When Ralph looked at it, it darkened and solidified into the cherry-stained magazine stand he had made her in woodshop during his sophomore year at Derry High. It was filled with *Reader's Digests* and *Life* magazines. And now the ground far below her began to disappear into a pattern of brown and dark-red squares that spread out from the rocker in a widening ring, like a pond-ripple. Ralph recognized it at once – the kitchen linoleum of the house on Richmond Street in Mary Mead, the one where he'd grown up. At first he could see the ground through it, geometries of farmland and, not far ahead, the Kenduskeag flowing through Derry, and then it solidified. A ghostly shape like a big milkweed puff became his mom's old Angora cat, Futzy, curled up on the windowsill and looking out at the gulls circling above the old dump in the Barrens. Futzy had died around the time Dean Martin and Jerry Lewis had stopped making movies together.

[*That old man was right, boy. You've no business messing into Long-Time affairs. Pay attention to your mother and stay out of what doesn't concern you. Mind me, now.*]

Pay attention to your mother . . . mind me, now. Those words had pretty well summed up Bertha Roberts's views on the art and science of child-rearing, hadn't they? Whether it was an order to wait an hour after eating before taking a swim or to make sure that old thief Butch Bowers didn't put a lot of rotten potatoes at the bottom of the peck basket she'd sent you to fetch, the prologue (*Pay attention to your mother*) and the epilogue (*Mind me, now*) were always the same. And if you *failed* to pay attention, if you *failed* to mind her, you had to face the Wrath of Mother, and God help you then.

She picked up the needles and began to knit again, running off scarlet stitches with fingers that looked faintly red themselves. Ralph supposed that was just an illusion. Or maybe the dye wasn't completely colorfast, and some of it was coming off on his fingers.

His fingers? What a silly mistake *that* was. Her fingers. Except . . .

Well, there were little bunches of whiskers at the corners of her mouth. *Long* ones. Nasty, somehow. And unfamiliar. Ralph could remember a fine down on her upper lip, but *whiskers*? No way. Those were new.

New? New? What are you thinking about? She died two days after Robert Kennedy was assassinated in Los Angeles, so what in the name of God can be new about her?

Two converging walls had bloomed on either side of Bertha Roberts, creating the kitchen corner where she had spent so much time. On one of them was a painting Ralph remembered well. It showed a family at supper — Dad, Mom, two kids. They were passing the potatoes and the corn, and looked like they were discussing their respective days. None of them noticed that there was a fifth person in the room — a white-robed man with a sandy beard and long hair. He was standing in the corner and watching them. CHRIST, THE UNSEEN VISITOR, the plaque beneath this painting read. Except the Christ Ralph remembered had looked both kind and a little embarrassed to be eavesdropping. This version, however, looked coldly thoughtful . . . evaluative . . . judgemental, perhaps. And his color was very high, almost choleric, as if he had heard something which had made him furious.

[*'Mom? Are you—'*]

She put the needles down again on the red blanket — that oddly *shiny* red blanket — and raised a hand to stop him.

[*Mom me no Moms, Ralph — just pay attention and mind. Stay out of this! It's too late for your muddling and meddling. You can only make things worse.*]

The voice was right, but the face was wrong and becoming wronger. Mostly it was her skin. Smooth and unlined, her skin had been Bertha Roberts's only vanity. The skin of the creature in the rocker was rough . . . more than rough, in fact. It was *scaly*. And there were two growths (or perhaps they were sores?) on the sides of her neck. At the sight of them, some terrible memory

(*get it off me Johnny oh please* GET IT OFF)

stirred far down in his mind. And—

Well, her aura. Where was her aura?

[*Never mind my aura and never mind about that fat old*

whore you've been running around with . . . although I'll bet Carolyn is just rolling in her grave.]

The mouth of the woman

(*not a woman that thing is not a woman*)

in the rocker was no longer small. The lower lip had spread, puffed outward and downward. The mouth itself had developed a drooping sneer. A strangely *familiar* drooping sneer.

(*Johnny it's biting me it's* BITING ME!)

Something horridly familiar about the bunches of whiskers bristling at the corners of the mouth, too.

(*Johnny please its eyes its black eyes*)

[*Johnny can't help you, boy. He didn't help you then and he can't help you now.*]

Of course he couldn't. His older brother Johnny had died six years ago. Ralph had been a pallbearer at his funeral. Johnny had died of a heart attack, possibly as Random as the one which had felled Bill McGovern, and—

Ralph looked to the left, but the pilot's side of the cockpit had also disappeared, and Ed Deepneau with it. Ralph saw the old combination gas and woodstove on which his mother had cooked in the house on Richmond Street (a job she had resented bitterly and done badly all her life) and the arch leading into the dining room. He saw their maple dining table. A glass pitcher stood in the center of it. The pitcher had been filled with a choke of lurid red roses. Each seemed to have a face . . . a blood-red, gasping face . . .

But that's wrong, he thought. *All wrong. She never had roses in the house — she was allergic to most blooms, and roses were the worst. She used to sneeze like crazy when she was*

813

around them. The only thing I ever saw her put on the dining room table was Indian Bouquet, and that wasn't anything but autumn grasses. I see roses because—

He looked back at the creature in the rocking chair, at red fingers which had now melted together into appendages that looked almost like fins. He regarded the scarlet mass which lay in the creature's lap, and the scar along his arm began to tingle again.

What in God's name is going on here?

But he knew, of course; he only had to look from the red thing in the rocking chair to the picture hanging on the wall, the picture of the scarlet-faced, malevolent Jesus watching the family eat their supper, to confirm it. He was not in his old house in Mary Mead, and he was not precisely in an aircraft over Derry, either.

He was in the Court of the Crimson King.

CHAPTER TWENTY-NINE

1

Without thinking about why he was doing it, Ralph slipped a hand into his sweater pocket and loosely cupped one of Lois's earrings. His hand felt far away, something which belonged to someone else. He was realizing an interesting thing: he had never been frightened in his life until now. Not once. He had *thought* he'd been frightened, of course, but it had been an illusion – the only time he'd even come close had been in the Derry Public Library, when Charlie Pickering stuck a knife into his armpit and said he was going to let Ralph's guts out all over the floor. That, however, was nothing but a mild moment of discomfort next to what he was feeling now.

A green man came . . . he felt good, but I could be wrong.

He hoped she wasn't; he most sincerely hoped she wasn't. Because the green man was about all he had left now.

The green man, and Lois's earrings.

[*Ralph! Stop woolgathering! Look at your mother when she's talking to you! Seventy years old and you still act like you were sixteen, with a bad case of pecker-rash!*]

815

He turned back to the red-finned thing slumped in the rocker. It now bore only a passing resemblance to his late mother.

['You're not my mother, and I'm still in the airplane.']

[You're not, boy. Don't make the mistake of thinking you are. Take one step out of my kitchen and you're in for a very long fall.]

['You might as well stop now. I can see what you are.']

The thing spoke in a bubbly, choked voice that turned Ralph's spine to a narrow line of ice.

[You don't. You may think you do, but you don't. And you don't want to. You don't ever want to see me with my disguises laid aside. Believe me, Ralph, you don't.]

He realized with mounting horror that the mother-thing had turned into an enormous female catfish, a hungry bottom-feeder with stubby teeth gleaming between its pendulous lips and whiskers which dangled almost to the collar of the dress it still wore. The gills in its neck opened and closed like razor-cuts, revealing troubled red inner flesh. Its eyes had grown round and purplish, and as Ralph watched, the sockets began to slide away from each other. This continued until the eyes bulged from the sides rather than the front of the creature's scaly face.

[Don't move so much as a single muscle, Ralph. You'll probably die in the explosion no matter what level you're on – the shockwaves travel here just as they do in any building – but that death will still be a great deal better than my death.]

The catfish opened its mouth. Its teeth ringed a blood-colored maw which looked full of strange guts and tumors. It seemed to be laughing at him.

['Who are you? Are you the Crimson King?']

[*That's Ed's name for me — we ought to have our own, don't you think? Let's see. If you don't want me to be Mom Roberts, why not call me the Kingfish? You remember the Kingfish from the radio, don't you?*]

Yes, of course he did . . . but the *real* Kingfish had never been on *Amos and Andy,* and it hadn't really been a kingfish at all. The real Kingfish had been a queenfish, and it had lived in the Barrens.

2

On a summer's day during the year when Ralph Roberts was seven he had hooked an enormous catfish out of the Kenduskeag while fishing with his brother John — this had been when it was still possible to eat what you caught down in the Barrens. Ralph had asked his older brother to take the convulsively flopping thing off his hook for him and put it in the bucket of fresh water they kept on the bank beside them. Johnny had refused, loftily citing what he called the Fisherman's Creed: good fishermen tie their own flies, dig their own worms, and unhook their own catches. It was only later that Ralph realized Johnny might have been trying to hide his own fear of the huge and somehow alien creature his kid brother had reeled out of the Kenduskeag's muddy, piss-warm water that day.

Ralph had at last brought himself to grasp the catfish's pulsing body, which was at the same time slick, scaly, and prickly. As he did, Johnny had added to his terror by telling him, in a low and ominous voice, to look out for the whiskers. *They're poison. Bobby Therriault told me if one of em sticks inya, you could get paralyzed. Spend the rest of your life in a wheelchair. So be careful, Ralphie.*

Ralph had twisted the creature this way and that, trying to free the hook from its dark, wet innards without getting his hand too near its whiskers (not believing Johnny about the poison and at the same time believing him completely), exquisitely aware of the gills, the eyes, the fishy smell that seemed to shimmer its way more deeply into his lungs each time he inhaled.

At last he'd heard a gristly ripping from deep within the catfish and felt the hook start to slide free. Fresh streamlets of blood trickled from the corners of its flexing, dying mouth. Ralph gave a little sigh of relief – prematurely, as it turned out. The catfish gave a tremendous flap of its tail as the hook came out. The hand Ralph had been using to free it slipped, and all at once the catfish's bleeding mouth clamped shut on his first two fingers. How much pain had there been? A lot? Some? Maybe none at all? Ralph couldn't remember. What he *did* remember was Johnny's completely unfeigned shriek of horror and his own surety that the catfish was going to make him pay for taking its life by eating two fingers off his right hand.

He remembered screaming himself, and shaking his hand, and begging Johnny to help him, but Johnny had been backing away, his face pale, his mouth a knotted line of revulsion. Ralph shook his hand in big, swooping arcs, but the catfish hung on like death, whiskers

(*poison whiskers put me in a wheelchair for the rest of my life*)

818

snapping and flapping against Ralph's wrist, black eyes staring.

At last he'd struck it against a nearby tree, breaking its back. It had dropped to the grass, still flopping, and Ralph had stamped on it with one foot, provoking the final horror. A spew of guts vomited from its mouth, and from the place where Ralph's heel had smashed it open had come a gluey torrent of bloody eggs. That was when he had realized that the Kingfish had really been the Queenfish, and only a day or two from roeing.

Ralph had stared from this freakish mess to his own bloody, scale-encrusted hand, and then howled like a banshee. When Johnny touched his arm in an effort to calm him, Ralph had bolted. He hadn't stopped running until he got home, and he'd refused to come out of his room for the rest of the day. It had been almost a year before he'd eaten another piece of fish, and he'd never had anything to do with catfish again.

Until now, that was.

3

[*'Ralph!'*]

That was Lois's voice . . . but distant! So distant!

[*'You have to do something* right away! *Don't let it stop you!'*]

Ralph now realized that what he'd taken for an afghan in his mother's lap was actually a mat of bloody eggs in the lap of the Crimson King. It was leaning toward him over this throbbing blanket, its thick lips quivering in a parody of concern.

[*Something wrong, Ralphie? Where does it hurt? Tell Mother.*]

[*'You're not my mother.'*]

[*No – I be the Queenfish! I be loud and I be proud! I got the walk and I got the talk! Actually, I can be whatever I want. You may not know it, but shape-changing is a time-honored custom in Derry.*]

[*'Do you know the green man Lois saw?'*]

[*Of course! I know all the neighborhood folks!*]

But Ralph sensed momentary puzzlement on that scaly face.

The heat along his forearm cranked up another notch, and Ralph had a sudden realization: if Lois were here now, she would hardly be able to see him. The Queenfish was putting out a pulsing, ever-brightening glow, and it was gradually surrounding him. The glow was red instead of black, but it was still a deathbag, and now he knew what it was like to be on the inside, caught in a web woven from your sickest fears and most traumatic experiences. There was no way to retreat from it, and no way to cut through it, as he had cut through the deathbag which had surrounded Ed's wedding ring.

If I'm going to escape, Ralph thought, *I'm going to have to do it by running forward so hard and fast I rip right out the other side.*

The earring was still in his hand. Now he shifted it so that the naked prong at the back was sticking out between the two fingers a catfish had tried to swallow sixty-three years ago. Then he said a brief prayer, not to God but to Lois's green man.

4

The catfish leaned further forward, a cartoon leer spreading across its noseless face. The teeth inside that flabby grin looked longer and sharper now. Ralph saw drops of colorless fluid beading the ends of the whiskers and thought, *Poison. Spend the rest of your life in a wheelchair. Man, I'm so scared. Scared to fucking death.*

Lois, screaming far away: [*'Hurry, Ralph! YOU HAVE TO HURRY!'*]

A little boy was screaming from somewhere a lot closer; screaming and waving his right hand, waving the fish clinging to the fingers buried inside the gullet of a pregnant monster that would not let go.

The catfish leaned closer yet. The dress it wore rustled. Ralph could smell his mother's perfume, Saint Elena, mixing obscenely with the fishy, garbagey aroma of bottom-feeder.

[*I intend Ed Deepneau's errand to end in success, Ralph; I intend that the boy your friends told you about should die in his mother's arms, and I want to see it happen. I've worked very hard here in Derry, and I don't feel that's too much to ask, but it means I have to finish with you right now. I—*]

Ralph took a step deeper into the thing's garbagey stink. And now he began to see a shape behind the shape of Mother, behind the shape of the Queenfish. He began to see a bright man, a *red* man with cold eyes and a merciless mouth. This man resembled the Christ he had seen only moments ago . . . but not the one which had really hung in his mother's kitchen corner.

An expression of surprise came into the lidless black

eyes of the Queenfish . . . and into the cold eyes of the red man beneath.

[*What do you think you're doing? Get away from me! Do you want to spend the rest of your life in a wheelchair?*]

[*'I can think of worse things, pal – my days of playing first base are pretty definitely over.'*]

The voice rose, becoming the voice of his mother when she was angry.

[*Pay attention to me, boy! Pay attention and mind me!*]

For a moment the old commands, given in a voice so eerily like his mother's, made him hesitate. Then he came on again. The Queenfish shrank back in the rocker, its tail flipping up and down below the hem of the old housedress.

[*JUST WHAT DO YOU THINK YOU'RE DOING?*]

[*'I don't know; maybe I just want to give your whiskers a tug. See for myself if they're real.'*]

And, exerting all of his willpower to keep from shrieking and fleeing, he reached out with his right hand. Lois's earring felt like a small, warm pebble closed within his fist. Lois herself seemed very close, and Ralph decided that wasn't surprising, considering how much of her aura he'd taken on. Perhaps she was even a part of him now. The feeling of her presence was deeply comforting.

[*No, you don't dare! You'll be paralyzed!*]

[*'Catfish aren't poisonous – that was the story of a ten-year-old boy who might have been even more scared than I was.'*]

Ralph reached for the whiskers with the hand concealing the metal thorn, and the massive, scaly head flinched away, as some part of him had known it would. It began to ripple and change, and its fearful red aura began to seep through. *If sickness and pain had a color,* Ralph thought, *that would be it.* And before the change could go any further, before that man he could now see – tall and coldly handsome with his blond hair and glaring red eyes – could step through the shimmer of the illusion it had cast, Ralph drove the sharp point of the earring into one black and bulging fisheye.

5

It made a terrible buzzing sound – like a cicada, Ralph thought – and tried to draw back. Its rapidly flipping tail produced a sound like a fan with a piece of paper caught in the blades. It slid down in the rocker, which was now changing into something that looked like a throne carved from dull orange rock. And then the tail was gone, the Queenfish was gone, and it was the Crimson King sitting there, his handsome face twisted into a snarl of pain and amazement. One of his eyes glared as red as the eye of a lynx in firelight; the other was filled with the fierce, splintered glow of diamonds.

Ralph reached into the blanket of eggs with his left hand, ripped it away, and saw nothing but blackness on the other side of the abortion. The other side of the deathbag. The way out.

[*You were warned, you Short-Time son of a bitch! You think you can pull my whiskers? Well, let's see, shall we? Let's just see!*]

The Crimson King leaned forward again on its throne, its mouth yawning, its remaining eye blazing with red light. Ralph fought the urge to yank his now-empty right hand away. Instead he pistoned it forward toward the mouth of the Crimson King, which yawned wide to engulf it, as that long-ago catfish had done that day in the Barrens.

Things – not flesh – first squirmed and jostled against his hand, then began to bite like horseflies. At the same time Ralph felt real teeth – no, *fangs* – sink into his arm. In a moment, two at the most, the Crimson King would bite through his wrist and swallow his hand whole.

Ralph closed his eyes and was at once able to find that pattern of thought and concentration which allowed movement between the levels – his pain and his fear were no bar to that. Only this time his purpose was not to *move* but to *trigger*. Clotho and Lachesis had planted a booby-trap inside his arm, and the time had come to set it off.

Ralph felt that sensation of *blink* inside his head. The scar on his arm immediately went white-hot and critical. That heat didn't burn Ralph but flew out from him in an expanding ripple of energy. He was aware of a titanic green flash, so bright that for one moment it was as if the Emerald City of Oz had exploded all around him. Something or someone was screaming. That high, jagged sound would have driven him mad if it had gone on for long, but it didn't. It was followed by a vast, hollow bang that made Ralph think of the time he had lit an M-80 firecracker and tossed it into a steel culvert.

A sudden rush of force blew past him in a fan of wind and fading green light. He caught a strange, skewed glimpse of the Crimson King, no longer handsome and no longer young but ancient and twisted and less human than the strangest creature to ever flop or hop its way along the Short-Time level of existence. Then something above them opened, revealing darkness shot through with conflicting swirls and rays of color. The wind seemed to blow the Crimson King up toward it, like a leaf in a chimney-flue. The colors began to brighten, and Ralph turned his face away, raising one hand to shield his eyes. He understood that a conduit had opened between the level where he was and the unimaginable levels stacked above it; he also understood that if he looked for long into that brightening glow, those

(*deadlights*)

swirling colors, then death would be not the worst thing that could happen to him but the best. He did not just squeeze his eyes shut; he squeezed his *mind* shut.

A moment later everything was gone – the creature which had identified itself to Ed as the Crimson King, the kitchen in the old house on Richmond Street, his mother's rocking chair. Ralph was kneeling on thin air about six feet to the right of the Cherokee's nose, his hands upraised as an oft-beaten child might raise his hands before the approach of a cruel parent, and when he looked between his knees, he saw the Civic Center and the adjacent parking lot directly below him. At first he thought his eyes were being fooled by an optical illusion, because the arc-sodiums in the parking lot seemed to be spreading apart. They almost looked like a crowd of very tall, very skinny people which is starting to break up because the excitement, whatever it was, is over. And the lot itself seemed to be . . . well . . . *expanding*.

Not expanding but getting closer, Ralph thought coldly. *He's going down. He's started his kamikaze run.*

6

For a moment Ralph was frozen in place, enchanted by the simple wonder of his position. He had become a mythical in-between creature, clearly no god (no god could be as tired and terrified as he was right now) but clearly no such earthbound creature as a man, either. This was what it was really like to fly; to see the earth from above, with no border around it. This—

[*'RALPH!'*]

Her scream was like a shotgun fired beside his ear. Ralph flinched from it, and the moment his gaze left the hypnotic sight of the ground swelling up toward him, he was able to move. He rose to his feet and walked back to the plane. He did this as easily and normally as a man walking down a hallway in his own home. No wind buffeted his face or blew his hair back from his brow, and when his left shoulder passed through the Cherokee's propeller, the whirling blade harmed him no more than it would have harmed smoke.

For a moment he saw Ed's pallid, handsome face – the face of the highwayman who'd come riding up to the old inn door in the poem which had always made Carolyn cry – and his previous feeling of mingled pity and regret was replaced by anger. It was difficult to become *really* infuriated with Ed – he was, after all, just another chess-piece being moved across the board – and yet the building he had aimed his airplane at was full of real people. *Innocent* people. Ralph saw something balky, childish, and willful about the dopey expression of disassociation on Ed's face, and as he passed through the thin skin of the cockpit wall,

Ralph thought, *I think that on some level, Ed, you knew the devil had come in. I think you might even have been able to put him out again . . . didn't Mr C and Mr L say there's always a choice? If there is, you have to own a piece of this, goddam you.*

For a moment Ralph's head poked through the ceiling as it had done before, and he knelt again. Now the Civic Center filled the entire windshield of the plane and he understood that it was too late to stop Ed from doing *something*.

He had pulled the doorbell free of the tape. He was holding it in his hand.

Ralph reached into his pocket and gripped the remaining earring, once again holding it between his fingers with the prong sticking out. He curled his other hand into a tube around the wires running between the cardboard carton and the doorbell. Then he closed his eyes and concentrated, creating that flexing sensation in the middle of his head again. There was a sudden hollow, fluttery sensation in his stomach, and he had time to think *Whoa! This is the express elevator!*

Then he was down on the Short-Time level where there were no gods or devils, no bald doctors with magic scissors and scalpels, no auras. Down where passing through walls and walking away from plane-crashes was an impossibility. Down on the Short-Time level where he could be seen . . . and Ed, Ralph realized, was doing just that.

'Ralph?' It was the drugged voice of a man just waking from his life's soundest sleep. 'Ralph Roberts? What are *you* doing here?'

'Oh, I was in the neighborhood and I thought I'd

drop in,' Ralph said. 'Drag up a rock, so to speak.' And with that, he closed his curled hand into a fist and tore the wires out of the box.

7

'*No!*' Ed shrieked. '*Oh no, don't, you'll spoil everything!*'

Yes indeed, Ralph thought, then reached over Ed's lap to grab the Cherokee's control-wheel. The Civic Center was now no more than twelve hundred feet below them, perhaps less. Ralph still didn't know for sure what was in the box strapped to the co-pilot's chair, but he had an idea it was probably the *plastique* stuff the terrorists always used in the martial arts movies starring Chuck Norris and Steven Seagal. It was supposed to be fairly stable – not like the nitro in Clouzot's *Wages of Fear,* certainly – but this was hardly the time to put his trust in the Gospel of Movieland. And even a stable explosive might go off without a deto- nator when dropped from a height of almost two miles.

He jammed the control-wheel as far over to the left as he could. Below them, the Civic Center began to wheel sickeningly around, as if it had been mounted on the spindle of a gigantic top.

'*No, you bastard!*' Ed yelled, and something that felt like the head of a small hammer struck Ralph in the side, almost paralyzing him with pain and making it all but impossible to breathe. His hand slid off the control-wheel as Ed hammered him again, this time in the armpit. Ed seized the wheel and yanked it savagely back over. The Civic Center, which had begun to slip toward the side of the windshield, began to rotate back toward dead center.

Ralph clawed at the wheel. Ed placed the heel of his hand on Ralph's forehead and shoved him backward. 'Why couldn't you stay out of it?' he snarled. 'Why'd you have to *meddle?*' His teeth were bared, his lips pulled back in a jealous snarl. Ralph's appearance in the cockpit should have incapacitated him with shock but hadn't.

Of course not, he's nuts, Ralph thought, and suddenly raised his interior voice in a panicked yell:

[*'Clotho! Lachesis! For Christ's sake, help me!'*]

Nothing. It didn't feel as if his shout were going *anywhere.* And why would it? He was back down on the Short-Time level, and that meant he was on his own.

The Civic Center was only eight or nine hundred feet below them now. Ralph could see every brick, every window, every person standing outside – he could almost even tell which ones were carrying signs. They were looking up, trying to figure out what this crazy plane was doing. Ralph couldn't see the fear on their faces, not yet, but in another three or four seconds—

He launched himself at Ed again, ignoring the throb in his left side and driving his right fist forward, using his thumb to ride the prong of the earring out beyond his fingers as far as possible.

The old Earring Gag had worked on the Crimson King, but Ralph had been higher then, and he'd had the element of surprise more firmly in hand. He went for the eye this time, too, but Ed snapped his head away at the last moment. The prong drove into the side of his face just above the cheekbone. Ed swatted at it as if it were a gnat, holding on tightly to the control-wheel with his left hand as he did it.

Ralph went for the wheel again. Ed lashed out at him. His fist connected above Ralph's left eye, driving him backward. A single loud tone, pure and silvery, filled Ralph's ears. It was as if there were a large tuning fork somewhere in between them, and someone had struck it. The world went as gray and grainy as a newsprint photograph.

[*'RALPH! HURRY!'*]

It was Lois, and now she was in terror. He knew why; time had all but run out. He had maybe ten seconds, twenty at most. He lunged forward again, this time not at Ed but at the picture of Helen and Nat that was taped above the altimeter. He snatched it, held it up . . . and then crumpled it between his fingers. He didn't know exactly what reaction he'd hoped for, but the one he got exceeded his wildest hopes.

'*GIVE THEM BACK!*' Ed screamed. He forgot about the control wheel and groped for the picture instead. As he did, Ralph again saw the man he had glimpsed on the day Ed had beaten Helen – a man who was desperately unhappy and afraid of the forces which had been set loose within him. There were tears not just in his eyes but running down his cheeks, and Ralph thought confusedly: *Has he been crying all along?*

'*GIVE THEM BACK!*' he bawled again, but Ralph was no longer sure he was the subject of that cry; he thought his former neighbor might be addressing the being which had stepped into his life, looked around itself to make sure it would do, and then simply taken it over. Lois's earring glittered in Ed's cheek like a barbaric funerary ornament. '*GIVE THEM BACK, THEY'RE MINE!*'

Ralph held the crumpled photograph just beyond the

reach of Ed's waving hands. Ed lunged, the seatbelt bit into his gut, and Ralph punched him in the throat as hard as he could, feeling an indescribable mixture of satisfaction and revulsion as the blow landed on the hard, gristly protuberance of Ed's Adam's apple. Ed fell back against the cockpit wall, eyes bulging with pain and dismay and bewilderment, hands going to his throat. A thick gagging noise came from somewhere deep inside him. It sounded like some heavy piece of machinery in the process of stripping its gears.

Ralph shoved himself forward over Ed's lap and saw the Civic Center now *leaping* up toward the airplane. He turned the wheel all the way to the left again and below him – *directly* below him – the Civic Center again began to rotate toward the side of the Cherokee's soon-to-be-defunct windshield . . . but it moved with agonizing slowness.

Ralph realized he could smell something in the cockpit – some faint aroma both sweet and familiar. Before he could think what it might be, he saw something that distracted him completely. It was the Hoodsie Ice Cream wagon that sometimes cruised along Harris Avenue, tinkling its cheery little bell.

My God, Ralph thought, more in awe than in fear. *I think I'm going to wind up in the deep freeze, along with the Creamsicles and Hoodsie Rockets.*

That sweet smell was stronger, and as hands suddenly seized his shoulders, Ralph realized it was Lois Chasse's perfume.

'*Come up!*' she screamed. '*Ralph, you dummy, you have to—*'

He didn't think about it; he just did it. The thing in

his mind clenched, the blink happened, and he heard the rest of what she had to say in that eerie, penetrating way that was more thought than speech.

[*– come up! Push with your feet!*]

Too late, he thought, but he did as she said nevertheless, planting his feet against the base of the radically canted instrument panel and shoving as hard as he could. He felt Lois rising up through the column of existence with him as the Cherokee shot through the last hundred feet between it and the ground, and as they zoomed upward, he felt a sudden blast of Lois-power wrap itself around him and yank him backward like a bungee cord. There was a brief, nauseating sensation of flying in two directions at the same time.

Ralph caught a final glimpse of Ed Deepneau slumped against the sidewall of the cockpit, but in a very real sense he did not see him at all. The thunderstruck yellow-gray aura was gone. Ed was also gone, buried in a deathbag as black as midnight in hell.

Then he and Lois were falling as well as flying.

CHAPTER THIRTY

1

Just before the explosion came, Susan Day, standing in a hot white spotlight at the front of the Civic Center and now living through the last few seconds of her fabulous, provocative life, was saying: 'I haven't come to Derry to heal you, hector you, or to incite you, but to mourn with you – this is a situation which has passed far beyond political considerations. There is no right in violence, nor refuge in self-righteousness. I am here to ask that you put your positions and your rhetoric aside and help each other find a way to help each other. To turn away from the attractions of—'

The high windows lining the south side of the auditorium suddenly lit up with a brilliant white glare and then blew inward.

2

The Cherokee missed the Hoodsie wagon, but that didn't save it. The plane took one final half-turn in the air and then screwed itself into the parking lot about twenty-five feet from the fence where, earlier that day, Lois had paused to yank up her troublesome half-slip. The wings snapped off. The cockpit made a quick and violent journey back through the passenger section. The fuselage blew out with the fury of a bottle of champagne in a microwave oven. Glass flew. The tail bent over the Cherokee's body like the stinger of a dying scorpion and impaled itself in the roof of a Dodge van with the words PROTECT WOMEN'S RIGHT TO CHOOSE! stencilled on the side. There was a bright and bitter crunch-clang that sounded like a dropped pile of scrap iron.

'Holy shi –' one of the cops posted on the edge of the parking lot began, and then the C-4 inside the cardboard box flew free like a big gray glob of phlegm and struck the remains of the instrument panel where several 'hot' wires rammed into it like hypo needles. The *plastique* exploded with an ear-crunching thud, flash-frying the Bassey Park racetrack and turning the parking lot into a hurricane of white light and shrapnel. John Leydecker, who had been standing under the Civic Center's cement canopy and talking to a State cop, was thrown through one of the open doors and all the way across the lobby. He struck the far wall and fell unconscious into the shattered glass from the harness-racing trophy case. At that, he was luckier than the man with whom he had been standing; the State cop was thrown into the post between two of the open doors and chopped in half.

The ranks of cars actually shielded the Civic Center from the worst of the hammering, concussive blow, but that blessing would only be counted later. Inside, over two thousand people at first sat stunned, unsure of what they should do and even more unsure of what most of them had just seen: America's most famous feminist decapitated by a jagged chunk of flying glass. Her head went flying into the sixth row like some strange white bowling ball with a blonde wig pasted on it.

They didn't erupt into panic until the lights went out.

3

Seventy-one people were killed in the trampling, panicked rush to the exits, and the next day's Derry *News* would trumpet the event with a forty-eight-point scare headline, calling it a terrible tragedy. Ralph Roberts could have told them that, all things considered, they had gotten off lucky. Very lucky, indeed.

4

Halfway up the north balcony, a woman named Sonia Danville – a woman with the bruises of the last beating any man would ever give her still fading from her face – sat with her arms around the shoulders of her son, Patrick. Patrick's McDonald's poster, showing Ronald and Mayor McCheese and the Hamburglar dancing the Boot-Scootin' Boogie just outside a drive-thru window, was on his lap, but he had hardly done more than color the golden arches before turning the poster over to the blank side. It wasn't that he had lost interest; it was just that he'd had an idea for a picture of his own, and it had come as such ideas often did to him, with the force of a compulsion. He had spent most of the day thinking about what had happened in the cellar at High Ridge – the smoke, the heat, the frightened women, and the two angels that had come to save them – but his splendid idea banished these disturbing thoughts, and he fell to work with silent enthusiasm. Soon Patrick felt almost as if he were living in the world he was drawing with his Crayolas.

He was an amazingly competent artist already, only four years old or not ('My little genius', Sonia sometimes called him), and his picture was much better than the color-it-in poster on the other side of the sheet. What he had managed before the lights went out was work a gifted first-year art student might have been proud of. In the middle of the poster-sheet, a tower of dark, soot-colored stone rose into a blue sky dotted with fat white clouds. Surrounding it was a field of roses so red they almost seemed to clamor aloud. Standing off to one side was a man dressed in faded blue jeans. A pair of gunbelts crossed his flat middle; a holster hung below each hip. At the very top of the tower, a man in a red robe was looking down at the gunfighter with an expression of mingled hate and fear. His hands, which were curled over the parapet, also appeared to be red.

Sonia had been mesmerized by the presence of Susan Day, who was sitting behind the lectern and listening to her introduction, but she had happened to glance down at her son's picture just before the introduction ended. She had known for two years that Patrick was what the child psychologists called a prodigy, and she sometimes told herself she had gotten used to his sophisticated drawings and the Play-Doh sculptures he called the Clay Family. Perhaps she even had to some degree, but this particular picture gave her a strange, deep chill that she could not entirely dismiss as emotional fallout from her long and stressful day.

'Who's that?' she asked, tapping the tiny figure peering jealously down from the top of the dark tower.

'Him's the Red King,' Patrick said.

'Oh, the Red King, I see. And who's this man with the guns?'

As he opened his mouth to answer, Roberta Harper, the woman at the podium, lifted her left arm (there was a black mourning band on it) toward the woman sitting behind her. 'My friends, Ms *Susan Day!*' she cried, and Patrick Danville's answer to his mother's second question was lost in the rising storm of applause.

Him's name is Roland, Mama. I dream about him, sometimes. Him's a King, too.

5

Now the two of them sat in the dark with their ears ringing, and two thoughts ran through Sonia's mind like rats chasing each other on a treadmill: *Won't this day ever end, I knew I shouldn't have brought him, won't this day ever end, I knew I shouldn't have brought him, won't this day—*

'Mommy, you're scrunching my *picture!*' Patrick said. He sounded a little out of breath, and Sonia realized she must be scrunching him, too. She eased up a little. A tattered skein of screams, shouts, and babbled questions came from the dark pit below them, where the people rich enough to pony up fifteen-dollar 'donations' had been seated in folding chairs. A rough howl of pain cut through this babble, making Sonia jump in her seat.

837

The thudding crump which had followed the initial explosion had pressed in painfully on their ears and shaken the building. The blasts which were still going on – cars exploding like firecrackers in the parking lot – sounded small and inconsequential in comparison, but Sonia felt Patrick flinch against her with each one.

'Stay calm, Pat,' she told him. 'Something bad's happened, but I think it happened outside.' Because her eyes had been drawn to the bright glare in the windows, Sonia had mercifully missed seeing her heroine's head leaving her shoulders, but she knew that somehow light-ning *had* struck in the same place

(*shouldn't have brought him, shouldn't have brought him*)

and that at least some of the people below them were panicking. If *she* panicked, she and Young Rembrandt were going to be in serious trouble.

But I'm not going to. I didn't get out of that deathbox this morning just to panic now. I'll be goddamned if I will.

She reached down and took one of Patrick's hands – the one that wasn't clutching his picture. It was very cold.

'Do you think the angels will come to save us again, Mama?' he asked in a voice that quivered slightly.

'Nah,' she said. 'I think this time we better do it ourselves. But we can do that. I mean, we're all right now, aren't we?'

'Yes,' he said, but then slumped against her. She had a terrible moment when she was sure he had fainted and she'd have to carry him from the Civic Center in her arms, but then he straightened up again. 'My books was on the floor,' he said. 'I didn't want to leave without my books,

838

especially the one about the boy who can't take off his hat. *Are* we leaving. Mama?'

'Yes. As soon as people stop running around. There'll be lights in the halls, ones that run on batteries, even though the ones in here are out. When I say, we're going to get up and walk – *walk!* – up the steps to the door. I'm not going to carry you, but I'm going to walk right behind you with both my hands on your shoulders. Do you understand, Pat?'

'Yes, Mama.' No questions. No blubbering. Just his books, thrust into her hands for safekeeping. He held onto the picture himself. She gave him a quick hug and kissed his cheek.

They waited in their seats five minutes by her slow count to three hundred. She sensed that most of their immediate neighbors were gone before she got to a hundred and fifty, but she made herself wait. She could now see a little, enough for her to believe that something was burning fiercely outside, but on the far side of the building. That was very lucky. She could hear the warble-wail of approaching police cars, ambulances, and fire-trucks.

Sonia got to her feet. 'Come on. Keep right in front of me.'

Pat Danville stepped into the aisle with his mother's hands pressed firmly down on his shoulders. He led her up the steps toward the dim yellow lights which marked the north balcony corridor, stopping only once as the dark shape of a running man hurtled toward them. His mother's hands tightened on his shoulders as she yanked him aside.

'Goddam right-to-lifers!' the running man cried. 'Fucking self-righteous *turds*! I'd like to kill them all!'

Then he was gone and Pat began walking up the stairs again. She felt a calmness in him now, a centered lack of fear, that touched her heart with love, and with some queer darkness, as well. He was so different, her son, so special . . . but the world did not love people like that. The world tried to root them out, like tares from a garden.

They emerged at last into the corridor. A few deeply shocked people wandered back and forth, eyes dazed and mouths agape, like zombies in a horror movie. Sonia hardly glanced at them, just got Pat moving toward the stairs. Three minutes later they exited into the fireshot night perfectly unscathed, and upon all the levels of the universe, matters both Random and Purposeful resumed their ordained courses. Worlds which had trembled for a moment in their orbits now steadied, and in one of those worlds, in a desert that was the apotheosis of all deserts, a man named Roland turned over in his bedroll and slept easily once again beneath the alien constellations.

6

Across town, in Strawford Park, the door of the Portosan marked MEN blew open. Lois Chasse and Ralph Roberts came flying out backwards in a haze of smoke, clutching each other. From within came the sound of the Cherokee hitting and then the *plastique* exploding. There was a flash of white light and the toilet's blue walls bulged outward, as if some giant had hammered them with his fists. A second later they heard the explosion all over again; this time it came rolling across the open air. The second version was fainter, but somehow more real.

Lois's feet stuttered and she thumped to the grass of the lower hillside with a cry which was partly relief. Ralph landed beside her, then pushed himself up to a sitting position. He stared unbelievingly at the Civic Center, where a fist of fire was now clenched on the horizon. A purple lump the size of a doorknob was rising on his forehead, where Ed had hit him. His left side still throbbed, but he thought maybe the ribs in there were only sprung, not broken.

[*Lois, are you all right?*]

She looked at him uncomprehendingly for a moment, then began to feel at her face and neck and shoulders. There was something so perfectly, sweetly *Our Lois* about this examination that Ralph laughed. He couldn't help it. Lois smiled tentatively back at him.

[*I think I'm fine. In fact, I'm quite sure I am.*]

[*What were you doing there? You could have been killed!*]

Lois, appearing somewhat rejuvenated (Ralph guessed that the handy wino had had something to do with that) looked him in the eye.

[*I may be old-fashioned, Ralph, but if you think I'm going to spend the next twenty years or so fainting and fluttering like the heroine's best friend in those Regency romances my friend Mina's always reading, you better pick another woman to chum around with.*]

He gaped for a moment, then pulled her to her feet and hugged her. Lois hugged back. She was incredibly warm, incredibly *there*. Ralph reflected for a moment on the similarities between loneliness and insomnia — how they were both insidious, cumulative, and divisive, the friends of despair and the enemies of love — and then he pushed those thoughts aside and kissed her.

841

Clotho and Lachesis, who had been standing at the top of the hill and looking as anxious as workmen who have wagered their Christmas bonuses on a prizefight underdog, now rushed down to where Ralph and Lois stood with their foreheads once more pressed together, looking into each other's eyes like lovestruck teenagers. From the far side of the Barrens, the sound of sirens rose like voices heard in uneasy dreams. The pillar of fire which marked the grave of Ed Deepneau's obsession was now too bright to look at without squinting. Ralph could hear the faint sound of cars exploding, and he thought of his car sitting abandoned somewhere out in the williwags. He decided that was okay. He was too old to drive.

7

Clotho: [*Are you both all right?*]

Ralph: [*'We're fine. Lois reeled me in. She saved my life.'*]

Lachesis: [*Yes. We saw her go in. It was very brave.*]

Also very perplexing, right, Mr L? Ralph thought. *You saw it and you admire it . . . but I don't think you have any idea of how or why she could bring herself to do it. I think that, to you and your friend, the concept of rescue must seem almost as foreign as the idea of love.*

For the first time, Ralph felt a kind of pity for the little bald doctors, and understood the central irony of their lives: they were aware that the Short-Timers whose existences they had been sent to prune lived powerful inner lives, but they did not in the least comprehend the reality of those lives, the emotions which drove them, or the actions − sometimes noble, sometimes foolish − which resulted. Mr C and Mr L had studied their Short-Time charges as certain rich but timid Englishmen had studied the maps brought back by the explorers of the Victorian Age, explorers who had in many cases been funded by these same rich but timid men. With their clipped nails and soft fingers the philanthropists had traced paper rivers upon which they would never ride and paper jungles through which they would never safari. They lived in fearful perplexity and passed it off as imagination.

Clotho and Lachesis had drafted them, and had used them with a certain crude effectiveness, but they understood neither the joy of risk nor the sorrow of loss – the best they had been able to manage in the way of emotion was a nagging fear that Ralph and Lois would try to take on the Crimson King's pet research chemist directly and be swatted like elderly flies for their pains. The little bald doctors lived long lives, but Ralph suspected that, brilliant dragonfly auras notwithstanding, they were *gray* lives. He looked at their unlined, oddly childish faces from the safe haven of Lois's arms and remembered how terrified of them he had been when he had first seen them coming out of May Locher's house in the early hours of the morning. Terror, he had since discovered, could not survive mere acquaintanceship, let alone knowledge, and now he had some of both.

Clotho and Lachesis returned his gaze with an uneasiness Ralph found he had absolutely no urge to allay. It seemed very right to him, somehow, that they should feel the way they were feeling.

Ralph: [*'Yes, she's very brave and I love her very much and I think we'll make each other very happy until—'*]

He broke off, and Lois stirred in his arms. He realized with a mixture of amusement and relief that she had been half asleep.

['Until what, Ralph?']

['Until you name it. I guess that there's always an until when you're a Short-Timer, and maybe that's okay.']

Lachesis: [Well, I guess this is goodbye.]

Ralph grinned in spite of himself, reminded of *The Lone Ranger* radio program, where almost every episode had ended with some version of that line. He reached out toward Lachesis and was sourly amused to see the little man recoil from him.

Ralph: ['Wait a minute . . . let's not be so hasty, fellas.']

Clotho, with a tinge of apprehension: [Is something wrong?]

['I don't think so, but after getting popped in the head, popped in the ribs, and then damned near roasted alive, I think I have a right to make sure that it's really over. Is it? Is your boy safe?']

Clotho, smiling and clearly relieved: [Yes. Can't you feel it? Eighteen years from now, just before his death, the boy is going to save the lives of two men who would otherwise die . . . and one of those men must not die, if the balance between the Random and the Purpose is to be maintained.]

Lois: ['Never mind all that. I just want to know if we can go back to being regular Short-Timers again.']

Lachesis: [Not only can, Lois, but must. If you and Ralph were to stay up here much longer, you wouldn't be able to go back down.]

Ralph felt Lois press more tightly against him.

['I wouldn't like that.']

Clotho and Lachesis turned toward each other and a subtle, perplexed glance — *how could anybody not like it up here?* their eyes asked — passed between them before they turned back to Ralph and Lois.

Lachesis: [*We really must be going. I'm sorry, but—*]

Ralph: [*'Hold on, neighbors — you're not going anywhere yet.'*]

They looked at him apprehensively while Ralph slowly pushed up the sleeve of his sweater — the cuff was now stiff with some fluid, perhaps catfish ichor, that he found he did not want to think about — and showed them the white, knotted line of scar on his forearm.

[*'Put away the constipated looks, guys. I just want to remind you that you gave me your word. Don't forget that part of it.'*]

Clotho, with obvious relief: [*You can depend on it, Ralph. What was your weapon is now our bond. The promise will not be forgotten.*]

Ralph was beginning to believe it really was over. And, crazy as it seemed, part of him regretted it. Now it was real life — life as it went on on the floors below this level — that seemed almost like a mirage, and he understood what Lachesis had meant when he told them that they would never be able to return to their normal lives if they stayed up here much longer.

Lachesis: [*We really must go. Fare you well, Ralph and Lois. We will never forget the service you have rendered us.*]

Ralph: [*'Did we ever have a choice? Did we really?'*]

Lachesis, very softly: [*We told you so, didn't we? For Short-Timers there is always a choice. We find that frightening . . . but we also find it beautiful.*]

Ralph: [*'Say — do you fellows ever shake hands?'*]

Clotho and Lachesis glanced at each other, startled, and Ralph sensed some quick dialogue flashing between them in a kind of telepathic shorthand. When they looked back at Ralph, they wore identical nervous smiles – the smiles of teenage boys who have decided that if they can't find enough courage to ride the *big* rollercoaster at the amusement park this summer, they will never truly be men.

Clotho: [*We have observed this custom many times, of course, but no – we have never shaken hands.*]

Ralph looked at Lois and saw she was smiling . . . but he thought he saw a shimmer of tears in her eyes, as well.

He offered his hand to Lachesis first, because Mr L seemed marginally less jumpy than his colleague.

[*'Put 'er there, Mr L.'*]

Lachesis looked at Ralph's hand for so long that Ralph began to think he wasn't going to be able to actually do it, although he clearly wanted to. Then, timidly, he put out his own small hand and allowed Ralph's larger one to close over it. There was a tingling vibration in Ralph's flesh as their auras first mingled, then merged . . . and in that merging he saw a series of swift, beautiful silver patterns. They reminded him of the Japanese characters on Ed's scarf.

He pumped Lachesis's hand twice, slowly and formally, then released it. Lachesis's look of apprehension had been replaced by a large goony smile. He turned to his partner.

[*His force is almost completely unguarded during this ceremony! I felt it! It's quite wonderful!*]

Clotho inched his own hand out to meet Ralph's, and in the instant before they touched, Mr C closed his eyes like a man expecting a painful injection. Lachesis, meanwhile, was shaking hands with Lois and grinning like a vaudeville hoofer taking an encore.

Clotho appeared to steel himself, then seized Ralph's hand. He flagged it once, firmly. Ralph grinned.

[*'Take her easy, Mr C.'*]

Clotho withdrew his hand. He seemed to be searching for the proper response.

[*Thank you, Ralph. I will take her any way I can get her. Correct?*]

Ralph burst out laughing. Clotho, now turning to shake hands with Lois, gave him a puzzled smile, and Ralph clapped him on the back.

[*'You got it right, Mr C – absolutely right.'*]

He slipped his arm around Lois and gave the little bald doctors a final curious look.

[*'I'll be seeing you fellows again, won't I?'*]

Clotho: [*Yes, Ralph.*]

Ralph: [*'Well, that's fine. About seventy years from now would be good for me; why don't you boys just put it down on your calendar?'*]

They responded with the smiles of politicians, which didn't surprise him much. Ralph gave them a little bow, then put his arms around Lois's shoulders and watched as Mr C and Mr L walked slowly down the hill. Lachesis opened the door of the slightly warped Portosan marked MEN; Clotho stood in the open doorway of WOMEN. Lachesis smiled and waved. Clotho lifted the long-bladed scissors in a queer sort of salute.

Ralph and Lois waved back.

The bald doctors stepped inside and closed the doors.

Lois wiped her streaming eyes and turned to Ralph.

[*Is that it? It is, isn't it?*]

Ralph nodded.

[*What do we do now?*]

He held out his arm.

[*May I see you home, madam?*]

Smiling, she clasped his forearm just below the elbow.

[*Thank you, sir. You may.*]

They left Strawford Park that way, returning to the Short-Time level as they came out on Harris Avenue, slipping back down to their normal place in the scheme of things with no fuss or bother – without, in fact, even being aware they were doing it until it was done.

8

Derry groaned with panic and sweated with excitement. Sirens wailed, people shouted from second-storey windows to friends on the sidewalks below, and on every street-corner people had clustered to watch the fire on the other side of the valley.

Ralph and Lois paid no attention to the tumult and hooraw. They walked slowly up Up-Mile Hill, increasingly aware of their exhaustion; it seemed to come piling into them like softly thrown bags of sand. The pool of white light marking the Red Apple Store's parking lot seemed an impossible distance away, although Ralph knew it was only three blocks, and short ones, at that.

To make matters worse, the temperature had dropped a good fifteen degrees since that morning, the wind was blowing hard, and neither of them was dressed for the weather. Ralph suspected this might be the leading edge of autumn's first big gale, and that in Derry, Indian summer was over.

Faye Chapin, Don Veazie, and Stan Eberly came hurrying down the hill toward them, obviously bound for Strawford Park. The field-glasses Old Dor sometimes used to watch planes taxi, land, and take off were bouncing around Faye's neck. With Don, who was balding and heavy set, in the middle, their resemblance to a more famous trio was inescapable. *The Three Stooges of the Apocalypse,* Ralph thought, and grinned.

'Ralph!' Faye exclaimed. He was breathing fast, almost panting. The wind blew his hair into his eyes and he raked it back impatiently. 'Goddam Civic Center blew up! Someone bombed it from a light plane! We heard there's a thousand people dead!'

'I heard about the same,' Ralph agreed gravely. 'In fact, Lois and I have just been down at the park, having a look. You can see straight across the valley from there, you know.'

'Christ, *I* know that, I've lived here all my damn life, haven't I? Where do you think we're going? Come on back with us!'

'Lois and I were just headed up to her house to see what they've got about it on TV. Maybe we'll join you later.'

'Okay, we – jeepers-creepers, Ralph, what'd you do to your head?'

For a moment Ralph drew a blank – what *had* he done to his head? – and then, in an instant of nightmarish recall, he saw Ed's snarling mouth and mad eyes. *Oh no, don't,* Ed had screamed at him. *You'll spoil everything.*

'We were running to get a better look and Ralph ran into a tree,' Lois said. 'He's lucky not to be in the hospital.'

Don laughed at that, but in the half-distracted manner of a fellow who has bigger fish to fry. Faye wasn't paying attention to them at all. Stan Eberly was, however, and Stan didn't laugh. He was looking at them with close, puzzled curiosity.

'Lois,' he said.

'What?'

'Did you know you've got a sneaker tied to your wrist?'

She looked down at it. Ralph looked down at it. Then Lois looked up and gave Stan a dazzling, eye-frying smile. 'Yes!' she said. 'It's an interesting look, isn't it? Sort of a . . . a life-sized charm bracelet!'

'Yeah,' Stan said. 'Sure.' But he wasn't looking at the sneaker anymore; now he was looking at Lois's face. Ralph wondered how in hell they were going to explain how they looked tomorrow, when there were no shadows between the streetlights to hide them.

'Come on!' Faye cried impatiently. 'Let's get going!'

They hurried off (Stan gave them one last doubtful glance over his shoulder as they went). Ralph listened after them, almost expecting Don Veazie to give out a *nyuck-nyuck* or two.

'Boy, that sounded so *dumb*,' Lois said, 'but I had to say something, didn't I?'

'You did fine.'

'Well, when I open my mouth, *something* always seems to fall out,' she said. 'It's one of my two great talents, the other being the ability to clean out an entire Whitman's Sampler during a two-hour TV movie.' She untied Helen's sneaker and looked at it. 'She's safe, isn't she?'

'Yes,' Ralph agreed, and reached for the sneaker. As he did, he realized he already had something in his left hand. The fingers had been clamped down so long that they were creaky and reluctant to open. When they finally did, he saw the marks of his nails pressed into the flesh of his palm. The first thing he was aware of was that, while his own wedding ring was still in its accustomed place, Ed's was gone. It had seemed a perfect fit, but apparently it had slipped off his finger at some point during the last half an hour, just the same.

Maybe not, a voice whispered, and Ralph was amused to realize that it wasn't Carolyn's this time. This time the voice in his head belonged to Bill McGovern. *Maybe it just disappeared. You know, poof.*

But he didn't think so. He had an idea that Ed's wedding band might have been invested with powers that hadn't necessarily died with Ed. The Ring Bilbo Baggins had found and reluctantly given up to his grandson, Frodo, had had a way of going where it wanted to . . . and when. Perhaps Ed's ring wasn't all that different.

Before he could consider this idea further, Lois traded Helen's sneaker for the thing in his hand: a small stiff crumple of paper. She smoothed it out and looked at it. Her curiosity slowly changed to solemnity.

'I remember this picture,' she said. 'The big one was on the mantel in their living room, in a fancy gold frame. It had pride of place.'

Ralph nodded. 'This must have been the one he

carried in his wallet. It was taped to the instrument panel of the plane. Until I took it, he was beating me, and not even breathing hard while he did it. Grabbing his picture was all I could think of to do. When I did, his focus switched from the Civic Center to them. The last thing I heard him say was "Give them back, they're mine."'

'And was he talking to you when he said it?'

Ralph stuck the sneaker into his back pocket and shook his head. 'Nope. Don't think so.'

'Helen was at the Civic Center tonight, wasn't she?'

'Yes.' Ralph thought of how she had looked out at High Ridge – her pale face and smoke-reddened, watering eyes. *If they stop us now, they win,* she'd said. *Don't you see that?*

And now he *did* see.

He took the picture from Lois's hand, crumpled it up again, and walked over to the litter-basket which stood on the corner of Harris Avenue and Kossuth Lane. 'We'll get another picture of them sometime, one we can keep on our own mantel. Something not quite so formal. This one, though . . . I don't want it.'

He tossed the little ball of paper at the litter-basket, an easy shot, two feet at the most, but the wind picked that moment to gust and the crumpled photo of Helen and Natalie which had been taped above the altimeter of Ed's plane flew away on its cold breath. The two of them watched it whirl up into the sky, almost hypnotized. It was Lois who looked away first. She glanced at Ralph with a trace of a smile curving her lips.

'Did I hear a backhand proposal of marriage from you, or am I just tired?' she asked.

He opened his mouth to reply and another gust of wind struck them, this one so hard it made them both wince their eyes shut. When he opened his, Lois had already started up the hill again.

'Anything's possible, Lois,' he said. 'I know that now.'

9

Five minutes later, Lois's key rattled in the lock of her front door. She led Ralph inside and shut it firmly behind them, closing out the windy, contentious night. He followed her into the living room and would have stopped there, but Lois never hesitated. Still holding his hand, not quite pulling him along (but perhaps meaning to do so if he began to lag), she showed him into her bedroom.

He looked at her. Lois looked calmly back . . . and suddenly he felt the blink happen again. He watched her aura bloom around her like a gray rose. It was still diminished, but it was already coming back, reknitting itself, healing itself.

[*Lois, are you sure this is what you want?*]

[*Of course it is! Did you think I was going to give you a pat on the head and send you home after all we've been through?*]

Suddenly she smiled – a wickedly mischievous smile.

[*Besides, Ralph – do you really feel like getting up to dickens tonight? Tell me the truth. Better still, don't flatter me.*]

He considered it, then laughed and drew her into his arms. Her mouth was sweet and slightly moist, like the skin of a ripe peach. That kiss seemed to tingle through his entire body, but the sensation was most concentrated in his mouth, where it felt almost like an electric shock. When their lips parted, he felt more excited than ever . . . but he also felt queerly drained.

[*'What if I say I do, Lois? What if I say I do want to get up to dickens?'*]

She stood back and looked at him critically, as if trying to decide whether he meant what he said or if it was just the usual male bluff and brag. At the same time her hands went to the buttons of her dress. As she began to slip them free, Ralph noticed a wonderful thing: she looked younger again. Not forty by any stretch of the imagination, but surely no more than fifty . . . and a *young* fifty. It had been the kiss, of course, and the really amusing thing was he didn't think she had the slightest idea that she had added a helping of Ralph to her earlier helping of wino. And what was wrong with that?

She finished her inspection, leaned forward, and kissed his cheek.

[*'I think that there'll be plenty of time for getting up to dickens later, Ralph – tonight's for sleeping.'*]

He supposed she was right. Five minutes ago he had been more than willing – he had always loved the act of physical love, and it had been a long time. For now, however, the spark was gone. Ralph didn't regret that in the least. He knew, after all, *where* it had gone.

[*'Okay, Lois – tonight's for sleeping.'*]

She went into the bathroom and the shower went on. A few minutes later, Ralph heard her brushing her teeth. It was nice to know she still had them. During the ten minutes she was gone he managed to do a certain amount of undressing, although his throbbing ribs made it slow work. He finally succeeded in wriggling McGovern's sweater off and pushing out of his shoes. His shirt came next, and he was fumbling ineffectually with the buckle of his belt when Lois came out with her hair tied back and her face shining. Ralph was stunned by her beauty, and suddenly felt much too big and stupid (not to mention old) for his own good. She was wearing a long rose-colored silk nightgown and he could smell the lotion she had used on her hands. It was a good smell.

'Let me do that,' she said, and had his belt unbuckled before he could say much, one way or the other. There was nothing erotic about it; she moved with the efficiency of a woman who had often helped her husband dress and undress during the last year of his life.

'We're down again,' he said. 'This time I didn't even feel it happening.'

'I did, while I was in the shower. I was glad, actually. Trying to wash your hair through an aura is very distracting.'

The wind gusted outside, shaking the house and blowing a long, shivering note across the mouth of a downspout. They looked toward the window, and although he was back down on the Short-Time level, Ralph was suddenly sure that Lois was sharing his own thought: Atropos was out there somewhere right now, no doubt disappointed by the way things had gone but by no means crushed, bloody but unbowed, down but not out. *From now on they can call him Old One-Ear,* Ralph thought, and shivered. He imagined Atropos swinging erratically through the scared, excited populace of the city like a rogue asteroid, peering and hiding, stealing souvenirs and slashing balloon-strings . . . taking

STEPHEN KING

solace in his work, in other words. Ralph found it almost impossible to believe that he had been sitting on top of that creature and slashing at him with his own scalpel not very long ago. *How did I ever find the courage?* he wondered, but he supposed he knew. The diamond earrings the little monster had been wearing had provided most of it. Did Atropos know those earrings had been his biggest mistake? Probably not. In his way, Doc #3 had proved even more ignorant of Short-Time motivations than Clotho and Lachesis.

He turned to Lois and grasped her hands. 'I lost your earrings again. This time they're gone for good, I think. I'm sorry.'

'Don't apologize. They were already lost, remember? And I'm not worried about Harold and Jan anymore, because now I've got a friend to help me when people don't treat me right, or when I just get scared. Don't I?'

'Yes. You most certainly do.'

She put her arms around him, hugged him tightly, and kissed him again. Lois had apparently not forgotten a single thing she'd ever learned about kissing, and it seemed to Ralph that she'd learned quite a lot. 'Go on and hop in the shower.' He started to say that he thought he'd fall asleep the moment he got his head under a stream of warm water, but then she added something which changed his mind in a hurry: 'Don't take offense, but there's a funny smell on you, especially on your hands. It's the way my brother Vic used to smell after he'd spent the day cleaning fish.'

Ralph was in the shower two minutes later, and in soapsuds up to his elbows.

10

When he came out, Lois was buried beneath two puffy quilts. Only her face showed, and that was visible only from the nose up. Ralph crossed the room quickly, wearing only his undershorts and painfully conscious of his spindly legs and potbelly. He tossed back the covers and slid in quickly, gasping a little as the cool sheets slid along his warm skin.

Lois slipped over to his side of the bed at once and put her arms around him. He put his face in her hair and let himself relax against her. It was very good, being with Lois under the quilts while the wind shrieked and gusted outside, sometimes hard enough to rattle the storm windows in their frames. It was, in fact, heaven.

'Thank God there's a man in my bed,' Lois said sleepily.

'Thank God it's me,' Ralph replied, and she laughed.

'Are your ribs okay? Do you want me to find you an aspirin?'

'Nope. I'm sure they'll hurt again in the morning, but right now the hot water seems to have loosened everything up.' The subject of what might or might not happen in the morning raised a question in his mind – one that had probably been waiting there all along. 'Lois?'

'Mmmmm?'

In his mind's eye Ralph could see himself snapping awake in the dark, deeply tired but not at all sleepy (it was surely one of the world's cruelest paradoxes), as the numbers on the digital clock turned wearily over from 3:47 a.m. to 3:48. F. Scott Fitzgerald's dark night of the soul, when every hour was long enough to build the Great Pyramid of Cheops.

'Do you think we'll sleep through?' he asked her.

'Yes,' she said unhesitatingly. 'I think we'll sleep just fine.'

A moment later, Lois was doing just that.

11

Ralph stayed awake for perhaps five minutes longer, holding her in his arms, smelling the wonderful interwoven scents rising from her warm skin, luxuriating in the smooth, sensuous glide of the silk under his hands, marvelling at where he was even more than the events which had brought him here. He was filled with some deep and simple emotion, one he recognized but could not immediately name, perhaps because it had been gone from his life too long.

The wind gusted and moaned outside, producing that hollow hooting sound over the top of the drainpipe again – like the world's biggest Nirvana Boy blowing over the mouth of the world's biggest pop-bottle – and it occurred to Ralph that maybe nothing in life was better than lying deep in a soft bed with a sleeping woman in your arms while the fall wind screamed outside your safe haven.

Except there *was* something better, one thing, at least, and that was the feeling of falling asleep, of going gently into that good night, slipping out into the currents of unknowing the way a canoe slips away from a dock and slides into the current of a wide, slow river on a bright summer day.

Of all the things which make up our Short-Time lives, sleep is surely the best, Ralph thought.

The wind gusted again outside (the sound of it now seeming to come from a great distance) and as he felt the tug of that great river take him, he was finally able to identify the emotion he had been feeling ever since Lois had put her arms around him and fallen asleep as easily and as trustingly as a child. It went under many different names – peace, serenity, fulfillment – but now, as the wind blew and Lois made some dark sound of sleeping contentment far back in her throat, it seemed to Ralph that it was one of those rare things which are known but essentially unnameable: a texture, an aura, perhaps a whole level of being in that column of existence. It was the smooth russet color of rest; it was the silence which follows the completion of some arduous but necessary task.

When the wind gusted again, bringing the sound of distant sirens with it, Ralph didn't hear it. He was asleep. Once he dreamed that he got up to use the bathroom, and he supposed that might not have been a dream. At another time he dreamed that he and Lois made slow, sweet love, and that might not have been a dream, either. If there were other dreams or moments of waking, he did not remember them, and this time there was no snapping awake at three or four o'clock in the morning. They slept – sometimes apart but mostly together – until just past seven o'clock on Saturday evening; about twenty-two hours, all told.

Lois made them breakfast at sunset – splendidly puffy waffles, bacon, home fries. While she cooked, Ralph tried to flex that muscle buried deep in his mind – to create that sensation of *blink*. He couldn't do it. When Lois tried, she was also unable, although Ralph could have sworn that just for a moment she flickered, and he could see the stove right through her.

'Just as well,' she said, bringing their plates to the table.

'I suppose,' Ralph agreed, but he still felt as he would have if he had lost the ring Carolyn had given him instead of the one he had taken from Atropos – as if some small but essential object had gone rolling out of his life with a wink and a gleam.

12

Following two more nights of sound, unbroken sleep, the auras had begun to fade, as well. By the following week they were gone, and Ralph began to wonder if perhaps the whole thing hadn't been some strange dream. He knew that wasn't so, but it became harder and harder to believe what he *did* know. There was the scar between the elbow and wrist of his right arm, of course, but he even began to wonder if that wasn't something he had acquired long ago, during those years of his life when there had been no white in his hair and he had still believed, deep in his heart, that old age was a myth, or a dream, or a thing reserved for people not as special as he was.

EPILOGUE

WINDING THE DEATHWATCH (II)

Glancing over my shoulder I see its shape
and so move forward, as someone in the woods
at night might hear the sound of approaching feet
and stop to listen; then, instead of silence
he hears some creature trying to be silent.
What else can he do but run? Rushing blindly
down the path, stumbling, struck in the face by
    sticks;
the other ever closer, yet not really
hurrying or out of breath, teasing its kill.

Stephen Dobyns
'Pursuit'

If I had some wings, I'd fly you all around;
If I had some money, I'd buy you the goddam
    town;
If I had the strength, then maybe I coulda pulled
    you through;

If I had a lantern, I'd light the way for you,
If I had a lantern, I'd light the way for you.
                                    Michael McDermott
                                          'Lantern'

1

On January 2nd, 1994, Lois Chasse became Lois Roberts. Her son, Harold, gave her away. Harold's wife did not attend the ceremony; she was up in Bangor with what Ralph considered a highly suspect case of bronchitis. He kept his suspicions to himself, however, being far from disappointed at Jan Chasse's failure to appear. The groom's best man was Detective John Leydecker, who still wore a cast on his right arm but otherwise showed no signs of the assignment which had nearly killed him. He had spent four days in a coma, but Leydecker knew how lucky he was; in addition to the State Trooper who had been standing beside him at the time of the explosion, six cops had died, two of them members of Leydecker's hand-picked team.

The bride's maid of honor was her friend Simone Castonguay, and at the reception, the first toast was made by a fellow who liked to say he used to be Joe Wyze but was now older and Wyzer. Trigger Vachon delivered a fractured but heartfelt follow-up, concluding with the wish that 'Dese two people gonna live to a hunnert and

fifty and never know a day of the rheumatiz or consti-
pations!'

When Ralph and Lois left the reception hall, their
hair still full of rice thrown for the most part by Faye
Chapin and the rest of the Harris Avenue Old Crocks, an
old man with a book in his hand and a fine cloud of white
hair floating around his head came walking up to them.
He had a wide smile on his face.

'Congratulations, Ralph,' he said. 'Congratulations, Lois.'

'Thanks, Dor,' Ralph said.

'We missed you,' Lois told him. 'Didn't you get your
invitation? Faye said he'd give it to you.'

'Oh, he gave it to me. Yes, oh yes, he did, but I don't
go to those things if they're inside. Too stuffy. Funerals are
even worse. Here, this is for you. I didn't wrap it, because
the arthritis is in my fingers too bad for stuff like that
now.'

Ralph took it. It was a book of poems called *Concurring
Beasts*. The poet's name, Stephen Dobyns, gave him a funny
little chill, but he wasn't quite sure why.

'Thanks,' he told Dorrance.

'Not as good as some of his later work, but good.
Dobyns is very good.'

'We'll read them to each other on our honeymoon,'
Lois said.

'That's a good time to read poetry,' Dorrance said.
'Maybe the best time. I'm sure you'll be very happy
together.'

He started off, then looked back.

'You did a great thing. The Long-Timers are very
pleased.'

864

He walked away.

Lois looked at Ralph. 'What was he talking about? Do you know?'

Ralph shook his head. He didn't, not for sure, although he felt as if he *should* know. The scar on his arm had begun to tingle as it sometimes did, a feeling which was almost like a deep-seated itch.

'Long-Timers,' she mused. 'Maybe he meant us, Ralph – after all, we're hardly spring chickens these days, are we?'

'That's probably just what he *did* mean,' Ralph agreed, but he knew better . . . and her eyes said that, somewhere deep down, so did she.

2

On that same day, and just as Ralph and Lois were saying their 'I do's, a certain wino with a bright green aura – one who actually *did* have an uncle in Dexter, although the uncle hadn't seen this ne'er-do-well nephew for five years or more – was tramping across Strawford Park, slitting his eyes against the formidable glare of sun on snow. He was looking for returnable cans and bottles. Enough to buy a pint of whiskey would be great, but a pint of Night Train wine would do.

Not far from the Portosan marked MEN, he saw a bright gleam of metal. It was probably just the sun reflecting off a bottle-cap, but such things needed to be checked out. It might be a dime . . . although to the wino, it actually seemed to have a goldy sort of gleam. It—

'Holy Judas!' he cried, snatching up the wedding ring which lay mysteriously on top of the snow. It was a broad

865

band, almost certainly gold. He tilted it to read the engraving on the inside: HD − ED 5–8–87.

A pint? Hell, no. This little baby was going to secure him a quart. *Several* quarts. Possibly a *week's* worth of quarts.

Hurrying across the intersection of Witcham and Jackson, the one where Ralph Roberts had once almost fainted, the wino never saw the approaching Green Line bus. The driver saw him, and put on his brakes, but the bus struck a patch of ice.

The wino never knew what hit him. At one moment he was debating between Old Crow and Old Grand Dad; at the next he had passed into the darkness which awaits us all. The ring rolled down the gutter and disappeared into a sewer grate, and there it remained for a long, long time. But not forever. In Derry, things that disappear into the sewer system have a way − an often unpleasant one − of turning up.

3

Ralph and Lois didn't live happily ever after.

There really *are* no evers in the Short-Time world, happy or otherwise, a fact which Clotho and Lachesis undoubtedly knew well. They *did* live happily for quite some time, though. Neither of them liked to come right out and say these were the happiest years of all, because both remembered their first partners in marriage with love and affection, but in their hearts, both *did* consider them the happiest. Ralph wasn't sure that autumn love was the richest love, but he came firmly to believe that it was the kindest, and the most fulfilling.

Our Lois, he often said, and laughed. Lois pretended to be irritated at this, but pretending was all it ever was; she saw the look in his eyes when he said it.

On their first Christmas morning as man and wife (they had moved into Lois's tidy little house and put his own white rhino up for sale), Lois gave him a beagle puppy. 'Do you like her?' she asked apprehensively. 'I almost didn't get her, Dear Abby says you should *never* give pets as presents, but she looked so sweet in the petshop window . . . and so *sad* . . . if you don't like her, or don't want to spend the rest of the winter trying to housebreak a puppy, just say so. We'll find someone—'

'Lois,' he said, giving his eyebrow what he hoped was that special ironic Bill McGovern lift, 'you're babbling.'

'I am?'

'You am. It's something you do when you're nervous, but you can stop being nervous right now. I'm crazy 'bout dis lady.' Nor was that an exaggeration; he fell in love with the black-and-tan beagle bitch almost at once.

'What will you name her?' Lois asked. 'Any idea?'

'Sure,' Ralph said. 'Rosalie.'

4

The next four years were, by and large, good ones for Helen and Nat Deepneau, as well. They lived frugally in an apartment on the east side of town for awhile, getting along on Helen's librarian's salary but not doing much more than that. The little Cape Cod up the street from Ralph's place had sold, but that money had gone to pay outstanding bills. Then, in June of 1994, Helen received an insurance windfall . . . only the wind that blew it her way was John Leydecker.

The Great Eastern Insurance Company had originally refused to pay off on Ed Deepneau's life insurance policy, claiming he had taken his own life. Then, after a great deal of harrumphing and muttering under their corporate breath, they had offered a substantial settlement. They were persuaded to do this by a poker-buddy of John Leydecker's named Howard Hayman. When he wasn't playing lowball, five-card stud, and three-card draw, Hayman was a lawyer who enjoyed lunching on insurance companies.

Leydecker had re-met Helen at Ralph and Lois's in February of 1994, had fallen head over heels in fascination with her ('It was never quite love,' he told Ralph and Lois later, 'which was probably just as well, considering how things turned out'), and had introduced her to Hayman because he thought the insurance company was trying to screw her. 'He was *insane,* not suicidal,' Leydecker said, and stuck to that long after Helen had handed him his hat and shown him the door.

After being faced with a suit in which Howard Hayman threatened to make Great Eastern look like Snidely Whiplash tying Little Nell to the railroad tracks, Helen had received a check for seventy thousand dollars. In the late fall of 1994 she had used most of this money to buy a house on Harris Avenue, just three doors up from her old place and right across from Harriet Bennigan's.

'I was never really happy on the east side,' she told Lois one day in November of that year. They were on their way back from the park, and Natalie had been sitting slumped and fast asleep in her stroller, her presence little more than a pink nose-tip and a fog of cold breath below a large ski-hat which Lois had knitted herself. 'I used to dream about Harris Avenue. Isn't that crazy?'

'I don't think dreams are *ever* crazy,' Lois replied.

Helen and John Leydecker dated for most of that summer, but neither Ralph nor Lois was particularly surprised when the courtship abruptly ended after Labor Day, or when Helen began to wear a discreet pink triangle pin on her prim, high-necked librarian's blouses. Perhaps they were not surprised because they were old enough to have seen everything at least once, or perhaps on some deep level they were still glimpsing the auras which surround things, creating a bright gateway opening on a secret city of hidden meanings, concealed motives, and camouflaged agendas.

5

Ralph and Lois babysat Natalie frequently after Helen moved back to Harris Avenue, and they enjoyed these stints tremendously. Nat was the child their marriage might have produced if it had happened thirty years sooner, and the coldest, most overcast winter day warmed and brightened when Natalie came toddling in, looking like a midget version of the Goodyear blimp in her pink quilted snowsuit with the mittens hanging from the cuffs, and yelled exuberantly: 'Hi, Walf! Hi, Roliss! I come to bizzit you!'

In June of 1995, Helen bought a reconditioned Volvo. On the back she put a sticker which read A

WOMAN NEEDS A MAN LIKE A FISH NEEDS A BICYCLE. This sentiment did not particularly surprise Ralph, either, but glimpsing that sticker always made him feel unhappy. He sometimes thought Ed's meanest legacy to his widow was summed up in its brittle, not-quite-funny sentiment, and when he saw it, Ralph often remembered how Ed had looked on that summer afternoon when he had walked up from the Red Apple Store to confront him. How Ed had been sitting, shirtless, in the spray thrown by the sprinkler. How there had been a drop of blood on one lens of his glasses. How he had leaned forward, looking at Ralph with his earnest, intelligent eyes, and said that once stupidity reached a certain level, it became hard to live with.

And after that, stuff started to happen, Ralph would sometimes think. Just what stuff was something he could no longer remember, though, and probably that was just as well. But his lapse of memory (if that was what it was) did not change his belief that Helen had been cheated in some obscure fashion . . . that some bad-tempered fate had tied a can to her tail, and she didn't even know it.

6

A month after Helen bought her Volvo, Faye Chapin suffered a heart attack while drafting a preliminary list of seeds for that fall's Runway 3 Classic. He was taken to Derry Home Hospital, where he died seven hours later. Ralph visited him shortly before the end, and when he saw the numbers on the door − 315 − a fierce sense of *déjà vu* washed over him. At first he thought it was because

Carolyn had finished her last illness just up the hall, and then he remembered that Jimmy V had died in this very room. He and Lois had visited Jimmy just before the end, and Ralph thought Jimmy had recognized them both, although he couldn't be sure; his memories of the time when he had first begun to really notice Lois were mixed up and hazy in his mind. He supposed some of that was love, and probably some of it had to do with getting on in years, but probably most of it had been the insomnia – he'd gone through a really bad patch of that in the months after Carolyn's death, although it had eventually cured itself, as such things sometimes did. Still, it seemed to him that something

([*hello woman hello man we've been waiting for you*])

far out of the ordinary had happened in this room, and as he took Faye's dry, strengthless hand and smiled into Faye's frightened, confused eyes, a strange thought came to him: *They're standing right over there in the corner and watching us.*

He looked over. There was no one at all in the corner, of course, but for a moment . . . for just a moment . . .

7

Life in the years between 1993 and 1998 went on as life in places like Derry always does: the buds of April became the brittle, blowing leaves of October; Christmas trees were brought into homes in mid-December and hauled off in the backs of Dumpsters with strands of tinsel still hanging sadly from their boughs during the first week of January; babies came in through the in door and old folks went out through the out door. Sometimes people in the prime of their lives went out through the out door, too.

In Derry there were five years of haircuts and permanents, storms and senior proms, coffee and cigarettes, steak dinners at Parker's Cove and hotdogs at the Little League field. Girls and boys fell in love, drunks fell out of cars, short skirts fell out of favor. People reshingled their roofs and repaved their driveways. Old bums were voted out of office; new bums were voted in. It was life, often unsatisfying, frequently cruel, usually boring, sometimes beautiful, once in awhile exhilarating. The fundamental things continued to apply as time went by.

In the early fall of 1996, Ralph became convinced he had colon cancer. He had begun to see more than trace amounts of blood in his stool, and when he finally went to see Dr Pickard (Dr Litchfield's cheerful, rumpled replacement), he did so with visions of hospital beds and chemotherapy IV-drips dancing bleakly in his head. Instead of cancer, the problem turned out to be a hemorrhoid which had, in Dr Pickard's memorable phrase, 'popped its top.' He wrote Ralph a prescription for suppositories, which Ralph took to the Rite Aid down the street. Joe Wyzer read it, then grinned cheerfully at Ralph. 'Lousy,' he said, 'but it beats the hell out of colon cancer, don't you think?'

'The thought of colon cancer never crossed my mind,' Ralph replied stiffly.

One day during the winter of 1997, Lois took it into her head to slide down her favorite hill in Strawford Park on Nat Deepneau's plastic flying-saucer sled. She went down 'faster'n a pig in a greased chute' (this was Don Veazie's phrase; he just happened to be there that day, watching the action) and crashed into the side of the Portosan marked WOMEN. She sprained her knee and twisted her back, and although Ralph knew he had no business doing so – it was unsympathetic to say the least – he laughed hilariously most of the way to the emergency room. The fact that Lois was also howling with laughter despite the pain did nothing to help Ralph regain control. He laughed until tears poured from his eyes and he thought he might have a stroke. She had just looked so goddamned *Our Lois* going down the hill on that thing, spinning around and around with her legs crossed like one of those yogis from the Mysterious East, and she had almost knocked the Portosan over when she hit it. She was completely recovered by the time spring rolled around, although that knee always ached on rainy nights and she *did* get tired of Don Veazie asking, almost every time he saw her, if she'd slid into any shithouses lately.

8

Just life, going on as it always does – which is to say mostly between the lines and outside the margins. It's what happens while we're making other plans, according to some sage or other, and if life was exceptionally good to Ralph Roberts during those years, it might have been because he had no other plans to make. He maintained friendships with Joe Wyzer and John Leydecker, but his best friend during those years was his wife. They went almost everywhere together, had no secrets, and fought so seldom one might just as well have said never. He also had Rosalie the beagle, the rocker that had once been Mr Chasse's and was now his, and almost daily visits from Natalie (who had begun calling them Ralph and Lois instead of Walf and Roliss, a change neither of them found to be an improvement). And he was healthy, which was maybe the best thing of all. It was just life, full of Short-Time rewards and setbacks, and Ralph lived it with enjoyment and serenity until mid-March of 1998, when he awoke one morning, glanced at the digital clock beside his bed, and saw it was 5:49 a.m.

He lay quietly beside Lois, not wanting to disturb her by getting up, and wondering what had awakened him.

You know what, Ralph.

No I don't.

Yes, you do. Listen.

So he listened. He listened very carefully. And after awhile he began to hear it in the walls: the low, soft ticking of the deathwatch.

9

Ralph awoke at 5:47 the following morning, and at 5:44 the morning after that. His sleep was whittled away, minute by minute, as winter slowly loosened its grip on Derry and allowed spring to find its way back in. By May he was hearing the tick of the deathwatch everywhere, but understood it was all coming from one place and simply projecting itself, as a good ventriloquist can project his voice. Before, it had been coming from Carolyn. Now it was coming from him.

He felt none of the terror that had gripped him when he'd been so sure he had developed cancer, and none of the desperation he vaguely remembered from his previous bout of insomnia. He tired more easily and began to find it more difficult to concentrate and remember even simple things, but he accepted what was happening calmly.

'Are you sleeping all right, Ralph?' Lois asked him one day. 'You're getting these big dark circles under your eyes.'

'It's the dope I take,' Ralph said.

'Very funny, you old poop.'

He took her in his arms and hugged her. 'Don't worry about me, sweetheart – I'm getting all the sleep I need.'

He awoke one morning a week later at 4:02 a.m. with a line of deep heat throbbing in his arm – throbbing in perfect sync with the sound of the deathwatch, which was, of course, nothing more or less than the beat of his own heart. But this new thing wasn't his heart, or at least Ralph didn't think it was; it felt as if an electric filament had been embedded in the flesh of his forearm.

It's the scar, he thought, and then: *No, it's the promise. The time of the promise is almost here.*

What promise, Ralph? What promise?

He didn't know.

10

One day in early June, Helen and Nat blew in to visit and tell Ralph and Lois about the trip they had taken to Boston with 'Aunt Melanie,' a bank teller with whom Helen had become close friends. Helen and Aunt Melanie had gone to some sort of feminist convention while Natalie networked with about a billion new kids in the day-care center, and then Aunt Melanie had left to do some more feminist things in New York and Washington. Helen and Nat had stayed on in Boston for a couple of days, just sightseeing.

'We went to see a movie cartoon,' Natalie said. 'It was about animals in the woods. They talked!' She pronounced this last word with Shakespearian grandiosity – *talked*.

'Movies where animals talk are neat, aren't they?' Lois asked.

'Yes! Also I got this new dress!'

'And a very pretty dress it is,' Lois said.

Helen was looking at Ralph. 'Are you okay, old chum? You look pale, and you haven't said boo.'

'Never better,' he said. 'I was just thinking how cute you two look in those caps. Did you get them at Fenway Park?'

Both Helen and Nat were wearing Boston Red Sox caps. These were common enough in New England during warm weather ('common as catdirt,' Lois would have said), but the sight of them on the heads of these two people filled Ralph with some deep, resonant feeling . . . and it was tied to a specific image, one he did not in the least understand: the front of the Red Apple Store.

Helen, meantime, had taken off her hat and was examining it. 'Yes,' she said. 'We went, but we only stayed for three innings. Men hitting balls and catching balls. I guess I just don't have much patience for men and their balls these days . . . but we like our nifty Bosox hats, don't we, Natalie?'

'Yes!' Nat agreed smartly, and when Ralph awoke the next morning at 4:01, the scar throbbed its thin line of heat inside his arm and the deathwatch seemed almost to have gained a voice, one which whispered a strange, foreign-sounding name over and over: *Atropos . . . Atropos . . . Atropos.*

I know that name.

Do you, Ralph?

Yes, he was the one wittth the rusty scalpel and the nasty disposition, the one who called me Shorts, the one who took . . . took . . .

Took what, Ralph?

He was getting used to these silent discussions; they seemed to come to him on some mental radio band, a pirate frequency that operated only during the little hours, the ones when he lay awake beside his sleeping wife, waiting for the sun to come up.

Took what? Do you remember?

He didn't *expect* to; the questions that voice asked him almost always went unanswered, but this time, unexpectedly, an answer came.

Bill McGovern's hat, of course. Atropos took Bill's hat, and once I made him so mad he actually took a bite out of the brim.

Who is he? Who is Atropos?

Of this he was not so sure. He only knew that Atropos had something to do with Helen, who now owned a Boston Red Sox cap of which she seemed very fond, and that he had a rusty scalpel.

Soon, thought Ralph Roberts as he lay in the dark,

listening to the soft, steady tick of the deathwatch in the walls. *I'll know soon.*

11

During the third week of that baking hot June, Ralph began to see the auras again.

12

As June slipped into July, Ralph found himself bursting into tears often, usually for no discernible reason at all. It was strange; he had no sense of depression or discontent, but sometimes he would look at something – maybe only a bird winging its solitary way across the sky – and his heart would vibrate with sorrow and loss.

It's almost over, the inside voice said. It no longer belonged to Carolyn or Bill or even his own younger self; it was all its own now, the voice of a stranger, although not necessarily an unkind one. *That's why you're sad, Ralph. It's perfectly normal to be sad as things start to wind down.*

Nothing's almost over! he cried back. *Why should it be? At my last checkup, Dr Pickard said I was sound as a drum! I'm fine! Never better!*

Silence from the voice inside. But it was a *knowing* silence.

13

'Okay,' Ralph said out loud one hot afternoon near the end of July. He was sitting on a bench not far from the place where the Derry Standpipe had stood until 1985, when the big storm had come along and knocked it down. At the base of the hill, near the birdbath, a young man (a serious birdwatcher, from the binoculars he wore and the thick stack of paperbacks on the grass beside him) was making careful notes in what looked like some sort of journal. 'Okay, tell me *why* it's almost over. Just tell me that.'

There was no immediate answer, but that was all right; Ralph was willing to wait. It had been quite a stroll over here, the day was hot, and he was tired. He was now waking around three-thirty every morning. He had begun taking long walks again, but not in any hope they would help him sleep better or longer; he thought he was making pilgrimages, visiting all his favorite spots in Derry one last time. Saying goodbye.

Because the time of the promise has almost come, the voice answered, and the scar began to throb with its deep, narrow heat again. *The one that was made to you, and the one you made in return.*

'What was it?' he asked, agitated. 'Please, if I made a promise, *why can't I remember what it was?*'

The serious birdwatcher heard that and looked up the hill. What he saw was a man sitting on a park bench and apparently having a conversation with himself. The corners of the serious birdwatcher's mouth turned down in disgust and he thought, *I hope I die before I get that old. I really do.* Then he turned back to the birdbath and began making notes again.

Deep inside Ralph's head, the clenching sensation – that feeling of *blink* – suddenly came again, and although he didn't stir from the bench, Ralph felt himself propelled rapidly upward none the less . . . faster and further than ever before.

Not at all, the voice said. *Once you were much higher than this, Ralph — Lois, too. But you're getting there. You'll be ready soon.*

The birdwatcher, who lived all unknowing in the center of a gorgeous spun-gold aura, looked around cautiously, perhaps wanting to make sure that the senile old man on the bench at the top of the hill wasn't creeping up on him with a blunt instrument. What he saw caused the tight, prissy line of his mouth to soften in astonishment. His eyes widened. Ralph observed sudden radiating spokes of indigo in the serious birdwatcher's aura and realized he was looking at shock.

What's the matter with him? What does he see?

But that was wrong. It wasn't what the birdwatcher *saw*; it was what he *didn't* see. He didn't see *Ralph,* because Ralph had gone up high enough to disappear from this level — had become the visual equivalent of a note blown on a dog-whistle.

If they were here now, I could see them easily.

Who, Ralph? If who was here?

Clotho. Lachesis. And Atropos.

All at once the pieces began to fly together in his mind, like the pieces of a jigsaw puzzle that had looked a great deal more complicated than it actually was.

Ralph, whispering: [*'Oh my God. Oh my God. Oh my God.'*]

14

Six days later, Ralph awoke at quarter past three in the morning and knew that the time of the promise had come.

15

'I think I'll walk upstreet to the Red Apple and get an ice-cream bar,' Ralph said. It was almost ten o'clock. His heart was beating much too fast, and his thoughts were hard to find under the constant white noise of terror which now filled him. He had never felt less like ice-cream in his entire life, but it was a reasonable enough excuse for a trip to the Red Apple; it was the first week of August, and the weatherman had said the mercury would probably top ninety by early afternoon, with thunderstorms to follow in the early evening.

Ralph thought he needn't worry about the thunderstorms.

A bookcase stood on a spread of newspapers by the kitchen door. Lois had been painting it barn-red. Now she got to her feet, put her hands into the small of her back, and stretched. Ralph could hear the minute crackling sounds of her spine. 'I'll go with you. My head'll ache tonight if I don't get away from that paint for awhile. I don't know why I wanted to paint on such a muggy day in the first place.'

The last thing on earth Ralph wanted was to be accompanied up to the Red Apple by Lois. 'You don't have to, honey; I'll bring you back one of those coconut Popsicles you like. I wasn't even planning on taking Rosalie, it's so humid. Go sit on the back porch, why don't you?'

'Any Popsicle you carry back from the store on a day like this will be falling off the stick by the time you get it here,' she said. 'Come on, let's go while there's still shade on this side of the . . .'

She trailed off. The little smile she'd been wearing slipped off her face. It was replaced by a look of dismay, and the gray of her aura, which had only darkened slightly during the years Ralph hadn't been able to see it, now began to glow with flocks of reddish-pink embers.

'Ralph, what's wrong? What are you really going to do?'

'Nothing,' he said, but the scar was glowing inside his arm and the tick of the deathwatch was everywhere, loud and everywhere. It was telling him he had an appointment to keep. A *promise* to keep.

'Yes, there is, and it's been wrong for the last two or three months, maybe longer. I'm a foolish woman – I knew something was happening, but I couldn't bring myself to look at it dead-on. Because I was afraid. And I was right to be afraid, wasn't I? I was right.'

'Lois—'

She was suddenly crossing the room to him, crossing fast, almost *leaping,* the old back injury not slowing her down in the least, and before he could stop her, she had seized his right arm and was holding it out, looking at it fixedly.

The scar was glowing a fierce bright red.

Ralph had a moment to hope that it was strictly an aural glow and she wouldn't be able to see it. Then she looked up, her eyes round and full of terror. Terror, and something else. Ralph thought that something else was recognition.

'Oh my God,' she whispered. 'The men in the park. The ones with the funny names . . . Clothes and Lashes, something like that . . . and one of them cut you. Oh Ralph, oh my God, *what are you supposed to do?*'

'Now, Lois, don't take on—'

'Don't you dare tell me not to take on!' she shrieked into his face. *'Don't you dare! Don't you DARE!'*

Hurry, the interior voice whispered. *You don't have time to stand around and discuss this; somewhere it's already begun to happen, and the deathwatch you hear may not be ticking just for you.*

'I have to go.' He turned and blundered toward the door. In his agitation he did not notice a certain Sherlock Holmesian circumstance attending this scene: a dog which should have barked – a dog which *always* barked her stern disapproval when voices were raised in this house – but did not. Rosalie was missing from her usual place by the screen door . . . and the door itself was standing ajar.

Rosalie was the furthest thing from Ralph's mind at that moment. He felt knee-deep in molasses, and thought he would be doing well just to make the porch, let alone the Red Apple up the street. His heart thumped and skidded in his chest; his eyes were burning.

'*No!*' Lois screamed. '*No, Ralph, please! Please don't leave me!*'

She ran after him, clutched his arm. She was still holding her paintbrush, and the fine red droplets which splattered his shirt looked like blood. Now she was crying, and her expression of utter, abject sorrow nearly broke his heart. He didn't want to leave her like this; wasn't sure he *could* leave her like this.

He turned and took her by her forearms. 'Lois, I *have* to go.'

'You haven't been sleeping,' she babbled, 'I knew that, and I knew it meant something was wrong, but it doesn't matter, we'll go away, we can leave right now, this minute, we'll just take Rosalie and our toothbrushes and go—'

He squeezed her arms and she stopped, looking up at him with her wet eyes. Her lips were trembling.

'Lois, listen to me. *I have to do this.*'

'*I lost Paul, I can't lose you, too!*' she wailed. '*I couldn't stand it! Oh Ralph, I couldn't stand it!*'

You'll be able to, he thought. *Short-Timers are a lot tougher than they look. They have to be.*

Ralph felt a couple of tears trickle down his cheeks. He suspected their source was more weariness than grief. If he could make her see that all this changed nothing, only made what he had to do harder . . .

He held her at arm's length. The scar on his arm was throbbing more fiercely than ever, and the feeling of time slipping relentlessly away had become overwhelming.

'Walk with me at least partway, if you want,' he said. 'Maybe you can even help me do what I have to do. I've *had* my life, Lois, and a fine one it was. But *she* hasn't really had anything yet, and I'll be damned if I'll let that son of a bitch have *her* just because he's got a score to settle with me.'

'What son of a bitch? Ralph, what in the world are you talking about?'

'I'm talking about Natalie Deepneau. She's supposed to die this morning, only I'm not going to let that happen.'

'*Nat?* Ralph, why would anyone want to hurt Nat?'

She looked very bewildered, very *our Lois* . . . but wasn't there something else beneath that daffy exterior? Something careful and calculating? Ralph thought the answer was yes. Ralph had an idea Lois wasn't half as bewildered as she was pretending to be. She had fooled Bill McGovern for years with that act – him, too, at least part of the time – and this was just another (and rather brilliant) variation of the same old scam.

What she was *really* trying to do was hold him here. She loved Nat deeply, but to Lois, a choice between her husband and the little girl who lived up the lane was no choice at all. She didn't consider either age or questions of fairness to have any bearing on the situation. Ralph was her man, and to Lois, that was all that mattered.

'It won't work,' he said, not unkindly. He disengaged himself and started for the door again. 'I made a promise, and I'm all out of time.'

'Break it, then!' she cried, and the mixture of terror and rage in her voice stunned him. 'I don't remember much about that time, but I remember we got involved with things that almost got us killed, and for reasons we couldn't even understand. So break it, Ralph! Better your promise than my heart!'

'And what about the kid? What about *Helen,* for that matter? Nat's all she lives for. Doesn't Helen deserve something better from me than a broken promise?'

'I don't *care* what she deserves! What *any* of them deserve!' she shouted, and then her face crumpled. 'Yes, all right, I suppose I do. But what about *us,* Ralph? Don't we count?' Her eyes, those dark and eloquent Spanish eyes of hers, pleaded with him. If he looked into them too long, it would become all too easy to cry it off, so Ralph looked away.

'I mean to do it, honey. Nat's going to get what you

and I have already had — another seventy years or so of days and nights.'

She looked at him helplessly, but made no attempt to stop him again. Instead, she began to cry. 'Foolish old man!' she whispered. 'Foolish, willful old man!'

'Yes, I suppose,' he said, and lifted her chin. 'But I'm a foolish, willful old man of my word. Come with me. I'd like that.'

'All right, Ralph.' She could hardly hear her own voice, and her skin was as cold as clay. Her aura had gone almost completely red. 'What is it? What's going to happen to her?'

'She's going to be hit by a green Ford sedan. Unless I take her place, she's going to be splashed all over Harris Avenue . . . and Helen's going to see it happen.'

16

As they walked up the hill toward the Red Apple (at first Lois kept falling behind, then trotting to catch up, but she quit when she saw she could not slow him with such a simple trick), Ralph told her what little more he could. She had some memory of being under the lightning-struck tree out by the Extension — a memory she had believed, at least until this morning, to be the memory of a dream — but of course she hadn't been there during Ralph's final confrontation with Atropos. Ralph told her of it now — of the random death Atropos intended Natalie to suffer if Ralph continued standing in the way of his plans. He told her of how he'd extracted a promise from Clotho and Lachesis that Atropos might in this case be overruled, and Nat saved.

'I have an idea that . . . the decision was made . . . very near the top of this crazy building . . . this Tower . . . they kept talking about. Maybe . . . at the *very* top.' He was panting out the words and his heart was beating more rapidly than ever, but he thought most of that could be attributed to the fast walk and the torrid day; his fear had subsided somewhat. Talking to Lois had done that much.

Now he could see the Red Apple. Mrs Perrine was at the bus stop half a block further up, standing straight as a general reviewing troops. Her net shopping bag hung over her arm. There was a bus shelter nearby, and it was shady inside, but Mrs Perrine stolidly ignored its existence. Even in the dazzling sunlight he could see that her aura was the same West Point gray as it had been on that October evening in 1993. Of Helen and Nat there was as yet no sign.

17

'Of course I knew who he was,' Esther Perrine later tells the reporter from the Derry News. 'Do I look incompetent to you, young man? Or senile? I've known Ralph Roberts for over twenty years. A good man. Not cut from the same cloth as his first wife, of course — Carolyn was a Satterwaite, from the Bangor Satterwaites — but a very fine man, just the same. I recognized the driver of that green Ford auto, too, right away. Pete Sullivan delivered my paper for six years, and he did a good job. The new one, the Morrison boy, always throws it in my flower-beds or up on the porch roof. Pete was driving with his mother, on his learner's permit, I understand. I hope he *won't take on too much about what happened, for he's a good lad, and it really wasn't his fault. I saw the whole thing, and I'll take my oath on it.*

'I suppose you think I'm rambling. Don't bother denying it; I can read your face just like it was your own newspaper. Never mind, though – I've said most of what I have to say. I knew it was Ralph right away, but here's something you'll get wrong even if you put it in your story . . . which you probably won't. He came from nowhere to save that little girl.'

Esther Perrine fixes the respectfully silent young reporter with a formidable glance – fixes him as a lepidopterist might fix a butterfly on a pin after administering the chloroform.

'I don't mean it was like he came from nowhere, young man, although I bet that's what you'll print.'

She leans toward the reporter, her eyes never leaving his face, and says it again.

'He came from nowhere to save that little girl. Do you follow me? From nowhere.'

18

The accident made the front page of the following day's Derry *News*. Esther Perrine was sufficiently colorful in her remarks to warrant a sidebar of her own, and staff photographer Tom Matthews got a picture to go with it that made her look like Ma Joad in *The Grapes of Wrath*. The headline of the sidebar read: 'IT WAS LIKE HE CAME FROM NOWHERE,' EYEWITNESS TO TRAGEDY SAYS.

When she read it, Mrs Perrine was not at all surprised.

19

'In the end I got what I wanted,' Ralph said, 'but only because Clotho and Lachesis – and whoever it is they work for on the upper levels – were desperate to stop Ed.'

'Upper levels? What upper levels? What *building*?'

'Never mind. You've forgotten, but remembering wouldn't change anything. The point is just this, Lois: they didn't want to stop Ed because thousands of people would have died if he'd hit the Civic Center dead-on. They wanted to stop him because there was one person whose life needed to be preserved at any cost . . . In *their* reckoning, anyway. When I was finally able to make them see that I felt the same about my kid as they did about theirs, arrangements were made.'

'That's when they cut you, wasn't it? And when you made the promise. The one you used to talk about in your sleep.'

He shot her a wide-eyed, startled, and heartbreakingly boyish glance. She only looked back.

'Yes,' he said, and wiped his forehead. 'I guess so.' The air lay in his lungs like metal shavings. 'A life for a life, that was the deal – Natalie's in exchange for mine. And—'

[*Hey! Quit tryin to wiggle away! Quit it, Rover, or I'll kick your asshole square!*]

Ralph broke off at the sound of that shrill, hectoring, horridly familiar voice – a voice no human being on Harris Avenue but him could hear – and looked across the street.

'Ralph? What—'

'Shhh!'

He pulled her back against the summer-dry hedge in front of the Applebaums' house. He wasn't doing anything so polite as perspiring now; his whole body was crawling with a stinking sweat as heavy as engine oil, and he could feel every gland in his body dumping a hot load into his blood. His underwear was trying to crawl up into the crack of his ass and disappear. His tongue tasted like a blown fuse.

Lois followed the direction of his gaze. 'Rosalie!' she cried. 'Rosalie, you bad dog! What are *you* doing over there?'

The black-and-tan beagle she had given Ralph on their first Christmas was across the street, standing (except *cringing* was actually the word for what she was doing) on the sidewalk in front of the house where Helen and Nat had lived until Ed had popped his wig. For the first time in the years they'd had her, the beagle reminded Lois of Rosalie #1. Rosalie #2 appeared to be all alone over there, but that did not allay Lois's sudden terror.

Oh, what have I done? she thought. *What have I done?*

'Rosalie!' she screamed. '*Rosalie, get over here!*'

The dog heard, Lois could see that she did, but she didn't move.

'Ralph? What's happening over there?'

'*Shhhh!*' he said again, and then, just a little further up the street, Lois saw something which stopped her breath. Her last, unstated hope that all this was happening only in Ralph's head, that it was a kind of flashback to their previous experience, disappeared, because now their dog had company.

Holding a skip-rope looped over her right arm,

six-year-old Nat Deepneau came to the end of her walk and looked down the street toward a house she didn't remember ever living in, toward a lawn where her shirtless father, an undesignated player named Ed Deepneau, had once sat among intersecting rainbows, listening to the Jefferson Airplane as a single spot of blood dried on his John Lennon spectacles. Natalie looked down the street and smiled happily at Rosalie, who was panting and watching her with miserable, frightened eyes.

20

Atropos doesn't see me, Ralph thought. *He's concentrating on Rosie . . . and on Natalie, of course . . . and he doesn't see me.*

Everything had come around with a sort of hideous perfection. The house was there, Rosalie was there, and Atropos was there, too, wearing a hat cocked back on his head and looking like a wiseacre news reporter in a 1950s B-picture — something directed by Ida Lupino, perhaps. Only this time it wasn't a Panama with a bite gone from the brim; this time it was a Boston Red Sox cap and it was too small even for Atropos because the adjustable band in the back had been pulled all the way over to the last hole. It had to be, in order to fit the head of the little girl who owned it.

All we need now is Pete the paperboy and the show would be perfect, Ralph thought. *The final scene of* Insomnia, or, Short-Time Life on Harris Avenue, a Tragi-Comedy in Three Acts. *Everyone takes a bow and then exits stage right.*

This dog was afraid of Atropos, just as Rosalie #1 had been, and the main reason the little bald doc hadn't

seen Ralph and Lois was that he was trying to keep her
from running off before he was ready. And here came Nat,
headed down the sidewalk toward her favorite dog in the
whole world, Ralph and Lois's Rosalie. Her jump-rope

(*three-six-nine, hon, the goose drank wine*)

was slung over her arm. She looked impossibly beau-
tiful and impossibly fragile in her sailor shirt and blue
shorts. Her pigtails bounced.

It's happening too fast, Ralph thought. *Everything is
happening much too fast.*

[*Not at all, Ralph! You did splendidly five years ago; you'll
do splendidly now.*]

It sounded like Clotho, but there was no time to
look. A green car was coming slowly down Harris Avenue
from the direction of the airport, moving with the sort of
agonized care which usually meant a driver who was very
old or very young. Agonized care or not, it was unques-
tionably *the* car; a dirty membrane hung over it like a
shroud.

Life is a wheel, Ralph thought, and it occurred to him
that this was not the first time the idea had occurred to
him. *Sooner or later everything you thought you'd left behind
comes around again. For good or ill, it comes around again.*

Rosie made another abortive lunge for freedom, and
as Atropos yanked her back, losing his hat, Nat knelt before
her and patted her. 'Are you lost, girl? Did you get out by
yourself? That's okay, I'll take you home.' She gave Rosie
a hug, her small arms passing through Atropos's arms, her
small, beautiful face only inches from his ugly, grinning
one. Then she got up. 'Come on, Rosie! Come on, sugarpie.'

Rosalie started down the sidewalk at Nat's heel,

looking back once at the grinning little man and whining uneasily. On the other side of Harris Avenue, Helen came out of the Red Apple, and the last condition of the vision Atropos had shown Ralph was fulfilled. Helen had a loaf of bread in one hand. Her Red Sox hat was on her head.

Ralph swept Lois into his arms and kissed her fiercely. 'I love you with all my heart,' he said. 'Remember that, Lois.'

'I know you do,' she said calmly. 'And I love *you*. That's why I can't let you do it.'

She seized him around the neck, her arms like bands of iron, and he felt her breasts push against him hard as she drew in all the breath her lungs would hold.

'*Go away, you rotten bastard!*' she screamed. '*I can't see you, but I know you're there! Go away! Go away and leave us alone!*'

Natalie stopped dead in her tracks and looked at Lois with wide-eyed surprise. Rosalie stopped beside her, ears pricking.

'*Don't go into the street, Nat!*' Lois screamed at her. '*Don't—*'

Then her hands, which had been laced together at the back of Ralph's neck, were holding nothing; her arms, which had been locked about his shoulders in a deathgrip, were empty.

He was gone like smoke.

21

Atropos looked toward the cry of alarm and saw Ralph and Lois standing on the other side of Harris Avenue. More important, he saw Ralph seeing *him*. His eyes widened; his lips parted in a hateful snarl. One hand flew to his bald pate – it was crisscrossed with old scars, the remnants of wounds made with his own scalpel – in an instinctive gesture of defense that was five years too late.

[*Fuck you, Shorts! This little bitch is mine!*]

Ralph saw Nat, looking at Lois with uncertainty and surprise. He heard Lois shrieking at her, telling her not to go into the street. Then it was Lachesis he heard, speaking from someplace close by.

[*Come up, Ralph! As far as you can! Quickly!*]

He felt the clench in the center of his head, felt that brief swoop of vertigo in his stomach, and suddenly the whole world brightened and filled with color. He half-saw and half-felt Lois's arms and locked hands collapse inward, through the place where his body had been a moment before, and then he was drawing away from her – no, being *carried* away from her. He felt the pull of some great current and understood, in a vague way, that if there was such a thing as a Higher Purpose, he had joined it and would soon be swept downriver with it.

Natalie and Rosalie were now standing directly in front of the house which Ralph had once shared with Bill McGovern before selling up and moving into Lois's house. Nat glanced doubtfully at Lois, then waved tentatively. 'She's okay, Lois – see, she's right here.' She patted Rosalie's head. 'I'll cross her safe, don't worry.' Then, as she started into the street, she called to her mother. 'I can't find my baseball cap! I think somebody stole it!'

Rosalie was still on the sidewalk. Nat turned to her impatiently. 'Come *on*, girl!'

The green car was moving in the child's direction, but very slowly. It did not at first look like much of a danger to her. Ralph recognized the driver at once, and he did not doubt his senses or suspect he was having a hallucination. In that instant it seemed very right that the approaching sedan should be piloted by his old paperboy.

'*Natalie!*' Lois screamed. '*Natalie, no!*'

Atropos darted forward and slapped Rosalie #2 on the rump.

[*Get outta here, mutt! G'wan! Before I change my mind!*]

Atropos spared Ralph one final grimacing leer as Rosie yelped and darted into the street . . . and into the path of the Ford driven by sixteen-year-old Pete Sullivan.

Natalie didn't see the car; she was looking at Lois, whose face was all red and scary. It had finally occurred to Nat that Lois wasn't screaming about Rosie at all, but something else entirely.

Pete registered the sprinting beagle; it was the little girl he didn't see. He swerved to avoid Rosalie, a maneuver that ended with the Ford aimed directly at Natalie. Ralph could see two frightened faces behind the windshield as the car veered, and he thought Mrs Sullivan was screaming.

Atropos was leaping up and down, doing an obscenely joyful hornpipe.

[*Yahh, Short-Time! Silly white-hair! Toldja I'd fix you!*]

In slow motion Helen dropped the loaf of bread she was holding. '*Natalie, LOOK OUUUUUUTTT!*' she shrieked.

Ralph ran. Again there was that clear sensation of moving by thought alone. And as he closed in on Nat, now diving forward with his hands stretched out, aware of the car looming just beyond her, kicking bright arrows of sun through its dark deathbag and into his eyes, he clenched his mind again, bringing himself back down to the Short-Time world for the last time.

He fell into a landscape that rang with splintered screams: Helen's mingled with Lois's mingled with the ones being made by the tires of the Ford. Weaving its way through them like an outlaw vine was the sound of Atropos's jeers. Ralph got a brief glimpse of Nat's wide blue eyes, and then he shoved her in the chest and stomach as hard as he could, sending her flying backwards with her hands and feet thrust out in front of her. She landed sitting up in the gutter, bruising her tailbone on the curb but breaking nothing. From some distant place, Ralph heard Atropos squawk in fury and disbelief.

Then two tons of Ford, still travelling at twenty miles an hour, struck Ralph and the soundtrack dropped dead. He was heaved upward and backward in a low, slow arc – it *felt* slow, anyway, from inside – and went with the Ford's hood ornament imprinted on his cheek like a tattoo and one broken leg trailing behind him. There was time to see his shadow sliding along the pavement beneath him in a shape like an X; there was time to see a spray of red droplets in the air just above him and to think that Lois must have splattered more paint on him than he had thought at first. And there was time to see Natalie sitting at the side of the street, weeping but all right . . . and to sense Atropos on the sidewalk behind her, shaking his fists and dancing with rage.

I believe I did pretty damned good for an old geezer, Ralph thought, *but now I think I could really do with a nap.*

Then he came back to earth with a terrible mortal

smack and rolled – skull fracturing, back breaking, lungs punctured by brittle thorns of bone as his ribcage exploded, liver turning to pulp, intestines first coming unanchored and then rupturing.

And nothing hurt.

Nothing at all.

22

Lois never forgot the awful thud that was the sound of Ralph's return to Harris Avenue, or the bloody splash-marks he left behind as he cartwheeled to a stop. She wanted to scream but dared not; some deep, true voice told her that if she did that, the combination of shock, horror, and summer heat would send her unconscious to the sidewalk, and when she came to again, Ralph would be beyond her.

She ran instead of screaming, losing one shoe, marginally aware that Pete Sullivan was getting out of the Ford, which had come to rest almost exactly where Joe Wyzer's car – also a Ford – had come to rest after Joe had hit Rosalie #1 all those years ago. She was also marginally aware that Pete was screaming.

She reached Ralph and fell on her knees beside him, seeing that his shape had somehow been changed by the green Ford, that the body beneath the familiar chino pants and paint-splattered shirt was fundamentally different from the body which had been pressed against hers less than a minute ago. But his eyes were open, and they were bright and aware.

'Ralph?'

'Yes.' His voice was clear and strong, unmarked by either confusion or pain. 'Yes, Lois, I hear you.'

She started to put her arms around him and hesitated, thinking about how you weren't supposed to move people who had been badly injured because you might hurt them even worse or kill them. Then she looked at him again, at the blood pouring from the sides of his mouth and the way his lower body seemed to have come unhinged from the upper part, and decided it would be impossible to hurt Ralph more than he had been hurt already. She hugged him, leaning close, leaning into the smells of disaster: blood and the sweet-sour acetone odor of spent adrenaline on the outrush of his breath.

'You did it this time, didn't you?' Lois asked. She kissed his cheek, his blood-soaked eyebrows, his bloody forehead where the skin had been peeled away from his skull in a flap. She began to cry. 'Look at you! Shirt torn, pants torn . . . do you think clothes grow on trees?'

'Is he all right?' Helen asked from behind her. Lois didn't turn around, but she saw the shadows on the street: Helen with her arm around her weeping daughter's shoulders, and Rosie standing by Helen's right leg. 'He saved Nat's life and I didn't even see where he came from. Please, Lois, say he's all r—'

Then the shadows shifted as Helen moved to a place where she could actually see Ralph, and she pulled Nat's face against her blouse and began to wail.

Lois leaned closer to Ralph, caressing his cheeks with the palms of her hands, wanting to tell him that she had meant to come with him – she had meant to, yes, but in the end he had been too quick for her. In the end he had left her behind.

'Love you, sweetheart,' Ralph said. He reached up and copied her gesture with his own palm. He tried to raise his left hand as well, but it would only lie on the pavement and twitch.

Lois took his hand and kissed it. 'Love you, too, Ralph. Always. So much.'

'I had to do it. You see?'

'Yes.' She didn't know if she *did* see, didn't know if she would *ever* see . . . but she knew he was dying. 'Yes, I see.'

He sighed harshly — that sweet acetone smell wafted up to her again — and smiled.

'Miz Chasse? Miz Roberts, I mean?' It was Pete, speaking in hitching gasps. 'Is Mr Roberts okay? Please say I didn't hurt him!'

'Stay away, Pete,' she said without turning around. 'Ralph is fine. He just tore his pants and shirt a little . . . didn't you, Ralph?'

'Yes,' he said. 'You bet. You'll just have to hosswhip me for—'

He broke off and looked to her left. No one was there, but Ralph smiled anyway. 'Lachesis!' he said.

He put out his trembling, blood-grimy right hand, and as Lois, Helen, and Pete Sullivan watched, it rose and fell twice in the empty air. Ralph's eyes moved again, this time to the right. Slowly, very slowly, he moved his hand in that direction. When he spoke this time, his voice had begun to fade. 'Hi, Clotho. Now remember: this . . . doesn't . . . hurt. Right?'

Ralph appeared to listen, and then smiled.

'Yep,' he whispered, 'any way you can get her.'

His hand rose and fell again in the air, then dropped back to his chest. He looked up at Lois with his fading blue eyes.

'Listen,' he said, speaking with great effort. Yet his eyes blazed, would not let hers go. 'Every day I woke up next to you was like waking up young and seeing . . . everything new.' He tried to raise his hand to her cheek again, and could not. 'Every day, Lois.'

'It was like that for me, too, Ralph – like waking up young.'

'Lois?'

'What?'

'The ticking,' he said. He swallowed and then said it again, enunciating the words with great effort. 'The ticking.'

'What ticking?'

'Never mind, it's stopped,' he said, and smiled brilliantly. Then Ralph stopped, too.

23

Clotho and Lachesis stood watching Lois weep over the man who lay dead in the street. In one hand Clotho held his scissors; he raised the other to eye-level and looked at it wonderingly.

It glowed and blazed with Ralph's aura.

Clotho: [*He's here . . . in here . . . how wonderful!*]

Lachesis raised his own right hand. Like Clotho's left, it looked as if someone had pulled a blue mitten over the normal green-gold aura which swaddled it.

Lachesis: [*Yes. He was a wonderful man.*]
Clotho: [*Shall we give him to her?*]
Lachesis: [*Can we?*]
Clotho: [*There's one way to find out.*]

They approached Lois. Each placed the hand Ralph had shaken on one side of Lois's face.

24

'Mommy!' Natalie Deepnau cried. In her agitation, she had reverted to the patois of her babyhood. 'Who those wittle men? Why they touchin Roliss?'

'Shh, honey,' Helen said, and buried Nat's head against her breast again. There were no men, little or otherwise, near Lois Roberts; she was kneeling alone in the street next to the man who had saved her daughter's life.

25

Lois looked up suddenly, her eyes wide and surprised, her grief forgotten as a gorgeous feeling of

(*light blue light*)

calmness and peace filled her. For a moment Harris Avenue was gone. She was in a dark place filled with the sweet smells of hay and cows, a dark place that was split by a hundred brilliant seams of light. She never forgot the fierce joy that leaped up in her at that moment, nor the sure sense that she was seeing a representation of a universe that Ralph wanted her to see, a universe where there was dazzling light behind the darkness . . . couldn't she see it through the cracks?

'Can you ever forgive me?' Pete was sobbing. 'Oh my God, can you ever forgive me?'

'Oh yes, I think so,' Lois said calmly.

She passed her hand down Ralph's face, closing his eyes, and then held his head in her lap and waited for the police to come. To Lois, Ralph looked as if he had gone to sleep. And, she saw, the long white scar on his right forearm was gone.

September 10, 1990 – November 10, 1993